Lecture Notes in Artificial Intelligence 8480

Subseries of Lecture Notes in Computer Science

LNAI Series Editors

Randy Goebel
University of Alberta, Edmonton, Canada

Yuzuru Tanaka
Hokkaido University, Sapporo, Japan

Wolfgang Wahlster
DFKI and Saarland University, Saarbrücken, Germany

LNAI Founding Series Editor

Joerg Siekmann
DFKI and Saarland University, Saarbrücken, Germany

Marios Polycarpou André C.P.L.F. de Carvalho
Jeng-Shyang Pan Michał Woźniak
Héctor Quintián Emilio Corchado (Eds.)

Hybrid Artificial Intelligence Systems

9th International Conference, HAIS 2014
Salamanca, Spain, June 11-13, 2014
Proceedings

Springer

Volume Editors

Marios Polycarpou
University of Cyprus, Nicosia, Cyprus
E-mail: mpolycar@ucy.ac.cy

André C.P.L.F. de Carvalho
University of Sao Paulo at Sao Carlos, SP, Brazil
E-mail: andre@icmc.usp.br

Jeng-Shyang Pan
Harbin Institute of Technology, Shenzhen Graduate School, China
E-mail: jengshyangpan@gmail.com

Michał Woźniak
Wroclaw University of Technology, Poland
E-mail: michal.wozniak@pwr.edu.pl

Héctor Quintián
University of Salamanca, Spain *and* University of A Coruna, Spain
E-mail: hector.quintian@usal.es *and* hector.quintian@udc.es

Emilio Corchado
University of Salamanca, Spain
E-mail: escorchado@usal.es

ISSN 0302-9743 e-ISSN 1611-3349
ISBN 978-3-319-07616-4 e-ISBN 978-3-319-07617-1
DOI 10.1007/978-3-319-07617-1
Springer Cham Heidelberg New York Dordrecht London

Library of Congress Control Number: 2014939509

LNCS Sublibrary: SL 7 – Artificial Intelligence

© Springer International Publishing Switzerland 2014
This work is subject to copyright. All rights are reserved by the Publisher, whether the whole or part of the material is concerned, specifically the rights of translation, reprinting, reuse of illustrations, recitation, broadcasting, reproduction on microfilms or in any other physical way, and transmission or information storage and retrieval, electronic adaptation, computer software, or by similar or dissimilar methodology now known or hereafter developed. Exempted from this legal reservation are brief excerpts in connection with reviews or scholarly analysis or material supplied specifically for the purpose of being entered and executed on a computer system, for exclusive use by the purchaser of the work. Duplication of this publication or parts thereof is permitted only under the provisions of the Copyright Law of the Publisher's location, in ist current version, and permission for use must always be obtained from Springer. Permissions for use may be obtained through RightsLink at the Copyright Clearance Center. Violations are liable to prosecution under the respective Copyright Law.
The use of general descriptive names, registered names, trademarks, service marks, etc. in this publication does not imply, even in the absence of a specific statement, that such names are exempt from the relevant protective laws and regulations and therefore free for general use.
While the advice and information in this book are believed to be true and accurate at the date of publication, neither the authors nor the editors nor the publisher can accept any legal responsibility for any errors or omissions that may be made. The publisher makes no warranty, express or implied, with respect to the material contained herein.

Typesetting: Camera-ready by author, data conversion by Scientific Publishing Services, Chennai, India

Printed on acid-free paper

Springer is part of Springer Science+Business Media (www.springer.com)

Preface

This volume of *Lecture Notes on Artificial Intelligence* (LNAI) includes the accepted papers presented at the 9th International Conference on Hybrid Artificial Intelligence Systems (HAIS 2014) held in the beautiful and historic city of Salamanca, Spain, in June 2014.

The International Conference on Hybrid Artificial Intelligence Systems has become a unique, established, and broad interdisciplinary forum for researchers and practitioners who are involved in developing and applying symbolic and sub-symbolic techniques aimed at the construction of highly robust and reliable problem-solving techniques and in bringing the most relevant achievements in this field.

Hybridization of intelligent techniques, coming from different computational intelligence areas, has become popular because of the growing awareness that such combinations frequently perform better than the individual techniques such as neurocomputing, fuzzy systems, rough sets, evolutionary algorithms, agents and multiagent systems, etc.

Practical experience has indicated that hybrid intelligence techniques might be helpful for solving some of the challenging real-world problems. In a hybrid intelligence system, a synergistic combination of multiple techniques is used to build an efficient solution to deal with a particular problem. This is, thus, the setting of the HAIS conference series, and its increasing success is the proof of the vitality of this exciting field.

HAIS 2014 received 199 technical submissions. After a rigorous peer-review process, the international Program Committee selected 61 papers, which are published in these conference proceedings.

The selection of papers was extremely rigorous in order to maintain the high quality of the conference and we would like to thank the Program Committee for their hard work in the reviewing process. This process is very important to the creation of a conference of high standard and the HAIS conference would not exist without their help.

The large number of submissions is certainly not only testimony to the vitality and attractiveness of the field but an indicator of the interest in the HAIS conferences themselves.

HAIS 2014 enjoyed outstanding keynote speeches by distinguished guest speakers: Prof. Amparo Alonso Betanzos, University of Coruña (Spain) and President Spanish Association for Artificial Intelligence (AEPIA), Prof. Sung-Bae Cho, Yonsei University (Korea), and Prof. André de Carvalho, University of Saõ Paulo (Brazil).

HAIS 2014 teamed up with the journals *Neurocomputing* (Elsevier) and the *Logic Journal of the IGPL* (Oxford Journals) for a set of special issues including selected papers from HAIS 2014.

Particular thanks go to the conference main Sponsors, IEEE-Sección España, IEEE Systems, Man and Cybernetics–Capítulo Español, AEPIA, Ayuntamiento de Salamanca, University of Salamanca, MIR Labs, The International Federation for Computational Logic, and project ENGINE (7th Marco Program, FP7-316097), who jointly contributed in an active and constructive manner to the success of this initiative.

We would like to thank Alfred Hofmann and Anna Kramer from Springer for their help and collaboration during this demanding publication project.

June 2014

Marios Polycarpou
André C.P.L.F. de Carvalho
Jeng-Shyang Pan
Michał Woźniak
Héctor Quintián
Emilio Corchado

Organization

Honorary Chairs

Alfonso Fernández Mañueco	Mayor of Salamanca
Amparo Alonso Betanzos	University of Coruña, Spain, President of the Spanish Association for Artificial Intelligence (AEPIA)
Costas Stasopoulos	Director-Elect, IEEE Region 8
Hojjat Adeli	The Ohio State University, USA

General Chair

Emilio Corchado	University of Salamanca, Spain

International Advisory Committee

Ajith Abraham	Machine Intelligence Research Labs, Europe
Antonio Bahamonde	President of the Spanish Association for Artificial Intelligence, AEPIA
Andre de Carvalho	University of São Paulo, Brazil
Sung-Bae Cho	Yonsei University, Korea
Juan M. Corchado	University of Salamanca, Spain
José R. Dorronsoro	Autonomous University of Madrid, Spain
Michael Gabbay	King's College London, UK
Ali A. Ghorbani	UNB, Canada
Mark A. Girolami	University of Glasgow, UK
Manuel Graña	University of País Vasco, Spain
Petro Gopych	Universal Power Systems USA-Ukraine LLC, Ukraine
Jon G. Hall	The Open University, UK
Francisco Herrera	University of Granada, Spain
César Hervás-Martínez	University of Córdoba, Spain
Tom Heskes	Radboud University Nijmegen, The Netherlands
Dusan Husek	Academy of Sciences of the Czech Republic, Czech Republic
Lakhmi Jain	University of South Australia, Australia
Samuel Kaski	Helsinki University of Technology, Finland
Daniel A. Keim	University of Konstanz, Germany

Isidro Laso	D.G. Information Society and Media, European Commission
Marios Polycarpou	University of Cyprus, Cyprus
Witold Pedrycz	University of Alberta, Canada
Václav Snášel	VSB-Technical University of Ostrava, Czech Republic
Xin Yao	University of Birmingham, UK
Hujun Yin	University of Manchester, UK
Michał Woźniak	Wroclaw University of Technology, Poland
Aditya Ghose	University of Wollongong, Australia
Ashraf Saad	Armstrong Atlantic State University, USA
Fanny Klett	German Workforce Advanced Distributed Learning Partnership Laboratory, Germany
Paulo Novais	Universidade do Minho, Portugal

Industrial Advisory Committee

Rajkumar Roy	The EPSRC Centre for Innovative Manufacturing in Through-life Engineering Services, UK
Amy Neustein	Linguistic Technology Systems, USA

Program Committee

Emilio Corchado	University of Salamanca, Spain (Co-chair)
Marios Polycarpou	University of Cyprus, Cyprus (Co-chair)
André C.P.L.F. de Carvalho	University of São Paulo, Brazil (Co-chair)
Jeng-Shyang Pan	National Kaohsiung University of Applied Sciences, Taiwan (Co-chair)
Michał Woźniak	Wroclaw University of Technology, Poland (Co-chair)
Abdel-Badeeh Salem	Ain Shams University, Egypt
Aboul Ella Hassanien	Cairo University, Egypt
Adolfo R. De Soto	University of Leon, Spain
Alberto Fernandez Gil	University Rey Juan Carlos, Spain
Alfredo Cuzzocrea	ICAR-CNR and University of Calabria, Italy
Alicia Troncoso	Universidad Pablo de Olavide, Spain
Alvaro Herrero	University of Burgos, Spain
Amelia Zafra Gómez	University of Cordoba, Spain
Ana M. Bernardos	Universidad Politécnica de Madrid, Spain

Ana Madureira	Polytechnic University of Porto, Portugal
Anca Andreica	Babes-Bolyai University, Romania
Andreea Vescan	Babes-Bolyai University, Romania
Andres Ortiz	University of Malaga, Spain
Angelos Amanatiadis	Democritus University of Thrace, Greece
Antonio Dourado	University of Coimbra, Portugal
Arkadiusz Kowalski	Wroclaw University of Technology, Poland
Arturo De La Escalera	Universidad Carlos III de Madrid, Spain
Barna Laszlo Iantovics	Petru Maior University of Tg. Mures, Romania
Bogdan Trawinski	Wroclaw University of Technology, Poland
Bozena Skolud	Silesian University of Technology, Poland
Bruno Baruque	University of Burgos, Spain
Camelia Pintea	North University of Baia-Mare, Romania
Carlos Carrascosa	Universidad Politecnica de Valencia, Spain
Carlos D. Barranco	Pablo de Olavide University, Spain
Carlos Laorden	University of Deusto, Spain
Carlos Pereira	ISEC, Portugal
Cerasela Crisan	Vasile Alecsandri University of Bacau, Romania
Cezary Grabowik	Silesian Technical University, Poland
Constantin Zopounidis	Technical University of Crete, Greece
Damian Krenczyk	Silesian University of Technology, Poland
Dario Landa-Silva	University of Nottingham, UK
Darya Chyzhyk	University of the Basque Country, Spain
David Iclanzan	Hungarian Science University of Transylvania, Romania
Diego P. Ruiz	University of Granada, Spain
Dimitris Mourtzis	University of Patras, Greece
Dragan Simic	University of Novi Sad, Serbia
Dragos Horvath	Université de Strassbourg, France
Eiji Uchino	Yamaguchi University, Japan
Eva Volna	Univerzity of Ostrava, Czech Republic
Fabrício Olivetti De França	Universidade Federal do ABC, Brazil
Fermin Segovia	University of Liège, Belgium
Fidel Aznar	Universidad de Alicante, Spain
Florentino Fdez-Riverola	University of Vigo, Spain
Francisco Cuevas	Centro de Investigaciones en Óptica, A.C., Mexico
Francisco Martínez-Álvarez	Universidad Pablo de Olavide, Spain
Frank Klawonn	Ostfalia University of Applied Sciences, Germany
George Papakostas	TEI of Kavala, Greece
Georgios Dounias	University of the Aegean, Greece
Giancarlo Mauri	University of Milano-Bicocca, Italy
Giorgio Fumera	University of Cagliari, Italy

Gonzalo A. Aranda-Corral	Universidad de Huelva, Spain
Guiomar Corral	Ramon Llull University, Spain
Guoyin Wang	Chongqing University of Posts and Telecommunications, China
Héctor Quintián	University of Salamanca, Spain
Henrietta Toman	University of Debrecen, Hungary
Ignacio Turias	Universidad de Cádiz, Spain
Ingo R. Keck	Dublin Institute of Technology, Ireland
Ioannis Hatzilygeroudis	University of Patras, Greece
Irene Diaz	University of Oviedo, Spain
Isabel Barbancho	University of Málaga, Spain
Isabel Nepomuceno	University of Seville, Spain
Jaume Bacardit	University of Nottingham, UK
Javier Bajo	Universidad Politécnica de Madrid, Spain
Javier De Lope	Universidad Politécnica de Madrid, Spain
Javier Sedano	Instituto tecnológico de Castilla y León, Spain
Joaquín Derrac	University of Cardiff, UK
Jorge García-Gutiérrez	University of Seville, Spain
José C. Riquelme	University of Seville, Spain
José Dorronsoro	Universidad Autónoma de Madrid, Spain
José Garcia-Rodriguez	University of Alicante, Spain
José Luis Calvo Rolle	Universidad de A Coruña, Spain
José Luis Verdegay	Universidad de Granada, Spain
José M. Molina	Universidad Carlos III de Madrid, Spain
Jose Manuel Lopez-Guede	Basque Country University, Spain
José María Armingol	Universidad Carlos III de Madrid, Spain
José Ramón Villar	University of Oviedo, Spain
José-Ramón Cano De Amo	University of Jaen, Spain
Joses Ranilla	University of Oviedo, Spain
Juan Álvaro Muñoz Naranjo	University of Almería, Spain
Juan Humberto Sossa Azuela	National Polytechnic Institute, Mexico
Juan J. Flores	Universidad Michoacana de San Nicolas de Hidalgo, Mexico
Juán Pavón	Universidad Complutense de Madrid, Spain
Julio Ponce	Universidad Autónoma de Aguascalientes, Mexico
Krzysztof Kalinowski	Silesian University of Technology, Poland
Lauro Snidaro	University of Udine, Italy
Lenka Lhotska	Czech Technical University in Prague, Czech Republic
Leocadio G. Casado	University of Almeria, Spain
Lourdes Sáiz	University of Burgos, Spain
Manuel Grana	University of the Basque Country, Spain
Marcilio De Souto	LIFO/University of Orleans, France

María Guijarro	Universidad Complutense de Madrid, Spain
María Jose Del Jesus	Universidad de Jaén, Spain
María Martínez Ballesteros	University of Seville, Spain
María R. Sierra	Universidad de Oviedo, Spain
Mario Köeppen	Kyushu Institute of Technology, Japan
Martí Navarro	Universidad Politécnica de Valencia, Spain
Martin Macas	Czech Technical University in Prague, Czech Republic
Matjaz Gams	Jozef Stefan Institute, Slovenia
Miguel Ángel Patricio	Universidad Carlos III de Madrid, Spain
Miguel Ángel Veganzones	GIPSA-lab, Grenoble-INP, France
Miroslav Bursa	Czech Technical University in Prague, Czech Republic
Mohammed Chadli	University of Picardie Jules Verne, France
Nicola Di Mauro	Università di Bari, Italy
Nima Hatami	University of California, USA
Noelia Sanchez-Maroño	University of A Coruña, Spain
Oscar Fontenla-Romero	University of A Coruña, Spain
Ozgur Koray Sahingoz	Turkish Air Force Academy, Turkey
Paula M. Castro Castro	University of A Coruña, Spain
Paulo Novais	University of Minho, Portugal
Pavel Brandstetter	VSB-Technical University of Ostrava, Czech Republic
Peter Rockett	University of Sheffield, UK
Petrica Claudiu Pop	North University of Baia Mare, Romania
Rafael Alcala	University of Granada, Spain
Ramón Moreno	Universidad del País Vasco, Spain
Ramon Rizo	Universidad de Alicante, Spain
Ricardo Del Olmo	Universidad de Burgos, Spain
Robert Burduk	Wroclaw University of Technology, Poland
Rodolfo Zunino	University of Genoa, Italy
Roman Senkerik	Tomas Bata University in Zlin, Czech Republic
Ronald Yager	Iona College, USA
Rubén Fuentes-Fernández	Universidad Complutense de Madrid, Spain
Sean Holden	University of Cambridge, UK
Sebastián Ventura	University of Cordoba, Spain
Stella Heras	Universidad Politécnica de Valencia, Spain
Theodore Pachidis	Kavala Institute of Technology, Greece
Tomasz Kajdanowicz	Wroclaw University of Technology, Poland
Urko Zurutuza	Mondragon University, Spain
Urszula Stanczyk	Silesian University of Technology, Poland
Václav Snášel	VSB-Technical University of Ostrava, Czech Republic

Vasile Palade	Oxford University, UK
Waldemar Małopolski	Cracow University of Technology, Poland
Wei-Chiang Hong	Oriental Institute of Technology, Taiwan
Wiesław Chmielnicki	Jagiellonian University, Poland
Yannis Marinakis	Technical University of Crete, Greece
Ying Tan	Peking University, China
Yusuke Nojima	Osaka Prefecture University, Japan
Zuzana Oplatkova	Tomas Bata University in Zlin, Czech Republic

Organizing Committee

Emilio Corchado	University of Salamanca, Spain
Álvaro Herrero	University of Burgos, Spain
Bruno Baruque	University of Burgos, Spain
Héctor Quintián	University of Salamanca, Spain
José Luis Calvo	University of Coruña, Spain

Table of Contents

HAIS Applications

Data Mining and Knowledge Discovery

Video and Image Analysis

Bio-inspired Models and Evolutionary Computation

Learning Algorithms

Hybrid Intelligent Systems for Data Mining and Applications

Classification and Cluster Analysis

Computer Aided Diagnosis of Schizophrenia Based on Local-Activity Measures of Resting-State fMRI

Alexandre Savio*, Darya Chyzhyk, and Manuel Graña

Computational Intelligence Group, University of the Basque Country (UPV/EHU), San Sebastián, Spain

Abstract. Resting state functional Magnetic Resonance Imaging (rs-fMRI) is increasingly used for the identification of image biomarkers of brain diseases or psychiatric conditions, such as Schizophrenia. One approach is to perform classification experiments on the data, using feature extraction methods that allow to localize the discriminant locations in the brain, so that further studies may assess the clinical value of such locations. The classification accuracy results ensure that the located brain regions have some relation to the disease. In this paper we explore the discriminant value of brain local activity measures for the classification of Schizophrenia patients. The extensive experimental work, carried out on a publicly available database, provides evidence that local activity measures such as Regional Homogeneity (ReHo) may be useful for such purposes.

1 Introduction

There is a growing research effort devoted to the development of automated diagnostic support tools that may help clinicians perform their work with greater accuracy and efficiency. In medicine, diseases are often diagnosed with the aid of biological markers, including laboratory tests and radiologic imaging. The process of diagnosis difficult increases when dealing with psychiatric disorders, in which diagnosis relies primarily on the patient's self-report of symptoms, the presence or absence of characteristic behavioral signs and clinical history. This paper falls in the line of work that looks for image biomarkers, which are non-invasive and may provide additional objective evidence to aid in the clinical decision process.

Specifically, we are looking at resting-state fMRI (rs-fMRI) data, which is functional brain MRI data acquired when a subject is not performing an explicit task. Slow fluctuations in activity measured by the functional MRI signal of the resting brain allows to find correlated activity between brain regions. Measures on the correlation of these fluctuations provide functional connectivity maps

* This research has been partially funded by the Ministerio de Ciencia e Innovación of the Spanish Government, and the Basque Government funds for the research group.

M. Polycarpou et al. (Eds.): HAIS 2014, LNAI 8480, pp. 1–12, 2014.
© Springer International Publishing Switzerland 2014

that may serve as biomarkers or discriminant features for individual variations or dysfunction.

The extremely high dimensionality of a fMRI volume is one of the main issues for machine learning because it is considerably higher than the number of volumes collected for one experiment, i.e., tens of thousands of voxels vs. tens or hundreds of volumes. This difference forces the use of further preprocessing and/or data dimensionality reduction methods losing the least amount of information possible within a manageable computational cost [6]. Most resting-state fMRI studies perform functional connectivity analysis looking for temporal correlations between the time series of the fMRI signal in different brain regions. Nonetheless, functional connectivity delivers little insight about local properties of spontaneous brain activity observer in singular regions. Local measurements of brain activity provide information which is complementary to functional connectivity [14], so that they are being considered to find disease biomarkers. Here, we explore their usefulness for classification purposes, because they provide scalar maps that are different from other dimensionality reduction approaches.

Schizophrenia is a disabling psychiatric disorder characterized by hallucinations, delusions, disordered thought/speech, disorganized behavior, emotional withdrawal, and functional decline [2]. A large number of magnetic resonance imaging (MRI) morphological studies have shown subtle brain abnormalities to be present in schizophrenia. Since 1984, the works of Wernicke proposed that schizophrenia might involve altered connectivity of distributed brain networks that are diverse in function and that work in concert to support various cognitive abilities and their constituent operations [23]. Consistent with this "disconnectivity hypothesis", functional connectivity studies have found correlations between prefrontal and temporal lobe volumes [24] and disruptions of functional connectivity between frontal and temporal lobes in schizophrenia [15].

Experiments based on functional MRI data have been reported with small datasets , e.g. [20] achieved a 93% of accuracy on 44 matched subjects. A novel kernel approach (BDopt) to Support Vector Machines (SVM) and global network measures of brain network complexity has been reported [8] to classify a 18 subjects schizophrenia vs. controls dataset with 100% accuracy. The diffusion data from the same database have been previously tested and we also obtained 100% accuracy [18].

This paper studies the discrimination between Schizophrenia patients and healthy controls on the basis of local activity measures computed on rs-fMRI data. The aim is to find out if these measures can also contribute to the identification of biomarkers for the Computer Aided Diagnosis of Schizophrenia. Feature selection is performed on voxel saliency measures. The experimental work carried out has explored all combinations of the experimental factors involving data preprocessing, brain local activity measures, voxel saliency, and feature extraction parameters, as well as the classifiers applied. This kind of experiments are useful to understand which pre-processing methods and extracted features can be eligible for a hybrid classification system [3, 25].

Section 2 describes the database used for the experiments, as well as the preprocessing previous to feature extraction and classification. Section 3 describes the feature extraction methods, including the description of the brain local activity measures. Section 4 reviews the classifier methods used for the experiments. Section 5 reports the summary results of the computational experiments. Finally, section 6 gives the conclusions of the paper.

2 Resting-State Data and Preprocessing

Subjects

The Center for Biomedical Research Excellence in Brain Function and Mental Illness (COBRE) [1] is contributing raw anatomical and functional MR data from 72 patients with Schizophrenia and 74 healthy controls (ages ranging from 18 to 65 in each group) [5]. All subjects were screened and excluded if they had: history of neurological disorder, history of mental retardation, history of severe head trauma with more than 5 minutes loss of consciousness, history of substance abuse or dependence within the last 12 months. Diagnostic information was collected using the Structured Clinical Interview used for DSM Disorders (SCID). A multi-echo MPRAGE (MEMPR) sequence was used with the following parameters: TR/TE/TI = 2530/[1.64, 3.5, 5.36, 7.22, 9.08]/900 ms, flip angle = 7°, FOV = 256x256 mm, slab thickness = 176 mm, Matrix = 256x256x176, voxel size = 1x1x1 mm, number of echoes = 5, pixel bandwidth =650 Hz, total scan time = 6 min. With 5 echoes, the TR, TI and time to encode partitions for the MEMPR are similar to that of a conventional MPRAGE, resulting in similar GM/WM/CSF contrast. Resting state functional MRI (rs-fMRI) data was collected with single-shot full k-space echo-planar imaging (EPI) with ramp sampling correction using the intercomissural line (AC-PC) as a reference (TR: 2s, TE: 29ms, matrix size: 64x64, 32 slices, voxel size: 3x3x4mm).

Preprocessing

Preprocessing has been performed using the open source software pipeline Configurable Pipeline for the Analysis of Connectomes (C-PAC) [2], built upon AFNI [7], FSL (the FMRIB Software Library) [12] and FreeSurfer. Individual functional and anatomical acquisitions have been spatially normalized using FSL FNIRT [13] to match the MNI152 template [9] provided by the Montreal Neurological Institute . In addition, AFNI SkullStrip and FSL FAST [28] have been used for brain extraction and tissue segmentation. The first 6 fMRI volumes were discarded for transient removal, leaving a sequence of 144 fMRI volumes. The data preprocessing pipeline follows slice timing, head motion correction (Friston's 24 parameters motion model [11, 21]) and nuisance corrections (principal components regression and linear detrending). Pre-processing variations tested

[1] `http://cobre.mrn.org/`

[2] `http://fcp-indi.github.io/`

correspond to the four combinations of band-pass temporal filtering (TPF) between 0.01 and 0.1Hz [1] and global signal regression (GSR) [10], i.e. TPF-GSR means that we have performed band-pass filtering and global signal regression.

3 Feature Extraction Methods

The general pipeline of our feature selection and extraction methods is shown in Figure 1. The process starts from the computation of voxel-based measures from the rs-fMRI signal, resulting in separate 3D scalar maps for each measure *per* subject, that will be processed independently, i.e. we are not performing any kind of fusion of these scalar maps. The 3D scalar maps are input to the computation of a voxel site saliency measure relative to the actual subject class labels (i.e. control vs. patient), resulting in a 3D saliency map for each measure. Feature selection consists in the selection of the voxel sites with saliency above some percentile of the empirical distribution of saliency values in the 3D map. The values of the voxel-based scalar measures of fMRI signal for these voxel sites are used to build the feature vector per subject. This schema produces as many datasets for experimentation as possible combinations of scalar measures of fMRI signal, voxel saliency measures, and percentile threshold selection.

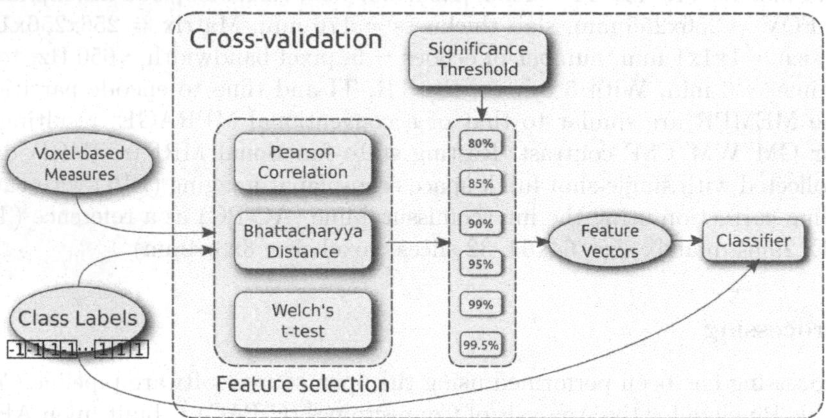

Fig. 1. Feature selection and extraction computational pipeline

3.1 Local Activity Measures from rs-fMRI

It has been proposed that local measurements of brain activity from rs-fMRI signal provide complementary information to functional connectivity analyses [14]. Measures on the slow fluctuations in activity in the resting brain may serve as discriminant features for individual dysfunction, as they can vary between brain regions and between subjects.

– *Amplitude of Low Frequency Fluctuations* (ALFF) [26] and *fractional Amplitude of Low Frequency Fluctuations* (fALFF) are measures of amplitude for low frequency oscillations (LFOs) of the fMRI signal. ALFF is defined as the total power within the frequency range between 0.01 and 0.1 Hz. fALFF is the relative contribution of specific LFO to the power of whole frequency range, defined as the power within the low-frequency range (0.01-0.1 Hz) split by the total power in the entire detectable frequency range [29].
– *Voxel-Mirrored Homotopic Connectivity* (VMHC) quantifies functional homotopy through a voxel-wise measure of connectivity between hemispheres, assuming the synchronization of spontaneous activity between homotopic (geometrically corresponding) regions at each hemisphere. The strength of these homotopic patterns can vary between regions [19], providing a fingerprint of the brain functional connectivity. An estimation of this connectivity is calculated between each voxel in one hemisphere and its mirrored counterpart in the other, assuming morphology symmetry between them. To ensure this property, a symmetric anatomical T1-weighted volume is created averaging the anatomical volume with its mirrored version. The fMRI data is registered to the symmetric anatomical volume.
– *Regional Homogeneity* (ReHo) is a voxel-based measure of brain activity which estimates the similarity between the time series of a given voxel and its nearest neighbors [27], requiring no *a priori* specification of ROIs. Similarity between voxel fMRI signal is computed as the Kendall's coefficient of concordance (KCC). In this paper the cluster size has been set to 27 neighboring voxels. The KCC values are standardized and smoothed (4mm FWHM) to build a voxel-based map for each subject.

3.2 Voxel Site Saliency Measures

Once we calculate the brain local activity measures, the following step is to select the most discriminant voxels in order to reduce the dimensionality of the data. We tackled this computing three distances between controls and patients, forming three independent experiments. The used voxel-wise distances were: the absolute value of the Pearson's Correlation Coefficient (PC) to the subject class labels, the univariate Gaussian Bhattacharyya distance (BD) and Welch's t-test (WT) between both groups [17].

4 Classification Algorithms

In this experiment we used Support Vector Machines [22] [3] and Random Forests [4] as classifiers [16].

[3] `http://www.csie.ntu.edu.tw/~cjlin/libsvm/`

Support Vector Machines (SVM). The kernel function chosen results in different kinds of SVM with different performance levels, and the choice of the appropriate kernel for a specific application is a difficult task. In this study two different kernels were tested: the linear and the radial basis function (RBF) kernel. The linear kernel function is defined as $K(\mathbf{x}_i, \mathbf{x}_j) = 1 + \mathbf{x}_i^T \mathbf{x}_j$, this kernel shows good performance for linearly separable data. The RBF kernel is defined as $K(\mathbf{x}_i, \mathbf{x}_j) = exp(-\frac{||\mathbf{x}_i - \mathbf{x}_j||^2}{2\sigma^2})$. This kernel is best suited to deal with data that have a class-conditional probability distribution function approaching the Gaussian distribution. The RBF kernel is largely used in the literature because it corresponds to the mapping into an infinite dimension feature space, and it can be tuned by its variance parameter σ.

Random Forests (RF) The critical parameters of the RF classifier for the experiments reported below are set as follows. The number of trees in the forest should be sufficiently large to ensure that each input class receives a number of predictions: we set it to 100. The number of variables randomly sampled at each split node is $\hat{d} = 5$.

Cross-Validation and Model Grid-Search. A 10-fold cross-validation was carried out to test the classification performance, we stratified training and test set in order to have proportional number of controls and patients in each random disjoint set. Class weights were set proportionally to the number of subjects in each group in the training set. In each validation fold, ten percent of the subjects are kept out to perform a grid search for model selection of classifiers parameters. We perform a 3-fold cross-validation on the training set using each possible combination of parameter values. In the parameter value grid for the linear SVM the only parameter to set is C, so that the grid search is performed in the set $\{1e-3, 1e-2, 1e-1, 1, 1e1, 1e2, 1e3\}$. For the RBF-SVM the parameters to be set are C and γ. For Random Forest this search is on the the number of trees in the set $\{3, 5, 10, 30, 50, 100\}$. Prior to analysis, each feature was normalized across subjects in the training sample via a Fisher z-score transformation. Normalization is required to avoid effects due to feature scale differences.

5 Results

The complete exposition of the experimental results would need more space than it is available here. It covers all combinations of four pre-processing processes, four local activity measures, three voxel saliency measures, six voxel selection percentiles (0.80, 0.90, 0.95, 0.99, 0.995 and 0.999), and three classifiers. We report only the mean and variance of the accuracy in the 10-fold cross-validation experiment, and the sensitivity, specificity, precision, F1-score, and Area under the Curve. First we present the summary of best classification results. Next, we present some feature localizations in the brain for the best combinations of experimental factors.

Summary Classification Results

Figures 2, 3 and 4 show the cross-validation performance its variance across all feature selection thresholds, for TPF-GSR and GSR ReHo data with Bhattacharyya's Distance and TPF-GSR ReHo with Pearson's correlation. The highest value reported is 80% with a 0.02 variance using on the TPF-GSR preprocessed ReHo data and Pearson's Correlation Coefficient voxels saliency for feature selection. In general terms, TPF-GSR preprocessing improves over all other preprocessing pipelines, ReHo is the best local activity measure, and the Pearson Correlation Coefficient is the best voxel saliency measure.

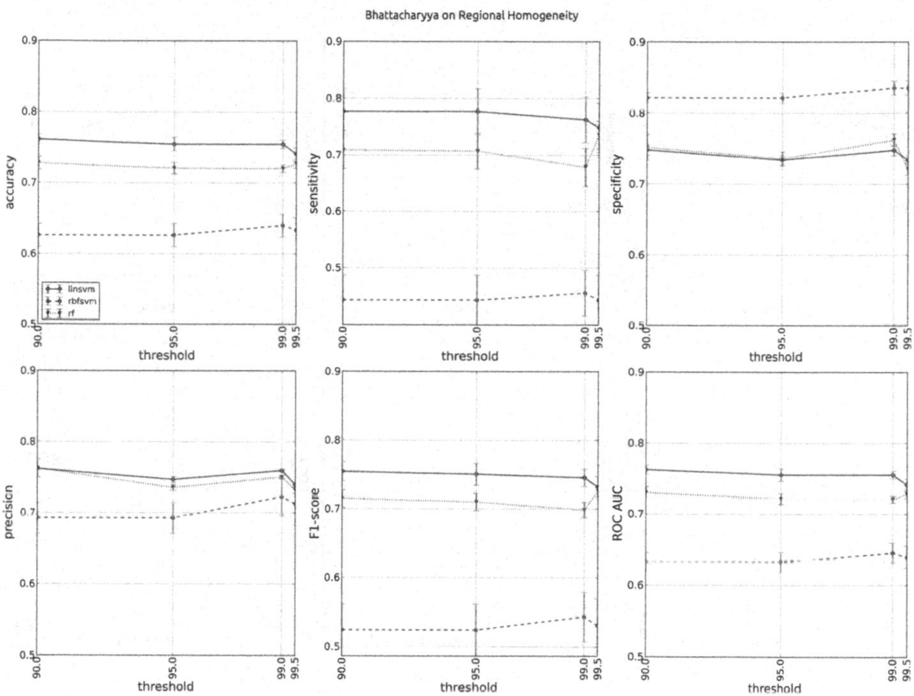

Fig. 2. Classification performance using TPF-GSR ReHo data and the Bhattacharyya's distance

Selected Features Localization

The extracted features sites can be seen as candidate to be discussed as biomarkers for the disease. Their localization on the Harvard-Oxford Cortical Structural Atlas of selected voxel clusters and the brain regions show high overlap with the Inferior Temporal Gyrus, anterior division of the Parahippocampal Gyrus, Planum Polare, Temporal Fusiform Cortex, and Left and Right Thalamus.

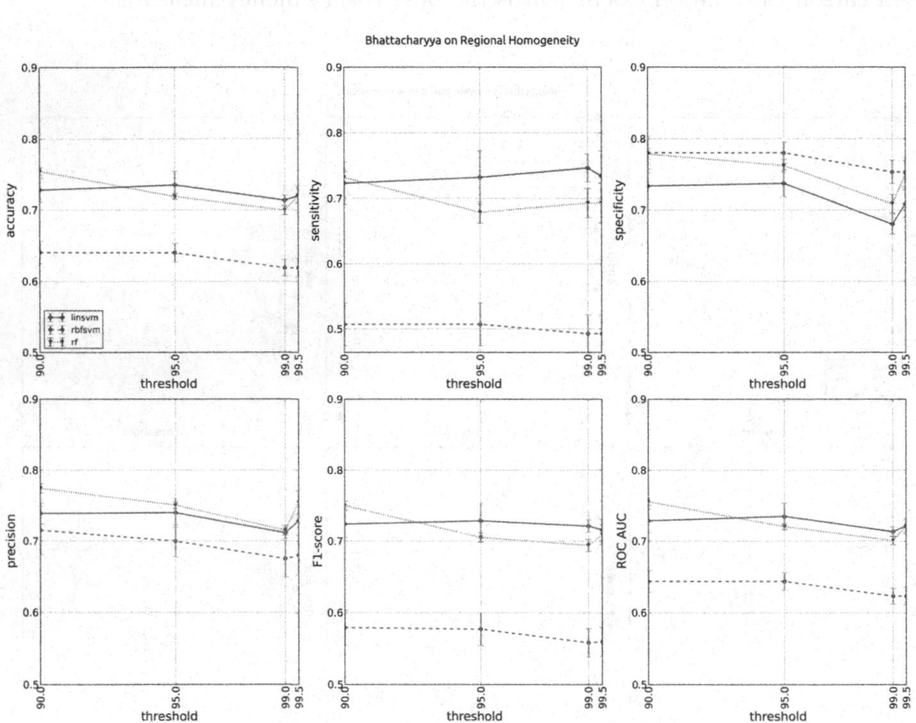

Fig. 3. Classification performance using GSR ReHo data and the Bhattacharyya's distance

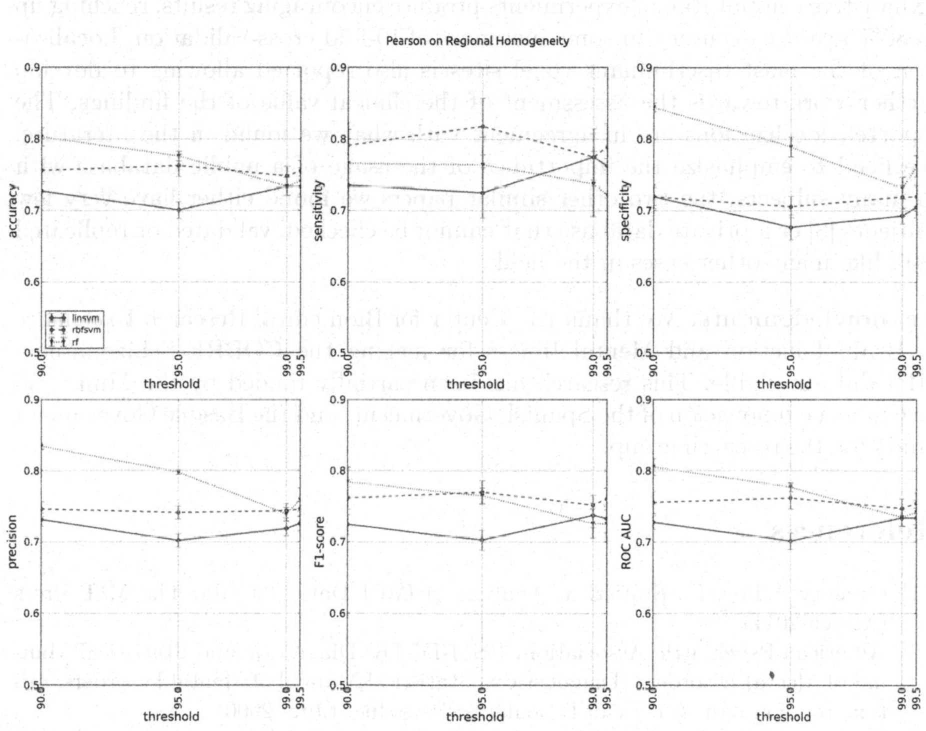

Fig. 4. Classification performance using TPF-GSR ReHo data and the Pearson's correlation

6 Conclusions

In this paper we report results on a Computer Aided Diagnosis (CAD) system based on features selected from brain local activity measures computed on resting-state fMRI data. The purpose of this work was to explore the discriminant power of brain local activity measures, so we have designed a classification experiment on a database of Schizophrenia patients and healthy controls, the COBRE database recently made available to the public. We have studied four local activity measures and three voxel saliency measures for feature selection. Exhaustive computational experiments produce encouraging results, reaching up to 80% average accuracy in some instances of 10-fold cross-validation. Localization of the most discriminant voxel sites is also reported allowing to develop further work towards the assessment of the clinical value of the findings. The reported localizations are in agreement with what we found in the literature. We need to emphasize the importance of the usage of a public database with so many subjects, the two other similar papers we found either have very few subjects [8] or a private database that cannot be checked, validated or replicated [20], like many other cases in the field.

Acknowledgments. We thank the Center for Biomedical Research Excellence in Brain Function and Mental Illness for making the COBRE Schizophrenia MRI data available. This research has been partially funded by the Ministerio de Ciencia e Innovación of the Spanish Government, and the Basque Government funds for the research group.

References

[1] Gregory Ashby, F.: Statistical Analysis of fMRI Data, 1st edn. The MIT Press (March 2011)

[2] American Psychiatric Association. DSM-IV-TR: Diagnostic and Statistical Manual of Mental Disorders (Diagnostic & Statistical Manual of Mental Disorders, 4th text revision edn. American Psychiatric Press Inc. (July 2000)

[3] Borrajo, M.L., Baruque, B., et al.: Hybrid neural intelligent system to predict business failure in small-to-medium size enterprise. International Journal of Neural Systems 21(04), 277–296 (2011) 00012

[4] Breiman, L.: Random forests. Machine Learning 45(1), 5–32 (2001)

[5] Calhoun, V.D., Sui, J., Kiehl, K., et al.: Exploring the psychosis functional connectome: aberrant intrinsic networks in schizophrenia and bipolar disorder. Frontiers in Neuropsychiatric Imaging and Stimulation 2, 75 (2012)

[6] Castro, E., et al.: Characterization of groups using composite kernels and multisource fMRI analysis data: Application to schizophrenia. NeuroImage 58(2), 526–536 (2011)

[7] Cox, R.W.: AFNI: what a long strange trip it's been. NeuroImage 62(2), 743–747 (2012)

[8] Fekete, T., et al.: Combining classification with fMRI-Derived complex network measures for potential neurodiagnostics. PLoS ONE 8(5), e62867 (2013)
[9] Fonov, V., Evans, A.C., Botteron, K., Almli, C.R., McKinstry, R.C., Collins, D.L.: Unbiased average age-appropriate atlases for pediatric studies. NeuroImage 54(1), 313–327 (2011) PMID: 20656036 PMCID: PMC2962759
[10] Fox, M.D., Zhang, D., Snyder, A.Z., Raichle, M.E.: The global signal and observed anticorrelated resting state brain networks. Journal of Neurophysiology 101(6), 3270–3283 (2009) PMID: 19339462
[11] Friston, K.J., Williams, S., Howard, R., Frackowiak, R.S., Turner, R.: Movement-related effects in fMRI time-series. Magnetic Resonance in Medicine: Official Journal of the Society of Magnetic Resonance in Medicine / Society of Magnetic Resonance in Medicine 35(3), 346–355 (1996) PMID: 8699946
[12] Jenkinson, M., et al.: FSL. NeuroImage 62(2), 782–790 (2012)
[13] Jenkinson, M., Smith, S.: A global optimisation method for robust affine registration of brain images. Medical Image Analysis 5(2), 143–156 (2001)
[14] Liu, D., Yan, C., Ren, J., Yao, L., Kiviniemi, V.J., Zang, Y.: Using coherence to measure regional homogeneity of restingstate fMRI signal. Frontiers in Systems Neuroscience 4, 24 (2010)
[15] McGuire, P.K., Frith, C.D.: Disordered functional connectivity in schizophrenia. Psychological Medicine 26(4), 663–667 (1996) PMID: 8817700
[16] Pedregosa, F., Varoquaux, G., Gramfort, A., Michel, V., Thirion, B., et al.: Scikit-learn: Machine learning in python. Journal of Machine Learning Research 12, 2825–2830 (2011)
[17] Savio, A., Graña, M.: Deformation based feature selection for computer aided diagnosis of alzheimer's disease. Expert Systems with Applications 40(5), 1619–1628 (2013) 00006
[18] Charpentier, J., Savio, A.: Neural classifiers for schizophrenia diagnostic support on diffusion imaging data. Neural Network World 20, 935–949 (2010) 00005
[19] Stark, D.E., Margulies, D.S., et al.: Regional variation in interhemispheric coordination of intrinsic hemodynamic fluctuations. The Journal of Neuroscience 28(51), 13754–13764 (2008)
[20] Tang, Y., Wang, L., Cao, F., Tan, L.: Identify schizophrenia using resting-state functional connectivity: an exploratory research and analysis. BioMedical Engineering OnLine 11(1), 50 (2012) PMID: 22898249
[21] Van Dijk, K.R.A., Sabuncu, M.R., Buckner, R.L.: The influence of head motion on intrinsic functional connectivity MRI. NeuroImage 59(1), 431–438 (2012)
[22] Vapnik, V.N.: Statistical Learning Theory. Wiley-Interscience (September 1998)
[23] Wernicke, C.: Grundriss der Psychiatrie in klinischen Vorlesungen / von Carl Wernicke. VDM Verlag Dr. Müller, Saarbrücken (2007)
[24] Wible, C.G., Shenton, M.E., Hokama, H., Kikinis, R., Jolesz, F.A., Metcalf, D., McCarley, R.W.: Prefrontal cortex and schizophrenia: A quantitative magnetic resonance imaging study. Archives of General Psychiatry 52(4), 279–288 (1995)
[25] Wozniak, M., Graña, M., Corchado, E.: A survey of multiple classifier systems as hybrid systems. Information Fusion 16, 3–17 (2014) 00010
[26] Zang, Y.-F., et al.: Altered baseline brain activity in children with ADHD revealed by resting-state functional MRI. Brain & Development 29(2), 83–91 (2007) PMID: 16919409

[27] Zang, Y., et al.: Regional homogeneity approach to fMRI data analysis. NeuroImage 22(1), 394–400 (2004)
[28] Zhang, Y., Brady, M., Smith, S.: Segmentation of brain MR images through a hidden markov random field model and the expectation-maximization algorithm. IEEE Transactions on Medical Imaging 20(1), 45–57 (2001)
[29] Zuo, X.-N., Martino, A.D., Kelly, C., et al.: The oscillating brain: Complex and reliable. NeuroImage 49(2), 1432–1445 (2010) PMID: 19782143 PMCID: PMC2856476

A Variable Neighborhood Search Approach for Solving the Generalized Vehicle Routing Problem

Petrică C. Pop[1], Levente Fuksz[2], and Andrei Horvat Marc[1]

[1] Department of Mathematics and Computer Science, Technical University of Cluj-Napoca, North University Center of Baia Mare, Romania
[2] Indeco Soft, Baia Mare, Romania

Abstract. Variable Neighborhood Search (VNS) is quite a recent metaheuristic used for solving optimization problems based on a systematic change of the neighborhoods structures within the search in order to avoid local optima. In this paper, we propose a VNS based heuristic for solving the generalized vehicle routing problem (GVRP) that uses different neighborhood structures which are adapted for the problem. Computational results for an often used collection of benchmark instances show that our proposed heuristic delivered competitive results compared to the existing state-of-the-art algorithms for solving the GVRP.

1 Introduction

The generalized vehicle routing problem (GVRP) was introduced by Ghiani and Improta [5] and belongs to the class of generalized network design problems, known as well as generalized combinatorial optimization problems, we refer to [10] for more details. Characteristic for this class of problems is the fact that it generalizes in a natural way many network design problems by considering a related problem on a clustered graph (i.e. graph where the nodes are replaced by node sets), where the original problem's feasibility constraints are expressed in terms of the clusters instead of individual nodes. In the literature several generalized network design problems have been already considered: the generalized minimum spanning tree problem, the generalized traveling salesman problem, the generalized vehicle routing problem, the generalized fixed-charge network design problem, the selective graph coloring problem, etc.

The GVRP consists of designing optimally delivery or collection routes, from a given depot to a number of predefined, mutually exclusive and exhaustive clusters (node sets) subject to capacity restrictions. The problem has several applications: some extended naturally from the Vehicle Routing Problem (VRP) or the generalized traveling salesman problem (GTSP) and others specific to GVRP: the design of tandem configurations for automated guided vehicles, the design of routes visiting a number of customers situated in some islands of an archipelago, health-care logistics, urban waste collection problem, etc.

M. Polycarpou et al. (Eds.): HAIS 2014, LNAI 8480, pp. 13–24, 2014.
© Springer International Publishing Switzerland 2014

Two variants of the GVRP have been considered: one in which at least one node has to be selected from each cluster [1] and the clustered GVRP in which all the nodes of each cluster must be visited consecutively [14].

Due to the complexity of the problem, efficient transformations of the GVRP into classical combinatorial optimization problems, for which exist heuristics, approximation algorithms or optimal solution methods, have been developed: Ghiani and Improta [5] considered a transformation of the GVRP into Capacitated Arc Routing Problem (CARP), while Pop and Pop Sitar [13] considered an efficient transformation of the GVRP into classical VRP.

Integer programming formulations have been developed by Pop et al. [14]: a so called node formulation and a flow based formulation and by Bektas et al. [1]: two based on multicommodity flow and the other two based on exponential sets of inequalities. The latter authors have proposed as well some branch-and-cut algorithms based on two of their models.

Due to its practical applications, the GVRP has generated a considerable interest in the last period. The difficulty of obtaining optimum solutions for the GVRP has led to the development of some metaheuristic approaches. The first such algorithms were: an ant colony system based algorithm developed by Pop et al. [11] and a genetic algorithm based heuristic [12]. Bektas et al. [2] proposed an adaptive large neighborhood search, an incremental tabu search heuristic was described by Moccia et al. [8] and a hybrid heuristic algorithm obtained by combining a genetic algorithm (GA) with a local-global approach to the GVRP and a powerful local search procedure was developed by Pop et al. [15].

The aim of this paper is to develop an efficient Variable Neighborhood Search (VNS) approach for the GVRP. VNS is quite a recent metaheuristic used for solving optimization problems based on a systematic change of the neighborhoods structures within the search in order to avoid local optima and to head for a global optimum. For more details on the VNS we refer to [6,7]. Our heuristic is tested against state-of-the-art algorithms on a set of 20 benchmark instances from the literature and as will be shown in the computational experiments section, the proposed approach provides high quality solutions.

The remainder of this article is organized as follows. In Section 2, we give the formal definition of the GVRP. Section 3 describes the components of our VNS approach in detail, Section 4 describes the instances used in our computational experiments and Section 5 presents the obtained computational results. Finally, Section 6 concludes our work and provides some future work plans.

2 Definition of the Generalized Vehicle Routing Problem

In this section we give a formal definition of the GVRP as a graph theoretic model. Let $G = (V, A)$ be a directed graph with $V = \{0, 1, 2, ..., n\}$ as the set of vertices and the set of arcs $A = \{(i, j) \mid i, j \in V, i \neq j\}$. The graph G must be strongly connected and in general it is assumed to be complete.

Vertices $i = 1, ..., n$ correspond to the customers and the vertex 0 corresponds to the depot. The entire set of vertices is partitioned into $k+1$ mutually exclusive nonempty subsets, called clusters, $V_0, V_1, ..., V_k$ (i.e. $V = V_0 \cup V_1 \cup ... \cup V_k$ and $V_l \cap V_p = \emptyset$ for all $l, p \in \{0, 1, ..., k\}$ and $l \neq p$). The cluster V_0 has only one vertex 0, which represents the depot, and remaining n vertices are belonging to the remaining k clusters. A nonnegative cost c_{ij} is associated with each arc $(i, j) \in A$ and represents the travel cost spent to go from vertex i to vertex j.

Each customer i $(i = 1, ..., n)$ is associated with a known nonnegative demand d_i to be delivered and the depot has a fictitious demand $d_0 = 0$. Given a cluster $V_p \subset V$, let $d(V_p) = \sum_{i \in V_p} d_i$ the total demand of the cluster V_p, $p = 1, ..., k$ and we assume that each cluster can be satisfied via any of its nodes.

There exist m identical vehicles, each with a capacity Q and to ensure feasibility we assume that $d_i \leq Q$ for each $i = 1, ..., n$. Each vehicle may perform at most one route.

The *generalized vehicle routing problem* (GVRP) consists in finding a collection of simple circuits (each corresponding to a vehicle route) with minimum cost, defined as the sum of the costs of the arcs belonging to the circuits and such that the following constraints hold: each circuit visits the depot vertex, each cluster should be visited exactly once by a circuit, the entering and leaving nodes of each of the clusters should be the same and the sum of the demands of the visited vertices by a circuit does not exceed the capacity of the vehicle, Q.

An illustrative scheme of the GVRP and a feasible tour is shown in the next figure.

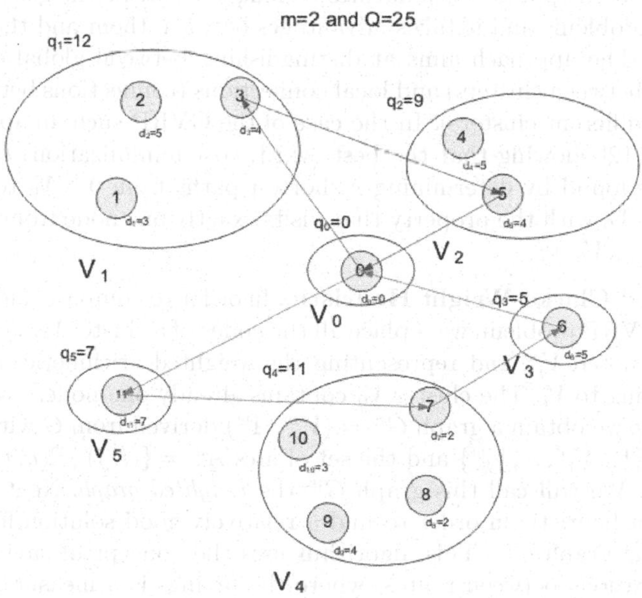

Fig. 1. An example of a feasible solution of the GVRP

A feasible solution of the GVRP consists of a collection of routes, each visiting the depot and exactly one node from each cluster. We will call such a route a *generalized route.* The order of visiting the clusters is called *global route.*

The GVRP reduces to the classical Vehicle Routing Problem (VRP) when all the clusters are singletons and to the Generalized Traveling Salesman Problem (GTSP) when $m = 1$ and $Q = \infty$. The GVRP is NP-hard because it includes GTSP as a special case when $m = 1$ and $Q = \infty$.

3 Variable Neighborhood Search (VNS) for the GVRP

In this section, we describe our VNS approach in detail. First, we consider a constructive heuristic based on the [3] heuristic for the classical VRP to produce initial solutions. In Section 3.2, we describe the neighborhoods and the search techniques applied to them and finally, Section 3.3 presents the VNS framework.

3.1 Creating Initial Solutions

Our strategy for determining an initial solution for the GVRP is inspired by the Clarke-Wright savings algorithm for the classical vehicle routing problem [3] and therefore is called the Adapted Clarke-Wright Heuristic (ACWH). Before describing the ACWH, we describe the local-global procedure that is going to be used in our heuristic for creating initial solutions and as well in all our neighborhoods as a subroutine.

The local-global approach is a natural technique to tackle the generalized network design problems and it takes advantages between them and their classical variants [10]. The approach aims at distinguishing between global connections (connections between clusters) and local connections (connections between nodes belonging to different clusters). In the case of the GVRP such an approach was presented in [12] showing that the best (w.r.t. cost minimization) collection of routes can be found by determining r shortest paths from $0 \in V_0$ to the corresponding $0' \in V_0$ with the property that visits exactly one node from each of the clusters $(V_{k_1}, ..., V_{k_p})$.

The Adapted Clarke-Wright Heuristic. In order to compute a feasible solution for the GVRP problem, we replace all the nodes of a cluster V_i, $\forall i \in \{1, ..., k\}$ by a node denoted V_i^w and representing the weighted arithmetic mean of the nodes belonging to V_i. The cluster V_0 contains already one node.

In this way, we obtain a graph $G^w = (V^w, A^w)$ derived from G with the set of nodes $V^w = \{V_0, V_1^w, ..., V_k^w\}$ and the set of arcs $A^w = \{(i,j) \mid \exists(u,v) \in A \wedge u \in V_i \wedge v \in V_j\}$. We will call this graph G^w the *weighted graph.* Next we use the Clarke-Wright heuristic in order to find a relatively good solution for the VRP defined on the graph G^w. This algorithm uses the concept of savings to rank merging operations between routes, where the savings is a measure of the cost reduction obtained by combining two small routes into one larger route.

The obtained feasible solution consists of a collection of routes on G^w that will provide us the sequence in which the corresponding clusters on G are visited.

Finally, having the sequences in which the clusters are visited, we use the local-global procedure in order to find the collection of best generalized routes, i.e. an initial feasible solution of the GVRP.

3.2 Neighborhoods

Our VNS algorithm applies 8 types of neighborhoods, each of them focusing on different aspects and properties of the solutions to the GVRP. We divided these neighborhoods into two classes depending if they operate on a single route or if they consider more than one route simultaneously. All the considered neighborhoods are defined at the level of the global graph.

The neighborhoods from the first class are obtained by moving one or more clusters from one position in the global route to another position in the same route and are called *intra-route* neighborhoods. We considered in our VNS three such neighborhoods: *Two-opt neighborhood, Three-opt neighborhood* and *Or-opt neighborhood.* The moves defined within the intra-route neighborhoods are used in order to reduce the overall distance.

The other class, called *inter-route neighborhoods* work with two global routes. They are used in order to reduce the overall distance and in some cases they can reduce as well the number of vehicles. We considered in our VNS five such neighborhoods: *1-0 Exchange neighborhood, 1-1 Exchange neighborhood, 1-2 Exchange neighborhood, Relocate neighborhood* and *Cross-exchange neighborhood.*

For each candidate solution provided by any of the mentioned neighborhoods, we apply the local-global procedure in order to find the best collection of routes (w.r.t. cost minimization) visiting the clusters according to the given sequences.

Two-opt Neighborhood. In the case of the GVRP, in a Two-opt neighborhood two global arcs corresponding to two arcs belonging to a single route are replaced by two other global arcs in order to improve the total cost of the route. Then using the local-global procedure, we find the best corresponding feasible solution and check if the cost of the route was improved. The size of the Two-opt neighborhood is quadratic (w.r.t. the number of clusters) and there is only one proper move type. The following figure illustrates this process.

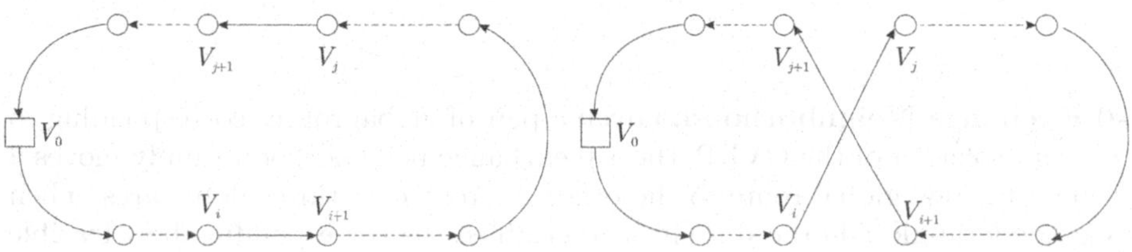

Fig. 2. Example showing a two-opt exchange move

Three-opt Neighborhood. The Three-opt neighborhood extends the Two-opt neighborhood and involves deleting three arcs in a route and reconnecting the three remaining paths in all other possible ways, and then evaluating each of the reconnecting methods in order to find the optimum one. The size of the Three-opt neighborhood is cubic and there are three proper move types. The following figure illustrates this process and an contains an example of a proper move.

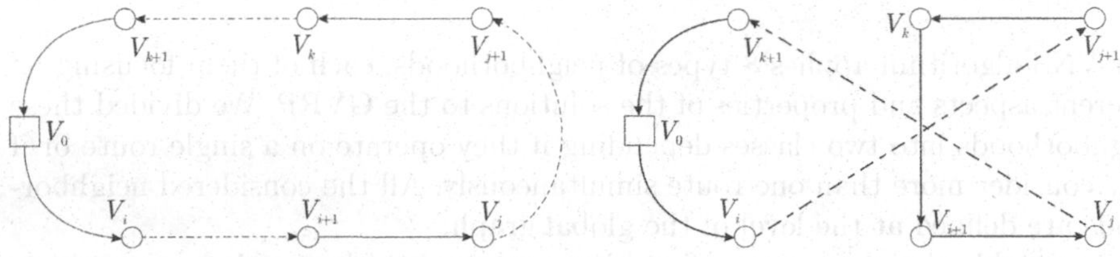

Fig. 3. Example showing a three-opt exchange move

Or-opt Neighborhood. The Or-opt heuristic designed in the case of TSP, is due to [9]. It attempts to improve the current tour by first moving a chain of three consecutive vertices in a different location (and possibly reversing it) until no further improvement can be obtained.

In the case of the GVRP, in a Or-opt neighborhood a sequence of consecutive customers, usually one, two or three, are relocated within the route. The size of the Or-opt neighborhood is quadratic with the condition that the length of the sequence is bounded. The following figure illustrates this process and an contains an example of a proper move.

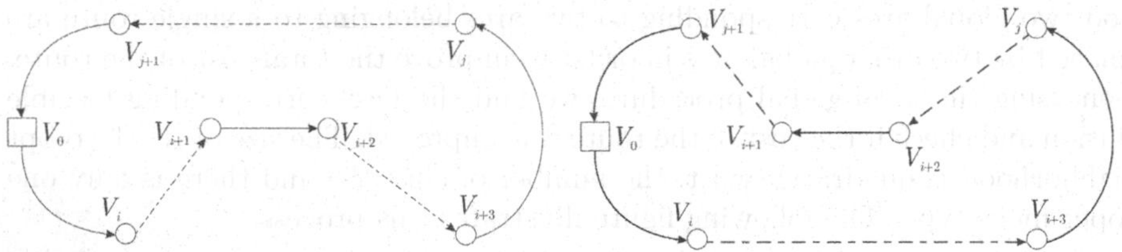

Fig. 4. Example showing a Or-opt exchange move

1-0 Exchange Neighborhood. Given a pair of global routes corresponding to a current solution of the GVRP, the 1-0 exchange neighborhood simply moves a cluster from one global route to the other, by replacing three global arcs. Then using the local-global procedure it is determined the corresponding best feasible solution of the GVRP w.r.t. the new collection of global routes. The following figure illustrates this process.

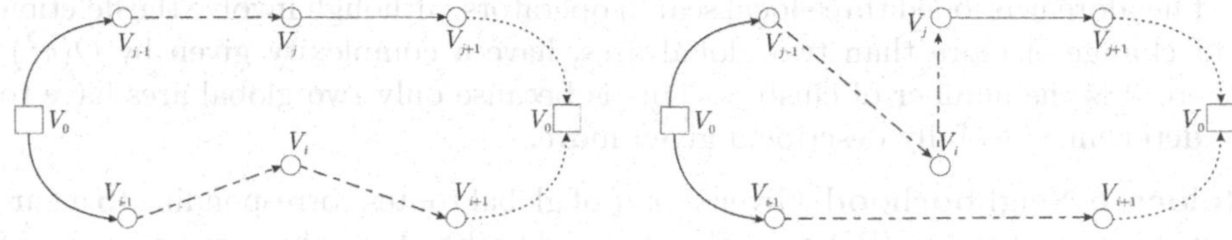

Fig. 5. Example showing a 1-0 Exchange move

1-1 Exchange Neighborhood. Given a pair of global routes corresponding to a current solution of the GVRP, the 1-1 exchange neighborhood swaps the positions of a cluster pair belonging to two different global routes, by removing four global arcs and creating four new ones. Then again using the local-global procedure it is determined the corresponding best feasible solution of the GVRP w.r.t. the new collection of global routes. The following figure illustrates this process.

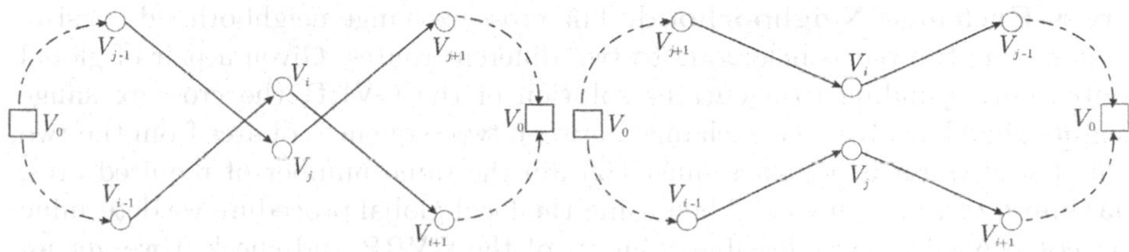

Fig. 6. Example showing a 1-1 Exchange move

1-2 Exchange Neighborhood. Given a pair of global routes corresponding to a current solution of the GVRP, the 1-2 exchange neighborhood swaps the positions of a cluster belonging to one global route with two consecutive clusters from the other global route, by removing four global arcs and creating four new ones. The following figure illustrates this process.

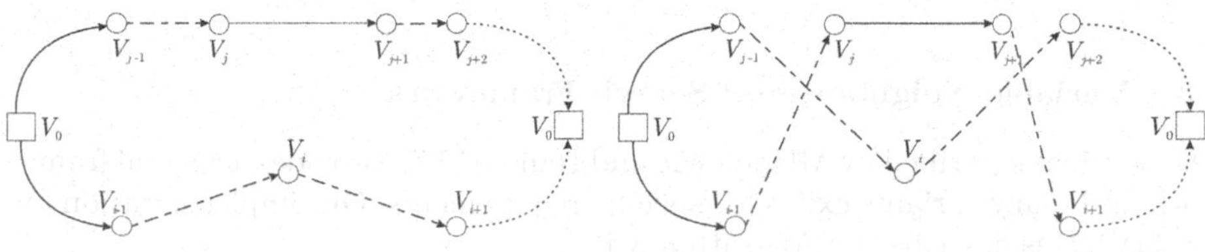

Fig. 7. Example showing a 1-2 Exchange move

The aforementioned three local search operators, although involve the deletion and change of more than two global arcs, have a complexity given by $O(k^2)$, where k is the number of clusters. This is because only two global arcs have to be determined to fully describe a given move.

Relocate Neighborhood. Given a pair of global routes corresponding to a current solution of the GVRP, the relocate neighborhood simply moves a sequence of 2,3 or 4 global arcs from one global route to another one. The following figure illustrates this process.

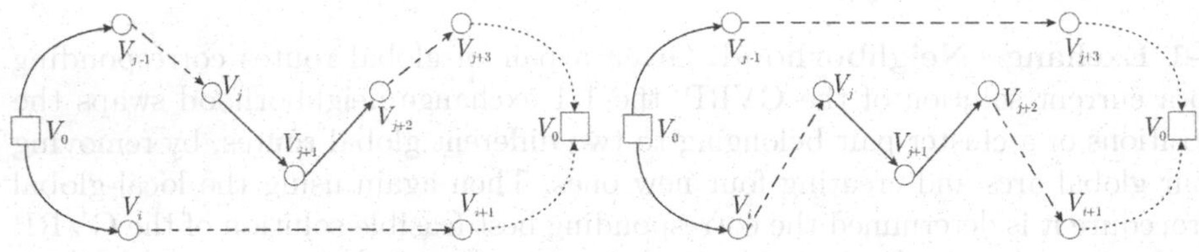

Fig. 8. Example showing a 1-2 Exchange move

Cross-Exchange Neighborhood. The cross-exchange neighborhood consists in swapping two paths belonging to two different routes. Given a pair of global routes corresponding to a current solution of the GVRP, the cross-exchange neighborhood involves the exchange between two sequences of arcs from the two global routes. Each sequence must contain the same number of required arcs, maximum three in our case. Then using the local-global procedure we determine the corresponding best feasible solution of the GVRP and check if we get an improvement of the solution. The following figure illustrates this process.

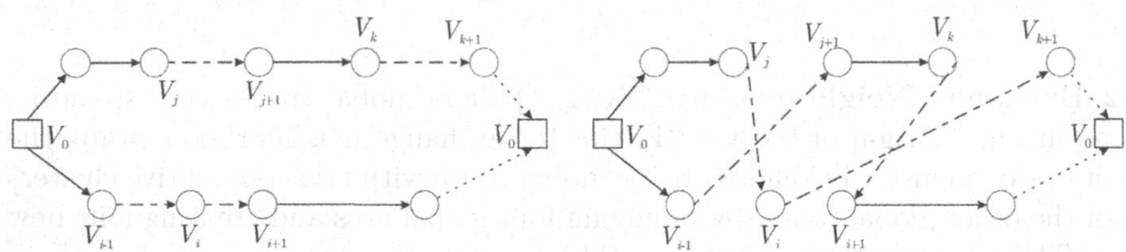

Fig. 9. Example showing a cross-exchange for $k = 2$

3.3 Variable Neighborhood Search Framework

The VNS, as described by Mladenovic and Hansen [6,7], provides a general framework and many variants exists for specific requirements. Our implementation for the GVRP is described in Algorithm 3.1.

Given a directed graph $G = (V, A)$ with n nodes partitioned into $k+1$ clusters, each node $i \in V$ having a nonnegative demand d_i, each arc $(i, j) \in A$ having a nonnegative cost c_{ij} and m vehicles of capacity Q, we want to find a collection of routes each visiting the depot and exactly one node from each cluster with minimum cost.

Variable Neighborhood Search Framework for GVRP
Initialization. Select a set of neighborhoods structures $\mathcal{N}=\{\mathcal{N}_l \mid l = 1,...,8\}$; find an initial solution x; choose a stopping criterion
Repeat the following sequence till the stopping criterion is met:
(1) Set $l = 1$;
(2) Repeat the following steps until $l = 8$:
Step 1 (Shaking): Generate $x' \in \mathcal{N}_l$ at random;
Step 2 (Local Search): Apply a local search method starting with x' as initial solution and denote by x'' the obtained local optimum ;
Step 3 (Move or not): If the local optimum x'' is better than the incumbent x, *then* move there ($x \leftarrow x''$) and continue the search with $\mathcal{N}_1$
otherwise set $l = l + 1$ (or if $l = 8$ set ($l = 1$);
Go back to Step 1.

According to this basic scheme, we can observe that our VNS is a random descent first improvement heuristic.

The algorithm starts from an initial feasible solution x generated by a heuristic adapted from the Clarke-Wright heuristic and with with the set of the following 8 nested neighborhood structures: 1-0 Exchange neighborhood ($\mathcal{N}_1$), 1-1 Exchange neighborhood ($\mathcal{N}_2$), 1-2 Exchange neighborhood ($\mathcal{N}_3$), Relocate neighborhood ($\mathcal{N}_4$), Two-opt neighborhood ($\mathcal{N}_5$), Three-opt neighborhood ($\mathcal{N}_6$), Or-opt neighborhood ($\mathcal{N}_7$) and Cross-Exchange neighborhood ($\mathcal{N}_8$). They have the property that their sizes are increasing. Then a point x' at random (in order to avoid cycling) is selected within the first neighborhood $\mathcal{N}_1(x)$ of x and a descent from x' is done with the local search routine. This will lead to a new local minimum x''. At this point, there exists three possibilities:

1) $x'' = x$, i.e. we are again at the bottom of the same valley and we continue the search using the next neighborhood $\mathcal{N}_l(x)$ with $l \geq 2$;
2) $x'' \neq x$ and $f(x'') \geq f(x)$, i.e. we found a new local optimum but which is worse than the previous incumbent solution. Also in this case, we will continue the search using the next neighborhood $\mathcal{N}_l(x)$ with $l \geq 2$;
3) $x'' \neq x$ and $f(x'') < f(x)$, i.e. we found a new local optimum but which is better than the previous incumbent solution. In this case, the search is re-centered around x'' and begins with the first neighborhood.

If the last neighborhood has been reached without finding a better solution than the incumbent, than the search begins again with the first neighborhood $\mathcal{N}_1(x)$ until a stopping criterion is satisfied. In our case, as stopping criterion we have chosen a maximum number of iterations since the last improvement.

4 Test Instances

In this section we present the test instances used in our computational experiments. We conducted computational experiments on two sets of instances.

The first set of instances were considered used by Pop et al. [11,12] in their computational experiments. These instances were generated in a similar manner to that of Fischetti et al. [4] who have derived the generalized traveling salesman problem (GTSP) instances from the existing TSP instances. These problems were drawn from *TSPLIB* library test problems and contain between 51 and 101 customers (nodes), which are partitioned into a given number of clusters, and in addition the depot. The second set of instances used in our computational experiments were generated through an adaptation of the existing instances in the CVRP-library available at *http://branchandcut.org/VRP/data/*.

Originally the set of nodes in these problems were not divided into clusters. Fischetti et al. [4] proposed a procedure to partition the nodes of the graph into clusters, called CLUSTERING. This procedure sets the number of clusters $s = [\frac{n}{\theta}]$, identifies the s farthest nodes from each other and finally assigns each remaining node to its nearest center. We considered for our instances as in [2,8] a clustering procedure with $\theta = 3$. However, the solution approach proposed in this paper is able to handle any cluster structure.

5 Computational Results

This section presents the obtained computational results for solving the generalized vehicle routing problem with our proposed VNS heuristic. The testing machine was an Intel Core 2 Quad Q6600 and 3.50 GB RAM with Windows 7 as operating system. The VNS algorithm has been developed in Microsoft .NET Framework 4 using C #.

In the next table are shown the computational results obtained for solving the *GVRP* using the proposed VNS based heuristic algorithm comparing with the GA [12] and ACS algorithm [11] using the first set of instances existing in the literature.

Table 1. Best values and computational times - *ACS*, *GA* and *VNS* algorithms for *GVRP*

Problem	*ACS*	*Time ACS*	*GA*	*Time GA*	*VNS*	*Time VNS*
11eil51	418.85	212	237.00	7	233.910	0.656
16eil76A	668.78	18	583.80	18	309.299	1.545
16eil76B	625.83	64	540.87	95	291.205	0.321
16eil76C	553.21	215.00	336.45	50	237.876	0.197
16eil76D	508.81	177.00	295.55	12	232.296	0.651

In the first column of Table 1 we presented the name of the instance followed by the best solutions obtained by using ACS algorithm [11], genetic algorithm [12] and our VNS heuristic together with the corresponding computational times.

Table 2. Computational results on small and medium instances with $\theta = 3$

Instance	*LB*	*ALNS*	*ITS*	*HA*	*VNS*
A-n32-k5-C11-V2	386	386	386	386	386
A-n33-k5-C11-V2	315	318	315	315	315
A-n34-k5-C12-V2	419	419	419	419	419
A-n45-k6-C15-V3	474	474	474	474	474
A-n55-k9-C19-V3	473	473	473	473	473
B-n31-k5-C11-V2	356	356	356	356	356
B-n34-k5-C12-V2	369	369	369	369	369
B-n35-k5-C12-V2	501	501	501	501	501
B-n39-k5-C13-V2	280	280	280	280	280
B-n50-k7-C17-V3	393	393	393	393	393
P-n16-k8-C6-V4	170	170	170	170	170
P-n20-k2-C7-V1	117	117	117	117	117
P-n22-k2-C8-V1	111	111	111	111	111
P-n23-k8-C8-V3	174	174	174	174	175
P-n50-k7-C17-V3	261	261	261	261	261

Analyzing the computational results, it results that the proposed VNS heuristic outperforms the ant colony algorithm [11] and the GA [12] in terms of both solution quality and computational times. As well, we can observe that our proposed algorithm has short computational running times.

In Table 2, we summarize the results of our VNS algorithm in comparison to the adaptive large neighborhood search [1], the incremental tabu search [8] and the hybrid algorithm [12] on 15 small to medium instances with $\theta = 3$.

The first column in the table give the name of the instances, the second column provides the values of the best lower bounds in the branch-and-cut tree [1]. Next three columns contains the values of the best solutions obtained using the adaptive large neighborhood search (ALNS), the incremental tabu search (ITS) and the hybrid algorithm. Finally, the last column contains the corresponding solutions provided by our proposed VNS based heuristic algorithm.

Analyzing the computational results reported in Table 2, we observe that our VNS based heuristic algorithms provides high-quality solutions, similar to those provided by the state-of-the-art algorithms for solving the GVRP.

6 Conclusions

In this paper we considered the generalized vehicle routing problem (GVRP) and we developed an efficient VNS algorithm for solving the GVRP based on a systematic change of eight neighborhoods structures, each of them focusing on different aspects and properties of the solutions to the GVRP. An important feature of our proposed approach is that the systematic change of the neighborhoods is applied to the associated global graph reducing considerable the size of the solutions space.

The preliminary computational results show that our VNS algorithm is robust and compares favorably in comparison to the existing approaches for solving the

GVRP providing high-quality solutions in reasonable computational running times. This analysis proves again the ability of Variable Neighborhood Search to deal with $\mathcal{NP}$-hard combinatorial optimization problems.

In the future, we plan to introduce a diversification procedure in order to explore other regions of the search space. In addition, we will need to asses the generality and scalability of the proposed heuristic by testing it on larger instances.

Acknowledgements. This work was supported by a grant of the Romanian National Authority for Scientific Research, CNCS - UEFISCDI, project number PN-II-RU-TE-2011-3-0113.

References

1. Baldacci, R., Bartolini, E., Laporte, G.: Some applications of the generalized vehicle routing problem. J. of the Operational Research Society 61(7), 1072–1077 (2010)
2. Bektas, T., Erdogan, G., Ropke, S.: Formulations and Branch-and-Cut Algorithms for the Generalized Vehicle Routing Problem. Transportation Science 45(3), 299–316 (2011)
3. Clarke, G., Wright, J.W.: Scheduling of Vehicles from a Central Depot to a Number of Delivery Points. Operations Research 12, 568–581 (1964)
4. Fischetti, M., Salazar, J.J., Toth, P.: A branch-and-cut algorithm for the symmetric generalized traveling salesman problem. Oper. Res. 45(3), 378–394 (1997)
5. Ghiani, G., Improta, G.: An efficient transformation of the generalized vehicle routing problem. European Journal of Operational Research 122(1), 11–17 (2000)
6. Hansen, P., Mladenovic, N.: Variable neighborhood search: Principles and applications. European Journal of Operational Research 130(3), 449–467 (2001)
7. Mladenovic, N., Hansen, P.: Variable neighborhood search. Computers & Operations Research 24(11), 1097–1100 (1997)
8. Moccia, L., Cordeau, J.-F., Laporte, G.: An incremental tabu search heuristic for the generalized vehicle routing problem with time windows. Journal of the Operational Research Society 63, 232–244 (2012)
9. Or, I.: Traveling Salesman-Type Combinatorial Problems and Their Relation to the Logistics of Regional Blood Banking. Ph.D. Thesis (1976)
10. Pop, P.C.: Generalized Network Design Problems, Modelling and Optimization. De Gruyter, Germany (2012)
11. Pop, P.C., Pintea, C., Zelina, I., Dumitrescu, D.: Solving the Generalized Vehicle Routing Problem with an ACS-based Algorithm. American Institute of Physics 1117, 157–162 (2009)
12. Pop, P.C., Matei, O., Pop Sitar, C., Chira, C.: A genetic algorithm for solving the generalized vehicle routing problem. In: Corchado, E., Graña Romay, M., Manhaes Savio, A. (eds.) HAIS 2010, Part II. LNCS (LNAI), vol. 6077, pp. 119–126. Springer, Heidelberg (2010)
13. Pop, P.C., Pop Sitar, C.: A new efficient transformation of the generalized vehicle routing problem into the classical vehicle routing problem. Yugoslav Journal of Operations Research 21(2), 187–198 (2011)
14. Pop, P.C., Kara, I., Horvat Marc, A.: New Mathematical Models of the Generalized Vehicle Routing Problem and Extensions. Applied Mathematical Modelling 36(1), 97–107 (2012)
15. Pop, P.C., Matei, O., Pop Sitar, C.: An improved hybrid algorithm for solving the generalized vehicle routing problem. Neurocomputing 109, 76–83 (2013)

A Framework to Develop Adaptive Multimodal Dialog Systems for Android-Based Mobile Devices*

David Griol and José Manuel Molina

Applied Artificial Intelligence Group
Computer Science Department
Carlos III University of Madrid
Avda. de la Universidad, 30, 28911 - Leganés, Spain
{david.griol,josemanuel.molina}@uc3m.es

Abstract. Mobile devices programming has emerged as a new trend in software development. The main developers of operating systems for such devices have provided APIs for developers to implement their own applications, including different solutions for developing voice control. Android, the most popular alternative among developers, offers libraries to build interfaces including different resources for graphical layouts as well as speech recognition and text-to-speech synthesis. Despite the usefulness of such classes, there are no strategies defined for multimodal interface development for Android systems, and developers create ad-hoc solutions that make apps costly to implement and difficult to compare and maintain. In this paper we propose a framework to facilitate the software engineering life cycle for multimodal interfaces in Android. Our proposal integrates the facilities of the Android API in a modular architecture that emphasizes interaction management and context-awareness to build sophisticated, robust and maintainable applications.

Keywords: Dialog systems, Multimodal interaction, Android, Mobile devices, User adaptation, Statistical methodologies.

1 Introduction

Continuous advances in the development of information technologies have currently led to the possibility of accessing information and services on the Internet from anywhere, at anytime and almost instantaneously. In addition, these technological advances have made possible the creation of powerful mobile devices capable of running network applications and accessing web services and information through wireless connections. Smartphones and tablets are widely used today to access the web, but mainly through web browsers or graphical user interfaces.

* This work was supported in part by Projects MINECO TEC2012-37832-C02-01, CICYT TEC2011-28626-C02-02, CAM CONTEXTS (S2009/TIC-1485).

M. Polycarpou et al. (Eds.): HAIS 2014, LNAI 8480, pp. 25–36, 2014.
© Springer International Publishing Switzerland 2014

Different technologies have recently emerged to facilitate the accessibility of these devices, which reduced size makes them difficult to operate in some situations and specially for some user groups. For example, multimodal dialog systems [1] can be employed to build more natural interaction with mobile devices by means of speech. They can be defined as computer programs designed to emulate communication capabilities of a human being including several communication modalities, such as speech, tactile and visual interaction.

In addition, these systems typically employ several output modalities to interact with the user, which allows to stimulate several of his senses simultaneously, and thus enhance the understanding of the messages generated by the system. This is particularly useful for people with visual or motor disabilities, allowing their integration and the elimination of barriers to Internet access [2]. For this reason, multimodal conversational agents are becoming a strong alternative to traditional graphical interfaces which might not be appropriate for all users and/or applications [1].

In this paper, we propose a domain-independent framework to develop multimodal dialog systems for mobile devices. Currently the 75% of smartphones and tablets operate with the Android OS [3]. Also, there is an active community of developers who use the Android Open Source Project and have made possible to have more than one million applications currently available at the official Play Store, many of them completely free. For these reasons, our framework makes use of different facilities integrated in Android-based devices.

The remainder of the paper is as follows. Section 2 briefly describes the motivation of our proposal and related work. Section 3 describes the proposed framework to develop adaptive multimodal dialogs systems for mobile devices. Section 4 presents the application of our proposal to developed an advanced multimodal city street guide for Android-based mobile devices. This section also presents the results of a preliminary evaluation of this system. Finally, Section 6 presents some conclusions and future research lines.

2 State of the Art

Although there are currently different approaches to make web contents available using multimodal interaction, they present important limitations. Some of them add a vocal interface to an existing web browser [4]. Others are focused on specific tasks, as e-commerce [5], chat functionalities [6], database access [7], etc. Finally, the solution could be restricted to access information of a limited domain, like in [8], where the dialog system works for selected on-line resources. Several traditional information retrieval systems have been also extended with a vocal interface. However, these applications usually emphasize on the search of documents and not on the interaction with the user.

Additionally, several studies have reported that providing applications with multimodal interfaces is becoming a way to achieve more efficient, pleasant and adapted interaction for mobile applications [9]. In human conversation, speakers adapt their message and the way they convey it to their interlocutors and to the context in which the dialog takes place. This way, information related to the environment and users presence and location is essential to achieve this adaptation. Recent portable devices (e.g. Android-based mobile devices) are equipped with a diversity of input and output technologies and sensors (accelerometers, multi-touch screens, compasses) and start using these to support some form of very basic multimodal interaction. They can be employed to adapt the operation of the multimodal system by taking into account both the context of the interaction and user's specific preferences and previous interactions with the system.

Our proposed framework allows an advance in this direction by considering these valuable sources of contextual information for the development of adaptive multimodal interfaces [10]. To do this, a statistical methodology is proposed to flexible adapt the operation of the system taking into account both user's specific interactions and preferences and also environmental conditions.

3 Proposed Framework to Develop Adaptive Multimodal Dialog Systems for Android-Based Mobile Devices

Figure 1 shows the proposed framework. A spoken dialog system integrates five main tasks to deal with user's spoken utterances: automatic speech recognition (ASR), natural language understanding (NLU), dialog management (DM), natural language generation (NLG), and text-to-speech synthesis (TTS).

Speech recognition is the process of obtaining the text string corresponding to an acoustic input. Our proposal integrates the Google Speech API to include the speech recognition functionality in a multimodal dialog system. Speech recognition services have been available on Android devices since Android 2.1 (API level 7). The ASR functionality is available by means of a microphone icon on the Android keyboard, which activates the Google speech recognition service. Language-configurable messages can be predefined for specific events like no speech detected, no suitable match for the user's utterance, or no Internet connection is available.

Using the Google Speech API (package *android.speech*), speech recognition can be carried out by means on a *RecognizerIntent*, or by creating an instance of *SpeechRecognizer*. The former starts the intent and process its results to complete the recognition, providing feedback to the user to inform that the ASR is ready or there were errors during the recognition process. The latter provides developers with different notifications of recognition related events, thus allowing a more fine-grained processing of the speech recognition process. In both cases, the results are presented in the form of an N-best list with confidence scores.

Once the conversational agent has recognized what the user uttered, it is necessary to understand what he said. Natural language processing generally involves morphological, lexical, syntactical, semantic, discourse and pragmatical knowledge. Lexical and morphological knowledge allow dividing the words in their constituents distinguishing lexemes and morphemes. We propose the use of grammars in order to carry the semantic interpretation of the user inputs.

As explained in the introduction section, a multimodal dialog system involves user inputs through two or more combined modes, which usually complement

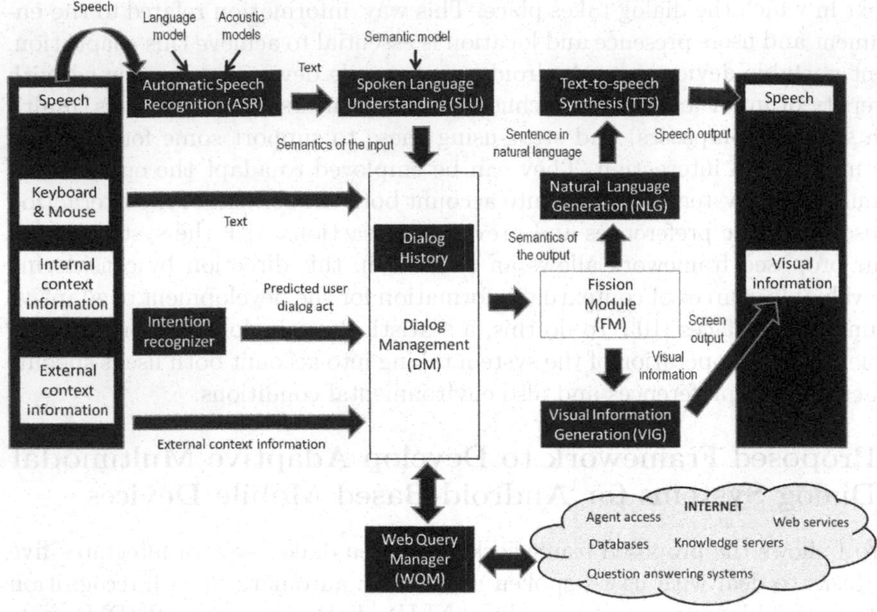

Fig. 1. Proposed framework for the generation of multimodal dialog systems in Android-based mobile devices

spoken interaction by also adding the possibility of textual and tactile inputs provided using physical or virtual keyboards and the screen. In our contribution, we want also to model the context of the interaction as an additional valuable information source to be considered in the fusion process.

We propose the acquisition of external context by means of the use of sensors currently supported by Android devices. Android allows applications to access location services using the classes in the *android.location* package. The central component of the location framework is the *LocationManager* system service, also the Google Maps Android API permits to add maps to the application, which are based on Google Maps data. This API automatically handles access to Google Maps servers, data downloading, map display, and touch gestures on the map. The API can also be used to add markers, polygons and overlays, and to change the user's view of a particular map area. To integrate this API into an application, is it required to install the Google Play services libraries.

Most Android-powered devices have built-in sensors that measure motion, orientation, and various environmental conditions. These sensors are capable of providing raw data with high precision and accuracy, and are useful to monitor three-dimensional device movement or positioning, or monitor changes in the ambient environment near a device. The Android platform supports three main categories of sensors. Motion sensors measure acceleration forces and rotational forces along three axes. This category includes accelerometers, gravity sensors, gyroscopes, and rotational vector sensors. Environmental sensors measure various environmental parameters, such as ambient air temperature and pressure, illumination, and humidity. This category includes barometers, photometers, and thermometers. Finally, position sensors measure the physical position of a device. This category includes orientation sensors and magnetometers.

The Android sensor framework (*android.hardware* package) allows to access these sensors and acquire raw sensor data. Some of these sensors are hardware-based and some are software-based. Hardware-based derive their data by directly measuring specific environmental properties, such as acceleration, geomagnetic field strength, or angular change. Software-based sensors derive their data from one or more of the hardware-based sensors (e.g., linear acceleration and gravity sensors).

Android also provides several sensors to monitor the motion of a device. Two of these sensors are always hardware-based (the accelerometer and gyroscope), and three of these sensors can be either hardware-based or software-based (the gravity, linear acceleration, and rotation vector sensors). Motion sensors are useful for monitoring device movement, such as tilt, shake, rotation, or swing. All of the motion sensors return multi-dimensional arrays of sensor values for each SensorEvent. Two additional sensors allow to determine the position of a device: the geomagnetic field sensor and the orientation sensor. The Android platform also provides a sensor to determine how close the face of a device is to an object (known as the proximity sensor). The geomagnetic field sensor and the proximity sensor are hardware-based. The orientation sensor is software-based and derives its data from the accelerometer and the geomagnetic field sensor.

Finally, four sensors allow monitoring various environmental properties: relative ambient humidity, light, ambient pressure, and ambient temperature near an Android-powered device. All four environment sensors are hardware-based and are available only if a device manufacturer has built them into a device. With the exception of the light sensor, which most device manufacturers use to control screen brightness, environment sensors are not always available on devices. Unlike most motion sensors and position sensors, environment sensors return a single sensor value for each data event.

Regarding internal context, our proposal is based on the traditional view of the dialog act theory, in which communicative acts are defined as intentions or goals. Our technique is based on a statistical model to predict user's intention during the dialog, which is automatically learned from a dialog corpus. This model is used by the system to anticipate the user's needs by dynamically adopting their goals and also providing them with unsolicited comments and suggestions, as well as responding immediately to interruptions and provide clarification questions. The model takes into account the complete history of the interaction and also the information stored in user profiles.

The dialog manager of the system has to deal with different sources of information such as the NLU results, database queries results, application domain knowledge, and knowledge about the users and the previous dialog history to select the next system action. We propose a statistical methodology that combines multimodal fusion and dialog management functionalities. To do this, a data structure is introduced to store the information provided by the user's inputs, the user's intention model, and the context of the interaction.

The modality fission module receives abstract, modality independent presentation goals from the dialog manager. The multimodal output depends on several constraints for the specific domain of the system, e.g., the current scenario, the display size, and user preferences like the currently applicable modality mix. This module applies presentation strategies that decompose the complex presentation goal into presentation tasks. It also decides whether an object description is to be uttered verbally or graphically. The result is a presentation script that is passed to the the Visual Information and Natural Language generation modules.

The visual generation module creates the visual arrangement of the content using dynamically created and filled graphical layout elements. Since many objects can be shown at the same time on the display, the manager re-arranges the objects on the screen and removes objects, if necessary. The visual structure of the user interface (UI) is defined in an Android-based multimodal application by means of layouts. Layouts can be defined by declaring UI elements in XML or instantiating layouts elements at runtime. Both alternatives can be combined in order to declare the application's default layouts in XML and add code that would modify the state of the screen objects at run time. Declaring the UI allows to better separate the presentation of the application from the code that controls its behavior.

UI layouts can be quickly designed in the same way a web page is generated. Android provides a wide variety of controls that can be incorporated to the UI, such as buttons, text fields, checkboxes, radio buttons, toggle buttons, spinners, and pickers. The View class provides the means to capture the events from the specific control that the user interacts with. The user interactions with the UI are captured by means of event listeners. The default event behaviors for the different controls can also been extended using the class event handlers.

Natural language generation is the process of obtaining texts in natural language from a non-linguistic representation. The simplest approach consists in using predefined text messages (e.g., error messages and warnings). Finally, a text-to-speech synthesizer is used to generate the voice signal that will be transmitted to the user. We propose the use of the Google TTS API to include the TTS functionality in an application.

The text-to-speech functionality has been available on Android devices since Android 1.6 (API Level 4). To listen a sample of the included TTS speech synthesizer, once located in the settings menu of the device, the option Settings of Speech Synthesis must be selected in the menu Speech Input and Output. This menu allows selecting the TTS engine, language, and speed used to read a text (from very low to very fast).

The *android.speech.tts* package includes the classes and interfaces required to integrate text-to-speech synthesis in an Android application. They allow the initialization of the TTS engine, a callback to return speech data synthesized by a TTS engine, and control the events related to completing and starting the synthesis of an utterance, among other functionalities.

3.1 Modeling User's Intention

The statistical technique that we propose to model user's intention is described in [11]. The proposed technique carries out the functions of the ASR and SLU modules, i.e., it estimates user's intention providing the semantic interpretation of the user utterance in the same format defined for the output of the SLU module. A data structure, that we call *User Register* (UR), contains the information provided by the user throughout the previous history of the dialog. For each time i, the proposed model estimates user's intention taking into account the sequence of dialog states that precede time i, the system answer at time i, and the objective of the dialog $\mathcal{O}$. The selection of the most probable user answer U_i is given by:

$$\hat{U}_i = \arg\max_{U_i \in \mathcal{U}} P(U_i | UR_{i-1}, A_i, \mathcal{O})$$

The information contained in UR_i is a summary of the information provided by the user up to time i. That is, the semantic interpretation of the user utterances during the dialog and the information that is contained in a user profile (e.g., user's name, gender, experience, skill level, most frequent objectives, additional information from previous interactions, user's neutral voice, and additional parameters that could be important for the specific domain of the system). We propose to solve the previous equation by means of a classification process, which takes the current state of the dialog (represented by means of the set $UR_{i-1}, A_i, \mathcal{O}$) as input and provides the probabilities of selecting the different user dialog acts.

3.2 Fusion of Input Modalities and Dialog Management

The methodology that we propose for the multimodal data fusion and dialog management processes considers the set of input information sources (spoken interaction, visual interaction, external context, and user intention modeling) by means of a machine-learning technique. As in our previous work on user modeling and dialog management [11], we propose the definition of a data structure similar to the *User Register* to store the values for the different concepts and attributes provided by means of the different input modalities along the dialog history, which we called Interaction Register (IR).

The information contained in the IR at each time i has been generated considering the values provided by the input modules of the system along the dialog history. Each slot in the IR can be usually completed by means of more tan one input modality. If just one value has been received for a specific dialog act, then it is stored at the corresponding slot in the IR using the described codification. Confidences scores provided by the modules processing each input modality are used in case of conflict among the values provided by several modalities for the same slot. Thus, a single input is generated for the dialog manager to consider the next system response.

As in our previous work on dialog management [12], we propose the use of a classification process to determine the next system response given the single input that is provided by the interaction register after the fusion of the input modalities and also considering the previous system response. This way, the current state of the dialog is represented by the term (IR_i, A_{i-1}), where A_{i-1} represents the last system response. The values of the output of the classifier can be viewed as the a posteriori probability of selecting the different system responses given the current situation of the dialog, as the following equation shows:

$$\hat{A}_i = \arg\max_{A_i \in \mathcal{A}} P(A_i | IR_i, A_{i-1})$$

4 Practical Application: An Advanced Multimodal City Street Guide for Android-Based Mobile Devices

We have applied our proposed framework to develop a practical multimodal system acting as an enhanced city street guide service for Android-base mobile devices. The app can be operated either visually or orally and is able to locate interesting sites near the current position of the user or a different starting point indicated by the user. It is able to locate sites such as banks, libraries or restaurants and to retrieve and display information about these sites, visualize their position in different maps, show routes, visit their webpages or phone them. The system is also able to initiate navigation to a selected spot considering different means of transportation, and to track the position where the user has parked and show a route to it if needed. This information is provided in Spanish.

To offer these functionalities the system uses Google Maps, Google Directions and Google Places. Google Maps Android API makes it possible to show an interactive map in response to a certain query. It is possible to add markers or zoom to a particular area, also to include images such as icons, highlighted areas and routes. Google Directions is a service that computes routes to reach a certain spot walking, on public transport or bicycle, and it is possible to specify the origin and destination as well as certain intermediate spots. Google Places shows detailed information about sites corresponding to number of categories currently including 80 million commerces and other interesting sites. Each of them include information verified by the owners and moderated contributors. The application also employs the android.speech and android.speech.tts libraries described in the previous section.

When the application is started, it displays a map centered in the current location of the user. The user can search for a place in three ways: spotting it with a finger in the map, introducing the address in a text field, indicating it orally. In any of the three cases, the user is indicating a destination, which will be marked in the map by the system with a red sign. The system also shows the route to the destination from the current location. It can be shown visually or orally, and it is possible to set the preferred transportation means.

The application offers the possibility to look for stores in a long list of options around the user position or a position selected previously. The search can be performed by touching the screen, using the graphical interface or orally. Once the stores are retrieved, e.g. restaurants in an area of 1km around the campus (Figure 2, left), the user can obtain further information about them. When a store is selected, the view is centered on it and an information box appears indicating the name of the store and its address (Figure 2, center). A new screen contains an HTML block comprised of an image representing the type of store, its name, geographic coordinates, complete address, punctuation in the Google+ social network, telephone, website, and its profile in Google+ (Figure 2, right).

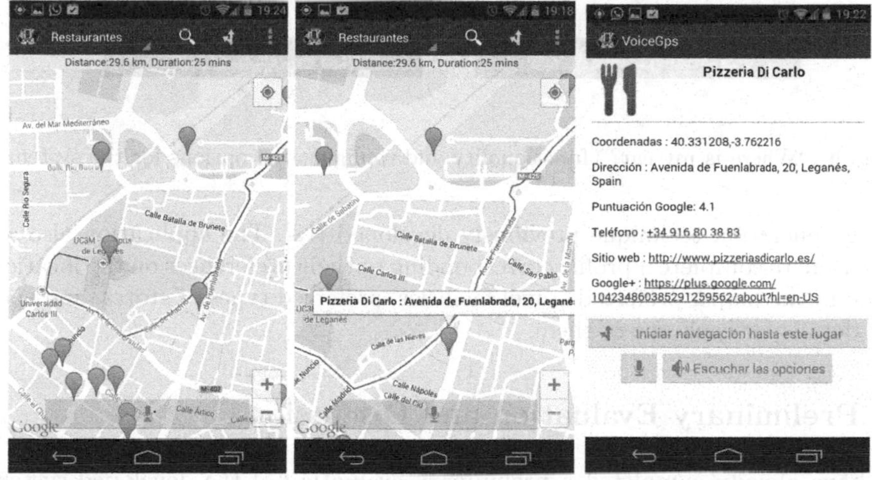

Fig. 2. System functionality to look for specific places and show the corresponding information

Finally, it is possible to store the location where the user parked his vehicle in order to be able to track it. Initially, the user must register the location using a drop-down menu with the visual option "I have parked here" or uttering this sentence after touching the microphone button. This way, the application stores the coordinates in which the user is at the moment and inserts a blue marker in the map. When the user wants to go back to the vehicle, he can press the option "Where is my car?" or utter the same sentence. Then, the application centers the map in the location registered indicating how to get there as shown in Figure 3.

The statistical models for the user's intention recognizer and dialog management modules were learned using a corpus acquired by means of an automatic

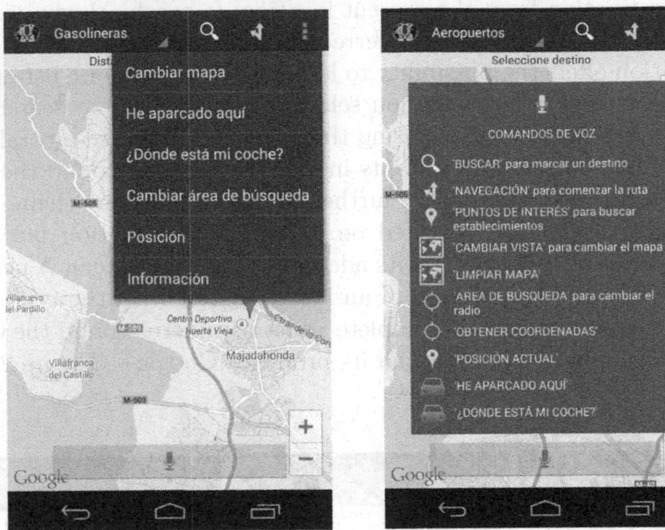

Fig. 3. "Where is my car?" functionality and configuration options for the system

dialog generation technique previously developed [13]. The application also allows users to complete a profile corresponding to their preferences on the location of the initial maps, preferred travel facilities, preferred types of stores, and specific details for each one of them.

5 Preliminary Evaluation and Discussion

We have already completed a preliminary evaluation of the developed system with recruited users and a set of scenarios covering the different functionalities of the system. A total of 150 dialogs for each agent was recorded from the interactions of 25 users. We asked the recruited users to complete a questionnaire to assess their opinion about the interaction. The questionnaire had seven questions: i) Q1: *How well did the system understand you?*; ii)Q2: *How well did you understand the system messages?*; iii) Q3: *Was it easy for you to get the requested information?*; iv) Q4: *Was the interaction with the system quick enough?*; v) Q5: *If there were system errors, was it easy for you to correct them?*; vi) Q6: *How did the system adapt to your preferences?*; vi) Q7: *In general, are you satisfied with the performance of the system?* The possible answers for each questions were the same: *Never/Not at all*, *Seldom/In some measure*, *Sometimes/Acceptably*, *Usually/Well*, and *Always/Very Well*. All the answers were assigned a numeric value between one and five (in the same order as they appear in the questionnaire).

Also, from the interactions of the users with the system we completed an objective evaluation of the application considering the following interaction parameters: i) question success rate (*SR*), percentage of successfully completed questions: system asks - user answers - system provides appropriate feedback about the answer; ii) confirmation rate (CR), computed as the ratio between the number of explicit confirmations turns and the total of turns; iii) error correction rate (ECR), percentage of corrected errors.

Table 1 shows the average results of the subjective evaluation using the described questionnaire. It can be observed that the users perceived that the system understood them correctly. Moreover, they expressed a similar opinion regarding the easiness to understand the system responses. In addition, they assessed that it was easier to obtain the information specified for the different objectives, and that the interaction with the system was adequate and adapted to their preferences. An important point remarked by the users was that it was difficult to correct the errors and misunderstandings generated by the ASR and NLU processes in some scenarios. Finally, the satisfaction level also shows the correct operation of the system.

The results of the objective evaluation for the described interactions show that the developed system could interact correctly with the users in most cases, achieving a success rate of 96.73%. The fact that the possible answers to the user's responses are restricted made it possible to have a very high success in speech recognition. Additionally, the approaches for error correction by means of confirming or re-asking for data were successful in 94.15% of the times when the speech recognizer did not provide the correct input.

Table 1. Results of the preliminary evaluation with recruited users (For the mean value M: 1=worst, 5=best evaluation)

Q1	M = 4.56, SD = 0.47
Q2	M = 4.67, SD = 0.35
Q3	M = 4.12, SD = 0.58
Q4	M = 3.74, SD = 0.39
Q5	M = 3.49, SD = 0.51
Q6	M = 3.97, SD = 0.55
Q7	M = 4.02, SD = 0.27

SR	CR	ECR
96.73%	11.00%	94.15%

6 Conclusions and Future Work

Multimodal interactive systems offer the user combinations of input and output modalities for interacting with the systems, taking advantage of the naturalness of speech. In particular, multimodal interfaces are a useful alternative to graphic user interfaces for mobile devices, allowing the use of other communication as an alternative to tapping through different menus. However, there are no guidelines for the development of multimodal interfaces for mobile devices. Different vendors offer APIs for the development of applications that use speech as a possible input and output modality, but developers have to design ad-hoc solutions to implement the interaction management. In this paper we have presented a general-purpose modular framework for the development of mobile speech applications in Android that integrates the libraries provided by the Android API.

Using our framework it is possible to develop multimodal interfaces that optimize interaction management and integrate different sources of information that make it possible for the application to adapt to the user and the context of the interaction. To show the pertinence of our proposal, we have implemented an evaluated an Android application that uses geographical context in order to provide different location services to its users. The results show that the users were satisfied with the interaction with the system, which achieved high performance rates. We are currently using the framework to build applications in other increasingly complex domains implying different web services and web services mashups.

References

1. Pieraccini, R.: The Voice in the Machine: Building Computers That Understand Speech. MIT Press (2012)
2. Agree, E.: The potential for technology to enhance independence for those aging with a disability. Disability and Health Journal 7(1), 33–39 (2014)
3. McTear, M., Callejas, Z.: Voice Application Development for Android. Packt Publishing (2013)
4. Vesnicer, B., Zibert, J., Dobrisek, S., Pavesic, N., Mihelic, F.: A voice-driven web browser for blind people. In: Proc. of Interspeech/ICSLP, pp. 1301–1304 (2003)
5. Tsai, M.: The VoiceXML dialog system for the e-commerce ordering service. In: Proc. of CSCWD 2009, pp. 95–100 (2005)
6. Kearns, M., Isbell, C., Singh, S., Litman, D., Howe, J.: CobotDS: A Spoken Dialogue System for Chat. In: Proc. of AAAI 2002, pp. 425–430 (2002)
7. Nishimoto, T., Kobayashi, Y., Niimi, Y.: Spoken Dialog System for Database Access on Internet. In: Proc. of AAAI 1997 (1997)
8. Polifroni, J., Chungand, G., Seneff, S.: Towards the Automatic Generation of Mixed-Initiative Dialogue Systems from Web Content. In: Proc. of Eurospeech 2003, pp. 193–196 (2003)
9. Gabbanini, F., Burzagli, L., Emiliani, P.: An innovative framework to support multimodal interaction with Smart Environments. Expert Systems with Applications 39, 2239–2246 (2012)
10. Corchado, E., Wozniak, M., Abraham, A., de Carvalho, A., Snásel, V.: Recent trends in intelligent data analysis. Neurocomputing 126, 1–2 (2014)
11. Griol, D., Carbó, J., Molina, J.: A statistical simulation technique to develop and evaluate conversational agents. AI Communication 26(4), 355–371 (2013)
12. Griol, D., Callejas, Z., López-Cózar, R., Riccardi, G.: A domain-independent statistical methodology for dialog management in spoken dialog systems. Computer Speech and Language 28(3), 743–768 (2014)
13. Griol, D., Carbó, J., Molina, J.: An Automatic Dialog Simulation Technique to Develop and Evaluate Interactive Conversational Agents. Applied Artificial Intelligence 27(9), 759–780 (2013)

Wind Power Ramp Event Prediction with Support Vector Machines

Oliver Kramer, Nils André Treiber, and Michael Sonnenschein

Computational Intelligence Group
Department of Computing Science
University of Oldenburg, Germany
forename.surname@uni-oldenburg.de

Abstract. Wind energy is playing an important part for ecologically friendly power supply. Important aspects for the integration of wind power into the grid are sudden and large changes known as wind power ramp events. In this work, we treat the wind power ramp event detection problem as classification problem, which we solve with support vector machines. Wind power features from neighbored turbines are employed in a spatio-temporal classification approach. Recursive feature selection illustrates how the number of neighbored turbines affects this approach. The problem of imbalanced training and test sets w.r.t. the number of no-ramp events is analyzed experimentally and the implications on practical ramp detection scenarios are discussed.

1 Introduction

Increasing natural energy resources, the reduction of emissions, climate change and rising energy costs lead to a change from classic carbon or nuclear-based power supply to a concentration on renewable energy resources. The movement to a system with a growing amount of renewables is a multidisciplinary objective. It affords the development and optimization of technologies, but also their integration and intelligent combination. Data mining and machine learning are important technologies in such smart power grids. The growing infrastructure of wind turbines and solar panels can also be seen as huge sensor system that allows monitoring and prediction of the renewable resources.

In case of wind power, its volatileness renders the integration to a difficult task. For the prediction of ramp events, there are many challenges from the data mining perspective, e.g., modeling of spatio-temporal wind time series as supervised learning problem and the necessity of real-time capabilities.

In this work, we concentrate on the challenge to predict the most critical aspects when integrating wind, i.e., ramp events that are sudden changes of wind power. Wind power ramp events can threaten the stability of the power grid. Ramp-up events have to be detected in order to save expensive reserve energy. As an example, at 2012/12/24 the feed-in of wind energy converters in the German power grid increased from 4 GW to 19 GW within eight hours [2], the difference is approximately 25% of the total average power demand of Germany.

M. Polycarpou et al. (Eds.): HAIS 2014, LNAI 8480, pp. 37–48, 2014.
© Springer International Publishing Switzerland 2014

Ramp-down events are also very critical, if no reserve energy is available that can compensate sudden drop outs. Prediction of ramps in the power supply from wind energy converters becomes an import aspect for grid stability and hence an important issue for operators in grid control centers [17].

In the past, we employed a spatio-temporal approach for the prediction of wind power for short time ranges based on support vector regression (SVR) [10]. We extend this approach to classification of wind power ramp events with support vector machines (SVMs). SVMs are very successful classification methods for non-linear data. Further, we extend the approach by preprocessing the high-dimensional patterns with dimensionality reduction (DR) methods. The introduced methods are part of WindML, a framework that connects wind energy data bases to data mining and machine learning methods.

The paper is structured as follows. In Section 2, we introduce the framework and data sets our analysis is based on. After an overview of related articles on wind power ramp event prediction in Section 4, ramps are introduced and defined in Section 5. We analyze the ramp prediction problem experimentally in Section 6 with an emphasis on ramp separation, prediction, and a discussion on imbalanced data sets. Further, we present hybrid approaches that combine SVMs with DR methods for preprocessing. Conclusions are drawn in Section 7.

2 WindML

The wind power ramp prediction module is part of the wind and data mining framework WindML that offers specialized techniques and easy-to-use data mining and machine learning methods based on Python and scikit-learn [12]. Classification, regression, clustering, and DR methods allow solving various prediction, planning, and optimization problems. We aim at minimizing the obstacles for research in the wind power domain. Numerous steps like accessing different data bases via interfaces, preprocessing, parameterizations of appropriate methods, and the statistical evaluation of the results can be automatized with WindML. With a framework that bounds specialized mining algorithms to data sets of a particular domain, frequent steps of the data mining process chain can be re-used and simplified. Modules of WindML for power prediction, visualization or statistical programs are illustrated with text and graphical output on the WindML website[1].

In our experimental study, we employ the NREL *Western Wind* data set that consists of wind energy time-series data of 32,043 wind turbines, each holding ten 3 MW turbines over a timespan of three years in 10-minute resolution. The data is based on a numerical weather prediction model, whose output has been modified with statistical methods in such a way, that the ramping characteristics are more comparable with those observed in reality [13]. WindML loads the data for the requested turbines and time range. Once the data is downloaded, the modules can re-use them and load them from the client's cache. Patterns are stored on the user's hard drive in the Numpy [18] binary file format, which

[1] `http://www.windML.org/`

allows an efficient storage and fast reading. The data set interface allows the encapsulation of different data sources, resulting in a flexible and enhanceable framework.

3 Support Vector Machines

We treat the prediction of wind power ramp events as classification problem. The classifiers we employ are SVMs [16] that belong to the state-of-the art techniques in machine learning. SVMs are based on optimizing a linear discriminant function based on a normal vector $\mathbf{w}$ with shift w_0 in data space. Given pattern $\mathbf{x} \in \mathbb{R}^d$ from a d-dimensional data space and label information $y \in \{+1, -1\}$, an SVM is seeking for the decision boundary that maximizes the distance to its closest patterns. This distance is also known as margin. Let $(\mathbf{x}_1, y_1), \ldots, (\mathbf{x}_N, y_N)$ be the set of pattern-label pairs the SVM has to learn. Slack variables $\xi_i \leq 0$ store the deviation from the margin. The SVM optimization problem with slack variables becomes:

$$L_p = \frac{1}{2}\|\mathbf{w}\|^2 + C\sum_{i=1}^{N} \xi_i \tag{1}$$

subject to the constraints

$$y_i(\mathbf{w}^T \mathbf{x}_i + w_0) \geq 1 - \xi_i \tag{2}$$

The optimization problem directly yields an error for the number of misclassification, which is $|\{\xi_i > 0\}|$. The soft error is defined via $\sum_{i=1}^{N} \xi_i$. Equation (1) can be transformed into the dual optimization problem employing the method of Lagrange multipliers:

$$L_d = \sum_{i=1}^{N} \alpha_i - \frac{1}{2}\sum_{i=1}^{N}\sum_{j=1}^{N} \alpha_i \alpha_j y_i y_j \mathbf{x}_i^T \tag{3}$$

with $\sum_{i=1}^{N} \alpha_i y_i = 0$ and $0 \leq \alpha_i \leq C, \forall i$. The penalty factor C is regularization parameter trading off complexity (L_2 norm of $\mathbf{w}$) and data misfit (number of non separable patterns). Patterns on the correct side of the boundary vanish with $\alpha_i = 0$, while support vectors have $\alpha_i > 0$ and define $\mathbf{w}$. Those support vectors with $\alpha < C$ are on the margin and can be used to compute w_0.

4 Related Work

Although state-of-the-art techniques in machine learning have already been applied to the domain of wind energy forecasting, the results are often limited to simplified case-studies. Mohandes *et al.* [11] compared an SVR approach for wind speed prediction to a multi-layer perceptron. The prediction is based on mean daily wind speed data from Saudi Arabia. Shi *et al.* [14] proposed an approach that combines an evolutionary algorithm for parameter tuning with SVR-based prediction. The technique allows a six hour ahead prediction, and is experimentally evaluated on wind data from North China. Recently, Zhao *et al.* [19] compared SVR models to backpropagation for a ten minutes prediction of wind speed. Kramer *et al.* [10] employed SVR-based prediction with a spatio-temporal approach to the NREL data for the first time. Most related work in ramp event prediction is based on numerical weather prediction (NWP) models [4,5]. Only few approaches concentrate on forecasts based on data mining methods. An example is the work of Zareipour *et al.* [9], who analyze the recognition of ramps on the Albert wind power data set that consists of wind time-series data from a park near the Rocky Mountains. The model takes into account univariate input variables and neglects the problem of unbalanced data sets.

5 Wind Power Ramp Events

A critical aspect for power grid stability when integrating wind is the occurrence of ramp events, i.e., sudden changes of wind power (up or down). In this section, we give a definition of ramp events and introduce the ramp event prediction problem as classification problem. In the experimental part of this work, we will concentrate on three reference turbines, i.e., in *Tehachapi* (CA, ID 4155), in *Palm Springs* (CA, ID 1175) and a turbine near *Reno* (NV, ID 11600).

In literature, ramps are not clearly defined [4,8] and may vary from turbine to turbine depending on locations and sizes (for parks respectively). Let $y(t)$ be the wind power time-series of the target turbine, for which we determine the forecast. A ramp event is defined as a wind energy change from time step $t \in \mathbb{N}$ to time step $t + \lambda$ with $\lambda \in \mathbb{N}$ by ramp height $\theta \in (0, y_{\max}]$, i.e., for a ramp-up event, it holds $y(t + \lambda) - y(t) > \theta$, for a ramp-down event it holds $y(t + \lambda) - y(t) < -\theta$.

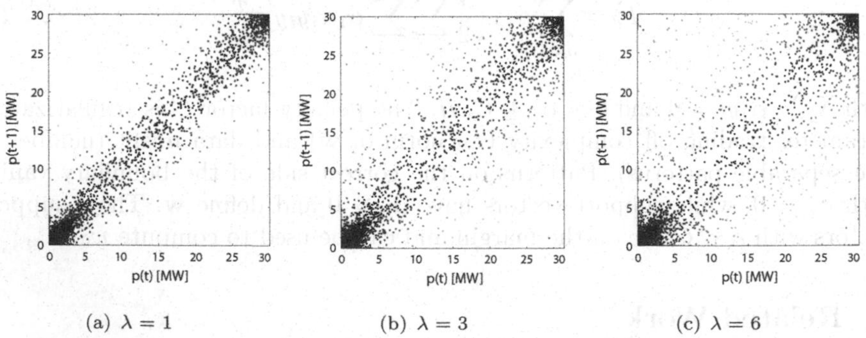

(a) $\lambda = 1$ (b) $\lambda = 3$ (c) $\lambda = 6$

Fig. 1. Plot of wind energy changes of reference turbine in *Tehachapi* for the three time ranges $\lambda = 1, 3, 6$

Figure 1 visualizes the differences of time-series of a test wind turbine in *Tehachapi*. The wind energy $y(t)$ at time t is plotted against $y(t + \lambda)$. If the wind does not change, dots are plotted on the main diagonal. Stable wind situations, i.e., dots near the main diagonal, occur more often than larger wind changes. Ramp events with height θ larger than 15% of the maximum power are comparably rare. The number of ramps increases with the time horizon λ, as a ramp event may appear multiple times. This holds for short time horizons, as a ramp-down may be followed by a ramp-up event over a longer horizon.

We define the ramp prediction problem as the task to predict, whether a ramp-up or a ramp-down event starts at time t, i.e., an energy change from time t to time $t + \lambda$. This problem can be defined as classification problem, for which we construct a pattern $\mathbf{x}_i \in \mathbb{R}^d$ from the wind power features of the target turbine and the surrounding turbines like introduced for the regression approach in [10]. The ramp event serves as label (e.g., 0 for no-ramp, +1 for ramp-up, and −1 for ramp-down). Figure 2 shows the construction of a pattern $\mathbf{x}_i$ based on the radius r around the target turbine.

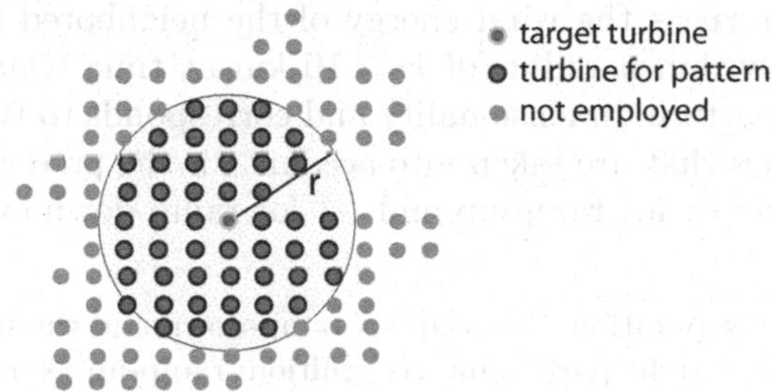

Fig. 2. Illustration of feature construction based on d turbines in a radius r around the target turbine resulting in a pattern $\mathbf{x}_i \in \mathbb{R}^d$ of wind power measurements

If we have observed a training set of such observations over a period of N time steps, i.e., $\{(\mathbf{x}_i, y_i)\}_{i=1}^N$, we train a classifier and predict the ramp for an unknown observation $\mathbf{x}'$. In the experimental section, we will employ an SVM as classifier. An alternative kind of way to predict ramps is to treat the problem as regression problem by determining ramps of the continuous power prediction of a target turbine.

Besides the classifier accuracy $\delta = \sum_{i=1}^N \mathcal{I}(f(\mathbf{x}_i) = y_i)/N$, i.e., the rate of correct classifications using indicator function $\mathcal{I}$ to compare model output and label, we will employ two quality measures to evaluate the quality of a ramp prediction method. We define the following quality parameters:

1. f_t is the number of true ramp forecasts ($[f(\mathbf{x}_i) = +1 \wedge y_i = +1] \vee [f(\mathbf{x}_i) = -1 \wedge y_i = -1]$)
2. f_f is the number of false forecasts ($f(\mathbf{x}_i) = \pm 1 \wedge y_i = 0$)
3. r_m is the number of missed ramps ($f(\mathbf{x}_i) = 0 \wedge y_i = \pm 1$)

Then, $f_a = f_t/(f_t + f_f)$ is the forecast accuracy, which is an indicator for the ability of the model to be correct in case of predicting a ramp. Another useful measure is the ramp capture $r_c = f_t/(f_t + r_m)$, which is an indicator for the ability of the model to hit each ramp.

6 Ramp Prediction

In this section, we treat the prediction of wind power ramp events as classification problem, which is solved with SVMs [16].

6.1 Ramp Separation

As first step, we learn a classifier that separates ramp-up from ramp-down events, i.e., we consider a two-class classification problem. For our reference turbines, ramp-up and ramp-down events of different heights, i.e., $\theta = 10, 15\,[MW]$ are detected. The left part of Table 1 shows the number of ramp events (up, down, no ramps) for each data set, i.e., wind turbines in *Tehachapi*, *Palm Springs*, and *Reno*. Further, the table shows the achieved classifier accuracy δ achieved by the SVM. We define a pattern as the wind energy of the neighbored turbines and the reference turbines within a radius of $r = 10$ km at time t and $t-1$. Parameter d is the input pattern dimensionality and corresponds to the number of neighbored wind turbines that are taken into account for the prediction process. The employed labels are +1 for ramp-up and −1 for ramp-down events.

Table 1. Left part: Ramp separation: ramp-up vs. ramp-down and classification accuracy, forecast horizon $\lambda = 2$, right part: ramp recognition: ramp-up vs. ramp-down vs. no-ramps and classification accuracy, forecast horizon $\lambda = 1$

park			separation				recognition					
location	height	d	up	down	no	δ	up	down	no	δ	f_a	r_c
Teha	10	132	139	93	0	0.93	40	28	75	0.76	0.81	0.77
Teha	15	132	50	42	0	0.96	13	13	28	0.74	0.82	0.88
Palm Sp.	10	84	140	90	0	0.92	38	18	54	0.75	0.86	0.64
Palm Sp.	15	84	48	20	0	0.95	13	3	14	0.73	0.90	0.63
Reno	10	120	158	168	0	0.90	50	55	78	0.65	0.82	0.58
Reno	15	120	48	56	0	0.98	10	13	32	0.73	0.87	0.62

The SVM is trained with grid search and 5-fold cross-validation (CV) on half of the data set. A linear kernel with regularization parameter C and an RBF kernel with C and kernel bandwidth σ are chosen from the set $C, \sigma \in \{10^{-20}, \ldots, 10^{20}\}$. Search in the parameter space of C is reasonable for unbalanced data sets. The other half of the data is employed for evaluation. The experimental results are summarized in Table 1 showing the classification accuracy δ. The results show that the classifiers are able to distinguish between ramp-up and ramp-down events with a comparatively high accuracy. The parameter tuning process chose an RBF-kernel in most of the trails. Ramp separation as first step to approach the ramp prediction problem can be solved satisfactorily.

6.2 Ramp Recognition

We enhance the classification problem to a three-class problem considering no-ramp patterns. We employ the same settings like in the previous section, i.e., 5-fold CV and the search in the parameter space specified above. The right part of Table 1 shows the description of training and test set and the experimental results. The classifier accuracy δ decreases to values between 0.65 and 0.76. But the forecast accuracy f_a is comparatively high with values over 0.8 and up to 0.9. The results for ramp capture depend on the turbine location. For *Tehachapi*, better ramp capture results are achieved than for *Palm Springs* and *Reno*.

The standard model employs all turbines in a specified radius to construct a pattern. To answer the question, if the concentration on a subset of features can improve the prediction, we employ the SCIKIT-LEARN implementation of recursive feature elimination (RFE) [6] for a linear SVM. RFE uses the weight magnitude as criterion for the elimination of dimensions. Successively, SVMs are trained and the features with the smallest ranking criterion based on the weight magnitude are removed. A description of the algorithm can be found in [6].

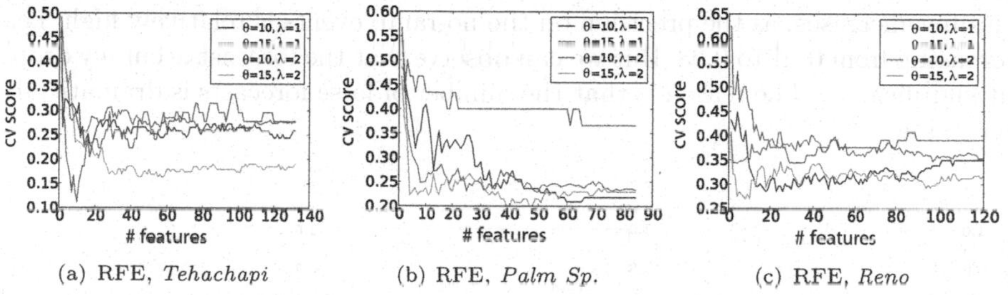

(a) RFE, *Tehachapi* (b) RFE, *Palm Sp.* (c) RFE, *Reno*

Fig. 3. RFE CV score for training of a linear SVM with 2-fold CV for (a) *Tehachapi*, (b) *Palm Springs*, and (c) *Reno* for $\theta = 10, 15$ and $\lambda = 1, 2$

Figure 3 shows the CV error (CV score) using RFE with a linear SVM and 2-fold cross-validation for three turbines, i.e., (a) in *Tehachapi*, (b) in *Palm Springs*, and (c) in *Reno* for two ramp heights and prediction horizons w.r.t. a varying number of features, which have been recursively eliminated from the learning setting. The plots show that the CV score is decreasing with increasing number of features between one to ten features. In many situations, the smallest CV score is achieved with a feature subset. On *Tehachapi*, there is a clear minimum in case of ramp height $\theta = 15$ and horizon $\lambda = 1$ (green line) at about ten features. The CV score is remarkably increasing for a larger number of features. The other training scenarios do not show such a clear minimum for a low number of features. The model learned for ramp height $\theta = 15$ and horizon $\lambda = 2$ achieves good results as of about 30 features and does not deteriorate significantly with a larger number. On *Palm Springs*, the model quality differs noticeably. The best results have been achieved for $\theta = 15, \lambda = 2$, where the error is minimal as of about 40 features. Adding further features leads to slight deteriorations, i.e., there exists an optimal subset of features that is remarkably smaller than the maximum number of considered wind turbines. Also on *Reno*, there is a minimum for two of four models ($\lambda = 2$), while the CV error is again increasing and later approximately constant for a larger number of features. For time critical applications, the reduction of the number of relevant features is an important aspect and can sufficiently be detected with RFE.

6.3 Imbalanced Training and Test Sets

The balance of labels in training and test sets significantly influences the learning and the evaluation result. For prediction of wind ramp events, this effect has an important implication for the ramp event prediction problem. First, we illustrate the imbalance problem for a classifier trained on a balanced training set, predicting the labels on an imbalanced set. Figure 4 shows the corresponding results for (a) *Tehachapi*, (b) *Palm Springs*, and (c) *Reno*. The ramp capture result r_c is independent of the number of no-ramp patterns, as no-ramp patterns do not affect the number of true forecasts f_t and the number of missed ramps r_m, when only increasing the number of no-ramps. The accuracy score of the classifier increases, as the precision on the no-ramp events is relatively high, i.e., increasing from 0.91 to 0.98. But we can observe that the forecast accuracy drops out significantly. The reason is that the number of false forecasts is dramatically increasing.

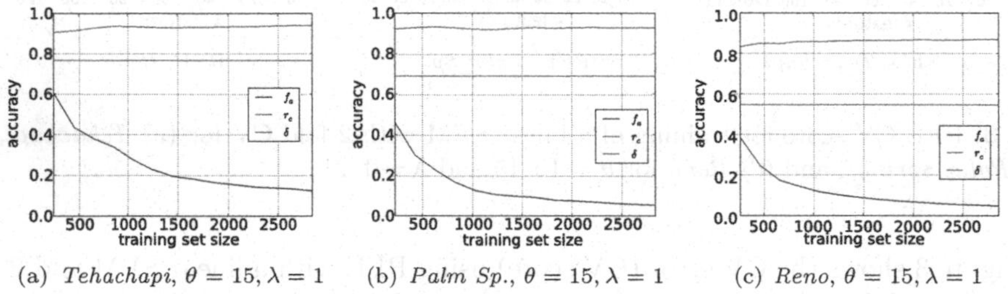

(a) *Tehachapi*, $\theta = 15, \lambda = 1$ (b) *Palm Sp.*, $\theta = 15, \lambda = 1$ (c) *Reno*, $\theta = 15, \lambda = 1$

Fig. 4. SVM ramp prediction with balanced training set and test set with increasing number of no-ramp patterns for references turbines in (a) *Tehachapi*, (b) *Palm Springs*, and (c) *Reno* with $\theta = 15$ and $\lambda = 1$

Figure 5 shows the result of SVM-based ramp event predictions w.r.t. a training set with increasing number of no-ramps. The plots show experiments for the *Tehachapi* data set with $\theta = 10, 15$ and $\lambda = 2$, and for *Palm Springs* with $\theta = 15, \lambda = 2$. We can observe that forecast accuracy f_a and the ramp capture r_c decrease with an increasing amount of no-ramps, while the accuracy score is even slightly increasing. But the forecast accuracy is still much better than in case of the balanced training set and the increasing test set. The reason is that the classifier better learns to distinguish ramp-events from each other and from

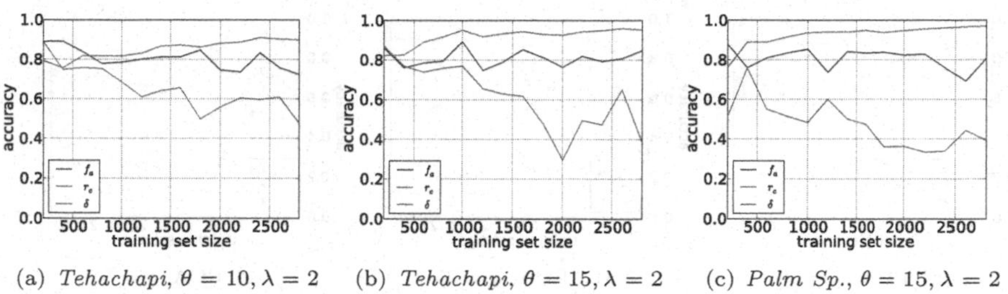

(a) *Tehachapi*, $\theta = 10, \lambda = 2$ (b) *Tehachapi*, $\theta = 15, \lambda = 2$ (c) *Palm Sp.*, $\theta = 15, \lambda = 2$

Fig. 5. SVM ramp prediction with unbalanced training sets, i.e., increasing number of no-ramp patterns in *Tehachapi* with (a) $\theta = 10, \lambda = 2$ and (b) $\theta = 15, \lambda = 2$, and (c) *Palm Springs* with $\theta = 15, \lambda = 2$

no-ramp events with more examples in the training set. But the cost that has to be paid is the ramp capture r_c, as the number of true forecasts f_t decreases.

The imbalance of class labels has a dramatic implication on the ramp prediction problem. Although SVMs turn out to be comparatively strong classifiers, the achieved accuracy may not be high enough to avoid false alarms. The number of false positives is too large in case of a strongly unbalanced test data set. In practical recognition scenarios, the number of no-ramps is significantly larger (about 150 to 300 times assuming 10-minute time steps) than the number of ramp events. Consequently, the accuracy of a classifier would have to exceed about $\delta = 1 - 365/52560 \approx 0.995$ to allow at most one false alarm a day. The spatio-temporal model based on the turbine infrastructure is not sufficient to achieve such an accuracy rate, and more explaining features must be added.

6.4 Dimensionality Reduction Preprocessing

The hybridization of methods has shown to be very successful to overcome limitation of individual techniques [3,1]. In this section, we analyze the preprocessing with DR methods, which is a successful procedure in machine learning to speed up SVM learning and to improve classification results. In the following, we compare principal component analysis (PCA) [7] and isometric mapping (ISOMAP) [15] as preprocessing methods. After the DR process, the patterns $\mathbf{x}_1, \ldots, \mathbf{x}_N \in \mathbb{R}^d$ are reduced to low-dimensional representations $\hat{\mathbf{x}}_1, \ldots, \hat{\mathbf{x}}_N \in \mathbb{R}^q$ with target dimensionality $q < d$. Figure 6 shows the experimental results on the data set *Tehachapi* with ramp height $\theta = 10$ and prediction horizon $\lambda = 2$. In comparison to the results without DR preprocessing, see Figure 5(a), PCA with $q = 25$ and $q = 50$ achieves similar results. The accuracy δ stays high with larger training sets, while the ramp capture r_c deteriorates moderately. This situation changes for $q = 5$, where valuable information is lost that is important for a high ramp capture accuracy. For ISOMAP, we choose the neighborhood size $K = 30$. The ISOMAP results for all target dimensions $q = 5, 25, 50$ are slightly worse than the PCA results and more fluctuating. In particular, the ramp capture is not satisfying for larger dimensions q. As ISOMAP is usually

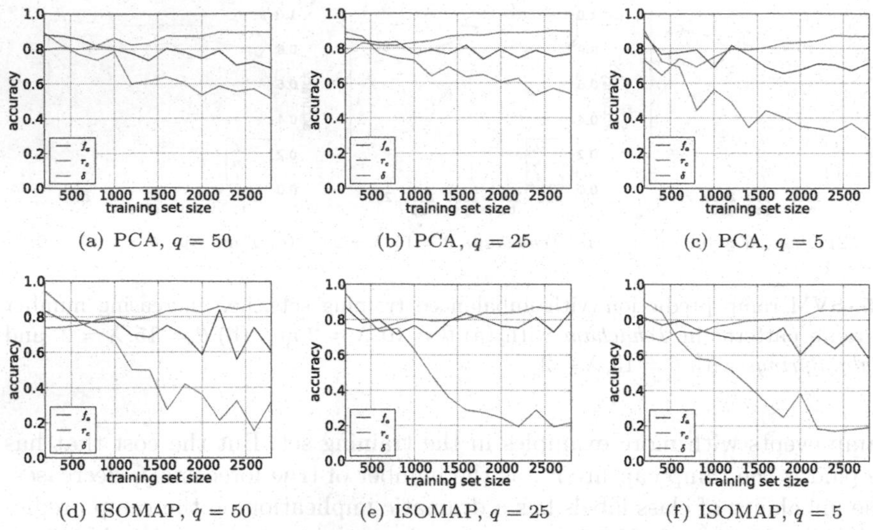

(a) PCA, $q = 50$ (b) PCA, $q = 25$ (c) PCA, $q = 5$

(d) ISOMAP, $q = 50$ (e) ISOMAP, $q = 25$ (f) ISOMAP, $q = 5$

Fig. 6. SVM ramp prediction with PCA and ISOMAP preprocessing to three dimensionalities ($q = 5, 20, 50$) for wind time series of *Tehachapi*, $\theta = 10, \lambda = 2$

computationally more expensive, we recommend to employ the PCA-SVM hybrid for ramp prediction.

7 Conclusion

Objective of this paper is to show that soft margin SVMs are appropriate methods for learning wind power ramp events. The combination of PCA and SVMs turned out to be the most promising hybridization in ramp prediction, which is also comparatively robust w.r.t. ramp accuracy. Although a high precision has been achieved in the classification process, the precision is not sufficient to reduce the number of false ramp event forecasts in practical applications. The reason is that ramp events are rare, which leads to an imbalanced data set. Ramp events may accidentally be predicted in normal situations. The only solution to this problem is a further increase of forecast accuracies, which – to our mind – cannot be achieved with the data available in the *Western Wind* data set. Instead, more data is necessary, e.g., with higher spatial and temporal resolutions. The combination with physical simulations, i.e., numerical weather predictions may also be a possibility to increase the classifier accuracy. With these attempts, it may be possible to improve the classifiers in order to reduce the number of false positive classifications to *one* a day, which seems to be tolerable for practical applications.

Further prospective future work is the prediction of wind ramp events based on regression. The spatio-temporal regression model for wind prediction [10] can easily be used for prediction of ramps. An ensemble of the classification with the regression approach might improve the prediction quality.

Acknowledgment. We thank the Präsidium of the Carl-von-Ossietzky University of Oldenburg and the EWE research institute NextEnergy for partly supporting this work. Further, we thank NREL for the *Western Wind* data set.

References

1. Abraham, A.: Special issue: Hybrid approaches for approximate reasoning. Journal of Intelligent and Fuzzy Systems 23(2-3), 41–42 (2012)
2. Bundesnetzagentur. Bericht zum Zustand der leitungsgebundenen Energieversorgung im Winter 2012/13 (2013)
3. Diz, M.L.B., Baruque, B., Corchado, E., Bajo, J., Corchado, J.M.: Hybrid neural intelligent system to predict business failure in small-to-medium-size enterprises. Int. J. Neural Syst. 21(4), 277–296 (2011)
4. Focken, U., Lange, M.: Wind power forecasting pilot project in alberta. In: Energy & Meteo Systems (2008)
5. Greaves, B., Collins, J., Parkes, J., Tindal, A.: Temporal forecast uncertainty for ramp events. In: Proceedings of the European Wind Energy Conference & Exhibition, EWEC (2009)
6. Guyon, I., Weston, J., Barnhill, S., Vapnik, V.: Gene selection for cancer classification using support vector machines. Machine Learning 46(1-3), 389–422 (2002)
7. Jolliffe, I.: Principal component analysis. Springer series in statistics. Springer, New York (1986)
8. Kamath, C.: Understanding wind ramp events through analysis of historical data. In: Proceedings of the IEEE PES Transmission and Distribution Conference and Expo, pp. 1–6 (2010)
9. Kamath, C., Fan, Y.J.: Using data mining to enable integration of wind resources on the power grid. Stat. Anal. Data Min. 5(5), 410–427 (2012)
10. Kramer, O., Gieseke, F., Satzger, B.: Wind energy prediction and monitoring with neural computation. Neurocomputing 109, 84–93 (2013)
11. Mohandes, M., Halawani, T., Rehman, S., Hussain, A.A.: Support vector machines for wind speed prediction. Renewable Energy 29(6), 939–947 (2004)
12. Pedregosa, F., Varoquaux, G., Gramfort, A., Michel, V., Thirion, B., Grisel, O., Blondel, M., Prettenhofer, P., Weiss, R., Dubourg, V., Vanderplas, J., Passos, A., Cournapeau, D., Brucher, M., Perrot, M., Duchesnay, E.: Scikit-learn: Machine learning in Python. Journal of Machine Learning Research 12, 2825–2830 (2011)
13. Potter, C.W., Lew, D., McCaa, J., Cheng, S., Eichelberger, S., Grimit, E.: Creating the dataset for the western wind and solar integration study (u.s.a.). In: 7th International Workshop on Large Scale Integration of Wind Power and on Transmission Networks for Offshore Wind Farms (2008)
14. Shi, J., Yang, Y., Wang, P., Liu, Y., Han, S.: Genetic algorithm-piecewise support vector machine model for short term wind power prediction. In: Proceedings of the 8th World Congress on Intelligent Control and Automation, pp. 2254–2258 (2010)
15. Tenenbaum, J.B., Silva, V.D., Langford, J.C.: A global geometric framework for nonlinear dimensionality reduction. Science 290, 2319–2323 (2000)
16. Vapnik, V.N.: The nature of statistical learning theory. Springer, New York (1995)

17. Waldl, H.-P., Brandt, P.: Anemos.rulez: Extreme event prediction and alarming to support stability of energy grids. In: Proceedings of the Annual EWEA 2011 Conference (2011)
18. van der Walt, S., Colbert, S.C., Varoquaux, G.: The numpy array: A structure for efficient numerical computation. Computing in Science and Eng. 13(2), 22–30 (2011)
19. Zhao, P., Xia, J., Dai, Y., He, J.: Wind speed prediction using support vector regression. In: Industrial Electronics and Applications (ICIEA), pp. 882–886 (2010)

An Ontology for Human-Machine Computation Workflow Specification

Nuno Luz[1], Carlos Pereira[2], Nuno Silva[1], Paulo Novais[3], António Teixeira[2], and Miguel Oliveira e Silva[2]

[1] GECAD (Knowledge Engineering and Decision Support Gro up), Polytechnic of Porto, Portugal
{nmalu,nps}@isep.ipp.pt

[2] DETI/IEETA (Department of Electronics Telecommunications and Informatics/ Institute of Electronics and Telematics Engineering of Aveiro), University of Aveiro, Portugal
{cepereira,ajst,mos}@ua.pt

[3] CCTC (Computer Science and Technology Center), University of Minho, Portugal
pjon@di.uminho.pt

Abstract. Lately, a focus has been given to the re-usability of workflow definitions and to flexible and re-usable workflow components, culminating with approaches that harness the benefits of the enriched semantics provided by ontologies. Following this trend and the needs of multiple application domains, such as micro-task crowdsourcing and ambient assisted living, of incorporating cooperation between the efforts of human and machine entities, this paper proposes an ontology and process for the definition, instantiation and execution of semantically enriched workflows.

Keywords: Workflow, Task, Ontology, Domain Knowledge.

1 Introduction

Extensive work exists regarding workflow specification languages and formalisms [1–5], which focus on the workflow definition and instantiation. Workflows are typically used to represent business processes with languages such as YAWL [2], and commercial languages such as XPDL (XML Process Definition Language) and BPEL (Business Process Execution Language), which lack semantics and formal definitions [6]. The standardization efforts that led to the emergence of these languages date back to 1993 with the emergence of the WfMC (Workflow Management Coalition), a coalition of several companies with the purpose of standardizing workflow model specification (or definitions) [5].

Lately, a focus has been given to the re-usability of workflow definitions and to giving some degree of adaptation and flexibility to workflow components, culminating with approaches that harness the benefits of the enriched semantics provided by ontologies [3, 5, 7]. Besides allowing re-usability, ontologies are conceptual models, closer to the human conceptual level, which provide structure and semantics understandable to machines [8, 9]. In this sense, ontologies are ideal for agile model development focuses on domain knowledge [10].

M. Polycarpou et al. (Eds.): HAIS 2014, LNAI 8480, pp. 49–60, 2014.
© Springer International Publishing Switzerland 2014

Particularly, in [5], OWL (Web Ontology Language) ontologies are used to capture the semantics of the workflow domain in order to provide inference and guide the workflow execution engine into the following steps of the workflow.

OWL-S (Semantic Markup for Web Services) [7] is a format that introduces the semantics of OWL to web service specification and composition (service workflows). Although it is not a format for workflow definition, services are represented as processes or workflows of atomic operations with input and output parameters. Thus, the specification of services shares many similarities with workflow definition specification languages.

Current workflow definition approaches lack or do not consider the semantics of the atomic operations performed throughout the workflow. They are usually limited to the specification of input and output parameters along with some identification of the type of operation. OWL-S, however, includes domain ontologies (with the inherent expressivity of Description Logic languages) in web service process definitions. Besides providing benefits in domain workflow extensibility, such semantics would aid in the interoperability of workflow engines and execution agents.

In this paper, a workflow specification ontology tailored for workflows of human-machine computations is proposed. The approach absorbs ideas from other workflow definition languages and retains the benefits of OWL-S.

Workflow definitions according to this approach inherit the benefits of Description Logic ontologies such as re-usability and extensibility. A focus on domain knowledge is given through domain concepts, which describe a specific task or work domain. These concepts can be re-used by multiple workflow definitions.

The ultimate purpose of this architecture is to allow not only the specification of workflow definitions, but also to include all knowledge and semantics of atomic tasks (not only the input and output, but also the full description of the operation itself) in the definition through Description Logics [11]. Furthermore, the reasoning and conceptualization capabilities given by ontologies are exploited in order to establish a human-machine environment for solving workflows of tasks.

Typical applications of this work include micro-task crowdsourcing [12], which benefits from the structure and semantics given by ontologies, and Ambient Assisted Living (AAL) approaches [13], which benefit from the inherent scalability and re-usability of the proposed solution.

This paper is organized as follows. Section 2 presents the proposed CompFlow process, which is followed by its formal definition on section 3. Section 4 provides a use case of CompFlow in the AAL domain. Section 5 concludes this work with some remarks on future work.

2 The CompFlow Process

The CompFlow is a process for (1) workflow definition, (2) instantiation and (3) execution (see fig. 1). The workflow definition phase (1) results in a workflow-definition ontology that extends the CompFlow upper ontology. The workflow-definition ontology represents a workflow-definition for a specific domain, which can be instantiated multiple times in the workflow instantiation phase (2). These instantiations are finally executed during the workflow execution phase (3). In this paper, a focus is given to the workflow definition phase. Phases 2 and 3 are considered in the context of an execution engine and are, thus, left outside the scope of this paper.

In some situations, an abstract workflow-definition may result from the workflow definition phase (1). These definitions capture only the domain knowledge and cannot be instantiated. They can, however, be extended by concrete workflow-definitions.

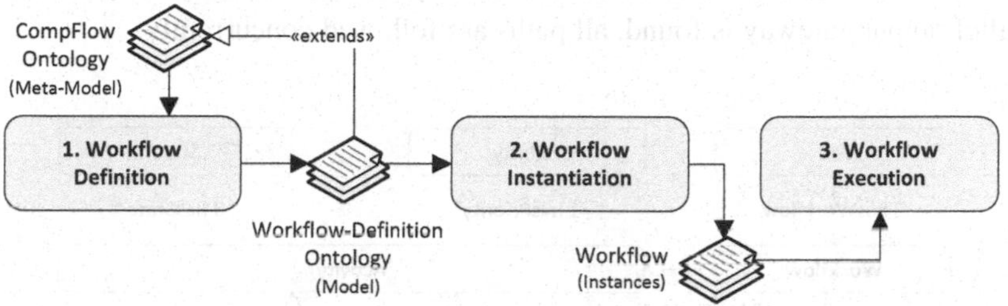

Fig. 1. The CompFlow workflow definition, instantiation and execution process

The workflow meta-model (see fig. 2) is fixed and defines the constructs required for workflow-definitions at the model level. In practice, the meta-model is represented through the CompFlow upper ontology.

A workflow is considered to be a set of tasks ordered according to a set of procedural rules in order to deliver a specific result in a specific domain of application or knowledge. The model or specification of a workflow is a workflow-definition, which contains elements called activity-definitions. Activity-definitions have an associated priority value that can be used to establish an execution order. There are four types of activity-definitions: task-definitions, event-definitions, gateway-definitions and workflow-definitions. Analogously, instantiations of a workflow-definition, for different units of work, are called workflows.

Task-definitions model tasks (the full atomic operations and their semantics) in a specific domain. Tasks (instances of a task-definition), inherently belonging to a workflow, perform atomic operations over data, which may have an associated (physical) effect on the state of the world.

Each task is performed by workers which can represent machines and/or humans. Workers have access to a task through a specific interface. Interface-definitions establish the different types of interfaces through which a task can be delivered to a worker. For instance, tasks can be delivered to a worker through a visual interface, sound interface, or simply through a web interface (the common case for crowdsourcing applications). The inclusion of an interface as an element within the ontology allows the customization of standard interfaces according to application scenarios. This customization enables the creation of mixed or multimodal interfaces, capable of merging and coordinating multiple interfaces, commonly used on user-centric environments.

Event-definitions specify events that may either (i) trigger the continuation of an existing workflow or (ii) trigger a new instantiation and execution of a workflow-definition. Events are received and handled through event interfaces that follow a publish-subscribe pattern [14].

Gateway-definitions establish flow control blocks in the workflow-definition. While input gateway-definitions establish different behaviors on the input of the gateway, output gateway-definitions establish different behaviors on the output of the gateway. For instance, regarding input gateways, if a merge input gateway is found during execution, the engine must simply wait for the first input in order to continue. Instead, if a sync input gateway is present, the engine must wait for all inputs to arrive. Regarding output gateways, if a decision output gateway is found, the gateway condition must be evaluated in order to decide which paths must be followed next. If a parallel output gateway is found, all paths are followed concurrently.

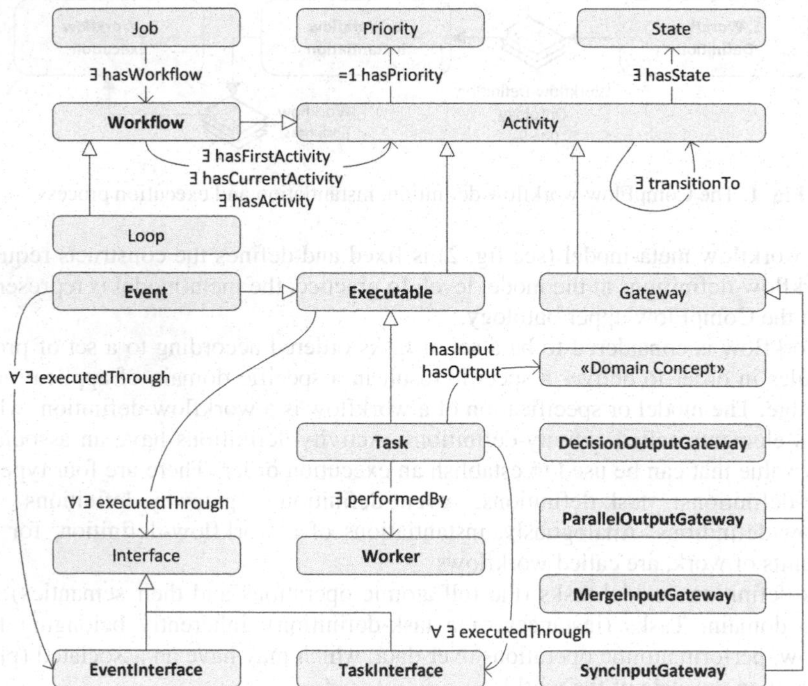

Fig. 2. The CompFlow upper ontology (meta-model)

3 CompFlow Formal Definition

A CompFlow structure is a singleton $CompFlow = (Z)$, where Z is the set of entities pertaining to $CompFlow$. A $CompFlow$ represents a self-contained unit of structured information. Elements in a $CompFlow$ are called workflow definition entities.

3.1 Workflow-Definition

A CompFlow extension, which represents a workflow-definition, is a 11-tuple $WFD(CompFlow) := (A, W, F, P, AR, ER, TR, C, CIN, COUT, \Omega)$ where:

- $A \sqsubseteq Z$ is a set of activity-definitions, where:
  - $E \sqsubseteq A$ is the set of executable-definitions;
    - o $T \sqsubseteq E$ is the set of task-definitions;
    - o $EV \sqsubseteq E$ is the set of event-definitions;
  - $G \sqsubseteq A$ is the set of gateway-definitions;
    - o $DOG \sqsubseteq G$ is the set of gateway-definitions corresponding to DecisionOutputGateways;
    - o $POG \sqsubseteq G$ is the set of gateway-definitions corresponding to ParallelOutputGateways;
    - o $MIG \sqsubseteq G$ is the set of gateway-definitions corresponding to MergeInput Gateways;
    - o $SIG \sqsubseteq G$ is the set of gateway-definitions corresponding to SyncInputGateways;
  - $SA \sqsubseteq A$ is the set of activity-definitions that start the workflow-definition;
    - o $ST \sqsubseteq T \sqcap SA$ is the set of task-definitions that start the workflow-definition;
    - o $SG \sqsubseteq G \sqcap SA$ is the set of gateway-definitions that start the workflow-definition;
    - o $SEV \sqsubseteq EV \sqcap SA$ is the set of event-definitions that start the workflow-definition;
- $W \sqsubseteq Z \wedge W \equiv MW \sqcup HW$ is a set of worker-definitions (or roles), where:
  - MW is the set of machine worker-definitions;
  - HW is the set of human worker-definitions;
- $F \sqsubseteq Z \wedge F \equiv EF \sqcup TF$ is a set of interface-definitions, where:
  - EF is the set of event interface-definitions;
  - TF is the set of task interface-definitions;
- $P \sqsubseteq (Z, \leq)$ is a totally ordered set of priority values;
- $AR : A \rightarrow 2^A \times P$ defines, for an activity-definition, (i) the following activity-definition (transition restriction) and (ii) a priority value, where:
  - $APR : A \rightarrow P$ is an injective function that defines the priority value for each activity-definition;
  - $AAR \sqsubseteq A \times A$ is relationship that defines a transition restriction between two activity-definitions;
- $ER : E \rightarrow F$ is a function that defines the interface-definition for each executable-definition;
- $TR : T \rightarrow W$ is a function that defines the worker-definition (or role) for each task-definition;
- $C \sqsubseteq Z$ is the set of domain concepts that define the input and output of task-definitions;
- $CIN \sqsubseteq T \times C$ is a relation that defines the input concept of the task-definition;
- $COUT \sqsubseteq T \times C$ is a relation that defines the output concept of the task-definition;

- $\Omega^\alpha \sqsubseteq \alpha \times \alpha$ is a subsumption relationship between elements of the same set $\alpha \sqsubseteq Z$, which maps to the sub-class-of relationship in Description Logics.

A workflow-definition consists in building a domain-specific workflow-definition ontology (model) that extends the CompFlow upper ontology (meta-model).

An activity-definition a is called abstract iff it doesn't belong to any workflow-definition, i.e., $a \notin SA$ and $\forall x \in A \Rightarrow a \notin AAR^+(a,x) \wedge a \notin AAR^+(x,a)$. Otherwise, it is called concrete.

For concrete workflow-definitions the following rules must be satisfied:

- A priority value must be specified for each activity-definition: $\forall a : a \in A \Rightarrow \exists p : p \in P \wedge APR(a) = p$;
- An input and output domain concept must be specified for each task-definition: $\forall t : t \in T \Rightarrow \exists c1, c2 : c1 \in C \wedge c2 \in C \wedge (t, c1) \in CIN \wedge (t, c2) \in COUT$;
- A worker-definition must be specified for each task-definition: $\forall t : t \in T \Rightarrow \exists w : w \in W \wedge TR(t) = w$;
- An interface-definition must be specified for every executable-definition: $\forall e : e \in E \Rightarrow \exists f : f \in F \wedge ER(e) = f$.

It is assumed that activity-definitions, interface-definitions and worker-definitions are concept descriptors according to Description Logic languages. This allows the specification of domain-specific abstract definitions, from which new subsumed definitions (through the Ω^α relationship) can be created in order to build new workflow-definition. The CI and CO relations can also be subsumed in order to represent specific domain relations between domain concepts. For instance, text constitutes the input and output of a translation task. However the *input* is referred to, specifically, as the *originalText*, and the *output* as the *translatedText*.

In this paper, Description Logic knowledge bases and ontologies are considered. A Description Logic knowledge base contains a TBox (terminological box) and an ABox (assertion box) [15], where the TBox contains all the concepts and relationships that define a specific domain (workflow-definition), and the ABox contains the instances or individuals defined according to the elements in the TBox (workflow instantiation).

3.2 Workflow-Definition Instantiation

An instantiation of a workflow consists in creating and preparing an instance of the workflow definition for future execution.

A CompFlow workflow-definition instantiation is a 10-tuple $WFDI(CompFlow)$ $:= (I, instA, instW, instF, S, \Sigma, execThrough, perfBy, instC, \Phi)$ where:

- $I \sqsubseteq Z$ is a set of instances;
- $instA : A \rightarrow 2^I$ is a function that relates an activity-definition (task-definition, event-definition or gateway-definition) with a set of instances. Consequently, the set of all activity instantiations AI is defined as $AI = \bigcup_{\forall x \in A} instA(x)$. Instantiations of the sub-sets of A are defined as:

- $instE : E \rightarrow 2^I$ is a function that relates an executable-definition with a set of instances. Consequently, the set of all executable instantiations EI is defined as $EI = \bigcup_{\forall x \in E} instE(x)$;
  - o $instT : T \rightarrow 2^I$ is a function that relates a task-definition with a set of instances (tasks). Consequently, the set of all tasks TI is defined as $TI = \bigcup_{\forall x \in T} instT(x)$;
  - o $instEV : EV \rightarrow 2^I$ is a function that relates an event-definition with a set of instances (events);
- $instG : G \rightarrow 2^I$ is a function that relates a gateway-definition with a set of instances (gateways);
- $instSA : SA \rightarrow 2^I$ is a function that relates an activity-definition that starts the workflow, with a set of activities that start the workflow;

- $instW : W \rightarrow 2^I$ is a function that relates a worker-definition with a set of instances (workers). Consequently, the set of all workers WI is defined as $WI = \bigcup_{\forall x \in W} instW(x)$;
- $instF : F \rightarrow 2^I$ is a function that relates an interface-definition with a set of instances (interfaces). Consequently, the set of all interfaces FI is defined as $FI = \bigcup_{\forall x \in F} instF(x)$;
- $S \sqsubseteq Z \wedge S \equiv \{notStarted, inProgress, withError, paused, canceled, finished\}$ is the set of possible states that an activity can have;
- $\Sigma : AI \rightarrow 2^{AI} \times P \times S$ is a function that defines for every activity (i) the following activities, (ii) its priority and (iii) its current state, where:
  - $transitionTo : AI \times AI$ is a relation that defines the following activities for every activity;
  - $hasPriority : AI \rightarrow P$ defines the priority value for every activity;
  - $hasState : AI \rightarrow S$ defines the current state for every activity;
- $execThrough : EI \rightarrow 2^{FI}$ is a function that defines, for every executable, the set of interfaces through which it was dispatched;
- $perfBy : TI \rightarrow 2^{WI}$ is a function that defines, for every task, the set of workers that participated in its execution;
- $instC : C \rightarrow 2^I$ is a function that relates a domain concepts with a set of instances. Consequently, the set of all domain instances CI is defined as $CI = \bigcup_{\forall x \in C} instCI(x)$;
- $\Phi : TI \rightarrow 2^{CI} \times 2^{CI}$ is a function that defines for every task (i) the input instances and (ii) the output instances, where:
  - $hasInput : TI \times CI$ is a relation that defines the input instances for every task;
  - $hasOutput : TI \times CI$ is a relation that defines the output instances for every task.

3.3 Interpretation

An interpretation of a CompFlow workflow-definition is a structure $\mathfrak{I} = (\Delta^{\mathfrak{I}}, A^{\mathfrak{I}}, W^{\mathfrak{I}}, F^{\mathfrak{I}}, P^{\mathfrak{I}}, S^{\mathfrak{I}}, C^{\mathfrak{I}}, I^{\mathfrak{I}})$, where:

- $\Delta^{\mathfrak{I}}$ is the domain set assumed to contain a single workflow;

- $A^{\mathfrak{I}} : A \rightarrow 2^{\Delta^{\mathfrak{I}}}$ is an activity-definition interpretation function that maps each activity-definition (task-definition, event-definition or gateway-definition) to a sub-set of the domain set. Accordingly, the following functions exist:
  - $E^{\mathfrak{I}} : E \rightarrow 2^{A^{\mathfrak{I}}}$ is an executable-definition interpretation function that maps each executable-definition to a sub-set of $A^{\mathfrak{I}}$;
    - $T^{\mathfrak{I}} : T \rightarrow 2^{E^{\mathfrak{I}}}$ is a task-definition interpretation function that maps each task-definition to a sub-set of $E^{\mathfrak{I}}$;
    - $EV^{\mathfrak{I}} : EV \rightarrow 2^{E^{\mathfrak{I}}}$ is an event-definition interpretation function that maps each event-definition to a sub-set of $E^{\mathfrak{I}}$;
  - $G^{\mathfrak{I}} : G \rightarrow 2^{A^{\mathfrak{I}}}$ is a gateway-definition interpretation function that maps each gateway-definition to a sub-set of $A^{\mathfrak{I}}$;
- $W^{\mathfrak{I}} : W \rightarrow 2^{\Delta^{\mathfrak{I}}}$ is a worker-definition interpretation function that maps each worker-definition to a sub-set of the domain set;
- $F^{\mathfrak{I}} : F \rightarrow 2^{\Delta^{\mathfrak{I}}}$ is an interface-definition interpretation function that maps each interface-definition to a sub-set of the domain set;
- $P^{\mathfrak{I}} : P \rightarrow \Delta^{\mathfrak{I}}$ is an instance interpretation function that maps each priority value to a single element in the domain set;
- $S^{\mathfrak{I}} : S \rightarrow \Delta^{\mathfrak{I}}$ is an instance interpretation function that maps each state to a single element in the domain set;
- $C^{\mathfrak{I}} : C \rightarrow 2^{\Delta^{\mathfrak{I}}}$ is an instance interpretation function that maps each domain concept to a sub-set of the domain set;
- $I^{\mathfrak{I}} : I \rightarrow \Delta^{\mathfrak{I}}$ is an instance interpretation function that maps each instance to a single element in the domain set.

An interpretation is a model of CompFlow if it satisfies the general set properties and instantiation properties. The general set properties are:

- $\forall a, i : a \in A \land i \in instA(a) \Rightarrow I^{\mathfrak{I}}(i) \in A^{\mathfrak{I}}(a)$, which implies:
  - $\forall e, i : e \in E \land i \in instE(e) \Rightarrow I^{\mathfrak{I}}(i) \in E^{\mathfrak{I}}(e)$;
    - $\forall t, i : t \in T \land i \in instT(t) \Rightarrow I^{\mathfrak{I}}(i) \in T^{\mathfrak{I}}(t)$;
    - $\forall ev, i : ev \in EV \land i \in instEV(ev) \Rightarrow I^{\mathfrak{I}}(i) \in EV^{\mathfrak{I}}(ev)$;
  - $\forall g, i : g \in G \land i \in instG(g) \Rightarrow I^{\mathfrak{I}}(i) \in G^{\mathfrak{I}}(g)$;
- $\forall w, i : w \in W \land i \in instW(w) \Rightarrow I^{\mathfrak{I}}(i) \in W^{\mathfrak{I}}(w)$;
- $\forall f, i : f \in F \land i \in instF(f) \Rightarrow I^{\mathfrak{I}}(i) \in F^{\mathfrak{I}}(f)$;
- $\forall c, i : c \in C \land i \in instC(c) \Rightarrow I^{\mathfrak{I}}(i) \in C^{\mathfrak{I}}(c)$.

The instantiation properties define the rules for workflow definition instantiations. They are:

- $\forall a1, a2, i, j : a1 \in A \land a2 \in A \land (a1, a2) \in AAR \land i \in instA(a1) \land j \in instA(a2) \Rightarrow transitionTo\left(I^{\mathfrak{I}}(i), I^{\mathfrak{I}}(j)\right)$;
- $\forall t, i, j : t \in T \land i \in instT(t) \land hasInput\left(I^{\mathfrak{I}}(i), I^{\mathfrak{I}}(j)\right) \Rightarrow \exists c : j \in c \land c \in C \land (t, c) \in CIN$;

- $\forall t, i, j : t \in T \wedge i \in instT(t) \wedge hasOutput\big(I^{\mathfrak{T}}(i), I^{\mathfrak{T}}(j)\big) \Rightarrow \exists c : j \in c \wedge c \in C \wedge (t, c) \in COUT$;
- $\forall t, i, j : t \in T \wedge i \in instT(t) \wedge perfBy\big(I^{\mathfrak{T}}(i), I^{\mathfrak{T}}(j)\big) \Rightarrow \exists w : j \in w \wedge w \in W \wedge (t, w) \in TR$;
- $\forall a, i, j : a \in A \wedge i \in instA(a) \wedge hasPriority\big(I^{\mathfrak{T}}(i), P^{\mathfrak{T}}(j)\big) \Rightarrow j \in P \wedge APR(a) = j$;
- $\forall e, i, j : e \in E \wedge i \in instE(e) \wedge execThrough\big(I^{\mathfrak{T}}(i), I^{\mathfrak{T}}(j)\big) \Rightarrow \exists f : j \in f \wedge f \in F \wedge (e, f) \in ER$.

4 Applications of CompFlow

The CompFlow upper ontology (as represented in the meta-model layer) establishes the building blocks for every workflow definition. With it, workflow-definition ontologies can be built by importing and extending the upper ontology to a specific domain while fully focusing on its specific logics. By extending tasks, events or interfaces, domain specific classes with different purposes can be created.

CompFlow can be applied to a variety of domains with several use case scenarios (e.g., human-machine computation scenarios and business workflows). In the scope of this work, a proof of concept will be presented regarding AAL. AAL scenarios normally incorporate a wide number of passive and active interaction modalities, such as sensors or actuators, touch, gestures or speech interfaces, or even location-tracking or fall-detection services [13, 16]. Given the highly dynamic nature of AAL environments, CompFlow provides the flexibility required to incorporate and maintain the cooperation of all the necessary components.

4.1 Scenario

For the purpose of a demonstration, imagine a scenario in which researchers want to assess the relevance of a help option within a certain application. For that, they establish the need to ask a simple question whenever the user interacts with the help option, thus building the workflow in fig. 3.

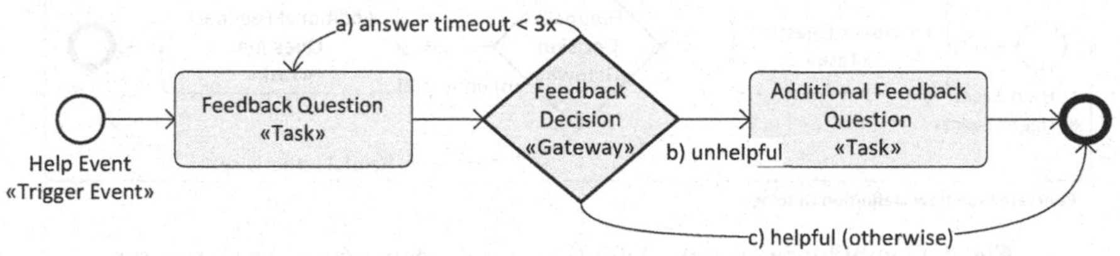

Fig. 3. AAL workflow for assessing the relevance of a help option in an application

Given the AAL paradigm, and to introduce some level of redundancy, interaction can be made via multiple interfaces such as speech and graphical interfaces. Furthermore, it is envisaged that similar additional workflows (placing questions to users) will be required as the AAL environment evolves.

4.2 Workflow-Definition

CompFlow allows a straightforward implementation of this scenario through ontologies. It establishes the building blocks for creating semantically enriched workflow-definitions, while leaving the specificities of the domain entirely up to the developer. A CompFlow execution engine is then used to instantiate and execute any concrete workflow-definition.

Fig. 4 shows the implementation of the help option AAL scenario using CompFlow. The abstract workflow-definition establishes all domain constructs required to place questions to users. At this level, and upon the initialization of the execution engine, the code blocks that handle and know the domain must be associated with each task-definition. Analogously, each interface-definition has an associated code block that handles the specificities of the interface. This not only allows the execution engine to scale through the inclusion of interface components, but also the re-usability of domain specific task-definitions that may be included in different concrete workflow-definitions. Furthermore, it is possible to define composite interface-definitions, which allow multimodal interaction through the aggregation of multiple interface-definitions. This, in turn, makes it possible to achieve concurrency, redundancy and cooperation between multiple interface components.

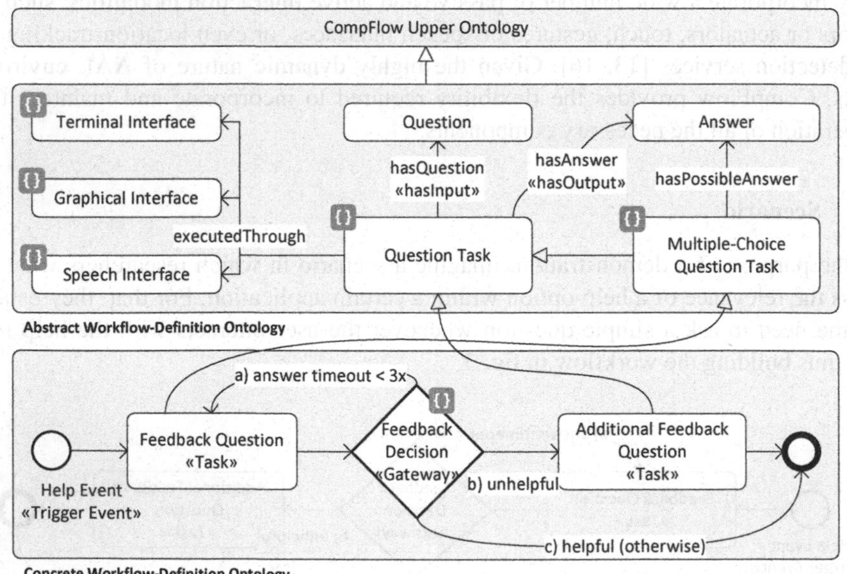

Fig. 4. CompFlow workflow-definitions for the help option AAL scenario

The execution flow starts by making the execution engine wait for a specified event. Since it is a trigger event, each manifestation of the event will result in a new instantiation of the concrete workflow-definition. The event reaches the execution engine through its associated interface, typically following a publish-subscribe pattern.

After the event is processed, a Feedback Question Task is triggered. At this stage, the task is delivered to workers (of the specified role or worker-definition) using one of two strategies: (i) the slave strategy or (ii) the agent strategy. If the engine follows the slave strategy (i), a worker is automatically selected from the set of available workers. Otherwise, if the engine follows the agent strategy (ii), the task must be delivered to all available workers, which in turn will decide if they want to participate in the task.

When an answer to the Feedback Question Task is received, the workflow continues onto the Feedback Decision Gateway. The Feedback Decision Gateway is a DecisionOutputGateway, meaning that each output path will only be followed if a specific condition is met. The logics that decide this are introduced in an associated code block that evaluates the answer from the previous task. Depending on the answer, the workflow may end, or the Additional Feedback Question may be triggered. The later results in a process very similar to that of the Feedback Question Task, although it refers to a free text question instead of a multiple-choice question.

5 Conclusions and Future Work

The CompFlow process and upper ontology represents an approach to workflow-definition, instantiation and execution that exploits the benefits of Description Logic ontologies and technologies. Its nature allows the straightforward definition of semantically enriched workflows that are scalable and re-usable. The benefits of the CompFlow are relevant to multiple application domains and scenarios such as human-machine computation in general and AAL, in particular.

A formal definition of the meta-model (upper ontology) is given, which can be followed for the implementation of CompFlow compatible workflow execution engines. The structure and semantics provided by the ontology definitions allow these execution engines to deliver tasks to both human and machine workers able to understand the domain of knowledge. An early implementation of the CompFlow execution engine proves the applicability of CompFlow in AAL environments through the given scenario.

Given the minimalistic structure of the CompFlow upper ontology, new features will be added in the near future, which can be either considered as an application of CompFlow or, if generic enough, be assimilated into the proposed upper ontology and process. In the particular case of the later, a more thorough definition of gateway and task is envisaged in order to avoid the requirement of code blocks in gateway-definitions and task-definitions.

Acknowledgements. This work is partially funded by FEDER Funds and by the ERDF (European Regional Development Fund) through the COMPETE Programme (operational programme for competitiveness) and by National Funds through the FCT (Portuguese Foundation for Science and Technology) under the projects AAL4ALL (QREN13852) and FCOMP-01-0124-FEDER-028980 (PTDC/EEI-SII/1386/2012).

References

1. Eshuis, R., Wieringa, R.: A formal semantics for UML Activity Diagrams-Formalising workflow models (2001)
2. Van Der Aalst, W.M., Ter Hofstede, A.H.: YAWL: yet another workflow language. Inf. Syst. 30, 245–275 (2005)
3. Weske, M.: Formal foundation and conceptual design of dynamic adaptations in a workflow management system. In: Proc. 34th Annu. Hawaii Int. Conf. on Syst. Sci. IEEE (2001)
4. Wodtke, D., Weikum, G.: A formal foundation for distributed workflow execution based on state charts. In: Afrati, F.N., Kolaitis, P.G. (eds.) ICDT 1997. LNCS, vol. 1186, pp. 230–246. Springer, Heidelberg (1996)
5. Vieira, T.A.S., Casanova, M.A., Ferrao, L.G.: An ontology-driven architecture for flexible workflow execution. In: WebMedia -Web 2004 Proc., pp. 70–77. IEEE (2004)
6. Van der Aalst, W.M.P.: Don't go with the flow: Web services composition standards exposed. IEEE Intell. Syst. 18, 72–76 (2003)
7. Martin, D., et al.: Bringing semantics to web services: The OWL-S approach. In: Cardoso, J., Sheth, A.P., et al. (eds.) SWSWPC 2004. LNCS, vol. 3387, pp. 26–42. Springer, Heidelberg (2005)
8. Obrst, L., Liu, H., Wray, R.: Ontologies for Corporate Web Applications. AI Mag. 24, 49 (2003)
9. Happel, H.-J., Seedorf, S.: Applications of ontologies in software engineering. In: Proc. Workshop Semat. Web Enabled Softw. Eng., ISWC, pp. 5–9. Citeseer (2006)
10. Oberle, D.: How ontologies benefit enterprise applications. Semantic Web Journal - Interoperability, Usability, Applicability (2009)
11. Luz, N., Silva, N., Novais, P.: Construction of Human-Computer Micro-Task Workflows using Domain Ontologies. In: ESWC 2014 (submitted, 2014)
12. Quinn, A.J., Bederson, B.B.: Human Computation: A Survey and Taxonomy of a Growing Field. In: Proc. SIGCHI Conf. Hum. Factors Comput. Syst., pp. 1403–1412. ACM, New York (2011)
13. Teixeira, A., Rocha, N., Pereira, C., et al.: The Living Lab Architecture: Support for the Development and Evaluation of New AAL Services for the Elderly. Ambient Assisted Living Book. Taylor and Francis, USA (2011) (accepted)
14. Eugster, P.T., Felber, P.A., Guerraoui, R., Kermarrec, A.-M.: The many faces of publish/subscribe. ACM Comput. Surv. CSUR 35, 114–131 (2003)
15. Baader, F., Calvanese, D., McGuinness, D.L., et al.: The Description Logic Handbook: Theory, Implementation, and Applications, 2nd edn. Cambridge University Press (2007)
16. Abraham, A.: Special Issue: Hybrid Approaches for Approximate Reasoning. Journal of Intelligent and Fuzzy Systems 23, 41–42 (2012)

A Fuzzy Reinforcement Learning Approach to QoS Provisioning Transmission in Cognitive Radio Networks

Jerzy Martyna

Institute of Computer Science, Faculty of Mathematics and Computer Science
Jagiellonian University, ul. Prof. S. Lojasiewicza 6, 30-348 Cracow, Poland

Abstract. In this paper, we introduce a new fuzzy reinforcement learning method to quality of service (QoS) provisioning cognitive transmission in cognitive radio networks. The cognitive transmissions under QoS constraints are treated here as the data sending at two different average power levels depending on the activity of the primary (licensed) users, which is determined by the secondary (unlicensed) users. For this transmission, the model is defined a state-transition model. The maximum throughput under these statistical QoS constraints is determined by using fuzzy QoS reinforcement learning techniques. The performance effectiveness of the proposed method is obtained in situations and comparison with the numerical method based on the effective capacity of the cognitive radio channel under various QoS constraints. It is shown that the hybrid AI method used outperforms comparable results obtained by the classical numerical method, including various situations with different QoS limitations.

1 Introduction

Hybrid artificial intelligence systems are defined as any combination of intelligent technologies (e.g. neuro-fuzzy approaches, evolutionary optimised networks, etc.), but particularly those that prove to have an obvious advantage in their performance. Therefore, hybrid artificial intelligence systems have been used in various application domains such as medical diagnoses from data images [14], industrial and environmental applications [5], strategic human resource management in high-technology companies [11], etc. Hybrid artificial intelligence can then be considered as the ability to act appropriately in an uncertain environment using artificial intelligence techniques such as learning, reasoning, adaptation, etc.

Cognitive radio (CR) [10], [7] deals with intelligent assignment and the use of the radio spectrum and cognitive networking [2], which deals with the intelligent routing of information through a network, and are new research fields for hybrid artificial intelligence applications. A cognitive radio network is defined by Thomas [13] as a computer network with a cognitive process that can detect current network conditions, learn from previous and current network environ-

M. Polycarpou et al. (Eds.): HAIS 2014, LNAI 8480, pp. 61–73, 2014.
© Springer International Publishing Switzerland 2014

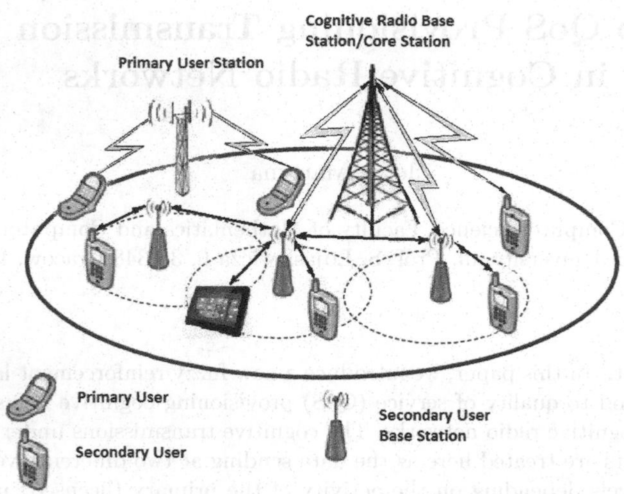

Fig. 1. An example of downlink/uplink cognitive radio

ments, and improve its network parameters. It can provide a better wireless network service by improving its network parameters through this cognitive process.

The resource allocation problem in downlink (Cognitive Radio Base Station/Core Station, CRBS/CS, to secondary users transmission) and uplink (secondary users to CRBS/CS) is depicted in Fig. 1. As shown in Fig. 1, the cognitive radio network coexists with the primary (licensed) system in the same geographical location. The cognitive radio network is able to opportunistically access the available unused spectrum bands without causing interference to the primary users. There is no synchronization between the primary system and cognitive radio network.

Providing quality of service (QoS) guarantees over cognitive radio channels has not been sufficiently studied yet. Multimedia services such as video and audio transmission require bounded delays or guaranteed bandwidth. A hard delay bound guarantee is infeasible due to the impact of the time varying fading cognitive channels. For example, over the Rayleigh fading channel, the only lower-bound of the system bandwidth that can be deterministically guaranteed is a bandwidth of zero.

Thus, we use an alternative solution by providing the statistical QoS constraints that guarantee a delay-bound with a small violation probability. Moreover, in cognitive radio channels in which access to the channel can be intermittent, or transmission occurs at lower power levels depending on the activity of the primary users (PUs). Furthermore, cognitive radios can suffer from errors in channel sensing as false alarms. Hence, the performance of cognitive radio systems under QoS constraints can be studied as a form of delay or buffer constraints.

It is our opinion that the QoS provisioning problem raising in cognitive radio networks can be properly solved using techniques based on artificial intelligence methods. In particular, we propose the application of fuzzy reinforcement learning methods to implement the decision making process in situations where inputs are generally uncertain, imprecise or qualitatively interpreted. As a result, in this paper, we propose a distributed algorithm that can be implemented in each of the secondary user stations. It allows the implementation of the QoS provisioning transmissions for each of the secondary users with low complexity from both hardware and software perspectives. Moreover, the proposed solutions can be used in many real-time applications such as mobile TV, TV distribution (e.g. Video on Demand over DTT), TV White Spaces, etc.

The main goal of this paper is as follows. We propose a novel fuzzy reinforcement learning for QoS provisioning transmission in cognitive radio networks. The suggested method includes the traditional fuzzy logic system with the determined membership function, as well as the reinforcement learning algorithm. Using simulation experiments, we have found the highest probability for QoS provisioning transmission to secondary users (SUs) for defined parameters of the CR network.

The remainder of the paper is organised as follows. Section 2 describes the system model. Section 3 gives an overview of the fuzzy reinforcement learning method applied to the QoS provisioning system in CR networks. Section 4 outlines the results of simulation experiment. In Section 5, we present the conclusion.

2 System Model

In this section, we present the model for QoS provisioning transmission in cognitive radio networks. We also formulate the radio channel model and provide the effective capacity term of the cognitive radio channel.

Consider a cognitive radio network with the secondary users and free radio channels available for use by multiple secondary users. Each channel can be used simultaneously by multiple secondary users. Moreover, a single secondary user can use several channels at the same time to achieve their requirements.

2.1 Cognitive Channel Model

Cognitive radio channel model allows the sending of information by a secondary transmitter to a secondary user, possibly in the presence of primary users. The cognitive radio channel will be tested by secondary users. If the secondary transmitter selects its transmission when the channel is busy, the average power is $\overline{P}_1$ and the rate is r_1. When the channel is idle, the average power is $\overline{P}_2$ and the rate is r_2. We assume that $\overline{P}_1 = 0$ denotes the stoppage of the secondary transmission in the presence of an active primary user. Both transmission rates, r_1 and r_2, can be fixed or time-variant depending on whether the transmitter has channel side information or not. In general, we assume that $\overline{P}_1 < \overline{P}_2$. In the

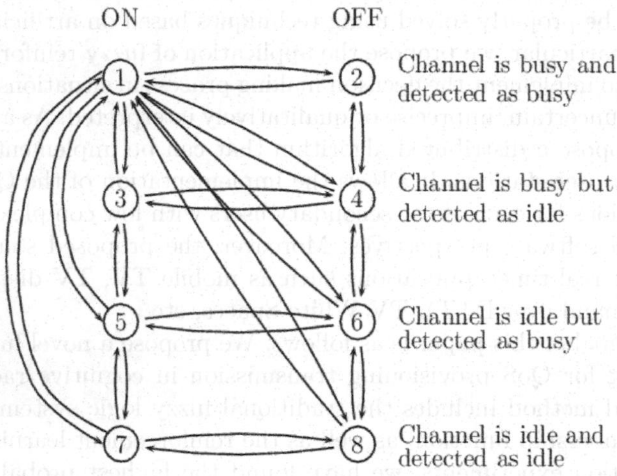

Fig. 2. State transition model for the cognitive radio channel

above model, the discrete-time channel input-output relation in the absence in the channel of the primary users is given by

$$y(i) = h(i)x(i) + n(i), \quad i = 1, 2, \ldots \tag{1}$$

where $h(i)$ is the channel coefficient, i is the symbol duration. If primary users are present in the channel, the discrete-time channel input-output relation is given by

$$y(i) = h(i)x(i) + s_p(i) + n(i), \quad i = 1, 2, \ldots \tag{2}$$

where $s_p(i)$ represents the sum of the active primary users' faded signals arriving at the secondary receiver $n(i)$ is the additive thermal noise at the receiver and is zero-mean, circularly symmetric, complex Gaussian random variable with variance $E\{|n(i)|^2\} = \sigma_n^2$ for all i.

We assume that the receiver knows the instantaneous lambda values $\{h(i)\}$, while the transmitter has no such knowledge. We construct a state-transition model for cognitive transmission by considering the cases in which the fixed transmission rates are lesser or greater than the instantaneous channel capacity values. In particular, the ON state is achieved if the fixed rate is smaller than the instantaneous channel capacity. Otherwise, the OFF state occurs.

We assume that the maximum throughput can be obtained in the state-throughput model [1], which is given in Fig. 2. Four possible scenarios are associated with the model, namely:

1) channel is busy, detected as busy (correct detection),
2) channel is busy, detected as idle (miss-detection),

3) channel is idle, detected as busy (false alarm),
4) channel is idle, detected as idle (correct detection).

If the channel is detected as busy, the secondary transmitter sends with power $\overline{P}_1$. Otherwise, it transmits with a larger power, $\overline{P}_2$. In the above four scenarios, we have the instantaneous channel capacity, namely

$$C_1 = B\log_2(1 + SNR_1 \cdot z(i)) \text{ channel is busy, detected as busy} \quad (3)$$

$$C_2 = B\log_2(1 + SNR_2 \cdot z(i)) \text{ channel is busy, detected as idle} \quad (4)$$

$$C_3 = B\log_2(1 + SNR_3 \cdot z(i)) \text{ channal is idle, detected as busy} \quad (5)$$

$$C_4 = B\log_2(1 + SNR_4 \cdot z(i)) \text{ channel is idle, detected as idle} \quad (6)$$

where B is the bandwidth available in the system, $z(i) = [h(i)]^2$, SNR_i for $i = 1, \ldots, 4$ denotes the average signal-to-noise ratio (SNR) values in each possible scenario.

The cognitive transmission is associated with the ON state in scenarios 1 and 3, when the fixed rates are below the instantaneous capacity values ($r_1 < C_1$ or $r_2 < C_2$). Otherwise, reliable communication is not obtained when the transmission is in the OFF state in scenarios 2 and 4. Thus, the fixed rates above are the instantaneous capacity values ($r_1 \geq C_1$ or $r_2 \geq C_2$). The above channel model has 8 states and is depicted in Fig. 2. In states 1, 3, 5 and 7, the transmission is in the ON state and is successfully realised. In the states 2, 4, 6 and 8 the transmission is in the OFF state and fails.

2.2 Effective Capacity

The statistical QoS constraints in cognitive radio networks can be identified through effective capacity. Effective capacity was introduced by Wu and Negi [16] as the maximum constant arrival rate that a given time-varying service process can support while meeting the QoS requirements.

We assume that the maximum throughput can be obtained in the state-transition model [1]. The effective capacity is expressed by:

$$E_c(\theta) = -\frac{1}{\theta}\log(E[e^{-\theta R}]) \quad (7)$$

where R is the independent identical distributed (i.i.d.) service process and $E[y]$ is taking expectation over y. Specifically, if $\theta \geq -\log \epsilon / D_{max}$, then:

$$\sup_t Pr\{D(t) \geq D_{max}\} \leq \epsilon \quad (8)$$

where D_{max} is the maximum tolerable delay of the traffic rate and $D(t)$ is the delay at time t. The Eq. (8) indicating that the probability that the traffic rate delay exceeds the maximum tolerable delay is below ϵ.

By using effective capacity Tang and Zhang [12] have determined that the optimal power and rate adaptation techniques that maximise the system throughput under QoS constraints. The effective capacity and resource allocation strategies for Markov wireless channel models were studied by Liu et al. [9]. In this study, the continuous Gilbert-Elliot channel model with ON and OFF states was used. The energy efficiency under QoS constraints was analysed by Gursoy et al. [6] in low power and wideband regions. Unfortunately, none of the above-mentioned papers have been not considered in the application of artificial intelligence systems to solve the formulated problem.

3 Fuzzy Reinforcement Learning Methods for QoS Provisioning Transmission in the Cognitive Radio Network

We assume that each secondary user possesses three sensors: one to detect the required SNR, the second to detect the primary user transmission and the third to define channel quality. For a two-dimensional environment, all of this information obtained by the j-th secondary user is given by Fig. 3.

The current SNR is defined by the membership function plotted in the Fig. 3(a) and 3(b). Fig. 3(c) and 3(d) show the membership function associated with the required SNR. The levels of acceptance of transmission realized by primary users are defined by the membership functions presented in Fig. 3(e) and Fig. 3(f). Fig. 3(g) and 3(h) show the membership function associated with channel transmission rate defined by the current value of r.

A membership value defining the fuzzy state of the j-th SU with reference to the k-th transmission channel in respect current SNR for a two-dimensional environment is given by:

$$\mu^{(j)}_{state}(current\ SNR^{(k)}) = \mu^{(j)}_{x}(current\ SNR^{(k)}) \cdot \mu^{(j)}_{y}(current\ SNR^{(k)}) \quad (9)$$

A membership function defining the fuzzy state of thhe j-th SU with reference to the k-th transmission channel in respect of the required SNR for a two-dimensional environment is as follows:

$$\mu^{(j)}_{state}(required\ SNR^{(k)}) = \mu^{(j)}_{x}(required\ SNR^{(k)}) \cdot \mu^{(j)}_{y}(required\ SNR^{(k)}) \quad (10)$$

A membership function defining the fuzzy state of the j-th SU defining its acceptance level of transmission realized by the l-th PU for a two-dimensional environment is as follows:

$$\mu^{(j)}_{state}(PU\ acceptance^{(l)}) = \mu^{(j)}_{x}(PU\ acceptance^{(l)}) \cdot \mu^{(j)}_{y}(PU\ acceptance^{(l)}) \quad (11)$$

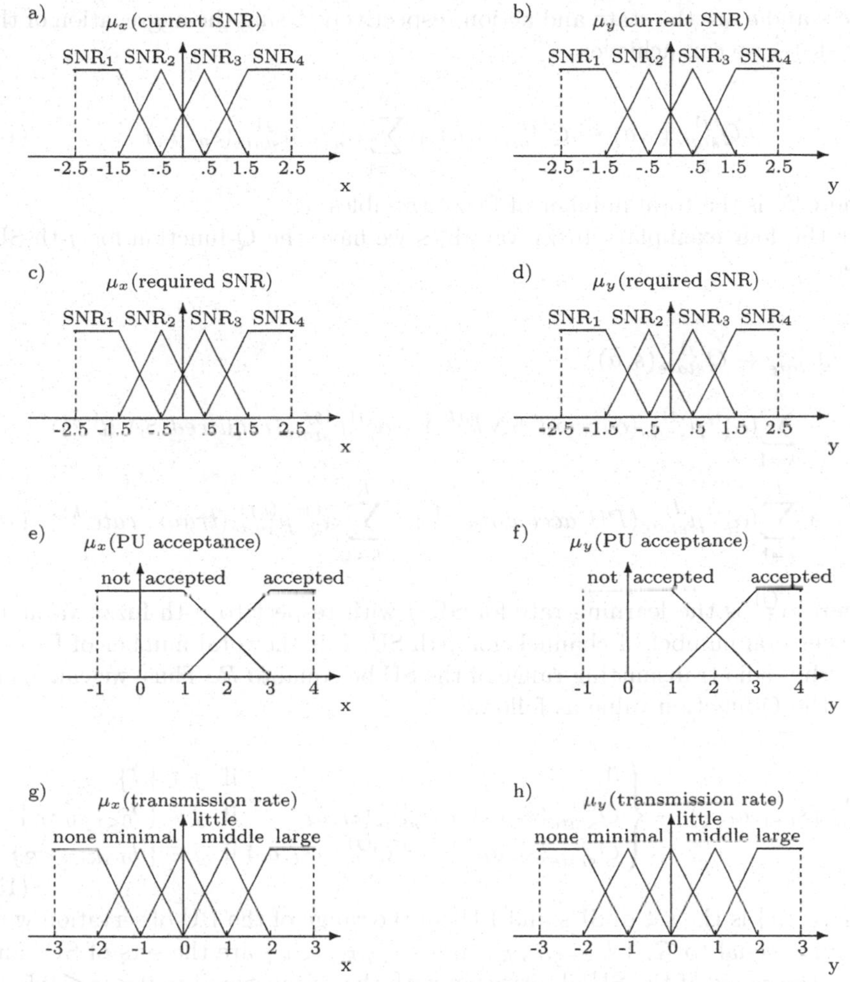

Fig. 3. Fuzzy sets for two-dimensional environment defining membership functions of *current SNR* (a, b), *required SNR* (c, d) with reference to the studied channel, *PU acceptance* (e, f) with respect to the nearest PU; *transmission rate* with reference to the studied channel

Similarly, the current transmission rate of j-th SU with reference to the k-th channel which also defines the fuzzy state for a two-dimensional environment is computed as:

$$\mu_{state}^{(j)}(trans.\ rate^{(m)} = \mu_x^{(j)}(trans.\ rate^{(k)}) \cdot \mu_y^{(j)}(trans.\ rate^{(k)}) \qquad (12)$$

The system model is described by the multidimensional membership function, which can be treated as a multidimensional hypercube. The fuzzy state for the

j-th SU can be defined by the fuzzy pair (s_n, a_n) for the n-th fuzzy variable, where s and a are the state and action respectively. Using the aggregation of the fuzzy state, we can achieve:

$$Q^{(j)}_{state}(s,a) \leftarrow Q^{(j)}_{state}(s,a) + \sum_{n=1}^{N} \alpha^{(j)}_n \cdot \mu^{(j)}_{state}(s_n, a_n) \tag{13}$$

where N is the total number of fuzzy variables.

For the four exemplary fuzzy variables we have the Q-function for j-th SU, namely

$$\begin{aligned} Q^{(j)}_{state} &\leftarrow Q^{(j)}_{state}(s,a) \\ &+ \sum_{k=1}^{K} (\alpha^{(j)}_k \mu^{(j)}_{state}(current\ SNR^{(k)}) + \alpha^{(j)}_k \mu^{(j)}_{state}(required\ SNR^{(k)})) \\ &+ \sum_{l=1}^{L} (\alpha^{(j)}_l \mu^{(l)}_{state}(PU\ acceptance^{(l)}) + \sum_{k=1}^{K} \alpha^{(j)}_k \mu^{(k)}_{state}(trans.\ rate^{(k)}) \end{aligned} \tag{14}$$

where $\alpha^{(j)}_n$ is the learning rate for SU j with respect to n-th fuzzy variable, K is the total number of channels for j-th SU, L is the total number of PUs.

Let the radio transmitting range of the SU be equal to $\mathcal{R}$. Thus, we can again define the Q-function value as follows:

$$Q^{(j)}_{state}(s_{t+1}, a_{t+1}) \leftarrow \begin{cases} 0 & \text{if } j \notin \{J\} \\ Q^{(j)}_{state}(s_t, a_t) + \alpha^{(j)}_{state}(s_t, a_t) & \text{if } j \in \{J_{0<\tau\leq 0.5\mathcal{R}}\} \\ Q^{(j)}_{state}(s_t, a_t) + \beta^{(j)} Q^{(j)}_{state}(s_t, a_t) & \text{if } j \in \{J_{0.5\mathcal{R}<\tau\leq\mathcal{R}}\} \end{cases} \tag{15}$$

where $\{J\}$ is the set of SUs and PUs in the range of the PU observation with the radius equal to $\mathcal{R}$, $\{J_{0<\tau\leq 0.5\cdot\mathcal{R}}\}$ and $\{J_{0.5\cdot\mathcal{R}<\tau\leq\mathcal{R}}\}$ are the sets of SUs and PUs in the range of the SU observation with the radius equal to $0 < \tau \leq 0.5 \cdot \mathcal{R}$ and $0.5 \cdot \mathcal{R} < \tau \leq \mathcal{R}$, respectively. $\beta^{(j)}$ are learning rate factors.

The state space in reinforcement learning can be treated as a stochastic problem. In the standard approach, we can generalise the Q-value across states using the function approximation $Q(s, a, f)$ for approximating $Q(s, a)$, where f is the set of all learned fuzzy logic mechanisms [3], [4]. To handle all the information, we can use the data mining approach.

Fig. 4 presents the system architecture used for the data mining process of a single SU station in the CR network. The data mining process referring to a single SU is given by the following procedure:

Procedure 1

1) The SU by use its sensors fixes the current values of all the membership functions. Further, it defines the actual value of state-action pair.

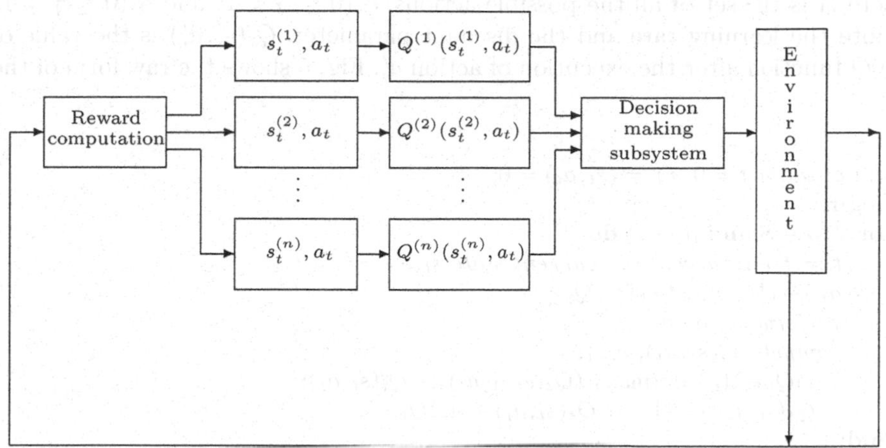

Fig. 4. A block diagram for an agent system architecture in case of data mining

2) The SU computes the learning rate α, which for the j-th SU is given as follows:

$$\alpha^{(j)} = \frac{1}{\sum_{n=1}^{N} \mu_{state}^{(n)}} \tag{16}$$

where N is the total number of fuzzy variables. Above equation shows that by increase of the number of fuzzy variables the learning rate becomes smaller.

3) The SU computes the Q-function for each fuzzy parameter. We applied the selection procedure based on Kóczy-Hirot method presented a.o. by Joó [8]. This method computes a conclusion as a weighted sum of vague consequent values b_n, which is given by

$$C(b_h) = \frac{\sum_{h=1}^{H} w_h \cdot dist(y_0, b_h)}{\sum_{h=1}^{H} w_h} \tag{17}$$

where w_h is the weight inverse proportional to the vague distance of the observation x from action a. For the h-th rule the weight is defined as

$$w_h = \frac{1}{dist(x, a)} \tag{18}$$

5) After the choice of the action by the SU the reward function $r_t(s_t, a_t)$ is computed. Further, it upgrades the ΔQ_t and computes $Q_t(s_t, a_t)$.

6) The computation goes to step 1. ■

The function Q is computed by the Q-learning algorithm; this algorithm was presented by Watkins and Watkins and Dayan [15]. We recall that the Q-function is given by:

$$Q_t(s_t, a_t) = (1 - \alpha)Q_t(s_t, a_t) + \alpha(r_t + \gamma \max_{a_t \in A} Q_t(s_t', a_t')) \tag{19}$$

where A is the set of all the possible actions, α $(0 \leq \alpha < 1)$ and γ $(0 \leq \gamma \leq 1)$ denote the learning rate and the discount parameter, $Q_t(s'_t, a'_t)$ is the value of the Q function after the execution of action a'_t. Fig. 5 shows the raw form of the

initialization $t = 0$, $r_T = (s_t, a_t) = 0$;
begin
for $\forall\ s_t \in S$ **and** $a_t \in A$ **do**
$t := t + 1$; *access the current state* s_t;
$a_t \leftarrow$ *choose_action*(s_t, Q_t);
perform_action a_t;
compute: $r_t(s_t, a_t)$, s_{t+1};
$\Delta Q_t \leftarrow (r_t + \gamma \max_{a_t}(Q_t(s_{t+1}, a_t)) - Q_t(s_t, a_t)$;
$Q_t(s_t, a_t) \leftarrow (1 - \alpha) Q_t(s_t, a_t) + \alpha \Delta Q_t$;
end;

Fig. 5. Q-learning algorithm estimates new state obtained by performing the chosen action at each time step

Q-learning algorithm. It can be seen that the Q-learning algorithm is an incremental reinforcement learning method. The choice of the action does not show how to obtain it. Therefore, the Q-learning algorithm can use other strategies that it learns, irrespective of the assumed strategy. This means that it does not need actions that would maximise the reward function.

4 Simulation Results

In this section, we highlight the performance of the learning framework presented in the previous sections.

We simulated the cognitive framework as an extension of wireless LANs with cognitive radio capability. We used an arrangement of 12 secondary transmitters and receivers randomly distributed on a quadrat equal to 200 m × 200 m. The maximum power of each of the secondary users is equal to 20 dBm. A primary unity with a maximum power equal to 30 dBm is located at the central point of the simulated area.

In this illustrative simulation, we assume that the highlight of the impact on the multimedia quality of all six pairs of secondary transmitters stream the multimedia data to their receivers. The primary user randomly disturbs their transmission.

For each pair of secondary users, we simulated 3000 samples of Rayleigh faded received signals. Analogously, for the primary user, we generated 3000 randomly distributed Rayleigh faded signal samples.

For the decision system, 12 rules with various heights have been used. For rules considering the required SNR values, we have a weight equal to 3. All four rules associated with the primary user have weights equal to 2. The weights

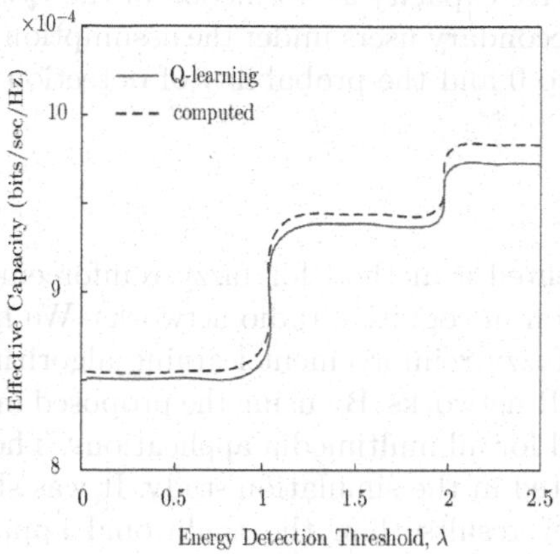

Fig. 6. Effective capacity as a function of the detection threshold value for the secondary users

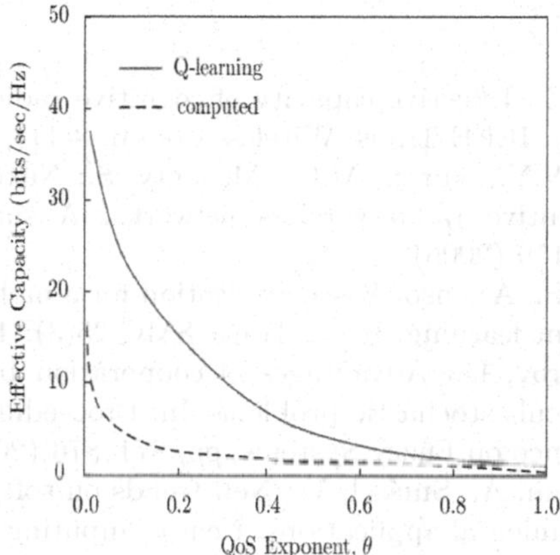

Fig. 7. Effective capacity versus QoS exponent θ for the secondary users

considering the current value of SNR have a value equal to 1. We assume that the radio transmitting range for secondary users is equal to 50 m. The channel bandwidth is equal to 100 kHz. The QoS exponent is equal to 0.001. The average SNR values when the channels are correctly detected are $\text{SNR}_1 = 0$ dBm and $\text{SNR}_4 = 1$ dBm for busy and idle channels respectively.

The results obtained by the simulation have been compared with the computational results achieved using the effective capacity method applied to the streaming multimedia data. Fig. 6 shows the effective capacity as a function of the detection threshold value λ. As we see in Fig. 6 the effective capacity is increasing with increasing the detection threshold value λ.

Fig. 7 plots the effective capacity as a function of the QoS exponent obtained for both classes of the secondary users under the assumption that the probability of false alarm is equal to 0 and the probability of detection is equal to 1.

5 Conclusion

In this paper, we presented a method for fuzzy reinforcement learning in QoS provisioning transmission in cognitive radio networks. We have also proposed a new algorithm for the fuzzy reinforcement learning algorithm that can be used by secondary users in CR networks. By using the proposed method, CR networks can offer great potential for all multimedia applications. The effectiveness of our technique is demonstrated in the simulation study. It was shown that presented solution provides better results than the traditional approach to QoS provisioning transmission in CR networks. Moreover, the proposed method could be viewed as a starting point in the design of other techniques such as neuro-fuzzy or type-2 fuzzy logic controllers.

References

1. Akin, S., Gursoy, M.C.: Effective capacity of cognitive radio channels for quality of service provisioning. IEEE Trans. Wireless Comm. 8(11), 3354–3364 (2010)
2. Akyildiz, I.F., Lee, W.Y., Vuran, M.C., Mohanty, S.: Next generation/dynamic spectrum access/cognitive radio wireless networks: A survey. Computer Networks 50(13), 2127–2159 (2006)
3. Beon, H.R., Chen, H.S.: A sensor-based navigation for a mobile robot using fuzzy-logic and reinforcement learning. IEEE Trans. SMC 25(3), 467–477 (1995)
4. Berenji, H.R., Vengerov, D.: Advantages of cooperation between reinforcement learning agent in difficult stochastic problems. In: Proceedings of the Ninth IEEE International Conference on Fuzzy Systems, pp. 871–876 (2000)
5. Corchado, E., Abraham, A., Smásel, V.: New trends on soft computing models in industrial and environmental applications. Neurocomputing 109, 1–2 (2013)
6. Gursoy, M.C., Deli, Q., Velipasalar, S.: Analysis of energy efficiency in fading channel under qos constraints. IEEE Trans. Wireless Comm. 8(8), 4252–4263 (2009)
7. Haykin, S.: Cognitive radio: Brain-empowered wireless communications. IEEE Journal on Selected Areas in Communications 23(2), 201–220 (2005)
8. Joó, L., Kóczy, L.T., Tikk, D., Varlaki, P.: On a stable interpretation method. In: Proceedings of the 7th International Fuzzy System Association World Congress, pp. 133–137 (1997)
9. Liu, L., Parag, P., Tang, J., Chen, W.Y., Chamberland, J.F.: Resource allocation and quality of service evaluation for wireless communication systems using fluid models. IEEE Trans. on Information Theory 53(5), 1767–1777 (2007)
10. Mitola, J.R., Maguire Jr., G.Q.: Cognitive radio: Making software radios more personal. IEEE Personal Communications 6(4), 13–18 (1999)
11. Sáiz, L., Manzanedo, M.A., Pérez, A., Herrero, Á., Corchado, E.: Hybrid visualization for deep insight into knowledge retention in firms. In: Pan, J.-S., Polycarpou, M.M., Woźniak, M., de Carvalho, A.C.P.L.F., Quintián, H., Corchado, E. (eds.) HAIS 2013. LNCS, vol. 8073, pp. 280–293. Springer, Heidelberg (2013)

12. Tang, J., Zhang, X.: Quality of service driven power and rate adaptation over wireless links. IEEE Trans. Wireless Comm. 6(8), 3058–3068 (2007)
13. Thomas, R.W., DaSilva, L.A., MacKenzie, A.B.: Cognitive networks. In: Proc. of the Dynamic Spectrum Access Networks, pp. 352–360 (2005)
14. Trzupek, M., Ogiela, M.R., Tadeusiewicz, R.: Intelligent image content semantic description for cardiac 3d visualisations. Eng. Appl. of AI 24(8), 1410–1418 (2011)
15. Watkins, C.J.C.H., Dayan, P.: Technical note: Q-learning. Machine Learning 8, 279–292 (1992)
16. Wu, D., Negi, R.: Effective capacity: A wireless link model for support of quality of service. IEEE Trans. Wireless Comm. 2(4), 630–643 (2003)

Time Series Segmentation and Statistical Characterisation of the Spanish Stock Market Ibex-35 Index

M. Cruz-Ramírez[1,*], M. de la Paz-Marín[2], M. Pérez-Ortiz[1], and C. Hervás-Martínez[1]

[1] Dept. of Computer Science and Numerical Analysis, University of Córdoba, Córdoba, Spain
{mcruz,i82perom,chervas}@uco.es

[2] Dept. of Management and Quantitative Methods, Loyola University, Córdoba, Spain
ma2pamam@uco.es

Abstract. The discovery of characteristic time series patterns is of fundamental importance in financial applications. Repetitive structures and common type of segments can provide very useful information of patterns in financial time series. In this paper, we introduce a time series segmentation and characterisation methodology combining a maximal likelihood optimisation procedure and a clustering technique to automatically segment common patterns from financial time series and address the problem of stock market prices trends. To do so, the obtained segments are transformed into a five-dimensional space composed of five typical statistical measures in order to group them according to their statistical properties. The experimental results show that it is possible to exploit the behaviour of the stock market Ibex-35 Spanish index (closing prices) to detect homogeneous segments of the time series.

Keywords: Clustering, Ibex-35 index, segmentation, stock market, time series.

1 Introduction

Time series are an important type of temporal data objects that are collected chronologically. Time series analysis is a challenging topic in the machine learning community because of the intrinsic characteristics of these data (e.g. the natural temporal ordering of the data or the potential random fluctuations of the underlying dynamics of the time series), which hampers their analysis. In this context, the term time series data mining [1] refers to a wide range of techniques which are used with the purpose of exploratory analysis, prediction and forecasting, hidden pattern discovery, segmentation or visualisation, among others. This paper is framed in the context of time series segmentation and pattern

* Corresponding author.

M. Polycarpou et al. (Eds.): HAIS 2014, LNAI 8480, pp. 74–85, 2014.
© Springer International Publishing Switzerland 2014

discovery. More specifically, the problem of segmenting a financial time series in order to group the resultant segments into similar clusters is considered.

Based on the work of Cheong *et al.* [2], this paper introduces the concept of maximal likelihood ratio (denoted as max-LR) for time series segmentation. This likelihood ratio can be used for dividing the time series considered (or part of it) until a predefined threshold is reached. As opposed to the original proposal, we also consider the problem of characterising the segments obtained from the previous segmentation step. To do so, firstly, five common statistical measures are computed for each segment and a clustering technique is used thereafter with the purpose of assigning a class label to each segment and automatically cluster common patterns within the framework of financial time series. As said, this two-fold technique is used for discovering stock market prices trends (see [3], which attempts in a similar way to detect macroeconomic phases based on the Dow Jones Industrial Average).

Concerning the analysis of stock prices, there are two main schools of thought, two different methods of answering to the questions of what and when to buy or sell that can be found in the financial literature: fundamental and technical analysis. Recently, a third approach, known as cyclical, has made rapid progress and promises to contribute a great deal to our understanding of economic trends. In this work, we move between the cyclical and the technical analysis[1] approaches as our analysis is based on charts and figures but we also search for characteristic cycles in a long time series. More specifically, the characteristics of the resultant segments from the segmentation algorithm (when considering the time period 1992-2013) are investigated following the analysis of the behaviour of 'bear', 'bull' and 'sluggish' markets, as defined by Pagan and Sossounov [5]. From this analysis, several patterns are identified as time periods[2] of a generalised upward trend (positive returns), periods of a generalised downward trend (negative returns) and accumulative/distribution phases, respectively, based on technical analysis. On both bases, we concentrate on aspects of the stock market behaviour by relating the resultant segments to several well-known financial patterns.

The research conducted in this paper corresponds to the first step of a two-phase time series study. As said, this paper focuses on the identification of characteristic temporal patterns associated to stock market time series (the Spanish Ibex-35). The second future step would correspond to event prediction or forecasting using the temporal patterns identified in the previous phase (as opposed to common prediction strategies in time series).

The rest of the paper is organized as follows. Section 2 presents a little state of the art about segmentation, while Section 3 presents and discusses the clustering

[1] Technical analysis is the science of recording, usually in graphic form, the actual history of trading (price changes, volume of transactions, etc.) in a certain stock and then deducing from that pictured history the probable future trend [4].

[2] Trend analysis studies also include the well-known Elliott Wave Principle, Dow Theory and related vocabulary as primary trend.

segmentation. In Section 4, some results are presented and analysed. The last section depicts the conclusions and future lines of research.

2 Overview of the Segmentation Problem

In general, time series segmentation consists of two interdependent steps: detecting nonstationarity and localising important or characteristic events in the time series. Most of the segmentation techniques can be subdivided into methods based on one distribution and methods based on two distributions.

The one-distribution or one-model method bases the segmentation on the presence of significant deviations of the residuals from its assumed behaviour (which is given by the selected distribution), i.e., these methods analyse whether the time series values follow the predefined distribution (where the choice of this function is an important step of these techniques). Typical one-model segmentation algorithms includes the online versions of CUSUM (Cumulative Sum) and GLR (Generalized Likelihood Ratio) tests [6], the sliding windows Algorithm, and its extension, the Sliding-Windows-And-Bottom-up (SWAB) algorithm [7].

In contrast, the two-distribution approach assumes that there exist a cut point in the time series where the distributions of the time values before and after this cut point differ. This kind of segmentation methods bases the segmentation on some convenient measures of differences between two distributions, which we denote as the reference distribution (hypothetical distribution before the cut point) and test distribution (the distribution after the cut point). Two main questions underlying the two-distribution segmentation arise: firstly, as in the case of one-distribution methods, how to identify the reference and test distributions; and secondly, how to measure the differences between the two distributions. Several statistics have been suggested to measure this difference such as the maximal generalised likelihood ratio (max-GLR) [2,8], the Chernoff's distance [9] or the maximal Vald statistic (max-W) [10]. The methodology used in this paper can be framed under the category of two-distributions methods (the assumed distribution is the Normal and it makes uses of the maximal likelihood ratio in order to measure the previously mentioned difference).

On the other hand, other time series segmentation works consider the discretisation of continuous time series (or segments) into meaningful labels/symbols [11,12] (an approach known as the "numeric-to-symbolic" conversion). This is usually done by considering the mean of each segment, but other statistical properties can be considered as well (such as the ones considered in this paper, where each segment is characterised using a clustering analysis process). This is a useful approach (which is used after segmenting the time series) when trying to detect similar patterns in the time series or for a prediction phase.

3 Time Series Segmentation and Clustering

The problem of time-series segmentation considered is the following: Given a time series $X = \{x_i \mid i = 1, \ldots, N\}$, partition the set of values x_i into m consecutive subsets/segments within which the behaviour of x_i is homogeneous. The segmentation algorithm should provide a partition of the time index set into subsets: $S_1 = \{x_1, \ldots, x_{t_1}\}, S_2 = \{x_{t_1}, \ldots, x_{t_2}\}, \ldots, S_m = \{x_{t_{m-1}}, \ldots, x_N\}$, where t's are the cut points and are subscripted in ascending order ($t_1 < t_2 < t_{m-1}$). Each subset $S_l, l = 1, \ldots, m$ is a segment. The integer m and the cut points $t_i, i = 1, \ldots, m-1$, have to be determined automatically by the algorithm. Furthermore, in the approach considered in this paper, the segments are grouped into k different classes ($k < m$), where k is a parameter defined by the user, in such a way that each S_l segment will be associated to a class label: $(S_1, \mathcal{C}_1)$, $(S_2, \mathcal{C}_2)$, ..., $(S_m, \mathcal{C}_m)$, where $\mathcal{C}_l, l = 1, \ldots, m$, is the class label of the l-th segment. The class label of each segment $\mathcal{C}_l$ has k possible values.

3.1 Likelihood-Based Segmentation

To find the $m-1$ unknown cut points t_l (separating segment l and $l+1$, where m is the number of segments) a recursive segmentation scheme could be considered as done in previous works [2,13,14]. This method is based on the likelihood-ratio test under an *i.i.d.* Gaussian distribution (assuming that each segment is sampled from a Gaussian distribution with different mean and variance) and a joint distribution consisting of two different Gaussian models for the complete time series.

Suppose a segment $\mathbf{s}_s$ with a number of elements n_s (where $\mathbf{s}_s = (x_{t_l}, \ldots, x_{t_{l+1}})$ and $s = 1, \ldots, m$) following a Gaussian distribution with parameters μ_s and σ_s^2. Then, let us denote a potential cut point for the observations $\mathbf{s}_s$ as u, in such a way that the observations on the left hand side are assumed to be sampled from a Normal distribution $N(\mu_{sL}, \sigma_{sL}^2)$ and the ones on the right hand side from a Normal distribution $N(\mu_{sR}, \sigma_{sR}^2)$ with different parameters. In this case, we define the likelihood-ratio between L_1 and $L_2(u)$ to contrast the null hypothesis that the n_s observations are sampled from the same Normal distribution (the alternative hypothesis being that the n_s observations are associated with two independent Normal distributions). L_1 and $L_2(u)$ can be defined as:

$$L_1 = \prod_{i=t_l}^{t_{l+1}} f(x_i; \mu_s, \sigma_s^2) \text{ and } L_2(u) = \prod_{i=t_l}^{t_l+u} f(x_i; \mu_{sL}, \sigma_{sL}^2) \prod_{i=t_l+u+1}^{t_{l+1}} f(x_i; \mu_{sR}, \sigma_{sR}^2)$$

The logarithmic likelihood-ratio between L_1 and $L_2(u)$ (i.e., $\log L(u)$) can be defined in the form:

$$\log L(u) = \log \frac{L_2(u)}{L_1} = \log L_2(u) - \log L_1 =$$

$$= \sum_{i=t_l}^{t_l+u} f(x_i; \mu_{sL}, \sigma_{sL}^2) + \sum_{i=t_l+u+1}^{t_{l+1}} f(x_i; \mu_{sR}, \sigma_{sR}^2) - \sum_{i=t_l}^{t_{l+1}} f(x_i; \mu_s, \sigma_s^2),$$

where for the Normal distributions hypothesis it holds that:

$$\log L(u) = n_s \log \sigma_s - u \log \sigma_{sL} - (n_s - u) \log \sigma_{sR},$$

where σ_s, σ_{sL} and σ_{sR} are approximated as the maximum likelihood estimators, based on a sufficiently large value of n_s, u and $(n_s - u)$ (in order to warranty that these estimators have good properties, such as consistency, efficiency and asymptotic normality). For this reason, the minimum size of the segments will be analysed in the experimental study (this parameter will be denoted as z in the subsequent paragraphs).

To find the optimal cut point u for a segment $\mathbf{s}_s$, the logarithmic likelihood-ratio between L_1 and $L_2(u)$ that has been defined previously can be used as an indicator to separate the observations into two segments. More specifically, an adequate way to separate the observations is to choose u so that $\log L(u)$ takes the maximum value. In other words, an adequate segmentation should be done at $u^* = \arg\max_u(\log L(u))$.

Note that, a predefined threshold p can be selected in order to restrict the divisions to be done. That is, if $\max(\log L(u))$ is less than p, then the segment is not divided. This is used as the stopping condition for the recursive segmentation procedure. As the asymptotic distribution of $2 \log L(u)$ is a χ^2_2 distributed with two degrees of freedom, then we can select $p = -2\log(1 - \alpha)$, where α is the level of significance. Then, the decision rule to divide a segment $\mathbf{s}_s$ is:

IF $\log L(u^*) > -2\log(1 - \alpha)$

THEN the initial segment $\mathbf{s}_s$ must be split at u^*. Continue to divide the resultant left subsegment $\mathbf{s}_{sL}$ provided that $u > 2z$ and/or the resultant right subsegment $\mathbf{s}_{sR}$ if $(n_s - u) > 2z$.

ELSE Stop the division procedure.

The defined segmentation procedure is a Top-Down technique, since the time series is recursively partitioned until the stopping criterion is met. Other approaches in the literature are the Bottom-Up and the Sliding Windows [7].

For the sake of understanding, the main steps of the proposed algorithm are summarized in Fig. 1. Note that, once that the segmentation step is finished, the next steps (which are defined in the next subsections) are the mapping to a five-dimensionality space and the clustering process.

Input: Time series, k, z, α

Output: Time series segments and labels.

1. Divide the time series according to the likelihood-based decision rule previously defined (recursive process).
2. Map the segments to a five-dimensional space via a predefined set of statistical functions.
3. Apply the k-means clustering algorithm.

Fig. 1. Pseudocode for the proposed methodology

3.2 Segment Characteristics for Clustering

As said, each segment provided by the segmentation algorithm is converted into a five-dimensional space by the computation of five statistical metrics. The metrics selected for the analysis are the following:

– Variance: it is a measure of variability of the values in the segment:

$$S_s^2 = \frac{1}{n_s} \sum_{i=t_l}^{t_{l+1}} (x_i - \mu_s)^2$$

– Skewness: it represents the asymmetry of the segment values distribution:

$$\gamma_{1s} = \frac{\frac{1}{n_s} \sum_{i=t_l}^{t_{l+1}} (x_i - \mu_s)^3}{S_s^3}$$

– Kurtosis: it measures the degree of concentration that the values present around the mean:

$$\gamma_{2s} = \frac{\frac{1}{n_s} \sum_{i=t_l}^{t_{l+1}} (x_i - \mu_s)^4}{S_s^4} - 3$$

– Slope of a linear regression over the points of the segment: A linear model is constructed for every segment trying to obtain the best linear approximation for the points. It is a measure of the general tendency of the segment:

$$\beta_s = \frac{\frac{1}{n_s} \sum_{i=t_l}^{t_{l+1}} (i - \overline{t}_s)(x_i - \mu_s)}{S_s^2},$$

where $\overline{t}_s = \frac{t_l + t_{l+1}}{2}$.

– Autocorrelation coefficient: it measures the degree of correlation between the current values of the time-series and the values of the time-series in the previous time stamp:

$$AC_s = \frac{\sum_{i=t_l}^{t_{l+1}} (x_i - \mu_s)(x_{i+1} - \mu_s)}{S_s^2}$$

3.3 Clustering Phase

In this step of the methodology, the segments (which are represented as patterns in the five-dimensional space) are grouped according to their similarity (considering their statistical properties) via a clustering algorithm. For the sake of simplicity, the well-known k-means algorithm is selected for this purpose [15]. Note that, before the clustering, the metrics have been normalised given the distance-based nature of the k-means clustering. In order to minimise the randomness of the results in the experiments (due to different centroids initialisations), we performed a deterministic process to select these values based on the metrics variability (similar to the one in [16]).

4 Experimental Results and Discussion

The experiments performed and the results obtained are analysed in this section.

4.1 Spanish Stock Market Index Dataset

As said, we analysed one of the official indexes of the Madrid Stock Market: the Ibex-35, an index composed of the 35 most liquid values listed in the Computer Assisted Trading System. For our study we considered the daily closing prices of the Spanish Ibex-35 stock index from 15 January 1992 to 29 October 2013, presenting thus a total of 5504 observations. The complete time series used in the experiments can be seen in Fig. 2a where the most relevant financial phases have been included.

4.2 Clustering Evaluation Metrics

To evaluate the segmentation (and the different parameters of the segmentation algorithm) several metrics [15] have been selected to measure the compactness of the clusters:

- The Davies-Bouldin index (DB): This index attempts to maximise the between-cluster distance while minimising the distance between the cluster centroids to the rest of points. It is obtained as:

$$DB = \frac{1}{k}\sum_{i=1}^{k} \max_{i \neq j} \frac{\overline{d_i} + \overline{d_j}}{d(\mathbf{c}_i, \mathbf{c}_j)}$$

  Where $\overline{d_i}$ is the average distance of all elements in cluster $\mathcal{C}_i$ to centroid $\mathbf{c}_i$, and $d(\mathbf{c}_i, \mathbf{c}_j)$ is the Euclidean distance between centroids $\mathbf{c}_i$ and $\mathbf{c}_j$.
- The Dunn index (DU): This index attempts to identify clusters that are compact and well-separated. In this case, the distance between two clusters is defined as: $d(\mathcal{C}_i, \mathcal{C}_j) = \min d(\mathbf{x}, \mathbf{y})$, $\forall \mathbf{x} \in \mathcal{C}_i$, $\forall \mathbf{y} \in \mathcal{C}_j$. Thus, the Dunn index is constructed as:

$$DU = \min_{i=1,\ldots,k}\left(\min_{j=i+1,\ldots,k}\left(\frac{d(\mathcal{C}_i, \mathcal{C}_j)}{\max_{l=1,\ldots,k} \mathtt{diam}(\mathcal{C}_l)}\right)\right),$$

  where

$$\mathtt{diam}(\mathcal{C}_i) = \frac{1}{n_{\mathcal{C}_i}(n_{\mathcal{C}_i} - 1)} \sum_{\mathbf{x},\mathbf{y} \in \mathcal{C}_i} d(\mathbf{x}, \mathbf{y}),$$

  being $n_{\mathcal{C}_i}$ the number of patterns belonging to cluster $\mathcal{C}_i$.

4.3 Experimental Results

For the experiments, several configurations of the algorithm are tested (changing the parameters k, z and α) in order to decide the optimal parameter combination. The obtained results can be seen in Table 1 for the two selected clustering evaluation metrics (DB and DU). Note that DB is intended to be minimised and DU to be maximised. The range for the parameters has been determined in the following manner: for α, values of 0.01 and 0.05 are considered, as they are the most common levels of significance in hypothesis tests. z is dependent on the time series analysed. In our case, values associated with 5, 6 and 7 workweeks ($z = 25, 30, 35$, respectively) have been considered. k is the most difficult parameter to obtain, for this reason, its grid is greater ($k = 4, 5, 6, 7$). Analysing the results, the best values for the DB and DU functions are achieved with the following parameter configuration: $\alpha = 0.01$, $z = 30$ and $k = 5$. The clustering obtained for these parameters identifies compact and well-separated clusters that maximise the between-cluster distances and minimise the intra-cluster distances.

Table 1. DB and DU values obtained for different parameter configurations

Davies-Bouldin index (DB)				Dunn index (DU)			
$\alpha = 0.01$	$z = 25$	$z = 30$	$z = 35$	$\alpha = 0.01$	$z = 25$	$z = 30$	$z = 35$
$k = 4$	0.9384	0.8886	0.9677	$k = 4$	0.2344	0.2653	0.4342
$k = 5$	0.8567	**0.7828**	0.9161	$k = 5$	0.2267	**0.4615**	0.3764
$k = 6$	1.0032	0.9142	0.9818	$k = 6$	0.2086	0.3683	0.4133
$k = 7$	1.0500	0.8083	0.9600	$k = 7$	0.1534	0.2690	0.4133
$\alpha = 0.05$	$z = 25$	$z = 30$	$z = 35$	$\alpha = 0.05$	$z = 25$	$z = 30$	$z = 35$
$k = 4$	0.9298	0.8685	0.9623	$k = 4$	0.2755	0.2653	0.4342
$k = 5$	0.8495	0.8139	0.9120	$k = 5$	0.2719	0.3280	0.3764
$k = 6$	1.0084	0.9055	0.9794	$k = 6$	0.2465	0.3683	0.4133
$k = 7$	1.0551	0.8034	0.9535	$k = 7$	0.1419	0.2690	0.4133

The characteristics of the centroids obtained by the clustering algorithm for the best segmentation can be seen in Table 2. In the following subsection, these clusters will be analysed, comparing some of them to some previous and well-known financial patterns.

Table 2. Characteristics of the obtained centroids

Cluster	Variance	Asymmetry	Kurtosis	Slope	Autocorrelation
C_1 (red)	53141.70	0.6843	0.3547	0.0964	31.9930
C_2 (green)	51103.79	-0.0112	-0.9191	6.4235	26.9927
C_3 (dark blue)	312073.39	0.0950	-0.7967	-49.1215	26.6318
C_4 (pink)	49860.80	0.0024	-0.6944	1.3271	51.3734
C_5 (cyan)	60948.96	-0.5927	-0.0685	2.2222	29.7812

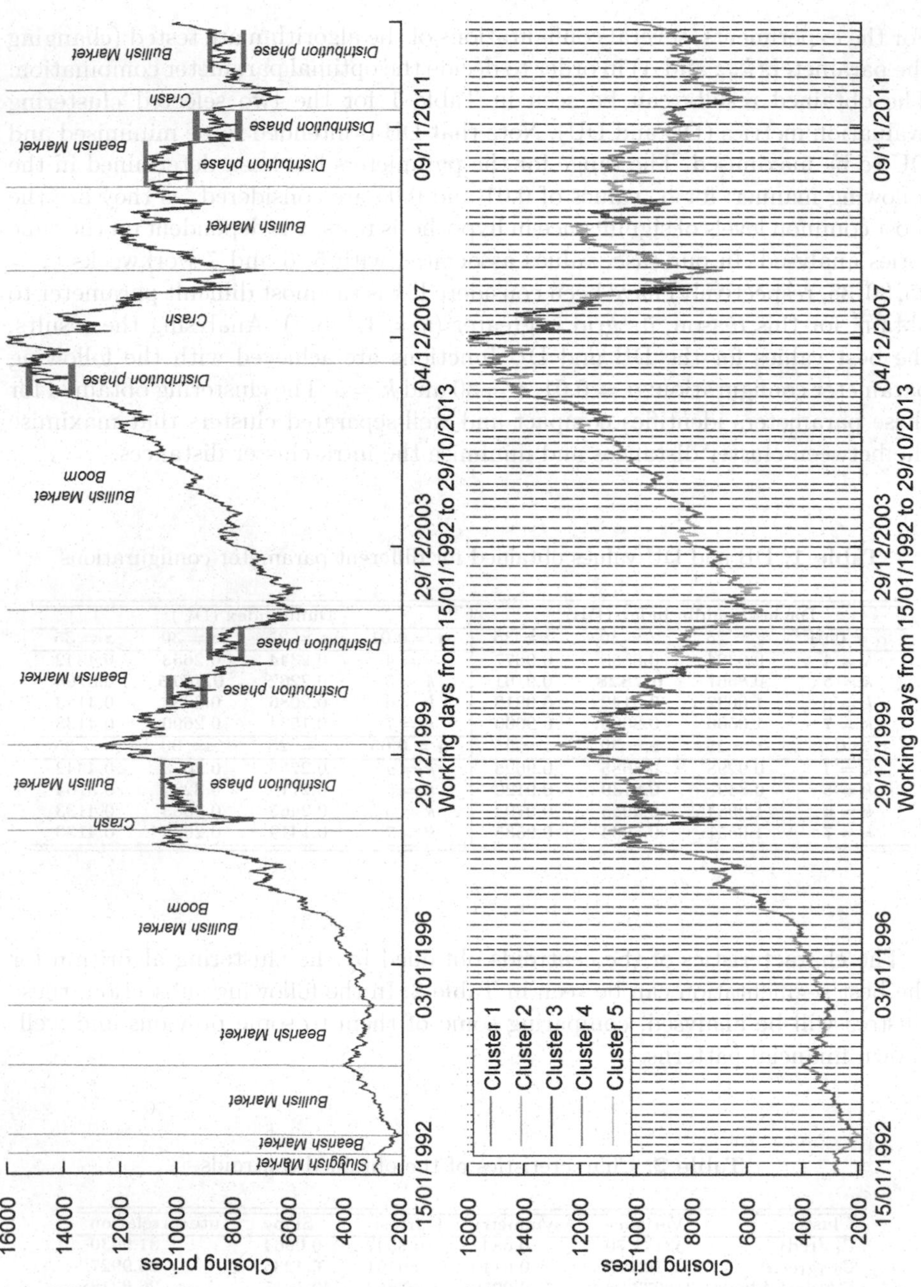

(a) The original sequence of the dataset used. **(b)** Best segmentation and clustering obtained.

Fig. 2. Original time series and the best segmentation

4.4 Discussion

The best segmentation, with a total of 134 segments, can be seen in Fig. 2b. The cut points obtained in the best segmentation are represented as vertical dashed lines and each segment is coloured according to its assigned cluster in the clustering process. Note that, given the nature of the used statistics for the clustering process, the shape of patterns belonging to the same cluster might differ (as patterns presenting different shapes can present similar statistical properties), instead, patterns in the same cluster will have similar trends and homogeneous characteristics. According to the centroids in Table 2, each cluster can be defined as follows:

- C_1 (red colour) groups segments with high variance (values far from the mean and with great differences between maximum and minimum values). The distribution presents a clear asymmetry to the right; kurtosis is slightly positive, which show that segments are little concentrated around the centroid; the slope is nearly null, so the segments in this cluster do not present a linear trend. As they have a high autocorrelation (although far from the fourth cluster), this means that values in time t are positive correlated with values in time $t-1$. The shape is as deep saw tooth pattern, but with some very low values. It corresponds to the broadening financial pattern (there are 24 well-known financial patterns [17], and these are used to verify the segmentation results).
- C_2 (green colour) presents segments with a similar variance to the previous cluster (values far from the mean and important differences between maximum and minimum values of the segments). The distribution is symmetric and the kurtosis is highly negative (the segments are built with a high number of values of the time series, nor concentrated around the centroid, and quite low). The slope is positive, which indicates the presence of an increasing linear trend in the segments, with a low autocorrelation, or systematic saw tooth patterns. This cluster is the most frequent in the time series and mainly appears in the bullish phases of the market, being clearly identified as the up-trend pattern.
- The segments with the greatest variance are included in C_3 (dark blue colour), where there can be appreciated the greatest differences between maximum and minimum values of the segments, with a symmetric distribution; kurtosis value is slightly negative and the slope is highly negative, representing a highly sloped decreasing linear trend, even with abrupt declines. The low autocorrelation indicates systemic saw tooth pattern. The segments in this cluster could easily be recognised as Downtrend financial pattern and it can be highlighted that they are clearly found in the crash phases (see Fig. 2a and 2b).
- C_4 (pink colour) presents the lowest variance, with symmetric distribution, and a slightly low kurtosis value. The segments in this cluster present a moderate increasing linear trend (slightly positive slope). The autocorrelation presents also increasing values for this cluster. These segments could

represent moderate oscillations around the trend line, as a period of generalised profit taking by investors.

- C_5 (cyan colour) is composed of segments with very high variance (high volatility of the market), with a clear left asymmetric distribution, that is, there are more values lower than the centroid or mean; kurtosis is nearly null (a number of values near to the centroid) which, considered along with the high variance presented, indicates that there might be few patterns but presenting very different values to the mean. As in the previous cluster, they present a moderate increasing linear trend (slight positive slope) but also a moderate autocorrelation (little saw tooth pattern or little oscillations as wedges financial pattern).

To summarize, the proposed approach allows us to group segments with similar statistical characteristics and trends. After the segments are analysed and grouped in clusters according to their statistical characteristics, these clusters are compared (or related) to the financial patterns defined in [17] and it can be observed that contain at least four different financial patterns, namely Downtrend (third cluster), Uptrend (second cluster), Broadening (first cluster) and Wedges (fifth cluster). The segments in the fourth cluster can not be clearly identified to a financial pattern, so one could state that belongs to some kind of distribution phase, and it can be regarded as new for future analysis. It can be observed that the segments obtained in each cluster generally mutate their shape in some way since 1998 (crisis in Brazil), and from that date peaks and troughs are more acute, being an additional obstacle for finding homogeneous patterns in this type of time series.

As it is shown in Fig. 2a and 2b, the presence of the corresponding segments in each phase agree well with the date of important market events, phases and changes of primary trends.

5 Conclusions

This paper presents a likelihood-based time series segmentation methodology. The segments obtained are used for a posterior clustering-based analysis (where these segments are mapped to a five-dimensional space representing their statistical properties and grouped according to their similarity). The characteristics of the resultant clusters and their relation to other well-known financial patterns is analysed in the discussion section of this paper. The segmentation obtained is consistent with the key milestones in this Ibex-35 index and describe this time series satisfactorily, which encourages us to further investigate in this hybrid data mining methodology.

The next step of this work corresponds to the prediction of complete time periods, using the temporal patterns identified in the segmentation/clustering phase. This prediction will allow us to determine the shape of the next period, which is especially useful in financial applications to identify future market behaviours ('bear', 'bull' and 'sluggish' periods or any other financial patterns that indicates a change of trend).

Acknowledgment. This work was supported in part by the TIN2011-22794 project of the Spanish Ministerial Commision of Science and Technology (MICYT), FEDER funds and the P2011-TIC-7508 project of the "Junta de Andalucía" (Spain). Manuel Cruz-Ramírez's research has been subsidized by the FPU Predoctoral Program (Spanish Ministry of Education and Science), grant reference AP2009-0487.

References

1. Fu, T.C.: A review on time series data mining. Eng. Appl. Artif. Intell. 24(1), 164–181 (2011)
2. Cheong, S.A., Fornia, R.P., Lee, G.H.T., Kok, J.L., Yim, W.S., Xu, D.Y., Zhang, Y.: The japanese economy in crises: A time series segmentation study. Economics: The Open-Access. Open-Assessment E-Journal 6(2012-5) (2012)
3. Wong, J., Lian, H., Cheong, S.: Detecting macroeconomic phases in the dow jones industrial average time series. Physica A 388(21), 4635–4645 (2009)
4. Edwards, R., Magee, J.: Technical analysis of stock trends. Magee, Springfield/Mass (2013)
5. Pagan, A.R., Sossounov, K.A.: A simple framework for analysing bull and bear markets. Journal of Applied Econometrics 18(1), 23–46 (2003)
6. Basseville, M., Nikiforov, I.V.: Detection of Abrupt Changes: Theory and Application. Prentice-Hall, Inc., Upper Saddle River (1993)
7. Keogh, E., Chu, S., Hart, D., Pazzani, M.: An online algorithm for segmenting time series. In: Proceedings of the IEEE International Conference on Data Mining, ICDM 2001, pp. 289–296 (2001)
8. Appel, U., Brandt, A.V.: Adaptive sequential segmentation of piecewise stationary time series. Information Sciences 29(1), 27–56 (1983)
9. Basseville, M., Benveniste, A.: Sequential segmentation of nonstationary digital signals using spectral analysis. Information Sciences 29(1), 57–73 (1983)
10. Hawkins, D.: A test for a change point in a parametric model based on a maximal Wald-type statistic. Sankhya 49, 368–376 (1987)
11. Das, G., Lin, K.I., Mannila, H., Renganathan, G., Smyth, P.: Rule discovery from time series, pp. 16–22. AAAI Press (1998)
12. Ou-Yang, K., Jia, W., Zhou, P., Meng, X.: A new approach to transforming time series into symbolic sequences. In: 21st Annual Conference on Engineering in Medicine and Biology and the 1999 Annual Fall Meetring of the Biomedical Engineering Society, Proceedings of the First Joint BMES/EMBS Conference, vol. 2, p. 974 (October 1999)
13. Bernaola-Galván, P., Román-Roldán, R., Oliver, J.L.: Compositional segmentation and long-range fractal correlations in dna sequences. Phys. Rev. E 53, 5181–5189 (1996)
14. Sato, A.H.: A comprehensive analysis of time series segmentation on japanese stock prices. Procedia Computer Science 24, 307–314 (2013); 17th Asia Pacific Symposium on Intelligent and Evolutionary Systems, IES 2013
15. Xu, R., Wunsch, D.: Clustering. IEEE Press Series on Computational Intelligence. Wiley (2008)
16. Cohen, S., Intrator, N.: Global optimization of rbf networks (2000)
17. Chung, F.L., Fu, T.C., Ng, V., Luk, R.W.: An evolutionary approach to pattern-based time series segmentation. IEEE Transactions on Evolutionary Computation 8(5), 471–489 (2004)

An Approach of Steel Plates Fault Diagnosis in Multiple Classes Decision Making

Dragan Simić[1,*], Vasa Svirčević[2], and Svetlana Simić[3]

[1] University of Novi Sad, Faculty of Technical Sciences, Trg Dositeja Obradovića 6, 21000 Novi Sad, Serbia
dsimic@eunet.rs

[2] Lames Ltd., Jarački put bb., 22000 Sremska Mitrovica, Serbia
vasasv@hotmail.com

[3] University of Novi Sad, Faculty of Medicine, Hajduk Veljkova 1–9, 21000 Novi Sad, Serbia
drdragansimic@gmail.com

Abstract. In the steel industry, specifically alloy steel, creating different defected product can impose a high cost for steel product manufacturer. This paper is focused on an intelligent multiple classes fault diagnosis in steel plates to help operational decision makers to organise an effective and efficient manufacturing production. Treebagger random forest, machine learning ensemble method, and support vector machine are proposed as multiple classifiers. The experimental results are further on compared with results in previous researches. Experimental results encourage further research in application intelligent fault diagnosis in steel plates decision support system.

Keywords: Fault diagnosis in steel, pattern classification, treebagger, support vector machine.

1 Introduction

A fault might be defined as non-optimal operation or an off-specification product as reference to an omission or error of a product or its specification and requests that it now be added or corrected. A "fault" or "problem" does not have to be the result of a complete failure of a piece of equipment, or even involve specific hardware. In process plants, faults can be categorized according to their sources, i.e. sensor faults affecting process measurements, actuator faults leading to errors in the operation of the plant, faults arising from erroneous operating policies or procedures as well as system component faults arising from changes in process equipment or human error [1].

In the alloy steel industry, creating different defected products imposes a high cost for steel product manufacturer. Pits & Blister defect is a common fault in producing low carbon steel grades. To remove this drawback, it is necessary to grind the surface of the steel product which represents waste of time and causes increased production cost.

* Corresponding author.

M. Polycarpou et al. (Eds.): HAIS 2014, LNAI 8480, pp. 86–97, 2014.
© Springer International Publishing Switzerland 2014

Fault detection and diagnosis is a key component of many operations management automation systems. A "root cause" fault is a fundamental, underlying problem that may lead to other problems and observable symptoms. A root cause is also generally associated with procedures for repair.

Intelligent fault diagnosis techniques can provide quick and correct systems that help to keep away from product quality problems and facilitates precautionary maintenance. These intelligent systems use different artificial intelligent and data mining models and they should be simple and efficient. Decision tree, support vector machine, fuzzy logic algorithm, neural network and statistical algorithms are alternative approaches that are commonly employed nowadays in the industrial context to detect the occurrence of failure or faults [2].

This research is focused on an intelligent multiple classes fault diagnosis in steel plates. Treebagger random forest, machine learning ensemble method, and support vector machine are proposed as multiple classifiers. The basic purpose of implementation multiple classifiers at fault diagnosis in steel plates is to help operational decision makers to organise an effective and efficient manufacturing production. The steel plates fault dataset investigated in this research is taken from the University of California at Irvine (UCI) machine learning repository [3]. The diagnosis performances of the proposed models are presented using statistical accuracy, specificity and sensitivity. The experimental results are further on discussed and compared with results in previous researches that use hybrid artificial intelligent techniques such as: decision tree with boosting, multi perception neural network with pruning and logistic regression with step forward [4]. Experimental results show that the statistical measures, classification accuracy and specificity, of proposed treebagger random forest model had the best success of all test samples classification. On the other side, statistical measure, sensitivity of treebagger random forest, SVM and decision tree with boosting models have achieved nearly the same amount.

The rest of the paper is organized in the following way: Section 2 provides better understanding for the relationship between hybrid intelligent systems approach and relationship with classifier models. Section 3 provides some approaches about methods for fault diagnosis in steel plates and related work. Section 4 presents general pattern classification and implemented techniques support vector machine and treebagger random forest. Section 5 introduces steel plates faults data set and examines three statistical measures: classification accuracy, sensitivity and specificity. Experimental results are presented in Section 6. Finally, Section 7 provides concluding remarks.

2 Hybrid Approaches and Multiple Classifier Systems

Artificial intelligence techniques have demonstrated a capability to solve real-word problems in sciences, business, technology, and commerce. The integration of different artificial intelligent learning techniques and their adaptation, which overcomes individual constraints and achieves synergetic effects through hybridisation or fusion, has in recent years contributed to a large number of new intelligent system designs [5].

Hybrid approaches seek to exploit the strengths of the individual components, obtaining enhanced performance by their combination. The hybridization of intelligent techniques, draws from different areas of computational intelligence, and has become prevalent because of the growing awareness that they outperform individual computational intelligence techniques. In a hybrid intelligence system, a synergy combination of multiple techniques is used to build an efficient solution to deal with a particular problem [6].

Multiple classifiers implementation in the intelligent decision process is subject to hybridization by various forms of combination [7]. A rough representation of the computational domains covered by the hybrid intelligent systems approach and relationship with classifier models is presented in Fig. 1 [8].

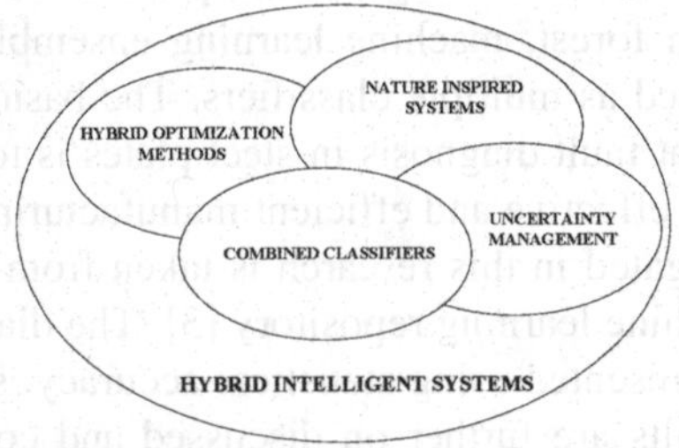

Fig. 1. Domains of hybrid intelligent systems (Source [8], p. 4)

To better understand relationship between hybrid intelligent systems approach and relationship with classifier models some important points will be determined [8]:

- Hybrid intelligent systems are free combinations of computational intelligence techniques for solving a given problem, covering all computational phases from data normalization up to final decision making. Specifically, they mix heterogeneous fundamental views blending them into one effective working system.
- Information fusion covers the ways to combine information sources in a view providing new properties that may allow better or more efficient solving of a proposed problem. Information sources can be the result of additional computational processes.
- Multi-Classifier Systems (MCS) focus on the combination of classifiers form heterogenous or homogeneous modelling backgrounds to give the final decision. MCS are therefore a subcategory of HIS.

Intelligent data analysis deals with the visualization, pre-processing, pattern recognition and knowledge discovery tools and applications using various computational intelligence techniques. Recent trends in intelligent data analysis are focused to, and engaged in developing and applying, advanced hybrid artificial intelligence system from a theoretical point of view and also for solving real-world problems [9]. One of real-world problems facing manufacturing industry is modelling classifier for fault diagnosis in steel plates.

3 Fault Diagnosis in Steel Plates and Related Work

Globalization and increased competition put pressure on profit margins of companies. This has led to the development of quality control management methodologies and other management programs to assist organizations in addressing some of these challenges. Faults diagnosis problems are representing challenging and attracting applications for experts and researchers.

The "Steel Plates Faults data set" which is used in this research is from the University of California at Irvine (*UCI*) machine learning repository donated in October 2010 [3]. The first used data set is in 2010 [10]. It presents the usage of artificial intelligent models: (1) decision tree with boosting; (2) multi perception neural network with pruning; (3) logistic regression with step forward; to create classifier for fault diagnosing in steel plates. The same data set, also, used by the same authors in 2012 [11]. The experimental results of this case are in part presented and in detail discussed in Section 6.

The application of random forest model, the identification of defects in hot rolled steel plates on an industrial plant is considered in [12]. In this case, historic plant data are used to construct a model that contributes to defects in the steel plate, such as inclusions and delamination of the steel. A data set consisting of 26 operating variables and 3017 sample was used to calibrate an ensemble of boosted trees. Each sample represented a rolled steel plate that was inspected and identified as normal (i.e. no defects) or defective (containing a defect of one type or another). The random forest model could predict the quality of the steel plates with an overall accuracy of approximately 76.6%. Defect-free plates could be identified with an accuracy of 89.9 %, while defective plates could be identified in 51.7 % of the cases. Although not highly reliable, the performance of the random forest model is significant, given that 34.3 % of the samples in the data were defective.

The application of fault diagnosis on steel structures using artificial neural networks in generally and particularly supervised feed forward network with *Levenberg-Marquardt* back-propagation algorithm is applied in [13]. The system is a three-layer net which has: 42 input neurons, one hidden level with 7 neurons, and only a 1 output neuron. The output neuron classifies the beams into damaged or not damaged. The net is trained to learn the weights ($w_1 = 1.2$, $w_2 = 21.7$, $w_3 = 7.1$). After applying the training on a limited number of training data, the neural network is able to identify the damaged beams with considerable accuracy. The net converges to the final system in less than twenty epochs in average. But, in this paper is not given any numerical result of that research.

In the next research, data set consists of 1080 steel structures achieved from the production line of the "Mobarake Steel Manufacturing" [14]. The data set contributes 680 defects which belong to four common defect types in steel industry: scratch, roll imprint, edge strain, and pit. The training set for each defect type was used to train support vector machine with different kernel type: linear, polynomial, Gaussian, and quadratic; based on one-against-one method. Experimental results for multiclass classification of the steel surface defects for statistical measure accuracy could be shown: Scratch: 92.94%, Roll Imprint: 96.47%, Edge Strain: 95.88%, Pit: 97.64%.

4 Pattern Classification

In a typical statistical pattern recognition setting, a set of patterns *S* is given, also referred to as a *training set*. The labels of the patterns in *S* are known and the goal is to construct an algorithm in order to label new patterns. A classification algorithm is also known as an *inducer* and an instance of an inducer for a specific training set is called a *classifier*.

The training set is described by a vector of feature values. Each vector belongs to a single class and is associated with the class label. The training set is stored in a table where each row consists of a different pattern. Let *A* and y denote the set of n features: *A* = *{a1, . . . , ai, . . . , an}* and the class label, respectively. In a similar way, *dom (y)* = *{c1, c2, . . . , ck}* constitutes the set of labels.

The dataset contains seven classes that correspond to seven types of steel plates fault: *dom (y) = {Pastry, Z_Scratch, K_Scatch, Stains, Dirtiness, Bumps, Other_Faults}*. Each pattern is characterized by twenty-seven numeric features: *A* = *{X_Minimum, X_Maximum, Y_Minimum, ... Luminosity_Index, Sigmoid_ofAreas, Steel_Plate_Thickness}*. The instance space, the set of all possible examples is defined as a *Cartesian product* of all the input attributes domains: $X = dom\ (a_1) \times dom(a_2) \times \ldots \times dom(a_n)$. The universal instance space *U* is defined as a *Cartesian product* of all input attribute domains and the target attribute domain, i.e.: $U = X \times dom(y)$.

4.1 Support Vector Machine

The concept of support vector machine (SVM) was presented in [15] and then extended in [16] [17], and finally which are formed a complete theory in [18]. Basically, SVMs consist of a set of related supervised learning methods for the purpose of two-class classification tasks. The goal of SVM is to produce a model which predicts target value of data instances in the learning set. SVM works on the principle that it tries to form the hyperplane between the data points, which separates these data points into two sets by mapping these data points into the high-dimension space, using the feature vectors that are obtained by the attributes of the data [19].

SVM map the input space into a high-dimensional feature space through a nonlinear mapping that is chosen *a priori* [20]. An optimal separating hyper-plane is then constructed in the new feature space. The method searches for a hyper-plane that is optimal according the *VC–Dimension* (*Vapnik–Chervonenkis*) dimension theory. Detail SVM description is presented in [19]

4.2 TreeBagger Random Forest

Random forests are an ensemble learning method for classification or regression that operate by constructing a multitude of decision trees at training time and outputting the class that is the mode of the classes output by individual trees [21]. The term came from "random decision forests" and was first proposed in [22]. Random forests are a combination of tree predictors such that each tree depends on the values of a random vector sampled independently and with the same distribution for all trees in the forest.

Bagging - bootstrap aggregating, is a machine learning ensemble meta-algorithm, and is designed to improve the stability and accuracy of random forest learning algorithm. Bagging works by taking uniform random samples of a training set and using the ensemble average to form the final decision. It is also reduced variance and helps to avoid over-fitting. Although it is usually applied to decision tree methods, such as random forest, it can be combined with any type of other machine learning method.

Treebagger random forests method implements both bagging and random forests [23]. A treebagger random forests method presents one of random forest ensembles models in parallel. Treebagger random forests classifier, in this research, works by using bootstrap aggregation to form a collection of decision trees. In this research, 150 decision trees were used on a training set with the feature set as a predictors and the actual label as the response. Bagging only leads to minor improvements in error, in order to construct a collection of decision trees with controlled variance, as errors in the individual models are most likely highly correlated.

5 Multiple Classes Steel Plates Fault Diagnosis

The Steel Plates Faults data set which is used in this research is from the University of California at Irvine (*UCI*) machine learning repository [3], and the goal of Repository is to train machine learning for automatic pattern recognition. "Steel Plates Faults" is one of the datasets in the Repository, which classifies steel plates' faults into 7 different types: *Pastry*, *Z_Scratch*, *K_Scatch*, *Stains*, *Dirtiness*, *Bumps* and *Other_Faults*. The dataset includes 1941 instances, which have been labelled by different fault types. Table 1 shows output class distribution and list of predictive attributes. Each instance of the dataset owns 27 independent variables and one fault type.

The classification performance of each model is evaluated using three statistical measures: classification accuracy, sensitivity and specificity which are described in Eq. (1) (2) and (3). These measures are defined using the values of True Positive (*TP*), True Negative (*TN*), False Positive (*FP*) and False Negative (*FN*). A true positive decision occurs when the positive prediction of the classifier coincided with a positive prediction of the expert. A true negative (*TN*) decision occurs when both the classifier and the expert suggested the absence of a positive prediction. False positive (*FP*) occurs when the classifier labels a negative case as a positive one.

Finally, false negative (*FN*) occurs when the system labels a positive case as negative one. Classification accuracy is defined as the ratio of the number of correctly classified cases and is equal to the sum of *TP* and *TN* divided by the total number of cases *N*:

$$Accuracy = (TP + TN) / N \tag{1}$$

Sensitivity refers to the rate of correctly classified positive and is equal to *TP* divided by the sum of *TP* and *FN*. Sensitivity may be referred as a True Positive Rate:

$$Sensitivity = TP / (TP + FN) \tag{2}$$

Specificity refers to the rate of correctly classified negative and is equal to the ratio of *TN* to the sum of *TN* and *FP*. False Positive Rate equals (100-specificity):

$$Specificity = TN / (TN + FP) \tag{3}$$

Table 1. Steel plates dataset; class distribution and predictive attributes

Output Class	# of Cases	Predictive attributes			
Pastry	158	Attrib. 1	X_Minimum	Attrib. 14	Steel_Plate_Thickness
Z_Scratch	190	Attrib. 2	X_Maximum	Attrib. 15	Edges_Index
K_Scatch	391	Attrib. 3	Y_Minimum	Attrib. 16	Empty_Index
Stains	72	Attrib. 4	Y_Maximum	Attrib. 17	Square_Index
Dirtiness	55	Attrib. 5	Pixels_Areas	Attrib. 18	Outside_X_Index
Bumps	402	Attrib. 6	X_Perimeter	Attrib. 19	Edges_X_Index
Other Faults	673	Attrib. 7	Y_Perimeter	Attrib. 20	Edges_Y_Index
		Attrib. 8	Sum_of_Luminosity	Attrib. 21	Outside_Global_Index
		Attrib. 9	Minimum_of_Luminosity	Attrib. 22	Log_Of_Areas
		Attrib. 10	Maximum_of_Luminosity	Attrib. 23	Log_X_Index
		Attrib. 11	Length_of_Conveyer	Attrib. 24	Orientation_Index
		Attrib. 12	TypeOfSteel_A300	Attrib. 25	Luminosity_Index
		Attrib. 13	TypeOfSteel_A400	Attrib. 26	Sigmoid_Of_Areas
				Attrib. 27	Steel_Plate_Thickness

Sensitivity in Eq. (2) measures the proportion of actual positives which are correctly identified as such while specificity in Eq. (3) measures the proportion of negatives which are correctly identified. Finally, accuracy in Eq. (1) is the proportion of true results, either true positive or true negative, in a population. It measures the degree of veracity of a diagnostic test on a condition.

6 Experimental Results and Discussion

The steel plate's faults dataset is partitioned for training the models and test them by the ratio of 70:30% respectively, 1359 instances test set and 582 instances training sub. The training set will be used to calibrate/train the model parameters. The training set is used to estimate the model parameters, while the test set is used to assess, independently, the individual model. The trained model is then used to make a prediction on the test set. These models are applied again to the entire dataset and to any new data. Cross validation is almost an inherent part of machine learning. Cross validation is used to compare the performance of different predictive modelling techniques, and holdout validation method is used. Predicted values will be compared with actual data to compute the confusion matrix (Table 2).

Table 2. Cross validation confusion matrix for training and test subset

Class		Cross validation			
		Training Set		Test Set	
	Value	0	1	0	1
Pastry	Count	1252	107	531	51
	%	*92.13*	*7.87*	*91.24*	*8.76*
Z_Scratch	Count	1223	136	528	54
	%	*89.99*	*10.01*	*90.72*	*9.28*
K_Scratch	Count	1082	277	468	114
	%	*79.62*	*20.38*	*80.41*	*19.59*
Stains	Count	1311	48	558	24
	%	*96.47*	*3.53*	*95.88*	*4.12*
Dirtiness	Count	1327	32	559	23
	%	*97.65*	*2.35*	*96.05*	*3.95*
Bumps	Count	1083	276	456	126
	%	*79.69*	*20.31*	*78.35*	*21.65*
Other_Faults	Count	876	483	392	190
	%	*64.46*	*35.54*	*67.35*	*32.65*

Table 3. Confusion matrix of individual models and their ensemble for training and test subset (582 testing data samples)

Class	Support vector machine				Treebagger			
	Count		%		Count		%	
Pastry	46	5	*90.19*	*9.80*	51	0	*100.0*	*0*
	1	530	*0.18*	*99.81*	4	527	*0.75*	*99.24*
Z_Scratch	49	5	*90.74*	*9.25*	54	0	*100.0*	*0*
	0	528	*0*	*100.0*	2	526	*0.37*	*99.62*
K_Scratch	90	24	*78.94*	*21.05*	114	0	*100.0*	*0*
	0	468	*0*	*100.0*	0	468	*0*	*100.0*
Stains	16	8	*66.66*	*33.33*	22	2	*91.66*	*8.33*
	0	558	*0*	*100.0*	9	549	*1.61*	*98.38*
Dirtiness	18	5	*78.26*	*21.73*	23	0	*100.0*	*0*
	1	558	*0.17*	*99.82*	1	558	*0.17*	*99.82*
Bumps	103	23	*81.74*	*18.25*	456	0	*100.0*	*0*
	9	447	1.97	*98.02*	*0*	*126*	*0*	*100.0*
Other_ Faults	135	55	*71.05*	*28.9*	190	0	*100.0*	*0*
	31	361	*7.90*	*92.09*	0	392	*0*	*100.0*

The predictions of all models, support vector machine and treebager random forest, are compared to the original classes to identify the values of true positives, true negatives, false positives and false negative. These values have been computed to construct the confusion matrix as shown in Table 3.

The values of the statistical measures, sensitivity, specificity and total classification accuracy, of the both models were computed and presented in Table 4. Sensitivity and specificity approximate the probability of the positive and negative labels being true. They assess the usefulness of the algorithm on a single model. Using the results shown in Table 4, it can be seen that the sensitivity, specificity and classification accuracy of treebagger model has achieved the best success of test samples classification.

Table 4. Values of the statistical measures for test subset

Classifier	Class	Statistical measures		
		Accuracy	**Specificity**	**Sensitivity**
SVM	Pastry	98.96	90.19	**99.81**
	Z_Scratch	99.14	90.74	**100.0**
	K_Scratch	95.87	78.94	**100.0**
	Stains	**98.62**	66.66	**100.0**
	Dirtiness	98.96	78.26	**99.82**
	Bumps	94.50	81.74	98.02
	Other_Faults	85.22	71.05	92.09
	Average	*95.89*	*79.65*	*98.53*
Treebagger	Pastry	**99.31**	**100.0**	99.24
	Z_Scratch	**99.65**	**100.0**	99.62
	K_Scratch	**100.0**	**100.0**	**100.0**
	Stains	98.10	**91.66**	98.38
	Dirtiness	**99.82**	**100.0**	**99.82**
	Bumps	**100.0**	**100.0**	**100.0**
	Other_Faults	**100.0**	**100.0**	**100.0**
	Average	*99.55*	*98.80*	*99.58*

The time required to build each model with the dataset is variable; ranging from few seconds, four seconds (elapsed time is 3.72 sec.) for support vector machine, up to four min (elapsed time is 222.00 sec.) for the treebagger random forest.

The experimental results are further on compared with results in previous researches that use hybrid artificial intelligent techniques: logistic regression with step forward (LR), multi perception neural network with pruning (MLPNN), decision tree with boosting (C5.0) [4]. The compared results for five systems are presented in Table 5. The shown results, demonstrate that the classification accuracy and specificity of treebagger model has achieved the best success of test samples classification. On the other hand, statistical measure, sensitivity of SVM, treebagger random forest and decision tree with boosting models, have achieved nearly the same.

Table 5. Values of the statistical measures for test subset

	Class	Classifier				
		SVM	**Treebagger**	**LR**	**MLPNN**	**C5.0**
Accuracy	**Pastry**	98.96	99.31	91.78	93.68	**99.50**
	Z_Scratch	99.14	**99.65**	91.27	96.79	99.50
	K_Scratch	95.87	**100.0**	97.29	98.60	99.90
	Stains	98.62	98.10	97.29	99.60	**99.90**
	Dirtiness	98.96	**99.82**	95.79	98.50	99.80
	Bumps	94.50	**100.0**	83.05	87.56	99.20
	Other_Faults	85.22	**100.0**	73.42	60.18	98.40
Specificity	**Pastry**	90.19	**100.0**	94.21	98.36	96.34
	Z_Scratch	90.74	**100.0**	91.36	97.56	94.68
	K_Scratch	78.94	**100.0**	99.01	99.63	99.48
	Stains	66.66	91.66	93.16	**100.00**	**100.00**
	Dirtiness	78.26	**100.0**	96.10	99.18	95.65
	Bumps	81.74	**100.0**	90.98	91.11	96.67
	Other_Faults	71.05	**100.0**	91.36	86.11	99.43
Sensitivity	**Pastry**	**99.81**	99.24	64.63	41.46	99.78
	Z_Scratch	**100.0**	99.62	90.43	89.36	**100.00**
	K_Scratch	**100.0**	**100.0**	90.10	94.27	**100.00**
	Stains	**100.0**	98.38	97.87	91.49	99.89
	Dirtiness	99.82	99.82	82.61	69.57	**99.90**
	Bumps	98.02	**100.0**	53.33	74.29	99.87
	Other_Faults	92.09	**100.0**	40.11	12.03	97.84

The time required to build each model with the dataset is variable; ranging from few seconds for LR and SVM (four seconds) up to two minutes for the neural network with pruning. In C5.0 decision tree model with boosting can significantly improve the classification accuracy and specificity compare with previous models, but it requires longer training, more then two minutes. Also, the time required for building the treebagger random forest model which can significantly improve the classification accuracy, specificity and to have same sensitivity as previous discussed models is up to four minutes which is the model that is the most time consuming.

7 Conclusion and Future Work

This paper presents an approach to steel plates fault diagnosis in multiple classes, two models for decision making, pattern classification models in general and particularly support vector machine and treebagger random forest. The values of the statistical measures, sensitivity, specificity and total classification accuracy, of the both models were computed and presented. Treebagger classification model has been proven to have significantly better statistical measures. On the other hand, there are significantly better results in computation and time cost with 4 sec. (support vector machine) as opposed to 222 sec (treebagger) model.

The compared experimental results for five models: treebager random forest, support vector machine, logistic regression with step forward, multi perception neural network with pruning, decision tree with boosting have been shown, that the classification accuracy and specificity of the proposed treebagger random forest model had the best success of all test sample classifications. On the other hand statistical measure, sensitivity of SVM, treebagger random forest, and decision tree with boosting models, have achieved nearly the same. But, the time required to build each model with the dataset is variable; ranging from few seconds for LR and SVM (four seconds) up to two minutes for the neural network with pruning, decision tree model with boosting more than two minutes and treebagger random forest model up to four minutes which is a model that is the most time consuming. Although, the time required to build the proposed treebagger random forest is the model that is the most time consuming, the best experimental results encourage further research in application intelligent fault diagnosis in steel plates decision support system.

Acknowledgments. The authors acknowledge the support for research project TR 36030, funded by the Ministry of Science and Technological Development of Serbia.

References

1. Aldrich, C., Auret, L.: Unsupervised process monitoring and fault diagnosis with machine learning methods. Springer (2013)
2. Deng, S., Lin, S.Y., Chang, W.L.: Application of multiclass support vector machines for fault diagnosis of field air defence gun. Expert Systems with Applications 38(5), 6007–6013 (2011)
3. Semeion, Research Center of Sciences of Communication, Via Sersale 117, 00128, Rome, Italy, UCI Machine Learning Repository (2010), `http://archive.ics.uci.edu/ml` (accessed July 29, 2013)
4. Fakhr, M., Elsayad, A.M.: Steel Plates Faults Diagnosis with Data Mining Models. Journal of Computer Science 8(4), 506–514 (2012)
5. Abraham, A., Corchado, E., Corchado, J.M.: Hybrid Learning Machines. Neurocomputing 72(13-15), 2729–2730 (2009)
6. Corchado, E., Abraham, A., de Carvalho, A.: Hybrid intelligent algorithms and applications. Information Science 180, 2633–2634 (2010)
7. Simić, D., Kovačević, I., Simić, S.: Insolvency Prediction for Assessing Corporate Financial Health. Logic Journal of the IGPL 20(3), 536–549 (2012)
8. Wozniak, M., Grana, M., Corchado, E.: A survey of multiple classifier systems as hybrid systems. Information Fusion 16, 3–17 (2014)
9. Corchado, E., Wozniak, M., Abraham, A., de Carvalho, A., Snašel, V.: Recent trends in intelligent data analysis. Neurocomputing 126, 1–2 (2014)
10. Buscema, M., Terzi, S., Tastle, W.: A new meta-classifier. In: Proceedings of the North American Fuzzy Information Processing Society (NAFIPS), pp. 1–7 (2010)

11. Buscema, M., Tastle, W.J., Terzi, S.: Meta Net: A New Meta-Classifier Family. In: Tastle, W.J. (ed.) Data Mining Applications Using Artificial Adaptive Systems, pp. 141–182. Springer (2012)
12. Aldrich, C., Auret, L.: Unsupervised Process Monitoring and Fault Diagnosis with Machine Learning Methods. Springer (2013)
13. Zapico, A., Molisani, L.: Fault Diagnosis on Steel Structures Using Artificial Neural Networks. Mecanica Computacional 28(3), 181–188 (2009)
14. Amid, E., Aghdam, S.R., Amindavar, H.: Enhanced Performance for Support Vector Machines as Multi-class Classifiers in Steel Surface Defect Detection. World Academy of Science, Engineering and Technology 6(7), 1096–1100 (2012)
15. Vapnik, V.N.: Estimation of Dependences Based on Empirical Data. Springer Series in Statistics. Springer-Verlag New York, Inc., Secaucus (1982)
16. Vapnik, V.N.: The nature of statistical learning theory. Springer-Verlag New York, Inc., New York (1995)
17. Vapnik, V.N.: Statistical learning theory. Wiley (1998)
18. Burges, C.J.C.: A tutorial on support vector machines for pattern recognition. Data Mining Knowledge Discovery 2(2), 121–167 (1998)
19. Wozniak, M.: Hybrid Classifiers: Methods of Data, Knowledge, and Classifier Combination. Springer Series in Studies in Computational Intelligence (2013)
20. Corte, C., Vapnik, V.: Support–Vector Networks. Machine Learning 20(3), 273–297 (1995)
21. Breiman, L.: Random Forests. Machine Learning 45(1), 5–32 (2001)
22. Ho, T.K.: Random decision forests. In: Proceedings of 3rd International Conference on Document Analysis & Recognition, Montreal, Canada, vol. 1, pp. 278–282 (1995)
23. Okun, O.: Feature Selection and Ensemble Methods for Bioinformatics: Algorithmic Classification and Implementations. Medical Information Science Reference (2011)

Developing Adaptive Agents Situated in Intelligent Virtual Environments

J.A. Rincon, Emilia Garcia, V. Julian, and C. Carrascosa

Universitat Politècnica de València
Departamento de Sistemas Informáticos y Computación (DSIC)
Camino de Vera s/n, Valencia, Spain
{jrincon,mgarcia,vinglada,carrasco}@dsic.upv.es

Abstract. This paper presents a framework specially designed for the execution and adaptation of Intelligent Virtual Environments. This framework, called JACALIVE, facilitates the development of this kind of environments managing in an efficient and realistic way the evolution of parameters for the adaptation of the physical world. The framework includes a design method and a physical simulator which is in charge of giving the Intelligent Virtual Environment the look of the real or physical world, allowing to simulate physical phenomena such as gravity or collision detection. The paper also includes a case study which illustrates the use of the proposed framework.

1 Introduction

Nowadays, having software solutions at one's disposal that enforce autonomy, robustness, flexibility and adaptability of the system to develop is completely necessary. The dynamic agents organizations that auto-adjust themselves to obtain advantages from their environment seems a more than suitable technology to cope with the development of this type of systems. These organizations could appear in emergent or dynamic agent societies, such as grid domains, peer-to-peer networks or other contexts where agents dynamically group together to offer compound services as in Intelligent Virtual Environments (IVE). An IVE is a virtual environment simulating a physical (or real) world, inhabited by autonomous intelligent entities[1].

Today, this kind of applications are between the most demanded ones, not only as being the key for multi-user games such as *World Of Warcraft*[1] (with more than 7 million of users in 2013)[2] but also for immersive social networks such as *Second Life*[3] (with 36 million accounts created in its 10 years of history)[4]. It is

1 http://eu.battle.net/wow

2 http://www.statista.com/statistics/276601/number-of-world-of-warcraft-subscribers-by-quarter/

3 http://www.secondlife.com

4 http://massively.joystiq.com/2013/06/20/second-life-readies-for-10th-anniversary-celebrates-a-million-a/

M. Polycarpou et al. (Eds.): HAIS 2014, LNAI 8480, pp. 98–109, 2014.
© Springer International Publishing Switzerland 2014

in the development of these huge IVEs where the need of a quick and easy-to-use modelling toolkit arises.

These kinds of IVEs are addressed to a huge number of simultaneous entities, so they must be supported by highly scalable software. This software has also to be able to adapt to changes, not only of the amount of entities but also of their users needs. Technology currently used to develop this kind of products lacks of elements facilitating the adaptation and management of the system. Traditionally, this kind of applications use the client/server paradigm, but due to their features, a distributed approach such as multi-agent systems (MAS) seems to fit in the development of components that will evolve in an autonomous way and coordinated with the own environment's evolution.

This paper presents the JaCalIVE[5] (Jason Cartago implemented Intelligent Virtual Environment) framework. It provides a method to develop this kind of IVEs along with a supporting platform to execute them. JaCalIVE is based on the MAM5 meta-model [2] which describes a method to design IVEs.

MAM5 is based in the A & A meta-model [3] that describes environments for MAS as populated not only by agents, but also for other entities that are called *artifacts*. According to this, an IVE is composed of three important parts: artifacts, agents and physical simulation. Artifacts are the elements in which the environment is modelled. Agents are the IVE intelligent part. The physical simulation is in charge of giving the IVE the look of the real or physical world, allowing to simulate physical fenomenal such as gravity or collision detection.

The rest of the paper is organized as follows: Section 2 summarizes the most important related work. Section 3 describes the JaCalIVE framework. Section 4 summarizes the development process of an IVE based on modular robotics developed using JaCalIVE. Finally, Section 5 summarizes the main conclusions of this work.

2 Related work

This section summarizes the most relevant techniques and technology that the JACALIVE framework integrates in order to design and simulate IVEs. These techniques allow JACALIVE to develop IVEs that are realistic, complex, adaptable, and with autonomous and rational entities. First, some concepts about IVEs are presented, to continue commenting about Multi-Agent Systems concepts, as platforms and methodologies relevant to the present work. Finally, this section presents the MAM5 meta-model, as it is the starting point for the present work to model IVEs in MAS terms.

2.1 IVE

Currently, there is an increasing interest in the application of IVEs in a wide variety of domains. IVEs have been used to create advanced simulated environments [4,5,6] in so different domains as education [7], entertainment [8,9,10,11], e-commerce[12], health [13,14] and use to VR-based simulations[15].

[5] `http://jacalive.gti-ia.dsic.upv.es/`

One of the key features of any IVE is to offer a high level of user immersion. In order to achieve that, it is necessary that the IVE has the ability of simulating physical conditions of the real world such as gravity, friction and collisions. Besides, in order to increase the graphical realism, the physical simulators should include dynamic and static objects that inhabitate the IVE in a three-dimensional environment. Some of the most important developed physical simulation tools are *JBullet*[6] and *Open Dynamic Engine (ODE)*[7].

Another important feature of any IVE is to offer a high level of graphical realism. Currenly there are in the market some well-developed graphical simulators like *Unity 3D*[8], *Unrealengine UDK*[9] y *Cryengine*[10]. Although they were initially designed for videogames, they can be applied to simulate IVEs.

2.2 Multi-Agent Systems

Until now, we have highlighted the importance of giving *realism* to IVEs, which would enable the user to have the desired level of immersion. This realism is provided by the physical simulation and 3D visualization, but this is only one part of a virtual environment. To be an IVE, a virtual environment needs to give entities with the intelligence to enhance the user's immersion.

MAS is one of the most employed artificial intelligence technique for modeling IVEs. This is mainly due to the characteristics that agents have, such as autonomy, proactivity, reactivity and sociability. But this does not mean that no other AI techniques can be used within MAS for IVE development. An agent can include as a decision-making mechanism other algorithms that improve the deliberative process such as reinforcement learning [16], genetic algorithms [17], markov models [18], classification[19,20], neuronal networks [21] or use any method to hybrid artificial intelligence systems[22] etc.

However, when modeling an environment it is necessary to take into account that not all the entities are agents. The A&A meta-model [23,24] describes a methodology for modeling environments using artifacts. Artifacts represent the first level of abstraction when modeling environments. This is mainly due to the clear differentiation of the entities which are in systems of this kind. This differentiation can determine which items are objects (Artifacts) and which are intelligent entities (Agents).

The BDI model (Belief - Desire - Intention)[25,26,27] is the most well-known and used agent model when designing intelligent agents. This model is based on logic and psychology, which creates symbolic representations of beliefs, desires and intentions of the agents. The beliefs are the information the agent has about the environment. This information can be updated at each time step or not. This obsolescence of the used information forces the agent to perform deliberative

---

[6] `http://jbullet.advel.cz/`
[7] `http://www.ode.org/`
[8] `http://unity3d.com/unity`
[9] `http://www.unrealengine.com/udk/`
[10] `http://www.crytek.com/cryengine`

processes. Desires are the possible actions that the agent could make. This does not mean that every desire of an agent has to be performed. Finally, intentions represent the actions that the agent has decided to perform. These actions may be goals that have been delegated to the agent or may be the result of previous deliberation processes.

Different approaches have been devised in order to develop MAS. One of the first tools used for implementing agents is the JADE platform. JADE has been used for the development of *JGOMAS (Game Oriented Multi -Agent System based on Jade)* [28,29,30]. JADE does not directly provide a BDI model but there exist an extension called *JADEX* allowing developers to design BDI-oriented MAs incorporating the representation of beliefs, desires and intentions. JADEX has been used for modeling environments like the presented in [31]. *Jason* is another development tool used for MAS programming which also integrates the BDI model.

In our proposal we employ Jason as the programming toolkit for our BDI agents [32]. The main reason to employ JASON is its full integration with CArtAgO (Common ARTifact infrastructure for AGents Open environments)[33]. CArtAgO is a framework/infrastructure for modeling artifacts which can run virtual environments. This framework allows the implementation of open work-spaces, which facilitates the creation of distributed environments.

2.3 MAM5

MAM5[2] is a model to design IVEs based in the A&A meta-model. It is addressed to be used by an IVE designer, that wants to design an IVE based on a multi-agent system. As it is intended to be distributed, the human interface part of the system is decoupled from the intelligent part, being only this last one the part designed by means of MAM5. To have this two parts distributed facilitates the developing, gives more flexibility to the final applications (allowing different interfaces to be connected and at the same time) and allows to scale the final system (thinking on massive applications with a huge number of users and/or agents).

This model classifies the entities in the design into two different sets (as seen in Figure 1). The first one is related to all the entities that do not have any physical representation in the IVE (Non Virtually Physical Situated), whilst the second one is formed by all the entities having a representation inside the IVE (Virtually Physical Situated). Inside the former set there are Agents, Artifacts, and Workspaces following the A&A definition. In a similar way, inside the last set there are IVE Artifacts and Inhabitant Agents that are situated in the virtual environment (in fact, the Inhabitant Agent will have an IVE Artifact representing its body in the IVE), and IVE Workspaces, representing the virtual place, and the laws defining and governing such places.

MAM5 meta-model not only allows to diferenciate between virtual represented entities and not virtual represented, but it also incorporates the definition of the physical restrictions and properties in the modelling of the environment and of their inhabiting entities, respectively. That is, the designer may define the

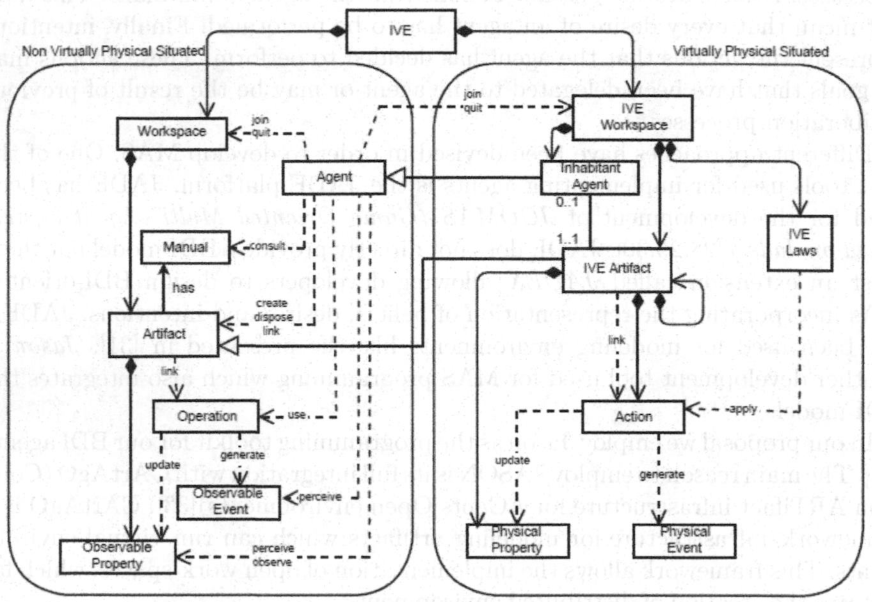

Fig. 1. Meta-modelo MAM5 de un IVE basado en A&A

different IVE Laws governing the different IVE Workspaces in the IVE (representing the physical laws of the real world) and, he may also define the different physical properties of the entities populating such virtual environment (mass, length, ...).

3 JaCalIVE (Jason Cartago Implemented Intelligent Virtual Environment)

In the last years, there have been different approaches for using MAS as a paradigm for modelling and engineering IVEs, but they have some open issues: low generality and then reusability; weak support for handling full open and dynamic environments where objects are dynamically created and destroyed.

As a way to tackle these open issues, and based on the MAM5 meta-model, we have developed the JaCalIVE framework. It provides a method to develop this kind of applications along with a supporting platform to execute them. Figure 2 shows the steps that should be followed in order to develop an IVE according to the JaCalIVE framework.

1. Model: The first step is to design the IVE. JaCalIVE provides an XSD based on MAM5 meta-model. According to it, an IVE can be composed of two different types of workspaces depending on whether they specify the location

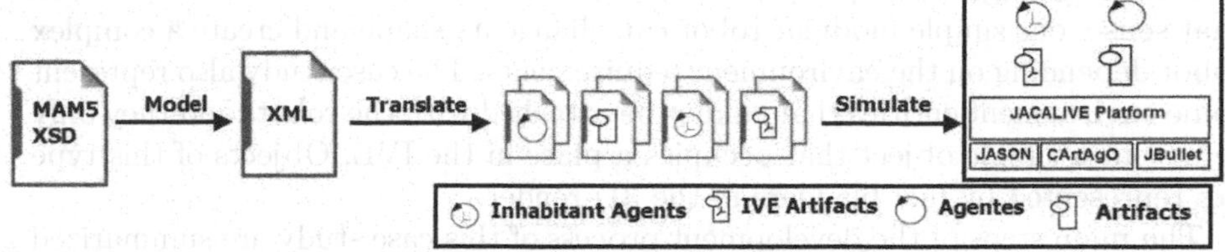

Fig. 2. General Scheme, JaCalIVE

of its entities (`IVE_Workspaces`) or not (`Workspaces`). It also includes the specification of agents, artifacts and the norms that regulate the physical laws of the IVE Workspaces.

2. Translate: The second step is to automatically generate code templates from design. One file template is generated for each agent and artifact. JaCalIVE agents are rational agents based on JASON. The artifacts representing the virtual environment are based on CArtAgO. The developer must complete these templates and then the IVE is ready to be executed.
3. Simulate: Finally the IVE is simulated. As is shown in Figure 2, JaCalIVE platform uses JASON, CArtAgO and JBullet. JASON offers support for BDI agents that can reason about their beliefs, desires and intentions. CArtAgO offers support for the creation and management of artifacts. JBullet offers support for physical simulation. JaCalIVE platform also includes internal agents (JASON based) to manage the virtual environment.

4 Case Study

In this section a case study based on modular robots is described to show the versatility of JaCalIVE framework. Modular robots [34,35,36] are robots mainly characterized by their ability to reconfigure their modules and changing its shape [37,38]. Each module of a robot is an independent entity that can be joined to other modules. This feature allows each robot to adapt its shape dynamically to changes in the environment. Currently, a wide range of domains of application are using modular robotics. For example, they are being used to search for missing persons in earthquakes [39] and to space exploration [40]. These domains need advanced virtual simulation environments like the ones MAM5 and JaCalIVE allow to test their implementations. Moreover, simulations as the one presented in this paper can be used as test beds for new adaptive algorithms, cooperative algorithms, Swarm Robotics, and so on.

Our case study implements a modular robot simulation that is composed of seven 3D modular robots models and one 3D camera model that that behave autonomously and interact with the environment. The environment is composed of a simple map without any wall. The map length and width is configured on the modeling process, in our case is 500X500. Robots can interact among them in order to change its shape by joining other modules or environment objects. In that sense, one simple modular robot can change its shape and create a complex robot depending on the environment requirements. The case study also represent some environment entities that cannot be attached with the robots and they only represent a simple object that occupies a place in the IVE. Objects of this type are represented by fuel bladders in the 3D render.

The main steps of the development process of this case study are summarized below:

1. Model: The design of the IVE is described in terms of IVE Artifacts, Inhabitant Agents and IVE Workspaces using an XML as based on the JaCalIVE XSD. The main parts of this XML are: (i) An `IVE_Workspace` called `apodoRobot_Workspaces` as show in Figure 3.

```
<VIRTUAL>
 <IVE_WORKSPACE NAME="apodRobot_workspace">
  <IVE_ARTIFACTS>
   <ITEM NAME="BodyLeft"/>
   <ITEM NAME="BodyRight"/>
   <ITEM NAME="linkedArtifact"/>
   <ITEM NAME="unlinkedArtifact"/>
  </IVE_ARTIFACTS>
  <INHABITANT_AGENTS>
   <ITEM NAME="Robot"/>
  </INHABITANT_AGENTS>
  <IVE_LAWS>
   <ITEM NAME="Gravity"/>
  </IVE_LAWS>
 </IVE_WORKSPACE>
```

Fig. 3. XML that configures the IVE_Workspace

   (ii) Nine `IVE_Artifacts`. One of the attributes of these artifacts is whether they are linkable or not, that is, if they can be joined to other artifacts or not. Three of these artifacts are linkable; two are unlinkable and the other ten form the bodies of the inhabitant agents as show in Figure 4.

   (iii) Five `Inhabitant_Agent`. Each one of them models one modular robot, that initially is associated to two of the previously defined IVE artifacts as show in Figure 5.

2. Translate: From the XML file that represents the design of the system, the JaCalIVE framework automatically generates the following files: (i) Fifteen java files representing the IVE artifacts (Ten files representing the agent bodies, three files corresponding to linkable artifacts and two files correspond to unlinkable artifacts). (ii) Six JASON files that correspond to the agents. (iii) A file called `jacalive.asl`, where the developer programs the communication between agents and artifacts.

```
<IVE_ARTIFACT NAME="linkedArtifact" LINKEABLE="true">
 <ATTRIBUTES/>
 <PHYSICAL_PROPERTIES>
  <PERCEIVABLE>
    <VECTOR3D NAME ="position">
  <DOUBLE NAME ="x"> 100.0 </DOUBLE>
  <DOUBLE NAME ="y"> 80.0 </DOUBLE>
  <DOUBLE NAME ="z"> 0.0 </DOUBLE>
 </VECTOR3D>
 <VECTOR3D NAME ="velocity">
  <DOUBLE NAME ="x"> 1.0 </DOUBLE>
  <DOUBLE NAME ="y"> 1.0 </DOUBLE>
  <DOUBLE NAME ="z"> 1.0 </DOUBLE>
 </VECTOR3D>
 <VECTOR3D NAME ="orientation">
  <DOUBLE NAME ="x"> 1.0 </DOUBLE>
  <DOUBLE NAME ="y"> 0.0 </DOUBLE>
  <DOUBLE NAME ="z"> 0.0 </DOUBLE>
 </VECTOR3D>
    <VECTOR3D NAME ="joint">
  <DOUBLE NAME ="x"> 0.0 </DOUBLE>
  <DOUBLE NAME ="y"> 0.0 </DOUBLE>
  <DOUBLE NAME ="z"> 0.0 </DOUBLE>
```

Fig. 4. XML that configures the IVE_Artifacts

```
<INHABITANT_AGENT NAME="Robot">
 <ATTRIBUTES/>
 <BODY_ARTIFACT>
  <ITEM ID="0"/>
  <ITEM ID="1"/>
 </BODY_ARTIFACT>
 <FILE NAME="apodRobotJason.asl"/>
</INHABITANT_AGENT>...

<IVE_LAW NAME="Gravity">
 <VECTOR3D NAME="gravity">
  <DOUBLE NAME="x"> 0.0 </DOUBLE>
  <DOUBLE NAME="y"> -9.8 </DOUBLE>
  <DOUBLE NAME="z"> 0.0 </DOUBLE>...
 </VECTOR3D>
 <ACTIONS>
  <ITEM NAME="move"/>
 </ACTIONS>
</IVE_LAW>
```

Fig. 5. XML that configures the Inhabitant Agents

3. Simulate: Entities that have been modeled and programmed in the previous steps are simulated. Since JaCalIVE physical engine handles the IVE physics simulation, any visualization engine can be used to view the simulation. In this case study the render used is implemented with Unity 3D. Figure 6 shows an snapshot excerpt of the simulation.

Figure 7 shows an example of a construction sequence to show the adaptability feature of such robots. In the sequence 1, the robot (the inhabitant agent) is

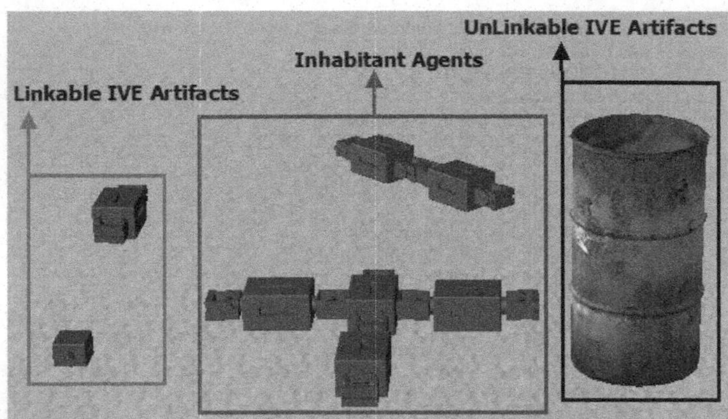

Fig. 6. Excerpt of the case study simulation using Unity 3D

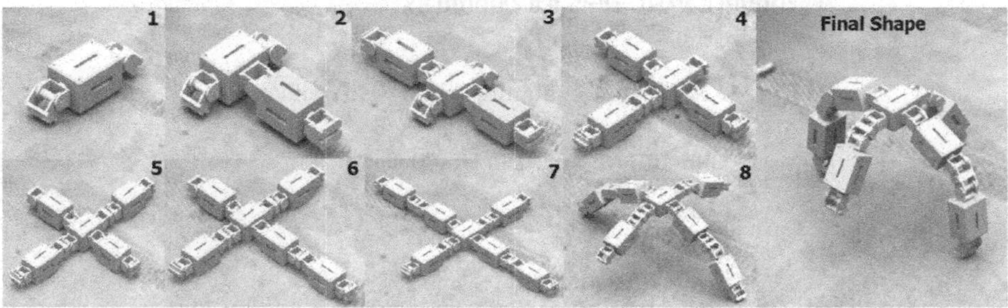

Fig. 7. Modular robotic sequence

displayed as a single module. This fact reduces its mobility, i.e., the robot will advance slowly. In sequence 2, an IVE Artifact has been adhered to its body changing its shape helping to improve its movement. During sequences 3, 4, 5, 6, and 7 the inhabitant agent adheres more IVE Artifacts in order to build a complex body. The final shape of the final robot allows it to improve its performance when its moving through the environment.

5 Conclusions

In this paper we present a framework for the design and simulation of IVEs. This framework differs from other works in the sense that it integrates the concepts of agents, artifacts and physical simulation. Besides, IVEs developed using the JaCalIVE framework can be easily modified thanks to the XML modellation and the automatic code generation.

Following the MAM5 perspective, the modules used to interact with the developed IVEs are uncoupled from the rest of the system. It allows to easily integrate different kinds of modules as needed. For example, it allows to adapt the visualization render to the requirements of the specific IVE we want to simulate.

To show the possibilities of such approach, a case study based on modular robotics is presented. These robots can adapt its shape to changing environment conditions. In the developed scenario, there are different modules in the environment that the agents can incorporate to their body, changing the way they move.

Acknowledgements. This work is partially supported by the TIN2009-13839-C03-01, TIN2011-27652-C03-01, CSD2007-00022, COST Action IC0801, FP7-294931 and the FPI grant AP2013-01276 awarded to Jaime-Andres Rincon.

References

1. Aylett, R., Luck, M.: Applying artificial intelligence to virtual reality: Intelligent virtual environments. Applied Artificial Intelligence 14, 3–32 (2000)
2. Barella, A., Ricci, A., Boissier, O., Carrascosa, C.: MAM5: Multi-Agent Model For Intelligent Virtual Environments. In: 10th European Workshop on Multi-Agent Systems (EUMAS 2012), pp. 16–30 (2012)
3. Omicini, A., Ricci, A., Viroli, M.: Artifacts in the A&A meta-model for multi-agent systems. Autonomous Agents and Multi-Agent Systems 17(3), 432–456 (2008)
4. Yu, C.-H., Nagpal, R.: Distributed consensus and self-adapting modular robots. In: IROS 2008 Workshop on Self-Reconfigurable Robots and Applications (2008)
5. Lidoris, G., Buss, M.: A multi-agent system architecture for modular robotic mobility aids. In: European Robotics Symposium 2006, pp. 15–26 (2006)
6. Yu, C.-H., Nagpal, R.: A self-adaptive framework for modular robots in a dynamic environment: theory and applications. The International Journal of Robotics Research 30(8), 1015–1036 (2011)
7. Barbero, A., González-Rodríguez, M.S., de Lara, J., Alfonseca, M.: Multi-agent simulation of an educational collaborative web system. In: European Simulation and Modelling Conference (2007)
8. Ranathunga, S., Cranefield, S., Purvis, M.K.: Interfacing a cognitive agent platform with a virtual world: a case study using second life. In: AAMAS, pp. 1181–1182 (2011)
9. Andreoli, R., De Chiara, R., Erra, U., Scarano, V.: Interactive 3d environments by using videogame engines. In: Proceedings of the Ninth International Conference on Information Visualisation, pp. 515–520. IEEE (2005)
10. Roncancio, C., Gómez G-B, J., Zalama, E.: Modeling virtual agent behavior in a computer game to be used in a real enviroment. In: Demazeau, Y., et al. (eds.) Trends in PAAMS. AISC, vol. 71, pp. 623–630. Springer, Heidelberg (2010)
11. Dignum, F.: Agents for games and simulations. Autonomous Agents and Multi-Agent Systems 24(2), 217–220 (2011)
12. dos Santos, C.T., Osorio, F.S.: AdapTIVE: an intelligent virtual environment and its application in e-commerce. In: Proceedings of the 28th Annual International Computer Software and Applications Conference, COMPSAC 2004, vol. 1, pp. 468–473 (September 2004)
13. Tian, J., Tianfield, H.: A multi-agent approach to the design of an E-medicine system. In: Schillo, M., Klusch, M., Müller, J., Tianfield, H. (eds.) MATES 2003. LNCS (LNAI), vol. 2831, pp. 85–94. Springer, Heidelberg (2003)

14. Mago, V.K., Syamala Devi, M.: A multi-agent medical system for indian rural infant and child care. In: IJCAI, pp. 1396–1401 (2007)
15. Anastassakis, G., Ritchings, T., Panayiotopoulos, T.: Multi-agent systems as intelligent virtual environments. In: Baader, F., Brewka, G., Eiter, T. (eds.) KI 2001. LNCS (LNAI), vol. 2174, pp. 381–395. Springer, Heidelberg (2001)
16. Garcá-Pardo, J.A., Carrascosa, C.: Social Welfare for Automatic Innovation. In: Klügl, F., Ossowski, S. (eds.) MATES 2011. LNCS, vol. 6973, pp. 29–40. Springer, Heidelberg (2011)
17. Kazemi, A., Fazel Zarandi, M.H., Moattar Husseini, S.M.: A multi-agent system to solve the production-distribution planning problem for a supply chain: a genetic algorithm approach. Int. J. Adv. Manuf. Technol. 44(1-2), 180–193 (2009)
18. Dimuro, G.P., da Rocha Costa, A.C., Gonçalves, L.V., Hubner, A.: Interval-valued hidden markov models for recognizing personality traits in social exchanges in open multiagent systems (2008)
19. Orkin, J., Roy, D.: Semi-automated dialogue act classification for situated social agents in games. In: Dignum, F. (ed.) Agents for Games and Simulations II. LNCS (LNAI), vol. 6525, pp. 148–162. Springer, Heidelberg (2011)
20. Woźniak, M., Graña, M., Corchado, E.: A survey of multiple classifier systems as hybrid systems. Information Fusion 16, 3–17 (2014)
21. Jia, L., Zhenjiang, M.: Entertainment oriented intelligent virtual environment with agent and neural networks. In: IEEE International Workshop on Haptic, Audio and Visual Environments and Games, HAVE 2007, pp. 90–95 (October 2007)
22. Corchado, E., Wonźiak, M., Abraham, A., de Carvalho, A.C.P.L.F., Snásel, V.: Recent trends in intelligent data analysis. Neurocomputing 126, 1–2 (2014); Recent trends in Intelligent Data Analysis Selected papers of the The 6th International Conference on Hybrid Artificial Intelligence Systems (HAIS 2011); Online Data Processing Including a selection of papers from the International Conference on Adaptive and Intelligent Systems 2011 (ICAIS 2011)
23. Ricci, A., Viroli, M., Omicini, A.: The A&A programming model and technology for developing agent environments in MAS. In: Dastani, M., El Fallah Seghrouchni, A., Ricci, A., Winikoff, M. (eds.) ProMAS 2007. LNCS (LNAI), vol. 4908, pp. 89–106. Springer, Heidelberg (2008)
24. Ricci, A., Viroli, M., Omicini, A.: Give agents their artifacts: the A&A approach for engineering working environments in MAS. In: Proceedings of the 6th International Joint Conference on Autonomous Agents and Multiagent Systems, p. 150 (2007)
25. Bordini, R.H., Hübner, J.F., Wooldridge, M.J.: Programming multi-agent systems in AgentSpeak using Jason. J. Wiley, Chichester (2007)
26. Rehman, S.U., Nadeem, A.: AgentSpeak (L) based testing of autonomous agents. In: Kim, T.-H., Adeli, H., Kim, H.-K., Kang, H.-J., Kim, K.J., Kiumi, A., Kang, B.-H. (eds.) ASEA 2011. CCIS, vol. 257, pp. 11–20. Springer, Heidelberg (2011)
27. Go, C.A.L., Lee, W.-H.: An intelligent belief-desire-intention agent for digital game-based learning. In: Analysis and Design of Intelligent Systems Using Soft Computing Techniques, pp. 677–685. Springer (2007)
28. Barella, A., Valero, S., Carrascosa, C.: JGOMAS: new approach to AI teaching. IEEE Transactions on Education 52(2), 228–235 (2009)
29. Barella, A., Carrascosa, C., Botti, V.: Agent architectures for intelligent virtual environments, pp. 532–535. IEEE (November 2007)
30. Barella, A., Carrascosa, C., Botti, V., Martí, M.: Multi-agent systems applied to virtual environments: A case study. In: Proceedings of the 2007 ACM Symposium on Virtual Reality Software and Technology, pp. 237–238. ACM (2007)

31. Behrens, T.M., Hindriks, K.V., Dix, J.: Towards an environment interface standard for agent platforms. Ann. Math. Artif. Intell. 61(4), 261–295 (2011)
32. van Oijen, J., van Doesburg, W., Dignum, F.: Goal-based communication using BDI agents as virtual humans in training: An ontology driven dialogue system. In: Dignum, F. (ed.) Agents for Games and Simulations II. LNCS, vol. 6525, pp. 38–52. Springer, Heidelberg (2011)
33. Ricci, A., Viroli, M., Omicini, A.: A general purpose programming model & technology for developing working environments in MAS. In: 5th International Workshop "Programming Multi-Agent System" (PROMAS 2007), pp. 54–69 (2007)
34. Schmickl, T.: How to engineer robotic organisms and swarms? In: Meng, Y., Jin, Y. (eds.) Bio-Inspired Self-Organizing Robotic Systems. SCI, vol. 355, pp. 25–52. Springer, Heidelberg (2011)
35. Modular self-reconfigurable robots
36. Yu, C.-H., Nagpal, R.: Sensing-based shape formation on modular multi-robot systems: a theoretical study. In: Proceedings of the 7th International Joint Conference on Autonomous Agents and Multiagent Systems, vol. 1, pp. 71–78 (2008)
37. Yim, M., White, P.J., Park, M., Sastra, J.: Modular Self-Reconfigurable Robots (2009)
38. Park, M., Chitta, S., Teichman, A., Yim, M.: Automatic configuration recognition methods in modular robots. The International Journal of Robotics Research 27(3-4), 403–421 (2008)
39. Gonzalez-Gomez, J., Gonzalez-Quijano, J., Zhang, H., Abderrahim, M.: Toward the sense of touch in snake modular robots for search and rescue operations. In: Proc. ICRA 2010 Workshop on Modular Robots: State of the Art, pp. 63–68 (2010)
40. A modular robotic system with applications to space exploration. In: IEEE International Conference on Space Mission Challenges for Information Technology, 0:8 p. (2006)

Concurrence among Imbalanced Labels and Its Influence on Multilabel Resampling Algorithms

Francisco Charte[1], Antonio Rivera[2],
María José del Jesus[2], and Francisco Herrera[1]

[1] Dep. of Computer Science and Artificial Intelligence, University of Granada, Granada, Spain
[2] Dep. of Computer Science, University of Jaén, Jaén, Spain
{fcharte,herrera}@ugr.es, {arivera,mjjesus}@ujaen.es
http://simidat.ujaen.es, http://sci2s.ugr.es

Abstract. In the context of multilabel classification, the learning from imbalanced data is getting considerable attention recently. Several algorithms to face this problem have been proposed in the late five years, as well as various measures to assess the imbalance level. Some of the proposed methods are based on resampling techniques, a very well-known approach whose utility in traditional classification has been proven.

This paper aims to describe how a specific characteristic of multilabel datasets (MLDs), the level of concurrence among imbalanced labels, could have a great impact in resampling algorithms behavior. Towards this goal, a measure named *SCUMBLE*, designed to evaluate this concurrence level, is proposed and its usefulness is experimentally tested. As a result, a straightforward guideline on the effectiveness of multilabel resampling algorithms depending on MLDs characteristics can be inferred.

Keywords: Multilabel Classification, Imbalanced Learning, Resampling, Measures.

1 Introduction

Multilabel classification (MLC) [1] models are designed to predict the subset of labels associated to each instance in an MLD, instead of only one class as traditional classifiers do. It is a task useful in fields such as automated tag suggestion [2], protein classification [3], and object recognition in images [4], among others. Many different methods have been proposed lately to accomplish this problem.

The number of instances in which each label appears is not homogeneous. In fact, most MLDs show big differences in label frequencies. This peculiarity is known as imbalance [5], and it has been profoundly studied in traditional classification. In the context of MLC, several proposals to deal with imbalanced MLDs [6–12] have been made lately. Despite these efforts, there are still some aspects regarding imbalanced learning in MLC that would need additional analysis.

M. Polycarpou et al. (Eds.): HAIS 2014, LNAI 8480, pp. 110–121, 2014.
© Springer International Publishing Switzerland 2014

Resampling techniques are commonly used in non-MLDs [13], hence they are an obvious choice to face the same problem with MLDs. Notwithstanding, the nature of MLDs can be a challenge for resampling algorithms. In this paper we will show how a specific characteristic of these datasets, the joint presence of labels with different frequencies in the same instance, could prevent the goal of these algorithms. We hypothesized that this symptom, the concurrence among imbalanced labels, would influence the resampling algorithms behavior. A new measure, named *SCUMBLE* (*Score of ConcUrrence among iMBalanced LabEls*) and designed explicitly to assess this causality, will be proposed. Its effectiveness will be experimentally demonstrated.

The *SCUMBLE* measure was conceived aiming to know how difficult would be to work with a certain MLD for resampling algorithms. Its goal is to appraise the concurrence among imbalanced labels, giving as result a score easily interpretable. This score will be in the range [0,1]. A low score would denote an MLD with not much concurrence among imbalanced labels, whereas a high one would evidence the opposite case. Our hypothesis was that the lower the score obtained, the better the resampling algorithms would work. In the future, some recently published ideas, such as the modularity-based label grouping introduced in [14], could be included in our framework as additional means to obtain label concurrence data.

The rest of this paper is structured as follows. Section 2 offers a brief introduction to MLC, as well as a description on how the learning from imbalanced MLDs has been faced. In Section 3 the problem of concurrence among imbalanced level in MLDs will be defined, and how to assess this concurrence using the proposed measured will be explained. Section 4 describes the experimental framework used, as well as the obtained results from experimentation. Finally, Section 5 will offer the conclusions.

2 Preliminaries

In this section a concise introduction to multilabel classification is offered, along with a description on how the learning from imbalanced MLDs has been faced until now.

2.1 Multilabel Classification

Currently, there are many domains [3, 4, 15–18] in which each instance is not associated to an exclusive class, but to a group of them. In this context the classes are named labels, and the set of labels that belongs to a data sample is called labelset. Let D be an MLD, D_i the *i-th* instance, and L the full set on labels on D. The goal of a multilabel classifier is to predict a set $Z_i \subseteq L$ with the labelset for D_i.

Multilabel classification has been traditionally faced through two different approaches [1]. The first one, called data transformation, aims to produce binary or multiclass datasets from an MLD, allowing the use of non-MLC algorithms. The second, known as algorithm adaptation, has the goal of adapting established algorithms to work natively with MLDs. The two most common transformation methods are Binary Relevance (BR) [19] and Label Powerset (LP) [20]. The former produces several binary datasets from an MLD, one for each label. The latter transforms the MLD in a multiclass dataset, taking each labelset as class identifier. Regarding adapted algorithms, the number of proposals is quite high. There are multilabel KNN classifiers such as ML-kNN [21], multilabel trees based on C4.5 [22], and multilabel SVMs such as [17], as well as a profusion of algorithms based on ensembles of BR and LP classifiers. A recent review on multilabel classification algorithms can be found in [23].

Thus far, most proposed multilabel measures are focused in assessing the number of labels and labelsets. The most common are the total number of labels $|L|$, label cardinality (*Card*), which is the average number of labels per instance, and label density, obtained as $Card/|L|$.

2.2 Learning from Imbalanced Data

Imbalanced learning is a well-known problem in traditional classification [5], having been faced through three main approaches [24]. First, through algorithmic adaptations [25] of existent classifiers, the imbalance is taken into account in the classification process. Second, the preprocessing approach aims to balance class distributions by way of data resampling, creating [26] (oversampling) or removing [27] (undersampling) data samples. Third, cost sensitive classification [28] is a combination of the two previous approaches. The data resampling approach has the advantage of being classifier independent, and its effectiveness has been proven in many scenarios.

In the MLC field, both the algorithmic adaptation and the data resampling approaches have been applied. The former is present in [6–8], while the latter appears in [10–12]. There are also proposals based on the use of ensemble of classifiers, such as [9].

When it comes to assess the imbalance level in MLDs, the measures in Equation 1 and Equation 2 are proposed in [11]. Let D be an MLD, Y the full set of labels in it, y the label being analyzed, and Y_i the labelset of *i-th* instance in D. *IRLbl* is a measure calculated individually for each label. The higher is the *IRLbl* the larger would be the imbalance, allowing to know what labels are in minority or majority. *MeanIR* is the average *IRLbl* for an MLD, useful to estimate the global imbalance level.

$$IRLbl(y) = \frac{\underset{y'=Y_1}{\overset{Y_{|Y|}}{\text{argmax}}}(\sum_{i=1}^{|D|} h(y', Y_i))}{\sum_{i=1}^{|D|} h(y, Y_i)}, \quad h(y, Y_i) = \begin{cases} 1 & y \in Y_i \\ 0 & y \notin Y_i \end{cases}. \tag{1}$$

$$MeanIR = \frac{1}{|Y|} \sum_{y=Y_1}^{Y_{|Y|}} (IRLbl(y)). \tag{2}$$

Even though the previously cited proposals for facing imbalanced learning in MLC achieve some good results, their behavior is heavily influenced by MLDs characteristics. In the following we will focus in this topic, specifically in regard to data resampling solutions.

3 MLDs and Resampling Algorithms Behavior

Most traditional resampling methods do their job by removing instances with the most frequent class, or creating new samples from instances associated to the least frequent one. Since each instance can belong to one class only, these actions would effectively balance the classes frequencies. However, this is not necessarily the case when working with MLDs.

3.1 Concurrence among Imbalanced Labels in MLDs

The instances in a MLD are usually associated simultaneously to two or more labels. It is entirely possible that one of those labels is the minority label, while other is the majority one. In the most extreme situation, all the appearances of the minority label could be jointly with the majority one, into the same instances. In practice the scenario would be more complicated, as commonly there are more than one minority/majority label in an MLD. Therefore, the potential existence of instances associated to minority and majority labels at once is very high. This fact is what we called concurrence among imbalanced labels.

A multilabel oversampling algorithm that clones minority instances, such as the proposed in [11], or that generates new samples from existing ones preserving the labelsets, as is the case in [12], could be also increasing the number of instances associated to majority labels. Thus, the imbalance level would be hardly reduced if there is a high level of concurrence among imbalanced labels. In the same way, a multilabel undersampling algorithm designed to remove instances from the majority labels, such as the proposed in [11], could inadvertently cause also a loss of samples associated to the minority ones.

The ineffectiveness of these resampling methods, when they are used with certain MLDs, would be noticed once the preprocessing is applied and the classification results are evaluated. This process will need computing power and time. For that reason, it would be desirable to know in advance the level of concurrence among imbalanced labels that each MLD suffers, saving these valuable resources.

3.2 The SCUMBLE Measure

The concurrence of labels in an MLD can be visually explored in some cases, as shown in Figure 1. Each arc represents a label, being the arc's length proportional to the number of instances in which this label is present. The top diagram corresponds to the genbase dataset. At the position of twelve o'clock appears a label called *P750* which is clearly a minority label. All the samples associated to

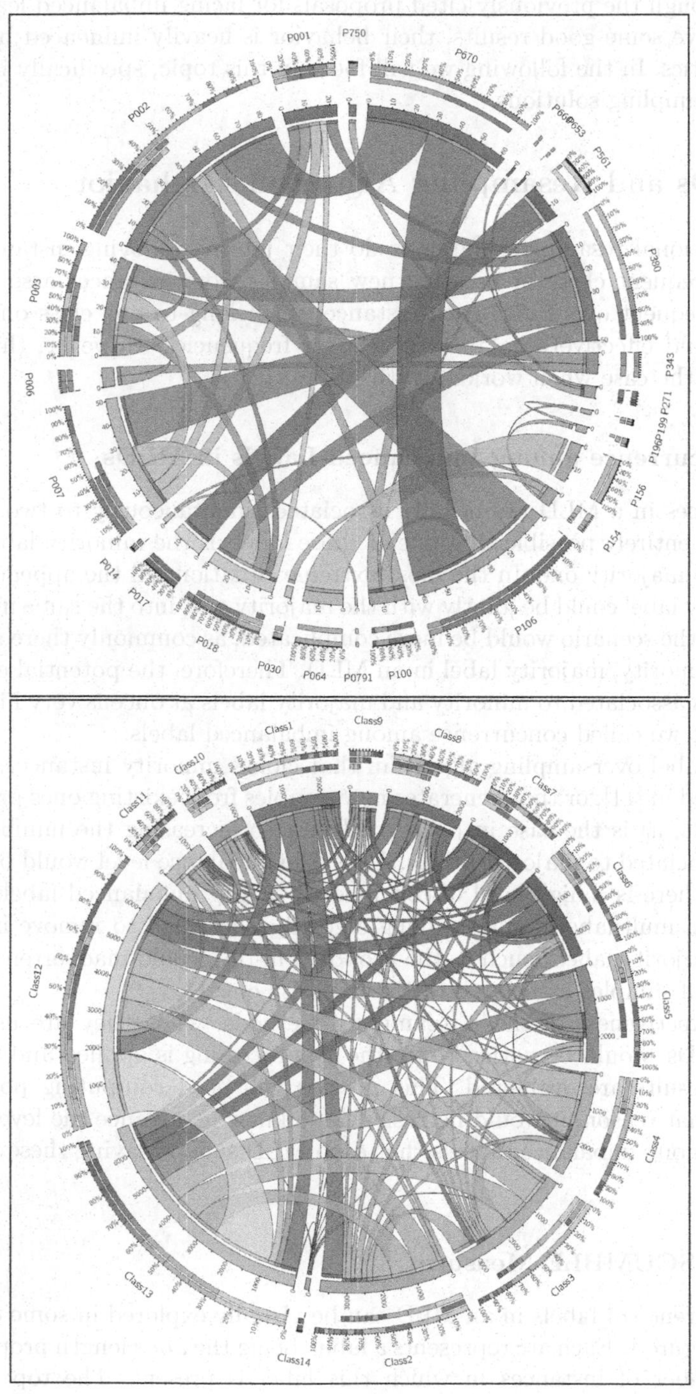

Fig. 1. Label concurrence in genbase (top) and yeast MLDs

this label also contains *P271*, another minority label. The same situation can be seen with label *P154*. By contrast, in the yeast MLD (bottom diagram) is easy to see that the samples associated to minority labels, such as *Class14* and *Class9*, appear always together with one or more majority labels. At first sight, that the concurrence between imbalanced labels is higher in yeast than in genbase could be concluded. However, this visual exploratory technique is not useful with MLDs having more than a few dozens labels.

The *SCUMBLE* measure aims to quantify the imbalance variance among the labels present in each data sample. This measure (Equation 3) is based on the Atkinson index [29] and the *IRLbl* measure (Equation 1) proposed in [11]. The former is an econometric measure directed to assess social inequalities among individuals in a population. The latter is the measure that lets us know the imbalance ratio of each label in an MLD. The Atkinson index is used to know the diversity among people's earnings, while our objective is to assess the extend to which labels with different imbalance levels appear jointly. Our hypothesis is that the higher is the concurrence level the harder would be the work for resampling algorithms, and therefore the worse they would perform.

The Atkinson index is calculated using incomes, we used the imbalance level of each label instead, taking each instance D_i in the MLD D as a population, and the active labels in D_i as the individuals. If the label l is present in the instance i then $IRLbl_{il} = IRLbl(l)$. On the contrary, $IRLbl_{il} = 0$. $\overline{IRLbl_i}$ stands for the average imbalance level of the labels appearing in instance i. The scores for every sample are averaged, obtaining the final *SCUMBLE* value.

$$SCUMBLE(D) = \frac{1}{|D|}\sum_{i=1}^{|D|}[1 - \frac{1}{\overline{IRLbl_i}}(\prod_{l=1}^{|L|} IRLbl_{il})^{(1/|L|)}] \tag{3}$$

Whether our initial hypothesis was correct or wrong, and therefore this measure is able to predict the difficulty that an MLD implies for resampling algorithms or not, is something to be proven experimentally.

4 Experimentation and Analysis

This section starts describing the experimental framework used to assess the usefulness of the *SCUMBLE* measure, and follows giving all the details about the obtained results and their analysis.

4.1 Experimental Framework

To determine the usefulness of the *SCUMBLE* measure the six MLDs shown in Table 1 were used. The rightmost column indicates each dataset's origin. All of them are imbalanced, so theoretically they could benefit from the application of a resampling algorithm. Aside from the *SCUMBLE* measure, the *MaxIR* and *MeanIR* values are also shown. These will be taken as reference point to the

Table 1. Measures about imbalance on datasets before preprocessing

Dataset	SCUMBLE	MaxIR	MeanIR	Ref.
corel5k	0.3932	896.0000	168.7806	[4]
cal500	0.3369	133.1917	21.2736	[15]
enron	0.3023	657.0500	72.7730	[16]
yeast	0.1044	53.6894	7.2180	[17]
medical	0.0465	212.8000	72.1674	[18]
genbase	0.0283	136.8000	32.4130	[3]

posterior analysis. All the measures are average values from training partitions[1] using a 2x5 folds scheme. The datasets appear in Table 1 sorted by *SCUMBLE* value, from higher to lower. According to this measure, corel5k and cal500 would be the most difficult MLDs, since they have a high level of concurrence among labels with different imbalance levels. On the other hand, medical and genbase would be the most benefited from resampling.

Regarding the resampling algorithms, the two proposed in [11] were applied. Both are based on the LP transformation. LP-ROS does oversampling by cloning instances with minority labelsets, whereas LP-RUS performs undersampling removing samples associated to majority labelsets. All the dataset partitions were preprocessed, and the imbalance measures were calculated for each algorithm.

4.2 Results and Analysis

Once the LP-ROS and LP-RUS resampling algorithm were applied, the imbalance levels on the preprocessed MLDs were reevaluated. Table 2 shows the new *MaxIR* and *MeanIR* values for each dataset. Comparing these values with the ones shown in Table 1, it can be verified that a general improvement in the imbalance levels has been achieved. Although there are some exceptions, in most cases both *MaxIR* and *MeanIR* are lower after applying the resampling algorithms.

Table 2. Imbalance levels after applying resampling algorithms

	LP-ROS		LP-RUS	
Dataset	MaxIR	MeanIR	MaxIR	MeanIR
corel5k	969.4000	140.7429	817.1000	155.0324
cal500	179.35838	25.4685	620.0500	68.6716
enron	710.9667	53.2547	133.1917	21.2736
yeast	15.4180	2.6116	83.8000	19.8844
medical	39.9633	10.5558	46.5698	6.3706
genbase	13.7030	4.5004	150.8000	51.1567

[1] The dataset partitions used in this experimentation, as well as color version of all figures, are available to download at `http://simidat.ujaen.es/SCUMBLE`.

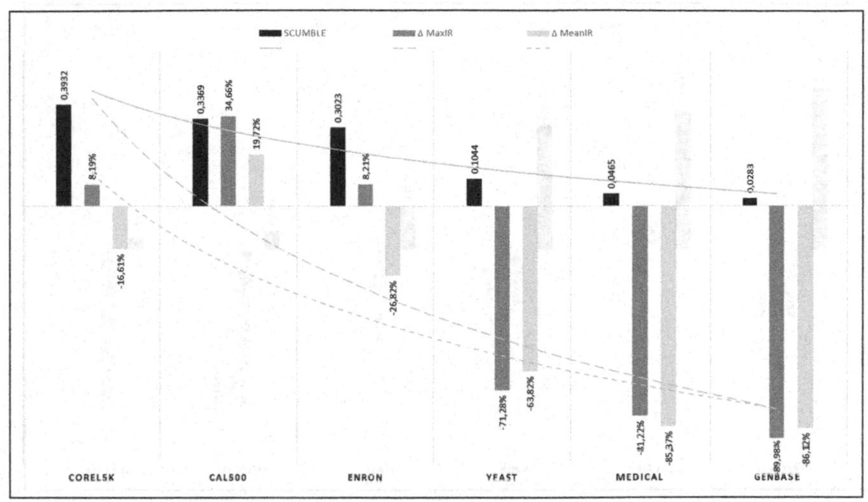

Fig. 2. SCUMBLE vs changes in imbalance level after applying LP-ROS

It would be interesting to know if the imbalance reduction is proportionally coherent with the values obtained from the *SCUMBLE* measure. The graphs in Figure 2 and Figure 3 are aimed to visually illustrate the connection between *SCUMBLE* values and the relative variations in imbalance levels. For each MLD, the *SCUMBLE* value from Table 1 is represented along with the percentage change in *MaxIR* and *MeanIR* after applying the LP-ROS/LP-RUS resampling methods. The tendency for the three values among all the MLDs is depicted by three logarithmic lines. As can be seen, a clear parallelism exists between the continuous line, which corresponds to *SCUMBLE*, and the dashed lines. This affinity is specially remarkable with the LP-RUS algorithm (Figure 3).

Although the previous figures allow to infer that an important correlation between the *SCUMBLE* measure and the success of the resampling algorithms exists, this relationship must be formally analyzed. To this end, a Pearson correlation test was applied over the *SCUMBLE* values and the relative changes in imbalance levels for each resampling algorithm. The resulting correlation coefficients and *p-values* are shown in Table 3. It can be seen that all the coefficients are above 80%, and all the *p-values* are under 0.05. Therefore, a statistical correlation between the *SCUMBLE* measure and the behavior of the tested resampling algorithms can be concluded.

Following this analysis, it seems reasonable to avoid resampling algorithms when the *SCUMBLE* measure for an MLD is well above 0.1, such as is the case with corel5k, cal500 and enron. In this situation the benefits obtained from resampling, if any, are very small. The result can even be a worsening of the imbalance level. In average, the *MeanIR* for the three MLDs with *SCUMBLE* > 0.3 has been reduced only a 6%, while the *MaxIR* is actually increasing in the same percentage. By contrast, the average *MeanIR* reduction for the other three MLDs, with *SCUMBLE* $\lesssim 0.1$, reaches 52% and the *MaxIR* reduction 54%.

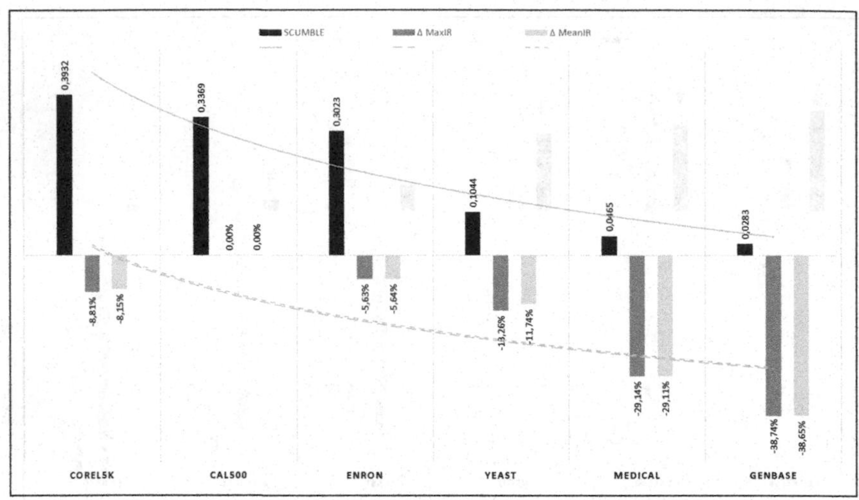

Fig. 3. SCUMBLE vs changes in imbalance level after applying LP-RUS

Table 3. Results from the Pearson correlation tests

	SCUMBLE vs ΔMaxIR		SCUMBLE vs ΔMeanIR	
Algorithm	Cor	p-value	Cor	p-value
LP-ROS	0.8120	0.0497	0.9189	0.0096
LP-RUS	0.8607	0.0278	0.8517	0.0314

Aiming to know how these changes in the imbalance levels would influence classification results, and if a correlation with *SCUMBLE* values exists, the HOMER [30] algorithm was used, following a 2x5 folds cross-validation scheme. It must be highlighted that the interest here is not in the raw performance values, but in how they change after a resampling algorithm has been applied and how this change correlates with *SCUMBLE* values. Therefore, the HOMER algorithm is used only as a tool to obtain classification results before and after applying the resampling. Any other MLC algorithm could be used for this task. Additionally, the proposed *SCUMBLE* measure is not used in the experimentation to influence the behavior of LP-ROS, LP-RUS or HOMER by any means. The goal is to theoretically explore the correlation between changes in classification results and *SCUMBLE* values.

Table 4 shows these results assessed with the F-measure, the harmonic mean of precision and recall measures. It can be seen that with the three MLDs which show high *SCUMBLE* values, the preprocessing has produced a remarkable deterioration in classification results. Among the other three MLDs the resampling has improved them in some cases, while producing a slight worsening (less than 1%) in others. Therefore, even though the MLC algorithm behavior would be also affected by other dataset characteristics, that the *SCUMBLE* measure would offer valuable information to determine the convenience of applying a resampling method can be concluded.

Table 4. F-Measure values obtained by HOMER MLC algorithm

Dataset	Base	LP-RUS	LP-ROS	ΔRUS	ΔROS
corel5k	0.3857	0.2828	0.2920	-26.6788	-24.2935
cal500	0.3944	0.3127	0.3134	-20.7150	-20.5375
enron	0.5992	0.5761	0.5874	-3.8551	-1.9693
yeast	0.6071	0.6950	0.6966	14.4787	14.7422
medical	0.9238	0.9158	0.9162	-0.8660	-0.8227
genbase	0.9896	0.9818	0.9912	-0.7882	0.1617

5 Conclusions

Multilabel classification has many applications nowadays, but usually MLDs are imbalanced. This is a fact that challenges most MLC algorithms, and several approaches to face it have been proposed lately. Some of them rely on resampling techniques, through adaptations of algorithms that have proven their usefulness in traditional classification. However, the specific nature of MLDs has to be taken into account, since some of their characteristics could influence these algorithms behavior.

In this paper the concurrence among imbalanced labels has been explained and *SCUMBLE*, a new measure designed to assess this characteristic, has been proposed. The suitability of this measure has been experimentally demonstrated against six MLDs and two resampling algorithms. The conducted correlation analysis, summarized in Table 3, has shown that the *SCUMBLE* measure can be used to know in advance if resampling would be positive for a certain MLD or not. This assumption has been corroborated by classification results, shown in Table 4, which experiment a remarkable worsening when used with MLDs with the highest *SCUMBLE* values.

Given this reality, a further and deeper analysis should be directed, involving additional MLDs and other resampling algorithms. Notwithstanding it could be concluded that basic resampling algorithms, which clone the labelsets in new instances or remove samples, are not a general solution in the multilabel field. More sophisticated approaches, which take into account the concurrence among imbalanced labels, would be needed.

Acknowledgments. F. Charte is supported by the Spanish Ministry of Education under the FPU National Program (Ref. AP2010-0068). This work was partially supported by the Spanish Ministry of Science and Technology under projects TIN2011-28488 and TIN2012-33856, and the Andalusian regional projects P10-TIC-06858 and P11-TIC-9704.

References

1. Tsoumakas, G., Katakis, I., Vlahavas, I.: Mining Multi-label Data. In: Maimon, O., Rokach, L. (eds.) Data Mining and Knowledge Discovery Handbook, ch. 34, pp. 667–685. Springer US, Boston (2010)

2. Katakis, I., Tsoumakas, G., Vlahavas, I.: Multilabel Text Classification for Automated Tag Suggestion. In: Proc. ECML PKDD 2008 Discovery Challenge, Antwerp, Belgium, pp. 75–83 (2008)
3. Diplaris, S., Tsoumakas, G., Mitkas, P.A., Vlahavas, I.: Protein Classification with Multiple Algorithms. In: Bozanis, P., Houstis, E.N. (eds.) PCI 2005. LNCS, vol. 3746, pp. 448–456. Springer, Heidelberg (2005)
4. Duygulu, P., Barnard, K., de Freitas, J.F.G., Forsyth, D.: Object Recognition as Machine Translation: Learning a Lexicon for a Fixed Image Vocabulary. In: Heyden, A., Sparr, G., Nielsen, M., Johansen, P. (eds.) ECCV 2002, Part IV. LNCS, vol. 2353, pp. 97–112. Springer, Heidelberg (2002)
5. Chawla, N.V., Japkowicz, N., Kotcz, A.: Editorial: special issue on learning from imbalanced data sets. SIGKDD Explor. Newsl. 6(1), 1–6 (2004)
6. He, J., Gu, H., Liu, W.: Imbalanced multi-modal multi-label learning for subcellular localization prediction of human proteins with both single and multiple sites. PloS One 7(6), 7155 (2012)
7. Li, C., Shi, G.: Improvement of learning algorithm for the multi-instance multi-label rbf neural networks trained with imbalanced samples. J. Inf. Sci. Eng. 29(4), 765–776 (2013)
8. Tepvorachai, G., Papachristou, C.: Multi-label imbalanced data enrichment process in neural net classifier training. In: IEEE Int. Joint Conf. on Neural Networks, IJCNN, 2008, pp. 1301–1307 (2008)
9. Tahir, M.A., Kittler, J., Bouridane, A.: Multilabel classification using heterogeneous ensemble of multi-label classifiers. Pattern Recognit. Lett. 33(5), 513–523 (2012)
10. Tahir, M.A., Kittler, J., Yan, F.: Inverse random under sampling for class imbalance problem and its application to multi-label classification. Pattern Recognit. 45(10), 3738–3750 (2012)
11. Charte, F., Rivera, A., del Jesus, M.J., Herrera, F.: A first approach to deal with imbalance in multi-label datasets. In: Pan, J.-S., Polycarpou, M.M., Woźniak, M., de Carvalho, A.C.P.L.F., Quintián, H., Corchado, E. (eds.) HAIS 2013. LNCS, vol. 8073, pp. 150–160. Springer, Heidelberg (2013)
12. Giraldo-Forero, A.F., Jaramillo-Garzón, J.A., Ruiz-Muñoz, J.F., Castellanos-Domínguez, C.G.: Managing imbalanced data sets in multi-label problems: A case study with the smote algorithm. In: Ruiz-Shulcloper, J., Sanniti di Baja, G. (eds.) CIARP 2013, Part I. LNCS, vol. 8258, pp. 334–342. Springer, Heidelberg (2013)
13. García, V., Sánchez, J., Mollineda, R.: On the effectiveness of preprocessing methods when dealing with different levels of class imbalance. Knowl. Based Systems 25(1), 13–21 (2012)
14. Szymański, P., Kajdanowicz, T.: MLG: Enchancing multi-label classification with modularity-based label grouping. In: Pan, J.-S., Polycarpou, M.M., Woźniak, M., de Carvalho, A.C.P.L.F., Quintián, H., Corchado, E. (eds.) HAIS 2013. LNCS, vol. 8073, pp. 431–440. Springer, Heidelberg (2013)
15. Turnbull, D., Barrington, L., Torres, D., Lanckriet, G.: Semantic Annotation and Retrieval of Music and Sound Effects. IEEE Audio, Speech, Language Process. 16(2), 467–476 (2008)
16. Klimt, B., Yang, Y.: The Enron Corpus: A New Dataset for Email Classification Research. In: Boulicaut, J.-F., Esposito, F., Giannotti, F., Pedreschi, D. (eds.) ECML 2004. LNCS (LNAI), vol. 3201, pp. 217–226. Springer, Heidelberg (2004)
17. Elisseeff, A., Weston, J.: A Kernel Method for Multi-Labelled Classification. In: Advances in Neural Information Processing Systems 14, vol. 14, pp. 681–687. MIT Press (2001)

18. Crammer, K., Dredze, M., Ganchev, K., Talukdar, P.P., Carroll, S.: Automatic Code Assignment to Medical Text. In: Proc. Workshop on Biological, Translational, and Clinical Language Processing, BioNLP 2007, Prague, Czech Republic, pp. 129–136 (2007)
19. Godbole, S., Sarawagi, S.: Discriminative Methods for Multi-labeled Classification. In: Dai, H., Srikant, R., Zhang, C.(eds.) PAKDD 2004. LNCS (LNAI), vol. 3056, pp. 22–30. Springer, Heidelberg (2004)
20. Boutell, M., Luo, J., Shen, X., Brown, C.: Learning multi-label scene classification. Pattern Recognit. 37(9), 1757–1771 (2004)
21. Zhang, M., Zhou, Z.: ML-KNN: A lazy learning approach to multi-label learning. Pattern Recognit. 40(7), 2038–2048 (2007)
22. Clare, A.J., King, R.D.: Knowledge discovery in multi-label phenotype data. In: Siebes, A., De Raedt, L. (eds.) PKDD 2001. LNCS (LNAI), vol. 2168, pp. 42–53. Springer, Heidelberg (2001)
23. Zhang, M., Zhou, Z.: A Review on Multi-Label Learning Algorithms. IEEE Trans. Knowl. Data Eng., doi:10.1109/TKDE.2013.39
24. López, V., Fernández, A., García, S., Palade, V., Herrera, F.: An insight into classification with imbalanced data: Empirical results and current trends on using data intrinsic characteristics. Inf. Sciences 250, 113–141 (2013)
25. Fernández, A., López, V., Galar, M., del Jesus, M.J., Herrera, F.: Analysing the classification of imbalanced data-sets with multiple classes: Binarization techniques and ad-hoc approaches. Knowl. Based Systems 42, 97–110 (2013)
26. Chawla, N.V., Bowyer, K.W., Hall, L.O., Kegelmeyer, W.P.: Smote: Synthetic minority over-sampling technique. J. Artificial Intelligence Res. 16, 321–357 (2002)
27. Kotsiantis, S.B., Pintelas, P.E.: Mixture of expert agents for handling imbalanced data sets. Annals of Mathematics, Computing & Teleinformatics 1, 46–55 (2003)
28. Provost, F., Fawcett, T.: Robust classification for imprecise environments. Mach. Learn. 42, 203–231 (2001)
29. Atkinson, A.B.: On the measurement of inequality. Journal of Economic Theory 2(3), 244–263 (1970)
30. Tsoumakas, G., Katakis, I., Vlahavas, I.: Effective and Efficient Multilabel Classification in Domains with Large Number of Labels. In: Proc. ECML/PKDD Workshop on Mining Multidimensional Data, MMD 2008, Antwerp, Belgium, pp. 30–44 (2008)

Depth-Based Outlier Detection Algorithm

Miguel Cárdenas-Montes

Centro de Investigaciones Energéticas Medioambientales y Tecnológicas,
Department of Fundamental Research, Madrid, Spain
miguel.cardenas@ciemat.es

Abstract. Nowadays society confronts to a huge volume of information which has to be transformed into knowledge. One of the most relevant aspect of the knowledge extraction is the detection of outliers. Numerous algorithms have been proposed with this purpose. However, not all of them are suitable to deal with very large data sets. In this work, a new approach aimed to detect outliers in very large data sets with a limited execution time is presented. This algorithm visualizes the tuples as N-dimensional particles able to create a potential well around them. Later, the potential created by all the particles is used to discriminate the outliers from the objects composing clusters. Besides, the capacity to be parallelized has been a key point in the design of this algorithm. In this proof-of-concept, the algorithm is tested by using sequential and parallel implementations. The results demonstrate that the algorithm is able to process large data sets with an affordable execution time, so that it overcomes the curse of dimensionality.

Keywords: Outlier Detection, Parallel and Distributed Data Mining, Big Data, Large-Scale Learning, Scalability.

1 Introduction

The modern society is tackling with a deluge of information. The challenge is to convert this huge and increasing volume of information into useful knowledge. In order to achieve this purpose, numerous techniques have been developed to extract pieces of knowledge from large data sets. In the past, this area has been termed as knowledge discover or data mining, and nowadays it is moving toward a blurry set of techniques [1,2] which are termed big data.

One of the typical problems in data mining is to identify in a data set, the tuples or objects that can be considered as special or anomalous elements. Usually these elements are labelled as outliers. Outlier detection is an important task in fraud detection, intrusion detection or simply for cleaning noisy data.

Many techniques have been proposed to detect the tuples or objects which do not belong to groups or clusters in a given data set. For example, there are techniques based on the distance or the angle between the objects. However, these techniques suffer from the curse of dimensionality. This means that for high-dimensional spaces, the objects are by almost equally distant from other object. If the techniques are based on the angles between the objects, then the angle between any two objects is close to 90 degree [3].

Therefore, the curse of dimensionality degrades the performance of certain algorithms for outlier detection. For this reason, alternative strategies are mandatory to process large data sets.

M. Polycarpou et al. (Eds.): HAIS 2014, LNAI 8480, pp. 122–132, 2014.
© Springer International Publishing Switzerland 2014

For other algorithms, the difficulty arises from the computational complexity of the method. Any method with computational complexity larger than linear one results into infeasible for large data sets. In these cases, when incrementing the data size, very large increments in the execution time are produced.

A second source of difficulties arises from the algorithms that analyse the information monolithically. In these cases, the appearance of new tuples forces to perform a new analysis of the complete volume of information. When a large volume of information is involved, this severely impacts over the efficiency of the algorithm. In order to overcome these difficulties, the proposed algorithm performs outlier detection based on a well potential created by each particle in the feature space.

In this algorithm, each tuple is visualized as a particle in a space of N dimensions, being N the number of attributes. Each particle is able to create a squared-well around its position in this N-dimensional space. The well created by each particle is characterized by two parameters: the radius and the depth. All the particles additively contribute to create in the N-dimensional space a potential map. In the positions where more particles concentrate, the potential map has a larger depth.

This model is inspired in the nuclear potential created by nucleons (protons and neutrons) in the nucleus of the atoms. The nucleons in the nucleus create a well potential which bound them together.

The parameters which govern the behaviour of the algorithm are briefly described in the followings:

Radius of the well. This parameter indicates the distance of influence of the presence of the particle. By increasing the radius, distant particles will belong to the same cluster. On the contrary, if the radius is shortened, then more particles will be considered as outliers instead of forming a cluster. The radius gives an notion about the neighbourhood size of a particle.

Depth of the well. This parameter marks the sensitiveness level of the algorithm. If the well formed by a single particle is very depth, then few particles in the neighbourhood of a position will be necessary to form a cluster. Oppositely, if the well is shallow, then more particles in the neighbourhood will be necessary to form a cluster.

Threshold outlier level. This parameter gives to the practitioners the capacity to select the threshold level for outlier-cluster discrimination. The threshold value is subtracted to the final potential in all the feature space to determine which particles form clusters and which are outliers. By defining a low value for the threshold, with the appropriate values for the two former parameters, few particles will be necessary to form a cluster. On the contrary, if the threshold level has a high value, many particles grouped in the neighbourhood of a position will be mandatory to be considered as a cluster.

Although the depth of the well and the threshold outlier level seem to have a similar function, they have been proposed for different purposes. The depth of the well is conceived for the creation of the potential map in the feature space. By varying the radius and the depth, different potential maps are generated. However, this task is considered as computationally intensive. Therefore, for big data, the generation of the potential map is a task which should be performed once.

On the other hand, the threshold outlier level is a parameter that ought to be handled by the practitioner for discriminating clusters and outliers. This task can be performed many times, with different threshold outlier levels, over a previously generated potential map; so that, it provides different sensitiveness in the outlier detection.

This approach provides diverse advantages and potential capacities to process the information in distributed computing infrastructures (grid and cloud computing), by processing the information by parts and later by gathering the partial information pieces; or to process in parallel platform such as clusters or accelerator cards (GPU or Xeon Phi). Besides, this can be executed with horizontal data fragmentation, in subsets of tuples; or with vertical data fragmentation, in subsets of attributes [4]. These advantages are developed in the following points.

- Series of data sets can be compared against a potential map conceived as standard or correct. This allows distinguishing changes in data.
- The potential maps can be compared among them. This comparison allows distinguishing if the clusters or the outliers locations evolve.
- In most of the problems, the data set is composed by a large number of objects with multiple attributes. The approach allows processing the data set by taking into consideration only a sub-set of the attributes, and when finishing the task to continue with the remaining attributes. If some attributes are considered as more important than others, the approach supports to tackle the analysis as a "feature selection" mode. Firstly, the more important attributes are analysed, and the objects marked as outliers based on this initial consideration. Thus, the practitioners can start to extract conclusions from the subset of data analysed. In parallel, the second order of importance attributes can generate their potential maps, and the remaining outliers analysed against these new maps.
- Taking into account that the objective is to process large data sets, the practitioners aim to execute the analysis in high-performance computing platforms (clusters or accelerator cards) or in distributed computing infrastructures (grid or cloud computing). The modularity of the approach allows easily adapting the algorithm to distributed computing infrastructures. Subsets divided by attributes can be processed in different nodes. The execution of the work can be performed in an asynchronous and elastic way (cloud or grid platforms). As far as the partial units are processed, information about the outliers found in this partial processing can be presented as partial conclusions. Moreover, the variation of the number of computational resources available does not impede to process the data set, but it will accelerate or slow down.
- If the main bulk of data but not the complete set is accessible by the practitioners at determined time, the data can be analysed, and the remaining part be incorporated later when possible. This kind of disaggregate analysis is supported by the approach. The potential maps are additive, so that when a set of data are available its potential map can be created, and later be incorporated. The work done with the initial part of the data is not wasted since the potential map does not need to be completely regenerated, only the contribution of the new objects are processed.

The final aim for designing this algorithm is to process the log-files of the cluster Tier-2 at CIEMAT. This infrastructure is devoted to analyse the data of the CMS detector.

This cluster is composed of 1300 cores (roughly 8 cores per node) with 1 PB storage capacity on disk. The analysis of these logs-files might provide clues about fails in the systems, types of job rejected, errors in connections, etc, which currently are concealed in the huge volume of data generated.

The rest of the paper is organized as follows: Section 2 summarizes the Related Work and previous efforts done. An in-depth description of the implementation of the algorithm is presented at Section 3. The Analysis is presented in Section 4, including the asymptotic analysis of the algorithm proposed (Section 4.1) and the study of an MPI implementation (Section 4.2). And finally, the Conclusions and Future Work are presented in Section 5.

2 Related Work

In [3] a brief sub-section describing "depth-based methods" for outlier detection is presented. In this book, the authors express as follows for presenting this type of methods: "The idea is that the points in the outer boundaries of the data lie at the corners of the convex hull". These points in the outer boundaries are identified as likely to be outliers. Although the word "depth-based" is employed in this description of the convex hull algorithm, it is not related at all with the approach presented in the present article. Different meanings to the concept "depth" are given in both works.

Some other studies [5,6] underline that the main drawback of this convex hull-based approach is the large execution time. So that, it makes impractical for processing large data set, and therefore, in big data. Furthermore, by studying the pseudo-code of the algorithm, it is not intuitive how it can be parallelized in order to accelerate the execution.

In [7] an excellent recap of the clustering strategies as well as a discussion about the curse of dimensionality can be found. This is relevant because one of the main drawbacks of outlier detection is the degradation of the performance when incrementing the data size. Other classification of the clustering methods can be found in [8]. Further comparison with the categories presented in these books will be done when describing in-depth the proposed algorithm. In the clustering algorithms, the outlier detection depends on the efficiency of the clustering method, in such way that the outliers are considered as a sub-product of the cluster structure.

Finally, the classifications presented in [4] have been used along this work to categorize both the algorithm and the data fragmentation.

3 Implementation

The schema of the algorithm (Algorithm 1) is as follows: from a zero-level potential map, iteratively for each particle the depth is subtracted in the points inner to the radius of influence of the particle. This process is executed for all feature-space and all particles. The visual result of this process for an one-dimensional example is presented at Fig. 1(a) (continuous line).

At Fig. 1(a), a set of objects (points at horizontal axis) is drawn. Each object generates a squared-well potential of radius 10 and depth 0.1. The dotted horizontal line

Algorithm 1. The outlier detection algorithm pseudocode

```
for Each object in the data set do
    while The distance to the object is lower than the radius do
        Subtract to the potential map, the value of the depth of the well;
    end
end
Once the potential map has been created, add in all the feature space the threshold
outlier level;
for Each object in the data set do
    if The object is below the zero level then
        This object is member of a cluster;
    end
    else
        This object is an outlier;
    end
end
```

marks the threshold outlier level. This level discriminates the objects which are member of a cluster from the outliers (marked with stripped vertical lines at Fig. 1(a)).

Visually it can be identified the effect over the analysis of the variation of the algorithm parameters. If the absolute value of the threshold outlier level is incremented, then the horizontal line will go down, and as a consequence more objects will be classified as outlier (Fig. 1(b)). As an example, the two points around the position 400 will be classified as outliers if this threshold goes slightly down. In essence, the threshold outlier level marks how many objects in a close area are necessary to be classified as members of a cluster, or on the contrary, as outlier.

Both the threshold outlier level and the depth of the well are connected. If both parameters are modified in the same direction (both are incremented or both are reduced), then no net effect will be produced. For this reason, it is useful to define the threshold outlier level as a multiple of the depth of the well. Then, it can be visualized as the minimum number of objects in a reduced neighbourhood area to conform a cluster. At Fig. 1(c), the reduction of the radius produces an increment of the objects labelled as outlier. This effect is specially significant in the outer border of the clusters.

Finally, the radius of the well created by an object can visually understood as the size of the area to be considered as the neighbourhood of an object. By enlarging this parameter, scatter objects might be considered as being member of a cluster. Oppositely, by reducing the radius, the objects should be really close to be considered as a cluster.

If the problem is computationally intensive (large number of tuples and large number of attributes), then the process can be performed iteratively for each feature. In this case, for one feature and all particles, the one-dimensional potential map is created. Next, all objects are checked against this one-dimensional potential map while retaining the outliers list after the attribute analysed. Once again, iteratively for each feature and the remaining list of outliers, coming from the previous steps, the mentioned procedure is followed, so that, at the end of the process all the features have been checked.

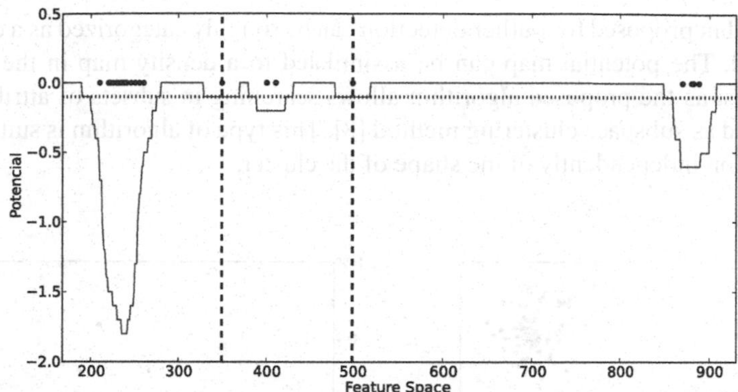

(a) The configuration is: radius = 20; depth =0.1; and threshold outlier level = -0.1.

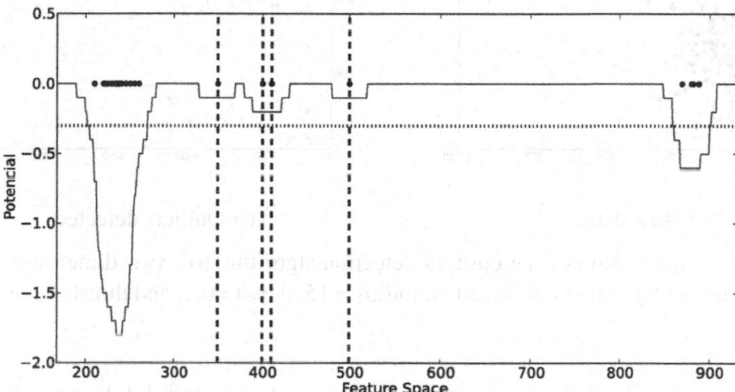

(b) The configuration is: radius = 20; depth =0.1; and threshold outlier level = -0.3.

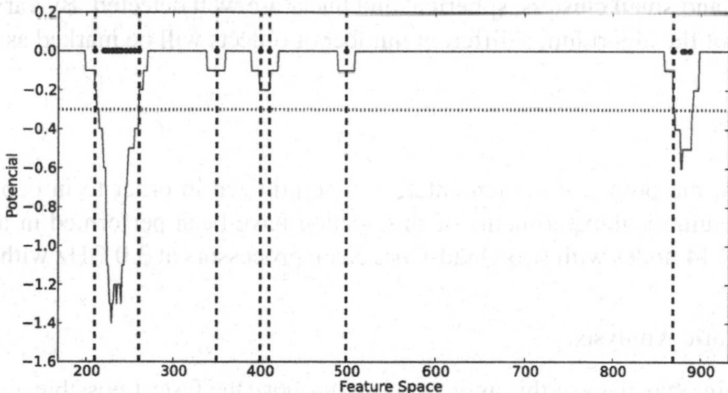

(c) The configuration is: radius = 10; depth =0.1; and threshold outlier level = -0.3.

Fig. 1. In this plot, the potential map for a set of points (points in x-axis), the threshold outlier level (dotted horizontal line), and the outlier positions (dashed vertical lines) for one-dimensional problem are presented

The algorithm proposed for outlier detection can be roughly categorized as a density-based method. The potential map can be assimilated to a density map in the feature space. Besides, as the proposed algorithm allows searching in subsets of attributes, it can be labelled as subspace clustering method [8]. This type of algorithm is suitable for outlier detection independently of the shape of the cluster.

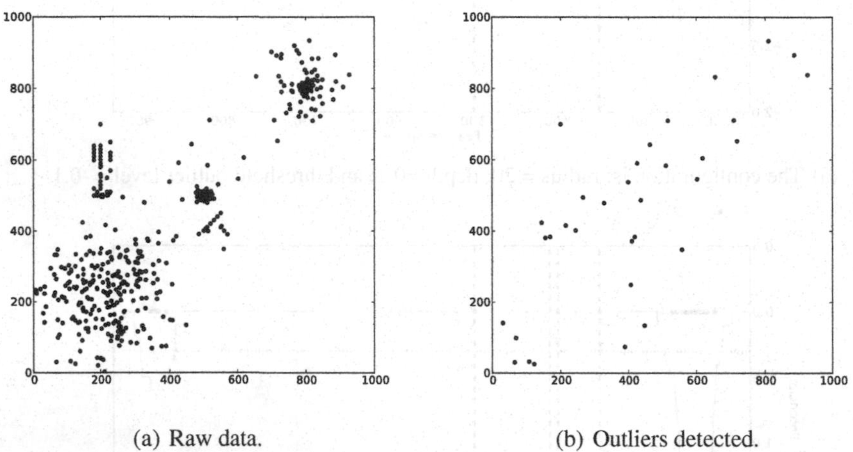

(a) Raw data. (b) Outliers detected.

Fig. 2. Example of application of the outliers detection algorithm to a two-dimensional data set (600 objects). The configuration employed is: radius = 15; depth =0.2; and threshold outlier level = 0.4.

At Fig. 2, an example of data processing for a two-dimensional data set is presented. On the left figure (Fig. 2(a)), the original data set is plotted, whereas the tuples labelled as outliers are plotted at Fig. 2(b). As be can appreciated, both compact and scatter clusters, large and small clusters, spherical and linear are well detected. By varying the configuration of the algorithm, a different number of objects will be marked as outlier.

4 Analysis

In this section, the proposed implementation is scrutinized in order to in-depth characterize. The numerical experiments of this section have been performed in a cluster composed by 144 nodes with two Quad-Core Xeon processors at 3.0 GHz with 8 GB.

4.1 Asymptotic Analysis

One of the main objectives of this approach is to propose the fastest possible algorithm. This premise was considered in the initial design phase. For this reason, the implementation is tested against an incremental number of tuples (Fig. 3(a) for 2 attributes) and an incremental number of attributes (Fig. 3(b) for 1 million objects, and Fig. 3(c) for 10 million objects). For each configuration, 20 executions are performed and the worst execution time divided by the varying parameter (tuples or attributes) is plotted.

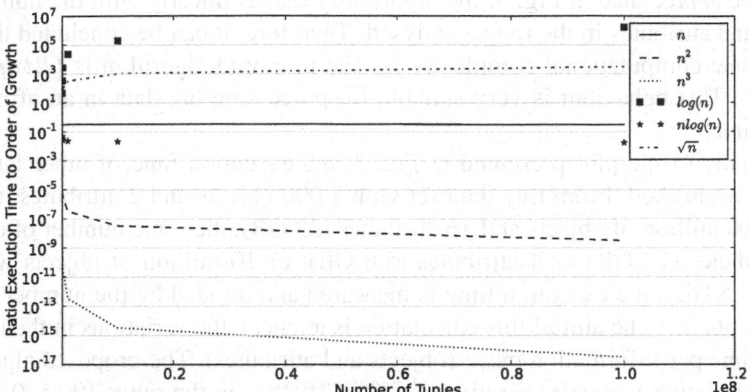

(a) Asymptotic behaviour (worst execution time divided by the number of tuples) of the algorithm when incrementing the number of tuples (two attributes).

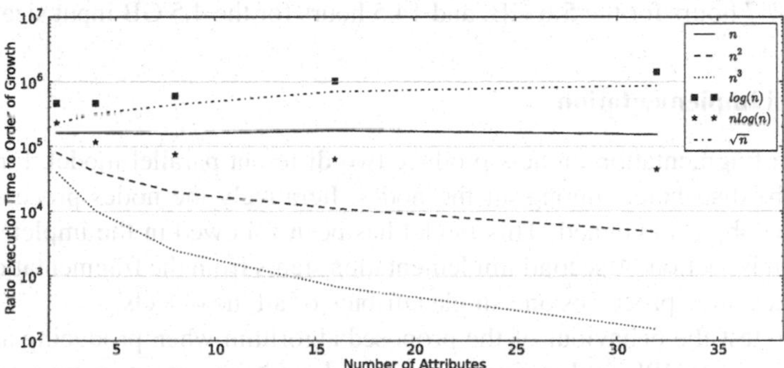

(b) Asymptotic behaviour (execution time divided by the number of attributes) of the algorithm when incrementing the number of attributes (1M objects).

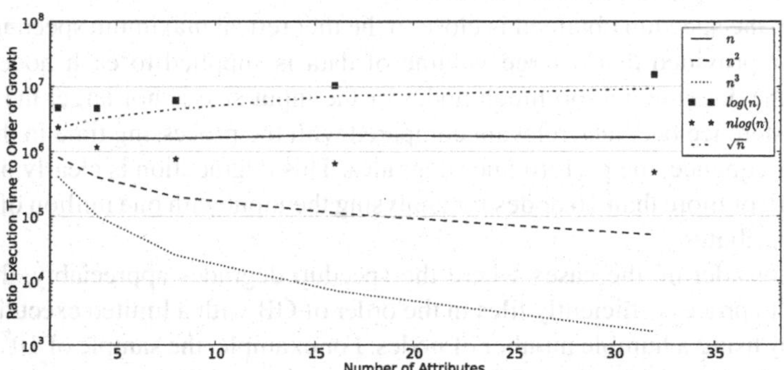

(c) Asymptotic behaviour (worst execution time divided by the number of attributes) of the algorithm when incrementing the number of attributes (10M objects).

Fig. 3. Asymptotic analyses of the proposed algorithm for outlier detection. The worst execution time of 20 runs is employed. The plots demonstrate that the computational complexity is $O(tuples \times attributes)$.

As can be appreciated at Fig. 3, the algorithm behaves linearly with the number of the tuples and attributes in the range analysed. Therefore, it can be concluded that the most adequate computational complexity for the proposed algorithm is $O(tuples \times attributes)$. This behaviour is very suitable for processing big data in an affordable execution time.

Additionally to the plot presented at Fig. 3, the execution time of other large input sizes was checked. From tiny data set with 1,000 objects and 2 attributes, to data sets with 100 million of objects and 16 attributes (23 GB), the same number of objects with 8 attributes (12 GB) or 4 attributes (5.6 GB); or 10 million of objects with 32 attributes (4.5 GB), the execution time is measured and divided by the number of objects and attributes. The aim of this calculation is to check the variations in the unitary execution time per information piece (objects and attributes). The proposed algorithm for outlier detection maintains a ratio $\frac{Execution\,time}{Objects \times Atrributes}$ in the range [0.15–0.18] for the inputs processed. This stability in the unitary execution time is an excellent feature when intending to process large data sets. As a consequence, the execution times[1] keeps affordable even for large input sizes: 74 hours for the 23 GB input size, 36.8 hours for the 12 GB, 17.7 hours for the 5.6 GB, and 14.5 hours for the 4.5 GB input size.

4.2 Parallel Implementation

The two data fragmentation models produce two different parallel model. Firstly, the objects can be distributed among all the nodes. Iteratively the nodes process the attributes of the objects assigned. This model has been followed in the implementation described in this section. A second implementation stems from the fragmentation of the attributes. Each node processes one single attribute of all the objects.

In order to test the behaviour of the proposed algorithm when producing a parallel implementation, an MPI implementation is coded, and the execution time tested for diverse number of objects and attributes, and number of cores (Table 1). As can be appreciated in this survey, the algorithm behaves differently in function of the problem size, and number of nodes used to process it.

In general, the speedup obtained is close to the theoretical maximum speedup (number of nodes) provided that a large volume of data is supplied to each node. When distributing the data among too much nodes or the input size is not large, the time of the data transference becomes relevant compared with the processing time in the node, and, as a consequence, the performance degrades. This degradation is clearly observed when using 16 or more than 16 nodes for analysing the input with one million of objects and up to 8 attributes.

Without considering the cases where the speedup degrades appreciably, the algorithm is able to process efficiently files in the order of GB with a limited execution time budget and by using a humble number of nodes. For example, the sample of 10^7 objects and 16 attributes has a size of 2.3 GB, and it can be analysed in less than one hour in 8 cores.

[1] The worst execution time after 20 runs is employed.

Table 1. Mean execution times in seconds (20 executions) and speedup of the MPI implementation of the outlier detection algorithm for diverse input sizes: number of tuples from 10^6 to 10^7 and number of attributes from 2 to 16

Number of Nodes	Number of Objects			
	10^6		10^7	
	Execution Time	Speed-up	Execution Time	Speed-up
2A				
1	319.17		3099.46	
2	167.09	1.91	1560.92	1.99
4	90.56	3.52	791.85	3.91
8	53.13	6.01	408.75	7.58
16	34.76	9.18	218.66	14.17
32	25.96	12.30	136.20	22.76
64	23.55	13.55	88.42	35.05
4A				
1	631.32		6220.18	
2	326.40	1.93	3138.17	1.98
4	173.02	3.65	1598.82	3.89
8	94.82	6.66	805.38	7.72
16	57.03	11.07	421.27	14.77
32	37.57	16.81	234.24	26.56
64	30.46	20.73	142.44	43.67
8A				
1	1285.33		12368.90	
2	648.60	1.98	6206.87	1.99
4	333.40	3.86	3130.69	3.95
8	175.36	7.33	1592.99	7.76
16	99.15	12.96	830.10	14.90
32	50.81	25.30	457.38	27.04
64	42.29	30.39	274.92	44.99
16A				
1	2530.92		25961.52	
2	1313.64	3.71	12532.01	2.07
4	682.46	3.71	6500.17	3.99
8	342.07	7.40	3208.67	8.09
16	180.78	14.00	1602.08	16.20
32	108.00	23.44	895.33	29.00
64	71.29	35.50	522.27	49.71

5 Conclusions and Future Work

In this paper, a new approach to detect outliers based on squared-well has been proposed. This approach has been designed to be able to deal with large data sets, at the same time that it keeps an affordable execution time. Besides, in the design phase, it has been taken into account to be suitable for diverse computational infrastructures.

The proposed approach is fully additive. This allows disaggregating the calculation by objects and by attributes. This property eases the adaptation of the algorithm to distributed computational infrastructures, such as: cloud and grid; as well as to parallel platforms, such as: cluster and GPU.

Furthermore, the approach has demonstrated that the sequential implementation behaves linearly with the number of objects and the number of attributes, $O(objects \times attributes)$, which is an excellent feature when intending to process large data sets. For testing the approach, artificial very large data sets (in the order of GB input size) have been successfully processed while maintaining a limited execution time budget.

Additionally to the sequential version, a parallel implementation (MPI) has been created and tested. The speedup achieved for large data sets is close to theoretical maximum speedup. This demonstrates that the approach is able to deal with these large data sets.

As future work, more comparative works are proposed. On the one hand, the approach will be tested for other computational platforms, preferentially cloud and GPU. On the other hand, other data sets are considered for comparing with other algorithms devoted to outlier detection. Finally, the aim of this approach is to process the log-files of the cluster Tier-2 at CIEMAT for processing the data of CMS detector. So that, once the approach has been successfully tested against artificial data sets, to analyse the data sets generated by the CMS Tier-2 infrastructure.

Acknowledgement. The research leading to these results has received funding by the Spanish Ministry of Economy and Competitiveness (MINECO) for funding support through the grant FPA2010-21638-C02-02, together with the European Community's Seventh Framework Programme (FP7/2007-2013) via the project EGI-InSPIRE under the grant agreement number RI-261323.

References

1. Corchado, E., Wozniak, M., Abraham, A., de Carvalho, A.C.P.L.F., Snášel, V.: Recent trends in intelligent data analysis. Neurocomputing 126, 1–2 (2014)
2. Abraham, A.: Special issue: Hybrid approaches for approximate reasoning. Journal of Intelligent and Fuzzy Systems 23(2-3), 41–42 (2012)
3. Aggarwal, C.C.: Outlier Analysis. Springer (2013)
4. Peteiro-Barral, D., Guijarro-Berdiñas, B.: A survey of methods for distributed machine learning. Progress in AI 2(1), 1–11 (2013)
5. Johnson, T., Kwok, I., Ng, R.T.: Fast computation of 2-dimensional depth contours. In: Agrawal, R., Stolorz, P.E., Piatetsky-Shapiro, G. (eds.) Proceedings of the Fourth International Conference on Knowledge Discovery and Data Mining (KDD 1998), pp. 224–228. AAAI Press (1998)
6. Struyf, A., Rousseeuw, P.J.: High-dimensional computation of the deepest location. Computational Statistics and Data Analysis 34, 415–426 (1999)
7. Rajaraman, A., Ullman, J.D.: Mining of massive datasets. Cambridge University Press, Cambridge (2012)
8. Han, J., Kamber, M.: Data Mining: Concepts and Techniques. Morgan Kaufmann (2000)

Symbolic Regression for Precrash Accident Severity Prediction

Andreas Meier[1], Mark Gonter[2], and Rudolf Kruse[3]

[1] Volkswagen AG, Group Research, Germany
andreas.meier1@volkswagen.de
[2] Volkswagen AG, Germany
[3] University of Magdeburg, Faculty of Computer Science, Germany
kruse@iws.cs.uni-magdeburg.de

Abstract. New advanced safety systems like accident-adaptive restraint systems have the potential to improve vehicle safety. However, these systems may require a function predicting the crash severity prior to a collision. This means that only with accident parameters gathered by precrash car sensors the severity of the upcoming collision has to be predicted. In this work, we present the first known approach based on symbolic regression that finds a solution for this challenging problem automatically. For that, we process crash simulation data and apply Prioritized Grammar Enumeration (PGE) for the first time in a real-world application. In the evaluation, we show that the found model is fast, compact and interpretable yet achieving a good prediction performance. We conclude this paper with a discussion and research questions, which may lead to an application of this approach for future, safer vehicles.

1 Introduction

Improving vehicle safety is a major challenge in the development of new cars. New safety assessments as they are continuously established by governments and customer organizations, e.g. Euro NCAP, should be fulfilled [17]. Additionally, automobile manufacturers and suppliers develop more advanced safety systems to address long-term ambitions like *Vision Zero*, which aims at having no killed or seriously injured people on the road anymore [24]. Furthermore, also customer demands influence the development of new and improved safety systems.

Future advanced safety systems like accident-adaptive restraint systems may help to fulfill some of these upcoming requirements [20,21]. These systems adapt their behavior on crash severity which, in some cases, must be predicted within a few hundred milliseconds at maximum prior to a collision for a timely adaption. This means that only with accident parameters gathered by precrash car sensors, e.g. cameras, radar, etc., the severity of the upcoming collision has to be predicted.

In this work, we present a new algorithm, which finds a crash severity prediction function that takes estimated accident parameters as inputs and predicts the crash severity prior to a collision. We use *Prioritized Grammar Enumeration* (PGE) for performing symbolic regression to find a fast, universal and interpretable model achieving a good prediction performance. The major advantage

M. Polycarpou et al. (Eds.): HAIS 2014, LNAI 8480, pp. 133–144, 2014.
© Springer International Publishing Switzerland 2014

of this data-driven approach is that the algorithm can find prediction models automatically without direct inclusion of expert knowledge, e.g. physical formulae or a regression model. This is beneficial, because the physical modeling of vehicle collisions with different angles, hit locations, velocities, etc. is very difficult and we do not know any work that solves this problem at this complexity with expert knowledge. To our knowledge, this is also the first real-world application of PGE and also the first work on solving this problem with symbolic regression.

The paper is structured as follows. After explaining necessary background in vehicle safety and symbolic regression, we describe our approach about finding crash severity prediction models. Then, we evaluate PGE-based models in comparison with models obtained by another symbolic regression algorithm, discuss the results and finish with a conclusion and future research questions.

2 Background

In this section, we give an overview of vehicle safety and symbolic regression that helps to understand this work. Furthermore, we describe relevant literature.

2.1 Vehicle Safety

In vehicle safety, the ultimate goal is to protect persons in case of a car accident. There are different types of crash severity, but we focus on the effect of the collision on the vehicle [14].

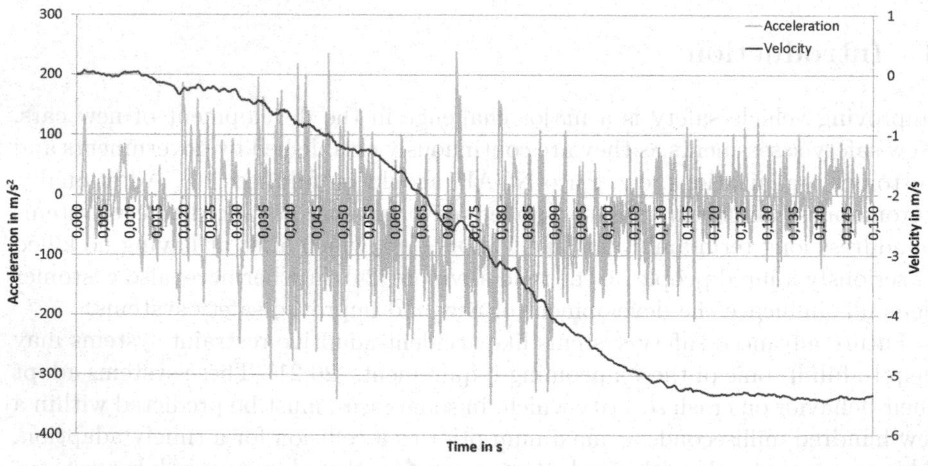

Fig. 1. Acceleration and velocity sensor signals of a car crash

We want to output a universal crash severity measure which allows the adaptation of many different safety systems that protect persons within a vehicle. In today's vehicles, an electronic control unit (ECU) detects crashes with sensitive accelerometers measuring accelerations of vehicle structures. In figure 1, we show such an acceleration signal for a 20 km/h head-on collision and its integral called *velocity curve*, which describes the change in velocity of the vehicle. The acceleration signal is very noisy and chaotic which is caused by the deceleration of the vehicle superimposed by vibrations and tensions in the vehicle structure. Instead, velocity curves are robust so that they can be used as universal indicators for crash severity, because multiple crash severity measures can be extracted [7,10]. Meier et al. describe the extraction of several crash severity measures in more detail [12]. For instance, Δv_{max} describes the maximum change in velocity and is calculated by identifying the largest difference between the initial collision velocity and one velocity value. Also various acceleration-based measures like decelerations over sliding windows may be extracted by calculating the differential of the curve. According to our knowledge, there is no ultimate severity measure, which describes crash severity and can be used for all safety systems. Therefore, we want to predict velocity curves prior to collisions as they should enable us to extract the recommended crash severity measure for every safety systems.

In literature, there is only little work about predicting crash severity. Pawlus, Robbersmyr and Karimi do not predict crash severities, but use a feedforward neural network for reproducing acceleration, velocity and displacement signals of a vehicle-pole crash test [16]. Sala and Wang as well as Cho, Choi and Lee use accelerometers to predict a crash severity after the collision has started in order to adapt the airbag [18,3]. Wallner, Eichberger and Hirschberg perform a multi-body simulation with masses, dampers and non-linear springs to predict acceleration signals prior to a collision [25]. However, the used springs are not suitable for large angles or low overlaps, so that this approach is not able to handle the accident severity prediction problem at our desired complexity. Overall, most previous work addresses a specific safety system instead of providing a *universal* prediction model for multiple safety systems. Furthermore, complex regression models or artificial neural networks are difficult to interpret. In contrast, we present the first work on finding a universal crash severity prediction model with symbolic regression.

2.2 Symbolic Regression

Symbolic regression seeks to find interpretable equations describing the relationship between input and output data. In contrast to parametrical regression, there is no need to specify an underlying regression model. Instead, symbolic regression algorithms combine input variables and functions (+ - * / log sin tan, etc.) to more complex formulae. Schmidt and Lipson used symbolic regression to determine the natural laws of different oscillators based on experimental data [19]. Another more vehicle-related work was published by Otte who designed an airbag control algorithm with symbolic regression [15].

Due to Koza's work, symbolic regression is often connected with genetic programming (GP) [8]. GP is a generalization of symbolic regression as it allows the automatic creation of programs [9]. Programs are often modelled with parse trees, but there are also other representations like stacks or a Cartesian grid [13,11]. Independently of the chosen program representation, most GP algorithms rely on evolutionary algorithms with different genetic operators and fitness functions. There also exist a lot of modifications and extensions to improve the expressive power of GP like self-modifying code [6] or integrating memory [23]. In this work, we use the new PGE algorithm proposed by Worm and Chiu [26] because it is able to find the best solution deterministically yet avoiding a complete search in the solution space.

3 System Approach

In this section, we describe our system approach shown in figure 2 including the database, an approximation method for compressing velocity curves, the chosen symbolic regression algorithm and the final building of the prediction model.

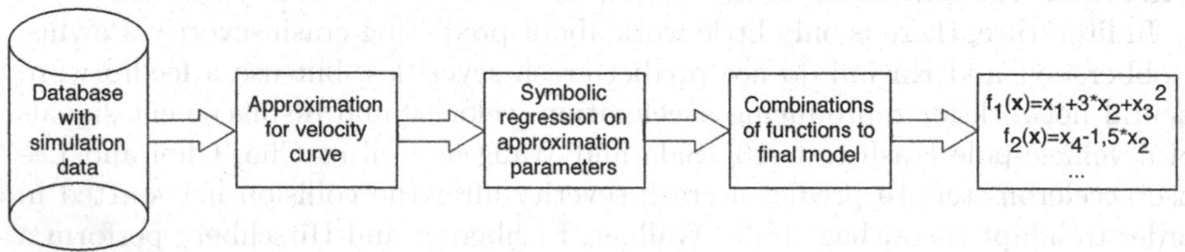

Fig. 2. System approach for developing the crash severity prediction model

3.1 Database

Our approach uses symbolic regression to find a crash severity prediction model which can be integrated into an ECU inside a vehicle later. In order to perform this data-driven process, we use a database consisting of *Finite element method* (FEM) simulation data.

The simulations cover head-on collisions of two vehicles, which can be a small car, a compact car or an SUV each. Besides the vehicle pair, we varied collision angles, impact points at the vehicle front as well as velocities. We choose these accident parameters because they affect crash severity significantly [2,22]. For each vehicle, we store the measured velocity curves in the database.

3.2 Similarity Function

For finding a prediction function, we need to determine how similar a predicted velocity curve is compared to the original velocity curve which was obtained by FEM simulation. Thus, a similarity function for velocity curves is required.

At first, we used the Minkowski metric, e.g. Manhattan and Euclidean distance, which did not perform well. Using the Minkowski metric, the learning system tends to favor prediction models that estimate the long constant parts at the end of a velocity curve well by losing much accuracy for the other parts.

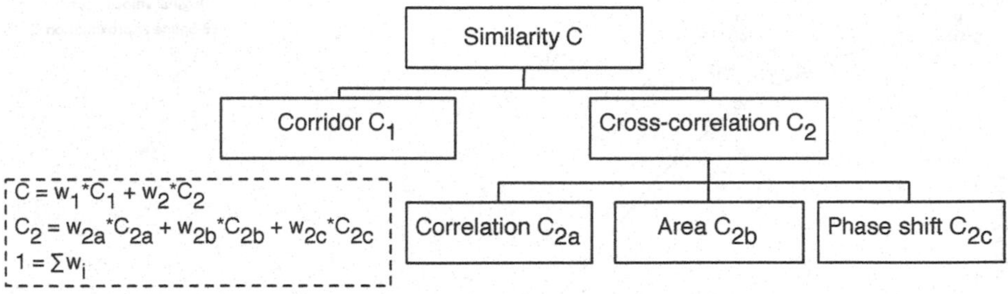

Fig. 3. Similarity function with its different ratings based on [12]

We use the similarity function presented in figure 3, which was proposed by Meier et al. [12]. This function calculates the weighted average of multiple ratings leading to a value C between 0 (no similarity) and 1 (perfect match). At first, the function limits all calculations to relevant beginnings of velocity curves thus ignoring long constant parts at the end. Then, it spans an inner and outer corridor around the defined reference curve for the *Corridor rating* and calculates, how well the test curve is located inside each corridor. The more often the test curve is close to the inner corridor, the higher the Corridor rating is. As for the *Phase shift rating*, the reference curve is shifted to the test curve relatively to the position where the cross-correlation value of these two curves is maximal. The smaller the shift is, the higher the Phase shift rating. Afterwards, the *Correlation rating* is calculated from the maximal cross-correlation value, which is at the phase shift position. The higher the cross-correlation value, the higher the Correlation rating. As the last rating, the *Area rating* calculates the integral of both curves and it scores a high value, if the ratio between the two integrals is close to 1. In order to get the final similarity rating C, the Correlation rating is weighted at C_{2a}, the Area rating at C_{2b} and the Phase shift at C_{2c} which leads to the *Cross-correlation rating.* The final *Similarity rating* C is obtained by weighting the Corridor rating at C_1 and the Cross-correlation rating at C_2. Since some ratings depend on the definition of a reference curve, we average the similarity values of two similarity calculations in which the reference and test curves have been interchanged. In that way, we guarantee the compliance with the symmetry property of similarity functions. All in all, the major benefit of this similarity function is that it also considers macroscopic curve properties.

3.3 B-Spline Curve as Approximation Method

Each velocity curve covers a crash duration of 300 ms sampled at 10 KHz so that it consists of 3,000 data points. Since we need to process hundreds of curves, performing a regression on this amount of data is computationally demanding. However, velocity curves for head-on collisions always have a similar shape so that we can utilize this property by using approximations, which describe each curve with very few parameters. This helps to accelerate learning and to filter

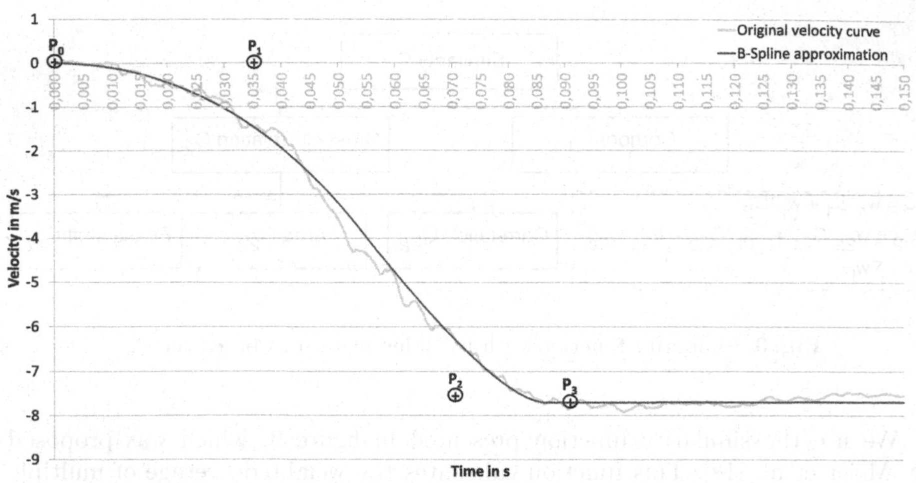

Fig. 4. Velocity curve and its B-Spline approximation

noisy data, so that we use B-Spline curves as approximations for velocity curves as it was proposed by Meier et al. [12]. They also showed that despite this strong compression of the curve, the B-Spline approximation still maintains nearly all relevant crash severity measures derivable from a velocity curve.

In figure 4, we show a velocity curve and its B-Spline curve approximation. The given curves express the change in velocity due to the head-on collision of the vehicle, which always results in a deceleration and thus negative velocity change. Each B-Spline curve is constructed by the control points P_0, P_1, P_2 and P_3, which define the shape of the curve. The curve segment after P_3 is a linear extrapolation over P_2 and P_3. P_0 is always located at $(0, 0)$ so that the three remaining points with two parameters each describe the approximated curve. We determine the control points P_1, P_2 and P_3 for each velocity curve by fitting the corresponding B-Spline curve with the help of the described similarity function and Covariance Matrix Adaption Evolution Strategy (CMA-ES) [5,12]. Afterwards, the algorithm stores these parameters in the database so that this fitting only needs to be performed once. The main advantage is the simplification of the regression problem because we only need to find a model which outputs the six B-Spline parameters instead of 3,000 data points per curve. Although the additional CMA-ES calculation takes three to four minutes per curve, we speed up the training process in comparison to training a model which predicts 3,000 data points per curve. The reason is that by reducing the number of points, we reduce the number of time-consuming evaluations of the prediction model in the same way. Subsampling the curve may also be an option, but even reducing the number to 300 does not offer the same speed improvement and leads to a loss in prediction performance. Therefore, we use such a hybrid artificial intelligence system, which is often a suitable approach for solving difficult problems [1,4].

3.4 Symbolic Regression

We want to find a fast and interpretable model which estimates the six B-spline parameters from accident parameters for curve construction. Symbolic regression is a suitable approach because it outputs an equation for each B-Spline parameter. Equations are fast to execute, do not require much memory and analyzing them helps us to identify limitations of a prediction model.

Symbolic regression requires us to define operands and functions working on them. Besides self-determined constants, the algorithm can use the following accident parameters of each of the two vehicles taking part in the collision:

- Vehicle mass m
- Velocity v at the beginning of the collision
- Normalized point of impact p at the vehicle front
- Sine, cosine and tangent of collision angle α

Since basic physical laws underline the importance of closing velocity $v_{relative}$, we provide it directly as an operand to accelerate learning. This decision as well as the usage of B-Spline curves can be regarded as some kind of expert knowledge integrated into our prediction system. We do not provide any predefined constants, because we have no knowledge about which constants might be beneficial. Furthermore, the symbolic regression algorithm is able to determine useful constants on its own. Besides the given operands, the symbolic regression may use the following functions to connect these operands with each other:

- *Basic operators*: addition, negation, absolute value, multiplication, division
- *Additional functions*: exponential function *exp*, square root

As already mentioned, we use PGE as symbolic regression algorithm that was proposed by Worm and Chiu [26]. This algorithm represents equations with n-ary program trees in which operands and constants are stored in leafs whereas inner nodes encode functions to perform on their child nodes. Due to space limitations, we only describe it very brief, but focus on its special properties.

In contrast to classic, probabilistic GP-based symbolic regression, PGE explores the solution space deterministically. Grammar production rules create program trees of increasing complexity iteratively instead of mutating or recombining trees. After evaluating the trees using a L1-norm, PGE modifies and evaluates the trees again so that the solution space is explored.

In order to avoid evaluating all possible trees, PGE uses dynamic programming with a Pareto priority queue storing the best tree for any possible tree size. In that way, search is guided by performance and parsimony simultaneously. It also uses a memory so that every tree is evaluated only once. Furthermore, it transforms trees to a standard form so that isomorphic trees are eliminated. Last, PGE determines values of constants with a Levenberg-Marquardt optimizer before a formula gets evaluated which separates the optimization of form from the optimization of constants. Therefore, PGE will not perform an exhaustive search because equivalent solutions are never evaluated. Furthermore, the depth of trees may be restricted so that the length of formulae is limited. However, if the tree depth is set to infinity, PGE will find the best possible solution.

PGE offers significant advantages over classic, probabilistic GP-based symbolic regression. Although PGE might seem slower due to its determinism, it avoids multiple runs with different random seeds because there is no pseudo-random number generator. It is also able to cover solution spaces fully to find exact solutions. Last, PGE is simple to use since it is almost parameter-free.

3.5 Generating Final Prediction Model

The last step is to generate the final prediction model. As explained, PGE seeks to find six formulae each connecting accident parameters with one B-Spline parameter. After learning, PGE outputs the best 32 formulae for each of the B-Spline parameters ranked by L1-norm. Now, the final model can be built by taking the best six formulae with the smallest error on L1-norm. However, this combination does not necessarily maximize our similarity function. Thus, another way may be to find the combination of six formulae that achieves the highest value on the similarity function compared with original velocity curves.

4 Evaluation

In this section, we describe our evaluation methodology and compare two symbolic regression algorithms for finding a crash severity prediction model.

4.1 Methodology

In order to evaluate symbolic regression algorithms, we use 190 FEM simulations of our database comprising a compact car colliding with other vehicles and varying accident parameters. As training set, we use 75% of these simulations whereas the remaining 25% form the evaluation set. Each symbolic regression algorithm learns a crash severity prediction model on the training set. After learning, we evaluate each prediction model on the training and evaluation set separately. We measure the performance by comparing predicted B-Spline approximation curves with original velocity curves using our similarity function of section 3.2. The average similarity describes the performance of each model.

We compare four models obtained with PGE and *Cartesian Genetic Programming* (CGP) [13]. CGP uses no trees but a Cartesian grid instead, which represents programs as a graph in which every node can be connected with every preceding node. We choose CGP for comparison because it can learn a model that outputs all six B-Spline parameters simultaneously. Thus, CGP may be able to find relationships between the B-Spline parameters as well, which may lead to a higher performance. Additionally, we use CGP to learn an equation for each B-Spline parameter. We create two models with PGE, but use different strategies to create the final prediction model. One model comprises the best six equations for the B-Spline parameters output by PGE. The other model is the combination of six equations achieving the best training performance on our similarity function. For CGP, we use an own Java implementation whereas we use the reference implementation of Worm and Chiu for PGE [26].

We configure the algorithms as follows. As for CGP, we found the configuration with multiple test runs. We set the population size to 100 and the number of generations to 500. Each individual has 500 nodes for program representation. We use a uniform crossover (probability = 0.5), a mutation operator which resets arbitrary genes (probability = 0.2) and a tournament selection (size = 5). Furthermore, we use elitism of size 1 to achieve monotony. As for PGE, we use the default configuration, which performs 400 iterations, allows a maximum program size of 100 operands and operators and has a maximum depth of 8.

4.2 Results

In table 1, we show average performances and standard deviations for the training and evaluation set. The best CGP-based symbolic regression model achieves an average evaluation performance of 0.606 and the best PGE-based symbolic regression model scores 0.805. With the exception of the CGP solution comprising six equations, the standard deviations do not differ notably.

Table 1. Average performance and standard deviations of learned prediction models

Algorithm	Training performance	Evaluation performance
CGP (six equations)	0.469 ± 0.219	0.487 ± 0.253
CGP (one equation)	0.607 ± 0.117	0.606 ± 0.118
PGE (best equation)	0.794 ± 0.126	0.788 ± 0.126
PGE (best combination)	0.800 ± 0.118	0.805 ± 0.123

$$\begin{aligned}
x_1 &= 0.00225 + \frac{0.003684 * |p_2|}{v_{relative}} + 0.0006 * \sqrt{m_2} \\
y_1 &= -2.985431 * exp(0.376616 * \cos\alpha_1 * |p_2 + 9.034628 * |\sin\alpha_1||) \\
x_2 &= 0.000092 * (646.555477 + \frac{m_2 + 57.285781 * |p_2|}{v_{relative}}) \\
y_2 &= -1.960664 + 0.023319 * |p_1| + 0.012447 * \cos\alpha_2 * v_{relative} * \sqrt{m_2} \\
x_3 &= 0.000082 * (1102.860176 + \frac{m_1 + 88.096884 * |p_1|}{v_{relative}}) \\
y_3 &= -2.179486 + 0.025837 * |p_1| + 0.012183 * \cos\alpha_1 * v_{relative} * \sqrt{m_2}
\end{aligned} \tag{1}$$

In equation 1, we show the best crash severity prediction model for the compact car found by PGE. Each equation outputs a component for the B-Spline control point P_1, P_2 or P_3 for the approximation. Accident parameters with index 1 belong to the compact car, parameters with index 2 to the other vehicle.

4.3 Discussion

The evaluation results indicate that symbolic regression is able to solve this prediction problem. Models found by PGE outperform CGP-based models with a good, average training and evaluation performance of 0.800 or 80 %. In order to explain this difference in performance, we have some assumptions. First, our CGP implementation should be correct, because it finds solutions for many standard symbolic regression problems. Maybe the parameterization of genetic operators was not optimal although we performed multiple runs to find the best parameter set. We believe that this difference is caused by a rugged fitness landscape with many local optima spanned by our similarity function. Probabilistic approaches like CGP are sensitive to initialization and may not overcome these optima. Instead, PGE seems to overcome these issues due to its determinism.

Our approach to find a prediction model takes very long. Calculating approximations to obtain B-Spline parameters for all 190 velocity curves takes about 11 hours on a 12-core workstation. Finding prediction models with PGE takes about 6 hours. However, better parallelization may accelerate training significantly.

The model in equation 1 is simple, compact and achieves a good prediction performance so that it could be integrated into an ECU in a vehicle. It is also very fast as it takes less than 2 ms on average to predict crash severity on a single core. The model also seems to follow basic physical laws because the closing velocity, which influences crash severity significantly, is often represented in the formulae. Although the model does not use typical physical expressions due to its constants which look like "magic numbers", we believe that it encodes physical relationships. We assume that these constants average other accident parameters which are not given as inputs. However, we think that due to its simplicity, the model should be interpretable so that limitations can be found easily. For instance, we are able to identify discontinuities for each parameter mathematically which allows us to limit the usage of this model to the *safe* parts of accident parameter domains. We are also able to analyze how sensitive the precrash sensors must be for estimating the accident parameters at the required accuracy. This interpretation of the formulae will be a future research question.

Although the presented evaluation sounds rather theoretical like the usual symbolic regression benchmark problems [8], it is indeed a real-world application. The simulation data was obtained with sophisticated FEM models, which are also used for the development of vehicle safety systems. Furthermore, the usage of simulations is possibly the only realistic way to create the necessary amount of detailed crash data for finding and evaluating a crash severity prediction model.

5 Conclusion

Accident-adaptive safety systems could improve road safety, but may require models which predict crash severity up to a few hundred milliseconds prior to a collision. In this work, we present the first known approach for this problem that builds on symbolic regression to find a fast, interpretable and universal model. It is also the first real-world application of PGE for performing symbolic regression. In our experiments, PGE outperforms CGP-based symbolic regression notably by achieving a prediction performance of 80 % on average. Additionally, the model is simple, compact and able to predict crash severity in less than 2 ms on average undercutting the time limitation by orders of magnitude. As future research questions, we want to improve prediction performance. We also plan to interpret prediction models comprehensively and evaluate them in conjunction with accident-adaptive safety systems. In case of successful evaluation, we may have found a new technology for safer vehicles with artificial intelligence.

References

1. Abraham, A.: Special Issue: Hybrid Approaches for Approximate Reasoning. Journal of Intelligent and Fuzzy Systems 23(2), 41–42 (2012)
2. Angel, A., Hickman, M.: Analysis of the Factors Affecting the Severity of Two-Vehicle Crashes. Ingeniería y Desarollo 24, 176–194 (2008)
3. Cho, K., Choi, S.B., Shin, K., Yun, Y.: A Pre-Crash Discrimination System for an Airbag Deployment Algorithm. In: American Control Conference (ACC), 2010, pp. 6949–6954. IEEE (July 2010)
4. Corchado, E., Woniak, M., Abraham, A., De Carvalho, A.C., Snášel, V.: Editorial: Recent Trends in Intelligent Data Analysis. Neurocomputing 126, 1–2 (2014)
5. Hansen, N., Ostermeier, A.: Adapting Arbitrary Normal Mutation Distributions in Evolution Strategies: The Covariance Matrix Adaptation. In: Proceedings of International Conference on Evolutionary Computation, pp. 312–317. IEEE (1996)
6. Harding, S., Miller, J.F., Banzhaf, W.: Developments in Cartesian Genetic Programming: self-modifying CGP. Genetic Programming and Evolvable Machines 11(3-4), 397–439 (2010)
7. Kübler, L., Gargallo, S., Elsäßer, K.: Characterization and Evaluation of Frontal Crash Pulses with Respect to Occupant Safety. In: Airbag. 9th International Symposium and Exhibition on Sophisticated Car Occupant Safety Systems, ICT (2008)
8. Koza, J.R.: Genetic Programming: A Paradigm for Genetically Breeding Populations of Computer Programs to Solve Problems. Stanford University, Department of Computer Science (1990)
9. Kruse, R., Borgelt, C., Klawonn, F., Moewes, C., Steinbrecher, M., Held, P.: Computational Intelligence: A Methodological Introduction. Springer Publishing Company, Incorporated (2013)
10. Marsh IV, J.C., Campbell, K.L., Shah, U.: A Review and Investigation of Better Crash Severity Measures: An Annotated Bibliography. Tech. rep., Highway Safety Research Institute, The University of Michigan (1977)
11. Meier, A., Gonter, M., Kruse, R.: Accelerating Convergence in Cartesian Genetic Programming by Using a New Genetic Operator. In: Proceeding of the 15th Annual Conference on Genetic and Evolutionary Computation Conference, GECCO 2013, pp. 981–988. ACM (2013)

12. Meier, A., Gonter, M., Kruse, R.: Approximation Methods for Velocity Curves Caused by Collisions (Original title: Approximationsverfahren für kollisionsbedingte Geschwindigkeitskurven). In: Proceedings of 23rd Workshop on Computational Intelligence. KIT Scientific Publishing (2013)
13. Miller, J.F., Thomson, P.: Cartesian Genetic Programming. In: Poli, R., Banzhaf, W., Langdon, W.B., Miller, J., Nordin, P., Fogarty, T.C. (eds.) EuroGP 2000. LNCS, vol. 1802, pp. 121–132. Springer, Heidelberg (2000)
14. Niederer, P.F., Walz, F., Muser, M.H., Zollinger, U.: What is a Severe, What is a Minor Traffic Accident (Original title: Was ist ein "schwerer", was ist ein "leichter" Verkehrsunfall?). Schweizerische Ärztezeitung 82(28), 1535–1539 (2001)
15. Otte, C.: Safe and interpretable machine learning: A methodological review. In: Moewes, C., Nürnberger, A. (eds.) Computational Intelligence in Intelligent Data Analysis. SCI, vol. 445, pp. 111–122. Springer, Heidelberg (2013)
16. Pawlus, W., Robbersmyr, K.G., Karimi, H.R.: Performance Evaluation of Feedforward Neural Networks for Modeling a Vehicle to Pole Central Collision. In: Proceedings of the 4th International Conference on Energy and Development - Environment - Biomedicine, pp. 467–472. WSEAS (2011)
17. van Ratingen, M., Williams, A., Castaing, P., Lie, A., Frost, B., Sandner, V., Sferco, R., Segers, E., Weimer, C.: Beyond NCAP: Promoting New Advancements in Safety. In: Proceedings of the 22nd International Technical Conference on the Enhanced Safety of Vehicles (2011)
18. Sala, D.M., Wang, J.T.: Continuously Predicting Crash Severity. In: Proceedings of 18th International Technical Conference on the Enhanced Safety of Vehicles (2003)
19. Schmidt, M., Lipson, H.: Distilling Free-Form Natural Laws from Experimental Data. Science 324(5923), 81–85 (2009)
20. Schramm, C., Fürst, F., van den Hove, M., Gonter, M.: Adaptive restraint systems - the restraint systems of the future. In: Proceedings of 8th International Symposium Airbag 2006 (2006)
21. Seiffert, U.W., Gonter, M.: Integrated Automotive Safety Handbook. SAE International (2013)
22. Sohnke, T., Sangorrin, J.S., Hötzel, J.: Adaptable Approach of Precrash Functions. In: 5th European Congress on ITS (2005)
23. Teller, A.: Turing Completeness in the Language of Genetic Programming With Indexed Memory. In: Proceedings of the First Conference on Evolutionary Computation. World Congress on Computational Intelligence, pp. 136–141. IEEE (1994)
24. Tingvall, C., Haworth, N.: Vision Zero: an Ethical Approach to Safety and Mobility. In: 6th ITE International Conference Road Safety & Traffic Enforcement: Beyond 2000, pp. 6–7 (1999)
25. Wallner, D., Eichberger, A., Hirschberg, W.: A Novel Control Algorithm for Integration of Active and Passive Vehicle Safety Systems in Frontal Collisions. Journal of Systemics, Cybernetics and Informatics 8(5), 6–11 (2010)
26. Worm, T., Chiu, K.: Prioritized grammar enumeration: Symbolic regression by dynamic programming. In: Proceeding of the 15th Annual Conference on Genetic and Evolutionary Computation Conference, pp. 1021–1028. ACM (2013)

Constraint and Preference Modelling for Spatial Decision Making with Use of Possibility Theory

Jan Caha, Veronika Nevtípilová, and Jiří Dvorský

Department of Geoinformatics, Faculty of Science, Palacký University in Olomouc
17. listopadu 50, 771 46, Olomouc, Czech Republic
{jan.caha,veronika.nevtipilova01,jiri.dvorsky}@upol.cz

Abstract. Decision making support is one of the main objectives of geographical information systems. So far mainly boolean queries and boolean logic are used for spatial decision making problems. The study presents utilization of Possibility theory for modelling constraints and preferences for spatial data. The importance of aggregation operators in decision making is discussed as well. The case study involving a simple decision making problem is presented: selection of a waste disposal site based on three parameters - slope, distance from water and landuse. The results are presented and discussed. The main aim is focused on providing more information to the decision maker that will allow him to select the most suitable alternative.

Keywords: Possibility theory, decision making, spatial query.

1 Introduction

The decision support for problems that involve spatial data is among the most important aims of geographical information systems (GIS). When users think about these spatial decision problems, they commonly think in rather vague and imprecise language terms instead of precise numerical values [17,18]. For example if the user is reasoning about distance he/she will most likely think in terms "far", "near" and "very close" instead of numerical thresholds that specify such terms. However for representations in GIS the language terms must be translated into precise mathematical expressions [17] in order to allow the data query that will return results that fulfil the criterion. This approach can theoretically lead to very rigid queries that can negatively affect the query result [5]. For example some problems may have so many constraints that the solution does not even exist. In such cases some constraints need to be either removed or relaxed to obtain solutions, but this process can be quite time consuming [11]. In other cases several solutions may exist without a clear preference for any of those solutions. This state is a result of using Boolean logic in a traditional querying tools. To overcome this undesired property several alternative querying tools that utilize instruments of the fuzzy set theory [8,17] and the possibility theory [6,7] were introduced. The main aim of all these tools is to enrich the modelling of constraints and preferences and thus data queries with new possibilities that

M. Polycarpou et al. (Eds.): HAIS 2014, LNAI 8480, pp. 145–155, 2014.
© Springer International Publishing Switzerland 2014

would allow the decision maker to obtain more informative results [4] that will help him/her to adopt better solution to the problem. These new techniques are products of combination of soft and hard computing, that allow modelling of decision maker's uncertainty and vagueness, when expressing his/her knowledge about constraints and preferences for the decision making problem.

The presented research utilizes the possibility theory to expand possibilities of the spatial queries and the decision making based on them. The structure of the article is as follows: Section 2 provides brief introduction to the decision making, section 3 summarizes necessary details about possibilistic queries. The case study is presented in section 4 and a conclusion is done in section 5.

2 Decision Making

The decision making process is a procedure where a set of alternatives A_i, $i = 1, \dots, m$ is evaluated with respect to a set of criteria C_j, $j = 1, \dots, n$. Each alternative can be described by a set of criterion values a_{ij}, so that $A_i = [a_{i1}, \dots, a_{in}]$ and $a_{ij} \in [0, 1]$ [3]. In such decision making the utility or value functions assign values to each a_{ij} according to the relevant criterion C_j. These criteria evaluations are further used in an aggregation process that determines overall ranking of the alternative A_i. The selection of the aggregation function is an important part of the process, because the function can significantly affect the outcome of the aggregation process [2].

When a decision maker is specifying the criteria for the decision making problem he/she often do so in terms of constraints. Constraints represent requirements that an alternative can not violate in order to be acceptable. However besides specifying the constraints the decision maker can also express preferences. The former can be viewed as strong conditions that has to be satisfied and the latter can be seen as weak (optional) conditions [2]. Constraints and preferences are often modelled jointly. Such approach leads to what is called bipolar scales in [12]. However as noted in [7] if there are negative and positive parts of the information (constraints and preferences), then they should be processed in parallel and not as one piece of information. Otherwise undesirable shuffle of the constraints and preferences may occur. Ideally the decision maker should obtain a set of solutions that meet the constraints and a set of solutions that satisfy even the preferences. Naturally it should apply that the solutions with preference are a subset of the solutions that satisfy the constraints.

Usually the utility/value functions are used to evaluate the alternatives on the interval $[0, 1]$, or some other interval that can be scaled to this range. Such scale is usually bipolar, because 1 denotes completely acceptable alternative, 0 denotes absolutely unacceptable alternative and the midpoint m marks neutral (indefinite) solutions. The midpoint plays an important role of a boundary between the positive and negative values [12]. This approach can be viewed as a classic example of processing constraints and preferences as one piece of information. An alternative approach to this problem is to create two scales, one that is negative unipolar, where 0 means unacceptable and 1 denotes neutral ranking of the alternative, and positive unipolar scale, where 0 denotes neutral and 1 means absolutely acceptable solution [12]. In this case each scale is modelled and processed separately [7], which leads to the ranking of alternatives in terms of acceptability and desirability. As examples of these dual scales the measures of possibility or loss functions and necessity or gain functions can be mentioned [12].

2.1 Aggregation of Criteria Fulfilment

To obtain overall ranking of the alternative A_i, an operator that summarizes values of a_{ij} into one value providing overall evaluation of A_i is needed. Such aggregation operators can be t-norms, averaging operators, OWA operator [19] or even t-conorm, depending on the behaviour the operator should model [7]. Generally the aggregation function has a form:

$$A_i = f(a_{i1}, \ldots, a_{in}). \tag{1}$$

The most commonly used t-norm and t-conorm are the min and max operators, that also form limits for Yager's OWA operators [19]. The overview of the t-norms, t-conorms and averaging operators is provided in [21].

Criteria for selecting an aggregation operator were summarized by Zimmermann [21] as following: axiomatic strength, empirical fit, adaptability, numerical efficiency, compensation, range of compensation, aggregation behavior, required scale level of membership functions. For a practical use especially empirical fit, adaptability and compensation are the most important. Often the use of aggregation operator is not discussed and the min, max operators are used when working with fuzzy sets. But as noted in [12] there are problems of a negligibility effect and a drowning effect. The first describes situation when many high values cannot compensate for one small - so $\min(0.8, 0.6, 0.1) < \min(0.2, 0.2, 0.2)$ and the other describes situation $\min(0.5, 0.7, 0.1) = \min(0.1, 0.1, 0.1)$. Obviously neither one of those is correct nor does it model human thinking about ranking of alternatives, as humans would be able to distinguish between such alternatives and decide which one is better.

2.2 Ranking of the Alternatives

As mentioned above if constraints and preferences are present in the decision making process, each of them should be processed separately. This means that for each A_i the constraint and preference raking have to be established independently, so that we have a_{ij}^C denoting ranking of the alternative i according to the criterion j of constraints and in the same sense a_{ij}^P that denotes ranking according to the preference. Aggregated ranking of the alternatives is than denoted as A_i^C and A_i^P respectively.

Since each alternative has two rankings A_i^C and A_i^P the ranking process is slightly more complex. Let A_a and A_b be the alternatives from A_i. A_a is better than A_b only if $A_a^C > A_b^C$ and at the same time $A_a^P > A_b^P$, the alternatives are equal if $A_a^C = A_b^C$ and at the same time $A_a^P = A_b^P$, otherwise A_b is better than A_a. Verbally expressed it means that one alternative is better than the other if and only if it has higher values of ranking in terms of both constraints and preferences. Since the constraints are viewed as a stronger criterion they are used as the main ranking criterion. So the alternatives are first ranked by A_i^C and then A_i^P.

3 Possibilistic Queries

In this section the elementary definitions of Possibility Theory that are needed for possibilistic queries will be given. The complete overview of Possibility theory is provided in [10,20]. Possibility theory provides new approaches and tools for handling fuzzy sets. Among those the comparison of a crisp number and a fuzzy number is of special interest for our research.

In geography vague specifications of queries are often encountered, because binary queries are usually too restrictive for geographical data [5]. In such cases an expert provides information about what are unacceptable solutions, which solutions might be used, what are rather suitable solutions and finally what solutions would be the best. Lets take an example of selecting a construction site for new houses with respect to slope of the terrain. The expert specifies that values of slope higher than 20° are off limits because of the costs associated with preparation of the terrain. He also specifies that it would be good if slope higher than 10° could be avoided. He also mentions that anything below 5° is perfect as there are almost no costs associated with the preparation of the construction site. What the expert actually provided is a description of so called possibilistic query [6]. Possibilistic queries are modelled as fuzzy numbers and utilizes Possibility theory for comparison with crisp data values.

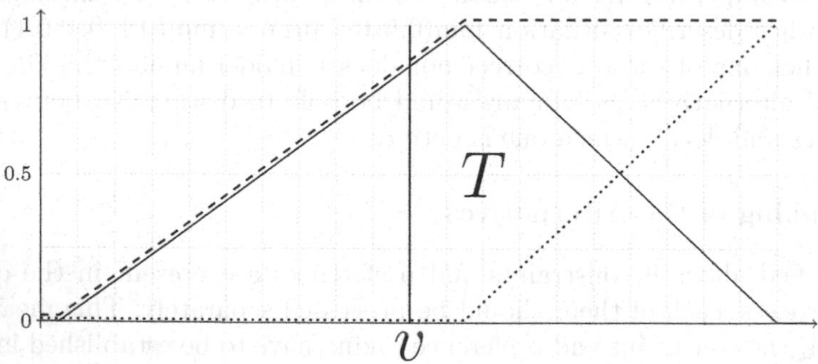

Fig. 1. Measures of possibility (dashed) and necessity (dotted) of $v \geq T$

Fuzzy number is a special case of a normal convex fuzzy set that is defined on $\mathbb{R}$ (real numbers) and represents vague, ill-known or imprecise value. For more details about fuzzy numbers please see [13]. In the framework of Possibility theory the fuzzy number can be viewed as a possibility distribution [10], that specifies values the number can possibly take. Uncertain parameters/values are often modelled as fuzzy numbers [1,9,16]. The possibility distribution is an appropriate tool for the modelling of soft constraints, that form soft queries [20]. These soft (or possibilistic) queries offer the decision maker much more flexible way of querying the data [5,6].

Let T be a triangular fuzzy number that represents a vague threshold. Triangular fuzzy numbers are defined by three values - minimum, modal value and maximum. The membership function μ_T of a triangular fuzzy number is a simple linear function [13]. Crisp value v can be compared to this soft threshold. The outcome of such comparison are measures of possibility Π and necessity N. For use in queries the possibility measure can be viewed as a measure of fulfilment of constraint, while necessity is a measurement of preference [12].

The comparison $v \geq T$ is done according to equations (Fig. 1):

$$\mu_{[T,+\infty)}(v) = \Pi_T((-\infty, v]) = \sup_{u \leq v} \mu_T(u), \tag{2}$$

$$\mu_{]T,+\infty)}(v) = \mathcal{N}_T((-\infty, v[) = \inf_{u \geq v} (1 - \mu_T(u)). \tag{3}$$

And the counterpart $v \leq T$:

$$\mu_{(-\infty,T]}(v) = \Pi_T([v, +\infty)) = \sup_{u \geq v} \mu_T(u), \tag{4}$$

$$\mu_{(-\infty,T[}(v) = \mathcal{N}_T(]v, +\infty)) = \inf_{u \leq v} (1 - \mu_T(u)). \tag{5}$$

In both cases the growth of possibility represents the rising fulfilment of constraints while the growth of necessity represents the rising fulfilment of preference.

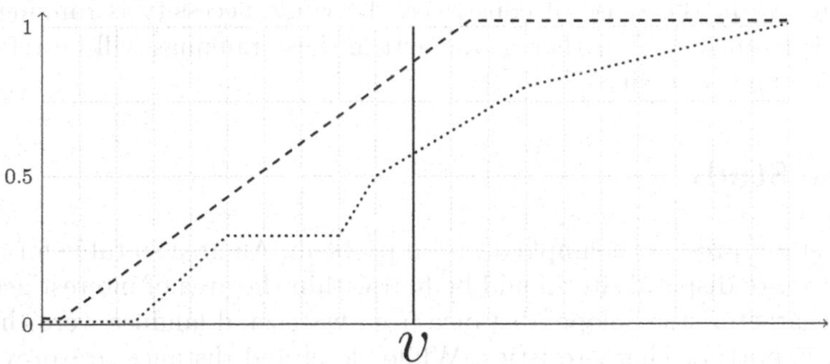

Fig. 2. Measures of possibility (dashed) and necessity (dotted) specified as functions

3.1 Alternative Specifications of the Possibility and Necessity Measures

Previously it was shown how possibility and necessity measures can be obtained from so called soft thresholds, that were modelled as fuzzy numbers. There are situations in which alternative approaches to defining these measures might be a good idea.

The expert may be able to specify the definitions of possibility and necessity measures directly as functions (Fig. 2). Reasons for such definition can be various, it is only necessary that always $\mathbb{N} \leq \Pi$. This direct definition of the measures allows expert to freely express his opinions and knowledge of the problem.

Another specific case are categorical (ordinal) data. In such case the expert should provide values of possibility and necessity for each category (Fig. 3).

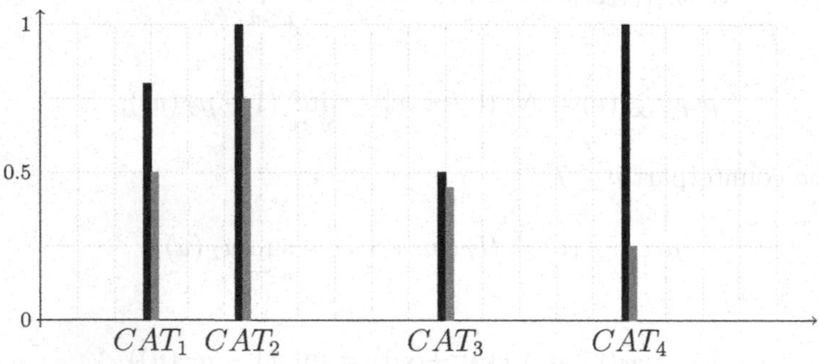

Fig. 3. Measures of possibility (black) and necessity (grey) for categorical data

The described approaches provide necessary methods for querying all types of data with possibilistic queries. Obviously possibility value is than ranking of the alternative in the sense of constraint A_i^C while necessity is ranking in the sense of preference A_i^P. Further in the article these rankings will be referred as a possibility and necessity.

4 Case Study

The case study presents a simple decision problem. An area suitable for a placement of a waste disposal site should be find within the area of interest according to three characteristics. Slope, distance from water and landuse were chosen as the most important characteristics. While slope and distance are provided as rational data, the landuse is provided as ordinal data.

All the datasets are so called field models [14]. That means that they are stored as grids with M rows and N columns (alternatives). So for each data layer there are $M \times N$ cells. This representation of data is rather common in GIS.

The queries on distance from water and slope were specified as triangular fuzzy numbers, which allows possibility and necessity to be calculated directly from those soft thresholds. In case of the distance we are searching for values beyond specific threshold ($v \geq T$ Eqs. (2, 3)) because the waste disposal site cannot be close to water. In case of slope we are searching for values smaller than certain threshold, because the site cannot be even on medium slope ($v \leq T$ Eqs. (4, 5)). Definitions of the fuzzy numbers are provided in Table 1 the visualizations of the possibility and necessity are in Figures 4 and 5.

Table 1. Definition of triangular fuzzy numbers for possibilistic thresholds

characteristic	minimum	core	maximum
distance from water	150 m	500 m	750 m
slope	0°	1°	3°

As a comparison the same task was done using classic boolean approach. With values 1° and 500 m used as thresholds for slope and distance from water. Landuse categories grassland, cropland and forest land with bushed were selected as suitable in the query. The result was obtained as spatial intersection of these three queries. The data outcomes from the classic query are shown in Figs. (4,5,6,7) as shaded area.

As is visible from the Figure 4 quite a big part of the area of interest fulfils the constraint with some specific membership value $\Pi > 0$. However the area that has $\mathbb{N} > 0$ is much smaller and also more broken into smaller clusters.

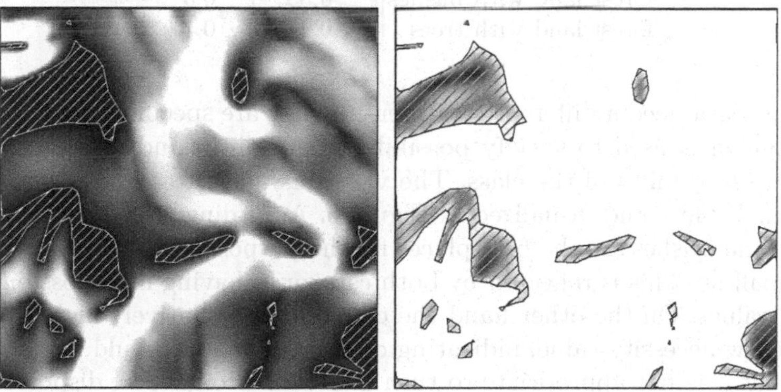

Fig. 4. Possibility (right) and necessity (left) of slope being smaller than specified threshold. White color represents value 0 and black value 1. The shaded area was selected by respective crisp query.

The distance from the water is a linear variable that forms a buffer zone around the water. The possibility and necessity of distance being bigger than the soft threshold also reflects this fact (Fig. 5). Obviously the area that would fulfil the preference measure on the distance is rather small.

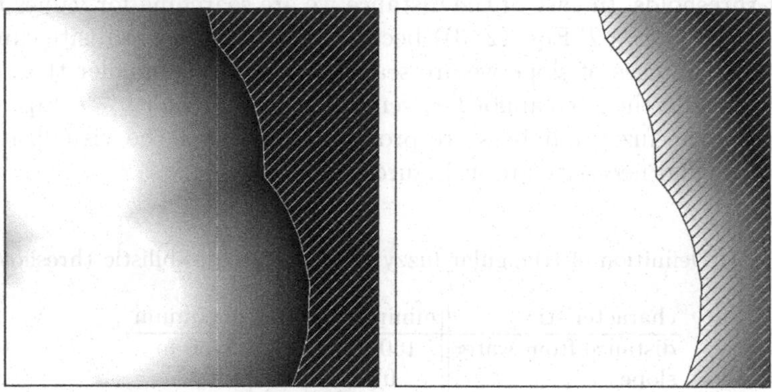

Fig. 5. Possibility (right) and necessity (left) of distance being higher than specified threshold. White color represents value 0 and black value 1. The shaded area was selected by respective crisp query.

Table 2. Definition of possibility and necessity for landuse types

landuse type	possibility	necessity
water	0	0
grassland	1	1
cropland	0.75	0.25
forest land with bushes	0.85	0.5
forest land with trees	0.4	0.1

Landuse data need a different treatment as they are specified as classes. Here expert opinion is used to specify possibility (feasibility) and necessity (attractiveness) of suitability of the class. The values assigned to the classes are summarized in Table 2 and visualized in Figure 6. According to expert opinion the grassland and bushes are the best places for the purpose as the costs of their use will be smallest. This is reflected by both categories having high possibility and necessity values. On the other hand the cropland has relatively high possibility value but low necessity value, indicating conflict. The land would be fine for the purpose but it is not appropriate to turn a cropland to a waste disposal site.

Hamacher product [21] was used as aggregation operator:

$$t(a,b) = \begin{cases} 0 & \text{if } a = b = 0 \\ \frac{ab}{a+b-ab} & \text{otherwise} \end{cases} . \tag{6}$$

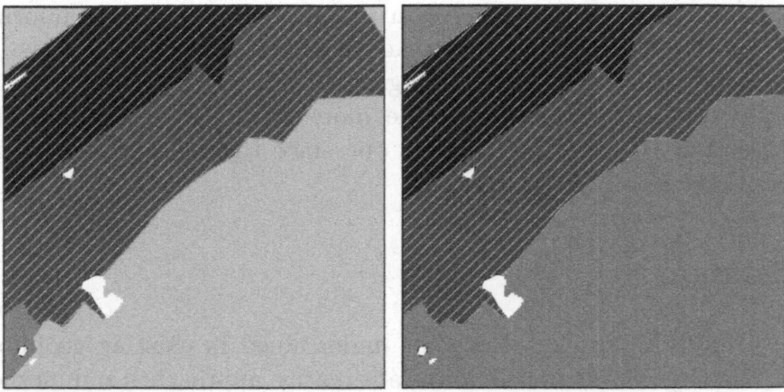

Fig. 6. Possibility (right) and necessity (left) values specified for landuse. White color represents value 0 and black value 1. The shaded area was selected by respective crisp query.

The operator selection was based on expert's opinion as being the most suitable in terms of compensation and aggregation behaviour.

The results are visualized in Figure 7. The highest possibility value was 0.85 which means that there is no solution that would fit all the constraints completely, however some solutions are rather close to it. The highest necessity value was only 0.1 which means that there are none attractive solutions. This is rather common outcome in geographical analysis, as usually the data does quite fit together.

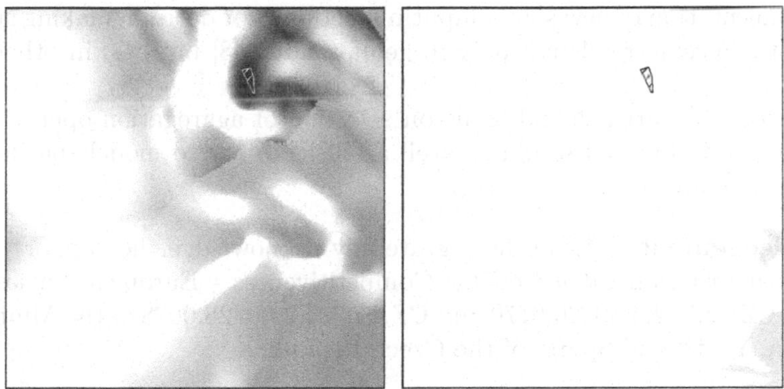

Fig. 7. Possibility (right) and necessity (left) of the result. White color represents value 0 and black value 1. The shaded area is result of combination of crisp data queries.

Visual comparison of the results obtained by possiblistic and classic query in Fig. 7 shows that classic query selected only small area, where high values of possibility occur for the possibilistic query. It is visible from the example that the possibilistic query provided decision maker with much more information. Such outcome should allow him/her to adopt better solution.

In the case of this case study it might be reasonable to the expand area of interest to find out if there are some more attractive solutions nearby, or completely switch the area for another one since there are no solutions that would completely fit all the constraints.

5 Conclusion

The topic of decision support is rather undervalued in existing geoinformatic literature. Even less is mentioned about alternative approaches and methods for modelling constraints and preferences, for example [15] does not mention them at all. Geoinformatics is a part of Information Sciences and as such exploration of new trends and methods of decision support should be one of the crucial topics. The presented method can be used to for all types of spatial queries in order to enrich the results and provide users with more information. It also handles uncertainty of the user's point of view on threshold selection.

In this research we present approach for modelling constraints and preferences for spatial data that would allow the decision maker to obtain more complex evaluation of the data and easily integrate even vague definitions provided by field experts. The paper presents utilization of Possibility theory for spatial decision making, which was not presented so far. This approach enriches the results of classic data queries that are based on boolean expressions. Modelling vague definitions provided by experts also addresses the issue of expert's uncertainty when specifying values used as a thresholds. The topic of aggregation of the results is also mentioned, which can be crucial for the whole decision making problem. The implementation of new soft computing methods for decision making support is one of the recent trends not only in geoiformatics [8] but also in other fields [4].

The further research should focus on selection of aggregation operators and their impact on obtained results as well as their ability to model specific ways of human reasoning.

Acknowledgement. The authors gratefully acknowledge the support by the Operational Program Education for Competitiveness - European Social Fund (projects CZ.1.07/2.3.00/20.0170 and CZ.1.07/2.2.00/28.0078 of the Ministry of Education, Youth and Sports of the Czech Republic).

References

1. Abraham, A.: Special issue: Hybrid approaches for approximate reasoning. Journal of Intelligent and Fuzzy Systems 23(2-3), 41–42 (2012)
2. Benferhat, S., Dubois, D., Kaci, S., Prade, H.: Bipolar possibility theory in preference modeling: Representation, fusion and optimal solutions. Information Fusion 7(1), 135–150 (2006)

3. Boroushaki, S., Malczewski, J.: Using the fuzzy majority approach for GIS-based multicriteria group decision-making. Computers & Geosciences 36(3), 302–312 (2010)
4. Borrajo, M.L., Baruque, B., Corchado, E., Bajo, J., Corchado, J.M.: Hybrid Neural Intelligent System to Predict Business Failure in SMEs. International Journal of Neural Systems 21(4) (2011)
5. Caha, J., Dvorský, J.: Querying on Fuzzy Surfaces with Vague Queries. In: Pan, J.-S., Polycarpou, M.M., Woźniak, M., de Carvalho, A.C.P.L.F., Quintián, H., Corchado, E. (eds.) HAIS 2013. LNCS, vol. 8073, pp. 548–557. Springer, Heidelberg (2013)
6. Caha, J., Vondráková, A., Dvorský, J.: Comparison of Crisp, Fuzzy and Possibilistic Threshold in Spatial Queries. In: Abraham, A., Krömer, P., Snášel, V. (eds.) Innovations in Bio-inspired Computing and Applications. AISC, vol. 237, pp. 239–248. Springer, Heidelberg (2014)
7. Destercke, S., Buche, P., Guillard, V.: A flexible bipolar querying approach with imprecise data and guaranteed results. Fuzzy Sets and Systems 169(1), 51–64 (2011)
8. De Bruin, S.: Querying probabilistic land cover data using fuzzy set theory. International Journal of Geographical Information Science 14(4), 359–372 (2000)
9. Dubois, D., Prade, H.: Ranking Fuzzy Numbers in the Setting of Possibility Theory. Information Sciences 30(3), 183–224 (1983)
10. Dubois, D., Prade, H.: Possibility Theory: An approach to Computerized Processing of Uncertainty. Plenum Press, New York (1986)
11. Dubois, D., Fargier, H., Prade, H.: Possibility theory in constraint satisfaction problems: Handling priority, preference and uncertainty. Applied Intelligence 6, 287–309 (2006)
12. Dubois, D.: The role of fuzzy sets in decision sciences: Old techniques and new directions. Fuzzy Sets and Systems 184(1), 3–28 (2011)
13. Hanss, M.: Applied fuzzy arithmetic: An introduction with engineering applications. Springer, Berlin (2005)
14. Janoška, Z., Dvorský, J.: P systems: State of the art with respect to representation of geographical space. In: CEUR Workshop Proceedings - 12th Annual Workshop on Databases, Texts, Specifications and Objects, DATESO 2012, pp. 13–24 (2012)
15. Sugumaran, R., Degroote, J.: Spatial decision support systems: principles and practices. Taylor & Francis, Boca Raton (2011)
16. Vinotha, J.M., Ritha, W., Abraham, A.: Total time minimization of fuzzy transportation problem. Journal of Intelligent and Fuzzy Systems 23(2), 93–99 (2012)
17. Wang, F.J.: A fuzzy grammar and possibility theory-based natural language user interface for spatial queries. Fuzzy Sets and Systems 113(1), 147–159 (2000)
18. Witlox, F., Derudder, B.: Spatial Decision-Making Using Fuzzy Decision Tables: Theory, Application and Limitations. In: Petry, F., Robinson, V.B., Cobb, M.A. (eds.) Fuzzy Modeling with Spatial Information for Geographic Problems, pp. 120–142. Springer, Berlin (2005)
19. Yager, R.R.: On ordered weighted averaging aggregation operators in multicriteria decisionmaking. IEEE Transactions on Systems, Man and Cybernetics 18(1), 183–190 (1988)
20. Zadeh, L.A.: Possibility theory and soft data analysis. In: Klir, G.J., Yuan, B. (eds.) Fuzzy Sets, Fuzzy Logic, and Fuzzy Systems, pp. 481–541. World Scientific Publishing Co., Inc. (1996)
21. Zimmermann, H.J.: Fuzzy set theory - and its applications, 2nd rev. edn. Kluwer Academic Publishers, Boston (1991)

Mining Incomplete Data with Attribute-Concept Values and "Do Not Care" Conditions

Patrick G. Clark[1] and Jerzy W. Grzymala-Busse[1,2]

[1] Department of Electrical Engineering and Computer Science, University of Kansas, Lawrence, KS 66045, USA
[2] Department of Expert Systems and Artificial Intelligence, University of Information Technology and Management, 35-225 Rzeszow, Poland
patrick.g.clark@gmail.com, jerzy@ku.edu

Abstract. In this paper we present novel experimental results on comparing two interpretations of missing attribute values: attribute-concept values and "do not care" conditions. Experiments were conducted on 176 data sets, with preprocessing using three kinds of probabilistic approximations (lower, middle and upper) and the MLEM2 rule induction system. The performance was evaluated using the error rate computed by ten-fold cross validation. At 5% statistical significance level, in four cases attribute-concept values and in two cases "do not care" conditions performed better (out of 24 cases). At 10% statistical significance level, in five cases attribute-concept values and in three cases "do not care" conditions performed better. In the remaining cases the differences were not statistically significant.

1 Introduction

Hybrid intelligent systems are an area of research that seeks to combine many single classifier approaches to pattern recognition such that the resulting collective performance improves on the performance of any single part [21]. The idea that no single computational view solves all problems was presented in [19]. In our work we combine two areas of intelligent systems, rule learner classification systems and uncertainty management in the form of rough set methodology.

Lower and upper approximations are the basic ideas of rough set theory. A probabilistic approximation, defined using a probability α, is an extension of standard lower and upper approximations. If α is equal to 1, the probabilistic approximation is reduced to the lower approximation; if α is slightly larger than 0, the probabilistic approximation becomes the upper approximation. Probabilistic approximations have been investigated in Bayesian rough sets, decision-theoretic rough sets, variable precision rough sets, etc., see, e.g., [12, 15–17, 20, 22–25].

Until recently, research on probabilistic approximations focused on theoretical properties of such approximations. Additionally, it was restricted to complete data sets (with no missing attribute values). For incomplete data sets standard approximations were extended to probabilistic approximations in [11]. The first papers reporting experimental results on probabilistic approximations were [1, 4].

M. Polycarpou et al. (Eds.): HAIS 2014, LNAI 8480, pp. 156–167, 2014.
© Springer International Publishing Switzerland 2014

In this paper we study two interpretations of missing attribute values: attribute-concept values and "do not care" conditions. Our research is a continuation of [5]. In [5] three interpretations of missing attribute values: lost values, attribute-concept values and "do not care" conditions were discussed; however, data sets used for experiments in [5] were very restricted: only eight data sets were considered, all with 35% of missing attribute values. In this paper we consider a spectrum of data sets with various percentages of missing attribute values, starting from 0 (complete data sets), and ending with saturated incomplete data sets, with 5% as an increment of missing attribute values, for details see Section 4.

Our main objective was to check which interpretation of missing attribute values: attribute-concept values and "do not care" conditions is better in terms of the error rate. Our secondary objective was to compare three types of approximations, lower, middle and upper, where middle approximations are probabilistic approximation associated with the parameter $\alpha = 0.5$ [2, 3]. In this paper we study usefulness of all three types of probabilistic approximations applied for rule induction from incomplete data.

There exist many definitions of approximations [9] for data sets with missing attribute values, we use one of the most successful options (from the view point of rule induction) called *concept* approximations [9]. Concept approximations were generalized to concept probabilistic approximations in [11].

Our experiments on rule induction on 176 data sets (with two types of missing attribute values) and with three probabilistic approximations (lower, middle and upper) show that an error rate, evaluated by ten-fold cross validation, depends on a choice of the data set. Our main conclusion is that for a specific data set both choices, for an interpretation of missing attribute values and for an approximation type, should be taken into account in order to find the best combination used for data mining.

2 Incomplete Data

We assume that the input data sets are presented in the form of a *decision table*. An example of a decision table is shown in Table 1. Rows of the decision table represent *cases*, while columns are labeled by *variables*. The set of all cases will be denoted by U. In Table 1, $U = \{1, 2, 3, 4, 5, 6, 7, 8\}$. Independent variables are called *attributes* and a dependent variable is called a *decision* and is denoted by d. The set of all attributes will be denoted by A. In Table 1, $A = \{$*Education*, *Skills*, *Experience*$\}$. The value for a case x and an attribute a will be denoted by $a(x)$.

In this paper we distinguish between two interpretations of missing attribute values: attribute-concept values and "do not care" conditions. *Attribute-concept values*, denoted by "–", mean that the original attribute value is unknown; however, because we know the concept to which a case belongs, we know all possible attribute values. For example, if we know that a patient is sick with flu and if typical temperature values for such patients is high or very high, then we will use these values for rule induction, for details see [10]. *"Do not care" conditions* , denoted by "*", mean that the original attribute values are irrelevant, so we may replace them by any attribute value, for details see [6, 13, 18]. Table 1 presents an incomplete data set affected by both lost values and attribute-concept values.

Table 1. A decision table

	Attributes			Decision
Case	Education	Skills	Experience	Productivity
1	higher	high	–	high
2	*	high	low	high
3	secondary	–	high	high
4	higher	*	high	high
5	elementary	high	low	low
6	secondary	–	high	low
7	–	low	high	low
8	elementary	*	–	low

One of the most important ideas of rough set theory [14] is an indiscernibility relation, defined for complete data sets. Let B be a nonempty subset of A. The indiscernibility relation $R(B)$ is a relation on U defined for $x, y \in U$ as follows:

$$(x, y) \in R(B) \text{ if and only if } \forall a \in B\ (a(x) = a(y)).$$

The indiscernibility relation $R(B)$ is an equivalence relation. Equivalence classes of $R(B)$ are called *elementary sets* of B and are denoted by $[x]_B$. A subset of U is called *B-definable* if it is a union of elementary sets of B.

The set X of all cases defined by the same value of the decision d is called a *concept.* For example, a concept associated with the value *low* of the decision *Productivity* is the set {1, 2, 3, 4}. The largest B-definable set contained in X is called the *B-lower approximation* of X, denoted by $\underline{appr}_B(X)$, and defined as follows

$$\cup\{[x]_B \mid [x]_B \subseteq X\},$$

while the smallest B-definable set containing X, denoted by $\overline{appr}_B(X)$ is called the *B-upper approximation* of X, and is defined as follows

$$\cup\{[x]_B \mid [x]_B \cap X \neq \emptyset\}.$$

For a variable a and its value v, (a, v) is called a variable-value pair. A *block* of (a, v), denoted by $[(a, v)]$, is the set $\{x \in U \mid a(x) = v\}$ [7].

For incomplete decision tables the definition of a block of an attribute-value pair is modified in the following way.

- If for an attribute a there exists a case x such that $a(x) = -$, then the corresponding case x should be included in blocks $[(a, v)]$ for all specified values $v \in V(x, a)$ of attribute a, where

$$V(x, a) = \{a(y) \mid a(y) \textit{ is specified}, \; y \in U, \; d(y) = d(x)\},$$

- If for an attribute a there exists a case x such that $a(x) = *$, then the case x should be included in blocks $[(a, v)]$ for all specified values v of the attribute a.

For the data set from Table 1, $V(1, Experience) = \{low, high\}$, $V(3, Skills) = \{high\}$, $V(6, Skills) = \{low, high\}$, $V(7, Education) = \{elementary, secondary\}$, and $V(8, Experience) = \{low, high\}$.

For the data set from Table 1 the blocks of attribute-value pairs are:

[(Education, elementary)] = {2, 5, 7, 8},
[(Education, secondary)] = {2, 3, 6, 7},
[(Education, higher)] = {1, 2, 4},
[(Skills, low)] = {4, 6, 7, 8},
[(Skills, high)] = {1, 2, 3, 4, 5, 6, 8},
[(Experience, low)] = {1, 2, 5, 8},
[(Experience, high)] = {1, 3, 4, 6, 7, 8}.

For a case $x \in U$ and $B \subseteq A$, the *characteristic set* $K_B(x)$ is defined as the intersection of the sets $K(x, a)$, for all $a \in B$, where the set $K(x, a)$ is defined in the following way:

- If $a(x)$ is specified, then $K(x, a)$ is the block $[(a, a(x))]$ of attribute a and its value $a(x)$,
- If $a(x) = -$, then the corresponding set $K(x, a)$ is equal to the union of all blocks of attribute-value pairs (a, v), where $v \in V(x, a)$ if $V(x, a)$ is nonempty. If $V(x, a)$ is empty, $K(x, a) = U$,
- If $a(x) = *$ then the set $K(x, a) = U$, where U is the set of all cases.

For Table 1 and $B = A$,

$K_A(1) = \{1, 2, 4\}$,
$K_A(2) = \{1, 2, 5, 8\}$,
$K_A(3) = \{3, 6\}$,
$K_A(4) = \{1, 4\}$,
$K_A(5) = \{2, 5, 8\}$,
$K_A(6) = \{3, 6, 7\}$,
$K_A(7) = \{6, 7, 8\}$,
$K_A(8) = \{2, 5, 7, 8\}$.

Note that for incomplete data there are a few possible ways to define approximations [9], we used *concept* approximations [11] since our previous experiments indicated that such approximations are most efficient [11]. A B-*concept lower approximation* of the concept X is defined as follows:

$$\underline{B}X = \cup\{K_B(x) \mid x \in X, K_B(x) \subseteq X\},$$

while a *B-concept upper approximation* of the concept X is defined by:

$$\overline{B}X = \cup\{K_B(x) \mid x \in X, K_B(x) \cap X \neq \emptyset\} = \cup\{K_B(x) \mid x \in X\}.$$

For Table 1, A-concept lower and A-concept upper approximations of the concept {5, 6, 7, 8} are:

$\underline{A}\{5, 6, 7, 8\} = \{6, 7, 8\}$,
$\overline{A}\{5, 6, 7, 8\} = \{2, 3, 5, 6, 7, 8\}$.

3 Probabilistic Approximations

For completely specified data sets a *probabilistic approximation* is defined as follows

$$appr_\alpha(X) = \cup\{[x] \mid x \in U, P(X \mid [x]) \geq \alpha\},$$

α is a parameter, $0 < \alpha \leq 1$, see [11, 12, 16, 20, 22, 24]. Additionally, for simplicity, the elementary sets $[x]_A$ are denoted by $[x]$. For discussion on how this definition is related to the value precision asymmetric rough sets see [1, 11].

Note that if $\alpha = 1$, the probabilistic approximation becomes the standard lower approximation and if α is small, close to 0, in our experiments it was 0.001, the same definition describes the standard upper approximation.

For incomplete data sets, a *B-concept probabilistic approximation* is defined by the following formula [11]

$$\cup\{K_B(x) \mid x \in X,\ Pr(X|K_B(x)) \geq \alpha\}.$$

For simplicity, we will denote $K_A(x)$ by $K(x)$ and the *A-concept probabilistic approximation* will be called a *probabilistic approximation.*

For Table 1 and the concept X = [(*Productivity*, *low*)] = {5, 6, 7, 8}, there exist three distinct three distinct probabilistic approximations:

$appr_{1.0}(\{5, 6, 7, 8\}) = \{6, 7, 8\}$,
$appr_{0.75}(\{5, 6, 7, 8\}) = \{2, 5, 6, 7, 8\}$,
and
$appr_{0.001}(\{5, 6, 7, 8\}) = \{2, 3, 5, 6, 7, 8\}$.

The special probabilistic approximations with the parameter $\alpha = 0.5$ will be called a *middle* approximation.

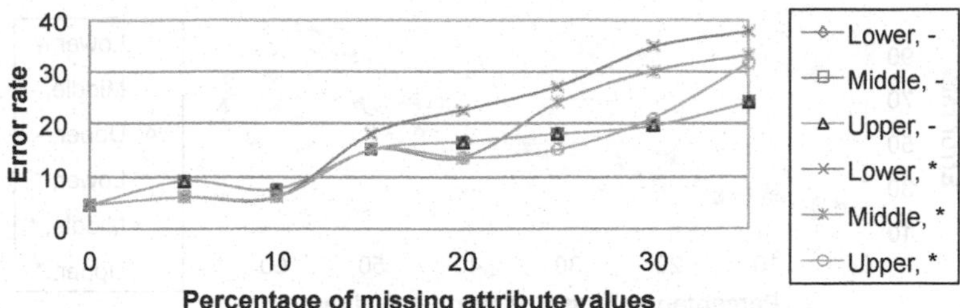

Fig. 1. Error rate for the *bankruptcy* data set

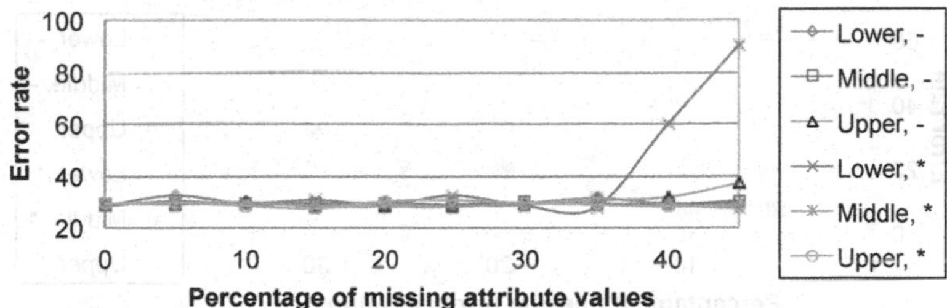

Fig. 2. Error rate for the *breast cancer* data set

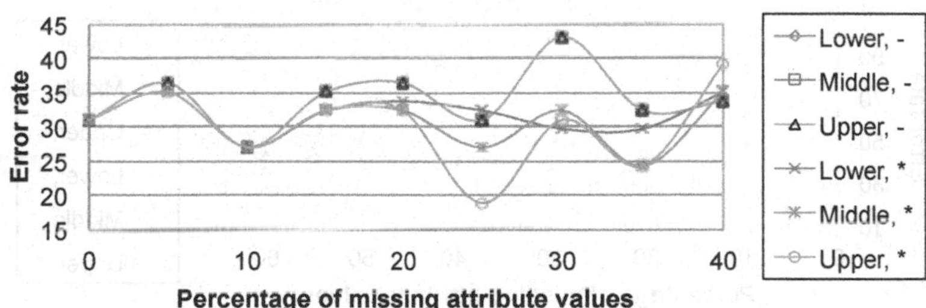

Fig. 3. Error rate for the *echocardiogram* data set

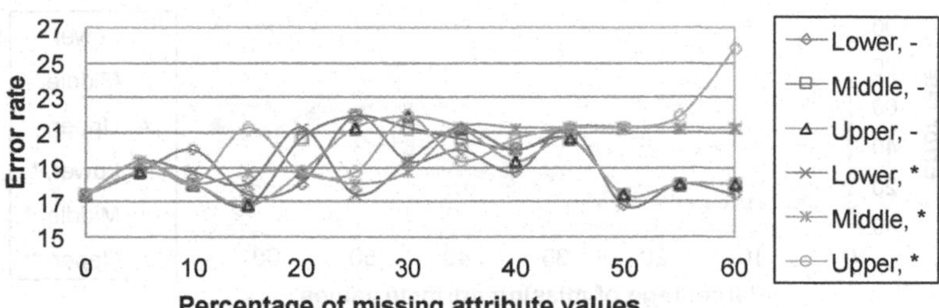

Fig. 4. Error rate for the *hepatitis* data set

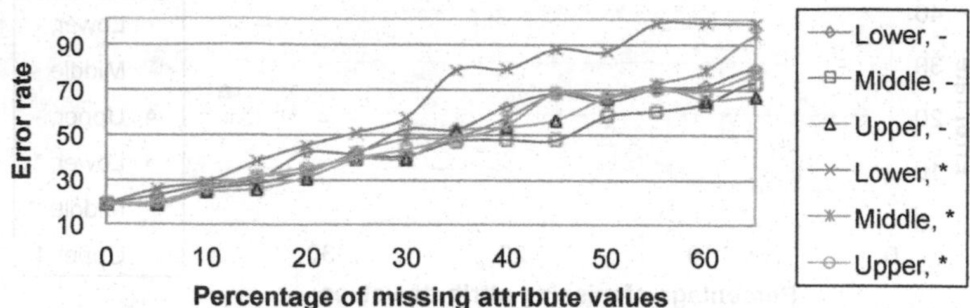

Fig. 5. Error rate for the *image segmentation* data set

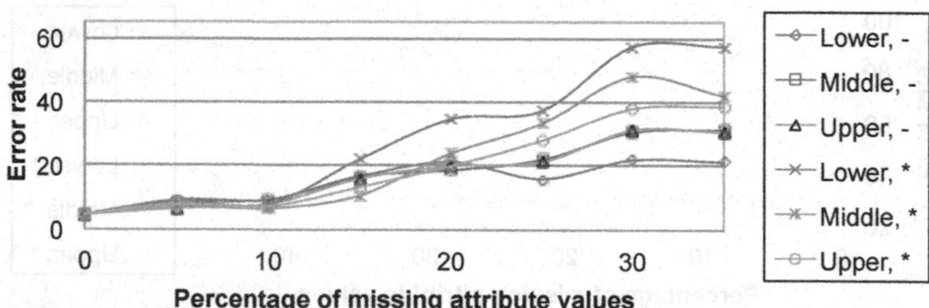

Fig. 6. Error rate for the *iris* data set

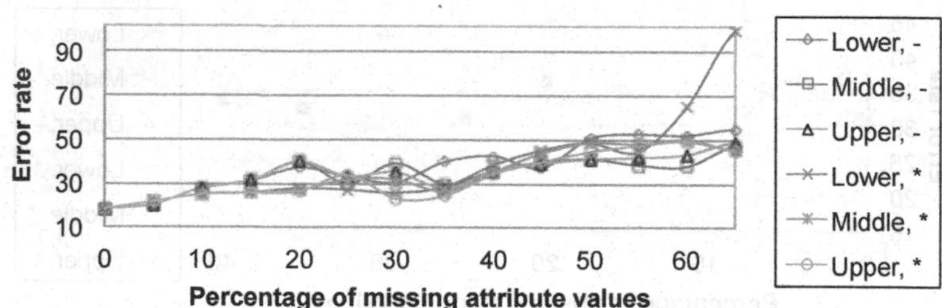

Fig. 7. Error rate for the *lymphography* data set

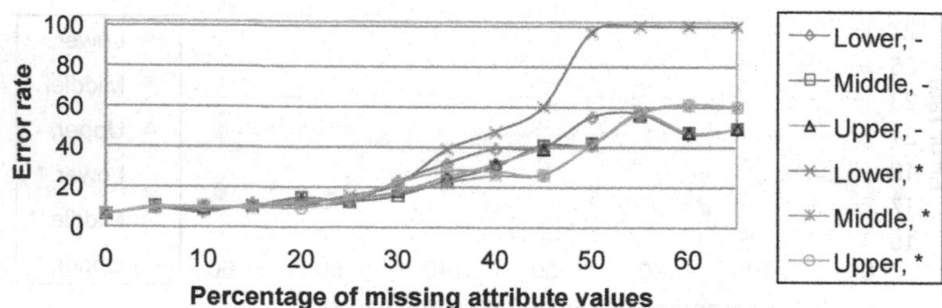

Fig. 8. Error rate for the *wine recognition* data set

4 Experiments

For our experiments we used eight types of data sets from the University of California at Irvine *Machine Learning Repository*.

Our main objective was to check which interpretation of missing attribute values: attribute-concept values or "do not care" conditions is better in terms of the error rate. Our secondary objective was to test which of the three probabilistic approximations: lower, middle or upper provides the best results, again in terms of the error rate.

In our experiments two parameters were used: the percentage of missing attribute values and the probability α used in the definition of probabilistic approximations. Both parameters have many possible values.

For practical reasons, we restricted both parameters, for the percentage of missing attribute values we considered numbers 0, 5%, 10% and so on. We have replaced randomly and incrementally existing attribute values by symbols of missing attribute values, first using – and then we replaced all symbols of attribute-concept values by *, with the increment 5% until replacing another 5% of existing attribute values by symbols of missing attribute values caused in the incomplete data set the entire row full of missing attribute values (i.e., there was a case x such that $a(x)$, for all $a \in A$, was a symbol of the missing attribute value). If so, we retracted the last replacement and tried another random replacement. If this attempt was unsuccessful, we tried yet another random replacement. If this third attempt was unsuccessful, we ended the process of creating incomplete data sets.

For example, for the *bankruptcy* data set, the maximum number of missing attribute values is 35%, since with three random tries of replacing yet another 5% of attribute values, all three data sets with 40% of missing attribute values had a row labeled by some $x \in U$ with $a(x)$ being a symbol of missing attribute values for all $a \in A$.

For the *bankruptcy* data set, replacing existing attribute values by symbols of attribute-concept values, resulted in seven new data sets (with 5%, 10%,..., 35%) of attribute-concept values. Then we created another seven data sets by replacing all symbols of attribute-concept values by symbols of "do not care" conditions. Thus for *bankruptcy* data sets, 15 data sets were used in experiments. Since we used eight types of data sets, the total number of all data sets used in experiments was 176.

We restricted our attention to three probabilistic approximations: lower ($\alpha = 1$), upper ($\alpha = 0.001$) and the most typical probabilistic approximation, for $\alpha = 0.5$, called the middle approximation. Therefore the total number of ten-fold cross validation experiments was $176 \times 3 = 528$.

Results of our experiments are presented on Figures 1–8. First, for all eight types of data sets we computed error rate associated with two interpretations of missing attribute values: attribute-concept values and "do not care" conditions. Then we evaluated the statistical significance of the results using the Wilcoxon matched-pairs signed rank test, with the 5% level of significance for two-tailed test, separately for lower, middle and upper approximations. For the *echocardiogram*, for middle and upper approximations, the "do not care" condition interpretation of missing attribute values was better than the attribute-concept interpretation of missing attribute values.

On the other hand, for the *image segmentation* data set, for all three types of approximations and for the *wine recognition* data set with lower approximation, the attribute-concept value interpretation of missing attribute values was better than the "do not care" condition interpretation of missing attribute values. Thus, for two combinations of data set and type of approximation, the "do not care" condition interpretation of missing attribute values was better than the attribute-concept value interpretation of missing attribute values. For other four combinations of data set and type of approximation, the attribute-concept value interpretation of missing attribute values was better than the "do not care" condition interpretation of missing attribute values. For remaining 18 combinations of data set and type of approximation, the difference in performance between attribute-concept values and "do not care" condition interpretation of missing attribute was not statistically significant (5% significance level).

When we changed the level of significance in the Wilcoxon test to 10%, we observed additionally that for the *echocardiogram*, for lower approximations, the "do not care" condition interpretation of missing attribute values was better than the attribute-concept value interpretation of missing attribute values. However, for the *iris* data set and lower approximations, the attribute-concept value interpretation of missing attribute values was better than the "do not care" condition interpretation of missing attribute values.

Thus, for three combinations of data set and type of approximation, the "do not care" condition interpretation of missing attribute values was better than the attribute-concept value interpretation of missing attribute values. For other five combinations of data set and type of approximation, the attribute-concept value interpretation of missing attribute values was better than the "do not care" condition interpretation of missing attribute values. For the remaining 16 combinations of data set and type of approximation, the difference in performance between attribute-concept values and "do not care" condition interpretation of missing attribute was not statistically significant (10% significance level).

Then we compared the three kinds of approximations, separately for attribute-concept values and for "do not care" conditions, using the Friedman Rank Sums test, again, with 5% of significance level. The total number of tests was 16 (eight types of data sets with two interpretations of missing attribute values). For *image segmentation* data set with attribute-concept values and with "do not care" conditions, for the *iris* data set with "do not care" conditions and for the *wine recognition* data set with "do not care" conditions there was a strong evidence to reject the null hypothesis that all three approximations are equivalent.

Using the test for ordered alternatives based on the Friedman rank sums test we conclude that, with 5% of significance level, the middle and upper approximations are better than the lower approximations both *image segmentation* data sets, while for remaining two data sets: *iris* and *wine recognition*, both with "do not care" conditions, upper approximations are better than lower approximations. The difference in performance between the middle and upper approximations is not statistically significant. For the remaining 10 combinations of data set and type of missing attribute value, the difference in performance between approximations was not significant.

Again, when we changed the level of significance in the Friedman test to 10%, we may observe additionally that for the *bankruptcy* and *lymphography* data sets, both with "do not care" conditions, upper approximations are better than lower, while for the *iris* and *wine recognition* data sets, both with "do not care" conditions, middle approximations are better than lower. Thus, upper approximations were better than lower approximations for six combinations of data set and type of missing attribute values, and middle approximations were better than lower approximations for other two such combinations. For the remaining six combinations of data set and type of missing attribute value, the difference in performance between approximations was not significant.

A summary of the results of the experiments indicate that for the majority of the experiments performed, the results did not show a statistically significant difference in performance between the interpretation of missing attribute values and approximation types. However, there is strong evidence that there are situations where varying these values would yield better results with certain data sets.

For rule induction we used the MLEM2 (Modified Learning from Examples Module version 2) rule induction algorithm, a component of the LERS (Learning from Examples based on Rough Sets) data mining system [7, 8].

5 Conclusions

Our primary objective was to compare the quality of rule sets induced from incomplete data sets with attribute-concept values and "do not care" conditions using three types of probabilistic approximations: lower, middle and upper. There is some evidence that attribute-concept values are better than "do not care" conditions in terms of the error rate measured by ten-fold cross validation.

This work is a continuation of the experiments in [5]. The primary focus of [5] was to identify the best interpretation of missing attribute values with a secondary objective of testing the usefulness of concept probabilistic approximations in mining incomplete data. In this work we expanded our investigation to 176 data sets while in [5] only 24 data sets were considered. However, because of the experiment size, we restricted the number of interpretations from three to two. In addition, while a primary objective was an investigation of two interpretations of missing attribute values, this work also compared three approximations in an effort to identify the most effective between lower, middle and upper.

Our experiments on rule induction on 176 data sets (with two types of missing attribute values) and with three probabilistic approximations (lower, middle and upper) show that an error rate, evaluated by ten-fold cross validation, depends on a choice of the data set. In the majority of the data experimented with resulted in insignificant differences between the methods.

Our main conclusion is that for a specific data set both choices, for an interpretation of missing attribute values and for an approximation type, should be taken into account in order to find the best combination used for data mining.

Data sets with large percentage of "do not care" conditions may cause the error rate for lower approximation to increase up to 100% due to large characteristic sets, and, consequently, empty corresponding lower approximations and empty rule sets.

Our secondary objective was to compare three approximations: lower, middle, and upper. In six combinations, out of 16, lower approximations were worse than middle or upper (5% significance level). In addition, in ten combinations, out of 16, lower approximations were worse than middle or upper approximations. Hence lower approximations should be avoided for mining incomplete data with attribute-concept values or "do not care" conditions.

References

1. Clark, P.G., Grzymala-Busse, J.W.: Experiments on probabilistic approximations. In: Proceedings of the 2011 IEEE International Conference on Granular Computing, pp. 144–149 (2011)
2. Clark, P.G., Grzymala-Busse, J.W.: Experiments on rule induction from incomplete data using three probabilistic approximations. In: Proceedings of the 2012 IEEE International Conference on Granular Computing, pp. 90–95 (2012)
3. Clark, P.G., Grzymala-Busse, J.W.: Experiments using three probabilistic approximations for rule induction from incomplete data sets. In: Proceeedings of the MCCSIS 2012, IADIS European Conference on Data Mining, ECDM 2012, pp. 72–78 (2012)
4. Clark, P.G., Grzymala-Busse, J.W.: Rule induction using probabilistic approximations and data with missing attribute values. Proceedings of the 15th IASTED International Conference on Artificial Intelligence and Soft Computing, ASC 2012, pp. 235–242 (2012)
5. Clark, P.G., Grzymała-Busse, J.W.: An experimental comparison of three interpretations of missing attribute values using probabilistic approximations. In: Ciucci, D., Inuiguchi, M., Yao, Y., Ślęzak, D., Wang, G. (eds.) RSFDGrC 2013. LNCS, vol. 8170, pp. 77–86. Springer, Heidelberg (2013)
6. Grzymala-Busse, J.W.: On the unknown attribute values in learning from examples. In: Raś, Z.W., Zemankova, M. (eds.) ISMIS 1991. LNCS, vol. 542, pp. 368–377. Springer, Heidelberg (1991)
7. Grzymala-Busse, J.W.: LERS—a system for learning from examples based on rough sets. In: Slowinski, R. (ed.) Intelligent Decision Support. Handbook of Applications and Advances of the Rough Set Theory, pp. 3–18. Kluwer Academic Publishers, Dordrecht (1992)
8. Grzymala-Busse, J.W.: MLEM2: A new algorithm for rule induction from imperfect data. In: Proceedings of the 9th International Conference on Information Processing and Management of Uncertainty in Knowledge-Based Systems, pp. 243–250 (2002)

9. Grzymala-Busse, J.W.: Rough set strategies to data with missing attribute values. In: Workshop Notes, Foundations and New Directions of Data Mining, in conjunction with the 3rd International Conference on Data Mining, pp. 56–63 (2003)
10. Grzymala-Busse, J.W.: Three approaches to missing attribute values—a rough set perspective. In: Proceedings of the Workshop on Foundation of Data Mining, in conjunction with the Fourth IEEE International Conference on Data Mining, pp. 55–62 (2004)
11. Grzymała-Busse, J.W.: Generalized parameterized approximations. In: Yao, J., Ramanna, S., Wang, G., Suraj, Z. (eds.) RSKT 2011. LNCS, vol. 6954, pp. 136–145. Springer, Heidelberg (2011)
12. Grzymala-Busse, J.W., Ziarko, W.: Data mining based on rough sets. In: Wang, J. (ed.) Data Mining: Opportunities and Challenges, pp. 142–173. Idea Group Publ., Hershey (2003)
13. Kryszkiewicz, M.: Rough set approach to incomplete information systems. In: Proceedings of the Second Annual Joint Conference on Information Sciences, pp. 194–197 (1995)
14. Pawlak, Z.: Rough sets. International Journal of Computer and Information Sciences 11, 341–356 (1982)
15. Pawlak, Z., Skowron, A.: Rough sets: Some extensions. Information Sciences 177, 28–40 (2007)
16. Pawlak, Z., Wong, S.K.M., Ziarko, W.: Rough sets: probabilistic versus deterministic approach. International Journal of Man-Machine Studies 29, 81–95 (1988)
17. Ślęzak, D., Ziarko, W.: The investigation of the bayesian rough set model. International Journal of Approximate Reasoning 40, 81–91 (2005)
18. Stefanowski, J., Tsoukiàs, A.: On the extension of rough sets under incomplete information. In: Zhong, N., Skowron, A., Ohsuga, S. (eds.) RSFDGrC 1999. LNCS (LNAI), vol. 1711, pp. 73–82. Springer, Heidelberg (1999)
19. Wolpert, D.H.: The supervised learning no-free-lunch theorems. In: Soft Computing and Industry, pp. 25–42. Springer (2002)
20. Wong, S.K.M., Ziarko, W.: INFER—an adaptive decision support system based on the probabilistic approximate classification. In: Proceedings of the 6th International Workshop on Expert Systems and their Applications, pp. 713–726 (1986)
21. Wozniak, M., Graña, M., Corchado, E.: A survey of multiple classifier systems as hybrid systems. Information Fusion 16, 3–17 (2014)
22. Yao, Y.Y.: Probabilistic rough set approximations. International Journal of Approximate Reasoning 49, 255–271 (2008)
23. Yao, Y.Y., Wong, S.K.M.: A decision theoretic framework for approximate concepts. International Journal of Man-Machine Studies 37, 793–809 (1992)
24. Ziarko, W.: Variable precision rough set model. Journal of Computer and System Sciences 46(1), 39–59 (1993)
25. Ziarko, W.: Probabilistic approach to rough sets. International Journal of Approximate Reasoning 49, 272–284 (2008)

An Approach to Sentiment Analysis of Movie Reviews: Lexicon Based vs. Classification

Lukasz Augustyniak, Tomasz Kajdanowicz, Przemyslaw Kazienko, Marcin Kulisiewicz, and Wlodzimierz Tuliglowicz

Faculty of Computer Science and Management, Institute of Informatics, Wroclaw University of Technology, Wroclaw, Poland
{lukasz.augustyniak,tomasz.kajdanowicz,przemyslaw.kazienko, marcin.kulisiewicz,wlodzimierz.tuliglowicz}@pwr.edu.pl

Abstract. The paper examines two approaches to sentiment analysis: lexicon-based vs. supervised learning in the domain of movie reviews. In evaluation, the methods were compared using a standard movie review test collection. The results show that lexicon-based approach is easily outperformed by classification approach.

Keywords: Sentiment Analysis, Opinion Mining, Sentiment Lexicon.

1 Introduction

Sentiment analysis is usually described as a classyfyeing problem, where text units (such as documents, paragraphs, sentences) are classified into one of three groups (e.g., "positive", "neutral", or "negative"). Nowadays, it is becoming more and more popular mainly because of the popularity of social media. Individuals and organizations want to know what is said about them on the Web, companies want to know the attitudes towards their products, services and brands expressed in social media like Facebook, Twitter, blogs, and other Web 2.0 content. Sentiment analysis is used in various domains such as banking, finances, travels, news, etc. It can be applied to all kinds of services and product reviews, including sentiment analysis of internal situation of company and risk evaluation. Although, it is still evolving area, vast volume of research was conducted on the basis of similar approaches such as multi-agent systems, e.g. [1]. Tools and methods supporting sentiment analysis, are becoming increasingly complex and achieve better results. However, still one of the most popular methods to assign sentiment to documents are lexicon-based approaches. They use specific types of lexicons with sentiment orientation assigned to each word. The major goal of this paper is to present the comparison of the sentiment analysis results of two distinct approaches: lexicon-based and based on classification.

What needs to be emphasized is that sentiment lexicons are mostly available for English, which is mainly caused by the availability of resources for analysis, such as manually labelled corpora, e.g., OpinionFinder [2]. Additionally, even if lexicons exist for other languages, they are partial, incomplete and usually developed for specific purposes (particular domain or problem). Moreover, it should be noted that results of

M. Polycarpou et al. (Eds.): HAIS 2014, LNAI 8480, pp. 168–178, 2014.
© Springer International Publishing Switzerland 2014

lexicon-based approaches may be affected by errors which occur in lexicons creation process. For instance one of the most recognizable lexicon - SentiWordNet[1], named as general (or global) lexicon, where scores are deemed to be of general application regardless of the specific domain [3] contains some errors. Due to the fact that SentiWordNet is an automatically generated resource, it contains incorrect triplets of values (positive, negative or neutral). Hence, the correctness of this sentiment lexicon is doubtful, despite the fact that authors added to SentiWordNet possibility to submit feedback of polarity entries.

To summarize, it is impossible to build universal sentiment lexicon for all purposes, because sentiment expressions often behave with strong domain-specific nature. Remedy for this problem could be domain-specific sentiment lexicons, which have played an important role in most real sentiment analysis systems. Due to the omnipresent domain diversity and absence of domain-specific prior knowledge, automatic construction of domain-specific sentiment lexicon has become a challenging research topic in recent years [4, 5]. Domain-depended sentiment lexicons are needed and they should contain semantic orientations of opinion expressions specific to particular domain, i.e., the word "predictable" has opposite polarity, in context of car driving experience and in movie context.

As outlined above, lexicons are still very important for sentiment analysis purposes. However, is it possible to build usefull lexicons based on any dataset? Is movie reviews corpus good for building such lexicon? Up to now, movie reviews have been analysed for opinion mining in numerous papers [6, 7, 8, 9, 10]. This paper is focused on the issue of sentiment lexicon construction from a corpus of movie reviews. The dataset used in this paper is from Amazon[2]. Furthermore, the results obtained by lexicon-based sentiment annotation method are compared to classification-based one.

This paper is organized by follows: Section 2 provides concise presentation of related work in the field of sentiment lexicons creations and methods based on supervised learning. Section 3.1 presents a description of examined approach of lexicon-based sentiment analysis and the one based on supervised learning. The experimental scenarios as well as the results of their execution are described in Section 4. The paper is concluded in Section 5.

2 Related Work

The issues related to building sentiment lexicons appeared in many publications so far.

Hatzivassiloglou and McKeown [11] constructed lexical network and determined polarity of adjectives, by using pairs of adjectives conjoined by *and, but, either-or*, or *neither-nor* for research, such as *fair and legitimate* or *simplistic but well-received* to separate similarly and oppositely connoted words. Hatzivassiloglou and McKeown have used the 1987 Wall Street Journal corpus, consisted of 21 million words, which were automatically annotated with part-of-speech tags. Another classic approach was presented by Turney [12]. He determined polarity values of words based on the number

[1] `http://sentiwordnet.isti.cnr.it/`

[2] `http://snap.stanford.edu/data/web-Movies.html`

of documents with their co-occurrence with seed words found in internet (with the AltaVista search engine). Seven positive words (good, nice, excellent, positive, fortunate, correct, and superior) and seven negative words (bad, nasty, poor, negative, unfortunate, wrong, and inferior) as representatives for positive and negative orientation were used. Extended Turneys approach presented Gamon and Aue [13]. They added assumption, that sentiment words with opposite orientation should not co-occur at the level of single sentence.

Recently, automatic construction strategy of domain-specific sentiment lexicon based on constrained label propagation were presented in [4]. Earlier, technique to build domain-specific, feature-level opinion lexicons in a semi-supervised manner for three different domains (headphones, hotels and cars) were described in [5].

Other approach to building sentiment lexicons involves automatic machine translation of existing sentiment lexicons (English and Spanish lexicons for [14]) into other languages. The new language lexicon is formed by the overlap of the mentioned translations (triangulation). Mihalcea et al. [15] proposed similar method to learn multilingual subjective language via cross-language projections. They used The Subjectivity Lexicon from OpinionFinder [2] and two bilingual English-Romanian dictionaries to translate the words in the lexicon. They have developed it using method that automatically builds text classifiers in a new language by training on already labeled data in another language [16].

Another approach to lexicon construction is based on thesaurus. This method utilizes synonyms or glosses of a thesaurus to determine polarities of words. One of the approach [17] was based on the synonym and antonym lists obtained from Wordnet to compute the probability of a word given a sentiment class. Kamps et al. [18] made a hypothesis that synonyms have the same polarity. They linked synonyms from thesaurus to build network. Word polarities were determined by the distance from seed words (*good* and *bad*) in the network. Extended approach was described by Hu and Liu [19]. They used synonyms and also antonyms to build sentiment lexicon. Esuli and Sebastiani [20] presented method for determining the polarity of terms based on the quantitative analysis of the glosses of such terms, i.e. the definitions that these terms are given in on-line dictionaries.

In general, co-occurrence of words along documents implies their similar polarity as a whole. Similar polarity might stand for distinct meaning but within this paper, in movie reviews domain, it means that reviews with similar text units should have similar polarity, which was expressed in similar star assignment for movie review (see Section 4.2 for dataset description). This is associated with rating-inference problem [10], where rather than simply decide whether a review is "thumbs up" or "thumbs down" [6] it should be determined an author's evaluation score. This makes the problem a multi-class text classification problem. Pang and Lee examined human accuracy at estimating number of stars "stars" assigned to reviews in different subjects. As it is depicted in Table 1, humans are able to correctly classify reviews with accuracy from 47% to 80% (0 rating difference). Thus, it can easily noticed that humans recognize small differences in evaluation scores.

Sentiment analysis can be treated as a classification problem, hence it is possible to use machine learning methods such as classification. Sentiment analysis by classification,

Table 1. Human accuracy at determining "stars" score [10]. Rating differences are given in "notches". Parentheses enclose the number of pairs attempted.

Rating diff.	Pooled	Subject 1	Subject 2
3 or more	100%	100% (35)	100% (15)
2 (e.g., 1 star)	83%	77% (30)	100% (11)
1 (e.g., 1/2 star)	69%	65% (57)	90% (10)
0	55%	47% (15)	80% (5)

a supervised learning task, is an approach that is using a classifier (such as Nave Bayes, SVM or any other) and extracted features of text to classify it as of positive, negative or neutral sentiment orientation [21]. In this approach no sentiment lexicon is needed, so it can be treated as an alternative to lexicon-based sentiment analysis. Pang et al. [22] were among the first to explore the sentiment analysis of reviews based on machine-learning approaches. They experimented with three different algorithms: Support Vector Machines (SVMs), Nave Bayes, and Maximum Entropy classifiers. They used, e.g., unigrams and bigrams, POS (part-of-speech) tags and term frequency weight features. The best accuracy attained with a movie reviews dataset was obtained with SVM classifier, although all three classifiers had very similar accuracy. They used three-fold cross-validation. In [23] there were proposed features extracted from text, e.g., terms and their frequency in text, parts of speech, opinion phrases, negation, syntactic dependencies. Pang and Lee [8] described another approach based on detecting and removing the objective parts of documents. Turney and Littman [12] presented similar an approach which resulted with a slight improvement over the baseline using only unigrams. Some other authors tried to combine machine-learning techniques with lexical-based methods. One of that work presented Ortigosa et al. [24] for data from Facebook. They reached the best result while combining methods.

3 Sentiment Analysis Methods

Two distinct approaches to sentiment analysis: lexicon-based and the one based on classification are compared in the domain of movie reviews. Following Section introduces the concept of both of approaches.

3.1 Lexicon-Based Approach to Sentiment Analysis

The goal of the method is to enable the assignment of sentiment orientation to the textual units from test set T, that have unknown sentiment. It is obtained by creation and application of lexicon L using information extracted from dataset D with priory known sentiment. The lexicon contains the mean sentiment orientation of words that occur in that dataset. The dataset D, T and lexicon L are sets of tuples defined as below:

$$D = \{< t, s(t) >:\ t\ is\ a\ text\ unit\ \wedge s(t) \in S\} \quad (1)$$

$$L = \{< w, \bar{s}(w), c >:\ w\ is\ a\ word\ stem\ \wedge \bar{s}(w) \in\ [min(S), max(S)] \wedge\ c \in N_+\} \quad (2)$$

$$T = \{< t, \hat{s}(t) > : \ t \ is \ a \ test \ text \ unit \ \wedge \hat{s}(t) \in [min(S), max(S)]\} \tag{3}$$

where S is an ordered set of sentiment orientations expressed by numbers (e.g. 1- negative, 2- neutral, 3-positive), $s(t)$ is a number from S that represents a single sentiment orientation of text unit t in the original dataset D, $\bar{s}(w)$ denotes mean sentiment orientation of text units t from the entire dataset D that correspond to a given stem w and c is their count. Mean sentiment orientation of word stem $\bar{s}(w)$ is denoted by the range of S limits, i.e. $\bar{s} \in [min(S), max(S)]$. A text unit is a textual statement that contains subjective opinion with sentiment orientation, e.g. a sentence, review, paragraph.

The main steps of the method used in this research are:

1. Text preprocessing,
2. Lexicon creation,
3. Application of the aggregated sentiment from lexicon to a test dataset T.

In the first step the textual content is processed according to the following rules in order: punctuations are removed, all characters are converted into lower case, text is tokenized into words, all words of length less than three are removed, also stop words are eliminated and as the last step stemming is performed on each word.

In the second step a lexicon is built by splitting all reviews into single and unique stems with assigned count of occurrence of that stem in whole dataset. Optional task is to select only these stems that have count of appearance greater or equal to a given threshold. To each stem a number $\bar{s}$ is computed and assigned, which represents the mean value of sentiment orientations of all reviews in the whole dataset D in which words of that stem are present.

In the third step all text units in dataset T are preprocessed in the same way as in step one. As an output each text unit from T has the sentiment orientations computed. For particular text unit it is calculated as a mean of sentiment orientations of all stems in that text unit, that were present in the lexicon L. All stems from text units in T that were absent in lexicon L are not taken into consideration while calculating sentiment orientation. All, above mentioned steps in the lexicon-based method have been presented in the Figure 1.

3.2 Sentiment Classification Using Classification

In this section the method for sentiment analysis based on classification, a task of supervised learning techniques, is presented. The goal of this method is similar to lexicon-based approach but obtained in different way: based on collection of features derived from analysed text and using classification algorithm classify sentiment polarity of document. The method allows practically every characteristic of the document to be taken as classification feature, e.g., terms and their frequency, POS (part-of-speech), sentiment words and phrases, sentiment shifters such as negations, syntactic features. All these features can be utilized with any of supervised learning methods. Three most commonly used in the field are: SVM, nave Bayes and Maximum Entropy. In order to train the classifiers it is required a dataset with assigned sentiment orientation to the

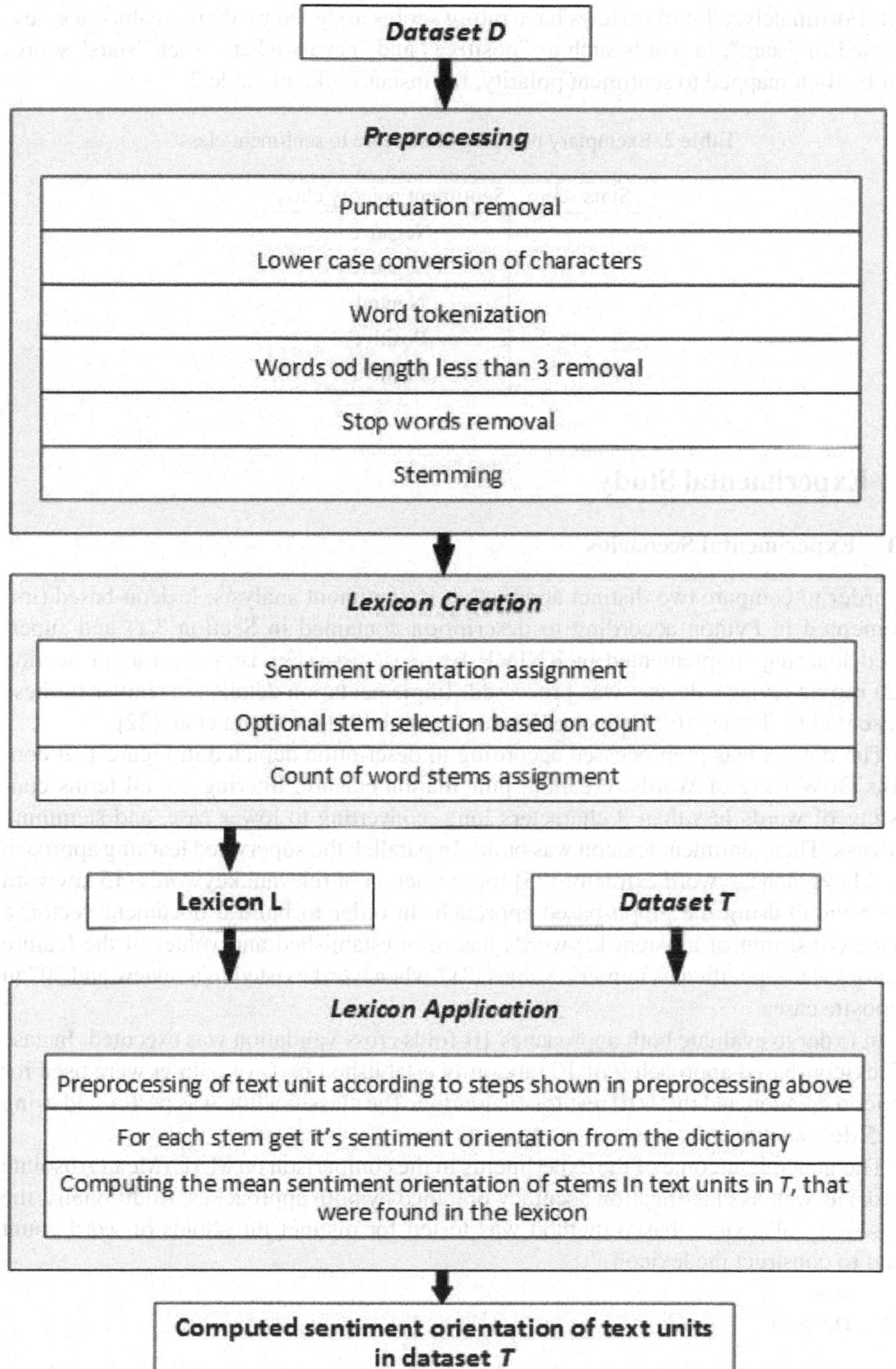

Fig. 1. Method description

text. Fortunately, a lot of reviews have rating scores assigned by their creators, e.g., expressed in "stars", in words such as "positive" and "negative" etc. Such "stars" scores can be then mapped to sentiment polarity, for instance like in Table 2.

Table 2. Exemplary mapping stars score to sentiment class

Stars score	Sentiment polarity class
★	Negative
★★	Negative
★★★	Neutral
★★★★	Positive
★★★★★	Positive

4 Experimental Study

4.1 Experimental Scenarios

In order to compare two distinct approaches to sentiment analysis: lexicon-based (implemented in Python according to description contained in Section 3.1) and supervised learning (implemented in KNIME `http://www.knime.org` as in Section 3.2) movie reviews dataset was processed. Implementation details are similar to these presented by Turney [6], Ortigosa-Hernandez et al. [24] and Pang et al. [22].

The dataset was preprocessed according to description depicted in Figure 1. It contains BoW (Bag of Words) creation, punctuation erasure, filtering out all terms consisting of words less than 3 characters long, converting to lower case, and stemming process. Then sentiment lexicon was build. In parallel, the supervised learning approach used keygraph keyword extractor [25] for extraction of relevant keywords (15 keyword per review) using the graph-based approach. In order to build a document vector, a space consisting of all stem keywords has been established and values of the feature vectors were specified as numeric values, "1" when word existed in a review and "0" in opposite case.

In order to evaluate both approaches 10-folds cross validation was executed. In case of lexicon-based approach 9 of 10 randomly established parts of dataset were used for lexicon creation and the 1/10 rest for evaluation. The classification was performed using C4.5 decision tree.

The general outcome of the experiments in the comparison on MAE (Mean Absolute Error) as well as classification accuracy obtained by both approaches. Additionally, the sensitivity of lexicon-based method was tested for distinct thresholds of word count used to construct the lexicon.

4.2 Dataset

The experiments have been conducted using large set of movie reviews from Amazon.com. The dataset contains 34,686,770. Reviews of 2,441,053 movies issued by 6,643,669 users of which 16,341 have issued more then 50 reviews. The data comes from a time period between June 1995 and March 2013. Each review contains 8 fields - *productId, userId, profileName, helpfulness, score, time, summary, text*. In the experiment there were used only *score* and *text*, where *text* is a text unit of review and *score* is overall sentiment orientation of the movie expressed in stars - 1 to 5. The median number of words per review is 82. The dataset is unbalanced in terms of score distribution, see Figure 2. The majority of scores are highly positive (5 stars). Due to the fact that it would be beneficial to build a balanced lexicon, the dataset has been randomly sampled to have balanced distribution of scores. Three examples of the reviews taken from the dataset are presented in Table 3.

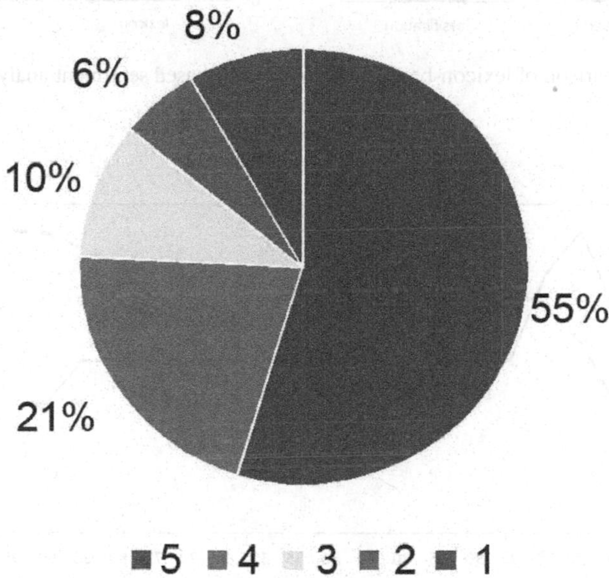

Fig. 2. Review score distribution in the original dataset

Table 3. Exemplary reviews (text units) with assigned score, which represents sentiment orientation

Movie review	Score
Don't waste your money and time for this garbage	★
This movie was not what expect but was still cute show	★★★
Excellent movie and can't wait until it comes out on dvd	★★★★★

4.3 Results

Due to the fact that the sentiment orientation had 5-values scale the Mean Absolute Error (MAE) as well as classification accuracy was calculated. As it can been seen in Figure 4 the lexicon-based sentiment annotation method was outperformed by classification one both in terms of classification accuracy and MAE. Supervised learning

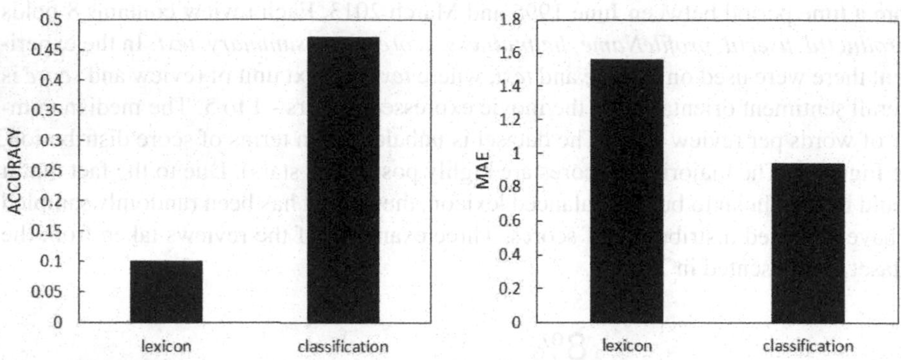

Fig. 3. The comparison of lexicon-based and classifiation-based sentiment analysis approach

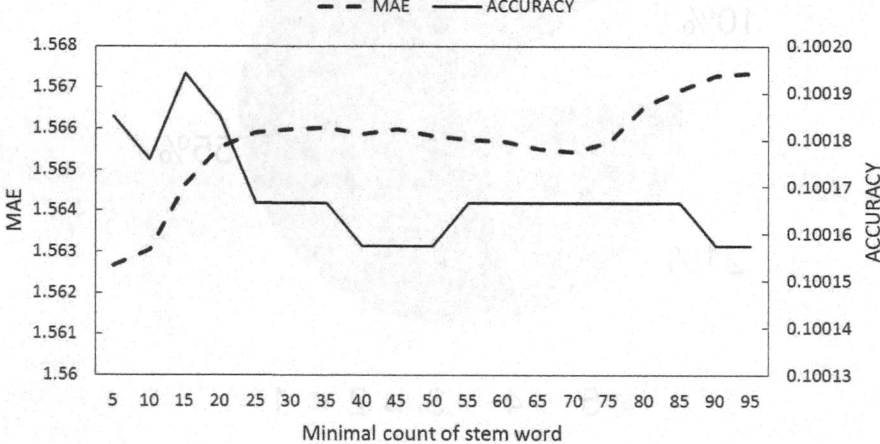

Fig. 4. The results of lexicon-based sentiment analysis approach for distinct word count thresholds in lexicon construction

technique resulted with 0.47 accuracy, whereas lexicon-based with 0.10. Additionally, MAE for classification is bellow 1, which means it rarely happen that the classification error is greater than one class in the 5 classes target. The lexicon-based approach has much higher MAE equal to 1.56. According to findings presented in Figure 3, lexicon-based approach with the settings as described in Section 3 and 4.1 hardly depends on the threshold of minimal word count used in lexicon creation. Both, MAE and classification accuracy change only imperceptibly with distinct threshold value.

5 Conclusions and Future Works

The main goal of the paper was to compare two distinct approaches to sentiment analysis: lexicon-based vs. supervised learning in the domain of movie reviews. As it was observed in the experimental results the approach based on lexicon creation is easily outperformed by classification approach. This makes the latter algorithm more applicable for accurate sentiment annotation. Generally, better results can be obtained with more sophisticated method, which is able to capture the nature of sentiment. Summarizing, the usage of supervised learning algorithms as well as underlying feature space representation of text and sentiment is a powerful modelling tool that should be extensively address in sentiment analysis.

The future work will focus on further analysis of supervised learning schemes in sentiment analysis as well as on the analysis of computation efficiency of considered algorithms.

Acknowledgement. The work was partially supported by The National Science Centre, decision no. DEC-2013/09/B/ST6/02317 and the European Commission under the 7th Framework Programme, Coordination and Support Action, Grant Agreement Number 316097, Engine project.

References

[1] Diz, M.L.B., Baruque, B., Corchado, E., Bajo, J., Corchado, J.M.: Hybrid neural intelligent system to predict business failure in small-to-medium-size enterprises. Int. J. Neural Syst. 21(4), 277–296 (2011)

[2] Wilson, T., Wiebe, J., Hoffmann, P.: Recognizing contextual polarity in phrase-level sentiment analysis. In: Proceedings of the Conference on Human Language Technology and Empirical Methods in Natural Language Processing, HLT 2005, pp. 347–354. Association for Computational Linguistics, Stroudsburg (2005)

[3] Esuli, A.: The user feedback on sentiwordnet. CoRR abs/1306.1343 (2013)

[4] Huang, S., Niu, Z., Shi, C.: Automatic construction of domain-specific sentiment lexicon based on constrained label propagation. Knowl.-Based Syst. 56, 191–200 (2014)

[5] Cruz, F.L., Troyano, J.A., Ortega, F.J., Enríquez, F.: Automatic expansion of feature-level opinion lexicons. In: Proceedings of the 2nd Workshop on Computational Approaches to Subjectivity and Sentiment Analysis, WASSA 2011, pp. 125–131. Association for Computational Linguistics, Stroudsburg (2011)

[6] Turney, P.D.: Thumbs up or thumbs down?: Semantic orientation applied to unsupervised classification of reviews. In: Proceedings of the 40th Annual Meeting on Association for Computational Linguistics, ACL 2002, pp. 417–424. Association for Computational Linguistics, Stroudsburg (2002)

[7] Thet, T.T., Na, J.C., Khoo, C.S.: Aspect-based sentiment analysis of movie reviews on discussion boards. J. Inf. Sci. 36(6), 823–848 (2010)

[8] Pang, B., Lee, L.: A sentimental education: Sentiment analysis using subjectivity summarization based on minimum cuts. In: Proceedings of the 42nd Annual Meeting on Association for Computational Linguistics, ACL 2004. Association for Computational Linguistics, Stroudsburg (2004)

[9] Basari, A.S.H., Hussin, B., Ananta, I.G.P., Zeniarja, J.: Opinion mining of movie review using hybrid method of support vector machine and particle swarm optimization. Procedia Engineering 53, 453–462 (2013)

[10] Pang, B., Lee, L.: Seeing stars: Exploiting class relationships for sentiment categorization with respect to rating scales. In: Proceedings of ACL, pp. 115–124 (2005)

[11] Hatzivassiloglou, V., McKeown, K.R.: Predicting the semantic orientation of adjectives. In: Proceedings of the 35th Annual Meeting of the Association for Computational Linguistics and Eighth Conference of the European Chapter of the Association for Computational Linguistics, ACL 1998, pp. 174–181. Association for Computational Linguistics, Stroudsburg (1997)

[12] Turney, P., Littman, M.: Unsupervised learning of semantic orientation from a hundred-billion-word corpus. Technical report nrc technical report erb-1094, Institute for Information Technology, National Research Council Canada (2002)

[13] Gamon, M., Aue, A.: Automatic identification of sentiment vocabulary: exploiting low association with known sentiment terms. In: Proceedings of the ACL 2005 Workshop on Feature Engineering for Machine Learning in NLP, ACL, pp. 57–64 (2005)

[14] Steinberger, J., Ebrahim, M., Ehrmann, M., Hurriyetoglu, A., Kabadjov, M., Lenkova, P., Steinberger, R., Tanev, H, Vázquez, S., Zavarella, V.: Creating sentiment dictionaries via triangulation. Decision Support Systems 53(4), 689–694 (2012) (Computational Approaches to Subjectivity and Sentiment Analysis 2) Service Science in Information Systems Research: Special Issue on {PACIS} (2010)

[15] Mihalcea, R., Banea, C., Wiebe, J.: Learning multilingual subjective language via cross-lingual projections. In: Proceedings of the 45th Annual Meeting of the Association of Computational Linguistics, pp. 976–983. Association for Computational Linguistics, Prague (2007)

[16] Shi, L., Mihalcea, R., Tian, M.: Cross language text classification by model translation and semi-supervised learning. In: Proceedings of the 2010 Conference on Empirical Methods in Natural Language Processing, EMNLP 2010, pp. 1057–1067. Association for Computational Linguistics, Stroudsburg (2010)

[17] Min Kim, S.: Determining the sentiment of opinions. In: Proceedings of COLING, pp. 1367–1373 (2004)

[18] Kamps, J., Marx, M., Mokken, R.J., Rijke, M.D.: Using wordnet to measure semantic orientation of adjectives. In: National Institute for, pp. 1115–1118 (2004)

[19] Hu, M., Liu, B.: Mining and summarizing customer reviews. In: Proceedings of the Tenth ACM SIGKDD International Conference on Knowledge Discovery and Data Mining, KDD 2004, pp. 168–177. ACM, New York (2004)

[20] Esuli, A., Sebastiani, F.: Determining the semantic orientation of terms through gloss classification. In: Proceedings of the 14th ACM International Conference on Information and Knowledge Management, CIKM 2005, pp. 617–624. ACM, New York (2005)

[21] Liu, B.: Sentiment Analysis and Opinion Mining. Synthesis Lectures on Human Language Technologies. Morgan & Claypool Publishers (2012)

[22] Pang, B., Lee, L., Vaithyanathan, S.: Thumbs up?: sentiment classification using machine learningtechniques. In: Proceedings of the ACL 2002 Conference on Empirical Methods Innatural Language Processing, EMNLP 2002, vol. 10, pp. 79–86. Association for Computational Linguistics, Stroudsburg (2002)

[23] Pang, B., Lee, L.: Opinion mining and sentiment analysis. Found. Trends Inf. Retr. 2(1-2), 1–135 (2008)

[24] Ortigosa-Hernández, J., Rodríguez, J.D., Alzate, L., Lucania, M., Inza, I., Lozano, J.A.: Approaching sentiment analysis by using semi-supervised learning of multi-dimensional classifiers. Neurocomputing 92, 98–115 (2012)

[25] Ohsawa, Y., Benson, N.E., Yachida, M.: Keygraph: Automatic indexing by co-occurrence graph based on building construction metaphor. In: ADL 1998: Proceedings of the Advances in Digital Libraries Conference, p. 12. IEEE Computer Society, Washington, DC (1998)

Scalable Uncertainty-Tolerant Business Rules

Alfredo Cuzzocrea[1], Hendrik Decker[2,⋆], and Francesc D. Muñoz-Escoí[2,⋆]

[1] ICAR-CNR and University of Calabria, 87036 Cosenza, Italy
[2] Instituto Tecnológico de Informática, UPV, 46022 Valencia, Spain
cuzzocrea@si.deis.unical.it, {hendrik,fmunyoz}@iti.upv.es

Abstract. Business rules are of key importance for maintaining the correctness of business data. They also can help to contain the amount of uncertainty associated to business data and decisions based on them. However, business rule enforcement does not scale up easily to concurrent systems. That is due to two common exigencies: the postulates of total and of isolated business rule satisfaction. In order to limit the accumulation of uncertainty, we outline how measure-based uncertainty-tolerant business rules maintenance scales up to concurrent transactions, by refraining from the postulates of total and isolated rule satisfaction.

1 Introduction

For fully automating the reasoning and processing of business workflows, arguably the best choice is to invest in business rules and represent them as integrity constraints. That point of view has been convincingly argued for in [9].

Another important application domain of integrity constraints is data quality [30]. In [12] we have argued that, to a large extent, conditions deemed necessary by the database designer for the data to have quality can be represented by integrity constraints. Consequently, data quality can be equated to the degree by which the data satisfy the constraints that capture quality. Hence, such constraints can be conveniently called *quality constraints* [14].

Uncertainty in databases can be understood as a lack of data quality, and quality conditions can conveniently be represented as integrity constraints. It has been pointed out in [8] that the violation of constraints corresponds to the uncertainty of the data items. On the other hand, it is well-known that many database applications may involve considerable amounts of uncertain data.

Business rules can be used to avoid uncertainty. Nevertheless, they need to be able to tolerate it, i.e., to perform reasonably well in the presence of uncertain data. The specific problem addressed in this paper is to make uncertainty-tolerant business rules work not only with regard to isolated updates of the database, but also when arbitrarily many database transactions are executed concurrently. Concurrency of transactions is typical for most OLTP applications, for distributed systems and for transactions in the cloud. In [8], the scale-up of uncertainty tolerance to concurrent transactions was addressed as a side issue. In this paper, it receives unabridged attention.

⋆ Supported by ERDF/FEDER and the MEC grant TIN2012-37719-C03-01 .

M. Polycarpou et al. (Eds.): HAIS 2014, LNAI 8480, pp. 179–190, 2014.
© Springer International Publishing Switzerland 2014

There is a large amount of methods for evaluating declarative integrity constraints [26]. Also the use of business rules for data quality management has been documented, e.g., in [27] [31]. Moreover, the management of concurrent transactions has been broadly covered in the literature [18] [5] [38].

This paper addresses two characteristic difficulties that impede a combination of approaches to control data uncertainty by checking quality constraints, on one hand, and uncertainty-containing processing of concurrent transactions, on the other. One of the two difficulties corresponds to a particular requirement that is traditionally imposed on all methods of integrity checking. The other corresponds to a particular requirement traditionally imposed on the design, implementation and use of concurrent transactions. It will turn out that both requirements are unrealistic and indeed not necessary to their full extent in practice.

The first requirement is that an update can be efficiently checked for integrity only if the state before the update totally satisfies all constraints, without exception. We call this requirement *the total integrity postulate*. The second is that, for guaranteeing integrity preservation by serializable concurrent transactions, each transaction is supposed to preserve integrity when executed in isolation. We call this requirement *the isolated integrity postulate*.

We point out that the isolated integrity postulate must not be confused with the well-known requirement of an isolated execution of transactions for avoiding update anomalies. That requirement usually is complied with by ensuring the serializability of schedules, or some relaxation thereof [38,35]. However, serializability is independent of the isolated integrity postulate, requiring that integrity be preserved in isolation: while serializability can be guaranteed automatically by the scheduler of the DBMS, the isolated integrity postulate is usually expected to be complied with by the designers, programmers and users of transactions.

The dispensability of the total integrity postulate has been unveiled in [15], and the isolated integrity requirement has been relaxed in [16], both by a concept of inconsistency-tolerant integrity checking. That concept was based 'cases', i.e., instances of integrity constraints. Their violation can be tolerated as long as integrity checking can guarantee that the amount of violated cases does not increase. In [12], a generalization of inconsistency-tolerant integrity checking, based on inconsistency measures, has been presented. It tolerantes integrity violation as long as the amount of measured inconsistency is not increased by given updates. In this paper, we show that measure-based uncertainty checking also enables a significant weakening of the isolated integrity postulate.

In section 2, we characterize the postulates of total and isolated integrity. In section 3, we recapitulate measure-based uncertainty checking, which serves to get rid of total integrity as well as to relax isolated integrity. In section 4, we address related work, with an emphasis on integrity checking for concurrent transactions. If not specified otherwise, we use conventional terminology and notations for logic databases [1] and transaction concurrency [5].

2 Bad Postulates

The total integrity postulate is explained in Subsection 2.1, the isolated integrity postulate in Subsection 2.2.

2.1 Integrity Checking with Totality

Integrity checking can be exceedingly costly, unless some simplification method is used [29]. That can be illustrated as follows. (As usual, lower-case letters x, y, z denote variables, in the example below.)

Example 2.1. *Let* emp *be a relation about employees, whose first column is a unique name and the second a project assigned to the employee. The formula* $I = \leftarrow \text{proj}(x, y), \text{proj}(x, z), y \neq z$ *is a primary key constraint on the first column of* proj, *a relation about projects, with unique identifiers in the first column. The foreign key constraint* $I' = \forall x, y\, \exists z\, (\text{emp}(x, y) \rightarrow \text{proj}(y, z))$ *on the second column of* emp *references the primary key of* proj. *Now, assume a transaction* T *that inserts* emp(Jack, p)*. Most integrity checking methods* $\mathcal{M}$ *ignore* I *for checking* T*, since* I *does not constrain* emp. *Rather, they only evaluate the case* $\exists z\, (\text{emp}(Jack, p) \rightarrow \text{proj}(p, z))$ *of* I'*, or its simplification* $\exists z\ \text{proj}(p, z)$*, since* emp(Jack, p) *becomes* true *by the transaction. If, e.g.,* (p, e) *is a row in* proj, $\mathcal{M}$ *accepts the insertion. If there is no tuple matching* (p, z) *in* proj, *then* $\mathcal{M}$ *signals a violation of integrity.* □

Proofs of the correctness of methods for simplified constraints checking in the literature all rely on the total integrity postulate, i.e., that integrity always be totally satisfied, before updates are checked for preserving consistency. In practice, however, it is rather the exception than the rule that this postulate is complied with. In particular for applications such as business intelligence, distributed and replicated databases, legacy data maintenance, data warehousing, data federation, etc, a certain amount of uncertain data that violate constraints in committed states has to be lived with, at least temporarily.

Suppose that, for instance, the constraint I' in Example 2.1 is violated due to *emp*(*Jack*, *OO*) $\in D$ and a previous deletion of the *OO* project. Thus, by definition, no method that requires total integrity is equipped to check T, since not all constraints are satisfied. In practice however, if the project that *Jack* is assigned to is stored in the *proj* relation, T is rightfully sanctioned by all common implementations of integrity checking, as already indicated in Example 2.1. Example 3.1 in Subsection 3.1 will illustrate essentially the same point.

Hence, the total integrity postulate, which conventionally has always been imposed, does not approve the correctness of integrity checking in practice, since the latter often is performed in the presence of consistency violations. Fortunately, however, that postulate can be abolished without incurring any cost and without losing its essential guarantees, as shown in 3.1.

2.2 Integrity Checking with Isolation

We cite from [18]: "*it is assumed that each transaction, when executed alone, transforms a consistent state into a consistent state; that is, transactions preserve consistency*". This is what we have called the isolated integrity postulate. Clearly, it presupposes the total integrity postulate. From the isolated integrity postulate, [18] [5] and many others have inferred that then, also all serializable schedules of concurrent transactions preserve 'consistency', i.e., integrity.

The requirements of total and isolated integrity often are illusionary, particularly for distributed databases, let alone for transactions in the cloud, where 'eventual consistency' [36] may compromise both integrity and isolation. Actually, it is hard to imagine than any agent who issues a transaction T would blindly believe in a consistency-preserving outcome of T by naïvely assuming that all concurrent transactions had been programmed with sufficient care to preserve integrity in isolation. Hitherto, there has been no theory to justify such optimism in the presence of uncertainty. Now, such a justification is given in Section 3. In particular, we show in 3.4 that the consistency guarantees of uncertainty-tolerant integrity checking scale up to concurrent transactions.

3 Uncertainty Tolerance

The purpose of business rules (i.e., integrity constraints) is to state and enforce quality properties of business data. However, uncertainty (i.e., violations of quality constraints that take the form of logical inconsistencies) are unavoidable in practice. Rather than insisting that all business rules must be totally satisfied at all times, it is necessary to tolerate unavoidable constraint violations.

Whenever time permits, attempts of reducing or repairing such manifestations of uncertainty can be made, while such attempts often are not affordable at update time. Thus, updates should be checkable for quality preservation, even if there are extant constraint violations, which can be dealt with later. That is the philosophy behind uncertainty-tolerant constraint checking, as revisited in 3.1. Technically speaking, constraint preservation means that the amount of measured uncertainty that manifests itself in constraint violations is not increased by a checked and approved transaction. In 3.4, we outline a generalization of the results in 3.1 to concurrent transactions.

Throughout the remainder, let D, I, $\mathcal{IC}$, T, $\mathcal{M}$ stand for a database, an integrity constraint, a set of constraints, a transaction and, resp., an integrity checking method. By $D(\mathcal{IC}) = TRUE$ and $D(\mathcal{IC}) = FALSE$, we denote that $\mathcal{IC}$ is satisfied or, resp., violated in D. Moreover, we suppose that all constraints are represented in prenex form, i.e., all quantifiers of variables appear leftmost.

In general, each method $\mathcal{M}$ can be conceived as a mapping which takes triples $(D, \mathcal{IC}, T)$ as input, and returns either OK, which means that $\mathcal{M}$ sanctions T as integrity-preserving, or KO, which indicates that executing T would violate some constraint. Further, let D^T denote the database state obtained by applying the write set of T to D.

3.1 Removing the Total Integrity Constraint

In [15], it is shown that, contrary to common belief, one may get rid of the total integrity postulate for most approaches to integrity checking without any trade-off. Methods which continue to function well when this postulate is renounced are called inconsistency-tolerant. The basic idea is illustrated below.

Example 3.1. *Let I and I' be as in Example 2.1. Most integrity checking methods $\mathcal{M}$ accept the update* insert *(*Jack, p*) if, e.g., (p, e) is a row in* proj. *Now, the positive outcome of this integrity check is not disturbed if, e.g., also the tuple (p, f) is a row in* proj. *At first sight, that may be somewhat irritating, since I then is violated by two tuples about project p in the relation* proj. *In fact, the case $\leftarrow$ proj(p, e), proj(p, f), $e \neq f$ indicates an integrity violation. However, this violation has not been caused by the insertion just checked. It has been there before, and the assignment of* Jack *to p should not be rejected just because the data about p are not consistent. After all, it may be part of* Jack*'s new job to cleanse potentially inconsistent project data. In general, a transaction T that preserves the integrity of all consistent data without increasing the amount of extant inconsistency should not be rejected. And that is exactly what $\mathcal{M}$'s output indicates: no instance of any constraint that is satisfied in the state before T is committed is violated after T has been committed.* □

3.2 Uncertainty Measures

Example 3.1 conveys that each update which does not increase the amount of inconsistency (i.e., integrity violation) can and should be accepted. For making precise what it means to have an increase of inconsistency or not, inconsistency needs to be measured. That can be formalized as follows.

Definition 3.1. *We say that $(\mu, \preceq)$ is an* uncertainty measure *(in short, a* measure*) if μ maps tuples $(D, \mathcal{IC})$ to a metric space that is partially ordered by $\preceq$. If $\preceq$ is understood, we simply identify a measure $(\mu, \preceq)$ with μ.* □

Example 3.2. *A binary border-case measure β is given by $\beta(D, \mathcal{IC}) = D(\mathcal{IC})$, with the natural ordering $TRUE \prec FALSE$ of the range of β, i.e., quality constraint satisfaction ($D(\mathcal{IC}) = TRUE$) means lower uncertainty than quality constraint violation ($D(\mathcal{IC}) = FALSE$). In fact, β is used by all conventional integrity checking methods, for deciding whether a given transaction T on a database D that satisfies its constraints $\mathcal{IC}$ should be accepted (if $D^T(\mathcal{IC}) = TRUE$) or rejected (if $D^T(\mathcal{IC}) = FALSE$).* □

More, less trivial uncertainty measures are defined and discussed in [8]. For instance, the function that maps pairs $(D, \mathcal{IC})$ to the cardinality of the set of cases (instances) of violated constraints is a convenient uncertainty measure. Inconsistency can also be measured by taking such sets themselves, as elements of the powerset of all cases of $\mathcal{IC}$, together with the subset ordering.

3.3 Integrity Checking with Uncertainty: Generalizing the Process

In accordance with [8], uncertainty-tolerant integrity checking can now be defined as follows, for databases D, integrity theories $\mathcal{IC}$ and transactions T.

Definition 3.2. *Let $\mathcal{M}$ be a mapping from triples $(D, \mathcal{IC}, T)$ to $\{OK, KO\}$, so that T is either accepted or, resp. rejected, and $(\mu, \preceq)$ an uncertainty measure. $\mathcal{M}$ is called a* sound, *resp.,* complete *method for integrity checking if, for each triple $(D, \mathcal{IC}, T)$, (1) or, resp., (2) holds.*

$$\mathcal{M}(D, \mathcal{IC}, T) = OK \Rightarrow \mu(D^T, \mathcal{IC}) \preceq \mu(D, \mathcal{IC}). \quad (1)$$

$$\mu(D^T, \mathcal{IC}) \preceq \mu(D, \mathcal{IC}) \Rightarrow \mathcal{M}(D, \mathcal{IC}, T) = OK. \quad (2)$$

If (1) holds, then $\mathcal{M}$ is also called measure-based, *or* μ-based. □

Definition 3.2 generalizes the traditional definition of sound and complete integrity checking significantly, in two ways. The first essential upgrade is that, traditionally, the measure used for sizing constraint violations in a database with regard to its associated integrity theory is binary, and thus very coarse: $\mathcal{IC}$ is either *violated* or *satisfied* in D, i.e., there is no distinction with regard to different amounts of uncertainty. As opposed to that, the range of an uncertainty measure μ may be arbitrarily fine-grained. The second upgrade is equally significant: traditionally, the total integrity postulate is imposed, i.e., $D(\mathcal{IC}) = TRUE$ is required. As opposed to that, this postulate is absent in Definition 3.2, i.e., $\mathcal{M}$ does not need to worry about extant constraint violations.

Definition 3.2 formalizes that a method $\mathcal{M}$ is uncertainty-tolerant if its output OK for a given transaction T guarantees that the amount of uncertainty in $(D, \mathcal{IC})$ as measured by μ is not increased by executing T on D. Moreover, each transaction that, on purpose or by happenstance, repairs some inconsistent instance(s) of any constraint without introducing any new violation will be OK-ed too by $\mathcal{M}$. This means that, over time, the amount of integrity violations will decrease, as long as an uncertainty-tolerant method is used for checking each transaction for integrity preservation.

Note that it follows by the definition above that each uncertainty-tolerant $\mathcal{M}$ returns KO for any transaction the commitment of which would violate a hitherto satisfied instance of some constraint. It is then up to the agent who has called $\mathcal{M}$ for checking integrity to react appropriately to the output KO

A defensive reaction is to simply cancel and reject the transaction. A more offensive reaction could be to modify ('repair') the database, the constraints or the transaction, so that an increase of the amount of integrity violations is undone. Such measure-based database repairs are dealt with in [13].

3.4 Relaxed Integrity Checking with Isolation

To say, as the isolated integrity postulate does, that a transaction T "preserves integrity in isolation", means the following: For a given set $\mathcal{IC}$ of integrity constraints and each state D of a given database schema, each $I \in \mathcal{IC}$ is satisfied in D^T if I is satisfied in D.

We now apply uncertainty-tolerant constraint checking not only to transactions executed in isolation, but also to concurrent transactions. Thus, we abandon the above postulate "if I is satisfied in D" and weaken the consequence "each $I \in \mathcal{IC}$ is satisfied in D^T" according to Definition 3.2. In [16], we could show that this is possible for integrity checking methods that preserve all satisfied cases of integrity constraints, while tolerating cases that are violated in the state before executing a given transaction. By an analogous (though more abstract) argument, the isolated integrity postulate can be weakened as follows.

For each state $(D, \mathcal{IC})$ of a given database schema, each uncertainty measure $(\mu, \preceq)$ and each transaction T,

$$\mu(D^T, \mathcal{IC}) \preceq \mu(D, \mathcal{IC}) \tag{3}$$

must hold whenever T is executed in isolation.

Under this postulate, we can infer the result that (3) will continue to hold if T and all transaction that are concurrent with T are serializable, and (3)' holds for each transaction T' that is concurrent with T whenever T' is executed in isolation, where (3)' is obtained from (3) by replacing T with T'.

Note that this result does not endorse that each case should be checked individually. On the contrary, integrity checking can proceed as for non-concurrent transactions, i.e., no built-in nor any external routine that takes part in the integrity checking process needs to be modified. The result just says that, if the method returns OK, then everything that was satisfied in the state before the transaction will remain satisfied after the transaction has committed.

The difference between this relaxation and the traditional result which imposes the general isolated integrity postulate, is the following. In the relaxed result, isolated integrity preservation only is asked to hold for individual cases. Simplified integrity checking focuses on cases that are relevant for the write set of a given transaction T. Hence, only those cases are guaranteed to remain satisfied by a successful integrity check. All non-relevant cases may possibly be violated by concurrent or preceding transactions. Such violations are detected only if the respective transactions are checked too. If not, such violations are tolerated by each uncertainty-tolerant method that checks T.

Note that the above relaxation of isolated integrity still asks for the serializability of all concurrent transactions. This means that we cannot expect that integrity guarantees of the form (3) would continue to hold in general if the isolation level is lowered. In upcoming work, we shall investigate possible isolation level relaxations such that sufficient integrity guarantees can still be given.

The generalized form of uncertainty-tolerant integrity checking, as presented in 3.3, is further generalizable for transactions that also involve schema updates including changes of the quality constraints [11]. Unfortunately, that is not the case for the consequences obtained from the relaxed isolated integrity postulate in 3.4. In fact, already the guarantees provided by the traditional isolated integrity postulate cannot be maintained for changes in the set of constraints.

Thus, more work is necessary in order to establish sufficiently general conditions under which any integrity guarantees can be made for concurrent transactions across evolving database schemata.

4 Related Work

Most papers about the maintenance of constraints do not deal with transaction concurrency. On the other hand, most papers that do address concurrent transactions take it for granted that, if transaction were checked for constraint preservation in isolation, then it would pass that test successfully, i.e., they do not care how integrity is ensured.

As an exception, the work documented in [25], addresses both problem areas. However, the proposed solutions are application-specific (flight reservation) and seem to be quite ad-hoc. Also the author of [33] is aware of the problem, and argues convincingly to not be careless about consistency issues. However, with regard to semantic integrity violations in concurrent scenarios, he only exhibits a negative result (the CAP theorem [20]), but does not investigate uncertainty-tolerant solutions. There do exists solutions for reconciling consistency, availability and partition tolerance in distributed systems, e.g., [36] [34]. However, the consistency they are concerned with is either transaction consistency (i.e., the avoidance of dirty reads, unrepeatable reads and phantom updates) or replication consistency (i.e., that all replicas consist of identical copies, so that there are no stale data), not the semantic consistency that is the contrary of uncertainty.

In the seminal papers [21,17,23,18,3,19], a distinction is made between integrity violations caused either by anomalies of concurrency or by semantic errors. In [17,23], concurrency is not dealt with in depth. In [21,18,3,19], integrity is not looked at in detail.

For replicated database systems, the interplay of built-in integrity checking, concurrency and replication consistency has been studied in [28]. Integrity checking is enabled even in systems where the isolation level of transactions is lowered to *snapshot isolation* [4]. However, uncertainty tolerance has not been considered in [28]. Thus, for the snapshot-isolation-based replication of databases, more research is necessary in order to clarify which consistency guarantees can be given when inconsistency-tolerant integrity checking methods are used in the presence of inconsistent cases of constraints.

5 Discussion

Since the beginnings of the field of computational databases, the obligation of maintaining the integrity of business rules in multi-user systems, and thus the avoidance of uncertainty, has remained with the designers, implementers, administrators and end users of transaction processing. More precisely, integrity maintenance in concurrency-enabled systems is delegated to a multitude of individual human actors who, on one hand, have to trust on each other's unfailing compliance with the integrity requirements, but, on the other hand, usually do not know each other.

We expect that, in the long run, this unfortunate distribution of responsibilities will give way to declarative specifications of integrity constraints that can be supported automatically, just the way some fairly simple kinds of constraints are supported already for serial schedules in centralized, non-distributed database systems. An early attempt in this direction is reported in [22], where, however, concurrency is hardly an issue. Likewise, the work in [24] largely passes by concurrency.

Anyway, we have aimed in our work on uncertainty-containing transactions to keep as close to the declarative paradigm as possible. The advantage of declarativity is to free users and application programmers from having to worry about quality preservation. That is, the database designer should formalize business rules as declarative integrity constraints in SQL and leave everything else to the integrity checking module of the DBMS. That module may be built into the DBMS core or run on top of it. In any case, the enforcement of the business rules should be as transparent to the user as concurrency, distribution and replication.

However, as seen above, well-known authors of concurrency theory require what is virtually impossible, on a grand scale: that all transactions should be programmed such that they guarantee the preservation of all constraints in isolation [5] [38]. So, database designers and users are asked to program transactions in a way such that all semantically uncertain situations are avoided. This obviously may amount to a formidable task in complex systems.

Hence, the motivating objective of this paper has been to enable an automated enforcement of business rules for concurrent transactions. We have identified two obstacles that, in the past, have prevented to attain that goal: the postulates of total and isolated integrity.

For overcoming the traditional misbelief that integrity can be checked efficiently for a transaction T only if the state before T totally complies with all constraints, we have revisited the work in [15]. There, it has been shown that the total integrity postulate can be waived without further ado, for most (though not all) integrity checking methods. Fortunately, the postulate also is unnecessary for deferred checking of key constraints and other common built-in integrity constructs in DBMSs on the market.

We have seen that the advantages of making the total integrity postulate dispensable even extend to relaxing the isolated integrity postulate. More precisely, the use of an uncertainty-tolerant quality checking method to enforce business rules for concurrent serializable transactions guarantees that no transaction can violate any instance of any constraint that has been satisfied in the state before committing if all transactions preserve the integrity of the same instance in isolation. Conversely stated, our result guarantees that, if any violation happens, then no transaction that has been correctly and successfully checked for integrity preservation by an inconsistency-tolerant method can be held responsible for that. The most interesting aspect of this result is that it even holds in the presence of extant uncertain data that violates any integrity constraint.

6 Outlook to Future Work

Important contemporary areas where uncertainty tolerance is paramount are systems for streaming data [6], linked data [7] and big data [37], as well as hybrid approaches for approximate reasoning [2]. In the data stores of such systems, data integrity and the isolation level of concurrent transactions usually is severely compromised. We have seen that, in general, more research is needed for systems involving such compromises. In particular, for non-serializable histories of concurrent transactions, it should be interesting to elaborate a precise theory of different kinds of database states. Such a theory should allow to differentiate between states that are committed, states that are "seen" by a transaction and states that are "seen" by (human or programmed) agents that have issued the transaction. and which consistency guarantees can be made by which methods for transitions between those states. This area of research is important because most commercial database management systems compromise the isolation level of transactions in favor of a higher transaction throughput, while leaving the problem of integrity preservation to the application programmers. First steps in this direction have been proposed in [16].

Another important, possibly even more difficult area of upcoming research is that of providing uncertainty-containing transactions not only in distributed and replicated systems with remote clients and servers, but also for databases in the cloud, for big volumes of data and for No-SQL data stores. These are going to be the objectives of impending projects. So far, there are only some special-purpose solutions (e.g., [39]), which lack genericity (or, at least, the generalizability of which is less than obvious). After all, a move away from the universality-obsessed attitude toward solutions to technical problems in the field of databases will be the way of the future [32].

References

1. Abiteboul, S., Hull, R., Vianu, V.: Foundations of Databases. Addison-Wesley (1995)
2. Abraham, A.: Hybrid approaches for approximate reasoning. Journal of Intelligent and Fuzzy Systems 23(2-3), 41–42 (2012)
3. Bayer, R.: Integrity, concurrency, and recovery in databases. In: Samelson, K. (ed.) ECI 1976. LNCS, vol. 44, pp. 79–106. Springer, Heidelberg (1976)
4. Berenson, H., Bernstein, P.A., Gray, J., Melton, J., O'Neil, E.J., O'Neil, P.E.: A critique of ansi sql isolation levels. In: SIGMOD Conference, pp. 1–10 (1995)
5. Bernstein, P.A., Hadzilacos, V., Goodman, N.: Concurrency Control and Recovery in Database Systems. Addison-Wesley (1987)
6. Cuzzocrea, A.: Optimization issues of querying and evolving sensor and stream databases. Information Systems 39, 196–198 (2014)
7. Cuzzocrea, A., Leung, C.K.-S., Tanbeer, S.K.: Mining of Diverse Social Entities from Linked Data. In: Selçuk Candan, K., Amer-Yahia, S., Schweikardt, N., Christophides, V., Leroy, V. (eds.) Proc. Workshops of the EDBT/ICDT 2014 Joint Conference. CEUR Workshop Proceedings, pp. 269–274 (2014)

8. Cuzzocrea, A., de Juan Marín, R., Decker, H., Muñoz-Escoí, F.D.: Managing uncertainty in databases and scaling it up to concurrent transactions. In: Hüllermeier, E., Link, S., Fober, T., Seeger, B. (eds.) SUM 2012. LNCS, vol. 7520, pp. 30–43. Springer, Heidelberg (2012)
9. Date, C.J.: What not how: the business rules approach to application development. Addison-Wesley Longman Publishing Co., Inc., Boston (2000)
10. Decan, A., Pijcke, F., Wijsen, J.: Certain conjunctive query answering in SQL. In: Hüllermeier, E., Link, S., Fober, T., Seeger, B. (eds.) SUM 2012. LNCS, vol. 7520, pp. 154–167. Springer, Heidelberg (2012)
11. Decker, H.: Causes for inconsistency-tolerant schema update management. In: ICDE Workshops, pp. 157–161 (2011)
12. Decker, H.: Causes of the violation of integrity constraints for supporting the quality of databases. In: Murgante, B., Gervasi, O., Iglesias, A., Taniar, D., Apduhan, B.O. (eds.) ICCSA 2011, Part V. LNCS, vol. 6786, pp. 283–292. Springer, Heidelberg (2011)
13. Decker, H.: Partial repairs that tolerate inconsistency. In: Eder, J., Bielikova, M., Tjoa, A.M. (eds.) ADBIS 2011. LNCS, vol. 6909, pp. 389–400. Springer, Heidelberg (2011)
14. Decker, H.: Answers that have quality. In: Murgante, B., Misra, S., Carlini, M., Torre, C.M., Nguyen, H.-Q., Taniar, D., Apduhan, B.O., Gervasi, O. (eds.) ICCSA 2013, Part II. LNCS, vol. 7972, pp. 543–558. Springer, Heidelberg (2013)
15. Decker, H., Martinenghi, D.: Inconsistency-tolerant integrity checking. IEEE Trans. Knowl. Data Eng. 23(2), 218–234 (2011)
16. Decker, H., Muñoz-Escoí, F.D.: Revisiting and improving a result on integrity preservation by concurrent transactions. In: Meersman, R., Dillon, T., Herrero, P. (eds.) OTM 2010. LNCS, vol. 6428, pp. 297–306. Springer, Heidelberg (2010)
17. Eswaran, K.P., Chamberlin, D.D.: Functional specifications of subsystem for database integrity. In: Kerr, D.S. (ed.) Proceedings of the International Conference on Very Large Data Bases, Framingham, Massachusetts, USA, September 22-24, pp. 48–68. ACM (1975)
18. Eswaran, K.P., Gray, J., Lorie, R.A., Traiger, I.L.: The notions of consistency and predicate locks in a database system. Commun. ACM 19(11), 624–633 (1976)
19. Gardarin, G.: Integrity, consistency, concurrency, reliability in distributed database management systems. In: Distributed Databases, pp. 335–351 (1980)
20. Gilbert, S., Lynch, N.A.: Brewer's conjecture and the feasibility of consistent, available, partition-tolerant web services. SIGACT News 33(2), 51–59 (2002)
21. Gray, J., Lorie, R., Putzolu, G.: Granularity of locks in a shared data base. In: 1st International Conference on Very Large Data Bases, pp. 428–451. ACM Press (1975)
22. Grefen, P.W.P.J.: Combining theory and practice in integrity control: A declarative approach to the specification of a transaction modification subsystem. In: Agrawal, R., Baker, S., Bell, D.A. (eds.) 19th International Conference on Very Large Data Bases, Dublin, Ireland, August 24-27, pp. 581–591. Morgan Kaufmann (1993)
23. Hammer, M., McLeod, D.: Semantic integrity in a relational data base system. In: 1st International Conference on Very Large Data Bases, pp. 25–47. ACM Press (1975)
24. Ibrahim, H.: Checking integrity constraints - how it differs in centralized, distributed and parallel databases. In: DEXA Workshops, pp. 563–568 (2006)
25. Lynch, N.A., Blaustein, B.T., Siegel, M.: Correctness conditions for highly available replicated databases. In: PODC, pp. 11–28 (1986)

26. Martinenghi, D., Christiansen, H., Decker, H.: Integrity checking and maintenance in relational and deductive databases and beyond. In: Ma, Z. (ed.) Intelligent Databases: Technologies and Applications, pp. 238–285. Idea Group Publishing (2006)
27. Morgan, T.: Business Rules and Information Systems: Aligning IT with Business Goals (Unisys Series). Addison-Wesley Professional (2002)
28. Muñoz-Escoí, F.D., Ruiz-Fuertes, M.I., Decker, H., Armendáriz-Íñigo, J.E., de Mendívil, J.R.G.: Extending middleware protocols for database replication with integrity support. In: Meersman, R., Tari, Z. (eds.) OTM 2008, Part I. LNCS, vol. 5331, pp. 607–624. Springer, Heidelberg (2008)
29. Nicolas, J.-M.: Logic for improving integrity checking in relational data bases. Acta Informatica (18), 227–253 (1982)
30. Pipino, L., Lee, Y., Yang, R.: Data quality assessment. Commun. ACM 45(4), 211–218 (2002)
31. Ross, R.G.: Business Rule Concepts: Getting to the Point of Knowledge, 2nd edn. (1998)
32. Stonebraker, M.: Technical perspective - one size fits all: an idea whose time has come and gone. Commun. ACM 51(12), 76 (2008)
33. Stonebraker, M.: Errors in Database Systems, Eventual Consistency, and the CAP Theorem (2010)
34. Stonebraker, M.: In search of database consistency. Commun. ACM 53(10), 8–9 (2010)
35. Vidyasankar, K.: Serializability. In: Encyclopedia of Database Systems, pp. 2626–2632 (2009)
36. Vogels, W.: Eventually consistent. Commun. ACM 52(1), 40–44 (2009)
37. Weikum, G.: Where's the Data in the Big Data Wave? ACM SIGMOD Blog (2013), `http://wp.sigmod.org/?p=786`
38. Weikum, G., Vossen, G.: Transactional Information Systems: Theory, Algorithms, and the Practice of Concurrency Control and Recovery. Morgan Kaufmann (2002)
39. Ziwich, R.P., Duarte Jr., E.P., Albini, L.C.P.: Distributed integrity checking for systems with replicated data. In: ICPADS (1), pp. 363–369 (2005)

Incorporating Belief Function in SVM for Phoneme Recognition

Rimah Amami, Dorra Ben Ayed, and Nouerddine Ellouze

Department of Electrical Engineering, National School of Engineering of Tunis (ENIT), Tunisia
{rimah.amami,dorrainst}@yahoo.fr, n.ellouze@enit.tn

Abstract. The Support Vector Machine (SVM) method has been widely used in numerous classification tasks. The main idea of this algorithm is based on the principle of the margin maximization to find an hyperplane which separates the data into two different classes.In this paper, SVM is applied to phoneme recognition task. However, in many real-world problems, each phoneme in the data set for recognition problems may differ in the degree of significance due to noise, inaccuracies, or abnormal characteristics; All those problems can lead to the inaccuracies in the prediction phase. Unfortunately, the standard formulation of SVM does not take into account all those problems and, in particular, the variation in the speech input.

This paper presents a new formulation of SVM (B-SVM) that attributes to each phoneme a confidence degree computed based on its geometric position in the space. Then, this degree is used in order to strengthen the class membership of the tested phoneme. Hence, we introduce a reformulation of the standard SVM that incorporates the degree of belief. Experimental performance on TIMIT database shows the effectiveness of the proposed method B-SVM on a phoneme recognition problem.

Keywords: SVM, Phoneme, Belief, TIMIT.

1 Introduction

Support Vector Machine (SVM) was, at first, introduced by Vladimir [2] for a binary classification tasks in order to construct, in the input space, the decision functions based on the theory of Structural Risk Minimization, ([3] and [4]). Afterwards, SVM has been extended to support either the multi-class classification and regression tasks. SVM consists of constructing one or several hyperplanes in order to separate the data into the different classes. Nevertheless, an optimal hyperplane must be found in order to separate accurately the data into two classes.

[3] defined the optimal hyperplane as the decision function with maximal margin. Indeed, the margin can be defined as the shortest distance from the separating hyperplane and the closest vectors to the couple of classes. The application of SVM to the automatic speech recognition (ASR) problem has shown

M. Polycarpou et al. (Eds.): HAIS 2014, LNAI 8480, pp. 191–199, 2014.
© Springer International Publishing Switzerland 2014

a competitive performance and accurate recognition rates. In the sound system of a language, a phoneme is considered as the smallest distinctive unit which is able to communicate a possible meaning. Thus, the success of the phoneme recognition task is important to the development of language systems. Nevertheless, during the signal acquisition process, the speech signal may be affected by the speaker characteristics such as his gender, accent, and style of speech. Also, there are other external factors which can admittedly have an impact on the speech recognition such as the noise coming from a microphone or the variation in the vocal tract shape.

The standard formulation of SVM may not determine accurately the identity of the tested phoneme. Indeed, the speech signal is accompanied by all sorts of unpleasant variations during the acquisition. Those variations affect badly the recognition rates since the recognition mechanism may not be taken into account those changes in the phoneme data. For example, in the real-application problems, the English pronunciation differences and the differences in accents may lead to increase significantly the error rate of any learning algorithm since all phoneme data are handled identically. Thus, the standard SVM may find an optimal hyperplane without considering the influences of the differences accompanied by the speech signals. Thus, the identified optimal hyperplane can lead to loss of accuracies.

In this paper, we propose a novel approach in order to incorporate a belief function into the standard SVM algorithm which involves integrating confidence degree of each phoneme data. To fulfill this new formulation, we have, beforehand, compute the geometric distance between the centers of each possible class of the tested phoneme. Indeed, the benefit of hybrid approaches relies in their support to the decision-making and their ability to confirm the robustness of the recognition system [12], [13]. The experimental results with all phoneme datasets issued from the TIMIT database [5] show that the B-SVM outperforms the standard SVM and produces a better recognition rates. The rest of this paper is organized as follows: Section 2 presents an overview of the method Support Vector Machines (SVM). Section 3 presents the steps of the phoneme processing and the problems which accompanying the speech processing. Section 4 presents the new formulation B-SVM algorithm; Section 5 describes the hierarchical phoneme recognition system; Section 6 presents the experimental results and a comparison between the standard SVM and B-SVM in a multi-class phoneme recognition problem. The final section is the conclusion.

2 Support Vector Machines

The Support Vector Machines (SVM) is a learning algorithm for pattern recognition and regression problems [9] whose approaches the classification problem as an approximate implementation of the Structural Risk Minimization(SRM) induction principle [3].

SVM approximates the solution to the minimization problem of SRM through a Quadratic Programming optimization. It aims to maximize the margin which is the distance from a separating hyperplane to the closest positive or negative sample between classes.

Hence the hyperplane that optimally separates the data is the one that minimises:

$$\frac{1}{2}\|w^{ij}\|^2 + C\sum_{i=1}^{m}\xi^{ij} \tag{1}$$

Where C is a penalty to errors and ξ is a positive slack variable which measures the degree of misclassification.

subject to the constraints:

$$\begin{aligned} (w^{ij})\phi(x_t) + b^{ij} &\geq 1 - \xi^{ij}, \text{si } \ y = i \\ (w^{ij})\phi(x_t) + b^{ij} &\leq 1 - \xi^{ij}, \text{si } \ y = j \\ \xi_t^{ij} &\geq 0 \end{aligned} \tag{2}$$

For the phoneme classification, the decision function of SVM is expressed as:

$$f(x) = sign(\sum_{i=1}^{m} \alpha_i y_i K(x_i, x) + b) \tag{3}$$

The above decision function gives a signed distance from a phoneme x to the hyperplane.

However, when the data set is linearly non-separable, solving the parameters of this decision function becomes a quadratic programming problem. The solution to this optimization problem can be cast to the Lagrange functional and the use of Lagrange multipliers α_i, we obtain the Lagrangian of the dual objective function:

$$L_d = \max_{\alpha_i} \sum_{i=1}^{m} \alpha_i - \sum_{i=1}^{m}\sum_{j=1}^{m} \alpha_i \alpha_j y_i y_j K(x_i, x_j). \tag{4}$$

where $K(x_i, x_j)$ is the kernel of data x_i and x_j and the coefficients α_i are the lagrange multipliers and are computed for each phoneme of the data set. They must be maximised with respect to $\alpha_i \geq 0$. It must be pointed out that the data with nonzero coefficients α_i are called support vectors. They determine the decision boundary hyperplane of the classifier.

Moreover, applying a kernel trick that maps an input vector into a higher dimensional feature sapce, allows to SVM to approximate a non-linear function [3] and [7]. In this paper, we use SVM with the radial basis function kernel (RBF).This kernel choice was made after doing a case study in order to find the suitable kernel with which SVM may achieve good generalization performance as well as the parameters to use [11]. Based on this principle, the SVM adopts a systematic approach to find a linear function that belongs to a set of functions with lowest VC dimension (the VapnikChervonenkis dimension measure the capacity of a statistical classification algorithm).

3 Phoneme Processing

Speech recognition is the process of converting an acoustic signal, captured by a microphone , to a set of words, syllables or phonemes. The speech recognition systems can be used for applications such as mobiles applications, commands, control, data entry, and document preparation. The steps of the speech processing are described in the figure 1:

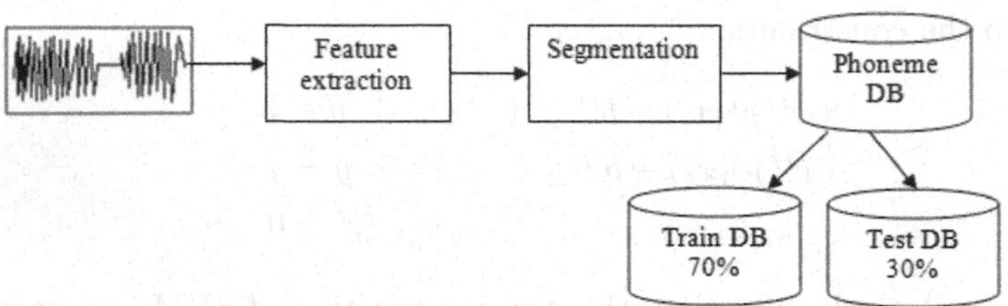

Fig. 1. Phoneme processing steps

The phoneme processing consists, first, on converting the speech captured by a microphone to a sequence of feature vectors. Then, a segmentation step is applied consisting on converting the continued speech signal to a set of units such as phonemes. Once the train and test data sets are prepared, a classifier is applied to classify the unknown phonemes. However, the phoneme recognition systems can be characterised by many parameters and problems which have the effect of making the task of recognition more difficult. Those factors can not be taking into account by the classifier since their accompanying the captured speech.

In fact, the speech contains disfluencies, or periods of silence, and is much more difficult for the classifier to recognise than speech periods. In the other hand, the speaker is not able to say phrases in the same or similar manner each time. Thus, the phoneme recognition systems learn barely to recognize correctly the phoneme. The speaker's voice quality, such as volume and pitch, and breath control should also be taken into account since they distorted the speech. Hence, the physiological elements must be taken into account in order to construct a robust phoneme recognition.

Regrettably, the classifier is not able to take into account all those external factors which are inherent in the signal speech in the recognition process which may lead to a confusion inter-phonemes problem. In this paper, we propose to incorporate a confidence degree which will help the standard classifier SVM to find the optimal hyperplane and classify the phoneme into its class.

4 Belief SVM (B-SVM)

The formulation of the proposed method B-SVM is described in three steps; the first step consists of computing the Euclidean distance $d(Y_i, X_i)$ between the center of the different classes and the phoneme to be classified x_i. The second step is to compute the confidence degree of the membership of the phoneme x_i into the class y_i. Then, those confidence degrees are incorporated into SVM to help to find the optimal hyperplane.

4.1 Geometric Distance

We propose to calculate the geometric distance between X_i and the center of the class CY_i where $i \in (1, \ldots, k)$. We consider that there is a possibility to which the phoneme X_i belongs to one of the classes Y_i. The geometric distance noted $d(CY_i, X_i)$ is calculated using euclidian distance.

The higher value of $d(CY_i, X_i)$ is assigned to the most distant class Y_i from the phoneme X_i and the lower value is associated with the closer class to the phoneme X_i.

4.2 Confidence Degree

This step consists on calculating the confidence degree $m_i(X)$ of each phoneme X_i. It tells the possibility that X_i belongs to the class Y_i. This proposed algorithm allows the generation of confidence degree for each phoneme:
Calculate confidence degrees $m_i(X_i)$

```
begin
   Set of phoneme samples with lables {(X_1,Y_1),...,(X_n,Y_k)};
Initialize confidence degree m_i of samples:
1 if X_i in the ith class, 0 Otherwise;
 C_i:= Center of the ith class;
 m_i(X) := 1/d(C_i, X_i)
 end.
```

4.3 Formulation of Belief SVM

In a space where the data sets are not linearly separable and a multi-class classification problem, SVM constructs $k(k-1)/2$ classifiers for the training data set. In order to convert the multi-class problem into multiple binary problems, the approach one-against-one is used.

In the proposed B-SVM, we incorporate the confidence degree of each phoneme samples into the constraints since the identity is not affected by a scalar multiplication. We normalized the hyperplane to satisfy:

$$\begin{aligned} \mathbf{m(x)}(w^{ij})^T\phi(x_t) + b^{ij} &\geq 1 - \xi_t^{ij}, \text{if } y_t = i \\ \mathbf{m(x)}(w^{ij})^T\phi(x_t) + b^{ij} &\leq 1 - \xi_t^{ij}, \text{if } y_t = j \\ \xi_t^{ij} &\geq 0 \end{aligned} \tag{5}$$

In fact, the incorporation of the confidence degree allows to to reduce the restrictions when the phoneme have a high degree into the class.

In the other hand, the dual representation of the standard SVM allows to maximise the α_L of each phoneme. Thus, with high value of the confidence degree, the subject to $\alpha_i \geq 0$ can be easily satisfied which allows to consider this one as support vector which be helping to decide on the hyperplane.

In the proposed B-SVM, we optimize this formulation to obtain a new dual representation:

$$L_d = \max_{\alpha_i} \sum_{i=1}^{m} \alpha_i - \sum_{i=1}^{m} \sum_{j=1}^{m} m(x_i) m(x_j) \alpha_i \alpha_j y_i y_j \Phi(x_i) \Phi(x_j). \tag{6}$$

In the standard SVM, the class Y_i of a phoneme X is determined by the sign of the decision function. In the proposed B-SVM, the new decision function thus becomes:

$$\sum_{i=1}^{m} \mathbf{m}(\mathbf{x}) \alpha_i y_i \Phi(x_i) + b \tag{7}$$

This new formulation will help for the decision making on the sign of phoneme in order to classify into its class.

5 Hierarchical Phoneme Recognition System

The architecture of our Hierarchical phoneme recognition systems is described in the figure 2:

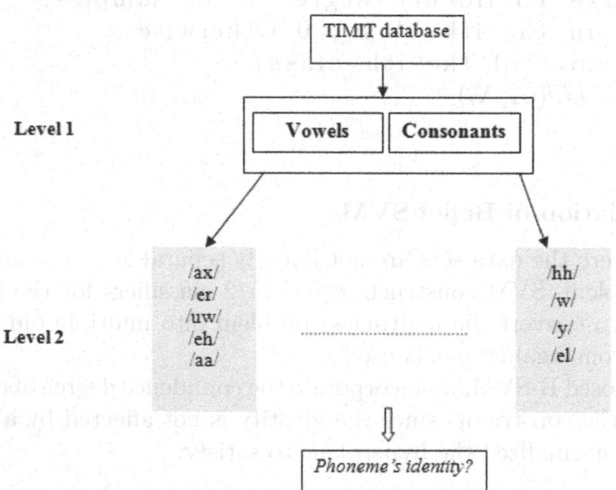

Fig. 2. Hierarchical phoneme recognition system

The recognition system proceeds as follows: (1) conversion from the speech waveform to a spectrogram (2) transforming the spectogram to a Mel-frequency cepstral coefficients (MFCC) spectrum using the Spectral analysis (3) segmentation of the phoneme data sets to sub-phoneme data sets (4) initiating the phoneme recognition at the first level of the system using B-SVM to recognize the class of the unknown phoneme (vowels or consonant) (5) and, finally, initiate the phoneme recognition at the second level of the system using B-SVM to recognize the identity of the unknown phoneme (i.e. aa, ae, ih , etc) [6].

For the proposed recognition system, we have used the MEL frequency cepstral coefficients (MFCC) feature extractor in order to convert the speech waveform to a set of parametric representation.

Davis and Mermelstein were the first who introduced the MFCC concept for automatic speech recognition [8]. The main idea of this algorithm consider that the MFCC are the cepstral coefficients calculated from the mel-frequency warped Fourier transform representation of the log magnitude spectrum. The Delta and the Delta-Delta cepstral coefficients are an estimation of the time derivative of the MFCCs. Including the temporal cepstral derivative aim to improve the performance of speech recognition system.

Those coefficients have shown a determinant capability to capture the transitional characteristics of the speech signal that can contribute to ameliorate the recognition task. The experiments using SVM are done using LibSVM toolbox [10]. The table 1 recapitulate our main choice of experiments conditions:

Table 1. Experimental setup

Method	SVM
γ	1/117
Cost	10
Kernel trick	RBF
Windowing	3-middle aligned Windows
Corpus	TIMIT
Dialect	New England
Frame rate	125/s
Features technique	MFCC
Features number	39
Sampling frequency	16ms

It should be noted that, for the nonlinear B-SVM method, we chose the RBF Kernel and the one-against-one strategy to carry out a multi-class SVM classification. Furthermore, the input speech signal is segmented into frames of 16 ms with optional overlap of $1/3 \sim 1/2$ of the frame size. If the sample rate is 16 kHz and the frame size is 256 sample points, then the frame duration is $16ms$. In addition, the frame rate is 125 frames per second. Each frame has to be multiplied with a Hamming window in order to keep the continuity of the first and the last points in the frame.

6 Experimental Results

The table 2 shows prediction accuracies at both first and second levels of the hierarchical recognition system using seven different phoneme classes.

Table 2. Accuracies of B-SVM and standard SVM

Method	B-SVM			Standard SVM		
	Acc. %	Precision %	Recall %	Acc. %	Precision %	Recall %
Level 1:	95	97	92	93	89	88
Level 2:	84	83	80	78	75	73
Vowels	83	86	82	76	77	71
Occlusives	85	88	82	82	86	81
Nasals	80	78	69	75	63	60
Fricatives	87	76	78	83	69	70
Semi-vowels	87	91	91	84	91	87
Silences	83	71	69	75	62	68
Affricates	83	88	88	71	78	77

To investigate the accuracy of the proposed method B-SVM, we applied the standard SVM and B-SVM to Timit database. It must be pointed out that for the prediction, we used a test samples which were not included in the training stage. We compare the performance of both methods and we note that the performance of B-SVM is better than the standard SVM for all data sets used.

Thus, the following results in the table 1 provides a summary through which we note that the proposed B-SVM shows a remarkable improvement over standard SVM.

7 Conclusion

In our paper, we have proposed a new formulation of SVM using the confidence degree for each object. We have, also, built an hierarchical phoneme recognition system.

The new method B-SVM seems to be more effective than the standard SVM for all tested data sets. The new formulation of SVM succeeded in improving phoneme recognition since the allocation of belief weights for each phoneme have the ability for modeling the similarity between phonemes in order to reduce the confusions inter-phonemes. We compare the performance of both methods and we note that the performance of B-SVM is better than the standard SVM for all data sets used.

References

1. Foster, I., Kesselman, C.: The Grid: Blueprint for a New Computing Infrastructure. Morgan Kaufmann, San Francisco (1999)

2. Vapnik, V.: The nature of statistical learning theory, vol. 8(6), p. 188. Springer, New York (1995)
3. Cortes, C., Vapnik, V.: Support-Vector Networks. Machine Learning 20(3), 273–297 (1995)
4. Schölkopf, B., Burges, C., Vapnik, V.: Extracting Support Data for a Given Task. In: Conference on Knowledge Discovery and Data Mining (1995)
5. Garofolo, J.S., Lamel, L.F., Fisher, W.M., Fiscus, J.G., Pallett, D.S., Dahlgren, N.L., Zue, V.: TIMIT Acoustic-Phonetic Continuous Speech Corpus. In Texas Instruments (TI) and Massachusetts Institute of Technology, MIT (1993)
6. Amami, R., Ben Ayed, D., Ellouze, N.: Phoneme Recognition Using Support Vector Machine and Different Features Representations. In: Omatu, S., Paz Santana, J.F., González, S.R., Molina, J.M., Bernardos, A.M., Rodríguez, J.M.C. (eds.) Distributed Computing and Artificial Intelligence. AISC, vol. 151, pp. 587–595. Springer, Heidelberg (2012)
7. Li, X., Wang, L., Sung, E.: Adaboost with SVM-based compnent classifers. Engineering Applications of Artificial Intelligence 21, 785–795 (2008)
8. Davis, S.B., Mermelstein, P.: Comparison of parametric representations for monosyllabic word recognition in continuously spoken sentences. Acoust Speech Signal Processing 28(4), 357–366 (1980)
9. Schapire, R.E., Singer, Y.: Improved Boosting Algorithms Using Confidence-rated Predictions. Machine Learning 37(3), 297–336 (1999)
10. Chang, C.C., Lin, C.J.: LIBSVM: a Library for Support Vector Machines, Department of Computer Science National Taiwan University, Taipei, Taiwan (2011)
11. Amami, R., Ben Ayed, D., Ellouze, N.: Practical Selection of SVM Supervised Parameters with Different Feature Representations for Vowel Recognition. International Journal of Digital Content Technology and its Applications 7, 418–424 (2013)
12. Borrajo, M.L., Baruque, B., Corchado, E., Bajo, J., Corchado, J.M.: Hybrid neural intelligent system to predict business failure in small-to-medium-size enterprises. International Journal of Neural Systems 21(04), 277–296 (2011)
13. Abraham, A.: Special issue: Hybrid approaches for approximate reasoning. Journal of Intelligent and Fuzzy Systems 23(2-3), 41–42 (2012)

Evaluation of Bounding Box Level Fusion of Single Target Video Object Trackers

Rafael Martín and José M. Martínez

Video Processing and Understanding Lab, Universidad Autónoma de Madrid, Spain
{rafael.martinn,josem.martinez}@uam.es
www-vpu.eps.uam.es

Abstract. The main objective of this work is to evaluate a simple fusion system which improves the performance of several object trackers, within a methodological and rigorous evaluation framework. The considered algorithms are monocamera single target trackers.

After analyzing in detail the state of the art, an evaluation framework is selected and presented. The sequences selected in this evaluation try to represent different real scenes and conditions. Then, clasical and modern tracking algorithms are selected and evaluated individually, in order to understand their performance in different scenarios and problems. Finally, some fusion methods are described and evaluated, comparing their results with the results of the individual tracking algorithms.

Keywords: Computer Vision, Object Tracking, Fusion, Evaluation.

1 Introduction

Computer Vision is a field whose goal is to automate the processing of images to understand their content. This information is used to solve specific tasks or to understand what happens in the scene. Object tracking is one of the most important tasks in computer vision.

There are many algorithms for object tracking in the state of the art, but none of the algorithms works correctly in all situations. Furthermore, there is no common evaluation framework, so most of the authors usually evaluate their algorithms using their own criteria. As each traker works well depending on the scenario, the fusion of multiple tracking algorithms can help to solve this problem.

The final objective of this work is to create a fusion system which improves the performance of several single target object trackers, within a methodological and rigorous evaluation framework. Therefore, the work is divided in three main steps. Firstly, an evaluation framework will be proposed. Secondly, some individual video object tracking algorithms, extracted from the state of the art, will be selected. Finally, some fusion methods will be tested with the aim of improving the individual tracker results.

M. Polycarpou et al. (Eds.): HAIS 2014, LNAI 8480, pp. 200–210, 2014.
© Springer International Publishing Switzerland 2014

2 State of the Art

Video object tracking[1] is the process of locating (or estimating) one or more moving objects of interest over time using sequences acquired by one or more cameras. In [2], the problem is defined as the task of following one or more objects in a scene, from their first appearance to their exit. In its simplest form, tracking can be defined[3] as the problem of estimating the trajectory of an object in the image plane as it moves around a scene. Since the amount of data to be processed is very large, object tracking is a task of hight complexity and great processing time consumption.

An object may be anything of interest within the scene that can be detected, and depends on the requirements of the application. In a real tracking situation, both background and tracked object(s) are allowed to vary, what difficults the tracking task. A set of constraints can be put to make this problem solvable. The more the constraints, the easier to solve the problem. Some of the constraints that are generally considered during object tracking are[2]: object motion is smooth with no abrupt changes, there are no sudden changes in the background, changes in the appearance of the object are gradual, fixed camera scenarios, limited number and size of objects or limited amount of occlusions.

There are different stages of analysis in the video analysis systems, some of them are presented below. The image segmentation is the partitioning of a digital image into two or more regions. Video tracking is the process of locating one or more moving objects over time. Event detection involves detecting specific actions that occur in a sequence. In practice, the results of the different stages of analysis are interconnected (for example, an erroneous foreground/background segmentation significantly complicates tracking objects). This has led to the development of techniques using the results of the steps of high-level analysis to improve the results obtained in low-level stages[4].

2.1 Individual Tracking Algorithms

There are multiple tracking algorithms in the state of the art. The trackers used in this work are: Template Matching (TM)[5], Mean-Shift (MS)[6], Particle Filter-based Colour tracking (PFC)[7], Lucas-Kanade tracking (LK)[8], Incremental learning for robust Visual Tracking (IVT) [9], Tracking Learning Detection (TLD)[10], Corrected Background Weighted Histogram tracker (CBWH) [11] and Scale and Orientation Adaptive Mean-Shift Tracking (SOAMST) [12]. The first four tracking algorithms have been selected because they are classical and general tracking systems. The last four have been chosen because they are modern trackers with contrasted and remarkable results. Below is a summary describing each of them.

The Template Matching tracking algorithm (TM)[5] represents the target model by the subimage corresponding to the given rectangular region of interest to be tracked.

The Mean-Shift tracking algorithm (MS)[6] represents the target model by the colour histogram of all pixels belonging to the given elliptical or rectangular region of interest to be tracked. Pixels close to the target center have a larger weight than those away from it..

Similarly to the colour-based mean shift tracker summarized above, the Particle Filter-based Colour tracking algorithm (PFC)[7] represents the target model by the colour histogram. However, differently to the mean shift tracker, the candidate position of the target model in the current video frame is found as a weighted average of alternative candidate positions, each referred to as a particle.

The Lukas-Kanade tracking algorithm (LK)[8] can be considered to be a generalization of the above template matching algorithm that allows for small affine transformations (translation, rotation, scaling, shear mapping, etc.) of the target model.

The Incremental learning for robust Visual Tracking algorithm (IVT)[9] incrementally learns a low dimensional eigenbasis representation, adapting online to changes in the appearance of the target. The model update, based on incremental algorithms for principal component analysis, includes two features: a method for updating the sample mean, and a forgetting factor to ensure less modelling power is expended fitting older observations.

The Tracking Learning Detection algorithm (TLD)[10] can be seen as a combination of tracking and detection. The tracking component estimates the object motion between consecutive frames. Detector treats every frame as independent and performs full scanning of the image to localize all appearances that have been observed and learned in the past.

The Corrected Background-Weighted Histogram tracking algorithm (CBWH) [11] is a variation of the original colour-based mean-shift technique [6] that modifies the stage that reduces the interference of background pixels. This algorithm transforms the histogram of the target model using information of a neighborhood of the initial object position.

The last algorithm considered is the Scale and Orientation Adaptive Mean-Shift Tracking algorithm (SOAMST) [12]. This algorithm is a variation of the original colour-based mean-shift technique [6] that is able to update the scale and orientation of the target model during the tracking process.

2.2 Fusion

Multiply and as much independent as possible sources of information are commonly combined in signal processing to improve the result of an algorithm creating hybrid systems[13][14]. Using multiple independent features also improves the performance and the robustness of a video tracker. The fusion strategies (for video object tracking) can be classified in two different architectures[15][1], parallel and sequential, and in two main levels[1], tracker-level fusion and measurement level fusion.

In the parallel architecture, each tracker is executed independently and the result of the fusion is the most confident tracker or the best combination of trackers. In the sequential or cascade architecture, trackers are evaluated sequentially: if the first tracker returns a high confidence[1], its result is chosen as the fusion result; otherwise, the next tracker is evaluated and the process applied is repeated.

Fusion at tracker level models single-feature tracking algorithms as black boxes. The video tracking fusion problem is redefined by modeling the interaction between outputs of each tracker, which can run in parallel or in cascade (sequentially). Fusion can use classical combination techniques (average, maximum, minimum, median,...)[16], combine the resulting Probability Density Function (PDF) of each algorithm[17], consider variable weights for the algorithms[17][18], use a probabilistic approach[19][20], add a later prediction stage[21], combine the resulting bounding box of each tracker[20][22] or combine results at pixel (segmentation) level[4]. For the fusion of multiple features at measurement level, the measurements are combined internally by the tracking algorithm. Measurement level fusion can take place with a variety of mechanisms, such as using Bayesian methods[23][24], particle filtering[25], estimating mutual information[9][26] or calculating correlation[27].

There are many classical simple fusion techniques that can be applied to object tracking, as those described in [16], where a detailed study of several possible combinations is presented. Although this reference is not focused on visual tracking, many of the combinations presented can be applied to it. The main classic combination techniques presented are majority vote, weighted majority vote, naive bayes combination, multinomial methods and other approximations such as those mentioned previously (mean, median, ...).

3 Evaluation Framework

The evaluation of object tracking algorithms is necessary to validate their correct performance and robustness. This section presents the content set and the metrics considered.

To create the dataset used in this work, the authors have collected a large pool of the sequences that have been used by various authors in the tracking community. Then, the most interesting ones have been selected, focusing on the main problems that the developed trackers can face. This is why this dataset has been selected instead of others from the state of the art, as SPEVI[28], ETISEO[29], PETS[30], CAVIAR[31] or VISOR[32].

For the selection of the evaluation metrics, multiple metrics from the state of the art have been considered (SFDA[33], ATA[33], Overlap[34], AUC[34], CT[35], TC[35] and CoTPS[36]). As indicated in the corresponding subsection, a correlation study has been performed, resulting in a very high correlation among them.

[1] This confidence measure must be given by the tracker.

3.1 Dataset

The content set used was provided by the VOT2013 challenge[2] trying to independently address the different problems that a tracker can face. The main criteria for dataset selection was that the dataset should represent various realistic scenes and conditions, including occlusions, illumination changes, scale changes, rotations, etc. The dataset contains 16 videos with a duration between 172 and 770 frames. More information of each one of the sequences can be obtained from the dataset website.

The VOT2013 dataset also provides the ground truth files. The relevant target in each sequence has been manually annotated by placing a bounding box over the object in each frame.

3.2 Metrics

The metrics that have been considered for the evaluation framework are: Sequence Frame Detection Accuracy[33], Average Tracking Accuracy[33], Overlap [34], Area Under the lost track ratio Curve[34], Closeness of Track[35], Track Completeness[35] and Combined Tracking Performance Score[36]. A metric correlation study has been performed[37], obtaining redundancy between all the metrics presented (correlation around 0,9). Therefore, the chosen metric is the SFDA, defined below. This metric has been chosen for two main reasons: its correlation with respect to other metrics is one of the the highest. SFDA also considers and penalizes both false positives and false negatives.

The Sequence Frame Detection Accuracy (SFDA)[33] measure calculates in each frame the spatial overlap between the estimated target location and the ground-truth annotation. This mapping is optimized on a frame-by-frame basis. It contains information regarding the number of objects detected, missed detections, false positives and spatial overlap, providing a ratio of the spatial intersection and union between two object locations. The total sum of data from the Frame Detection Accuracy (FDA) is then normalized to the number of frames including ground-truth targets. Therefore, SFDA can be seen as the average of the FDA over all the relevant frames in the sequence. SFDA ranges from 0 to 1; the higher the value, the better.

$$\mathbf{SFDA} = \frac{\sum_{t=1}^{t=Nframes} FDA(t)}{\sum_{t=1}^{t=Nframes} \exists(N_G^{(t)} OR\, N_D^{(t)})} \tag{1}$$

$$FDA(t) = \frac{Overlap\, ratio}{N_G^{(t)} + N_D^{(t)}} \tag{2}$$

$$Overlap\, ratio = \sum_{i=1}^{N_{mapped}^{(t)}} \frac{|G_i^{(t)} \cap D_i^{(t)}|}{|G_i^{(t)} \cup D_i^{(t)}|} \tag{3}$$

[2] http://votchallenge.net/

Where:
$G_i^{(t)}$ denotes the i-th ground-truth object in frame t.
$D_i^{(t)}$ denotes the i-th detected object in frame t.
$N_G^{(t)}$ and $N_D^{(t)}$ denote the number of ground-truth objects and the number of detected objects in frame t, respectively.
N_{frames} is the number of frames in the sequence.
$N_{mapped}^{(t)}$ is the number of mapped ground truth and detected object pairs in frame t (frame level mapping).

4 Fusion

In this section, the fusion methods considered in this work are described. After defining them, tracking results on the dataset are presented.

The implemented fusion methods have been selected based on its simplicity and independence(i.e., only using its outputs - bounding boxes).

Fusion considered uses only the resulting bounding box of each of the individual trackers. For each frame, the bounding box resulting from the processing of each single tracking algorithm is extracted, and then the corresponding fusion is performed. As only the resulting bounding box from each tracker is used for the fusion, no matter what kind of single tracker is used for the fusion and any tracker can be used for these types of fusion. As the cost of fusing the outputs of each tracker is significantly lower than the cost of processing a frame for each independent tracker, the final cost would be similar to the cost of the slower independent tracker if they are properly parallelized.

The first considered fusion method (F1_Mean) is based on calculating the mean of the bounding box values. Starting from all available resulting bounding boxes, the mean of the center coordinates of the bounding boxes (x0, y0), and of the height and width of the bounding boxes are calculated. These values are rounded to the nearest pixel value. In this way the new values that define the bounding box resulting from the fusion are obtained.

The second considered fusion method (F2_Median) is the median fusion. This method is very similar to media fusion method, except that in this case the operation performed is the median: the median of the center coordinates of the bounding boxes (x0, y0), and of the height and width of the bounding boxes are calculated. As in the previous fusion method, the values are rounded to the nearest pixel value.

Majority voting fusion (F3_Major1 to F10_Major8) is based on the selection of the resulting bounding box from the areas of the frame in which a minimum number of individual trackers (N) coincide in indicating that the object is present. For a ≥N majority voting, the fusion resulting bounding box corresponds to the rectangle which contains all the areas in which at least N trackers agree that the object is located in that area.

There are other works in the state of the art which also use the resulting bounding boxes from each tracker to estimate the fusion. In the work presented in [20], a crowdsourcing tracking method is proposed. Under the sequential Monte

Carlo framework, both the hidden ground truth bounding box and the confidence of each tracker is inferred. The other work that uses the resulting bounding boxes of the trackers is [22]. Similarly to the previous case, a confidence score is estimated based on the tracking performance of each tracker and the consistency performance among different trackers. The bounding box selected is the one with the maximum confidence score. In the case of the fusion presented in this paper, the method is simpler than the two cited works, as a confidence measure is not calculated but simply combining different bounding boxes in the most efficient possible way, avoiding assumptions which may be erroneous. Unlike [22], in the proposed fusion method the resulting bounding box, instead of being the output of a single tracker, is a combination of the output of individual trackers.

5 Experimental Results

Figure 1 shows the SFDA score of the ten fusion methods considered: mean, median and eight possible majority voting (N from ≥1 to ≥8). Majority voting ≥ 1 corresponds to logical OR, and majority voting $\geq N_{max}$ corresponds to logical AND, where N_{max} is the maximum number of considered trackers. The results of the individual trackers have been added to facilitate the comparison between all the scores.

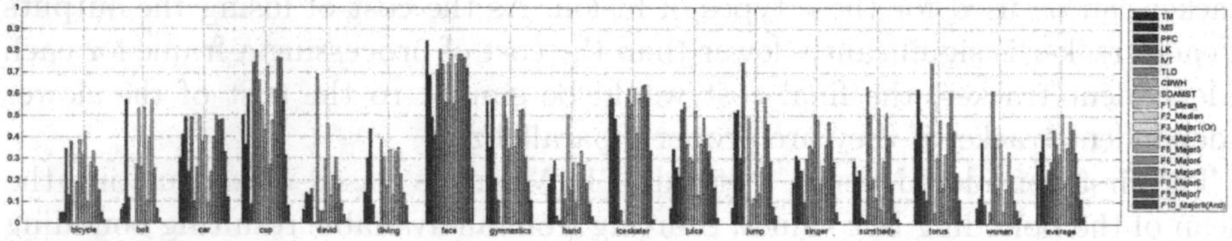

Fig. 1. Fusion SFDA result

As shown in figure 1, the results of individual trackers present high variations depending on the evaluated sequence. The individual trackers with the best performance are CBWH and PFC. In the case of the fusion trackers, the best scores are observed for the median fusion and the majority voting fusion (in this last case, for the central N values, in particular N=3 and N=4).

When any of the individual tracking algorithms obtains a significantly better score than the others, the fusion scores do not reach such level, so in these cases the fusion does not improve that individual performance. This situation occurs in the sequences *david*, *hand*, *jump*, *sunshade*, *torus* and *woman*.

Another situation that occurs in some sequences is that many of the individual algoritgms perform best with similar values among them. In these cases, the best fusion scores are similar to those obtained by the best individual algorithms, equaling their performance closely. This situation occurs in the sequences *car*, *gymnastics* and *iceskater*.

An interesting result is obtained with the sequence *bolt*. In this case, just two (PFC and SOAMST) of the eight individual tracking algorithms present scores around 5.5, being the third score below 0.3. Two fusions are obtained with similar values to the best of the individual algorithm scores. A majority of the algorithms working correctly is not necessary for obtaining a good fusion result. Another example of such situations is the case of the *singer* sequence, where there are three fusion scores which are 0,1 higher than the best score of the independent tracking algorithms.

After analyzing the obtained results, the most interesting aspect of the studied fusions is the versatility of some of them. The tracking fusions considered, as a combination of individual trackers, work well in most cases.

The tables contained in this section present the individual average scores for each metric and each individual tracker or fusion. These average scores are obtained as the average value of each tracker in all the evaluated sequences.

Table 1 presents the average scores of both individual trackers as fusions.

Table 1. Average SFDA scores

	TM	MS	PFC	LK	IVT	TLD	CBWH	SOAMST
SFDA	0,273	0,333	0,412	0,183	0,251	0,287	0,433	0,368

	F1	**F2**	**F3**	**F4**	**F5**	**F6**	**F7**	**F8**	**F9**	**F10**
SFDA	0,323	0,508	0,188	0,352	0,475	0,435	0,329	0,221	0,113	0,032

To facilitate the results comparison, table 2 shows the percentual difference between the individual trackers and fusions, obtained using equation 4.

$$Perc.diff. = \frac{fusion\ score - individual\ score}{individual\ score} \tag{4}$$

Table 2. Percentual difference (percentage) SFDA average score between fusion trackers and individual algorithms trackers

	TM	MS	PFC	LK	IVT	TLD	CBWH	SOAMST
F1_Mean	18,1	-3,0	-21,6	76,8	28,5	12,6	-25,4	-12,3
F2_Median	**85,9**	**52,7**	**23,4**	**178,4**	**102,3**	**77,2**	**17,5**	**38,1**
F3_Major1	-31,1	-43,4	-54,3	3,1	-25,1	-34,4	-56,5	-48,9
F4_Major2	28,9	5,9	-14,4	93,0	40,2	22,8	-18,6	-4,3
F5_Major3	73,8	42,8	15,4	160,3	89,1	65,7	9,8	29,1
F6_Major4	59,3	30,9	5,8	138,6	73,3	51,8	0,7	18,3
F7_Major5	20,3	-1,2	-20,1	80,1	30,9	14,7	-24,0	-10,7
F8_Major6	-19,2	-33,6	-46,3	21,1	-12,0	-23,0	-48,9	-40,0
F9_Major7	-58,5	-65,9	-72,5	-37,9	-54,9	-60,5	-73,8	-69,2
F10_Major8	-88,1	-90,2	-92,1	-82,2	-87,1	-88,7	-92,5	-91,2

6 Conclusion

The work presented in this paper is focused on video object tracking. This field of study is one of the most popular in Computer Vision, so there is abundant literature, algorithms, metrics, datasets, etc., about this subject.

There are multiple datasets for video object tracking. Depending on the objective of your work, there are some appropriate datasets. One possibility is to combine these datasets to form a new one that suits your needs, as is the case of the dataset used in this work. About the metrics, there are also multiple possibilities for evaluating a video object tracker. The main differences between the metrics are based on the penalties that are attributed to the errors (false positives, false negatives, target losses ...).

About tracking algorithms, there are many publications that present their own tracking algorithms, and many others which try to improve some aspect or limitation of existing algorithms. As observed in the results of individual trackers, all tracking algorithms have limitations in certain scenarios, and only work correctly in those scenarios for which they were designed.

With the (simple) fusions performed, more generalized tracking approaches have been obtained, which are able to function reasonably well in most situations (covered by the selected dataset), overcoming the problem of specialization observed in the individual trackers.

The work described in this paper analyzes several tracking algorithms from the state of the art and presents methods to combine them efficiently. Despite this, a tracker that performs properly in all possible situations has not yet been achieved, as there are problems which are not solved with the used algorithms. Moreover, there are new scenarios not covered in this work. We identify some main areas for future work. With respect to individual trackers, new algorithms can be analyzed and their results can be compared with the previous algoritms and be incoporated in the fusion approaches. Thanks to the evaluation framework, the results of the new algorithm sets can be easily compared with the reference algorithm set results, presented in this paper. Also, new fusion methods can be studied and evaluated, for example, by adding weights to the different algorithms depending on its accuracy. Another possibility is to add feedback to the system, so that the result of each frame can be used to adjust the analysis of the subsequent frames. In this last case, special attention should be paid to the learning-based algorithms as, after correcting the position of the object, the learning must be performed with the corrected region position of the object.

Acknowledgment. This work has been partially supported by the Spanish Government (TEC2011-25995).

References

1. Maggio, E., Cavallaro, A.: Video Tracking: Theory and Practice. Wiley (2011)
2. Jalal, A.S., Singh, V.: The state-of-the-art in visual object tracking. Informatica 36(3), 227–248 (2012)

3. Yilmaz, A., Javed, O., Shah, M.: Object tracking: A survey. ACM Computing Surveys 38(4), 1–45 (2006)
4. Heber, M., Godec, M., Rüther, M., Roth, P.M., Bischof, H.: Segmentation-based tracking by support fusion. Computer Vision and Image Understanding 117(6), 573–586 (2013)
5. Fukunaga, K., Hostetler, L.: The estimation of the gradient of a density function, with applications in pattern recognition. IEEE Trans. on Information Theory 21(1), 32–40 (1975)
6. Comaniciu, D., Ramesh, V., Meer, P.: Kernel-based object tracking. IEEE Trans. on Pattern Analysis and Machine Intelligence 25(5), 564–577 (2003)
7. Nummiaro, K., Koller-Meier, E., Gool, L.V.: An adaptive colour-based particle filter. Image and Vision Computing 21(1), 99–110 (2002)
8. Baker, S., Matthews, I.: Lucas-kanade 20 years on: A unifying framework. International Journal of Computer Vision 56(3), 221–255 (2004)
9. Ross, D.A., Lim, J., Lin, R.S., Yang, M.H.: Incremental learning for robust visual tracking. International Journal of Computer Vision 77(1-3), 125–141 (2008)
10. Kalal, Z., Mikolajczyk, K., Matas, J.: Tracking-learning-detection. IEEE Trans. on Pattern Analysis and Machine Intelligence 34(7), 1409–1422 (2011)
11. Ning, J., Zhang, L., Zhang, D., Wu, C.: Robust mean-shift tracking with corrected background-weighted histogram. IET Computer Vision 6(1), 62–69 (2012)
12. Ning, J., Zhang, L., Zhang, D., Wu, C.: Scale and orientation adaptive mean shift tracking. IET Computer Vision 6(1), 52–61 (2012)
13. Corchado, E., Wozniak, M., Abraham, A., de Carvalho, A.C.P.L.F., Snásel, V.: Special issue: Recent trends in intelligent data analysis. Neurocomputing 126, 1–2 (2014)
14. Abraham, A.: Special issue: Hybrid approaches for approximate reasoning. Journal of Intelligent and Fuzzy Systems 23(2), 41–42 (2012)
15. Stenger, B., Woodley, T., Cipolla, R.: Learning to track with multiple observers. In: Proc of. Computer Vision and Pattern Recognition, pp. 2647–2654 (2009)
16. Kuncheva, L.I.: Combining Pattern Classifiers: Methods and Algorithms. Wiley-Interscience (2004)
17. Leichter, I., Lindenbaum, M., Rivlin, E.: A general framework for combining visual trackers, the black boxes approach. International Journal of Computer Vision 67, 343–363 (2006)
18. Avidan, S.: Ensemble tracking. IEEE Trans. on Pattern Analysis and Machine Intelligence 29(2), 261–271 (2007)
19. Zhong, B., Yao, H., Chen, S., Ji, R., Yuan, X., Liu, S., Gao, W.: Visual tracking via weakly supervised learning from multiple imperfect oracles. In: Proc of. Computer Vision and Pattern Recognition, pp. 1323–1330 (2010)
20. Liu, W., Hauptmann, A.G.: A crowdsourcing approach to tracker fusion. Tech. rep., Carnegie Mellon University (2011)
21. McCane, B., Galvin, B., Novins, K.: Algorithmic fusion for more robust feature tracking. International Journal of Computer Vision 49(1), 79–89 (2002)
22. Zhang, L., Gao, Y., Hauptmann, A., Ji, R., Ding, G., Super, B.: Symbiotic black-box tracker. In: Proc. of Advances in Multimedia Modeling, pp. 126–137 (2012)
23. Kwon, J., Lee, K.M.: Visual tracking decomposition. In: Proc. of Computer Vision and Pattern Recognition, pp. 1269–1276 (2010)
24. Kwon, J., Lee, K.M.: Tracking by sampling trackers. In: Proc. of International Conference on Computer Vision, pp. 1195–1202 (2011)

25. Wang, H., Liu, C., Xu, L., Tang, M., Wu, X.: Multiple feature fusion for tracking of moving objects in video surveillance. Computational Intelligence and Security 1, 554–559 (2008)
26. Conaire, C.O., O'Connor, N.E., Smeaton, A.F.: Detector adaptation by maximising agreement between independent data sources. In: Proc. of Computer Vision and Pattern Recognition, pp. 1–6 (2007)
27. SanMiguel, J.C., Martinez, J.M.: Shadow detection in video surveillance by maximizing agreement between indep. detectors. In: Proc. of International Conference on Image Processing, pp. 1141–1144 (2009)
28. SPEVI, surveillance performance evaluation initiative, `http://www.eecs.qmul.ac.uk/andrea/spevi.html`
29. Munder, S., Gavrila, D.M.: An experimental study on pedestrian classification. IEEE Trans. on Pattern Analysis and Machine Intelligence 28(11), 1863–1868 (2006)
30. PETS, IEEE int. workshop perform. eval. trackking surveillance
31. CAVIAR, Context aware vision using image-based active recognition, `http://homepages.inf.ed.ac.uk/rbf/caviar/`
32. Vezzani, R., Cucchiara, R.: Video surveillance online repository (visor): an integrated framework. Multimedia Tools and Applications 50(2), 359–380 (2010)
33. Kasturi, R., Goldgof, D., Soundararajan, P., Manohar, V., Garofolo, J., Bowers, R., Boonstra, M., Korzhova, V., Zhang, J.: Framework for performance evaluation of face, text, and vehicle detection and tracking in video: Data, metrics, and protocol. IEEE Trans. on Pattern Analysis and Machine Intelligence 31(2), 319–336 (2009)
34. Nawaz, T., Cavallaro, A.: Pft: A protocol for evaluating video trackers. In: Proc. of International Conference on Image Processing, pp. 2325–2328 (2011)
35. Yin, F., Makris, D., Velastin, S.A.: Performance evaluation of object tracking algorithms. In: PETS, pp. 17–24 (2007)
36. Nawaz, T., Cavallaro, A.: A protocol for evaluating video trackers under real-world conditions. IEEE Trans. on Image Processing 22, 1354–1361 (2012)
37. Martín, R., Martínez, J.M.: Correlation study of video object trackers evaluation metrics. IET Electronics Letters 50(5), 361–363 (2014)

A Hybrid System of Signature Recognition Using Video and Similarity Measures

Rafal Doroz, Krzysztof Wrobel, and Mateusz Watroba

Institute of Computer Science, University of Silesia,
ul. Bedzinska 39, 41-200 Sosnowiec, Poland
{rafal.doroz,krzysztof.wrobel}@us.edu.pl,
http://zsk.tech.us.edu.pl,http://www.biometrics.us.edu.pl

Abstract. The method proposed in this paper uses signatures recorded with the use of four webcams. In the method a different sets of signature features and similarity measures can be used. Additionally, the influence of individual features on the signature similarity value has been examined. Practical experiments were also conducted with the own signatures' database and confirmed that results obtained are promising.

Keywords: biometrics hybrid system, signature recognition, dynamic features, similarity measures.

1 Introduction

Hybrid intelligent systems are today very popular due to their capabilities in handling many real world complex problems. They have the opportunity to use both, knowledge and raw data to solve problems in many multidisciplinary researches - for example in analyzing of medical images, biometrics patterns and so on [3], [7], [12], [13], [31]. In preseted work, a biometrics hybrid system based on signature recognition has been proposed.

Biometrics is a field of science that uses biological and behavioural features to recognize and verify the identity of people [4], [8], [11], [27]. Biometric authentication becomes a more and more popular alternative to the security systems based e.g. on passwords or magnetic cards.

Handwritten signature is one of the oldest and longest used methods for personal verification and identification [1], [8], [27]. Thanks to wide public acceptance, it has become an indispensable form of reliable identification confirmation. There are two methods for authentication with the use of a signature: the static method based on the image of a previously put signature and the dynamic method, which will be the main subject of this study. Dynamic method consists in registration of the moment of putting a signature, while the relevant features obtained in this way, such as the time of signing or pen position, are compared with the reference features. For this purpose a many techniques are used, e.g. methods based on neural networks or Hidden Markov Models (HMM) [10], [20]. There are also methods, which compare signatures with the use of specific similarity measures (distances) [6], [27].

M. Polycarpou et al. (Eds.): HAIS 2014, LNAI 8480, pp. 211–220, 2014.
© Springer International Publishing Switzerland 2014

Digital cameras in recent years have become more and more widely used in different spheres of life. Image recording, as their primary task, has not changed radically, however the use itself has changed. Cameras perform their function well not only for private purposes, but also in monitoring systems and industry as webcams, as well as in various fields of science, inter alia, in problems associated with biometrics.

Solutions that use cameras in the signature acquisition process have also applications in biometric systems. Their use for signature recognition is described in [21], [35]. One and seven webcams have been used for data acquisition under these studies. The Monte Carlo method was employed to track the tip of a ballpoint pen.

The method for personal recognition proposed in this paper uses signatures recorded with the use of four webcams. Novelty is the proposed new similarity coefficient that takes into account the impact of the data acquired from individual cameras on a signature recognition effectiveness.

2 The Proposed Research Method

2.1 The Test Bench

In the first stage of the study, a test bench for registration of signatures with the use of webcams was built. The main assumption for the test bench was its simple, cheap and easy to make construction. A photo and a diagram of the test bench are shown in Fig. 1.

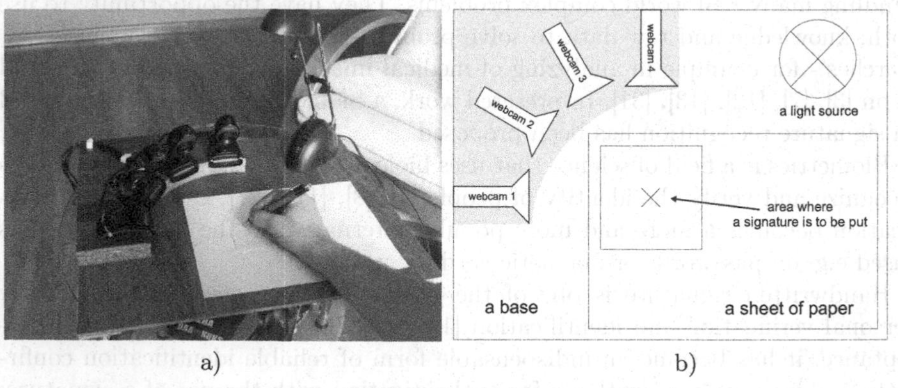

Fig. 1. a) Photo of the test bench, b) pictorial diagram of the test bench (top view)

The test bench consists of the following components:

- A base,
- Four webcams,
- A light source,
- A sheet of paper representing the area where a signature is to be put.

Fig. 2. A sample image obtained from one of the cameras

The base of the test bench is made from a 50 cm wide and 40 cm long plate. An adequate thickness of the plate ensures a proper stiffness for the whole structure and a solid base for the remaining components mounted on it. Four cameras were used for data acquisition. These are standard webcams. Fig. 2 shows a sample image obtained from one of the cameras.

The cameras were mounted at a height of 3 cm above the level of the area on which a signature is to be put. In this way, the problem of covering the pen tip by the hand of a right-handed user was eliminated. The arrangement of individual cameras on the test bench is shown in Fig. 1b. Each camera was set in such a way, so that the centre of the image recorded by it coincides with the centre of the area, on which a signature is to be put. Signatures were put on sheets sized 7.5 cm x 7.5 cm. The remaining area of the base was covered with a white sheet of paper. The purpose of it was to standardize the background recorded by the cameras and to eliminate the unnecessary interferences or noise caused by e.g. the colour of the base. The lighting conditions during the system operation constitute another important aspect of the test bench. They have a huge impact on the quality of the image recorded by the cameras. Based on the tests performed, it was found that the test bench must be evenly illuminated. The lighting conditions should not change radically during the data acquisition, as this leads to distortions and errors. Fixed lighting conditions were ensured by adding an additional, constant source of light. A lamp with a power of 20 watts along with a boom that allows placing the bulb over the centre of the signature was installed in the upper right corner of the test bench. During the signature acquisition, the area of the image containing the tip of the pen was detected in images obtained from the cameras. This area was treated then as the reference image. A sample image from a camera with a marked area containing the template is shown in Fig. 3.

Detection of the template on the recorded images consisted in finding their fragment corresponding to the template. For this purpose, the Template Matching method was used [5], [17]. The centre of an image fragment, which matches best the template, was used to calculate the coordinates of the pen position.

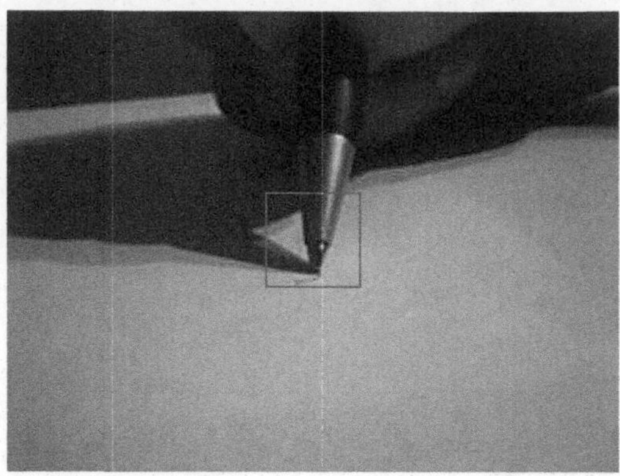

Fig. 3. Sample image with a marked area containing the template

2.2 Data Acquisition

A database of user signatures has been created with the use of the test bench presented earlier. The signatures were stored in the database in the form of data files. Each row of the file contains the information obtained from the processed image for each of the four cameras. It consists of a set of numbers separated by spaces, which in turn mean:

- the coordinate x of the registered signature point,
- the coordinate y of the registered signature point,
- the time t of registering a point with the coordinates (x, y),
- the velocity v of marker's movement between two points.

Table 1 presents a sample file containing the data of a signature.

2.3 Determining the Similarity of Signatures

The values of the similarity between signatures were determined separately for each of the three features: X, Y, V and four cameras designated as: C_1, C_2, C_3, C_4. For such assumptions, the formula for the similarity between the P and S signatures is as follows:

$$sim(P, S) = M_f^{C_n}(P, S), \tag{1}$$

where:
M - similarity coefficient or other signature comparison method,
C_n - camera number, $C_n \in \{C_1, C_2, C_3, C_4\}$,
f - the feature being compared $f \in \{X, Y, V\}$.

For example, the similarity between signatures determined on the basis of the feature Y registered by the camera C_2 takes the following form:

$$sim(P, S) = M_Y^{C_2}(P, S). \tag{2}$$

Table 1. File containing the data of a signature

camera	1			camera	2			camera	3			camera	4		
x	y	t	v	x	y	t	v	x	y	t	v	x	y	t	v
149	151	92	0.00	184	151	92	0.00	208	135	92	0.35	215	123	92	0.00
155	151	96	0.25	184	151	96	0.00	208	135	96	0.00	215	121	96	0.00
155	151	100	0.00	189	150	100	0.56	208	135	100	0.35	215	121	100	0.00
160	151	104	0.75	189	150	104	0.79	210	133	104	0.00	215	119	104	0.56
160	151	108	0.00	193	148	108	0.00	212	131	108	0.90	215	119	108	0.00
160	151	112	1.50	193	148	112	0.00	212	131	112	0.00	214	117	112	0.50
160	151	116	0.00	196	147	116	1.28	212	131	116	0.00	214	117	116	0.00
165	151	120	1.25	196	147	120	0.00	213	131	120	0.71	214	117	120	0.50
165	151	124	0.00	196	147	124	1.12	213	131	124	0.71	214	116	124	0.00
165	151	128	0.00	196	147	128	0.00	213	130	128	0.00	214	116	128	0.56
167	151	132	0.00	196	147	132	0.79	213	130	132	0.00	214	116	132	0.00
167	151	136	1.25	196	147	136	0.00	213	130	136	0.25	214	116	136	0.00
		⋮				⋮				⋮				⋮	

Images recorded by individual cameras differ from each other. This is affected by the location of the cameras. In order to determine the influence of the data from each camera on the effectiveness of signature recognition, the wC_1, wC_2, wC_3, and wC_4 weights were assigned respectively to each camera. It has been assumed that the values of individual weights must meet the following conditions:

1. $wC_1, wC_2, wC_3, wC_4 \in [0, 1]$,
2. $wC_1 + wC_2 + wC_3 + wC_4 = 1$.

The final formula for the similarity between the P and S signatures for a given feature f is as follows:

$$sim_f(P, S) = \sum_{i=1}^{4} wC_i * M_f^{C_i}(P, S). \tag{3}$$

A comparison of signatures using the coefficient given by the formula (3) is possible only if the signatures are of an equal length. In practice, this condition is not always fulfilled. In order to eliminate this problem, the DTW method was used in the study. This method is described in detail in [26].

The advantage of the presented approach is the possibility of using any similarity coefficients or data comparison methods. Under the research part, 10 similarity coefficients had been tested and then those were selected, which allowed obtaining the smallest classification error.

3 The Course and Results of the Studies

The studies were carried out on the basis of 200 signatures collected from 40 people. Each person put four reference signatures and one test signature. EER [4] was

Table 2. The best results obtained for all combinations of weights, methods and features

Weights				Method	Feature	EER [%]
wC_1	wC_2	wC_3	wC_4			
0.25	0.75	0.00	0.00	R^2	X	7.0
0.00	1.00	0.00	0.00	R^2	X	7.8
0.50	0.50	0.00	0.00	R^2	X	8.0
0.00	0.75	0.00	0.25	R^2	Y	8.0
0.25	0.25	0.00	0.50	Soergel	Y	8.0
0.50	0.25	0.00	0.25	Gower	Y	8.0
0.00	0.50	0.00	0.50	Soergel	Y	8.4
0.25	0.50	0.00	0.25	R^2	Y	8.5
0.75	0.00	0.00	0.25	Gower	Y	8.6
0.00	0.25	0.00	0.75	Soergel	Y	8.7
0.25	0.25	0.25	0.25	Gower	Y	10.0

adopted as criterion for assessing the effectiveness of this method. The similarity between signatures was determined separately for each of the three registered signature features: the X and Y coordinates, and the velocity V. It was determined also separately for the following similarity coefficients: R^2, Euclidean, Gower, Soergel, Cosine, Jaccard, Dice, Matusita, Clark, Jensen [6], [16].

The first stage of the studies consisted in calculating the EER value, taking account of the weights assigned to the data obtained for each of the 4 cameras. To this end, the similarity between each signature of a given person and other signatures in the database was determined by changing the values of weights assigned to the cameras. A list containing 10 results obtained for all the combinations of weights, methods and features characterized by the smallest error is presented in Table 2. In addition, the Table 2 includes the result (marked grey) obtained in a special case, where the value of all weights assigned to the cameras was 0.25. This meant that the data from each camera had equal influence on the error. This allowed examining the influence of the number of cameras on the results achieved. As it appears from the data presented in Table 2, from among the 10 best results, the first three were obtained for the R^2 measure and the feature of comparison in relation to the X coordinates of signatures. The smallest error equal to 7% was obtained for the combination of the following weights: $wC_1 = 0.25, wC_2 = 0.75, wC_3 = 0, wC_4 = 0$. The next 7 results were obtained for the Y feature and the R^2, Soergel's and Gower's similarity measures. It should be noted that the weight assigned to the camera 3 for each of these 10 cases was 0, while for the best 3 results the weight assigned to the camera 4 was also 0. In addition, a large share of the weight of the camera 2 was observed in the obtained results, which may indicate its significance in the signature acquisition process. The camera No. 2 was positioned at an angle of

Table 3. Average EERs for a given number of cameras

Number of cameras	The average EER [%]
1	22.1
2	20.1
3	18.7
4	17.7

Table 4. Different online signature verification methods

Method	EER [%]
Proposed method	7.00
Barkoula, Economou and Fotopoulos [2]	5.33
Flores-Mendez and Bernal-Urima [9]	10.63
Kostorz and Doroz [14]	4.14
Lei H., Govindaraju V. [15]	33.00
Lumini A., Nanni L. [18]	4.50
Maiorana E. [19]	8.33
Meshoul and Batouche [20]	6.44
Mohammadi and Faez [22]	6.33
Nanni L., Lumini A. [23]	21.00
Nanni L., Maiorana E.,Lumini A., Campisi P. [24]	3.00
Ong et al. [25]	6.08
Piyush Shanker A.,Rajagopalan A. N. [26]	2.00
Saeidi et al. [28]	4.50
Vargas J. F., Ferrer M. A., Travieso C. M., Alonso J. B. [29]	12.82
Vélez J., Sánchez Á., Moreno B., Esteban J. L. [30]	12.5
Wang et al. [32]	6.65
Wen J., Fang B., Tang Y. Y., Zhang T. [33]	11.4
Wrobel and Doroz [34]	6.50

30 degrees to area, in which the signatures were put, thanks to which the pen movements were recorded both in relation to the X and Y axes.

Table 3 shows averaged values of EER obtained for a different number of cameras. An analysis of the Table 3 shows that an increase in the number of cameras reduces the average EER determined for all the features and similarity measures.

4 Conclusions

The signature recognition method described in the paper appeared to be a fully functional solution. The smallest EER of the method was 7%, which is comparable with other results known from the literature (see Table 4).

A satisfactory effectiveness of recognition was obtained using well-known similarity measures which are easy to implement. It should be emphasized that these results were obtained with the use of only four cameras. It is a unquestionable advantage of this method, since it does not require the use of specialized tablets, which are often expensive. The determination of the similarity between signatures was based on the use of only three basic dynamic signature features. All this facts indicate that the results obtained, despite their preliminary nature, are promising and that this method can be further developed, so it is worth to continue working on it.

Disadvantages of this method may include the possibility of registering only signatures obtained from right-handed individuals. This inconvenience can be easily eliminated by creating a mirrored version of the proposed test bench.

In future studies it is planned to implement and analyse other dynamic signature features (e.g. pen acceleration) and their impact on the value of errors obtained. Other advanced data classification methods and voting systems will also be used in the signature recognition process. The work will also focus on increasing the number of signatures in the database.

References

1. Ahrary, A., Chiang, H.-J., Kamata, S.-I.: On-line signature matching based on Hilbert scanning patterns. In: Tistarelli, M., Nixon, M.S. (eds.) ICB 2009. LNCS, vol. 5558, pp. 1190–1199. Springer, Heidelberg (2009)
2. Barkoula, K., Economou, G., Fotopoulos, S.: Online signature verification based on signatures turning angle representation using longest common subsequence matching. International Journal on Document Analysis and Recognition (IJDAR) 16(3), 261–272 (2013)
3. Barroso, N., López de Ipiña, K., Ezeiza, A., Barroso, O., Susperregi, U.: Hybrid Approach for Language Identification Oriented to Multilingual Speech Recognition in the Basque Context. In: Graña Romay, M., Corchado, E., Garcia Sebastian, M.T. (eds.) HAIS 2010, Part I. LNCS, vol. 6076, pp. 196–204. Springer, Heidelberg (2010)
4. Bolle, R., Connell, J., Pankanti, S., Ratha, N., Senior, A.: Guide to Biometrics. Springer, New York (2004)
5. Brunelli, R.: Template Matching Techniques in Computer Vision: Theory and Practice. Wiley (2009)
6. Cha, S.C.: Comprehensive Survey on Distance/Similarity Measures between Probability Density Functions. International Journal of Mathematical Models and Methods in Applied Sciences 1(4), 300–307 (2007)
7. Cyganek, B., Gruszczynski, S.: Hybrid computer vision system for drivers' eye recognition and fatigue monitoring. In: 6th International Conference on Hybrid Artificial Intelligence Systems (HAIS), Wroclaw, pp. 78–94 (2011)
8. Doroz, R., Porwik, P.: Handwritten Signature Recognition with Adaptive Selection of Behavioral Features. In: Chaki, N., Cortesi, A. (eds.) CISIM 2011. CCIS, vol. 245, pp. 128–136. Springer, Heidelberg (2011)
9. Flores-Mendez, A., Bernal-Urbina, M.: Dynamic signature verification through the longest common subsequence problem and genetic algorithms. In: Proceedings of the IEEE Congress Evol. Computing, pp. 1–6 (2010)
10. Gupta, G.K., Joyce, R.C.: Using position extreme points to capture shape in on-line handwritten signature verification. Pattern Recognition 40, 2811–2817 (2007)
11. Jain, A.K., et al.: Handbook of biometrics. Springer, New York (2007)

12. Koprowski, R., Wrobel, Z., Wilczynski, S.: Methods of measuring the iridocorneal angle in tomographic images of the anterior segment of the eye. Biomedical Engineering Online 12, Article Number: 40 (2013)
13. Koprowski, R., Wrobel, Z., Zieleznik, W.: Automatic Ultrasound Image Analysis in Hashimoto's Disease. In: Martínez-Trinidad, J.F., Carrasco-Ochoa, J.A., Kittler, J. (eds.) MCPR 2010. LNCS, vol. 6256, pp. 98–106. Springer, Heidelberg (2010)
14. Kostorz, I., Doroz, R.: On-line signature recognition based on reduced set of points. In: Burduk, R., Kurzyński, M., Woźniak, M., Żołnierek, A. (eds.) Computer Recognition Systems 4. AISC, vol. 95, pp. 3–11. Springer, Heidelberg (2011)
15. Lei, H., Govindaraju, V.: A comparative study on the consistency of features in online signature verification. Pattern Recognition Letters 26(15), 2483–2489 (2005)
16. Lei, H., Palla, S., Govindaraju, V.: ER^2: an intuitive similarity measure for on-line signature verification. In: Ninth International Workshop on Frontiers in Handwriting Recognition, pp. 191–195. IEEE Computer Society (2004)
17. Lin, Y.H., Chen, C.H.: Template Matching Using the Parametric Template Vector with Translation, Rotation and Scale Invariance. Pattern Recognition 41(7), 2413–2421 (2008)
18. Lumini, A., Nanni, L.: Ensemble of on-line signature matchers based on OverComplete feature generation. Expert Systems With Applications 36(3), 5291–5296 (2009)
19. Maiorana, E.: Biometric cryptosystem using function based on-line signature recognition. Expert Systems With Applications 37(4), 3454–3461 (2010)
20. Meshoul, S., Batouche, M.: A novel approach for online signature verification using Fisher based probabilistic neural network. In: Proceedings of the IEEE Symposium on Comp. Comm., pp. 314–319 (2010)
21. Muramatsu, D., Yasuda, K., Matsumoto, T.: Biometric Person Authentication Method Using Camera-Based Online Signature Acquisition. In: Document Analysis and Recognition, pp. I46–I50 (2009)
22. Mohammadi, M.H., Faez, K.: Matching between important points using dynamic time warping for online signature verification. J. Sel. Areas Bioinf. (JBIO) (2012)
23. Nanni, L., Lumini, A.: Ensemble of Parzen window classifiers for on-line signature verification. Neurocomputing 68, 217–224 (2005)
24. Nanni, L., Maiorana, E., Lumini, A., Campisi, P.: Combining local, regional and global matchers for a template protected on-line signature verification system. Expert Systems With Applications 37(5), 3676–3684 (2010)
25. Ong, T.S., Khoh, W.H., Teoh, A.: Dynamic handwritten signature verification based on statistical quantization mechanism. In: Proceedings of the International Conference on Comput. Engineering Technology, pp. 312–316 (2009)
26. Piyush Shanker, A., Rajagopalan, A.N.: Off-line signature verification using DTW. Pattern Recognition Letters 28(12), 1407–1414 (2007)
27. Porwik, P., Doroz, R., Wrobel, K.: A new signature similarity measure. In: World Congress on Nature & Biologically Inspired Computing (NABIC 2009), pp. 1021–1026 (2009)
28. Saeidi, M., Amirfattahi, R., Amini, A., Sajadi, M.: Online signature verification using combination of two classifiers. In: Proceedings of the 6th Iran Mach. Vis. Image. Proc., pp. 1–4 (2010)
29. Vargas, J.F., Ferrer, M.A., Travieso, C.M., Alonso, J.B.: Off-line signature verification based on grey level information using texture features. Pattern Recognition 44(2), 375–385 (2011)

30. Vélez, J., Sánchez, Á., Moreno, B., Esteban, J.L.: Fuzzy shape-memory snakes for the automatic off-line signature verification problem. Fuzzy Sets and Systems 160(2), 182–197 (2009)
31. Villaverde, I., Graña, M.: A Hybrid Intelligent System for Robot Ego Motion Estimation with a 3D Camera. In: Corchado, E., Abraham, A., Pedrycz, W. (eds.) HAIS 2008. LNCS (LNAI), vol. 5271, pp. 657–664. Springer, Heidelberg (2008)
32. Wang, K., Wang, Y., Zhang, Z.: On-line signature verification using wavelet packet. In: Proceedings of the International Joint Confrenece on Biom. (IJCB), pp. 1–6 (2011)
33. Wen, J., Fang, B., Tang, Y.Y., Zhang, T.: Model-based signature verification with rotation invariant features. Pattern Recognition 42(7), 1458–1466 (2009)
34. Wrobel, K., Doroz, R.: The new method of signature recognition based on least squares contour alignment. In: International Conference on Biometrics and Kansei Engineering (ICBAKE 2009), pp. 80–83 (2009)
35. Yasuda, K., Matsumoto, T., Muramatsu, D.: Visual-based online signature verification using features extracted from video. Journal of Network and Computer Applications Archive, 333–341 (2010)

Automatic Lane Correction in DGGE Images by Using Hybrid Genetic Algorithms

M. Angélica Pinninghoff[1], Macarena Valenzuela[1], Ricardo Contreras[1], and Marco Mora[2]

[1] Department of Computer Science
University of Concepción
Concepción, Chile
{mpinning,rcontrer}@udec.cl

[2] Department of Computer Science
Catholic University of Maule
Talca, Chile

Abstract. DGGE (denaturing gradient gel electrophoresis) images are a particular type of images obtained by electrophoresis, that are used with different purposes. One of them is to study microbial biodiversity. Processing of this kind of images is a quite difficult problem, affected by various factors. Among these factors, the noise and distortion affect the quality of images, and subsequently, accuracy in interpreting the data. One of the problems this process presents is that lanes on the image are not perfectly aligned, and so the automatic processing of these images, e.g., for detection and quantification of bands, is not reliable. We present some methods for processing DGGE images that allow to improve their quality and thereof, improving biological conclusions. Results obtained with pure genetic algorithms, genetic algorithms hybridized with Tabu Search and genetic algorithms combined with Simulated Annealing are presented.

Keywords: DGGE Images, Genetic algorithms, Image proccessing, Tabu Search, Simulated Annealing.

1 Introduction

Denaturing Gradient Gel Electrophoresis (DGGE) [2,7], is a DNA-based technique which generates a genetic profile or *fingerprint* which can be used to identify the dominant members of the microbial community. DGGE has been used to investigate microbial responses in a wide variety of applications, including bioremediation assessment, wastewater treatment, drinking water treatment, biofilm formation, microbial induced corrosion, among others.

DGGE separates mixtures of amplified 16SrRNA gene segments, which are all the same size, based on nucleotide sequence. Denaturing breaks apart the two strands of the DNA molecule. Gradient Gel, is a gel with an increasing concentration of a chemical (denaturant) which breaks apart the DNA molecule.

M. Polycarpou et al. (Eds.): HAIS 2014, LNAI 8480, pp. 221–232, 2014.
© Springer International Publishing Switzerland 2014

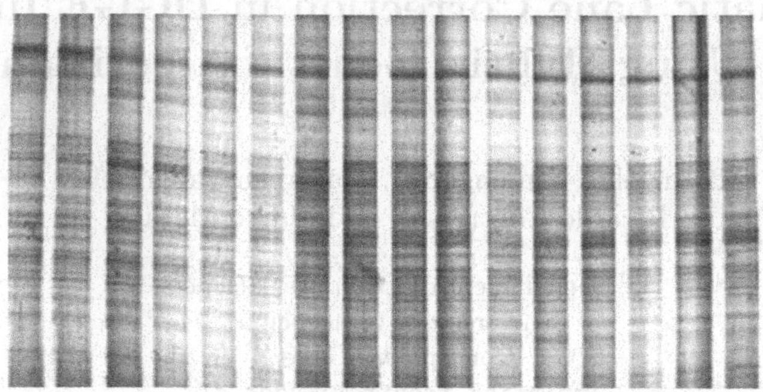

Fig. 1. A sample DGGE image with two reference lanes

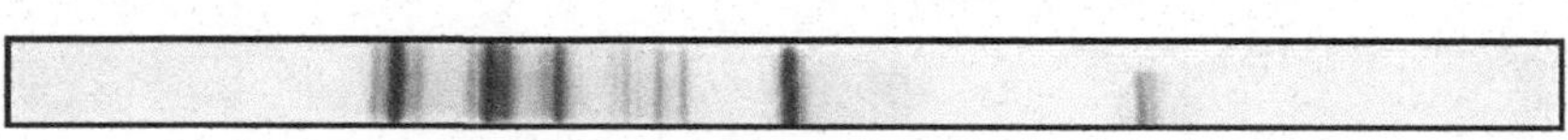

Fig. 2. A sample of a lane in a DGGE image

Electrophoresis is the application of an electric current across a gel. In response to the current, double-stranded DNA migrates (moves down) the gel. Denaturing the DNA molecule forms Y and T-shaped structures greatly slowing migration. Finally, this process allows to obtain, as a result, an image composed of bands and lanes [1].

Lanes are the vertical columns shown in Figure 1 and each one of them represents a DNA sample, except the reference lanes which are the leftmost and the rightmost lanes. Reference lanes are used to indicate the molecular weight, measured in base pairs (*bp*), of the DNA. The bands are the horizontal lines in each lane that represent the segments agglomeration of a DNA sample with the same *bp* value (see Figure 2).

By using DGGE, it is possible to detect the similarity or difference among individuals, and in doing so, it is necessary to know the location of a band in a lane. However, there are some problems when processing this type of images. One common problem when dealing with DGGE images is the lack of accuracy in band detection. To solve this problem we propose an automatic detection process, which is the starting point for the following step, to correct distortions in an image. When comparing images it is not only necessary to exactly match corresponding bands, but to realize this comparison among bands having the same slope. Otherwise, the conclusion could be not reliable.

Our proposal introduces genetic algorithms as a basic mechanism to correct images, and this means to correct a key parameter in each band: their slope. To improve this process that involves a global search, in a second step we hybridize the genetic algorithm with Tabu Search, and we hybridize also this genetic algorithm with Simulated Annealing. This allows to find better results, if there exist, in the neighborhood of the global solution founded by using only genetic algorithms. In doing so, we have the chance to compare different approaches, giving that the set of images is the same for the three solving methods.

Hybrid systems are free combinations of computational intelligence techniques, mixing heterogeneous fundamental views blending them into effective working systems, as shown in [11], a survey that summarizes the main research streams on multiple classifier systems. The use of innovative tools is illustrated in [1], describing an implementation for predicting business failure, supported by a neural-based multi-agent system that models the different actors of the companies as agents.

Image processing mechanisms have been developed in recent years for a wide number of computerized applications. Many applications are available for dealing with images, but only a reduced number of these applications to specific images as DNA images or, the particular issue that motivates this work, DGGE images. Etemad et al. [4] use an algorithm called *Ant-based Correlation for Edge Detection* (ACED), that is based on the Ant Colony System algorithm. It is expected that at the end of the processing, the trails marked by the ants represent the edges of a particular image. Results depend strongly on the set of chosen parameters, and the algorithm performs well in presence of noise.

The use of Ant Colony System for Edge Detection in DGGE Images is also described in [8]. In this experience, noisy images are not well recognized by the proposed algorithm. Another approach [9] deals with RAPD (Random Amplified Polymorphism DNA) images, that are similar to DGGE images. This work introduces the use of genetic algorithms hybridized with tabu search. In [3] there is a similar proposal, working with RAPD images, that combines genetic algorithms and simulated annealing. Unfortunately, both proposals uses a different set of images for testing. This work uses the same set of images for testing, aiming to obtain an objective comparison.

This article is structured as follows; the first section is made up of the present introduction; the second section describes the hybrid mechanisms considered in this work, the third section shows the proposal we are dealing with; the fourth section describes experiments we conducted and the results we obtained. The final section is devoted to the conclusions of the work.

2 Hybrid Genetic Algorithms

Hybrid genetic algorithms combine GA for a global search of solutions with metaheuristics for a local search, to find optimal solutions in the neighborhood. It has been shown that this combination provides best solutions to certain optimization problems.

The structure of a genetic algorithm consists of a simple iterative procedure on a population of genetically different individuals. The phenotypes are evaluated according to a predefined fitness function, the genotypes of the best individuals are copied several times and modified by genetic operators, and the newly obtained genotypes are inserted in the population in place of the old ones. This procedure is continued until a *good enough* solution is found [5].

We introduce the concept of template, that is a schematic representation of a DGGE image. The template is an image, computationally created, that contains a set of vertical lines. We say that a template is an acceptable representation of a DGGE image if lines in this template correspond in number and slope to the lanes in the image under consideration. In other words, as the template lines approach to the lanes, a higher matching degree is obtained. This is that we call similarity . In Section 3 can be found a more formal description for template.

In this work, the templates are the chromosomes, lines in a template are the genes, and a line having a particular slope represents the value (allele) that a gene has. Elitism was considered to keep a reduced set of the best individuals through different generations. A good fitness means that a particular template fits better to the original image. To evaluate a template, the template and the image are put together, and a function of fitness measures the similarity.

Genetic Operators: Different genetic operators were considered for this work. These genetic operators are briefly described bellow:

- Selection. Selection is accomplished by using the roulette wheel mechanism [5]. It means that individuals with a best fitness value will have a higher probability to be chosen as parents. In other words, those templates that are not a good representation of the lane image are less likely selected.
- Cross-over. Cross-over is used to exchange genetic material, allowing part of the genetic information that one individual to be combined with part of the genetic information of a different individual. It allows us to increase genetic variety, in order to search for better solutions. In other words, if we have two templates each containing $r+s+t$ curves, where r, s and t represent different regions of the template, generated by randomly choosing two points. First point is the limit between regions r and s and the second point is the limit between regions s and t. The two point cross-over is achieved by exchanging the s region. After cross-over, the generated children result in: children 1 will have the s region that corresponds to the second parent, and children 2 will have the s region that corresponds to parent 1.
- Mutation. By using this genetic operator, a slight variation is introduced into the population so that a new genetic material is created. In this work, mutation is accomplished by randomly replacing, with a low probability, a particular line in a template.

Tabu Search is one of the meta-heuristics used to hybridize the GA, is characterized for using adaptive memory to save some movements as taboo (are not allow to use this movements) and responsive exploration meaning that a bad strategic choice can yield the search to promising areas.

Tabu search (TS) is a meta-heuristic that guides a local heuristic search procedure to explore the solution space beyond local optimality. The local procedure is a search that uses an operation called *move* to define the neighborhood of any given solution. One of the main components of TS is its use of adaptive memory, which creates a more flexible search behavior. In a few words, this procedure iteratively moves from a solution x to a solution x' in the neighborhood of x, until some stopping criterion has been satisfied. In order to explore regions of the search space that would be left unexplored by the local search procedure, tabu search modifies the neighborhood structure of each solution as the search progresses [6].

A solution is a template representing a set of lane images, let us say the x solution; then to move from a solution x to a solution x' means that the template is modified. To modify a template we have chosen the change in the value of the slope, or the position for one or more lines in the template.

To avoid repeated movements during a certain bounded period of time, TS stores each movement in a temporal memory, which is called *tabu list*. Each element in the *tabu list* contains one band and its corresponding movement. A particular band in the list may occur more than once, but the associated movement needs to be different.

The other meta-heuristics used to hybridize the GA is Simulated Annealing (SA). This is a function optimization procedure based on random perturbations of a candidate solution and a probabilistic decision to retain the mutated solution. Simulated annealing takes inspiration from the process of shaping hot metals into stable forms through a gradual cooling process whereby the material transits from a disordered, unstable, high-energy state to an ordered, stable, low-energy state. In simulated annealing, the material is a candidate solution (equivalent to individual phenotype of an evolutionary algorithm) whose parameters are randomly initialized.

The solution undergoes a mutation and if its energy is lower than that at the previous stage, the mutated solution replaces the old one.

The temperature of the system is lowered every n evaluations, effectively reproducing the probability of retaining mutated solutions with a higher energy states. The procedure stops when the annealing temperature approaches the zero value [5].

In genetic algorithms the problem of local optimum is always present. By taking into account this issue, we decided to *hybridize* the procedure, i.e., to combine genetic algorithms with another strategy, in this specific work with Tabu Search and Simulated Annealing, to let potential solutions avoid those local optimum points. Both hybridization procedures consider the following strategy: the main objective of this process is to gradually improve individuals belonging to the population the genetic algorithm is working with. When the fitness measured during a certain number of iterations accomplished by the genetic algorithm doesn't vary; a reduced number of individuals is selected from the current population. One of them, at least, is the best individual of the population, while the others are randomly selected. Each one of these individuals acts as an input for triggering a tabu search procedure or a simulated annealing procedure.

Once the tabu search (simulated annealing) process is finished, the resulting individuals are re-inserted into the genetic population, and the process continues with the genetic algorithm procedure, as before. The complete process is repeated several times depending on the quality of the genetic population and the stopping process condition.

3 The Proposal

The problem addressed in this paper can be formally stated as follows.

Consider an image (matrix) $A = \{a_{ij}\}, i = 1, \ldots, n$ and $j = 1, \ldots, m$, where $a_{ij} \in Z^+$, and A is a DGGE image. Usually, a_{ij} is in the range [0..255] in a grey scale image, and we use a a_{ij} to refer to an element $A(x, y)$, where x and y are the pixel coordinates.

To deal with lane distortions, a set of templates is used. These templates are randomly created images with different distortion degrees, having lines that are in a one-to-one correspondence with lanes in the original DGGE image. A good template is the one that reflects in a more precise degree the distortions that the DGGE image under consideration has.

The template we consider is a matrix L (lanes) where $L = \{l_{ij}\}, i = 1, \ldots, n$ and $j = 1 \ldots, m$, $l_{ij} = 0$ or $l_{ij} = 1$ (a binary image), with 1 meaning that l_{ij} belongs to a line and 0 otherwise [10]. The generation of matrix L is limited to those regions that correspond to lanes in matrix A. Due to the rotation of the lanes, it is necessary to consider different alternate configurations. If we are dealing with an image with 12 lanes, and if for each lane we consider 14 possible rotations, we are considering 12^{14} different configurations to evaluate. This causes a combinatorial explosion, which justifies the use of genetic algorithms.

Genetic algorithms allow to manage a large number of templates, and those that are similar to the original image are chosen. Thus, it is necessary to seek for an objective function that reflects this similarity in a precise way. This function is used as a measure for the quality for the selected template. A template contains non-intersecting vertical lines, which are not necessarily parallel. A typical template is shown in Figure 3.

For automatically determining the limits of each lane, it is supposed that different lanes use similar areas, measured in number of pixels; and that they are uniformly distributed in the image. So, the image is partitioned in a number of regions that correspond to the number of observed lanes. At this point some pixels are out of the estimated limits for a lane. Then, the process of setting new limits is triggered: i) lines that are parallel to the original limit are considered, by taking into account a distance Δ to the right and to the left of the original limit (i.e., Δ determines the number of lines to be considered); ii) for each line obtained in this searching process, we take the sum of the values that have every pixel belonging to that line, and iii) the line that obtains the higher value in the sum, is the new limit. The higher the value, the higher the probability that the line corresponds to the background of the image.

In Figure 4 two images are shown, the first one is a DGGE image before the process of correcting limits, the second one is the same image, after the correction process.

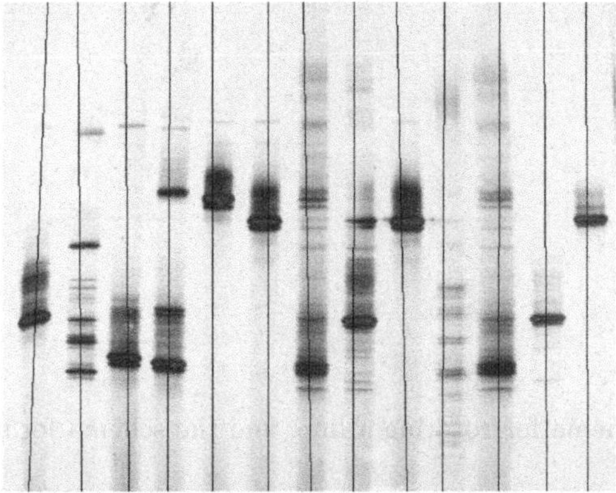

Fig. 3. A sample template for lane correction

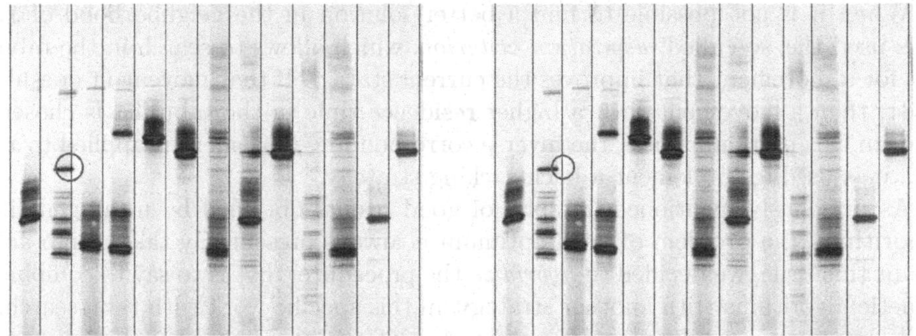

Fig. 4. A DGGE image, before and after correcting limits

A solution is a template representing a DGGE image, let us say the x solution; then to move from a solution x to a solution x' means that the template is modified. To modify a template we have chosen two possibilities: the first one is the change in the value of the slope for one or more lines in the template, i.e., a rotation movement; the second one is a shifting movement, the line is moved to the left or to the right, without changing the value of the slope for that line. In other words, if we call x_{inf} and x_{sup} the bottom and top points in a line respectively, a rotation movement is realized by changing these points to $x_{inf} - \delta$ and $x_{sup} + \delta$ (or changing to $x_{inf} + \delta$ and $x_{sup} - \delta$). In an analogous way, the shifting movement is accomplished by changing the original points to $x_{inf} + \delta$ and $x_{sup} + \delta$ (changing to minus if the movement is towards the opposite side of the image). Figure 5 illustrates the rotation movement and the shifting movement. The values allowed in both, shifting and rotation movements, are gradually diminished to avoid dramatic changes in the quality of the solutions.

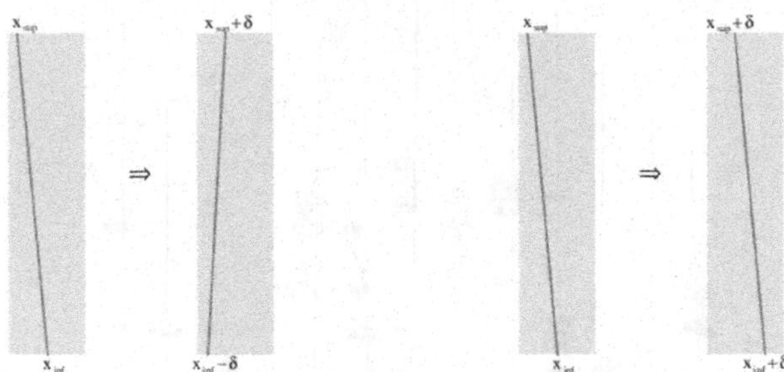

Fig. 5. The schema for rotating a line, and the schema for shifting a line

A particular lane in the list may occur more than once, but the associated movement needs to be different. In this work, the size of the tabu list is bounded by the number of lanes in the particular image under treatment.

When it is not possible to find a better solution in the neighborhood of x, it is used the, so-called, *aspiration criterion*, which allows to search in the tabu list for a movement that improves the current state x. If that movement doesn't exist, then a movement with a higher residence time in the tabu list is chosen and, in this particular case, the inverse corresponding movement is applied to x; i.e., it is used to implement a backtracking strategy.

As previously mentioned, in spite of good results obtained by using genetic algorithms, the problem of local optimum is always present. By taking into account this issue, we decided to *hybridize* the procedure, that is to say to combine genetic algorithms with another strategy, in this specific work with tabu search, and simulated annealing, to let potential solutions avoid those local optimum points. The hybridization procedure considers the following strategy: the main objective of this process is to gradually improve individuals belonging to the population the genetic algorithm is working with. When the fitness measured during a certain number of iterations accomplished by the genetic algorithm doesn't vary; a reduced number of individuals is selected from current population. One of them is the best individual of the population, while the others are randomly selected. Each one of these individuals acts as an input for triggering a tabu search procedure.

Once the tabu search (or simulated annealing) process is finished, the resulting individuals are re-inserted into the genetic population, and the process continues with the genetic algorithm procedure, as before. The complete process is repeated several times depending on the quality of the genetic population and the stopping process condition. The latter is specified as a time condition (number of iterations) or as a specific fitness value.

4 Experiments and Results

For testing, the first step considered only genetic algorithms. In this case the emphasis was on determining the best parameters, i.e., population size, cross-over

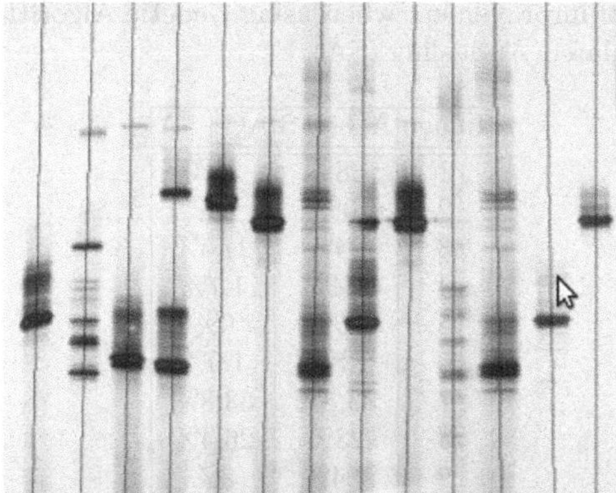

Fig. 6. Before processing the DGGE image

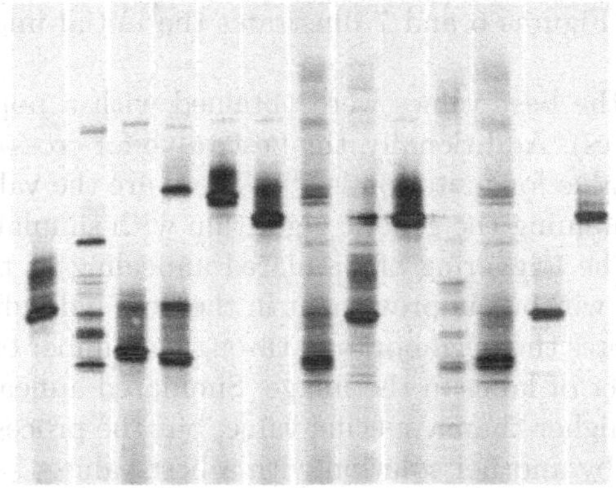

Fig. 7. The same DGGE image after processing

probability and mutation probability. An important set of experiments was conducted for determining the best combination of parameters, checking a great number of combinations ranging from very small size populations (e.g., ten individuals) to big size populations (e.g., over two thousands individuals), and combing this parameter with different cross-over percentage, and mutation probability. Then the strategy was to hybridize this best genetic algorithm configuration with tabu search and simulated annealing. In the case of hybridizing, the corresponding technique is triggered after the genetic algorithm reaches a steady state in which no improvements are detected during an arbitrary number of generations.

A set of 10 images was selected as a representative sample of available images for final tests. Each one of these images represents different image features, as brightness, contrast, noise presence, sharpness, and so on. For a particular group, lets say noisy images, differences among particular members are not significative. These images contains different slopes, and a different number of lanes. Additionally, the set contains images of different sizes and different grey values

Table 1. Percentage of improvement when using Genetic Algorithms (GA) with Tabu Search (TS) and Simulated Annealing (SA)

Image	AG+TS	AG+SA
1	38%	38%
2	0%	0%
3	24%	24.5%
4	5.4%	1.7%
5	0%,	0%
6	1.8%	1.9%
7	33.8%	33.8%
8	23%	26.4%
9	2.4%	3%
10	1.7%	1.4%

in the [0,255] scale. Figures 6 and 7 illustrates the initial image and the image after correction.

In all the cases, the best values were obtained with a population size of 50 individuals (templates). Additionally, the best value for cross-over probability is 70%, and the best value for mutation is 2%. These are the values that are going to be used when combining the genetic algorithm with simulated annealing, and with tabu search. The triggering of simulated annealing or tabu search occurs after 30 generations without improvement in the best individual.

Tabu search explores the neighborhood through a number of moves arbitrarily chosen as the number of lanes in the image. Simulated annealing iterates while the temperature is higher than a specific value, but the process stops if the best solution is replaced by another solution with a best value.

As expected in most of cases, hybridizing the genetic algorithm generates best solutions than using only genetic algorithms. Results obtained by using the combination genetic algorithms and tabu search are similar to results obtained using the other alternative. In two cases there is no improvement, a condition due to the fact that are good quality images, which probably by the single application of the genetic algorithm have reached an optimum result. Table 1 shows the percentage of improvement when using hybrid algorithms with respect to simple genetic algorithm. A good result implies that most of pixels corresponding to a lane are effectively considered as part of the lane. It depends on how close to the lane slope on the DGGE image is the line in the template. An ideal image will show a background with no dark pixels at all. In a real case, the number of dark pixels can be, eventually, reduced. In other word, figures in the table show the reduction of dark pixels that can be found as part of the background.

Additionally, the time involved in the process is lower for simple genetic algorithm, increases when tabu search is considered, and increases again in the case of simulated annealing.

Table 2 illustrates some execution times.

Table 2. Execution time (in seconds)

Case	AG	AG + TS	AG + SA
1	9.76	22.15	25.27
2	10.88	21.30	22.53
3	5.99	15.82	12.79
4	9.85	19.18	19.44
5	11.45	21.44	27.59
6	11.41	24.95	31.18
7	11.67	26.17	30.36
8	12.94	27.05	30.63
9	12.78	32.73	36.42
10	10.45	27.70	28.60

5 Conclusions

In this work we have presented three different models for dealing with lane correction in DGGE images. Genetic algorithms, as the classic approach; and the hybrid alternatives that include tabu search and a simulated annealing.

Genetic algorithms, working as the only technique, have shown to be a useful mechanism for dealing with this specific problem. With the particular values arbitrarily assigned to different parameters, the hybrid combination obtained best values in most of cases. Simulated annealing did not help to obtain better values that those obtained with tabu search with a significative difference, but computational time involved was a 20% higher, on the average, than the time involved when dealing with tabu search.

This results are important because the image correcting process may be very tedious, and highly time consuming for a person; and to automate this process requires a large number of templates, that cover the large number of alternatives. Due to its combinatorial nature, when generating an important number of templates, an heuristic procedure that considers a high number of possibilities to be explored is to be considered as a valid paradigm.

It is necessary to consider that, after implementing the procedures, testing was a very time demanding task. Taking this issue into account, it is clear that future work has to seek for a best mechanism to evaluate individuals, that is the most consuming task in the whole process.

References

1. Borrajo, M.L., Baruque, B., Corchado, E., Bajo, J., Corchado, J.M.: Hybrid neural intelligent system to predict business failure in SMEs. International Journal of Neural Systems 21(04), 277–296 (2011)
2. Borresem, A.L., Hovig, E., Brogger, A.: Detection of base mutations in genomic DNA using denaturing gradient gel electrophoresis (DGGE) followed by transfer and hybridization with gene-specific probes. Mutation Research/Fundamental and Molecular Mechanisms of Mutagenesis 202, 77–83 (1988)

3. Contreras, R., Pinninghoff, M.A., Alvarado, A.: Proposal of an hybrid algorithm for correcting RAPD images. Research in Computer Science. Avances en Inteligencia Artificial 55, 321–331 (2012)
4. Etemad, S.A., White, T.: An ant-inspired algorithm for detection of image edge features. Applied Soft Computing 11(8), 4883–4893 (2011)
5. Floreano, D., Mattiusi, C.: Bio-inspired Artificial Intelligence, 1st edn. MIT Press (2008)
6. Glover, M., Laguna, F.: Tabu Search, 1st edn. Springer (1997)
7. Muyzer, G., de Waal, E.C.: Uitterlinden A.G. Profiling of complex microbial populations by denaturing gradient gel electrophoresis analysis of polymerase chain reaction-amplified genes coding for 16SrRNA. Applied and Environmental Microbiology 59(3), 695–700 (1993)
8. Pinninghoff, M.A., Figueroa, C., Urrutia, H.: Using ant colony system for edge detection in DGGE images. In: Strategies for a Creative Future with Computer Science, Quality Design and Communicability (2012)
9. Pinninghoff, M.J.A., Venegas, Q.D., Contreras, A.R.: Genetic algorithms and tabu search for correcting lanes in DNA images. In: Martínez-Trinidad, J.F., Carrasco-Ochoa, J.A., Kittler, J. (eds.) MCPR 2010. LNCS, vol. 6256, pp. 144–153. Springer, Heidelberg (2010)
10. Rueda, L., Uyarte, O., Valenzuela, S., Rodriguez, J.: Processing random amplified polymorphysm DNA images using the radon transform and mathematical morphology. In: Kamel, M.S., Campilho, A. (eds.) ICIAR 2007. LNCS, vol. 4633, pp. 1071–1081. Springer, Heidelberg (2007)
11. Woźniak, M., Graña, M., Corchado, E.: A survey of multiple classifier systems as hybrid systems. Information Fusion 16, 3–17 (2014)

Augmented Reality: An Observational Study Considering the MuCy Model to Develop Communication Skills on Deaf Children

Jonathan Cadeñanes and María Angélica González Arrieta

Department of Computer Science and Automation - Faculty of Science, University of Salamanca, Spain

Abstract. To develop different Communication Skills (CS) on deaf children (such as making signs, reading, writing or speaking) we propose a Sign Language Teaching Model (SLTM) called Multi-language Cycle for Sign Language Understanding (MuCy). Also, we conduct an observational study at the Association of Parents of Deaf Children of Salamanca (ASPAS) in order to measure the development of CS on deaf children by using a kit of Sign Language Pedagogical Materials (SLPMs), as well as the use of Augmented Reality (AR) as complementary tools for teaching Sign Language (SL) within a Collaborative Learning Environment with Mixed-Reality (CLEMR).

Keywords: Augmented Reality, Sign Language, MuCy model, Mixed-Reality Learning Environment, Unity3D.

1 Introduction

To teach SL in preschool and primary education it is essential to identify the different individual learning needs of each deaf student in order to improve their school achievement and social integration [18]. Teachers have to adapt their classes to develop Sign Language Communication Skills (SLCS) on deaf children. An adequate alternative teaching tool that suits these needs is the AR, since it allows teachers and students to collaborate towards gaining knowledge in a Teaching-Learning Process [14].

One of the most important features of the AR is the overlay of images in the real world. This allows interaction with digital media in real time through tangible devices such as PCs screens, AR eye-wear displays or glove-based input recognition systems. With all this, deaf students can learn interactively. First, they can visualize within their minds the SL concepts given in their classes. Second, they can explore the motions of signs in a 3D view, so they can reproduce those signs and learn by imitation from the body, face and lips.

This article is presented as follows: In Section 2 we mention two current educational projects based on AR to analyze their technical features, since they are appropriate references to design our kit of SLPMs. In Section 3 we describe

M. Polycarpou et al. (Eds.): HAIS 2014, LNAI 8480, pp. 233–240, 2014.
© Springer International Publishing Switzerland 2014

two SL pilot lessons implemented at ASPAS [2]. The observational study design, the methodology and the results are also presented here. Then, in Section 4 we draw conclusions. Finally, in Section 5, a brief description of future research is mentioned taking into account possible alternatives to improve our approach technologically.

2 Related Works

Mathsigner™[1] is an AR project aimed to teach SL that can be used for non-immersive or immersive systems such as Flex™and reFex™, so deaf students can learn mathematical concepts and American Sign Language (ASL). This technology has several advantages: First, it is able to produce a highly realistic and fluid environment where 3D characters perform signs in real time. Second, it promotes interaction between users and 3D avatars via a simple glove-based gesture control system. Finally, a desktop version can be used at homes or at schools.

Another tool that can be considered a standard teaching method based on AR is the MagicBook [5,6,7]. It can be adapted to teach SL because it covers three levels of collaboration [15]: The first, is the Reality. A group of users can gather around to learn and interact with a book by changing its pages and by sharing their learning experience.

The second level is Augmented Reality (AR). A networked application is installed on several PCs where animated avatars and virtual environments can be seen projected on PC screens. The users' interactions are with AR devices and tangible books. The last level is Virtual Reality (VR). The AR device allows users to be connected within the workstation. Their learning experience is no longer in the real world, their digital interactions (through virtual avatars) are by sharing information within the immersive and interactive system.

With Mathsigner™and the MagicBook, teachers have the possibility to design their classes with different topics by adapting them to their students' learning needs. They can choose the learning experience through moving from one reality to another according with the specific skills or knowledge they want to develop in their students. What is missing in these two AR educational projects regarding deaf children is the existence of statistical data demonstrating the level of SL learning achievement in students. To solve this, we conducted two SL pilot lessons at a local deaf people Association in the province of Salamanca (Spain) in order to determine the Percentage of Development of SLCS and other CS such as reading, writing and speaking.

3 Study Design and Method

The objective of the observational study is to measure the development of CS on deaf children by the use of AR as a complementary tool for SL teaching based on the SLTM MuCy. The study was conducted at the Association of Parents of Deaf Children of Salamanca [2] along with a kit of Sign Language Pedagogical Materials (SLPMs) designed for this purpose (Fig.2).

3.1 SLTM MuCy, SLPMs, Software Architecture and Pilot Lessons

The Multi-language Cycle for Sign Language Understanding (MuCy) (Fig.1) is a continuous psychomotor cycle to teach SL to deaf people (signers and non-signers) and to students that require knowledge of SL because they have similar communication disabilities.

The theoretical background of the MuCy model is based on the Lev's Semionovich Vigotsky Zone of Proximal Development (ZPD) [9,12], the Principles of Social Education of deaf and dumb children [18] and the Milgram's Reality-Virtuality Continuum [15]. To design the model we are based on the neuropsychological findings that have shown that deaf children can develop reading and speaking skills by training at an early-age [13]. The criteria to validate the design are according to The Principles of Learning and Teaching [11] and on the Danielson's Group Teaching Framework [10].

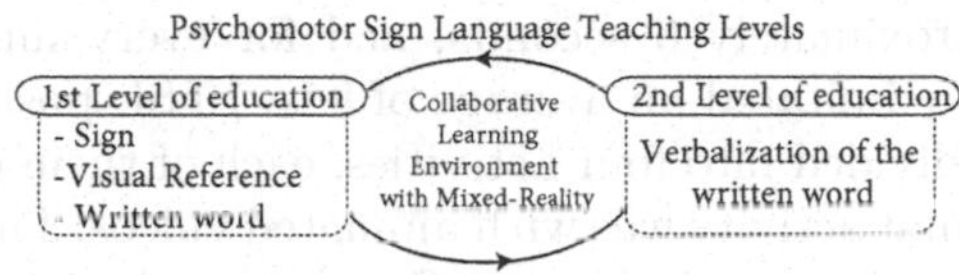

Fig. 1. Multi-language Cycle for Sign Language Understanding (MuCy model)

The first level of education in the MuCy model refers to learning the proper use of signs in relationship with their visual references (words or phrases) and their written versions. The second level refers to the practice of speaking those words by imitating the face, mouth and tongue movements. The SLPMs (Fig.2) are: 1) A *SL Book* which allows the use of the Vuforia marker-based tracking system for Unity3D [16,17]. A set of images of 3D avatars performing signs are printed on the book. Their respective meanings in words or phrases are presented in text format which makes possible to practice the reading and writing skills. 2) *Animated videos* that help deaf children to learn by imitation. 3) A Unity3D *SL AR desktop application* that displays on virtual scenes animated avatars which can be seen with AR devices such as the Vuzix eye-wear [19] or on PC screens. The modeling and animation process was made with Blender 2.69 [3].

Fig. 2. A) An Avatar performing the sign for the concept Colors, B) SL Fingerspelling Alphabet Book with sections for reading and writing exercises, C) AR Avatar in Unity3D, D) Vuzix eye-wear display for AR, E) Animations displayed on a Tablet

The AR SL application's architecture and design's flowchart explain the process we used to implement Unity3D for educational SL purposes (Fig.3). The two research instruments chosen to collect data for this study were observations and interviews. For the observations, the data collected was from two SL pilot lessons: The Fingerspelling Alphabet and the Rainbow Colors. For the interviews, we use a Smiley-face Likert's scale of five points to validate the SLTM and the SLPMs, as well as to know the parents and teachers attitudes about the usability, satisfaction and learning achievement they though the children reached by using our MuCy model and SLPMs (Table 2).

The two SL pilot lessons were conducted at ASPAS in order to measure the Percentage of Development of SLCS and other CS (such as reading, writing and speaking) reached by four children (two aged six and the other two aged seven) (Fig.4A). Each lesson had a duration of one hour with students located in the same classroom using the CLEMR (Table 1A,1B). For the Alphabet lesson we made 30 videos of words from A to Z and for the Colors lesson we made 16 videos (including the signs for the concepts of light, dark and color). The duration of each video was approximately 6 seconds, and for every minute each student watched a video, they imitated an average of 8 to 10 SL positions.

The lessons were divided into four activities, each of them corresponding to a specific SLPM. The first activity was with animated videos. The children watched the avatars performing signs on the Tablet (Group A) and on the PC screen (Group B). Then, they had to imitate SL positions right after the avatars. The second and third activities were with the SL book with images of avatars showing the correct SL positions printed on it. The students practiced reading the words (colors and alphabet). Then, they had to write these words down on the book. Immediately after, they had to perform the SL positions corresponding to those words. For the last activity, at first the children had to use the markers printed on the pages to display the animated 3D avatars on the PC screen. After visualizing the avatars they had to imitate the SL positions individually and then in a group. Finally they practiced speech facing each other and their teachers. The students also learned to move their lips to make sounds similar to those we use to speak.

3.2 Data Analysis and Results

According to the Percentage of Development of SLCS and other CS (Making signs: MS, Reading: RD, Writing: WR and Speaking: SP) in relationship with the SLPMs as complementary tools within a CLEMR, the results were as follows (Table 1A,1B and Fig.4A):

1) *For the Rainbow Colors lesson.* The use of videos in Activity one had shown an 91.76% improvement of making signs, activities two and three showed a 89.13% increase in improvement of reading skills and an 86.36% improvement in writing skills. In Activity four, the use of AR to develop speaking skills while performing signs showed a 95.60% increase in improvement.

2) *For the Fingerspelling Alphabet lesson*, Activity one showed a 90.53% in improvement, the development of reading skills 87.93%, writing skills 90.48%, and speaking skills 93.68%.

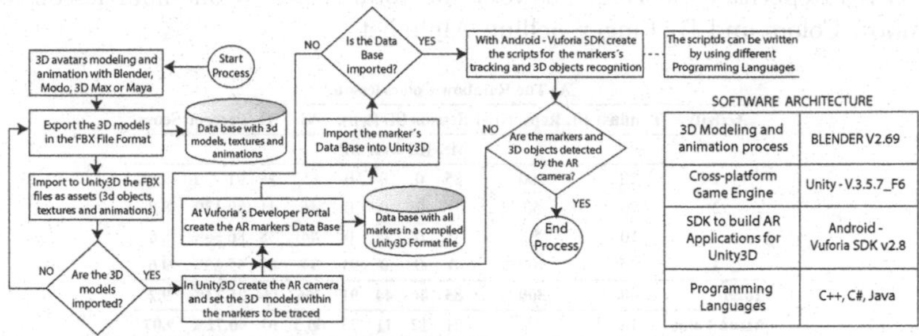

Fig. 3. AR SL application's architecture and design's flowchart

For the Colors lesson, the two students' Total Mean Value of SL Correct Answers was 90.72%, while for the Alphabet lesson 90.65%. These Mean Values has demonstrated that by using ICT Technology such as AR avatars increases the SLCS and the interest in speech on deaf children in primary education (Table 2, Q3 and Q9).

The Pearson's analysis has shown in both lessons a strong correlation coefficient of 0.99 between the two variables (Fig.4B): 1) The total number of SL Repetitions (Xi:SLR), and 2) the number of the Correct SL Answers (Yi:CA) given by the children once they had taken the two lessons of one hour duration each. This indicates that a greater number of SL repetitions with SLPMs produce more Correct SL Answers and learning achievement.

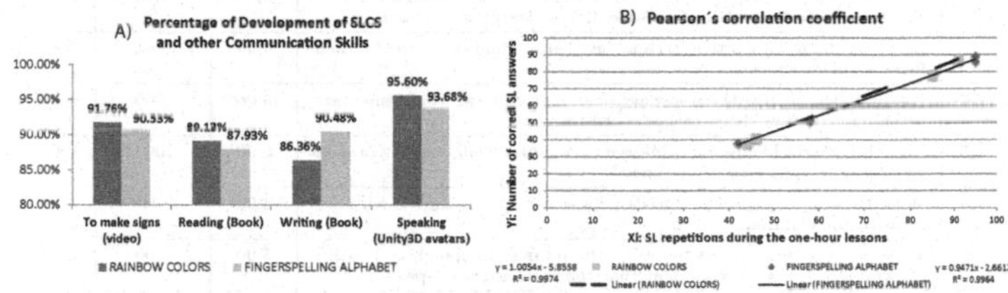

Fig. 4. A) Percent of Development of Communication Skills in relationship with the Pedagogical Materials, B) Correlation between the average of SL repetitions and the average of the Correct SL Answers given by the children

As for the Likert's scale, it is observed that all respondents strongly agree with our SL teaching approach (Table 2: Q2,Q6 and Q11). For the *Usability* variable (Table 2: Q3,Q4,Q6,Q7 and Q11) all the answers had a 100% approval which means that SLPMs promote the Collaborative Learning Experience, and that to learn in a CLEMR helps deaf students to understand complex situations in parts in order to create diverse learning solutions. Also both parents and teachers wanted to use these Pedagogical Materials at their homes or in schools

Table 1. SL Repetitions, correct answers and total scores in one-hour lesson for the A) Rainbow Colors and B) Fingerspelling Alphabet

A) The Rainbow Colors lesson.

Activity	T (mins)	SL Reps. Goal	Session SL Reps.				Xi	Yi	Percent	Score
			MS	RD	WR	SP				
1	20	100	85	0	0	0	85	78	91.76%	9.2
2	10	50	0	46	0	0	46	41	89.13%	8.9
3	10	50	0	0	44	0	44	38	86.36%	8.6
4	20	100	0	0	0	91	91	87	95.60%	9.6
Total	**60**	**300**	**85**	**46**	**44**	**91**	**266**	**244**	**91.73%**	**9.2**
Mean Value	15	75	21	12	11	23	66.5	61	**90.72%**	**9.07**
Std. Dev										**0.39**

B) Fingerspelling Alphabet lesson

Activity	T (mins)	SL Reps. Goal	Session SL Reps.				Xi	Yi	Percent	Score
			MS	RD	WR	SP				
1	20	130	95	0	0	0	95	86	90.53%	9.1
2	10	65	0	58	0	0	58	51	87.93%	8.8
3	10	50	0	0	42	0	42	38	90.48%	9.0
4	20	110	0	0	0	95	95	89	93.68%	9.4
Total	**60**	**355**	**95**	**58**	**42**	**95**	**290**	**264**	**91.03%**	**9.1**
Mean Value	15	88.75	24	15	11	24	72.50	66	**90.65%**	**9.07**
Std. Dev										**0.24**

Table 2. Likert's scale survey to validate the MuCy model and the SLPMs

i	Question	Mean	Std.Dev.	%
Q1	The SLPMs help deaf children to remember information through memorization.	4.00	1.414	80%
Q2	The two educational levels of the MuCy model help deaf students to cognitively understand relevant information from the SL.	5.00	.000	100%
Q3	Teaching Communication Skills such as reading , writing and speaking help deaf students to create solutions to the socio-cultural problems they face.	5.00	.000	100%
Q4	Learning with a CLEMR helps deaf students to understand a complex situation in parts in order to create diverse learning solutions.	5.00	.000	100%
Q5	Learning with interactive technology helps children increase their learning achievement.	4.50	.707	90%
Q6	I would like to use these pedagogical materials as complementary teaching resources either at home or at school.	5.00	.000	100%
Q7	The MuCy model helps deaf children to organize their learning process according to their educational needs.	5.00	.000	100%
Q8	With these pedagogical materials it is easier to explain the SL positions to the children.	4.00	1.414	80%
Q9	To learn with AR avatars increases the interest in speech and makes the children feel more confident that they will learn to speak.	5.00	.000	100%
Q10	The SL book is an adequate tool for teaching the reading and writing for an specific topic.	4.50	.707	90%
Q11	The SLPMs promote the collaborative learning experience with Mixed-Reality (CLEMR).	5.00	.000	100%

because the MuCy model helps deaf children to organize their learning process according to their educational needs.

For the *Satisfaction* variable (Table 2: Q8,Q9 and Q10), Q9 had a 100% approval which shows that learning with AR avatars increases the interest in speech and makes children feel more confident. Also, Q8 with 80% in positive responses has shown that parents and teachers thought that using our SLPMs made it easier to explain SL positions to children. Q10 with 90% in positive responses demonstrated that the SL book is an adequate tool for teaching the reading and writing skill for an specific topic.

Finally, the *Learning Achievement* variable (Table 2: Q1,Q2 and Q5) has shown that the two educational levels of the MuCy model help deaf students to cognitively understand relevant information from the SL, that they can remember information through memorization (Q1) and that learning with interactive technology children increase their learning achievement (Q5).

4 Conclusions

We have presented in this paper a SLTM and a kit of SLPMs that have been implemented at ASPAS for two SL lessons. With the collected data we have demonstrated that by using ICT (such as AR) and by promoting the CLEMR deaf children have developed a high percentage of SLCS and other CS. Also, a brief explanation of the process we used to create the AR SL application based on the Cross-platform Unity3D is provided. So it can be reproduced by any teacher that wanted to use the MuCy model and AR as a complementary teaching resource.

With all the above, we have concluded that the Teaching-Learning Process within a CLEMR reinforces social interactions and CS in deaf children. Also, we have proved that teachers can adapt their classes to the educational needs of their students for a specific topic. The MuCy model along with the SLPMs also have proved to be an adequate complementary tool for teaching SL and developing different CS in a continuous psychomotor cycle.

5 Future Research

To improve technologically our model and to create an Interactive-networked desktop application with Mixed-Reality, we consider the convergence of technologies such as motion capture and voice recognition. Since they are appropriate to design collaborative and remote SL lessons.

For the motion capture of face, body and SL hands movements we will use the OpenKinect camera [8], and for the voice recognition system the Carnegie's Mellon Open Source *Sphinx Speech Recognition Toolkit* [4]. With these technologies interacting with each other synergistically in a desktop application, deaf people will be able to learn SL by translating movements and sounds into text and Animated-outputs (3D avatars in AR) within a remote CLEMR in real time.

Acknowledgments. The authors would like to thank the Association of Parents of Deaf Children of Salamanca which gave us the opportunity to provide a SLTM to their students. Also, we thank the parents for their positive feedback and for their collaboration.

References

1. Adamo-Villani, N., Carpenter, E., Arns, L.: 3D Sign Language Mathematics in Immersive Environment. In: Proc. of ASM 2006 - 15th International Conference on Applied Simulation and Modeling, Rhodes, Greece (2006)

2. Association of Parents of Deaf Children of Salamanca, ASPAS, Spain (2014), http://www.aspas-salamanca.es/ (viewed on July 6, 2013)
3. Blender, Blender 2.69 (2014), http://www.blender.org/ (viewed on September 1, 2013)
4. Carnegie Mellon University. Sphinx Speech Recognition Toolkit (2014), http://cmusphinx.sourceforge.net/ (viewed on March 15, 2014)
5. Billinghurst, M., Kato, H., Poupyrev, I.: The Magic Book: A Transitional AR Interface. Computers and Graphics 25(5), 745–753 (2001)
6. Billinghurst, M., Kato, H., Poupyrev, I.: The MagicBook. Moving Seamlessly between Reality and Virtuality. Human Interface Technology Laboratory, University of Washington, Hiroshima City University and Sony Computer Science Laboratories (2001)
7. Billinghurst, M., Kato, H., Poupyrev, I.: MagicBook: Transitioning between Reality and Virtuality. In: Proceeding of the Extended Abstracts on Human Factors in Computing Systems, New York, pp. 25–26 (2001)
8. Chai, X., Li, G., Lin, Y., Xu, Z., Tang, Y., Chen, X.: Sign Language Recognition and Translation with Kinect. Key Lab of Intelligent Information Processing of Chinese Academy of Sciences (CAS), Institute of Computing Technology. Microsoft Research Asia. Beijing, China (2013)
9. Chaiklin, S.: Vygotsky's educational theory and practice in cultural context. The zone of proximal development in Vygotsky's analysis of learning and instruction. Cambridge University Press (2003)
10. Danielson, C.: The framework for teaching. Evaluation instrument. The Danielson Group (2013), http://www.danielsongroup.org (viewed on December 1, 2013)
11. Department of Education and Early Childhood Development. The Principles of Learning and Teaching P–12 Unpacked (2014), http://www.education.vic.gov.au (viewed on January 10, 2014)
12. Ivic, I.: Lev Semionovich Vygotsky. UNESCO 24(3-4), 773–799 (1994)
13. Mayberry, R.I.: Cognitive development in deaf children: the interface of language and perception in neuropsychology. In: Segalowitz, S.J., Rapin, I. (eds.) Handbook of Neuropsychology, 2nd edn., vol. 8, Part II (2002)
14. Mertzani, M.: Considering Sign Language and Deaf Culture in Computer Mediated Communication Environments: Initial Explorations and Concerns. In: 9th Theoretical Issues in Sign Language Research Conference, Florianopolis, Brazil (2008)
15. Milgram, P., Takemura, H., Utsumi, A., Kishino, F.: Augmented Reality: A class of displays on the reality-virtuality continuum. ATR Communication Systems Research Laboratories, Telemanipulator and Telepresence Technologies, Kyoto, Japan. SPIE, vol. 2351 (1994)
16. Unity Techs, Unity3D V4.3 (2014), http://unity3d.com (viewed on October 5, 2013)
17. Vuforia Developer, Vuforia™SDK, Unity extension Vuforia–2.8. (2014), https://developer.vuforia.com/resources/sdk/unity (viewed on December 22, 2013)
18. Vygotsky, L.: The principles of social education of deaf and dumb children in Russia. In: Proceedings of the International Conference on the Education of the Deaf, London, pp. 227–237 (1925)
19. Vuzix Corporation. Wrap 920AR and 1200DXAR Eyewear (2014), http://www.vuzix.com/ (viewed on December 22, 2013)

A 3D Facial Recognition System Using Structured Light Projection

Miguel A. Vázquez and Francisco J. Cuevas

Centro de Investigaciones en Óptica, A.C.
Loma del Bosque 115, Col. Lomas del Campestre, CP. 37150
León, Guanajuato, México
{mvazquez,fjcuevas}@cio.mx

Abstract. In this paper, a facial recognition system is described, which carry out the classification process by analyzing 3D information of the face. The process begins with the acquisition of the 3D face using light structured projection and the phase shifting technique. The faces are aligned respect a face profile and the region of front, eyes and nose is segmented. The descriptors are obtained using the eigenfaces approach and the classification is performed by linear discriminant analysis. The main contributions of this work are: a) the application of techniques of structured light projection for the calculation of the cloud of points related to the face, b) the use of the phase of the signal to perform recognition with 97% reliability, c) the use of the profile of the face in the alignment process and d) the robustness in the recognition process in the presence of gestures and facial expressions.

Keywords: Biometrics, facial recognition, structured light projection, pattern recognition, artificial vision, 3D face, 3d recovery.

1 Introduction

The face recognition is one of the main ways of personal identification in our everyday social interaction; people focus the visual attention in features and facial expressions. Humans are able to recognize up to hundreds of faces including people that have not seen for a long time or with different lighting conditions, pose, facial expressions or face with accessories (Turk & Petland, 1991). The development of automatic facial recognition system had been a challenge of several disciplines such as computer science, artificial vision, pattern recognition and biometrics. Under controlled conditions, the automatic face recognition systems are fast, accurate, economical and non-invasive. In the other hand, under non-controlled conditions it fails since they have different kind of problems such as variations in scale, orientation, facial expression, lighting conditions, occlusions, presence or absence of accessories among others (Cabello Pardos, 2004; Chenghua, Yunhong, Tieniu, & Long, 2004; Hwanjong, Ukil, Sangyoun, & Kwanghoon, 2006; Xue, Jianming, & Takashi, 2005; Zhang, 2010).

M. Polycarpou et al. (Eds.): HAIS 2014, LNAI 8480, pp. 241–253, 2014.
© Springer International Publishing Switzerland 2014

Traditionally, there are several methods to carry out the automatic identification of people such as passwords, personal identification numbers (PIN), radio frequency identification cards (RFID), keys, passport, driving license, among others. The disadvantage of these methods is that they use resources that can be lost, forgotten, shared, manipulated or stolen. It can have consequences either economic, illegal access, cloning of cards among others (Arun, Karthik, & Anil, 2006; Saeed & Nagashima, 2012). In the other hand, identification techniques based on biometrics offer a more robust solution since using physical or behavioral traits that are unique, permanent and non-transferable in the individual. Physical features can be extracted from the eyes (iris, retina), hands (fingerprints, hand geometry, vascular patterns) or face, so it can be used the behavioral traits gait, bell speech, writing, signing, press dynamics keyboards, etc. (Zhang, 2010; Jain, Flynn, & Ross, 2008; Wayman, 2011).

In this paper, it is presented the design of a facial recognition system, which uses the depth information of the face as biometric pattern. This is made up of modules of a typical pattern recognition system and implements techniques of different areas such as: biometrics, optics, machine vision, patter recognition, geometry and statistical difference (Woz, Graña, & Corchado, 2014).

2 Development of the Face Verification System

The proposed face verification system is composed of several modules that operate systematically over the three-dimensional information of the face. It is described in Figure 1.

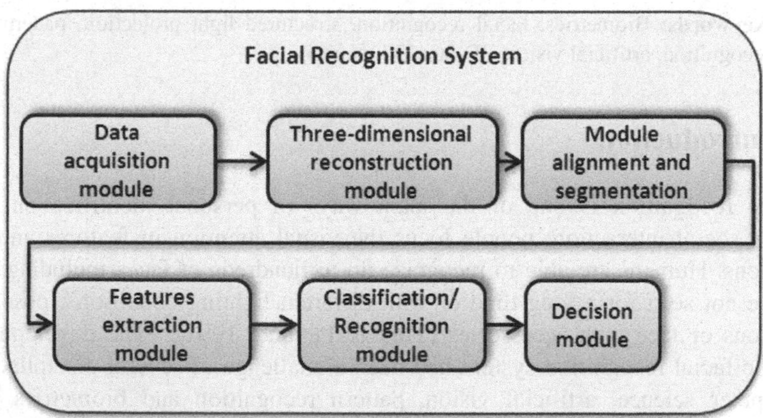

Fig. 1. Design of the facial recognition system

2.1 Data Acquisition Module

The data acquisition module aims to record a set of four intensity images by binary fringe projection and the 3D face data is recovered by four-step phase shifting method (Fu & Luo, 2011; Siva Gorthi & Rastogi, 2009).

The optical arrangement of structured light projection system is shown in Figure 2. It requires a digital camera, a multimedia projector and a reference plane C, P and R, respectively. The optical axes of the camera and projector are parallel, coplanar and normal to the reference plane.

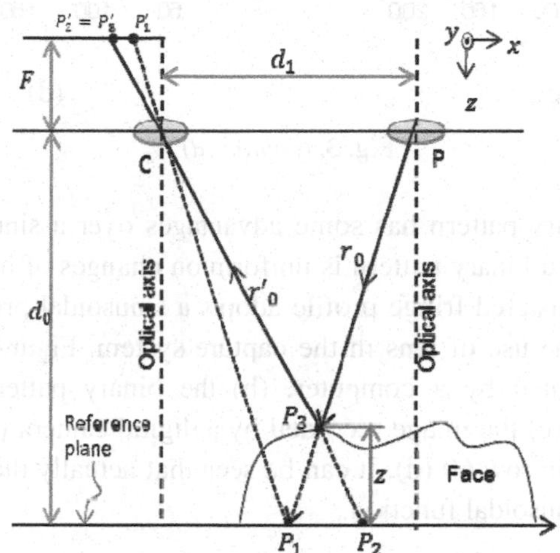

Fig. 2. Structured light projection setup

The binary pattern profile, generated by computer, is described by Equation (1).

$$I_k(x,y) = \begin{cases} 0 \quad si \quad [x-(p/4)*k]\ mod(p) < (^p/_2 - 1) \\ 1 \quad si \quad [x-(p/4)*k] mod\ (p) > (^p/_2 - 1) \end{cases} \tag{1}$$

where k is the sequential number of the fringe pattern, and p is the period of the signal, *mod(p)* is the module of the signal period. Fringe patterns generated by the Equation (1) are consecutively projected on the reference plane and the surface of the face, while they are recorded by a digital camera.

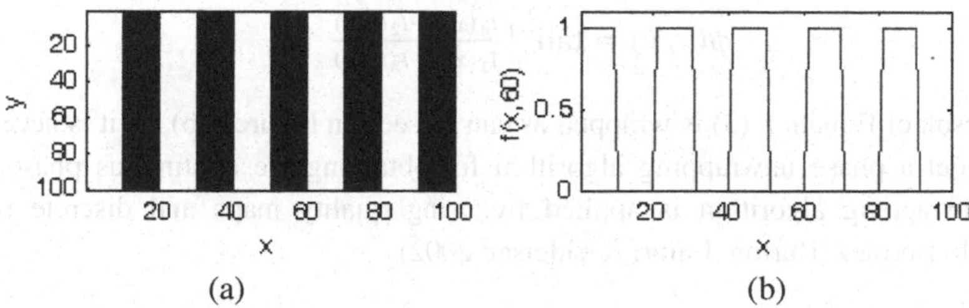

(a) (b)

Fig. 3. (a) Binary fringe pattern generate by computer, (b) Computer-generate binary fringe pattern profile in row 60, (c) image acquired by a digital camera and (d) Fringe sinusoidal profile acquired in row 60

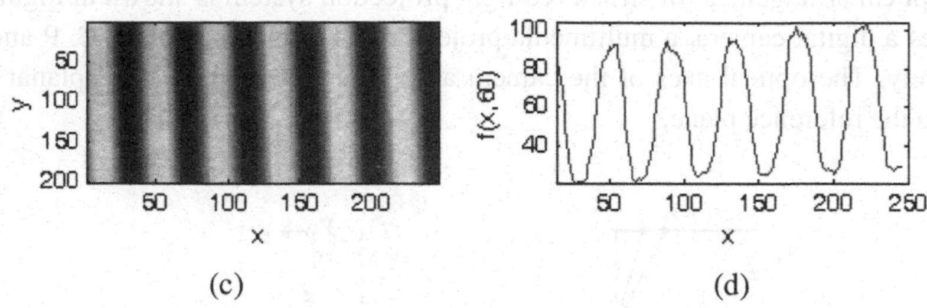

(c) (d)

Fig. 3. *(continued)*

The projected binary pattern has some advantages over a sinusoidal light pattern projection. A projected binary pattern is uniform on changes of intensity of the video projector, and the registered fringe profile adopts a sinusoidal profile due to blurring effect provoked by the use of lens in the capture system. Figure 3 (a) describes the binary pattern generated by a computer, (b) the binary pattern profile computer generated in row 60, (c) the image recorded by a digital camera (c) and (d) profile of the image recorded in row 60 (d). It can be seen that actually the profile of acquired pattern describes a sinusoidal function.

2.2 Three-Dimensional Reconstruction Module

The goal of this module is to obtain three-dimensional model of the face (3D model). It is approximated by the fringe projection technique with four-step phase-shifting method (Fu & Luo, 2011). Each image is described by the following Equation (2):

$$I_k(x,y) = a(x,y) + b(x,y)\cos\left(\phi(x,y) + (k-1)\nabla\psi\right) \tag{2}$$

where $a(x,y)$ is the background illumination, $b(x,y)$ is the modulation factor, $\phi(x,y)$ is the initial phase associate with the form of the face, $\nabla\psi$ is the phase shift between each fringe pattern, k is the sequential number of the phase shift and capture. The phase of the signal is demodulated to detect the face shape from Equation (3):

$$\phi(x,y) = \tan^{-1}\frac{I_4(x,y) - I_2(x,y)}{I_1(x,y) - I_3(x,y)} \tag{3}$$

The result of Equation (3) is wrapped as can be seen in Figure 4(b), so it is necessary to carry out a phase unwrapping algorithm for obtaining the continuous phase. The phase unwrapping algorithm is applied by using quality maps and discrete routes (Arevallilo Herráez, Burton, Lalor, & Gdeisat, 2002).

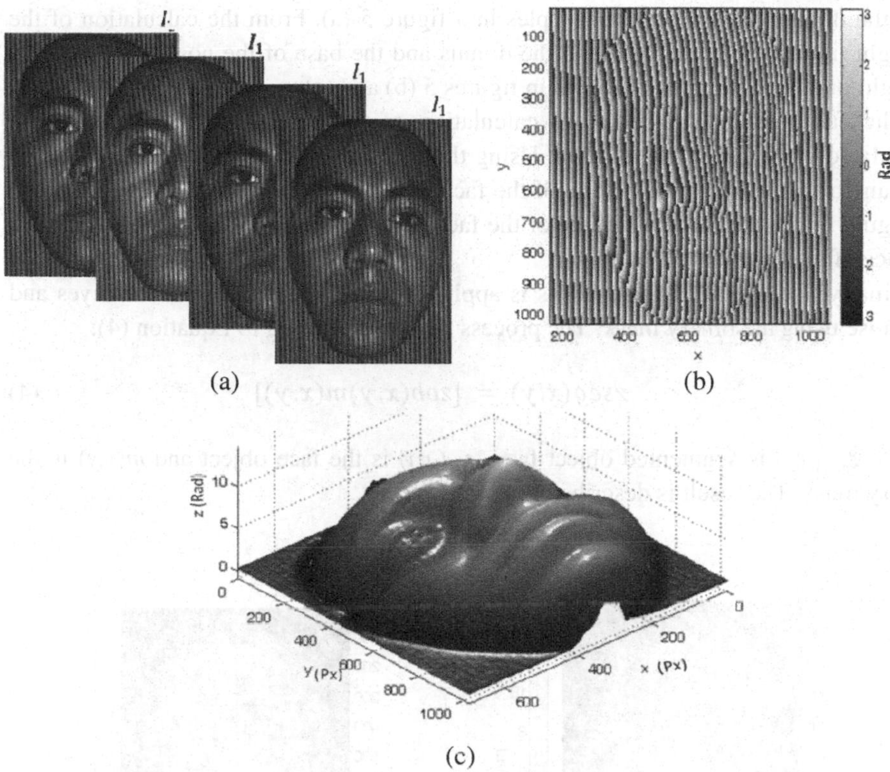

Fig. 4. (a) Images recorded with phase shifting method, (b) wrapped phase associated with the surface of the face and (c) phase unwrapped associated with the surface of the face (3D model)

The phase of the face is denoted by $\phi_I(x,y)$ and the phase of the reference plane as $\phi_R(x,y)$. When the difference of the unwrapped phases $\theta(x,y) = (\phi_I - \phi_R)$ is calculated, the three dimensional model of the face is gotten (Figure 4(c)).

2.3 Alignment and Segmentation Module

The alignment process allows orient the position of the faces with respect to a reference face, this process is carried out by means of the ICP algorithm, which minimizes the distance between the face object and the face model from the iterative calculation of the transformation matrix (Besl & McKay, 1992). The transformation matrix is calculated from the vertical profile of a face model and the tear ducts of the eyes, instead of using all points on the surface of the face.

The tear ducts of the eyes are located from the analysis of the surface by using the classifier of median and Gaussian (Colombo, Cusano, & Schettini, 2006). The base and the domus of the nose are samples in a figure 5 (a). From the calculation of the straight line which passes through the domus and the base of the nose is defined the upright profile of the face as shown in figures 5 (b) and (c).

The face model is aligned by calculating of the matrix of transformation is calculated using the ICP algorithm. Using the algorithm ICP is calculated the matrix of transformation from the profile of the face to align and the face model, as shown in figure 6 where (a) is the surface of the face before alignment and (b) is the surface of face after alignment.

Finally, the segmentation process is applied to determinate the forehead eyes and the nose using the binary mask. The process is done according to Equation (4):

$$zseg(x,y) = [zob(x,y)m(x,y)] \tag{4}$$

where $z_{seg}(x,y)$ is segmented object face, $z_{ob}(x,y)$ is the face object and $m(x,y)$ is the binary mask. The result is described in Figure 7.

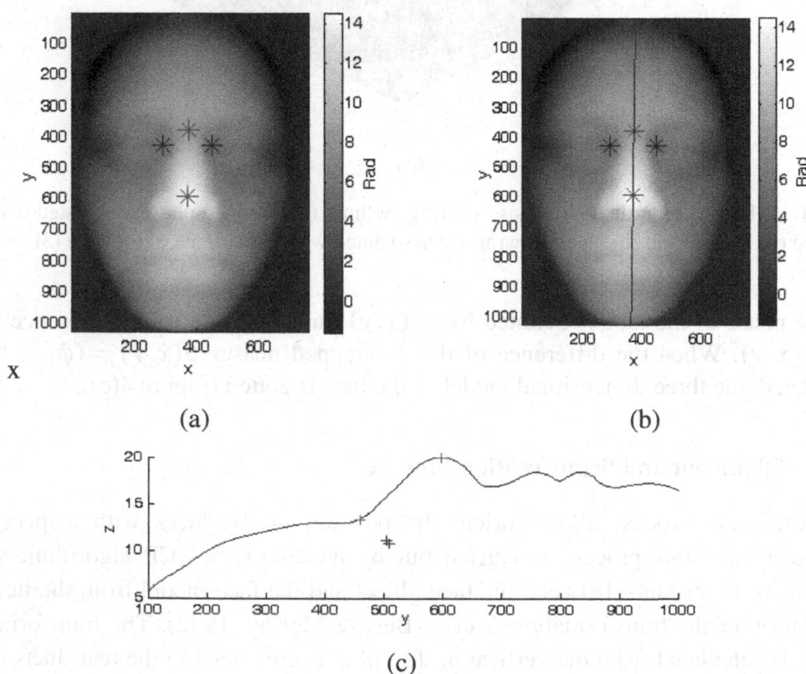

Fig. 5. (a) Landmark over the face, (b) profile overlapped on face and (c) deep of the face profile

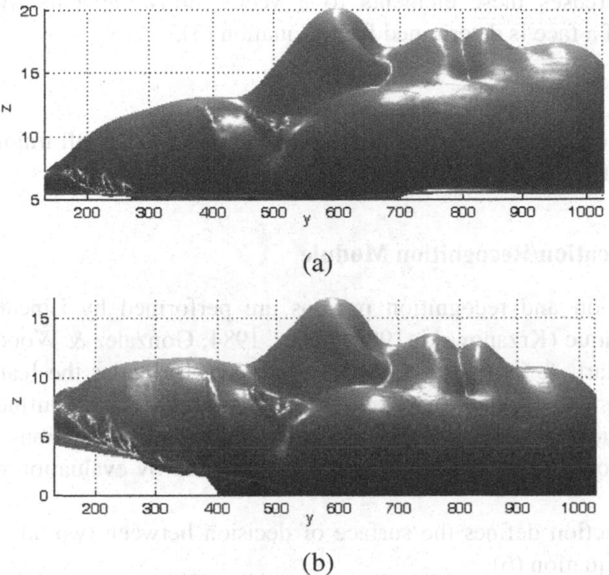

Fig. 5. Example of a face surface (a) before alignment and (b) after alignment

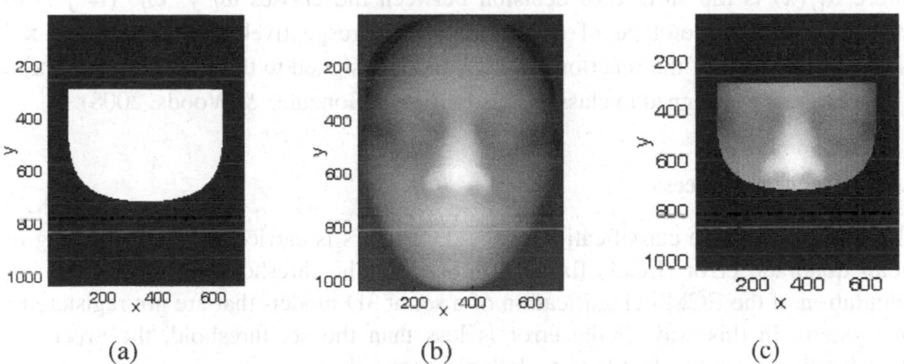

Fig. 6. Face segmentation process. (a) Binary mask, (b) 3D model before performing the segmentation, (c) 3D model after enhance segmentation

2.4 Feature Extraction Module

The descriptors of the face are obtained using the technique of Principal Component Analysis (PCA) or eigenfaces (Turk & Petland, 1991; Chenghua, Yunhong, Tieniu, & Long, 2004; Xue, Jianming, & Takashi, 2005). It is based on the analysis of the variability of the depth information of the face, which reduces the dimension of the original data set. Initially, the 3D face data is stored in a matrix of M elements, and then PCA decreases these elements to a vector of *N* elements (*N* << *M*). The descriptor **x** of a face is determined from Equation (5).

$$\mathbf{x} = \boldsymbol{UZ} \tag{5}$$

where **U** are the main components of the covariance matrix of all training faces, ***Z*** is the data of the face (Turk & Petland, 1991).

2.5 Classification/Recognition Module

The classification and recognition process are performed by Linear Discriminant Analysis technique (Krzanowski, 1988; Seber, 1984; Gonzalez & Woods, 2008; Bow, 1984; Duda, Hart, & Stork, 2001; Andrews, 1972). It divides the feature space into mutually exclusive regions, where each region defines the area of influence of a class. The classification process identifies a set of discriminant functions for calculated decision functions. Then, the descriptors are classified by evaluation of the decision functions.

A linear function defines the surface of decision between two adjacent classes is described by Equation (6).

$$d_{ij}(\mathbf{x}) = \mathbf{x}^T(\boldsymbol{m}_j - \boldsymbol{m}_i) + \tfrac{1}{2}(\boldsymbol{m}_i - \boldsymbol{m}_j)^T(\boldsymbol{m}_i + \boldsymbol{m}_j) \tag{6}$$

where $d_{ij}(\mathbf{x})$ is the surface of decision between the classes ω_i y ω_j (i≠ *j*), $\boldsymbol{m}_i$ and $\boldsymbol{m}_j$ are the prototype of classes ω_i y ω_j respectively. The descriptor **x** is evaluated for each of the functions $d_{ij}(\mathbf{x})$ and is assigned to the class ω_i if $d_{ij}(\mathbf{x}) > 0$ otherwise it is assigned in class ω_j (Bow, 1984; Gonzalez & Woods, 2008).

2.6 Decision Process

The validation of the classification of the descriptors is carried out by comparing the mean quadratic error (ECM) fixing a threshold. The threshold is defined from the calculation of the ECM's classification of a set of 3D models that are not registered in the system. In this way, if the error is less than the set threshold, the process of identification considers that face $\mathbf{x}_i$ belongs to the class ω_j.

$$\left(\mathbf{x}_i \in \omega_j \mid ECM(\mathbf{x}_i) < \text{threshold}\right) \tag{7}$$

3 Results

In the Facial verification system were recorded 173 facial models corresponding to 47 users with an average of 4 faces per person. Figure 8 corresponds to samples of the recorded 3D models, they are encoded in grey levels for viewing in 2D.

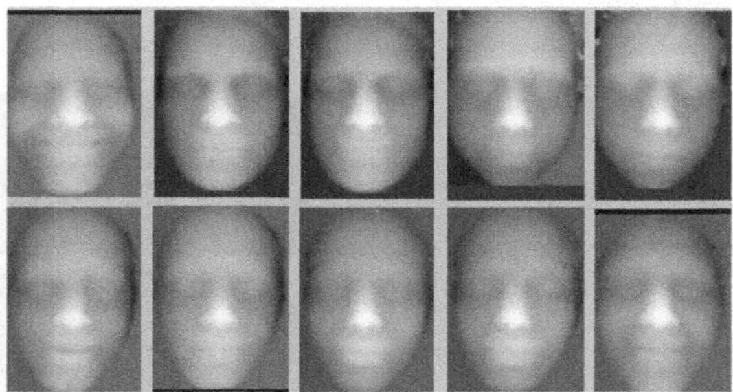

Fig. 7. Sample of three-dimensional models

They were considered two sets for the identification tests: Set A, consisting of 9 users not registered in the system; and set B, consisting of all the users registered in the system. Table 1 summarizes the results.

Table 1. Results of the classification of users registered and unregistered in the facial recognition system

Set	Num. of users	Acceptance		Reject		False positive		False negative	
		Num.	%	Num.	%	Num.	%	Num.	%
A	9	0	0	9	100	0	0	0	0
B	47	46	97.87	0	0	0	0	1	2.13

The system is capable of classifying people with different facial expressions positively since analysis of the face is only done with regions that suffer minimal variations to these changes as shown in the next four examples. It was included images with facial expressions or people wearing accessories such as glasses.

Example 1. User ID: 0047

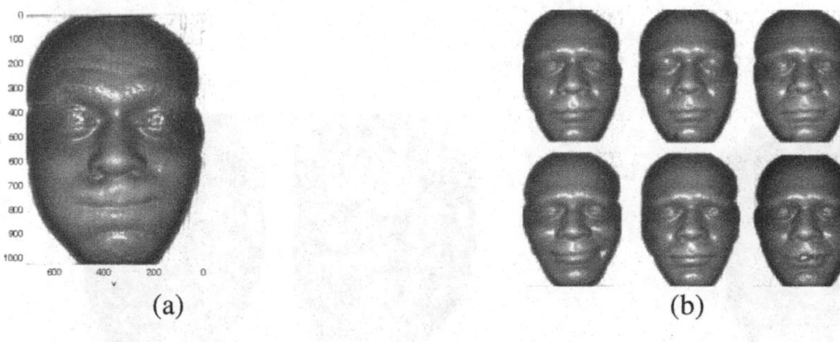

Fig. 8. a) Face object and (b) set of faces of training

Example 2. User ID: 0022.

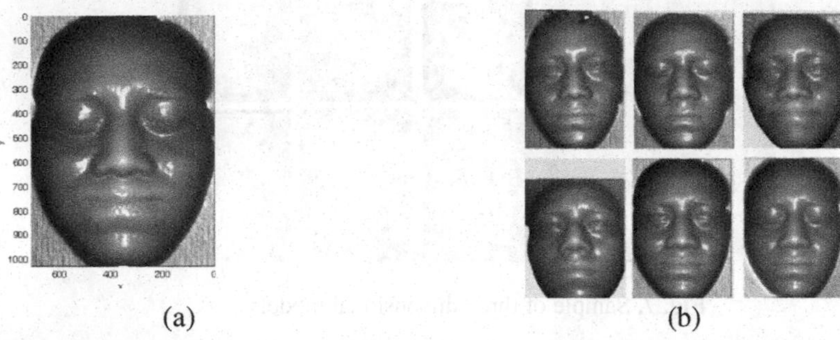

Fig. 9. a) Face object and (b) set of faces of training

Example 3. User ID: 0031.

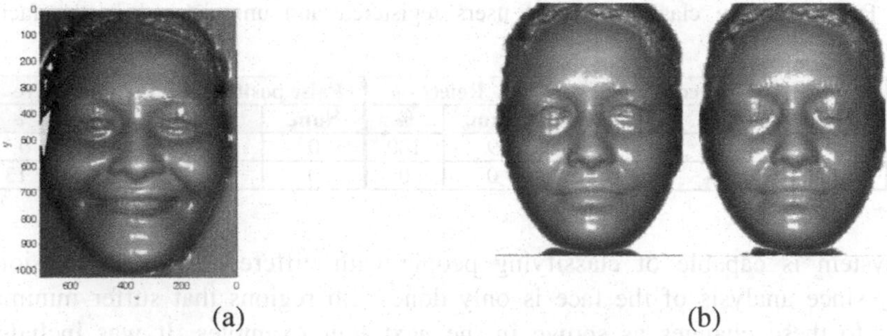

Fig. 10. a) Face object and (b) set of faces of training

Example 4. User ID: 0004.

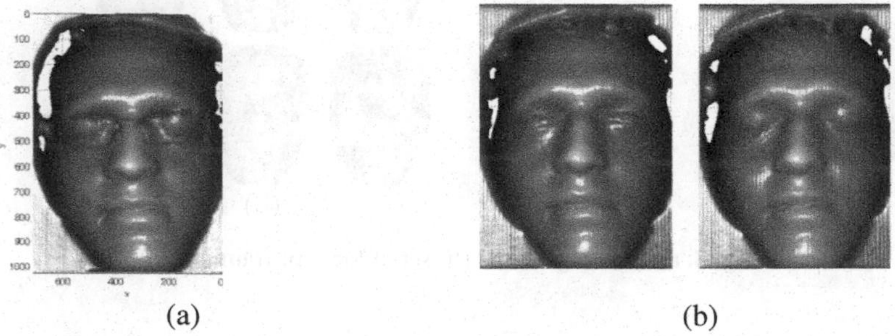

Fig. 11. a) Face object and (b) set of faces of training

The results of the classification are presented in table 2. It is worth mentioning that the error threshold for rejection is ECM=0.3682. The threshold was computed from the classification of faces whose identity is not registered in the system.

Table 2. Results of the classification of examples 1-4

Example	ID_User	ID_find	ECM	Result	Num. of training faces.
1	0022	0022	0.2547	Positive	20
2	0047	0047	0.3109	Positive	6
3	0031	0031	0.1809	Positive	2
4	0004	0004	0.2279	Positive	3

In example 1, it can be seen that one of the faces of the training set has errors of reconstruction on the side of the cheek, jaw and lips, this is because that at the time of scanning the user made any movement by altering the pattern of stripes. Even so, it qualify right way. In example 2, the important aspect to highlight is one of the faces of training has a slight rotation. The classification is positive. For example 3 and 4, the user only has two training images; despite this was one that generated a lower ECM. In example 4 the face was digitized with glasses, while those of training were digitized without this, despite the combination of variations between the object face and the training faces the classification is satisfactory.

4 Conclusions

It was introduced a facial recognition system that assigns the user identity from the analysis of the variation of the depth information from the surface of the face, which is obtained by using structured light projection and the phase shifting technique. The facial recognition system has proven to be a reliable and robust to identify effective users. It was able to identify effectively the 97.87% of users registered in the database, while 2.13% turned out with a false negative error. It is important to emphasize that the system is able to assign the (Heseltine, Pears, & Austin, 2004)identity of persons with different facial expressions, because effectively to the analysis of the information of the chamfer is only done in the regions of the face in which presents minimum variation. It is worth mentioning that the proposed alignment process allows optimize the computational load and processing time to find the optimal transformation matrix. Applications of the developed system, in principle, can be used from the control of entry/exit in the business area, control of virtual access to computer resources to control physical access in restricted areas only to personnel authorized.

In the last decade many systems related with the 3D facial recognition have been developed, such as systems that analyze points, lines and regions in the face surface (G. Gordon, 1991) with verification rates of 83.3% - 91.7%. In other hand also have developed systems that analyzes the entire information of face like in X. Chenghua, et al; Russ, et al; Yunqui, et al; and Heseltine et al. all this systems can recognize between 69 % - 100 %, however these use the entire information of face that requires many computational resources. The system that we propose use only a small region of the face that allows optimizes time and computational resources.

References

Song, H., Yang, U., Lee, S., Sohn, K.: 3D Face Recognition Based on Facial Shape Indexes with Dynamic Programming. In: Zhang, D., Jain, A.K. (eds.) ICB 2005. LNCS, vol. 3832, pp. 99–105. Springer, Heidelberg (2005)

Andrews, H.C.: Introduction to mathematical techniques in pattern recognition. Wiley-Interscience, Canada (1972)

Arevallilo Herráez, M., Burton, D.R., Lalor, M.J., Gdeisat, M.A.: Fast two-dimensional phase-unwrapping algorithm based on sorting by reliability following a noncontinuous path. Applied Optics 41(35), 7437–7444 (2002)

Arun, A.R., Karthik, N., Anil, K.J.: Hand book of multibiometrics. Springer, New York (2006)

Besl, P.J., McKay, N.D.: A method for registration of 3-D shapes. IEEE Transactions on Pattern Analysis and Machine Intelligence 14(2), 39–256 (1992)

Bow, S.-T.: Pattern recognition. Aplication to data-set problems. Electrocal Engineering and Electronics, Pennsylvania (1984)

Cabello Pardos, E.: Técnicas de reconocimiento facial mediante redes neuronales. Departamento de tecnología fotonica, facultad de informática, Madrid (2004)

Chenghua, X., Yunhong, W., Tieniu, T., Long, Q.: A new attempt to face recognition using 3d eigenfaces. In: Proc. ACCV 2004, pp. 884–889 (2004)

Colombo, A., Cusano, C., Schettini, R.: 3D face detection using curvature analysis. Pattern Recognition. The Journal of the Pattern Recognition Society 39(3), 445–455 (2006)

Duda, R., Hart, P., Stork, D.: Pattern clasification. A Wiley International Publication (2001)

Fu, Y., Luo, Q.: Fringe projection profilometry based on a novel phase shift method. Optics Express 19(22) (2011)

Gordon, G.G.: Face Recognition from depth maps and surface curvature. In: Conference on Geometric Methods in Computer Vision, pp. 234–247. SPIE, San Diego (1991)

Gonzalez, R., Woods, R.: Digital image proscessing. Pearson Pretince Hall, New Jersey (2008)

Heseltine, T., Pears, N., Austin, J.: Three-dimensional Face Recognition: an Eigensurface Approach. In: International Conference on Image Processing. IEEE, Singapore (2004)

Jain, A., Flynn, P., Ross, A.: Handbook of biometrics. Springer, New York (2008)

Krzanowski, W.J.: Principles of Multivariate Analysis: A User's Perspective. Oxford University Press, New York (1988)

Kyong, K.I., Bowyer, K.W., Flynn, P.J.: Multiple Nose Region Matching for 3D Face Recognition Under Varying Facial Expression. Transactions on Pattern Analisysis and machine Intelligence, 1695–1700 (2006)

Russ, T., Boehen, C., Peters, T.: 3D Face Recognition Using 3D Alignment for PCA. In: Conference on Computer Vision and Pattern Recognition. IEEE Computer Society (2006)

Saeed, K., Nagashima, T.: Biometrics and Kansei Enginering. Springer, New York (2012)

Seber, G.: Multivariate Observations. John Wiley & Sons, Inc., Hoboken (1984)

Siva Gorthi, S., Rastogi, P.: Fringe Projection Techniques: Whither we are? Optics and Lasers in Engineering 48(2), 133–140 (2009)

Turk, M., Petland, A.: Eigenfaces for recognition. Journal of Cognitive Neurosience 3(1), 71–86 (1991)

Wayman, J.: Introduction to biometrics. Springer, New York (2011)

Woz, M., Graña, M., Corchado, E.: A survey of multiple classifier systems as hybrid systems. Information Fusion 16, 3–17 (2014)

Xue, Y., Jianming, L., Takashi, Y.: A method of 3D face recognition based on principal component analysis algorithm. In: IEEE International Symposium on Circuits and Systems, ISCAS 2005 (2005)

Yunqui, L., Haibin, L., Qingmin, L.: Geometric Features of 3D Face and Recognition of It by PCA. Journal of Multimedia 6(2) (April 2002)

Zhang, C.: A survey of recent advances in face detecction. Microsoft corporation (2010)

Ear Recognition with Neural Networks Based on Fisher and Surf Algorithms

Pedro Luis Galdámez, María Angélica González Arrieta, and Miguel Ramón Ramón

University of Salamanca, Plaza de los Caídos, 37008 Salamanca, Spain
{peter.galdamez,angelica}@usal.es, miguel.ramon@dgp.mir.es

Abstract. This paper offers an approach to biometric analysis using ears for recognition. The ear has all the assets that a biometric trait should possess. Because it is a study field in potential growth, this research offers an approach using Speeded Up Robust Features (SURF) and Fisher Linear Discriminant Analysis (LDA) as an input of two neural networks with the purpose to detect and recognize a person by the patterns of its ear. It also includes the development of an application with .net to show experimental results of the applied theory. In the preprocessing task, the system adds sturdiness using Hausdorff distance to increase the performance filtering for the subjects to use in the testing stage of the neural network. To perform this study, we worked with the help of Ávila's police school (Spain), where we built a database with approximately 300 ears. The investigation results shown that the integration of LDA and SURF in neural networks can improve the ear recognition process and provide robustness in changes of illumination and perception.

Keywords: Neural Network, Fisher, SURF Algorithm, Ear Recognition.

1 Introduction

The ear has been used as a mean of human recognition in forensic activities for long time. During the investigation of several crime scenes, earprints commonly have been used to identify a suspect when there is no information of fingerprints. A recognition system based on images of the ears is very similar to a typical face recognition system, however, the ears have some advantages over the face; for instance, their appearance does not change due its expression is less affected by the aging process; indeed, their details and internal form are maintained over the years, although its size is changing over the years, their color is usually uniform and their background is predictable.

Although the use of information from ear identification of individuals has been studied, it is still debatable whether or not the ear can be considered unique or unique enough to be used as a biometric. However, any physical or behavioural trait can be used as biometric identification mechanism if it is universal, that every human being possesses an identifier, being distinctive and unique to each individual, invariant in time, and measurable automatically or manually; the ear accomplish all these characteristics.

M. Polycarpou et al. (Eds.): HAIS 2014, LNAI 8480, pp. 254–265, 2014.
© Springer International Publishing Switzerland 2014

2 Brief Review of the Literature

Significant progress has been made in the past few years in ear biometrics field. One of the most important techniques which are known to detect the ears is raised by Burge and Burger [17] who have made the process of detection using deformable contours with the observation that initialization contour requires user interaction. Therefore, the location of the ear is not fully automatic. Meanwhile Hurley et al. [9] used the technique of force field, this process ensures that it is not required to know the location of the ear to perform recognition. However, only applies when the technique has the specific image of the ear out of noise. In [19], Yan and Bowyer have used manual technique based on two previous lines for detection, where takes a line along the border between the ear and face while another line crosses up and down the ear.

A. Cummings et al. [3] show a strategy using the image ray transform which is capable of highlighting the ear tubular structures. The technique exploits the helix elliptical shape to calculate the localization. Kumar et al [2], have introduced a proposal where uses skin segmentation and edge map detection to find the ear, once they find the ear region apply an active contour technique [20] to get the exact location of ear contours, the technique has been tested over 700 ear images. As well as these techniques there are many other significant proposals.

In other terms a biometric recognition system requires the discovery of unique features that can be measured and compared in order to correctly identify subjects. There are some known techniques for ear recognition specially in 2D and 3D images, as the strategies based on appearance, force transformation, geometrical features, and the use of neural networks. The most used technique for face recognition [18], principal component analysis (PCA), is also suitable for use in ear recognition. PCA [12] is an orthogonal transform of a dataset which exploits the training data with the propose to find out a set of orthogonal basis vectors or a new axes that causes the projection onto the first axis (principal component) to represent one greatest variance in data, subsequent orthogonal axes to represent decreasing amounts of variance with minimum reconstruction mean square error. This strategy fall under appearance based techniques.

The first application for ear recognition was the PCA by Victor et al. [4] they used PCA to perform an comparative analysis between face and ear recognition, concluding that the face performs better than the ear. However, Chang et al. [16] also have accomplished a comparison using PCA and found that ears provided similar performance to faces, they concluded that ears are essentially just as good as faces for biometric recognition. There are many proposals to solve the problem, in this paper only has done a small review from some of them, the next section introduce an intent to solve the problem of ear recognition using a practical way, applying some interesting concepts for 2D images and real time video.

3 Ear Recognition System

Most of ear biometric articles have centered their attention on recognition using manually cropped ear images. This is due to the fact that ear detection is a complicated problem, especially because ear images vary in pose and scale under different conditions. However, for a robust and efficient ear recognition system is desired to detect the ear from the image face profile in an automatic way.

Recognition systems traditionally follow a set of standards, such as, acquiring images, pre-processing, feature extraction, and the classification. Nevertheless, it is important to notice that the process that we are about to describe is based in the combination of some existing methods in order to build a robust system. In this way, the system combines a series of algorithms that give significant results individually, and when they are combined, achieve a higher degree of robustness with improving in problems such as changes in brightness and perspective.

The chart one shows the workflow that the project will follow; describing how face profile is captured and how we tried to detect the ear. Once it has been detected is extracted removing the background; here the Hausdorff distance is used to filter the candidates, the next step is the feature extraction using SURF and LDA, features are used as input in two neural networks defining a threshold to determine the precision required. If both neural networks compute different results or the result does not exceed the threshold, the system will reject the ear which will be classified as unrecognized. These tasks will be deepened in upcoming sections.

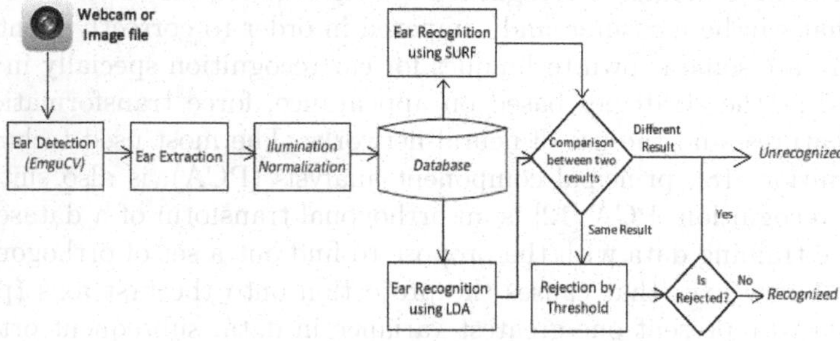

Fig. 1. System flow chart

4 Detecting and Tracking the Ear

There are some techniques which could be used to detect ear automatically. In fact, these techniques usually can detect the ear only when a profile face image does not contain a noisy around the ear. These techniques are not useful, when profile face images are affected by scaling and rotation. This section proposes an useful ear localization technique which attempts to solve these issues.

4.1 Ear Localization

OpenCV and its wrapper for .net framework EmguCV includes different object detectors based on the Viola-Jones framework, most of them are been constructed to deal with different patterns as frontal face, eyes, nose, etc. Modesto

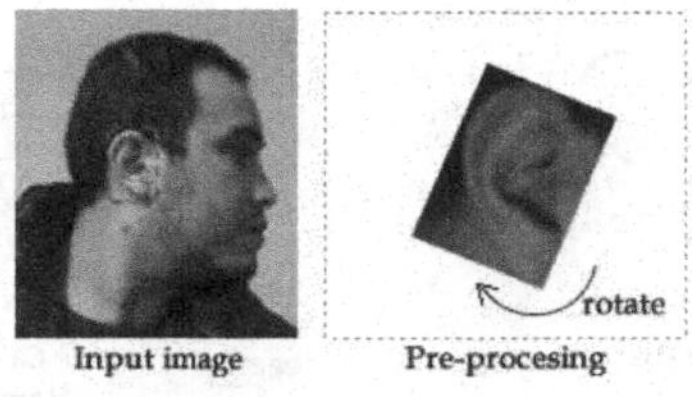

Fig. 2. Ear detection

Castellón-Santana et al. [7] have developed a Haarcascade classifier to be used with OpenCV to detect left and right ears. This classifier represents a first step to create a robust ear detection and tracking system. The application is developed in C#.

With the ear identified we proceed to perform the pre-processing task, converting the image to gray scale and begin the normalization process, the first step is to perform the segmentation of the image applying a mask to extract only the ear, then the image is converted to an edge map using the canny edge filter. If w is the width of the image in pixels and h is the height of the image in pixels, the canny edge detector takes as input an array $w \times h$ of gray values and sigma. The output is a binary image with a value 1 for edge pixels, i.e., the pixel which constitute an edge and a value 0 for all other pixels. We calculate a line between major and minor y value in the edge image to rotate and normalize each image, trying to put the lobule of the ear in the centre. This process is to try to get all the images whose shape is similar to the image to identify. We identify some points on the external shape of the ear and the angle created by the center of the line drawn before and the section in the ear's tragus with the major x value.

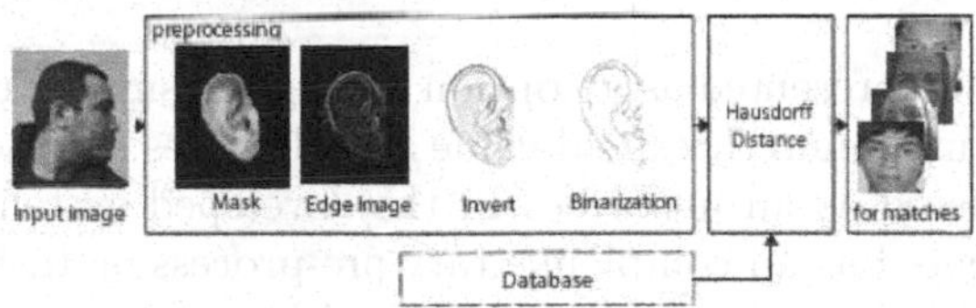

Fig. 3. Image preprocessing

4.2 Application of the Hausdorff Distance

The Hausdorff distance measure used in this document is based on the assumption that the ear regions have different degrees of importance, where characteristics such as helix, antihelix, tragus, antitragus, concha, lobe and ear contour; play the most important role in ear recognition. The algorithm applied is based on what is stated in [15].

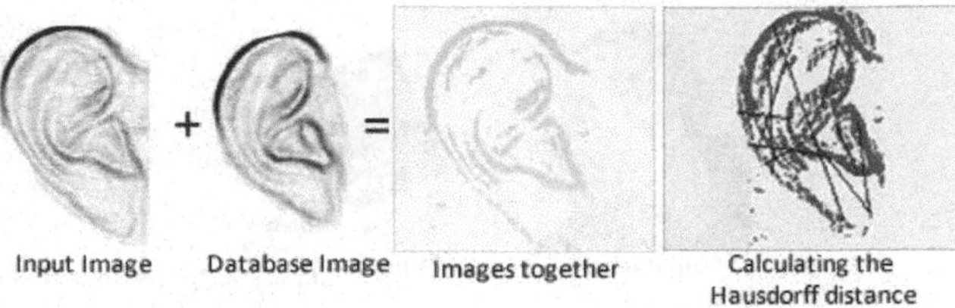

Fig. 4. Hausdorff preprocessing

In applying the Hausdorff distance, basically operates the comparison of edge maps. The advantage of using edges to match two objects, is that this representation is robust to illumination change. Accordingly, the edge detection algorithm used will have a significant effect on performance. Figure 3 shows the flow used in the application of the algorithm, and figure 4 represent an example of the Hausdorff distance trying to put together two images, in this case is not important that two images have been taken in different perspectives because the algorithm try to calculate the distance between the points and with this distance we choose a group of image of our database, this task works like a filter choosing and discarding some images in order to strengthen the classification system.

The procedure involves removing the background of the image as it was performed in the preprocessing original, added some steps after image masking, we proceed to obtain the edges using the canny and sobel filter, the image is reversed to operate with a white background, then the ear is binarized, similar procedure is applied to each image stored in the database. With the obtained objects we compare pixels to get how similar are the two figures, as if they were geometric figures performing a comparison process, calculating the Hausdorff distance, we compare pixels to get how similar are the two figures, resulting in a collection of values that contain the distance of the input image with respect to each item in the database.

The object can be presented as an option having the smaller relative distance; if not exceeds the minimum threshold value and identifies the user, otherwise the problem is considered as an unsolved. In the developed system, the Hausdorff algorithm is presented as an complementary pre-processing task to increase the performance of the neural network and recognition process using SURF algorithm, if the system procedures identify that the user is the same, even without exceeding the thresholds defined in each process, the image is accepted to belong to user input identified by all three techniques combined. In this stage we also compute the SURF features to track the ear in the video.

4.3 Tracking the Ear

Speeded Up Robust Features (SURF)[11] is a scale and rotation invariant interest point detector and descriptor. It has been designed for extracting highly distinctive and invariant feature points (also called interest points or key-points) from images.

One of the basic reasons to use SURF for the feature representation is to analyse how the distinctive characteristics works in images, and at the same time is to found more robust with respect to change, taking into account the point of view, rotation and scale, illumination changes and occlusion [11] as compared to other scale and rotation invariant shape descriptors such as SIFT [8] and GLOH [14]. In addition for the extracting SURF features from an image there are two main steps, which describe how to find key points and the calculation of their descriptor vectors. The result for the feature vectors SURF is the relative measured to the dominant orientation to generate each vector that represent an invariant with respect to rotation of the image.

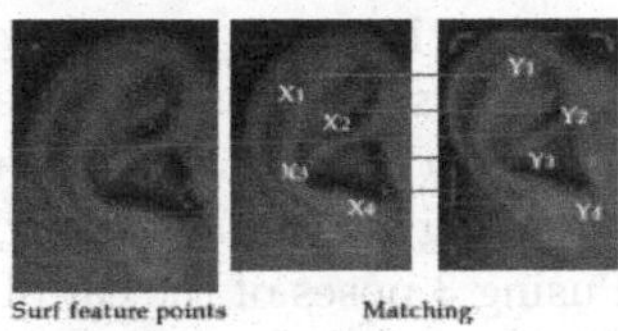

Fig. 5. Example of SURF features

The way SURF process pairing is using the most proximate neighbour ratio pairing. To get the greatest pairing match for a key-point of a picture inside in another picture is elucidated by detecting the most proximate neighbour in the other key-points from a second picture where the most proximate neighbour is defined as the key-point with the least Euclidean distance from the known key-point of the first picture between their characteristic unidirectional matrices. Due to the fact that these SURF vectors are invariant to the image rotation, the process of ear detection combining the previous viola-jones approach with the SURF vectors becomes robust and efficient.

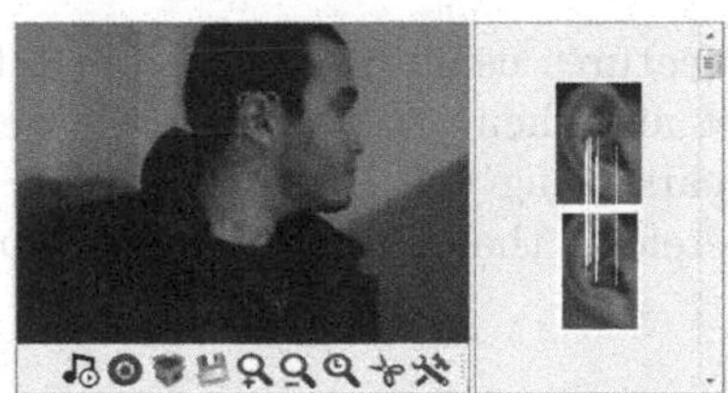

Fig. 6. Tracking ear using SURF features

The approach to isolate the ear in the image, the prototype we used for the ear identification should reveal the characteristics of scale and rotation immutability. To calculate such prototypes in a suggested method, an invariant shape characteristic to rotation and scale was used. Among numerous scale and rotation invariant shape characteristics, SURF [13] offers respectable distinctive features and at the same time it is robust to variations in viewing circumstances, rotations and scales. SURF denotes a picture by detecting some exclusive feature points in it and then by describing them with the support of a unidirectional feature descriptor matrix.

5 Ear Recognition Using Neural Networks

Neural networks provide a great alternative to many other conventional classifiers. This type of algorithms represent powerful tools that can be trained to perform complex tasks and functions in computer vision applications, either in pre-processing tasks, feature extraction and pattern recognition. Two neural networks are used in the system, the first one based on the SURF algorithm we have been talking and the second using a classification based on LDA, both networks have been trained and proven using the database of the police college of Ávila. The training was performed using 3 poses of the ear of each person and the tests were done with 10-n poses of the same people.

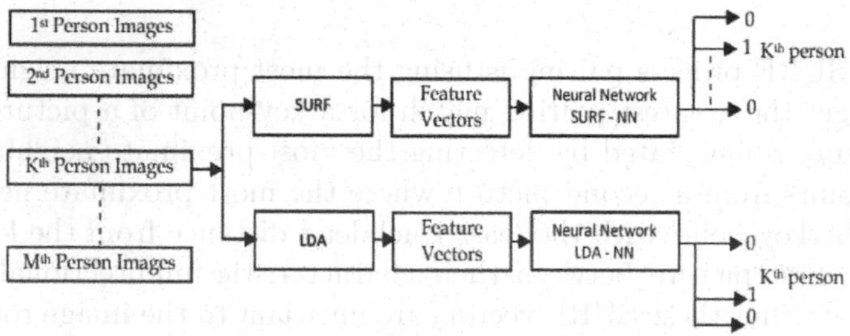

Fig. 7. Training phase of both Neural Networks

After calculating the features using SURF the projection vectors are calculated for the training set and then used to train the network. Similarly, after calculation of the fisherears using the LDA, projection vectors are calculated for the training set. Therefore, the second neural network is trained by these vectors.

5.1 SURF Neural Network

The ear image is recreated through the SURF algorithm as a set of salient points, where each on is associated with a vector descriptor. Each can be of 64 or 128 dimensions. If 128 dimensional vector is chosen, it is more exacting in comparison to the 64 vector. So the 128 dimensional descriptor vector is considered the most exacting feature based in the knowledge that is always best to represent the image with the most powerful discriminative features.

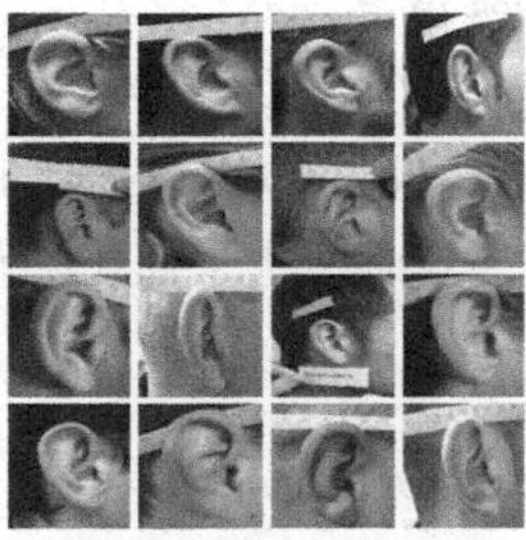

Fig. 8. Avila's Police School Database

A method to obtain unique characteristic fusion of one sole individual is proposed by combining characteristics acquired from various training instances of the individual. If we have n ear images of an individual for training, a fused prototype is gained by fusing the feature descriptor array of all training images collected, considering the redundant descriptor array only once. We had to use a small database made for the training purpose with 309 pictures matching to 3 ear captures from 103 persons. Having all the images processed, a collection was made with their respective tags describing the images and fusion vector calculated before indicating to whom the image belongs.

The parameter settings of the neural network used in this method are dynamic, the output neurons depends on Hausdorff Distance filter stage where the algorithm selects some possible answers to the recognition problem in order to reduce the amount of candidates. The hidden layer is created dynamically, respecting that the number of hidden neurons should be between the size of the input layer and the size of the output layer, should be 2/3 the size of the input layer, plus the size of the output layer; and less than twice the size of the input layer based on the research of Jeff Heaton [10].

5.2 Linear Discriminant Analysis Neural Network

Linear discriminant analysis or fisherears method in our case, overcomes the limitations of PCA method by applying the fisher's linear discriminant criterion. This criterion tries to maximize the ratio of the determinant of the between-class scatter matrix of the projected samples to the determinant of the within-class. The LDA approach is similar to the eigenears method which projects the training images into a subspace. The test images are projected into the same subspace and identified using a similarity measure. The ear which has the minimum distance with the test ear image is labelled with the identity of that image. The minimum distance can be calculated using the Euclidian distance. The Fisher algorithm that we implement basically goes like the version exposed in [5,21].

We construct the image matrix x with each column representing an image. Each image is assigned to a class in the corresponding class vector c. Then, we proceed to project x into the $(N-c)$ dimensional subspace as P with the rotation matrix $WPca$ identified by a PCA, where:

- N is the number of samples in x.
- c is unique number of classes $(length(unique(C)))$

In the next step we calculate the between-classes scatter of the projection P as $Sb = \sum_{i=1}^{c} N_i * (mean_i - mean) * (mean_i - mean)^T$ where:

- $mean$ is the total mean of P
- $mean_i$ is the mean of class i in P
- N_i is the number of samples for class i

Also, we proceed to calculate the within-classes scatter of P using the next formula $Sw = \sum_{i=1}^{c} \sum_{x_k \in X_i} (x_k - mean_i) * (x_k - mean_i)^T$ where:

- x_i are the samples of class i
- x_k is a sample of x_i
- $mean_i$ is the mean of class i in P.

We apply a standard linear discriminant analysis and maximize the ratio of the determinant of between-class scatter and within-class scatter. The solution is given by the set of generalized eigenvectors $Wfld$ of Sb and Sw corresponding to their eigenvalue. The rank of Sb is almost $(c-1)$, so there are only $(c-1)$ non-zero eigenvalues, cut off the rest. Finally we obtain the fisherears by $W = WPca * Wfld$ [21].

These vectors are used as inputs to train our neural network. In the training algorithm, the unidirectional vectors belonging to an individual, are taken as positive returning 1 as the neuron output assigned to that user and 0 to other neurons when the new image has been captured, we compute new descriptors. These descriptors are entered into the neural network, the outputs of individual neurons are compared, and if the maximum output level exceeds the predefined threshold, then it is determined that the user belongs to the ear assigned to the neuron with the index activated.

6 Experimental Results

The results obtained in the process of detection and recognition of the ear are presented in this section, table 1 shows the percentages of accuracy when only using the Viola-Jones classifier included in OpenCV vs the potentiation accomplished by adding the tracking with SURF features. That can be seen in 2D images or photographs the difference are not so evident, however when the process is done on video, the difference is almost 10 percentage points, and is only done when considering the location of the ear in the video in different pose and lighting conditions. If we take into consideration the time it succeeds in maintaining trying to identify the object, the algorithm combined with SURF tracking is much more accurate because these features allow you to place the image even if it has a 180 degrees event that does not happen with the ears.

In table 2 and figure 9 we can observe the results of the recognition process and system performance. At this stage we have compared the results obtained

Table 1. Ear Detection (Haar-Cascade and adding SURF tracking)

	#Attemps	*EarLocalization(%)*	
		Haar − Cascade	*with SURF tracking*
2D Images	308	92.53	98.70
Real Time Video	314	86.69	95.13

Table 2. (%)Performance of Conventional PCA vs LDA-NN and SURF-NN

Training Images	Testing Images	*PCA*	*LDA − NN*	*SURF − NN*
20	80	73	81	82
30	71	77	83	84
50	87	78	88	84
80	104	83	88	89
100	149	83	89	93
120	186	85	90	94
150	305	86	93	97

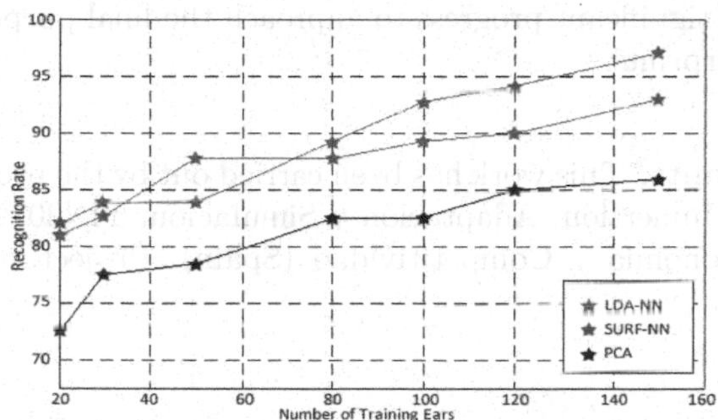

Fig. 9. Recognition rate vs number of training ears

with traditional algorithms such as PCA and our propose using the two neural networks with SURF and LDA to check the validity of our work. In this sense the results are encouraging, using SURF features as input of a neural network with different test subjects, we get a recognition percentage higher than the traditional algorithms in video. Summarizing with perspective and illumination in normal conditions, we get 86% of succeed in recognition with PCA, 93% with LDA-NN algorithm, using the neural network with SURF descriptors, the percentage increased to 97%, over more than 300 attempts of different individuals.

7 Conclusion and Future Work

The integration of two algorithms is the main result of this paper. the first technique is based on the SURF preprocessing followed by a feed forward neural network based classifier (SURF-NN), and the second is based on the LDA with another feed forward neural network (LDA-NN). The feature projection vectors obtained through the SURF and LDA techniques are used as input values in the training and testing stages in both architectures. The proposed system shows improvement on the recognition rates over the conventional fisher and PCA that use the Euclidean distance. Additionally, the recognition performance of SURF-NN is higher than the LDA-NN among the proposed system.

The neural network using SURF descriptors as input appears to be better over variation in lighting. The LDA-NN and SURF-NN perform better than the PCA traditional method over changes on illumination and perspective. Changes in preprocessing process allows better results specially using Hausdorff distance as a filter stage. Results have shown that approximately 95.03% of ear recognition accuracy is achieved with a simple 3-layer feed-forward neural network with back-propagation training even if the images contains some noise.

As future work, the most interesting and useful tool for the police is to achieve the development of an application not only able to propose candidates from the image of an ear, but also to achieve the identification and recognition of a criminal using an earprint. The results of this research are pointing towards that goal, they show a significant progress to approach the final purpose, recognition based on these earprints.

Acknowledgements. This work has been carried out by the project Sociedades Humano-Agente: Inmersión, Adaptación y Simulación. TIN2012-36586-C03-03. Ministerio de Economía y Competitividad (Spain). Project co-financed with FEDER funds.

References

1. Abraham, A.: Special issue: Hybrid approaches for approximate reasoning. Journal of Intelligent and Fuzzy Systems 23(2-3), 41–42 (2012)
2. Kumar, A., Hanmandlu, M., Kuldeep, M., Gupta, H.M.: Automatic ear detection for online biometric applications. In: Proceedings of National Conference on Computer Vision, Pattern Recognition, Image Processing and Graphics, NCVPRIPG 2011, pp. 146–149 (2011)
3. Cummings, A., Nixon, M., Carter, J.: A novel ray analogy for enrolment of ear biometrics. In: Proceedings of International Conference on Biometrics: Theory, Applications and Systems (BTAS 2010), pp. 1–6 (2010)
4. Victor, B., Bowyer, K., Sarkar, S.: An evaluation of face and ear biometrics. In: Proceedings of International Conference on Pattern Recognition (ICPR 2002), vol. 1, pp. 429–432 (2002)
5. Belhumeur, P.N., Hespanha, J.P., Kriegman, D.J.: Eigenfaces vs. Fisherfaces: Recognition Using Class Specific Linear Projection. IEEE Transactions on Pattern Analysis and Machine Intelligence (1997)
6. Borrajo, M.L., Baruque, B., Corchado, E., Bajo, J., Corchado, J.M.: Hybrid neural intelligent system to predict business failure in small-to-medium-size enterprises. International Journal of Neural Systems 21(04), 277–296

7. Castrillón-Santana, M., Lorenzo-Navarro, J., Hernández-Sosa, D.: An Study on Ear Detection and Its Applications to Face Detection. In: Lozano, J.A., Gámez, J.A., Moreno, J.A. (eds.) CAEPIA 2011. LNCS, vol. 7023, pp. 313–322. Springer, Heidelberg (2011)
8. Lowe, D.G.: Distinctive image features from scale-invariant keypoints. International Journal of Computer Vision 60(2), 91–110 (2004)
9. Hurley, D.J., Nixon, M.S., Carter, J.N.: Force field feature extraction for ear biometrics. In: Computer Vision and Image Understanding (2005)
10. Heaton, J.: Introduction to Neural Networks for C#, 2nd edn. (2010)
11. Bay, H., Ess, A., Tuytelaars, T., Van Gool, L.: Speeded-up robust features (SURF). In: Computer Vision and Image Understanding (2008)
12. Jolliffe, I.T.: Principal Components Analysis, 2nd edn. Springer, New York (2002)
13. Bustard, J., Nixon, M.: 3D morphable model construction for robust ear and face recognition. In: Proceedings of International Conference on Computer Vision and Pattern Recognition (CVPR 2010), pp. 2582–2589 (2010)
14. Mikolajczyk, K., Schmid, C.: A performance evaluation of local descriptors. IEEE Pattern Analysis and Machine Intelligence (2005)
15. Lin, K.-H., Lam, K.-M., Siu, W.-C.: Spatially eigen-weighted Hausdorff distances for human face recognition, Polytechnic University, Hong Kong (2002)
16. Chang, K., Bowyer, K.W., Sarkar, S., Victor, B.: Comparison and combination of ear and face images in appearance-based biometrics. IEEE Transactions on Pattern Analysis and Machine Intelligence 25(9), 1160–1165 (2003)
17. Burge, M., Burger, W.: Ear biometrics in computer vision. In: Proceedings of International Conference on Pattern Recognition, ICPR 2000 (2000)
18. Turk, M., Pentland, A.: Eigenfaces for recognition. Journal of Cognitive Neuroscience 3(1), 71–86 (1991)
19. Yan, P., Bowyer, K.W.: Empirical evaluation of advanced ear biometrics. In: Conference on Computer Vision and Pattern Recognition-Workshop, vol. 3 (2005)
20. Lankton, S., Tannenbaum, A.: Localizing region-based active contours. IEEE Transactions on Image Processing 17(11), 2029–2039 (2008)
21. Wagner, P.: Fisherfaces (January 13, 2013), `http://www.bytefish.de/blog/fisherfaces/`

Hybrid Sparse Linear and Lattice Method for Hyperspectral Image Unmixing

Ion Marques* and Manuel Graña

Computational Intelligence Group, University of the Basque Country, UPV/EHU, Spain

Abstract. Linear spectral unmixing aims to estimate the fractional abundances of spectral signatures in each pixel. The Linear Mixing Model (LMM) of hyperspectral images assumes that pixel spectra are affine combinations of fundamental spectral signatures called endmembers. Endmember induction algorithms (EIA) extract the endmembers from the hyperspectral data. The WM algorithm assumes that a set of Affine Independent vectors can be extracted from the rows and columns of dual Lattice Autoassociative Memories (LAAM) built on the image spectra. Indeed, the set of endmembers induced by this algorithm defines a convex polytope covering the hyperspectral image data. However, the number of endmembers extracted can be huge. This calls for additional endmember selection steps, and to approaching the unmixing problem with linear sparse regression techniques. In this paper, we combine WM algorithm with clustering techniques and Conjugate Gradient Pursuit (CGP) for endmember induction. Our experiments are conducted using hyperspectral imaging obtained by the Airborne Visible/Infrared Imaging Spectometer of the NASA Jet Propulsion Laboratory. The limited length of the paper limits the experimental depth to the confirmation of the validity of the proposed method.

1 Introduction

The Linear Mixing Model (LMM) [7] assumes that the spectral signature of one pixel of the hyperspectral image is a linear combination of the endmember spectra corresponding to the aggregation of materials in the scene due to reduced sensor spatial resolution. Given a hyperspectral image $\mathbf{H}$, whose pixels are vectors in L-dimensional space, it spectral signature is characterized by a set of endmembers, $\mathbf{E} = \{\mathbf{e}_1, \mathbf{e}_2, ..., \mathbf{e}_q\}$. The spatial-spectral characterization is a tuple $(\mathbf{E}, \alpha)$, where , α is an $q \times 1$ vector of fractional abundances resulting from the unmixing process. For each pixel, the linear model is written as

$$\mathbf{x} = \mathbf{E}\alpha + \mathbf{n} \tag{1}$$

where $\mathbf{x}$ is a is a $L \times 1$ column vector of measured reflectance values and n represents the noise affecting each band.

* Ion Marques has a predoctoral grant from the Basque Goverment.

M. Polycarpou et al. (Eds.): HAIS 2014, LNAI 8480, pp. 266–273, 2014.
© Springer International Publishing Switzerland 2014

The typical unsupervised hyperspectral scenario involves two steps: a) Inducing a set of endmembers $\mathbf{E}$ from the hyperspectral image and b) estimating the fractional abundances α. Contrarily to this unsupervised approach, a semi-supervised proposition would involve obtaining endmembers from some spectral library by an expert user. The unsupervised approach has the advantage of not requiring user expertise, and of being automatically fitted to the image content. For instance, endmembers can be used as features for content based image retrieval [2].

The WM algorithm [10] is a Lattice Computing based EIA finding a collection of affine independent vectors that define a convex polytope covering the data of the image in high dimensional spectral space. The algorithm is very fast, using only lattice operators and the resulting endmember set has a direct relation with the image data. However, it has the inconvenient of producing too many endmembers, which are strongly correlated. Therefore, some endmember selection method is needed to find the relevant endmembers which produce the most parsimonious explanation of the data. In this paper we propose a clustering step followed by the application of greedy sparse methods, based on gradient pursuit [1]. The aim of the sparse methods is to find the minimal set of contributions from a dictionary that make up the data with minimal loss. Formally, if we denote a sparse fractional abundance vector α, the unmixing problem is then

$$\min_{\alpha} \|\alpha\|_0 \text{ subject to } \|\mathbf{x} - \mathbf{E}\alpha\|_2 \leq \delta,\ \alpha \geq 0,\ \mathbf{1}^T\alpha = 1, \tag{2}$$

where $\mathbf{1}^T$ is a line vector of 1's, $\|\alpha\|_0$ denotes the number of nonzero components of α, and $\delta \geq 0$ is the error tolerance.

In this regard, the WM provides the data dictionary, and sparse method performs the selection of the endmembers for the optimal unmixing of the image.

The contents of the paper are the following: Section 2 recalls the definition of the WM algorithm. Section 3 recalls the endember selction step and sparse estimation process based on gradient pursuit. Section 4 gives some experimental results on a well known hyperspectral image. Finally, Section 5 gives some conclusions of our work.

2 WM Algorithm

2.1 Method

The WM algorithm was proposed in [10,11,3]. Given an hyperspectral image $\mathbf{H}$, it is reshaped to form a matrix $\mathbf{X}$ of dimension $N \times L$, where N is the number of image pixels, and L is the number of spectral bands. The algorithm starts by computing the minimal hyperbox covering the data, $\mathcal{B}(\mathbf{v}, \mathbf{u})$, where $\mathbf{v}$ and $\mathbf{u}$ are the *minimal* and *maximal corners,* respectively, whose components are computed as follows:

$$v_k = \min_{\xi} x_k^{\xi} \text{ and } u_k = \max_{\xi} x_k^{\xi};\ k = 1, \ldots, L;\ \xi = 1, \ldots, N. \tag{3}$$

Next, the WM algorithm computes the dual erosive and dilative Lattice Auto-Associative Memories (LAAMs), $\mathbf{W}_{XX}$ and $\mathbf{M}_{XX}$ [9]. The columns of $\mathbf{W}_{XX}$ and $\mathbf{M}_{XX}$ are scaled by $\mathbf{v}$ and $\mathbf{u}$, forming the additive scaled sets $W = \left\{\mathbf{w}^k\right\}_{k=1}^L$ and $M = \left\{\mathbf{m}^k\right\}_{k=1}^L$:

$$\mathbf{w}^k = u_k + \mathbf{W}^k;\ \mathbf{m}^k = v_k + \mathbf{M}^k,\ \forall k = 1, \ldots, L, \tag{4}$$

where $\mathbf{W}^k$ and $\mathbf{M}^k$ denote the k-th column of $\mathbf{W}_{XX}$ and $\mathbf{M}_{XX}$, respectively. Finally, the set $\mathbf{V} = W \cup M \cup \{\mathbf{v}, \mathbf{u}\}$ contains the vertices of the convex polytope covering all the image pixel spectra represented as points in the high dimensional space. The algorithm is simple and fast but the number of induced endmembers, the amount of column vectors in V, can be too large for practical purposes. Furthermore, some of the endmembers induced that way can show high correlation even if they are affine independent. To obtain a meaningful set of endmembers, we search for an optimal subset of V in the sense of minimizing the unmixing residual error and the number of endmembers.

3 Endmember Selection and Sparse Unmixing

3.1 Enbmember Selection via k-means

Lets have a set $\mathbf{E}$ of induced endmembers with WM algorithm. We assume that several endmember will be highly correlated, therefore the convex polytope that covers all the data could be defined by fewer endmembers. Thus, surplus endmembers will be occupying nearby positions in the high dimensional space. We aim to induce a new set of endmembers $\mathbf{E}^\star \subset \mathbf{E}$. To achieve this goal, we perform k-means with k equal to the number of endmembers we want to retain. We propose the use of two "closeness" measurements in the clustering process:

1. Pearson correlation distance between endmembers $\boldsymbol{x}$ and $\boldsymbol{y}$, i.e $\mathbf{dist}\left(\boldsymbol{x}, \boldsymbol{y}\right) = 1 - \mathbf{corr}\left(\boldsymbol{x}, \boldsymbol{y}\right) = 1 - \frac{\sum_{i=1}^n (x_i - \mu_x)(y_i - \mu_y)}{(n-1)\sigma_x \sigma_y}$. Each centroid is the mean of the points in that cluster, after normalizing those points to unit Euclidean length.
2. Cosine dissimilarity between endmembers $\boldsymbol{x}$ and $\boldsymbol{y}$, i.e $\mathbf{dist}\left(\boldsymbol{x}, \boldsymbol{y}\right) = 1 - \cos\theta = 1 - \frac{\sum_{i=1}^n (x_i \cdot y_i)}{\sqrt{\sum_{i=1}^n x_i^2}\sqrt{\sum_{i=1}^n y_i^2}}$. Each centroid is the component-wise mean of the points in that cluster, after centering and normalizing those points to zero mean and unit standard deviation.

We perform the clustering l times, selecting random initial cluster points at each iteration. We choose the iteration whose the sum of distances is minimum. This high number of repetition works towards reaching the global minimum. The set $\mathbf{E}^\star$ will consist of the endmembers that are closer to the centroids of said clusters.

3.2 Sparse Unmixing Using CGP

The sparse signal approximation problem can be summarized as follows: Let have a data matrix $\mathbf{X}$ (i.e. as defined as in section 2). We define a matrix $\boldsymbol{\Phi} \in \mathbb{R}^{q \times L}$

called the dictionary. The q columns of $\mathbf{\Phi}$ are referred as atoms.Therefore, each of the q induced endmembers corresponds to one atom of the dictionary. The problem is to find a mixing matrix $\mathbf{M}$ so that

$$\mathbf{X} = \mathbf{\Phi}\mathbf{M} + \varepsilon, \tag{5}$$

where matrix $\mathbf{M}$ optimizes certain sparsity measure. In terms of hyperspectral unmixing and in the context of our proposed method, Ritter's WM algorithm and the clustering method defined in section 3.1 provide the dictionary $\mathbf{\Phi}$, thus $\mathbf{\Phi} = \mathbf{E}^{\star}$. The matrix $\mathbf{M}$ is in fact the collection of abundance images obtained by the unmixing process.

There are several sparse unmixing approaches that have been recently used with hyperspectral data, like sparsity-constrained Nonnegative Matrix Factorization [6,8], Pursuit algorithms [5] or iterative spectral mixture analysis[12]. One of many methods to achieve this sparsification is to use Conjugate Gradient Pursuit [1].

Conjugate Gradient Pursuit The conjugate gradient method is a popular directional optimization method. This method is guaranteed to solve quadratic problems in as many steps as the dimension of the problem. It calculates a similar decomposition as the QR factorization.

4 Experimental Design and Results

We test our method using a sub-image of the AVIRIS Cuprite dataset[4]. It corresponds to the flight f970619t01p02_r02, run 2, section 3. I has a size with 512×614 pixels. A false grayscale image can be sen in figure 1 The scene consists of 224 spectral bands between 0.4 μm and 2.5 μm, with spectral resolution of 10 nm. Before the analysis, bands 1–3, 105–115, 150–170 and 223–224 were removed due to water absorption, artifacts and low SNR in those bands, leaving a total of 187 spectral bands. The Cuprite site is well understood mineralogically and is broadly used as a trusted benchmark for hyperspectral research.

One of the problems that the proposed method aims to solve is the excessive number of endmembers and the too high correlation between many of them. The WM algorithm drops 376 endmember candidates, which are plotted in figure ??. We perform the k-means algorithm, as presented in section 3.1, with $k = 10$ and $l = 200$. The motivation of choosing k is to have a small enough number of endmembers, validating the method while being able to show the visual results. The high number of repetitions are sufficient as to ensure that no local maximum is achieved by k-means. We center and scale the data prior to k-means, in order to achieve certain numeral stability. The resulting 10 endmembers showed significant variability.

The next step is to calculate the sparse representation of the hyperspectral image. We use the selected endmembers as a dictionary and the hyperspectral image the signal, to obtain the aforementioned sparse abundances applying CGP. We allow a maximum representation error of 0.05. The result is a sparse mixing

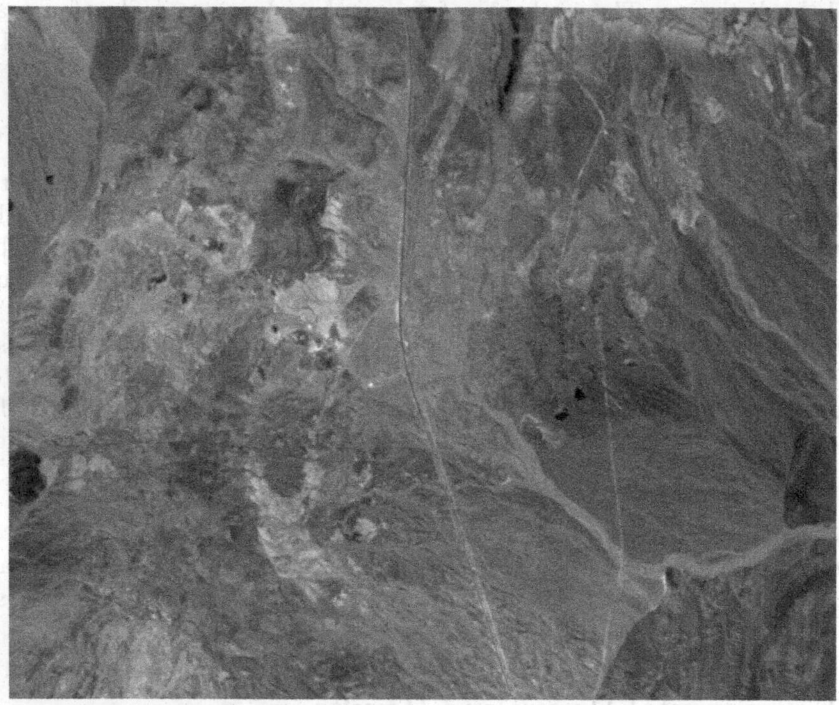

Fig. 1. False grayscale image of the Cuprite subsection used for this experiment

Table 1. Endmembers selected with the proposed method

Pearson Correlation										
Distance (x10^{-3})	3.639	5.176	3.991	3.133	1.386	1.431	21.994	22.904	2.561	1.522
Endmember	183	106	35	245	87	67	1	362	274	313
Cosine dissimilarity										
Distance(x10^{-3})	4.373	1.992	8.752	7.123	0.771	2.295	8.460	2.209	1.772	0.648
Endmember	292	101	362	371	153	258	174	32	232	275

matrix which corresponds to the abundance images for each selected endmember. Figures 2 and 3 illustrates the 10 endmembers abundances. Whiter regions imply higher abundance. Each endmember is more abundant in different regions, as can be observed. The scarce white pixels illustrate the sparse nature of the hyperspectral unmixing problem.

5 Discussion and Future Work

One fast and effective procedure to obtain endmembers is the WM Algorithm proposed by Ritter at al. [10,11]. The output is a set of affine independent vectors

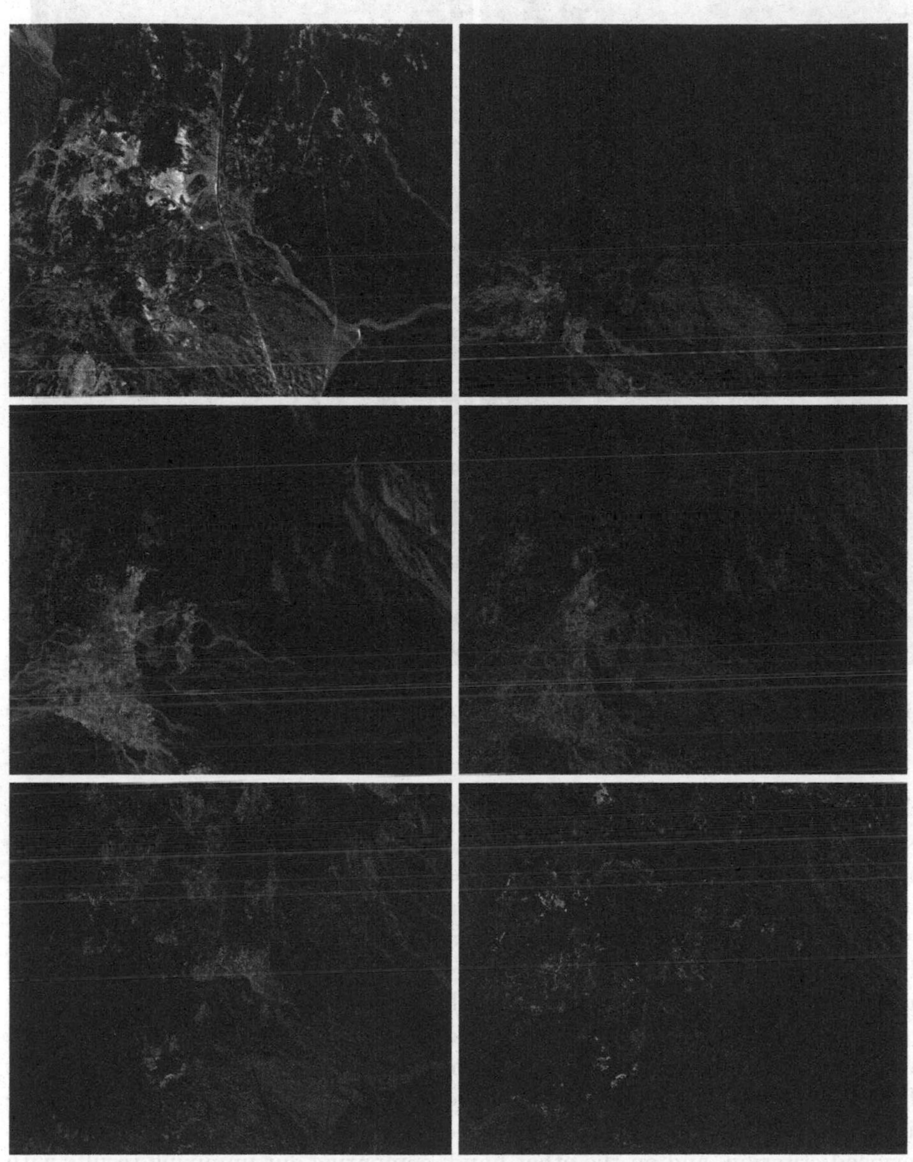

Fig. 2. Resulting abundances of applying CGP on 10-means WM induced first six endmembers of Cuprite scene, ordered left to right, top to bottom

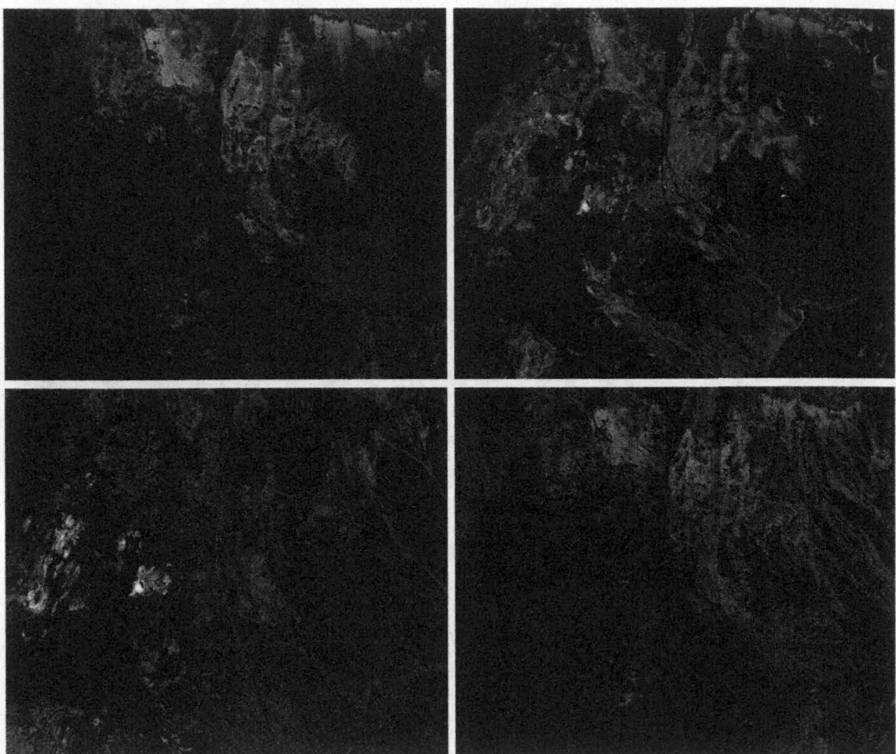

Fig. 3. Resulting abundances of applying CGP on 10-means WM induced las four endmembers of Cuprite scene, ordered left to right, top to bottom

which are the vertices of a convex polytope covering the sample data. We have experimentally proven that this method, like many others, is able to induce too many endmembers. These endmembers can be highly correlated. We propose a clustering step to reduce the number of endmember prior to the unmixing process. Proposing the unmixing problem as a linear regression problem, we use CGP algorithm to calculate sparse abundances. Experiments on a complex and well documented hyperspectral image show that the approach is able to select a few endmembers that are not highly correlated. The non-linearity is introduced by the WM algorithm, which a Lattice Computing base algorithm. The visual assessment of the results disjoint endmembers that are present in disparate abundances on the pixels of the scene. Future work involves, on one side, selecting k with some unsupervised criterion, and on the other hand, comparing our unmixing results with those obtained using USGS Spectral Library as the sparse algorithm's dictionary. This last step, which would greatly extend further from the limited scope of this paper, could demonstrate with ground truth the utility of the whole unsupervised unmixing method.

References

1. Blumensath, T., Davies, M.E.: Gradient pursuits. IEEE Transactions on Signal Processing 56(6), 2370–2382 (2008)
2. Graña, M., Veganzones, M.A.: An endmember-based distance for content based hyperspectral image retrieval. Pattern Recognition 49(9), 3472–3489 (2012)
3. Graña, M., Veganzones, M.A.: Endmember induction by lattice associative memories and multi-objective genetic algorithms. EURASIP Journal on Advances in Signal Processing 2012, 64 (2012)
4. Green, R.O., Eastwood, M.L., Sarture, C.M., Chrien, T.G., Aronsson, M., Chippendale, B.J., Faust, J.A., Pavri, B.E., Chovit, C.J., Solis, M., Olah, M.R., Williams, O.: Imaging spectroscopy and the airborne visible/infrared imaging spectrometer (aviris). Remo 65(3), 227–248 (1998)
5. Iordache, M.-D., Bioucas-Dias, J.M., Plaza, A.: Sparse unmixing of hyperspectral data. IEEE Transactions on Geoscience and Remote Sensing 49(6), 2014–2039 (2011)
6. Jia, S., Qian, Y.: Constrained nonnegative matrix factorization for hyperspectral unmixing. IEEE Transactions on Geoscience and Remote Sensing 47(1), 161–173 (2009)
7. Keshava, N., Mustard, J.F.: Spectral unmixing. IEEE Signal Processing Magazine 19(1), 44–57 (2002)
8. Paul Pauca, V., Piper, J., Plemmons, R.J.: Nonnegative matrix factorization for spectral data analysis. Linear Algebra and its Applications 416(1), 29–47 (2006); Special Issue devoted to the Haifa 2005 conference on matrix theory
9. Ritter, G.X., Sussner, P., Diaz-de-Leon, J.L.: Morphological associative memories. IEEE Transactions on Neural Networks 9(2), 281–293 (1998)
10. Ritter, G.X., Urcid, G.: A lattice matrix method for hyperspectral image unmixing. Information Sciences 181(10), 1787–1803 (2010)
11. Ritter, G.X., Urcid, G.: Lattice algebra approach to endmember determination in hyperspectral imagery. In: Hawkes, P.W. (ed.) Advances in Imaging and Electron Physics, vol. 160, pp. 113–169. Academic Press, Burlington (2010)
12. Rogge, D.M., Rivard, B., Zhang, J., Feng, J.: Iterative spectral unmixing for optimizing Per-Pixel endmember sets. IEEE Transactions on Geoscience and Remote Sensing 44(12), 3725–3736 (2006)

Hyperspectral Image Analysis Based on Color Channels and Ensemble Classifier

Bartosz Krawczyk, Paweł Ksieniewicz, and Michał Woźniak

Department of Systems and Computer Networks,
Wrocław University of Technology, Wrocław, Poland
{bartosz.krawczyk,pawel.ksieniewicz,michal.wozniak}@pwr.wroc.pl

Abstract. Hyperspectral image analysis is a dynamically developing branch of computer vision due to the numerous practical applications and high complexity of data. There exist a need for introducing novel machine learning methods, that can tackle high dimensionality and large number of classes in these images. In this paper, we introduce a novel ensemble method for classification of hyperspectral data. The pool of classifiers is built on the basis of color decomposition of the given image. Each base classifier corresponds to a single color channel that is extracted. We propose a new method for decomposing hyperspectral image into 11 different color channels. As not all of the channels may bear as useful information as other, we need to promote the most relevant ones. For this, our ensemble uses a weighted trained fuser, which uses a neural methods for establishing weights. We show, that the proposed ensemble can outperform other state-of-the-art classifiers in the given task.

Keywords: machine learning, classifier ensemble, multiple classifier system, hyperspectral image, image segmentation, color channels.

1 Introduction

Hyperspectral image is a collection of high-resolution monochromatic pictures covering large spacial region for broad range of wavelengths. From structural point of view it is a three-dimensional matrix of brightness. First two dimensions are width and length of flat projection. Third one is a number of spectral band. Main idea of hyperspectral imaging is minimization of range covered by every band with maximization of band number. Commonly hyperspectral images consist of at least 100 of such bands.

Taking a slice (two-dimensional matrix) from a hyperspectral cube can provide us information of brightness of the area for a given spectral band (Figure 1(a)). Taking a vector alongside the spectral band axis provides us information about brightness of one particular pixels for every covered spectral band. Such a vector is commonly named a *signature*. Example *signature* is presented on Figure 1(b).

Signatures are used to detect type of material represented by pixel on an image. It is possible to distinguish type of ground, vegetation, used building material, rock strata or many other.

M. Polycarpou et al. (Eds.): HAIS 2014, LNAI 8480, pp. 274–284, 2014.
© Springer International Publishing Switzerland 2014

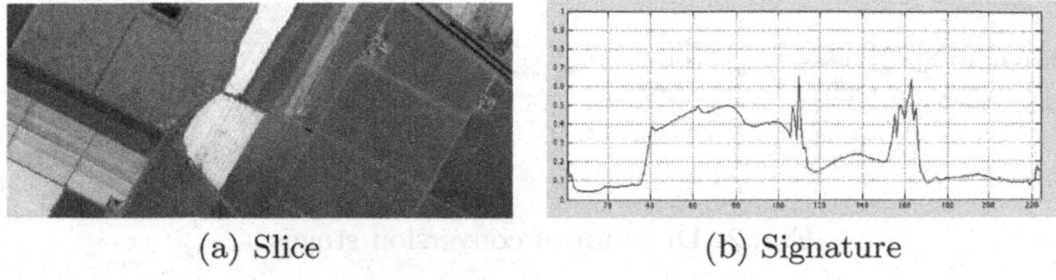

(a) Slice (b) Signature

Fig. 1. Hyperspectral image elements

Method of separation of an hyperspectral image into channels is based on human perception of colorful images. Its main base is to replace a *reading* from *photoreceptors* with metric, doing e.g. elementary statistical operations on signature vector. Monochromatic image from this kind of metric can turn into channel used to construct colorful picture or, after posterization, set of labels. It also implements a method of separation of homogenous areas on image, used also to filter noisy ranges of spectrum.

After the image color decomposition, we need to apply machine learning algorithms in order to conduct segmentation or classification. Among a plethora of classification methods, ensembles has gained a significant interest of researchers over the last decade [7]. Combining multiple classifiers can lead to a significant improvement of the accuracy in comparison to single learner. There are many different methods for forming efficient ensembles [14], but they all share several fundamental ideas. In order for the ensemble to work, we need to have more than one classifiers at our disposal. They can be trained on the given dataset, or supplied by heterogeneous sources (e.g., from different sensors [10]). A special attention should be paid to the properties of used classifiers. For an ensemble to work properly, it must consist of classifiers that at the same time display a high individual accuracy and are mutually complementary with each other. As, in most cases, not all of the available classifiers satisfy this condition, one needs to discard the irrelevant models. This step has a crucial impact on the quality of the formed committee and is known as classifier selection or ensemble pruning [4]. Another important part of ensemble design is the combination rule. It will fuse the individual outputs of base classifiers into a single committee decision. This task can be tackled in two different ways: with untrained or trained fuser. Untrained fusers (such as voting) [13] are simple and straightforward to use, but can be subject of performance limitations. Trained fusers adapt their behavior to the analyzed data, but require some time to establish their rules and a dedicated training set [9].

In this work, we propose a novel ensemble dedicated to analysis of hyperspectral data. Its base classifiers are being built on the basis of decomposed color channels. This assures their initial diversity, as every color channel carries different information. We further augment this idea by using a trained fuser, based on perceptron learning. This allows us to assign higher weights to more competent classifiers. As not all of the channels carry equally useful features, we boost the

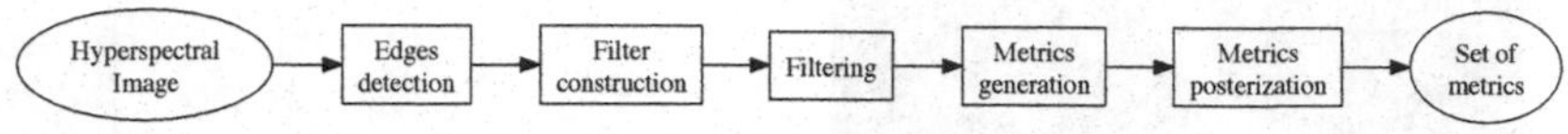

Fig. 2. Diagram of conversion stages

influence of the most relevant ones on the final decision of the ensemble. Experimental results show, that the proposed method can outperform state-of-the-art classifiers in hyperspectral data analysis.

2 Separation of Color Channels in Hyperspectral Images

Most common method of generating false-color pictures from hyperspectral data is maping three bands from a wide signature into RGB channels. For case of spectral depth reduction, the most popular standard is PCA[1] [1]. Three, richest in information, principal components from hyperspectral cube are mapped to various color models chanels (RGB, HSL, HSV) [12].

Some works suggest to balance S/N[2] to enhance contrast of an image [6] and reduce noise impact.

Main motivation behind the proposed method was to introduce a new representation, preserving as much information as possible, that is acceptable for human color perception, with possibly simple, low time-consuming method. As for the classification step this method allows us to use more information than is carried by three standard color channels, while maintaining a more compact representation than full spectral singature.

From mathematical angle, we can percept a *matrix of cone cells* of same type as a *function*, projecting three-dimensional input onto two-dimensional output. *Hyperspectrals* are nothing more than discrete form of this three-dimensional input. So, an hyperspectral cube gives us enough information to obtain other functions generating monochromatic image. One may describe them as *artifictial cone cells matrixes*. Later in this paper we are calling them, as well as theires outpus, the *metrics*.

There are five phases of metrics generation process. Chain of consecutive steps is presented with diagram on Figure 2.

2.1 Edges Detection

Calculation of a difference between maximal and minimal values in nearest neighbourhood of every pixel of image can be used to detect borders between present areas [5].

---

[1] Principal Components Analysis.

[2] Signal-to-noise ratio.

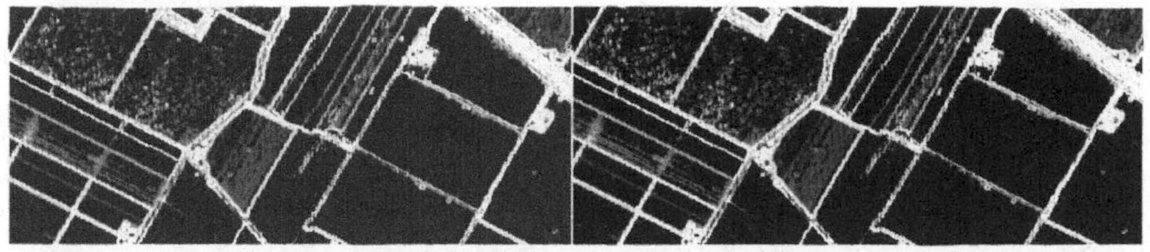

Fig. 3. Mask of region borders for *Salinas* (a) before and (b) after filtering

This can be implemented in a form of bigger, four-dimensional image. An additional dimension would be a shift of each layer by unit vector for every direction achievable on a surface. This allows us to fuse a new image without transformations in a form of four dimensional matrix from nine three dimensional images

In the next step we calculate a difference between maximal and minimal value in a fourth dimension to compress an image back into three dimensions. Values of single pixels of obtained cube are differentiation of theires nearest neighbourhood.

A flat mask would be less complex for later operations, than three-dimensional array. To achieve it as an output of this stage, we are flattering image alongside axis of wavelengths. Mask generated with this method is presented on Figure 3.

2.2 Filter Construction

As the side effect of conducted edge detection method we are receiving measurement of *entropy* ($\bar{\mathrm{H}}$) for every layer of image. Dividing amount of all values (ρ) from every layer by calculations of pixels per layer (*ppl*) gives us an vector with normalized value of entropy (Figure 4(a)).

$$\bar{\mathrm{H}} = \frac{\sum \rho}{ppl} \tag{1}$$

Assuming that every hyperspectral cube contains wavelengths with high noise ratio (which is absolutely right for AVIRIS-sourced images) adequate threshold for drain most of them would be *mean value of entropy* (Figure 4(b)). Nonetheless, filter like this is not separating hills of entropy changes.

To caulk filter, entropy vector was build up build from information about its *dynamics* ($\bar{DH}$) (Figure 4(c)). An vector of *dinamics* was made in a way analogous to edge detection, by calculating discrepancy between actual ($\bar{H}$) and next value ($\bar{H}'$) on the vector of entropy.

$$\bar{\mathrm{DH}} = |\bar{H} - \bar{H}'| \tag{2}$$

Mean dinamics filter was generated in an analogous way as the one for entropy (Figure 4(d)). Concluding filter was the *blend* of mean entropy and mean dinamics filters. Figure 4(f) shows ability of segregation informations from noises

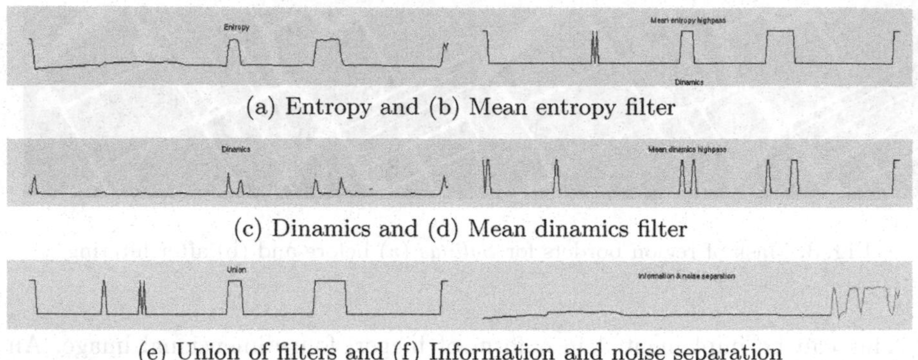

(a) Entropy and (b) Mean entropy filter

(c) Dinamics and (d) Mean dinamics filter

(e) Union of filters and (f) Information and noise separation

Fig. 4. Filtering process

crosswise the spectrum. Figure 3 presents difference between unfiltered and filtered mask of region borders.

2.3 Metrics

By using signatures with filtered-out noise, we can effectively use simple statistical operations like *maximum* or *minimum*, and improve the precision of *average* and *median value*. We propose a set of eleven example metrics. Figure 5 provides color visualization[3] for all of them.

First three metrics are three equal ranges from whole spectrum coverted to HSV. Filtered *hyperspectral cube* was divided into three smaller, equal cubes. Every cube was flattered with mean value function. Three layers was combined as channels into RGB image, later converted into HSV. Output, HSV image was divided into three metrics, one per every parameter. Metrics 4—7 are minimal or maximal value and indexes. Minimal and maximal values and indexes for full filtered spectral signature was computed. Metrics 8—9 are mean and median values for full filtered spectral signature. Last two metrics are differences between masks 4—7.

2.4 Smart Posterization

Posterization of an image is a process of color quantization of image. It allows grouping similar pixels of image with very low computational cost [11].

We can assign one from n labels on the image for its every pixel only by multiplicating its matrix by n and round it to the floor. Unfortunately, using this method we must pay attention for the risk of dividing original region classes into many quants. To avoid this hazard, a simple method was implemented.

[3] Visualizations are generated as HSV images, with metric as *hue* and edges mask as *value* channel.

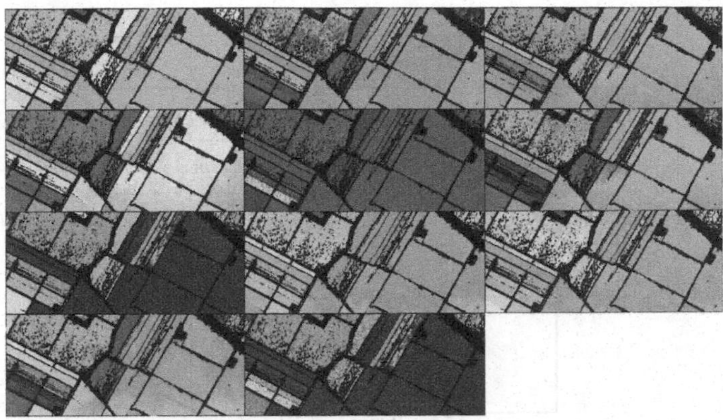

Fig. 5. Color visualization of proposed metrics

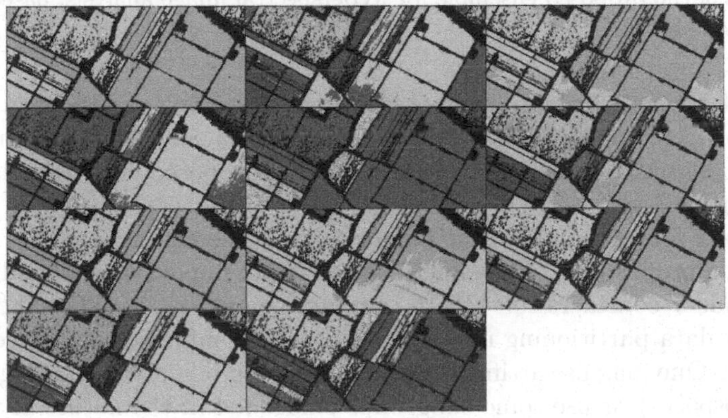

Fig. 6. Color visualization of proposed metrics after smart posterization

We calculate mean signature for every quant of posterization and comparing it with every other quant. If the mean value of difference for some comparison is lower than an arbitrary treshold, labels of both quants are unified. Result of this, enhanced proposition of posterization of metrics is presented on Figure 6.

3 Proposed Ensemble Classifier

In the paper, we propose a novel classification algorithm for tackling complex hyperspectral data. We want to propose an ensemble classifier for this task. We need to have a pool of efficient classifiers, that are mutually complementary to each other.

The general idea behind this approach is as follows. For constructing base classifiers, we use the proposed color channel decomposition. The input image is separated into 11 different channels, each serving as an input training set for

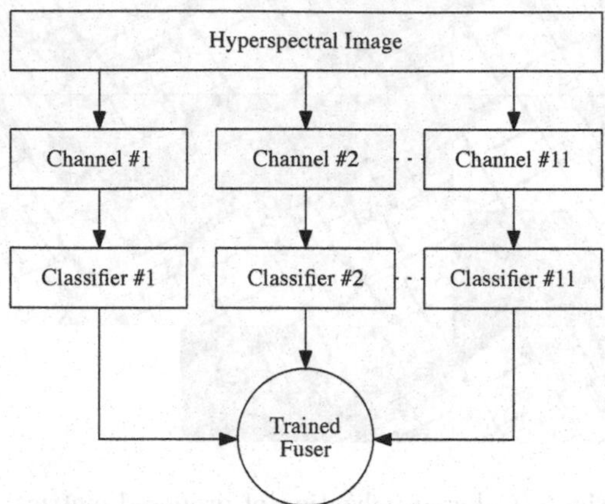

Fig. 7. Idea of the proposed ensemble for hyperspectral image analysis, based on color channel decomposition

individual learner. In order to promote the best classifiers, coming from the most relevant color channels, we use a trained fuser that can adapt its combination rule to the analyzed dataset. The schema of the proposed ensemble classifier is given in Figure 7.

Let us take a closer look on the components of the ensemble.

Forming a proper pool of classifiers has a crucial impact on the quality of the ensemble under consideration [3]. In our previous works, we have shown, that using input data partitioning may have a beneficial influence on the committee classifier [8]. One may use artificial data partitioning (e.g., bootstraping, random feature subspaces) or use some subgroups embedded in the nature of the data. Here, we propose to use different color channels as basis for classifiers in the committee. By this, from 11 different color channels we form 11 base classifiers. As each of them uses different decomposition of input hyperspectral image, they should use different information and be supplementary to each other. With this, we assure initial diversity among the pool of classifiers, which is one of the principles in ensemble approach [14].

At the same time, we should have in mind that the proposed color decomposition scheme does not assure in any explicit way that extracted channels carry significantly different information. Therefore, there is no way to say beforehand which of these channels should be used and which discarded. We need to enhance the influence of the better channels on the quality of recognition system, by promoting classifiers trained on them. For this, we propose to utilize a trained fuser, based on discriminants and neural methods of training. Such a trained fuser can adapt its combination rules to the data at hand, resulting in high-quality combined classifier. Additionally, the fuser's weights are dependent on class, so each classifier may have different weights associated for each class. This is especially important for problems with significant number of classes, and hyperspectral images tend to have large number of different class labels.

Assume we have N classifiers $\Psi^{(1)}$, $\Psi^{(2)}$, ..., $\Psi^{(N)}$. For a given sample $x \in \mathcal{X}$, each individual classifier make a decision regarding class $i \in \mathcal{M} = \{1, ..., M\}$. Let $F^{(l)}(i, x)$ denote this decision of the l-th classifier $\Psi^{(l)}$, then a combined classifier Ψ can reach a decision based on [15]

$$\Psi(x) = i \quad \text{if} \quad \hat{F}(i, x) = \max_{k \in M} \hat{F}(k, x), \tag{3}$$

where

$$\hat{F}(i, x) = \sum_{l=1}^{N} w^{(l)(i)} F^{(l)}(i, x) \text{ and } \sum_{i=1}^{N} w^{(l)(i)} = 1, \tag{4}$$

and the weights w are dependent on the classifier and the class, i.e. $w^{(l)}(i)$ is assigned to the l-th classifier and the i-th class.

We employ a perceptron as a trained classifier fusion approach based on decisions obtained from discriminant functions for the classifiers [15]. One perceptron fuser is constructed for each of the classes under consideration. Once trained (we employ the Quickprop algorithm in our implementation), the input weights established during the learning process are then the weights assigned to each of the base classifiers.

4 Experimental Evaluation

In this section, we experimentally analyze the usefulness of our ensemble method and compare it to several state-of-the-art machine learning methods for hyperspectral data analysis.

4.1 Used Hyperspectral Images

Illustrations of channel separation method and all experimental evaluation was obtained using example, benchmark *Salinas* dataset. This hyperspectral image was taken over *Valley of Salinas* in USA, CA.

Pictured terrain include bare soils, vegetables and vineyard fields, labeled in 16 classes. Image have a high noise ratio in some ranges, so it can be easily used as an example for noise filtering. Entire scene was used to present example metrics set on Figure 5.

Side of every pixel square is about 3.7 m on real surface. Image consist of 217 x 512 pixels and 224 spectral bands from 0.4 to 2.5 μm, with nominal spectral resolution of 10 nm.

4.2 Set-up

Our ensemble uses a Support Vector Machine with RBF kernel as a base classifier. We use 11 base classifiers, as there are 11 color channels after decomposition.

For comparison, we used thee different popular classifiers: *Support Vector Machine* (SVM), *Random Forest* and *Boosted* SVM. We trained them on normal pixel data and entire data after decomposition. With this, we can see what influence has the color decomposition on the performance of classifiers and does the proposed ensemble is better than pixel-based and color-based standard classifiers. The details of the used classifiers are given in Table 1.

Table 1. Segment table representation

Classifier	Parameter
SVM	SMO training, RBF kernel, C = 1.2, $\gamma = 0.5$
Random Forest	80 trees, 12 features in tree
Boosted SVM	10 classifier, majority voting

For testing, we used a statistical test to compare the results and judge if their differences were statistically significant. For this purpose, we used a combined 5 × 2 cv F Test [2], where preprocessing procedures were run independently for each of the folds.

4.3 Results

The results of the experiment are presented in the Table 2. They show the classifiers' accuracy. Each classifier has assigned its index number (in the row with classifier names). These indexes correspond with numbers in the *statistical test* row and indicates in comparison with which other tested classification methods (represented by their indexes) the considered classifier is statistically superior.

Table 2. Results of the experiment with respect to accuracy [%]

SVM[1]	RandF[2]	BoostSVM[3]	SVM+color[4]	RandF+color[5]	BoostSVM+color[6]	Proposed[7]
64.85	68.53	67.22	60.13	66.23	60.87	72.86
4, 6	1, 3, 4, 5, 6	1, 4, 6	–	1, 4, 6	–	*All*

4.4 Discussion

From the experimental results, we may draw several interesting conclusions.

First of all, let us take a look on the differences between using standard pixel-based representation and color channel-based representation. What is very interesting, all of the methods work significantly worse when using color space as an input. This can be explained by a great increase of the feature space size. For standard pixel-based representation, we have one set of features. For color-based channel decomposition, we have 11 set of features. Using their intersection as input, we get a 11 times bigger feature space with the same number of objects. This may lead to a significant drop of classifier's performance, as we have no control over what features are used for classification. Some of channel information can be irrelevant and mislead the constructed classifier. Therefore, simple usage of decomposed image into color channels is not a good direction.

However, our proposed method can outperform all other reference methods in a significant way. This can be explained by the fact, how the ensemble is formed. It uses all the beneficial information from the decomposed color channels, while being robust to increased feature space. Our ensemble uses 11 different feature sets, but each of them is delegated to a single classifier. Therefore, at one hand we do not increase the complexity of single classifier, while at the same time giving more information to the committee. By using trained fuser, we are able to boost the influence of certain channels on the final decision, while discarding irrelevant ones.

5 Conclusions

In this paper, we proposed two novel approaches for handling hyperspectral images. We showed a new method for decomposing hyperspectral images, based on selecting different color channels. Each of them can be used for efficient visualization of hyperspectral images, or as a data pre-processing step. We use this as a feature extraction procedure, to get more information about the image. We introduce a novel ensemble classifier, in which base learners are formed on the basis of each color channel. This assures initial diversity among classifiers. We further augment this approach by applying trained fuser, based on discriminant functions and perceptron training methods. This allows us to assign higher weights to classifiers carrying more discriminant power and boost their influence on the final aggregated output.

Experimental analysis proves the quality of our method. We showed, that the proposed ensemble can outperform several state-of-the-art methods in a statistically significant way.

In our future works, we would like to add ensemble pruning approach to discard irrelevant classifiers and reduce the complexity of our method.

Acknowledgment. The work was supported by the statutory funds of the Department of Systems and Computer Networks, Wroclaw University of Technology and by The Polish National Science Centre under the grant agreement no. DEC-2013/09/B/ST6/02264.

References

1. Agarwal, A., El-Ghazawi, T., El-Askary, H., Le-Moigne, J.: Efficient hierarchical-PCA dimension reduction for hyperspectral imagery. In: 2007 IEEE International Symposium on Signal Processing and Information Technology, pp. 353–356 (December 2007)
2. Alpaydin, E.: Combined 5 x 2 cv f test for comparing supervised classification learning algorithms. Neural Computation 11(8), 1885–1892 (1999)

3. Cyganek, B.: One-class support vector ensembles for image segmentation and classification. Journal of Mathematical Imaging and Vision 42(2-3), 103–117 (2012)
4. Dai, Q.: A competitive ensemble pruning approach based on cross-validation technique. Knowledge-Based Systems 37, 394–414 (2013)
5. Davies, E.R.: Machine Vision: Theory, Algorithms, Practicalities. Elsevier (December 2004)
6. Durand, J.M., Kerr, Y.H.: An improved decorrelation method for the efficient display of multispectral data. IEEE Transactions on Geoscience and Remote Sensing 27(5), 611–619 (1989)
7. Jain, A.K., Duin, R.P.W., Mao, J.: Statistical pattern recognition: a review. IEEE Transactions on Pattern Analysis and Machine Intelligence 22(1), 4–37 (2000)
8. Krawczyk, B., Woźniak, M., Cyganek, B.: Clustering-based ensembles for one-class classification. Inf. Sci. 264, 182–195 (2014)
9. Kuncheva, L.I., Jain, L.C.: Designing classifier fusion systems by genetic algorithms. IEEE Transactions on Evolutionary Computation 4(4), 327–336 (2000)
10. Szczurek, A., Krawczyk, B., Maciejewska, M.: Vocs classification based on the committee of classifiers coupled with single sensor signals. Chemometrics and Intelligent Laboratory Systems 125, 1–10 (2013)
11. Tamai, S.: Image processing suitable for changing the number of colors in an image, U.S. Classification: 358/518; 358/501; 358/520; 358/530 International Classification: G03F 308 (September 1999)
12. Tyo, J.S., Konsolakis, A., Diersen, D.I., Olsen, R.C.: Principal-components-based display strategy for spectral imagery. IEEE Transactions on Geoscience and Remote Sensing 41(3), 708–718 (2003)
13. van Erp, M., Vuurpijl, L., Schomaker, L.: An overview and comparison of voting methods for pattern recognition. In: Proceedings. Eighth International Workshop on Frontiers in Handwriting Recognition 2002, pp. 195–200 (2002)
14. Woźniak, M., Graña, M., Corchado, E.: A survey of multiple classifier systems as hybrid systems. Information Fusion 16, 3–17 (2014)
15. Woźniak, M., Zmyslony, M.: Designing combining classifier with trained fuser - analytical and experimental evaluation. Neural Network World 20(7), 925–934 (2010)

Non-dominated Sorting and a Novel Formulation in the Reporting Cells Planning

Víctor Berrocal-Plaza*, Miguel A. Vega-Rodríguez, and Juan M. Sánchez-Pérez

Dept. of Computers & Communications Technologies, University of Extremadura
Escuela Politécnica, Campus Universitario S/N, 10003, Cáceres, Spain
{vicberpla,mavega,sanperez}@unex.es

Abstract. In this paper, we study the Reporting Cells scheme, a popular strategy used to control the movement of mobile terminals in the Public Land Mobile Networks. In contrast to previously published works, we propose a multiobjective approach that allows us to avoid the drawbacks of the linear aggregation of the objective functions. Furthermore, we provide a novel formulation to take into account aspects of the Reporting Cells that have not been considered in previous works. Experimental results show that our proposal outperforms other optimization techniques published in the literature.

Keywords: Reporting Cells Planning Problem, Mobile Location Management, Multiobjective Optimization, Non-dominated Sorting Genetic Algorithm 2.

1 Introduction

One of the most important management tasks in the Public Land Mobile Networks (PLMNs) is the mobile location management. In fact, D. Nowoswiat and G. Milliken show in [1] that the signaling traffic generated by this management task is more than 33% of the total signaling load. That is why the use of soft computing to minimize the signaling traffic associated with the mobile location management is a very interesting research line.

In the PLMNs, the network operator divides the coverage area into several smaller regions (known as network cells) with the goal of providing mobile services with few radio-electric resources (the available resources are distributed and reused among the different network cells) [2]. And therefore, every mobile network should have a system to automatically track the movement of its subscribers across the different cells. Commonly, a mobile location management strategy consists of two main procedures: the subscriber's location update (LU), and the paging (PA). The first procedure is initiated by the mobile terminals to

* This work was partially funded by the Spanish Ministry of Economy and Competitiveness and the ERDF (European Regional Development Fund), under the contract TIN2012-30685 (BIO project). The work of Víctor Berrocal-Plaza has been developed under the Grant FPU-AP2010-5841 from the Spanish Government.

M. Polycarpou et al. (Eds.): HAIS 2014, LNAI 8480, pp. 285–295, 2014.
© Springer International Publishing Switzerland 2014

notify the network that they have changed their location (in terms of network cells). And the second one is used by the mobile network to know the exact cell in which a callee terminal is located.

This work addresses the Reporting Cells Planning Problem (RCPP), a popular strategy proposed by A. Bar-Noy and I. Kessler in [3] to control the subscribers' movement. In their work, A. Bar-Noy and I. Kessler demonstrated that the RCPP is in general an NP-complete optimization problem. Though the RCPP belongs to the multiobjective optimization field (see Section 2), this problem has not been yet tackled with multiobjective optimization techniques. A. Hac and X. Zhou proposed a heuristic method in which the paging cost was considered as a constraint [4]. R. Subrata and A. Y. Zomaya developed three single-objective metaheuristics in [5], where the objective functions were linearly combined. The same technique (the linear aggregation of objective functions, see Section 4.1) was used in [6,7,8], where the RCPP was also studied with single-objective metaheuristics. However, the linear aggregation has several drawbacks: the weight coefficient ($\beta \in \Re$) should be configured properly, the proper value of β might be different for different states of the signaling network, and a single-objective optimizer must perform an independent run per each value of this coefficient. With the aim of avoiding such drawbacks, we propose our version (in terms of our evolutionary operators specific to solve the RCPP) of the Non-dominated Sorting Genetic Algorithm II (NSGAII, a well-known multiobjective metaheuristic [9]). This is a novel contribution of our work because, to the best of our knowledge, there are no other authors that tackle the RCPP with a multiobjective approach. Furthermore, we provide a novel formulation to take into account aspects of the RCPP that have not been considered in the formulation defined in [5,6,7,8].

The paper is organized as follows. Section 2 presents a detailed explanation of the RCPP. The main features of a multiobjective optimization problem and our version of the NSGAII are shown in Section 3. An in-depth analysis of our proposal and a comparison with other works published in the literature are discussed in Section 4. Our conclusion and future work are summarized in Section 5.

2 Reporting Cells Planning Problem

The Reporting Cells scheme is a static strategy to control the subscribers' movement across the network cells. In this strategy, a mobile station only updates its location when it moves to a new Reporting Cell (RC), and the paging is only performed in the vicinity of the last updated Reporting Cell (for the mobile station in question) [3]. For definition, the vicinity of a RC (V) is the set of network cells in which it is possible to find the callee's mobile station. Therefore, this vicinity consists of the RC in question and the set of non-Reporting Cells (nRCs) that are reachable from this RC without passing over other RC (because a mobile station is free to move among non-Reporting Cells (nRCs) without updating its location). It should be noted that, when all the network cells are nRCs, the callee's mobile station must be searched in the whole mobile network.

According to this location management strategy, the main challenge consists in finding the configurations of RCs that reduce to the minimum the number of location updates (or location update cost) and the number of paging messages (or paging cost). These two objective functions can be formulated as Equation 1 and Equation 2 respectively.

$$\boldsymbol{f}_1 = \min\left\{\sum_{t=T_{ini}}^{T_{fin}} \sum_{i=1}^{N_{user}} \gamma_{t,i}\right\}, \quad (1)$$

$$\boldsymbol{f}_2 = \min\left\{\sum_{t=T_{ini}}^{T_{fin}} \sum_{i=1}^{N_{user}} \rho_{t,i} \cdot VF_{t,i}\right\}. \quad (2)$$

In these equations, $[T_{ini}, T_{fin}]$ is the time interval during which the location update cost and the paging cost are calculated. N_{user} is the number of mobile subscribers. $\gamma_{t,i}$ is a binary variable that is equal to 1 when the mobile station i moves to a new Reporting Cell in the time t, otherwise $\gamma_{t,i}$ is equal to 0. $\rho_{t,i}$ is a binary variable that is equal to 1 when the mobile station i has an incoming call in the time t, otherwise this variable is equal to 0. And $VF_{t,i}$ is the Vicinity Factor associated with the mobile station i in the time t. This last variable will be equal to the network size (number of network cells, N_{cell}) if there is no any RC in the network, otherwise this variable will be equal to the vicinity (V) of the last updated RC (for the mobile station i). Note that these two objective functions are conflicting (and hence, they define a multiobjective optimization problem). For example, if we would minimize the location update cost, we should configure all the network cells as nRC (i.e. $\gamma_{t,i} = 0, \forall t \in [T_{ini}, T_{fin}], \forall i \in [1, N_{user}]$). However, this configuration maximizes the paging cost because every callee's mobile station must be searched in the whole network (i.e. $VF_{t,i} = N_{cell}, \forall t \in [T_{ini}, T_{fin}], \forall i \in [1, N_{user}]$). On the other hand, if we would minimize the paging cost, all the network cells should be configured as RC (i.e. $VF_{t,i} = 1, \forall t \in [T_{ini}, T_{fin}], \forall i \in [1, N_{user}]$), but this configuration maximizes the location update cost (because a location update will be performed whenever a mobile station moves to a new network cell).

3 Multiobjective Optimization

There are many engineering problems in which two or more conflicting objective functions must be optimized simultaneously, e.g. the Reporting Cells Planning Problem (RCPP). In this kind of problems (commonly known as Multiobjective Optimization Problems, MOPs), the main challenge consists in finding the best possible set of non-dominated solutions (where every non-dominated solution is associated with a specific trade-off among objectives). If we assume a bi-objective MOP in which the two objective functions must be minimized (as the RCPP), a solution $\mathbf{x}^1$ is said to dominate the solution $\mathbf{x}^2$ (expressed as $\mathbf{x}^1 \prec \mathbf{x}^2$) when $\forall k \in [1,2], \mathbf{z}_k^1 = \boldsymbol{f}_k(\mathbf{x}^1) \leq \mathbf{z}_k^2 = \boldsymbol{f}_k(\mathbf{x}^2) \wedge \exists k \in [1,2] : \mathbf{z}_k^1 < \mathbf{z}_k^2$. Commonly, the image (in the objective space $\boldsymbol{Z} = \boldsymbol{f}(\boldsymbol{X})$) of this set of non-dominated solutions

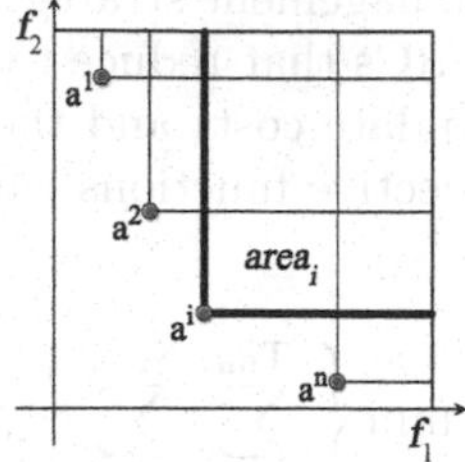

Fig. 1. Hypervolume for a minimization problem with two objectives

is referred as Pareto Front (PF). In the literature, we can find several indicators to estimate the quality of a set of non-dominated solutions [10]. One of the most accepted indicators is the Hypervolume (I_H). This indicator measures the area of the objective space that is dominated by the Pareto Front and is bounded by the reference points (see Fig. 1). In the RCPP, these reference points are calculated by means of the two extreme configurations of RCs: when all the network cells are RCs (or Always Update, $[f_1^{max}, f_2^{min}]$), and when all the network cells are nRCs (or Never Update, $[f_1^{min}, f_2^{max}]$). A formal definition of this indicator is presented in Equation 3. According to this definition and taking into account that the main target of any multiobjective optimization algorithm is to find a diverse set of non-dominated solutions, the set A will be better than the set B when $I_H(A) > I_H(B)$. With the aim of finding the best possible sets of non-dominated solutions, we have adapted the Non-dominated Sorting Genetic Algorithm II (NSGAII, a well-known metaheuristic) [9]. A detailed explanation of our version of the NSGAII (in terms of our evolutionary operators specific to solve the RCPP) is presented in Section 3.1.

$$I_H(A) = \left\{ \bigcup_i \text{area}_i \mid \mathbf{a}^i \in A \right\}. \tag{3}$$

3.1 The Non-dominated Sorting Genetic Algorithm II

The Non-dominated Sorting Genetic Algorithm II (NSGAII) is the multiobjective evolutionary algorithm proposed by K. Deb et al. in [9]. This algorithm is a population-based metaheuristic (i.e. where every individual is an encoded solution of the problem) in which the evolutionary operators of biological systems (i.e. recombination of parents or crossover, mutation and natural selection) are iteratively applied during N_G generations with the aim of finding the best possible set of non-dominated solutions (see Fig. 2). As we can see in Fig. 2, the first step of NSGAII consists in generating and evaluating the first population of parents (of N_{pop} individuals). Then, the crossover and mutation operations are used to generate a new population of N_{pop} individuals (offspring). And finally, the natural selection is applied with the goal of selecting the best individuals found so far as the parent population of the next generation.

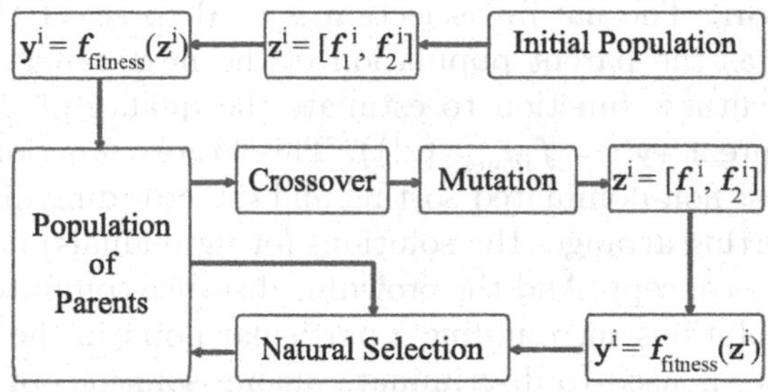

Fig. 2. Main tasks of the Non-dominated Sorting Genetic Algorithm II

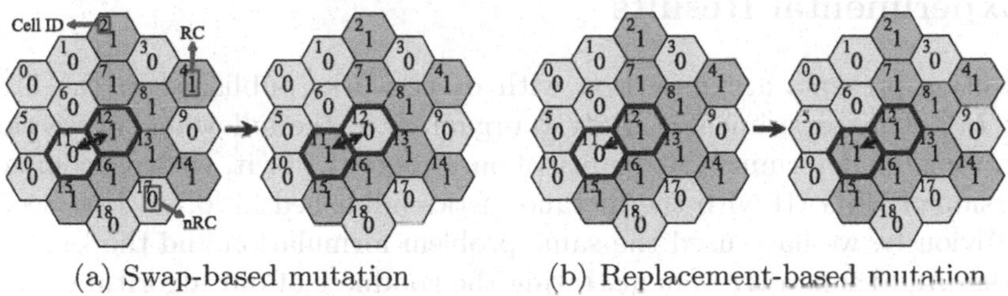

(a) Swap-based mutation (b) Replacement-based mutation

Fig. 3. Mutation operations

Individual Representation. Every individual (i.e. an encoded solution of the problem, $\mathbf{x}^{\mathrm{i}}$) is a vector in which we store whether a network cell is a Reporting Cell ($\mathrm{x}^{\mathrm{i}}_{\mathrm{j}} = 1$) or a non-Reporting Cell ($\mathrm{x}^{\mathrm{i}}_{\mathrm{j}} = 0$). On the other hand, the first population of parents is randomly generated by means of a discrete uniform distribution.

Crossover Operation. This operation is performed with probability $\mathrm{P_C}$ in order to generate a new population of $\mathrm{N_{pop}}$ offspring by recombining the parent population [10]. In this work, we have implemented an elitist multi-point crossover in which the maximum number of crossover points is equal to 4.

Mutation Operations. This evolutionary operator is performed with probability $\mathrm{P_M}$ over the offspring population. With this operation, we slightly change the genetic information of the offspring with the aim of exploring unknown regions of the objective space. In this work, we propose two mutation operations specific to solve the RCPP. The first mutation operation consists in swapping the value of two neighboring cells (they have to belong to different states, i.e. RC and nRC). Fig. 3(a) shows an example of this operation. And the second one consists in replacing the value of a network cell by the value of one of its neighboring cells of the other state. An example of this last operation is shown in Fig. 3(b).

Natural Selection. The natural selection is used to select the best individuals found so far as the parent population of the next generation. K. Deb et al. define in [9] a fitness function to estimate the quality of a solution in the multiobjective context ($\mathbf{y}^{\mathrm{i}} = \boldsymbol{f}_{\mathrm{fitness}}(\mathbf{z}^{\mathrm{i}})$). This fitness function has two main procedures: the fast non-dominated sorting and the crowding distance. The fast non-dominated sorting arranges the solutions (or individuals) in fronts by using the non-dominance concept. And the crowding distance computes an estimation of the density of solutions surrounding a particular point in the objective space. This last procedure is used to discriminate among solutions of the same front. For further information about these two procedures, please consult [9].

4 Experimental Results

This section presents a comparison with other works published in the literature [6,7,8]. This experimental study is organized in the following two sections. Firstly, we must determine the quality of our proposal. For it, we have compared our version of NSGAII with the metaheuristics published in [6,7,8] (see Section 4.1). Obviously, we have used the same problem formulation and the same test networks. And then, after demonstrating the goodness of our algorithm, we analyze the differences between the formulation proposed in this manuscript and the formulation defined in [6,7,8]. This last is shown in Section 4.2.

4.1 Comparison with Other Optimization Techniques

In this section, we compare our proposal with other algorithms published in the literature: Geometric Particle Swarm Optimization (GPSO) [6], a hybridized Hopfield Neural Network with the Ball Dropping technique (HNN-BD) [6], Differential Evolution (DE) [7], and Scatter Search (SS) [8]. All of these algorithms are single-objective metaheuristics with the following objective function:

$$\boldsymbol{f}_3^{\mathrm{SO}}\left(\beta = 10\right) = 10 \cdot \boldsymbol{f}_4 + \boldsymbol{f}_5, \tag{4}$$

where

$$\boldsymbol{f}_4 = \min \left\{ \sum_{\mathrm{i}=0}^{\mathrm{N_{cell}}-1} \lambda_{\mathrm{i}} \cdot \mathrm{N_{LU}}\left(\mathrm{i}\right) \right\}, \tag{5}$$

$$\boldsymbol{f}_5 = \min \left\{ \sum_{\mathrm{i}=0}^{\mathrm{N_{cell}}-1} \mathrm{N_P}\left(\mathrm{i}\right) \cdot \nu\left(\mathrm{i}\right) \right\}. \tag{6}$$

In these equations, λ_{i} is a binary variable that is equal to 1 when the network cell i is a RC, otherwise λ_{i} is equal to 0. $\mathrm{N_{LU}}(\mathrm{i})$ is the number of location updates of the cell i. $\mathrm{N_P}(\mathrm{i})$ is the number of incoming calls in the cell i. And $\nu(\mathrm{i})$ is equal to the vicinity of the cell i when this cell is a RC, otherwise $\nu(\mathrm{i})$ is equal to the maximum vicinity of all the RC reachable from this nRC. The main differences with respect to our formulation will be explained in Section 4.2.

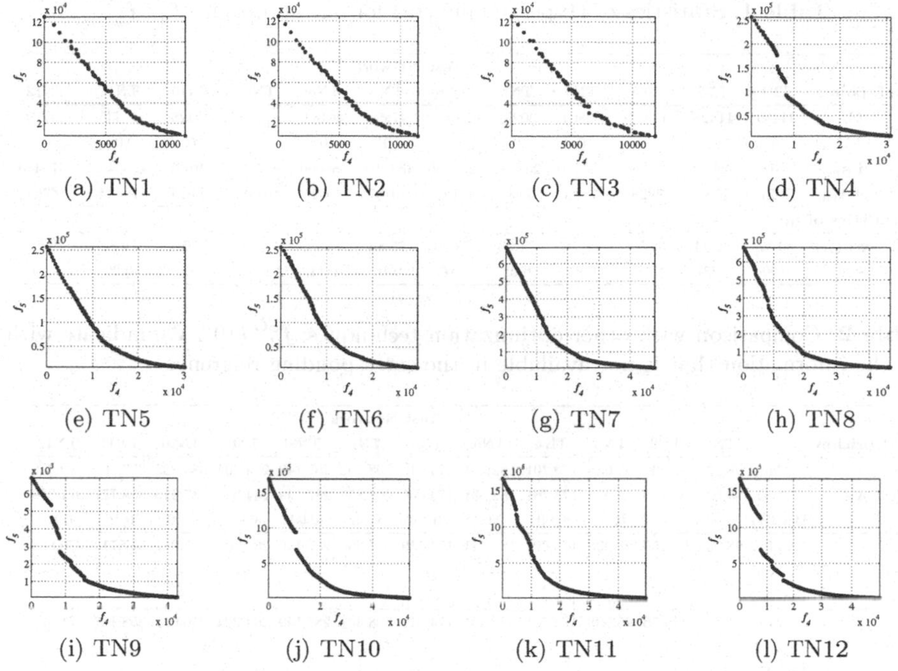

Fig. 4. Pareto Fronts associated with the median Hypervolume. $[\boldsymbol{f}_4, \boldsymbol{f}_5]$

With the aim of performing a fair comparison with these works, we have used the same formulation, the same test networks (12 test networks of different complexity that have been generated by using realistic call and mobility patterns [6]), the same population size ($N_{pop} = 175$), and the same number of generations ($N_G = 1000$). The other parameters of our version of NSGAII have been configured by means of a parametric study of 31 independent runs per experiment. We have chosen the parameter configuration that maximizes the Hypervolume: $P_C = 0.75$ and $P_M = 0.25$. Table 1 shows statistical data of the Hypervolume (mean and standard deviation of 31 independent runs) and the reference points for these 12 test networks. And Fig. 4(a)-Fig.4(l) present the Pareto Fronts associated with the median Hypervolume. In this figure, we can see that our proposal achieves good sets of non-dominated solutions, which extend between the two extreme configurations of Reporting Cells. On the other hand, Table 2 gathers the results of the comparison with the algorithms published in [6,7,8]. In this table, we present: the minimum cost (Min.), the average cost (Aver.), and the deviation percentage (Dev.(%)) from the minimum cost [6]. It should be noted that these algorithms are single-objective metaheuristics (i.e. they provide only one solution, the one that best optimizes Equation 4) and that our proposal is a multiobjective evolutionary algorithm (i.e. it provides a diverse set of non-dominated solutions). Therefore, in order to compare our version of NSGAII with these single-objective metaheuristics, we must search in

Table 1. Statistics of Hypervolume (I_H) for our approach. [$\boldsymbol{f}_4$, $\boldsymbol{f}_5$]

	Test Network											
Ref. points	TN1	TN2	TN3	TN4	TN5	TN6	TN7	TN8	TN9	TN10	TN11	TN12
LU_{max}	11480	11428	11867	30861	30237	29864	47854	46184	42970	54428	49336	49775
LU_{min}	0	0	0	0	0	0	0	0	0	0	0	0
PA_{max}	125184	124576	125248	256500	256788	255636	691008	680000	690112	1691300	1666400	1676400
PA_{min}	7824	7786	7828	7125	7133	7101	10797	10625	10783	16913	16664	16764
Statistics of I_H												
Aver.(%)	60.59	61.44	62.58	71.78	71.93	72.73	75.89	76.71	76.95	78.50	79.80	79.65
Dev.(%)	0.00	0.00	0.00	0.04	0.01	0.03	0.16	0.11	0.17	0.28	0.26	0.30

Table 2. Comparison with other optimization techniques: $\boldsymbol{f}_3^{SO}$ (10). We indicate with "-" the information that is not available in the corresponding reference

		Test Network											
Algorithm		TN1	TN2	TN3	TN4	TN5	TN6	TN7	TN8	TN9	TN10	TN11	TN12
	Min.	98,535	97,156	95,038	173,701	182,331	174,519	308,702	287,149	264,204	385,927	357,368	370,868
NSGAII	Aver.	98,535	97,156	95,038	173,701	182,331	174,605	308,859	287,149	264,396	387,416	358,777	371,349
	Dev.(%)	0.00	0.00	0.00	0.00	0.00	0.13	0.05	0.00	0.09	0.20	0.16	0.15
	Min.	98,535	97,156	95,038	173,701	182,331	174,519	307,695	287,149	264,204	385,927	357,714	370,868
SS[8]	Aver.	-	-	-	-	-	-	-	-	-	-	-	-
	Dev.(%)	-	-	-	-	-	-	-	-	-	-	-	-
	Min.	98,535	97,156	95,038	173,701	182,331	174,519	308,401	287,149	264,204	386,681	358,167	371,829
DE[7]	Aver.	-	-	-	-	-	-	-	-	-	-	-	-
	Dev.(%)	-	-	-	-	-	-	-	-	-	-	-	-
	Min.	98,535	97,156	95,038	173,701	182,331	174,519	308,929	287,149	264,204	386,351	358,167	370,868
HNN-BD[6]	Aver.	98,627	97,655	95,751	174,690	182,430	176,050	311,351	287,149	264,695	387,820	359,036	374,205
	Dev.(%)	0.09	0.51	0.75	0.56	0.05	0.87	0.78	0.00	0.18	0.38	0.24	0.89
	Min.	98,535	97,156	95,038	173,701	182,331	174,519	308,401	287,149	264,204	385,972	359,191	370,868
GPSO[6]	Aver.	98,535	97,156	95,038	174,090	182,331	175,080	310,062	287,805	264,475	387,825	359,928	373,722
	Dev.(%)	0.00	0.00	0.00	0.22	0.00	0.32	0.53	0.22	0.10	0.48	0.20	0.76

our Pareto Fronts the solution that best optimizes the objective function used in [6,7,8] (see Equation 4). Table 2 shows that our proposal achieves better and more stable results (in average) than the algorithms published in [6], and also better results than DE [7] in the most difficult test networks (TN10-TN12).

In summary, we could conclude that our proposal is very interesting because it achieves a wide range of non-dominated solutions and, at the same time, equals or outperforms the single-objective metaheuristics published in [6,7,8]. This last is far from trivial, because these are algorithms specialized in the search of only one solution.

4.2 Comparison between Formulations

In this section, we present a comparison between the formulation proposed in this manuscript (Equation 1 and Equation 2) and the formulation defined in [6,7,8] (Equation 5 and Equation 6). We provide a new formulation because Equation 5 and Equation 6 do not adjust to the Reporting Cells strategy proposed by A. Bar-Noy and I. Kessler in [3]. Firstly, the Never Update configuration

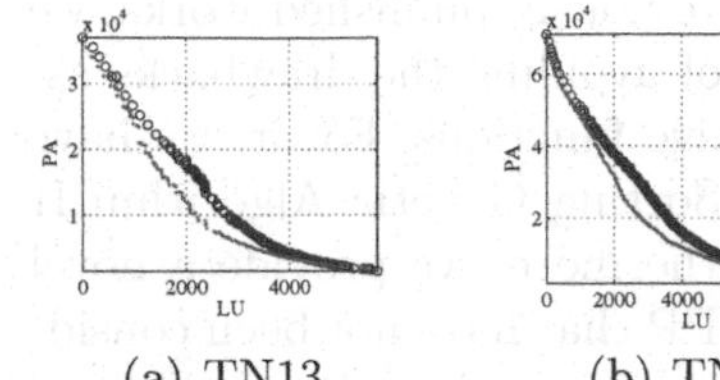
(a) TN13

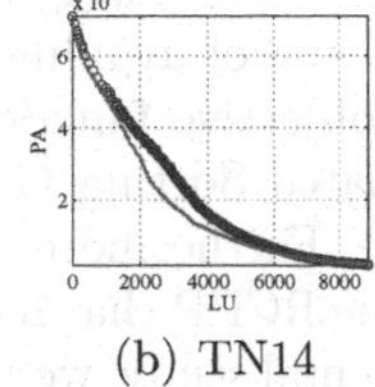
(b) TN14

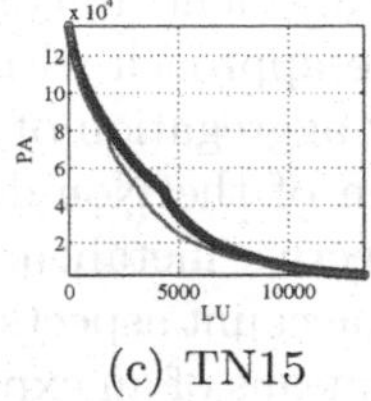
(c) TN15

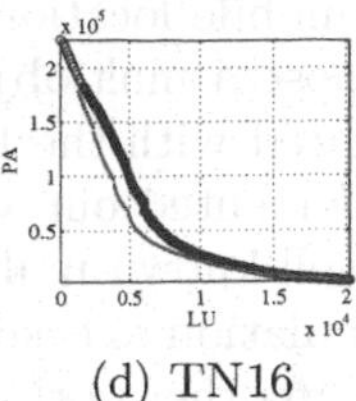
(d) TN16

Fig. 5. Pareto Fronts associated with the median Hypervolume. Open dot: $[f_4, f_5]$. Dot: $[f_1, f_2]$

Table 3. Comparison between formulations

	Ref. points				$[f_1, f_2]$		$[f_4, f_5]$	
Test Network	LU_{max}	LU_{min}	PA_{max}	PA_{min}	Aver.(%)	Dev.(%)	Aver.(%)	Dev.(%)
TN13	5,719	0	37,075	1,483	72.40	0.00	65.59	0.01
TN14	8,852	0	71,015	2,029	76.38	0.01	71.69	0.03
TN15	13,401	0	135,926	2,774	79.58	0.06	75.57	0.03
TN16	20,238	0	225,225	3,575	79,88	0.03	74.64	0.10

(i.e. when all the network cells are nRCs) is not considered in Equation 6. Secondly, the authors of the works [6,7,8] did not take into account that a mobile station only updates its location when it moves to a new RC (i.e. a RC different to the last updated RC). And thirdly, due to the fact that the mobile network knows the last updated RC of every mobile station, the callee's mobile station must be searched in the vicinity of its last updated RC. This is not reflected in the definition of the variable $\nu(i)$ in Equation 6. With the goal of comparing these two formulations, we have used the network simulator published in [11] to generate other four test networks (TN13 (5x5 cells), TN14 (5x7 cells), TN15 (7x7 cells), and TN16 (7x9 cells)). We have generated these new test networks because the test networks TN1-TN12 do not provide a mobile activity trace per subscriber (they only provide the variables $N_{LU}(i)$ and $N_P(i)$). TN13-TN16 are hosted on `http://arco.unex.es/vicberpla/RC-MLM.html`. Note that the authors of this network simulator also proposed the test networks studied in Section 4.1. The results of this comparative study are gathered in Table 3, where we present statistical data of the Hypervolume (mean and standard deviation of 31 independent runs) and the reference points for every test network. And Fig. 5(a)-Fig. 5(d) show the Pareto Fronts associated with the median Hypervolume. Table 3 and Fig. 5(a)-Fig. 5(d) highlight that, with a more realistic formulation, we are able to improve considerably the results obtained by our proposal. In this study we have used the same configuration of NSGAII as in Section 4.1, so the improvement is only due to the new formulation.

5 Conclusion and Future Work

This paper addresses the Reporting Cells Planning Problem, a popular strategy to manage one of the most important tasks in any Public Land Mobile Network:

the mobile location management. In contrast to previously published works, we propose a multiobjective approach with the aim of avoiding the drawbacks associated with the linear aggregation of the objective functions. For it, we have implemented our version of the Non-dominated Sorting Genetic Algorithm II (a well-known multiobjective metaheuristic). Furthermore, we provide a novel formulation to take into account aspects of the RCPP that have not been considered in other works. By means of an experimental study, we have shown that our NSGAII is very competitive, because it achieves good Pareto Fronts and, at the same time, it outperforms (in average) the results obtained with single-objective metaheuristics. Moreover, we have illustrated the benefits of our formulation. As a future work, it would be a good challenge to implement other multiobjective optimization techniques (e.g. SPEA2). Furthermore, the study of other mobile location management strategies could be an interesting research line.

References

1. Nowoswiat, D., Milliken, G.: Managing LTE core network signaling traffic. Alcatel-Lucent, Techzine (2013)
2. Kyamakya, K., Jobmann, K.: Location management in cellular networks: classification of the most important paradigms, realistic simulation framework, and relative performance analysis. IEEE Transactions on Vehicular Technology 54(2), 687–708 (2005)
3. Bar-Noy, A., Kessler, I.: Tracking mobile users in wireless communications networks. IEEE Transactions on Information Theory 39(6), 1877–1886 (1993)
4. Hac, A., Zhou, X.: Locating strategies for Personal Communication Networks: A novel tracking strategy. IEEE Journal on Selected Areas in Communications 15(8), 1425–1436 (1997)
5. Subrata, R., Zomaya, A.Y.: A comparison of three artificial life techniques for Reporting Cell planning in mobile computing. IEEE Trans. Parallel Distrib. Syst. 14(2), 142–153 (2003)
6. Alba, E., García-Nieto, J., Taheri, J., Zomaya, A.Y.: New research in nature inspired algorithms for mobility management in GSM networks. In: Giacobini, M., Brabazon, A., Cagnoni, S., Di Caro, G.A., Drechsler, R., Ekárt, A., Esparcia-Alcázar, A.I., Farooq, M., Fink, A., McCormack, J., O'Neill, M., Romero, J., Rothlauf, F., Squillero, G., Uyar, A.Ş., Yang, S. (eds.) EvoWorkshops 2008. LNCS, vol. 4974, pp. 1–10. Springer, Heidelberg (2008)
7. Almeida-Luz, S.M., Vega-Rodríguez, M.A., Gómez-Pulido, J.A., Sánchez-Pérez, J.M.: Applying differential evolution to the Reporting Cells problem. In: International Multiconference on Computer Science and Information Technology, pp. 65–71 (2008)
8. Almeida-Luz, S.M., Vega-Rodríguez, M.A., Gómez-Pulido, J.A., Sánchez-Pérez, J.M.: Solving the reporting cells problem using a scatter search based algorithm. In: Szczuka, M., Kryszkiewicz, M., Ramanna, S., Jensen, R., Hu, Q. (eds.) RSCTC 2010. LNCS, vol. 6086, pp. 534–543. Springer, Heidelberg (2010)
9. Deb, K., Pratap, A., Agarwal, S., Meyarivan, T.: A fast and elitist multiobjective genetic algorithm: NSGA-II. IEEE Transactions on Evolutionary Computation 6(2), 182–197 (2002)

10. Coello, C.A.C., Lamont, G.B., Veldhuizen, D.A.V.: Evolutionary Algorithms for Solving Multi-Objective Problems (Genetic and Evolutionary Computation). Springer-Verlag New York, Inc., Secaucus (2006)
11. Taheri, J., Zomaya, A.Y.: A simulation tool for mobility management experiments. Int. J. Pervasive Computing and Communications 5(3), 360–379 (2009)
12. Corchado, E., Wozniak, M., Abraham, A., de Carvalho, A.C.P.L.F., Snásel, V.: Recent trends in intelligent data analysis. Neurocomputing 126, 1–2 (2014)

Improving the k-Nearest Neighbour Rule by an Evolutionary Voting Approach

Jorge García-Gutiérrez, Daniel Mateos-García, and José C. Riquelme-Santos

Department of Computer Science,
Avda. Reina Mercedes S/N, 41012 Seville, Spain
{jorgarcia,mateosg,riquelme}@us.es
http://www.lsi.us.es

Abstract. This work presents an evolutionary approach to modify the voting system of the k-Nearest Neighbours (kNN). The main novelty of this article lies on the optimization process of voting regardless of the distance of every neighbour. The calculated real-valued vector through the evolutionary process can be seen as the relative contribution of every neighbour to select the label of an unclassified example. We have tested our approach on 30 datasets of the UCI repository and results have been compared with those obtained from other 6 variants of the kNN predictor, resulting in a realistic improvement statistically supported.

Keywords: kNN voting, evolutionary computation, fuzzy kNN.

1 Introduction

Weighting models are common techniques in hybrid approaches [1,2] and more specifically they are usually applied to classification problems. A proper fit of weights in the training step can thus improve the accuracy of a model. Artificial Neural Networks (ANNs) and Support Vector Machines (SVMs) might be the most evident examples of using weights in learning models, although it is also usual in the k-Nearest Neighbours rule (kNN). In any case, the main goal of weighting systems is to optimize a set of weights in the training step to obtain the highest accuracy and avoid overfitting in the resulting model.

If we focus on kNN weighting methods, most proposals are based on features or instances weighting by mean of a global or local procedure. An example of global methods can be found in [3] where authors select and remove features through a kNN-based genetic algorithm. That system optimizes a weighting vector to scale the feature space and also, it uses a bit vector to select features simultaneously. In a later work, the same authors show a hybrid evolutionary algorithm based on the Bayesian discriminant function [4]. The goal of this proposal is to isolate characteristics belonging to large datasets of biomedical origin by selecting and extracting features. Other heuristics can be found in the literature. Thus, in [5] the authors present an approach that is able of both selecting and weighting features simultaneously by using tabu search.

M. Polycarpou et al. (Eds.): HAIS 2014, LNAI 8480, pp. 296–305, 2014.
© Springer International Publishing Switzerland 2014

Regarding weighted decision regions, Fernández et al. propose a local weighting system besides a prototype-based classifier [6]. After a data normalization based on the position of the instances regarding the prototype (or region) which they belong to, the weights are iteratively calculated. Alsukker et al. use differential evolution to find weights for different features of data [7]. They describe four approaches: feature weighting, neighbour weighting, class weighting and mixed weighting (features and classes), with the latter being the one providing the best results. Mohemmed et al. present a nearest-centroid-based classifier [8]. The basis of this method lies in the calculation of prototypical instances by considering the arithmetic average of the training data. When an unlabeled instance has to be classified, the distance to every prototype is calculated and the nearest one is selected. The optimization of the best centroids that minimize the classification error is carried out through particle swarm.

Moreover, Paredes et al. use different similarity functions to improve the behaviour of nearest neighbour [9]. In a first approximation they consider a weight by feature and instance on training data, resulting in a non-viable number of parameters in the learning process. Thus, the authors present three types of reduction: a weight by class and feature (label dependency), a weight by prototype (prototype dependency) and a combination of the previous ones. The optimization process is carried out by descendant gradient.

Another work based on label dependency is described in [10]. This approach shows an evolutionary algorithm to find a weighted matrix (a weight by feature and class) besides an optimum number (k) of neighbours. Furthermore, the results are statistically tested beyond the classical cross-validation method. There are also references about the use of weights on unbalanced data. Liu et al. define a new measure called Class Confidence Weight (CCW) to gauge the probability that a feature value belong to a class [11]. The CCW estimation is performed by mixture models for numeric features and Bayesian nets for categorical data.

We can find another point of view in the use of weights by applying fuzzy sets theory to the kNN rule. The basis of this idea lies in the modulation of the class membership by the neighbours and the adaptation of the predictive voting system. This approach is called Fuzzy k Nearest Neighbour (Fuzzy kNN) and it presents good results in many classification problems [12]. The main handicap of this paradigm is the fuzzy membership definition, because although it can be established by the expert or even deducted from data analysis, the assignment of fuzzy values remains an open problem nowadays [13,14].

With all the previous in mind, we consider the use of a weighted system to improve the kNN rule to relativize the class membership in the training phase. Concretely, we work with the idea that the k neighbours contribute with different weights in the voting process of the kNN rule. Thus, we have designed an evolutionary system, called *Evolutionary Voting of Neighbours* (EVoN), to calculate the optimum vote weight of every neighbour from the training data and the application of the subsequent k-NN. Unlike most of the approaches in the literature our vector of weights is calculated independently of the neighbours distance. Furthermore, its performance has been statistically validated on UCI datasets [15].

The remaining of this study is organized as follows. Section 2 presents the elements of the evolutionary algorithm designed to calculate the contribution of the k nearest neighbours. The results and a number of statistical tests are specified in Section 3. And finally, Section 4 presents the conclusions and future work.

2 Method

In this section our voting optimization system called *Evolutionary Voting of Neighbours* (EVoN) is described. For this, in subsection 2.1 we present the purpose of this work and how the weighting vector from the learning process is used. The subsection 2.2 exposes the optimization algorithm in detail.

2.1 Purpose and Functionality

As previously described, the aim of our work is to find a set of weights to modify the influence of every neighbour when they vote. Thus, we try to improve the class prediction of an unlabelled instance and therefore improve the kNN rule. Whilst there are many references of approaches that use weighting votes, as far as we know, most of the studies focus on the distance between instances. In this way, the nearest neighbours are "heavier" than the furthest ones and therefore, their influence is greater. In our case, weights are calculated by an evolutionary algorithm regardless the distance. Obtaining a real-valued vector could transform the influence of every neighbour regarding the class to predict in the classification step. This means that the vote of a labeled neighbour is a real value instead of the typical absolute value of 1. Thus, the label that classifies a new instance is the maximum of the sums of the calculated weights for the existing labels into the k nearest neighbours.

To show the learning process, we assume that the set of classes (or labels) is represented by the natural numbers from 1 to b, with b being the number of labels. Thus, let $D = \{(e, l) \mid e \in \mathbb{R}^f \text{ and } l \in \{1, 2, ..., b\}\}$ be the dataset under study with f being the number of features and b the number of labels. Let *label* be an application that assigns to every element e the class to which it belongs to. Let's suppose that D is divided in the sets TR and TS with each of them being the training set and the testing set respectively, such that $D = TR \cup TS$ and $TR \cap TS = \emptyset$. In this manner, the instances of TS (testing set) will be used to evaluate the fitness of EVoN and therefore, they are not been considered for the weights calculation. As will be detailed in subsection 2.2, obtaining a vector $W = (\omega_1, \omega_2, ..., \omega_k)$ is carried out from the instances of TR exclusively. To classify the instance y from TS, the k nearest instances to y are calculated from TR. If x_i is each neighbour, the assigned label to the instance y is given by:

$$label(y) = \arg\max_{l \in \{1..b\}} \sum_{i=1}^{k} \omega_i \delta(l, label(x_i)) \tag{1}$$

where $\delta(l, label(x_i))$ is 1 if $label(x_i) = l$ and 0 in other case.

2.2 Voting Optimization

This subsection details the search algorithm to calculate the optimum contribution of k nearest neighbours. As mentioned above, this task is done by an evolutionary algorithm and therefore, it is necessary to define its main characteristics i.e., individual encoding, genetic operators, fitness function and generational replacement policy.

Individual Encoding. In our approach, an individual is a real-valued vector symbolizing the relative contribution of every neighbour in the voting system of the kNN rule. In the chosen design, the value at first position is associated with the nearest neighbour, and the one at position i affects to the *i-th* neighbour. In addition, a constraint is established to ensure that the closest neighbours are more important i.e., $\omega_1 \geq \omega_2 \geq ...\omega_k$.

Regarding the initial population, it integrates individuals with k sorted values between 0 and 1. To include the classic kNN, we include several vectors with the first k values set to 1 and the remaining set to 0 in the initial population e.g., $(1.0, 0.0, ..., 0.0)$ for $k = 1$, $(1.0, 1.0, ..., 0.0)$ for $k = 2$, and so on. Finally, the maximum value of 1 for a weight may be surpassed during the evolutionary process to highlight the importance of a concrete neighbour regarding the rest.

Crossover and Mutation. As we have mentioned in subsection 2.2 there is a constraint in the order of the genes. On the other hand, the main goal of the crossover operator is building a new individual ($offspring$) from the genotypic characteristics of two parents ($parent1$ and $parent2$). To achieve both aims, the crossover operator in the *i-th* gene is defined as follows:

$$offspring(i) = \begin{cases} BLX - \alpha & \text{if } i = 1 \\ (max - min) * \gamma + min & \text{in other case} \end{cases}$$

Where:

$BLX - \alpha$ is the crossover operator defined in Eshelman and Schaffer [16]
γ is a random value between 0 and 1
$max = offspring(i - 1)$
$min = minimum(parent1(i), parent2(i), offspring(i - 1))$

Regarding the mutation operator, if we consider the individual *indiv*, the i-th gene can change according to the following equation:

$$indiv'(i) = \begin{cases} indiv(i) + indiv(i) * \delta & \text{if } i = 1 \\ indiv(i) - indiv(i) * \delta & \text{if } i = k \\ (indiv(i-1) - indiv(i+1)) * \gamma + indiv(i+1) & \text{otherwise} \end{cases}$$

Where δ is a random value between 0 and 1 at the beginning. Later, the upper limit is reduced in g/G with G being the number of generations of the evolutionary algorithm and g the current generation. This reduction is used to improve the fit across generations. Thus, for $G = 100$ and $g = 10$, the δ upper limit is 1 in the first ten generations. In the following ten, it is 0.9. After another ten generations, it is 0.8 and so on.

Fitness Function. The evolutionary algorithm uses $TR \subset D$ exclusively to obtain the contributions of the neighbours in the training step. Because of we know the labels of the instances from TR, the fitness function is based on the cross-validation error rate by using kNN and the weighted voting system.

The Figure 1 shows the fitness calculation with $m \times s$ cross validations, where m is the number of iterations of the validation process (line 3) and s being the number of partitions of training data TR (line 4). Thus, the set TR is divided in the bags $B_1, B_2...B_s$ for each validation. Then, every bag B_j is evaluated through a classification process by using $TR - B_j$ as a training set. This evaluation is driven by the function *Evaluate* which we will describe later. The classification error on every B_j is accumulated on average by *partialError* (lines 7 and 9), and by *error* in every validation (line 10). Finally, the fitness value is the result of calculating the average of all validations (line 12).

The input parameters of the function *Evaluate* are the weighted vector W, the k value, and the subsets $TR - B_j$ and B_j (line 7). Therefore, the result of this function is the error rate on B_j taking $TR - B_j$ as reference to calculate the neighbours.

For every single instance from the set used to measure the fitness (line 16), the returned label by the function *NearestN* is the majority one according to the k nearest instances belonging to the set used as training data (line 17). If the returned label does not correspond to the real label of the testing instance, the error is increased by 1 (line 19). Then, the resulting error is normalized with the size of the set used as testing data (line 22). Therefore, the value returned by *Evaluate* is a real number between 0 (all instances are well-classified) and 1 (all instances are misclassified).

The function *NearestN* calculates the nearest instances to the example y belonging to the set under evaluation (line 24 and seq.). Every example of the neighbours bag is then inserted in a sorted set according to the distance to y. Thus, the example at the first position will be the nearest to y and the one at the last position will be the furthest (line 27). When we select the k nearest neighbours from the sorted set (line 29), the majority label is returned according

```
1: Fitness(W, k, TR) : error
2: error = 0
3: for i = 1 to m do
4:    Divide TR in s bags: B_1...B_s
5:    partialError = 0
6:    for j = 1 to s do
7:       partialError = partialError + Evaluate(W, k, TR − B_j, B_j)
8:    end for
9:    partialError = partialError/s
10:   error = error + partialError
11: end for
12: error = error/m
13: return error

14: Evaluate(W, k, Train, Test) : error
15: error = 0
16: for each instTest in Test do
17:    lab = NearestN(W, k, Train, instTest)
18:    if lab ≠ label(insTest) then
19:       error = error + 1
20:    end if
21: end for
22: error = error/size(Test)
23: return error

24: NearestN(W, k, Train, y) : labY
25: sortedInst and kNeighbours are empty sorted sets
26: for each x in Train do
27:    insert x in sortedInst sorted by d(x, y)
28: end for
29: kNeighbours = sortedInst.get(k)
30: labY = majorityLabel(kneighbours, W)
31: return labY
```

Fig. 1. Fitness function

to the relative contribution of each neighbour expressed by the vector W and by applying the equation 1 (lines 30 and 31).

Generational Policy. Regarding the transition between generations, we chose an elitist design where the best individual is transferred from one generation to the next but without being affected by the mutation operator. The remaining population is built as follows: being N the number of individuals, $C-1$ individuals are created by cloning the best individual from the previous generation, and the next $N-C$ individuals result from the crossover operation. The selection of the individuals to cross is carried out by the tournament method. All individuals except the first one is affected by the mutation operation with a probability of p.

3 Results

To measure the quality of our approach, we have compared EVoN with IBk (implementation of kNN in the framework WEKA[17]) with k=1, 3 and 5. In addition, we have used an implementation of Fuzzy kNN that can be downloaded from [18].

Table 1. Accuracy of every studied algorithm

	EVoN	IB1	IB3	IB5	FNN1	FNN3	FNN5
australian	**85.6 ± 1.3**	80.2 ± 2.2	83.5 ± 1.9	84.3 ± 1.2	80.2 ± 2.2	83.8 ± 1.9	84.3 ± 1.1
balance s.	**89.6 ± 0.6**	86.8 ± 0.9	86.9 ± 1.1	88.2 ± 0.9	78.2 ± 3.5	82.3 ± 2.4	84.6 ± 1.3
breast t.	66.5 ± 5.3	68.2 ± 5.0	63.9 ± 5.9	65.3 ± 7.6	**68.5 ± 5.0**	65.9 ± 5.3	68.2 ± 5.5
breast w.	96.9 ± 1.1	95.6 ± 1.0	96.6 ± 0.9	97.1 ± 1.0	95.9 ± 1.0	96.6 ± 0.9	**97.3 ± 1.0**
car	**93.4 ± 0.5**	93.1 ± 0.5	93.1 ± 0.5	93.1 ± 0.5	76.9 ± 1.5	82.2 ± 1.5	85.9 ± 1.4
cmc	46.6 ± 1.5	44.3 ± 1.3	**47.0 ± 1.6**	45.9 ± 1.5	43.8 ± 1.3	45.4 ± 1.8	45.8 ± 1.4
diabetes	**75.1 ± 1.6**	70.9 ± 2.1	74.3 ± 2.2	74.7 ± 1.5	71.0 ± 1.8	74.2 ± 2.3	74.6 ± 1.5
ecoli	**87.1 ± 2.1**	80.2 ± 2.8	84.8 ± 2.1	86.4 ± 1.9	80.2 ± 2.8	84.8 ± 2.0	87.0 ± 1.9
glass	69.1 ± 2.8	70.0 ± 3.3	68.6 ± 3.4	66.1 ± 4.6	**70.0 ± 3.4**	68.9 ± 2.9	68.3 ± 3.5
haberman	70.9 ± 1.9	67.0 ± 2.5	**71.5 ± 2.7**	71.0 ± 1.7	66.2 ± 2.3	71.4 ± 2.3	70.5 ± 1.8
heart s.	**80.6 ± 2.5**	75.2 ± 3.1	78.5 ± 3.3	78.3 ± 3.1	75.4 ± 3.2	78.5 ± 3.3	78.4 ± 3.0
hill v.	49.0 ± 1.4	50.3 ± 1.5	51.1 ± 2.4	51.3 ± 2.5	50.2 ± 1.4	50.9 ± 2.2	**51.4 ± 2.6**
ionosphere	86.0 ± 2.4	**86.8 ± 2.4**	86.1 ± 1.7	85.6 ± 1.5	**86.8 ± 2.4**	86.1 ± 1.7	85.6 ± 1.5
liver d.	**63.2 ± 5.2**	59.3 ± 3.9	61.8 ± 3.8	58.3 ± 3.7	59.7 ± 4.0	62.1 ± 4.0	58.7 ± 3.9
lymphoma	**83.3 ± 2.7**	81.7 ± 3.0	78.7 ± 4.1	78.5 ± 4.3	82.1 ± 3.3	80.4 ± 4.0	79.4 ± 3.6
mammogr.	**82.4 ± 1.6**	76.8 ± 1.8	80.9 ± 1.8	82.2 ± 1.5	76.1 ± 2.0	80.6 ± 1.9	81.4 ± 1.4
mfeat m.	**73.2 ± 1.3**	65.8 ± 1.4	69.6 ± 1.3	71.0 ± 1.1	66.0 ± 1.6	69.7 ± 1.2	71.6 ± 1
ozone	**94.1 ± 0.2**	92.2 ± 0.9	93.9 ± 0.3	94.0 ± 0.3	92.2 ± 0.9	93.9 ± 0.3	94.0 ± 0.3
pendigits	99.3 ± 0.1	99.3 ± 0.1	99.3 ± 0.0	99.2 ± 0.0	99.3 ± 0.1	**99.4 ± 0.0**	99.2 ± 0.0
postoper.	**72.6 ± 3.7**	62.8 ± 3.0	69.2 ± 4.3	72.4 ± 3.8	56.5 ± 6.9	63.0 ± 5.6	64.9 ± 5.0
sonar	84.3 ± 3.6	84.8 ± 3.4	83.0 ± 4.9	82.5 ± 3.6	**85.2 ± 3.2**	82.3 ± 5.0	82.8 ± 3.7
sponge	88.7 ± 1.7	**92.3 ± 3.0**	88.7 ± 1.7	88.7 ± 1.7	91.7 ± 3.6	90.2 ± 2.2	88.7 ± 1.7
tae	**63.3 ± 4.8**	60.9 ± 6.1	50.3 ± 7.7	53.6 ± 5.8	62.4 ± 5.5	57.1 ± 5.2	54.4 ± 5.3
transfusion	**78.3 ± 1.3**	69.4 ± 2.0	73.8 ± 1.5	75.9 ± 1.6	68.9 ± 1.6	73.0 ± 1.3	75.6 ± 1.7
vehicle	71.3 ± 1.6	70.0 ± 1.4	70.5 ± 1.5	70.9 ± 1.5	69.8 ± 1.5	71.2 ± 1.7	**72.3 ± 1.4**
vote	93.1 ± 1.6	93.0 ± 1.5	93.9 ± 1.8	94.0 ± 2.3	93.1 ± 1.2	93.1 ± 1.7	**94.0 ± 2.3**
vowel	99.0 ± 0.3	**99.0 ± 0.3**	96.4 ± 1.4	92.7 ± 1.3	**99.0 ± 0.3**	96.4 ± 1.4	93.2 ± 1.3
wine	**96.6 ± 1.6**	94.5 ± 1.8	95.6 ± 2.2	95.4 ± 2.3	94.4 ± 1.8	95.7 ± 2.2	95.3 ± 2.3
yeast	**60.4 ± 1.1**	52.9 ± 1.4	55.2 ± 1.1	57.5 ± 1.3	53.0 ± 1.4	55.9 ± 1.3	57.6 ± 1.1
zoo	94.6 ± 2.2	95.3 ± 2.8	92.7 ± 2.7	94.6 ± 2.1	**96.2 ± 2.1**	92.7 ± 2.7	94.6 ± 2.1
	79.8 ± 2.0	**77.3 ± 2.2**	**78.0 ± 2.4**	**78.3 ± 2.3**	**76.3 ± 2.4**	**77.6 ± 2.4**	**78.0 ± 2.2**

In the experiments we have chosen 30 datasets from the repository UCI[15] with different types of features and classes. Furthermore, all data had the same preprocessing profile i.e., binarization of nominal features, normalization and replacement of missing values by the average. Regarding the evolutionary search configuration we have used a population of 100 individuals, 100 generations, 10% of elitism and a mutation probability of 0.1. In relation to the parameters α (crossover) and g (mutation) their values were 0.5 and 20 respectively. With previous parameters and using four Intel Xeon Processors E7-4820, the computation time for one execution of the evolutionary algorithm with the biggest data file (ozone dataset) with 2534 instances and 73 features was 40 minutes aproximately.

Table 1 shows the results of the analyzed algorithms for each dataset and the global averaged accuracy reached. Every dataset was evaluated with 10CV using 5 different seeds (50 executions in total). We can verify that the performance of our algorithm was the best in 16 out of the 30 datasets, and the second best in 4 out of the remaining 14. Although our approach seems to outperform the rest of competitors, the results have to be statistically validated to reinforce that conclusion. Thus, we have carried out a non-parametric Friedman test and a Holm post-hoc procedure to find out if the performances of the different algorithms are statistically different. The reason for using non-parametric tests lies in the high vulnerability of the necessary conditions to apply parametric tests, specially for the sphericity condition [19,20].

After applying the Friedman' test we obtain the first position in the resulting ranking of algorithms. This fact is consistent with the averaged results obtained by each algorithm. After the calculation of the Friedman statistic, a $p - value$ of $2.679E - 4$ was reached. Therefore, the null hypothesis (no statistical difference among the different algorithms) can be refused with $\alpha = 0.05$. Notice that Friedman' test is not capable of stand out the best method. Thus, the Holm post-hoc procedure allows to compare a control algorithm (in this case EVoN, the best approach candidate) with the remaining. In this case all hypothesis of equivalent performance were also rejected, so we can say that our algorithm is significantly better than its competitors from a statistical point of view.

4 Conclusions

This work presents an method able of calculating the optimum contribution of the k nearest neighbours. Unlike the classical approach that assigns an unitary vote to each neighbour, our algorithm consider a real value (a weight). The main novelty is that, to the best of our knowledge, there are not previous works that consider a distance-independent kNN voting system. Thus, we use evolutionary computation to search a weighted-vector representing the contribution of every instance from the training data. This process is carried out through the genetic operators and without the intervention of the distance function. Our voting approach was tested on 30 datasets from the UCI repository against another 6 kNN-based algorithms, with the results showing a realistic improvement that was statistically supported. In future work, we will focus in the improvement of the fitness function of the evolutionary algorithm to avoid the full dependence with the classification error rate. The main goal of this idea is to achieve a smoothing effect of the learning curve, and therefore accomplish a more accurate searching task of solutions.

References

1. Corchado, E., Wozniak, M., Abraham, A., de Carvalho, A.C.P.L.F., Snásel, V.: Recent trends in intelligent data analysis. Neurocomputing 126, 1–2 (2014)
2. Abraham, A.: Special issue: Hybrid approaches for approximate reasoning. Journal of Intelligent and Fuzzy Systems 23(2-3), 41–42 (2012)
3. Raymer, M.L., Punch, W.F., Goodman, E.D., Kuhn, L.A., Jain, A.K.: Dimensionality reduction using genetic algorithms. IEEE Transactions on Evolutionary Computation 4(2), 164–171 (2000)
4. Raymer, M., Doom, T., Kuhn, L., Punch, W.: Knowledge discovery in medical and biological datasets using a hybrid bayes classifier/evolutionary algorithm. IEEE Transactions on Systems, Man, and Cybernetics, Part B: Cybernetics 33(5), 802–813 (2003)
5. Tahir, M.A., Bouridane, A., Kurugollu, F.: Simultaneous feature selection and feature weighting using hybrid tabu search/k-nearest neighbor classifier. Pattern Recognition Letters 28(4), 438–446 (2007)
6. Fernandez, F., Isasi, P.: Local feature weighting in nearest prototype classification. IEEE Transactions on Neural Networks 19(1), 40 (2008)
7. AlSukker, A., Khushaba, R., Al-Ani, A.: Optimizing the k-nn metric weights using differential evolution. In: 2010 International Conference on Multimedia Computing and Information Technology (MCIT), pp. 89–92 (2010)
8. Mohemmed, A.W., Zhang, M.: Evaluation of particle swarm optimization based centroid classifier with different distance metrics. In: IEEE Congress on Evolutionary Computation 2008, pp. 2929–2932 (2008)
9. Paredes, R., Vidal, E.: Learning weighted metrics to minimize nearest-neighbor classification error. IEEE Transactions on Pattern Analysis and Machine Intelligence 28(7), 1100–1110 (2006)
10. Mateos-García, D., García-Gutiérrez, J., Riquelme-Santos, J.C.: On the evolutionary optimization of k-nn by label-dependent feature weighting. Pattern Recognition Letters 33(16), 2232–2238 (2012)
11. Liu, W., Chawla, S.: Class confidence weighted *k*NN algorithms for imbalanced data sets. In: Huang, J.Z., Cao, L., Srivastava, J. (eds.) PAKDD 2011, Part II. LNCS, vol. 6635, pp. 345–356. Springer, Heidelberg (2011)
12. Keller, J.M., Gray Jr., M.R.: A fuzzy k-nearest neighbor algorithm. IEEE Transactions on Systems, Man, and Cybernetics 15, 580–585 (1985)
13. Mendel, J.M.: Advances in type-2 fuzzy sets and systems. Information Sciences 177(1), 84 (2007)
14. Sanz, J., Fernández, A., Bustince, H., Herrera, F.: A genetic tuning to improve the performance of fuzzy rule-based classification systems with interval-valued fuzzy sets: Degree of ignorance and lateral position. International Journal of Approximate Reasoning 52(6), 751–766 (2011)
15. Asuncion, A., Newman, D.: UCI machine learning repository (2007)

16. Eshelman, L.J., Schaffer, J.D.: Real-coded genetic algorithms and interval-schemata. In: Whitley, D.L. (ed.) Foundation of Genetic Algorithms 2, San Mateo, CA, pp. 187–202. Morgan Kaufmann (1993)
17. Hall, M., Frank, E., Holmes, G., Pfahringer, B., Reutemann, P., Witten, I.H.: The WEKA data mining software: An update. SIGKDD Explorations 11(1) (2009)
18. Jensen, R., Shen, Q.: Computational intelligence and feature selection: Rough and fuzzy approaches (2008), `http://users.aber.ac.uk/rkj/book/programs.php`
19. Demšar, J.: Statistical comparisons of classifiers over multiple data sets. J. Mach. Learn. Res. 7, 1–30 (2006)
20. García, S., Herrera, F.: An Extension on "Statistical Comparisons of Classifiers over Multiple Data Sets" for all Pairwise Comparisons. Journal of Machine Learning Research 9, 2677–2694 (2008)

Performance Testing of Multi-Chaotic Differential Evolution Concept on Shifted Benchmark Functions

Roman Senkerik[1], Michal Pluhacek[1], Donald Davendra[2], Ivan Zelinka[2], and Zuzana Kominkova Oplatkova[1]

[1] Tomas Bata University in Zlin , Faculty of Applied Informatics, Nam T.G. Masaryka 5555, 760 01 Zlin, Czech Republic
{senkerik,pluhacek,oplatkova}@fai.utb.cz

[2] Technical University of Ostrava, Faculty of Electrical Engineering and Computer Science, 17. listopadu 15,708 33 Ostrava-Poruba, Czech Republic
{donald.davendra,ivan.zelinka}@fai.utb.cz

Abstract. This research deals with the hybridization of the two softcomputing fields, which are chaos theory and evolutionary computation. This paper aims on the investigations on the multi-chaos-driven evolutionary algorithm Differential Evolution (DE) concept. This paper is aimed at the embedding and alternating of set of two discrete dissipative chaotic systems in the form of chaos pseudo random number generators for the DE. In this paper the novel initial concept of DE/rand/1/bin strategy driven alternately by two chaotic maps (systems) is introduced. From the previous research, it follows that very promising results were obtained through the utilization of different chaotic maps, which have unique properties with connection to DE. The idea is then to connect these two different influences to the performance of DE into the one multi-chaotic concept. Repeated simulations were performed on the selected set of shifted benchmark functions in higher dimensions. Finally, the obtained results are compared with canonical DE.

Keywords: Differential Evolution, Deterministic chaos, Dissipative systems, Optimization.

1 Introduction

These days the methods based on soft computing such as neural networks, evolutionary algorithms (EA's), fuzzy logic, and genetic programming are known as powerful tool for almost any difficult and complex optimization problem. Differential Evolution (DE) [1] is one of the most potent heuristics available.

This research deals with the hybridization of the two softcomputing fields, which are chaos theory and evolutionary computation. This paper is aimed at investigating the novel concept of multi-chaos driven DE. Although a number of DE variants have been recently developed, the focus of this paper is the embedding of chaotic systems in the form of Chaos Pseudo Random Number Generator (CPRNG) for the DE.

M. Polycarpou et al. (Eds.): HAIS 2014, LNAI 8480, pp. 306–317, 2014.
© Springer International Publishing Switzerland 2014

Firstly, the motivation for this research is proposed. The next sections are focused on the description of evolutionary algorithm DE, the concept of chaos driven DE and the used test function. Results and conclusion follow afterwards.

2 Motivation

This research is an extension and continuation of the previous successful initial experiment with chaos driven DE (ChaosDE) [2], [3] with test functions in higher dimensions.

In this paper the novel initial concept of DE/rand/1/bin strategy driven alternately by two chaotic maps (systems) is introduced. From the previous research it follows, that very promising results were obtained through the utilization of Delayed Logistic, Lozi, Burgers and Tinkerbelt maps. The last two mentioned chaotic maps have unique properties with connection to DE: strong progress towards global extreme, but weak overall statistical results, like average cost function (CF) value and std. dev., and tendency to premature stagnation. While through the utilization of the Lozi and Delayed Logistic map the continuously stable and very satisfactory performance of ChaosDE was achieved. The idea is then to connect these two different influences to the performance of DE into the one multi-chaotic concept.

A chaotic approach generally uses the chaotic map in the place of a pseudo random number generator [4]. This causes the heuristic to map unique regions, since the chaotic map iterates to new regions. The task is then to select a very good chaotic map as the pseudo random number generator.

The focus of our research is the embedding of chaotic systems in the form of CPRNG for evolutionary algorithms. The initial concept of embedding chaotic dynamics into the evolutionary algorithms is given in [5]. Later, the initial study [6] was focused on the simple embedding of chaotic systems in the form of chaos pseudo random number generator (CPRNG) for DE and Self Organizing Migration Algorithm (SOMA) [7] in the task of optimal PID tuning. Also the PSO (Particle Swarm Optimization) algorithm with elements of chaos was introduced as CPSO [8]. The concept of ChaosDE proved itself to be a powerful heuristic also in combinatorial problems domain [9]. At the same time the chaos embedded PSO with inertia weigh strategy was closely investigated [10], followed by the introduction of a PSO strategy driven alternately by two chaotic systems [11].

The primary aim of this work is to use and test the implementation of natural chaotic dynamics into evolutionary algorithm as a multi-chaotic pseudo random number generator.

3 Differential Evolution

DE is a population-based optimization method that works on real-number-coded individuals [1]. For each individual $\vec{x}_{i,G}$ in the current generation G, DE generates a new trial individual $\vec{x}'_{i,G}$ by adding the weighted difference between two randomly selected individuals $\vec{x}_{r1,G}$ and $\vec{x}_{r2,G}$ to a randomly selected third individual $\vec{x}_{r3,G}$. The resulting individual $\vec{x}'_{i,G}$ is crossed-over with the original individual $\vec{x}_{i,G}$. The fitness of the resulting individual, referred to as a perturbed vector $\vec{u}_{i,G+1}$, is then compared with the fitness of $\vec{x}_{i,G}$. If the fitness of $\vec{u}_{i,G+1}$ is greater than the fitness of $\vec{x}_{i,G}$, then $\vec{x}_{i,G}$ is replaced with $\vec{u}_{i,G+1}$; otherwise, $\vec{x}_{i,G}$ remains in the population as $\vec{x}_{i,G+1}$. DE is quite robust, fast, and effective, with global optimization ability. It does not require the objective function to be differentiable, and it works well even with noisy and time-dependent objective functions. Please refer to [1], [12] for the detailed description of the used DERand1Bin strategy (1) (both for ChaosDE and Canonical DE) as well as for the complete description of all other strategies.

$$u_{i,G+1} = x_{r1,G} + F \cdot \left(x_{r2,G} - x_{r3,G}\right) \tag{1}$$

4 The Concept of ChaosDE

The general idea of ChaosDE and CPRNG is to replace the default pseudorandom number generator (PRNG) with the discrete chaotic map. As the discrete chaotic map is a set of equations with a static start position, we created a random start position of the map, in order to have different start position for different experiments (runs of EA's). This random position is initialized with the default PRNG, as a one-off randomizer. Once the start position of the chaotic map has been obtained, the map generates the next sequence using its current position.

The first possible way is to generate and store a long data sequence (approx. 50-500 thousands numbers) during the evolutionary process initialization and keep the pointer to the actual used value in the memory. In case of the using up of the whole sequence, the new one will be generated with the last known value as the new initial one.

The second approach is that the chaotic map is not re-initialized during the experiment and any long data series is not stored, thus it is imperative to keep the current state of the map in memory to obtain the new output values.

As two different types of numbers are required in ChaosDE; real and integers, the use of modulo operators is used to obtain values between the specified ranges, as given in the following equations (2) and (3):

$$rndreal = \text{mod}\ (\text{abs}\ (rndChaos)\ ,\ 1.0) \tag{2}$$

$$rndint = \text{mod}\ (\text{abs}\ (rndChaos)\ ,\ 1.0) \times Range + 1 \tag{3}$$

Where *abs* refers to the absolute portion of the chaotic map generated number *rndChaos*, and *mod* is the modulo operator. *Range* specifies the value (inclusive) till where the number is to be scaled.

5 Chaotic Maps

This section contains the description of discrete dissipative chaotic maps used as the chaotic pseudo random generators for DE. In this research, direct output iterations of the chaotic maps were used for the generation of real numbers in the process of crossover based on the user defined CR value and for the generation of the integer values used for selection of individuals. Following chaotic maps were used: Burgers (4), and Lozi map (5).

The Burgers mapping is a discretization of a pair of coupled differential equations which were used by Burgers [13] to illustrate the relevance of the concept of bifurcation to the study of hydrodynamics flows. The map equations are given in (4) with control parameters $a = 0.75$ and $b = 1.75$ as suggested in [14].

$$\begin{aligned} X_{n+1} &= aX_n - Y_n^2 \\ Y_{n+1} &= bY_n + X_nY_n \end{aligned} \tag{4}$$

The Lozi map is a discrete two-dimensional chaotic map. The map equations are given in (5). The parameters used in this work are: $a = 1.7$ and $b = 0.5$ as suggested in [14]. For these values, the system exhibits typical chaotic behavior and with this parameter setting it is used in the most research papers and other literature sources.

$$\begin{aligned} X_{n+1} &= 1 - a|X_n| + bY_n \\ Y_{n+1} &= X_n \end{aligned} \tag{5}$$

5.1 Graphical Example – Lozi Map and Burgers Map

The illustrative histograms of the distribution of real numbers transferred into the range <0 - 1> generated by means of studied chaotic maps are in Figures 1 and 2.

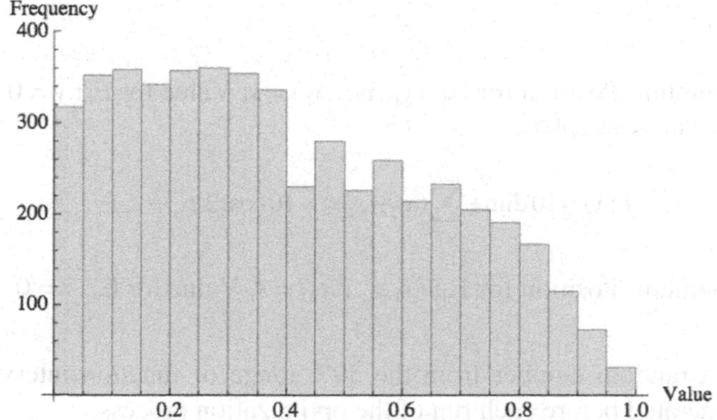

Fig. 1. Histogram of the distribution of real numbers transferred into the range <0 - 1> generated by means of the chaotic Lozi map – 5000 samples

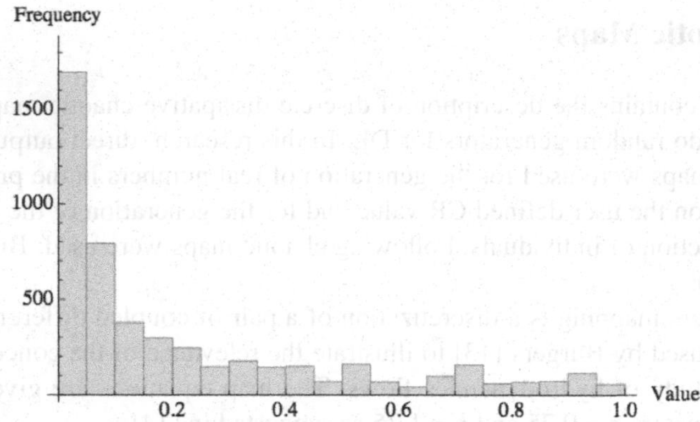

Fig. 2. Histogram of the distribution of real numbers transferred into the range <0 - 1> generated by means of the chaotic Burgers map – 5000 samples

6 Benchmark Functions

For the purpose of evolutionary algorithms performance comparison within this initial research, the shifted 1st De Jong's function (6), shifted Ackley's original function in the form (7) and shifted Rastrigin`s function (8) were utilized.

$$f(x) = \sum_{i=1}^{\dim} (x_i - s_i)^2 \tag{6}$$

Function minimum: Position for E_n: $(x_1, x_2 \ldots x_n) = \boldsymbol{s}$; Value for E_n: $y = 0$
Function interval: <-5.12, 5.12>.

$$f(x) = -20\exp\left(-0.02\sqrt{\frac{1}{D}\sum_{i=1}^{D}(x_i - s_i)^2}\right) - \exp\left(\frac{1}{D}\sum_{i=1}^{D}\cos 2\pi(x_i - s_i)\right) + \tag{7}$$

$$+ 20 + \exp(1)$$

Function minimum: Position for E_n: $(x_1, x_2 \ldots x_n) = \boldsymbol{s}$; Value for E_n: $y = 0$
Function interval: <-30, 30>.

$$f(x) = 10\dim + \sum_{i=1}^{\dim}(x_i - s_i)^2 - 10\cos(2\pi x_i - s_i) \tag{8}$$

Function minimum: Position for E_n: $(x_1, x_2 \ldots x_n) = \boldsymbol{s}$, Value for E_n: $y = 0$

Where s_i is a random number from the 50% range of function interval; $\boldsymbol{s}$ vector is randomly generated before each run of the optimization process.

7 Results

The novelty of this approach represents the utilization of discrete chaotic maps as the multi-chaotic pseudo random number generator for the DE. In this paper, the canonical DE strategy DERand1Bin and the Multi-Chaos DERand1Bin strategy driven alternately by two different chaotic maps (ChaosDE) were used.

The previous research [2], [3] showed that through utilization of Burgers and Tinkerbelt map the unique properties with connection to DE were achieved: strong progress towards global extreme, but weak overall statistical results, like average (benchmark function) Cost Function (CF) value and std. dev. Whereas through the utilization of the Lozi and Delayed Logistic map the continuously stable and very satisfactory performance of ChaosDE was achieved. The idea is then to connect these two different influences to the performance of DE into the one novel multi-chaotic concept. The moment of manual switching over between two chaotic maps as well as the parameter settings for both canonical DE and ChaosDE were obtained analytically based on numerous experiments and simulations (see Table 1)

Table 1. Parameter set up for canonical DE and ChaosDE

DE Parameter	Value
Popsize	75
F	0.8
Cr	0.8
Dimensions	30
Generations	100•D = 3000
Max Cost Function Evaluations (CFE)	225000

Experiments were performed in the combined environments of *Wolfram Mathematica* and *C language*, canonical DE therefore used the built-in *C language* pseudo random number generator *Mersenne Twister C* representing traditional pseudorandom number generators in comparisons. All experiments used different initialization, i.e. different initial population was generated in each run of Canonical or Chaos driven DE.

Within this initial research, one type of experiment was performed. It utilizes the maximum number of generations fixed at 3000 generations. This allowed the possibility to analyze the progress of DE within a limited number of generations and cost function evaluations.

The statistical results of the experiments are shown in Tables 2, 4, 6, which represent the simple statistics for cost function values, e.g. average, median, maximum values, standard deviations and minimum values representing the best individual solution for all 50 repeated runs of canonical DE and several versions of ChaosDE and Multi-ChaosDE.

Tables 3, 5 and 7 compare the progress of several versions of ChaosDE, Multi-ChaosDE and Canonical DE. These tables contain the average CF values for the generation No. 750, 1500, 2250 and 3000 from all 50 runs. The bold values within the all Tables 2 - 7 depict the best obtained result. The graphical comparison of the time evolution of average CF values for all 50 runs of ChaosDE/Multi-ChaosDE and canonical DERand1Bin strategy is depicted in Fig. 3 - 5. Following versions of Multi-ChaosDE were studied:

- *Burgers-Lozi-Switch-500*: Start with Burgers map CPRNG, switch to the Lozi map CPRNG after 500 generations.
- *Lozi-Burgers-Switch-1500*: Start with Lozi map CPRNG, switch to the Burgers map CPRNG after 1500 generations.

Table 2. Simple results statistics for the shifted 1st De Jong's function – 30D

DE Version	Avg CF	Median CF	Max CF	Min CF	StdDev
Canonical DE	5.929778	5.435726	11.69084	2.53501	2.432546
Lozi-No-Switch	3.73E-05	2.27E-05	0.000222	1.54E-06	4.17E-05
Burger-No-Switch	**1.02E-14**	**2.88E-15**	**5.73E-14**	**5.98E-17**	**1.49E-14**
Burger-Lozi-Switch-500	1.78E-06	4.2E-07	2.95E-05	1.59E-08	4.61E-06
Lozi-Burger-Switch-1500	8.34E-10	2.75E-10	1.2E-08	2.81E-11	1.76E-09

Table 3. Comparison of progress towards the minimum for the shifted 1st De Jong's function

DE Version	Generation No. 750	Generation No. 1500	Generation No. 2250	Generation No. 3000
Canonical DE	482.4017	114.3075	26.34619	5.929778
Lozi-No-Switch	90.40304	0.74516	0.004854	3.73E-05
Burger-No-Switch	**0.531726**	**1.33E-05**	**4.32E-10**	**1.02E-14**
Burger-Lozi-Switch-500	2.764289	0.022319	0.000201	1.78E-06
Lozi-Burger-Switch-1500	87.49406	0.709014	3.15E-05	8.34E-10

Table 4. Simple results statistics for the shifted Ackley's original function – 30D

DE Version	Avg CF	Median CF	Max CF	Min CF	StdDev
Canonical DE	3.791676	3.841045	4.518592	2.95934	0.341008
Lozi-No-Switch	0.005533	0.00452	0.014929	0.00154	0.003334
Burger-No-Switch	0.067287	**6.34E-08**	1.501747	**5.47E-09**	0.27714
Burger-Lozi-Switch-500	8.04E-04	7.24E-04	0.002667	1.85 E-04	4.84E-04
Lozi-Burger-Switch-1500	**1.77E-05**	1.03E-05	**7.6E-05**	1.95E-06	**1.46E-05**

Table 5. Comparison of progress towards the min. for the shifted Ackley's original function

DE Version	Generation No. 750	Generation No. 1500	Generation No. 2250	Generation No. 3000
Canonical DE	13.16276	8.511778	5.506989	3.791676
Lozi-No-Switch	8.199525	1.79389	0.081797	0.005533
Burger-No-Switch	**1.548046**	**0.071167**	0.067307	0.067287
Burger-Lozi-Switch-500	2.797948	0.168713	0.009855	8.04E-04
Lozi-Burger-Switch-1500	7.852258	1.621723	**0.003654**	**1.77E-05**

Table 6. Simple results statistics for the shifted Rastrigin`s function – 30D

DE Version	Avg CF	Median CF	Max CF	Min CF	StdDev
Canonical DE	270.9612	273.2324	305.4176	234.2218	15.99992
Lozi-No-Switch	50.68194	45.70853	110.4599	21.52906	21.71585
Burger-No-Switch	44.36785	43.06218	80.76961	16.9143	15.17985
Burger-Lozi-Switch-500	**38.67436**	**36.68143**	82.46749	**16.18175**	**11.82373**
Lozi-Burger-Switch-1500	42.94927	43.09553	**72.74598**	20.8219	13.53718

Table 7. Comparison of progress towards the minimum for the shifted Rastrigin`s function

DE Version	Generation No. 750	Generation No. 1500	Generation No. 2250	Generation No. 3000
Canonical DE	790.1378	404.8734	308.3072	270.9612
Lozi-No-Switch	370.954	177.9286	93.68944	50.68194
Burger-No-Switch	**189.6604**	**55.04461**	**44.56468**	44.36785
Burger-Lozi-Switch-500	221.8914	116.8081	60.55444	**38.67436**
Lozi-Burger-Switch-1500	365.1778	171.6624	57.50722	42.94927

Obtained numerical results given in Tables 2 - 7 and graphical comparisons in Figures 3 - 5 support the claim that all Multi-Chaos/ChaosDE versions have given better overall results in comparison with the canonical DE version. Although the shifted benchmark functions were utilized, from the presented data for the unimodal 1st De Jong's function it follows, that Multi-Chaos DE versions driven by Lozi/Burgers Map have given very satisfactory results, nevertheless the single-chaos concept of original ChaosDE has given the best overall results. High sensitivity of the differential evolution on the selection, settings and internal dynamics of the chaotic PRNG is fully manifested in the case of multi-modal functions. The influence of different internal chaotic dynamics and the exact moment of switching over of two different CPRNGs are clearly visible from Fig. 4 and Fig. 5. Multi-ChaosDE concept has reached the best results from all 50 runs.

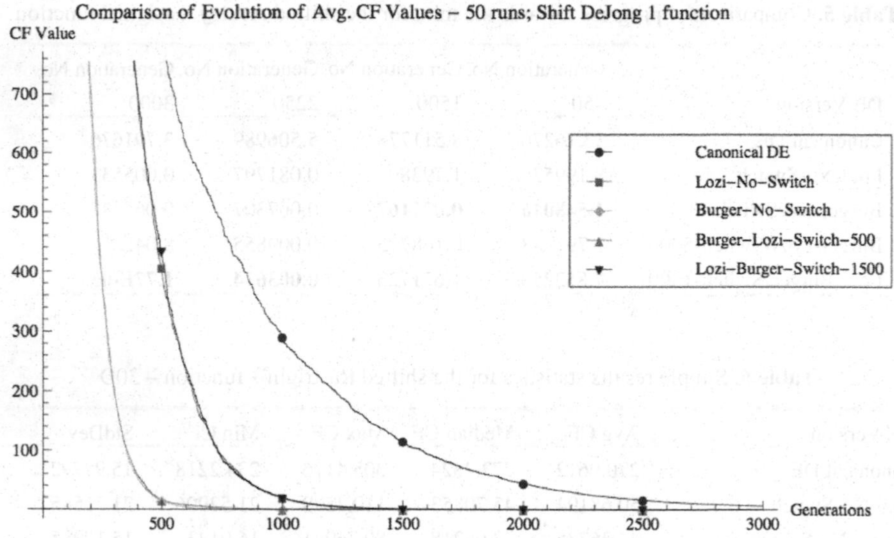

Fig. 3. Comparison of the time evolution of avg. CF values for the all 50 runs of Canonical DE, ChaosDE and Multi-ChaosDE. shifted 1st De Jong's function, $D = 30$.

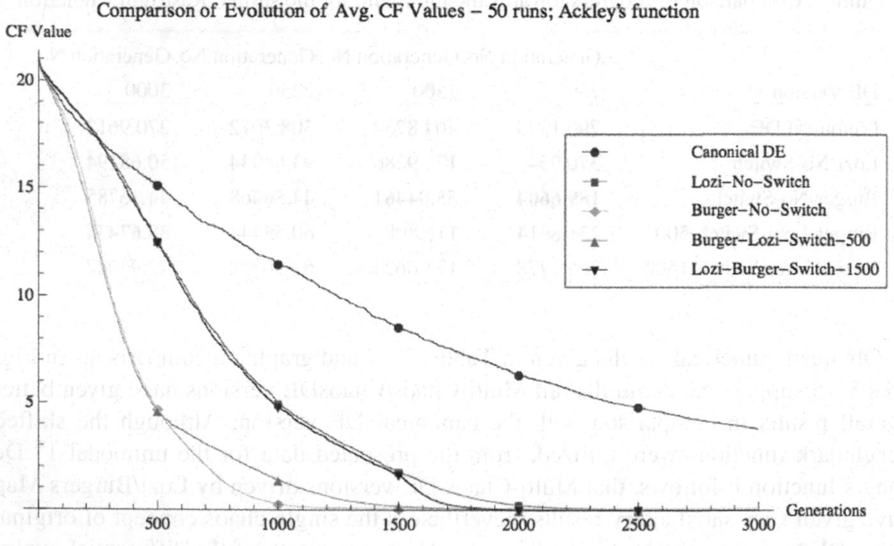

Fig. 4. Comparison of the time evolution of avg. CF values for the all 50 runs of Canonical DE, ChaosDE and Multi-ChaosDE. shifted Ackley's original function, $D = 30$.

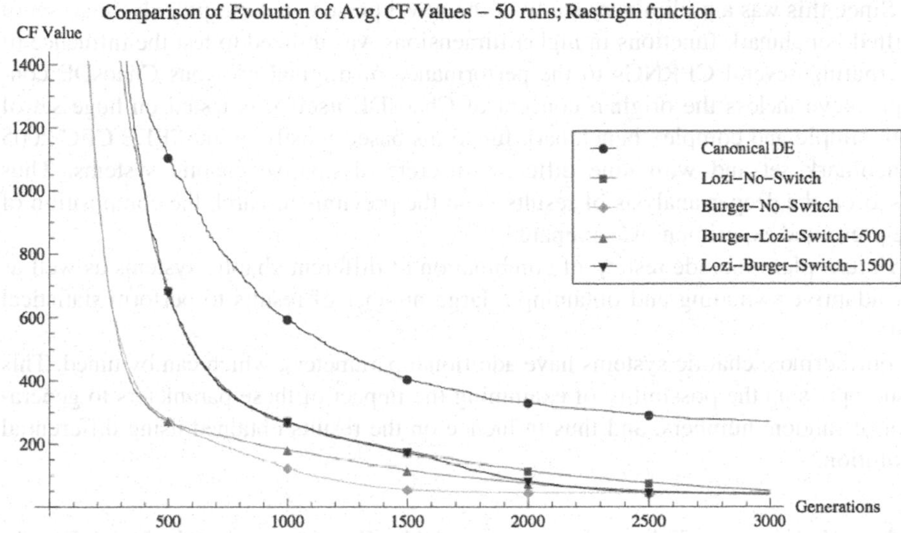

Fig. 5. Comparison of the time evolution of avg. CF values for the all 50 runs of Canonical DE, ChaosDE and Multi-ChaosDE. shifted Rastrigin`s function, $D = 30$.

For the *Burgers-Lozi-Switch-500* version the progressive Burgers map CPRNG secured the faster approaching towards the global extreme from the very beginning of evolutionary process. The very fast switch over to the Lozi map based CPRNG helped to avoid the Burgers map based CPRNG weak spots, which are the weak overall statistical results, like average CF value and std. dev.; and tendency to stagnation. The initial faster convergence (starting of evolutionary process) and subsequent continuously stable searching process without premature stagnation issues is visible from Figures 3 - 5 (magenta lines).

Through the utilization of *Lozi Burgers-Switch-1500* version, the strong progress towards global extreme given by Burgers map CPRNG helped to the evolutionary process driven from the start by mans of Lozi map CPRNG to achieve almost the best avg. CF and median CF values. The moment of switch (at 1500 generations) is clearly visible from Figures 3 - 5 (black lines).

8 Conclusion

In this paper, the novel concept of multi-chaos driven DERand1Bin strategy was tested and compared with the canonical DERand1Bin strategy on the selected benchmark function in higher dimension. Based on obtained results, it may be claimed, that the developed Multi-ChaosDE gives considerably better results than other compared heuristics in cases of complex multimodal benchmark functions.

This research represents the example of hybridizing of two discrete chaotic systems as a multi-chaotic pseudo-random number generator with evolutionary algorithms. Presented data shows the high sensitivity of DE to the selection and internal dynamics of used CPRNG.

Since this was a preliminary study of the novel presented concept, only small set of shifted benchmark functions in higher dimensions was utilized to test the influence of alternating several CPRNGs to the performance of original previous ChaosDE concept. Nevertheless the original concept of ChaosDE itself was tested on huge set of both simple and complex benchmark functions based mostly on the IEEE CEC 2005 benchmark set and with nine different discrete dissipative chaotic systems. Thus based on the deeper analysis of results from the previous research the composition of the presented experiment was prepared.

Future plans include testing of combination of different chaotic systems as well as the adaptive switching and obtaining a large number of results to perform statistical tests.

Furthermore chaotic systems have additional parameters, which can by tuned. This issue opens up the possibility of examining the impact of these parameters to generation of random numbers, and thus influence on the results obtained using differential evolution.

Acknowledgements. This work was supported by Grant Agency of the Czech Republic - GACR P103/13/08195S, partially supported by Grants of SGS No. SP2014/159 and SP2014/170 VŠB - Technical University of Ostrava, Czech Republic, by the Development of human resources in research and development of latest soft computing methods and their application in practice project, reg. no. CZ.1.07/2.3.00/20.0072 funded by Operational Programme Education for Competitiveness, co-financed by ESF and state budget of the Czech Republic, further was supported by European Regional Development Fund under the project CEBIA-Tech No. CZ.1.05/2.1.00/03.0089 and by Internal Grant Agency of Tomas Bata University under the project No. IGA/FAI/2014/010.

References

1. Price, K.V.: An Introduction to Differential Evolution. In: Corne, D., Dorigo, M., Glover, F. (eds.) New Ideas in Optimization, pp. 79–108. McGraw-Hill Ltd. (1999)
2. Senkerik, R., Pluhacek, M., Zelinka, I., Oplatkova, Z.K., Vala, R., Jasek, R.: Performance of Chaos Driven Differential Evolution on Shifted Benchmark Functions Set. In: Herrero, A., Baruque, B., Klett, F., Abraham, A., Snasel, V., de Carvalho, A.C.P.L.F., Bringas, P.G., Zelinka, I., Quintian, H., Corchado, E., et al. (eds.) International Joint Conference SOCO 2013-CISIS 2013-ICEUTE 20113. AISC, vol. 239, pp. 41–50. Springer, Heidelberg (2014)
3. Senkerik, R., Davendra, D., Zelinka, I., Pluhacek, M., Kominkova Oplatkova, Z.: On the Differential Evolution Drivan by Selected Discrete Chaotic Systems: Extended Study. In: 19th International Conference on Soft Computing, MENDEL 2013, pp. 137–144 (2013)
4. Aydin, I., Karakose, M., Akin, E.: Chaotic-based hybrid negative selection algorithm and its applications in fault and anomaly detection. Expert Systems with Applications 37(7), 5285–5294 (2010)

5. Caponetto, R., Fortuna, L., Fazzino, S., Xibilia, M.G.: Chaotic sequences to improve the performance of evolutionary algorithms. IEEE Transactions on Evolutionary Computation 7(3), 289–304 (2003)
6. Davendra, D., Zelinka, I., Senkerik, R.: Chaos driven evolutionary algorithms for the task of PID control. Computers & Mathematics with Applications 60(4), 1088–1104 (2010)
7. Zelinka, I.: SOMA — Self-Organizing Migrating Algorithm. In: New Optimization Techniques in Engineering, vol. 141, pp. 167–217. Springer, Heidelberg (2004)
8. Coelho, L.D., Mariani, V.C.: A novel chaotic particle swarm optimization approach using Hénon map and implicit filtering local search for economic load dispatch. Chaos, Solitons & Fractals 39(2), 510–518 (2009)
9. Davendra, D., Bialic-Davendra, M., Senkerik, R.: Scheduling the Lot-Streaming Flowshop scheduling problem with setup time with the chaos-induced Enhanced Differential Evolution. In: 2013 IEEE Symposium on Differential Evolution (SDE), April 16-19, pp. 119–126 (2013)
10. Pluhacek, M., Senkerik, R., Davendra, D., Kominkova Oplatkova, Z., Zelinka, I.: On the behavior and performance of chaos driven PSO algorithm with inertia weight. Computers & Mathematics with Applications 66(2), 122–134 (2013)
11. Pluhacek, M., Senkerik, R., Zelinka, I., Davendra, D., Chaos, P.S.O.: algorithm driven alternately by two different chaotic maps - An initial study. In: 2013 IEEE Congress on Evolutionary Computation (CEC), June 20-23, pp. 2444–2449 (2013)
12. Price, K.V., Storn, R.M., Lampinen, J.A.: Differential Evolution - A Practical Approach to Global Optimization. Natural Computing Series. Springer, Heidelberg (2005)
13. ELabbasy, E., Agiza, H., EL-Metwally, H., Elsadany, A.: Bifurcation Analysis, Chaos and Control in the Burgers Mapping. International Journal of Nonlinear Science 4(3), 171–185 (2007)
14. Sprott, J.C.: Chaos and Time-Series Analysis. Oxford University Press (2003)

Time Series Segmentation of Paleoclimate Tipping Points by an Evolutionary Algorithm*

M. Pérez-Ortiz[1], P.A. Gutiérrez[1], J. Sánchez-Monedero[1], C. Hervás-Martínez[1], Athanasia Nikolaou[2], Isabelle Dicaire[2], and Francisco Fernández-Navarro[2]

[1] University of Córdoba, Dept. of Computer Science and Numerical Analysis, Rabanales Campus, Albert Einstein building, 14071 - Córdoba, Spain
{i82perom,pagutierrez,jsanchezm,chervas}@uco.es

[2] Advanced Concepts Team, European Space Research and Technology Centre (ESTEC), European Space Agency (ESA), Noordwijk, Netherlands
{athanasia.nikolaou,isabelle.dicaire,francisco.fernandez.navarro}@esa.int

Abstract. Recent studies propose that some dynamical systems, such as climate, ecological and financial systems, among others, present critical transition points named to as *tipping points* (TP). Climate TPs can severely affect millions of lives on Earth so that an active scientific community is working on finding early warning signals. This paper deals with the segmentation of a paleoclimate time series to find segments sharing common patterns with the purpose of finding one or more kinds of segments corresponding to TPs. Due to the limitations of classical statistical methods, we propose the use of a genetic algorithm to automatically segment the series together with a method to perform time series segmentation comparisons. Without a priori information, the method clusters together most of the TPs and avoids false positives, which is a promising result given the challenging nature of the problem.

Keywords: Time series segmentation, genetic algorithms, clustering, paleoclimate data, tipping points, abrupt climate change.

1 Introduction

In contrast to the famous statement of Linnaeus (1751) "*natura non facit saltus*" (or nature makes no leaps), it has been proven that some points of no return, thresholds and phase changes are widespread in nature and these are often non linear [1]. Such events can be rarely anticipated and some of them can have detrimental consequences on Earth's climate and large-scale impacts on human and ecological systems. Therefore, this increases the imperious necessity of studying, analysing and developing techniques for characterizing them in order to

* This work has been subsidized by the Ariadna project 13-9202 of the European Space Agency. The research work of M. Pérez-Ortiz, P.A. Gutiérrez, J. Sánchez-Monedero and C. Hervás-Martínez is partially funded by the TIN2011-22794 project of the Spanish Ministerial Commission of Science and Technology (MICYT), FEDER funds and the P11-TIC-7508 project of the "Junta de Andalucía" (Spain).

M. Polycarpou et al. (Eds.): HAIS 2014, LNAI 8480, pp. 318–329, 2014.
© Springer International Publishing Switzerland 2014

construct reliable early warning systems. Although the human being have influenced their local environment for millennia, e.g. reducing biodiversity, it is now, since the industrial revolution, that truly global changes are been noticed [2]. Examples that are currently receiving attention include the potential collapse of the Atlantic thermohaline circulation, the dieback of the Amazon rainforest or the decay of the Greenland ice sheet [1]. Formally, a climate "tipping point" (also known as "little things can make a big difference") occurs when a small change in forcing triggers a strongly nonlinear response in the internal dynamics of part of the climate system, qualitatively changing its future state.

The critical relevance of early TPs detection has produced a growing attention of the scientific community. Lenton differences between several types of TPs, and presents some indicators that can help to detect them, such as the increase of autocorrelation of the series values [3]. In [4], more concrete techniques regarding data processing and indicators are presented. They study a bank of methods using only simulated ecological data concluding, in concordance with the literature, that there is no unique best indicator for identifying an upcoming transition. They also conclude that all the methods require specific data-treatment. Up to our knowledge, all previous works tackle the TPs detection with statistical methods trying to select (by trial and error) the method more suitable to detect those transitions. They require an intensive data preprocessing that include, for instance, the use of Gaussian filters or rolling windows that introduces extra parameters (such as the width of the Gaussian function or size of the window) that need to be optimised [3,4]. The main limitation behind these methods is that different TPs and different statistical descriptors require different and specific treatments.

This paper deals with climate time series segmentation. We introduce a segmentation method as a first step to better understand the time series. This segmentation provides a more compact representation of the time series through splitting it into segments with similar behaviour [5]. A segmentation analysis avoids the necessity of specifying predefined sliding windows for the different TPs, which is one of the main difficulties of previous TP detection methods [4]. Moreover, the segmentation algorithm is able to detect differences between the TPs. We address the segmentation problem as a heuristic search problem with the proposal of a Genetic Algorithm (GA) to overcome the limitations of traditional statistical methods. The GA segments the data trying to obtain diverse clusters of segments based on six statistical properties. Measuring the quality of a segmentation can be only achieved by expert evaluation of the solutions given by the algorithm. An important contribution of this paper is a quantitative method to perform comparisons with respect to an expected ideal segmentation of the series to assess the robustness and stability of the method. This method allows evaluating a segmentation algorithm with a minimal effort by the expert, who has only to provide the ideal segmentation. We test the proposal with data collected within the North Greenland Ice Core Project δ^{18}O ice core data [6,15] which includes climate records from -60,000 years to the present.

The rest of the paper is organised as follows. Section 2 presents the segmentation algorithm, while Section 3 presents a proposal for segmentation comparison and discusses the experimental results. The last section depicts the conclusions.

2 Segmentation Algorithm

Given a time series $Y = \{y_n\}_{n=1}^{N}$, our objective is to divide the values of y_n into m consecutive subsets or segments. These segments should present a homogeneous behaviour regarding the values of y_n. This is done by partitioning the time indexes ($n = 1, \ldots, N$) into segments: $s_1 = \{y_1, \ldots, y_{t_1}\}, s_2 = \{y_{t_1}, \ldots, y_{t_2}\}, \ldots, s_m = \{y_{t_{m-1}}, \ldots, y_N\}$, where t's are the cut points and are subscripted in ascending order ($t_1 < t_2 < t_{m-1}$). The cut points belong to two segments (the one before and the one after, which allows to analyse consistently the transition from one segment to the next). The integer m and the cut points $t_i, i = 1, \ldots, m-1$, are the parameters to be determined by the algorithm. As done in [7], we extend this setting by trying to group the segments into k different classes or clusters ($k < m$), where k is a parameter defined by the user. In this way, each s_l segment will be associated to a class label: (s_1, z_1), ... ,(s_m, z_m), where z_l, $l = 1, \ldots, m$, is the class label of the l-th segment and takes values in a set of k different labels, $z_l \in \{\mathcal{C}_1, \ldots, \mathcal{C}_k\}$.

2.1 Summary of the Algorithm

The Genetic Algorithm considered in this paper can be included in the area of time series segmentation [5,8,9,10]. Each possible segmentation is represented as an array of binary values (chromosome representation), where a value of 1 represents a cut point. The evolution starts from a population of randomly generated segmentations. Mutation and crossover operators are applied to explore and exploit the search space. This procedure is repeated g generations. To evaluate a solution (or segmentation), we select a set of statistics to be calculated for each segment. Then, similar segments are grouped using a clustering process. The different characteristics of the GA are defined in the following subsections.

2.2 Chromosome Representation

As stated before, each individual chromosome consists of an array of binary values, where the length of the chromosome is the time series length, N. Each position c_i stores whether the time index t_i of the time series represents a cut point for the evaluated solution[1]. In this sense, for a given segment s_i delimited by the cut points t_{i-1} and t_i ($t_{i-1} < t_i$), the corresponding chromosome values will be $c_{i-1} = 1$, $c_i = 1$ and $c_l = 0, \forall l | t_{i-1} < l < t_i$.

[1] Note that the first and last points of the chromosome are considered as cut points.

2.3 Initial Population

The population of the GA is a set of binary vectors of length N. In order to initialise the population, an average segment length has to be specified by the user ($\overline{sl}$). Taking into account that the cut points belong to two segments, the number of cut points will be $\overline{m} = \lceil \frac{N}{\overline{sl}-1} \rceil$, so the chromosomes are binary arrays where $\overline{m}$ random positions are 1s and the rest are 0s.

2.4 Fitness Evaluation

Evaluation of the quality of a segmentation consists of three different steps: extracting the characteristics of the segments, applying a clustering process and measuring the quality of this clustering.

Extracting Segment Characteristics. Given that the segments in a chromosome can have different length, an approach is designed to project all the segments into the same dimensional space. Six statistical metrics are considered and measured for all chromosome segments. Then, the similarities between segments can be calculated in the 6-dimensional space. Consider s_s as a segment fulfilling the previously stated conditions (i.e., s_s is a segment delimited by the cut points t_{s-1} and t_s, where the segment length is $t_s - t_{s-1} + 1$). The mapping is done by the function $f : \mathbb{R}^{(t_s - t_{s-1}+1)} \rightarrow \mathbb{R}^6$, in the following way:

$$f(s_s) = (S_s^2, \gamma_{1s}, \gamma_{2s}, a_s, MSE_s, AC_s) \quad (1)$$

where the different characteristics are defined as:

1. Variance (S_s^2): It measures the variability of the segment:

$$S_s^2 = \frac{1}{t_s - t_{s-1}+1} \sum_{i=t_{s-1}}^{t_s} (y_i - \overline{y_s})^2, \quad (2)$$

   where y_i are the time series values of the segment, and $\overline{y_s}$ is the average value of the segment.
2. Skewness (γ_{1s}): It represents the (vertical) asymmetry of the distribution of the series values in the segment with respect to the arithmetic mean:

$$\gamma_{1s} = \frac{\frac{1}{t_s - t_{s-1}+1} \sum_{i=t_{s-1}}^{t_s} (y_i - \overline{y_s})^3}{S_s^3}, \quad (3)$$

   where S_s is the standard deviation of the s-th segment.
3. Kurtosis (γ_{2s}): This statistic is related to the degree of concentration that the values present around the mean of the distribution:

$$\gamma_{2s} = \frac{\frac{1}{t_s - t_{s-1}+1} \sum_{i=t_{s-1}}^{t_s} (y_i - \overline{y_s})^4}{S_s^4} - 3. \quad (4)$$

4. Slope of a linear regression over the points of the segment (a_s): A linear model is constructed for every segment trying to achieve the best linear

approximation of the points of the time series in the evaluated segment. The slope is a measure of the general tendency of the segment:

$$a_s = \frac{S_s^{yt}}{(S_s^t)^2}, \tag{5}$$

where, for the s-th segment, S_s^{yt} is the covariance between the time indexes, t, and the time series values, y; and S_s^t is the standard deviation of the time values. Covariance S_s^{yt} is defined by:

$$S_s^{yt} = \frac{1}{t_s - t_{s-1} + 1} \sum_{i=t_{s-1}}^{t_s} (i - \overline{t_s}) \cdot (y_i - \overline{y_s}). \tag{6}$$

5. Mean Squared Error (MSE_s): Considering the same linear model than the one used for the slope, we measure the error (MSE_s) of this linear fitting:

$$MSE_s = S_s^2 \cdot (1 - r_s^2), \text{ where } r_s^2 = \frac{S_s^{yt}}{S_s^2 \cdot (S_s^t)^2}. \tag{7}$$

6. Autocorrelation coefficient (AC_s): This a measure of the correlation between the current values of the time series and the previous ones:

$$AC_s = \frac{\sum_{i=t_{s-1}}^{t_s} (y_i - \overline{y_s}) \cdot (y_{i+1} - \overline{y_s})}{S_s^2}. \tag{8}$$

Clustering Process: *k*-means. A clustering process is applied to group similar segments (taking into account the six selected statistical measures). For simplicity, the algorithm chosen for the clustering step is the well-known k-means. Before the clustering algorithm, note that a normalisation of the values of the segment metrics is conducted, as the distance from each segment to its centroid strongly depends on the range of values of each metric (e.g. variance can have a much broader range of variation than skewness).

In the classic k-means, the initial centroids are randomly chosen from the set of patterns. Instead, we have developed a deterministic process to select these centroids which ensures that a chromosome will always present the same fitness. First, we choose the feature with the maximum standard deviation. The first initial centroid will be the segment with the highest value for this feature. The second one will be the segment with the highest Euclidean distance from the first centroid. The third centroid will be that which is farthest from both, and so on. This assures a deterministic initialisation, at the same time that the initial centroids are as far as possible from each other, favouring centroids diversity.

Measuring the Quality of the Clustering Process. The last step of the evaluation of the chromosome is to measure how well the segments are grouped (compactness of the clustering). It is clear that different clustering algorithms usually lead to different clusters or reveal different clustering structures. In this sense, the problem of objectively and quantitatively evaluating the clustering results is particularly important and this is known in the literature as cluster validation. There are two different testing criteria for this purpose [11]:

external criteria and internal criteria. When a clustering result is evaluated based on the data that was clustered itself, this is called internal evaluation. In external evaluation, clustering results are evaluated using for example known class labels. Based on these concepts, the internal criteria evaluation metrics will be a suitable option for the evolution, because the GA is not given any a priori information of the segments to be found. Note that the segments metrics are normalised at this step as well. We have considered four different metrics:

1. *Sum of squared errors (SSE)*: The simplest error measure is the sum of squared errors (considering errors as the distance from each point to their centroid), i.e.:
$$SSE = \frac{1}{N}\sum_{i=1}^{k}\sum_{\mathbf{x}\in\mathcal{C}_i} d(\mathbf{x},\mathbf{c}_i)^2, \tag{9}$$
where k is the number of clusters, $\mathbf{c}_i$ is the centroid of cluster $\mathcal{C}_i$ and $d(\mathbf{x},\mathbf{c}_i)$ is the Euclidean distance between pattern $\mathbf{x}$ and centroid $\mathbf{c}_i$. This function does not prevent clusters to fall very close in the clustering space. As this index has to be minimised, the fitness will be defined as $f = \frac{1}{1+SSE}$.
2. *Caliński and Harabasz index (CH)*: This index has been found to be one of the best performing ones for adjusting the value of k. It is defined as:
$$CH = \frac{\mathtt{Tr}(\mathbf{S}_B)\cdot(N-k)}{\mathtt{Tr}(\mathbf{S}_W)\cdot(k-1)}, \tag{10}$$
where N is the number of patterns, and $\mathtt{Tr}(\mathbf{S}_B)$ and $\mathtt{Tr}(\mathbf{S}_W)$ are the trace of the between and within-class scatter matrix, respectively. Note that the value of k will be fixed in our algorithm. As this index has to be maximised, the fitness will be defined as $f = CH$.
3. *Davies-Bouldin index (DB)*: This index also attempts to maximize the between-cluster distance while minimising the distance between the cluster centroids to the rest of points. It is calculated as follows:
$$DB = \frac{1}{k}\sum_{i=1}^{k}\max_{i\neq j}\frac{\alpha_i+\alpha_j}{d(\mathbf{c}_i,\mathbf{c}_j)}, \tag{11}$$
where α_i is the average distance of all elements in cluster $\mathcal{C}_i$ to centroid $\mathbf{c}_i$, and $d(\mathbf{c}_i,\mathbf{c}_j)$ is the distance between centroids $\mathbf{c}_i$ and $\mathbf{c}_j$. As this index has to be minimised, the fitness will be defined as $f = \frac{1}{1+DB}$.
4. *Dunn index (DU)*: The Dunn index attempts to identify clusters that are compact and and well-separated. In this case, the distance between two clusters is defined as $d(\mathcal{C}_i,\mathcal{C}_j) = \min_{\mathbf{x}\in\mathcal{C}_i,\mathbf{y}\in\mathcal{C}_j} d(\mathbf{x},\mathbf{y})$, that is, the minimum distance between a pair of points $\mathbf{x}$ and $\mathbf{y}$ belonging to $\mathcal{C}_i$ and $\mathcal{C}_j$. Furthermore, we could define the diameter $\mathtt{diam}(\mathcal{C}_i)$ of cluster $\mathcal{C}_i$ as the maximum distance between two of its members, such as: $\mathtt{diam}(\mathcal{C}_i) = \max_{\mathbf{x},\mathbf{y}\in\mathcal{C}_i} d(\mathbf{x},\mathbf{y})$. Then, the Dunn index is constructed as:
$$DU = \min_{i=1,\ldots,k}\left(\min_{j=i+1,\ldots,k}\left(\frac{d(\mathcal{C}_i,\mathcal{C}_j)}{\max_{l=1,\ldots,k}\mathtt{diam}(\mathcal{C}_l)}\right)\right). \tag{12}$$
The Dunn index has been found to be very sensitive to noise, but this disadvantage can be avoided by considering different definitions of cluster distance

or cluster diameter. For example, as suggested in [11], the cluster diameter can be computed as:

$$\mathtt{diam}(C_i) = \frac{1}{N_{C_i}(N_{C_i}-1)} \sum_{\mathbf{x},\mathbf{y}\in C_i} d(\mathbf{x},\mathbf{y}), \quad (13)$$

where N_{C_i} is the number of patterns belonging to cluster C_i. This cluster diameter estimation has been found to be more robust in the presence of noise. As this index has to be maximised, the fitness will be $f = DU$.

2.5 Selection and Replacement Processes

All individuals will be considered for reproduction and generation of offspring, promoting a greater diversity because all individuals are possible parents. After the application of the genetic operators, the offspring and the parent population are joined and a replacement process is performed by roulette wheel selection. The selection probability for each individual chromosome is calculated from its fitness value. The roulette wheel process is repeated as many times as the population size minus one, and the last place is kept for the best segmentation of the previous generation, thus being an elitist algorithm. As can be seen, the selection process promotes diversity, while the replacement process promotes elitism.

2.6 Mutation Operator

Two mutation operators are included in the GA with the aim of reducing the dependency with respect to the initial population and escaping from local optima. The probability p_{m} of performing any mutation is decided by the user. Once a mutation is decided to be performed, the kind of perturbation applied to the chromosome is randomly selected from the following two: 1) add or remove (with the same probability) a given number of cut points of the segmentation; and 2) move a given number of cut points of the segmentation towards the left or the right (with the same probability).

For all the mutations, the number of cut points to be mutated is decided by a user parameter as a percentage of the current number of cut points. When moving cut points to the right or the left, each selected cut point is randomly pushed towards the previous or the following cut point (with the constraint that it never reaches the previous or the next point).

2.7 Crossover Operator

The algorithm includes a crossover operator, whose main function is to perform an exploitation of the existing solutions. For each parent individual, the crossover operator is applied with a given probability p_{c}. The operator randomly selects the other parent and a time index. It interchanges the left and right parts of the chromosomes selected with respect to the time index.

3 Experiments

The dataset chosen for this study is the North Greenland Ice Core Project (NGRIP) δ^{18}O ice core data [6,15]. The δ^{18}O water isotope record is used as a proxy for past atmospheric temperature. We focus on the 20-yr resolution δ^{18}O isotope records. The dataset is pre-processed by obtaining a 5-point average in order to reduce short-term fluctuations within the data. In this way, the time series we have considered is $\{y_n^*\}_{n=1}^{N/5}$ with $y_i^* = \frac{1}{5}\sum_{j=5i}^{5i+4} y_i$.

3.1 Experimental Setting

The experimental design is presented in this subsection. The GA was configured with the following parameters: the number of individuals of the population is $P = 100$. The crossover probability is $p_c = 0.8$ and the mutation probability $p_m = 0.2$. The percentage of cut points to be mutated is the integer part of the 20% of the number of cut points, and the average segment length for the initialisation is $\overline{sl} = 4$. The maximum number of generations is set to $g = 100$, and the k-means clustering process is allowed a maximum of 20 iterations. These parameters were optimised by a trial and error procedure, although the algorithm showed a very robust performance to their values. The most important parameters for the final performance of the algorithm were $\overline{sl}$ and k.

We performed different experiments considering the 4 different fitness functions presented in Section 2.4 and different values of k for the k-means algorithm ($k = 2, \ldots, 6$). It is important to recall that the algorithm estimates the optimal segments and clusters them without any prior information of the DO events. The only information given to the algorithm is the time series and the statistic characteristics to use for the clustering in order to validate whether the statistics proposed in the literature are useful for characterising paleoclimate TPs in general. Given the stochastic nature of GAs, the algorithm was run 30 times with different seeds to evaluate its stability and robustness.

3.2 Evaluation Metrics

In order to evaluate the results of the algorithm, two evaluation metrics were used. These measures analyse both the homogeneity of cluster assignation with respect to the DO events and the robustness of the results obtained from different seeds. They are not included in the fitness function, serving only as an automatic way of evaluating the quality of the segmentation, avoiding the intervention of the expert. Both are indexes comparing two different clustering partitions:

1. *Rand index (RI)* This metric is particularly useful for data clustering evaluation [12]. It is related to the accuracy, but is applicable even when class labels are not available for the data, as in our case. A set $Y = \{y_n\}_{n=1}^{N}$ is given (in our case, the time series), and two clustering partitions of Y are to be compared: $X = \{X_1, \ldots, X_r\}$ and $Z = \{Z_1, \ldots, Z_s\}$. For a given segmentation, the partitions are defined in the following way: X_l is a set containing

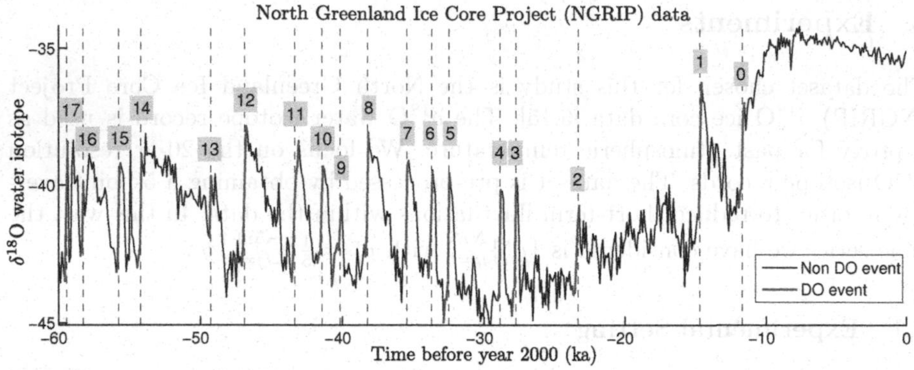

Fig. 1. Representation of the ideal segmentation and the different DO events

every $y_i \in s_s, s_s \in \mathcal{C}_l$, i.e. the partitions are based on the label assigned to each time series value y_i from the current segmentation. The following two numbers are defined: a (number of pairs in Y that are in the same set in X and Z) and b (number of pairs in Y that are in different sets in X and Z). Then, the Rand index is defined as: $RI = (a+b)/\binom{n}{2}$. This metric has a value between 0 and 1, with 0 indicating that the two partitions do not agree on any pair of points and 1 indicating that they are exactly the same.

2. *Adjusted rand index (ARI)*: It is a corrected version of the RI [13] trying to fix some known problems with the RI, e.g. the expected value of the RI of two random partitions does not take a constant value and it approaches its upper limit of unity as the number of clusters increases. ARI values range from −1 to +1, yielding negative values if the index is less than the expected index. The detailed formulation can be found in [13].

In order to evaluate the segmentation returned by the algorithm, we compare it with an ideal segmentation[2]. The ideal segmentation (Fig. 1) has been designed by examining the literature about Dansgaard-Oeschger (DO) events, which are associated to TPs. In the Figure, the onsets of the DO events (in a first approximation, we do not consider the error margin) reported in [15] are represented by vertical lines and the segments covering the period precursor to the DO events (which we hypothesize as TP) are delimited by the slope close to the corresponding onset. The closer the segmentation returned by the GA is to this ideal segmentation, the better the segmentation. To perform this comparison, RI and ARI indexes will be used (ARI_Ideal and RI_Ideal).

Given that the wishful ideal segmentation would be binary (non DO event or DO event) and the segmentation returned by the GA can have a value of $k > 2$, we need to binarise the segmentation of the GA (i.e. decide which clusters

[2] Hypothetically ideal segmentation, based on the available data. The hypothesis is that the onset of the DO events is detected from combined analysis of benthic sediment data and ice core analysis [14]. Those data do not always agree, therefore part of the error margin. The method of timing contributes the rest of the error.

Table 1. NGRIP average segmentation results for different algorithm settings

Fitness	k	ARI_Ideal	RI_Ideal	ARI_Seeds	RI_Seeds
DB	5	**0.315 ± 0.060**	*0.777 ± 0.015*	**0.346 ± 0.078**	**0.727 ± 0.040**
DU	5	*0.308 ± 0.067*	**0.788 ± 0.018**	*0.341 ± 0.092*	**0.727 ± 0.046**
CH	5	0.260 ± 0.073	0.772 ± 0.008	0.223 ± 0.105	0.644 ± 0.074
SSE	5	0.279 ± 0.048	0.770 ± 0.018	0.057 ± 0.018	0.638 ± 0.017
Fitness	k	ARI_TPs	RI_TPs	ARI_Seeds	RI_Seeds
DB	2	0.171 ± 0.132	0.766 ± 0.001	0.258 ± 0.292	**0.821 ± 0.081**
DB	3	0.257 ± 0.081	0.758 ± 0.013	*0.411 ± 0.152*	*0.780 ± 0.046*
DB	4	*0.304 ± 0.045*	0.773 ± 0.009	**0.412 ± 0.080**	0.761 ± 0.037
DB	5	**0.315 ± 0.060**	*0.777 ± 0.015*	0.346 ± 0.078	0.727 ± 0.040
DB	6	0.286 ± 0.075	**0.779 ± 0.014**	0.214 ± 0.109	0.615 ± 0.084

represent the DO events and which not). Preliminary experiments revealed that DO events were usually grouped under one or two clusters, so we evaluated ARI_Ideal and RI_Ideal for all possible combinations of one or two clusters. The final value was the maximum ARI_Ideal and RI_Ideal values of all these combinations. Moreover, the stability of the GA was estimated by comparing the 30 segmentations from the different runs. This was done by averaging RI and ARI comparing all possible pairs of segmentations (ARI_Seeds and RI_Seeds).

3.3 Results

All these results are included in Table 1. The first part of the table compares the different fitness functions for a predefined value of $k = 5$ (as we initially observed that this was obtaining suitable results). As can be seen, both DB and DU fitness functions obtain very good segmentation quality and stability, although DB performs slightly better. In contrast, CH and SSE are performing poorly in both scenarios (it is noteworthy the very low stability obtained by the SSE fitness function, which may be due to the fact that it only minimises the intra-cluster distances and obviates the inter-cluster distances). The result that the algorithm is robust and stable to different initialisations is crucial for the following parts of the study (i.e. develop an early warning system for TPs of climatic component). Concerning the experiment that studies different values of k, it can be seen that $k = 5$ is indeed the optimal value for the segmentation. This result indicates that the concept and nature of DO events is too complex to only consider a binary approach (TPs versus non TPs). The climate system exhibits a dynamical behaviour with intrinsic variability hence a binary approach is not able to encompass all features present within a DO event, being $k = 5$ a reasonable choice. Moreover, the method can group several DO events together and is still a useful tool to better understand the behaviour of DO events.

The segmentation obtaining the highest ARI_Ideal metric (with a value of 0.498) for the fitness function DB, along with a representation of the 18 DO events can be seen in Fig. 2. The segments have been coloured according to their cluster assignation. The clusters associated to the DO events are $\mathcal{C}_1$ and $\mathcal{C}_5$. If we compare this segmentation to the one in Fig. 1, we can see that almost all DO

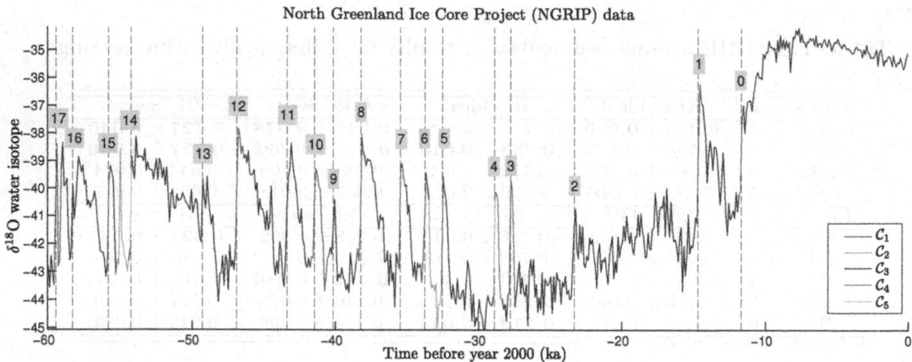

Fig. 2. Best time series cluster assignation after the evolutionary process

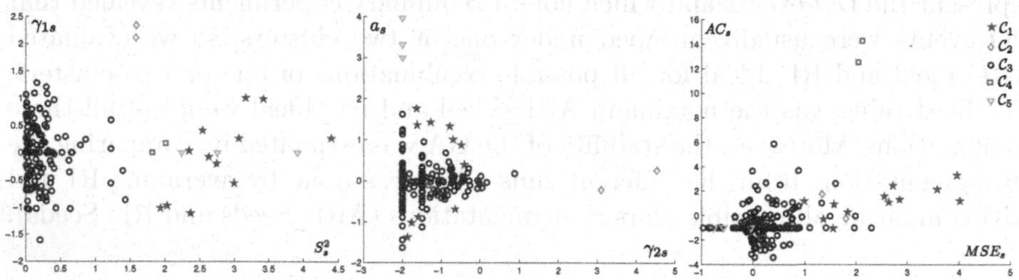

Fig. 3. Clustering space for the six metrics (each point represents a segment)

events are correctly segmented by the algorithm ($\mathcal{C}_1$ and $\mathcal{C}_5$ segments are always close to the DO onset) and that there are not "false positives" labels ($\mathcal{C}_1$ and $\mathcal{C}_5$ segments are not found in a non DO event part of the series). However, five events are not detected: 2, 9, 11, 13 and 16 (some of which have been found in the literature to be caused by random fluctuations of the dynamics of the time series and for which there is no evidence of increase in the selected statistics). The clustering space of this segmentation can be analysed in Fig. 3. This Figure confirms that there are some differences between the two clusters associated to the DO events ($\mathcal{C}_1$ and $\mathcal{C}_5$), mainly from the values of the S_s^2 metric.

4 Conclusions

This work tackles the problem of time series segmentation in the context of paleoclimate time series analysis. We propose a Genetic Algorithm to perform the segmentation and clustering of the time series by using six statistic characteristics that have been found to reveal incoming tipping points (TPs). The results have shown that the method clusters together most of the TPs avoiding "false positives", which is a promising result because it demonstrates that most of the TPs can be segmented with the same data analysis, as opposed to other proposals in the literature, which design TP-specific descriptors. Future work includes extending the method to find early warning signals and considering other time series datasets, mutation and crossover operators and fitness functions.

References

1. Wassmann, P., Lenton, T.: Arctic tipping points in an earth system perspective. AMBIO 41(1), 1–9 (2012)
2. Allen, M.: Planetary boundaries: Tangible targets are critical. Nature Reports Climate Change, 114–115 (2009)
3. Lenton, T.M.: Early warning of climate tipping points. Nature Climate Change 1(4), 201–209 (2011)
4. Dakos, V., Carpenter, S.R., Brock, W.A., Ellison, A.M., Guttal, V., Ives, A.R., Kefi, S., Livina, V., Seekell, D.A., Van Nes, E.H., et al.: Methods for detecting early warnings of critical transitions in time series illustrated using simulated ecological data. PLoS One 7(7), e41010 (2012)
5. Keogh, E., Chu, S., Hart, D., Pazzani, M.: An online algorithm for segmenting time series. In: Proceedings IEEE International Conference on Data Mining, ICDM 2001, pp. 289–296 (2001)
6. Andersen, K.K., Azuma, N., Barnola, J.M., Bigler, M., Biscaye, P., Caillon, N., Chappellaz, J., Clausen, H.B., Dahl-Jensen, D., Fischer, H., et al.: High-resolution record of northern hemisphere climate extending into the last interglacial period. Nature 431(7005), 147–151 (2004)
7. Tseng, V.S., Chen, C.H., Huang, P.C., Hong, T.P.: Cluster-based genetic segmentation of time series with dwt. Pattern Recognition Letters 30(13), 1190–1197 (2009)
8. Sclove, S.L.: Time-series segmentation: A model and a method. Information Sciences 29(1), 7–25 (1983)
9. Himberg, J., Korpiaho, K., Mannila, H., Tikanmaki, J., Toivonen, H.T.: Time series segmentation for context recognition in mobile devices. In: Proceedings IEEE International Conference on Data Mining, ICDM 2001, pp. 203–210 (2001)
10. Chung, F.L., Fu, T.C., Ng, V., Luk, R.W.: An evolutionary approach to pattern-based time series segmentation. IEEE Transactions on Evolutionary Computation 8(5), 471–489 (2004)
11. Xu, R., Wunsch, D.: Clustering. IEEE Press Series on Computational Intelligence. Wiley (2008)
12. Rand, W.M.: Objective Criteria for the Evaluation of Clustering Methods. Journal of the American Statistical Association 66(336), 846–850 (1971)
13. Hubert, L., Arabie, P.: Comparing partitions. Journal of Classification 2(1), 193–218 (1985)
14. Peterson, L.C., Haug, G.H., Hughen, K.A., Röhl, U.: Rapid changes in the hydrologic cycle of the tropical atlantic during the last glacial. Science 290(5498), 1947–1951 (2000)
15. Svensson, A., Andersen, K.K., Bigler, M., Clausen, H.B., Dahl-Jensen, D., Davies, S.M., Johnsen, S.J., Muscheler, R., Parrenin, F., Rasmussen, S.O., Röthlisberger, R., Seierstad, I., Steffensen, J.P., Vinther, B.M.: A 60 000 year greenland stratigraphic ice core chronology. Climate of the Past 4(1), 47–57 (2008)

Mutual Information-Based Feature Selection in Fuzzy Databases Applied to Searching for the Best Code Metrics in Automatic Grading

José Otero, Rosario Suárez, and Luciano Sánchez

Universidad de Oviedo. Departamento de Informática. Edificio Departamental Oeste, Campus de Viesques, Gijón 33204, Asturias, Spain

Abstract. Massive open online courses have a large impact in developing countries, helping to improve education in poor regions. However, instructors cannot review open-ended work from students as they do in smaller class settings. In the context of computer science courses where students' code is reviewed, there are some methods that use code metrics for automatically providing the student with a qualification. Notwithstanding this, a high number of incomplete and conflicting sources of information must be combined in the prediction process, and it may happen that there are too many variables involved to make any meaningful predictions. In this work a new method is proposed for sorting a set of metrics by their relevance in the prediction of student qualifications that can cope with incomplete and imprecise results. Measurements taken on variable-sized sets of assignments are aggregated into fuzzy values, and a fuzzy random variable-based definition of mutual information is used to build a partial ranking of metrics according to their predictive power. The most relevant metrics are fed to a genetic fuzzy system that models the dependence between the fuzzy code metrics and the qualifications of the corresponding students. A set comprising 800 source code files, collected in classroom Computer Science lectures taught between 2013 and 2014, was used for validating the hypotheses of this research, and it was found that the new ranking method significantly improves the predictive capability of the models.

1 Introduction

On-line courses are ubiquitous nowadays. Almost every institution, university, college or high-school offers freely accessible on-line courses. Massive Open Online Courses (MOOCs) and Distance Learning have a large impact in developing countries, helping to improve education in poor regions.

Learning Management Systems or Content Management Systems are used to provide the students with different kinds of material and also allow students and teachers to interact via lectures, assignments, exams or gradings. However, the resources needed for tracking students and taking examination are time consuming for the organizing institutions, thus there is demand for intelligent techniques that help the instructor to manage large groups of students. In particular, procedures are seeked that partial or completely automate the grading

M. Polycarpou et al. (Eds.): HAIS 2014, LNAI 8480, pp. 330–341, 2014.
© Springer International Publishing Switzerland 2014

process, understood as taking standardized measurements of varying levels of achievement in a course [3].

There are topics, however, whose qualification is troublesome. Think for instance in computer programming, where the usual examination procedure consists in challenging the students with a set of problems to be solved. In online courses, the student's solutions, comprising one or more source code files, are uploaded to the platform, where the person at charge scores the task. This needs a long time and it is also difficult for the teacher to be objective and unbiased. If the grading depends not only on the program output correctness (using a set of sample data inputs) but also on the structure of the solution (data types, control flow, efficiency) or the documentation quality, the situation is even worse. In addition to this, the students should follow the usual software developing process and thus the solution of each assignment should pass through several stages until it reaches a maturity level such that it can be submitted as a completed task. Those intermediate stages could provide a valuable feedback to the teacher, regarding individual students' needs and also teacher's lectures, materials or strategies quality.

This problem has been addressed before by different researchers. In [22] a semi automated system for task submission and grading is proposed, but the grading itself must be done manually by the teacher. Other systems exist that are able to check submitted source code automatically, for instance the *WebToTeach* system [3]. Similar to this, and focused on programming, the methods in [19] or [11] achieve an automatic grading by comparing the output of each student program with the output of a correct program. There is no measurement of the internals of the source code, which it is labelled as correct if the output is correct, regardless of the solution strategy. The *AutoLEP* system [28] is more recent. One of the salient points of this last work is a procedure to compare any implementation of an algorithm against a single model. Furthermore, in [27] a methodology is presented that accomplishes automatic grading by testing the program results against a predefined set of inputs, and also by formally verifying the source code or by measuring the similarities between the control flow graph and the teacher's solution. The parameters of a linear model are found that averages the influence of the three techniques in order to match teacher's and automatic grading in a corpus of manually graded exercises. Finally, in [16], software metrics are used to measure the properties of the students' programs and a fuzzy rule-based system is used to determine how close the programs submitted by students and the solutions provided by the teacher are, partially achieving an automatic grading.

However, these approaches are not without problems. Automatic grading may not only be intended to compare students' and teacher's solutions to a particular problem but also to determine the level of achievement of each programming concept, as mentioned before. But programming concepts are, generally speaking, related to *sets* of different source code files written by the students. The metrics of all source codes in these sets should be jointly considered by the grading system. Since these sets may be of different sizes for different students and some of its elements may be missing, a robust combination method is needed.

Furthermore, not all metrics are equally informative for each programming concept, thus a procedure is needed for chosing the most relevant ones. Because of this, in this paper:

- A method is proposed for building a fuzzy compound value that summarizes the values of the software metrics of different source files that are related to the same programming concept. This compound value takes into account both the average value and the dispersion of the different metrics.
- The relevance of the different metrics is assessed with an extension of the Mutual Information (MI) criterion to fuzzy data. It will be shown that the extension described in this paper exploits better the available data and significantly improves the crisp definition of MI for this problem.
- A genetic fuzzy system that can learn rules from interval and fuzzy data is used to build the fuzzy rule based system that performs the automatic grading on the basis of the metrics that have been selected in the preceding step.

This paper is organized as follows: in Section 2, a brief state of the art in software metrics for software analysis is given. In Section 3, a method for combining the values of a metric over a set of different source files is proposed. In Section 4, a method for ranking the importance of the fuzzy aggregated metric values is proposed, and in Section 5 the rule learning algorithm is described. In Section 6 numerical results are provided that validate the claims of this paper with actual data collected in classroom lectures in 2013 and 2014. Section 7 concludes the paper and highlights future research lines.

2 Software Metrics for Software Analysis

Software metrics have been actively researched since the early stages of Computer Science, and an extensive amount of results are available; see for instance [1] or [18], where comprehensive surveys about Software Metrics are performed.

In this work, software metrics will be used to measure the quality of the students' submitted source code. It will be assumed that better coding leads to higher scoring, but static analysis is also used to obtain additional insights about the student's programs. According to [24], the most relevant software metrics in this context are:

- Number of lines of code: a naive measurement of the code size.
- Ratio between lines of comments and lines of code: a measurement of code documentation.
- Halstead metrics [13]: these metrics have been reported to be useful to evaluate students programs [2].
- Cyclomatic number [20]: often related to *complexity* measures and thus usually referred to as cyclomatic complexity number, but there is not a full agreement about the subject [2]. The cyclomatic number is a graph theory concept that has been translated to software because a program can be modeled as a strongly connected graph [30].

Most of the software analysis tools[1] provide these features and many other indexes. As the number of software metrics increases, the odds that some of them are closely related or overlap in the property being measured increases too. For instance, it is hard to conceive an increase of the cyclomatic number without a simultaneous increase of the lines of code. Moreover, an increase in the value of a metric is not always consistent with an improvement in the code quality. For instance, it may happen that the complexity of a given problem solution is too low, because the student is unwinding a loop, or the complexity may be greater than expected because the student is using a quadratic algorithm for a problem with linear solution. In either case, the dependence between the metric value and the desired solution is highly problem dependent. Because of this, some researchers propose to use feature selection techniques for finding the best software metrics for the problem at hand. In [21], a stochastic procedure is employed to select the subset of quantitative measures that bring out the best software quality prediction. Another example is [17], where eighteen filter based feature selection procedures are tested against sixteen software datasets, in this case searching for fault prone modules.

In this paper, a set of software metrics that are commonly used to measure student's source code properties [16] with some additions from [23] for extracting information related with style and structure will be used, and feature selection techniques will be developed that help to select the best set of metrics for each programming concept.

3 Fuzzy Data as an Aggregate of Disperse Information

As mentioned, the grading process is intended to determine the level of achievement of each programming concept, which in turn is assessed by means of a set of source code files written by the students. The metrics of all files in these sets are jointly considered by the grading system. Given that these sets are of different sizes for different students and some of its elements may be missing, a robust combination method is needed.

The proposed combination is based on the assumption that the application of a software metric to a given source code can be assimilated to the process of measuring the value of an observable variable or *item* that provides partial information to describe an unobservable or *latent* variable. In this case, the latent variable is the degree of assessment of a given programming concept. It is remarked that the information provided by different items may be in conflict.

The conversion of a set of items into a compound value that can be fed into a model has been solved in different ways in other contexts. For instance, in marketing problems certain models have been designed where sets of items are preprocessed and aggregated into a characteristic value [6]. The most commonly used aggregation operator is the mean, although many different functions may be used instead [7].

[1] `http://www.webappsec.org/`

In [26], however, a different approach was used: it was assumed that there exists a true value for the latent variable, but also that this value cannot be precised further than a set that contains it. The same idea will be adopted in this paper. Observe that this method is compatible with a possibilistic view of the uncertainty, where fuzzy sets are used for describing partial knowledge about the data. This interpretation is grounded in the result that the contour function of a possibility distribution is a fuzzy set [12], and α-cuts of fuzzy sets are linked to confidence intervals about the unknown value of the feature with significance levels $1 - \alpha$ (see reference [10]). This last property supports the use of intervals or fuzzy data for modelling uncertain data: a fuzzy set is found such that their α-cuts are confidence intervals with degree $1 - \alpha$ of the expected value of the observation error. In this paper, bootstrap estimates of these confidence intervals have been used, that are stacked to form the fuzzy membership functions describing the aggregated value of the metrics.

4 Feature Selection for Fuzzy Data

In this section, a method for ranking the importance of the fuzzy aggregated metrics in relation to the grading problem is presented. The importances of the different metrics will be ordered by means of an estimation of the degree of independence between the scores assigned by the teacher to the members of a control group and the fuzzy aggregated values of the metric in the set of source files. This degree of independence is based on an estimation of the mutual information between a random variable (the grades) and a fuzzy random variable (each aggregated metric).

A fuzzy random variable will be regarded as a nested family of random sets, $(\Lambda_\alpha)_{\alpha\in(0,1)}$, each one associated to a confidence level $1-\alpha$ [9]. A random set is a mapping where the images of the outcomes of the random experiment are crisp sets. A random variable X is a selection of a random set Γ when the image of any outcome by X is contained in the image of the same outcome by Γ. For a random variable $X : \Omega \to \mathbf{R}$ and a random set $\Gamma : \Omega \to \mathcal{P}(\mathbf{R})$, X is a selection of Γ (written $X \in S(\Gamma)$) when

$$X(\omega) \in \Gamma(\omega) \quad \text{for all } \omega \in \Omega. \tag{1}$$

In turn, a random set can be viewed as a family of random variables (its selections.)

The mutual information between a random variable X and a random set Γ is defined as the set of all the values of mutual information between the variable X and each one of the selections of Γ:

$$\mathrm{MI}(X,\Gamma) = \{\mathrm{MI}(X,T) \mid T \in S(\Gamma)\}. \tag{2}$$

and the mutual information between a random variable X and a fuzzy random variable Λ is the fuzzy set defined by the membership function

$$\widetilde{\mathrm{MI}}(X,\Lambda)(t) = \sup\{\alpha \mid t \in \mathrm{MI}(X,\Lambda_\alpha)\}. \tag{3}$$

Let $M+1$ paired samples $(X_1^k, X_2^k, \ldots, X_N^k)$, and $(Y_1, Y_2, \ldots, Y_N)$, with $k = 1, \ldots, M$, from $M+1$ standard random variables $X^1, X^2, \ldots, X^M$ and Y. It will be assumed that all universes of discourse are finite. Let $p_1^k, p_2^k, \ldots, p_n^k$ and $q_1, q_2, \ldots, q_m$ be the relative frequencies of the values of the samples of X^k and Y, respectively, and let $r_1^k, r_2^k \ldots, r_s^k$ be the frequencies of the values of the joint sample $X^k \times Y$. The mutual information between the variables X^k and Y is estimated as follows:

$$\begin{array}{l} \mathrm{MI}(k) = \mathrm{MI}((X_1^k, \ldots, X_N^k), (Y_1, \ldots, Y_N)) = \\ -\sum_{i=1}^n p_i^k \log p_i^k - \sum_{i=1}^m q_i \log q_i + \sum_{i=1}^s r_i^k \log r_i^k. \end{array}$$

Let

$$\Sigma(X^1, \ldots, X^M, Y) = (\sigma_1, \sigma_2, \ldots, \sigma_M) \tag{4}$$

be a ranking of the variables $(X^1, X^2, \ldots, X^M)$ according to their relevance. The notation

$$\Sigma(X^1, \ldots, X^M, Y)(k) = \sigma_k \tag{5}$$

will be used in the following. In this paper, the ranking Σ is a permutation of the M elements $1, \ldots, M$ fulfilling that[2]

$$\mathrm{MI}(\sigma_1) \leq \mathrm{MI}(\sigma_2) \leq \ldots \leq \mathrm{MI}(\sigma_M). \tag{6}$$

Now let be $M+1$ fuzzy paired samples $(\widetilde{X}_1^k, \widetilde{X}_2^k, \ldots, \widetilde{X}_N^k)$, and an also paired crisp sample $(Y_1, Y_2, \ldots, Y_N)$ from $M+1$ fuzzy random variables $\widetilde{X}^1, \widetilde{X}^2, \ldots, \widetilde{X}^M$ and the standard random variable Y. It is proposed that the ranking of the variables $\widetilde{X}^1, \widetilde{X}^2, \ldots, \widetilde{X}^M$ is the fuzzy permutation $\widetilde{\Sigma}$ defined as follows:

$$\begin{array}{l} \left[\widetilde{\Sigma}(\widetilde{X}^1, \ldots, \widetilde{X}^M, Y)(k)\right]_\alpha = \\ \left\{\Sigma(X^1, \ldots, X^M, Y)(k) \mid X^1 \in S([\widetilde{X}^1(\omega)]_\alpha) \ldots X^M \in S([\widetilde{X}^M(\omega)]_\alpha)\right\}. \end{array} \tag{7}$$

Each element of $\widetilde{\Sigma}$ is a fuzzy set describing the set of ranks of each fuzzy aggregated metric $\widetilde{X}^k$. In this paper the metrics will be ordered according to the modal points of this fuzzy permutation; see Section 6 for a detailed practical case.

5 Genetic Learning of Fuzzy Rules from Imprecise Data in Modeling Problems

The fuzzy aggregated metrics are the inputs of a rule-based model that predicts the grades of a student. In this section the rule learning algorithm introduced in [25] is briefly described for the convenience of the reader. Fuzzy models comprise R rules with the form

$$\texttt{If } x \texttt{ is } A_r \texttt{ then } y \texttt{ is } B_r \texttt{ with weight } w_r, \tag{8}$$

[2] Alternatively, Σ could also be thought of as the outcome of any suitable feature selection algorithm, for instance [4].

where x and y are the feature and the output vectors, respectively, and A_r are conjunctions of linguistic labels, which in turn are associated to fuzzy sets. B_r is a singleton or a fuzzy number. In this paper, A_r and B_r are not modified during the learning, to preserve the linguistic interpretability, but each rule is assigned a weight w_r. The output $\widetilde{Y}$ of the fuzzy model for a fuzzy input $\widetilde{X}$ is defined through the membership function

$$\widetilde{Y}(y) = \sup\left\{\widetilde{X}(x) \mid Y = \sum_{r=1}^{R} f_r(x)\right\} \tag{9}$$

where each function $f_r(x)$ is a product $\beta_r A_r(x)$. $A_r(x)$ is the membership of x to a linguistic expression whose terms are labels of the linguistic variables defined over the input variables, connected by the operators "AND" and "OR". β_r is the product of the centroid of B_r and the weight w_r assigned to the rule.

5.1 NMIC: A Multiobjective Michigan-Style Genetic Fuzzy Model for Imprecise Data

The NMIC learning method is based on the hypothesis that the best model will comprise rules that are in nondominated sets under confidence and support measures [15]. An extension of the NSGA-II algorithm to fuzzy data is repeatedly launched to obtain Pareto fronts containing nondominated rules in terms of confidence and support. Every front is regarded as a population of a Michigan-type algorithm, where each individual is an antecedent of a fuzzy rule and the whole population is a fuzzy model. Individuals (rules) are weighted and selected by means of a procedure called *SVD select* that will be explained later in this section. The pseudocode of the NMIC algorithm is shown in Figure 1. The codification and genetic operators are described in reference [25].

```
Initialize P
Evaluate confidence and support in P
SVD select P
Create Intermediate Population Q
while iter ≤ maxiter
    Evaluate confidence and support in P+Q
    SVD select P+Q
    non dominated sort P+Q
    compute crowding distance P+Q
    P ← selection of P+Q
    SVD select P
    non dominated sort P
    Create Intermediate Population Q
end while
Output the nondominated elements of P
```

Fig. 1. Pseudocode of the NMIC algorithm

The fitness of an individual has three components: the support of the antecedent of the rule, its confidence and the weight of the rule. The support is the fuzzy arithmetic-based sum of the memberships of the antecedent for all the points in the sample. The confidence is used to compare the degree to which a rule explains all the examples that it covers. In this case, this is understood as the inverse of the (fuzzy) variance of the examples covered by the rule, i.e. all examples in the dataset, weighed by their memberships to the antecedent of the rule.

The *SVD select* procedure consists in assigning each rule in the Pareto front a weight, with the purpose of obtaining a compact rulebase, while at the same time these weights achieve the best matching between the data and the model. Let A be the matrix of the memberships of the antecedents of all rules in the Pareto front, at the centerpoint of the inputs. Let Y be a column vector with the centers of the desired outputs of the model, and let W be another column vector formed by the weights of these rules, those that we want to obtain. The assignment of weights that minimizes the error (and therefore solves the cooperation problem) is

$$K = (A^tA)^{-1}A^tY \tag{10}$$

provided that the rank r_A of A coincides with its number of columns, the number of individuals in the Pareto front. In most cases, r_A is lower than this, therefore $C = A^tA$ does not have inverse. In this particular case, the eigenvalues of all the submatrices A' of A formed by removing only one of its columns are computed. When it is found a submatrix A' whose non null eigenvalues are the same as those of A, the column is removed and the process restarted from A'. At the end of the process, a matrix with r_A columns and full rank is obtained and Eq. 10 can be applied.

6 Numerical Results

Fourty six volunteering students from the first course of an Engineering Degree in Computer Science at Oviedo University, Spain, participated in this study. The Python programming language was used. Students were allowed to upload as many source code files as they wished, ranging from none to more than a solution for each problem. 800 files were uploaded. Seven programming concepts were studied: Standard I/O, Conditionals, While loop, For loop, Functions, File I/O and Lists. The evaluation of the students comprised both theoretical and practice skills, with two exams each, at the midterm and at the end of the term. The uploaded exercises were not part of the exams and had no impact on the final grading. 23 software metrics and properties were measured for each source file, thus the feature selection stage has to choose between 161 different combinations of programming concept and software metric.

The most relevant metrics, and the supports of their fuzzy ranks, are shown in the following table:

Programming concept	Description of the metric	Average rank
Conditional	Number of warnings and errors	2.00 ± 0.11
Iteration	Code documentation	3.17 ± 0.46
Conditional	Number of Characters	4.58 ± 0.67
Conditional	Code ratio	4.77 ± 1.40
Functions	Style convention adherence	6.54 ± 2.38
Conditional	Style convention adherence	7.47 ± 0.66
Conditional	Number of tokens	9.88 ± 1.60

The first conclusion that may be drawn from this selection is that the best students seem to have better coding style and produce a larger documentation. However, these indicators arguably have a limited practical use for automatic gradings; further work is needed to find a different set of software metrics with a higher descriptive power.

Notwithstanding this, from a methodological point of view the proposed technique is robust and the available information is better exploited with the combination of the fuzzy feature selection and NMIC than it is with alternate feature selection and model learning algorithms. To prove this fact, neural networks, generalized additive models [14], regression trees [5] and the NMIC algorithm were launched over subsets comprising the first 6, 8 and 10 metrics chosen by the both the fuzzy feature selection algorithm and their crisp version operating on the centerpoints of the aggregated data. The combination of the NMIC algorithm with fuzzy data was consistently better in all cases (statistically relevant results, according to Friedman/Wilcoxon tests).

	6 var		8 var		10 var	
Algorithm	Crisp IM	Fuzzy IM	Crisp IM	Fuzzy IM	Crisp IM	Fuzzy IM
NEU	12.69	8.52	14.70	20.34	19.77	12.72
GAM	7.09	7.24	9.25	8.25	10.94	10.36
TREE	7.60	7.19	8.58	8.30	8.33	7.31
NMIC	7.35	**6.94**	8.40	**7.88**	6.55	**6.54**
AVG RANK	1.75	**1.25**	1.75	**1.25**	2	**1**

In the left part of Figure 2 a set of boxplots is drawn containing the paired differences of linear regression (LIN), neural networks (NET), generalized additive models (GAM), regression trees (TRE), the NMIC algorithm applied to the centerpoints of the fuzzy data (NMC) and the same algorithm applied to the fuzzy aggregated metrics (NMI). Values lower than zero mean than the fuzzy feature selection algorithm is better than the crisp selection, and positive values mean the opposite. Again, the ranking proposed in this paper is significantly better than the same estimator applied to the average value of the metrics, demonstrating that the fuzzy aggregation loses less information than the alternatives and also that the proposed method is able to exploit this extra information.

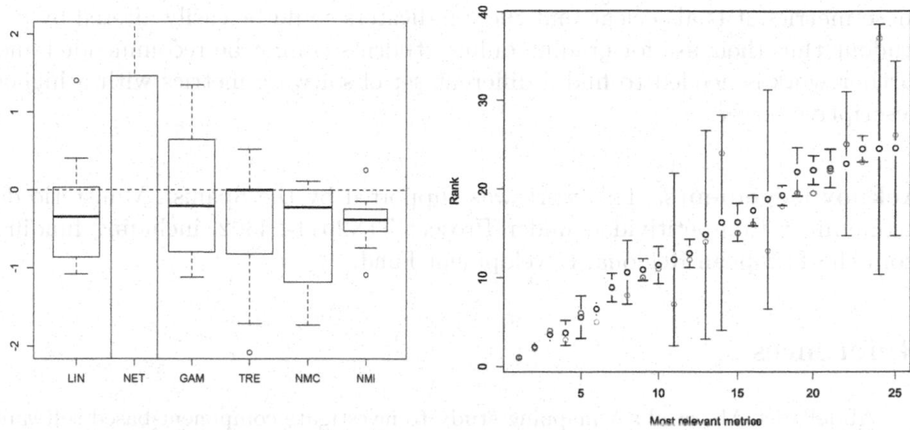

Fig. 2. Left part: paired differences of linear regression (LIN), neural networks (NET), generalized additive models (GAM), regression trees (TRE), the NMIC algorithm applied to the centerpoints of the fuzzy data (NMC) and the same algorithm applied to the fuzzy aggregated metrics (NMI). Right part: most relevant metrics according to the proposed algorithm (black circles and bars) and according to a MI-based ranking estimated on the centerpoints of the data (red circles).

Finally, in the right part of the same Figure 2 the rank of the most relevant metrics, according to the proposed algorithm, are graphically displayed with black circles and bars. The ranking of the same metrics, according to a MI-based ordering which is based on the centerpoints of the data (red circles) is superimposed. In this practical case, the first three metrics are the same for both methods, but at the fourth position both ranks begin to differ. The black error bars mean that the dispersion of the fuzzy data is high enough so that the rank of the metric changes for different selections of the data; this information would have been lost if a crisp feature selection method was used.

7 Concluding Remarks

A method for ranking software tests according to their relevance in an automatic grading systems has been proposed. The main innovation of the new method lies in the development of a set of techniques that can make use of a fuzzy aggregation of the information contained in a variable number of exercises about the same learning subject.

The technique has proven to be effective, as the fuzzy aggregation clearly preserves information that would be lost with crisp aggregations. From a methodological point of view, the new algorithm is a solid alternative. However, from the point of view of the automated grading techniques for MOOCs, the results are less convincing, as the most powerful metrics found in the available list were related to the quality of the documentation, the programming style and the size of the code. While it is clear that the best students consistently perform better in these metrics, it is also clear that these indicators could be easily altered by the student thus their use for grading online students cannot be recommended and further work is needed to find a different set of software metrics with a higher descriptive power.

Acknowledgements. This work was supported by the Spanish Ministerio de Economía y Competitividad under Project TIN2011-24302, including funding from the European Regional Development Fund.

References

1. Abdellatief, M., et al.: A mapping study to investigate component-based software system metrics. Journal of Systems and Software 86(3), 587–603 (2013)
2. Abran, A.: Software Metrics and Software Metrology. Wiley-IEEE Computer Society Press (2010)
3. Arnow, D., Barshay, O.: On-line programming examinations using Web to teach. In: Proceedings of the 4th Annual SIGCSE/SIGCUE ITiCSE Conference on Innovation and Technology in Computer Science Education (ITiCSE 1999), pp. 21–24 (1999)
4. Battiti, R.: Using mutual information for selecting features in supervised neural net learning. IEEE Trans. Neural Nets. 5(4) (July 1994)
5. Breiman, L., Friedman, L.J., Olshen, A., Stone, C.: Classification and Regression Trees. Wadsworth (1984)
6. Casillas, J., Martinez-Lopez, F., Martinez, F.: Fuzzy association rules for estimating consumer behaviour models and their application to explaining trust in internet shopping. Fuzzy Economic Review IX(2), 3–26 (2004)
7. Casillas, J., Martinez-Lopez, F.: Mining uncertain data with multiobjective genetic fuzzy systems to be applied in consumer behaviour modelling. Expert Systems with Applications 36(2), 1645–1659 (2009)
8. Corchado, E., Wozniak, M., Abraham, A., de Carvalho, A., Snásel, V.: Recent trends in intelligent data analysis. Neurocomputing 126, 1–2 (2014)
9. Couso, I., Montes, S., Gil, P.: The necessity of the strong alpha-cuts of a fuzzy set. International Journal of Uncertainty, Fuzziness and Knowledge-Based Systems 9(2), 249–262 (2001)
10. Couso, I., Sanchez, L.: Higher order models for fuzzy random variables. Fuzzy Sets and Systems 159(3), 237–258 (2008)
11. Cheang, B., Kurnia, A., Lim, A., Oon, W.: On automated grading of programming assignments in an academic institution. Comput. Educ. 41(2), 121–131 (2003)
12. Dubois, D., Prade, H.: Fuzzy sets - a convenient fiction for modeling vagueness and possibility. IEEE Transactions on Fuzzy Systems 2(1), 16–21 (1994)
13. Halstead, M.: Elements of Software Science. Elsevier, North-Holland (1975)
14. Hastie, T., Tibshirani, R.: Generalized Additive Models. Chapman and Hall, London (1990)
15. Ishibuchi, H., Kuwajima, O., Nojima, Y.: Relation between Pareto-optimal fuzzy rules and Pareto-optimal fuzzy rule sets. In: Proc. 2007 IEEE Symp. on Comp. Int. in Multicriteria Decision Making, Honolulu, USA (2007)

16. Jurado, F., Redondo, M., Ortega, M.: Using fuzzy logic applied to software metrics and test cases to assess programming assignments and give advice. J. Netw. Comput. Appl. 35(2) (2012)
17. Khoshgoftaar, T., Gao, K., Napolitano, A.: A Comparative Study of Different Strategies for Predicting Software Quality. SEKE 2011, 65–70 (2011)
18. Kitchenham, B.: What's up with software metrics? - A preliminary mapping study. J. Syst. Softw. 83(1) (2010)
19. Kurnia, A., Lim, A., Cheang, B.: Online judge. Comput. Educ. 36(4), 299–315 (2001)
20. McCabe, T.: A complexity measure. IEEE Trans. on Software Engineering 2(4), 308–320 (1976)
21. Pizzi, N., Demko, A., Pedrycz, W.: The Analysis of Software Complexity Using Stochastic Metric Selection. Journal of Pattern Recognition Research 6(1), 19–31 (2011)
22. Reek, K.A.: A software infrastructure to support introductory computer science courses. In: Klee, K.J. (ed.) Proceedings of the Twenty-Seventh SIGCSE Technical Symposium on Computer Science Education (SIGCSE 1996), pp. 125–129. ACM, New York (1996)
23. Sallis, P., Aakjaer, A., MacDonell, S.: Software forensics: old methods for a new science. In: Proceedings of the 1996 International Conference on Software Engineering: Education and Practice (SEEP 1996), pp. 481–484. IEEE Computer Society Press, Washington, DC (1996)
24. Samoladas, I., Stamelos, I., Angelis, L., Oikonomou, A.: Open source software development should strive for even greater code maintainability. Communications of the ACM 47(10), 83–87 (2004)
25. Sanchez, L., Otero, J., Couso, I.: Obtaining linguistic fuzzy rule-based regression models from imprecise data with multiobjective genetic algorithms. Soft. Comput. 13(5), 467–479 (2008)
26. Sanchez, L., Couso, I., Casillas, J.: Genetic learning of fuzzy rules on low quality data. Fuzzy Sets and Systems 160(17), 2524–2552 (2009)
27. Vujosevic-Janicica, M., Nikolica, M., Tosica, D., Kuncak, V.: Software verification and graph similarity for automated evaluation of students assignments. Information and Software Technology 55(6), 1004–1016 (2013)
28. Wang, T., Su, X., Ma, P., Wang, Y., Wang, K.: Ability-training-oriented automated assessment in introductory programming course. Comput. Educ. 56(1), 220–226 (2011)
29. Wozniak, M., Graña, M., Corchado, E.: A survey of multiple classifier systems as hybrid systems. Information Fusion 16, 3–17 (2014)
30. Watson, A.H.: McCabe Complexity, Software Development Systems Management Development, Auerbach (1995)

Optimizing Objective Functions with Non-Linearly Correlated Variables Using Evolution Strategies with Kernel-Based Dimensionality Reduction

Piotr Lipinski

Computational Intelligence Research Group,
Institute of Computer Science,
University of Wroclaw, Wroclaw, Poland
lipinski@ii.uni.wroc.pl

Abstract. This paper proposes an improvement of Evolutionary Strategies for objective functions with non-linearly correlated variables. It focuses on detecting non-linear local dependencies among variables of the objective function by analyzing the manifold in the search space that contains the current population and transforming individuals to a reduced search space defined by the Kernel Principal Components. Experiments performed on some popular benchmark functions confirm that the method may significantly improve the search process, especially in the case of complex objective functions with a large number of variables, which usually occur in many practical applications.

1 Introduction

Evolutionary Algorithms (EAs), [1], [5], [12], are an increasingly popular technique of solving optimization problems, which try to find an optimum of an objective function on a search space by maintaining a population of candidate solutions, representing data points in the search space, and moving it towards more and more promising regions using some evolutionary operators.

Many contemporary applications of EAs concern complex optimization problems with objective functions of a large number of variables defined on highly dimensional search spaces. Classic EAs usually do not inspect neither the real dimensionality of the search space nor the dependencies between variables of the objective function. However, in many practical applications, such as decision support systems, classifier systems, image analysis or signal processing systems, where the dimension of the search space often exceeds one hundred, some correlations between variables of the objective function exist. Discovering such correlations provides an opportunity to reduce the dimensionality of the optimization problem and its complexity.

Although there are numerous techniques of detecting global dependencies among variables over the entire search space [14], usually in a preprocessing phase, there has been little research on local dependencies over neighborhoods of optimal solutions and detecting them during runtime. It includes Correlation Matrix Adaptation - Evolutionary Strategies (CMA-ES) [6] or Evolution Strategies with Internal Dimensionality Reduction (ESIDR) [9].

M. Polycarpou et al. (Eds.): HAIS 2014, LNAI 8480, pp. 342–353, 2014.
© Springer International Publishing Switzerland 2014

The most popular techniques for exploring linear dependencies include the Principal Component Analysis (PCA) [7] and the Multidimensional Scaling (MDS) [4]. PCA tries to transform the original coordinate system to a new system with orthogonal axes ordered by the amount of variance of the original data sample that they describe. It uses the covariance matrix of the data sample and compute its eigenvalues and eigenvectors that defines the principal components being the axes of the new coordinate system. Ignoring the principal components with the lowest values of the corresponding eigenvalues leads to the dimensionality reduction. MDS tries to find a transformation from the original data space to a reduced one that preserve the distances between particular data points. It is similar to PCA, if the distance is euclidean, but may work with other distance functions. MDS is often used to visualize data samples on the plane, especially if the data sample contains non-numeric variables, which does not allow to use euclidean distances.

Exploring non-linear dependencies is more challenging [2]. Some methods, rather simple but efficient in many cases, extend PCA. For instance, the Kernel Principal Component Analysis (KPCA) [11], which maps the data sample to a higher dimensional space by a non-linear transformation and then tries to apply PCA to the mapped data sample and reduce its dimensionality. It uses the so-called kernel trick to avoid computing distances in the higher dimensional space. Other methods, such as Isomap [13], extend MDS with additional distance measures. Some techniques, such as the Locally Linear Embedding (LLE) [10], focus on preserving some local characteristics of the data sample. LLE defines each data point in the data sample as a linear combination of its neighbors and tries to find a transformation of the original data space to a reduced one in such a way that each mapped data point will be a linear combination of its mapped neighbors with the same coefficients as in the original data space.

Some recent Evolutionary Algorithms, called Estimation of Distribution Algorithms (EDAs) [8], try to regard the population of candidate solutions as a data sample with a probability distribution approximating the probability distribution describing optimal solutions. A similar approach is presented in this paper to detect correlations among variables – it treats the current population as the data sample from a neighborhood of optimal solutions and endeavours to discover dependencies among variables in such a neighborhood using KPCA.

In the approach, first, a number of iterations of the main evolution is performed in the entire original search space to move the population to some promising regions of the search space. Next, a number of subevolution iterations is performed in a manifold, defined by the current population of the main evolution - usually lower dimensional than the original search space, and then the population is restored back to the original search space in order to ensure whether the manifold corresponded to a neighborhood of the global optima or not. Few next main iterations may correct the population and move it to some other promising regions of the search space, and then a number of subevolution iterations exploit the new manifold.

This paper is structured in the following manner: Section 2 concerns the kernel-based mappings and the population dimensionality reduction. Section 3 introduces the improvement of Evolutionary Strategies for objective functions with non-linearly correlated variables. Section 4 discusses the experimental evaluation of the approach. Finally, Section 5 concludes the paper.

2 Kernel-Based Mappings and Population Dimensionality Reduction

Let $\mathcal{P} = \{\mathbf{x}_1, \mathbf{x}_2, \ldots, \mathbf{x}_N\} \subset \mathbb{R}^d$ be a population of N individuals, where each individual $\mathbf{x}_i = (x_{i1}, x_{i2}, \ldots, x_{id})^T \in \mathbb{R}^d$, for $i = 1, 2, \ldots, N$, is a data point in the search space $\Omega = \mathbb{R}^d$, where d is the dimensionality of the optimization problem.

We may investigate the manifolds in Ω that contain the population. In the pessimistic case, the population is chaotic and widespread across the entire search space without any significant dependencies, so the only one reasonable manifold to consider is the entire search space itself. In the optimistic case, the population may be chaotic, but focused on a certain manifold in the search space, possibly of a lower dimensionality than the entire search space. It may happen when some variables of the objective function are correlated, so there are some dependencies between values of genes in the chromosome.

It is worth noticing that such dependencies may be local, occurring only in a certain region of the search space, e.g. in the neighborhood of a local or global optimum of the objective function, where the current population focuses on, so they usually cannot be discovered by popular preprocessing methods before the evolution process starts.

Figure 1 presents an example illustrating the approach. Figure 1(a) presents an objective function of two correlated variables and its values for a hypothetical population. Figure 1(b) presents the population in the original search space, where it focuses on a circle manifold. Figure 1(c) presents the population after a non-linear transformation to a new search space. It is easy to see that the population may be quite well described by only one variable. Figure 2 presents a similar example with another objective function.

Assume that the population lies in a certain manifold in the search space. Although the manifold is embedded in the d-dimensional search space, it may be homeomorphic to another manifold of a lower dimensionality. However, the homeomorphism may not be obvious and discovering it may not be simple, especially in the case of local and non-linear dependencies.

One of the possible approaches, based on the Kernel Principal Component Analysis (KPCA) [11], is first to transform the search space to a highly dimensional data space, where it is easier to separate data points, i.e. to simplify the geometry of the manifold, and then to reduce the dimensionality of the highly dimensional mapping of the population by transforming it to a new lower dimensional search space.

Let $\Phi : \Omega \to \Pi$ be a mapping, not necessarily linear, from the original search space Ω to a hypothetical highly dimensional data space Π, which may be even of the infinite dimensionality, assumed only to be a Hilbert space. At the beginning, assume that the population $\mathcal{P}$ mapped by the transformation Φ is centered, i.e.

$$\sum_{i=1}^{N} \Phi(\mathbf{x}_i) = 0, \tag{1}$$

where $\Phi(\mathbf{x}_i)$ is the mapping of the individual $\mathbf{x}_i$ in the data space Π.

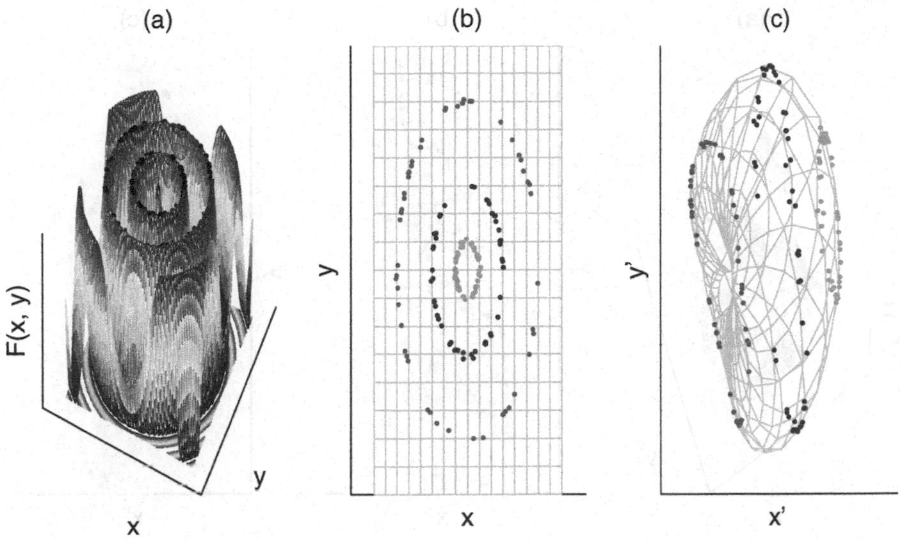

Fig. 1. An objective function with two correlated variables and its values for a hypothetical population (subplot (a)), the population in the original search space (subplot (b)) and in the reduced search space (subplot (c)), where the second variable seems to be redundant

In order to try to reduce the dimensionality of the mapped population in the highly dimensional data space Π, one may try to perform the classic Principal Component Analysis (PCA) [7] and to find eigenvalues and eigenvectors of the covariance matrix

$$\boldsymbol{\Sigma} = \frac{1}{N} \sum_{l=1}^{N} \Phi(\mathbf{x}_l)\Phi(\mathbf{x}_l)^T. \tag{2}$$

It is obvious that all the eigenvectors must be linear combinations of $\Phi(\mathbf{x}_1)$, $\Phi(\mathbf{x}_2)$, ..., $\Phi(\mathbf{x}_N)$ and lie in the span of $\Phi(\mathbf{x}_1)$, $\Phi(\mathbf{x}_2)$, ..., $\Phi(\mathbf{x}_N)$, so the eigenvalue equation

$$\lambda \mathbf{v} = \boldsymbol{\Sigma}\mathbf{v}, \tag{3}$$

where λ denotes the eigenvalue and $\mathbf{v}$ denotes the corresponding eigenvector of the matrix $\boldsymbol{\Sigma}$, is equivalent to a system of linear equations

$$\Phi(\mathbf{x}_i)^T(\lambda_k \mathbf{v}_k) = \Phi(\mathbf{x}_i)^T(\boldsymbol{\Sigma}\mathbf{v}_k), \qquad \text{for each } i = 1, 2, \ldots, N, \tag{4}$$

for $k = 1, 2, \ldots, K$, where $\lambda_1, \lambda_2, \ldots, \lambda_K$ are non-zero eigenvalues and $\mathbf{v}_1, \mathbf{v}_2, \ldots, \mathbf{v}_K$ are corresponding eigenvectors of the matrix $\boldsymbol{\Sigma}$. As each eigenvector $\mathbf{v}_k$ is a linear combination of $\Phi(\mathbf{x}_1)$, $\Phi(\mathbf{x}_2)$, ..., $\Phi(\mathbf{x}_N)$, let

$$\mathbf{v}_k = \sum_{j=1}^{N} \alpha_{kj} \Phi(\mathbf{x}_j), \tag{5}$$

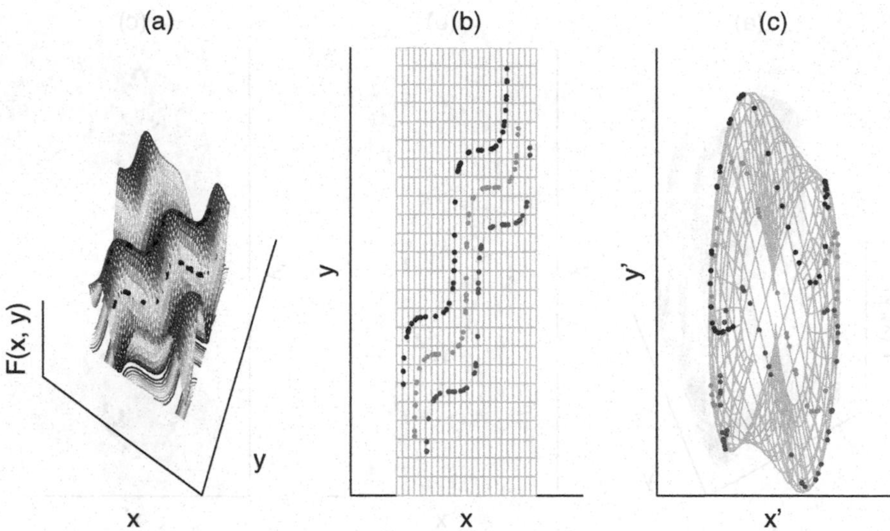

Fig. 2. An objective function with two correlated variables and its values for a hypothetical population (subplot (a)), the population in the original search space (subplot (b)) and in the reduced search space (subplot (c)), where the second variable seems to be redundant

where $\boldsymbol{\alpha}_k = (\alpha_{k1}, \alpha_{k2}, \ldots, \alpha_{kN})^T \in \mathbb{R}^N$ is a vector of linear coefficients. Therefore, the system of linear equations (4) reduces to

$$\lambda_k \sum_{j=1}^{N} \alpha_{kj} \Phi(\mathbf{x}_i)^T \Phi(\mathbf{x}_j) = \sum_{j=1}^{N} \alpha_{kj} \Phi(\mathbf{x}_i)^T \boldsymbol{\Sigma} \Phi(\mathbf{x}_j), \qquad \text{for each } i = 1, 2, \ldots, N, \tag{6}$$

and using (2) to

$$\lambda_k \sum_{j=1}^{N} \alpha_{kj} \Phi(\mathbf{x}_i)^T \Phi(\mathbf{x}_j) = \frac{1}{N} \sum_{j=1}^{N} \sum_{l=1}^{N} \alpha_{kj} \Phi(\mathbf{x}_i)^T \Phi(\mathbf{x}_l) \Phi(\mathbf{x}_l)^T \Phi(\mathbf{x}_j), \tag{7}$$

thus after defining a matrix $\mathbf{K} \in \mathbb{R}^{N \times N}$ with elements $k_{ij} = \Phi(\mathbf{x}_i)^T \Phi(\mathbf{x}_j)$, the system of linear equations (4) is equivalent to

$$N \lambda_k \boldsymbol{\alpha}_k \mathbf{K} = \mathbf{K}^2 \boldsymbol{\alpha}_k. \tag{8}$$

Finally, it may be shown that the solution to the system of linear equations (4) are the eigenvalues $N\lambda_k$ and corresponding eigenvectors $\boldsymbol{\alpha}_k$ of the matrix $\mathbf{K}$. Therefore, the mappings $\Phi(\mathbf{x}_i)$ of individuals $\mathbf{x}_i$ may be reduced to $\mathbf{y}_i = (y_{i1}, y_{i2}, \ldots, y_{iq}) \in \mathbb{R}^K$ by projecting $\Phi(\mathbf{x}_i)$ onto the K eigenvectors $\mathbf{v}_1, \mathbf{v}_2, \ldots, \mathbf{v}_q$ corresponding to the K non-zero eigenvalues, so

$$y_{ik} = \mathbf{v}_k^T \Phi(\mathbf{x}_i) = \sum_{j=1}^{N} \alpha_{kj} \Phi((\mathbf{x}_j)^T \Phi((\mathbf{x}_i) = \sum_{j=1}^{N} \alpha_{kj} k_{ji}. \tag{9}$$

In the approach proposed in this paper, based on the KPCA, the so-called *kernel trick* allowed to avoid the direct evaluation of the mappings $\Phi(\mathbf{x}_i)$ of the individuals $\mathbf{x}_i$ in the highly dimensional data space Π with evaluation only their dot products $\Phi(\mathbf{x}_i)^T\Phi(\mathbf{x}_j)$, i.e. the kernel values k_{ij}.

Regarding the assumption (1) that mappings are centered, it may be relaxed with transforming the arbitrary kernel matrix $\mathbf{K}$ into

$$\mathbf{K} = \mathbf{K} - \mathbf{1K} - \mathbf{K1} + \mathbf{1K1}, \tag{10}$$

where $\mathbf{1}$ is a matrix of ones divided by N of the same size than the matrix $\mathbf{K}$.

In the literature, a number of different kernel functions has been proposed, among the others, the polynomial kernels, the gaussian or radial basis kernels, the sigmoid kernels and the kernels constructed from particular mappings. In this paper, we focus on gaussian kernels defined by the gaussian kernel function $k : \mathbb{R}^d \times \mathbb{R}^d \to \mathbb{R}$:

$$k(\mathbf{x}, \mathbf{y}) = \exp(-\frac{||\mathbf{x} - \mathbf{y}||^2}{2\sigma^2}), \tag{11}$$

where σ is a parameter and the kernel matrix $\mathbf{K}$ defined by $k_{ij} = k(\mathbf{x}_i, \mathbf{y}_j)$.

3 Evolution Strategy with Kernel Principal Components Dimensionality Reduction

Algorithm 1 presents an overview of the Evolution Strategy with Kernel Principal Components Dimensionality Reduction (ESwKPCDR) for an objective function $F : \mathbb{R}^n \to \mathbb{R}$ of non-linearly correlated variables.

ESwKPCDR begins with generating a random population $\mathcal{P}_0$ of N individuals and evaluating it. In the main evolution loop, a parent population $\mathcal{P}_t^{(P)}$ of M individuals is selected with the roulette wheel method, recombined with the local intermediary recombination and mutated with adding some gaussian noise to each gene of each chromosome independently, as in classic ES [12]. It finally forms an offspring population $\mathcal{P}_t^{(O)}$ of M individuals, which is compared with the current population $\mathcal{P}_t$ and selected to the new population $\mathcal{P}_{t+1}$. In some main evolution iterations, ESwKPCDR performs a subevolution, which analyses the current population, transforms it to a reduced search space, and performs the same routine as the main evolution, but on the selected manifold only.

The main evolution and the subevolution is run in such a way that first a number of main iterations is performed in the entire original search space to move the population to some promising regions of the search space, then a number of subevolution iterations is performed in a selected manifold and then the population is restored to the original search space in order to ensure whether the manifold corresponded to a neighborhood of the global optima or not. Few next main iterations may correct the population and move it to some other promising regions of the search space, and then a number of subevolution iterations exploit the new manifold.

Algorithm 1. Evolution Strategy with Kernel Principal Components Dimensionality Reduction (ESwKPCDR)

```
P_0 = Random-Population(N, M)
Population-Evaluation(P_0, F)
t = 0
while not Termination-Condition(P_t) do
    P_t^(P) = Parent-Selection(P_t, M)
    P_t^(O) = Recombination(P_t^(P), M)
    P_t^(O) = Mutation(P_t^(O), M)
    Population-Evaluation(P_t^(O), F)
    P_{t+1} = New-Population-Selection(P_t, P_t^(O))
    t = t + 1
    if Subevolution-Starting-Condition() then
        Search-Space-Reduction()
        R_0 = Population-Reduction(P_t)
        s = 0;
        while not Subevolution-Termination-Condition(R_s) do
            R_s^(P) = Parent-Selection(R_s, M)
            R_s^(O) = Recombination(R_s^(P), M)
            R_s^(O) = Mutation(R_s^(O), M)
            Reduced-Population-Evaluation(R_s^(O), F)
            R_{s+1} = New-Population-Selection(R_s, R_s^(O))
            s = s + 1
        end while
        Search-Space-Restoring()
        P_t = Population-Restoring(R_{s-1})
    end if
end while
```

3.1 Search Space and Population Reduction

The subevolution starts with determining the manifold in the search space $\mathbb{R}^d$ that contains the current population $\mathcal{P}_t$ and transforming it to a reduced population $\mathcal{R}_0$ by projecting it onto a number of kernel principal components, as described in the previous section, usually smaller than the dimensionality of the original search space.

It is worthy noticing that although the original population is transformed to the reduced one, the mapping Φ itself, which transform the original search space Ω to the highly dimensional data space Π still remains unknown, as only the dot products in the data space Π are evaluated (by the kernel function, without prior evaluating the mapping Φ).

3.2 Reduced Population Evaluation

Although the evolutionary operators of the subevolution are derived from the main evolution without modifications, i.e. only the chromosome length changes, the problem occurs in evaluating the reduced population. As the mapping Φ remains unknown, as well as its inverse mapping, the new reduced individuals cannot be straightly evaluated by the original objective function.

In the literature concerning the kernel-based mappings, [11], a few solutions are suggested to restore a point from the reduced data space to the original one. They are usually based on some approximation or regression methods, beside the case of the kernel functions constructed from particular mappings.

In the algorithm proposed, a mechanism derived from restoring in Locally Linear Embedding [10], based on local linear dependencies, is used. In order to evaluate a reduced individual $\mathbf{y} \in \mathbb{R}^K$, first, we find k mappings of the original data points nearest to the reduced individual. Then, we try to approximate the reduced individual by a linear combination of the k nearest mappings. Finally, we define the restored individual as a linear combination of the k original data points corresponding to the k nearest mappings with the same linear coefficients and evaluate the objective function for the restored individual.

3.3 Search Space and Population Restoring

After termination of the subevolution, the current reduced population $\mathcal{R}_t$ is restored to the original search space by applying the same procedure as during the reduced population evaluation, described in the previous subsection.

4 Experimental Evaluation of the Approach

A number of experiments were performed in order to validate the approach proposed in this paper by comparing the algorithm that uses kernel principal components and works on the reduced search space with the original algorithm that works on the original search space.

Each experiment concerned a deceptive objective function being a transformation of one of the classic benchmark functions usually used in testing evolutionary algorithms for continuous problems [15]. Such a transformation extends the original benchmark function to a function of a larger number of correlated variables, otherwise, the comparison would not make any sense, because the original benchmark functions have usually independent variables and the improvement mechanism proposed in this paper would not be certainly capable of reducing the search space.

Some experiments were also performed on real-world problems, such as constructing optimal weights for a rule-based decision support system, where the weights are highly dependent due to existing similarities in the decision rules, but are not discussed here due to the size constraint of the paper.

4.1 Classic Benchmark Functions

The first part of benchmark functions concerns the classic De Jong test suite composed of the unimodal function F_1, the discontinuous function F_3 and the noisy function F_4 [15].

$$F_1(\mathbf{x}) = \sum_{i=1}^{n} x_i^2 \tag{12}$$

$$F_3(\mathbf{x}) = \sum_{i=1}^{n} \lfloor x_i \rfloor \tag{13}$$

$$F_4(\mathbf{x}) = \sum_{i=1}^{n} i x_i^4 + \mathcal{N}(0,1) \tag{14}$$

The second part of the benchmark functions includes other popular benchmark functions, such as the Rastrigin function F_6, the Schwefel function F_7, and the Griewangk function F_8 [15].

$$F_6(\mathbf{x}) = 10n + \sum_{i=1}^{n} (x_i^2 - 10\cos(2\pi x_i)) \tag{15}$$

$$F_7(\mathbf{x}) = 418.9829n - \sum_{i=1}^{n} x_i \sin(\sqrt{|x_i|}) \tag{16}$$

$$F_8(\mathbf{x}) = 1 + \sum_{i=1}^{n} \frac{x_i^2}{4000} - \prod_{i=1}^{n} \cos(x_i/\sqrt{i}) \tag{17}$$

4.2 Deceptive and k-Deceptive Benchmark Functions

Each classic benchmark function $F : \mathbb{R}^n \to \mathbb{R}$ was extended by a mapping $\Psi : \mathbb{R}^m \to \mathbb{R}^n$, for $m > n$, so that the actual objective function $f : \mathbb{R}^m \to \mathbb{R}$, called the m-dimensional deceptive objective function, was a composition of the mapping Ψ and the classic benchmark function F, i.e. $f(\mathbf{x}) = F(\Psi(\mathbf{x}))$. It is easy to see that variables of the final objective function f were correlated (although the objective function f was formally a function of m variables, the real dimensionality of the optimization problem was $n < m$) and the improvement mechanism proposed in this paper might have a chance to reduce the search space.

Both, the linear mappings Ψ with a random matrix $\mathbf{A} \in \mathbb{R}^{n \times m}$ and a random vector $\mathbf{b} \in \mathbb{R}^n$, where

$$\Psi(\mathbf{x}) = \mathbf{A}\mathbf{x} + \mathbf{b}, \tag{18}$$

and the non-linear mappings Ψ based on polynomial functions with random parameters, were considered.

Furthermore, k-deceptive objective functions were defined by the analogy to the k-deceptive objective functions used for evaluating the ECGA algorithm: the entire chromosome $\mathbf{x}$ was divided into blocks of successive k genes, then a chosen k-dimensional deceptive objective function was evaluated on each block, next the values of the deceptive objective function on all the blocks was summed and finally returned as the results of the k-deceptive objective function.

4.3 Results

Each experiment concerned a classic benchmark function transformed to a k-deceptive benchmark function with the final chromosome length $d = 50, 100$, or 250, divided into blocks of $k = 25$ genes, where on each block, the k-dimensional deceptive benchmark function based on a n-dimensional classic benchmark function, for $n = 5, 10$, or 15, was evaluated. Parameters of the transformation Ψ extending the n-dimensional classic benchmark function to a k-dimensional deceptive benchmark function were generated randomly for each experiment. Such an optimization problem was solved twice: once with the kernel mappings mechanism turned off, and once with turned on. In both cases, the population size was $N = 500$ and the number of offspring was $2N$. The original algorithm run for 5000 iterations. The improved algorithm run for 5000 iterations in total: main evolution was run for 100 iterations, then subevolutions was run for 400 iterations, and it was repeated 10 times. Thus, during their run, both algorithms evaluated the same number of individuals.

Figure 3 illustrates the typical behavior of these two algorithms on the benchmark function based on F_1 with $k = 50, 100$, and 250 (subplots (a), (b), and (c), respectively) and $n = 5$. It presents the best values of the objective function (the vertical axis) in successive iterations of the evolutionary algorithm (the horizontal axis), for the original algorithm (the red line) and the improved one (the black line). It is easy to see that the improved algorithm outperformed the original one. One may also see the effect of the search space reduction and restoring on the black line.

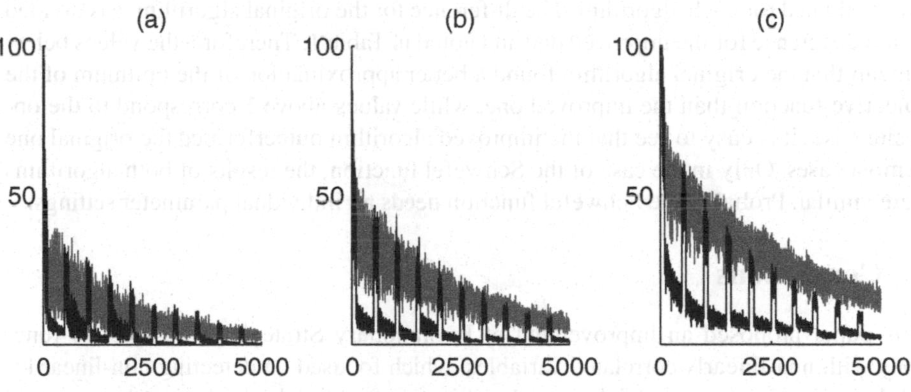

Fig. 3. A comparison of the original algorithm with the improved one on the benchmark function based on F_1 with $k = 50, 100$, or 250 (subplots (a), (b) and (c), respectively) and $r = 5$: the best values of the objective function (the vertical axis) in successive iterations of the evolutionary algorithm (the horizontal axis), for the original algorithm (the red line) and the improved one (the black line)

Table 1 presents a summary of results for all the benchmark functions. In order to compare the original algorithm with the improved one, for each experiment, the difference between the best found solution and the actual optimum of the objective function

Table 1. Summary of results

experiments with linear mappings Ψ							
d	n	f_1	f_3	f_4	f_6	f_7	f_8
50	5	15.75	84.53	235.53	1.86	1.00	4.73
50	10	11.33	79.24	372.24	1.38	0.99	4.54
50	15	3.00	78.61	192.51	1.30	1.00	3.28
100	5	9.89	83.19	119.53	1.19	1.01	3.86
100	10	9.84	57.34	58.17	1.31	1.01	2.89
100	15	4.37	64.23	16.47	1.23	0.99	2.67
250	5	7.26	36.00	101.58	1.48	0.99	1.94
250	10	8.63	8.25	55.12	1.43	1.00	2.03
250	15	6.48	7.57	43.73	1.36	1.00	1.51
experiments with non-linear mappings Ψ							
50	5	7.00	72.53	78.24	1.96	0.99	9.38
50	10	4.81	75.24	64.54	1.48	1.00	6.68
50	15	6.61	69.37	53.24	1.10	0.99	3.83
100	5	14.29	79.84	130.97	1.78	1.00	6.56
100	10	9.03	53.12	32.53	1.37	0.99	2.98
100	15	4.83	12.50	16.23	1.25	1.00	2.61
250	5	7.69	8.60	79.57	1.56	1.00	2.28
250	10	7.05	9.55	25.28	1.48	1.00	1.73
250	15	3.82	5.00	42.54	1.28	1.00	1.47

was evaluated for each algorithm. The difference for the original algorithm was divided by the difference for the improved one and noted in Table 1. Therefore, the values below 1 mean that the original algorithm found a better approximation of the optimum of the objective function than the improved one, while values above 1 correspond to the opposite case. It is easy to see that the improved algorithm outperformed the original one in most cases. Only in the case of the Schwefel function, the results of both algorithms were similar. Probably the Schwefel function needs an individual parameter settings.

5 Conclusions

This paper proposed an improvement of Evolutionary Strategies for objective functions with non-linearly correlated variables, which focused on detecting non-linear local dependencies among variables of the objective function by analyzing the manifold in the search space that contains the current population and transforming individuals to a reduced search space defined by the Kernel Principal Components. Experiments performed on some popular benchmark functions confirm that the method may significantly improve the search process, especially in the case of complex objective functions with a large number of variables, which usually occur in many practical applications.

Certainly, the improvement proposed requires some additional computational effort and resources, and consequently increases the computational complexity of the algorithm. However, in many practical applications, such as training decision support systems, classifier systems or signal processing, the main computational cost is the evaluation of the objective function that usually needs performing a kind of a simulation or validation. Therefore, in such applications, the computational cost of dimensionality reduction is low comparing to the rest of the algorithm.

References

1. Back, T.: Evolutionary Algorithms in Theory and Practice. Oxford University Press (1995)
2. Bishop, C., Svensen, M., Williams, C.: GTM: the Generative Topographic Mapping. Neural Computation 10, 215–234 (1998)
3. Brockhoff, D., Zitzler, E., Dimensionality Reduction in Multiobjective Optimization with (Partial) Dominance Structure Preservation: Generalized Minimum Objective Subset Problems, TIK Report, no. 247, ETH Zurich (2006)
4. Cox, T., Cox, M., Multidimensional Scaling. Chapman & Hall (2001)
5. Goldberg, D.,E., Genetic Algorithms in Search, Optimization and Machine Learning. Addison Wesley (1989)
6. Hansen, N., Ostermeier, A.: Adapting arbitrary normal mutation distributions in evolution strategies: The covariance matrix adaptation. CEC, 312–317 (1996)
7. Jolliffe, I.T.: Principal Component Analysis, Springer (1986)
8. Larranaga, P., Lozano, J. A.: Estimation of Distribution Algorithms. Kluwer Academic Publishers (2002)
9. Lipinski, P.: Evolution strategies for objective functions with locally correlated variables. In: Fyfe, C., Tino, P., Charles, D., Garcia-Osorio, C., Yin, H. (eds.) IDEAL 2010. LNCS, vol. 6283, pp. 352–359. Springer, Heidelberg (2010)
10. Roweis, S., Saul, L.: Nonlinear Dimensionality Reduction by Locally Linear Embedding. Science 290, 2323–2326 (2000)
11. Schoelkopf, B., Smola, A. J., Mueller, K.-R.: Nonlinear component analysis as a kernel eigenvalue problem, Technical Report, no. 44, Max Planck Institute (1996)
12. Schwefel, H.-P., Evolution and Optimum Seeking. John Wiley and Sons (1995)
13. Tenenbaum, J.B., de Silva, V., Langford, J.C.: A Global Geometric Framework for Nonlinear Dimensionality Reduction. Science 290, 2319–2323 (2000)
14. Webb, A.: Statistical Pattern Recognition. John Wiley, London (2002)
15. Whitley, D., Rana, S., Dzubera, J., Mathias, K.: Evaluating evolutionary algorithms. Artificial Intelligence 85(1-2), 245–276 (1996)

Visual Behavior Definition for 3D Crowd Animation through Neuro-evolution

Bruno Fernandez, Juan Monroy, Francisco Bellas, and Richard J. Duro

Integrated Group for Engineering Research,
Universidade da Coruña, 15403, Ferrol, Spain
{bruno.fernandez,jmonroy,fran,richard}@udc.es
http://www.gii.udc.es

Abstract. This paper addresses the problem of creating crowd based scenes in animated films automatically. The main problem in this area is how to provide a natural way for the animator or director to define what they want the crowd to do. To this end, we propose here a hybrid neuro-evolutionary scheme where the artists regulate the behavior that is desired from the crowd by drawing colored lines and areas within a scenario. These elements are then transformed into energy based aggregative fitness functions that can be used to evaluate the behaviors of the individuals within the crowd during the evolutionary process that produces the controller for all the characters and, consequently, determines the behavior of the crowd as a whole. The approach has been tested on several different real scenes within the workflow of a local animation film company and the results it produced were very satisfactory.

Keywords: Neuro-evolution, collective intelligence, behavior specification, crowd animation, visual interfaces.

1 Introduction

The 3D animation film industry has been increasing the technical quality of its productions in the last two decades due to the improvements in computational capabilities, both in software and hardware. Designers now have powerful tools that run in powerful computers, so they can carry out better work from an artistic point of view in an affordable amount of time. Nevertheless, a higher realism level is still possible and there are several open issues.

One of the most challenging topics is crowd animation [14]. The original procedure of animating a small set of characters and then copying this animation to other characters in the crowd is not valid for the current quality requirements. As a consequence, researchers have devoted much effort to automatically obtain the behavior of the characters with the aim of producing crowds made up of real independent characters, with independent "brains" [8][1]. Thus, we can find several approaches in the literature that differ in the computational technique used to control each character, resulting in different levels of autonomy and "intelligence". Most of them come from the collective intelligence field due to the similarities between a crowd in a scene and a multiagent system [15][2].

M. Polycarpou et al. (Eds.): HAIS 2014, LNAI 8480, pp. 354–364, 2014.
© Springer International Publishing Switzerland 2014

On one hand, we can find authors that use physics-based models like particle-flows, force fields, etc. [9][14] to determine the movement of the elements in the crowd. With these approaches, realistic results can be produced, but limited to motion scenes, and where all the characters are homogeneous and perform a slightly different movement most of the time. At a higher level of autonomy we can find rule-based systems, where the designer can specify the behavior of one character in a more general way [13][12][10]. The "brain" follows the same rules for all the characters, but the result is different depending on the different state variables of each individual in the scene. The main problem of these approaches is that, again, the variability is limited because it depends on the number and complexity of the implemented rules, which could grow exponentially with the number of characters and as their heterogeneity increases. The other problem with these approaches is the complexity of the behavior definition, requiring expert users or an intensive formation period.

In this work, we describe a crowd animation system called *Multitude* that uses a neuro-evolutionary approach in order to automate the crowd animation and to provide the characters with a higher level of autonomy. Other authors have used genetic algorithms for crowd animation like [7] and [6], but their application in real productions is still marginal. *Multitude* has been developed in collaboration with a 3D animation company to be applied in its productions, so applicability, reliability and usability have been very relevant issues. In fact, the main contributions of this paper are in the design decisions that have been made to make a neuro-evolutionary approach practical for real applications, especially in terms of how the artists have to express what they want from the scene in a natural manner so that the neuro-evolutionary system can really produce appropriate results. The resulting system is a combination of a powerful search procedure with a visual design technique that shows the practical potentially of intelligent hybrid approaches [16][4].

The remainder of the paper is structured as follows: section 2 is devoted to the description of the Multitude system, including the details about scene specification, the neuro-evolutionary approach proposed here, the visual behavior definition tool and the fitness assignment method. Section 3 contains the details of a prototypical crowd scene solved using Multitude and, finally, section 4 comments on the main conclusions of this work.

2 The Multitude Tool

2.1 Scene Specification

In order to provide some context, it is necessary to explain the elements and processes involved in the manual creation of a scene in the basic *Multitude* tool. All the information required to specify a scene is represented in the *scene specification* file. This file defines, along with other important information, all the types of characters that appear in the scene. Each type contains the common information to all the characters of the same group, such as its 3D model or the textures. Also, each type of character will have an associated definition of its brain, that is, the subsystem devoted to the execution of actions. Once a character type is defined, instances of it can be created and placed in the scene. Each character has a particular set of attributes, which are different from those of other characters, like its starting position or height. The brain is defined at a character-type level, so every character of the same type in the scene will have its own implementation of the same brain.

The brain of a character returns the actions the character should execute every frame, depending on its previous state. For example, *if the character is facing a wall, turn 180 degrees* could be an action. In order to simplify the behavior definition, the brain can be programmed using a node-based graphical language. Each node is a box representing a command with inputs and outputs. Inputs and outputs from different nodes can be connected to create commands that are more complex. There are three kind of nodes: sensors, actuators and operators. The sensors return information about the character or the environment, such as the speed of the character or the current frame. The actuators create a response in the character. For example, *double speed or turn 45 degrees* could be actuator outputs. Finally, the operators allow creating complex programs transforming the outputs of the sensors into the desired inputs for the actuators. Some operator examples could be arithmetic operators, such as sums or multiplications; logic operators such as or, and, etc.

Once the scene specification file is created, the scene can be executed. As a result, we obtain a visual representation of the situation and a *scene summary* file. This file contains all the information about the simulation, like the distance covered by each character, the number of jumps performed, etc. This information is computationally costly to obtain, but it is very important for the automatic evaluation of a scene.

2.2 Neuro-evolutionary Design

In general terms, our objective in this work was to provide each character with an ANN in the brain subsystem. The ANN node is a black box impossible to manipulate and transform into a nodes network, consequently, it will not be equivalent to any network created manually. Performance is a priority in this system, so for the brains we have implemented a multilayer perceptron with two hidden layers and with the weights as the only variable parameters. This architecture is flexible enough for the purpose we have in mind and minimizes the number of values to find. Ideally, the ANN-node should have all the sensors as inputs and all the actuators as outputs, but if some are not going to be used in a scene (for example a jump is not always allowed) they can be removed to reduce the number of parameters to improve performance.

In order to produce the appropriate values for the parameters of the ANNs, we are going to evolve them [5]. That is we are going to evolve the ANNs starting from a random population of chromosomes that encode the weights of the ANN using the Differential Evolution (DE) algorithm. This algorithm provides fast convergence with small populations [3], making it the most suitable for our task given the fact that a simulation needs to be run for each chromosome and the simulations are the bottleneck of this system. The specific version of DE that has been used is the DE/rand/1/bin described in the original work of Storn and Price [11].

The fitness required by the evolutionary algorithm for each individual in the population will be obtained by running a simulation and determining how good the scene is in terms of how similar the behavior of the crowd is to the one that is desired. This is the key aspect of this work, as for a director or an artist to express how they want the crowd to behave in terms of something the evolutionary algorithm can use in order to calculate fitness is not obvious.

2.3 Visual Behavior Definition and Fitness Assignment

As indicated, the main problem of any automatic behavior generation approach to produce scenes that are going to be part of films resides in evaluating if a scene is what the director wants. Obviously, the ideal way for evaluating it would be for the director to see it and directly score how good she considers the scene. However, scoring by hand all the scenes that are generated by simulating the operation of each possible brain in the evolutionary algorithm population is a very inefficient procedure. It would take much longer than obtaining the scene in the traditional way. An alternative method needs to be found to evaluate a scene from objective data, so that it can be carried out automatically. In the end this implies that the director or animator needs to somehow specify what he wants in a way that is natural to him and this specification can then be used to score the different scenes produced by relating it to the information from the scene summary file. In other words, the real challenge of this application, is finding a way of converting the desires of the user (director) on how the scene should pan out into something understandable by the system without using a programming language. This software is aimed at artists and computer animators that usually do not have these kinds of skills, so we will try to demand from them what they do better: to draw.

Thus, the way to represent how the user wants a crowd behavior to take place in an environment is going to be by drawing what the user expects from the crowd. However, the behaviors a director requires are in general complex, that is, they usually involve a series of basic behaviors that are carried out simultaneously or sequentially.

To calculate the fitness value, the main behavior is going to be divided into different sub-behaviors, and each one will be evaluated separately. For instance, let's consider a scene where we want the characters to walk to a point in the environment avoiding any obstacles such as pillars they main find, and, once there, sit down. This complex behavior can be divided into three simpler ones: walk to the target point, sit down and avoid obstacles. The scene will be better if all the objectives are achieved than if only some of them are. Also, each objective can be evaluated independently from the others.

Additionally, whenever possible, each sub-behavior should should not evaluate characteristics of the crowd but characteristics of a single character that affect the behavior of the crowd. The reason being that a character should act reacting to its own situation. It is easy to see, for instance, that if you want the center of mass of the crowd to reach a given point, some characters may be far from it and the scene achieve a high fitness value.

Obviously, this division into sub-behaviors that are evaluated independently converts the problem into a multi-objective problem. As such, two approaches can be used to evolve the populations of ANNs: use a dominance based evolutionary algorithm or integrate the objectives through some type of weighed combination function and use more traditional evolutionary algorithms. Here we have chosen the second approach as one of the requirements was for the users to be able to decide on the importance of the different objectives and try them out easily. Thus, the users are provided with sliders that allow them to assign a relevance to each objective. This relevance will correspond to the weight with which the objective will be weighed in a sum that produces the global fitness of the scene. They are also provided with a checkbox that allows them to indicate whether a sub-behavior is mandatory (that is, for instance, the character must jump, otherwise the scene is not valid) and these will be used as product terms over the fitness value.

Thus, for the animator the procedure is quite simple. A set of the most common types of behaviors are defined and each one of them is assigned a way of representing it as the intensity of color in a line or area. For example, if the objective is for the crowd to move from one area of the environment to another, a "go to" behavior is defined. To represent it, the user should associate a color channel to the behavior and draw a path from the origin to the target with growing intensity. The character should interpret that it should move in the direction of the increasing gradient. Once the behavior is defined, a fitness function is constructed to evaluate it as a function of color intensity. In this case, the fitness for one character could be the normalized value of the sum of the intensities of the color under the character in each frame of the scene. The nearer to the target the character finishes the scene, the higher the fitness value will be.

In order to recognize the colors in the environment, each character is provided with a sensor for each behavior that is painted. Those sensors sense the following information: the color intensity under the character, the angle to the direction of highest increasing intensity and the angle to the direction of least intensity in his surroundings. The information about the different color channels under the characters in each frame will be stored in the scene summary file. Although new behaviors can be added as needed, the user must have a set of the most common ones. To use one of them it only needs to select it from the list, assign it a color channel, and paint in the environment the desired behavior.

For the sake of making how the system works more understandable, a set of basic behaviors are described in what follows:

- Go to: We already talked about this behavior earlier.
- Path: The characters should stay during the whole scene within areas painted with the highest intensity of the associated color. This behavior is useful to draw paths or areas where the characters can move freely. The fitness value for each character (FC) is obtained, as in the previous example, by adding

the value of the channel under it in each frame and normalizing it between 0 and 1.
- Border: Complementary to paths, characters should not cross borders. Although it is similar to path, users find it more intuitive to split complementary behaviors.
- Acceleration: Characters should increase speed when they are over the color associated to this behavior. The speed can have values between 0 and 1, and the intensity of the channel is the desired increase of speed. To calculate the fitness, the speed in the next frame should be the speed in the current frame plus the intensity of the acceleration channel. The fitness value will be the normalized average of the differences between observed and desired values.
- Deceleration: The complementary channel to acceleration.
- Dispersion: If the value of the dispersion channel is larger than zero, the characters must try to separate from each other. The more intense the color, the larger the separation. Being together or separate from one another is not an absolute concept and it depends on the size of the characters. To calculate this fitness value, the user needs to define two extra parameters indicating the distances that can be considered close and far (an approximation could be obtained from the measurements of the scenery and the characters). To calculate the fitness value, the user should proceed as in the previous examples but using the difference between the current distance to the closest character and the new one.
- Concentration: The complementary channel to dispersion.
- Jump: The characters must jump if they detect the jump channel. The more intense the associated color, the higher the fitness. The fitness value is the average of the intensities of the channel in the frames where the character jumps.
- Animation: Similar to jump but for changing the animation cycle. For example, run, walk, dance, sit down...

This way of representing behaviors is easy to understand and does not require much training. Also, it is easily extendable in the case of users with programming skills. Adding a new behavior only requires creating a new class defining how the fitness value should be calculated for a character.

3 Practical Example

In what follows we will present an example of the operation of *Multitude* in a particular scene. In the stage, as we can see in figure 4, there are two adjacent rooms and one door connecting them. A crowd, which is standing in a room, has to walk over to the second room avoiding collisions among the characters and with the walls. Obviously, the behavior has to be realistic, and, therefore, the characters must get closer together as they approach the door. In the same way, the characters must move away from each other after going through the door. Besides, if a character goes through the left side of the door it should keep on walking on the left side and not cross over to the right side of the scenario.

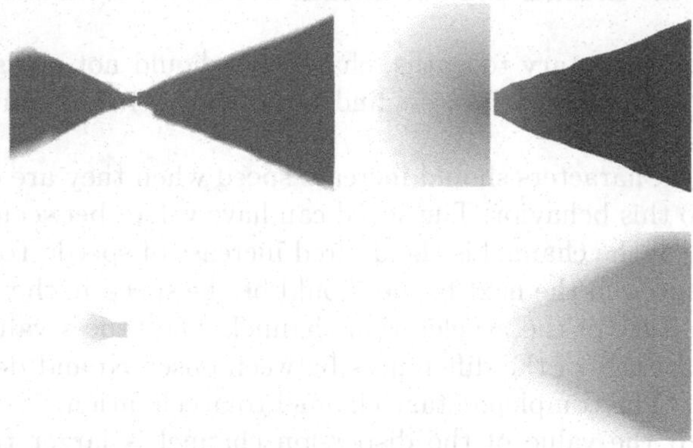

Fig. 1. Gradients that determine the behavior of the crowd for the scene

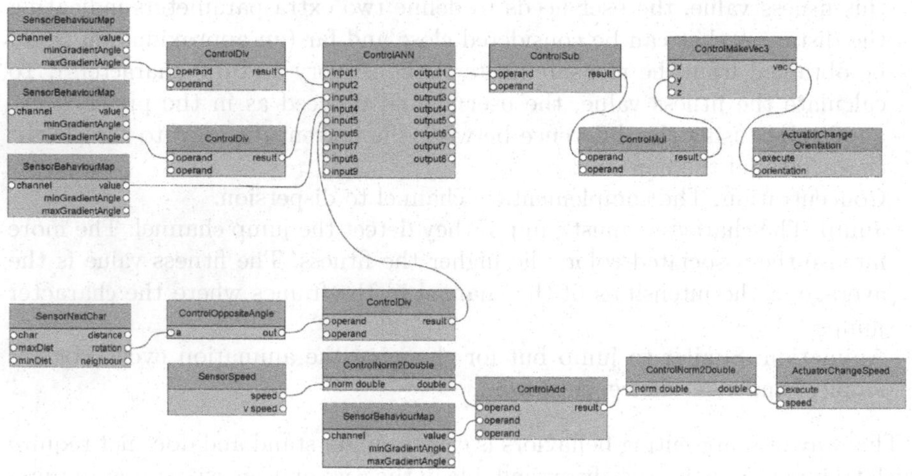

Fig. 2. The behavior node network for the two rooms scene

To produce this scene we have used a node network with one output and four inputs. The output will determine the turning angle for the character in each frame and the inputs are:

- Direction of the greatest intensity of the path.
- Direction of the greatest intensity of the destination.
- Dispersion intensity at the current position.
- Angle to the nearest character.

The first step is to determine the desired behavior for the characters by painting behavior gradients onto the scene. To achieve this, the artist used four different gradients as shown in figure 1:

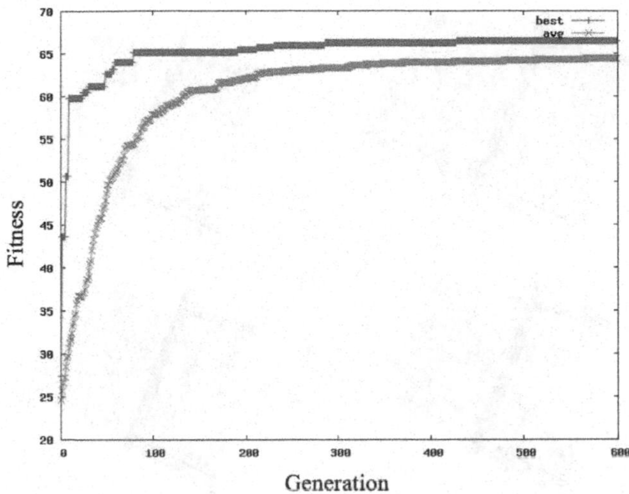

Fig. 3. Evolution results for the scene

1. A path gradient, to indicate which path the crowd must follow (top left gradient in the figure).
2. A destination gradient, to determine that the door is the destination in the first room (top right gradient).
3. An acceleration gradient indicating that the crowd must increase its speed when getting close to the door, just before going through it (bottom left gradient).
4. A dispersion gradient to make the characters move away from each other after going through the door (bottom right).

Three fitness terms are taken into account in order to score the solutions: following the path, reaching the destination and finishing the scene with enough distance between all of the characters. We consider that speed is a non evolvable parameter. The speed changes are solved by using a simple behavior node network that fulfills the requirements provided by the acceleration gradient. With this in mind, the following formula is used to evaluate the fitness of a solution S:

$$fitness(S) = \frac{Path + Destination}{2} \times 0.6 + Dispersion \times 0.4$$

Figure 2 displays the ANN node in the top network with the four inputs and one output commented above. Specifically, this ANN was made up of 4 inputs, two hidden layers of 4 and 3 neurons and one output neuron. The bottom network displayed in figure 2 is created to manage the speed.

On the other hand, figure 3 shows the results of the evolutionary process in terms of the evolution of the fitness value with growing generations of evolution. The best individual fitness as well as the population average improves with the number of generations.

Fig. 4. Different frames of the final scene

The maximum theoretical fitness is 100 but, due to the nature of the problem, there is no way to know if the best scene will ever achieve that value. In fact, in most cases it will achieve a very low value well below this maximum. This test, which achieved a fitness value of 64.43, ran on 35 processors, considering a population of 35 individuals and 600 generations, for 168 minutes. The scene length was 300 frames.

In figure 4 we display four frames of the final scene obtained with *Multitude*, showing the potentiality of the tool for future productions.

4 Conclusion

This paper deals with the problem of automating the generation of crowd behaviors in animated films. To this end, we propose a neuro-evolutionary approach that is integrated with the traditional way in which artists and animators do their work. Thus, the different characters that make up the crowd in a scene are controlled by a brain consisting of a neural network based node that controls those behaviors whose generation need to be automated, together with any additional nodes the designer wants to introduce with respect to behaviors he knows how to obtain. The network based behavior controller is the same for all the individuals in the crowd and it is evolved using as fitness a composition of the fitness of the individual sub-behaviors that make it up. The most important element for artists and animators within the field is that these fitness functions are defined by the user as drawings of colored lines or areas in the environment which, through their color intensity and its gradients, provide an energy based aggregative fitness value for the individuals in the crowd. The approach presented here has been tested in the creation of different scenes within the animation department of a local film company and the results have been very promising. It produces realistic results and, what is more important for them, it provides a very simple way to define what the director wants from the scene and to manipulate the different objectives in order to achieve the desired result precisely.

Acknowledgments. This work was partially funded by the Xunta de Galicia and European Regional Development Funds through projects 09DPI012166PR and 10DPI005CT.

References

1. Ali, S., Nishino, K., Manocha, D., Shah, M.: Modeling, Simulation and Visual Analysis of Crowds: A Multidisciplinary Perspective, vol. 11. Springer, Heidelberg (2013)
2. Banerjee, B., Kraemer, L.: Evaluation and Comparison of Multi-agent Based Crowd Simulation Systems. In: Dignum, F. (ed.) Agents for Games and Simulations II. LNCS, vol. 6525, pp. 53–66. Springer, Heidelberg (2011)
3. Caamaño, P., Bellas, F., Becerra, J.A., Duro, R.J.: Evolutionary algorithm characterization in real parameter optimization problems. Applied Soft Computing 13(4), 1902–1921 (2013)
4. Corchado, E., Wóniak, M., Abraham, A., de Carvalho, A.C.P.L.F., Snášel, V.: Recent trends in intelligent data analysis. Neurocomputing 126, 1–2 (2011); Recent trends in Intelligent Data Analysis Selected papers of the The 6th International Conference on Hybrid Artificial Intelligence Systems (HAIS 2011) Online Data Processing Including a selection of papers from the International Conference on Adaptive and Intelligent Systems 2011 (ICAIS 2011)
5. Floreano, D., Dürr, P., Mattiussi, C.: Neuroevolution: from architectures to learning. Evolutionary Intelligence 1(1), 47–62 (2008)
6. Yu, H., Liu, H., Yang, X.: Evolutionary modeling approach for crowd animation. In: 2012 International Conference on Computer Science and Information Processing (CSIP), pp. 237–241. IEEE (2012)
7. Li, T.-Y., Wang, C.-C.: An evolutionary approach to crowd simulation. In: Autonomous Robots and Agents, pp. 119–126. Springer, Heidelberg (2007)
8. Parent, R.: Computer animation: algorithms and techniques. Newnes (2012)
9. Patil, S., Berg, J.V.D., Curtis, S., Lin, M.C., Manocha, D.: Directing crowd simulations using navigation fields. IEEE Transactions on Visualization and Computer Graphics 17(2), 244–254 (2011)
10. Pelechano, N., Allbeck, J.M., Badler, N.I.: Controlling individual agents in high-density crowd simulation. In: Proceedings of the 2007 ACM SIGGRAPH/Eurographics Symposium on Computer Animation, pp. 99–108. Eurographics Association (2007)
11. Storn, R., Price, K.: Differential evolution–a simple and efficient heuristic for global optimization over continuous spaces. Journal of global optimization 11(4), 341–359 (1997)
12. Sung, M., Gleicher, M., Chenney, S.: Scalable behaviors for crowd simulation. In: Computer Graphics Forum, vol. 23, pp. 519–528. Wiley Online Library (2004)

13. Szarowicz, A., Amiguet-Vercher, J., Forte, P., Briggs, J., Gelepithis, P., Remagnino, P.: The Application of AI to Automatically Generated Animation. In: Stumptner, M., Corbett, D.R., Brooks, M. (eds.) Canadian AI 2001. LNCS (LNAI), vol. 2256, pp. 487–494. Springer, Heidelberg (2001)
14. Thalmann, D.: Crowd Simulation. John Wiley & Sons, Inc. (2007)
15. Vigueras, G., Orduña, J.M., Lozano, M., Jégou, Y.: A scalable multiagent system architecture for interactive applications. Science of Computer Programming 78(6), 715–724 (2013)
16. Woźniak, M., Graña, M., Corchado, E.: A survey of multiple classifier systems as hybrid systems. Information Fusion 16, 3–17 (2014)

Hybrid System for Mobile Image Recognition through Convolutional Neural Networks and Discrete Graphical Models

William Raveane and María Angélica González Arrieta

Universidad de Salamanca, Salamanca, Spain

Abstract. A system is presented which combines deep neural networks with discrete inference techniques for the successful recognition of an image. The system presented builds upon the classical sliding window method but applied in parallel over an entire input image. The result is discretized by treating each classified window as a node in a markov random field and applying a minimization of its associated energy levels. Two important benefits are observed with this system: a gain in performance by virtue of the system's parallel nature, and an improvement in the localization precision due to the inherent connectivity between classified windows.

Keywords: computer vision, deep neural networks, graphical models.

1 Introduction

Hybrid intelligent systems have consistently shown benefits that outperform those of their individual components in many tasks, especially when used along neural computing [1]. In recent years, two main areas of computer vision have gained considerable strength and support: On one side, soft computing techniques based on non-exact but very accurate machine learning models like neural networks, which have been successful for high level image classification [7]. Contrasting these systems, computer vision techniques modeled by graphical models have enjoyed great reception when performing low level image processing tasks such as image completion [6]. In this paper, we combine both of these techniques to successfully classify and localize a region of interest within an input image.

We use Convolutional Neural Networks (CNN) [3] for the classification of image content. CNNs have become a general solution for image recognition with variable input data, as their results have outclassed other machine learning approaches in large scale image recognition tasks [4]. Paired to this CNN classifier, we use energy minimization of a Markov Random Field (MRF) [8] for inference and localization of the target within the image space. Graphical models such as this have been implemented in areas of computer vision where the relationship between neighboring regions plays a crucial role [2].

We review the implementation of this system specifically within a mobile device. With the increasing use of mobile hardware, it has become a priority to

M. Polycarpou et al. (Eds.): HAIS 2014, LNAI 8480, pp. 365–376, 2014.
© Springer International Publishing Switzerland 2014

provide these devices with computer vision capabilities. Due to the high computational requirements, this need has mostly been met by outsourcing the analysis to a remote server over the internet. This approach introduces large delays and is hardly appropriate when interactivity and responsiveness are paramount. Embedded environments have intrinsic architecture constraints which require algorithms to make the best use of the available computing capacity. The proposed system exploits this specific platform by reducing the overall required memory throughput via a parallel execution approach. This is achieved by applying layer computations over the entire image space, as opposed to running smaller patches individually, as is common with the sliding window approach normally used in this type of image classification.

2 Background

The network on which our system is based upon is a standard CNN. Figure 1 depicts the layer structure of such a network, and it is the reference architecture used throughout this paper to describe the concepts of the framework presented.

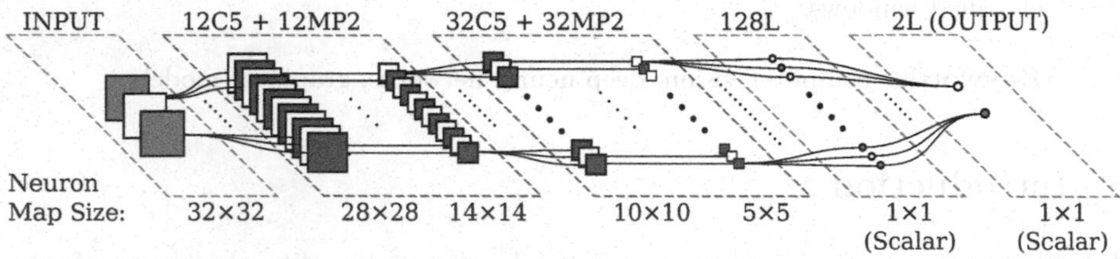

Fig. 1. A typical convolutional neural network architecture, with three input neurons for each color channel of an analyzed image patch, two feature extraction stages of convolutional and max-pooling layers, and two linear layers to produce a final one-vs-all classification output

In the initial stages of the CNN, a neuron consists of a two-dimensional grid of independent computing units, each producing an output value. As a result, every neuron will itself output a grid of numerical values, a data structure in $\mathbb{R}^2$ referred to as a map. When applying CNNs to image analysis, these maps represent an internal state of the image after being processed through a connective path leading to that particular neuron. Consequently, maps will usually bear a direct positonal and feature-wise relationship to the input image space. As data progresses through the network, however, this represenation turns more abstract as the dimentionality is reduced. Eventually, these maps are passed through one or more linear classifiers, layers consisting of traditional single unit neurons which output a single value each. For consistency, the outputs of these neurons are treated as 1×1 single pixel image maps, although they are nothing more than scalar values in $\mathbb{R}^0$.

2.1 CNN Layer Types

The first layer in the network consists of the image data to be analyzed, usually composed as the three color channels. The notation $N_j X K_j$ is used to describe all subsequent layers, where N_j is the neuron map count of layer j, $X \in \{\mathcal{C}, \mathcal{MP}, \mathcal{L}\}$ denotes the layer type group (Convolutional, Max-Pooling, and Linear), and K_j is the parameter value for that layer.

The first part of every $\mathcal{C} \rightarrow \mathcal{MP}$ feature extraction stage is a convolutional layer. Here, each neuron linearly combines the convolution of one or more preceding maps. The result is a map slightly smaller than the input size by an amount known as the kernel padding, which arises from the boundary conditions of the valid convolution algorithm. It is defined as ${}^{K_j}/_2 - 1$, where K_j is convolutional kernels size of layer j. Therefore, the layer's map size will be given by $M_j = M_{j-1} - {}^{K_j}/_2 - 1$, where M_{j-1} is the the preceding layer's map size.

A max-pooling neuron acts on a single map from a preceding convolutional neuron, and its task is to subsample a pooled region of size K_j. The result is a map size that is inversely proportional to said parameter by $M_j = {}^{M_{j-1}}/_{K_j}$.

Linear layers classify feature maps extracted on preceding layers through a linear combination as in a perceptron – always working with scalar values – such that $M_j = 1$ at every layer of this type.

Finally, the output of the final classification layer decides the best matching label describing the input image. Fig. 2 shows the information flow leading to this classification for a given image patch, where the CNN has been trained to identify a particular company logo.

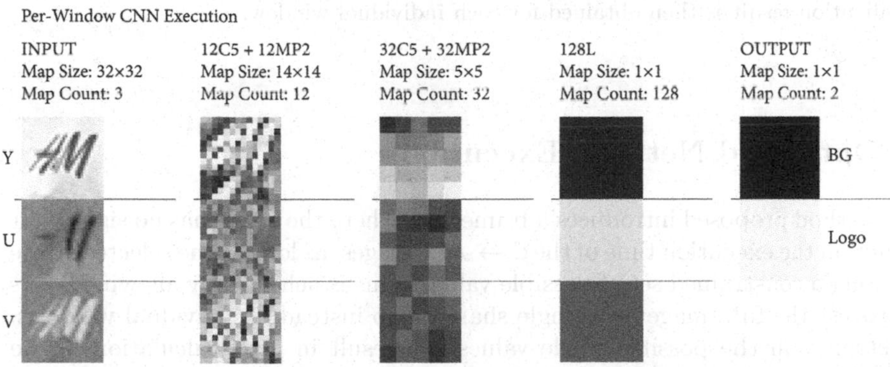

Fig. 2. Visualization of the first three neuron maps at each stage of the CNN. Note the data size reduction induced at each stage. The output of this execution consists of two scalar values, each one representing the likelihood that the analyzed input image belongs to that neuron's corresponding class. In this case the logo has been successfully recognized by the higher valued output neuron for class "Logo".

2.2 The Sliding Window Method

Recognition of images larger than the CNN input size is achieved by the sliding window approach. This algorithm is defined by two quantities, the window size S, usually fixed to match the CNN's designed input size; and the window stride T, which specifies the distance at which consecutive windows are spaced apart. This stride distance establishes the total number of windows analyzed W for a given input image. For an image of size $I_w \times I_h$, the window count is given by:

$$W = \left(\frac{I_w - S}{T} + 1\right)\left(\frac{I_h - S}{T} + 1\right) \quad \Longrightarrow \quad W \propto \frac{I_w I_h}{T^2} \tag{1}$$

Figure 3 shows this method applied on an input image downsampled to 144×92, extracting windows of $S = 32$ for the simple case where $T = {}^{S}\!/_{2}$. A network analyzing this image would require 40 executions to fully analyze all extracted windows. The computational requirement is further compounded when a smaller stride is selected – an action necessary to improve the resolving power of the classifier: at $T = {}^{S}\!/_{8}$, 464 separate CNN executions would be required.

Fig. 3. An overview of the sliding window method, where an input image is subdivided into smaller overlapping image patches, each being individually analyzed by a CNN. A classification result is then obtained for each individual window.

3 Optimized Network Execution

The method proposed introduces a framework where the stride has no significant impact on the execution time of the $\mathcal{C} \rightarrow \mathcal{MP}$ stages, as long as the selected stride is among a constrained set of possible values. This is achieved by allowing layers to process the full image as a single shared map instead of individual windows. Constraints in the possible stride values will result in pixel calculations to be correctly aligned throughout the layers.

3.1 Shared Window Maps

CNNs have a built-in positional tolerance due to the reuse of the same convolutional kernels over the entire neuron map. As a result of this behavior, their output is independent of any pixel offset within the map, such that overlapping windows will share convolved values. This is demonstrated in Fig. 4.

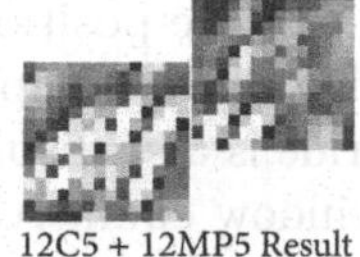

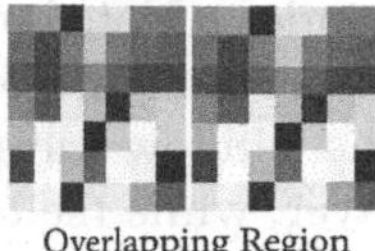

Fig. 4. Two adjacent windows extracted from an input image, passed through the 12C5 + 12MP5 feature extractor. A detailed view of the convolved maps in the overlapping top-right and bottom-left quarters of each window shows that these areas fully match.

This leads to the possibility of streamlining the feature extractors by running their algorithms over the full input image at once. Hence, each $\mathcal{C} \to \mathcal{MP}$ neuron will output a single map shared among all windows. This greatly reduces the expense of calculating again convolutions on overlapping regions of each window. Figure 5 shows an overview of the shared map process, which passes the input image in its entirety through each stage of the network.

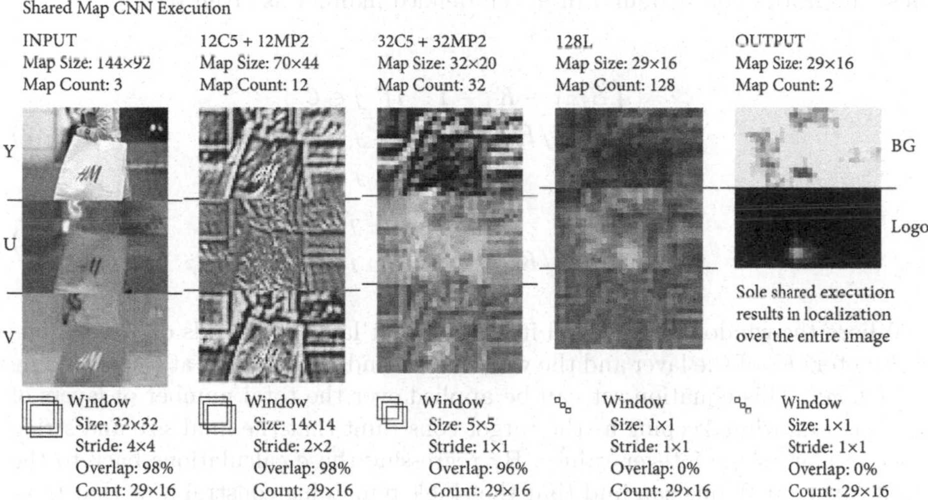

Fig. 5. The shared map execution method for a convolutional neural network, where each layer processes an entire image in a single pass, and each neuron is now able to process maps with dimensions that far exceed the layer's designed input size

By doing this, the output layer now produces a continuous and localized class distribution over the image space, a result which contrasts greatly to that of a single classification value as was previously seen in Fig. 2. The output of this execution consists of image maps where each pixel yields the relative position of all simultaneously classified windows.

Similar to the per-window execution method, the intensity value of a pixel in the output map represents the classification likelihood of the corresponding window. Note how the relative position of the logo in the input image has been discovered after only one shared map execution of the network. An account of the window size and stride is also displayed, illustrating how it evolves after each layer, while the total window count remains the same. Here, the correspondence of each 32×32 window in the input image can be traced to each one of the pixels in the output maps.

3.2 Window Configuration

The operation of the shared map process relies greatly on the details of the dimensionality reduction occurring at each layer within the network. For this reason, it is necessary to lay certain constraints that must be enforced when choosing the optimum sliding window stride.

At each layer, the window size and stride are reduced until they eventually become single pixel values at the final linear layers. The amount of reduction at each stage varies according to the type of the layer and its parameters. All of these quantities can be found in a well defined manner as given by:

$$S_j = \begin{cases} S_{j-1} - K_j - 1 & if\ j \in \mathcal{C} \\ S_{j-1}/K_j & if\ j \in \mathcal{MP} \\ S_{j-1} & if\ j \in \mathcal{L} \end{cases} \tag{2}$$

$$T_j = \begin{cases} T_{j-1} & if\ j \in \mathcal{C} \cup \mathcal{L} \\ T_{j-1}/K_j & if\ j \in \mathcal{MP} \end{cases} \tag{3}$$

Where the window size S_j and its stride T_j at layer j depends on the various parameters K_j of the layer and the window size and stride values at the preceding $j-1$ layer. This equation set can be applied over the total number of layers of the network, while keeping as the target constraint that the final size and stride must remain whole integer values. By regressing these calculations back to the input layer $j = 0$, one can find that the single remaining constraint at that layer is given by:

$$T_0 \equiv 0 \bmod \prod_{j \in \mathcal{MP}} K_j \tag{4}$$

In other words, the input window stride must be perfectly divisible by the product of the pooling size of all max-pooling layers in the network. Choosing the initial window stride in this manner, will ensure that every pixel in the final output map is correctly aligned thoughout all shared maps and corresponds to exactly one input window. Fig. 6 follows the evolution of the window image data along the various layers of the sample network architecture, showing this pixel alignment throughout the CNN.

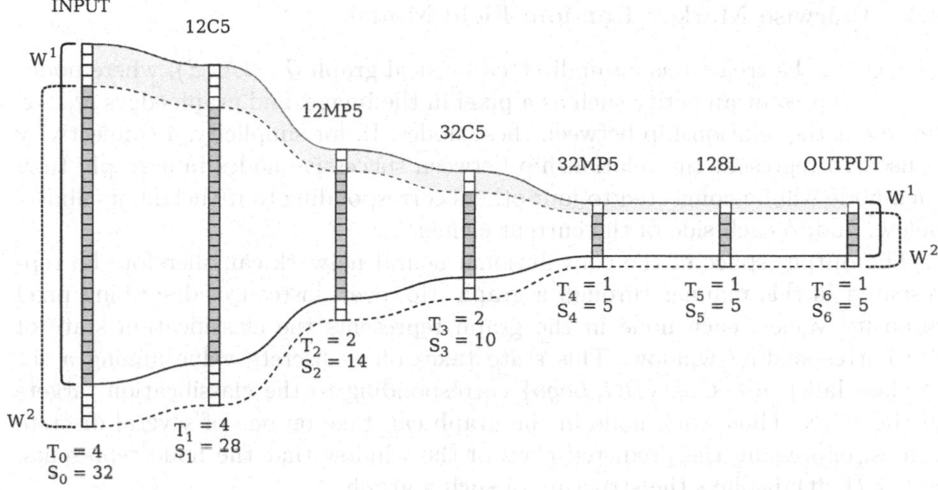

Fig. 6. The CNN layers and their effect on the window pixel space, illustrated in one dimension for simplicity. Two successive 32×32 windows W^1 and W^2 are shown. Overlapping pixels at each layer are shaded. Starting with an input layer window stride $T_0 = 4$, the final output layer results in a packed $T_6 = 1$ window stride, so that each output map pixel corresponds to a positional shift of 4 pixels in the input windows, a relationship depicted by the darkened column path traversing all layers.

4 Discrete Inference of CNN Output

The common practice to obtain a final classification from an output value set as seen in Fig. 5 is to identify which class has a higher output value from the CNN at each each window (here, each pixel in the output map). While efficient, results from this procedure are not always ideal because they only take into account each window separately.

Furthermore, maximum value inference is prone to false positives over the full image area. Due to their non-exact nature, neural network accuracy can decrease by finding patterns in random stimuli which eventually trigger neurons in the final classification layer. However, such occurrences tend to appear in isolation around other successfully classified image regions. It is therefore possible to improve the performance of the classifier by taking into account nearby windows.

There exist many statistical approaches in which this can be implemented, such as (i) influencing the value of each window by a weighted average of neighboring windows, or (ii) boosting output values by the presence of similarly classified windows in the surrounding area. However, we propose discrete energy minimization through belief propagation as a more general method to determine the final classification within a set of CNN output maps. The main reason being that graphical models are more flexible in adapting to image conditions and can usually converge on a globally optimal solution.

4.1 Pairwise Markov Random Field Model

Images can be treated as an undirected cyclical graph $\mathcal{G} = (\mathcal{N}, \mathcal{E})$, where nodes $n_i \in \mathcal{N}$ represent an entity such as a pixel in the image, and graph edges $e_{ij} \in \mathcal{E}$ represent the relationship between these nodes. If, for simplicity, 4-connectivity is used to represent the relationship between successive nodes in a graph; then each node will be connected to four others corresponding to its neighbors above, below, and to each side of the current element.

The output space of the convolutional neural network can therefore be represented in this manner through a graph. However, instead of describing pixel intensity values, each node in the graph represents the classification state of the corresponding window. This state takes on a discrete value among a set of class labels $c \in \mathcal{C} \equiv \{BG, Logo\}$ corresponding to the classification targets of the CNN. Thus, each node in the graph can take on one of several discrete values, expressing the predicted class of the window that the node represents. Fig. 7 (Left) displays the structure of such a graph.

It can be seen that if nodes represent classification outcomes, there is a strong relationship between them. The reason is that continuity throughout a map tends to be preserved over neighboring regions due to strong local correlation in in input images. This inflicts a Markovian property in the graph nodes where there is a dependency between successive nodes. Therefore, this graph follows the same structure as an MRF, and any operations available to this kind of structure will be likewise applicable to the output map.

4.2 Energy Allocation

To implement energy minimization on an MRF, it is necessary to assign energy potentials to each node and edge. These energies are usually adapted from observed variables, and in this case, they correspond to the values of the output maps and combinations thereof. Therefore, MRF optimization over a graph $\mathcal{G}$ can be carried out by minimizing its Markov random energy E, given by:

$$E(\mathcal{G}) = E(\mathcal{N}, \mathcal{E}) = \sum_{n_i \in \mathcal{N}} \Theta_i(n_i) + \sum_{e_{ij} \in \mathcal{E}} \Theta_{ij}(e_{ij}) \tag{5}$$

Here, $\Theta_i(\cdot)$ corresponds to the singleton energy potential of node n_i, and $\Theta_{ij}(\cdot)$ is a pairwise potential between nodes n_i and n_j. Starting from the CNN output map observations, the singleton potentials can be assigned as:

$$\Theta_i = \begin{bmatrix} \omega_i^0 \\ \omega_i^1 \\ \vdots \\ \omega_i^C \end{bmatrix} \tag{6}$$

$$\omega_i^a = \sum_{c \in C} \begin{cases} 1 - (O_i^c)^2 & if\ a = c \\ (O_i^c)^2 & otherwise \end{cases} \tag{7}$$

Where C is the total number of classes in set $\mathcal{C}$ (2 in the sample CNN architecture), and O_i^c is the observed CNN value for window $n_i \in \mathcal{N}$ and class $c \in \mathcal{C}$. In this manner, each ω_i^a value is an MSE-like metric that measures how far off from ideal training target values did the CNN classify window n_i as. Thus, a lower potential value will be assigned to the most likely class, while a higher potential value will be given to other possible classes at this node.

Pairwise potentials can be defined as:

$$\Theta_{ij} = \begin{bmatrix} \delta_{ij}^{00} & \delta_{ij}^{01} & \cdots & \delta_{ij}^{0C} \\ \delta_{ij}^{10} & \delta_{ij}^{11} & & \delta_{ij}^{1C} \\ \vdots & & \ddots & \\ \delta_{ij}^{C0} & \delta_{ij}^{C1} & & \delta_{ij}^{CC} \end{bmatrix} \tag{8}$$

$$\delta_{ij}^{ab} = | O_i^a - O_j^b | \tag{9}$$

Where each value δ_{ij}^{ab} is a straightforward distance metric that measures the *jump* in CNN output values when switching from class a to class b between windows n_i and n_j. Thus, these potentials will be small if the same class is assigned to both nodes, and large otherwise. Fig. 7 (Right) shows all energy assignments per node pair.

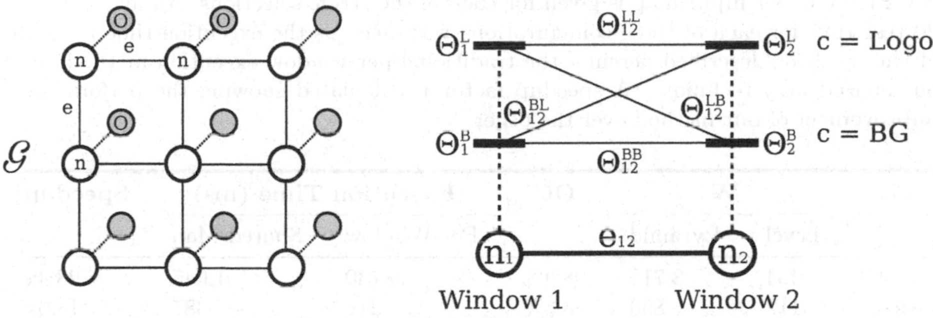

Fig. 7. Left: A subset of the MRF graph $\mathcal{G}$ formed by the CNN output space, where each node n_i represents the classification state of a corresponding window analyzed with the network, whose outputs are implemented into this system as the observed hidden variables O. Nodes have a 4-connectivity relationship with each other represented by the edges e_{ij} thus forming a grid-like cyclical graph. **Right:** A detail of the potential energies assigned to each of two nodes $\{n_1, n_2\}$ connected by edge e_{12}. The singleton potentials Θ_i^a correspond to the energy associated with node i if assigned to class a, and the pairwise potentials $\Theta_{ij}{}^{ab}$ are the changes in energy that occur by assigning class a to node n_i and class b to node n_j.

Applying Belief Propagation [5] to find the lowest possible energy state of the graph will now yield an equilibrium of class assignments throughout the image output space.

5 Results

The test application is developed for the Android mobile OS as an OpenGL ES shader which makes use of the available computing capabilities of the device GPU. The main logic of the system is placed within a fragment shader running the CNN per-pixel over a Surface Texture memory object. The test device is equipped with a quad core 1.3 GHz Cortex-A9 CPU with a 12-core 520 MHz Tegra 3 GPU. This SoC architecture embeds 1 Gb of DDR2 RAM shared by both the CPU and GPU.

The test system executes the same CNN architecture described in Fig. 1, except for the classification layer having 32 output neurons corresponding to one background label and 31 different logo labels. This network is exectued over 8 simultaneous 144×92 images forming a multi-scale image pyramid. The energy minimization technique as described in Section 4 is then applied, but over a 3D graph formed with 6-connectivity between nodes such that each window is also aware of window classifications at the corresponding larger and smaller scale steps. Table 1 gives a summary of the results obtained from this setup.

Table 1. Results of tests with several input layer stride T_0 configurations, from the closest packed 4×4 to the non-overlapping 32×32 layouts. A total window count W at each pyramid level and over the full 8 level pyramid, as well as the window overlap coverage OC per input map is given for each of the stride selections. An average over 20 test runs for each of these configurations was taken as the execution time for each of the methods described herein – the traditional per-window execution method, and our shared map technique. A speedup factor is calculated showing the performance improvement of our method over the other.

T_0	W		OC	Execution Time (ms)		Speedup
	Level	Pyramid		Per-Window	Shared Map	
4×4	464	3,712	98.4%	29,730	1,047	28.4x
8×8	112	896	93.8%	7,211	387	18.6x
12×12	60	480	85.9%	3,798	311	12.2x
16×16	32	256	75.0%	2,051	240	8.5x
20×20	24	192	60.9%	1,536	252	6.1x
24×24	15	120	43.8%	945	203	4.7x
28×28	15	120	23.4%	949	200	4.7x
32×32	8	64	0.00%	514	171	3.0x

It is of great interest to note the final 32×32 configuration. Regardless of the fact that there is no overlap at this stride, a 3.0 speedup is still observed over running the windows individually. This is due to the inherent reduction in memory bandwidth through the system's pipelined execution approach, where the entire image needs to be loaded only once per execution. This contrasts the traditional approach where loading separate windows into memory at different times requires each to be individually sliced from the original memory block – a very expensive operation in the limited memory throughput of mobile devices.

The results of the inference system are more of a qualitative nature, as it is difficult to objectively establish a ground truth basis for such experiments. This system aims to localize classified windows, therefore it is subject to an interpretation of which windows cover enough of the recognition target to be counted as a true positive. Regardless, Table 2 gives an indicative comparison of the system against the competing techniques previousy described. Fig. 8 shows a visual comparison.

Table 2. Results of various inference algorithms for the final classification, describing the Accuracy ($^{TP+TN}/_{ALL}$), PPV ($^{TP}/_{TP+FP}$), and F_1 ($^{2TP}/_{2TP+FP+FN}$) metrics

Algorithm	**Accuracy**	**PPV**	$\mathbf{F_1}$
Maximum Value	0.942	0.341	0.498
Weighted Average	0.964	0.391	0.430
Neighbor Boosting	0.972	0.489	0.591
Energy Minimization	**0.981**	**0.747**	**0.694**

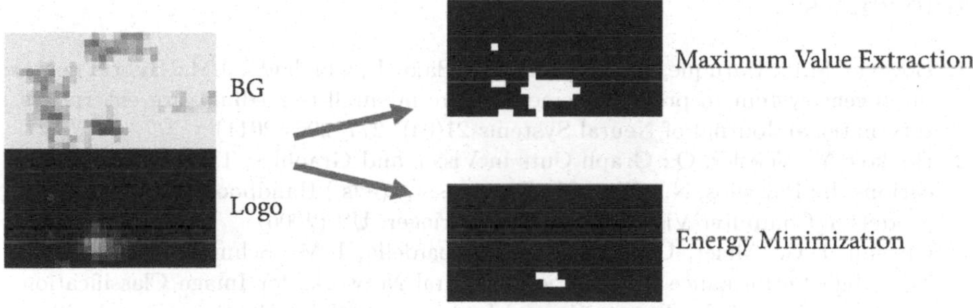

Fig. 8. Comparison of the final "Logo" classification and localization, applying the classical maximum value per class extraction vs. our proposed energy minimization inference method on the two CNN output maps introduced in Figure 5

6 Conclusions

A system for the optimization of convolutional neural networks has been presented for the particular application of mobile image recognition. Although a simple logo classification task was used here as a sample application, CNNs allow for many other image recognition tasks to be carried out. Most of these processes would have great impact on end users if implemented as real time mobile applications. Some examples where CNNs have been successfully used and their possible mobile implementations would be (i) text recognition for visually interactive language translators, (ii) human action recognition for increased user interactivity in social applications, or even (iii) traffic sign recognition for embedded automotive applications. Any of these applications could be similarly optimized and discretized by the system presented here.

In addition to the CNN classifier, the MRF model is very flexible as well and its implementation can be adjusted to domain-specific requirements as needed by each application. For example, a visual text recognizer might implement pairwise energy potentials which are modeled with the probabilistic distribution of character bigrams or n-grams over a corpus of text, thereby increasing the overall text recognition accuracy.

Therefore, we believe this to be a general purpose mobile computer vision framework which can be deployed for many different uses within the restrictions imposed by embedded hardware, but also encouraging the limitless possibilities of mobile applications.

Acknowledgements. This work has been carried out by the project Sociedades Humano-Agente: Inmersión, Adaptación y Simulación. TIN2012-36586-C03-03. Ministerio de Economa y Competitividad (Spain). Project co-financed with FEDER funds.

References

1. Borrajo, M.L., Baruque, B., Corchado, E., Bajo, J., Corchado, J.M.: Hybrid neural intelligent system to predict business failure in small-to-medium-size enterprises. International Journal of Neural Systems 21(04), 277–296 (2011)
2. Boykov, Y., Veksler, O.: Graph Cuts in Vision and Graphics: Theories and Applications. In: Paragios, N., Chen, Y., Faugeras, O. (eds.) Handbook of Mathematical Models in Computer Vision, pp. 79–96. Springer, US (2006)
3. Ciresan, D.C., Meier, U., Masci, J., Gambardella, L.M., Schmidhuber, J.: Flexible, High Performance Convolutional Neural Networks for Image Classification. In: Proceedings of the Twenty-Second International Joint Conference on Artificial Intelligence, pp. 1237–1242 (2011)
4. Ciresan, D.C., Meier, U., Gambardella, L.M., Schmidhuber, J.: Convolutional Neural Network Committees For Handwritten Character Classification. In: 11th International Conference on Document Analysis and Recognition, ICDAR (2011)
5. Felzenszwalb, P.F., Huttenlocher, D.P.: Efficient Belief Propagation for Early Vision. International Journal of Computer Vision 70(1), 41–54 (2006)
6. Komodakis, N., Tziritas, G.: Image completion using efficient belief propagation via priority scheduling and dynamic pruning. IEEE Transactions onImage Processing 16(11), 2649–2661 (2007)
7. Krizhevsky, A., Sutskever, I., Hinton, G.E.: ImageNet Classification with Deep Convolutional Neural Networks. In: Advances in Neural Information Processing Systems, vol. (25), pp. 1106–1114 (2012)
8. Wang, C., Paragios, N.: Markov Random Fields in Vision Perception: A Survey. Rapport de recherche RR-7945, INRIA (September 2012)

Self-adaptive Biometric Classifier Working on the Reduced Dataset

Piotr Porwik and Rafal Doroz

Institute of Computer Science
41-200 Sosnowiec, ul Bedzinska 39
University of Silesia, Katowice, Poland
{piotr.porwik,rafal.doroz}.us.edu.pl

Abstract. The paper presents a method of object recognition by means of a reduced data set. These data are specially prepared. The proposed method was also compared with two other well-known data reduction techniques, Principal Component Analysis (PCA) and Singular Value Decomposition (SVD). Objects can mostly be described through many features but these features can have different discriminant powers. The Hotelling's statistical method, allows determining the best discriminatory features and similarity measures which can be simultaneously selected.

Keywords: Hotelling's statistics, classification, recognition, biometrics.

1 Introduction

Any object can be characterized by means of features. The choice of features is an important criterion in the recognition process because the selection of features can change the recognition level accuracy and also allows a reduction in the number of features which should be taken into consideration [14], [16]. Features are selected by analyzing the efficacy of a feature in grouping objects of the same class and discriminating it from the members of other classes. The algorithm presented in this work performs the selection of the features but also indicates the best similarity measures which should be used in the recognition process (from the set of available measures), allowing the object recognition error to be minimized.

Today, many features of objects can be captured. For this reason there is a question of which features should be preferred in object recognition. In other words we ask which features have the greatest discriminant factors. A reduced number of features also ultimately reduces the computation time required for the recognition process and the size of databases can be smaller. The approach can be applied especially in recognition, classification, computer vision, and biometric systems. From a practical point of view a biometric system is a pattern recognition system which recognizes a user based on anatomical or behavioral characteristics [4], [5], [22]. Depending on the context, a biometric system can operate in either verification or identification mode. Verification involves confirming or denying a person's claimed

M. Polycarpou et al. (Eds.): HAIS 2014, LNAI 8480, pp. 377–388, 2014.
© Springer International Publishing Switzerland 2014

identity. In this paper only the object verification problem will be considered. In this study, we present a Hotelling's T^2 test that utilizes data to identify objects in two test groups [9], [12], [17]. The Hotelling method has been applied to various aspects of life, including genome association studies, microarray process control, charts or human liver cancers [13].

If a similarity measure is inappropriately selected, the object can be incorrectly recognized and assigned to the wrong class. If the grouping result is unsatisfactory due to the wrong choice of features describing the object, it will be necessary to the new feature selection through the removal of certain features and possibly the addition of others.

Various statistical methods have been proposed for the differentiation of objects on the basis of features analysis [4], [10], [15], [16], [18], [21]. A common characteristic of these methods is that they are essentially of univariate nature. Multivariate analyses take advantage of the correlation information and analyze the data from multiple objects jointly. However, applications of well-established multivariate statistical techniques for data analyses are not straightforward because of high dimensionality.

2 A New Method of Objects' Features Preparation

The main goal of the paper is to analyze two kinds of objects – original and forged signatures. In the first step two sets of signatures are formed. In the first step two sets of signatures are formed for every person. Let the set containing the original signatures be denoted as follows:

$$\pi_1 = \{S_1, S_2, ..., S_c\}. \tag{1}$$

Let the set containing the forged signatures of the same person be denoted as:

$$\pi_2 = \{S_1^{\Delta}, S_2^{\Delta}, ..., S_d^{\Delta}\}. \tag{2}$$

In the recording process, the discrete biometric features are sampled by a device (tablet), so signature S can be represented as a set of z points:

$$S = \{s(1), s(2), \ldots, s(z)\}, \tag{3}$$

where:
$s(t)$ – the tth point of the signature S,
z – the total number of signature points.

During signing, the tablet is capable of measuring many dynamic parameters such as a pressure of a pen on the tablet surface, the pen's position, velocity, and acceleration, and so on. This implies that each discrete point $s(t)$ is associated with many features recorded by the device. Let the set of attainable features be denoted as $F = \{f_1, f_2, ..., f_u\}$. Hence, each discrete point $s(t) = [f_1^t, f_2^t, ..., f_u^t]$ is a vector of the features. The most popular features [1], [8], [15] present Table 1.

Table 1. List of analysed features

Feature f_i, i=	Name	Feature f_i, i=	Name
1	Pressure	6	*x*-coordinate
2	Acceleration	7	*y*-coordinate
3	*x*-velocity	8	Time of measurement
4	*y*-velocity	9	Pen-up time
5	*x,y* – velocity	10	Pen-down time

Objects can be compared by means of the different similarity coefficients. Let a set of these methods be labeled as $M = \{\omega_1, \omega_2, ..., \omega_k\}$. This means that the set M contains methods and mathematical rules which can be included in the classification process. In this paper different similarity coefficients are taken into consideration. Table 2 presents various similarity computation methods. The similarities from Table 2 were utilized in the practical tests performed in this paper.

Table 2. List of similarity measures or coefficients [7]

Measure/coeff. ω_i, i=	Name	Measure/coeff. ω_i, i=	Name
1	Euclidean	6	Jaccard
2	Gower	7	Fidelity
3	Minkowski	8	Bhattacharyya
4	City Block	9	Hellinger
5	Cosine	10	Matusita

The similarity of the two objects can be determined by means of the same feature $f_m \in F$ which occurs in these objects. The similarity of objects can be computed by means of the method $\omega_j \in M$. For this assumption we can construct a set FM of all possible combinations of "feature–method" pairs:

$$FM = \{\varepsilon_i \prec (f_m, \omega_j)_i : f_m \in F, \omega_j \in M\}, \quad i = 1,...,u \cdot k, \tag{4}$$

where:

$(f_m, \omega_j)_i$ – the ith pair: "object's feature (f_m) – analysis method (ω_j)", $m = 1,...,u$, $j = 1,...,k$, $i = 1,...,u \cdot k$,

u – number of features of the object,

k – number of methods used in a comparison of the features.

Data prepared can be appropriately ordered in matrix form. The matrix $\mathbf{X}$ is built on the basis of the set π_1 of objects, while the matrix $\mathbf{Y}$ is created on the basis of the set $\pi_1 \cup \pi_2$. It can be observed that matrix $\mathbf{X}$ is constructed on the basis of original signatures of a given person (say person Q) when matrix $\mathbf{Y}$ consists of data from original and forged signatures of the same person. The matrices contain values of the similarity coefficient *Sim* calculated between pairs of objects:

$$\mathbf{X}=\left[[S_1 \leftrightarrow S_2],...,[S_1 \leftrightarrow S_c],...,[S_{c-1} \leftrightarrow S_c]\right]_{(u\cdot k)\times\binom{c}{2}}=[\mathbf{x}_1,...,\mathbf{x}_{\binom{c}{2}}] \tag{5}$$

$$\mathbf{Y}=\left[[S_1 \leftrightarrow S_1^{\Delta}],...,[S_1 \leftrightarrow S_d^{\Delta}],...,[S_c \leftrightarrow S_d^{\Delta}]\right]_{(u\cdot k)\times(c\cdot d)}=[\mathbf{y}_1,...,\mathbf{y}_{c\cdot d}] \tag{6}$$

where:

S_i, S_j – the ith and j^{th} original signatures of a given person,
c – the number of all genuine signatures of a given person,
S_i, S_j^{Δ} – the ith genuine and the jth forged signature of a given person,
d – the number of all unauthorized (falsified) signatures of a given person.

The similarity coefficients are computed using all combinations of "feature-method" pairs. The first columnar vector of the matrix **X** and **Y** is shown below:

$$\mathbf{X}\ni\mathbf{x}_1=[S_1\leftrightarrow S_2]=\begin{bmatrix} Sim(S_1,S_2)^{(f_1,\omega_1)_{1\cdot 1}} \\ \vdots \\ Sim(S_1,S_2)^{(f_1,\omega_k)_{1\cdot k}} \\ \vdots \\ Sim(S_1,S_2)^{(f_u,\omega_1)_{u\cdot 1}} \\ \vdots \\ Sim(S_1,S_2)^{(f_u,\omega_k)_{u\cdot k}} \end{bmatrix}_{(u\cdot k)\times 1} \qquad \mathbf{Y}\ni\mathbf{y}_1=[S_1\leftrightarrow S^{\Delta}{}_1]=\begin{bmatrix} Sim(S_1,S_1^{\Delta})^{(f_1,\omega_1)_{1\cdot 1}} \\ \vdots \\ Sim(S_1,S_1^{\Delta})^{(f_1,\omega_k)_{1\cdot k}} \\ \vdots \\ Sim(S_1,S_1^{\Delta})^{(f_u,\omega_1)_{1\cdot u}} \\ \vdots \\ Sim(S_1,S_1^{\Delta})^{(f_u,\omega_k)_{u\cdot k}} \end{bmatrix}_{(u\cdot k)\times 1} \tag{7}$$

where:

$Sim(S_a,S_b)^{(f_m,\omega_j)_i}$ – the ith similarity coefficient of the feature f_m of the objects $S_a, S_b \in \pi_1$ which was determined by means of the method ω_j,

$Sim(S_a,S_b^{\Delta})^{(f_m,\omega_j)_i}$ – the ith similarity coefficient of the feature f_m of the objects $S_a \in \pi_1$ and $S_b \in \pi_2$ which was determined by means of the method ω_j.

3 The Object Feature Reduction Method

The main goal of the investigation is to select the features that allow different objects to be distinguished. Features with low impact on the recognition process should be removed if possible. Features (Table 1) can be compared by means of different methods (Table 2). The features selection and reduction methods are frequently used in practice. One of these methods is Hotelling's discriminant analysis where feature reduction can be conducted automatically [2], [6], [10]. In the basic definition of the one-sample Hotelling's statistics we have n independent vectors of dimension p, observed over time, where p is the number of dependent characteristics (features) of the objects which are being measured. In the approach considered in this paper only a two-class problem will be examined. For a two-class problem, the two-sample T^2 statistics will be performed. In such a case we have two sets of independent vectors of features which form the two observation matrices **X** and **Y**.

$$\mathbf{X}=\begin{bmatrix} x_{11} & x_{12} & \cdots & x_{1n} \\ x_{21} & x_{22} & \cdots & x_{2n} \\ \vdots & \vdots & \vdots & \vdots \\ x_{p1} & x_{p2} & \cdots & x_{pn} \end{bmatrix}=[\mathbf{x}_1,\mathbf{x}_2,...,\mathbf{x}_n],\quad \mathbf{Y}=\begin{bmatrix} y_{11} & y_{12} & \cdots & y_{1m} \\ y_{21} & y_{22} & \cdots & y_{2m} \\ \vdots & \vdots & \vdots & \vdots \\ y_{p1} & y_{p2} & \cdots & y_{pm} \end{bmatrix}=[\mathbf{y}_1,\mathbf{y}_2,...,\mathbf{y}_m]\ , \tag{8}$$

where:

$\mathbf{x}_i = [x_{1i}, x_{2i},...x_{pi}]^T$,

$\mathbf{y}_j = [y_{1j}, y_{2j},..., y_{pj}]^T$.

In the basic version of Hotelling's approach, the ith row of the matrix **X** or **Y** means the ith feature among all of the p features in all observations, while the jth column means the jth observation among all of the n observations. The object's features create the vectors $\mathbf{x}_i$, $\mathbf{y}_j$ and should form a p-dimensional normally distributed population $\mathbf{x}_i \sim N_p(\boldsymbol{\mu},\boldsymbol{\Sigma})$, $\mathbf{y}_i \sim N_p(\boldsymbol{\mu},\boldsymbol{\Sigma})$ [16]. The parameters $\boldsymbol{\mu}$ and $\boldsymbol{\Sigma}$ are unknown, and they have to be estimated. The parameter $\boldsymbol{\mu}$ can be expressed by the mean vectors, separately for the matrix **X** or **Y**:

$$\overline{\mathbf{x}} = \frac{1}{n}\mathbf{Y} = \frac{1}{n}\sum_{i=1}^{n}\mathbf{x}_i = [\overline{x}_1, \overline{x}_2,...,\overline{x}_p]^T , \qquad \overline{\mathbf{y}} = \frac{1}{m}\mathbf{Y} = \frac{1}{m}\sum_{i=1}^{m}\mathbf{y}_i = [\overline{y}_1, \overline{y}_2,...,\overline{y}_p]^T , \tag{9}$$

The variance-covariance matrix $\boldsymbol{\Sigma}$, of dimension $p \times p$, can be estimated by unbiased estimators, separately for the matrix **X** or **Y**:

$$S_1 = \frac{1}{n-1}\sum_{i=1}^{n}(\mathbf{x}_i - \overline{\mathbf{x}})(\mathbf{x}_i - \overline{\mathbf{x}})^T , \qquad S_2 = \frac{1}{m-1}\sum_{i=1}^{m}(\mathbf{y}_i - \overline{\mathbf{y}})(\mathbf{y}_i - \overline{\mathbf{y}})^T \tag{10}$$

In Hotelling's primary, fundamental definition it is assumed that the mean vectors and covariance matrices are the same for both populations. Both of the homogeneous covariance matrices, S_1 and S_2 , are estimators of the common covariance matrix $\boldsymbol{\Sigma}$. A better estimate can be obtained by pooling the two estimates. Hence, for the two-class case, the pooled common variance-covariance matrix will be formed as a maximum likelihood estimator:

$$S = \frac{S_1(n-1) + S_2(m-1)}{n+m-2} \tag{11}$$

$$S = \frac{1}{n+m-2}\left(\sum_{i=1}^{n}(\mathbf{x}_i-\overline{\mathbf{x}})(\mathbf{x}_i-\overline{\mathbf{x}})^T + \sum_{i=1}^{m}(\mathbf{y}_i-\overline{\mathbf{y}})(\mathbf{y}_i-\overline{\mathbf{y}})^T\right) \tag{12}$$

For such an assumption a two-sample Hotelling's T^2 statistic is defined as follows:

$$T^2 = (\overline{\mathbf{x}}-\overline{\mathbf{y}})^T\left[S\left(\frac{1}{n}+\frac{1}{m}\right)\right]^{-1}(\overline{\mathbf{x}}-\overline{\mathbf{y}}) = \frac{n\cdot m}{n+m}(\overline{\mathbf{x}}-\overline{\mathbf{y}})^T S^{-1}(\overline{\mathbf{x}}-\overline{\mathbf{y}}) \tag{13}$$

$$\tilde{F} = \frac{n+m-p-1}{p(n+m-2)}T^2 . \tag{14}$$

The Hotelling's T^2 statistics can be approximated well by means of Snedecor's distribution: $\tilde{F} \sim F_{p,n+m-p-1,\alpha}$, where α denotes an established significance level.

For a given signature, Hotelling's approach allows the removal of the features which have the smallest discriminant power. In practice, discriminant analysis is useful to decide whether a selected "feature-method" pair (f,ω) is important for the classification process. In this procedure, among all possible pairs only pairs with the greatest discriminant power will be left. This method will be called FMS (Feature-Method Selection). For a given signature only its best discriminant features and methods recognizing them will be ultimately selected. The reduction of features can be carried out gradually. In each successive step the feature that causes the smallest reduction of a multidimensional measure of discrimination is eliminated. In practice, it leads to data reduction in the matrices **X** and **Y**. Reduction of the matrices was performed step by step for every accessible "feature-method" pair [6], [10].

1. Taking into consideration the absence of the ith "feature–method" pair, the discriminant measure is computed:

$$\forall\, i \in \{1,\ldots,\#FM,\}\;\; T_i^2(\varepsilon_1,\ldots,\varepsilon_{i-1},\varepsilon_{i+1},\ldots,\varepsilon_q)\,, \tag{15}$$

where q denotes the number of all possible combinations of the "feature-method" pairs and ε_i, as before, denotes an element of the set *FM*. In the first step of the algorithm we assume that $q = u\cdot k$. The reduction procedure always concerns the current pair $\varepsilon_i \prec (f,\omega)_i$, mentioned in Eq. (4).

2. The need for the ith "feature–method" pair can be checked as follows:

$$U_i = T^2(\varepsilon_1,\ldots,\varepsilon_q) - T^2(\varepsilon_1,\ldots,\varepsilon_{i-1},\varepsilon_{i+1},\ldots,\varepsilon_q)\,. \tag{16}$$

3. The value $\tilde{F}$ is calculated:

$$\tilde{F} = (n+m-p-1)\cdot\frac{U_i}{1+T^2(\varepsilon_1,\ldots,\varepsilon_q)-U_i}. \tag{17}$$

Because we have only two classes, the ith pair is redundant if the following condition is fulfilled $\tilde{F} < F_{1,n+m-p-1,\alpha}$. If condition is not satisfied then the similarity factor computed for the actual "feature-method" pair is important and cannot be ignored. If the value of F does not fall into the critical region, the current i^{th} row of the matrices **X** and **Y** is removed. In the successive step the parameter q is decreased, and the algorithm always starts with the new value of the parameter q from the beginning, that is, for $q-1, q-2, \ldots$. Hence, the dimension of the matrices is successively reduced.

4 Object Verification

In the proposed approach the *k*-Nearest Neighbor (*k-NN*) method was applied [4], [19-20]. Genuine signatures came from the database, so these signatures form the first class π_1. The falsified signatures form the second class π_2. Let $\mathbf{S}^{\Omega}$ be a signature of a person Ω which needs to be verified. This person appears himself or herself as a person *Q*, for example. This should be automatically verified. Let the reduced matrixes **X** and **Y** be denoted as $\tilde{\mathbf{X}}$ and $\tilde{\mathbf{Y}}$. After reduction these matrices have the same number of rows (say $r \le u \cdot k$). Both matrices $\tilde{\mathbf{X}}$ and $\tilde{\mathbf{Y}}$ form a new matrix $\mathbf{H} = \left[\tilde{\mathbf{X}}\,\tilde{\mathbf{Y}}\right]_{r \times l}$. The matrix $\mathbf{H}$ includes similarities between all signatures (say person *Q*) stored in the database. Columns of the matrix $\mathbf{H}$ can be treated separately as the vectors **h**. Let the dimension of the matrix $\mathbf{H}$ be defined as $r \times l$, where $l = \binom{c}{2} + (c \cdot d)$; then:

$$\mathbf{H} = \left[\mathbf{h}^1, \mathbf{h}^2, \ldots, \mathbf{h}^l\right] \qquad \mathbf{h}^i = \left[h_1^i, h_2^i, \ldots, h_r^i\right]^T, \tag{18}$$

Hence, if $\mathbf{h}^j \in \tilde{\mathbf{X}} \to \mathbf{h}^j \in \pi_1$ and if $\mathbf{h}^j \in \tilde{\mathbf{Y}} \to \mathbf{h}^j \in \pi_2$, $j = 1, \ldots, l$.

Because the classifier works in the verification mode, the classified person Ω appears in person as a person *Q*, for example. In this stage of verification, the common most distinctive features and signature similarity measures of the person *Q* have just been established. This means that matrix **H** for this signature is known. For this reason only a new vector $\mathbf{h}^{\Omega} = \left[h_1^{\Omega}, h_2^{\Omega}, \ldots, h_r^{\Omega}\right]^T$ of the person Ω is only created:

$$h_i^{\Omega} = Sim(S^{\Omega}, S^{Q})^{(f,\omega)_i}, \qquad i = 1, \ldots, r \tag{19}$$

where:

S^{Ω} – signature to be verified,

S^{Q} – randomly selected original signature of the person *Q*,

$h_i^{\Omega} = Sim(S^{\Omega}, S^{Q})^{(f,\omega)_i}$ – similarity between the signatures S^{Ω} and signature S^{Q}. The similarity was determined with use of the ith pair.

In the next stage, the set D of Euclidean distances between vector $\mathbf{h}^{\Omega}$ and all successive vectors $\mathbf{h}^{i} \in \mathbf{H}$ is determined:

$$D = \left\{ d(\mathbf{h}^{\Omega}, \mathbf{h}^{j} = \left[\sum_{i=1}^{r} \left(h_i - h_i^{j} \right)^2 \right]^{1/2}, \quad j = 1,\ldots,l \right\}. \tag{20}$$

The verified signature S^{Ω} is classified into the class π_1 or π_2. The final classification results are established on the basis of a voting score, which depends on the number of *k* neighbors which belong to the class π_1 or π_2. The works [3] reports that the most suitable value of *k* should be approximated by the square root of the number of complete cases. Hence, in our case, $k = l^{1/2}$. Let $D1$ and $D2$ be the sets of numbers which show how many times signature S^{Ω} has been classified into class π_1 or π_2:

$$d(\mathbf{h}^{\Omega}, \mathbf{h}^{j}) \in D1 \ \text{ if } \ : \mathbf{h}^{j} \to \pi_1, \qquad d(\mathbf{h}^{\Omega}, \mathbf{h}^{j}) \in D2 \ \text{ if } \ : \mathbf{h}^{j} \to \pi_2 \tag{21}$$

Let the cardinality of the sets be denoted by the symbol #, then the classification voting principle can be formulated as follows:

$$S^{\Omega} : \begin{cases} \text{genuine signature of the person } Q & \text{for } \ \#D1 > \#D2 \\ \text{forged signature of the person } Q & \text{for } \ \#D1 \le \#D2 \end{cases} \tag{22}$$

5 Interpretation of the Data

In this section, the verification attempt of a person Ω will be performed. This individual claims to be a person *Q*. Signatures of the person *Q* were divided into two groups – original and forged subjects. The *k*-NN classifier works with the nine neighbors. Let during reduction process the best two discriminant pairs (f_6, ω_2) and (f_3, ω_1) have been selected. It means that $\mathbf{h}^{i}$ vectors have dimensionality of *r*=2. Fig. 2 plots the similarity distribution between all signatures of the person *Q*. In practice, each point (triangle or circle) in this plot has an individual label. For example, label (1-5) represents the similarity between original signatures no. 1 and no. 5 of the person *Q*, while label (8-5F) represents the similarity between original signature no. 8 and forged signature no. 5 of this person. For simplicity, only selected labels are shown. Fig. 2 plots the *k*-NN classifier decision area during classification of the individual Ω and presents the decision-making areas for the trained classifier and shows the class to which a point with specific coordinates would be assigned. Fig. 2 clearly shows that all original and forged signatures of the individual *Q* are distinguished well by means of the clearly visible separation border. Fig. 2 plots also the *k*-NN classifier decision area during classification of the individual Ω. The signature of the person Ω will be recognized as the signature of an individual who wants to obtain unauthorized access to the resources.

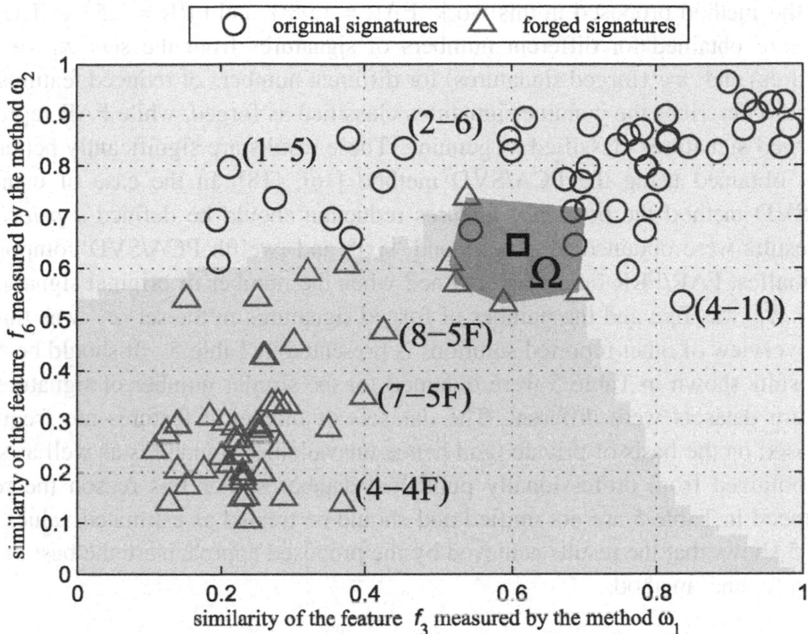

Fig. 1. Mutual similarities between signatures of the person Q and *k-NN* verification area of the person Ω

In practice, the above-presented graphic interpretation is not needed and the main goal of this representation is to show the basic ideas of the method. In practice all computations boil down to determination of the matrix **H**. In the proposed Hotelling reduction approach it is very convenient that appropriate signature features and similarity coefficients (Tables 1 and 2) are always automatically selected

6 Results Obtained

Researches were carried out using 600 signatures obtained from 40 people. For each person 20 genuine and 20 forged signatures have been captured. For each person, ten original ($c = 10$) and five forged ($d = 5$) signatures were taken into consideration. These signatures have been randomly selected from the whole set of signatures. In the experiments all elements of Tables 1 and 2 have been utilized. The analyzed signatures came from the SVC2004 database [11], which contains both genuine signatures and skilled forgeries. In the experiments conducted the captured signatures' features and similarity coefficients, which could be obtained from Tables 1 and 2, were taken into consideration. The achieved levels of the False Acceptance Rate (FAR) and False Rejection Rate (FRR) errors for different methods of features reduction are shown in Tables 3 and 4. Tables show that the smallest FAR/FRR coefficients were obtained using the method proposed in this work: FAR = 1.08% and FRR = 2.53%. These results were obtained for different numbers of signatures from the sets π_1 (original signatures) and π_2 (forged signatures) for different numbers of reduced features. The FRR ratio describes the genuine signatures classified as forged, while FAR represents the forged signatures classified as genuine. These results are significantly better than results obtained using the PCA/SVD method [16], [18]. In the case of using the PCA/SVD method the boundary features reduction should be defined *a priori*. The best results were obtained for the second, sixth and twelfth PCA/SVD components. The smallest FAR/FRR ratio was obtained when the number of original signatures in the set π_1 was five and the number of forged signatures in the set π_2 was three. A brief overview of other reported solutions is presented in Table 5. It should be noted, that results shown in Table 5 were obtained for the similar number of signatures but signature datasets were different. The datasets of biometric features are frequently composed on the basis of private (and hence unavailable) signatures as well as signatures obtained from professionally published databases. For this reason the results announced in Table 5 are not unified and should be treated as estimated values only. Table 5 shows that the results achieved by the proposed approach are the best in comparison to other methods.

Table 3. False Accepted Rate (FAR) different number of reference signatures, and different dimension of features vectors

Number of signatures in the set $\pi_1 \cup \pi_2$		FAR [%]						
π_1 (*genuine*)	π_2 (*forged*)	FMS	Vector dimension after using PCA			Vector dimension after using SVD		
			2	6	12	2	6	12
3	1	6.34	8.14	6.32	6.75	6.14	7.12	**5.62**
5	3	**1.08**	2.22	2.62	2.21	2.52	2.12	2.25
10	4	**1.67**	3.14	3.44	3.29	3.15	3.21	3.94

Table 4. False Rejection Rate (FRR) different number of reference signatures, and different dimension of features vectors

Number of signatures in the set $\pi_1 \cup \pi_2$		FRR [%]						
π_1 (*genuine*)	π_2 (*forged*)	FMS	Vector dimension after using PCA			Vector dimension after using SVD		
			2	6	12	2	6	12
3	1	7.14	5.31	6.55	5.40	6.33	5.60	**4.90**
5	3	**2.53**	2.58	2.78	4.94	4.35	4.78	4.05
10	4	**2.60**	2.83	3.06	5.25	3.96	4.84	4.60

Table 5. Comparison of performance of various signature recognition systems[1)]

The approach	FAR	FRR	Signature recognition system *off-line*	*on-line*
Proposed approach – Hotelling's reduction and k-NN	**1.08**	**2.53**	+	+
Exterior Contours and Shape Features	6.90	6.50	+	
HMM and Graphometric Features	23.00	1.00	+	
Virtual Support Vector Machine	13.00	16.00	+	
Genetic Algorithm	1.80	8.51	+	
Variable Length Segmentation and HMM	4.00	12.00		+
Dynamic Feature of Pressure	6.80	10.80		+
Consistency Functions	1.00	7.00		+
On line SRS - Digitizer Tablet	1.10	3.09		+

1) The selected best results based on the report [8].

7 Conclusions

The originality of the proposed approach follows from the fact that the classifier utilizes not only extracted features, but also the best similarity measures which are dedicated to a given problem. From the investigation conducted it follows that the FMS method gives the best object recognition level compared to the two other popular methods, where object features are analyzed. It should be noticed that the described FMS method can be applied to any domain where feature reduction needs to be done, where the number of features is large and only some of them have discriminant properties. In the proposed approach space features are precisely connected with the set of similarity measures which can be used in the recognition process. Such an approach has not yet been applied.

References

1. Porwik, P., Doroz, R., Wrobel, K.: A new signature similarity measure. In: World Congress on Nature and Biologically Inspired Computing (NABIC 2009), pp. 1021–1026 (2009)
2. Ibrahi, M.T., Kyan, M.T.L., Guan, L.: On-line signature verification using most discriminating features and Fisher linear discriminant analysis. In: 10th IEEE Int. Symposium on Multimedia, Berkeley CA, pp. 172–177 (2008)
3. Józwik, A., Serpico, S.B., Roli, F.: A parallel network of modified 1-NN and k-NN classifiers-application to remote-sensing image classification. Pattern Recognition Letters 19(1), 57–62 (1998)
4. Koprowski, R., Wrobel, Z., Zieleznik, W.: Automatic Ultrasound Image Analysis in Hashimoto's Disease. In: Martínez-Trinidad, J.F., Carrasco-Ochoa, J.A., Kittler, J. (eds.) MCPR 2010. LNCS, vol. 6256, pp. 98–106. Springer, Heidelberg (2010)

5. Porwik, P., Wróbel, K., Doroz, R.: Signature recognition method by means of the windows technique. Int. J. Image Processing and Communication 14(2/3), 43–50 (2009)
6. Guyon, I., Elisseeff, A.: An introduction to variable and feature selection. Journal of Machine Learning Research 3, 1157–1182 (2003)
7. Sung-Hyug, C.: Comprehensive survey on distance/similarity Measures between probability density functions. Int. J. of Mathematical Models and Methods in Applied Sciences 1, 300–307 (2007)
8. Bharadi, V.A., Kekre, H.B.: Off-line signature recognition systems. Int. J. of Computer Applications 1(27), 48–56 (2010)
9. Jolliffe, I.T.: Principal component analysis. Springer Series in Statistics. Springer (2002)
10. Ryan, T.P.: Statistical methods for quality improvement. John Wiley and Sons (2011)
11. http://www.cse.ust.hk/svc2004
12. Demšar, J.: Statistical comparisons of classifiers over multiple data sets. Journal of Machine Learning Research 7, 1–30 (2006)
13. Model, F., Konig, T., Piepenbrock, C., Adorjan, P.: Statistical process control for large scale microarray experiments. Bioinformatics 18, 155S–163S (2002)
14. Kurzyński, M., Wozniak, M.: Combining classifiers under probabilistic models: experimental comparative analysis of methods. Expert Systems 29(4), 374–393 (2012)
15. Kudlacik, P., Porwik, P.: A new approach to signature recognition using the fuzzy method. Pattern Anaysis and Applications, 1–13 (2012), DOI: 10.1007/s10044-012-0283-9
16. Hardle, W., Simar, L.: Applied multivariate statistical analysis. Springer, Heidelberg (2003)
17. Williams, J.D., Woodall, W.H., Birch, J.B., Sullivan, J.H.: Distributional properties of the multivariate T^2 statistic based on the successive differences covariance matrix estimator. Technical Report no. 04-5, Department of Statistics, Virginia Polytechnic Institute and State University (2004)
18. Kirkwood, B.R., Sterne, J.A.C.: Essentials of medical statistics. 2nd edn. Wiley-Blackwell (2003)
19. Shakhnarovich, G., Darrell, T., Indyk, P.: Nearest-neighbor methods in learning and vision: theory and practice. In: Neural Information Processing. The MIT Press (2006)
20. Ougiaroglou, S., Evangelidis, G., Dervos, D.A.: An Adaptive Hybrid and Cluster-Based Model for Speeding Up the *k*-NN Classifier. In: Corchado, E., Snášel, V., Abraham, A., Woźniak, M., Graña, M., Cho, S.-B. (eds.) HAIS 2012, Part II. LNCS, vol. 7209, pp. 163–175. Springer, Heidelberg (2012)
21. Koprowski, R., Teper, S.J., Weglarz, B., et al.: Fully automatic algorithm for the analysis of vessels in the angiographic image of the eye fundus. Biomedical Engineering on Line 11(35), doi:10.1186/1475-925X-11-35
22. Doroz, R., Wrobel, K.: Method of Signature Recognition with the Use of the Mean Differences. In: 31st International Conference on Information Technology Interfaces (ITI 2009), Croatia, pp. 231–235 (2009)

Analysis of Human Performance as a Measure of Mental Fatigue

André Pimenta, Davide Carneiro, Paulo Novais, and José Neves

CCTC/DI - Universidade do Minho
Braga, Portugal
{apimenta,dcarneiro,pjon,jneves}@di.uminho.pt

Abstract. In our daily life, we often have the feeling of being exhausted due to mental or physical work, and a sense of performance degradation in the execution of simple tasks. The maximum capacity of operation and performance of an individual, whether physical or mental, usually also decreases gradually as the day progresses. The loss of these resources is linked to the onset of fatigue, which is particularly noticeable in long and demanding tasks or repetitive jobs. However, good management of the working time and effort invested in each task, as well as the effect of breaks at work, can result in better performance and better mental health, delaying the effects of fatigue. This paper details a non-invasive approach on the monitoring of fatigue of a human being, based on the analysis of the performance of his interaction with the computer.

Keywords: Fatigue, Mental Fatigue, Performance, Behavioural Analysis, Classification.

1 Introduction

In today's busy society, people push their limits in order to find a balance between ever ambitious goals and time to dedicate to enjoyable moments, family or personal projects [1]. This balance, when it comes to exist, is generally obtained at the expenses of less time for rest and sleep, with an impact on the well-being and health of the individual. Fatigue, above all others, must be considered here. The effects of fatigue may not be felt immediately. Nonetheless, when prolonged it may have serious consequences on health and safety at the workplace as well as on labour productivity [2]. Ultimately, fatigue can put people who have safety-sensitive occupations at risk, as any mistake can lead to the loss of their own lives or those of others [3].

This paper presents a new approach on the problem of fatigue detection and monitoring, that can be included in the umbrella of Hybrid Artificial Intelligent Systems [4,5]. It looks at the effects of fatigue on the performance of the individual's interaction with the computer. This approach can be deemed both non-invasive and non-intrusive as it relies on the observation of the individual's use of the mouse and keyboard. It builds on a previous study, now to address the evolution of fatigue throughout the day and the role that task complexity and Circadian Rhythm play in the degradation of performance.

M. Polycarpou et al. (Eds.): HAIS 2014, LNAI 8480, pp. 389–401, 2014.
© Springer International Publishing Switzerland 2014

1.1 Circadian Rhythm, Environment and Their Role on Fatigue

In studying fatigue one must acknowledge the major role of the biological clock, i.e., one cannot expect to beat one's rhythm and biological need to rest. Indeed, the role of our biological clock goes beyond compelling the body to fall asleep and to wake up again. It also modulates our hour-to-hour waking behaviour, which in turn affects our sense of fatigue, alertness and performance, generating circadian rhythmicity in almost all neuro-behavioural variables [6]. This means that there is a natural fluctuation of the level of fatigue we experience during the day, that is independent of the intensity of the tasks we perform. It can be seen as a base-level of fatigue.

The context and environment in which the individual carries out the activity are also very important in determining the level of fatigue during the day. Indeed, factors such as workload, distractions, periods of boredom, motivational factors, stress, food intake, posture, ambient temperature, background noise, lighting conditions or drug intake (e.g., caffeine) are examples of contextual variables that can have a positive or negative influence on the level of fatigue of a human being [7]. Smith and Miles conducted a study which analyses the effects of lunch on cognitive vigilance tasks [8]. The authors analysed the performance of individuals who did not take lunch before performing tasks compared to those who took, to show some differences between morning and afternoon performance in subjects who abstained from eating lunch.

Figure 1 details the influence of several environment variables and external factors in task performance, as well as their relationship. Black boxes depict task characteristics and while red ones depict characteristics of the Human operator. The dotted line indicates a positive correlation (measured with the Pearson product-moment correlation coefficient) between actual, measurable task workload and the worker's perception of that workload (estimated with a mental workload tool such as NASA-TLX [9] or SWAT [10]).

1.2 Human Performance as a Measure of Fatigue

When under the effect of prolonged excessive mental workload, inadequate sleep patterns, or circadian effects, Humans may exhibit slowed cognitive processes or may not respond at all to the stimuli and information received. This is generally due to the amount of information exceeding the brain's processing capacity at that moment. In contrast, when the mental workload is significantly below the adequate level, the individual tends to get tired and bored, which will likely result in an increase in the number of errors in the tasks being performed [12]. Performance as a measure of fatigue has been used previously as an objective measure of fatigue in humans. Morris & Miller, for example, conducted a study which analysed the performance of pilots during simulated flight as a means of detecting and measuring fatigue [13]. The authors have shown that the decrease in flight performance occurs due to fatigue.

Consequently, the measurement of the performance of the individual while performing a task results in an objective way of measuring fatigue in the human being as a relationship between the two exists. Usually, tasks that imply

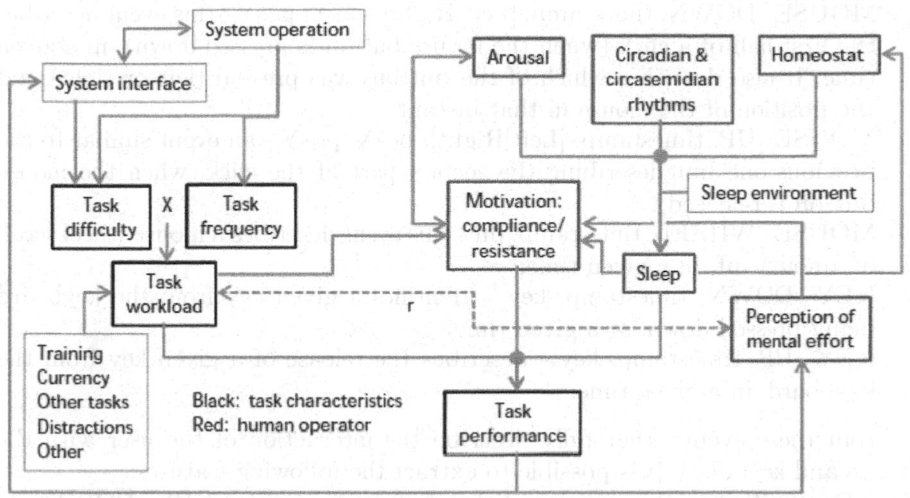

Fig. 1. Environment variables and external factors on Mental Performance Task (Source: [11])

excessive mental and physical workload as well as very low workload (observed in monotonous and repetitive activities) result in significant performance decrements. Thus being, the loss of performance due to fatigue can be studied as a function that takes as input the duration of the task and the quantity and/or quality of the work carried out [2,14].

The challenge lies in the fact that a decrease in the performance is often not "seen" immediately, which may be explained by the concept of *reverse capacity* [15]. The theory of reverse capacity states that an individual rarely works at his maximum capacity, and can thus temporarily absorb the load of cognitive or physical additional work while still maintaining performance indicators, as long as their inverse capacity is not exceeded. For this reason, the effects of fatigue may not be immediately visible [15]. The effects of fatigue on performance, in particular, may only be felt in the course of time, when it may be to late to avoid them.

2 A Non-Invasive Approach to Fatigue Monitoring

This paper introduces a system for detecting and monitoring mental fatigue through the analysis and measurement of human performance indicators. As previously postulated in [16] it uses the keyboard and mouse as sensors of user performance. Specifically, the user is monitored through particular Operating System events fired from the use of the computer's mouse and keyboard:

- MOV, timestamp, posX, posY - an event describing the movement of the mouse, in a given time, to coordinates (posX, posY) in the screen;

- MOUSE_DOWN, timestamp, [Left|Right], posX, posY - this event describes the first half of a click (when the mouse button is pressed down), in a given time. It also describes which of the buttons was pressed (left or right) and the position of the mouse in that instant;
- MOUSE_UP, timestamp, [Left|Right], posX, posY - an event similar to the previous one but describing the second part of the click, when the mouse button is released;
- MOUSE_WHEEL, timestamp, dif - this event describes a mouse wheel scroll of amount dif, in a given time;
- KEY_DOWN, timestamp, key - identifies a given key from the keyboard being pressed down, at a given time;
- KEY_UP, timestamp, key - describes the release of a given key from the keyboard, in a given time;

From these events, that fully describe the interaction of the user with the mouse and keyboard, it is possible to extract the following features:
KEY DOWN TIME - the timespan between two consecutive KEY_DOWN and KEY_UP events, i.e., for how long was a given key pressed.
UNITS - milliseconds

TIME BETWEEN KEYS - the timespan between two consecutive KEY_UP and KEY_DOWN events, i.e., how long did the individual took to press another key.
UNITS - milliseconds

MOUSE VELOCITY - The distance travelled by the mouse (in pixels) over the time (in milliseconds). The velocity is computed for each interval defined by two consecutive MOUSE_UP and MOUSE_DOWN events. Let us assume two consecutive MOUSE_UP and MOUSE_DOWN events, *mup* and *mdo*, respectively in the coordinates $(x1, y1)$ and $(x2, y2)$, that took place respectively in the instants $time_1$ and $time_2$. Let us also assume two vectors *posx* and *posy*, of size n, holding the coordinates of the consecutive MOUSE_MOV events between *mup* and *mdo*. The velocity between the two clicks is given by $r\_dist/(time_2 - time_1)$, in which r_dist represents the distance travelled by the mouse and is given by equation 1.
UNITS - pixels/milliseconds

$$r\_dist = \sum_{i=0}^{n-1} \sqrt{(posx_{i+1} - posx_i)^2 + (posy_{i+1} - posy_i)^2} \tag{1}$$

MOUSE ACCELERATION - The velocity of the mouse (in pixels/milliseconds) over the time (in milliseconds). A value of acceleration is computed for each interval defined by two consecutive MOUSE_UP and MOUSE_DOWN events, using the intervals and data computed for the Velocity.
UNITS - pixels/milliseconds^2

TIME BETWEEN CLICKS - the timespan between two consecutive MOUSE_UP and MOUSE_DOWN events, i.e., how long did it took the individual to perform

another click.
UNITS - milliseconds

DOUBLE CLICK DURATION - the timespan between two consecutive MOUSE_UP events, whenever this timespan is inferior to 200 milliseconds. Wider timespans are not considered double clicks.
UNITS - milliseconds

AVERAGE EXCESS OF DISTANCE - this feature measures the average excess of distance that the mouse travelled between each two consecutive MOUSE_UP and MOUSE_DOWN events. Let us assume two consecutive MOUSE_UP and MOUSE_DOWN events, *mup* and *mdo*, respectively in the coordinates $(x1, y1)$ and $(x2, y2)$. To compute this feature, first it is measured the distance in straight line between the coordinates of *mup* and *mdo* as depicted in equation 2.

$$s\_dist = \sqrt{(x2 - x1)^2 + (y2 - y1)^2} \tag{2}$$

Then, it is measured the distance actually travelled by the mouse by summing the distance between each two consecutive MOUSE_MV events. Let us assume two vectors *posx* and *posy*, of size n, holding the coordinates of the consecutive MOUSE_MV events between *mup* and *mdo*. The distance actually travelled by the mouse, *real_dist* is given by equation 1. The average excess of distance between the two consecutive clicks is thus given by r_dist/s_dist.
UNITS - pixels

AVERAGE DISTANCE OF THE MOUSE TO THE STRAIGHT LINE - in a few words, this feature measures the average distance of the mouse to the straight line defined between two consecutive clicks. Let us assume two consecutive MOUSE_UP and MOUSE_DOWN events, *mup* and *mdo*, respectively in the coordinates $(x1, y1)$ and $(x2, y2)$. Let us also assume two vectors *posx* and *posy*, of size n, holding the coordinates of the consecutive MOUSE_MOV events between *mup* and *mdo*. The sum of the distances between each position and the straight line defined by the points $(x1, y1)$ and $(x2, y2)$ is given by equation 3, in which *ptLineDist* returns the distance between the specified point and the closest point on the infinitely-extended line defined by $(x1, y1)$ and $(x2, y2)$. The average distance of the mouse to the straight line defined by two consecutive clicks is this given by s_dists/n.
UNITS - pixels

$$s\_dists = \sum_{i=0}^{n-1} ptLineDist(posx_i, posy_i) \tag{3}$$

DISTANCE OF THE MOUSE TO THE STRAIGHT LINE - this feature is similar to the previous one in the sense that it will compute the *s_dists* between two consecutive MOUSE_UP and MOUSE_DOWN events, *mup* and *mdo*, according to equation 3. However, it returns this sum rather than the average value during

the path.
UNITS - pixels

SIGNED SUM OF ANGLES - with this feature the aim is to determine if the movement of the mouse tends to "turn" more to the right or to the left. Let us assume three consecutive MOUSE_MOVE events, $mov1, mov2$ and $mov3$, respectively in the coordinates $(x1, y1)$, $(x2, y2)$ and $(x3, y3)$. The angle α between the first line (defined by $(x1, y1)$ and $(x2, y2)$) and the second line (defined by $(x2, y2)$ and $(x3, y3)$) is given by $degree(x1, y1, x2, y2, x3, y3) = \tan(y3 - y2, x3 - x2) - \tan(y2 - y1, x2 - x1)$. Let us now assume two consecutive MOUSE_UP and MOUSE_DOWN events, mup and mdo. Let us also assume two vectors $posx$ and $posy$, of size n, holding the coordinates of the consecutive MOUSE_MOV events between mup and mdo. The signed sum of angles between these two clicks is given by equation 4.
UNITS - degrees

$$s\_angle = \sum_{i=0}^{n-2} degree(posx_i, posy_i, posx_{i+1}, posy_{i+1}, posx_{i+2}, posy_{i+2}) \quad (4)$$

ABSOLUTE SUM OF ANGLES - this feature is very similar to the previous one. However, it seeks to find only how much the mouse "turned", independently of the direction to which it turned. In that sense, the only difference is the use of the absolute of the value returned by function $degree(x1, y1, x2, y2, x3, y3)$, as depicted in equation 5.
UNITS - degrees

$$s\_angle = \sum_{i=0}^{n-2} \mid degree(posx_i, posy_i, posx_{i+1}, posy_{i+1}, posx_{i+2}, posy_{i+2}) \mid \quad (5)$$

DISTANCE BETWEEN CLICKS - represents the total distance travelled by the mouse between two consecutive clicks, i.e., between each two consecutive MOUSE_UP and MOUSE_DOWN events. Let us assume two consecutive MOUSE_UP and MOUSE_DOWN events, mup and mdo, respectively in the coordinates $(x1, y1)$ and $(x2, y2)$. Let us also assume two vectors $posx$ and $posy$, of size n, holding the coordinates of the consecutive MOUSE_MOV events between mup and mdo. The total distance travelled by the mouse is given by equation 1.

From these features it is possible to obtain a measure of the user's performance (e.g. an increased distance between clicks or sum of angles represents decreased performance). Once information about the individual's performance exists in these terms, it is possible to start monitoring his fatigue, in real-time, and without the need for any explicit or conscious interaction. This makes this approach especially suited to be used in work environments in which people use computers as it requires no change in their working routines. This is the main advantage of this work, especially when compared to more traditional approaches that still rely on questionnaires (with issues concerning wording or question construction), specific hardware (that has additional costs and is frequently intrusive) or the availability of human experts.

3 Case Study

In order to assess the validity of the approach described in the previous section a case study was implemented aimed at collecting data over a relatively long period of time. This allowed us to determine if and how people are affected by fatigue in each of the mentioned features.

3.1 Participants

The participants, twenty seven in total (20 men, 7 women) were students from the University of Minho who volunteered to participate. Their age ranged between 18 and 30. The following requirements were established to select, among all the volunteers, the ones that participated: (1) familiarity and proficiency with the use of the computer; (2) use of the computer on a daily basis and throughout the day; (3) owning at least one personal computer. These restrictions constituted no problem as a large slice of the population of out institution, and particularly the ones affiliated to the Department of Informatics, fulfil the requirements.

3.2 Methodology

The methodology followed to implement the study was devised to be as minimally intrusive as the approach it aims to support. Participants were provided with an application for logging the previously mentioned events of the mouse and keyboard. This application, which maintained the confidentiality of the keys used, needed only to be installed in the participant's primary computer and would run on the background, starting automatically with the Operating System. The only explicit interaction needed from the part of the user was the input of very basic information on the first run, including the identification and age.

This application was kept running for approximately one month, collecting interaction data whenever there was interaction with the computer. During the whole process, participants did not need to perform any additional task and were asked to perform their activities regularly, whether they were work or leisure-related, as they would if they were not participating on the study.

Finally, when the period of one month ended, participants were asked to send in the file containing the log of their interaction during the duration of the study. The data collected was used to build the features described previously. The resulting dataset as well as the process by means of which data were analysed is described in the following sub-sections.

3.3 Data Selection

As previously stated, the data collected spans a period of approximately 30 complete days of computer use, in a work context as well as in a leisure one. From this data, we extracted particular moments for analysis.

Specifically, four distinct periods of one our each were selected in order to analyze the effect of Circadian rhythm and the effect of acute fatigue in a work day: (1) the start of the day, when the user is mentally fresh; (2) immediately before lunch break; (3) after lunch break; and (4) the end of the day, when the individual is most fatigued. This selection stems from the willingness to study the differences between the beginning and end of the day as well the potential effect of a lunch break. Lunch break is automatically inferred from the lack of interaction during a relative long time in a given period.

3.4 Statistical Data Analysis

To determine the effects of acute fatigue on the interaction patterns of an individual it is necessary to determine that the distributions of the data collected in each moment are statistically and significantly different. To this aim, the following approach was implemented.

First, it was determined, using the Pearson's chi-squared test, that most of the distributions of the data collected are not normal. Given this, the Kruskal-Wallis test was used in the subsequent analysis. This test is a non-parametric statistical method for testing whether samples originate from the same distribution. It is used for comparing more than two samples that are independent, and thus prove the existence of distinct behaviours. The null hypothesis considered is: H_0 : all samples have identical distribution functions against the alternative hypothesis that at least two samples have different distribution functions. For each set of samples compared, the test returns a $p-value$, with a small $p-value$ suggesting that it is unlikely that H_0 is true. Thus, for every Kruskal-wallis test whose $p-value < \alpha$, the difference is considered to be statistically significant, i.e., H_0 is rejected. In this work a value of $\alpha = 0.05$ is considered, a standard value generally accepted by research.

This statistical test is performed for each of the features considered, with the intention of determining if there are statistically significant differences between the several distributions of data, which will in turn confirm the existence of effects of fatigue on the interaction patterns.

Table 1 details, for each feature, the percentage of participants whose interaction patterns were significantly affected by fatigue and the average value of the $p-value$.

After having determined that a large majority of the participants were indeed significantly affected by acute fatigue, it was analysed the evolution of user performance throughout the day. Figure 2 shows these effects for a particular participant, in two different features and in each of the four previously mentioned moments. It is possible to see how, during the day, the excess of distance between clicks and the time between keys increases gradually. Both examples essentially depict a significant loss of performance.

Table 1. Percentage of participants whose interaction patterns were significantly affected by fatigue, in each feature, and the average value of the $p - value$

Metric	significant	p-value
Time between keys	100%	9.88e-74
Key down time	88.0%	7.42e-16
Mouse Acceleration	100%	3.83e-284
Mouse Velocity	100%	1.02e-126
Average Excess of Distance	94.4%	1.36e-13
Distance Between Clicks	94.4%	2.83e-07
Click Durations	94.4%	4.46e-143
Errors per key	77.7%	6.54e-21

In order to understand the effects of fatigue during the day it is useful to look at the evolution of the features. Figures 3 and 4 depict, respectively, the evolution of the velocity of the mouse and the key down time during the day, for a particular participant. They essentially depict the same trend of decreasing efficiency: the velocity of the mouse decreases from nearly 0.9 pixels/ms to 0.6 pixels/ms while the key down time increases from 86 ms to more than 90 ms. Both pictures belong to the same participant and the same day, between 9:27 AM to 5:50 PM.

Both the statistical differences and the trend identified show that there is indeed a gradual loss of performance over the day. Moreover, it is also proved that this loss of performance can be detected through non-invasive methods, specifically by looking at how the user interacts with the computer.

3.5 Classification Results

Having proved the existence of a change on the behaviours over the day due to fatigue, as well as the loss of performance in the use of mouse and keyboard, the final step is to train a classifier that can accurately quantify the level of fatigue of an individual.

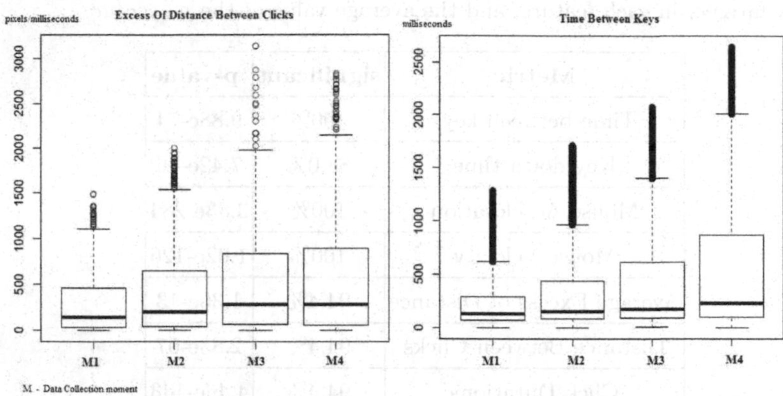

Fig. 2. The effects of fatigue on the excess of distance (left) and on the time between keys (right) for a participant, in each of the four moments

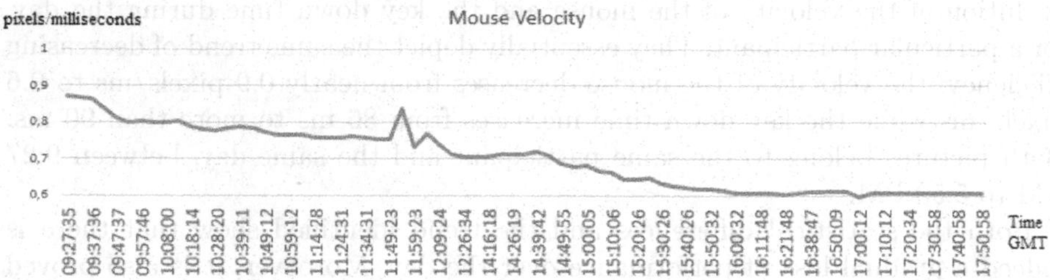

Fig. 3. Fatigue causes a gradual and consistent decrease in the mouse velocity over the day

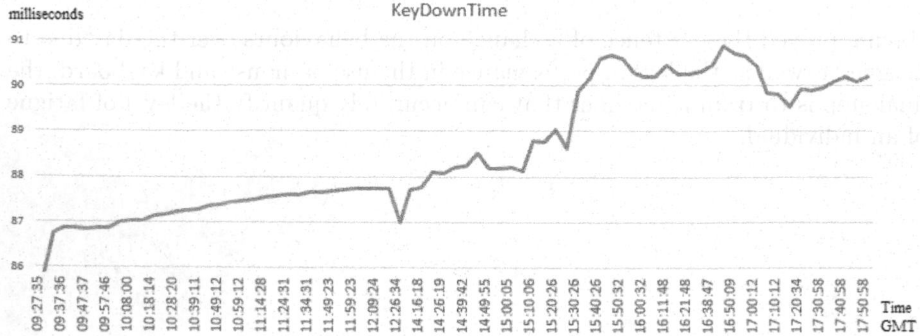

Fig. 4. Fatigue causes a gradual and consistent increase in the key down time over the day

Table 2. Results of several classifiers on WEKA

data set	Correctly Classified	Incorrectly Classified	Kappa s	MAE	ROC Area	RMSE
MultilayerPerceptron	92,97%	7.03%	0.83	0.09	0.939	0.240
KNN (k=10)	**96,85%**	**3.15%**	**0.92**	**0.04**	**0.992**	**0.155**
BayesNet	88,68%	11.31%	0.71	0.13	0.887	0.292
Regression	96,89%	3.10%	0.92	0.07	0.981	0.167

To this aim, the performance of several classifiers using the data collected was assessed. Table 2 depicts the performance of these classifiers, with the KNN holding the best results although all of them behave fairly good. These tests were performed with a dataset with a total of 2514 instances and 10-fold cross method.

To build the dataset it was used part of the data collected in the case study described. Specifically, we selected instances from the two most different distributions: instances resulting from periods where the performance is lower(M4) were labelled as *Fatigue*, and instances resulting from periods of better performance (M1) were labelled as *Normal*. The dataset describes 10 attributes: key down time, time between keys, error per key, mouse acceleration, mouse velocity, distance between clicks, click duration and average excess of distance. These attributes were selected to represent the features that revealed, in the overall, to be more significantly affected by fatigue in the moments considered.

Given this, we are currently using the k-Nearest Neighbor algorithm (k-NN) for classifying the interaction of a user with the computer in terms of fatigue. This is a non-parametric method that consists of a majority vote of its neighbours, with the object being assigned to the most common class among its k nearest neighbours. In this specific case, a value of $k = 10$ was used.

4 Conclusion

This paper presented an approach for measuring the level of fatigue of an individual through the analysis of his performance. This is achieved by analysing the interaction patterns of the individual with the mouse and keyboard. Thus being, it relies on behavioural analysis rather on traditional physiological sensors or questionnaires, being non-invasive, non-intrusive and objective.

The results achieved from the implementation of the case study detail prove that it is indeed possible to analyse and quantify human performance through the use of the mouse and keyboard, and this is a valid way to measure fatigue. It was also observed that the trend is towards the decrease in the performance of the interaction, visible through a generalized slower use of both the mouse and the keyboard or an increased distance between consecutive clicks.

This work opens the door to the development of real-time systems for fatigue monitoring through performance indicators. These can contribute to the development of healthier habits and even improve the quantity and quality of the work produced. All in all, such approaches can have a positive effect on both the worker and the institution. Nonetheless, we acknowledge that more accurate approaches can be developed when considering more specific context information not yet considered, such as the type of the task or workload, as well as environment information. This will be essential to develop accurate approaches to very specific domains in which the interaction with the peripherals is necessarily different than the one we studied in this paper. Moreover, we will also validate this approach against other existing ones, namely self-report mechanisms and EEG.

Acknowledgments. This work was developed in the context of the project CAMCoF - Context-aware Multimodal Communication Framework funded by ERDF - European Regional Development Fund through the COMPETE Programme (operational programme for competitiveness) and by National Funds through the FCT - Fundação para a Ciência e a Tecnologia (Portuguese Foundation for Science and Technology) within project FCOMP-01-0124-FEDER-028980. The work of Davide Carneiro is supported by an FCT post-doctoral grant (PTDC/EEI-SII/1386/2012).

References

1. Williamson, R.J., Purcell, S., Sterne, A., Wessely, S., Hotopf, M., Farmer, A., Sham, P.C.: The relationship of fatigue to mental and physical health in a community sample. Social psychiatry and psychiatric epidemiology 40(2), 126–132 (2005)
2. Tucker, P.: The impact of rest breaks upon accident risk, fatigue and performance: a review. Work & Stress 17(2), 123–137 (2003)
3. Jaber, M.Y., Neumann, W.P.: Modelling worker fatigue and recovery in dual-resource constrained systems. Computers & Industrial Engineering 59(1), 75–84 (2010)
4. Woźniak, M., Graña, M., Corchado, E.: A survey of multiple classifier systems as hybrid systems. Information Fusion 16(0), 3–17 (2014); Special Issue on Information Fusion in Hybrid Intelligent Fusion Systems
5. Borrajo, M., B.B.C.E.B.J.C.J.: Hybrid neural intelligent system to predict business failure in small-to-medium-size enterprises. International Journal of Neural Systems 21(04), 277–296 (2011); PMID: 21809475
6. Harris, W.: Fatigue, circadian rhythm, and truck accidents. In: Vigilance, pp. 133–146. Springer, Heidelberg (1977)
7. Folkard, S., Tucker, P.: Shift work, safety and productivity. Occupational Medicine 53(2), 95–101 (2003)
8. Smith, A.P., Miles, C.: The effects of lunch on cognitive vigilance tasks. Ergonomics 29(10), 1251–1261 (1986)
9. Hart, S.G., Staveland, L.E.: Development of nasa-tlx (task load index): Results of empirical and theoretical research. Advances in Psychology 52, 139–183 (1988)
10. Reid, G.B., Nygren, T.E.: The subjective workload assessment technique: A scaling procedure for measuring mental workload. Advances in Psychology 52, 185–218 (1988)
11. Turner, R.: The handbook of operator fatigue. Ergonomics 56(9), 1486–1486 (2013)

12. McClernon, C.K., Miller, J.C.: Variance as a measure of performance in an aviation context. The International Journal of Aviation Psychology 21(4), 397–412 (2011)
13. Morris, T., Miller, J.C.: Electrooculographic and performance indices of fatigue during simulated flight. Biological Psychology 42(3), 343–360 (1996)
14. Tanabe, S., Nishihara, N.: Productivity and fatigue. Indoor Air 14(s7), 126–133 (2004)
15. Kahneman, D.: Remarks on attention control. Acta Psychologica 33, 118–131 (1970)
16. Pimenta, A., Carneiro, D., Novais, P., Neves, J.: Monitoring mental fatigue through the analysis of keyboard and mouse interaction patterns. In: Pan, J.-S., Polycarpou, M.M., Woźniak, M., de Carvalho, A.C.P.L.F., Quintián, H., Corchado, E. (eds.) HAIS 2013. LNCS, vol. 8073, pp. 222–231. Springer, Heidelberg (2013)

CA-Based Model for Hantavirus Disease between Host Rodents

E. García Merino[1], E. García Sánchez[2], J.E. García Sánchez[2], and A. Martín del Rey[3]

[1] Department of Health
IES Martínez Uribarri, Salamanca, Spain
engarme@gmail.com

[2] Department of Preventive Medicine, Public Health and Clinic Microbiology
Faculty of Medicine, University of Salamanca, Salamanca, Spain
{engarsan,joegas}@usal.es

[3] Department of Applied Mathematics
Institute of Fundamental Physics and Mathematics,
University of Salamanca, Salamanca, Spain
delrey@usal.es

Abstract. A new mathematical model to simulate the hantavirus disease between a population of rodents is introduced. It is based on the use of a two-dimensional cellular automaton where the cells stand for uniform portions of the terrain and the state of each cell can be either empty (without any rodent), susceptible (there is only one susceptible rodent placed in it) or infected (there is one infected rodent in the cell). Simulations about the evolution of the different classes of cells and the number of susceptible and infected rodents are obtained and analyzed.

Keywords: Cellular automata, Hantavirus, Epidemic disease, Mathematical modelling.

1 Introduction

Hantavirus Pulmonary Syndrome (HPS for short) is a severe, and sometimes lethal, respiratory disease in humans which is caused by infection with the hantavirus. This disease is transmitted to humans by rodents, specially deer mice (*Peromyscus maniculatus*), cotton rats (genus *Sigmodon*), rice rats (*Oryzomys palustris*) and white-footed mice (*Peromyscus leucopus*). Fortunately, the virus does not spread between humans or, at least, no cases of HPS have been reported in which the virus was transmitted from one person to another ([7]). The hantavirus is found in rodent urine, saliva and droppings and consequently human infection occurs through contact with any of these contaminents. Human infection occurs sporadically and specially in rural areas (the suitable habitat for rodent hosts); cases of HPS have been confirmed elsewhere in North and South America (see [5,10]).

The hantaviruses are members of the family *Bunyaviridae*, which are enveloped, single-stranded, mostly negative-sense RNA viruses. They have three

M. Polycarpou et al. (Eds.): HAIS 2014, LNAI 8480, pp. 402–414, 2014.
© Springer International Publishing Switzerland 2014

genomic segments: large, medium, and small, including three structural proteins: glycoproteins G1 and G2, and nucleoprotein N. The hantavirus does not appear to have an arthropod vector. The hantavirus causes persistent asymptomatic infections in the host rodents, and each hantavirus strain is perpetuated in only its single or few specific genus or species of rodent. There are several distinct, regional hantaviruses: Hantaan virus the causative agent of the Korean hemorrhagic fever, Seoul virus, Sin Nombre virus (previously, Muerto Canyon virus, and also known as Four Corners virus), Puumala virus, Dobrava or Belgrade virus, Baltimore rat virus or New York virus, Thai virus, etc.

In nature, the transmission of hantavirus among rodents is exclusively horizontal and it occurs via inhalation of infected aerosols, through saliva or excreta, biting, and other aggressive behavioral interactions (see, for example, [4]). Transmission of virus between laboratory rodents is also horizontal: the hantavirus can spread from an infected rodent to a susceptible one within the same cage or through infected bedding (see, for example [6]). The viral infection is defined by two phases: (1) an acute phase which is associated with high virus titers, and (2) a chronic phase associated with lower virus titers and the continued shedding of virus in rodent's excreta.

Hantavirus is associated with seasonal changes which concur with the life cycle of the host rodent population. Rodent peaks appears when nuts of trees (which provide abundant nutrients to rodents) accumulate on the ground; usually population density has a minimum in spring and a maximum in late autumn-winter. Moreover, the landscape composition is an important cause in the ecology of the infected host rodents by hantavirus. Large continuous forests might favor the spread of the virus in the reservoir population in comparison to fragmented forests; there is a positive relationship between anthropogenic land cover disturbances (deforestation, agricultural land cover conversion, etc.) and the presence of hantavirus (see, for example, [10]). Such situations benefit the opportunistic rodent species that may be reservoirs for hantavirus. Moreover, environmental changes commonly decrease the rodent diversity which could enhance interactions between more rodent species and, as a consequence, more virus transmission through aggressive encounters between species.

Taking into account the argument mentioned above, it seems of interest the design and study of mathematical models that allow one to simulate virus spread. Unfortunately, few models have appeared in the scientific literature related to hantavirus spread among host rodents. The majority are based on the use of differential equations (see [1,2,9,11]). However, these models do not take into account spatial factors such as population density, they neglect the local character of the spread process or they cannot comprehensively depict complex contagion patterns (which are mostly caused by the host rodent interaction), etc. As a consequence it is very interesting to study the use of discrete models (agent-based models, cellular automata, etc.) that can eliminate some of these shortcomings. Furthermore, discrete models are also specially suitable for computer simulations (see [3]).

Cellular automata (CA for short) are finite state machines formed by a collection of n memory units called cells. At each time step, they are endowed with a state from a finite state set that are synchronously updated according to a specified rule function whose variables are the states of the neighbor cells at the previous time step (see, for example, [13,14]). Cellular automata have been widely used to simulate several physical, chemical, social and biological phenomena (see [12]) and there is no doubt about its efficiency in mathematical modeling.

To the best of our knowledge, there is only one work dealing with the use of cellular automata to simulate hantavirus spread; a model developed by Karim *et al.* (see [8]). In this work, the authors propose a simple and interesting model to analyzed the spatiotemporal patterns of hantavirus infection. It is based on the use of a two-dimensional cellular automata with periodic boundary conditions. Each cell is endowed with a state: susceptible (if there is a susceptible mice placed on it), infected (if the mice placed is infected) and empty (there is no mouse in the cell). As Von Neumann neighborhoods are considered, the rodents can move in four directions (north, east, south and west) and their movement is cyclic starting from north. Births and death are considered and environmental conditions are defined in one parameter K. The transition rule between the susceptible and the infected state is defined in terms of a probability: a susceptible rodent with at least one infected rodent in its neighborhood will become infected with probability 1/8.

The main goal of this work is to propose an improvement of the model by Karim *et al.* Specifically it is based on two-dimensional cellular automata and it can be considered as a compartmental one since the population of rodents is divided into two classes: susceptible and infected. In order to improve the last mentioned model and to obtain a more realistic one, we will consider the following:

i. In order to define the movement, Moore neighborhoods are considered; consequently there will be 8 possible neighbors instead of the 4 neighbor cells considered in the paper of Karim *et al.*, and the movement of each rodent can be in one of these eight possible directions. Moreover, in the model proposed in this work the movement is not cyclic: it depends on the amount of nutrients of each cell (when the food resources of the cell where the rodent is are finished, the rodent moves to the empty neighbor cell with highest nutrient parameter).
ii. Null boundary conditions instead of periodic conditions are considered, that is, the neighborhood of the cells placed in the border of the cellular space are endowed with a reduce neighborhood whose elements are the possible cells of the cellular space around it.
iii. As the time needed to reach an endemic equilibrium is short, no births or deaths are taken into account: the population of rodents remains constant all along.
iv. The environmental conditions considered depends on two parameters: the nutrient parameter f (resource food) and the contaminant waste parameter

w (excreta and saliva). These parameters could be different from one cell to other and vary with time: when a rodent is placed in a cell the food resources decreases and excreta and/or saliva is deposited in it.

v. The transition rule (between susceptible and infected states) used in the new model takes into account: (1) the number of infected neighbor rodents and the probability to get infected after a bite, and (2) the nutrients resources which are contaminated by wastes due to infected rodents.

The rest of the work is organized as follows: In section 2 the mathematical background about cellular automata is introduced; the model of hantavirus spreading among host rodents is shown in section 3. Several simulations and the discussion is presented in section 4. Finally the conclusions are stated in section 5.

2 Cellular Automata

Two-dimensional cellular automata (CA for short) are discrete dynamical systems formed by a finite number of identical objects called cells which are arranged uniformly in a two-dimensional space. At every step of time, they are endowed with a state that changes sincronously according to a local transition rule. More precisely, a CA can be defined as the 4-uplet $\mathcal{A} = (\mathcal{C}, \mathcal{S}, V, f)$, where C is the cellular space formed by a two-dimensional array of $r \times c$ cells:

$$\mathcal{C} = \{(i,j),\quad 1 \leq i \leq r, 1 \leq j \leq c\}, \tag{1}$$

The standard paradigm for cellular space states that the cells are represented by means of identical square areas defining a rectangular cellular space (see Figure 1).

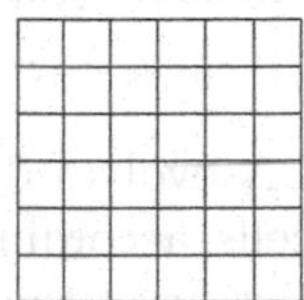

Fig. 1. Rectangular cellular space $\mathcal{C}$

The state of each cell is an element of a finite state set $\mathcal{S}$. In this sense, the state of the cell (a, b) at time t is denoted by $s_{ab}^t \in \mathcal{S}$. When CA are used to simulate natural phenomena, the state of every cell stand for the variable or feature to be analyzed.

The neighborhood of each cell is defined by means of the (ordered finite) set of indices $V \subset \mathbb{Z} \times \mathbb{Z}$, $|V| = m$, such that for every cell (a, b), its neighborhood $V_{(a,b)}$ is the following set of m cells:

$$V_{(a,b)} = \{(a + \alpha_1, b + \beta_1), \ldots, (a + \alpha_m, b + \beta_m) : (\alpha_k, \beta_k) \in V\}. \tag{2}$$

When rectangular cellular space is taken, usually two types of neighborhoods are considered: Von Neumann and Moore neighborhoods. The Von Neumann neighborhood of a cell c is formed by the main cell itself and the four cells orthogonally surrounding it (see Figure 2-(a)). Note that in this case: $V = \{(-1,0),(0,1),(0,0),(1,0),(0,-1)\}$, that is:

$$V_{(a,b)} = \{N = (a-1,b), E = (a,b+1), c = (a,b), \\ S = (a+1,b), W = (a,b-1)\}. \tag{3}$$

The Moore neighborhood of the central cell c is constituted by the eight nearest cells around it and c (see Figure 2-(b)). Consequently:

$$V = \{(-1,-1),(-1,0),(-1,1),(0,-1),(0,0),(0,1)(1,-1),(1,0),(1,1)\}, \tag{4}$$

that is:

$$V_{(a,b)} = \{NW = (a-1,b-1), N = (a-1,b), NE = (a-1,b+1) \\ W = (a,b-1), c = (a,b), E = (a,b+1), SW = (a+1,b-1), \\ S = (a+1,b), SE = (a+1,b+1)\}. \tag{5}$$

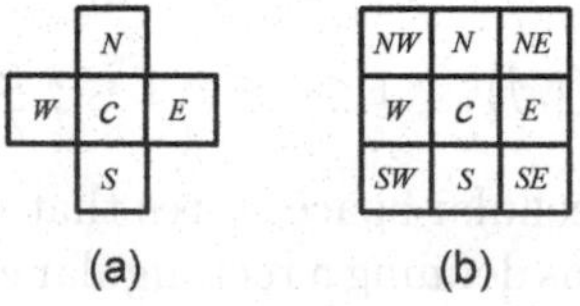

Fig. 2. (a) Von Neumann neighborhood; (b) Moore neighborhood

As was mentioned above, the CA evolves deterministically in discrete time steps, changing the states of all cells according to a local transition function $f\colon \mathcal{S}^m \to \mathcal{S}$. That is, the updated state of the main cell (a,b) depends on the m variables of the local transition function, which are the previous states of the cells constituting its neighborhood, that is:

$$s_{ab}^{t+1} = f\left(s_{a+\alpha_1,b+\beta_1}^t, \ldots, s_{a+\alpha_m,b+\beta_m}^t\right) \in \mathcal{S}. \tag{6}$$

Moreover, the matrix

$$C^{(t)} = \begin{pmatrix} s_{11}^t & s_{12}^t & \ldots & s_{1c}^t \\ s_{21}^t & s_{22}^t & \ldots & s_{2c}^t \\ \vdots & \vdots & \ddots & \vdots \\ s_{r1}^t & s_{r2}^t & \ldots & s_{rc}^t \end{pmatrix}, \tag{7}$$

is called the configuration at time t of the CA, where $C^{(0)}$ is the initial configuration of the CA.

As the number of cells of the CA is finite, boundary conditions must be considered in order to assure the well-defined dynamics of the CA. One can state several boundary conditions depending on the nature of the phenomenon to be simulated. In this work we will consider null boundary conditions, that is: if $(a,b) \notin C$ then $s_{ab}^t = 0$.

3 The Model of Hantavirus Spreading

The model for hantavirus virus spreading shown in this work is a compartmental model, that is, each rodent can be in one of the following two states: susceptible or infected. Susceptible rodents are those that have not been infected by the hantavirus, whereas infected rodents are those reached by the virus and which are able to propagate it to susceptible rodent.

In the model proposed in this work, some assumptions will be done related to environmental situation, rodent behavior and virus spreading.

3.1 Environmental Considerations

The following environmental suggestions must be considered in the model:

1. Each cell of the cellular space stands for a portion of the landscape habitat of rodent population.
2. Each cell, (a,b), of the cellular space is endowed with the nutrient parameter, $f_{ab}^t \in \mathbb{N}$, which estimates the food sources at every step of time for the possible rodent placed in this cell at this time.
3. At every step of time there will be rodent wastes due to their saliva, urine and/or droppings: set $w_{ab}^t \in \mathbb{N}$ the total contaminated waste (the waste due to infected rodents) at time t in the cell (a,b).

3.2 Host Rodent Considerations

The following suggestions are made related to rodent behavior:

1. At every step of time there can not be more than two rodents in each cell, that is, the number of rodents in one cell could be 0 (the cell is empty) or 1 (the cell is occupied). As a consequence, the physical interaction between rodents is considered when they are placed in neighbor cells.
2. The number of rodents in the system remains constant throughout time.
3. At a particular time each rodent will be endowed with one of the following two states: susceptible or infected.
4. When a rodent is placed in a cell, the nutrient parameter of such cell decreases in $\alpha \in \mathbb{N}$ units at every step of time. Consequently, if there is a rodent in the cell (a,b) at time t then $f_{ab}^{t+1} = f_{ab}^t - \alpha$.
5. When a rodent is placed in a cell, it deposits excreta and saliva uniformly throughout the cell and, as a consequence, the remaining nutrients could be contaminated if the rodent is infected. If $\beta \in \mathbb{N}$ are the units of excreta and saliva deposited by an infected rodent in the cell (a,b) at time t, then $w_{ab}^{t+1} = w_{ab}^t + \beta$.

6. A rodent moves from its cell to a neighbor cell when the food resources corresponding to the main cell are finished. In this case, the rodent moves to the empty neighbor cell with highest nutrient parameter.

3.3 Virus Spreading Considerations

The hantavirus is transmitted to a susceptible rodent by means of two ways:

i) When the susceptible rodent inhales infected aerosols or ingests contaminated food. This occurs with probability $\frac{w_{ab}^t}{f_{ab}^t} \leq 1$ in the cell (a,b) at time t.
ii) When the susceptible rodent is bitten by an infected rodent. The probability to become infected after a bite is δ for each contact, and only contacts between the susceptible rodent and infected rodents placed in the neighbor cells are considered.

3.4 The Local Transition Function

Let $s_{ab}^t \in \mathcal{S}$ be the state of the cell (a,b) at time t and set $\mathcal{S} = \{X,Y,Z\}$ the state set. Thus:

$$s_{ab}^t = \begin{cases} X, & \text{if there is a susceptible rodent in the cell } (a,b) \text{ at time } t \\ Y, & \text{if there is an infected rodent in the cell } (a,b) \text{ at time } t \\ Z, & \text{if there is not any rodent located at cell } (a,b) \text{ at time } t \end{cases} \quad (8)$$

Note that the state of cell (susceptible, infected or empty) depends on the state of the rodent (susceptible or infected). Taking into account the suggestions stated in subsection 3.2, it follows:

i) A susceptible rodent at time t will be infected at time $t+1$ with probability $\frac{w_{ab}^t}{f_{ab}^t}$ or with probability δ per contact. Otherwise, the rodent remains susceptible.
ii) An infected rodent at time t remains infected at time $t+1$.

Consequently, the local transition function is given by the following rules:

1. $s_{ab}^{t+1} = X$ if one of the following two conditions hold:
   (i) $s_{ab}^t = X$ and the rodent placed in (a,b) has not been infected and it does not move from (a,b) to other neighbor cell at time t.
   (ii) $s_{ab}^t = Z$ and a susceptible rodent moved to cell (a,b) at time t.
2. $s_{ab}^{t+1} = Y$ if one of the following three conditions hold:
   (i) $s_{ab}^t = X$ and the rodent placed in (a,b) has been infected and it does not move from (a,b) to other neighbor cell at time t.
   (ii) $s_{ab}^t = Y$ and the rodent does not move from (a,b) to other neighbor cell at time t.

   (iii) $s_{ab}^{t} = Z$ and an infected rodent moved to the cell (a, b) at time t.
3. $s_{ab}^{t+1} = Z$ if one of the following two conditions hold:
   (i) $s_{ab}^{t} = Z$ and any rodent does not move to cell (a, b) at time t.
   (ii) If $s_{ab}^{t} \neq Z$ and the rodent placed in (a, b) moved from this cell to a neighbor cell at time t.

4 Simulations and Discussion

The computational implementation of the model introduced in this work has been made using the computer algebra system *Mathematica* (version 9.0). Several simulations have been performed for 100 iterations, all of then with a lattice of 10×10 cells. The rest of parameters (number of rodents, amount of nutrients and infection rate) are varied in order to study the behavior of the model.

In Figure 3 an illustrative example of the simulations obtained from the model proposed in the last section is shown. In this example 50 rodents are randomly placed in a lattice of 10×10 cells; 10 of them are infected at time $t = 0$. Moreover the initial nutrient parameter of each cell satisfies $75 \leq f_{ab}^{0} \leq 85$ and $\delta = 0.05$.

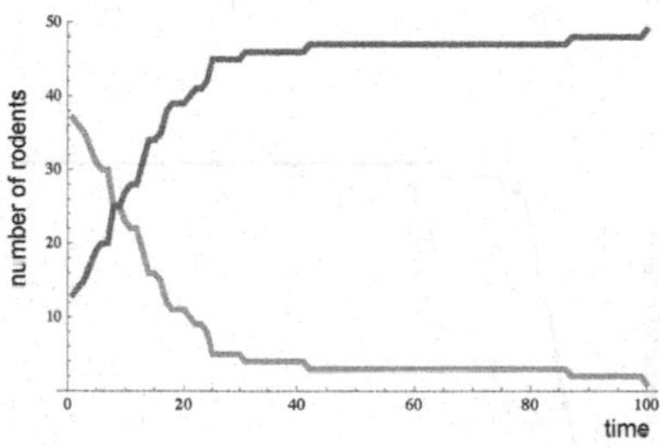

Fig. 3. Evolution of the number of infected and susceptible rodents in a 10×10 grid with a total number of rodents 50. At time $t = 0$, 10 infected hosts are considered and the nutrient parameter varies between 75 to 85.

In what follows we analyze the model considering several initial conditions and parameters values.

4.1 Variation of the Infection Rate Probability

First of all, we will consider a constant population of 50 rodents which are randomly distributed over the grid (0.5 rodents per cell). At the initial time $3 - 5$ rodents are considered infected ($6 - 10\%$ of total rodents) and the nutrient parameter associated to every cell is equal to 25.

Six different values of the infection rate probability will be considered: $\delta = 0, 0.05, 0.1, 0.15, 0.2$ and 0.3. The evolution for the infected population in all these cases is introduced in Figure 4. As is shown, with independence of the value of the infection probability rate, the total number of infected individuals gradually increases to reach an equilibrium stable value (endemic equilibrium). The step of time at which this endemic equilibrium value is obtained is $t = 96, 63, 37, 39, 58$ and 28, respectively.

Note that there is a notable growth of the population of infected individuals in the first steps of the evolution in all the cases with the except of $\delta = 0$. The period of this trend generally lasts over a period between $t = 0$ to $t = 30$, depending on the value of the infection rate: as δ increases, the growth is more defined. After this fast and stressed increasing, the evolution produces by the model exhibits a short period of slow growth and finally the endemic equilibrium is reached.

Note that it is not necessary to consider higher values of δ to obtain an endemic situation: even when $\delta = 0$ this scenario occurs although there is a significant difference: an initial period without infections appears (from $t = 0$ to $t = 50$) since the rodents do not bite due to there is not a fight for the food.

Similar results are obtained if we slightly vary the values of nutrient parameters: in Figure 5 the evolution of infected population in the same cases than those considered in Figure 4 is shown. Note that the trends are the same although the differences between the particular evolutions (for each value of δ) are reduced. This also occurs if we consider a non-constant distribution of the nutrient; see for example Figure 6.

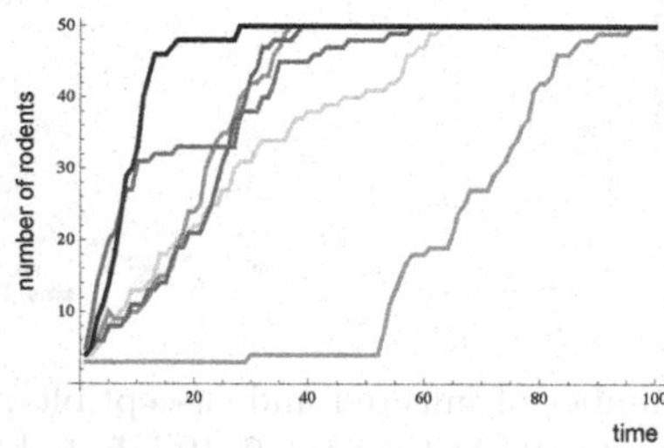

Fig. 4. Evolution of the number of infected rodents for different values of the infection rate δ. The color code is as follows: green for $\delta = 0$, yellow for $\delta = 0.05$, orange for $\delta = 0.1$, red for $\delta = 0.15$, brown for $\delta = 0.2$, and black for $\delta = 0.3$.

Consequently, the infection rate probability has an accelerant effect on the evolution of infected population.

4.2 Variation of the Density Population: Both Global and Infected

Suppose that a total population of 50 individuals are considered and there is an initial constant distribution of the nutrient parameter (the value of such parameter in each cell is 25 at $t = 0$); moreover set $\delta = 0$ (recall that this parameter affects to the speed of convergence to endemic equilibrium, not to the trend). The simulations obtained for different values of the initial density of

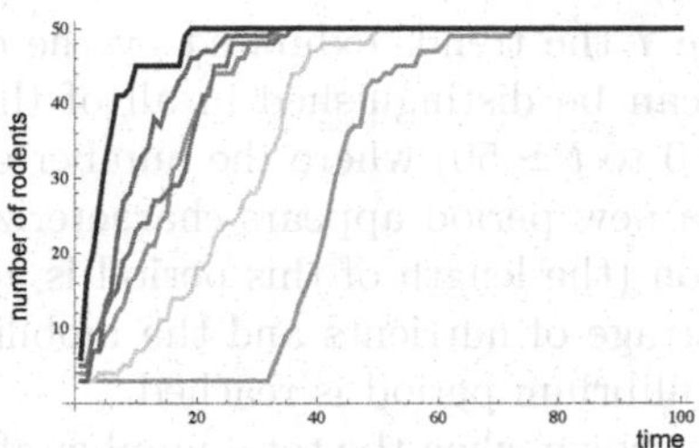

Fig. 5. Evolution of the number of infected and susceptible rodents for different values of the infection rate δ when the nutrient parameter is constant and equal to 15

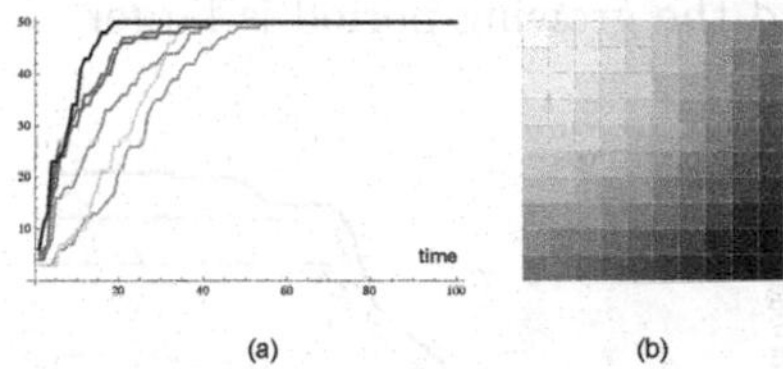

Fig. 6. (a) Evolution of the number of infected and susceptible rodents for different values of the infection rate δ when the nutrient parameter is distributed following a non-constant function. (b) Distribution of the nutrients in the grid (the gray level denotes the total amount of nutrients).

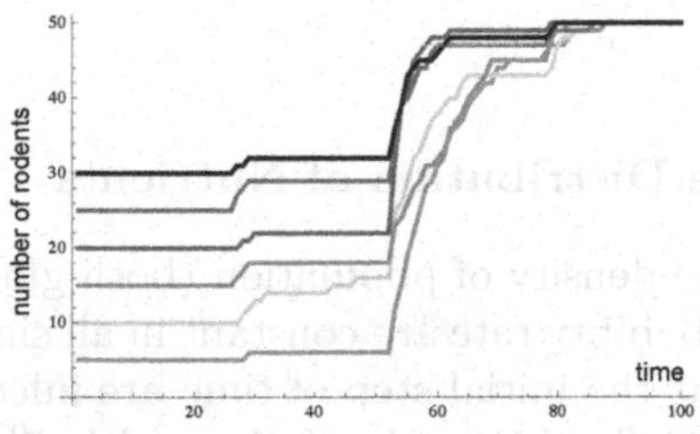

Fig. 7. Evolution of the number of infected rodents when different values of the density of infected population are considered. The color code is as follows: green for 10%, yellow for 20%, orange for 30%, red for 40%, brown for 50%, and black for 60%.

infected rodents are given in Figure 7. Specifically the densities considered are 10%, 20%, 30%, 40%, 50%, and 60%.

As is shown in Figure 7 the trends exhibited by the different evolutions are similar. Three periods can be distinguished in all of them: The first one is a stable period (from $t = 0$ to $t \simeq 50$) where the number of new infected cases is very small. After that, a new period appears characterized by a strong growth of the infected population (the length of this period is about 20 steps of time), which is due to the shortage of nutrients and the mobility of infected rodents. Finally, the endemic equilibrium period is reached.

Similar evolutions are shown when the total number of rodents varies and the percentage of initial infected hosts remains constant. For example, in Figure 8 the simulations obtained when 20, 30, 50, 70, 80 and 90 rodents are placed in the grid and the 10% of these rodents are infected at time $t = 0$ are shown. Moreover, the infection rate probability is taken equal to 0 and the initial nutrient parameters are all equal to 25. Note that in this case the evolution is very similar to the previous case since there are three distinct periods (with the same behavior than in the last case) but their lengths vary when the global population increases: The first period is shorter and the growing period is larger.

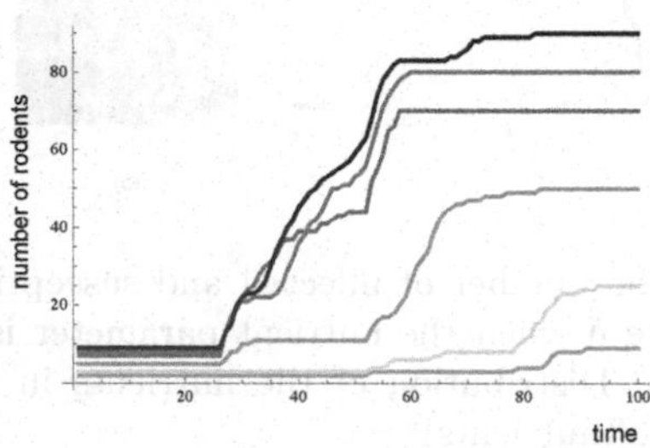

Fig. 8. Evolution of the number of infected rodents when different values of the global density of population are considered (with a 10% of initial infected rodents considered). The color code is as follows: green for 20 rodents, yellow for 30 rodents, orange for 50 rodents, red for 70 rodents, brown for 80 rodents, and black for 90 rodents.

4.3 Variation of the Distribution of Nutrients

Finally, suppose that the density of population (both global and infected at $t = 0$) and the infection probability rate are constant in all simulations: $\delta = 0.05$ and 10% of the population at the initial step of time are infected. If initial constant nutrient parameters are defined then simulations with $f_{ab}^0 = 10, 20, 30, 40, 50$ are computed ($1 \leq a, b \leq 10$) and the results are shown in Figure 9. The evolutions obtained are similar, there is a constant growth from the first time ($t = 0$) to the endemic value. As it could be expected the force of the growth of the number of infected rodents is inversely proportional to the total amount of nutrients.

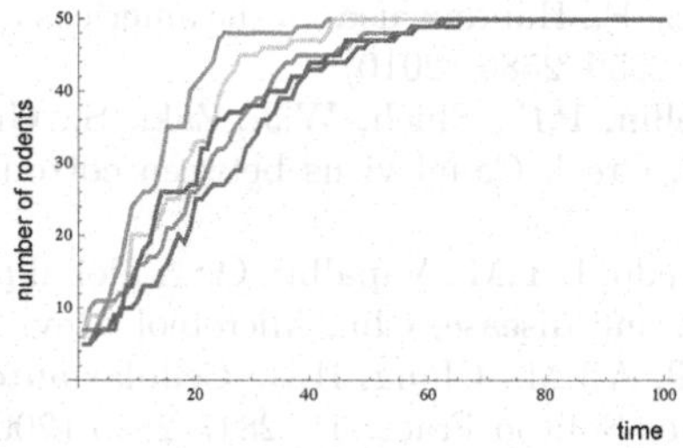

Fig. 9. Evolution of the number of infected rodents when different values of the nutrients are considered (and the other parameters remain constant). The color code is as follows: green for $f = 10$, yellow for $f = 20$, orange for $f = 30$, red for $f = 40$, and brown for $f = 50$.

5 Conclusions

In this work a novel mathematical model to simulate the spreading of hantavirus disease between a population of rodents is proposed. It is a improvement of the model proposed by Karim, Ismail and Ching in 2009. The improvements are related to boundary conditions, neighborhood and environmental conditions that defines the local transition function.

Several simulations have been obtained starting from different initial conditions (population density, infected probability rate, nutrient distribution) and in all of them an endemic equilibrium is obtained, that is, the population of infected rodents grows up to an endemic value. The strength of this growth depends on the behavior of the parameters: it is inversely proportional to the amount of nutrients and directly proportional to the initial density of infected rodents and the infected probability rate.

Acknowledgements. This work has been supported by Consejería de Educación (Junta de Castilla y León, Spain).

References

1. Abramson, G., Kenkre, V.M.: Spatiotemporal patterns in the hantavirus infection. Phys. Rev. E 66, 011912 (2002)
2. Abramson, G., Kenkre, V.M., Yates, T.L., Parmenter, B.R.: Traveling waves of infection in the hantavirus epidemics. Bull. Math. Biol. 65, 519–534 (2003)
3. Bauer, A.L., Beauchemin, C.A.A., Perelson, A.S.: Agent-based modeling of host-pathogen systems: The successes and challenges. Inform. Sci. 179, 1379–1389 (2009)
4. Hinson, E.R., Shone, S.M., Zink, M.C., Glass, G.E., Klein, S.L.: Wounding: The primary mode of Seoul virus transmission among male Norway rats. Am. J. Trop. Med. Hig. 70, 310–317 (2004)

5. Hjelle, B., Torres-Pérez, F.: Hantaviruses in the americas and their role as emerging pathogens. Viruses 2, 2559–2586 (2010)
6. Hutchinson, K.L., Rollin, P.E., Shieh, W.J., Zaki, S., Greer, P.W., Peters, C.J.: Transmission of Black Creek Canal virus between cotton rats. J. Med. Virol. 60, 70–76 (2000)
7. Jonsson, C.B., Figueiredo, L.T.M., Vapalhti, O.: A global perspective on hantavirus ecology, epidemiology, and disease. Clin. Microbiol. Rev. 23(2), 412–441 (2010)
8. Karim, M.F.A., Ismail, A.I.M., Ching, H.B.: Cellular automata modelling of hantavirus infection. Chaos Soliton Fract. 41, 2847–2853 (2009)
9. Kenkre, V.M., Giuggioli, L., Abramson, G., Camelo-Neto, G.: Theory of hantavirus infection spread incorporating localized adult and itinerant juvenile mice. Eur. Phys. J. B 55, 461–470 (2007)
10. Mackelprang, R., Dearing, M.D., Jeor, S.: High prevalence of Sin Nombre virus in rodent populations, central Utah: a consequence of human disturbance? Emerg. Infect. Dis. 7, 480–482 (2001)
11. Peixoto, I.D., Abramson, G.: The effect of biodiversity on the hantavirus epizootic. Ecology 87(4), 873–879 (2006)
12. Sarkar, P.: A brief history of cellular automata. ACM Comput. Surv. 32(1), 80–107 (2000)
13. Toffoli, T., Margolus, N.: Cellular Automata Machines: A New Environment for Modeling. The MIT Press, Cambridge (1987)
14. Wolfram, S.: A New Kind of Science. Wolfram Media Inc., Champaign (2002)

DHGN Network with Mode-Based Receptive Fields for 2-Dimensional Binary Pattern Recognition

Anang Hudaya Muhamad Amin[1], Asad I. Khan[2], and Benny B. Nasution[3]

[1] Thundercloud Research Lab, FIST, Multimedia University, Jalan Ayer Keroh Lama, 75450 Melaka, Malaysia
anang.amin@mmu.edu.my

[2] Faculty of Information Technology, Monash University, Clayton, 3168 VIC, Australia
asad.khan@monash.edu

[3] Politeknik Negeri Medan, Jalan Almamater No. 1, Kampus USU, Padang Bulan, Medan 20155, Indonesia
benny.nasution@polmed.ac.id

Abstract. We introduce an extension to existing Distributed Hierarchical Graph Neuron (DHGN) network for 2-dimensional binary pattern recognition. The new form of DHGN network, termed as receptive field DHGN network (RF-DHGN) is a hybrid of a receptive field layer for 2D feature extraction, and one or more DHGN subnets for feature recognition. All inputs to the network, in the form of synaptic weights are automatically determined through mode-based activation function within the RF neurons. The proposed scheme minimizes the need for large number of neurons as compared to the normal DHGN scheme. Furthermore, the results of preliminary recognition tests indicate high recognition accuracy, similar to existing DHGN approach for distributed pattern recognition.

Keywords: Hybrid system, receptive field, bio-inspired algorithm, parallel pattern recognition.

1 Introduction

Pattern recognition is a process of identifying similar characteristics or features of given objects or entities. Living organisms have been providing many examples of how recognition of patterns can be performed in efficient ways. Small organisms such as honeybees and fruit flies exhibit effective mechanisms of pattern recognition. Honeybees have the ability to recognize fairly complex features in flowers, while fruit flies can conduct flight stunts using minuscule amounts of energy. Both honeybees and fruit flies are able to perform such intricate operations using such miniature-sized brains.

The ability to recognize patterns using biologically-inspired mechanisms such as neural networks have been commonly used to memorize patterns. Apart from

M. Polycarpou et al. (Eds.): HAIS 2014, LNAI 8480, pp. 415–426, 2014.
© Springer International Publishing Switzerland 2014

statistical and syntactical approaches, neural networks have been shown to produce higher recall accuracy as compared to the aforementioned techniques [1]. Nevertheless, most of the existing schemes do not scale up to the increase in the size and complexity of patterns.

An important concept in bio-inspired computations is the hierarchical structure of learning. Neural system in human brain for example, consists of numerous hierarchical structures with feedback loops between the levels of hierarchy. According to Dileep [2], this multiple levels of neurons within the brain creates a far more compact and flexible recognition engine, controller or model. Distributed Hierarchical Graph Neuron (DHGN) [3] is a variant of parallel and distributed neural network scheme for pattern recognition. DHGN implements a hierarchical learning mechanism that allows generalizations of structures from specific combination of elements within patterns. The DHGN approach has been derived from both Graph Neuron (GN) [4] and Hierarchical Graph Neuron (HGN) [5] approaches. GN is a scalable associative memory scheme for memorizing patterns of various forms, ranging from generic sensor stimuli to pixel intensities in images. GN offers better resource utilization by changing the emphasis of computation from sequential CPU processing to parallel in-network processing. HGN on the other hand, extends the capabilities and effectiveness of GN recognition, by introducing the bird's eye view of pattern formations through its hierarchical learning structures.

DHGN implements similar functions as HGN and GN recognition schemes. However, DHGN reduces the learning cycle and complexity of HGN through decomposition of HGN large structure into several DHGN sub-structures. Learning in DHGN involves the use of collaborative-comparison learning function [6] that implements adjacency comparison of input values in pattern memorization. This kind of learning exhibits a one-shot learning capability without the needs for re-training. Although DHGN is able to reduce the complexity of HGN hierarchical structure, the size of its network structure can substantially increase for larger and complex patterns.

In this paper, we propose a neural activation-like function to reduce the size of DHGN network composition for recognition of 2-dimensional binary patterns. The use of modal values for activation of neuron within the network is considered. This work has been inspired by a number of researches done in receptive field [7,8] of a sensory neuron that react on specific stimulus that provides a firing mechanism within the neuron. The receptive field acts as a feature extraction mechanism for the input patterns. In this approach, mode calculation has been used to identify the frequent appearances of dominant elements within a given pattern. The proposed approach minimizes the number of DHGN subnets required, by reducing the size of the input space for recognition purposes. The preliminary results indicate that the scheme offers comparable levels of accuracy as original DHGN scheme.

The article is structured as follows. Section 2 presents some of the related works on DHGN pattern recognition and other related components. The fundamental concept of mode-based activation function for DHGN will be discussed in Section 3.

The results of simple recognition test on 2-dimensional binary character patterns are further presented in Section 4, followed by conclusions presented in Section 5.

2 Related Works

2.1 Distributed Hierarchical Graph Neuron (DHGN)

DHGN is a pattern recognition network that comprises a number of DHGN subnets (HGN sub-composition) and a Stimulator/Interpreter Module (SI Module) node, as described by Muhamad Amin and Khan [6]. Fig. 1 shows a complete architecture of DHGN network. This figure illustrates a decomposition of binary image pattern 'K' into subpatterns. This decomposition is performed by the SI Module node. The input activates the neurons corresponding to the bits of the input pattern. In doing so each pattern element within a subpattern is mapped to relevant neurons in the respective subnet. Each subnet integrates its responses and sends the results to the SI Module to form overall network responses.

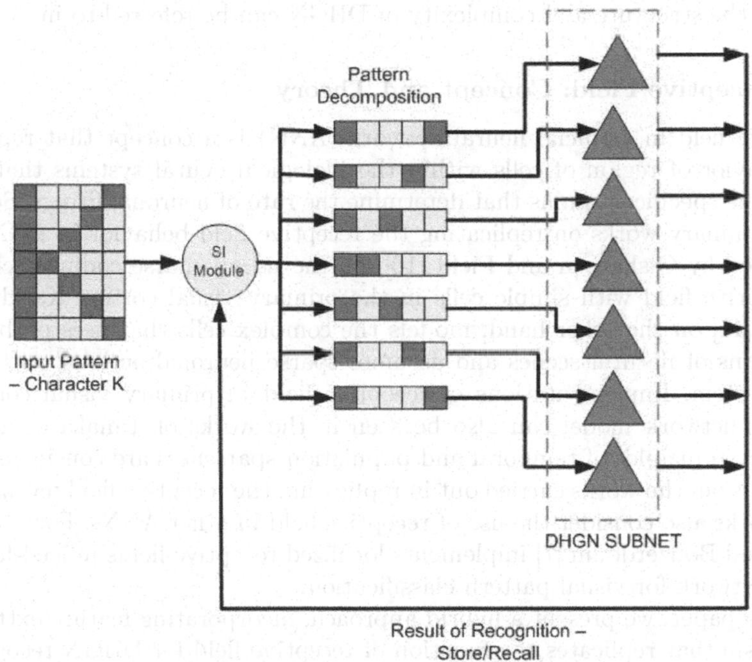

Fig. 1. DHGN network architecture for pattern recognition (adopted from [9])

Learning within DHGN network occurs in a one-shot environment, in which each pattern is passed through the network only once. Recognition result, in terms of recall (pattern is known) or store (pattern is memorized). Within each

DHGN subnet, the recognition process involving communication between neurons also happening once for each subpattern. In this point of view, DHGN offers fast recognition procedure by eliminating the needs for iterative mechanism to recall or store patterns. The size of subnet depends on the size of the subpattern used in the system and the number of different elements in the subpattern. Therefore, to define the size of each subnet, we consider the number of neurons, N_{gn} required for subpattern with size p and v different element as shown in the following equation:

$$N_{gn} = v\left(\frac{p+1}{2}\right)^2 \quad (1)$$

Consequently, the total number of GNs, N_{gn}^T required for M size pattern can be calculated as:

$$N_{gn}^T = \frac{M}{p}\left[v\left(\frac{p+1}{2}\right)^2\right] \quad (2)$$

It is best to note that for binary patterns, the value of $v = 2$. Further descriptions on the structure and complexity of DHGN can be referred to in [3,6].

2.2 Receptive Field: Concept and Theory

Receptive field in artificial neural network (ANN) is a concept that replicates the behavior of region of cells within the biological neural systems that react upon some specific stimulus that determine the rate of neuronal firings. Some of the preliminary works on replicating the receptive field behavior in ANN were introduced by Olshausen and Field [10], on the use of sparse coding technique for receptive field with simple cells in the primary visual cortex. Karklin and Lewicki [11] on the other hand, models the complex cells that uses probability estimations of natural scenes and assumes sparse neuronal activity within the visual system. Implementations of receptive field in primary visual cortex of neuronal network model can also be seen in the works of Tanaka et al. [12], where the principles of temporal and population sparseness are considered.

Apart from the works carried out in replicating the receptive field mechanism, other works also consider the use of receptive field in other ANNs. For example, Phung and Bouzerdoum [7] implements localized receptive fields in feed-forward neural network for visual pattern classification.

In this paper, we present a hybrid approach, incorporating feature extraction mechanism that replicates the function of receptive field for DHGN recognition scheme involving 2-dimensional binary patterns. Our work introduces the modal-value calculation as an activation function to determine the types of input to the DHGN network. By acquiring this capability of receptive field, the size of DHGN network could substantially be reduced. The work being carried out resembles some of the hybrid system approaches by Bouaziz et al. [13] and Wozniak et al. [14]

In the next section, we will describe our proposed feature extraction approach using receptive field (RF) mode-based activation function for DHGN network.

3 Mode-Based RF-DHGN Network

In this section, we will describe the feature extraction technique that has been deployed for DHGN network. The use of receptive field concept in capturing important feature of a given pattern will be presented. The proposed DHGN scheme mainly consists of two important components, namely mode-based RF neurons and DHGN network.

3.1 Mode-Based RF Neurons

Generally, mode is a value that represents the frequency of similar elements in a set of data. According to Yule and Kendall [15], mode is the value of the variable that corresponds to the maximum of the ideal curve which gives the closest possible fit to the actual distribution. Mode can be used as a tool to identify dominant elements in a given pattern. Past works on mode-based RF can be seen in the works of Ramirez and Pedrycz [16] on the receptive fields of Radial-Basis Function (RBF) neural network.

The proposed receptive field mechanism within DHGN network implements a mode-based analysis of a given input pattern. In normal DHGN network, an input pattern will be divided into a series of subpatterns, and each of these subpatterns will be used in each of the DHGN subnets. The learning mechanism deployed in each DHGN subnet follows the collaborative-comparison learning as described in Muhamad Amin and Khan [6]. In RF-DHGN, additional array of neurons will be used for feature extraction purposes, prior to DHGN recognition procedure. Fig. 2 shows the composition of DHGN subnet and RF neurons in the proposed distributed recognition scheme.

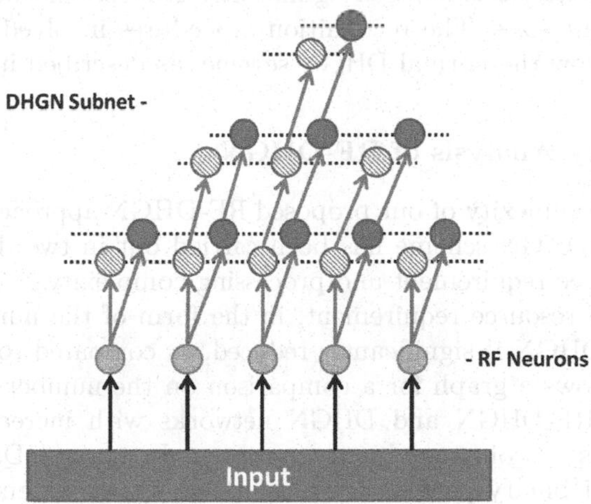

Fig. 2. RF-DHGN network composition comprising DHGN subnet and RF neurons

In the proposed scheme, the firing of RF neuron will be determined by the modal value obtained from the input pattern/subpattern. For example, considering binary pattern as input to the network. If the frequency of bit 1 is higher than bit 0, then the neuron will activate bit 1 as the input for the base layer of DHGN subnet. Otherwise, bit 0 will be generated. The number of RF neurons for feature extraction is determined based on the dimension and size of the input patterns. Given the pattern length d for each dimension D, where $d \in D$, the number of RF neurons, N_{rf} required could be derived from the following equation:

$$N_{rf} = \prod_{i=1}^{D} d_i \tag{3}$$

The important aspect of the RF neurons deployment in DHGN network is that it allows different other feature extraction mechanisms to be applied, instead of only depending upon actual input values such as pixels and sensor readings. The capability of having a simple pre-processing of input patterns enables recognition to be performed more effectively. The use of these neurons in DHGN perspective is such that it allows less number of DHGN neurons to be deployed for large-scale and multi-dimensional pattern recognition.

3.2 RF-DHGN Network Architecture

Fig. 3 illustrates the overall view of DHGN network with RF neurons for 2-dimensional binary character pattern 'A'.

Note that the network layout for the proposed approach is different from the original DHGN network as shown in Fig. 1. With additional RF neurons for feature extraction, the amount of DHGN subnets required for recognizing binary character patterns is reduced significantly, from seven subnets to only two subnets of different sizes. The recognition procedures involved in each DHGN subnet simply follow the normal DHGN scheme, as described in [6].

3.3 Complexity Analysis of RF-DHGN

To estimate the complexity of our proposed RF-DHGN approach, a comparison between existing DHGN scheme has been carried out in two different criteria, namely the resource requirement and processing complexity.

Computational resource requirement, in the form of the number of neurons required for RF-DHGN is significantly reduced, as compared to current DHGN scheme. Fig. 4 shows a graph for a comparison on the number of neurons generated for both RF-DHGN and DHGN networks with increasing size for 2-dimensional (rows × columns) binary patterns. In normal DHGN approach, the 2-dimensional binary pattern is transformed into 1-dimensional (1-row × n-columns) bit string and recognition is performed on this bit string.

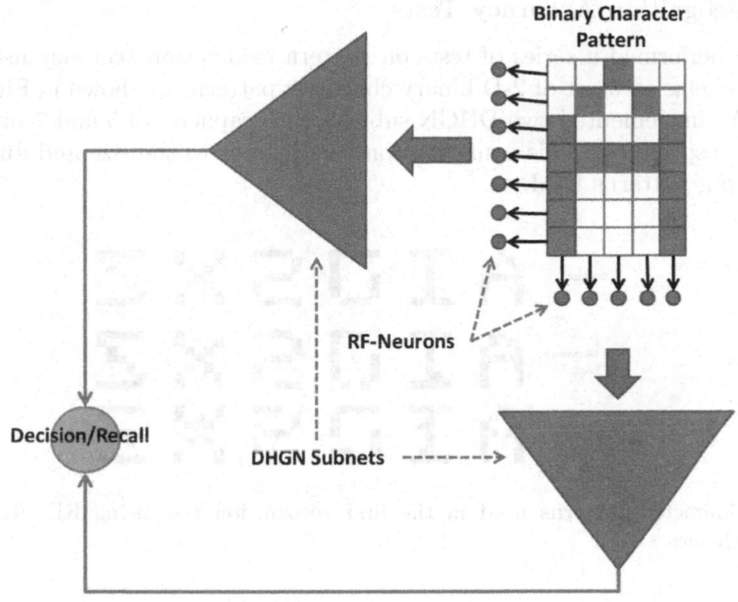

Fig. 3. RF-DHGN network for 2-D binary pattern recognition of character 'A'

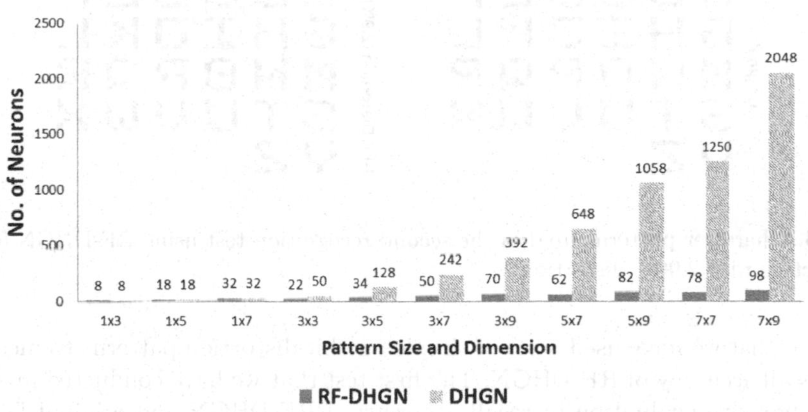

Fig. 4. A comparison on the number of neurons generated in DHGN and RF-DHGN for pattern recognition involving 2-dimensional binary patterns

In regards to the processing complexity of the proposed approach, the RF neurons function only focuses on determining the modal value from the elements within the input subpattern. The complexity of this process can be defined as $O(n)$, where the value estimation process only involve passing a single-cycle within the entire bit pattern. It is best to note that the processing complexity of the DHGN network does not change and remains as $O(n)$.

3.4 Recognition Accuracy Tests

We have performed a series of tests on pattern recognition accuracy using RF-DHGN scheme on a set of 2-D binary character patterns as shown in Fig. 5 and Fig. 6. We implemented two DHGN subnets with capacity of 5 and 7-bits input patterns respectively. This configuration corresponds to the size and dimension of the input patterns used.

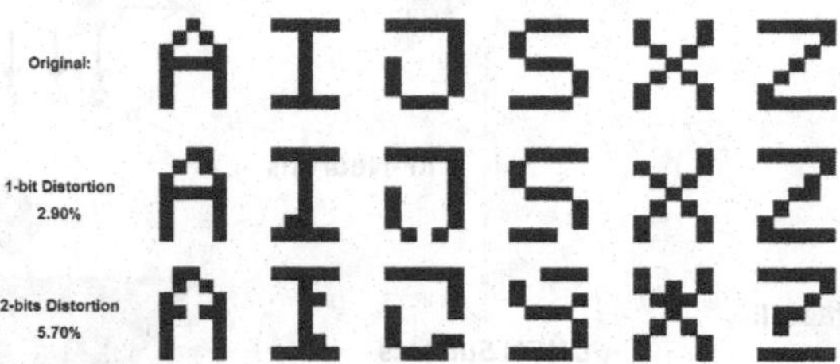

Fig. 5. Character patterns used in the first recognition test using RF-DHGN and DHGN schemes

Fig. 6. Character patterns used in the second recognition test using RF-DHGN for all characters with 2.90% distortion

Note that we have used a set of simple one-bit distortion patterns to measure the recall accuracy of RF-DHGN. The first test that we have conducted involves a comparative evaluation of recall accuracy of RF-DHGN and original DHGN implementations. In the second test, we perform a recognition procedure on 26 binary alphabet characters (with 2.90% distortion (1-bit)) as shown in Fig. 6. Results of these tests will be further presented in the following section.

The RF-DHGN code was developed using C programming language with MPICH-2 library for message-passing interface (MPI) parallel processing capability.

4 Results and Discussion

Fig. 7 and 8 show the recall accuracy rates of RF-DHGN and normal DHGN scheme for recognition of binary character patterns with 2.90% (1-bit) and 5.70%

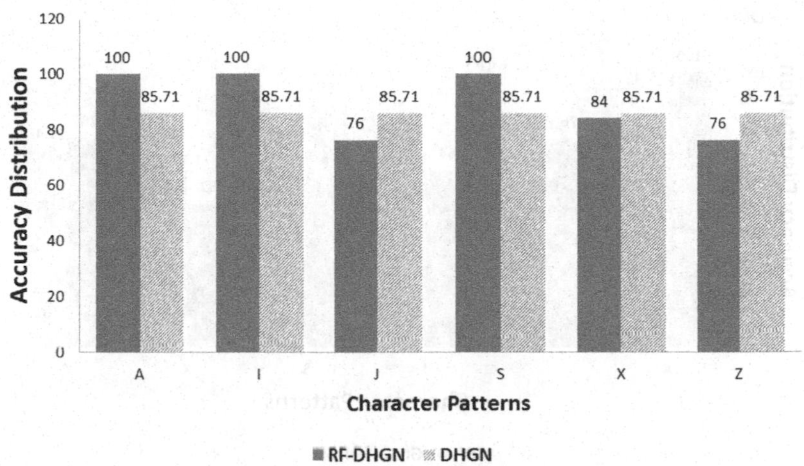

Fig. 7. Recall accuracy comparison between RF-DHGN and DHGN schemes for 1-bit (2.90%) distorted patterns

(2-bit) distortions respectively. The recall accuracy rate for both schemes were obtained by calculating the recall indices of each subnet as described in the original HGN scheme by Nasution and Khan [5].

Note that RF-DHGN produces comparatively similar accuracy rates as the original DHGN network. However, as described in the previous section, RF-DHGN minimizes the resource requirement by generating less number of neurons for similar pattern size and dimension used in normal DHGN.

For the recognition test involving 26 alphabet characters with 1-bit distortion, it is best to note that the storing of the original alphabet characters (without distortion) using RF-DHGN approach has revealed similar spatial structure for some of the characters. These characters are *A* and *H*; *E* and *G*; *F*, *P*, and *R*; *D*, *J*, and *O*; and *X* and *Y*. Fig. 9 shows the result of recall accuracy test conducted on the 1-bit distorted alphabet characters. Note that about 53% of the alphabet characters have been perfectly recalled by the scheme.

An important element in determining the accuracy of RF-DHGN lies in the mechanism used for feature extraction. In this paper, we have implemented a mode-based RF activation function for extracting features of binary patterns. Modal-value for binary pattern is used, based on the hypothesis that changes in the number of dominant bit may not significantly affect the overall representation of the patterns. Consider the following example as shown in Fig. 10.

Note that flipping a bit from bit 1 (dark square) (dominant) to bit 0 (light square) does not affect the modal value of the given pattern. However, when significant changes to the bit values experienced, the pattern information will totally be changed. Hence the original pattern information will be lost.

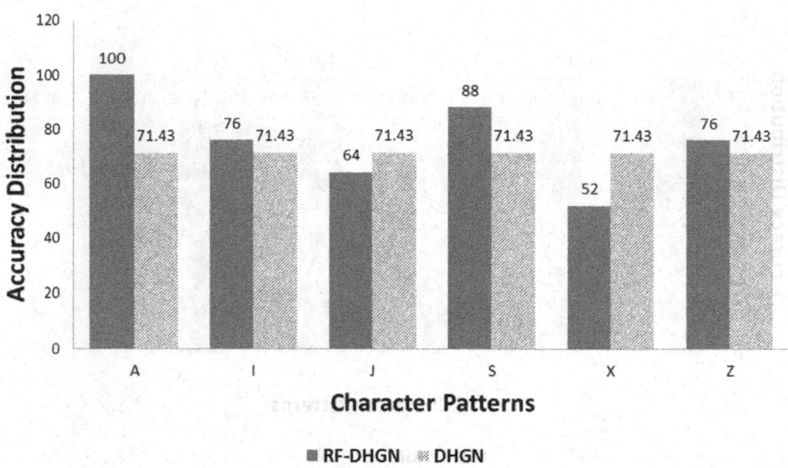

Fig. 8. Recall accuracy comparison between RF-DHGN and DHGN schemes for 2-bit (5.70%) distorted patterns

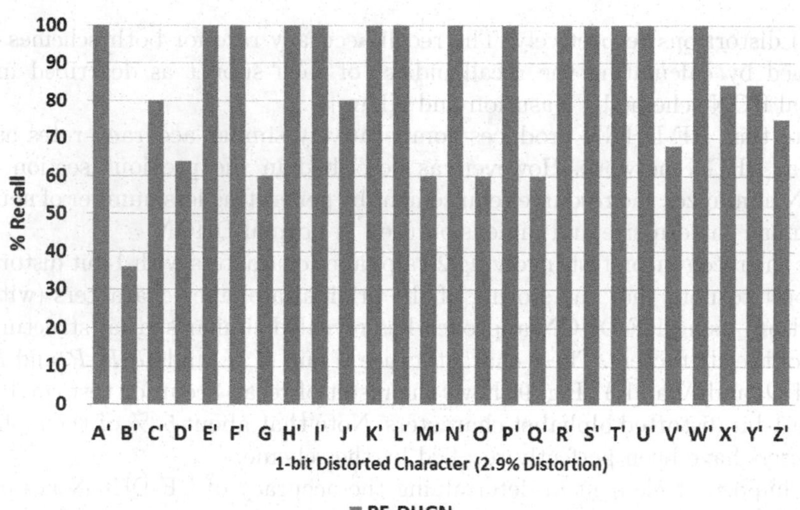

Fig. 9. Recall accuracy percentages for RF-DHGN scheme on 1-bit (2.90%) distorted alphabet characters

It is best to consider that the use of modal value may not be the best activation function to be used for different forms of patterns. Nevertheless, the RF-DHGN structure allows different types of feature extraction mechanism to be deployed prior to the recognition procedures performed using DHGN network.

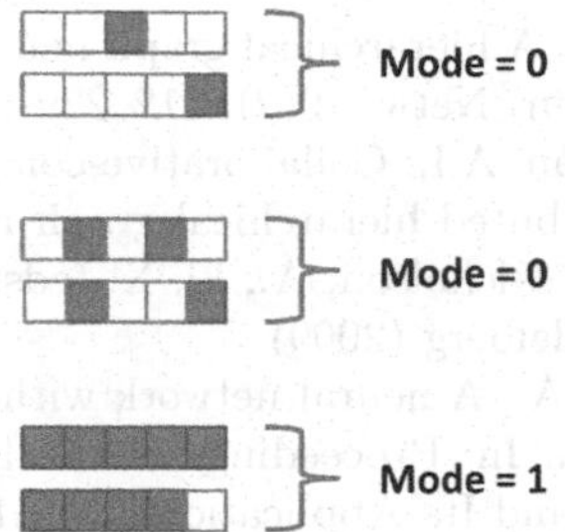

Fig. 10. Examples of the effect of bit flipping in modal value of a given pattern

5 Conclusions

In this paper, we present our work on implementing receptive field (RF) mechanism for binary pattern recognition using DHGN network. Arrays of RF neurons were implemented for feature extraction using mode-based activation on binary patterns. The hybrid RF-DHGN scheme allows recognition of patterns to be performed with minimum number of DHGN subnets, while exhibits comparative recognition accuracy of existing DHGN scheme. The proposed approach also offers a flexible mechanism of feature extraction, by allowing different activation function to be used prior to DHGN recognition. The use of receptive field for feature extraction also provides an adaptive approach to different forms of available feature extraction methods to be used on DHGN network. Our future works will be focusing on developing different extraction modules for receptive field function within the DHGN composition. In addition, more complex patterns that incorporate multi-dimensional features will be used to analyze the capability of the recognition scheme.

Acknowledgments. This work supported by the Fundamental Research Grant Scheme (FRGS) under the Ministry of Education, Malaysia. It is also partially supported by the Swedish Foundation for International Cooperation in Research and Higher Education (STINT), institutional grant IG2011-2025.

References

1. Schalkoff, R.J.: Pattern recognition - statistical, structural and neural approaches. Wiley (1992)
2. George, D.: How the Brain Might Work: A Hierarchical and Temporal Model for Learning and Recognition. PhD thesis, Stanford, CA, USA (2008) AAI3313576
3. Khan, A., Muhamad Amin, A.H.: One shot associative memory method for distorted pattern recognition. In: Orgun, M.A., Thornton, J. (eds.) AI 2007. LNCS (LNAI), vol. 4830, pp. 705–709. Springer, Heidelberg (2007)
4. Khan, A.I., Mihailescu, P.: Parallel pattern recognition computations within a wireless sensor network. In: Proceedings of the 17th International Conference on Pattern Recognition, ICPR 2004, vol. 1, pp. 777–780 (August 2004)

5. Nasution, B.B., Khan, A.I.: A hierarchical graph neuron scheme for real-time pattern recognition. Trans. Neur. Netw. 19(2), 212–229 (2008)
6. Muhamad Amin, A.H., Khan, A.I.: Collaborative-comparison learning for complex event detection using distributed hierarchical graph neuron (DHGN) approach in wireless sensor network. In: Nicholson, A., Li, X. (eds.) AI 2009. LNCS, vol. 5866, pp. 111–120. Springer, Heidelberg (2009)
7. Phung, S.L., Bouzerdoum, A.: A neural network with localized receptive fields for visual pattern classification. In: Proceedings of the Eighth International Symposium on Signal Processing and Its Applications, vol. 1, pp. 94–97 (August 2005)
8. Coates, A., Ng, A.Y.: Selecting receptive fields in deep networks. In: Shawe-Taylor, J., Zemel, R., Bartlett, P., Pereira, F., Weinberger, K. (eds.) Advances in Neural Information Processing Systems 24, pp. 2528–2536 (2011)
9. Muhamad Amin, A.H., Khan, A.I.: Single-cycle image recognition using an adaptive granularity associative memory network. In: Wobcke, W., Zhang, M. (eds.) AI 2008. LNCS (LNAI), vol. 5360, pp. 386–392. Springer, Heidelberg (2008)
10. Olshausen, B.A., Field, D.J.: Emergence of simple-cell receptive field properties by learning a sparse code for natural images. Nature 381(6583), 607–609 (1996)
11. Karklin, Y., Lewicki, M.S.: Emergence of complex cell properties by learning to generalize in natural scenes. Nature 457(7225), 83–86 (2009)
12. Tanaka, T., Aoyagi, T., Kaneko, T.: Replicating receptive fields of simple and complex cells in primary visual cortex in a neuronal network model with temporal and population sparseness and reliability. Neural Comput. 24(10), 2700–2725 (2012)
13. Bouaziz, S., Dhahri, H., Alimi, A.M., Abraham, A.: A hybrid learning algorithm for evolving flexible beta basis function neural tree model. Neurocomputing 97, 131–140 (2013)
14. Wozniak, M., Graña, M., Corchado, E.: A survey of multiple classifier systems as hybrid systems. Information Fusion 16, 3–17 (2014)
15. Yule, G., Kendall, M.G.: An Introduction to the Theory of Statistics. Charles Griffin and Company (1950)
16. Ramirez, L., Pedrycz, W.: Prototypes stability analysis in the design of radial basis function neural networks. In: Benítez, J., Cordón, O., Hoffmann, F., Roy, R. (eds.) Advances in Soft Computing, pp. 13–20. Springer, London (2003)

Extending Qualitative Spatial Theories with Emergent Spatial Concepts*

An Automated Reasoning Approach

Gonzalo A. Aranda-Corral[1], Joaquín Borrego-Díaz[2], and Antonia M. Chávez-González[2]

[1] Departamento de Tecnologías de la Información.
Escuela Técnica Superior de Ingeniería - Universidad de Huelva.
Crta. Palos de La Frontera s/n. 21819 Palos de La Frontera. Spain

[2] Departamento de Ciencias de la Computación e Inteligencia Artificial.
E.T.S. Ingeniería Informática-Universidad de Sevilla.
Avda. Reina Mercedes s.n. 41012-Sevilla, Spain

Abstract. Qualitative Spatial Reasoning is an exciting research field of the Knowledge Representation and Reasoning paradigm whose application often requires the extension, refinement or combination of existent theories (as well as the associated calculus). This paper addresses the issue of the sound spatial interpretation of formal extensions of such theories; particularly the interpretation of the extension and the desired representational features. The paper shows how to interpret certain kinds of extensions of Region Connection Calculus (RCC) theory. We also show how to rebuild the qualitative calculus of these extensions.

1 Introduction

One of the main challenges in Qualitative Spatial Reasoning (QSR) is the need to combine or extend the existing theories to include new aspects in the same formalism [18,12]. In order to face the problem, several features and viewpoints must be considered.

The focus here is the logical aspect of the challenge, particularly the relationship among models of initial theories and that of the new ones. A key aspect to consider in Artificial Intelligence in general is the feasibility/complexity of the reasoning process, by providing, for example, a qualitative calculus. This approach contrasts with the qualitative and nature inspired one [14]. Several of the purely logical features could be solved if a sound methodology is adopted, for example the *definitional methodology* for building formal ontologies [4]. It can be too rigid because of strong requirements such as logical categoricity. In contrast with this framework, in QSR the (characterization of) the class from *intended models* is more important than the general class of models. In fact, a sound interpretation of the revised ontology/theory for preserving those models is a key step especially if previous definitions have to be changed. For example, any extension by definition of a new concept/relationship should be supported by a

* Partially supported by Excelence project of *Junta de Andalucía* TIC 6064, cofinanced with FEDER founds.

M. Polycarpou et al. (Eds.): HAIS 2014, LNAI 8480, pp. 427–438, 2014.
© Springer International Publishing Switzerland 2014

good theory about its relationship with the original theory, as well as by a nice way of expanding a representative class of models of the source theory to the new one.

From this point of view, the use of automated reasoning systems can ensure the correctness of the results as well as that it has not been used spatial intuitions which are not formalized in the theory (c.f. [21]). It is very important both the soundness of the associated calculus and the use of a spatial theory as basis for building and reasoning with ontologies [17].

The aim of the paper is to show how the assistance of automated reasoning systems (ARS) can help to classify, interpret and compute abstract extensions of QSR theories, required to accommodate new concepts and insights which Knowledge Engineering problems induces. The use of ARS provides an formal framework where contrast hypothesis, specifications and axioms.

Specifically, the case of the extension of RCC theory [12,18] by insertion of an undefined relationship is analyzed. In a broad scope, the aim is to describe how rudiments of First Order Model Theory (and computational logic) can be used for increasing the knowledge on generic extensions of the QSR theory: On the one hand, by providing a formal support to the reasoning both from lattice of spatial relationships and transition tables. On the other hand, since the computing of the extensions is assisted by automated reasoning, it provides information to the designer which comes from the logical entailment. In this way the designer only has to re-interpret if necessary, elements from the older theory in order to satisfy those information requirements. This task, non algorithmic in essence, is the responsibility of experts in the domain represented by the ontology. In fact, such re-interpretation can force us to reconsider the initial ontological commitments. This paper addresses these issues.

The rest of the paper proceeds as follows. Next section motivates the need of qualitative reasoning on abstract extensions of standard theories. Section 3 introduces basic features of lattice categorical extensions, a formal notion for extending theories and it recalls a result on extensions of RCC. Sections 4,5,6 represent the main contributions of the paper. In Section 4 the interpretation of the extensions by means topological pulsation is described. Section 5 shows how the transition table for the extensions from interpretation can be rebuilt. Section 6 shows other interpretation framework (egg-yolk approach). Conclusions and new insights are summarized in Section 7.

2 Interpretation of Generic Extensions

The paper addresses in first place the problem of obtaining a sound interpretation (by providing a spatial meaning) of the extensions obtained by means automated reasoning; and, in the second one, it studies how from that interpretation, other tools for QSR (as transition tables) can be deduced. Formally:

Definition 1. *Let Ω be a topological space and T be a mereotopological theory. An* **interpretation** *on Ω is an interpretation of the language of T whose universe is Ω. T is* **interpretable** *on Ω if there exists an interpretation on Ω which is model of T.*

Roughly speaking, an interpretation is a (logical) interpretation which interprets spatial entities as open sets in the space, and relations as spatial relations, often on spatial regular regions. If an abstract extension of a standard QSR theory is obtained, it

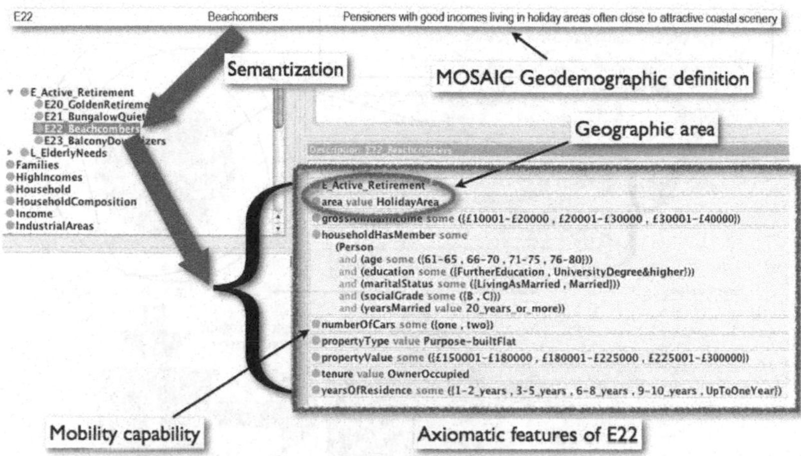

Fig. 1. Semantic approach to a geodemographic class [11]

is necessary to extend the standard interpretation by interpreting the new concepts or relationships as spatial regions and relations respectively.

2.1 A Motivating Example

The needs of generic extensions of (classic) qualitative reasoning theories comes from the analysis of spatial relationships partially defined by different specifications. For example, in [11] authors show how to build a (semantic web) ontology from a state-of-art geodemographic system. Such kind of systems are composed by high-level specifications of spatio-temporal and geodemographic features. Geodemographic classes extracted from the system are underspecified by the formalization of a number of geographic, demographic and sociological restrictions that really do not define the intent of geodemographic specialist (see Fig. 1). Therefore, when automated reasoning work on specifications poor results are obtained: formal class can not soundly interpreted as geodemographic expert desires, which really represents a vague region contained in the intersection of a number of anonymous classes.

The refinement of geodemographic ontologies can not be sufficient if the system can not reason with rough, generic spatial relations which provides a basic spatial calculus. The selection of QSR for refining ontologies was showed in a range of papers [6,9,2,3] in which are presented both the foundational issues as well as their applications. The paper [3] describes an intelligent interface (called Paella), based on qualitative spatial reasoning which is designed to (spatially) reason with ontology classes (see [2] for an application). The refining cycle to be applied (once extended standard qualitative reasoning to work with the new kind of spatial entities) is represented in Fig. 2. It can be considered other possibility consisting on the refinement of the definition by means of the combined use of two or more classifier systems (and the sound topology) [24]. However the qualitative nature of ontological definitions discourages this approach. Standard mereotopological interpretation leads an abstract spatial configuration which

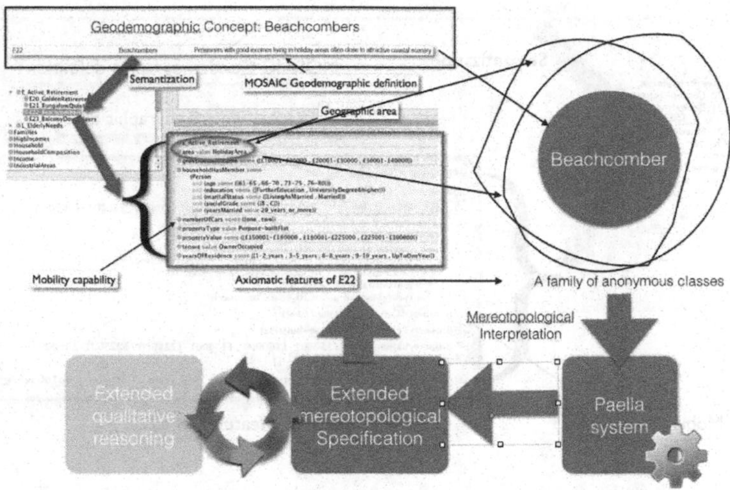

Fig. 2. Augmenting reasoning cycle with extended spatial reasoning [3]

has to be used by purely formal methods (because the spatial intuition may fail on these new relationships). Therefore, it needs a new formal framework where the reasoning is founded with strong logical theories on spatial reasoning, which must be topologically interpretable in turn.

2.2 The Mereotopological Theory RCC

RCC theory [12], a mereotopological approach to QSR, describes topological features of the spatial relations. It has been useful in several fields of Artificial Intelligence such as Geographic Information Systems (GIS) and Spatial Databases (see e.g. [16]) It allows us both to reason on spatial regions and to interchange knowledge between ontologies and their spatial models. We consider a ground relation, the connection between two regions, which enjoys the reflexive and symmetrical properties. The meaning of connection is: the topological closures of two connected regions intersect. The set of axioms expressing the properties and definitions of the remaining relations (Fig. 3 (left) conforms the set of axioms of RCC (see [12]).

On one hand, the set of the eight binary relations depicted in Fig. 3 is denoted by RCC8. These relations are jointly exhaustive and pairwise disjoint (JEPD) and RCC8 is regarded a calculus for Constraints Satisfaction Problems (CSP) (see e.g. [22]). On the other hand, there is another interesting calculus, $RCC5 = \{DR, PO, PP, PPi, EQ\}$. The difference between them is that while the former allows us to enrich the representation of knowledge by using frontiers of the regions, the latter do not. This fact will be discussed next. Although it has been empirically established [19] that RCC8 is more suitable than RCC5 for the representation of topological relations discriminated by humans, both of them are used here: RCC5 is appropriate for solving CSPs associate to

$DC(x,y) \leftrightarrow \neg C(x,y)$	(x is disconnected from y)
$P(x,y) \leftrightarrow \forall z[C(z,x) \rightarrow C(z,y)]$	(x is part of y)
$PP(x,y) \leftrightarrow P(x,y) \wedge \neg P(y,x)$	(x is proper part of y)
$EQ(x,y) \leftrightarrow P(x,y) \wedge P(y,x)$	(x is identical with y)
$O(x,y) \leftrightarrow \exists z[P(z,x) \wedge P(z,y)]$	(x overlaps y)
$DR(x,y) \leftrightarrow \neg O(x,y)$	(x is discrete from y)
$PO(x,y) \leftrightarrow O(x,y) \wedge \neg P(x,y) \wedge \neg P(y,x)$	(x partially overlaps y)
$EC(x,y) \leftrightarrow C(x,y) \wedge \neg O(x,y)$	(x is externally connected to y)
$TPP(x,y) \leftrightarrow PP(x,y) \wedge \exists z[EC(z,x) \wedge EC(z,y)]$	(x is a tangential prop. part of y)
$NTPP(x,y) \leftrightarrow PP(x,y) \wedge \neg\exists z[EC(z,x) \wedge EC(z,y)]$	(x is a non-tang. prop. part of y)

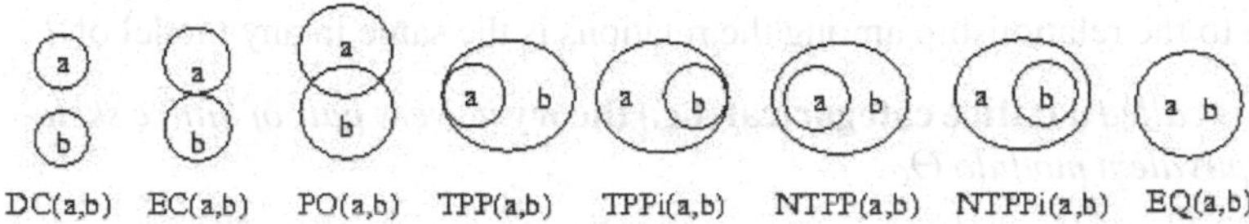

Fig. 3. Axioms of RCC (top) and RCC8 spatial relations (bottom)

a mereotopological representation and RCC8 is useful to design a rich translation of a spatial representation to the ontology code.

Models of RCC have been deeply studied from different viewpoints [20,22]. The study of the lattice of spatial relationships of extensions of RCC was made in [10]. The last work raise several questions about the relation between the original theory and its extensions. This can be studied from the QSR paradigm, or from the logical consequences of the extension of the theory (see e.g. [15] for the combination of RCC and reasoning about qualitative size and [9] for the same problem).

3 Background: Lattice-Categorical Extensions

An essential requirement to a qualitative theory should be that if it is possible to entail the basic relationships among the concepts considered. For example, RCC entails both the relationship between the spatial defined relations (which has lattice structure) and the transition calculus [21]. Likewise the extension should satisfy the same requirement. Inspired by foundational questions on the Semantic Web [1], in [10] a formal definition of *robust ontology* is proposed, called *lattice categorical extension* [8] used for computing a range of RCC-extensions used in the paper.

A *lattice categorical* theory is the one that proves the lattice structure of its basic relations. Formally, given a fixed language, let $\mathcal{C} = \{C_1, \ldots, C_n\}$ be a (finite) set of concept symbols, let T be a theory. Given M a model of T, $M \models T$, we consider the structure $L(M, \mathcal{C})$, in the language $L_{\mathcal{C}} = \{\top, \bot, \leq\} \cup \{c_1, \ldots, c_n\}$, whose universe are the interpretations in M of the concepts (interpreting c_i as C_i^M), $\top$ is M, $\bot$ is $\emptyset$ and $\leq$ is the subset relation. We assume that $L(M, \mathcal{C})$ is requested to have a lattice structure for every theory we consider.

The relationship between $L(M, \mathcal{C})$ and the model M itself is based on that the lattice L can be characterized by a finite set of equations E_L, plus a set of formulas $\Theta_{\mathcal{C}}$

categorizing the lattice under completion, that is, $\Theta_{\mathcal{C}}$ includes the domain closure axiom, the unique names axioms and, additionally, the axioms of lattice theory.

Definition 2. *Let E be a $L_{\mathcal{C}}$-theory. We say that E is a* **lattice skeleton** *(l.s.) for a theory T if E verifies that*

- *There is $M \models T$ such that $L(M, \mathcal{C}) \models E \cup \Theta_{\mathcal{C}}$, and*
- *$E \cup \Theta_{\mathcal{C}}$ has an unique model (modulo isomorphism).*

Every consistent theory has a lattice skeleton [10]. The existence of non equivalent l.s. makes it difficult to reason with the relations, while the existence of only one would make it easy due to the relationship among the relations is the same in any model of T.

Definition 3. *T is called a* **lattice categorical (l.c.) theory** *if every pair of lattice skeletons for T are equivalent modulo $\Theta_{\mathcal{C}}$.*

Note also that every consistent theory T has an extension T' which is lattice categorical: it suffices to consider a model $M \models T$, and then to find a set E of equations such that $\Theta_{\mathcal{C}} \cup E$ has $L(M, \mathcal{C})$ as only model.

A method -assisted by ATP an MF- for obtaining the skeleton is described [10].

Finally, we can give a formalization of *robust ontological extension*, based in the categorical extension of the ontology:

Definition 4. *Given two pairs $(T_1, E_1), (T_2, E_2)$ we will say that (T_2, E_2) is a* **lattice categorical extension** *of (T_1, E_1) with respect to the sets of concepts $\mathcal{C}_1$ and $\mathcal{C}_2$ respectively, if $\mathcal{C}_1 \sqsubseteq \mathcal{C}_2$ and $L(T_2, \mathcal{C}_2)$ is an E_1-conservative extension of $L(T_1, \mathcal{C}_1)$.*

The most important feature of l.c. theories is that this allows use only the lattice relationships for reasoning with the relations. Lattice categoricity has been used for extending ontologies by decision of the user [10], motivated by data and designed by the user [8], data-driven [7] and ontology merging [9].

In [10] l.c. extensions of RCC for supporting undefinition are computed: those that insert the undefinition into RCC8 calculus, so obtaining a new JEPD set. There exist other kind of extensions designed for other uses. See [8] for details.

Theorem 1. *[10] There are only eight l.c. extensions of the lattice of RCC by insertion of a new relation D such that $RCC8 \cup \{D\}$ is a JEPD set.*

The analysis of the extensions (fig. 4) suggests us that the new relations represent *undefinition up to a degree.*

4 Interpreting with Pulsation/Contraction

The above result is an example of a purely logical result obtained by automated reasoning. As it is commented the method ensures the correctness of the result. It is necessary to complete the study by interpreting (if possible) the new elements (and the reinterpreting the older ones). This way it qualifies the designer to use it as QSR theory. In order to obtain specific interpretations, it need to work with concrete spaces. In this section we illustrate this idea by using $\mathcal{R}(\Omega)$ as the set of regular sets of the topological space Ω.

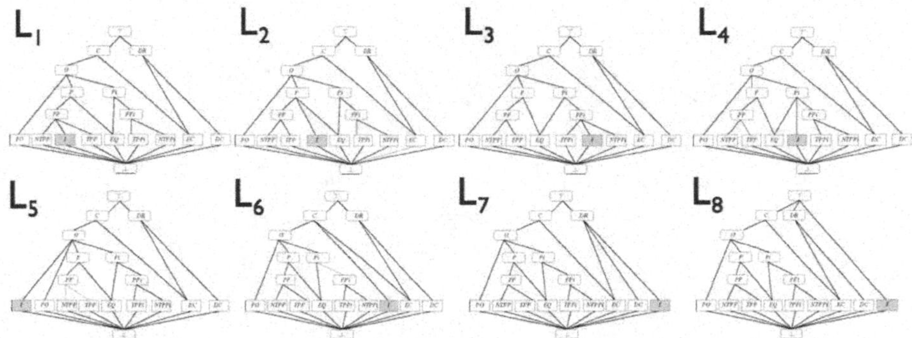

Fig. 4. The eight lattice describing the l.c. extensions of RCC by a undefinition relation

Definition 5. *A* **pulsation** *on a topological space* $\Omega = (\mathcal{X}, \mathcal{T})$ *is a map* $\sigma : \mathcal{R}(\Omega) \longmapsto \mathcal{R}(\Omega)$ *such that the closure of* $\sigma(X)$ *contains that of* X*;* $\overline{X} \subset \overline{\sigma(X)}$*. The pair* (Ω, σ) *where* Ω *is nontrivial, connected and regular is a* **topological space with pulsation**.

The interpretation on these spaces is based on considering the pairs $(x, \sigma(x))$.

Theorem 2. *Seven of the eight extensions from theorem 1 are interpretable in topological spaces with pulsation.*

Proof. We denote by R^{Ω} ($R \in RCC$) the natural interpretation of R in the topological space Ω. For the sake of simplicity, we make use of the following conventions,

$$R^{\sigma}(a,b) := R(\sigma(a), \sigma(b)) \text{ and } \bigvee RCC8^{\sigma} := \bigcup_{R \in RCC8} R^{\sigma}$$

Let (Ω, σ) be a topological space with pulsation σ. Ω_k is defined like the structure on the language of $RCC + \{I_k\}$ where $k \in \{1,2,3,4,5,7,8\}$, and for every $R \in \mathcal{R}_{RCC}$, the interpretation of R in Ω_k is obtained by combination of regions. It only shows two of such interpretations. The others explanations are similar.

$$\begin{aligned} L_1: \ & R^{\Omega_1} = R^{\Omega} \text{ if } R \in \mathcal{R}_{RCC} \setminus \{NTPP, TPP\}, \quad TPP^{\Omega_1} = TPP^{\Omega} \cap TPP^{\sigma}, \\ & NTPP^{\Omega_1} = NTPP^{\Omega} \cap NTPP^{\sigma} \text{ and} \\ & I_1{}^{\Omega_1} = (TPP^{\Omega} \cap (\bigvee RCC8^{\sigma} \setminus \{TPP^{\sigma}\})) \cup (NTPP^{\Omega} \cap (\bigvee RCC8^{\sigma} \setminus \{NTPP^{\sigma}\})) \\ L_3: \ & R^{\Omega_3} = R^{\Omega} \text{ if } R \in \mathcal{R}_{RCC} \setminus \{TPPi, NTPPi\}, TPPi^{\Omega_3} = TPPi^{\Omega} \cap TPPi^{\sigma}, \\ & NTPPi^{\Omega_3} = NTPPi^{\Omega} \cap NTPPi^{\sigma} \text{and} \\ & I_3{}^{\Omega_3} = (TPPi^{\Omega} \cap (\bigvee RCC8^{\sigma} \setminus \{TPPi^{\sigma}\})) \cup (NTPPi^{\Omega} \cap (\bigvee RCC8^{\sigma} \setminus \{NTPPi^{\sigma}\})) \end{aligned}$$

The relation I_6 does not have interpretation on pulsation. It has to use *contraction*.

Definition 6. *A* **contraction** *in a topological space* $\Omega = (\mathcal{X}, \mathcal{T})$ *is a map* $\sigma : \mathcal{R}(\Omega) \longmapsto \mathcal{R}(\Omega)$ *such that* $\overline{(\xi(A))} \subset \overline{A}$ *for each* A *with nonempty inner. The pair* (Ω, ξ) *where* Ω *is nontrivial, connected is called a* **topological space with contraction**.

Theorem 3. I_6 *is interpretable in a topological space with contraction*

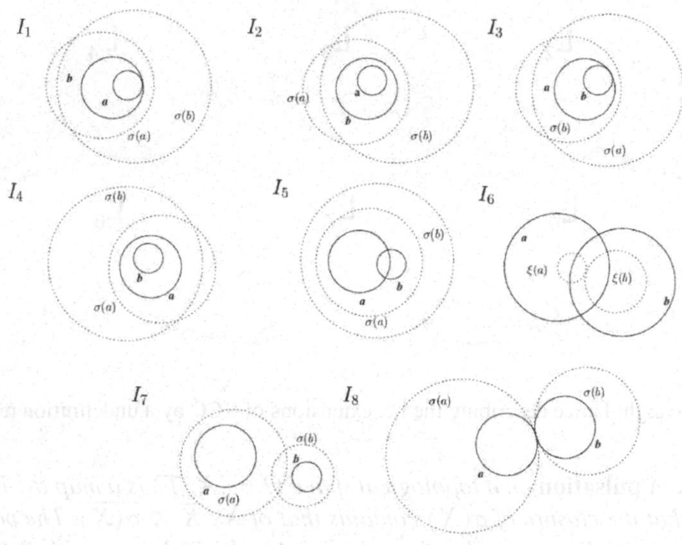

Fig. 5. Interpretation of the relations by undefintion (I_6 by contraction.The rest by pulsation)

Proof. Given (Ω, ξ) define Ω_6 the structure of the language $RCC + \{I_6\}$ as follows:

- $R^{\Omega_6} = R^{\Omega}$ if $R \in \{C, DR, EC, DC\}$
- $R^{\Omega_6} = R^{\Omega} \cap O^{\xi}$ if $R \in \mathcal{R}_{RCC} \setminus \{C, DR, EC, DC\}$
- $I_6{}^{\Omega_6} = O^{\Omega} \cap DR^{\xi}$

Fig. 5 summarizes the interpretations. In fact, it verifies:

Theorem 4. *The set of interpretations Ω_k, $k \in \{1, 2, \ldots, 8\}$ defined above entails the lattice structure L_k depicted in the Fig. 4.*

It suffices to check exhaustively the properties of the reticle according to the corresponding interpretation. The details of such long and tedious process are omitted.

Corollary 1. *The set $RCC8 + \{I_k\}$ is a JEPD set under the interpretation Ω_k, for $k = \{1, 2, \ldots, 8\}$.*

The interpretations correspond, in essence, to a skeleton of every possible extension of RCC. The skeleton (the set of lattice equations characterizing the lattice) can be obtained by using a model finder (MACE4 in our case), but the calculus is out of the scope of this paper.

5 Building the New Transition Tables

One of the advantages of interpreting l.c. extensions is that it allows to build a transition table for the new theory, particularly in the case of the news JEPDs. As for RCC8, it is

Table 1. Composition table for the extension corresponding to L_1

R2(b, c) / R1(a, b)	DC	EC	PO	TPP	NTPP	TPPi	NTPPi	EQ	I_1
DC	RCC8[I_1]	DC, EC, PO, TPP, NTPP, I_1	DC, EC, PO, TPP, NTPP, I_1	DC, EC, PO, TPP, NTPP, I_1	DC, EC, PO, TPP, NTPP, I_1	DC	DC	DC	DC, EC, PO, TPP, NTPP, I_1
EC	DC, EC, PO, TPPi, NTPPi	DC, EC, PO, TPP, TPPi, EQ, I_1	DC, EC, PO, TPP, NTPP, I_1	EC, PO, TPP NTPP, I_1	PO, TPP NTPP, I_1	DC, EC	DC	EC	EC, PO, TPP NTPP, I_1
PO	DC, EC, PO, TPPi, NTPPi	DC, EC, PO, TPPi NTPPi	RCC8[I_1]	PO, TPP NTPP, I_1	PO, TPP NTPP, I_1	DC, EC, PO, TPPi NTPPi	DC, EC, PO, TPPi NTPPi	PO	PO, TPP NTPP, I_1
TPP	DC	DC, EC	DC, EC, PO, TPP NTPP, I_1	TPP NTPP, I_1	NTPP	DC, EC, PO, TPP TPPi, EQ I_1	DC, EC, PO, TPPi NTPPi	TPP	TPP NTPP, I_1
NTPP	DC	DC	DC, EC, PO, TPP NTPP, I_1	NTPP	NTPP	DC, EC, PO, TPP NTPP, I_1	RCC8[I_1]	NTPP	NTPP, I_1
TPPi	DC, EC, PO, TPPi, NTPPi	EC, PO, TPPi, NTPPi	PO, TPPi, NTPPi	PO, EQ TPP, TPPi	PO, TPP NTPP I_1	TPPi NTPPi	NTPPi	TPPi	PO, EQ TPP, TPPi, NTPP, I_1
NTPPi	DC, EC, PO, TPPi, NTPPi	PO, TPPi, NTPPi	PO, TPPi, NTPPi	PO, TPPi, NTPPi	PO, TPPi TPP, NTPP NTPPi, EQ I_1	NTPPi	NTPPi	NTPPi	PO, TPPi TPP, NTPP NTPPi, EQ I_1
EQ	DC	EC	PO	TPP	NTPP	TPPi	NTPPi	EQ	I_1
I_1	DC	DC, EC	DC, EC, PO, TPP NTPP, I_1	TPP NTPP, I_1	NTPP, I_1	DC, EC, PO, TPP EQ NTPP, I_1	RCC8[I_1]	I_1	TPP, NTPP, I_1

possible to prove the transition table for the new JEPD sets $RCC8+I_k, k = \{1, \ldots, 8\}$. To illustrate the method, the table for $RCC8 + \{I_1\}$ is computed.

Table 1 shows the transition table for $RCC8 + \{I_1\}$.

The part of the table that corresponds(fits) to the composition of relations $R_1^{\Omega}, R_2^{\Omega}$ where $R_1, R_2 \in RCC8$, coincides with the table we obtain for $RCC8$, except:

- If from the composition of two relations R_1, R_2 in $RCC8$ is obtained TPP or $NTPP$ (or both of them),then it will appear TPP or $NTPP$ (or both of them), besides the relation I_1.
- As a consequence of that, if in the composition table of $RCC8$ the result of composing two relations is $RCC8$, then, the result is the set $RCC8 + \{I_1\}$, which we have denoted as $RCC8[I_1]$.

In table 2 it shows an example of calculus.

6 Interpretation in the "egg-yolk" Approach

In this section another interpretation, in the egg-yolk paradigm [13] is studied. This is naturally related with the pulsation one. A complete picture of the relationship between undefinition relations is given (as well as with RCC5) instead of a separate interpretation for each one. In egg-yolk paradigm, regions (which we call *e-y regions*) have undetermined boundaries (a 'vague region'), and they are represented by a pair of concentric regions with determinate boundaries ('crisp regions'), which provide limits (not necessarily the tightest limits possible) on the range of indeterminacy. In this paradigm

Table 2. Computing $I_1 \circ I_1 \equiv NTPP \vee TPP \vee I_1$ under interpretation with pulsation

$$
\begin{aligned}
& I_1^{\Omega_1}(a,b) \wedge I_1^{\Omega_1}(b,c) = \\
& = ((TPP^{\Omega}(a,b) \cap (\bigvee RCC8^{\sigma} \setminus \{TPP^{\sigma}\})(a,b)) \cup (NTPP^{\Omega}(a,b) \cap (\bigvee RCC8^{\sigma} \setminus \{NTPP^{\sigma}\})(a,b))) \\
& \quad \cap ((TPP^{\Omega}(b,c) \cap (\bigvee RCC8^{\sigma} \setminus \{TPP^{\sigma}\})(b,c)) \cup (NTPP^{\Omega}(b,c) \cap (\bigvee RCC8^{\sigma} \setminus \{NTPP^{\sigma}\})(b,c))) = \\
& \quad = (NTPP^{\Omega}(a,c) \cap (\bigvee RCC8^{\sigma}(a,c))) \cup (TPP^{\Omega}(a,c) \cap (\bigvee RCC8^{\sigma}(a,c))) = \\
& \quad = (NTPP^{\Omega}(a,c) \cap (NTPP^{\sigma}(a,b) \cup (\bigvee RCC8^{\sigma} \setminus \{NTPP^{\sigma}\})(a,c))) \cup \\
& \quad \cup (TPP^{\Omega}(a,c) \cap (TPP^{\sigma}(a,b) \cup (\bigvee RCC8^{\sigma} \setminus \{TPP^{\sigma}\})(a,c))) = \\
& \quad = (NTPP^{\Omega}(a,c) \cap NTPP^{\sigma}(a,b)) \cup (NTPP^{\Omega}(a,c) \cap (\bigvee RCC8^{\sigma} \setminus \{NTPP^{\sigma}\})(a,c)) \cup \\
& \qquad \cup (TPP^{\Omega}(a,c) \cap TPP^{\sigma}(a,b)) \cup (TPP^{\Omega}(a,c) \cap (\bigvee RCC8^{\sigma} \setminus \{TPP^{\sigma}\})(a,c)) = \\
& \quad = NTPP^{\Omega_1}(a,c) \cup (NTPP^{\Omega}(a,c) \cap (\bigvee RCC8^{\sigma} \setminus \{NTPP^{\sigma}\})(a,c)) \cup \\
& \quad \cup TPP^{\Omega_1}(a,c) \cup (TPP^{\Omega}(a,c) \cap (\bigvee RCC8^{\sigma} \setminus \{TPP^{\sigma}\})(a,c)) = \\
& \quad = NTPP^{\Omega_1}(a,c) \vee TPP^{\Omega_1}(a,c) \vee {I_1}^{\Omega_1}(a,c)
\end{aligned}
$$

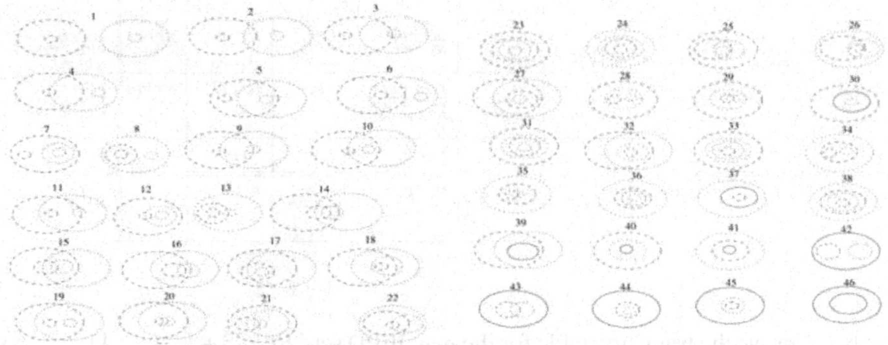

Fig. 6. Egg-yolk relations [13]

RCC5 is used instead of RCC8 by evident reasons. In Fig. 6 a complete description of e-y relations is shown.

Given two e-y regions $A = (a, \overline{a})$, $B = (b, \overline{b})$ and $R \in RCC5$ define $\overline{R}$ by: $(A, B) \in \overline{R} \iff (\overline{a}, \overline{b}) \in R$. Thus the interpretation of $\{I_1, \ldots, I_5, I_7, I_8\} \cup RCC5$ is

- $\overline{DR} = \{1\}$ and $\overline{EQ} = \{42, 43, 44, 45, 46\}$
- $\overline{PP} = \{(A, B) : PP(\overline{a}, \overline{b})\}$ which agree with I_1 (acording to lattice L_1). Thus, $I_1 = \overline{PP} = \{8, 13, 22, 24, 26, 34, 35, 36, 37, 38, 41\}$.
- $I_2 = \overline{PP} \cup \overline{EQ} = \{8, 13, 22, 24, 26, 34, 35, 36, 37, 38, 41, 42, 43, 44, 45, 46\}$,
- By symmetry, $I_3 = \overline{PPi} = \{7, 12, 21, 23, 25, 28, 29, 30, 31, 33, 40\}$ and $I_4 = \overline{PPi} \cup \overline{EQ} = \{7, 12, 21, 23, 25, 28, 29, 30, 31, 33, 40, 42, 43, 44, 45, 46\}$.
- $\overline{PO} = \{2, 3, 4, 5, 6, 9, 10, 11, 14, 15, 16, 17, 18, 19, 20, 27, 32, 39\}$, thus
- $I_5 = I_2 \cup I_4 \cup \overline{PO} = \{2, \ldots, 46\}$
- $I_7 = \overline{DR} = \{1\}$.
- $I_8 = \{1, 2, \ldots, 46\} = \bigcup_{k \in \{1,2,3,4,5,7\}} I_k = I_5 \cup I_7$

Theorem 5. *$RCC5 \cup \{I_1, \ldots, I_5, I_7, I_8\}$ have the lattice structure depicted in 7 in the egg-yolk interpretation.*

Therefore, the set $\{I_1, \overline{EQ}, I_3, \overline{PO}, I_7\}$ is JEPD, and also $\{I_2, I_4, \overline{PO}, I_7\}$ y $\{I_5, I_7\}$. Likewise it is possible to build transition tables for these calculus.

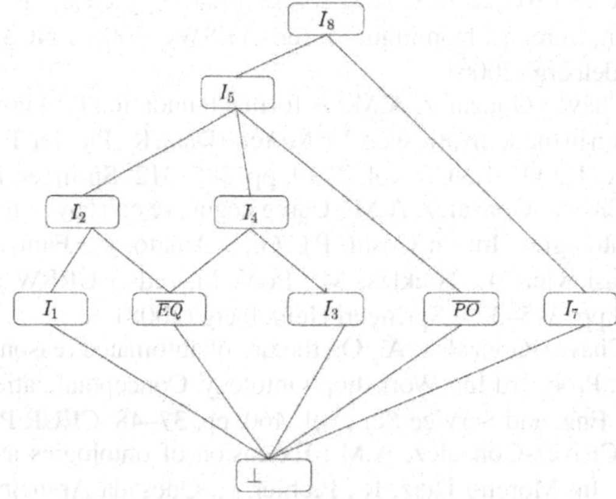

Fig. 7. Lattice of egg-yolk interpretations of new relationships

7 Conclusions and Future Work

The paper is a first step towards the classification/interpretation of generic kind of extensions of RCC as well as the computing of their transition tables. They represent the logical side of the extensions of RCC used in [6], and it is the basis of the associated tool [2,3]. The method for obtaining all the extensions was shown in [10]. The main contribution (sections 4,5 and 6) rest unpublished by now.

Due the lack of space, we do not present related interpretation based on rough sets [23]. This approach is based on totally disconnected topological spaces as models. Thus it starts from a different class of intended models. Also, the approach described in [5] can be used as a basis for a interpretation. The future work is to implement the abstract interpretations as an extended feature of Paella system, in order to specify ontologies which vaguely represent specialized concepts (as for example in the geodemography field).

References

1. Alonso-Jiménez, J., Borrego-Díaz, J., Chávez-González, A., Martín-Mateos, F.J.: Foundational challenges in automated semantic web data and ontology cleaning. IEEE Intelligent Systems 21(1), 42–52 (2006)
2. Aranda-Corral, G.A., Borrego-Díaz, J.: Mereotopological analysis of formal concepts in security ontologies. In: Herrero, Á., Corchado, E., Redondo, C., Alonso, Á. (eds.) CISIS 2010. AISC, vol. 85, pp. 33–40. Springer, Heidelberg (2010)
3. Aranda-Corral, G., Borrego-Díaz, J., Chávez-González, A.: Repairing conceptual relations in ontologies by means of an interactive visual reasoning: Cognitive and design principles. In: Proc. 3rd IEEE Int. Conf. on Cognitive Infocommunications, pp. 739–744 (2012)
4. Bennett, B.: The role of definitions in construction and analysis of formal ontologies. In: Logical Formalization of Commonsense Reasoning 2003. AAAI Press (2003)
5. Bittner, T., Stell, J.G.: Rough sets in approximate spatial reasoning. In: Ziarko, W.P., Yao, Y. (eds.) RSCTC 2000. LNCS (LNAI), vol. 2005, pp. 445–553. Springer, Heidelberg (2001)

6. Borrego-Díaz, J., Chávez-González, A.M.: Visual ontology cleaning: Cognitive principles and applicability. In: Sure, Y., Domingue, J. (eds.) ESWC 2006. LNCS, vol. 4011, pp. 317–331. Springer, Heidelberg (2006)
7. Borrego-Díaz, J., Chávez-González, A.M.: A formal foundation for knowledge integration of defficent information in the semantic web. In: Moreno Díaz, R., Pichler, F., Quesada Arencibia, A. (eds.) EUROCAST 2007. LNCS, vol. 4739, pp. 305–312. Springer, Heidelberg (2007)
8. Borrego-Díaz, J., Chávez-González, A.M.: Using cognitive entropy to manage uncertain concepts in formal ontologies. In: da Costa, P.C.G., d'Amato, C., Fanizzi, N., Laskey, K.B., Laskey, K.J., Lukasiewicz, T., Nickles, M., Pool, M. (eds.) URSW 2005 - 2007. LNCS (LNAI), vol. 5327, pp. 315–329. Springer, Heidelberg (2008)
9. Borrego-Díaz, J., Chávez-González, A.: On the use of automated reasoning systems in ontology integration. In: Proc. 3rd Int. Workshop Ontology, Conceptualization and Epistemology for Inf. Syst., Soft. Eng. and Service Sci., vol. 460, pp. 37–48. CEUR Proceedings (2009)
10. Borrego-Díaz, J., Chávez-González, A.M.: Extension of ontologies assisted by automated reasoning systems. In: Moreno Díaz, R., Pichler, F., Quesada Arencibia, A. (eds.) EUROCAST 2005. LNCS, vol. 3643, pp. 247–253. Springer, Heidelberg (2005)
11. Borrego-Díaz, J., Chávez-González, A.M., Martín-Pérez, M.A., Zamora-Aguilera, J.A.: Semantic geodemography and urban interoperability. In: Dodero, J.M., Palomo-Duarte, M., Karampiperis, P. (eds.) MTSR 2012. CCIS, vol. 343, pp. 1–12. Springer, Heidelberg (2012)
12. Cohn, A.G., Renz, J.: Qualitative spatial reasoning. In: Handbook of Knowledge Representation. Elsevier (2007)
13. Cohn, A., Gotts, N.: The 'egg-yolk' representation of regions with indeterminate boundaries. In: Proc. Specialist Meeting on Geographical Objects with Undetermined Boundaries. GISDATA Series, vol. 3, pp. 171–187. Taylor and Francis (1995)
14. Corchado, E., Woźniak, M., Abraham, A., de Carvalho, A.A.C.P.L.F., Snásel, V.: Recent trends in intelligent data analysis. Neurocomputing 126, 1–2 (2014)
15. Gerevini, A., Renz, J.: Combining topological and size information for spatial reasoning. Artif. Intell. 137(1-2), 1–42 (2002)
16. Grohe, M., Segoufin, L.: On first-order topological queries. ACM Trans. Comput. Logic 3(3), 336–358 (2002), http://doi.acm.org/10.1145/507382.507384
17. Grütter, R., Scharrenbach, T., Bauer-Messmer, B.: Improving an RCC-derived geospatial approximation by OWL axioms. In: Sheth, A.P., Staab, S., Dean, M., Paolucci, M., Maynard, D., Finin, T., Thirunarayan, K. (eds.) ISWC 2008. LNCS, vol. 5318, pp. 293–306. Springer, Heidelberg (2008)
18. Hernández, D.: Qualitative Representation of Spatial Knowledge. LNCS, vol. 804. Springer, Heidelberg (1994)
19. Knauff, M., Rauh, R., Renz, J.: A cognitive assessment of topological spatial relations: Results from an empirical investigation. In: Frank, A.U. (ed.) COSIT 1997. LNCS, vol. 1329, pp. 193–206. Springer, Heidelberg (1997)
20. Li, S., Ying, M.: Region connection calculus: Its models and composition table. Artificial Intelligence 145(1-2), 121–146 (2003)
21. Randell, D., Cohn, A., Cui, Z.: Computing transitivity tables: A challenge for automated theorem provers. In: Kapur, D. (ed.) CADE 1992. LNCS, vol. 607, pp. 786–790. Springer, Heidelberg (1992)
22. Renz, J.: Qualitative Spatial Reasoning with Topological Information. LNCS (LNAI), vol. 2293. Springer, Heidelberg (2002)
23. Vigneron, L., Wasilewska, A.: Rough Diagrams. In: 6th Int. Workshop Rough Sets, Data Mining & Granular Computing, p. 4 (1998), http://hal.inria.fr/inria-00098493/en/
24. Woźniak, M., Graña, M., Corchado, E.: A survey of multiple classifier systems as hybrid systems. Information Fusion 16, 3–17 (2004)

Theory-Inspired Optimizations for Privacy Preserving Distributed OLAP Algorithms*

Alfredo Cuzzocrea and Elisa Bertino

ICAR-CNR and University of Calabria
Cosenza, Italy
cuzzocrea@si.deis.unical.it
CERIAS and Purdue University
West Lafayette, IN, USA
bertino@cs.purdue.edu

Abstract. Actually, a lot of attention focusing on the problem of *computing privacy-preserving OLAP cubes* effectively and efficiently arises. State-of-the-art proposals rather focus on an *algorithmic vision* of the problem, and neglect relevant *theoretical aspects* the investigated problem introduces naturally. In order to fulfill this gap, in this paper we provide *algorithms for supporting privacy-preserving OLAP in distributed environments*, based on the well-known *CUR matrix decomposition method*, enriched by some relevant *theory-inspired optimizations* that look at the intrinsic nature of the investigated problem in order to gain significant benefits, at both the (privacy-preserving) cube computation level and the (privacy-preserving) cube delivery level.

1 Introduction

The problem of effectively and efficiently supporting *Privacy Preserving Distributed OLAP* [1,26,14,19,2,18,6] plays a leading role in modern organizations due to the fact the latter need to collaboratively harness the potential of "big data" analytics for decision making while at the same time assuring the privacy and confidentiality of their own data sets. This reference scenario example adheres to the *Secure Multiparty Computation* (SMC) [23] model, which is well-known in the context of *Privacy Preserving Distributed Data Mining research* [3,16], with respect to which Privacy Preserving Distributed OLAP can be considered a major, yet-independent, research area. In order to solve the challenging problem of *computing and managing privacy preserving data cubes in distributed environments*, in our previous work [5] we introduced an innovative privacy preserving distributed OLAP framework that relies on the novel concept of *secure distributed OLAP aggregation task*. Basically, this framework is based on the idea of performing OLAP across multiple distributed *SUM-based two-dimensional OLAP views* extracted from data cubes

* The work reported in this paper has been partially supported by the US National Science Foundation under grants CNS-1111512 and CNS-1016722.

M. Polycarpou et al. (Eds.): HAIS 2014, LNAI 8480, pp. 439–453, 2014.
© Springer International Publishing Switzerland 2014

under the SMC requirements [5]. In a sense, our approach follows *hybrid artificial intelligence methodologies*, whose fundamentals can be found in [30,31].

In this paper, we further extend the proposed privacy preserving distributed OLAP framework [5] by providing a number of theoretical results that nicely extend the capabilities of the framework: (*i*) *privacy preserving capabilities of the CUR decomposition method*, where we prove that the two-dimensional OLAP views computed via this method are privacy preserving according to a theoretically-sound probabilistic interpretation; (*ii*) *re-construction capabilities of the CUR decomposition method*, where we prove that the privacy preserving two-dimensional OLAP views can be used for re-constructing the original OLAP views in a theoretically-sound manner; (*iii*) *independence capabilities of the CUR decomposition method*, where we prove that the final two-dimensional OLAP view obtained from the target distributed OLAP aggregation task can be obtained from the two-dimensional OLAP views of the first and the last node of the reference environment, respectively, without dependency on the OLAP views of the remaining nodes, still in a theoretically-sound manner. A preliminary version of this paper appears in [11] as short paper.

2 Privacy Preserving Two-Dimensional OLAP Views Based on the CUR Matrix Decomposition Technique

Given the local OLAP view V_0 at the first node N_0 of the target distributed environment, a critical phase of our proposed secure distributed OLAP aggregation protocol [5] is the computation of the privacy preserving version of V_0, V_0^{PP}, which is then aggregated with the local view V_0 of the node N_1 that "follows" N_0 in the fixed node ordering. It is easy to understand how this first-step operation heavily impacts the overall degree of privacy achieved by the distributed OLAP aggregation protocol.

Therefore, the critical issue is how to effectively and efficiently compute a privacy preserving two-dimensional OLAP view from a given two-dimensional OLAP view. This problem has received great attention with equal emphasis on both ROLAP (e.g., [15,27,28,29]) and MOLAP (e.g., [7,24,8,20]) cubes. Despite this proliferation, state-of-the-art proposals cannot be directly integrated in our privacy preserving distributed OLAP framework, as they are inherently resource-consuming, hence unsuitable for a distributed computation task.

Based on this motivation, we propose exploiting the *CUR matrix decomposition* [10] to compute privacy preserving two-dimensional OLAP views. As argued by Drineas *et al.* [9], the CUR matrix decomposition can be used for privacy preservation purposes. In more detail, CUR is a matrix decomposition method for computing *approximate representations* of large matrices. It can be applied to several application contexts ranging from classification problems to similarity search problems, from analysis of biological data to compression of hyper-spectral data for image processing, and so forth [10]. Formally, given a large $m \times n$ matrix **A**, a CUR matrix decomposition is a *low-rank approximation* of **A**, denoted by **A'**, that represents **A** *in terms of a small number of columns and rows of* **A**, as follows:

$$\left[\mathbf{A}\right] \approx \left[\mathbf{C}\right] \cdot \left[\mathbf{U}\right] \cdot \left[\mathbf{R}\right] \equiv \left[\mathbf{A'}\right] \tag{1}$$

where: (*i*) **C** is an $m \times c$ matrix *that* stores $O(1)$ columns of **A**; (*ii*) **R** is an $r \times n$ matrix that stores $O(1)$ rows of **A**; (*iii*) **U** is a $c \times r$ carefully-chosen matrix. In particular, the number of columns of **C** consists of $c = \Theta(1/\varepsilon^2)$ columns of **A**, and the number of rows of **R** consists of $r = \Theta(1/\varepsilon^2)$ rows of **A**, respectively, with $\varepsilon > 0$ arbitrarily small. **C** and **R** are built by means of *adaptive sampling* [25], via *c* (*r*, respectively) trials by picking a column (a row, respectively) of **A** with probability p_j defined as follows:

$$p_j = \frac{\left|\mathbf{A}[\bullet][j]\right|^2}{\sum_j \left|\mathbf{A}[\bullet][j]\right|^2} \tag{2}$$

whereas the probability p_i for rows is defined as follows:

$$p_i = \frac{\left|\mathbf{A}[i]\right|^2}{\sum_i \left|\mathbf{A}[i]\right|^2} \tag{3}$$

respectively.

Given a *matrix* **A**, computing a CUR decomposition of **A** is a difficult problem [10]. With respect to complexity, the *upper bound* of the complexity of computing a CUR decomposition of an $m \times n$ matrix **A** is represented by the complexity of computing the *Singular Value Decomposition* (SVD) [13] of **A**, which is $O(min\{m \cdot n^2, m^2 \cdot n\})$ in time [10]. This cost can be prohibitive for large matrices one can find in real-world applications. Therefore, several approaches for effectively and efficiently computing CUR decompositions of large matrices have been proposed.

Given an $m \times n$ matrix **A**, Drineas *et al.* [10] address the problem of computing an effective and efficient CUR decomposition of **A** such that the deriving approximate representation of **A**, **A'**, satisfies the following constraints: (*i*) **A'** is a *"good" approximation* of **A**; (*ii*) **A'** can be computed after *very few* scans of **A**; (*iii*) **A'** can be stored in $O(m + n)$ space. [10] provides a very nice theoretical result consisting of an algorithm that allows us to compute **A'** *with rank k* after *two scans* of **A** in $O(c^2 \cdot m + c^3 + r^3)$ time, by picking $r = O(k/\varepsilon^2)$ rows of **A** and $c = O(k/\varepsilon^2)$ columns of **A**, for any $\varepsilon > 0$ arbitrarily small, such that the following inequality holds (error bound):

$$\left\|\mathbf{A} - \mathbf{A'}\right\|_2^2 \leq \left\|\mathbf{A} - \mathbf{A}_k\right\|_F^2 + \varepsilon \cdot \left\|\mathbf{A}\right\|_F^2 \tag{4}$$

where: (*i*) $\left\|\mathbf{A}\right\|_2$ denotes the *spectral norm* [13] of **A**, which is defined as follows:

$$\left\|\mathbf{A}\right\|_2 = \sqrt{\max_{\lambda_p}\{\Lambda_{\mathbf{A}^H \cdot \mathbf{A}}\}} \tag{5}$$

such that that $\mathbf{A}^H$ denotes the *conjugate transpose* matrix of **A**, and $\Lambda_{\mathbf{A}}$ the set of *eigenvalues* of **A**, respectively; (*ii*) $\|\mathbf{A}\|_F$ denotes the *Frobenius norm* [13] of **A**, which is defined as follows:

$$\|\mathbf{A}\|_F = \sqrt{\sum_{i=0}^{m-1}\sum_{j=0}^{n-1}|\mathbf{A}[i][j]|^2} \tag{6}$$

(*iii*) $\mathbf{A}_k$ denotes the rank-k approximation of **A** given by the SVD [10], such that $k \in \{1, \ldots, rank(\mathbf{A})\}$. For $k = k^*$ *"best"* rank-k approximation of **A** given by the SVD (low-rank approximation), i.e. by picking $r = O(1/\varepsilon^2)$ rows of **A** and $c = O(1/\varepsilon^2)$ columns of **A**, (4) can be re-formulated as follows [10]:

$$\|\mathbf{A} - \mathbf{A'}\|_2^2 \leq \varepsilon \cdot \|\mathbf{A}\|_F^2 \tag{7}$$

The satisfaction of inequality (7) ensures that **A'** provides *a "good" approximation of* **A**, *while being still different from* **A**. At the same, **A'** can be computed in $O(m)$ time, in terms of an asymptotic approximation of $O(c^2 \cdot m + c^3 + r^3)$. According to Drineas *et al.* [9], we clearly state that both properties are suitable to Privacy Preserving Data Mining, and, in particular, to our main goal of computing a privacy preserving two-dimensional OLAP view. Such view can be reasonably represented by the output $m \times n$ matrix **A'** provided by the CUR decomposition, from a given two-dimensional OLAP view, which can be reasonably represented by the input $m \times n$ matrix **A** in the CUR decomposition process.

3 A Privacy Preservation Theory Extending the Capabilities of the CUR Matrix Decomposition Technique

Inequality (7) also embeds a *probabilistic interpretation*, which can be derived from results in [10]. For each pair of $\varepsilon > 0$ and $\delta > 0$ arbitrarily small, *with high probability* the following inequality holds [22]:

$$P\left(\|\mathbf{A} - \mathbf{A'}\|_2^2 \leq \varepsilon \cdot \|\mathbf{A}\|_F^2\right) \geq 1 - \delta \tag{8}$$

More precisely, (8) gives us a probabilistic (lower) bound on the probability of *event* e^D = **A** ≠ **A'**, which models the case of obtaining the approximate matrix **A'** as *different* from the input matrix **A**. We denote as $P(e^D)$ the probability associated with this event. In our privacy preserving distributed OLAP framework, we are indeed interested in formally estimating the probability of the *complementary* (*probabilistic*) *event* of e^D, namely e^E = **A** ≡ **A'**, which models the case of obtaining the approximate matrix **A'** as *equal* to the input matrix **A**. We denote as $P(e^E)$ the probability associated with this event. $P(e^E)$ formally models the *privacy risk* of our framework, which is the probability of the occurrence of privacy breaches, which, in our reference framework, are represented by the event such that **A'** (cell partitions of **A'**) is equal to **A** (are equal to cell partitions of **A**). Furthermore, this model allows us to study how much our proposed framework is secure against these possible privacy breaches, again in a probabilistic manner. By recalling that $P(e^E) = 1 - P(e^D)$, the following probabilistic (upper) bound on the probability of event $e^E = \mathbf{A} \equiv \mathbf{A'}$ can be derived, as stated by Theorem 1:

$$P\left(\|\mathbf{A}\|_2^2 = \|\mathbf{A'}\|_2^2\right) \leq \frac{1-\delta}{\varepsilon \cdot \|\mathbf{A}\|_F^2} \tag{9}$$

Theorem 1. *Given an* $m \times n$ *matrix* $\mathbf{A}$*, such that* $m > 0$ *and* $n > 0$*, and its CUR-based approximating matrix* $\mathbf{A'}$*, for each pair* $\langle \varepsilon, \delta \rangle$*, such that* $\varepsilon > 0$ *and* $\delta > 0$ *arbitrarily small, the probability of the event* $e^E = \mathbf{A} \equiv \mathbf{A'}$ *is superiorly bounded by the quantity* $\frac{1-\delta}{\varepsilon \cdot \|\mathbf{A}\|_F^2}$*, i.e.* $P\left(\|\mathbf{A}\|_2^2 = \|\mathbf{A'}\|_2^2\right) \leq \frac{1-\delta}{\varepsilon \cdot \|\mathbf{A}\|_F^2}$.

Proof. (8) can be re-written as follows:

$$-1 + P\left(\|\mathbf{A} - \mathbf{A'}\|_2^2 \leq \varepsilon \cdot \|\mathbf{A}\|_F^2\right) \geq -\delta \tag{10}$$

By simple sign inversion, (10) can be re-written as follows:

$$1 - P\left(\|\mathbf{A} - \mathbf{A'}\|_2^2 \leq \varepsilon \cdot \|\mathbf{A}\|_F^2\right) \leq \delta \tag{11}$$

i.e.:

$$-P\left(\|\mathbf{A} - \mathbf{A'}\|_2^2 \leq \varepsilon \cdot \|\mathbf{A}\|_F^2\right) \leq \delta - 1 \tag{12}$$

By noticing that, for this theoretical probabilistic setting, $P(e^D)$ is defined as follows:

$$P(e^D) = P\left(\|\mathbf{A} - \mathbf{A'}\|_2^2 \leq \varepsilon \cdot \|\mathbf{A}\|_F^2\right) \tag{13}$$

and $P(e^E)$ is defined as follows:

$$P(e^E) = 1 - P(e^D) = P\left(\|\mathbf{A}\|_2^2 = \|\mathbf{A'}\|_2^2\right) \tag{14}$$

respectively, thanks to the *central limit theorem* and the *complementary-event's probability theorem* [22], (12) can be re-formulated as follows:

$$P\left(\|\mathbf{A}\|_2^2 = \|\mathbf{A'}\|_2^2\right) \leq \frac{1-\delta}{\varepsilon \cdot \|\mathbf{A}\|_F^2} \tag{15}$$

which is equal to (9).

Theorem 1 is a relevant theoretical result of our research. It further confirms us the suitability of the CUR decomposition method [10] in supporting Privacy Preserving Data Mining, as argued in [9], since the probability of obtaining two equal matrices is negligible in practice. Thanks to Theorem 1, in our research we achieve an effective, efficient and, above all, theoretically-sound approach for computing a privacy preserving two-dimensional OLAP view from the input two-dimensional OLAP view, which is a fundamental and critical step of the secure distributed OLAP aggregation task.

4 Getting-Back the Original Two-Dimensional OLAP Views

Another critical property that is central to theoretical aspects of the CUR decomposition method is related to assessing the capabilities of the method in re-constructing the original matrix **A** from the approximating matrix **A'** that is retrieved by the method itself. In order to prove the re-construction property ensured by the CUR decomposition method, which also guarantees the theoretical convergence of the framework, we provide Theorem 2 (see next) whose proof is characterized by a structure inspired by the theoretical model proposed by Agrawal *et al.* [1]. In more detail, with respect to the re-construction property ensured by the proposed *Retention Replacement Perturbation* algorithm [1], Agrawal *et al.* provide rigorous probabilistic bounds over aggregates that are re-constructed from a relational table that has been perturbed by means of their algorithm. These aggregates are defined in terms of input range queries over the perturbed relational table, and their values are compared with the values of aggregates retrieved by the same queries over the original relational table. Here, we follow a similar approach, i.e. we study the re-construction property of the CUR decomposition method by considering the aggregate values of range queries over the approximating matrix **A'** in comparison with the aggregate values of the same queries over the original matrix **A**.

Before introducing Theorem 2, some definitions are necessary. First, we define a two-dimensional range query Q over the $m \times n$ matrix **A** (**A'**, respectively) as follows:

$$Q = [\langle l_1{:}u_1\rangle; \langle l_2{:}u_2\rangle] \tag{16}$$

where: (*i*) l_1 denotes a lower bound on the dimension d_1 of **A** (**A'**, respectively); (*ii*) u_1 denotes an upper bound on the dimension d_1 of **A** (**A'**, respectively); (*iii*) $l_1 < u_1$; (*iv*) l_2 denotes a lower bound on the dimension d_2 of **A** (**A'**, respectively); (*v*) u_2 denotes an upper bound on the dimension d_2 of **A** (**A'**, respectively); (*vi*) $l_2 < u_2$. On the basis of well-understood matrix algebra [13] principles, the evaluation of Q over **A** (**A'**, respectively) can be expressed as follows:

$$\mathbf{x}^T \cdot \mathbf{A} \cdot \mathbf{y} = z \tag{17}$$

where: (*i*) **x** models an m-dimensional vector whose elements $\mathbf{x}[i]$, with $0 \leq i \leq m-1$, are defined as follows:

$$\mathbf{x}[i] = \begin{cases} 1 & \text{if } l_1 \leq i \leq u_1 \\ 0 & \text{otherwise} \end{cases} \tag{18}$$

(*ii*) **y** models an n-dimensional vector whose elements $\mathbf{y}[j]$, with $0 \leq j \leq n-1$, are defined as follows:

$$\mathbf{y}[j] = \begin{cases} 1 & \text{if } l_2 \leq j \leq u_2 \\ 0 & \text{otherwise} \end{cases} \tag{19}$$

and (*iii*) z models the answer to Q (z' models the approximate answer to Q, respectively).

For the sake of clarity, Theorem 2 proves that the approximate answer to Q, z', is *probabilistically-close* to the exact answer to Q, z, or, in other words, the reconstruction property of the CUR decomposition method.

Second, we introduce the concept of *re-constructible function*, also inspired by [1], whose formal definition is provided in Definition 1. Intuitively, a numeric function γ is said to be re-constructible iff it allows us to "invert" the transformation of the original matrix **A** (cell partitions of **A**) in the perturbed matrix **A'** (cell partitions of **A'**) due to the CUR decomposition method, in our case. In our theoretical analysis, we interpret numeric functions γ as the data distributions associated with elements of the original matrix **A** (the approximating matrix **A'**, respectively). A relevant property of a re-constructible function γ is that of verifying whether it is $\langle n,\varepsilon,\delta\rangle$*-re-constructible* by means of the so-called *re-constructing function* γ', such that n is the number of items in γ, and ε and δ are positive integer arbitrarily small. In other words, this corresponds to verifying whether an *unbiased estimator* [22] γ' for γ exists. If this is the case, γ' gives us theoretically-proofed probabilistic bounds on the error we commit in reconstructing the function γ (by means of γ').

Definition 1. *Let* $\alpha : \mathbb{R}^m \rightarrow \mathbb{R}^n$ *be a perturbation function converting a matrix* **A** *into the approximating matrix* **A'**; *a numeric function* γ *on* **A** *is said to be* $\langle n,\varepsilon,\delta\rangle$*-re-constructible by means of a re-constructing function* γ', *such that n is the number of items in* γ, *and* ε *and* δ *are positive integers arbitrarily small, iff* γ' *can be evaluated on* **A'** *and the following condition holds:* $|\gamma - \gamma'| = max\{\varepsilon, \varepsilon\cdot\gamma\}$, *such that* $max\{I\}$ *denotes the operator max over a given item set I.*

Based on these theoretical constructs and concepts, we now focus on reconstructing the answer z to a given range query $Q = [\langle l_1{:}u_1\rangle; \langle l_2{:}u_2\rangle]$ over **A** from the approximating matrix **A'** (or, equally, retrieving the approximate answer to Q, z') and the probabilities p_i (3) and p_j (2) exploited by the CUR decomposition method to obtain **A'** from **A**. For this theoretical setting, the re-constructing function γ' we adopt is defined as follows:

$$\gamma'(Q = [\langle l_1 : u_1\rangle; \langle l_2 : u_2\rangle]) = \sum_{i=l_1}^{u_1}\sum_{j=l_2}^{u_1}\left[\mathbf{A'}[i][j] - \frac{(1-p_i)\cdot p_j}{p_i\cdot(1-p_j)}\cdot b\right] \tag{20}$$

where: (*i*) **A'**[i][j] denotes an element of **A'**; (*ii*) p_i (3) denotes the probability of picking the i-th row of **A** during the CUR decomposition method; (*iii*) p_j (2) denotes the probability of picking the j-th column of **A** during the CUR decomposition method; (*iv*) b is defined as follows:

$$b = \frac{max\{\mathbf{A'}\} - min\{\mathbf{A'}\}}{max\{\mathbf{A}\} - min\{\mathbf{A}\}} \quad (21)$$

where that $max\{\mathbf{B}\}$ denotes the operator *max* over the elements of **B**, with **B** in {**A**, **A'**}, and $min\{\mathbf{B}\}$ denotes the operator *min* over the elements of **B**, with **B** in {**A**, **A'**}, respectively. Theorem 2 states that the re-constructing function γ' (20) is an unbiased estimator for the function γ determined by the CUR decomposition method, under the following condition:

$$n \geq 4 \cdot \log(\frac{2}{\delta}) \cdot (p_i \cdot p_j \cdot \varepsilon)^{-2} \quad (22)$$

where: (*i*) n denotes the number of elements of **A** involved in the evaluation of Q; (*ii*) ε and δ are positive integers arbitrarily small; (*iii*) p_i and p_j are the probabilities (3) and (2), respectively, exploited by the CUR decomposition method.

Theorem 2. *Let the value* $\mathbf{A}[i][j]$ *in* $[min\{\mathbf{A'}\}, max\{\mathbf{A'}\}]$ *be estimated by the re-constructing function* γ'*; then* γ' *is a* $\langle n,\varepsilon,\delta\rangle$*-unbiased-estimator for* γ *if the following condition holds:* $n \geq 4 \cdot \log(\frac{2}{\delta}) \cdot (p_i \cdot p_j \cdot \varepsilon)^{-2}$.

Proof. Let $\mathcal{X}_{ij}$ denote a *random variable* [22] for the event that element $\mathbf{A}[i][j]$ of **A** is perturbed, and the perturbed element $\mathbf{A'}[i][j]$ is contained by the interval $[min\{\mathbf{A'}\}, max\{\mathbf{A'}\}]$. It should be noted that the collection of random variables $\mathcal{X}_{ij}$ are i.i.d. [22], and that the probability that element $\mathbf{A}[i][j]$ of **A** is perturbed is given by the following expression:

$$P(\mathcal{X}_{ij} = 1) = (1 - p_i) \cdot (1 - p_j) \cdot b \quad (23)$$

As a consequence, the following equality holds:

$$P(\mathcal{X}_{ij} = 0) = 1 - P(\mathcal{X}_{ij} = 1) = 1 - (1 - p_i) \cdot (1 - p_j) \cdot b \quad (24)$$

Likewise, let $\mathcal{Y}_{ij}$ denote a random variable for the event that element $\mathbf{A}[i][j]$ of **A** is *not* perturbed, and it is contained by the interval $[min\{\mathbf{A'}\}, max\{\mathbf{A'}\}]$. Similarly to the case of random variables $\mathcal{Y}_{ij}$, it should be clear that the collection of random variables $\mathcal{Y}_{ij}$ are i.i.d. and that the probability that element $\mathbf{A}[i][j]$ of **A** is not perturbed is given by the following expression:

$$P(\mathcal{Y}_{ij} = 1) = p_i \cdot p_j \quad (25)$$

In turn, the following expression holds:

$$P(\mathcal{Y}_{ij} = 0) = 1 - P(\mathcal{Y}_{ij} = 1) = 1 - p_i \cdot p_j \quad (26)$$

Now, let $\mathcal{Z}_{ij}$ denote a random variable for the event that, during the CUR decomposition method, element $\mathbf{A}[i][j]$ of **A** falls within the interval $[min\{\mathbf{A'}\}, max\{\mathbf{A'}\}]$.

It follows that $\mathcal{Z}_{ij}$ can be defined in terms of the previous random variable $\mathcal{X}_{ij}$ and $\mathcal{Y}_{ij}$, as follows:

$$\mathcal{Z}_{ij} = \mathcal{X}_{ij} + \mathcal{Y}_{ij} \tag{27}$$

due to the fact that, during the CUR decomposition method, an arbitrary element $\mathbf{A}[i][j]$ of $\mathbf{A}$ may be contained (i.e., $\mathcal{X}_{ij} = 1$ and $\mathcal{Y}_{ij} = 0$) or not (i.e., $\mathcal{X}_{ij} = 0$ and $\mathcal{Y}_{ij} = 1$) by the interval $[min\{\mathbf{A'}\}, max\{\mathbf{A'}\}]$. From (27), it follows that the collection of random variables $\mathcal{Z}_{ij}$ are i.i.d. and that the probability that element $\mathbf{A}[i][j]$ of $\mathbf{A}$ falls within the interval $[min\{\mathbf{A'}\}, max\{\mathbf{A'}\}]$ is given by the following expression:

$$P(\mathcal{Z}_{ij} = 1) = P((\mathcal{X}_{ij} + \mathcal{Y}_{ij}) = 1) = P(\mathcal{X}_{ij} = 1) + P(\mathcal{Y}_{ij} = 1) \tag{28}$$

From (23) and (25), (28) we finally obtain the following expression:

$$P(\mathcal{Z}_{ij} = 1) = (1 - p_i) \cdot (1 - p_j) \cdot b + p_i \cdot p_j \tag{29}$$

As a consequence, the following formula holds:

$$P(\mathcal{Z}_{ij} = 0) = 1 - P(\mathcal{Z}_{ij} = 1) = 1 - (1 - p_i) \cdot (1 - p_j) \cdot b + p_i \cdot p_j \tag{30}$$

Furthermore, let Δ_1 denote the range of Q on the dimension d_1 of $\mathbf{A}$ ($\mathbf{A'}$, respectively). From (16), it clearly follows that the cardinality of Δ_1, $\|\Delta_1\|$, is given by the following expression:

$$\|\Delta_1\| = u_1 - l_1 \tag{31}$$

Similarly, let Δ_2 denote the range of Q on the dimension d_2 of $\mathbf{A}$ ($\mathbf{A'}$, respectively). From (16), it clearly follows again that the cardinality of Δ_2, $\|\Delta_2\|$, is given by the following expression:

$$\|\Delta_2\| = u_2 - l_2 \tag{32}$$

Also, let $\|Q\|$ denote the *volume* (or *selectivity* [4]) of Q. Based on (16), (31) and (32), $\|Q\|$ is given by the following expression:

$$\|Q\| = \|\Delta_1\| \cdot \|\Delta_2\| \tag{33}$$

such that $\|\Delta_1\|$ denotes the cardinality of Δ_1, and $\|\Delta_2\|$ denotes the cardinality of Δ_2, respectively.

Now, let $\mathcal{U}_{ij}$ denote a random variable defined as the *summation of random variables* $\mathcal{Z}_{ij}$ [P] over the two-dimensional domain of $\mathbf{A}$ ($\mathbf{A'}$, respectively) modeling the range of Q, i.e. $[\langle l_1{:}u_1\rangle; \langle l_2{:}u_2\rangle]$ that is defined as follows:

$$\mathcal{U}_{ij}(\Delta_1, \Delta_2) = \sum_{h=i}^{i+\Delta_1-1} \sum_{k=j}^{j+\Delta_2-1} \mathcal{Z}_{hk} \cdot \mathbf{A'}[h][k] \tag{34}$$

It should be noted that random variables $\mathcal{U}_{ij}$ are those associated with the evaluation of the approximate answer to Q, z', and they underlie the definition of the re-constructing function γ' (20). The number of elements of **A'** involved in the Q's evaluation process, n (or, equally, the number of items of $\gamma' - \gamma$, respectively), is given by the following expression:

$$n = \|Q\| = \|\Delta_1\| \cdot \|\Delta_2\| \tag{35}$$

How to model the approximate evaluation of Q over **A'** *in a probabilistic manner?* In order to answer this critical question, first note that each one among the n elements **A'**[i][j] of **A'** may contribute (i.e., $\mathcal{U}_{ij} = 1$) or not (i.e., $\mathcal{U}_{ij} = 0$) to the approximate answer to Q, z'. Our final aim is to find probabilistic bounds for the probability P($\mathcal{U}_{ij} = 1$). Since the random variables Z_{ij} are i.i.d. and the random variables $\mathcal{U}_{ij}$ are defined as the summation of Z_{ij}, *then* $\mathcal{U}_{ij}$ *are independent Bernoulli random variables* [22]. Under the condition (22), by applying the well-known *Chernoff bound* [22], the following inequality holds:

$$P\left[\left|\mathcal{U}_{ij}(\Delta_1,\Delta_2) - n \cdot t \cdot \mathsf{AVG}(\Delta_1,\Delta_2)\right| > n \cdot \theta\right] < 2e^{\frac{-n\cdot\theta^2}{4\cdot t}} \leq \delta \tag{36}$$

such that (*i*) $t = \mathrm{P}(Z_{ij} = 1)$ (29); (*ii*) AVG(Δ_1,Δ_2) denotes the average value of elements **A'**[i][j] of **A'** contained by the two-dimensional range of Q, $[\langle l_1:u_1\rangle; \langle l_2:u_2\rangle]$; (*iii*) θ is defined as follows:

$$\theta = \prod_{i=l_1}^{u_1}\prod_{j=l_2}^{u_2} p_i \cdot p_j \cdot \varepsilon \tag{37}$$

where p_i and p_j are the probabilities (3) and (2), respectively, exploited by the CUR decomposition method, and ε is a positive integer arbitrarily small; (*iv*) δ is a positive integer arbitrarily small. From (36), it follows that, with probability greater than $1 - \delta$, the following inequality holds:

$$\gamma - \varepsilon < \sum_{i=l_1}^{u_1}\sum_{j=l_2}^{u_1}\left[\mathbf{A'}[i][j] - \frac{(1-p_i)\cdot p_j}{p_i\cdot(1-p_j)}\cdot b\right] < \gamma + \varepsilon \tag{38}$$

from which it follows that $/\gamma - \gamma'/ < \varepsilon$ with probability $1 - \delta$, and that re-constructing function γ' (20) is an unbiased estimator for the function γ determined by the CUR decomposition method.

5 CUR-Based Distributed OLAP Aggregation Task

Based on the results in [5] and the fact that SUM-based OLAP aggregation is a *non-holistic* operator [12], it is easy to demonstrate that the final global result of the target distributed OLAP aggregation task, i.e. the view V^{GLOBAL}, can be reconstructed as follows (as formally stated by Theorem 3):

$$V^{GLOBAL} = V_0 + \left(V_{n-1}^{PP} - V_0^{PP}\right) \tag{39}$$

Theorem 3. *The final global OLAP view V^{GLOBAL} obtained from any arbitrary SUM-based secure OLAP aggregation task over a distributed environment populated by n nodes can be retrieved from combining the local OLAP view V_0 at node N_0, the privacy preserving OLAP view V_0^{PP} at node N_0 and the privacy preserving OLAP view V_{n-1}^{PP} at node N_{n-1} without dependency on the OLAP views located at other nodes N_i, with $1 \leq i \leq n-2$, of the reference distributed environment, i.e.* $V^{GLOBAL} = V_0 + \left(V_{n-1}^{PP} - V_0^{PP}\right)$.

Proof. Take as reference a distributed environment populated by n nodes. First, note that, given two consecutive nodes N_{i-1} and N_i in the fixed node ordering, such that $1 \leq i \leq n-2$, since we focus on SUM-based OLAP aggregations, the privacy preserving view V_i^{PP} at node N_i is obtained by combining the local view V_i at node N_i with the privacy preserving view V_{i-1}^{PP} returned to node N_i from node N_{i-1}, as follows (see Section 1):

$$V_i^{PP} = V_i + V_{i-1}^{PP} \tag{40}$$

By contrast, for the *sole* instance represented by the first node N_0, the privacy preserving view V_0^{PP} is directly obtained from the local view V_0 (see Section 1) via the CUR-based approximation method (see Section 2). Hence, with respect to privacy preserving views located at nodes of the reference distributed environment, the following equalities hold:

$$\begin{aligned} & V_0^{PP} = \mathrm{CUR}(V_0) \\ & V_1^{PP} = V_1 + V_0^{PP} \\ & V_2^{PP} = V_2 + V_1^{PP} \\ & \ldots \\ & V_{n-1}^{PP} = V_{n-1} + V_{n-2}^{PP} \end{aligned} \tag{41}$$

Based on (40), by applying simple mathematical substitutions, (41) can be rewritten as follows:

$$\begin{aligned} & V_0^{PP} = \mathrm{CUR}(V_0) \\ & V_1^{PP} = V_1 + V_0^{PP} \\ & V_2^{PP} = V_2 + V_1^{PP} = V_2 + V_1 + V_0^{PP} \\ & \ldots \\ & V_{n-1}^{PP} = V_{n-1} + V_{n-2} + \ldots + V_1 + V_0^{PP} \end{aligned} \tag{42}$$

Based on (42), (39) can be expanded as follows:

$$\begin{aligned} V^{GLOBAL} &= V_0 + \left(V_{n-1}^{PP} - V_0^{PP}\right) \\ &= V_0 + \left(\left(V_{n-1} + V_{n-2} + \ldots + V_1 + V_0^{PP}\right) - V_0^{PP}\right) \end{aligned} \tag{43}$$

i.e.:

$$V^{GLOBAL} = V_0 + V_1 + V_2 + \ldots + V_{n-1} \tag{44}$$

which, from Section 1, represents the (exact) final result of the target distributed OLAP aggregation task.

Theorem 3 is another relevant theoretical result of our research. It allows us to obtain the final global result of the target secure distributed OLAP aggregation task, V^{GLOBAL} from the OLAP views stored at the first node N_0 of the reference distributed environment, V_0 and V_0^{PP}, respectively, one exact (i.e., V_0) and one privacy preserving (i.e., V_0^{PP}), and from the privacy preserving OLAP view V_{n-1}^{PP} returned to node N_0 from node N_{n-1}, *without dependency on the OLAP views* (local and privacy preserving) *of other nodes* N_i, with $1 \leq i \leq n-2$, of the reference distributed environment. Intuitively, this phenomenon opens interesting theoretical as well as query-optimization opportunities for enhancing our privacy preserving distributed OLAP framework.

6 Related Work

Distributed Privacy Preserving OLAP techniques solve the problem of making distributed OLAP data cubes (i.e., OLAP data cubes populating a distributed environment) able to preserve the privacy of data during common (data) management tasks (e.g., computing data cubes, querying data cubes etc) or, under an alternative interpretation, generating a privacy preserving OLAP data cube from distributed data sources. With respect to the first problem, to the best of our knowledge, no approaches exist addressing this problem, beyond our framework [5], whereas concerning the second problem, the approach by Agrawal *et al.* [1] is the state-of-the-art approach.

By looking at the recent literature, while a plethora of initiatives focusing on Privacy Preserving Distributed Data Mining [3,16] exist, to the best of our knowledge, only [1,26,14,19,2,18] deal with the problem of effectively and efficiently supporting privacy preserving OLAP over distributed data sources. Agrawal *et al.* [1] define a privacy preserving OLAP model over data partitioned across multiple clients using a *randomization approach*, which is implemented by the so-called *Retention Replacement Perturbation* algorithm, on the basis of which (*i*) clients perturb tuples which they contribute to the partition in order to achieve *row-level privacy*, and (*ii*) the server is capable of evaluating OLAP queries against perturbed tables via *reconstructing* the original distributions of attributes involved by such queries. Agrawal *et al.* prove that the proposed distributed privacy preserving OLAP model is safe against privacy breaches. The approach by Tong *et al.* [26] is another distributed privacy preserving OLAP approach that is reminiscent of ours. More specifically, they [26] propose the idea of obtaining a privacy preserving OLAP data cube from *distributed data sources across multiple sites* via applying perturbation-based techniques on *aggregate data* that are retrieved from each single site as a baseline step of the main (distributed) OLAP computation task. Other approaches [14,2,19] focus on the significant issue of providing efficient data aggregation while preserving privacy over *Wireless Sensor Networks* (WSN). In more details, He *et al.* [14] propose a solution based on two privacy-preserving data aggregation schemes that make use of innovative *additive aggregation functions*. These schemes are called *Cluster-based Private Data Aggregation* (CPDA) and *Slice-Mix-AggRegaTe* (SMART), respectively. The proposed aggregation functions fully-exploit topology and dynamics of the underlying wireless sensor network, and bridge the gap between collaborative data collection over such networks and data privacy needs. Chan and Castelluccia [2] focus on a formal treatment of a *Private Data Aggregation* (PDA) security model over WSN; this contribution is general enough to cover most cases of security-demanding scenarios over WSN and from a practical perspective allow one to execute privacy preserving data aggregation operations over WSN. The work by Lin *et al.* [19] is an incremental contribution aiming at improving security and saving energy consumption of the privacy preserving data aggregation task over WSN; the main idea of such an approach consists in integrating the super-increasing sequence and perturbation techniques into compressed data aggregations in order to gain efficiency. Li *et al.* [18] propose a novel incremental method for supporting secure and privacy preserving information aggregation over smart grids; this method introduces a novel scheme according to which data aggregation is performed at all smart meters involved in routing the data from the source meter to the collector unit, and the user privacy is provided by the use of *homomorphic encryption* on the transmitted data. Finally, there are more recent efforts that clearly confirm the interest from the research community for the issues investigated in this paper. Among others, Jurezyk and Xiong [17] propose a fully-decentralized anonymization protocol over horizontally-partitioned distributed databases, which supports privacy-preserving aggregate query answering in a distributed fashion, whereas Mohammed *et al.* [21] propose *LKC-privacy*, a new privacy model for achieving anonymization over distributed high-dimensional *healthcare data*, which is perfectly compliant with the privacy preserving distributed OLAP scenario we investigate in our research, as high-dimensional data smoothly resemble data cube cells.

7 Conclusions and Future Work

Starting from our previous research [5], which defined and experimentally evaluated a privacy preserving distributed OLAP framework, in this paper we have introduced a number of theoretical results that nicely extend the capabilities and the potentialities of our framework, mainly related to some relevant capabilities of the CUR matrix decomposition method. Future work is mainly oriented to extend the theoretical results presented here as to make them more robust in order to cover two "difficult" privacy preserving distributed OLAP scenarios of the main framework [5], i.e. (*i*) the need for *multi-resolution OLAP analysis across suitable dimensional hierarchies*, and (*ii*) the presence of *coalition of attackers* that may share *partial knowledge* in order to magnify the capabilities of sensitive data cell inference tasks.

References

1. Agrawal, R., et al.: Privacy-Preserving OLAP. In: Proc. of SIGMOD, pp. 251–262 (2005)
2. Chan, A.C.-F., Castelluccia, C.: A Security Framework for Privacy-Preserving Data Aggregation in Wireless Sensor Networks. ACM Transactions on Sensor Networks 7(4), art. 29 (2011)
3. Clifton, C., et al.: Tools for Privacy Preserving Distributed Data Mining. SIGKDD Explorations 4(2), 28–34 (2002)
4. Cuzzocrea, A.: Accuracy Control in Compressed Multidimensional Data Cubes for Quality of Answer-based OLAP Tools. In: Proc. of SSDBM 2006, pp. 301–310 (2006)
5. Cuzzocrea, A., Bertino, E.: A Secure Multiparty Computation Privacy Preserving OLAP Framework over Distributed XML Data. In: Proc. of SAC, pp. 1666–1673 (2010)
6. Cuzzocrea, A., Russo, V.: Privacy Preserving OLAP and OLAP Security. In: Wang, J. (ed.) Encyclopedia of Data Warehousing and Mining, 2nd edn., pp. 1575–1581. IGI Global (2009)
7. Cuzzocrea, A., Russo, V., Saccà, D.: A Robust Sampling-based Framework for Privacy Preserving OLAP. In: Song, I.-Y., Eder, J., Nguyen, T.M. (eds.) DaWaK 2008. LNCS, vol. 5182, pp. 97–114. Springer, Heidelberg (2008)
8. Cuzzocrea, A., Saccà, D.: Balancing Accuracy and Privacy of OLAP Aggregations on Data Cubes. In: Proc. of DOLAP, pp. 93–98 (2010)
9. Drineas, P., et al.: Computing Sketches of Matrices Efficiently and Privacy Preserving Data Mining. In: Proc. of DIMACS PPDM (2004)
10. Drineas, P., et al.: Fast Monte Carlo algorithms for Matrices III: Computing a Compressed Approximate Matrix Decomposition. SIAM Journal on Computing 36(1), 184–206 (2006)
11. Cuzzocrea, A., Bertino, E.: Further Theoretical Contributions to a Privacy Preserving Distributed OLAP Framework. In: Proc. of COMPSAC, pp. 234–239 (2013)
12. Gray, J., et al.: Data Cube: A Relational Aggregation Operator Generalizing Group-By, Cross-Tab, and Sub-Totals. Data Mining and Knowledge Discovery 1(1), 29–53 (1997)
13. Golub, G.H., Van Loan, C.F.: Matrix Computations. Johns Hopkins University Press (1989)
14. He, W., et al.: PDA: Privacy-Preserving Data Aggregation for Information Collection. ACM Transactions on Sensor Networks 8(1), art. 6 (2011)
15. Hua, M., Zhang, S., Wang, W., Zhou, H., Shi, B.-L.: FMC: An Approach for Privacy Preserving OLAP. In: Tjoa, A.M., Trujillo, J. (eds.) DaWaK 2005. LNCS, vol. 3589, pp. 408–417. Springer, Heidelberg (2005)
16. Jiang, W., Clifton, C.: A Secure Distributed Framework for Achieving k-Anonymity. Very Large Data Bases Journal 15(4), 316–333 (2006)
17. Jurczyk, P., Xiong, L.: Distributed Anonymization: Achieving Privacy for Both Data Subjects and Data Providers. In: Gudes, E., Vaidya, J. (eds.) Data and Applications Security XXIII. LNCS, vol. 5645, pp. 191–207. Springer, Heidelberg (2009)
18. Li, F., et al.: Secure and Privacy-Preserving Information Aggregation for Smart Grids. International Journal of Security and Networks 6(1), 28–39 (2011)
19. Lin, X., et al.: MDPA: Multidimensional Privacy-Preserving Aggregation Scheme for Wireless Sensor Networks. Wireless Communications and Mobile Computing 10(6), 843–856 (2010)
20. Liu, Y., et al.: A Cubic-Wise Balance Approach for Privacy Preservation in Data Cubes. Information Sciences 176(9), 1215–1240 (2006)

21. Mohammed, N., et al.: Centralized and Distributed Anonymization for High-Dimensional Healthcare Data. ACM Transactions on Knowledge Discovery from Data 4(4), art. 18 (2010)
22. Papoulis, A.: Probability, Random Variables, and Stochastic Processes. McGraw-Hill (1984)
23. Pinkas, B.: Cryptographic Techniques for Privacy-Preserving Data Mining. SIGKDD Explorations 4(2), 12–19 (2002)
24. Sung, S.Y., et al.: Privacy Preservation for Data Cubes. Knowledge and Information Systems 9(1), 38–61 (2006)
25. Thompson, S.K., Seber, G.A.F.: Adaptive Sampling. John Wiley & Sons (1996)
26. Tong, Y., et al.: Privacy-Preserving OLAP based on Output Perturbation Across Multiple Sites. In: Proc. of PST, p. 46 (2006)
27. Wang, L., et al.: Securing OLAP Data Cubes against Privacy Breaches. In: Proc. of SP, pp. 161–175 (2004)
28. Wang, L., et al.: Cardinality-based Inference Control in Data Cubes. Journal of Computer Security 12(5), 655–692 (2004)
29. Zhang, N., et al.: Cardinality-based Inference Control in OLAP Systems: An Information Theoretic Approach. In: Proc. of DOLAP, pp. 59–64 (2004)
30. Borrajo, M.L., et al.: Hybrid Neural Intelligent System to Predict Business Failure in Small-To-Medium-Size Enterprises. International Journal of Neural Systems 21(4), 277–296 (2011)
31. Abraham, A.: Special Issue: Hybrid Approaches for Approximate Reasoning. Journal of Intelligent and Fuzzy Systems 23(2-3), 41–42 (2012)

Log-Gamma Distribution Optimisation via Maximum Likelihood for Ordered Probability Estimates*

M. Pérez-Ortiz, P.A. Gutiérrez, and C. Hervás-Martínez

University of Córdoba, Dept. of Computer Science and Numerical Analysis, Rabanales Campus, Albert Einstein building, 14071 - Córdoba, Spain
{i82perom,pagutierrez,chervas}@uco.es

Abstract. Ordinal regression considers classification problems where there exist a natural ordering between the categories. In this learning setting, thresholds models are one of the most used and successful techniques. These models are based on the idea of projecting the patterns to a line, which is thereafter divided into intervals using a set of biases or thresholds. This paper proposes a general likelihood-based optimisation framework to better fit probability distributions for ordered categories. To do so, a specific probability distribution (log-gamma) is used, which generalises three commonly used link functions (log-log, probit and complementary log-log). The experiments show that the methodology is not only useful to provide a probabilistic output of the classifier but also to improve the performance of threshold models when reformulating the prediction rule to take these probabilities into account.

Keywords: Ordinal regression, discriminant learning, log-gamma, probability estimation, maximum likelihood.

1 Introduction

The classification of patterns into naturally ordered labels is referred to as ordinal regression or ordinal classification. This learning paradigm, although still mostly unexplored, is spreading rapidly and receiving a lot of attention from the pattern recognition and machine learning communities [1], given its applicability to real world problems. Thresholds models [1,2,4] are one of the most common methodologies for classification problems where the categories exhibit an ordering. The main assumption made by these methods is that an underlying real-valued outcome (also known as latent variable) exists for the ordered crisp categories, although it is unobservable. Consequently, these methodologies try to estimate two elements:

– A function $g(\mathbf{x})$ to predict the nature of the latent variable.

* This work has been subsidized by the TIN2011-22794 project of the Spanish Ministerial Commission of Science and Technology (MICYT), FEDER funds and the P11-TIC-7508 project of the "Junta de Andalucía" (Spain).

M. Polycarpou et al. (Eds.): HAIS 2014, LNAI 8480, pp. 454–465, 2014.
© Springer International Publishing Switzerland 2014

– A vector of thresholds $\mathbf{b} = (b_1, b_2, \ldots, b_{K-1}) \in \mathbb{R}^{K-1}$ (where K is the number of classes in the problem) to represent the intervals in the range of $g(\mathbf{x})$, where $b_1 \leq b_2 \leq \ldots \leq b_{K-1}$.

For example, if the categories of an ordinal regression problem of age estimation are {*young*, *adult*, *old*}, a threshold model would try to uncover the latent variable related to the actual age of the person and the thresholds would divide this latent variable into the considered categories.

There has been a great deal of work of probabilistic linear regression models for ordinal response variables [4,3]. These models are known as Cumulative Link Models (CLMs) and they are based on the idea of modelling the cumulative probability of each pattern to belong to a class lower than the class which is being considered. The proportional odds model (POM) [4] is the first model in this category, being a probabilistic model which leads to linear decision boundaries, given that the latent function $g(\cdot)$ is a linear model. This probabilistic model resembles the threshold model structure, although the linearity of $g(\cdot)$ can limit its applicability for real datasets. Other threshold models have been considered in the literature for ordinal regression, such as the support vector machine (SVM) reformulation [5] or the kernel discriminant learning one [2], which result into nonlinear decision boundaries based on a nonlinear latent function $g(\cdot)$. For these models, the thresholds are chosen so as to perform the classification task, without directly providing probability estimates for the patterns. In this sense, the motivation for the optimisation method proposed in this paper is to derive a general probability estimation framework for projected patterns obtained by $g(\cdot)$ which can be used in conjunction with all threshold models (linear or nonlinear).

In CLMs, the final response depends on the link function considered (logit, probit, complementary log-log, negative log-log or cauchit functions) [3]. The optimal choice of this distribution will directly depend on the distribution of the patterns itself. A more suitable option, which is barely explored in the literature, is a generalised link function (such as the one used in this paper: the log-gamma distribution [6], which generalises the probit, log-log and complementary log-log links). The log-gamma distribution depends on a parameter, q, which modifies the shape of the function. Usually, the value of q is the same for all classes [6]. We propose to consider this generalised cumulative distribution function for modelling probabilities of projected patterns, but allowing a different q for each class which will ideally provide better probability estimates for ordered categories.

The rest of the paper is organised as follows: Section 2 presents the methodology proposed, while Section 3 presents and discusses the experimental results. The last section summarises the main contributions of the paper.

2 Methodology

The goal in ordinal classification is to assign an input vector $\mathbf{x}$ to one of K discrete classes $\mathcal{C}_k, k \in \{1, \ldots, K\}$ where there exists a given ordering between the labels $\mathcal{C}_1 \prec \mathcal{C}_2 \prec \cdots \prec \mathcal{C}_K$, $\prec$ denoting this order information. Hence the objective is to find a prediction rule $C : \mathcal{X} \rightarrow \mathcal{Y}$ by using an i.i.d. training sample $X = \{\mathbf{x}_i, y_i\}_{i=1}^{N}$ where N is the number of training patterns, $\mathbf{x}_i \in \mathcal{X}$, $y_i \in \mathcal{Y}$, $\mathcal{X} \subset \mathbb{R}^k$ is the k-dimensional input space and $\mathcal{Y} = \{\mathcal{C}_1, \mathcal{C}_2, \ldots, \mathcal{C}_K\}$ is the label space. For convenience, denote by $\mathbf{X}_i$ to the set of patterns belonging to $\mathcal{C}_i$.

The optimisation methodology presented in this paper can be used with a wide range of ordinal regression models in order to obtain probability estimates, provided they resemble the threshold model structure. However, there are some methods that could benefit more from the proposed strategy, such as the reformulation of the Kernel Discriminant Analysis to ordinal regression (KDLOR) [2]. This method, which is the one chosen for the experimental part of the study, makes a very strong assumption when fixing the bias terms and does not include them in the optimisation of the model (while they are indeed a extremely important part of the model, that could lead to poor results when not optimised correctly). We propose to include both the parameters associated to the log-gamma distribution and the thresholds of the model in the proposed probability estimation optimisation step. In the next subsection, we will include some introductory notions of this method for the sake of understanding.

2.1 Discriminant Learning

We briefly introduce some notions of discriminant learning in this subsection. Its main objective is to find the optimal projection for the data (which allows the classes of the problem to be easily separated). To do so, the algorithm analyses two objectives: the maximisation of the between-class distances, and the minimisation of the within-class distances, by using variance-covariance matrices ($\mathbf{S}_b$ and $\mathbf{S}_w$ respectively) and the so-called Rayleigh coefficient ($J(\boldsymbol{\beta}) = \frac{\boldsymbol{\beta}^{\mathrm{T}}\mathbf{S}_b\boldsymbol{\beta}}{\boldsymbol{\beta}^{\mathrm{T}}\mathbf{S}_w\boldsymbol{\beta}}$, where $\boldsymbol{\beta}$ is the projection to be found). To achieve these objectives, the $K-1$ eigenvectors associated with the highest eigenvalues of $\mathbf{S}_w^{-1} \cdot \mathbf{S}_b$ are computed, and these will be the mapping functions which project the data to a lower-dimensional space, which will be used as the discriminant function. As stated before, this learning methodology has also been adapted to ordinal classification [2] by imposing a constraint on the projection to be computed, so that it will preserve and take advantage of the ordinal information. This constraint forces the projected classes to be ordered according to their rank, which is useful for minimising ordinal misclassification errors. This method is known as Kernel Discriminant Learning for Ordinal Regression (KDLOR). Further information can be found in [2].

2.2 Bias Computation for the Discriminant Function

The bias terms (both in the original binary Discriminant Analysis and the ordinal version) can be derived from the Bayes theorem [7], assuming that the projected patterns follow a normal distribution with equal variance and a priori probabilities. That is,

$$P(y_i = \mathcal{C}_k | X = \mathbf{x}_i) = \frac{f_k(\mathbf{x}_i)\pi_k}{\sum_{l=1}^{K} f_l(\mathbf{x}_i)\pi_l} = \frac{\pi_k \frac{1}{\sqrt{2\pi\sigma}} \exp\left(-\frac{1}{2}\left(\frac{x-\mu_k}{\sigma}\right)^2\right)}{\sum_{l=1}^{K} \pi_l \frac{1}{\sqrt{2\pi\sigma}} \exp\left(-\frac{1}{2}\left(\frac{x-\mu_l}{\sigma}\right)^2\right)}, \quad (1)$$

where π_k is the prior probability of class k and $f_k(\mathbf{x}_i)$ the class-conditional density function of X for class y. Assuming that each class density function (f_k) can be modelled by a univariate Gaussian distribution (as done in the right part of Eq. 1), it can be seen that this is equivalent to assigning $\mathbf{x}_i$ to the class with the largest discriminant score (taking logs and discarding terms that do not depend on k):

$$\gamma_k(\mathbf{x}_i) = \mathbf{x}_i \cdot \frac{\mu_k}{\sigma^2} - \frac{\mu_k^2}{2\sigma^2} + \log(\pi_k), \quad (2)$$

where μ_k is the mean of $\boldsymbol{\beta}^{\mathrm{T}} X_k$ and σ the variance (assuming that all the variances for the classes are equal). For $K = 2$, the bias can be fixed to the point $\mathbf{x}$ where the discriminant scores for both classes are equal (decision boundary). This leads us to:

$$b = \frac{\mu_1 + \mu_2}{2} + \frac{\sigma^2 \cdot \log(\pi_2)}{\mu_1 - \mu_2} - \frac{\sigma^2 \cdot \log(\pi_1)}{\mu_1 - \mu_2}. \quad (3)$$

In the case of KDLOR, a priori probabilities π_1 and π_2 are assumed to be equal (therefore, $b = \frac{\mu_1 + \mu_2}{2}$). Moreover, each bias is computed considering the adjacent projected classes (e.g. b_1 is computed considering $\mathcal{C}_1$ and $\mathcal{C}_2$):

$$b_i = \frac{\mu_i + \mu_{i+1}}{2}. \quad (4)$$

In contrast, we propose to consider the full expression of (3), given that a priori probabilities are generally different, specially in the case of ordinal regression, where extreme classes are usually associated to infrequent events.

2.3 Maximum Likelihood Based Methodology

Instead of considering the technique introduced in previous subsection, we can perform a maximum likelihood estimation of the biases of the probability distributions, which will be introduced in this subsection. In order to do so, we will consider ordinal logistic regression models. The well-known binary logistic regression model can be easily generalised to handle an ordinal response [4,3], leading to cumulative link models (CLMs). Let h denote a given link function, then, the model:

$$h[(P(y_i \prec \mathcal{C}_j))] = b_j - \boldsymbol{\beta}^{\mathrm{T}} \mathbf{x}_i, \;\; j = 1, \ldots, K-1, \;\; b_1 < \ldots < b_{K-1}, \quad (5)$$

links the cumulative probabilities to a linear predictor based on the parameter vector $\boldsymbol{\beta}$. By definition, $P(y_i \prec \mathcal{C}_K) = 1$. Let $F = h^{-1}$ denote the inverse link function for the CLM (e.g. the normal cdf for the cumulative probit model). The log-likelihood function can be defined:

$$\mathcal{L}(\boldsymbol{\theta}) = \sum_{i=1}^{N}\sum_{j=1}^{K} y_{ij} \log[F(\boldsymbol{\beta}^{\mathrm{T}}\mathbf{x}_i, b_j, q_j) - F(\boldsymbol{\beta}^{\mathrm{T}}\mathbf{x}_i, b_{j-1}, q_{j-1})], \quad (6)$$

where, for $\mathbf{x}_i$, $y_{ij} = 1$ if $y_i = \mathcal{C}_j$ and $y_{ij} = 0$ otherwise, $\boldsymbol{\theta} = \{\boldsymbol{\beta}, \mathbf{b}, \mathbf{q}\}$ is the vector of parameters of the model, $\mathbf{b}$ is the vector containing the biases and $\mathbf{q}$ is the vector of possible distribution parameters. Note that, by definition, $F(\boldsymbol{\beta}^{\mathrm{T}}\mathbf{x}_i, b_0, q_0) = 0$ and $F(\boldsymbol{\beta}^{\mathrm{T}}\mathbf{x}_i, b_K, q_K) = 1$. Therefore, the probability of a pattern $\mathbf{x}_i$ belonging to a given class $\mathcal{C}_j$ is computed as follows:

$$P(y_i = \mathcal{C}_j|\mathbf{x}_i) = F(\boldsymbol{\beta}^{\mathrm{T}}\mathbf{x}_i, b_j, q_j) - F(\boldsymbol{\beta}^{\mathrm{T}}\mathbf{x}_i, b_{j-1}, q_{j-1}), \quad (7)$$

i.e. the difference of the cumulative probabilities.

There are multiple options for F [3]. However, in this paper we will consider the log-gamma function [6], which depends on a parameter q, generalising the log-log link function ($q > 0$), the probit link ($q = 0$) and the complementary log-log ($q < 0$). The log-gamma link can be written as follows:

$$F(z_i, b_j, q_j) = \begin{cases} 1 - \mathit{\Gamma}_{\mathrm{inc}}(q_j^{-2}, v_{ij}), & q_j < 0, \\ \mathit{\Phi}(b_j - z_i), & q_j = 0, \\ \mathit{\Gamma}_{\mathrm{inc}}(q_j^{-2}, v_{ij}), & q_j > 0, \end{cases} \quad (8)$$

where $v_{ij} \equiv q_j^{-2}\exp(q_j \cdot (b_j - z_i))$, $z_i = \boldsymbol{\beta}^{\mathrm{T}}\mathbf{x}_i$, $\mathit{\Gamma}_{\mathrm{inc}}(\cdot,\cdot)$ denotes the standardised incomplete gamma function $\mathit{\Gamma}_{\mathrm{inc}}(a, x) = \int_0^x \exp(-t) \cdot t^{a-1}dt \cdot \frac{1}{\mathit{\Gamma}(a)}$ and $\mathit{\Phi}$ corresponds to the standard normal distribution. Using the log-gamma link, the density is negatively skewed for $q < 0$, positively skewed for $q > 0$ and the absolute skewness and kurtosis increase monotonically in $|q|$ [6]. The cumulative and standard probabilities obtained using this function for different q values for a single class can be seen in Fig.1. On the contrary, Fig. 2 shows these probabilities for a problem with 4 ordered classes and different q values.

We will consider a nonlinear projection given by other ordinal regression model (in our case, KDLOR). Let z_i the projection of pattern $\mathbf{x}_i$, $g(\mathbf{x}_i) = z_i$. Consequently, the parameter vector will be $\boldsymbol{\theta} = \{\mathbf{b}, \mathbf{q}\}$. Because of the differentiability of the log-likelihood $\mathcal{L}(\{\mathbf{b}, \mathbf{q}\})$ with respect to the parameters $\mathbf{b}$ and $\mathbf{q}$, a gradient-ascent algorithm can be used to maximise it:

$$\{\mathbf{b}^*, \mathbf{q}^*\} = \arg\max_{\mathbf{b},\mathbf{q}} \mathcal{L}(\{\mathbf{b}, \mathbf{q}\}). \quad (9)$$

The gradient vector will be composed of partial derivatives $\nabla\mathcal{L} = \left[\frac{\partial\mathcal{L}}{\partial b_1}, \ldots, \frac{\partial\mathcal{L}}{\partial b_{K-1}}, \frac{\partial\mathcal{L}}{\partial q_1}, \ldots, \frac{\partial\mathcal{L}}{\partial q_{K-1}}\right]$. Note that the optimised parameters by our proposal are the bias terms $\mathbf{b}$ and the parameters $\mathbf{q}$ associated to the link function F (but not the projection model $\boldsymbol{\beta}$).

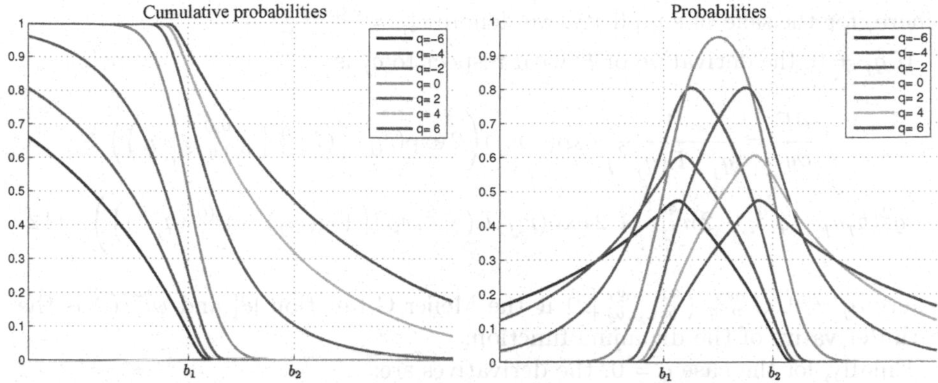

Fig. 1. Log-gamma probabilities for given b_1 and b_2 and different q values

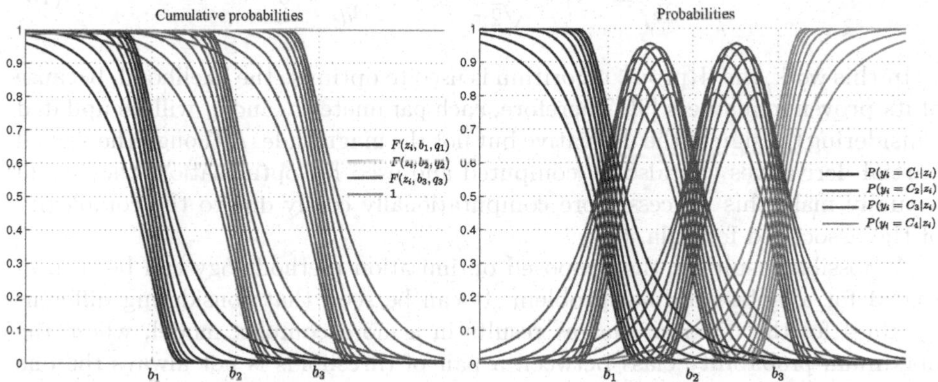

Fig. 2. Log-gamma computed probabilities for a 4-class problem and different q values

The derivatives of the likelihood with respect to the vector $\mathbf{b}$ and $\mathbf{q}$ are:

$$\frac{\partial \mathcal{L}}{\partial b_j} = \sum_{i=1}^{N}\sum_{j=1}^{K} y_{ij} \frac{\delta_{jk} \cdot \frac{\partial F}{\partial b_j}(z_i, b_j, q_j) - \delta_{j-1,k} \cdot \frac{\partial F}{\partial b_j}(z_i, b_{j-1}, q_{j-1})}{F(z_i, b_j, q_j) - F(z_i, b_{j-1}, q_{j-1})}, \tag{10a}$$

$$\frac{\partial \mathcal{L}}{\partial q_j} = \sum_{i=1}^{N}\sum_{j=1}^{K} y_{ij} \frac{\delta_{jk} \cdot \frac{\partial F}{\partial q_j}(z_i, b_j, q_j) - \delta_{j-1,k} \cdot \frac{\partial F}{\partial q_j}(z_i, b_{j-1}, q_{j-1})}{F(z_i, b_j, q_j) - F(z_i, b_{j-1}, q_{j-1})}, \tag{10b}$$

where f denotes the derivative of F, i.e. the probability density function corresponding to the cumulative density function F, and δ_{jk} is the Kronecker delta, i.e. $\delta_{jk} = 1$ if $j = k$ and $\delta_{jk} = 0$ otherwise.

If $q_j \neq 0$, the derivative of F with respect to b_j:

$$\frac{\partial F}{\partial b_j} = \frac{q_j \cdot \exp(-z) \cdot r_{ij}^{q_j^{-2}}}{\Gamma(q_j^{-2})}, \tag{11}$$

where, for the sake of simplicity, we denote $r_{ij} = \frac{\exp(q_j \cdot (b_j - z_i))}{q_j^2}$.

If $q_j \neq 0$, the derivative of F with respect to q_j is:

$$\frac{\partial F}{\partial q_j} = \frac{1}{q_j^3 \cdot \Gamma(q_j^{-2})} \exp(-r_{ij}) \Bigg(2 \exp(r_{ij}) \left(G^{3\,0}_{2\,3} \left({}^{0,0}_{0,0,q_j^{-2}} \middle| r_{ij} \right) \right) +$$

$$+ q_j^2 (b_j q_j - q_j z_i - 2) r_{ij}^{q_j^{-2}} + 2 \exp(r_{ij}) \Gamma(q_j^{-2}, r_{ij}) \Big(\log(r_{ij}) - \psi^{(0)}(q_j^{-2}) \Big) \Bigg), \quad (12)$$

where $q_j \neq 0$, $G^{m\;n}_{p\;q} \left({}^{a_1,\ldots,a_p}_{b_1,\ldots,b_q} \middle| z \right)$ it the Meijer G-function [8] and $\psi^{(n)}(\cdot)$ is the n-th derivative of the digamma function.

Finally, for the case $q = 0$, the derivatives are:

$$\frac{\partial F}{\partial b_j} = \frac{\exp\left(-\frac{(b_j - z_i)^2}{2}\right)}{\sqrt{2\pi}}, \quad \frac{\partial F}{\partial q_j} = 0. \quad (13)$$

In this work, the iRprop$^+$ algorithm is used to optimise the likelihood, because of its proven robustness [9]. Therefore, each parameter b_i and q_i will be updated considering the sign of the derivative but not the magnitude. Although the second partial derivatives can also be computed and used for optimisation, they could actually make this process more computationally costly due to the complexity of the associated formula.

A possible result for the proposed optimisation methodology can be seen in Fig. 3 for a 4-class ordinal problem. It can be seen that considering different q values for the different classes results in a more complex model, where the maximum probability class between a pair of thresholds is not always the one corresponding to the first threshold (contrary to standard CLMs such as the POM model).

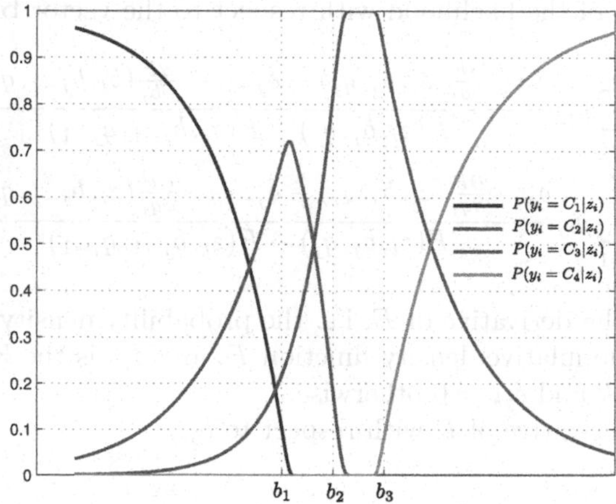

Fig. 3. Probabilistic distributions obtained for eucalyptus and ESL

Table 1. Characteristics of the benchmark datasets in alphabetical order

Dataset	#Pat.	#Attr.	#Classes	Class distribution
balance-scale	625	4	3	(288, 49, 288)
contact-lenses	24	6	3	(15, 5, 4)
ESL	488	4	9	(2, 12, 38, 100, 116, 135, 62, 19, 4)
eucalyptus	736	91	5	(180, 107, 130, 214, 105)
LEV	1000	4	5	(93, 280, 403, 197, 27)
pasture	36	25	3	(12, 12, 12)
squash-stored	52	51	3	(23, 21, 8)
SWD	1000	10	4	(32, 352, 399, 217)
tae	151	54	3	(49, 50, 52)
toy	300	2	5	(35, 87, 79, 68, 31)

The original prediction decision rule for the KDLOR method was the following: $y_i^* = \mathcal{C}_j$ if $b_{j-1} < z_i < b_j$, where $b_0 \equiv -\infty$ and $b_K \equiv \infty$. However, in this case it should be done considering the class associated to the maximum probability computed using the log-gamma function:

$$y_i^* = (\mathcal{C}_j | j = \arg\max_j (F(b_j - z_i, q_j) - F(b_{j-1} - z_i, q_{j-1}))). \tag{14}$$

3 Experiments

Several benchmark datasets with different characteristics have been tested in order to validate the methodology proposed. Table 1 shows the characteristics of these datasets, where the number of patterns, attributes, classes and the class distribution (number of patterns per class) can be seen.

The experiments were designed to compare three different methodologies. First of all, the KDLOR nonlinear projection is obtained and then the biases (and the parameters of the distributions) are learnt using one of the following methods:

- The original KDLOR method considering the methodology in Eq. (4) for setting the thresholds and assuming equal a priori probabilities (KDLOR).
- KDLOR considering the complete expression of Eq. (3) for setting the thresholds without assuming equal a priori probabilities (AP-KDLOR).
- KDLOR optimising the bias and the distribution parameters via maximum likelihood (ML-KDLOR) (see Section 2.3), with the parametrised log-gamma function.

3.1 Evaluation Metrics

Several measures can be considered for evaluating ordinal classifiers, e.g. the mean absolute error (MAE) and the well-known accuracy (Acc) [1,2]. While the

Acc measure is also intended to evaluate nominal classifiers, the MAE metric is the most common choice for ordinal methods.

The mean absolute error (MAE) is the average deviation in absolute value of the predicted class from the true class [10]: $MAE = \frac{1}{N}\sum_{i=1}^{N} e(\mathbf{x}_i)$, where $e(x_i) = |r(y_i) - r(y_i^*)|$ is the distance (in number of categories) between the true and the predicted ranks. $r(y)$ is the rank for a given target y (its position in the ordinal scale), so MAE values range from 0 to $K-1$ (maximum deviation in number of ranks between two labels).

3.2 Experimental Setting

Regarding the experimental setup, a holdout stratified technique was applied to divide the datasets 30 times, using 75% of the patterns for training and the remaining 25% for testing. The parameters of each algorithm are chosen using a nested validation for each of the training sets (k-fold method with $k = 3$) and the validation criteria is the MAE error (see Section 3.1), since it can be considered the most common one in ordinal regression. The kernel selected for KDLOR is the Gaussian one, $K(\mathbf{x}, \mathbf{y}) = \exp\left(-\frac{\|\mathbf{x}-\mathbf{y}\|^2}{\sigma^2}\right)$ where σ is the standard deviation and is cross-validated within the following values: $\{10^{-3}, \ldots, 10^{3}\}$.

As stated before, the optimisation of gradient-based methods is guaranteed only to find a local minimum; therefore, the quality of the solution can be sensitive to initialisation. The initial $\mathbf{b}$ value for the gradient-ascent was set to the original biases of the KDLOR method (Eq. (4)). The $\mathbf{q}$ vector associated to the log-gamma distribution parameters were randomly initialised between $[-1, 1]$ (recall that the thresholds were firstly computed assuming a normal distribution). The gradient norm stopping criterion was set at 10^{-8} and the maximum number of conjugate gradient steps at 10^2 [9].

3.3 Results

Table 2 shows the mean test results for the 10 datasets considered in terms of *Acc* and MAE. First of all, it can be appreciated from this Table that the results for KDLOR and AP-KDLOR are very similar. This indicates that the consideration of the a priori probabilities for the bias computation does not influence the results to a great extent and therefore it can be assumed that these are equal. On the other hand, one can appreciate that the optimisation via maximum likelihood results in a better performance of the algorithm in both metrics (specially if ones takes into account that the projections z_i remain unchanged and that the improvement is only due to the optimisation of the thresholds and distribution parameters). However, there are also some cases in which the capability of the proposal is limited (e.g. for the tae dataset, where the same results are obtained for the three methods).

Table 2. Mean test results for *Acc* and *MAE*. Best results are highlighted in boldface

Dataset	Method	*Acc*	*MAE*
balance-scale	KDLOR	82.55 ± 3.54	0.176 ± 0.040
	AP-KDLOR	82.55 ± 3.54	0.176 ± 0.040
	ML-KDLOR	$\mathbf{90.70 \pm 0.72}$	$\mathbf{0.103 \pm 0.014}$
contact-lenses	KDLOR	61.11 ± 18.74	0.533 ± 0.257
	AP-KDLOR	61.11 ± 18.74	0.533 ± 0.257
	ML-KDLOR	$\mathbf{65.00 \pm 12.65}$	$\mathbf{0.506 \pm 0.212}$
ESL	KDLOR	64.34 ± 3.41	0.374 ± 0.040
	AP-KDLOR	64.34 ± 3.41	0.374 ± 0.040
	ML-KDLOR	$\mathbf{68.47 \pm 2.85}$	$\mathbf{0.330 \pm 0.033}$
eucalyptus	KDLOR	59.91 ± 2.70	0.450 ± 0.037
	AP-KDLOR	59.91 ± 2.70	0.450 ± 0.037
	ML-KDLOR	$\mathbf{61.01 \pm 2.78}$	$\mathbf{0.437 \pm 0.035}$
LEV	KDLOR	55.12 ± 2.81	0.507 ± 0.033
	AP-KDLOR	55.12 ± 2.81	0.507 ± 0.033
	ML-KDLOR	$\mathbf{60.49 \pm 2.73}$	$\mathbf{0.436 \pm 0.031}$
pasture	KDLOR	61.85 ± 11.56	0.385 ± 0.119
	AP-KDLOR	61.69 ± 11.72	0.387 ± 0.121
	ML-KDLOR	$\mathbf{62.22 \pm 11.15}$	$\mathbf{0.381 \pm 0.116}$
squash-stored	KDLOR	62.86 ± 14.10	0.387 ± 0.150
	AP-KDLOR	$\mathbf{63.08 \pm 13.76}$	0.385 ± 0.147
	ML-KDLOR	$\mathbf{63.08 \pm 15.17}$	$\mathbf{0.377 \pm 0.161}$
SWD	KDLOR	48.87 ± 3.00	0.579 ± 0.036
	AP-KDLOR	48.87 ± 3.00	0.579 ± 0.036
	ML-KDLOR	$\mathbf{56.65 \pm 4.08}$	$\mathbf{0.462 \pm 0.046}$
tae	KDLOR	$\mathbf{56.67 \pm 5.30}$	$\mathbf{0.452 \pm 0.055}$
	AP-KDLOR	$\mathbf{56.67 \pm 5.30}$	$\mathbf{0.452 \pm 0.055}$
	ML-KDLOR	$\mathbf{56.67 \pm 5.30}$	$\mathbf{0.452 \pm 0.055}$
toy	KDLOR	88.67 ± 3.35	0.113 ± 0.034
	AP-KDLOR	88.67 ± 3.35	0.113 ± 0.034
	ML-KDLOR	$\mathbf{90.91 \pm 2.56}$	$\mathbf{0.092 \pm 0.026}$

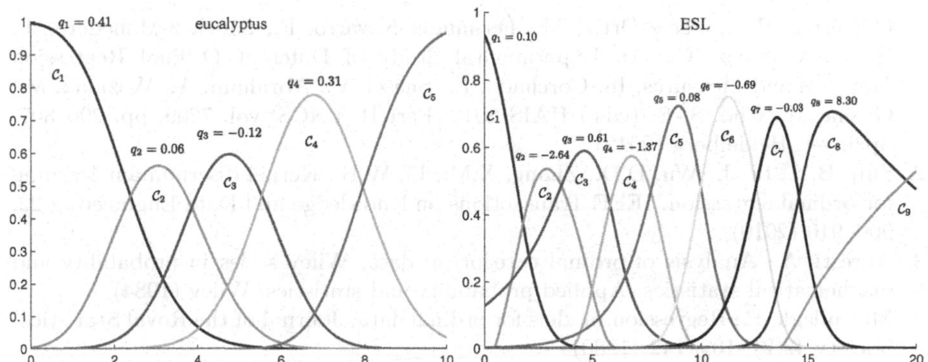

Fig. 4. Probabilistic distributions obtained for eucalyptus and ESL

Furthermore, it is important to note that the proposed methodology consider the optimisation of the thresholds and distribution parameters as a whole, taking into account all the classes in the problem. This is opposed to the bias computation used for KDLOR and AP-KDLOR, where these are computed considering adjacent classes only. To understand how this could influence the results in terms of the classes ordering, we can check the results for the squash-stored dataset, where both AP-KDLOR and ML-KDLOR obtained the same performance in *Acc*, while AP-KDLOR presented worse results for MAE.

Fig. 4 shows the resultant probability distributions for two of the considered datasets. It can be seen that the assumption of $q = 0$ for all probability distributions may not hold, and performing the proposed maximum likelihood optimisation results in a much higher flexibility (which also improves the generalisation performance, see Table 2).

4 Conclusions

In the context of ordinal regression threshold models, this paper proposes a gradient-ascent optimisation of the log-gamma distribution via maximum likelihood to obtain more accurate probabilistic predictions. The experimental results show a good synergy between the proposed technique and the reformulation of the well-known kernel discriminant analysis to ordinal regression problems. More specifically, the results suggests that a per-class bias and probability distribution optimisation is indeed a crucial step for the base methodology, leading to an improvement of the performance. As future work, the methodology proposed in this paper could be used in conjunction with some probabilistic ensemble methods for ordinal regression [11] or derived for and included in other statistical and ordinal link-based methodologies [4].

References

1. Gutiérrez, P.A., Pérez-Ortiz, M., Fernández-Navarro, F., Sánchez-Monedero, J., Hervás-Martínez, C.: An Experimental Study of Different Ordinal Regression Methods and Measures. In: Corchado, E., Snášel, V., Abraham, A., Woźniak, M., Graña, M., Cho, S.-B. (eds.) HAIS 2012, Part II. LNCS, vol. 7209, pp. 296–307. Springer, Heidelberg (2012)
2. Sun, B.Y., Li, J., Wu, D.D., Zhang, X.M., Li, W.B.: Kernel discriminant learning for ordinal regression. IEEE Transactions on Knowledge and Data Engineering 22, 906–910 (2010)
3. Agresti, A.: Analysis of ordinal categorical data. Wiley series in probability and mathematical statistics: Applied probability and statistics. Wiley (1984)
4. McCullagh, P.: Regression models for ordinal data. Journal of the Royal Statistical Society 42(2), 109–142 (1980)
5. Chu, W., Keerthi, S.S.: Support vector ordinal regression. Neural Computation 19, 792–815 (2007)
6. Lin, K.C.: Goodness-of-fit tests for modeling longitudinal ordinal data. Comput. Stat. Data Anal. 54(7), 1872–1880 (2010)

7. Hastie, T., Tibshirani, R., Friedman, J.: The elements of statistical learning: data mining, inference and prediction, 2nd edn. Springer (2008)
8. Askey, R.A., Daalhuis, A.B.O.: Generalized Hypergeometric Functions and Meijer G-Function. In: NIST Handbook of Mathematical Functions, pp. 403–418. Cambridge University Press (2010)
9. Igel, C., Hüsken, M.: Empirical evaluation of the improved rprop learning algorithms. Neurocomputing 50, 105–123 (2003)
10. Baccianella, S., Esuli, A., Sebastiani, F.: Evaluation measures for ordinal regression. In: Proceedings of the Ninth International Conference on Intelligent Systems Design and Applications (ISDA 2009), Pisa, Italy (2009)
11. Pérez-Ortiz, M., Gutiérrez, P.A., Hervás-Martínez, C.: Projection based ensemble learning for ordinal regression. IEEE Transactions on Cybernetics (99) (2013), `http://dx.doi.org/10.1109/TCYB.2013.2266336` (accepted)

A Relational Dual Tableau Decision Procedure for Multimodal and Description Logics

Domenico Cantone[1], Joanna Golińska-Pilarek[2], and Marianna Nicolosi-Asmundo[1]

[1] University of Catania, Dept. of Mathematics and Computer Science, Italy
{cantone,nicolosi}@dmi.unict.it

[2] University of Warsaw, Institute of Philosophy, Poland
j.golinska@uw.edu.pl

Abstract. We present a dual tableau based decision procedure for a class of fragments of the classical relational logic of binary relations. The logics considered share a common language involving a restricted composition operator and infinitely many relational constants which may have the properties of reflexivity, transitivity, and heredity. The construction of the dual tableau is carried out by applying in a deterministic way axioms and inference rules of the system without resorting to external tools. An important feature of the dual tableau procedure is a rule to handle the relational composition operator, that permits to decompose in a single step compositional formulae and negative compositional formulae with the same left object variable.

Our relational dual tableau can be used as a decision procedure for validity verification in the multimodal logic K, the description logic $\mathcal{ALC}$, and several non-classical logics for reasoning in various AI systems.

1 Introduction

Hybrid intelligent systems are crucial and essential in solving the real-world complex problems. In the last decades, the increasing need for hybrid methods which combine and integrate different techniques of representation and computation in AI has contributed to new approaches in hybrid artificial intelligence systems (cf. [1], [5]). As stated in [9], one of the main goals of hybrid system research is to increase the efficiency, expressive power, and reasoning power of intelligent systems. Hence, the development of a powerful language of representation and of an effective system of automated deduction is one of the most important and significant challenges in hybrid systems area.

The relational representation of states is very natural and has many benefits in hybrid intelligence systems that are complex and involve many objects which interact with each other. A homogeneous relational framework, based on the logic of binary relations RL introduced in [12], has proved to be a useful logical tool for relational representation and reasoning in various AI systems. Indeed, the general methodology of relational logics provides a means for a uniform and modular representation of three basic components of a formal system:

M. Polycarpou et al. (Eds.): HAIS 2014, LNAI 8480, pp. 466–477, 2014.
© Springer International Publishing Switzerland 2014

its syntax, semantics, and deduction system, called *relational dual tableau*. The relational formalization of many non-classical logics that have found applications in AI has been studied systematically in the last decades [11]. In particular, relational formalisms have been constructed for various applied theories of computational logic such as temporal and spatial reasoning, fuzzy-set- and rough-set-base based reasoning, order-of-magnitude and qualitative reasoning, dynamic reasoning about programs, etc.

One of the greatest advantages of the relational methodology is that, given a theory with a relational representation, we can build its deduction system in the form of a relational dual tableau in a systematic modular way. Though the relational logic RL is undecidable, it contains several decidable fragments of great expressive power. In many cases, however, dual tableau proof systems of such decidable fragments are not their decision procedures. This is mainly due to the way decomposition and specific rules are defined and to the strategy of proof construction.

Over the years, great efforts have been spent to define dual tableau proof systems for various logics known to be decidable, but little care has been taken to construct dual tableau-based decision procedures for them. On the other hand, it is clear that when a proof system is constructed and implemented, the existence of a decision procedure for a decidable logic is important. In [6], for instance, an optimized relational dual tableau for RL, based on Binary Decision Graphs, has been implemented. However, such an implementation turns out not to be effective with respect to decidable fragments.

To the best of our knowledge, relational dual tableau-based decision procedures can be found in [11] for fragments of RL corresponding to the class of first-order formulae in prenex normal form with universal quantifiers only, in [10,8] for the relational logic corresponding to the modal logic K, in [3,4] for fragments of RL characterized by some restrictions in terms of type $(R\,;S)$, and in [7] for a class of relational logics admitting just one relational constant with the properties of reflexivity, transitivity, and heredity.

In this paper we present an extension of the results achieved [7]. We construct a dual tableau decision procedure for relational fragments allowing an unbounded number of relational constants which may enjoy the properties of reflexivity, transitivity, and heredity. We show that our procedure always terminates and that it is sound and complete. The class of relational logics presented here is more expressive than the one introduced in [7]. In fact, while in [7] only some monomodal logics can be treated, in this paper it is shown that the multimodal logic with reflexive and transitive frames and the description logic $\mathcal{ALC}$ with transitive roles are expressible within relational fragments that can be decided by our procedure. Being able to express and reason on many modalities is important for AI deduction systems where propositional dynamic logic with actions and logics for qualitative reasoning are used.

The paper is organized as follows. In Sect. 2 we define the syntax and semantics of a class $\mathcal{RDL}^m$ of fragments of the logic RL. In Sect. 3 we present our dual tableau based decision procedures for the logics belonging to $\mathcal{RDL}^m$ and state its termination, soundness, and completeness. Then, in Sect. 4 we illustrate some applications of our decision procedures to well-known logics that can be expressed by the relational fragments belonging to $\mathcal{RDL}^m$. Finally, in Sect. 5, we draw our conclusions and give some hints for future work.

2 A Class of Decidable Fragments of Relational Logic

We consider a class of fragments of the relational logic RL, called $\mathcal{RDL}^m$, and exhibit a dual-tableau based decision procedure that can be applied to each logic belonging to it.

Fragments of $\mathcal{RDL}^m$ share a common language which admits only restricted forms of terms of type $R\,;S$. Relational constants are admitted only on the left hand side of terms of type $R\,;S$, and they can enjoy properties like reflexivity, transitivity, and heredity. In addition, the left part of terms of type $R;S$, namely R, is allowed to be a relational constant only.

2.1 Syntax

Let $\mathbb{RV}$ be a countably infinite set of *relational variables* $\mathsf{p}_1, \mathsf{p}_2, \ldots$, let $\mathbb{RC}$ be a countably infinite set of *relational constants* $R_1, R_2, \ldots$. The *relational operators* admitted in terms of $\mathbb{RT}_{\mathcal{RDL}^m}$ are complement '$-$', intersection '$\cap$', and composition '$;$'. Then, the set $\mathbb{RT}_{\mathcal{RDL}^m}$ of *relational terms* of $\mathcal{RDL}^m$ is the smallest set of terms (with respect to inclusion) containing all the relational variables in $\mathbb{RV}$ and satisfying the following closure condition: if $S, T \in \mathbb{RT}_{\mathcal{RDL}^m}$, then $-S$, $S \cap T, (R_i\,; T) \in \mathbb{RT}_{\mathcal{RDL}^m}$, for every $R_i \in \mathbb{RC}$.

Let $\mathbb{OV}$ be a countably infinite set of *object (individual) variables* $z_0, z_1, \ldots$ $\mathcal{RDL}^m$-formulae have the form $z_n T z_0$, where $T \in \mathbb{RT}_{\mathcal{RDL}^m}$, $z_n, z_0 \in \mathbb{OV}$, $n \geq 1$.

$\mathcal{RDL}^m$-formulae of type $z_n \mathsf{p}_j z_0$ are called *atomic $\mathcal{RDL}^m$-formulae.* A *literal formula* is either an atomic formula or its complement (namely a formula of type $z_n(-\mathsf{p}_j)z_0$). If $z_n T z_0$ is a literal formula, then the term T is said to be a *literal term.* A *Boolean formula* (resp., *compositional, negative-compositional formula*) is a relational formula either of the form $z_n(--T)z_0$, $z_n(T \cap T')z_0$, or $z_n(-(T \cap T'))z_0$ (resp., $z_n(R_i;T)z_0$, $z_n(-(R_i;T))z_0$). If $z_n T z_0$ is a Boolean formula (resp., compositional, negative-compositional formula), then T is a *Boolean term* (resp., *compositional, negative-compositional term*). A formula (resp., a term) which is not compositional is called *non-compositional.*

For every i, by $(R_i^s\,; T)$ we denote the term obtained from T and from the relational constant R_i, by applying the composition operator s times, where $s \geq 0$. Formally, $(R_i^0\,; T) =_{\text{Def}} T$ and $(R_i^{s+1}\,; T) =_{\text{Def}} (R_i\,; (R_i^s\,; T))$.

2.2 Semantics

$\mathcal{RDL}^m$-formulae are interpreted in *$\mathcal{RDL}^m$-models.* An $\mathcal{RDL}^m$-model is a structure $\mathcal{M} = (U, h, m)$, where U is a nonempty universe, h is a function mapping each relational constant of $\mathbb{RC}$ into a binary relation on U, namely $h : \mathbb{RC} \rightarrow \wp(U \times U)$, and m is a *meaning* function satisfying the following conditions:

- $m(\mathsf{p}_j) = X \times U$, where $X \subseteq U$, for every $\mathsf{p}_j \in \mathbb{RV}$; $m(R_i) = h(R_i)$, for every $R_i \in \mathbb{RC}$;
- $m(-T) = (U \times U) \setminus m(T)$; $m(T \cap T') = m(T) \cap m(T')$;
- $m(R_i\,;T) = m(R_i)\,;m(T)$
$= \{(a,b) \in U \times U : (a,c) \in m(R_i) \text{ and } (c,b) \in m(T), \text{ for some } c \in U\}$.

Given an $\mathcal{RDL}^m$-model $\mathcal{M} = (U, h, m)$, a *valuation* in $\mathcal{M}$ is any function $v : \mathbb{OV} \to U$.

Next we introduce the conditions (ref_i), (tran_i), and (her_i) on $h(R_i)$, for $R_i \in \mathbb{RC}$, with the following meaning:

(ref_i) $h(R_i)$ is reflexive, namely, for all $a \in U$, $(a,a) \in h(R_i)$;
(tran_i) $h(R_i)$ is transitive, namely, for all $a,b,c \in U$, if $(a,b) \in h(R_i)$ and $(b,c) \in h(R_i)$, then $(a,c) \in h(R_i)$;
(her_i) heredity condition: For all $a,b,c \in U$, $\mathsf{p}_j \in \mathbb{RV}$, if $(a,b) \subset h(R_i)$ and $(a,c) \in m(\mathsf{p}_j)$, then $(b,c) \in m(\mathsf{p}_j)$.

By $\mathcal{RDL}^m$ we denote the class of logics $\mathsf{RL_L}$ such that $\mathsf{L} \subseteq \{\mathsf{r}_i, \mathsf{t}_i, \mathsf{h}_i : i = 1, \ldots\}$ and whose set of relational terms is a subset of $\mathbb{RT}_{\mathcal{RDL}^m}$. The models of a logic $\mathsf{RL_L} \in \mathcal{RDL}^m$, referred to as $\mathsf{RL_L}$-*models*, are those $\mathcal{RDL}^m$-models that satisfy (ref_i), for $\mathsf{r}_i \in \mathsf{L}$, ($\mathsf{tran}_i$), for $\mathsf{t}_i \in \mathsf{L}$, and ($\mathsf{her}_i$), for $\mathsf{h}_i \in \mathsf{L}$.

An $\mathcal{RDL}^m$-formula (resp., $\mathsf{RL_L}$-formula) $z_n T z_0$ is said to be *satisfied* in an $\mathcal{RDL}^m$-model (resp., $\mathsf{RL_L}$-model) $\mathcal{M} = (U, h, m)$ by a valuation v if and only if $(v(z_n), v(z_0)) \in m(T)$. An $\mathcal{RDL}^m$-formula (resp., $\mathsf{RL_L}$-formula) is said to be *true* in an $\mathcal{RDL}^m$-model $\mathcal{M}$ (resp., $\mathsf{RL_L}$-model) if it is satisfied in $\mathcal{M}$ by all valuations. An $\mathcal{RDL}^m$-formula (resp., $\mathsf{RL_L}$-formula) is said to be $\mathcal{RDL}^m$-valid (resp., $\mathsf{RL_L}$-valid) if it is true in all $\mathcal{RDL}^m$-models (resp., $\mathsf{RL_L}$-models). A finite set of $\mathcal{RDL}^m$-formulae (resp., $\mathsf{RL_L}$-formulae) $\{\varphi_1, \ldots, \varphi_n\}$ is $\mathcal{RDL}^m$-valid (resp., $\mathsf{RL_L}$-valid) if and only if for every $\mathcal{RDL}^m$-model (resp., $\mathsf{RL_L}$-model) $\mathcal{M}$ and valuation v in $\mathcal{M}$, there exists $i \in \{1, \ldots, n\}$ such that $\mathcal{M}, v \models \varphi_i$.

3 A Dual Tableau Decision Procedure for the Relational Logics in $\mathcal{RDL}^m$

We introduce a dual tableau proof procedure, called $\mathsf{RDT_{RL_L}}$, to decide $\mathsf{RL_L}$-validity of relational formulae belonging to any logic $\mathsf{RL_L}$ in $\mathcal{RDL}^m$. The proof system is constructed along the lines of the dual tableau methodology described in [11]. It consists of decomposition rules to analyze the structure of the formulae to be proved, of specific rules to deal with properties that can be enjoyed by the relational constants occurring in the formulae to be proved (namely, reflexivity, transitivity, and heredity), and of axiomatic sets which specify the closure conditions.

An $\mathsf{RDT_{RL_L}}$-*axiomatic set* is any finite set of $\mathsf{RL_L}$-formulae including a subset of the form $\{z_n T z_0, z_n(-T)z_0\}$, for some $n \geq 1$ and $T \in \mathbb{RT}_{\mathcal{RDL}^m}$. Sets which are not axiomatic are referred to as *non-axiomatic*. It is evident that every $\mathsf{RDT_{RL_L}}$-axiomatic set is an $\mathsf{RL_L}$-valid set.

Table 1. Boolean decomposition rules for $\mathsf{RDT}_{\mathsf{RL_L}}$

$$(--)\,\frac{X \cup \{z_n(--T)z_0\}}{X \cup \{z_n T z_0\}}$$

$$(\cap)\,\frac{X \cup \{z_n(T \cap T')z_0\}}{X \cup \{z_n T z_0\} \mid X \cup \{z_n T' z_0\}} \qquad (-\cap)\,\frac{X \cup \{z_n(-(T \cap T'))z_0\}}{X \cup \{z_n(-R)z_0, z_n(-S)z_0\}},$$

where $n \geq 1$ and $T, T' \in \mathbb{RT}_{\mathcal{RDL}^m}$.

Each relational system considered in this paper admits the following rule schemas:

$$(A)\frac{X \cup \Gamma}{X \cup \Delta} \qquad (B)\,\frac{X \cup \Gamma}{X \cup \Delta_1 \mid X \cup \Delta_2},$$

where $\Gamma, \Delta, \Delta_1, \Delta_2$ are finite nonempty sets of formulae, and X is a finite, possibly empty, set of formulae. X and Δ (resp., X and Δ_i, for $i = 1, 2$) are assumed to be disjoint and $X \cup \Gamma \neq X \cup \Delta$ (resp., $X \cup \Gamma \neq X \cup \Delta_i$, for some $i \in \{1, 2\}$).

Table 2. Decomposition rule for compositional formulae in $\mathsf{RDT}_{\mathsf{RL_L}}$

$$(\mathsf{glob}\,;)\,\frac{X \cup Y \cup \bigcup_{i \in I_\Phi} \{z_n(-(R_i\,;S_{q_i}))z_0, z_n(R_i\,;T_{j_i})z_0 : q_i \in Q_i, j_i \in J_i\}}{X \cup \bigcup_{i \in I_\Phi} \{z_{n_{q_i}}(-S_{q_i})z_0, z_{n_{q_i}} T_{j_i} z_0 : q_i \in Q_i, j_i \in J_i\}}$$

where:

- $n \geq 1$ and Y is the set of literals with left variable z_n occurring in the current node;
- I_Φ is the set of indices of constants of $\mathbb{RC}$ occurring in the current node Φ;
- for all $T \in \mathbb{RT}_{\mathcal{RDL}^m}$, $z_n T z_0 \notin X$ (the only formulae in the premise that are neither compositional nor negative-compositional and have z_n as left variable are in Y);
- $Q = \bigcup_{i \in I_\Phi} Q_i$ and $J = \bigcup_{i \in I_\Phi} J_i$ are sets of indices such that $Q_i \neq \emptyset$, for some $i \in I_\Phi$ (by this condition, if in the current node there is a formula $z_n(R_i\,;T_{j_i})z_0$, for some $i \in I_\Phi$, and no formula of type $z_n(-(R_i\,;\,S_{q_i}))z_0$ occurs in the current node, then $z_n(R_i\,;T_{j_i})z_0$ cannot be decomposed anymore and therefore it is not repeated in the successive nodes of the dual tableau);
- $S_{q_i}, T_{j_i} \in \mathbb{RT}_{\mathcal{RDL}^m}$, for all $q_i \in Q_i$, $j_i \in J_i$, with $i \in I_\Phi$;
- the set $N = \{n_{q_i} : q_i \in Q_i, i \in I_\Phi\}$ satisfies the following conditions:
  - the elements of N are consecutive natural numbers,
  - $\min(N) = k+1$, where k is the largest number such that z_k occurs in the premise,
  - for all $n_{q_i}, n_{q'_{i'}} \in N$, we have $n_{q_i} < n_{q'_{i'}}$ if and only if $\langle R_i, S_{q_i}\rangle < \langle R_{i'}, S_{q'_{i'}}\rangle$;
- the pivot of $(\mathsf{glob}\,;)$ is the formula $z_n(-(R_i\,;S_{q_i}))z_0$ with the minimal pair $\langle R_i\,;S_{q_i}\rangle$.

Rules of type (B) are 'conjunctive' branching rules, and in fact, in the (B) rule schema the symbol '|' is interpreted as a conjunction. On the other hand, rules of type (A) are 'disjunctive'.

A variable z_n, with $n > 1$, which appears in a conclusion of a rule while it does not appear in its premise, is called a *new variable* (introduced by the rule application). In view of the definition of the dual tableau decision procedure, it is convenient to associate with every rule a specific element of the set of formulae Γ, called the pivot of the rule, to determine the order of application of the rules. Moreover, for a set of $\mathsf{RL_L}$-formulae S, we denote by I_S the set of indices of the relational constants of $\mathbb{RC}$ occurring in S.

In order to construct a deterministic decision procedure, we define an order on the set of the relational formulae. We begin with relational terms. For $\mathsf{p}_{j_1}, \mathsf{p}_{j_2} \in \mathbb{RV}$, $R_{i_1}, R_{i_2} \in \mathbb{RC}$, and $S_0, \ldots, S_6 \in \mathbb{RT}$, we put:

$$\mathsf{p}_{j_1} < (-\mathsf{p}_{j_2}) < (--S_0) < (-(S_1 \cap S_2)) < (S_3 \cap S_4) < (R_{i_1} \,; S_5) < -(R_{i_2} \,; S_6).$$

Next, we introduce an order also for the constants in $\mathbb{RC}$ by putting $R_{i_1} < R_{i_2}$ iff $i_1 < i_2$. For terms left unordered by the above, we define an order in the following way: $\mathsf{p}_{j_1} < \mathsf{p}_{j_2}$ iff $j_1 < j_2$; $(-T) < (-T')$ iff $T < T'$; $T \cap T' < S \cap S'$ iff $\langle T, T'\rangle < \langle S, S'\rangle$; $(R_{i_1};T) < (R_{i_2};T')$ iff $\langle R_{i_1}, T\rangle < \langle R_{i_2}, T'\rangle$, where $\langle a, b\rangle < \langle c, d\rangle$ if and only if either $a < c$, or both $a = c$ and $b < d$.

Finally, for formulae $z_n S z_0$ and $z_{n'} S' z_0$, we put $z_n S z_0 < z_{n'} S' z_0$ if and only if $\langle n, S\rangle < \langle n', S'\rangle$. It can easily be proved that $<$ linearly orders the set of all relational formulae.

Given a finite nonempty set of relational formulae X, *the minimal element of* X is the minimal element with respect to the order $<$ defined above. An immediate consequence of the above definition is that if $z_n S z_0$ is the minimal element of X then, for any formula $z_{n'} T' z_0$ in X, it holds that $n \leq n'$.

We also introduce a notion that is used in some restrictions on rule applications to avoid infinite loops. A finite set $\{z_n S_j z_0 : j \in J\}$ is said to be a *subcopy* of a set Y whenever there exists an $n' < n$ such that $\{z_{n'} S_j z_0 : j \in J\} \subseteq Y$.

3.1 The Decision Procedure $\mathsf{RDT}_{\mathsf{RL_L}}$

The decomposition rules of $\mathsf{RDT}_{\mathsf{RL_L}}$ are presented in Tables 1 and 2. Rules $(-)$, $(\cap)$, and $(-\cap)$, illustrated in Table 1, deal with Boolean operators, while rule (glob ;), depicted in Table 2, deals with the composition operator. Rule (glob ;) is a proper extension of rule $(R;)$, introduced in [7], because while rule $(R;)$ is applicable only to compositional and negative-compositional formulae with the same left object variable and with the same relational constant R, rule (glob ;) decomposes in a single step all the compositional formulae and negative-compositional formulae with the same left object variable occurring on the current node.

Rules (ref_i), (tran_i), and (her_i) defined in Table 3 reflect the reflexivity, transitivity, and heredity of R_i, respectively, for $i \in I_\Phi$, where Φ is the set of formulae labelling the current node.[1] They are generalizations of rules (ref), (tran), and (her), introduced in [7] to deal with the reflexivity, transitivity, and heredity of a single relational constant R. Clearly, rule (ref_i) (resp., (tran_i), (her_i)) can be applied to a pivot formula only if $h(R_i)$ is reflexive (resp., transitive, enjoys the heredity property).

Definition 1 (Proof tree). *An* $\mathsf{RDT}_{\mathsf{RL_L}}$*-proof tree of an* $\mathsf{RL_L}$*-formula* ψ *is a finitely branching tree satisfying the following conditions:*

[1] From now on, we identify nodes with the (disjunctive) sets labelling them.

Table 3. Reflexivity, transitivity, and heredity rules for $\mathsf{RDT}_{\mathsf{RL_L}}$

Reflexivity rule:

$$(\mathsf{ref}_i)\ \frac{X \cup \{z_n(R_i^s\,;T)z_0\}}{X \cup \{z_n(R_i^s\,;T)z_0\} \cup \{z_n(R_i^j\,;T)z_0 : j \in \{0,\dots,s-1\}\}}\,,$$

where $n, s \geq 1$ and $T \in \mathbb{RT}_{\mathcal{RDL}^m}$ is either a non-compositional term or a compositional term $(R_j\,;T')$, with $j \neq i$, and $z_n(R_i^t\,;T) \notin X$, for all $t > s$.

Transitivity rule:

$$(\mathsf{tran}_i)\ \frac{X \cup \{z_n(R_i\,;T)z_0\}}{X \cup \{z_n(R_i\,;T)z_0\} \cup \{z_n(R_i^2\,;T)z_0\}}\,,$$

where $n \geq 1$ and $T \in \mathbb{RT}_{\mathcal{RDL}^m}$ is either a non-compositional term or a compositional term $(R_j\,;T')$, with $j \neq i$.

Heredity rule:

$$(\mathsf{her}_i)\ \frac{X \cup \{z_n(-(R_i\,;T))z_0\} \cup \{z_n(-\mathsf{p}_j)z_0 : j \in J_\Phi\}}{X \cup \{z_n(-(R_i^s\,;T))z_0\} \cup \{z_n(-\mathsf{p}_j)z_0 : j \in J_\Phi\} \cup \{z_n(R_i\,;(-\mathsf{p}_j))z_0\ : j \in J_\Phi\}}$$

where: $n \geq 1$, $T \in \mathbb{RT}_{\mathcal{RDL}^m}$, and $z_n(-\mathsf{p}_j)z_0 \notin X$, for any $\mathsf{p}_j \in \mathbb{RV}$.
The pivot of the rule (her_i) is $z_n(-(R_i\,;T))z_0$.

1. *the root of the tree is the set* $\{\psi\}$;
2. *each node but the root is obtained by an application of an* $\mathsf{RDT}_{\mathsf{RL_L}}$*-rule to its direct predecessor node;*
3. *when more that one rule is applicable to a node* Φ*, the first possible schema from the following list is chosen:* $(-)$, $(-\cap)$, $(\cap)$, (ref_i), *for every* $i \in I_\Phi$ *chosen in increasing numerical order,* (her_i), *for every* $i \in I_\Phi$ *chosen in increasing numerical order,* (tran_i), *for every* $i \in I_\Phi$ *chosen in increasing numerical order, and finally the rule* $(\mathsf{glob}\,;)$;
4. *the rule* $(\mathsf{glob}\,;)$ *applies to a node* Φ *which has the form of the premise of the rule* $(\mathsf{glob}\,;)$, *provided that* $\Phi \setminus X$ *is not a subcopy of any of its predecessor nodes;*
5. *given* φ, *the rule* (ref_i) *with pivot* φ *applies in a given branch at most once;*
6. *a node does not have successors if and only if it is* $\mathsf{RDT}_{\mathsf{RL_L}}$*-axiomatic or none of the* $\mathsf{RDT}_{\mathsf{RL_L}}$*-rules applies to it.*

Definition 2. *A branch of an* $\mathsf{RDT}_{\mathsf{RL_L}}$*-proof tree is said to be* closed *whenever it ends with an axiomatic set of formulae. An* $\mathsf{RDT}_{\mathsf{RL_L}}$*-proof tree is closed if and only if all of its branches are closed. A formula is* $\mathsf{RDT}_{\mathsf{RL_L}}$-provable *whenever it has a closed* $\mathsf{RDT}_{\mathsf{RL_L}}$*-proof tree, which is then referred to as its* $\mathsf{RDT}_{\mathsf{RL_L}}$-proof.

It can easily be checked that, given a finite set of $\mathsf{RL_L}$-formulae Φ, for each rule schema and each $\varphi \in \Phi$, there is at most one instance of that schema whose premise equals Φ and pivot equals φ. As a consequence of what observed before and of the conditions in the definition of proof tree, one can show that, for every $\mathsf{RL_L}$-formula φ, there is exactly one $\mathsf{RDT}_{\mathsf{RL_L}}$-proof tree of φ.

It can be proved that the proof system $\mathsf{RDT}_{\mathsf{RL_L}}$ always terminates by showing that each proof tree that we can construct is finite.

Theorem 1 (Termination). *For every formula $\varphi \in \mathsf{RL_L}$ there is exactly one finite $\mathsf{RDT_{RL_L}}$-proof tree of φ.*

In addition, by using the proof techniques from [11] and [7], it can be shown that the proof system $\mathsf{RDT_{RL_L}}$ is sound and complete.

Theorem 2 (Soundness and Completeness of $\mathsf{RDT_{RL_L}}$). *Let φ be a relational formula. Then, φ is $\mathsf{RL_L}$-valid if and only if φ is $\mathsf{RDT_{RL_L}}$-provable.*

Theorems 1 and 2 readily imply:

Theorem 3. *An $\mathsf{RDT_{RL_L}}$-dual tableau is a sound and complete deterministic decision procedure for the logic $\mathsf{RL_L}$.*

4 Applications to Multimodal and Description Logics

Relational logics and their dual tableaux presented in Sects. 2 and 3, respectively, can be used as decision procedures for verification of validity in some multimodal and description logics.

To begin with, we discuss multimodal logics and their relational decision procedures in dual tableaux style. The class of multimodal logics considered in this section will be denoted by ML. The common vocabulary of logics in ML consists of the following pairwise disjoint sets of symbols: $\mathbb{V} = \{p_1, p_2, p_3, \ldots\}$, a countably infinite set of propositional variables, $\{\neg, \wedge\}$, the set of the classical operations of negation and conjunction, respectively, $\{[R_i], \langle R_i\rangle : i \in I\}$, a finite set of modal propositional operations of necessity and possibility, respectively. The set of modal formulae is then the smallest set including the set of propositional variables and closed with respect to all the propositional operations.

Let $\mathsf{L} \subseteq \{\mathsf{r}_i, \mathsf{t}_i, \mathsf{h}_i : i \in I\}$. Logics in the class ML are determined by $\mathsf{ML_L}$-models which are structures of the form $\mathcal{M} = (U, h, m)$ such that U is a nonempty set (of states), m is the meaning function such that $m(p) \subseteq U$, for every propositional variable $p \in \mathbb{V}$, and h is a function such that for every $i \in I$, $h(R_i)$ is a binary relation on U (referred to as the *i-th accessibility relation*) that satisfies conditions coded by L as in the definition of $\mathsf{RL_L}$-models given in Sect. 2. Therefore, any logic in ML is determined by the properties of the accessibility relation assumed in $\mathsf{ML_L}$-models. Given $\mathsf{L} \subseteq \{\mathsf{r}_i, \mathsf{t}_i, \mathsf{h}_i : i \in I\}$, a logic in ML will be denoted by $\mathsf{ML_L}$.

Observe that among logics in the class ML are multimodal temporal logics (for instance with transitive time orderings) and multi-agent epistemic logics (for instance with reflexive and transitive knowledge relation). The notions of satisfaction relation, truth, and validity are defined as usual in modal logics.

The *satisfaction relation* is defined as usual in modal logics, that is for the modal operators we set:

$\mathcal{M}, s \models [R_i]\varphi$ iff for every $s' \in U$, if $(s, s') \in h(R_i)$, then $\mathcal{M}, s' \models \varphi$.

$\mathcal{M}, s \models \langle R_i\rangle\varphi$ iff there is $s' \in U$ such that $(s, s') \in h(R_i)$ and $\mathcal{M}, s' \models \varphi$.

A modal formula is said to be *true* in an $\mathsf{ML_L}$-model $\mathcal{M}$ whenever it is satisfied in $\mathcal{M}$ by all $s \in U$, and it is $\mathsf{ML_L}$-*valid* whenever it is true in all $\mathsf{ML_L}$-models.

The translation τ of modal formulae into relational terms is defined as follows: $\tau(p_j) = \mathsf{p}_j$, for any propositional variable $p_j \in \mathbb{V}$; $\tau(\neg\varphi) = -\tau(\varphi)$; $\tau(\varphi \wedge \psi) = \tau(\varphi) \cap \tau(\psi)$; $\tau([R_i]\varphi) = -(R_i\,;-\tau(\varphi))$; $\tau(\langle R_i\rangle\varphi) = (R_i\,;\tau(\varphi))$. Translation τ preserves validity, as stated in the following theorem:

Theorem 4. *Let* $\mathsf{L} \subseteq \{\mathsf{r}_i, \mathsf{t}_i, \mathsf{h}_i : i \in I\}$ *and let* φ *be a modal formula. Then,* φ *is* ML_L*-valid if and only if* $z_1\tau(\varphi)z_0$ *is* RL_L*-valid.*

The proof of the above theorem is standard in the relational formalization of non-classical logics. For details see [11]. In view of this result, and by Theorems 2 and 3, we obtain:

Theorem 5. *Let* $\mathsf{L} \subseteq \{\mathsf{r}_i, \mathsf{t}_i, \mathsf{h}_i : i \in I\}$ *and let* φ *be a modal formula. Then,* φ *is* ML_L*-valid if and only if* $z_1\tau(\varphi)z_0$ *is* $\mathsf{RDT}_{\mathsf{RL}_\mathsf{L}}$*-provable. Moreover,* $\mathsf{RDT}_{\mathsf{RL}_\mathsf{L}}$ *is a deterministic decision procedure for a multimodal logic* ML_L.

Example 1. Let $I = \{1, 2\}$, and let φ be: $\langle R_1\rangle\langle R_1\rangle p_1 \rightarrow \langle R_2\rangle\langle R_1\rangle\neg(\neg p_1 \wedge p_2)$. The formula φ is valid in all Kripke frames with two accessibility relations: transitive $h(R_1)$ and reflexive $h(R_2)$. In order to show it, by Theorem 5, it suffices to construct a closed $\mathsf{RDT}_{\mathsf{RL}_\mathsf{L}}$-proof tree of a formula $z_1\tau(\varphi)z_0$, where $\mathsf{L} = \{\mathsf{t}_1, \mathsf{r}_2\}$ and $\tau(\varphi)$ is the relational translation of φ of the following form: $(-((R_1\,;(R_1\,;\mathsf{p}_1)) \cap -(R_2\,;(R_1\,;-(-\mathsf{p}_1 \cap \mathsf{p}_2)))))$. Figure 1 presents an $\mathsf{RDT}_{\mathsf{RL}_\mathsf{L}}$-proof of $z_1\tau(\varphi)z_0$, which proves the validity of φ in Kripke frames where the first accessibility relation is transitive and the second one reflexive. Recall that a $\mathsf{RDT}_{\mathsf{RL}_\mathsf{L}}$-dual tableau consists of rules for Boolean operators, rules (glob ;), (tran$_1$), and (ref$_2$).

Next we show how $\mathsf{RDT}_{\mathsf{RL}_\mathsf{L}}$-systems can decide validity for description logics, a family of logic-based formalisms which allow one to represent knowledge about a domain of interest in terms of *concepts*, which denote sets of elements, of *roles*, which represent relations between elements, and of *individuals*, which denote domain elements [2]. Each language in this family is characterized by its set of constructors, which allow one to form complex terms. Here, we focus on the well-known description logic $\mathcal{ALC}$, considering also the case in which $\mathcal{ALC}$ is provided with transitive roles [13].

Definition 3. *Let* $N_C = \{\mathsf{p}_1, \mathsf{p}_2, \ldots\}$ *be a countably infinite set of* concept names *and let* $N_R = \{R_1, R_2, \ldots\}$ *be a countably infinite set of* role names. *The set of* $\mathcal{ALC}$*-concepts is the smallest set such that: each concept name is an* $\mathcal{ALC}$*-concept, and if* C, D *are* $\mathcal{ALC}$*-concepts and* R_i *is a role name, then* $-C$, $C \sqcap D$, $\exists R_i.C$, *and* $\forall R_i.D$ *are* $\mathcal{ALC}$*-concepts.*

An interpretation $\mathcal{I} = (\Delta^\mathcal{I}, \cdot^\mathcal{I})$ consists of a nonempty set $\Delta^\mathcal{I}$, called the domain of $\mathcal{I}$, and of a function $\cdot^\mathcal{I}$ mapping each concept into a subset of $\Delta^\mathcal{I}$ and each role into a subset of $\Delta^\mathcal{I} \times \Delta^\mathcal{I}$. For space reasons, we report here only the interpretations of concepts of type $\exists R_i.C$ and $\forall R_i.C$:

$(\exists R_i.C)^\mathcal{I} = \{d \in \Delta^\mathcal{I} :$ there is some $e \in \Delta^\mathcal{I}$ with $(d, e) \in R_i^\mathcal{I}$ and $e \in C^\mathcal{I}\}$,

$(\forall R_i.C)^\mathcal{I} = \{d \in \Delta^\mathcal{I} :$ for all $e \in \Delta^\mathcal{I}$, if $(d, e) \in R_i^\mathcal{I}$, then $e \in C^\mathcal{I}\}$.

$$\underline{z_1(-((R_1 ; (R_1 ; \mathsf{p}_1)) \cap -(R_2 ; (R_1 ; -(-\mathsf{p}_1 \cap \mathsf{p}_2)))))z_0}$$

$(-\cap)$ and $(--)$

$$z_1-(R_1 ; (R_1 ; \mathsf{p}_1))z_0, \underline{z_1(R_2 ; (R_1 ; -(-\mathsf{p}_1 \cap \mathsf{p}_2)))z_0}$$

(ref_2)

$$z_1-(R_1 ; (R_1 ; \mathsf{p}_1))z_0, z_1(R_2 ; (R_1 ; -(-\mathsf{p}_1 \cap \mathsf{p}_2)))z_0, \underline{z_1(R_1 ; -(-\mathsf{p}_1 \cap \mathsf{p}_2))z_0}$$

(tran_1)

$$\underline{z_1-(R_1 ; (R_1 ; \mathsf{p}_1))z_0, z_1(R_2 ; (R_1 ; -(-\mathsf{p}_1 \cap \mathsf{p}_2)))z_0,}$$
$$\underline{z_1(R_1 ; -(-\mathsf{p}_1 \cap \mathsf{p}_2))z_0, z_1(R_1 ; (R_1 ; -(-\mathsf{p}_1 \cap \mathsf{p}_2)))z_0}$$

$(\mathsf{glob}\ ;)$ with a new variable z_2

$$z_2-(R_1 ; \mathsf{p}_1)z_0, z_2-(-\mathsf{p}_1 \cap \mathsf{p}_2)z_0, \underline{z_2(R_1 ; -(-\mathsf{p}_1 \cap \mathsf{p}_2))z_0}$$

(tran_1)

$$\underline{z_2-(R_1 ; \mathsf{p}_1)z_0, z_2(R_1 ; -(-\mathsf{p}_1 \cap \mathsf{p}_2))z_0, z_2(R_1 ; (R_1 ; -(-\mathsf{p}_1 \cap \mathsf{p}_2)))z_0, \ldots}$$

$(\mathsf{glob}\ ;)$ with a new variable z_3

$$z_3-\mathsf{p}_1 z_0, \underline{z_3-(-\mathsf{p}_1 \cap \mathsf{p}_2)z_0}, z_3(R_1 ; -(-\mathsf{p}_1 \cap \mathsf{p}_2))z_0, \ldots$$

$(-\cap)$ and $(--)$

$$z_3-\mathsf{p}_1 z_0, z_3\mathsf{p}_1 z_0, z_3-\mathsf{p}_2 z_0, z_3(R_1 ; -(-\mathsf{p}_1 \cap \mathsf{p}_2))z_0, \ldots$$

closed

Fig. 1. Relational proof of $\langle R_1\rangle\langle R_1\rangle p_1 \rightarrow \langle R_2\rangle\langle R_1\rangle\neg(\neg p_1 \wedge p_2)$.

A concept C is *satisfiable* if there is an interpretation $\mathcal{I}$ such that $C^{\mathcal{I}} \neq \emptyset$, namely if there is an $e \in \Delta^{\mathcal{I}}$ such that $e \in C^{\mathcal{I}}$. A concept C is *true* in an interpretation $\mathcal{I}$ if $C^{\mathcal{I}} = \Delta^{\mathcal{I}}$, namely if for every $e \in \Delta^{\mathcal{I}}$, it holds that $e \in C^{\mathcal{I}}$. A concept C is *valid* if it is true in every interpretation $\mathcal{I}$.

$\mathcal{ALC}_{R^+}$ is an extension of $\mathcal{ALC}$ obtained by allowing the presence of transitive roles inside concepts [13]. The set of role names of $\mathcal{ALC}_{R^+}$, N_R, is the union of two disjoint sets of role names, N_P and N_+. N_P is a set of non-transitive role names and N_+ is a set of transitive role names. Any interpretation $\mathcal{I} = (\Delta^{\mathcal{I}}, \cdot^{\mathcal{I}})$ for $\mathcal{ALC}_{R^+}$ has to satisfy the additional condition that if $(d, e) \in R_i^{\mathcal{I}}$ and $(e, f) \in R_i^{\mathcal{I}}$, then $(d, f) \in R_i^{\mathcal{I}}$, for each role $R_i \in N_+$.

It is well known that $\mathcal{ALC}$ is a notational variant of the multimodal logic $\mathbf{K}_n$. In fact, concepts of type $\exists R_i.C$ are syntactical variations of multimodal formulae of type $\langle R_i\rangle\varphi$ and concepts of type $\forall R_i.C$ are notational counterparts of multimodal formulae of type $[R_i]\varphi$. As a consequence, the translation of $\mathcal{ALC}$ and $\mathcal{ALC}_{R^+}$ in relational terms is analogous to the relational translation of any multimodal logic ML_L introduced above: $\mathcal{ALC}$ can be mapped into a multimodal logic ML_L such that $\mathsf{L} = \emptyset$, and $\mathcal{ALC}_{R^+}$ is a notational variant of a multimodal logic ML_L where $\mathsf{L} = \{\mathsf{t}_i : R_i \in N_+\}$.

Example 2. Consider the $\mathcal{ALC}_{R^+}$-formula:

$$\psi = \neg((\exists.R_1\neg\mathsf{p}_1 \sqcap \exists R_2.\mathsf{p}_2) \sqcap \neg((\exists R_1.\neg(\mathsf{p}_1 \sqcap \neg\mathsf{p}_2)) \sqcap (\exists R_2.\neg(\mathsf{p}_1 \sqcap \neg\mathsf{p}_2)))),$$

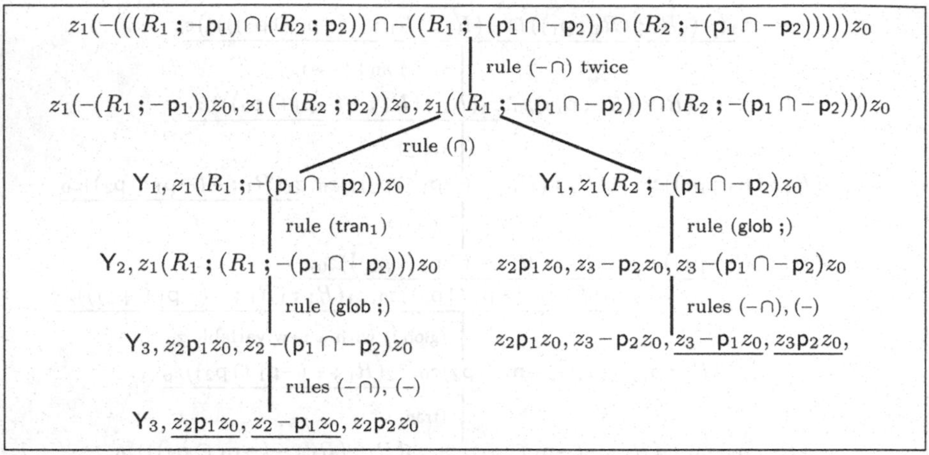

$$z_1(-(((R_1\,;-\mathsf{p}_1)\cap(R_2\,;\mathsf{p}_2))\cap-((R_1\,;-(\mathsf{p}_1\cap-\mathsf{p}_2))\cap(R_2\,;-(\mathsf{p}_1\cap-\mathsf{p}_2)))))z_0$$

rule $(-\cap)$ twice

$$z_1(-(R_1\,;-\mathsf{p}_1))z_0, z_1(-(R_2\,;\mathsf{p}_2))z_0, z_1((R_1\,;-(\mathsf{p}_1\cap-\mathsf{p}_2))\cap(R_2\,;-(\mathsf{p}_1\cap-\mathsf{p}_2)))z_0$$

rule $(\cap)$

Left branch:

$$\mathsf{Y}_1, z_1(R_1\,;-(\mathsf{p}_1\cap-\mathsf{p}_2))z_0$$

rule (tran_1)

$$\mathsf{Y}_2, z_1(R_1\,;(R_1\,;-(\mathsf{p}_1\cap-\mathsf{p}_2)))z_0$$

rule (glob ;)

$$\mathsf{Y}_3, z_2\mathsf{p}_1z_0, z_2-(\mathsf{p}_1\cap-\mathsf{p}_2)z_0$$

rules $(-\cap)$, $(-)$

$$\mathsf{Y}_3, \underline{z_2\mathsf{p}_1z_0}, \underline{z_2-\mathsf{p}_1z_0}, z_2\mathsf{p}_2z_0$$

Right branch:

$$\mathsf{Y}_1, z_1(R_2\,;-(\mathsf{p}_1\cap-\mathsf{p}_2)z_0$$

rule (glob ;)

$$z_2\mathsf{p}_1z_0, z_3-\mathsf{p}_2z_0, z_3-(\mathsf{p}_1\cap-\mathsf{p}_2)z_0$$

rules $(-\cap)$, $(-)$

$$z_2\mathsf{p}_1z_0, z_3-\mathsf{p}_2z_0, \underline{z_3-\mathsf{p}_1z_0}, \underline{z_3\mathsf{p}_2z_0},$$

Fig. 2. $\mathsf{RDT}_{\mathsf{RL_L}}$-proof tree of the formula $z_1\tau(\psi)z_0$.

where $R_1 \in N_+$ and $R_2 \in N_P$. The formula ψ is true in all interpretations $\mathcal{I} = (\Delta^{\mathcal{I}}, \cdot^{\mathcal{I}})$ for $\mathcal{ALC}_{R^+}$. Reasoning as in the previous example, in order to prove the validity of ψ in our relational setting, we just have to construct the closed $\mathsf{RDT}_{\mathsf{RL_L}}$-proof tree of the formula $z_1\tau(\psi)z_0$, with $\mathsf{L} = \{\mathsf{t}_1\}$. This is illustrated in Fig. 2. For space reasons, in the $\mathsf{RDT}_{\mathsf{RL_L}}$-proof tree of Fig. 2 we are using the following shorthands: Y_1 stands for $z_1(-(R_1\,;-\mathsf{p}_1))z_0, z_1(-(R_2\,;\mathsf{p}_2))z_0$, Y_2 stands for $z_1(-(R_1\,;-\mathsf{p}_1))z_0, z_1(-(R_2\,;\mathsf{p}_2))z_0, z_1(R_1\,;-(\mathsf{p}_1\cap-\mathsf{p}_2))z_0$, and Y_3 stands for $z_3-\mathsf{p}_2z_0, z_2(R_1\,;-(\mathsf{p}_1\cap-\mathsf{p}_2))z_0$.

5 Conclusions and Future Work

We have presented proof systems in the style of relational dual tableaux that can serve as decision procedures for some multimodal and description logics. By way of example, we showed how the systems can be used to verify validity in multimodal logic with one reflexive and one transitive accessibility relation and in a description logic corresponding to a multimodal logic with transitive accessibility relations. The results presented in the paper lead to some further questions about the possibility of extending these systems to decision procedures for other logics not captured by $\mathcal{RDL}^m$. In particular, we intend to work on dual tableau decision procedures for relational logics in which relational constants can also enjoy such properties as symmetry, seriality, Euclidean, partial functionality, functionality, weak density. In this way we would get relational decision procedures for a great variety of standard multimodal logics. Furthermore, we intend to develop decision procedures for those relational logics in which some constraints on interactions between relational constants are assumed. Such relational dual tableaux could be used as decision procedures for multimodal information logics with sufficiency modal operators, for propositional dynamic logic with actions, and for logics for qualitative reasoning. Finally, we plan to implement the decision procedures we have described, and to integrate them in the implementation of the dual tableau from [6], or in another relational theorem prover.

Acknowledgments. This work was supported by the Polish National Science Centre research project DEC-2011/02/A/HS1/00395.

References

1. Abraham, A.: Special issue: Hybrid approaches for approximate reasoning. J. Intell. Fuzzy Syst. 23(2,3), 41–42 (2012)
2. Baader, F., Calvanese, D., McGuinness, D.L., Nardi, D., Patel-Schneider, P.F. (eds.): The Description Logic Handbook: Theory, Implementation, and Applications. Cambridge University Press, New York (2003)
3. Cantone, D., Nicolosi-Asmundo, M., Orlowska, E.: Dual tableau-based decision procedures for some relational logics. In: Proceedings of the 25th Italian Conference on Computational Logic. CEUR Workshop Proceedings, vol. 598, pp. 1–16 (2010)
4. Cantone, D., Nicolosi-Asmundo, M., Orlowska, E.: Dual tableau-based decision procedures for relational logics with restricted composition operator. Journal of Applied Non-Classical Logics 21(2), 177–200 (2011)
5. Corchado, E., Wozniak, M., Abraham, A., de Carvalho, A.C.P.L.F., Snásel, V.: Recent trends in intelligent data analysis. Neurocomputing 126, 1–2 (2014)
6. Formisano, A., Nicolosi-Asmundo, M.: An efficient relational deductive system for propositional non-classical logics. Journal of Applied Non-Classical Logics 16(3,4), 367–408 (2006)
7. Golinska-Pilarek, J., Huuskonen, T., Muñoz-Velasco, E.: Relational dual tableau decision procedures and their applications to modal and intuitionistic logics. Ann. Pure Appl. Logic 165(2), 409–427 (2014)
8. Golinska-Pilarek, J., Muñoz-Velasco, E., Mora, A.: A new deduction system for deciding validity in modal logic k. Logic Journal of the IGPL 19(2), 425–434 (2011)
9. Medsker, L.R.: Hybrid intelligent systems. Kluwer (1995)
10. Mora, A., Muñoz-Velasco, E., Golinska-Pilarek, J.: Implementing a relational theorem prover for modal logic. Int. J. Comput. Math. 88(9), 1869–1884 (2011)
11. Orłowska, E., Golińska-Pilarek, J.: Dual Tableaux: Foundations, Methodology, Case Studies. Trends in Logic, vol. 36. Springer (2011)
12. Orłowska, E.: Relational interpretation of modal logics. In: Andreka, H., Monk, D., Nemeti, I. (eds.) Algebraic Logic. Colloquia Mathematica Societatis Janos Bolyai, vol. 54, pp. 443–471. North Holland (1988)
13. Sattler, U.: A concept language extended with different kinds of transitive roles. In: Görz, G., Hölldobler, S. (eds.) KI 1996. LNCS, vol. 1137, pp. 333–345. Springer, Heidelberg (1996)

Daily Power Load Forecasting Using the Differential Polynomial Neural Network

Ladislav Zjavka

VŠB-Technical University of Ostrava, IT4innovations Ostrava, Czech Republic
lzjavka@gmail.com

Abstract. The purpose of the short-term electricity demand prediction is to forecast in advance the system load, represented by the sum of all consumers load at the same time. Power demand forecasting is important for economically efficient operation and effective control of power systems and enables to plan the load of generating unit. A precise load forecasting is required to avoid high generation cost and the spinning reserve capacity. Under-prediction of the demands leads to an insufficient reserve capacity preparation and can threaten the system stability, on the other hand, over-prediction leads to an unnecessarily large reserve that leads to a high cost preparations. Differential polynomial neural network is a new neural network type, which forms and resolves an unknown general partial differential equation of an approximation of a searched function, described by data observations. It generates convergent sum series of relative polynomial derivative terms, which can substitute for the ordinary differential equation, describing 1-parametric function time-series with partial derivatives. A new method of the short-term power demand forecasting, based on similarity relations of subsequent day progress cycles at the same time points is presented and tested on 2 datasets. Comparisons were done with the artificial neural network using the same prediction method. Experimental results indicate that proposed method using the differential polynomial network is efficient.

Keywords: power demand prediction, week load cycle, differential polynomial neural network, sum relative derivative term.

1 Introduction

Short-term electric energy estimations of a future demand are needful for the planning of generating electricity of regional grid systems and operating power systems. Cooperation on the electricity grid requires from all providers to foresee the load within a sufficient accuracy. Forecasting methods in general might be classified into 2 types, the time-series models, in which the load is a function of its past observed values and causal models, which the load is a function of some exogenous factors, especially weather and social variables. Day-ahead load forecasting techniques can involve autoregressive integrated moving average (ARIMA) [5], chaotic dynamic non-linear models with evolutionary hybrid computation [12], exponential smoothing or interval time-series [6]. Regression analysis is considered as a conventional way in the power

M. Polycarpou et al. (Eds.): HAIS 2014, LNAI 8480, pp. 478–489, 2014.
© Springer International Publishing Switzerland 2014

load forecast. A real data 1-parametric function time-series is difficult to predict using deterministic methods as weather conditions as well as other extraneous factors can by far influence it. Artificial neural network (ANN) can define simple and robust models, which exact solution is problematic or impossible to get using standard regression techniques. The power demand model might be trained with similarity data relations of several corresponding days of previous weeks, as the daily power cycles of each following week are of a similar progress. After that the prediction is formed with respect to values of a few last days with the same denomination in the current week.

$$y = a_0 + \sum_{i=1}^{m} a_i x_i + \sum_{i=1}^{m}\sum_{j=1}^{m} a_{ij} x_i x_j + \sum_{i=1}^{m}\sum_{j=1}^{m}\sum_{k=1}^{m} a_{ijk} x_i x_j x_k + \ldots \qquad (1)$$

m – number of variables $X(x_1, x_2, \ldots, x_m)$ $\quad$ $A(a_1, a_2, \ldots, a_m), \ldots$ *- vectors of parameters*

Differential polynomial neural network (D-PNN) is a new neural network type designed by the author, which results from the GMDH (Group Method of Data Handling) polynomial neural network (PNN), created by a Ukrainian scientist Aleksey Ivakhnenko in 1968, when the back-propagation technique was not known yet [8]. It is possible to express a general connection between input and output variables by means of the Volterra functional series, a discrete analogue of which is the Kolmogorov-Gabor polynomial (1). This polynomial can approximate any stationary random sequence of observations and can be computed by either adaptive methods or a system of Gaussian normal equations. GMDH decomposes the complexity of a process into many simpler relationships each described by the low order polynomials (2) for every pair of the input values [10].

$$y = a_0 + a_1 x_i + a_2 x_j + a_3 x_i x_j + a_4 x_i^2 + a_5 x_j^2 \qquad (2)$$

D-PNN can combine the PNN functionality with some math techniques of differential equation (DE) solutions. Its models lie on the boundary of neural networks and exact computational techniques. D-PNN forms and resolves an unknown general DE description of an approximation of a searched function. It produces sum series of fractional polynomial derivative terms, which substitute for a DE, decomposing a system model into many partial derivative specifications of data relations. In contrast with the common neural network functionality, each neuron (i.e. derivative term) can take part directly in the total network output calculation, which is generated by the sum of the active neuron output values [13].

2 Forecasting Power Load

An overall electricity generation plan requires a forecast of total generation requirements and also peak demands. The inaccuracy in a forecast means that load matching is not optimized and consequently the generation and transmission systems are not being operated in an efficient manner. In order to guarantee a regular supply, it is necessary to keep a reserve. Over-estimating the future load results in an unused spinning reserve, being "burnt" for nothing. Under-estimating the future load is equally detrimental, because of high starting costs of cold reserves, buying at the last minute from other suppliers is obviously too expensive. The nature of parameters that affect this problem includes many uncertainties. The accuracy of a dispatching system is influenced by various conditional input parameters (weather, time, historical data and random disturbances), which can a prediction model involve, applying e.g. fuzzy logic [9]. ANN is able to model the non-linear nature of dynamic processes, reproduce an empirical relationship between some inputs and one or more outputs. It is applied for such purpose regarding to its approximation capability of any continuous nonlinear function with arbitrary accuracy that offer an effective alternative to more traditional statistical techniques. The application of hybrid systems, which consist typically of several different types of consolidated models, become recently very important to solve real world problems more accurately [1][4]. The load at a given hour is dependent not only on the load at the previous hour, but also on the load at the same hour on the previous day, and on the load at the same hour on the day with the same denomination in the previous week. There are also many important exogenous variables that should be considered, especially weather-related variables [7].

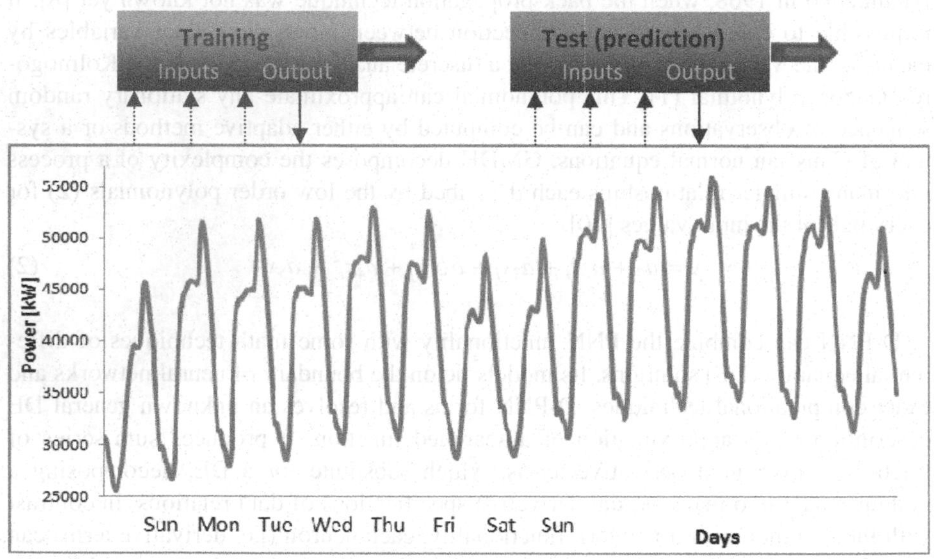

Fig. 1. Typical week cycles of power demands (January) [14]

$$y_t(d) = f(o_t(d-1), o_t(d-2), \ldots, o_t(d-n)) \qquad t = t_1, t_2, \ldots, t_k \tag{3}$$

$o_t(d)$ = *observation in time t and day d* $\qquad$ n = *number of inputs*

The proposed method keynote of the power load forecasting, using only 1-parametric function historical time-series, is to train a neural network model with actual daily cycle similarity relations of previous weeks, concerning several consecutive days with the same denomination, foregoing the 24-hour prediction. Power values of the 3 consequent days in previous weeks at the same time points form the input vector while the following day 24-hour shifted series define desired network outputs of the training data set (3). After training the network can estimate the following day power progress, using 3 input vector variables of 24-hour shifted time-series of the same time stamps of the current week last 3 days (Fig.1.). The model does not allow for weather or other disturbing effects, as these are not at disposal in most cases. The power demand day cycle progress is more variable in winter than summer months, which is influenced largely by using heating systems and temperature conditions [14].

3 General Differential Equation Composition

The D-PNN decomposes and substitutes for a general sum partial differential equation (4), in which an exact definition is not known in advance and which can generally describe a system model, with a sum of relative multi-parametric polynomial derivative convergent term series (5).

$$a+\sum_{i=1}^{n} b_i \frac{\partial u}{\partial x_i}+\sum_{i=1}^{n}\sum_{j=1}^{n} c_{ij}\frac{\partial^2 u}{\partial x_i \partial x_j}+\ldots=0 \qquad u=\sum_{k=1}^{\infty} u_k \tag{4}$$

$u = f(x_1, x_2, \ldots, x_n)$ – searched function of all input variables
$a, B(b_1, b_2, \ldots, b_n), C(c_{11}, c_{12}, \ldots)$ – polynomial parameters

Partial DE terms are formed according to the adapted method of integral analogues, which is a part of the similarity model analysis. It replaces mathematical operators and symbols of a DE by the ratio of the corresponding values. Derivatives are replaced by their integral analogues, i.e. derivative operators are removed and simultaneously along with all operators are replaced by similarly or proportion signs in equations to form dimensionless groups of variables [3].

$$u_i=\frac{\left(a_0+a_1x_1+a_2x_2+a_3x_1x_2+a_4x_1^2+a_5x_2^2+\ldots\right)^{m/n}}{b_0+b_1x_1+\ldots}=\frac{\partial^m f(x_1,\ldots,x_n)}{\partial x_1\partial x_2\ldots\partial x_m} \tag{5}$$

n – combination degree of a complete polynomial of n-variables
m – combination degree of denominator variables

The fractional polynomials (5), which substitute for the DE terms, describe partial relative derivative dependent changes of n-input variables. The numerator (5) is a polynomial of n-input variables and partly defines an unknown function u of eq. (4). The denominator includes an incomplete polynomial of the competent derivative combination of variables. The root function of the numerator decreases a combination degree of the input polynomial of a term (5), in order to get the dimensionless values [3]. In the case of time-series data observations an ordinary differential equation (6) is formed with time derivatives describing 1-parametric function progress using partial DE terms, analogous to the general partial DE (4) construction.

$$a+bf+\sum_{i=1}^{m} c_i\frac{df(t,x_i)}{dt}+\sum_{i=1}^{m}\sum_{j=1}^{m} d_{ij}\frac{d^2 f(t,x_i,x_j)}{dt^2}+\ldots=0 \tag{6}$$

$f(t, \mathbf{x})$ – function of time t and independent input variables $\mathbf{x}(x_1, x_2, \ldots, x_m)$

Blocks of the D-PNN (Fig.2.) consist of derivative neurons having the same inputs, one for each fractional polynomial derivative combination, so each neuron is considered a summation DE term (5). Each block contains a single output GMDH polynomial (2), without derivative part. Neurons do not affect the block output but can participate directly in the total network output sum calculation of a DE composition. Each block has *1* and neuron *2* vectors of adjustable parameters ***a***, then ***a, b***.

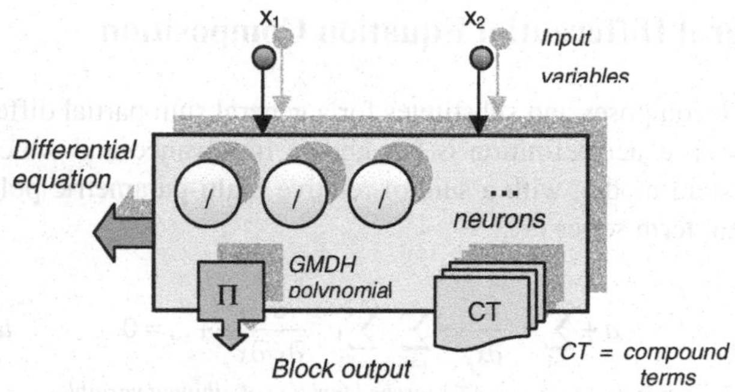

Fig. 2. D-PNN block includes basic and compound neurons (DE terms)

While using 2 input variables the 2nd order partial DE is formed (7), which involves derivative terms of all the variables of the GMDH polynomial (2). The D-PNN blocks form *5* simple neurons, which can substitute for the DE terms in respect of derivatives of the single x_1, x_2 (8) square x_1^2, x_2^2 (9) and combination x_1x_2 (10) variables of the 2nd order partial DE (7) solution, most often used to model physical or natural system non-linearities. Denominator coefficients of fractions (8)(9)(10) balance a length variety of the derivative polynomials.

$$F\left(x_1, x_2, u, \frac{\partial u}{\partial x_1}, \frac{\partial u}{\partial x_2}, \frac{\partial^2 u}{\partial x_1^2}, \frac{\partial^2 u}{\partial x_1 \partial x_2}, \frac{\partial^2 u}{\partial x_2^2}\right) = 0 \tag{7}$$

where $F(x_1, x_2, u, p, q, r, s, t)$ is a function of 8 variables

$$y_1 = \frac{\partial f(x_1, x_2)}{\partial x_1} = w_1 \frac{\left(a_0 + a_1x_1 + a_2x_2 + a_3x_1x_2 + a_4x_1^2 + a_5x_2^2\right)^{1/2}}{1.5 \cdot (b_0 + b_1x_1)} \tag{8}$$

$$y_4 = \frac{\partial^2 f(x_1, x_2)}{\partial x_2^2} = w_4 \frac{a_0 + a_1x_1 + a_2x_2 + a_3x_1x_2 + a_4x_1^2 + a_5x_2^2}{2.7 \cdot (b_0 + b_1x_2 + b_2x_2^2)} \tag{9}$$

$$y_5 = \frac{\partial^2 f(x_1, x_2)}{\partial x_1 \partial x_2} = w_5 \frac{a_0 + a_1x_1 + a_2x_2 + a_3x_1x_2 + a_4x_1^2 + a_5x_2^2}{2.3 \cdot (b_0 + b_1x_{11} + b_2x_{12} + b_3x_{11}x_{12})} \tag{10}$$

4 Differential Polynomial Neural Network

Multi-layer networks forms composite polynomial functions (Fig.3.). Compound terms (CT), i.e. derivatives in respect of variables of previous layer blocks, are calculated according to the composite function partial derivation rules (11)(12). They are formed by products of the partial derivatives of external and internal functions.

$$F(x_1, x_2, \ldots, x_n) = f(y_1, y_2, \ldots, y_m) = f(\phi_1(X), \phi_2(X), \ldots, \phi_m(X)) \tag{11}$$

$$\frac{\partial F}{\partial x_k} = \sum_{i=1}^{m} \frac{\partial f(y_1, y_2, \ldots, y_m)}{\partial y_i} \cdot \frac{\partial \phi_i(X)}{\partial x_k} \qquad k=1, \ldots, n \tag{12}$$

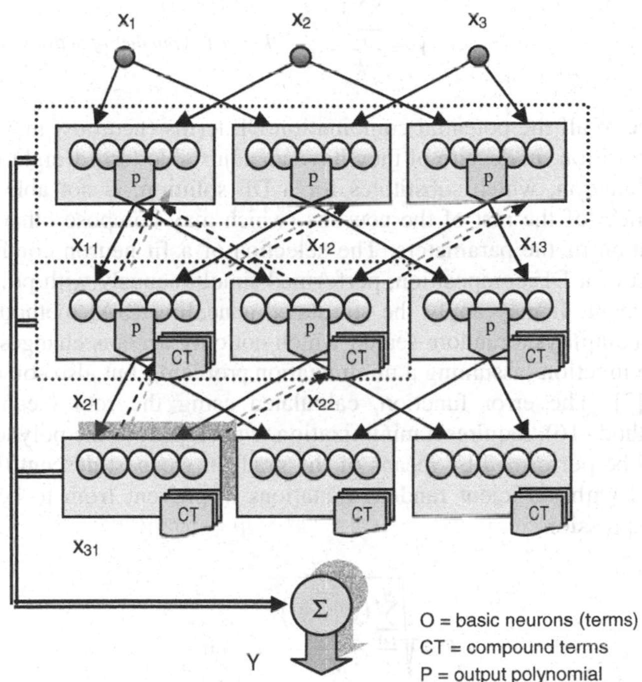

Fig. 3. 3-variable multi-layer D-PNN with 2-variable combination blocks

The blocks of the 2nd and following hidden layers are additionally extended with neurons, i.e. CT, which form composite derivatives with respect to the output and input variables of the back connected previous layer blocks, e.g. (13)(14). The number of neurons of blocks, which involve composite function derivatives, doubles each previous back-connected layer [13].

$$y_2 = \frac{\partial f(x_{21}, x_{22})}{\partial x_{11}} = w_2 \frac{(a_0 + a_1x_{21} + a_2x_{22} + a_3x_{21}x_{22} + a_4x_{21}^2 + a_5x_{22}^2)^{1/2}}{1.6 \cdot x_{22}} \cdot \frac{(x_{21})^{1/2}}{1.5 \cdot (b_0 + b_1x_{11})} \tag{13}$$

$$y_3 = \frac{\partial f(x_{21}, x_{22})}{\partial x_1} = w_3 \frac{(a_0 + a_1x_{21} + a_2x_{22} + a_3x_{21}x_{22} + a_4x_{21}^2 + a_5x_{22}^2)^{1/2}}{1.6 \cdot x_{22}} \cdot \frac{(x_{21})^{1/2}}{1.6 \cdot x_{12}} \cdot \frac{(x_{11})^{1/2}}{1.5 \cdot (b_0 + b_1x_1)} \quad (14)$$

The compound square and combination derivative terms are also calculated according to the composite function derivation rules. The number of the network hidden layers should coincide with the total number of input variables in order to enable the D-PNN to form all the possible derivative terms. D-PNN is trained with only a small set of input-output data samples, in a similar way to the GMDH algorithm [10]. The total output Y of the D-PNN is the arithmetical mean of all the active neuron output values (15) so as to prevent a changeable number of neurons (of a combination) from influencing the total network output value.

$$Y = \frac{\sum_{i=1}^{k} y_i}{k} \qquad k = \textit{actual number of active neurons} \quad (15)$$

Only some of all the potential combination DE terms (neurons) may participate in the DE composition, in despite of they have an adjustable term weight (w_i). A proper neuron combination, which substitutes for a DE solution, is not able to accept the disturbing effect of the rest of the neurons (which may compose other solutions) on the optimization of the parameters. The selection of a fit neuron combination is the principal part of a DE composition, performed simultaneously with polynomial parameter adjustment. It may apply the simulated annealing (SA) method in the initial phase, which employs a random search which not only accepts changes that decrease the objective function (assuming a minimization problem), but also some changes that increase it [2]. The error function, calculated using the root mean square error (RMSE) method (16), requires a minimization with respect to the polynomial parameters. It could be performed by means of the gradient steepest descent (GSD) method [11] supplied with sufficient random mutations to prevent from to be trapped to a local error depression.

$$E = \sqrt{\frac{\sum_{i=1}^{M} \left(y_i^d - y_i\right)^2}{M}} \rightarrow \min \quad (16)$$

y_i^d = *desired output* y_i = *estimated output for* i^{th} *training vector*

5 Power Load Forecast Model Experiments

The presented prediction method, based on daily similarity relations of the power demand cycles, applied the D-PNN (Fig.3.) model trained with 1-parametric historical time-series [14] to form following day estimations. 3 con-sequent day power values (foregoing the forecasting day denomination) of several previous weeks at the same time points form the network input vector; the 24-hour shifted time-series define desired

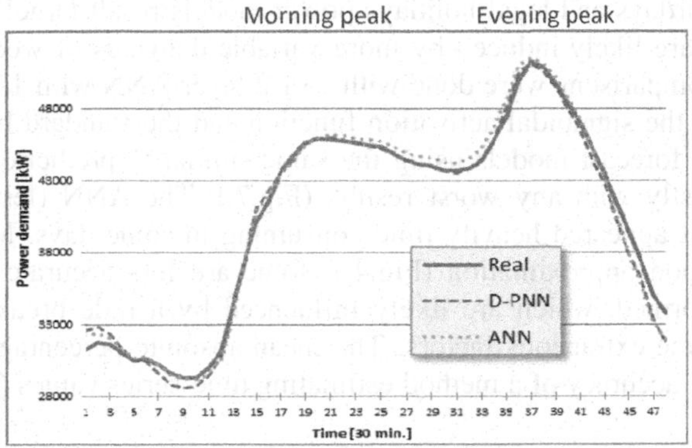

Fig. 4. National Grid : 18.02.2013 (Monday), D-PNN_{MAPE} = *1.32*, ANN_{MAPE} = *1.39*

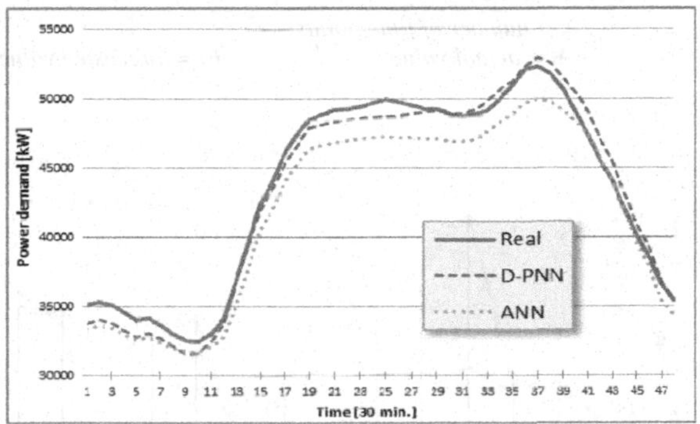

Fig. 5. National Grid : 22.2.2013 (Friday), D-PNN_{MAPE} = *1.83*, ANN_{MAPE} = *3.66*

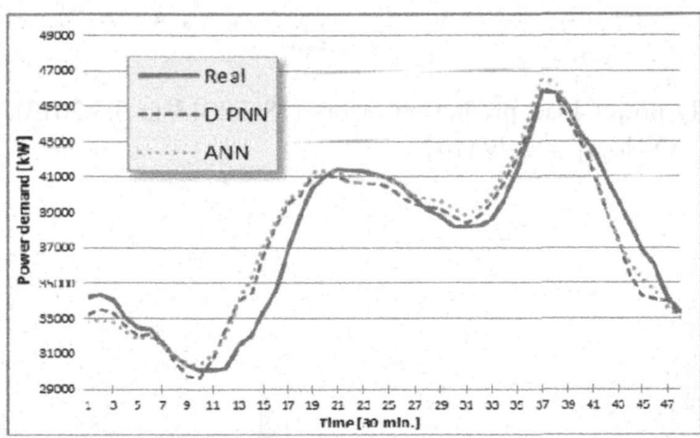

Fig. 6. National Grid : 2.3.2013 (Saturday), D-PNN_{MAPE} = *2.76*, ANN_{MAPE} = *3.06*

scalar outputs in the training data set. After training the network can predict the following day power series in respect of the current week last 3 day values in a uniform time (Fig.4.- Fig.6.). The training set can consist of 2-6 previous week periods; testing (prediction) applies the current week input data. A power demand daily period consists typically of 2 peak-hours, morning (midday) and evening peak consumptions (Fig.4.).

Sundays, Saturdays and legal holidays power models result largely in higher inaccuracies, which are likely induced by more variable demands of weekends and holidays (Fig.6.). Comparisons were done with 1 or 2-layer ANN with 15 neurons in hidden layers using the sigmoidal activation function and the standard back-propagation algorithm. ANN forecast models using the same similarity prediction method as the D-PNN, get mostly with any worst results (Fig.7.). The ANN (less commonly D-PNN) adjustment appeared heavily time-consuming in some days. Most models can obtain a very good approximation (Fig.4.), some are less accurate (Fig.6) or even difficult to be formed, which are likely influenced by a rude break in the weather conditions or some extraneous factors. The mean absolute percentage error (MAPE) is the measure of accuracy of a method estimating time-series values (17).

$$MAPE = \frac{100\%}{k} \sum_{t=1}^{k} \left| \frac{A_t - F_t}{A_t} \right| \tag{17}$$

k = number of time points
A_t = actual value *F_t = forecasted value*

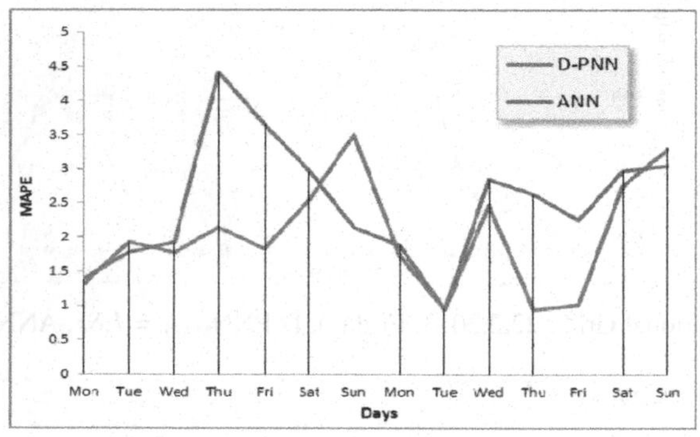

Fig. 7. 2-week daily power load prediction errors (18.2.2013 to 3.3.2013), Average MAPE : $DPNN_{MAPE}$ = *2.02*, ANN_{MAPE} = *2.49* [14]

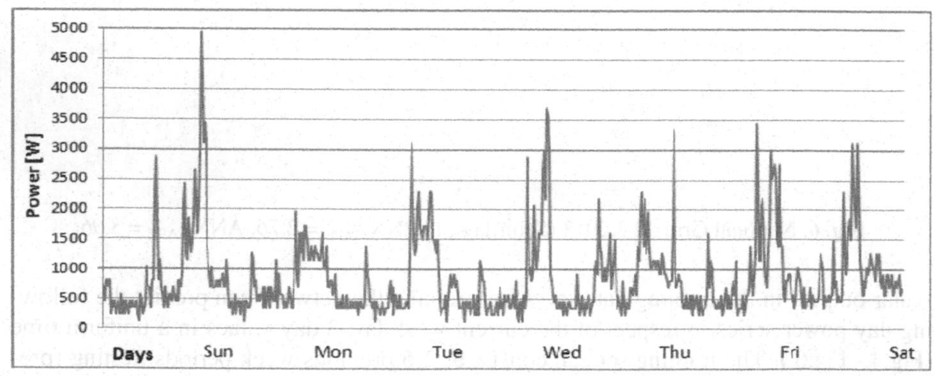

Fig. 8. A typical winter week period of the average domestic load profiles [15]

The 2nd data set comprises measured electric load profiles for Canadian detached houses [15], involving much more variable power progress (Fig.8.) of the average electric draw of the house (in Watts), evoked likely by a lower quantity in the customer demands and some more exogenous factors (Fig.9.-Fig.11). The Sundays and holidays are mostly peak consumption days, their models can also embody usual higher prediction errors.

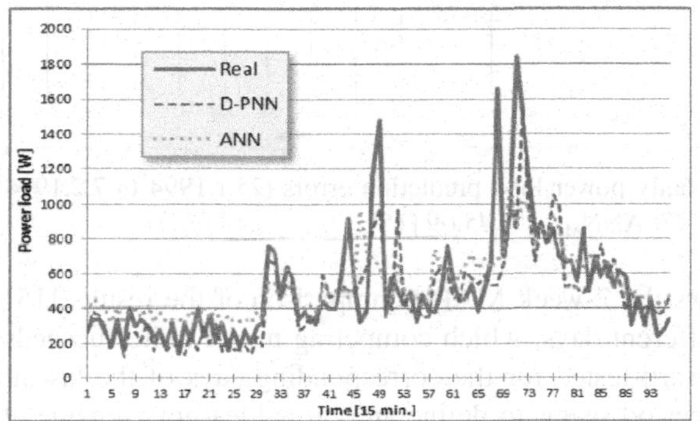

Fig. 9. ANEX, 25.1.1994 (Tuesday) low, D PNN$_{MAPE}$ = *26.07*, ANN$_{MAPE}$ = *23.65*

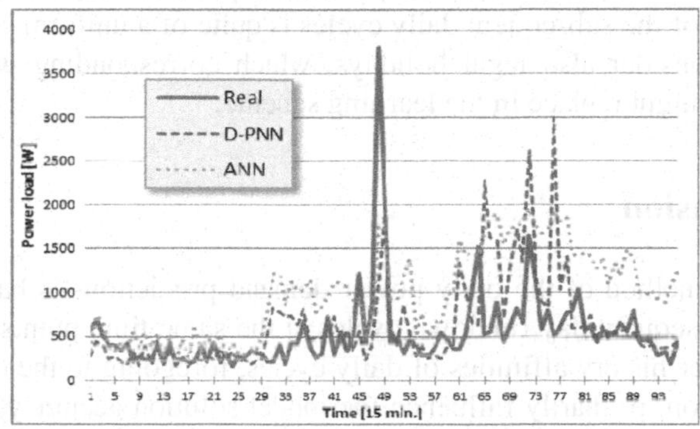

Fig. 10. ANEX,30.1.1994 (Sunday), D-PNN$_{MAPE}$ = *60.27*, ANN$_{MAPE}$ = *120.24*

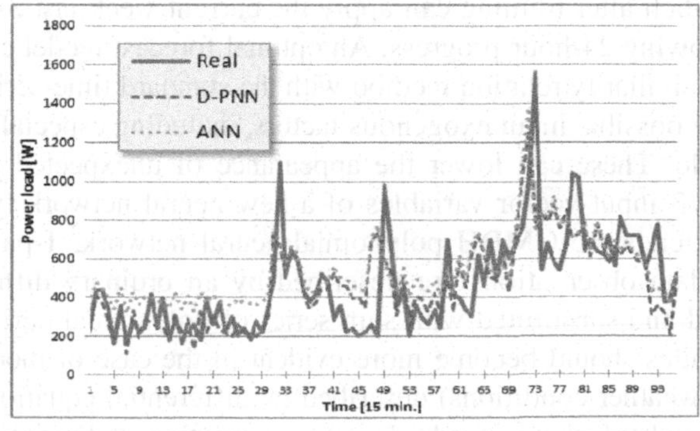

Fig. 11. ANEX, 4.2.1994 (Friday), D-PNN$_{MAPE}$ = *31.51*, ANN$_{MAPE}$ = *44.01*

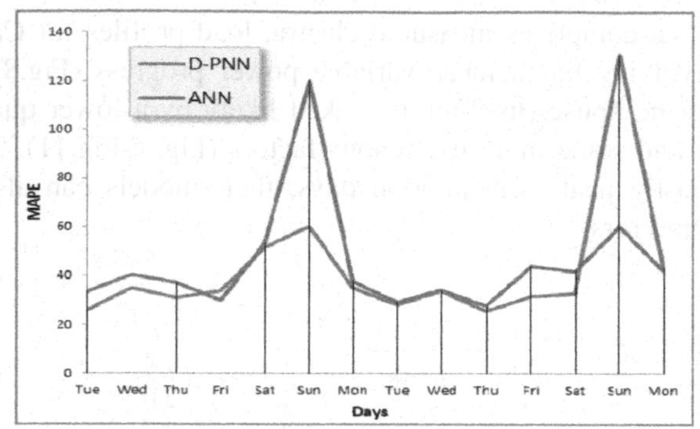

Fig. 12. 2-week daily power load prediction errors (25.1.1994 to 7.2.1994), Average MAPE : $DPNN_{MAPE} = 42.77$, $ANN_{MAPE} = 45.09$ [15]

Fig.12. shows the 2-week MAPE comparison of the results [15], both models fail notably in 2 different days, which competing model quite succeeds. The real models could be backward tested for the corresponding days of the last not trained week. 3 training week period seems to define an optimal learning scheme, it is better to apply less or more week-cycles in some cases. The valid number of training week periods could be estimated in practice with respect to the previous day(s) best testing results, as the progress of the subsequent daily cycles is quite of a uniform character. There is necessary to consider also legal holidays, which corresponding week Sundays (or working days) might replace in the learning scheme.

6 Conclusion

The presented method of the daily power demand predictions is based on similarity relations of subsequent day rundown cycles at the same time points in past week periods. The power history affinities of daily cycles, foregoing to the current week next day denomination, primarily influence the model solution accuracy, as no other considerable effects were taken into account, especially weather conditions. 3-day time interval series of several previous weeks define a learning scheme of the neural network model, which after training can apply the current week last 3-day power series to estimate following 24-hour progress. An optimal forecast model could combine the presented daily similarity relation method with the standard time-series prediction and apply also some possible input exogenous factors, including especially weather conditions if available. These can lower the appearance of unexpected prediction errors. The study used 3 input vector variables of a new neural network type called the D-PNN, which extends the GMDH polynomial neural network. 1-parametric function time-series of data observations are described by an ordinary differential equation, which is formed and substituted with sum series of polynomial derivative terms. The D-PNN advantages should become more evident in the case of modeling of systems (e.g. including weather conditions) described by differential equations, which are too complex to be solved using standard soft computation techniques. The increasing number of input factors, which can impact the power demand progress, might significantly influence the effect of the D-PNN application. The D-PNN operating principle is quite different from other soft-computing techniques. The experimental results proved the D-PNN can define comparable models, despite the fact the network structure, the selective and adjustment algorithms have not been completed yet.

Acknowledgement. The article has been elaborated in the framework of the IT4Innovations Centre of Excellence project, reg. no. CZ.1.05/1.1.00/02.0070 funded by Structural Funds of the European Union and state budget of the Czech Republic and in the framework of the project Opportunity for young researchers, reg. no. CZ.1.07/2.3.00/30.0016, supported by Operational Programme Education for Competitiveness and co-financed by the European Social Fund and the state budget of the Czech Republic.

References

1. Abraham, A.: Special issue: Hybrid approaches for approximate reasoning. Journal of Intelligent and Fuzzy Systems 23(2-3), 41–42 (2012)
2. Bertsimas, D., Tsitsiklis, J.: Simulated annealing. Statistical Science 8(1), 10–15 (1993)
3. Chan, K., Chau, W.Y.: Mathematical theory of reduction of physical parameters and similarity analysis. International Journal of Theoretical Physics 18, 835–844 (1979)
4. Corchado, E., Wozniak, M., Abraham, A., de Carvalho, A., Snášel, V.: Recent trends in intelligent data analysis. Neurocomputing 126, 1–2 (2014)
5. Darbellay, G.A., Slama, M.: Forecasting the short-term demand for electricity. International Journal of Forecasting 16, 71–83 (2000)
6. Garcıa-Ascanio, K., Mate, C.: Electric power demand forecasting using interval time series. Energy Policy 38, 715–725 (2010)
7. Hippert, H.S., Pedreira, C.E., Souza, R.C.: Neural Networks for Short-Term Load Forecasting: A Review and Evaluation. IEEE Transactions on Power Systems 16(1) (2001)
8. Ivakhnenko, A.G.: Polynomial theory of complex systems. IEEE Transactions on Systems, SMC-1(4) (1971)
9. Mamlook, R., Badran, O., Abdulhadi, E.: A fuzzy inference model for short-term load forecasting. Energy Policy 37, 1239–1248 (2009)
10. Nikolaev, N.Y., Iba, H.: Adaptive Learning of Polynomial Networks. Springer (2006)
11. Nikolaev, N.Y., Iba, H.: Polynomial harmonic GMDH learning networks for time series modelling. Neural Networks 16, 1527–1540 (2003)
12. Unsihuay-Vila, C., Zambroni, A.C., Marangon-Lima, J.W., Balestrassi, P.P.: Electricity demand and spot price forecasting using evolutionary computation combined with chaotic nonlinear dynamic model. Electrical Power and Energy Systems 32, 108–116 (2010)
13. Zjavka, L.: Recognition of Generalized Patterns by a Differential Polynomial Neural Network. Engineering, Technology & Applied Science Research 2(1) (2012)
14. National Grid, U.K. Electricity Transmission, `http://www2.nationalgrid.com/UK/Industry-information/Electricity-transmission-operational-data/Data-explorer/`
15. ANEX 54, Measured Canadian Occupant-driven Electrical Load Profiles, `http://www.iea-annex54.org/annex42/data.html`

Metaheuristics for Modelling Low-Resolution Galaxy Spectral Energy Distribution

Miguel Cárdenas-Montes[1], Miguel A. Vega-Rodríguez[2], and Mercedes Molla[1]

[1] Centro de Investigaciones Energéticas Medioambientales y Tecnológicas, Department of Fundamental Research, Madrid, Spain
(miguel.cardenas,mercedes.molla)@ciemat.es
[2] University of Extremadura, ARCO Research Group, Dept. Technologies of Computers and Communications, Cáceres, Spain
mavega@unex.es

Abstract. Astrophysics is entering in a new epoch characterized by a huge increment of the volume of data accessible. Consequently, scientists are modifying their traditional data analysis and simulation procedures to adapt them to this circumstance. As part of this increment, it should be underlined the number of high-quality galaxy spectra produced by the new instruments. Galaxy spectra are important in Astrophysics since they encode essential information, as the age and the metallicity, of the constituent stellar populations. These galaxy spectra can be modelled based on Simple Stellar Population. This procedure allows understanding the present state of the galaxy, and also inferring the evolution of the whole stellar system. However, this modelling requires to combine adequately more than one Simple Stellar Population to reproduce the galaxy spectral energy distribution. In order to deal with this modelling process, metaheuristics techniques are suitable, and for this reason, in this work diverse metaheuristics are implemented and tested to model the low resolution Spectral Energy Distribution of the M110 galaxy. The final purpose of this work is to pave the way to create and deliver a code based on metaheuristics techniques able to fit the Spectral Energy Distribution of a galaxy as a combination of predefined Simple Stellar Populations Spectra.

Keywords: Differential Evolution, Combinatorial Optimization, Particle Swarm Optimizer, Galaxy Spectral Energy Distribution.

1 Introduction

During the last decades Astrophysics has suffered from a deluge of high-quality data coming from new digital instruments. The forthcoming future will intensify this situation with the put into service of new projects as these ones using Integral Field Units (IFU's). For this reason, this discipline is incorporating new computational procedures to automatically deal with the storage, to handle and to analyse this high volume of data. In this scenario, where knowledge has to be extractged from large data volumes, evolutionary techniques have demonstrated to be productive [1,2], and for this reason, they

M. Polycarpou et al. (Eds.): HAIS 2014, LNAI 8480, pp. 490–501, 2014.
© Springer International Publishing Switzerland 2014

are used in this work to model the low-resolution galaxy spectra energy distribution of M110 galaxy[1].

The modelling techniques of spectra presently used in Astrophysics is based on Single Stellar Populations[2] (SSP). The idea is to model a given spectrum as a combination of spectra of SSPs defined by their different ages and metallicities[3]. Since the age and metallicity of the all components are obtained, it is also possible to determine the star formation and the enrichment histories of the galaxy or of the galaxy region. Due to the advances in the observed spectra, the researchers have a huge volume of accessible high-quality data. Theoretical stellar models have also greatly improved, mimicking to the real stellar evolution. At the same time, the fossil record methods based on spectral synthesis techniques have emerged and matured in the last decade [3,4,5,6]. These methods are very demanded in the community to analyse, when possible automatically, the galaxy spectra.

In the present work, the adjustment of the observational low-resolution Spectral Energy Distribution (SED, O_λ) of M110 galaxy to a set of SSPs is implemented and tested. Beyond of this immediate goal, the final purpose is to create and deliver to the community a code able to fit the SED of a galaxy using predefined SSPs, and this work tries to pave this way.

On the other hand, IFU facilities (e.g. CALIFA SURVEY) will enlarge the complexity of the problem since a complete spectrum will be produced per pixel of the image of the galaxy, instead of a single spectrum for the image of the galaxy. For this purpose, diverse Evolutionary Algorithms —EAs— are tested against the problem in order to find the most suitable one. Therefore, the scope of this work is far from this particular galaxy; being this one simply used as benchmark to test the approach. The evolutionary algorithms tested in this work are: Genetic Algorithm (GA), Particle Swarm Optimizer (PSO) and some variants: Inertial Weight PSO (IWPSO), and MeanPSO; and Differential Evolution (DE).

The low resolution spectra for the galaxy M110 given by the magnitudes in several broad band filters[4] are used as input to our code. The SSPs broad-band filter magnitudes are taken from the results of the evolutionary synthesis code POPSTAR [7], with which a set of models have been calculated for 6 different metallicities, Z, in the range [0.0001, 0.05], and 106 different stellar logarithmic ages ranging from 5.00 to 10.18. The final sample of SSPs employed consists in a set of 636 theoretical models.

Along this work, the galaxy spectra are modelled with two SSPs. By using SSP mechanism, some implicit considerations are usually assumed about the creation and evolution of the stars in the galaxy. In elliptical and spheroidal galaxies the conversion

---

[1] M110 is termed NGC205 in the New General Catalogue of Nebulae and Clusters of Stars. This galaxy is a dwarf spheroidal galaxy of the Local Group.

[2] Simple Stellar Population consists of a set of stars born at the same time and having the same initial chemical composition.

[3] Metallicity (Z) is the proportion in mass of chemical elements without taking into account H and He, H+He+Z=1

[4] Data have been extracted from NASA/IPAC Extragalactic Database; `http://ned.ipac.caltech.edu/`. These quantities have not necessarily been corrected for background extinction. This might introduce uncertainties which make difficult the fitting process.

of an amount of gas in a set of stars is considered a very rapid process, and in this way only two (or even one) SSPs may be valid to reproduce their spectra. Although this model can seem simple to describe correctly the spectrum of a galaxy — O_λ—, it is useful enough to show the general tendency of the galaxy, and therefore, to understand its evolutionary history.

Associated to the data, a wide range of difficulties are faced. From the most relevant to the less ones, it can be mentioned:

- Depending on the reference, the value of the energy can vary up to three orders of magnitude.
- Depending on the reference, the wavelength where the energy has been measured can differ up to two orders of magnitude in Angstroms.

The rest of the paper is organized as follows: Section 2 summarizes the Related Work and previous efforts done. In Section 3, the most relevant details about the methodology are presented. The Results and the Analysis are displayed in Section 4. And finally, the Conclusions and Future Work are presented in Section 5.

2 Related Work

Although it exists a wide list of works where the use of evolutionary computing is applied to problems in the area of Astronomy and Cosmology, cases where evolutionary algorithms are applied to this kind of studies have not been found in the literature; neither analysis of the galaxy spectral energy distribution performed based on simple stellar populations.

By observing the techniques employed to adjust the galaxy spectra, the closest example is the use of an heuristic for the fitting process [8]. In that work, the exploration of the parameter space is made by a Metropolis algorithm. However, more differences exist between the mentioned and the present work than the simple change of an heuristic by an evolutionary algorithm. In [8] the complete emission spectrum is used in the adjustment process, whereas in the present work only 5 wavelengths —from 3650 Å to 8600 Å– are employed. This makes the fitting process essentially different.

Therefore, to the best of our knowledge, this is the first approach to the analysis of galaxy spectral energy distribution using evolutionary algorithms.

3 Methodology

3.1 Structure of the Candidate Solutions

By considering that the objective of this work involves the fitting of observational galaxy spectrum and, that this objective requires to weight the SSPs through coefficients representing the amount of stellar masses of the selected SSPs, the first step is to propose an adequate structure for the candidate solutions.

The structure of the proposed candidate solutions is composed by a sum of terms (Eq. 1), where each term has two factors:

$$O_\lambda = \sum_{types\ of\ SSPs} C_i \cdot SSP_{[Z,logage]} \qquad (1)$$

- the first one is the amount of stars —measured in solar masses— of a particular SSP. Each SSP is a spectrum of a model of galaxy defined by the logarithm of the age and the metallicity.
- whereas, the second factor is the SSP itself. The spectrum of the SSP depends on two features of the stars: the age and the metallicity.

In adopting this structure for the solutions, two different types of optimizations have to be performed. On the one hand, the selection of the most suitable SSPs from the set of the SSPs constitutes a combinatorial optimization problem. On the other hand, the optimization of the weights, C_i, previously mentioned constitutes a continuous optimization problem. Due to the nature of the problem and the structure of the candidate solutions, both optimizations should not be untied. This double faced problem makes the fitting process challenging and appropriate to hybridize different evolutionary techniques [9,10].

Taking into account the standard fitting problem, where one is given a discrete set of N data points with associated measured errors σ, and is asked to construct the best possible fit to these data using a specific functional form, the most appropriated fitness function is the merit function χ^2, Eq. 2. The lower the χ^2, the closer the solution is to the experimental data.

$$\chi^2 = \sum_{all\ points} \left(\frac{y_{simulated} - y_{observed}}{\sigma}\right)^2 \tag{2}$$

Due that the experimental data used appear without errors, it has been established by the authors, in a realistic approximation, an error of the 10% for all the measures. This is a realistic estimation of the experimental errors of this kind of measures.

3.2 Statistical Inference

In this work, the usual statistical analysis in the numerical optimization works has been followed [11,12]. The analysis is based on non-parametric tests, such as: Kruskal-Wallis and Wilcoxon signed-rank tests. Non-parametric tests have been selected because they do not assume any explicit condition on the data, for example normality. In-depth description of the statistical tests is beyond of the scope of this paper.

3.3 Evolutionary Algorithm

Three EAs have been employed in this work: GA (only mutation operator) [13,14], PSO [15,16], as well as two variants of PSO: Inertial Weight PSO (IWPSO) [17] and MeanPSO [18]; and DE [19,20]. The two variants of PSO have been selected because, in a previous study, they outperform other variants of PSO [21]. In the DE implementation, the schema DE/rand/1/bin [22] has been followed. The mutation operator of GA is used for selecting the most suitable SSPs and for fitting the coefficients C_i, whereas the other EAs are only used for fitting the coefficients C_i. These EAs have been selected based on their wide applicability in optimization problems. In-depth description of the EAs can be found in the mentioned articles, being this purpose out of the scope of the present paper.

In all EAs used in this work, the population structure is panmictic. Thus, the canonical operators of each EA —mutation, reproduction, selection, replacement, etc.— take place globally over the whole population. Furthermore, in all cases the EAs follow a generational model, in which a whole new population of individuals replaces the old one [23]. In all cases where comparisons among the EAs are performed, 10 entities (individuals, vectors) and 1,000 cycles or generations are applied to the algorithms. As pseudorandom number generator, a subroutine based on Mersenne Twister [24] has been used.

4 Results and Analysis

4.1 Mutation Operator for SSP

As first attempt, a Genetic Algorithm (GA) —only with the mutation operator active— is implemented. GA holds numerous advantages, such as: flexibility and adaptability to many different types of problem. Moreover, the reduced number of parameters and the low complexity of the GA allow a quick implementation in order to obtain in a short period of time the first tentative solutions.

Initially, the GA is applied to the combinatorial part of the problem —the selection of the SSPs—. In this part of the problem, the SSPs of the candidate solutions change, being governed this modification by a mutation ratio. The mutation operator randomly replaces one of the two SSPs which compose the candidate solution, by other randomly selected among all the SSPs. If the muted individual is better than the ascendant, then the ascendant is replaced by the muted individual; otherwise, the ascendant is kept and the descendant rejected. This simple mechanism allows a selection of the most suitable SSPs for a particular galaxy spectrum.

Table 1. Mean fitness and standard deviation for 1,000 cycles, 10 individuals and diverse mutation ratios when using only mutation operator over the SSPs selection

Mutation Ratio	0.01	0.05	0.10
Mean Fitness	14.3±39.4	0.8±0.7	7.8±14.2

The results of this first strategy —when implementing mutation ratios: 0.01, 0.05, and 0.10— are presented at Table 1. Although these results are promising for an initial attempt, the dispersion (standard deviation) is too much high. To have a low dispersion when repeating the executions is considered as a valuable feature of the final implementation. Beyond the numerical results, the objective is to reproduce the SED of M110.

In order to understand the goodness of the final results produced by the algorithm, a comparison between the observed SED of the galaxy M110, and the modelled SED by the final best individual of each execution is performed. As can be observed the fitting of the SED is not optimum (Fig. 1(a)). This initial strategy is able to reproduce only the general tendency of the observed SED, however it still overestimates or underestimates

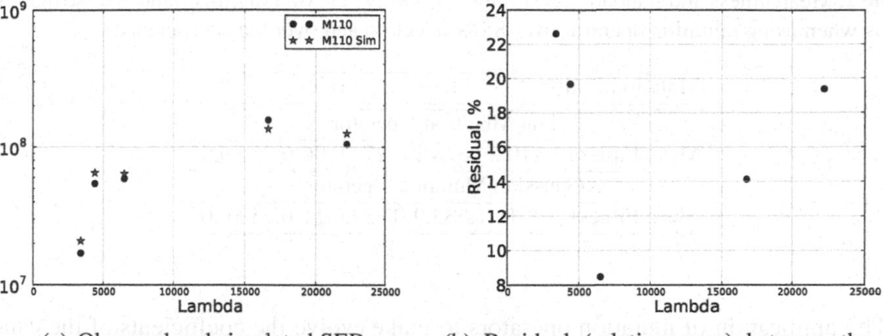

(a) Observed and simulated SED

(b) Residual (relative error) between the observed SED and the simulated SED.

Fig. 1. Results when applying the mutation operator only over the SSPs selection

some values. The relative differences, $(100 \times \frac{SED^{M100} - SED^{sim}}{SED^{M100}})$, reach up to 25% (Fig. 1(b)). Besides it is perceived the difficulty to fit values ranging up to 2 orders of magnitude. It is expected that more elaborated strategies will produce better adjustments between the SED observed and modelled. Better values of the fitness: lower mean and standard deviation, are expected when using more suitable metaheuristics.

4.2 Mutation Operator for Coefficients

Beyond the initial approach focussed on the combinatorial part of the problem, an additional mutation operator is implemented for the coefficients, C_i. Until now the algorithm keeps frozen the coefficients[5] from the initial generation and along the whole execution. This impedes the evolution of the stellar mass of a selected SSP in the galaxy. By implementing this new operator, the algorithm will be able to make them evolve. It is expected that this new mechanism improves the overall performance of the algorithm; overcoming the inherent flaws of the first approach.

In order to keep the same number of evaluations in the algorithm and to fairly compare with the previous implementation, the number of cycles is reduced to the half[6]. This is due that in each cycle the mutation operator over the SSPs selection is applied and evaluated, and next, the mutation operator over the coefficients is also applied and evaluated.

Two variants of the mutation operator for the coefficients have been tested. Firstly, a flat mutation probability distribution in which the mutation ratio is fixed as identical to the mutation ratio for SSPs; and secondly, a Gaussian probability distribution in which the mean and the standard deviation of the probability distribution is calculated over the coefficient values in each generation (Table 2).

[5] These coefficients are randomly created at the beginning of the algorithm.

[6] Hereafter, when two EAs are hybridized, a similar reduction in the number of cycles is applied in order to keep constant the number of evaluations.

Table 2. Mean fitness and standard deviation for 1,000 cycles, 10 individuals and diverse mutation ratios when using mutation operator over SSPs selection and over the coefficients

Mutation Ratio	0.01	0.05	0.10
Flat Mutation Operator			
Mean Fitness	110.2±334.1	0.27±0.06	0.25±0.03
Gaussian Mutation Operator			
Mean Fitness	16.1±33.9	0.33±0.11	0.25±0.05

The application of mutation operators to make evolve the coefficients of the candidate solutions improves significantly the best results obtained until now. However, better solutions (lower standard deviation and mean fitness) are expected if more refinements are applied. Therefore, other evolutionary algorithms are tested in the followings.

4.3 PSO for Coefficients

In order to check efficiency of other evolutionary algorithms, PSO is tested for optimizing the coefficients. Besides the standard PSO implementation, two variants are also checked: MeanPSO and IWPSO. The production includes the three algorithms: PSO, MeanPSO and IWPSO; three maximum velocities: 10^7, 10^8, and 10^9; and three mutation ratios for the GA: 0.01, 0.05 and 0.10. Unfortunately, the numerical results do not improve the previous results (mutation operator applied to the SSPs selection and to the coefficients), and for this reason, they have been omitted.

4.4 Differential Evolution for Coefficients

Differential Evolution is other EA specially suitable for optimizing continuous problems, and it has a large portfolio of cases where it outperforms both GA and PSO. For this reason, it is considered to optimize the continuous part of the candidate solutions, C_i. In this case, DE follows the schema DE/rand/1/bin with $\mu = CR = 0.5$. The main features of this algorithm are its flexibility to deal with many different types of problems, and the speed in the implementation and in the execution, which allows quickly obtaining high-quality suboptimal solutions.

First of all, the numerical results of the DE algorithm (Table 3) are compared with the results obtained in the previous best implementations (Table 2). As can be observed, the DE algorithm outperforms the previous best implementation, i.e. mutation operator acting over the SSPs selection and Gaussian mutation operator over the coefficients. By comparing, it can be concluded that the hybridization of the mutation operator acting over the SSPs with the DE algorithm acting over the coefficients (stellar masses) produces better results than any of the previous strategies tested. As an extra value, a low standard deviation is also achieved.

Table 3. Mean fitness and standard deviation for 1,000 cycles, 10 individuals and diverse mutation ratios when using mutation operator over SSPs selection and DE over the coefficients

Mutation Ratio	0.01	0.05	0.10
Mean Fitness	0.32±0.19	0.24±0.03	0.226±0.009

The application of the Kruskal-Wallis test, $p - value = 8.6 \cdot 10^{-6}$, indicates that the differences between the medians are significant[7]. The post-hoc analysis with the Wilcoxon signed-rank test with the Bonferroni correction shows that the differences between the cases with mutation ratio 0.01 and 0.05, $p - value = 0.0049$, are significant; whereas between the cases with mutation ratio 0.05 and 0.10, $p - value = 0.0926$, the differences are not significant.

Finally, in Fig. 2 the goodness of the numerical results are compared with the observed SED of the galaxy M110. By comparing Fig. 1 and Fig. 2, it can be appreciated the improvement in the fitting with the observational results. Considering that the data have not been corrected for background extinction, the adjustment can be considered as adequate for this phase of the work.

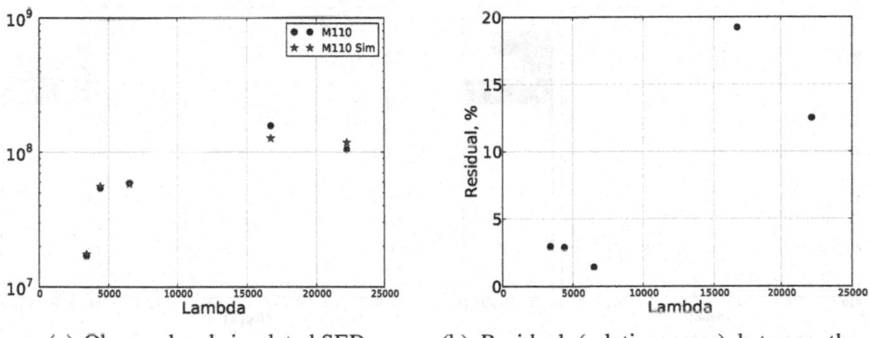

(a) Observed and simulated SED

(b) Residual (relative error) between the observed SED and the simulated SED.

Fig. 2. Results when applying the mutation operator to the SSPs and DE to the coefficients

Larger Number of Cycles. Until now the efforts have focussed on selecting the best evolutionary algorithms to produce high-quality suboptimal solutions. For comparison purposes, all the previous studies have been performed with 10^3 cycles. If the two SSPs obtained with the best solution of each execution are presented, a plot with some dispersion around the optimal SSPs appears (Fig. 3(a)). As much as the number of cycles grows up, a reduction of the dispersion is expected. Progressively, for 10^4 cycles (Fig. 3(b)) and for 10^5 cycles (Fig. 3(c)), the dispersion diminishes but still it is appreciated. For 10^6 cycles, the plot has reduced significantly the dispersion until an acceptable limit (Fig. 3(d)).

[7] A confidence level of 95% (p-value under 0.05) is used in this analysis. This means that the differences are unlikely to have occurred by chance with a probability of 95%.

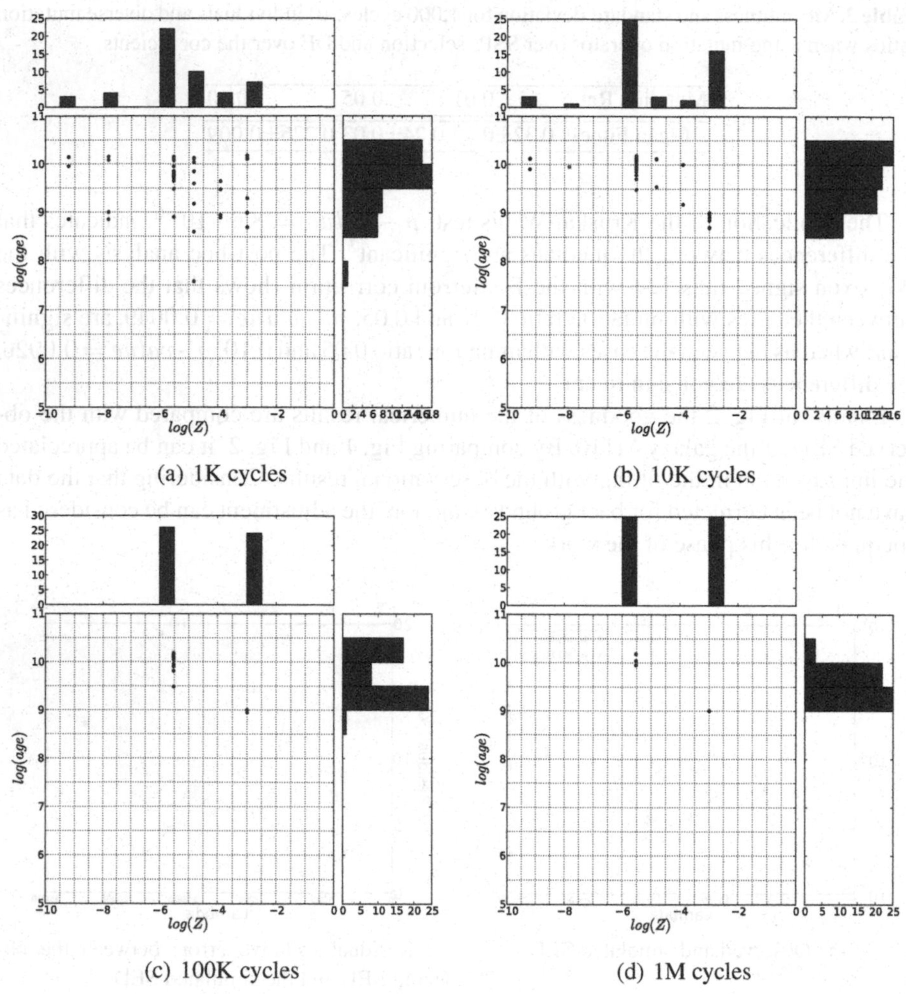

(a) 1K cycles (b) 10K cycles

(c) 100K cycles (d) 1M cycles

Fig. 3. Scatter plots and histograms of SSPs (2 per solution) solutions (25 solutions) when applying the mutation operator to the SSPs selection and DE to the coefficients

Furthermore, the increment in the number of cycles produces an improvement in the mean fitness (Table 4), as well as a reduction of the dispersion. This leads to select 10^6 cycles as an appropriate figure, which produces a low mean and standard deviation fitness, while keeping a limited processing time.

Alternatively, the dispersion can be analysed by clustering the points around centres. For clustering, k-means algorithm is used in this work [25]. The evolution of the coordinates of the two centres generated by k-means is presented at Table 5. It should be underlined that these centres might not coincide with a specific SSP. As can be appreciated, modification of the centres is not produced when executing more than 10^5. Therefore, from the two last studies, it can be concluded that a number of cycles in

Table 4. Mean fitness and standard deviation from 10^3 to 10^7 cycles and 10 individuals, when using mutation operator over SSPs and DE over the coefficients

Cycles	Mean Fitness
10^3	0.226±0.009
10^4	0.209±0.006
10^5	0.199±0.003
10^6	0.19548±0.00013
10^7	0.19535±0.00003

Table 5. Centres of the two clusters created by k-means algorithm for cycles from 10^3 to 10^7 and 10 individuals, when using mutation operator over SSPs selection and DE over the coefficients

Cycles	(log(Z), log(age))
10^3	(-7.82, 9.52), (-3.00, 9.00)
10^4	(-5.52, 9.54), (-3.00, 8.94)
10^5, 10^6, 10^7	(-5.52, 9.95), (-3.00, 9.00)

the range from 10^5 to 10^6 seems appropriate to balance efficiency in the numerical solutions and a reduced processing time.

5 Conclusions

In this paper, an approach based on metaheuristics to model the SED of M110 galaxy has been proposed. The fitting of the SED requires to implement two different evolutionary algorithms to cover the two parts of the problem: the combinatorial part of the optimization which corresponds to the selection of the SSPs; whereas the continuous part of the optimization corresponds to the coefficients indicating the stellar masses of each SSP selected. For obtaining the best fitting, the quality of the solutions provided by diverse evolutionary algorithms has been checked.

The adjustment between the experimental and the simulated SED indicates that this modelling approach in feasible. Besides, the numerical results demonstrate that the use of mutation operator for the selection of SSPs, and the use of DE for the coefficients produces the best fitting among the evolutionary algorithms tested in this work.

More comparative works, where other evolutionary algorithms are tested, is proposed as Future Work. Among others PBIL (Population-based Incremental Learning) is proposed for the combinatorial part of the problem; whereas ABC (Artificial Bee Colony) is proposed for the optimization of the coefficients. Besides, the excellent performance of DE indicates that other variants: DE/best/1/bin, DE/rand/2/bin or DE/rand-to-best/1/bin should be checked to verify if they improve the better solutions achieved.

Acknowledgement. This work has been partially supported by DGICYT grant AYA2010–21887–C04–02. Also, by the Comunidad de Madrid under grant CAM S2009/ESP-1496 (AstroMadrid) and by the Spanish MICINN under the Consolider-Ingenio 2010 Program grant CSD2006-00070: First Science with the GTC (http://www.iac.es/consolider-ingenio-gtc) which are acknowledged. The research leading to these results has received funding by the Spanish Ministry of Economy and Competitiveness (MINECO) for funding support through the grant FPA2010-21638-C02-02, together with the European Community's Seventh Framework Programme (FP7/2007-2013) via the project EGI-InSPIRE under the grant agreement number RI-261323.

References

1. Cárdenas-Montes, M., Mollá, M., Vega-Rodríguez, M.A., Rodríguez-Vázquez, J.J., Gómez-Iglesias, A.: Adjustment of observational data to specific functional forms using a particle swarm algorithm and differential evolution: Rotational curves of a spiral galaxy as case study. In: Sarro, L.M., Eyer, L., O'Mullane, W., De Ridder, J. (eds.) Astrostatistics and Data Mining. Springer Series in Astrostatistics, vol. 2, pp. 81–88. Springer, New York (2012)
2. Charbonneau, P.: Genetic algorithms in astronomy and astrophysics. The Astrophysical Journal Supplement Series 101, 309–334 (1995)
3. Conroy, C.: Modeling the panchromatic spectral energy distributions of galaxies. To appear in Annual Review of Astronomy and Astrophysics (ARAA) 51, 66 pages, 14 figures (2013), cite arxiv:1301.7095
4. Walcher, C.J., Groves, B., Budavari, T., Dale, D.: Fitting the integrated Spectral Energy Distributions of Galaxies. Astrophysics and Space Science 331(1), 1–51 (2011)
5. Mateus, A., Sodré, L., Fernandes, R.C., Stasińska, G., Schoenell, W., Gomes, J.M.: Semi-empirical analysis of sloan digital sky survey galaxies – II. The bimodality of the galaxy population revisited. Monthly Notices of the Royal Astronomical Society 370(2), 721–737 (2006)
6. Fernandes, R.C., Perez, E., Benito, R.G., Delgado, R.M.G., de Amorim, A.L., Sanchez, S.F., Husemann, B., Barroso, J.F., Sanchez-Blazquez, P., Walcher, C.J., Mast, D.: Resolving galaxies in time and space: I: Applying starlight to califa data cubes. Technical Report arXiv:1304.5788 (April 2013)
7. Mollá, M., García-Vargas, M.L., Bressan, A.: PopStar I: evolutionary synthesis model description. Monthly Notices of the Royal Astronomical Society 398, 451–470 (2009)
8. Cid Fernandes, R., Mateus, A., Sodré, L., Stasińska, G., Gomes, J.M.: Semi-empirical analysis of Sloan Digital Sky Survey galaxies - I. Spectral synthesis method. Monthly Notices of the Royal Astronomical Society 358, 363–378 (2005)
9. Corchado, E., Wozniak, M., Abraham, A., de Carvalho, A.C.P.L.F., Snásel, V.: Recent trends in intelligent data analysis. Neurocomputing 126, 1–2 (2014)
10. Abraham, A.: Special issue: Hybrid approaches for approximate reasoning. Journal of Intelligent and Fuzzy Systems 23(2-3), 41–42 (2012)
11. García, S., Molina, D., Lozano, M., Herrera, F.: A study on the use of non-parametric tests for analyzing the evolutionary algorithms' behaviour: a case study on the cec'2005 special session on real parameter optimization. J. Heuristics 15(6), 617–644 (2009)
12. García, S., Fernández, A., Luengo, J., Herrera, F.: A study of statistical techniques and performance measures for genetics-based machine learning: accuracy and interpretability. Soft Comput. 13(10), 959–977 (2009)
13. Michalewicz, Z.: Genetic Algorithms + Data Structures = Evolution Programs. Springer-Verlag New York, Inc. (1994)

14. Mitchell, M.: An Introduction to Genetic Algorithms. MIT Press, Cambridge (1998)
15. Kennedy, J., Eberhart, R.C.: Particle swarm optimization. In: Proceedings of the IEEE International Conference on Neural Networks, vol. IV, pp. 1942–1948 (1995)
16. Eberhart, R.C., Shi, Y., Kennedy, J.: Swarm Intelligence (The Morgan Kaufmann Series in Artificial Intelligence), 1st edn. Morgan Kaufmann (2001)
17. Eberhart, R.C.: Computational Intelligence: Concepts to Implementations. Morgan Kaufmann Publishers Inc., San Francisco (2007)
18. Deep, K., Bansal, J.C.: Mean particle swarm optimisation for function optimisation. Int. J. Comput. Intell. Stud. 1(1), 72–92 (2009)
19. Price, K.V., Storn, R.M., Lampinen, J.A.: Differential Evolution A Practical Approach to Global Optimization. Natural Computing Series. Springer, Berlin (2005)
20. Storn, R., Price, K.: Differential evolution – a simple and efficient heuristic for global optimization over continuous spaces. J. of Global Optimization 11(4), 341–359 (1997)
21. Cárdenas-Montes, M., Vega-Rodríguez, M.A., Gómez-Iglesias, A., Morales-Ramos, E.: Empirical study of performance of particle swarm optimization algorithms using grid computing. In: González, J.R., Pelta, D.A., Cruz, C., Terrazas, G., Krasnogor, N. (eds.) NICSO 2010. SCI, vol. 284, pp. 345–357. Springer, Heidelberg (2010)
22. Mezura-Montes, E., Velázquez-Reyes, J., Coello, C.A.C.: A comparative study of differential evolution variants for global optimization. In: GECCO, pp. 485–492 (2006)
23. Alba, E., Tomassini, M.: Parallelism and evolutionary algorithms. IEEE Trans. Evolutionary Computation 6(5), 443–462 (2002)
24. Matsumoto, M., Nishimura, T.: Mersenne twister: A 623-dimensionally equidistributed uniform pseudorandom number generator. ACM Transactions on Modeling and Computer Simulation 8(1), 3–30 (1999)
25. Han, J., Kamber, M.: Data Mining: Concepts and Techniques. Morgan Kaufmann (2000)

Hybrid Approaches of Support Vector Regression and SARIMA Models to Forecast the Inspections Volume

Juan J. Ruiz-Aguilar, Ignacio J. Turias, María J. Jiménez-Come, and M. Mar Cerbán

Intelligent Modelling of Systems Research Group, University of Cádiz,
Polytechnic School of Engineering, Algeciras, Spain
{juanjesus.ruiz,ignacio.turias,mariajesus.come,
mariadelmar.cerban}@uca.es

Abstract. The constant growth of air and maritime traffic of goods creates the need of increasing the number, the reliability and the security of inspections at the European borders. In this context of high security, this work applies a two-step procedure based on the hybridization of SARIMA and Support Vector Regression to forecast the inspection volume at the Border Inspection Post of Port of Algeciras Bay. Three hybrid approaches are proposed and two prediction horizons are evaluated. Based on several performance indexes to assess the goodness-of-fit of the models, the hybrid approaches perform better than the SARIMA and SVR models used separately. Hence, the study shows that the hybrid methodology improves the single methods. The experimental results can provide relevant information for resource planning and may become a decision-making tool in the inspection process of other European BIPs.

Keywords: Inspection process, SARIMA, support vector regression.

1 Introduction

Since the lifting of internal borders between European member States, and together with the general globalization trends, there has been a significant increase in cross-border freight transport. The European Union (EU) created the Border Inspections Posts (BIPs) in order to guarantee the quality and hygiene of all the products that come into the EU. BIPs are the facilities where goods are checked by an official inspector beforehand. When any goods pass the inspection in a satisfactory way, they can circulate freely within the EU without any controls or restrictions. Therefore, many of these entry points are under congestion problems due to the need of safe and reliable inspections. This situation may lead to the diversion of trade to some other ports with more competitive BIPs. To attack this problem, the application of forecasting methods in the inspection flow could avoid these bottlenecks, and thereby increase competitiveness. In this way, the inspection volume forecasting is a decisive component of a port system which can be used to improve the service quality, planning, facilities and operations or to optimize human and material resources.

The autoregressive integrated moving averages (ARIMA) is a well-known model of time series forecasting. Proposed by Box & Jenkins [3] in the early 70's, ARIMA

M. Polycarpou et al. (Eds.): HAIS 2014, LNAI 8480, pp. 502–514, 2014.
© Springer International Publishing Switzerland 2014

models have been successfully applied in many forecasting fields. Based on its principal assumption in which a time series is generated from a linear process, ARIMA models assume that the future values have a linear relationship with past and current values of the time series. However, real-world situations are more complex and they often show non-linearity [16]. Hence, classical methods show weaknesses when uncertainty or non-linear patterns are present in the data. On the other hand, intelligent models such as artificial neural networks (ANNs) have achieved considerable success in traffic flow prediction once they have demonstrated overcoming the problem of non-linearity [5,6]. In recent years support vector machines (SVMs) have gained special attention due to its relatively easy way to achieve a global minima and their great generalization ability [1]. Thus, SVMs can overcome the overfitting and local minima issues present in ANNs models. By introducing the ε-insensitive loss function, SVMs have been successfully used to solve regression problems, namely support vector regression (SVR). In terms of transport, SVR have been applied in several forecasting approaches such as travel time forecasting [13] or traffic speed forecasting [10]. In maritime transport, SVR have also been successfully used to forecast container throughput in a port [7].

Although ARIMA and SVR models have achieved successful results in their respective predictions fields, none of them is a universal technique to be applied in all conditions. Time series, indeed, frequently contain linear and non-linear patterns. On this basis, a hybrid methodology including both modelling capabilities in linear and non-linear conditions could lead in a good approach for predictions [15]. Particularly, several authors have proposed a methodology based on the hybridization of SARIMA and SVMs to overcome the limitations of the models used separately. Accordingly, [4] proposed a hybrid methodology which consists on ARIMA and SVMs to predict seasonal time series. In the same way, [17] and [14] presented novel hybrid approaches based on ARIMA and SVMs to predict carbon price and the container throughput of a port, respectively. In their respective domains, these authors of these hybrid approaches found that the use of a hybrid strategy based on ARIMA and SVR overcome the performance of the single models. Another use of a hybrid strategy can be found in [2,12].

To the best of our knowledge, the application of SVR or SARIMA in inspection process forecasting has not yet been studied in the research literature. In addition, the use of predictions models to forecast the inspection volume at BIP's inspection process has not been applied to date. Therefore, the final aim of this work is to assess the effectiveness and applicability of the use of hybrid models based on SARIMA and SVR in the prediction of the number of goods subject to inspection at BIPs, by comparing between hybrid SARIMA-SVR model and a single SVR and SARIMA model.

This paper is organized as follows: Section 2 exposes the forecasting models used in this work. In Section 3, an analysis of the database and the explanation of the methodology is presented: SARIMA, SVR and the hybrid SARIMA-SVR models are proposed. Section 4 analyses the results obtained by the proposed methodology and some related issues are discussed. Finally, Section 5 describes conclusions.

2 Methodology

2.1 Seasonal Autoregressive Integrated Moving Average Models (SARIMA)

ARIMA is a model based on three components: the autoregressive term AR, the integration term I and the moving average term MA. In the ARIMA model, the number of inspections should be a linear function of past values and error terms. The general model is expressed as ARIMA(*p*,*d*,*q*), where *p* is the order of the autoregressive terms, *q* is the order of the moving average terms and *d* is the degree of differencing. If the time series contains a seasonal component and the lag is coincident with the periodicity of the data, the model is called SARIMA(*p*,*d*,*q*)(*P*,*D*,*Q*)$_S$, where (*P*,*D*,*Q*) is the seasonal part of the model with the seasonal orders and *s* is the seasonality of the model. The linear expression can be written as Eq. (1):

$$y_t = \sum_{i=1}^{p} \phi_i y_{t-i} + \sum_{j=1}^{P} \Phi_j y_{t-j} + \sum_{k=1}^{q} \theta_k e_{t-k} + \sum_{l=1}^{Q} \Theta_l e_{t-l} + \varepsilon_t \tag{1}$$

where ϕi and Φ_j are the non-seasonal and seasonal autoregressive parameters respectively, θ_k and Θ_l are the non-seasonal and seasonal moving average parameters and ε_t is the error term at time *t*. The SARIMA modelling approach involves the following four-step iterative process: (1) identify the structure of SARIMA model, (2) estimate the parameter values, (3) check the estimated residuals and (4) predict future inspections. Residuals should satisfy the requirements of a white noise process (with mean of zero and a constant variance of σ^2). Here, in order to identify the model several parameters are iteratively used to select the best model by comparison of prediction results.

2.2 Support Vector Regression (SVR)

SVMs were developed by Vapnik [7]. This technique is focused on the principle of structural risk minimization (SRM) instead of empirical risk minimization (ERM) as other techniques such as ANNs. In recent years, the use of SVMs has spread into regression problems by introducing the ε-insensitive loss function defined by Eq. (2). The quality of the estimation is measured by this function.

$$L_\varepsilon(y) \begin{cases} 0, & \text{if } |f(x) - y| \le \varepsilon \\ |f(x) - y| - \varepsilon, & \text{otherwise} \end{cases} \tag{2}$$

Based on the SRM principle, SVMs aims to minimize an upper bound of the generalization error rather than minimizing the prediction error on the training set (empirical risk). First, the input data are mapped into a high dimensional feature space by choosing a non-linear mapping a priori. In the feature space, a linear regression function explaining the relationship between the input and the output data is identified. The linear regression in the new feature space tallies with the non-linear regression model in the original space. The linear regression function can be stated as:

$$y(x) = w^T \Phi(x) + b \tag{3}$$

where b is the bias term, w is the weight vector and $\phi(x)$ denotes the kernel function and it is responsible for mapping the input data into the new high dimensional space (see Fig. 1). In this work, Gaussian kernel has been selected as kernel function. Finally, the problem to be optimized is represented by the following form:

$$\min_{w,b,\xi} \frac{1}{2} \| w \|^2 + C \sum_{i=1}^{N} (\xi_i^+ + \xi_i^-) \tag{4}$$

with the constraints $w \cdot x_i + b - y_i \le \varepsilon + \xi_i^+$, $y_i - w \cdot x_i - b_i \le \varepsilon + \xi_i^-$ and $\xi_i^+, \xi_i^- \ge 0$ with $i = 1,...,l$. In Eq. (4), ξ_i^- and ξ_i^+ are the positive slack variables which denote the training error of the up and down sides, respectively. The slack variables assume non-zero values outside the {ε-, ε} region, previously defined by the loss function which is shown in Eq. (2). The first term $\|w\|^2/2$ in Eq. (4) is the Euclidean norm and it is related to the flatness of the model whereas the slack variables are related to the training error. Therefore, C is the parameter that governs the trade-off between these terms.

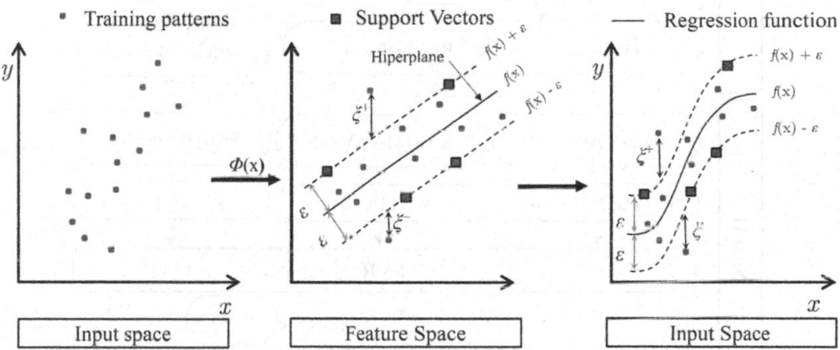

Fig. 1. SVR transformation process using the ε-intensive loss function (Gaussian kernel)

Finally, Lagrange multipliers are used to solve the dual optimization problem that satisfies the Karush-Kuhn-Tucker´s (KKT) conditions. Quadratic programming is applied to solve the problem. The observations with non-zero coefficients of Lagrangian multipliers obtained are referred to as the support vectors, which define the final decision function.

3 Experimental Procedure

The experimental database has been provided by Port Authority of Algeciras Bay. The time series comes from the inspection process at Border Inspection Post of Port of Algeciras Bay. The data collection is composed by daily records of number of goods subject to inspection during three consecutively years (January 2010 to December 2012). A previous analysis based on an autocorrelation analysis has been applied in order to find out a seasonal behavior. As a result, multiply-of-seven-day lags in the past are the points which present higher autocorrelation (weekly seasonality). Two prediction horizons have been taken into account: 1-day prediction horizon and 7-day prediction horizon. The prediction is one step ahead ($\hat{Y}_{t+nh}$), with *nh*=1 day ($\hat{Y}_{t+1}$), or *nh*=7 days ($\hat{Y}_{t+7}$). In this work, three hybrid models are proposed to better predict the number of inspections at BIPs (Fig. 2). In the first step, the time series is fitted by SARIMA model in order to capture the linear component of the inspections data series. Two data sets are defined: training and testing data. The first two years are chosen as training data and the last year (2012) is used as testing data. Due to the two prediction horizons, two different sets of predicted test values are obtained, called SARIMA-1 (comprising the $\hat{Y}_{t+1}$ values) and SARIMA-7 (containing the $\hat{Y}_{t+7}$ values).

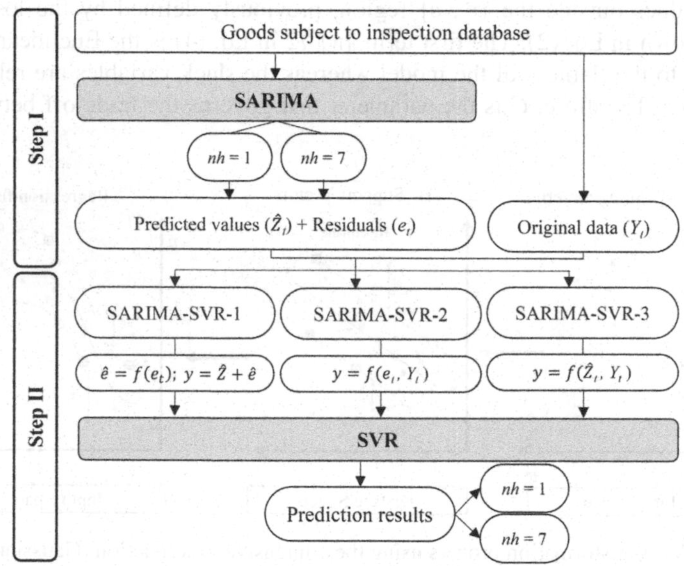

Fig. 2. The proposed hybrid forecasting approaches

In the second step, SVR models are applied using the three proposed configurations. Three models (three hybrid configurations using different autoregressive windows) for two prediction horizons were performed, resulting six possible configurations. Furthermore, the values used as the input of each of these six possible configurations were built using the two sets of predicted values obtained in the first stage (SARIMA-1 or SARIMA-7), resulting a total of twelve possible combinations. The prediction results of the three hybrid configurations were compared among them and the best one was also compared with the single SARIMA and SVR models. In both phases, to construct the SARIMA and SVR models a wide range of search has been considered in order to choose the best parameters. Table 1 collects these parameter ranges and the steps. For SVR models, the parameters *nres*, *ny* and *nZ* denote the autoregressive input window sizes of residuals (e), data (y) and predicted values of the data ($\hat{Z}$). The penalty factor C, tolerance ϵ and Gaussian kernel width γ are the specific SVR parameters.

Table 1. Parameter ranges used in the hybrid methodology

	SARIMA						SVR					
Parameters	p	d	q	P	D	Q	$nres$	ny	nZ	C	ϵ	γ
Values	0:3	0:1	0:3	0:3	0:3	0:1	1:20	1:20	1:20	1:10, 50:5000	2^{-3}:2^{-16}	2^{-3}:2^{-16}
Step	1	1	1	1	1	1	1	1	1	1, 50	2^1	2^1

Each data point related to the input values for SARIMA and SVR models were normalized into the range [0, 1].

3.1 The Hybrid Models

The application of SARIMA or SVR to model linear or nonlinear patterns may be inadequate, respectively. Hybridizing the two techniques can yield better results than the models separately and exploits the strengths of them in an individual way [9,15]. Therefore, a methodology based on the hybridization of SARIMA and SVR have been proposed to forecast the number of goods subject to inspections in a BIP.

The traditional hybrid approach considers that the data series can be decomposed as the sum of a linear and nonlinear component. Then, $Y_t = L_t + N_t$, where L_t is the linear component and N_t denotes the nonlinear component to be estimated. The methodology consists on two phases. In the first step, a SARIMA model is used to model the linear part and, thereby, to obtain the predicted value denoted as $\hat{Z}_t$. The generated residual at time t can be obtained by comparing the forecast value ($\hat{Z}_t$) with the real value (Y_t). That is, $e_t = Y_t - \hat{Z}_t$. This approach considers that the residuals of the first step (SARIMA model) might contain the nonlinear structure which linear models are not able to fit. In the second step, the aim is to recognize the nonlinear relationship of the residual by the application of SVR models. This leads to the first approach proposed:

Configuration 1: SARIMA-SVR 1.

$$\hat{N}_{t+nh} = \hat{e}_{t+nh} = f(e_t, e_{t-nh}, \ldots, e_{t-nres\cdot nh}) + \varepsilon_t \tag{5}$$

where f is the nonlinear function determined by the SVR model, ε_t is the random error and $\hat{e}_t$ is the forecast value and it corresponds to the predicted error of the model. Then, the final forecasted is calculated as:

$$\hat{Y}_{t+nh} = \hat{L}_{t+nh} + \hat{N}_{t+nh} \tag{6}$$

The prediction horizons are represented as *nh* with values of *nh*=1 and *nh*=7 respectively. Furthermore, the size of the autoregressive window (the input data of the SVR models) is indicated by the *nres* value.

Configuration 2: SARIMA-SVR 2.

The prediction can also be modelled by a function, generally nonlinear, of the n-samples in the past and an error term. The residuals (e) and the forecasted values ($\hat{Z}_t$) obtained in the first step (SARIMA) are used in the second step (SVR). In this way, the second hybrid approach is built with the following inputs:

$$\hat{Y}_{t+nh} = f(y_t, y_{t-nh}, ..., y_{t-ny \cdot nh}, e_t, e_{t-nh}, ..., e_{t-nres \cdot nh}) + \varepsilon_{t+nh} \tag{7}$$

where f is the nonlinear function determined by the SVR model, e_t is the residual from the linear SARIMA model, *ny* and *nres* are the size of the autoregressive window for *y* and *e* inputs, respectively.

Configuration 3: SARIMA-SVR 3.

$$\hat{Y}_{t+nh} = f(y_t, y_{t-nh}, ..., y_{t-ny \cdot nh}, \hat{Z}_t, \hat{Z}_{t-nh}, ..., \hat{Z}_{t-nZ \cdot nh}) + \varepsilon_{t+nh} \tag{8}$$

where $\hat{Z}_t$ is the predicted value from the SARIMA model and *nZ* is the size of the autoregressive window for the predicted $\hat{Z}$ values.

3.2 Performance Criteria

The estimation of generalization error has been calculated using three performance indexes: the index of agreement (d), the mean square error (MSE) and the mean absolute error (MAE). The definitions of these criteria are given in Table 2. O_i are the observed values, P_i are the predicted values in time *i* and *N* is the number of samples.

Table 2. Performance measures and their definitions

Metrics	Calculation
d	$d = 1 - \sum_{i=1}^{N}(P_i - O_i)^2 / \sum_{i=1}^{N}(\lvert P_i - \overline{O}\rvert + \lvert O_i - \overline{O}\rvert)^2$
MSE	$MSE = \frac{1}{N}\sum_{i=1}^{N}(O_i - P_i)^2$
MAE	$MAE = \frac{1}{N} \cdot \sum_{i=1}^{N}\lvert P_i - O_i\rvert$

MAE and MSE are among the best overall measures of model performance [11]. MAE is less sensitive to extreme values than MSE. In addition, to study the strength of the linear relationship existing between *O* and *P*, correlation coefficient (r) has been widely used. However, it presents some inconsistences and it is inadequate in certain situations. The index of agreement (d) are alternatively presented as superior indices for making comparisons [11].

4 Results and Discussions

In this section, the results from the hybrid models based on SARIMA and SVR for forecasting the number of goods subject to inspection at BIPs are presented and interpreted. Two different prediction horizons have been considered in the two steps of the two-phases procedure proposed: *nh*=1 day and *nh*=7 days. The model performance was evaluated by calculating the R, d and MSE measures of the testing data set.

In the first step, the SARIMA model was applied throughout the inspection database. A set of configurations based on different parameters were tested in order to find out the one with the best forecasting results. Initially, a power transformation has been used to stabilize the variance of the inspection series, which consists in a logarithmic transformation. Now, the time series is stationary in variance. An iterative process based on trial and error was carried out using the different adjustable parameters, obtaining several models for both prediction horizons. Table 3 shows the best models for *nh*=1 and *nh*=7 and their parameter setting. Considering one-day ahead prediction and based on the error measures, the best-fitted SARIMA model is $SARIMA(2,0,3)(2,1,3)_7$. As the model configuration shows, the test data were pre-processed by taking the first-order seasonal difference to remove the seasonality behavior. The data set, obtained called SARIMA-1 set, contains the one-day ahead prediction values of the test data. For seven-day ahead prediction, the optimal model generated from the data is also $SARIMA(2,0,3)(2,1,3)_7$, and provides the predicted data set called SARIMA-7. These two sets of predicted values were used in order to build the input data for the SVR models. Prior to initiating the second step, the residuals of the SARIMA model have been checked in order to guarantee the validation of the model.

Table 3. Results of the SARIMA models in the first step. In bold the best models obtained

nh	Model	Performance Index		
		d	MSE	MAPE
	$SARIMA(1,0,2)(3,1,3)_7$	0,8733	333,9599	27,7502
1	$SARIMA(2,0,3)(2,1,3)_7$	**0,8741**	**332,0910**	**27,5842**
	$SARIMA(3,0,2)(2,1,3)_7$	0,8734	332,9476	27,5935
	$SARIMA(2,0,2)(2,1,3)_7$	**0,8743**	327,2138	27,6103
7	$SARIMA(2,0,3)(2,1,3)_7$	0,8741	**327,1410**	**27,2354**
	$SARIMA(3,0,3)(2,1,3)_7$	0,8742	327,4970	27,7416

In the second step, SVR models with the three different hybrid configurations of input data were used in order to model the nonlinear (and linear) relationships existing in the original data and the SARIMA result sets (residuals and predicted values). Based on the value of the adjustable parameters of a SVR model (C, ϵ and γ), different networks architectures for each hybrid configuration are evaluated to compare the SVR performance. Furthermore, *nh*=1 and *nh*=7 were designated again as prediction horizons in this phase. The best architecture network was selected in terms of the performance indexes (R, d and MSE) and the best models for the two prediction horizons are collected in Table 4. The prediction results in the table are divided into two parts: inputs obtained from SARIMA-1 set (*nh*=1 in the first step) and inputs extracted from SARIMA-7 set (*nh*=7 in the first step). The models obtaining the best performance indexes are pointed out in bold (one for each prediction horizon).

For *nh*=1 day, the configuration 3 (SARIMA-SVR-3) provides the best performance indexes, followed by SARIMA-SVR-2 and SARIMA-SVR-1, in that order. This hybrid configuration includes an autoregressive window composed by past observations of the time series and the predicted values in the first step. The origin of the input values (the prediction horizon in the first step) has been integrated into the name of the model. Note that in this case the models which employed as input data the predicted values from SARIMA-1 set outperform the models which used the SARIMA-7 set. Related to the goodness-of-fit of the data, the values close to 0.90 in all configurations for the average d measure indicate the good performance achieved in the experiment.

Table 4. Comparison of the performance of the proposed hybrid models in the second step

h	SARIMA set	Configuration	Performance Indexes		
			d	**MSE**	**MAPE**
		SARIMA1-SVR-1	0.8852	308.8123	12.0692
	SARIMA-1	SARIMA1-SVR-2	0.8904	**300.0781**	12.2273
		SARIMA1-SVR-3	**0.8948**	305.3913	**12.0457**
		SARIMA7-SVR-1	0.8849	309.3312	12.0745
	SARIMA-7	SARIMA7-SVR-2	0.8910	305.6708	12.3260
		SARIMA7-SVR-3	0.8870	322.4543	12.5129
		SARIMA1-SVR-1	0.8832	313.6345	12.2340
	SARIMA-1	SARIMA1-SVR-2	0.8830	317.2347	12.3090
		SARIMA1-SVR-3	**0.8838**	**312.1224**	**12.2157**
		SARIMA7-SVR-1	0.8788	322.8398	12.4626
	SARIMA-7	SARIMA7-SVR-2	0.8764	324.1626	12.6835
		SARIMA7-SVR-3	0.8795	321.9089	12.4897

Although the best configuration for *nh*=1 seems to be the configuration number 3, a MSE value of 300.0781 obtained in the Configuration 2 (SARIMA1-SVR-2) leads to the best MSE value of the experiment and shows the good performance of this configuration. Indeed, the proposed two hybrid configurations (2 and 3) improve the traditional hybrid model (configuration 1) based on these performance criteria.

Similarly, the results obtained for *nh*=7 indicate that the performance of the three hybrid configurations using the SARIMA-1 set are better than the models which include values the SARIMA-7 set. Once again, the configuration number 3, called SARIMA7-SVR 3, outperforms the rest of the configurations in all of the performance indexes.

However, the models for *nh*=1 significantly outperform the models for *nh*=7 in the three proposed configurations. In conclusion, these results suggest that SARIMA-SVR-3 model as the optimal hybrid configuration. The structures of the best-fitted models for *nh*=1 and *nh*=7 are collected in Table 5.

Each best performance index value is achieved with a different set of parameters. As it can be seen in Table 5, *nh*=1 obtains the best results. 1-day ahead prediction requires relatively long sizes of auto-regressive windows (higher than 7) than 7-day ahead predictions (lower than 2). Thus, the autoregressive windows for *nh*=1 also contains some of the values of the autoregressive window for *nh*=7. This, together with the similar good results obtained for *nh*=7, suggests that variables located with a lag of seven days in the past contain the most relevant information.

Table 5. Best parameters for the best models of each prediction horizon

nh	Model	Performance index	Value	Parameters				
				ny	*nZ*	*C*	ϵ	γ
1	SARIMA1-SVR-3	*d*	0,8948	8	5	3150	2^{-16}	2^{-6}
		MSE	305,3913	8	5	3350	2^{-16}	2^{-6}
		MAE	12,0457	7	5	4950	2^{-7}	2^{-6}
7	SARIMA1-SVR-3	*d*	0,8838	1	1	4800	2^{-6}	2^{-8}
		MSE	312,1224	2	1	3850	2^{-14}	2^{-16}
		MAE	12,2157	1	2	1150	2^{-15}	2^{-9}

Finally, the results obtained from the best hybrid models have been compared with the forecasting results from the individual models (SARIMA and SVR). The comparisons of the number of predicted inspection values are summarized in Table 6. This table shows that the hybrid model outperformed the single SARIMA model and the single SVR model in either prediction horizon. For *nh*=1, SARIMA1-SVR-3 model from the SARIMA-1 predicted set (SARIMA1-SVR-3) provides a d value of 0.8948, which is clearly higher than those obtained with the single methods. This value shows an excellent correlation between observed and predicted values of the testing data. Furthermore, a MSE value close to 300 and a MAPE value of 12.0457 indicate the significant decrease of the error obtained.

Table 6. Comparison of prediction error of the different hybrid models and the individual models

nh	Model	Performance Indexes		
		d	*MSE*	*MAPE*
1	SARIMA	0,8741	332,0910	27,5842
	SVR	0,8822	389,1624	24,6060
	SARIMA1-SVR-2	0,8904	**300,0781**	12,2273
	SARIMA1-SVR-3	**0,8948**	305,3913	**12,0457**
7	SARIMA	0,8741	327,1410	27,2354
	SVR	0,8704	365,4109	22,9026
	SARIMA1-SVR-1	0,8832	313,6345	12,2340
	SARIMA1-SVR-3	**0,8838**	**312,1224**	**12,2157**

A point-to-point comparison between observed and predicted values for one-day ahead and seven-day-ahead prediction horizon are represented in Figs. 3 and 4, respectively. In both cases, SARIMA1-SVR-3 is selected as the hybrid model. The period between 1 February 2012 and 15 March 2012 has been represented as a prediction example in both figures. Under-predictions lead to underestimate the number of sanitary inspectors at BIPs which may cause delays in certain situations.

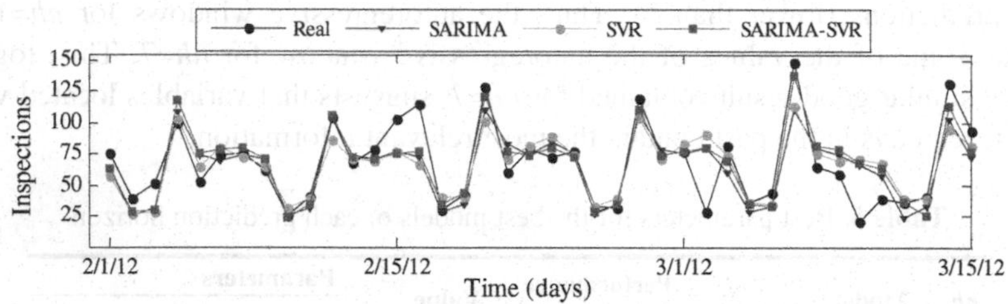

Fig. 3. Comparison of the real data and forecasts in the best models (*nh*=1)

As shown in these figures, the hybrid model is more efficient than single models in capturing data patterns. The introduction of an autoregressive window based on seven-day lags in the past does not improve the forecasting results of the hybrid model. Thus, the hybrid model with *nh*=1 provides a better fit to the data than *nh*=7.

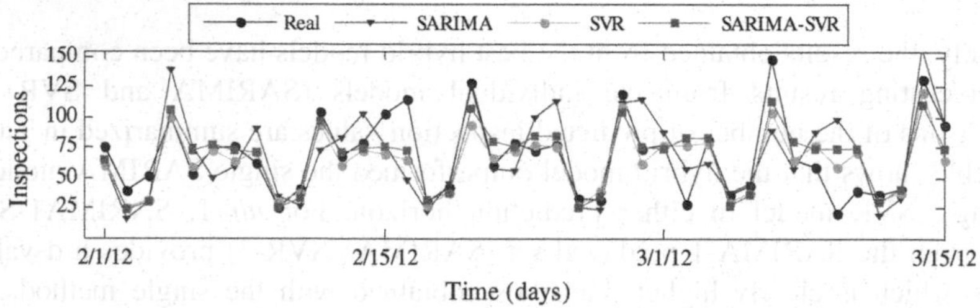

Fig. 4. Comparison of the real data and forecasts in the best models (*nh*=7)

5 Conclusions

The strong increase in global trade and common border between the Member States of the EU have created the need to increase the security and quality of the inspections at Border Inspection Posts. BIPs must be able to anticipate the workload in order to improve the level service of the port and to optimize human resources. The application of hybrid artificial intelligent systems can be a powerful decision-making tool.

The traditional hybrid approach based on ARIMA and a nonlinear forecasting technique consists on decomposing a time series into its linear and nonlinear components. Several studies reveal that this hybrid approach is able to outperform results obtained by either of the models used separately. Nevertheless, others works pointed out inconsistences arising from their underlying assumptions. Two additional hybrid approaches using SARIMA-SVR to forecast the number of goods subject to checks at BIPs are presented in order to overcome the limitations previously mentioned and achieve more accurate forecasting results. The SARIMA model is applied to capture the linear and seasonal patterns of the inspections data. Then, SVR are used to recognize the nonlinear patterns hidden in the time series, using obtained preprocessed data from SARIMA.

The present study compares the proposed approaches with the same methods used in an individual way. Using the d, MSE and MAE as performance criteria, the experiment results showed that the proposed hybrid model (SARIMA-SVR-3) is better than the single models (SARIMA and SVR) for both prediction horizons (nh=1 and nh=7). Similarly, this hybrid model is superior to the traditional hybrid approach of ARIMA-SVR (SARIMA-SVR 1). The results suggest that the proposed approaches are a promising methodology for forecasting the number of goods subject to inspection at BIPs. This application can be an excellent forecasting tool in the inspection process and can provide relevant information for decision making and resource planning.

References

1. Alenezi, A., Moses, S.A., Trafalis, T.B.: Real-Time Prediction of Order Flowtimes Using Support Vector Regression. Comput. Oper. Res. 35(11), 3489–3503 (2008)
2. Borrajo, M.L., Baruque, B., Corchado, E., Bajo, J., Corchado, J.M.: Hybrid Neural Intelligent System to Predict Business Failure in Small-to-Medium-Size Enterprises. Int. J. Neural Syst. 21(04), 277–296 (2011)
3. Box, G.E.P., Jenkins, G.M.: Time Series Analysis: Forecasting and Control. Holden-Day, Oakland (1976)
4. Chen, K., Wang, C.: A Hybrid SARIMA and Support Vector Machines in Forecasting the Production Values of the Machinery Industry in Taiwan. Expert Syst. Appl. 32(1), 254–264 (2007)
5. Dougherty, M.S., Cobbett, M.R.: Short-Term Inter-Urban Traffic Forecasts using Neural Networks. Int. J. Forecast. 13(1), 21–31 (1997)
6. Hornik, K., Stinchcombe, M., White, H.: Multilayer Feedforward Networks are Universal Approximators. Neural Networks 2(5), 359–366 (1989)
7. Mak, K., Yang, D.: Forecasting Hong Kong's Container Throughput with Approximate Least Squares Support Vector Machines. In: Proceedings of the World Congress on Engineering. Citeseer (2007)
8. Vapnik, V.N.: Statistical learning theory. John Wiley and Sons, New York (1998)
9. Wang, J., Wang, J., Zhang, Z., Guo, S.: Stock Index Forecasting Based on a Hybrid Model. Omega 40(6), 758–766 (2012)
10. Wang, J., Shi, Q.: Short-Term Traffic Speed Forecasting Hybrid Model Based on Chaos–Wavelet Analysis-Support Vector Machine Theory. Transportation Research Part C: Emerging Technologies 27, 219–232 (2013)
11. Willmott, C.J.: On the Validation of Models. Physical Geography 2(2), 184–194 (1981)
12. Woźniak, M., Graña, M., Corchado, E.: A Survey of Multiple Classifier Systems as Hybrid Systems. Information Fusion 16, 3–17 (2014)
13. Wu, C., Ho, J., Lee, D.: Travel-Time Prediction with Support Vector Regression. IEEE Transactions on Intelligent Transportation System 5(4), 276–281 (2004)

14. Xie, G., Wang, S., Zhao, Y., Lai, K.K.: Hybrid Approaches Based on LSSVR Model for Container Throughput Forecasting: A Comparative Study. Applied Soft Computing 13(5), 2232–2241 (2013)
15. Zhang, G.P.: Time Series Forecasting using a Hybrid ARIMA and Neural Network Model. Neurocomputing 50, 159–175 (2003)
16. Zhang, G., Eddy Patuwo, B., Hu, M.Y.: Forecasting with Artificial Neural Networks: The State of the Art. Int. J. Forecast. 14(1), 35–62 (1998)
17. Zhu, B., Wei, Y.: Carbon Price Forecasting with a Novel Hybrid ARIMA and Least Squares Support Vector Machines Methodology. Omega 41(3), 517–524 (2012)

A Hybrid Approach for Credibility Detection in Twitter

Alper Gün and Pınar Karagöz

Middle East Technical University,
Department of Computer Engineering, Ankara, Turkey
e182996@metu.edu.tr, karagoz@ceng.metu.edu.tr

Abstract. Nowadays, microblogging services are seen as a source of information. It brings us a question. Can we trust information in a microblogging service? In this paper, we focus on one of the popular microblogging services, Twitter, and try to answer which information in Twitter is credible. Newsworthiness, importance and correctness are the dimensions to be measured in this study. We propose a hybrid credibility analysis which combines feature based and graph based approaches. Our model is based on three types of structures, which are tweet, user and topic. Initially, we use feature based learning to construct a prediction model. In the second step, we use the results of this model as input to authority transfer and further refine the credibility scores for each type of node. The same process is used for measuring each of the dimensions of newsworthiness, importance and correctness. Experimental results show that the proposed hybrid method improves the prediction accuracy for each of these credibility dimensions.

Keywords: credibility, twitter, microblog, authority transfer, hybrid.

1 Introduction

Microblogging services are used by many people to share contents such as news, comments, images or videos. Generally they have a friendship mechanism and each user broadcasts his/her post to other people. As more people use a microblog service, service reaches more people by using friendship network of users. Twitter is one of the most popular microblogging and social networking services which is used worldwide by millions of people.

There are many academic studies that use huge amount of data in Twitter. For example, one of the popular research topics on Twitter is recommendation systems. There are various studies for recommending links, news [1], information sources [2] etc. Furthermore, there are studies about detection of important events such as earthquake [10]. However, these studies require picking proper ones among all tweets. For this reason, there is a need to investigate the credibility of users and tweets before using this massive amount of data. Credibility problem in microblogging services is studied in several studies. We can classify them into three groups. Studies in the first group build a machine learning model

M. Polycarpou et al. (Eds.): HAIS 2014, LNAI 8480, pp. 515–526, 2014.
© Springer International Publishing Switzerland 2014

and aim to learn credibility value from the data [4]. They generally use attributes of authors, posts and topics. The second group of studies measure credibility by utilizing friendship and retweeting network in Twitter [14]. Studies in the third group are hybrid solutions [8]. They use approaches in the first group and second group together to make a decision for credibility value in microblogging services.

In this study, we focus on classification of tweets and users in terms of their newsworthiness, importance and correctness. We propose a hybrid approach and apply a two-level process for ranking tweets in terms of these dimensions. In the first step, we build a machine learning scheme to classify tweets, users and topics with their attributes. We have in total 41 attributes for user, tweet and topic. In the second step we apply authority transfer, which gets initial scores from the first step. We have three different types of nodes which are user, tweet and topic. Each tweet is linked to a user and a topic. It provides us to transfer authority among user, tweet and topic nodes. The authority transfer makes use of the idea that if a user is important then we can conclude that tweets which are posted by this user are also important. Similarly if a topic is important, tweets in this topic are also important. Each node starts with initial score coming from feature evaluation. Besides, number of followers is added to the initial score to user nodes and number of retweets is added to the initial score to tweet nodes. After we transfer score between nodes, we obtain a final score for each node and if score of a node is more than a predefined threshold, then we label this node as newsworthy, important or correct.

This paper is organized as follows. Section 2 gives a summary of research in the literature about ranking and credibility in microblogs. Section 3 discusses the details of our proposed solution. Building our data set, user evaluation and proposed work are mentioned in this chapter. Section 4 explains experimental results of proposed solution and finally Section 5 gives a summary of study and possible improvements in the future.

2 Related Work

There are two common ways to rank tweets, which are feature based evaluation and graph based evaluation. There are also hybrid approaches that combine feature based and graph based solutions. In this section, we summarize the research in the literature for each of these approaches.

Feature based solutions generally aim to build a learning scheme such as decision tree, neural network, SVM or Bayes networks. They may use attributes of users, context and behavior. Research of Castillo et al. [4] is in this category and it is one of the basic studies which inspire us. They aim to classify tweets as credible and not credible and use wide range features that are grouped as message based, user based, topic based and propagation based. They categorize tweets into different topics. Each topic contains its own tweets. Another research investigates the spam issue [15]. This study aims to detect spam and promotional campaigns. They classify messages in Twitter as regular messages, promotional messages and spam messages. In order to detect spam and promotional messages, they analyze similarity of URLs by utilizing from tweet based attributes. Credibility of information in blog sites is investigated in [12]. This study focuses on the content and checks some credibility indicators such as spelling, timeliness, document length and comments. In [6], Gupta et al. use message based features and user based features to acquire trustworthy tweets in high impact events. They investigate tweets during 14 important events such as Libya crisis, hurricane Irene, earthquake in Virginia and UK Riots. Xia et al. [13] aim to measure trustworthiness of tweets in emergency situation and labels tweets as credible or incredible by using bayesian network. This study analyses author based, content based, topic based and diffusion based features.

The second common way for credibility ranking on Twitter is graph based solutions. Studies in this group build a graph with nodes of user, tweet and topic and then transfer score between nodes. TURank, which is one of the base studies for our research, uses actual information flow in Twitter to find authoritative users [14]. A similar approach for authority transfer is also used in our study. According to TURank, a user is more authoritative if this user is followed by an authoritative user. Similarly if a tweet is retweeted, retweet makes the original tweet more important. There are four ways to transfer authority in TURank. These are user to user, user to tweet, tweet to user and tweet to tweet transfers. User followership network is used by many studies to rank users in Twitter. The work of Armentano et al. [2] aims to recommend interesting users to follow. They utilize user's follower graph to improve recommendation quality. The same authors also perform another research which uses a user topology for recommending good information sources [3].

Hybrid approach which is refered in [16], can also be applied to credibility analysis. Several hybrid solutions which use feature based solution and graph based solution also exist in the literature. Kang et al. [8] provide a hybrid model solution and calculate a score by using 19 features in total and propagate this score in their network. They only use user friendship network and users sends their score to their followers. Another hybrid solution is proposed in [5]. This study ranks tweets in order to find the most retweetable posts. They use a hybrid model which uses small set of features. These feature scores are transferred to other nodes in their graph. The study of Huang et al. [7] proposes a hybrid strategy to calculate influence of users. They uses page ranking algorithm in user friendship network. Further, they utilize user behavioral attributes such as frequency of updating microblog, interaction with other users, and so on.

3 Proposed Solution

There exists many studies which concentrate on microblog credibility problem in the literature. Some of these studies aim to train and learn data and then predict credibility of tweets. Moreover, some of the studies in this area go with solution which utilize relationship of users, tweets etc.

Studies of Castillo [4] and Yamaguchi [14] form the basis of our hybrid solution. We start the training phase with machine learning schemes and then use authority transfer on our graph, which consists of user, tweet and topic relationship. Yamaguchi's study involves a graph with user - tweet relationship. In our work, we also use topic - tweet relationship because it is possible that some tweets may have more credibility if this tweet is in a credible topic. Therefore we also decided to transfer authority between tweet and topic. Studies of Castillo and Yamaguchi measure the credibility in terms of a single label. However, we use three labels which are newsworthiness, importance and correctness, and measure credibility in each of these dimensions. We used similar features with that of [4] to found our own prediction model but we eliminated some of features in Castillo's research that does not have any impact on our data set.

The proposed method basically builds a prediction model by using a learning scheme and then these prediction results are used in authority transfer. In order to build a prediction model, we needed to collect data and constructed a set of tweets annotated for newsworthiness, importance and correctness. In the rest of this section, we present the details of data collection and the user study as well as the proposed technique.

3.1 Data Collection

Since topic is used as one of the structure to measure credibility, we collected equal number of tweets for a set of selected topics. Therefore, we firstly determined the topics which will be used in our solution and then collected equal number of tweets for each topic. As the first step of data collection, 25 trend topics are determined. These are among the trend topics in Turkey which are announced by Twitter. Trend topics are selected in several time intervals between January 2013 and June 2013.

3.2 User Evaluation

To construct the ground truth, each tweet in our data set has been evaluated by four users. We designed an application with user interface to help users for their evaluation. In this application, users read each tweet one by one and mark the tweet for three criteria which are newsworthiness, importance and correctness. Users can answer as YES, NO or UNSURE. YES is answered for positive feedback such as newsworthy, important or correct. NO is for negative feedback and UNSURE is answered when user has no certain answer. Users are asked to answer YES for newsworthiness, if a tweet contains information which is significant enough to report as news, are asked to answer YES for importance, if a tweet has important information for evaluator and are asked to answer YES for correctness if a tweet seems to have true information for evaluator.

In order to construct the ground truth, we have used four different methods. Therefore, we have four different ground truths: GT_{avg}, GT_{4YES}, GT_{3YES}, GT_{1YES}.

- GT_{avg}: In this method, each YES answer is assigned two points, UNSURE answer is assigned one point and NO answer is assigned zero point. Four evaluations' scores are accumulated and total score is calculated. A tweet may have score between zero and eight points. If total score is more than four, we classified these tweet as YES, otherwise as NO for the given criterion.
- GT_{4YES}: If a tweet is answered YES by all four users for the given criterion, then we classified this tweet as YES for this criterion. Otherwise, we classified it as NO.
- GT_{3YES}: If a tweet is answered YES by at least three users for the given criterion, then we classified this tweet as YES for this criterion. Otherwise, we classified it as NO.
- GT_{1YES}: This is the most relaxed form of ground truth. If a tweet is answered YES by at least one user for the given criterion, then we classified this tweet as YES for this criterion. Otherwise, we classified it as NO.

Note that we do not use GT_{2YES} since its mechanism is similar to GT_{avg}.

Table 1. Agreement values between judges and ground truth types

Overlap	GT_{avg}	GT_{4YES}	GT_{3YES}	GT_{1YES}
Newsworthiness	0.9043	0.8585	0.9016	0.8371
Importance	0.8268	0.7592	0.8256	0.7232
Correctness	0.8517	0.7353	0.8443	0.8138

Table 2. Kappa values between judges and ground truth types

Kappa	GT_{avg}	GT_{4YES}	GT_{3YES}	GT_{1YES}
Newsworthiness	0.7257	0.5352	0.7135	0.6378
Importance	0.6194	0.4350	0.6159	0.4833
Correctness	0.5182	0.4133	0.5239	-0.0436

Table 1 represents the agreement rate between ground truth values and user answers. We see that GT_{avg} has the highest agreement level with user answers for each label. Table 2 gives the Cohen's Kappa values for the agreement between user answers and the ground truths. Cohen's Kappa measures the statistic value of agreement rate by considering the agreement occurring by chance. For newsworthiness and importance label, the best results are obtained with GT_{avg} and for correctness label, GT_{3YES} gives the best Kappa result. However, Kappa result for GT_{avg} is close to Kappa result for GT_{3YES} for correctness label. Since we generally obtained the best overlap and Kappa result from GT_{avg} evaluation method. Therefore, we will use it in our experiment.

21.12 % of tweets are regarded as newsworthy, 30.88 % of tweets are regarded as important and 73.52 % of tweets are regarded as correct according to GT_{avg} evaluation.

3.3 Features

In this phase, the features are grouped as tweet, user and topic features. In grouping and selecting the features, we followed the trend in the literature [4]. We aimed to benefit from many features used in the literature and then eliminated some of them since they have no impact on the result. Selected features are used for building a model to predict label of a tweet. We have total 41 features which contains 5 user features, 17 tweet features and 19 topic features as seen in Table 3. User features are collected by using Twitter API. Then we calculated value of tweet features by simple string parsing operations. For sentiment score calculation, SentiStrength libraries [11] are used to calculate negative and positive sentiment score. At the end, we calculated average scores for each topic feature. There are 100 tweets in each topic and average of features for these 100 tweets computed.

Table 3. List of features

Feature Type	Feature Name
User features	Registration age
	Number of total post
	Number of friends
	Has description in user profile
	Has URL in user profile
Tweet features	Number of characters in the tweet
	Number of words in the tweet
	Presence of question mark in the tweet
	Presence of exclamation mark in the tweet
	Presence of multiple marks in the tweet
	Presence of smile icon in the tweet
	Presence of frown icon in the tweet
	Presence of first pronoun in the tweet
	Presence of second pronoun in the tweet
	Fraction of uppercase letters among all letters
	Presence of URL in the tweet
	Presence of mention character in the tweet
	Presence of hashtag character in the tweet
	Is retweet
	Positive sentiment score
	Negative sentiment score
	Total sentiment score
Topic features	Average follower count in the topic
	Average friend count in the topic
	Average total post count in the topic
	Average registration age in the topic
	Average for presence of smile icon in the topic
	Average for presence of frown icon in the topic
	Average for presence of hashtag character in the topic
	Average for presence of mention character in the topic
	Average for presence of exclamation mark in the topic
	Average for presence of question mark in the topic
	Average for presence of multiple marks in the topic
	Fraction of retweets in the topic
	Average for presence of profile description in the topic
	Average for presence of URL in the tweet
	Average for presence of URL in user profile
	Average for presence of first pronoun in the topic
	Average for presence of second pronoun in the topic
	Average for presence of uppercase letters in the topic
	Average number of characters in the topic

3.4 Classification

After we have calculated feature values for tweet, user and topic, we constructed model by using various learning algorithms in KNIME and Weka data analysis tools. We used 10 folds cross validation in each learning scheme. GT_{avg} is used in all of our experiment and we applied same process for newsworthiness, importance and correctness labels. When predicting labels, we used two different methods as follow.

- We used all 43 features together to generate the model.
- We grouped the features as user features, tweet feature and topic features. Then we used each type of features separately to generate a model. Therefore, tweet features are used to predict labels of tweets, user features are used to predict label of users and topic features are used to predict labels of topics.

We used Random forest tree, J48 tree, ADTree, Random Tree, BFTree, Naive Bayes, KStar and AdaBoost machine learning algorithms to classify tweets.

3.5 Graph Based Approach

After feature based learning, we applied authority transfer between tweets, users and topics. At the end of the first phase, it is possible that a credible user may have low score. However, if this user has important tweets, then authority transfer enables that important tweets make their author more important. Similarly if an unreliable user has high score after the first phase, if this user has unimportant tweets, these tweets make author also less important. Furthermore, if we go through tweet - topic relationship, we see that if a topic has important tweets, tweets in this topic will also be more important. Similarly if a tweet is important, it makes its topic more important.

In our data set each tweet has a topic and a user. Figure 1 displays graph structure used in the authority transfer step of our solution. Nodes of the graph are *Tweet*, *User* and *Topic*, and the edges are *Tweet-User*, *User-Tweet*, *Tweet-Topic* and *Topic-Tweet* edges.

Fig. 1. Graph Structure of Our Study

Score of tweet node has influence on user and topic nodes. User nodes firstly affect tweet nodes then it affects topic nodes indirectly by transferring score from tweet to topic. Topic nodes send their scores to tweets and they also send their scores indirectly to users in the second step. Hence, these transfers implement the following effects.

- A tweet is more important if its author is important.
- A tweet is more important if its topic is important.

- An author is important if he/she posted important tweets.
- A topic is important if it contains important tweet.

We have initial scores for each tweet, user and topic from the result of the feature based learning phase. The number of retweets of a tweet is added to the feature score of each tweet node and the number of followers is added to the feature score of each user node.

Table 4. Definitions of Variables in Equations

Name	Definition
$S_{\#fol}$	Number of followers for each user
$S_{\#rt}$	Number of retweet for each tweet
w_1	Weight for User to Tweet Edge
w_2	Weight for Tweet to User Edge
w_3	Weight for Topic to Tweet Edge
w_4	Weight for Tweet to Topic Edge
S_{tweet0}	Initial score for tweet nodes
S_{user0}	Initial Score for user nodes
S_{topic0}	Initial Score for topic nodes

In our model, authority transfer is evaluated by using the Equations 1, 2 and 3 which are proposed for this problem. Definition of variables in equations is given in Table 4.

$$S_{tweet} = S_{tweet0} + w_1 \times S_{user0} + w_3 \times S_{topic0} \tag{1}$$

$$S_{user} = S_{user0} + ((w_3 \times S_{topic0}) + S_{tweet0}) \times w_2 \tag{2}$$

$$S_{topic} = S_{topic0} + ((w_1 \times S_{user0}) + S_{tweet0}) \times w_2 \tag{3}$$

Final score of a tweet is the sum of initial score of this tweet, score coming from user and score coming from topic. When we calculate the final score of a user, firstly topic score is transferred to tweet's initial score. Then tweet score is added to the initial score of this user. For the final score of topic score, firstly user score is transferred to tweet and then tweet score is added to initial score of this topic. At the end, we have final scores for each tweet, user and topic.

Scores are transmitted among the nodes according to values of weights. We experimented with several sets of weights and get the best result when w_1 is 0.1, w_2 is 10, w_3 is 1 and w_4 is 10. We can conclude that if the final score of a tweet is more than a predefined threshold, then tweet is newsworthy or important or correct. We also get best result when this predefined threshold is 10.

4 Experimental Evaluation

In this section, we describe the results of our experiments for each credibility dimension used in the study. In the feature based step, we used KNIME and Weka data analysis tools to generate prediction models. We tried two different ways to calculate initial score for nodes. The first way is giving all 41 features together to a learning scheme. Then each type of nodes is started with initial score of prediction results. The second way is giving features separately such as user related ones, tweet related ones and topic related ones. Therefore, at the end of this phase, each node has its own initial score from prediction results of its own type. For example, prediction results of user related features have only influence on user nodes.

In the rest of this section, we describe experiment result for each credibility label one by one. The overall result of the experiments in the first phase and second phase for the best results for each label is shown in Figure 2 and 3. These figures represent result of accuracy rate when training all features together.

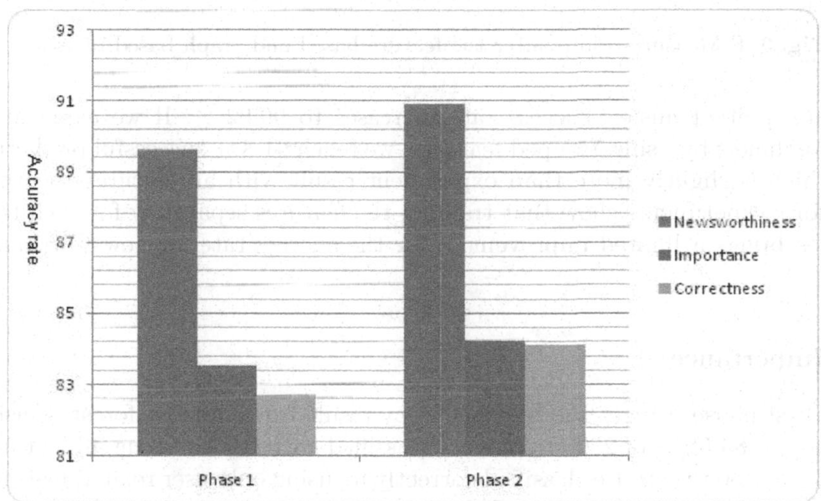

Fig. 2. Prediction accuracy results after the feature based and graph based phases

4.1 Newsworthiness

When we train data with all the features, we get the best accuracy result from random forest decision tree learner. 89.64 % of 2500 tweets are classified correctly by using all features. 82.68 % of 2500 tweets are classified correctly by using only user related features. 87.56 % of 2500 tweets are classified correctly by using only tweet related features and 85.84 % of 2500 tweets are classified correctly by using only topic related features. In the second phase we apply authority transfer.

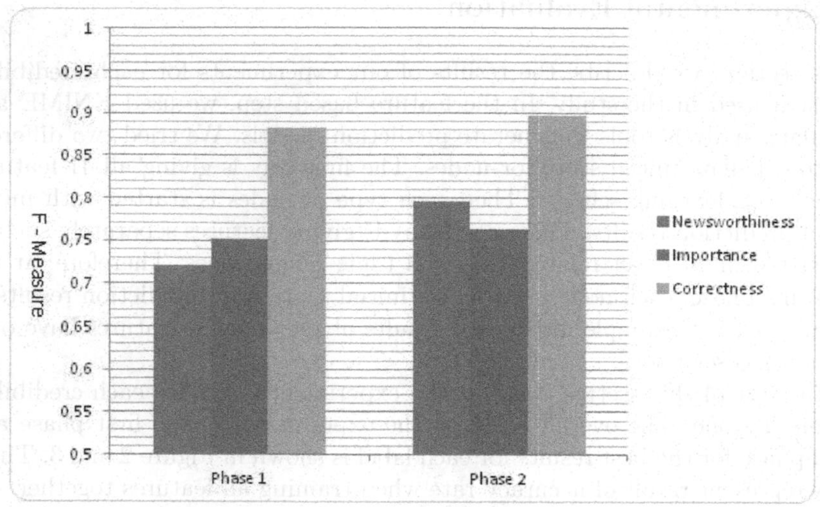

Fig. 3. F-Measure results after the feature based and graph based phases

After authority transfer, success rate increases to 90.92 %. If we experiment newsworthiness by using grouped features, we reach 91.8 % successful prediction rate which is slightly more than experiment result with all features together. Therefore, experiments show that training the features separately for each type of nodes brings a limited improvement for the success rate for newsworthiness label.

4.2 Importance

In the first phase, we get the best accuracy result from random forest decision tree learner. 83.52 % of 2500 tweets are classified correctly by using all features. 75.84 % of 2500 tweets are classified correctly by using only user related features. 81.20 % of 2500 tweets are classified correctly by using only tweet related features. 81.32 % of 2500 tweets are classified correctly by using only topic related features. In the second phase, after authority transfer, success rate reaches 84.24 % when we train all features together. If we train features separately for user, tweet and topic then we obtain success rate with 82.76 %.

4.3 Correctness

In the first phase, we get the best accuracy result from random forest decision tree learner for all features, tweet features and topic features. However, we get the best accuracy result from J48 decision tree for user features. 82.72 % of 2500 tweets are classified correctly by using all features. 79.88 % of 2500 tweets are classified correctly by using only user related features. 81.40 % of 2500 tweets are classified correctly by using only tweet related features. 81.88 % of 2500 tweets are classified correctly by using only topic related features. In the second phase, after applyinh authority transfer, success rate reaches 84.12 %. If we use features separately for nodes then we get 83.20 % success rate.

5 Conclusion and Future Work

5.1 Conclusion

In this study, we evaluated tweets in terms of three labels which are newsworthiness, importance and correctness. Initially, we asked our evaluators to get their feedback for these labels for each tweet. We used GT_{avg} evaluation method since it has better overlap and kappa results in comparison to our other ground truth methods. In the first phase, we trained our data set and obtained the best prediction result with random forest decision tree. When we trained all 41 features together, we obtained 89.64 % successful prediction rate for newsworthiness, 83.52 % for importance and 82.72 % for correctness label. In the second phase, we used the prediction results in the first phase and transferred this score in our graph. We defined three types of nodes which are user, tweet and topic. Users transfer their score to their tweets. Topics transfer their scores to tweets and tweets transfer score to their authors and their topics. After authority transfer, we obtained successful prediction rate between 80 % and 92 % for a range of experiments. For newsworthiness label, we obtained 91.80 % success rate when training features separately. For importance label, success rate is 84.24 %. Lastly for correctness label, we obtain 84.12 % success rate.

We see that if we apply authority transfer after feature based approach, prediction accuracy increases. Training features separately for user, tweet and topic increases success rate for newsworthiness but it does not affect other labels positively.

5.2 Future Work

We need to annotate each tweet for newsworthiness, importance and correctness in order to use these tweets in classification. Since this annotation process requires considerable time, we could not use larger data set in this study. However, we can increase the size of our data set as a future work. Therefore, users will get score from their friends and tweets will get their score from their retweets.

Acknowledgments. This work is supported by the research grant TUBITAK 112E275.

References

1. Abel, F., Gao, Q., Houben, G.-J., Tao, K.: Analyzing user modeling on twitter for personalized news recommendations. In: Konstan, J.A., Conejo, R., Marzo, J.L., Oliver, N. (eds.) UMAP 2011. LNCS, vol. 6787, pp. 1–12. Springer, Heidelberg (2011)

2. Armentano, M., Godoy, D., Amandi, A.: Recommending information sources to information seekers in twitter. In: International Workshop on Social Web Mining, UMAP 2011 (2011)
3. Armentano, M., Godoy, D., Amandi, A.: Topology-based recommendation of users in micro-blogging communities 27, 624–634 (2012)
4. Castillo, C., Mendoza, M., Poblete, B.: Information credibility on twitter. In: Proceedings of the 20th International Conference on World Wide Web, WWW 2011, pp. 675–684. ACM, New York (2011)
5. Feng, W., Wang, J.: Retweet or not?: Personalized tweet re-ranking. In: Proceedings of the Sixth ACM International Conference on Web Search and Data Mining, WSDM 2013, pp. 577–586. ACM, New York (2013)
6. Gupta, A., Kumaraguru, P.: Credibility ranking of tweets during high impact events. In: Proceedings of the 1st Workshop on Privacy and Security in Online Social Media, PSOSM 2012, pp. 2:2–2:8. ACM, New York (2012)
7. Huang, L., Yeming, X.: Evaluation of microblog users' influence based on pagerank and users behavior analysis. In: Advances in Internet of Things, pp. 34–40 (2013)
8. Kang, B., O'Donovan, J., Höllerer, T.: Modeling topic specific credibility on twitter. In: Proceedings of the 2012 ACM International Conference on Intelligent User Interfaces, IUI 2012, pp. 179–188. ACM, New York (2012)
9. O'Donovan, J., Kang, B., Meyer, G., Höllerer, T., Adalii, S.: Credibility in context: An analysis of feature distributions in twitter. In: SocialCom/PASSAT, pp. 293–301. IEEE (2012)
10. Sakaki, T., Okazaki, M., Matsuo, Y.: Earthquake shakes twitter users: Real-time event detection by social sensors. In: Proceedings of the 19th International Conference on World Wide Web, WWW 2010, pp. 851–860. ACM, New York (2010)
11. Sentistrength library source, `http://sentistrength.wlv.ac.uk` (last access: January 5, 2014)
12. Weerkamp, W., Rijke, M.: Credibility-inspired ranking for blog post retrieval 15, 243–277 (2012)
13. Xia, X., Yang, X., Wu, C., Li, S., Bao, L.: Information credibility on twitter in emergency situation. In: Chau, M., Wang, G.A., Yue, W.T., Chen, H. (eds.) PAISI 2012. LNCS, vol. 7299, pp. 45–59. Springer, Heidelberg (2012)
14. Yamaguchi, Y., Takahashi, T., Amagasa, T., Kitagawa, H.: TURank: Twitter user ranking based on user-tweet graph analysis. In: Chen, L., Triantafillou, P., Suel, T. (eds.) WISE 2010. LNCS, vol. 6488, pp. 240–253. Springer, Heidelberg (2010)
15. Zhang, X., Zhu, S., Liang, W.: Detecting spam and promoting campaigns in the twitter social network. In: 2012 IEEE 12th International Conference on Data Mining (ICDM), pp. 1194–1199 (2012)
16. Woniak, M., Graña, M., Corchado, E.: A survey of multiple classifier systems as hybrid systems. Inf. Fusion 16, 3–17 (2014)

A Hybrid Recommender System Based on AHP That Awares Contexts with Bayesian Networks for Smart TV

Ji-Chun Quan and Sung-Bae Cho

Department of Computer Science, Yonsei University
50 Yonsei-ro, Seodaemun-gu, Seoul 120-749, Korea
lean_quan@sclab.yonsei.ac.kr, sbcho@yonsei.ac.kr

Abstract. Recently, many researchers are paying close attention to TV program recommendation methods because of the enormous increase of available TV programs for users. As TV programs are often watched by multiple users like a family, this paper proposes a smart TV program recommendation method for multi-users using Bayesian networks and AHP (analytic hierarchy process). The proposed method uses Bayesian networks to infer each user's genre preference as well as program preference, and uses AHP to predict group genre preference and choose recommended programs. The accuracy of the Bayesian network model is improved through parameter learning from users' watching history. Experiments verify the inference accuracy of the Bayesian network and the accuracy of programs recommended by the proposed method.

Keywords: TV program recommendation, Bayesian network, Analytic hierarchy process, Group recommendation.

1 Introduction

As the technology of smart TV is rapidly developed, users can watch TV program not only from traditional television station but also from Internet [1]. Therefore a system which can recommend TV programs considering users' preference would help people to save time and energy [2, 3]. For this purpose, a number of researchers have proposed lots of TV program recommendation solutions. These solutions recommend TV programs according to users' preference which is predicted by users' profile or watching history. One drawback of these solutions is that they did not consider some information such as period (e.g., Olympic) and event (e.g., the last episode of a drama). Also, the cold start problem is another headache for these methods.

In this paper, we propose a TV program recommendation method for multiple users as well as single user using a hybrid recommendation method based on AHP (analytic hierarchy process) and Bayesian networks. A hybrid approach exploits the strengths of the individual method and enhances the performance by their combination [4, 5]. The proposed hybrid method can overcome several problems which cannot be addressed by single method. The contributions of this paper can be summarized as follows.

M. Polycarpou et al. (Eds.): HAIS 2014, LNAI 8480, pp. 527–536, 2014.
© Springer International Publishing Switzerland 2014

- A hybrid method of AHP and Bayesian networks: The proposed method predicts group preference using a hybrid method of AHP and Bayesian networks which can solve the consistency problem of AHP. Also, with this method, users do not need to provide the priority value of candidate decision when comparing each candidate decision with pairwise comparison in AHP.
- Solution of cold start problem: There are two kinds of cold start problem. One is happened when there are no data of user's watching history and the other is when all candidate programs are totally new program or have less watched time. The former problem is addressed by Bayesian networks and the latter is worked out by program audience rating from Internet.

The rest of this paper is organized as follows. Section 2 briefly reviews the related works for TV recommendation method and Section 3 presents the proposed recommendation method in detail. In Section 4, we conduct some experiments and analyze the results, and Section 5 concludes the work.

2 Related Works

At most of time, since there is more than one person watching TV, the research for TV program recommendation for multiple users is meaningful [6]. Yu *et al.* recommended TV programs by using a group profile which is constructed by aggregating all users' profile in that group [7]. Shin *et al.* integrated users' profile, watched TV program profile as well as watching history into a group file and recommend TV programs based on it [8]. Rafael *et al.* proposed a method which recommended TV programs using collaborative filtering and content-based method with a TV ontology model [9]. Thyagaraju *et al.* computed group preference using each user's preference in the group which was extracted from the user's watching history [10]. Wang *et al.* proposed a method which could estimate group preference based on external experts' preference [11].

These studies did not consider some program information which could affect the final decision. For example, during World Cup, user may watch football game instead of drama or other programs. Another drawback of these methods is that recommendation results of them are highly influenced by the number of users in the group. To address these problems, AHP is used to predict group preference and select TV program. AHP is one of the most widely used multi-criteria decision making method [12]. Chen *et al.* used AHP method to construct a context-aware mobile recommendation system [13]. Park *et al.* constructed a restaurant recommendation system for multiple users using AHP method [14]. Wu *et al.* proposed a web services selection method based on AHP and Wiki [15]. Because of using AHP, the proposed system could consider kinds of criteria when predicting group preference and selecting recommended TV program. However, they did not get over the cold start problem.

In this paper, the Bayesian network is used to address this problem. The Bayesian network is a directed acyclic graph which is a represantative method giving believable results predicted to users in uncertain environment [16]. It uses cause-effect relationship between parent nodes and children nodes to predict results through probability-based method [17]. Yang *et al.* constructed a context-aware system in smart TV using Bayesian networks with domain knowledge [18]. Park *et al.* design a Bayesian netwok with domain knowledge for context-aware robot in home service environment [19]. Park *et al.* developed a context-sharing system with Bayesian netwok [20]. One advantage of the Bayesian networks is that it could be constructed using domain knowledge, which means that we could construct a Bayesian network for a user without using the user's specific information. Although the accuracy may be lower, we could update the Bayesian network when we get enough information about the user's watching history.

3 A TV Program Recommendation Method for Multiple Users

As shown in Fig. 1, the program recommendation method consists of group genre preference inference part, candidate program integration part and program recommendation part.

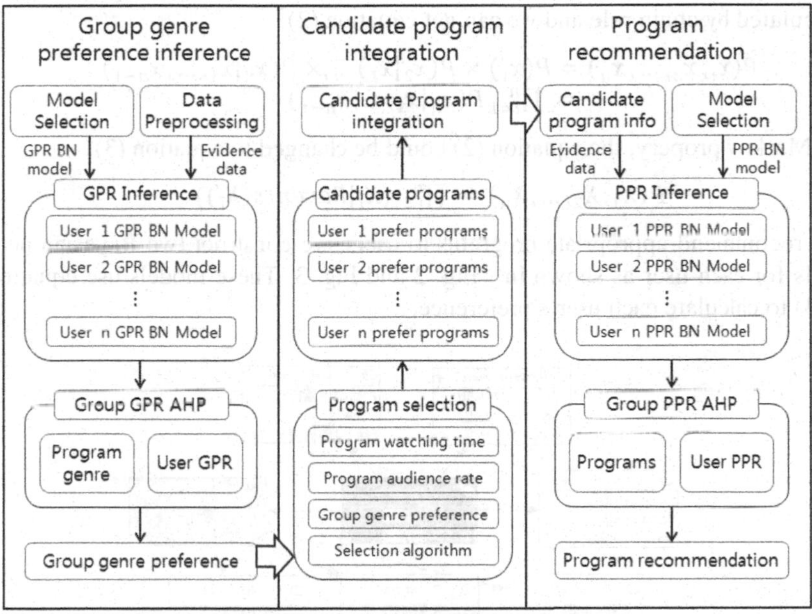

Fig. 1. Overview of the program recommendation method

- **Group Genre Preference Inference:** To predict group genre preference, first, each user's genre preference(GPR) is inferred by the GPR Bayesian network model. After that, the group's GPR is computed using GPR AHP model and each user's GPR which is inferred in the previous step. Finally, the top two genres are selected as the group's prefer genre.

- **Candidate Program Integration:** In this part, the method selects candidate programs based on the inferred group's GPR as well as each user's watching history in that group and a program selection algrorithm.
- **Program Recommendation:** To recommend the most attractable programs to users, firstly each user's preference to each candidate program is calculated by the program preference (PPR) Bayesian network model. Then, the group PPR AHP model is used to rank the cadidate programs and after that, the top *N* programs are recommended to the users. In this paper, we select 3 programs to users.

3.1 Inference with Bayesian Networks

In Bayesian networks, the belief of node *A* with evidence *B* is calculated by equation (1).

$$Bel(A) = P(A|B) = \frac{P(B|A) \times P(A)}{P(B)} \tag{1}$$

The joint probabilities of the Bayesian network $P(X_1 = x_1, X_2 = x_2, \dots, X_n = x_n)$ is calculated by chain rule and we can get equation (2).

$$\begin{aligned} P(x_1, x_2, \dots, x_n) &= P(x_1) \times P(x_2|x_1) \dots, \times P(x_n|x_1, \dots, x_{n-1}) \\ &= \prod_{i=1}^{n} P(x_n|x_1, \dots, x_{n-1}) \end{aligned} \tag{2}$$

With Markov propery, the equation (2) could be changed to equation (3).

$$P(X_1, X_2, \dots, X_n) = \prod_{i=1}^{n} (X_i|Parents(X_i)) \tag{3}$$

To recommend appropriate programs to users, we construct two Bayesian network models for each user as shown in Fig. 2 and Fig. 3. These models use equation (1) and (3) to calculate each user's preference.

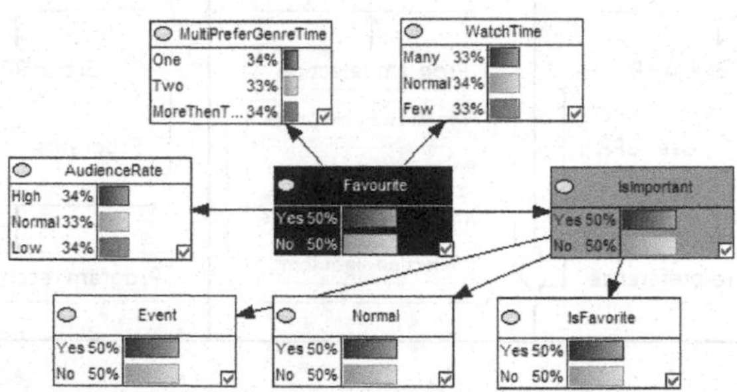

Fig. 2. The Bayesian network model for program preference inference

Fig. 2 is the Bayesian network model for program preference inference. It is calculated using the program's information, watching history of the program as well as the user's genre preference information. Fig. 3 is the genre preference inference Bayesian network model which represents the relationship between a user's genre preference and time.

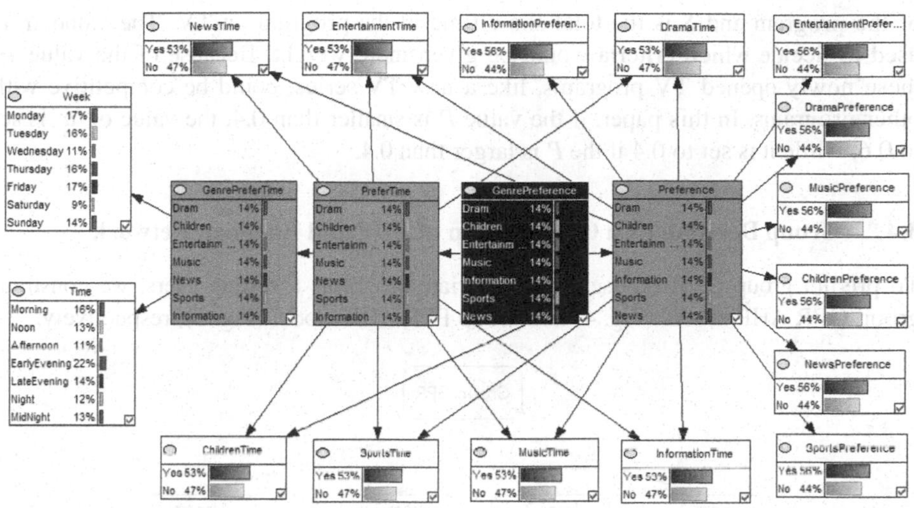

Fig. 3. The Bayesian network model for genre preference inference

3.2 Byesian Network Learning

Each user's genre preference Bayesian network model should be updated regularly to represent the user's patterns of watching TV. In this paper, the Maximum Likelihood (ML) estimation algorithm is applied to learn and update the Bayesian network model using one user's watching history and profile. ML algorithm is a parameter learning algorithm when the structure of a Bayesian network model is fixed [21]. The conditional probability table (CPT) of each Bayesian network model's node is generated by equation (4).

$$P(X = x|Parent(X) = y) = \frac{N(X=x,parent(X)=y)}{N(Parent(X)=y)} \tag{4}$$

In the equation (4), $N(X = x, Parent(X) = y)$is the number of occurrences that the $X = x$ and $Parent(X) = y$ come out at the same time in the data set. Here, $N(Parent(X) = y)$ is the appearance time of $Parent(X) = y$ in the data set.

3.3 Candidate Program Selection

To select candidate programs based on inferred group GPR, the equation (5) is used to rank the programs in the user's watching history.

$$R = \alpha \times E + (1 - \alpha) \times P \text{ where } P = \frac{T}{S} \tag{5}$$

In the proposed method, the top *N* programs are put into candidate program pool. In the equation (5), *R* is the score of the program, *E* is the audience rate of the program, and *P* is the watching ratio of that program. In addition, *T* is the watching time of the program and S is the total show time of the program on TV. The value α is used to decide which criteria would be given more weight. Because of the value α, these newly opened TV programs, like a new TV series, could be competitive with other programs. In this paper, if the value P is smaller than 0.4, the value of α is set to 0.6, while it is set to 0.4 if the P is larger than 0.4.

3.4 Group Decision by a Combination of AHP and Baeysian Network

To predict group GPR and select appropriate programs to group users, we constrcut group GPR AHP model (Fig. 4) and group PPR AHP model (Fig. 5), respectively.

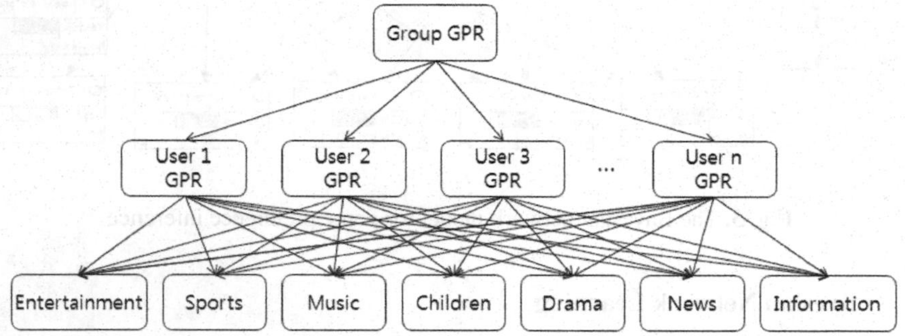

Fig. 4. AHP model for group genre preference

An AHP model consists of three hierarchies which are goal, criteria and alternatives. As shown in Fig. 4, the criteria of group GPR AHP model are each user's genre preference and the alternatives are the program genre. Similarly, as shown in Fig. 5, the criteria of group PPR AHP model are each user's program preference and the alternatives are candidate programs.

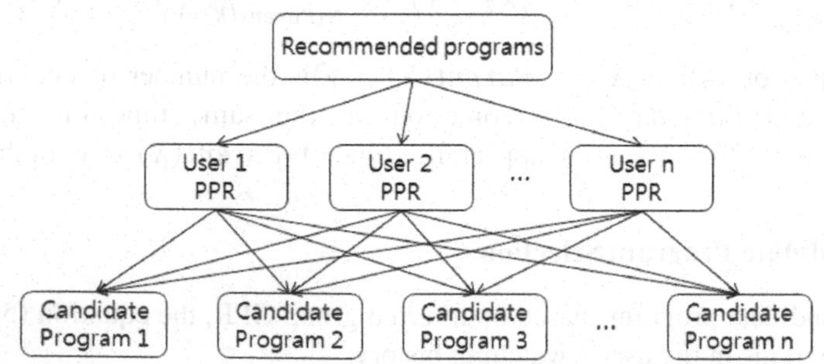

Fig. 5.AHP model for group program preference

In the original AHP method, users have to allocate the relative importance to each alternative decision with respect to each criterion. However, for TV program recommendation, the relative importance must be computed automatically as it is impossible to let users give it to every candidate program and genre by themselves. To address this problem, we use a hybrid method of AHP and Bayesian networks in which the importance value of each AHP alternative decision is calculated by a Bayesian network model and rank of these candidate decisions is computed by AHP method. Another advantage of this method is that there is no need to check the consistency of AHP as the comparison with numerical importance value will be always transitive. The process of the method consists of the following steps and the group GPR computation process will be used as an example to explain these steps.

At the first step, the comparison matrix is constructed for criteria and the alternatives with respect to each criterion through pairwise comparison. To construct the matrix for criteria of group GPR AHP model, like equation (6) , the users' relative importance value (pp_i in the equation) collected from user's profile will be used.

$$M_c = \begin{bmatrix} e_{11} & \cdots & e_{1j} \\ \vdots & \ddots & \vdots \\ e_{i1} & \cdots & e_{ij} \end{bmatrix}, e_{ij} = \frac{pp_i}{pp_j} \tag{6}$$

To construct the comparison matrix, $M_{gp} = \{M_{gp_1}, M_{gp_2}, M_{gp_3}, \dots, M_{gp_n}\}$ in which M_{gp_n} is representative of the alternative matrix with respect to criterion *n*, for candidate genres with respect to each criterion, like equation (7), each user's genre preference predicted by the Bayesian network model will be used. In the equation, $g_i p_n$ means user *n*'s preference regarding to genre *i*.

$$M_{gp_n} = \begin{bmatrix} e_{11} & \cdots & e_{1j} \\ \vdots & \ddots & \vdots \\ e_{i1} & \cdots & e_{ij} \end{bmatrix}, e_{ij} = \frac{g_i p_n}{g_j p_n} \tag{7}$$

At the second step, the priority of criterion and the alternatives with respect to each criterion is computed by equation (8). In the equation, *i* represents a criterion or an alternative and *n* and *m* represent the number of colums and rows in the matrix, respectively. For group GPR decision, a priority set, $\{Priority_{c_1}, Priority_{c_2}, \dots, Priority_{c_n}\}$, is constructed for criteria and a priority set, $\{Priority_{g_1c_1}, Priority_{g_1c_2}, \dots, Priority_{g_mc_n}\}$, is constructed for candidate genres.

$$priority_i = \sum_{k=1}^{n} {e_{ik}}/{\sum_{d=1}^{m} e_{dk}} \tag{8}$$

At the last step, the final priority of each alternative is computed by using equation (9).

$$GP_i = Priority_{g_ic_1} \times Priority_{c_1} + \cdots + Priority_{g_ic_n} \times Priority_{c_n} \tag{9}$$

After that, all alternatives are sorted by the final priority and top *N* alternatives are recommended to the users.

4 Experimental Results

In this section, we conduct two experiments to evaluate the accuracy of the genre Bayesian network model and the users' satisfaction about the recommended TV programs. The TV program information was downloaded from NAVER TV guide and 20 people attended out at the experiments. In addition, we collected the users' watching history for a month through survey.

4.1 Accuracy Evaluation of the Genre Bayesian Networks

In this experiment, we compared the result predicted by a Bayesian network model after learning from a user's watching history, a Bayesian network constructed by the domain knowledge, audience rate data from the internet, and rule-based inference method. We selected 5 times randomly to infer user's genre preference and the rule-based inference method always select the most watched TV program's genre as the predicted result. The accuracy is estimated by asking the participants in the experiment on which result is the most satisfied.

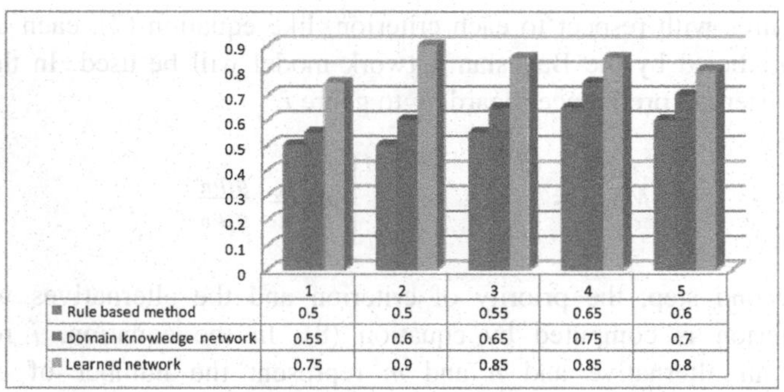

	1	2	3	4	5
Rule based method	0.5	0.5	0.55	0.65	0.6
Domain knowledge network	0.55	0.6	0.65	0.75	0.7
Learned network	0.75	0.9	0.85	0.85	0.8

Fig. 6. Accuracy of the genre preference Bayesian network model

As shown in Fig. 6, the learned network get the best accuracy. Through the learning process about one user's watching history, the Baeysian network could represent the user's watching pattern. For example, users select a drama which they have watched before instead of a drama which have the most audience rate.

4.2 Accuracy Evaluation of the Proposed Group Recommendation Method

In this experiment, participants were divided into ten 2-person groups, nine 3-person groups, seven 4-person groups as well as four 5-person groups. And we compared the proposed group recommendation method with a rule-based method and a neural network-based method. Rule-based method recommends the program which has the most audience rate while the neural network-based method is trained by all users' watching history.

As shown in Fig. 7, the proposed method has the best performance as it recommends TV programs considering group's genre preference, users' program preference and the relative importance of each user. After that is the neural network-based method and the rule-based method has the worst performance. It means that not all people prefer the program with higher audience rate, and some information like period and event of the program really affects the accuracy of the recommendation.

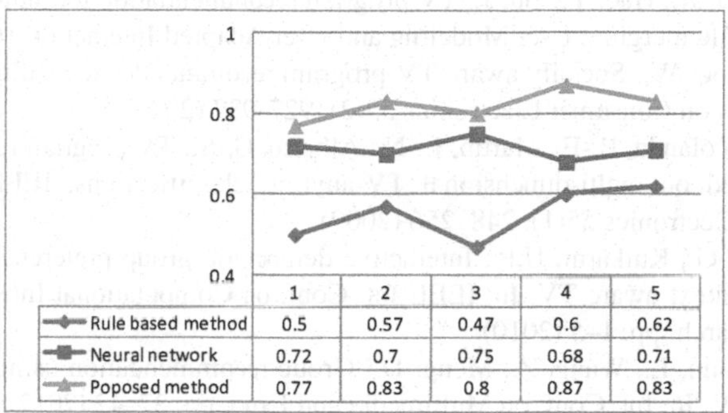

	1	2	3	4	5
Rule based method	0.5	0.57	0.47	0.6	0.62
Neural network	0.72	0.7	0.75	0.68	0.71
Poposed method	0.77	0.83	0.8	0.87	0.83

Fig. 7. Accuracy of the proposed group recommendation method

5 Concluding Remarks

In this paper, we have proposed a TV program recommendation method for group users. The proposed method uses a hybrid method of Bayesian networks and AHP to predict group's genre preference and recommend TV program to users from candidate program pool. Also, we propose a TV program selection algorithm to generate the candidate program pool. Furthermore, the cold start problem is addressed by applying Bayesian networks. Finally, we verify the advantage of the proposed method by two accuracy evaluation experiments.

As future work, we will develop a smart TV-based system which has user-friendly interface and can collect users' real watching history data. Also, more experiments will be done with these real data and more participants.

References

1. Kim, M.K., Park, J.H.: Demand forecasting and strategies for the successfully deployment of the smart TV in Korea. In: 13th Int. Conf. on Advanced Communication Technology (ICACT), pp. 1475–1478 (2011)
2. Kim, E.-H., Pyo, S.-J., Park, E.-Y., Kim, M.-C.: An automatic recommendation scheme of TV program contents for (IP)TV personalization. IEEE Transactions on Broadcasting 58(3), 674–684 (2011)
3. Kwon, H.-J., Hong, K.-S.: Personalized smart TV program recommender based on collaborative filtering and a novel similarity method. IEEE Transaction on Consumer Electronics 57(3), 1416–1423 (2011)

4. Wozniak, M., Graña, M., Corchado, E.: A survey of multiple classifier systems as hybrid systems. Information Fusion 16, 3–17 (2014)
5. Borrajo, M.L., Baruque, B., Corchado, E., Bajo, J., Corchado, J.: Hybrid neural intelligent system to predict business failure in small-to-medium-size enterprises. International Journal of Neural Systems 21(04), 277–296 (2011)
6. Konstantinos, C.: Personalized and mobile digital TV applications. Multimedia Tools and Applications 36(1-2), 1–10 (2008)
7. Yu, Z., Zhou, X., Hao, Y., Gu, J.: TV program recommendation for multiple viewers based on user profile merging. User Modeling and User-Adapted Interaction 16(1), 63–82 (2006)
8. Shin, C., Woo, W.: Socially aware TV program recommender for multiple viewers. IEEE Transactions on Consumer Electronics 55(2), 927–932 (2009)
9. Rafael, S., Yolanda, B.-F., Martin, L.-N., Alberto, G.-S.: TV program recommendation for groups based on multi-dimensional TV-anytime classifications. IEEE Transactions on Consumer Electronics 55(1), 248–256 (2009)
10. Thyagaraju, G., Kulkarni, U.P.: Interactive democratic group preference algorithm for interactive context aware TV. In: IEEE Int. Conf. on Computational Intelligence and Computing Research, pp. 1–5 (2010)
11. Wang, X., Sun, L., Wang, Z., Meng, D.: Group recommendation using external followee for social TV. In: Int. Conf. on Multimedia and Expo, pp. 37–42 (2012)
12. Saaty, T.L.: How to make a decision: The analytic hierarchy process. European Journal of Operational Research 48, 9–26 (1990)
13. Chen, D.-N., Hu, P.J.-H., Kuo, Y.-R., Liang, T.-P.: A web-based personalized recommendation system for mobile phone selection: Design, implementation, and evaluation. Expert Systems with Applications 37(12), 8201–8210 (2010)
14. Park, M.-H., Park, H.-S., Cho, S.-B.: Restaurant recommendation for group of people in mobile environments using probabilistic multi-criteria decision making. In: Lee, S., Choo, H., Ha, S., Shin, I.C. (eds.) APCHI 2008. LNCS, vol. 5068, pp. 114–122. Springer, Heidelberg (2008)
15. Wu, C., Chang, E.: Intelligent web services selection based on AHP and Wiki. In: Int. Conf. on Web Intelligence, pp. 767–770 (2007)
16. Charniak, E.: Bayesian networks without tears. AI Magazine 12, 50–63 (1991)
17. Kleiter, G.D.: Propagating imprecise probabilities in Bayesian networks. Artificial Intelligence 88(1-2), 143–161 (1996)
18. Yang, K.-M., Cho, S.-B.: Probabilistic modeling for context-aware service in smart TV. In: Intelligent Systems Modeling and Simulation, pp. 78–83 (2013)
19. Park, H.-S., Cho, S.-B.: A modular design of Bayesian networks using expert knowledge: Context-aware home service robot. Expert Systems with Applications 39(3), 2629–2642 (2012)
20. Park, H.-S., Oh, K.-H., Cho, S.-B.: Bayesian network-based high-level context recognition for mobile context sharing in cyber-physical system. Distributed Sensor Networks, 1–10 (2011)
21. David, H.: A tutorial on learning with Bayesian networks. In: Holmes, D.E., Jain, L.C. (eds.) Innovations in Bayesian Networks. SCI, vol. 156, pp. 33–82. Springer, Heidelberg (2008)

An Ontology-Based Recommender System Architecture for Semantic Searches in Vehicles Sales Portals

Fábio A.P. de Paiva[1], José Alfredo F. Costa[2], and Cláudio R.M. Silva[3]

[1] IFRN, Zona Norte Campus, Natal, Brazil
fabio.procopio@ifrn.edu.br
[2] UFRN, Department of Electrical Engineering, Natal, Brazil
jafcosta@gmail.com
[3] UFRN, Department of Communications Engineering, Natal, Brazil
claudio.rmsilva@gmail.com

Abstract. Internet has become an increasingly constant presence everywhere that people go. Particularly this reality is visible in social networks and selling portals scenarios. Whatever scenario, there is plenty of space to improve accuracy since big data is a problem when scale increases. Semantic search is an alternative to improve search accuracy by understanding the contextual meaning of terms as they appear in the searchable data space. Among the several approaches to Semantic Search methodologies, a variation of Ontology-based search (or Logic Approach) is the one adopted. In this methodology, the engine not only understands hierarchical relationships of entities, however also more complex inter-entities relationships defined inside ontologies. This paper proposes a hybrid approach for the problem using Ontology-based Recommender Systems and semantic profiles. A portal prototype is designed and implemented for the domain of online dealership's vehicle buyer's market. Precision and Recall measures are the two major indices of information retrieval. They have been used to evaluate the prototype results. After calculating these two metrics over some searches, we have seen that Precision is 86.66% and Recall is 68.42%. These final results have demonstrated an improvement in the searches, particularly with regard the precision of the results provided to the users.

Keywords: Recommender Systems, Ontology, Semantic Web Searches.

1 Introduction

It is a fact that Internet has become an increasingly constant presence everywhere that people go. A recent report [1] has estimated that 90% of the dealership's car buyers gather information on the Internet before heading to the store. Among this 90% dealership's car buyers, 20% to 30% of consumers used to cross-shop between various web portals in order to compare the information supplied in the different websites before buying a specific car. This increasing interest in Web is one of the reasons that motivate most of car dealers to dedicate a significant part of their

M. Polycarpou et al. (Eds.): HAIS 2014, LNAI 8480, pp. 537–548, 2014.
© Springer International Publishing Switzerland 2014

advertising budgets to attract the attention of customers using third-party automotive websites that list dealer inventory.

The report have also shown that the viewer interest of such listings depends on many things, particularly on the high-quality of the images, on the diversity of them and on the kind of special services available to efficiently help a potential seller or buyer user in finding the best result for their searches. Some of these services provide, for example, average prices for a specific vehicle, best buy option for a specified vehicle category or average selling price for a specific vehicle. These services are not simple web searches. Some of them may be so complexes that some of them are authentic Semantic Web Search Services.

Semantic search is a kind of data searching technique in a which a search query aims to not only find keywords matches, however essentially to determine the contextual meaning of the words that a user is using for search [29]. In general, search engines are evolving towards semantic search in two different ways. One way is the use of "tags" or label parts of a webpage to tell a computer what those parts are: a name, a birthdate, a medication, a concert venue, a friend, etc. These codes are not visible for human readers, however search engines and web browsers are able to work of them. The other way is computational intelligence or hybrid approaches combined with it. One of these hybrid approaches are the Hybrid Recommender System Guided by Semantic User Profiles for Search [2].

Recommender Systems are a special kind of filtering systems that seek to predict preferences that user would give to an item. They have emerged as one successful approach to tackle the problem of information overload [10][22]. In recent years, Recommender Systems have become extremely common and they have been applied in a variety of applications such as search queries, movies, online news, commercial services, online dating, Twitter and Facebook social networks. Some of these Recommender Systems may use optimization techniques such as machine learning, Particle swarm optimization or combinations of them to make recommendations [33-34].

The ontologies are one of the bases of the Semantic Web, since a semantic web vocabulary can be considered as a special form of ontology. They are also used to share common understanding of the structure of information among people or software agents, enable reuse of domain knowledge, make domain assumptions explicit, to separate domain knowledge from the operational knowledge and analyze domain knowledge [3-4]. The Semantic Web is well recognized as an effective infrastructure to enhance visibility of knowledge on the Web. Ontologies help extend recommender systems to a multi-class environment, allowing knowledge-based approaches to be used alongside classical machine learning algorithms. Moreover, they have been used routinely in recommender systems in combination with machine learning, statistical correlations, user profiling and domain specific heuristics [5].

This paper proposes a variant approach to Recommender Systems in which an ontology-based recommender system is built with a hierarchical layered architecture to implement semantic web searches to help dealership's vehicle buyers in finding "best buy opportunities" in Internet based on semantic profiles associated to the buyers (user) and to a set of portals such as dealership's vehicle sales, benchmarking and estimation portals of average price. The paper approach also considers a recommendation engine algorithm that extends a typical recommendation engine with machine learning capabilities. The paper is organized as follows. In Section 2, it is provided a brief background in order to introduce the basic concepts and technologies which are necessary for the reader's understanding. In Section 3, related works to Ontology-based Recommender Systems are presented. Section 4 shows the prototype architecture, the ontology model and a scenario of a semantic search in Web. And finally, in Section 5, the final considerations are presented to conclude the work.

2 Background

This section presents three essential concepts which are widely used in this paper: Ontology, Recommender Systems and Semantic Search. Ontology represents knowledge as a concepts set within a domain. Recommender Systems provide personalized recommendations to users based on their interests. Semantic Search may determine the contextual meaning of the words that a user is using for search.

2.1 Ontology

Ontology is a term "borrowed" from Philosophy and one can talk about ontology as a theory of the nature of existence. However, in the context of Computer and Information Sciences, ontology defines a set of representational primitives with which to model a domain of knowledge or discourse [3].

Ontologies play an important role in many knowledge spheres such as [4]: information retrieval, knowledge engineering, information modelling, knowledge representation, information integration, object-oriented analysis, information extraction, and others. Ontologies also are used in many applications, e.g., entertainment [11-12], e-commerce [13-14], nutrition [15], medicine [16-18], services [19-20], and etc.

The greatest contribution of ontology is that it can standardize one or more specific areas of concepts and terminology, provide convenience for the area or between areas to facilitate the practical application [6]. An ontology-based system can be used not only to improve the precision of search/retrieval mechanism but also to reduce search time [7]. For these reasons, as in [8], ontology-based approaches will likely be the core technology for the development of a next generation of semantically enhanced knowledge management solutions.

2.2 Recommender Systems

Recommender Systems provide items personalized suggestions to users according to their interests. "Item" is a general term used to represent what the system recommends. The recommendations relate to many decision-making processes, such as what book to read, what movie to watch, or what vehicle to buy.

In recent years, recommender systems is a research field which has attracted the attention of many researchers because [9] a) they play a relevant role in important websites such as Amazon.com, YouTube, Netflix, Yahoo, TripAdvisor, and IMDb; b) there are dedicated conferences and related workshops to this field; c) there are institutions of higher education around the world which offer undergraduate and graduate courses to Recommender Systems; d) there have been several special issues in academic journals covering research and developments in this field as well.

Burke [10] proposed a taxonomy that may be used to distinguish recommendation techniques. They are classified in six different categories: 1) Collaborative which applies the known preferences of a set of users to predicate the unknown preferences for new users; 2) Content-based which recommends item whose content is similar to the content that the user has previously viewed or selected; 3) Demographic which recommends items according to the user's demographic profile; 4) Knowledge-based which attempts to suggest objects based on inferences about user's preferences; 5) Community-based which recommends items based on the preferences of the user's friends and; 6) Hybrid approach which combines two or more techniques.

2.3 Semantic Search

As mentioned in previous section, a semantic search is normally defined as a kind of data searching technique in which a search query aims to not only find keywords matches, however essentially to determine the contextual meaning of the words that a user is using for search. Unlike typical search algorithms known in literature, semantic search approach is, essentially, based on the context of the searched phrase [29]. This is not the unique definition for semantic search. Some other authors [31], for example, primarily regard semantic search as a set of techniques for retrieving knowledge from richly structured data sources like ontologies as found on the Semantic Web. Such technologies enable the formal articulation of domain knowledge at a high level of expressiveness and could enable the user to specify his/her intent in more detail at query time.

Rather than using ranking algorithms to predict relevancy, a typical semantic search uses semantics to produce highly relevant search results [30]. In most cases, the goal is to deliver the information queried by a user rather than have a user sort through a list of loosely related keyword results. There are several methodologies to implement semantic search. The most commonly used methodologies in literature [32] are: RDF Path Traversal (it consists in traversing a net formed by a graph of information that uses the RDF data model); Keyword to Concept Mapping (it consists in dealing about the mapping of the textual materials to the well-defined information); Graph Patterns(it is generally used to formulate patterns for locating interesting connecting paths between resource); Logics (it consists in using inference based on OWL); and Fuzzy concepts (it is based in fuzzy relations, and fuzzy logics).

This work adopts a variant of Logic methodology, in which the search engine is implemented inside a recommender system architecture and the hierarchical relationships of entities and concepts (taxonomy) is defined inside ontologies.

3 Ontology-Based Recommender Systems

There are several studies that proposed the use of ontologies as a way to increase the performance of Recommender Systems. In this section, a brief survey about papers related to this field is presented to reader.

Rho *et al.* [11] proposed a Context-based Music Recommendation ontology for modeling user's musical preferences and context. The rules are defined according to user's musical preferences and from other situations, for example, an event, weather, mood and local.

Ge *et al.* [12] proposed the development of a personalized recommender system framework which is used to suggest movies. A domain ontology is used to integrate multi-source and heterogeneous data. Analysis of user's demographic characteristics, information about his/her personal preferences, and his/her browsing behavior were used to create an interest ontology.

Lin *et al.* [13] presented an algorithm of a User's Interest Model based on ontology which focus not only on the user's interest quality, but also the difference between long-time and short-time. The proposed system is used to recommend e-books.

Kang and Choi [14] presented a personalized system to recommend e-books. For this fact, they built two ontologies: a domain and another preference. By monitoring the visited web pages, the system constructs the user's preference ontology from associated weights to his/her preferences for long-term and short-term.

Sucksom *et al.* [15] proposed a system to recommend foods which provides suggestions based on user's dietary needs and his/her preferences. The rule-based knowledge was defined based on some recommendations from the clinical guideline for diabetes care issued by Thailand's Ministry of Public Health.

GalenOWL [16] is a recommender system for discovering drug recommendations and interactions. The rules are defined based on some patient's characteristics such as age, gender, and etc.

Chen *et al.* [17] presented a system to recommend anti-diabetics drugs which is based on fuzzy reasoning. Fuzzy rules have been used to represent knowledge in order to infer the usability of the classes of anti-diabetic drugs based on fuzzy reasoning techniques. The rules are defined to infer the usability degree of drug classes to treat diabetes.

The intelligent Ontology-based System for Cardiac Critical Care (iOSC3) [18] is a decision support system designed to supervise and to treat affected patients by acute cardiac disorders. The system provides recommendations about the treatment that should be administered to achieve the fastest possible recovery. The rules were extracted from interviews and meetings.

Mu *et al.* [19] proposed a model of vehicles recommendation system. Taking web pages about vehicles, results show that the model can to recommend effectively, and the results correspond to user's real and original interest.

Greenly *et al.* [20] developed a commercial system that offers contextual search for Volkswagen and the automotive industry based on ontology. The authors believe the use of ontologies will benefit the automotive web community at large.

4 Implementation and Analysis

Paiva, Costa and Silva [21] analyzed several works that are related to Ontology-based Recommender Systems. They observed that the functionalities of such systems may be organized in layers which interact with one another to implement the whole recommendation process. Therefore, according to Fig. 1, the authors proposed a hierarchical architecture for ontology-based recommender systems which is organized in four layers such as Context Layer, Discovery Layer, Recommendation Layer and Ontology Layer.

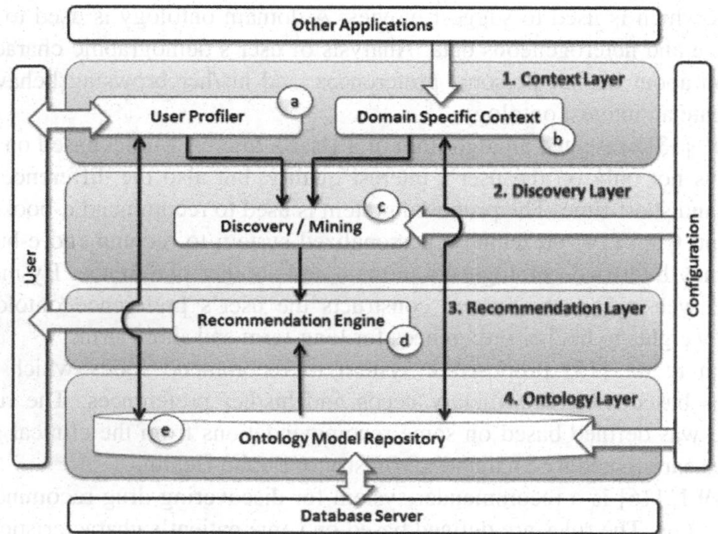

Fig. 1. Hierarchical Architecture for Ontology-based Recommender Systems

The shown layers in Fig. 1 have their own internal components, functionalities and relationships. They may be described as follows:

1. Context Layer – the User Profile (Fig. 1a) represents the related data to the user and the function of Domain Specific Context (Fig. 1b) is to represent the set of concepts used in a specific domain.
2. Discovery Layer – the user's feedbacks produced are delivered to the Discovery/Mining Component (Fig. 1c) which mines these data and the one sent by the Context Layer to compose the unified information to be submitted to the Recommendation Engine.
3. Recommendation Layer – this layer receives as an input the mined data by Discovery Layer and the Recommendation Engine component recommends an items list which meets the user's preferences.
4. Ontology Layer – the ontology repository (Fig. 1e) is the component responsible for the task of storing artifacts representations instances from models used ontologies in architecture.

Based on this architecture, a portal prototype is designed to recommend the best vehicles advertisements. However, there is an essential difference between the traditional portals and the proposed portal in this paper. The traditional portals search advertisements based on simple attributes such as price, model and brand. In addition to embody these attributes, our prototype considers others relevant information, for example, depreciation index and insurance price.

Traditional portals do not take into account these criteria however this information kind can be used to improve the recommendation quality. They perform searches only in their databases whereas our prototype visits traditional portals to collect various advertisement options in order to increase the possibility of finding good offers.

In most presented works in previous section, the ontologies are populated by means of data that are extracted from databases. In this paper, a web robot extracts advertisements from traditional portals (latter they will be called advertisements portals) and populates the ontology on-the-fly.

The prototype aims to identify and to recommend opportunities according to user's buying needs. It offers two services in the following scenarios: a) the best advertisements from a vehicles specific category and b) a good business opportunity considering the price that the user can disburse. In order to identify these offers, the prototype is integrated with three kinds of portals such as references, benchmarks and advertisements.

The references portal is used as parameter to evaluate the average price of a specific vehicle on the national market. The benchmarks portal is integrated to indicate the best vehicle from a specific category according to a set of defined criteria by this portal. The advertisements portals offer several opportunities to buy new and used vehicles. For each kind of portal, we choose some famous in Brazil such as FIPE [23], QuatroRodas [24], OLX [25], WebMotors [26] and MeuCarango [27].

The FIPE portal is used as reference to evaluate the average price of a specific vehicle. QuatroRodas portal has been used to acquire benchmarks. It evaluates many vehicles categories. The evaluation considers the following criteria: price, depreciation index, insurance price, parts replacements, satisfaction index with authorized dealer, reparability index and standard equipment. OLX, WebMotors and MeuCarango have been used to provide advertisements. OLX portal hosts advertisements in various categories such as vehicles, jobs, and etc. WebMotors offers the following services: buys, sales, insurance, and vehicle's financing. MeuCarango is a specialized portal in advertisements to buy and to sale new and semi-new vehicles.

To provide vehicles recommendation services, we need a set of concepts such as vehicle, advertisement, portal, and etc. We have developed ontology including related concepts to vehicles recommendation domain. The Vehicle Advertisements Ontology (VAO) has been built to be used in portal prototype. The UML class diagram which is shown in Fig. 2 illustrates the conceptual structures of the VAO.

It is crucial to take into account the concepts which have been built previously by others in order to evaluate the possibility of reuse them in a specific domain. Ontology reuse is the process in which available knowledge is used as an input to generate new ontologies. This process has several advantages [28] because a) it increases the quality of new ontologies because the components have been tested previously; b) it reduces human labor during the building of an ontology from scratch and; c) it facilitates the mapping of shared components between two ontologies.

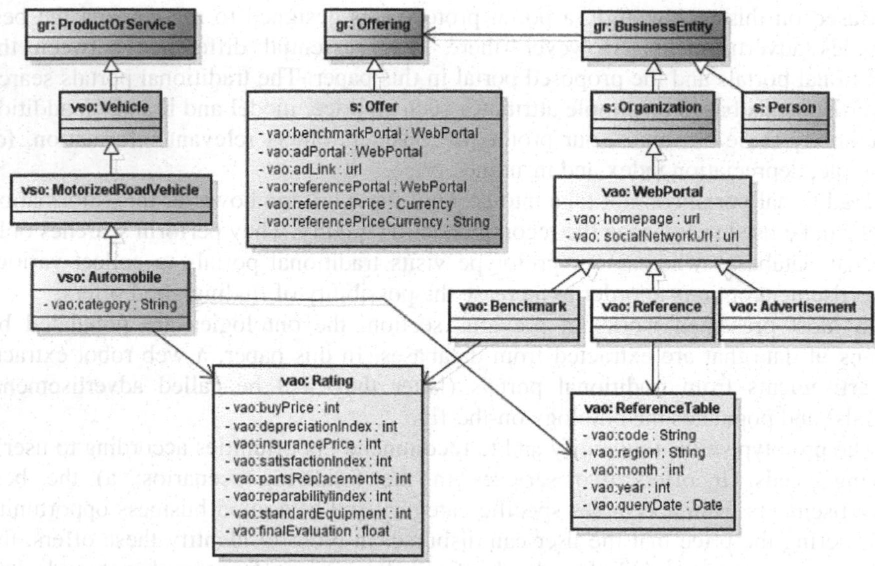

Fig. 2. Class diagram to illustrate conceptual structures of the VAO

Therefore some defined concepts in existing models have been reused in Vehicle Advertisements Ontology. These models are GoodRelations, Vehicle Sales Ontology and Schema. By convention, VAO assumes the following prefixes to reference the models: *vao:* for Vehicle Advertisements Ontology, *gr:* for GoodRelations, *vso:* for Vehicle Sales Ontology, and *s:* for Schema.org.

In proposed portal, only the administrator user may define the advertisements portals to be visited. Thereafter, the searches may be performed in portal. To begin his/her search, the user informs the advertisements kind (new or used vehicles), the vehicle category (e.g., SUV, Sedan, Van, and etc), how much he/she is intending to pay for it, and the advertisements portals to be visited, according to Fig. 3.

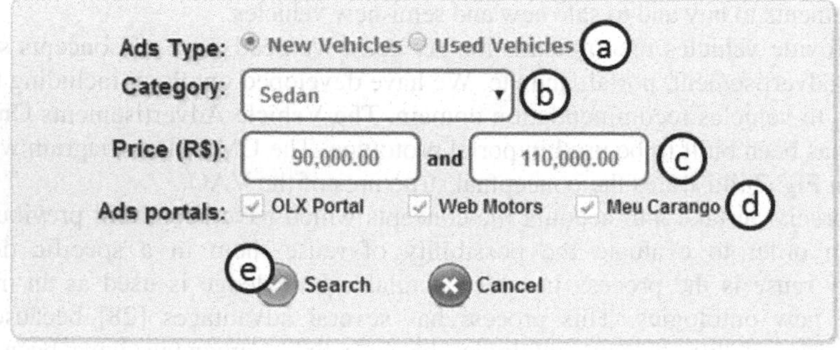

Fig. 3. Search for new vehicles from Sedan category

When the "Search" button is pressed, the user's request flow happens as follows:

1. The benchmarks portal is visited to recommend the best vehicle from the specified category;
2. To build a advertisements list that contains similar vehicles to that recommended by the benchmarks portal, three portals are visited;
3. A search range is created to present minimum and maximum prices from these three portals;
4. The references portal is visited to identify the average price of the recommended vehicle in step 1;
5. The search is performed within the defined range in step 3. For this propose, the algorithm considers the following conditions:

```
if (exists ads between MIN_PRICE(range) and REF_PRICE(avg)) then
 select this advertisements set;
 rank advertisements from MIN_PRICE(range) to REF_PRICE(avg);
else
 select this advertisements set;
 rank advertisements from REF_PRICE(avg) to MAX_PRICE(range);
end if
```

Fig. 4 displays 19 advertisements which were published in Portal 1, Portal 2 and Portal 3. Fig. 4a presents the MIN-MAX$_{PRICE}$ range which was informed in Fig. 3c. Fig. 4b represents the vehicle average price and it is used as reference to identify advertisements. If exists advertisements between minimum price (Fig. 4c) and the vehicle average price (Fig. 4b), the prototype ranks advertisements from MIN$_{PRICE(range)}$ to REF$_{PRICE(avg)}$. Otherwise, advertisements are ranked from REF$_{PRICE(avg)}$ to MAX$_{PRICE(range)}$. In our example, the first condition is true.

The presented advertisements in Fig. 4 are related to topic of user's interest. However, when the search is executed, only 15 advertisements arc found within the

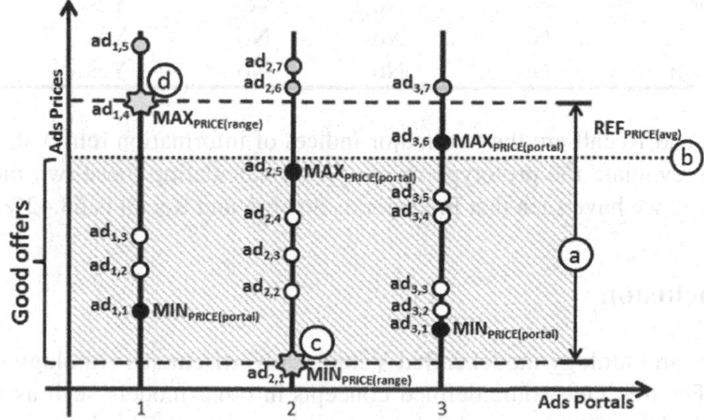

Fig. 4. Filtering of good offers to vehicle's buyers according to Fig. 3

Vehicle Image	Vehicle Description	Price	Source
	Ford Fusion White 16V 2.0 More details	R$ 90,000.00	Portal 2 View advertisement
	Ford Fusion White 16V 2.0 More details	R$ 96,000.00	Portal 2 View advertisement

Fig. 5. A web interface fragment that shows good offers based on user's search

range and therefore they are retrieved. From these found advertisements, 13 are selected as good offers to be recommended as seen in gray area in Fig. 4.

The selected advertisements as "good offers" are ranked according to price. Thereafter, they are listed to user in a web interface as shown in Fig. 5. In first column, the recommended vehicle image is shown. In next column, a brief description (model, color, and etc) is offered. The third column presents the advertised price in the portal. The last column indicates the portal and also it offers a hyperlink to advertisement.

In order to analyze our prototype compared to traditional portals of vehicle advertisements, we have defined some criteria. They are related to offered services such as: Criteria a) advertisements acquisition from others portals; Criteria b) best buy options by category; Criteria c) price comparison based on reference portals; Criteria d) search by new and used vehicles and; Criteria e) offer listing by price range. Table 1 lists the evaluated criteria and compares our proposal with the traditional portals.

Table 1. Comparision between the proposed prototype and the traditional portals

Portal	Criteria a	Criteria b	Criteria c	Criteria d	Criteria e
Our Prototype	Yes	Yes	Yes	Yes	Yes
Web Motors	No	No	Yes	Yes	Yes
OLX	No	No	No	Yes	Yes
Meu Carango	No	No	No	Yes	Yes

Precision and Recall are the two major indices of information retrieval. They have been used to evaluate the prototype results. After calculating these two metrics over some searches, we have seen that Precision is 86.66% and Recall is 68.42%.

5 Conclusion

In this paper, an ontology model called Vehicle Advertisements Ontology (VAO) has been built. For this fact, some defined concepts in other models such as GoodRelations, Vehicle Sales Ontology and Schema have been reused. This is essential because the ontology reuse process is one of the main features which justify its use.

Moreover a portal prototype to recommend the "best opportunities" to users which intend to buy a vehicle has been proposed in this paper. The offered service considers published advertisements in several portals. In order to recommend the best offers, the portal is integrated not only with advertisements portals, but also others kinds of portals such as references and benchmarks. The proposal is a variant approach to recommender systems that uses an ontology-based hierarchical layered architecture to implement semantic searches in Web.

References

1. McDonald, M.: Internet Reshapes How Dealers Sell Used Cars, `http://wardsauto.com/dealerships/internet-reshapes-how-dealers-sell-used-cars` (accessed February 05, 2014)
2. Zhuhadar, L., Nasraoui, O.: A Hybrid Recommender System Guided by Semantic User Profiles for Search in the E-learning Domain. Journal of Emerging Technologies in Web Intelligence 2 (2010)
3. Gruber, T.R.: A translation approach to portable ontology specifications. Journal Knowledge Acquisition Knowledge Acquisition 5, 199–220 (1993)
4. Guarino, N.: Formal ontology and information systems. In: Formal Ontology in Information Systems (1998)
5. Zikopoulos, P., Eaton, C., Deutsch, T., Deroos, D., Lapis, G.: Understanding Big Data: Analytics for Enterprise Class Hadoop and Streaming Data, p. 176. McGraw-Hill, NY (2012)
6. Yang, Q., Sun, J., Li, Y., Cai, K.: Domain ontology-based personalized recommendation research. In: Proceedings of 2nd International Conference on Future Computer and Communication, pp. 247–250 (2010)
7. Kim, H.H., Rieh, S.Y., Ahn, T.K., Chang, W.K.: Implementing an ontology-based knowledge management system in the Korean financial firm environment. In: Proceedings of 67th Annual Meeting of the American Society for Information Science and Technology, pp. 300–309 (2004)
8. Razmerita, L.: An ontology-based framework for modeling user behavior – A case study in Knowledge Management. IEEE Transactions on Systems, Man and Cybernetics, Part A: Systems and Humans 41, 772–783 (2011)
9. Ricci, F., Rokach, L., Shapira, B.: Introduction to Recommender Systems. In: Ricci, Rokach, Shapira (eds.) Recommender Systems Handbook, pp. 1–35. Springer, Berlin (2011)
10. Burke, R.: Hybrid web recommender systems. In: Brusilovsky, P., Kobsa, A., Nejdl, W. (eds.) Adaptive Web 2007. LNCS, vol. 4321, pp. 377–408. Springer, Heidelberg (2007)
11. Rho, S., Song, S., Hwang, E., Kim, M.: COMUS: Ontological and rule-based reasoning for music recommendation system. In: Theeramunkong, T., Kijsirikul, B., Cercone, N., Ho, T.-B. (eds.) PAKDD 2009. LNCS, vol. 5476, pp. 859–866. Springer, Heidelberg (2009)
12. Ge, J., Chen, Z., Peng, J., Li, T.: An ontology-based method for personalized recommendation. In: Proceedings of 11th International Conference on Cognitive Informatics & Cognitive Computing, pp. 522–526 (2012)
13. Lin, P., Yang, F., Yu, X., Xu, Q.: Personalized E-Commerce Recommendation Based on Ontology. In: Proceedings of International Conference on Computing in Science and Engineering, pp. 201–206 (2008)
14. Kang, J., Choi, J.: An ontology-based recommendation system using long-term and short-term preferences. In: Proceedings of International Conference on Information Science and Applications, pp. 1–8 (2011)

15. Suksom, N., Buranarach, M., Thein, Y.M., Supnithi, T., Netisopakul, P.: A Knowledge-based Framework for Development of Personalized Food Recommender System, School of Information Technology, King Mongkut's Institute of Technology Ladkrabang, Thailand
16. Doulaverakis, C., Nikolaidis, G., Kleontas, A., Kompatsiari, I.: GalenOWL: Ontology-based drug recommendations discovery. J. of Biomedical Semantics 3, 1–9 (2012)
17. Chen, S., Huang, Y., Chen, R.: A recommendation system for anti-diabetic drugs selection based on fuzzy reasoning and ontology techniques. International Journal of Pattern Recognition and Artificial Intelligence 27, 1–18 (2013)
18. Martínez-Romero, M., Vázquez-Naya, J.M., Pereira, J., Pereira, M., Pazos, A., Baños, G.: The iOSC3 System: Using Ontologies and SWRL Rules for Intelligent Supervision and Care of Patients with Acute Cardiac Disorders. Computational and Mathematical Methods in Medicine, pp. 1–13 (2013)
19. Mu, X., Chen, Y., Li, N., Jiang, J.: Modeling of Personalized Recommendation System Based on Ontology. In: Proceedings of International Conference on Management and Service Science, pp. 1–3 (2009)
20. Greenly, W., Sandeman-Craik, C., Otero, Y., Streit, J.: Case Study: Contextual Search for Volkswagen and the Automotive Industry, `http://www.w3.org/2001/sw/sweo/public/UseCases/Volkswagen/Volkswagen.pdf` (accessed March 19, 2013)
21. de Paiva, F.A.P., Costa, J.A.F., Silva, C.R.M.: A Hierarchical Architecture for Ontology-based Recommender Systems. In: Proceedings of BRICS Countries Congress (2013)
22. Manchale, P., Bilal, M.: Curated Content Based Recommender System. International Journal of Computer Science and Engineering 2, 66–72 (2013)
23. FIPE, `http://www.fipe.org.br/web/index.asp` (accessed February 03, 2014)
24. QuatroRodas, `http://quatrorodas.abril.com.br/melhorcompra/2013/` (accessed February 03, 2014)
25. O.L.X.: `http://natal.olx.com.br/carros-cat-378` (accessed February 03, 2014)
26. WebMotors, `http://www.webmotors.com.br/` (accessed February 03, 2014)
27. MeuCarango, `http://www.meucarango.com.br/carro.asp?pg=pesquisa.asp` (accessed February 03, 2014)
28. Yuan, J., Zhang, H., Ni, J.: A new ontology-based user modeling method for personalized recommendation. In: Proceedings of 3rd IEEE International Conference on Computer Science and Information Technology, pp. 363–367 (2010)
29. InformationWeek. Breakthrough Analysis: Two + Nine Types of Semantic Search, `http://www.informationweek.com/software/information-management/breakthrough-analysis-two-+-nine-types-of-semantic-search/d/d-id/1086310` (accessed February 01, 2014)
30. Guha, R., McCool, R., Miller, E.: Semantic Search, `http://WWW2003.org` (accessed January 2014)
31. Ruotsalo, T.: Domain Specific Data Retrieval on the Semantic Web. In: Simperl, E., Cimiano, P., Polleres, A., Corcho, O., Presutti, V. (eds.) ESWC 2012. LNCS, vol. 7295, pp. 422–436. Springer, Heidelberg (2012)
32. Mäkelä, E.: Survey of Semantic Search Research, `http://www.seco.tkk.fi/publications/2005/makela-semantic-search-2005.pdf` (accessed February 17, 2014)
33. Agarwal, D., Chen, B.: Machine Learning for Large Scale Recommender Systems, `http://pages.cs.wisc.edu/~beechung/icml11-tutorial` (accessed February 01, 2014)
34. Wozniak, M., Graña, M., Corchado, E.: A survey of multiple classifier systems as hybrid systems. Journal Information Fusion, 3–17 (2014)

Hybrid Systems for Analyzing the Movements during a Temporary Breath Inability Episode

María Luz Alonso Álvarez[1], Silvia González[2], Javier Sedano[2], Joaquín Terán[1], José Ramón Villar[3], Estrella Ordax Carbajo[1], and María Jesús Coma del Corral[1]

[1] Hospital Universitario de Burgos, 09006 Burgos, Unidad de Sueo y Unidad de Investigacin, Spain
joaquinteransantos@yahoo.es

[2] Instituto Tecnológico de Castilla y León. C/ López Bravo 70, Pol. Ind. Villalonquejar, 09001 Burgos, Spain
javier.sedano@itcl.es

[3] Computer Science Department, University of Oviedo, ETSIMO, c/Independencia 13, 33004 Oviedo, Spain
villarjose@uniovi.es

Abstract. This research is concerned with analyzing a real world problem: the detection of a sleep disorder called Obstructive Apnea Hypopnea Syndrome. The sleep apnea affects a significant number of adults, but children are affected as well. This study is focused on finding the apnea patterns using a well known time series representation method and several distance measures. In this preliminary work, the aim is twofold: on one hand, finding the most relevant features that characterize the apnea episodes; on the other hand, choosing the most promising distance measurements among patterns. The experiments were carried out at the Hospital Universitario de Burgos's Sleep Laboratory with real subjects and with technicians monitoring the Conventional Polysomnography.

Keywords: Sleep apnea, Sleep disorders breathing, Distances, Euclidean, DTW.

1 Introduction

The Spanish Society of Pneumology and Thoracic Surgery defines Obstructive Apnea Hypopnea Syndrome (OAHS) as "a picture of excessive sleepiness, cognitive-behavioral disorders, respiratory, cardiac, metabolic or inflammatory secondary to repeated episodes of obstruction of the upper airway during sleep". OAHS have to long-term consequences as sleep fragmentation and therefore daytime sleepiness and a reduction of oxygen levels, all these can increase risk of cardiovascular events. The frequency of the disease is similar on percentage throughout the world. These episodes are measured with the Respiratory Disturbance Index (RDI): an apnea diagnose is positive if the RDI value, computed for

M. Polycarpou et al. (Eds.): HAIS 2014, LNAI 8480, pp. 549–560, 2014.
© Springer International Publishing Switzerland 2014

those symptoms related with the apnea that have not been explained by other causes, is higher than 5. However, this definition is rather controversial.

The most referenced method for diagnosing sleep disorders, the OSAHS among them, is the Conventional Polysomnography (PSG), where technicians monitor subjects while sleeping in a specific sleep lab. The PSG quantifies both the amount and quality of sleep and breathing disorders as well as the physiological implications. In order to identify the sleep stages several variables are recorded with the PSG: the electroencephalogram, the electrooculogram, the chin electromyagram, the pulse oximetry, the naso-bucal airflow (by nasal cannula and thermistor), the thoracic and abdominal snoring movements and breathing disorders and the electrocardiogram. The PSG should be performed at night or during the subject's usual period of sleeping, recording at least 6.5 hours provided that more than 3 sleeping hours are included. The PSG is a relatively expensive, highly laborious and technically complex technique that is not universally available. Nowadays, the demand for centers exploration and the high prevalence of the OSAS make impossible to fulfill all the service appliances.

This study is devoted to tackle these problems using a novel method called Respiratory Polygraphy (RP) [1,2]. This method proposes the use of a set of two portable sensors in order to record the respiratory variables. According to the American Academy of Sleep Medicine [3,4,5,6], the RP is a Type 3 study, where breathing and pulse oximetry thoracoabdominal effort for a total between 4 to 7 channels are recorded. This research is a preliminary study for determining the most relevant features and distance algorithm in order to obtain a decision support system for determining apnea episodes. In order to choose the most promising solution, PSG tests have been carried out together and simultaneously with the RP tests: the detection error between the outcome of the model and the results from the PSG is used for choosing the best feature subset and the distance measurement that best discriminates among the relevant patterns. The rest of this paper is organized as follows. Section 2 includes the problem definition and describes both the distances measurements and features transformations. Section 3 introduces the experimentation results. The experiments and commented results are presented in Section 4. Finally, conclusions are drawn and future work is outlined.

2 Sleep Apnea Discovering

2.1 Detecting an Apnea from Signals

Apnea was defined as an absence or reduction higher than 90 % of the respiratory signal detected by thermistors, nasal cannula or pneumotachograph and a duration longer than 10 seconds in the presence of respiratory effort detected by thoraco-abdominal bands. The respiratory effort include abrupt inhalation and exhalation. In the inspiration, the outer intercostal muscles contract which raises the chest cavity or the ribs; in the exhalation, the inner intercostal muscles contract, bringing the ribs back to the original position while the diaphragm is also raised back.

All these movements, and subjects position can be determined by 3D accelerometers. Acceleration is caused by a net force and is decomposed along three axes. The accelerations are decompositions of the actual acceleration and the gravitational acceleration. As we know, when the sensor is static, the total acceleration of the sensor is due to the gravitational accelerations, this allows to determine the position of the body. Finally, knowing the position and actual acceleration, it is possible to detect signal patterns in normal conditions or respiratory effort.

Therefore, we proposed to detect anomalies in the values of the acceleration measured with two sensors, placed on the thorax and the abdomen, in order to detect episodes of apnea.

2.2 Human Movement Analysis

The analysis of human movements through triaxial accelerometers is well documented in the literature. The main part of the studies are devoted to human activity recognition using different techniques: Support Vector Machines and a specific set of sensors [7,8], using the accelerometer included in many smartphones [9], Hierarchical Hidden Markov [10], Fuzzy Basic Function [11], Genetic Fuzzy Finite State Machine (GFFSM) [12,13], Symbolic Aggregate ApproXimation (SAX) [14], Kohonen Self-Organizing Maps (SOM) [15] and wrapper GFFSM [16]. Moreover, the accelerometers have also been used for stress detection systems [17], as well as other illnesses onsets [18,19].

One of the main problems when dealing with accelerometers is the wide variety of transformations that can be applied to each of the acceleration components or to the aggregated signal as well. Each of the transformations is suitable for detecting a specific type of changes in the signal, and the ideal scenario is to choose the most satisfactory combinations of transformations for each problem.

Furthermore, pattern matching is always related with signal processing; thus a time series (TS) representation and a distance measurement are always needed. There are several studies in the literature concerning with these topics; choosing the most suitable TS representation and distance measurement is also a challenge when solving a real world problem. For the purposes of this study, a sliding window of size 120 samples without overlapping has been use; therefore, the distance measurement should be chosen. This topic will be analyze in Subsection 2.4.

2.3 Input Space Feature

Using triaxial accelerometers induces that the measurement obtained from the sensors acc_x, acc_y and acc_z, for the sake of the length of the paper, the transformations do not include a reference to the original contributions; interested readers can find all of them in a previous study [16], also use the feature Module.

$$Module = \sqrt{(acc_x)^2 + (acc_y)^2 + (acc_z)^2} \,. \tag{1}$$

2.4 Time Series Distance Measurements

When sliding windows of the raw data are used for TS representation, the most common distance measurements for matching patterns includes the following ones. Let A and B be 2D time-series with sizes m and n, respectively, where $A = ((a_{x,1}, a_{y,1}), \ldots, (a_{x,n}, a_{y,n}))$ and $B = ((b_{x,1}, b_{y,1}), \ldots, (b_{x,m}, b_{y,m}))$, $dist(a_i, b_i) = (a_{x,i} - b_{x,i})^2 + (a_{y,i} - b_{y,i})^2$ and $Rest(A) = (a_{x,2}, a_{y,2}), \ldots, (a_{x,n}, a_{y,n})$.

1. Euclidean distance. Typically some variation or extension of Euclidean is used. Euclidean is only defined for sequences of the same length [20].

$$Euclidean(A, B) = \sqrt{\sum_{i=1}^{n} dist(a_i, b_i)} \ . \tag{2}$$

2. Dynamic Time Warping (DTW) can successfully recognize sequences with noise and most importantly can recognize sequences contained within a longer sequence. DTW provides an elastic matching two sequences of time series by minimizing the distance between the two cumulative sequences [21,22,20].

$$DTW(A, B) = \begin{cases} 0 & \text{if } m = n = 0 \\ \inf & \text{if } m = 0 \text{ or } n = 0 \\ dist(a_1, b_1) + \\ min\{DTW(Rest(A), Rest(B)), \\ DTW(Rest(A), B), & \text{otherwise} \ . \\ DTW(A, Rest(B))\} \end{cases} \tag{3}$$

3. Continuous Dynamic Time Warping (CDTW) is the continuous counter-part of DTW [23].
4. Longest Common Subsequences (LCSS) has been applied with sensor failures and disturbance signals [20,24]. Constant ϵ is the matching threshold in space.

$$LCSS(A, B) \begin{cases} 0 & \text{if } m = 0 \text{ or } n = 0 \\ LCSS(Rest(A), Rest(B)) + 1 & \text{if } | a_{x,1} - b_{x,1} | \leq \epsilon \\ & \& \ | a_{y,1} - b_{y,1} | \leq \epsilon \\ max\{LCSS(Rest(A), B), LCSS(A, Rest(B)))\} & \text{other} \ . \end{cases} \tag{4}$$

5. Edit Distance on Real sequences (EDR) is robust and accurate in measuring the similarity between two trajectories [20], where subcost=0 if $match(a_1, b_1)$ = $true$ and subcost=1 otherwise.

$$EDR(A,B) = \begin{cases} n & \text{if } m = 0 \\ m & \text{if } n = 0 \\ min\{EDR(Rest(A), Rest(B)) + subcost, & \\ EDR(Rest(A), B) + 1, & \text{otherwise} \\ EDR(A, Rest(B)) + 1\} & \end{cases} . \quad (5)$$

6. Edit distance with Real Penalty (ERP) can be used to measured the similarity between trajectories with local shift, are sensitive to noise [20].

$$ERP(A,B) = \begin{cases} \sum_1^n dist(b_i, g) & \text{if } m = 0 \\ \sum_1^m dist(a_i, g) & \text{if } n = 0 \\ min\{ERP(Rest(A), Rest(B)) + dist(t_i, b_i), & \\ ERP(Rest(A), B) + dist(a_i, g), & \text{otherwise} \\ ERP(A, Rest(B)) + dist(b_i, g)\} & \end{cases} . \quad (6)$$

7. Online Smith-Waterman (OSW) can locate and accurately quantify embedded activities within a windowed sequence [21]. Where $d(a_i, b_i) = (a_{x,i} - b_{x,i})^2 + (a_{y,i} - b_{y,i})$, $\theta = 1.0$, $\alpha = 1$ and $\gamma = 1$.

$$SW(A,B) = \begin{cases} 0 & \text{if } m = 0 \text{ or } n = 0 \\ max\{SW(Rest(A), Rest(B)) + s(A,B), & \\ SW(Rest(A), B) - \gamma, & \text{otherwise} \\ SW(A, Rest(B)) - \gamma\,,\ 0\} & \end{cases} . \quad (7)$$

$$s(A,B) = \begin{cases} \alpha & d(A,B) < \theta \\ -d(A,B) & d(A,B) \geq \theta \end{cases} \quad (8)$$

8. Dissimilarity Metric (DISSIM) for the measurement of the spatiotemporal dissimilarity between two trajectories [25].

$$DISSIM(A,B) = \int_{i_1}^{i_n} Euclidean_{A,B}(i)\, di\,. \quad (9)$$

9. L_p Norms. Only one index structure is needed for all L_p norms, is faster than DTW [26].

$$L_p(A - B) = \left(\sum_{i=1}^{n} \mid a_i - b_i \mid^p \right)^{\frac{1}{p}} . \quad (10)$$

It is called Manhattan norm when $p = 1$, and the Euclidean norm when $p = 2$.

10. SpADe can be applied to both full sequence and subsequence matching. SpADe is a robust measure of distances between shape-based time series as it is not sensitive to shifting and scaling in temporal and amplitude dimensions of streaming time series [27].

3 Experimentation and Results

3.1 Experiment Setup

For this study a pair of belts have been developed. Each of the belts include a data collection devices with a sampling frequency of 16 Hz. Each device is a micro-controler unit with wireless capabilities integrated in a board with a triaxial accelerometer [28]. Consequently, for each sample a set of three values is obtained: the three components of the total acceleration $\{a_{i,j}\}$.

Two middle aged volunteers, a male and a female, have been enrolled in the study, which has been carried out in the sleep laboratory. The male subject suffers from several apneas during each monitored cycle, while the female presents an apnea-free profile. For the essay, the belts with the accelerometers were placed on the thorax and on the abdomen. Furthermore, the sensory for a conventional PSG was placed. Both the acceleration measurements and the PSG were carried out, this latter for evaluating and validating the acceleration discoveries. The data gathered from the subjects sleeping periods were monitored and stored. For each case, about 478.000 samples were registered. Due to the high computational cost, only the two most promising distance metrics among all the proposed ones have been used in this study: Euclidean and DTW.

Fig.1 depicts the pattern of breathing recovery in one specific position called *decubito supino*. This pattern has been codified by a PSG and one sleep medicine physician expert. The accelerometers were situated on abdomen, -upper figure- and thorax -figure below-. In this figure the x-axis represents the number of samples, while the y-axis represents the module.

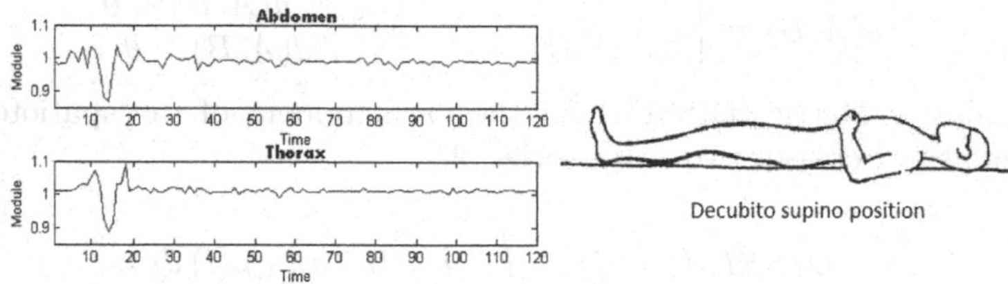

Fig. 1. Pattern of breathing recovery during a decubito supino position

3.2 Discussion of the Results

The first aim of this preliminary study has being to select the best combination between feature and distance algorithm in order to detect apnea episodes, but for that a total of 190 features have been used with Euclidean and DTW distances for analysing the data set. In all the cases, the sliding window size was fixed to 120 samples without overlapping. In this preliminary study the apneas to detect are accomplished for the decubito supino position.

In order to detect a situation of breathing recovery, we measure the distance between the apnea pattern and the current window using DTW and Euclidean.

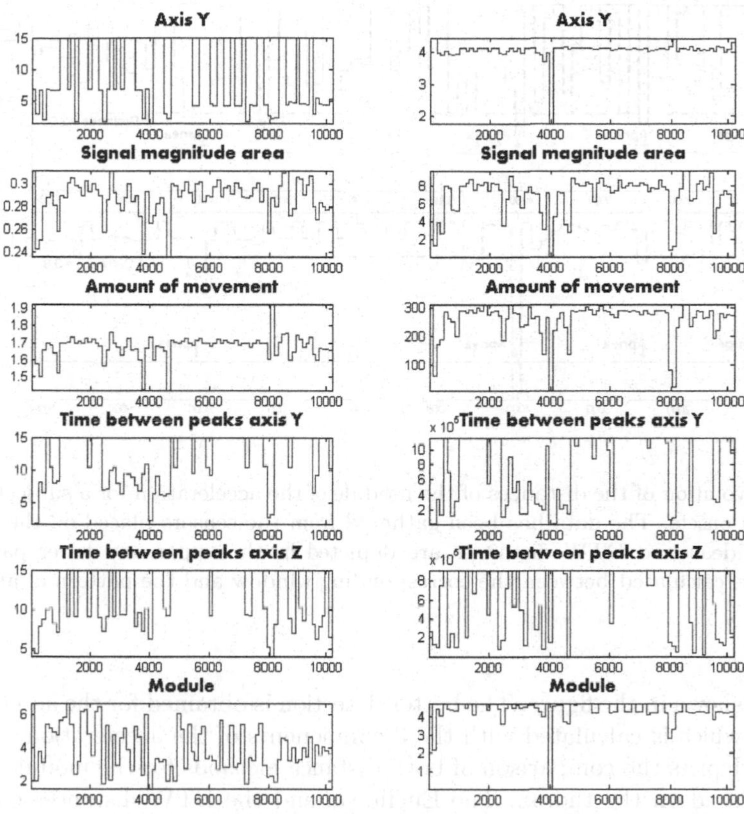

Fig. 2. Results of both distances for the several remarkable features, data gathered from the sensor placed on the thorax. The left part are patterns analyzed with the Euclidean distance, while on the right part the DTW was used instead.

If the distance is small than a threshold then it is a situation of breathing recovery. The breathing recovery pattern within a certain time interval is identified both by a PSG and one sleep medicine physician expert.

The results obtained for the male data from the sensor placed on the thorax for the Euclidean and DTW distance measurements for some of the features mentioned in the section 2.3 are shown in Fig.2. In this figure, the x-axis represents the number of samples, while the y-axis represents the distance magnitudes.

As can be seen, the scale varies from figure to figure so that the most interesting values (those closer to 0) can be displayed with higher detail, and the apnea episodes appear on x-axis positions 2300, 4000, 4400 and 8000. Clearly, the capabilities of certain set of features for discriminating an apnea pattern from that of the post-apnea are very limited or even negligible. However, some of them, the module, signal magnitude area and amount of movement among them, can be used for this detection task as they correctly detect the 4 different apneas

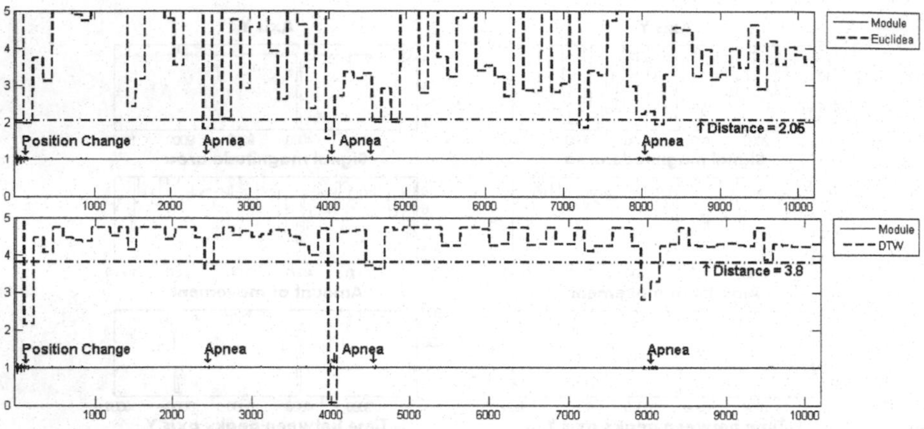

Fig. 3. Evolution of the distances of the module of the acceleration for a subject suffering apnea onsets. The data has been gathered from the sensors placed on the thorax. The Euclidean and DTW distances are depicted in the upper and lower part. The distance is calculated between the corresponding window and the pattern of an apnea episode.

episodes shown in the figure. The better detection is obtained for the acceleration module, which is calculated with the 3 components of the acceleration.

Fig.3 depicts the comparison of both distance methods for the module for the sensor placed on the thorax. The Euclidean and the DTW distances correctly detected all of the 4 apneas episodes for the male, but the Euclidean distance is also capable of discriminating between 2 false positive cases. We have found an upper bound for each of the distances in order to determine whether or not the subject is suffering an apnea: if the Euclidean (DTW) distance value is higher than 2.05 (3.8) then the current window corresponds with a normal sleeping scenario. With the same upper bound for both methods of distances, we determine that the female was having a normal sleeping scenario.

The DTW distance renders more effective apnea episode recognition than the Euclidean distance, hence only DTW distance is used on the second patient. As you can be seen in Fig.4 the DTW correctly detected that the patient female not suffer any apnea during this period of time.

Besides, neither the Euclidean distance nor the DTW distance are capable of differentiating between apneas and movements due to changes of position while sleeping. In the Fig.3, the first detection is a mistake due to the fact that in this moment is when the position change is produced. This is, the position of this patient before and after of decubito supino is a lateral decubitus position. In Fig.5 it can be seen how the gravity affects the accelerometers output, hence the orientation of the sensor with the gravitational acceleration can be known and we can therefore know which is the patient position. So, the orientation of the accelerometer will be different in the case of decubito supino or lateral

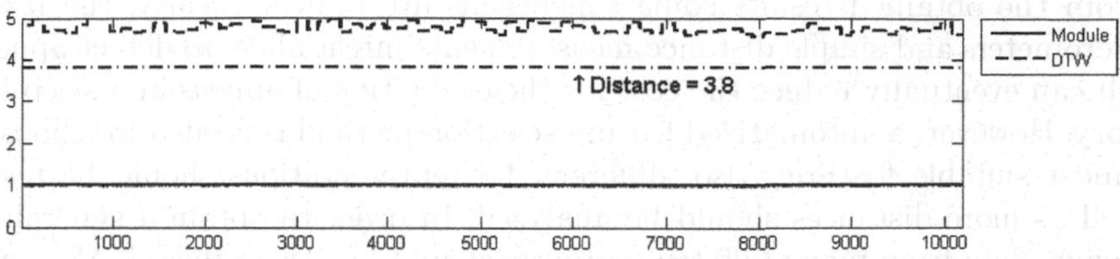

Fig. 4. Evolution of the distances of the module of the acceleration for a health subject wrt the pattern of an apnea onset. The data has been gathered from the sensors placed on the thorax. The Euclidean and DTW distances are depicted in the upper and lower part.

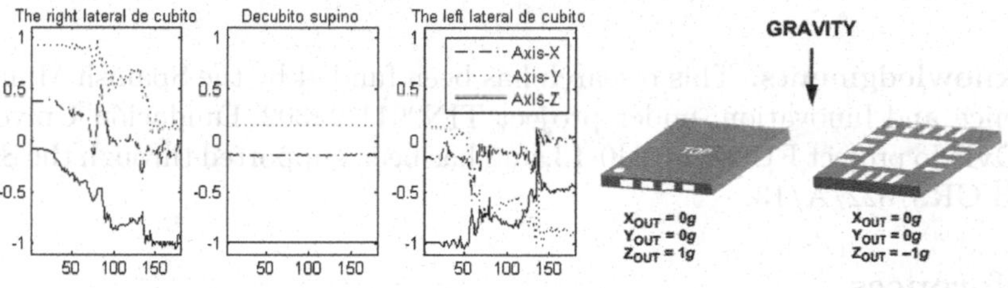

Fig. 5. The difference in the acceleration components according to the subject posture. Output response vs. orientation to gravity.

decubitus, where the Z axis will be close to -1, or the Y axis will be close to ± 1, respectively. The figure on the right the perfect lying position is depicted, where Z axis is 1 or -1 for a decubito supino or a decubito prono position, respectively.

Thus, determining both the current posture and the changes in the current posture is very interesting. However, using an accelerometer to find out the posture might introduce some fuzzyness in the position: the subject will rarely be in exactly perpendicular position with respect the bed and, even in this case, the sensors will surely be in a slightly different position that might introduce uncertainty. This is an intersting topic to study, introducing some decision support or alternative reasoning [29,30].

4 Conclusions and Future Research Lines

The fact that this study on an apnea detection method is a preliminary study was given by the restrictions imposed by the reduced number of patients, the use of only two distance metrics and the lack of clincal profiles available. The main objective of this study is to choose the best combination of features and distance algorithms. For these purpose several features obtained by means of transformations of the acceleration in a tri-axial accelerometer have been analysed. Besides, two different distance algorithms are used for detection the data set from an initial pattern of apnea. Finally, the results from the method presented are validated by an expert using Polysomnography by one expert.

From the obtained results some conclusions are drawn. Clearly, the use of accelerometers and simple distance measurements might allow to detect apneas, which can eventually reduce the cost for the evaluation of apneas in a sleep laboratory. However, a automatized feature selection method is needed for choosing the most suitable feature. Also, different TS representations should be tested as well as more distances should be analyzed. In order to obtain a generalized behavior, data from many different subjects should be also gathered. Moreover, the analysis should be extended to all the possible sleeping positions -including the hybrid positions, where the subject is not clearly decubito promo or in lateral decubito position, for instance-. Several distance metrics, with higher computational cost should also be included. All of these topics are included as future work of this research.

Acknowledgments. This research has been funded by the Spanish Ministry of Science and Innovation, under project TIN2011-24302, Fundación Universidad de Oviedo project FUO-EM-340-13, and has been supported through the SACYL 2013 GRS/822/A/13.

References

1. Alonso Álvarez, M.L., Terán Santos, J., Cordero Guevara, J., González Martínez, M., Rodríguez Pascual, L., Viejo Bañuelos, J.L., Marañón Cabello, A.: Fiabilidad de la poligrafía respiratoria domiciliaria para el diagnóstico del síndrome de apneas/hipopneas durante el sueño. análisis de costes. Arch. Bronconeumol. 44(1), 22–28 (2008)
2. Alonso Álvarez, M.L., Canet, T., Cubel Alarco, M., Estivill, E., Fernandez Julian, E., Gozal, D., Jurado Luqué, M.J., Lluch Roselló, A., Martínez Pérez, F., Merino-Andreu, M., Pin-Arboledas, G., Roure, N., Sanmartí, F., Sans Capdevila, O., Segarra Isern, F., Tomás Vila, M., Terán Santos, J.: Documento de consenso del síndrome de apneas-hipopneas durante el sueño en niños. Archivos de Bronconeumología 47(5), 1–18 (2011)
3. Somers, V.K., White, D.P., Amin, R., Abraham, W.T., Costa, F., Culebras, A., Daniels, S., Floras, J.S., Hunt, C.E., Olson, L.J., Pickering, T.G., Russell, R., Woo, M., Young, T.: Sleep apnea and cardiovascular diseasean american heart association/american college of cardiology foundation scientific statement from the american heart association council for high blood pressure research professional education committee, council on clinical cardiology, stroke council, and council on cardiovascular nursing in collaboration with the national heart, lung, and blood institute national center on sleep disorders research (national institutes of health). Journal of the American College of Cardiology 52, 686–717 (2008)
4. Kushida, C.A., Littner, M.R., Morgenthaler, T., Alessi, C.A., Bailey, D., Coleman, J.J., Friedman, L., Hirshkowitz, M., Kapen, S., Kramer, M., Lee-Chiong, T., Loube, D.L., Owens, J., Pancer, J.P., Wise, M.: Practice parameters for the indications for polysomnography and related procedures: an update for 2005, 28, 499–521 (2005)
5. Lloberes, P., Durán-Cantolla, J., Martínez-García, M.Á., Marín, J.M., Jaime Corralf, A., Masa, J.F., Parra, O., Alonso-Álvarez, M.L., Santos., J.T.: Normativa sobre diagnóstico y tratamiento del síndrome de apneas-hipopneas del sueño 47(3), 143–156 (2011)

6. Berry, R., Brooks, R., Gamaldo, C., Harding, S., Marcus, C., Vaughn, B., Tangredi, M.: The AASM Manual for the Scoring of Sleep and Associated Events: Rules, Terminology and Technical Specification. American Academy of Sleep Medicine, Darien (2012)
7. Banos, O., Damas, M., Pomares, H., Prieto, A., Rojas, I.: Daily living activity recognition based on statistical feature quality group selection. Expert Systems with Applications 39(9), 8013–8021 (2012)
8. Martiskainen, P., Järvinen, M., Skön, J.P., Tiirikainen, J., Kolehmainen, M., Mononen, J.: Cow behaviour pattern recognition using a three-dimensional accelerometer and support vector machines. Applied Animal Behaviour Science 119(1-2), 32–38 (2009)
9. Fuentes, D., Gonzalez-Abril, L., Angulo, C., Ortega, J.A.: Online motion recognition using an accelerometer in a mobile device. Expert Systems with Applications 39(3), 2461–2465 (2012)
10. Wang, J., Chen, R., Sun, X., She, M.F.H., Wu, Y.: Recognizing human daily activities from accelerometer signal. Procedia Engineering 15, 1780–1786 (2011)
11. Chen, Y.P., Yang, J.Y., Liou, S.N., Lee, G.Y., Wang, J.S.: Online classifier construction algorithm for human activity detection using a tri-axial accelerometer. Applied Mathematics and Computation 205(2), 849–860 (2008)
12. Ávarez-Álvarez, A., Triviño, G., Cordón, O.: Body posture recognition by means of a genetic fuzzy finite state machine. In: IEEE 5th International Workshop on Genetic and Evolutionary Fuzzy Systems (GEFS), pp. 60–65 (2011)
13. González, S., Villar, J.R., Sedano, J., Chira, C.: A preliminary study on early diagnosis of illnesses based on activity disturbances. In: Omatu, S., Neves, J., Rodriguez, J.M.C., Paz Santana, J.F., Gonzalez, S.R. (eds.) Distrib. Computing & Artificial Intelligence. AISC, vol. 217, pp. 521–527. Springer, Heidelberg (2013)
14. Villar, J.R., González, S., Sedano, J., Chira, C., Trejo, J.M.: Early diagnosis of stroke: bridging the gap through wearable sensors and computational models. In: Proceedings of the 9th International Conference on Applied Mathematics (2013)
15. Sedano, J., González, S., Baruque, B., Herrero, Á., Corchado, E.: Soft computing for the analysis of people movement classification. In: Snasel, V., Abraham, A., Corchado, E.S. (eds.) SOCO Models in Industrial & Environmental Appl. AISC, vol. 188, pp. 241–248. Springer, Heidelberg (2013)
16. Villar, J.R., González, S., Sedano, J., Chira, C., Trejo, J.M.: Human activity recognition and feature selection for stroke early diagnosis. In: Pan, J.-S., Polycarpou, M.M., Woźniak, M., de Carvalho, A.C.P.L.F., Quintián, H., Corchado, E. (eds.) HAIS 2013. LNCS, vol. 8073, pp. 659–668. Springer, Heidelberg (2013)
17. Sedano, J., Chira, C., Gonzalez, J., Villar, J.R.: Intelligent system to measuring stress: Stresstic. DYNA 87-3, 336–344 (2012)
18. Hausdorff, J.M., Schaafsma, J.D., Balash, Y., Bartels, A.L., Gurevich, T., Giladi, N.: Impaired regulation of stride variability in parkinson's disease subjects with freezing of gait 149, 187–194 (2003)
19. Shoeb, A., Edwards, H., Connolly, J., Bourgeois, B., Treves, S.T., Guttag, J.: Patient-specific seizure onset detection. Epilepsy & Behavior 5(4), 483–498 (2004)
20. Chen, L., Özsu, M.T., Oria, V.: Robust and fast similarity search for moving object trajectories. In: Proceedings of the 2005 ACM SIGMOD International Conference on Management of Data, SIGMOD 2005, pp. 491–502. ACM, New York (2005)
21. Riedel, D.E., Venkatesh, S., Liu, W.: Recognising online spatial activities using a bioinformatics inspired sequence alignment approach. Pattern Recognition 41(11), 3481–3492 (2008)

22. Tormene, P., Giorgino, T., Quaglini, S., Stefanelli, M.: Matching incomplete time series with dynamic time warping: an algorithm and an application to post-stroke rehabilitation. Artificial Intelligence in Medicine 45(1), 11–34 (2009)
23. Munich, M.E., Perona, P.: Continuous dynamic time warping for translation-invariant curve alignment with applications to signature verification. In: Proceedings of 7th International Conference on Computer Vision, pp. 108–115 (1999)
24. Vlachos, M., Hadjieleftheriou, M., Gunopulos, D., Keogh, E.J.: Indexing multidimensional time-series. VLDB J. 15(1), 1–20 (2006)
25. Frentzos, E., Gratsias, K., Theodoridis, Y., Frentzos, E., Gratsias, K., Theodoridis, Y.: 1 index-based most similar trajectory search (November 2006)
26. Yi, B.K., Faloutsos, C.: Fast time sequence indexing for arbitrary lp norms. In: Proceedings of the 26th International Conference on Very Large Data Bases, VLDB 2000, pp. 385–394. Morgan Kaufmann Publishers Inc., San Francisco (2000)
27. Chen, Y., Nascimento, M.A., Chin, B., Anthony, O., Tung, K.H.: Spade: On shape-based pattern detection in streaming time series. In: ICDE 2007, pp. 786–795 (2007)
28. Xie, H., Fedder, G.K., Sulouff, R.E.: 2.05 - accelerometers. In: Yogesh Gianchandani, E., Tabata, O., Zappe, H. (eds.) Comprehensive Microsystems, pp. 135–180. Elsevier, Oxford (2008)
29. Diz, M.L.B., Baruque, B., Corchado, E., Bajo, J., Corchado, J.M.: Hybrid neural intelligent system to predict business failure in small-to-medium-size enterprises. Int. J. Neural Syst. 21(4), 277–296 (2011)
30. Abraham, A.: Special issue: Hybrid approaches for approximate reasoning. Journal of Intelligent and Fuzzy Systems 23(2-3), 41–42 (2012)

Hybrid Intelligent Model to Predict the SOC of a LFP Power Cell Type

Luis Alfonso Fernández-Serantes[1], Raúl Estrada Vázquez[2], José Luis Casteleiro-Roca[1], José Luis Calvo-Rolle[1], and Emilio Corchado[3]

[1] Universidad de A Coruña,
Departamento de Ingeniería Industrial,
Avda. 19 de febrero s/n, 15495, Ferrol, A Coruña, España
luis.alfonso.fernandez.serantes@udc.es

[2] FH JOANNEUM University of Applied Sciences,
Institute for Electronic Engineering,
Werk-VI-Strasse 46, 8605, Kapfenberg, Austria

[3] Universidad de Salamanca,
Departamento de Informática y Automática,
Plaza de la Merced s/n, 37008, Salamanca, Salamanca, España

Abstract. Nowadays, batteries have two main purposes: to enable mobility and to buffer intermitent power generation facilities. Due to their electromechaminal nature, several tests are made to check battery performance, and it is very helpful to know a priori how it works in each case. Batteries, in general terms, have a complex behavior. This study describes a hybrid intelligent model aimed to predict the State Of Charge of a LFP (Lithium Iron Phosphate - LiFePO4) power cell type, deploying the results of a Capacity Confirmation Test of a battery. A large set of operating points is obtained from a real system to create the dataset for the operation range of the power cell. Clusters of the different behavior zones have been obtained to achieve the final solution. Several simple regression methods have been carried out for each cluster. Polynomial Regression, Artificial Neural Networks and Ensemble Regression were the combined techniques to develop the hybrid intelligent model proposed. The novel model allows achieving good results in all the operating range.

Keywords: Power cell, battery, clustering, neural networks.

1 Introduction

The variation of the energy production at renewable energy installations like wind farms, the necessity of finding a substitute for fossil fuels in vehicles or to supply energy to portable devices, are several reasons for which electric energy storage is one of the trending solutions [1].

At present, there are some researches with the aim of improving energy storage. For instance, Smart Grid is a good example where energy store systems are employed to face intermittent renewable generations [2], such as wind or solar

M. Polycarpou et al. (Eds.): HAIS 2014, LNAI 8480, pp. 561–572, 2014.
© Springer International Publishing Switzerland 2014

power production. In this way, portable devices require higher autonomy and lower weight with the purpose of improving people's quality of life [3].

In other terms, the current development of electric vehicles possesses the problem of storing energy, despite the fact that electric powertrains are more efficient than internal combustion engines [4]. Among the different energy storage technologies, this paper is focused on one of these technologies, the battery storage systems, specifically LFP (Lithium Iron Phosphate - LiFePO4) power cell type. Due to the relevance of this types of batteries, modeling them is really important, especially its behavior and its ageing prediction, as charging and discharging cycles reduce cell efficiency [5].

The classic regression models are based on Multiple Regression Analysis (MRA) methods [6]. MRA-based methods are useful due to their applications in different subjects [7,8]; the first cite shows a model for cost prediction in the early state of projects, the second one proposes a method to evaluate suppliers performance. The main problem of these methods is their limitations in certain cases. For instances in [6] and [9] the common trouble is its non linearity and the different ways followed to solve them with aproaches based on MRA techniques. Regression techniques based on Soft Computing could avoid some of the problems mentioned above. Several works have been developed with this goal. In [10] the prediction state of a model predictive control system is carried out by meta-classifiers. By combining multi regression analysis and artificial neural networks an optimizing overbreak prediction is made in [11]. In [12] failure detection and prediction in wind turbines is achieved by using intelligent techniques.

Despite the new methods to solve regression problems, there are cases where it is not possible to achieve a good performance of the model, for instances due to the high non-linearity of the system. Clustering could be a complementary solution as a previous step to apply regression to the dataset [13]. K-means clustering algorithms are often employed with this purpose [14,15]. With this method, all the dataset is divided into subsets (clusters), depending on the features of the input data. Then, regression is made over each cluster. Previous works like [16,17] used similar techniques to solve other physical systems.

This study implements a hybrid model to predict several parameters in one specific test of batteries. To develop the model, K-means clustering algorithm was used to make groups of data with the same behavior. Then, three different regression techniques were tested for each group to choose the best one based on the lowest mean squared error achieved.

This paper is organized in the following way. After this introduction, the case of study section describes the employed test and how the dataset was obtained. Then, the model approach and the tested algorithms taken into account in the research are presented. The results section shows the best configuration achieved by the hybrid model. After the results, the conclusions and future works are presented.

2 Case of Study

The model has been obtained to study the behavior of a LFP power cell type, by detecting its State Of Charge (SOC). The scheme of the practical implementation to carry out the test is shown on figure 1.

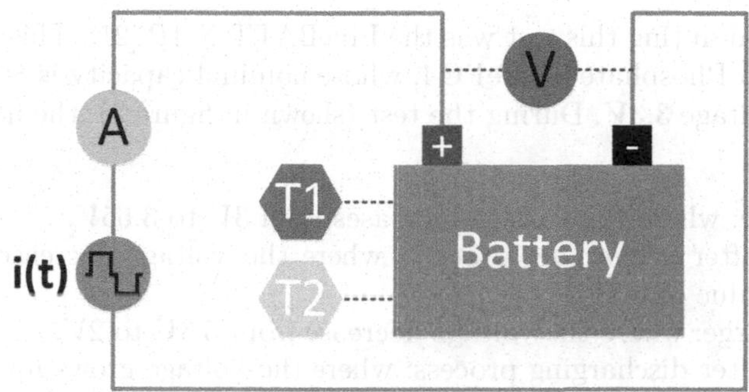

Fig. 1. Scheme of the capacity confirmation test

In the next subsections the test and the battery device are explained in detail.

2.1 The Battery

A battery is a device capable of storing electricity within a electrochemical medium and reconverting it to electrical energy by electrochemical reactions [1]. The operating principle is based on a redox reaction by reducing the cations at the cathode and oxiding the anions at the anode, during the discharge, and in the other way during the charge [1]. This cycle can be repeated for a certain number of times, after that capacity decreases to anymore usable levels [18].

Lithium-ion (Li-ion) cells are one type of rechargeable batteries that have traditionally been used to power consumer electronic devices, and more recently for electric vehicles [19]. These cells are characterized for their light weight and high energy densities [1], they also have no memory effect, long life cycle and a low selfdischarge [19,18].

2.2 Capacity Confirmation of the Battery Test

The developed test measures the device capacity in ampere-hour at a constant current [20]. The first step is to charge the cell to its maximum SOC. After that, the battery is discharged at constant current up to the discharge voltage limit specified by the manufacturer [20]. Once the cell is recharged to its maximum capacity, the battery capacity and the SOC are calculated at each moment.

The test was done with a battery tester that can charge and discharge the cells at constant current, and it is able to measure different parameters. These parameters are the voltage provided by the battery, the current flowing to and from the battery, its temperature and the time, while the test is running.

The test scheme is shown on figure 1. On it, it is possible to see different components like a voltmeter *(V)*, an amperemeter *(A)*, and two temperature sensors *(T1 & T2)* to measure the temperature value at two different places. Also, there is a current source that provides and absorbs the flowing current *(i(t))*.

The cell used during this test was the LiFeBATT X-1P [21]. This power cell is a Lithium Iron Phosphate - LiFePO4, whose nominal capacity is $8000mAh$ and its nominal voltage $3.3V$. During the test (shown in figure 2), the next steps are carried out:

- (1) Charge: where the voltage increases from $3V$ to $3.65V$.
- (2) Rest after a charging process: where the voltage decreases up to the nominal value of $3.3V$.
- (3) Discharge: where the voltage decrease from $3.3V$ to $2V$.
- (4) Rest after discharging process: where the voltage grows up to the value of $3V$, and then the cycle starts again.

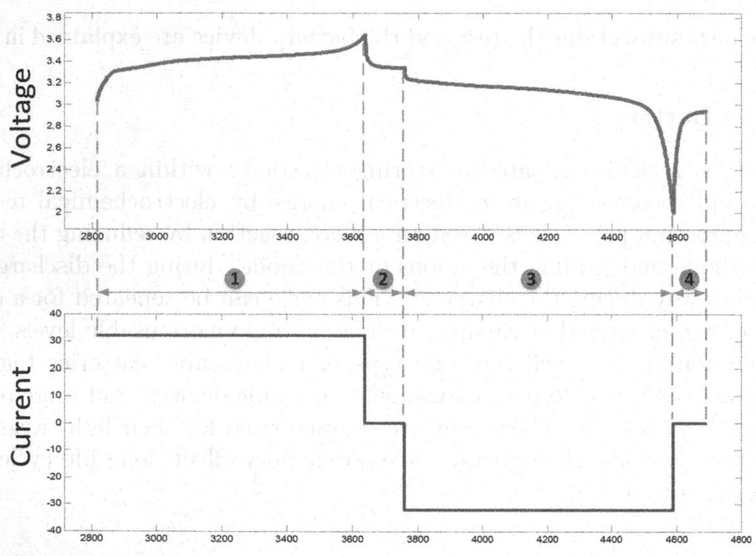

Fig. 2. Voltage and current during one cycle test

The analysis of voltage progress for one entire cycle is shown at the top of figure 2. The analysis of the current (bottom of figure 2) shows that the process carried out was done at a constant value of current. The current is positive when it flows from the source to the battery, and it is negative when it flows from the battery to the source.

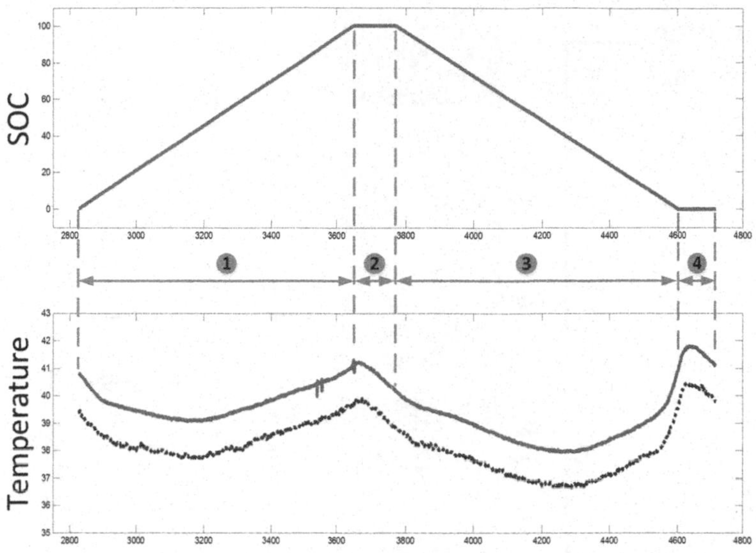

Fig. 3. Energy balance and temperatures during one cycle test

With the value of current at each time it is possible to obtain the energy provided or absorbed in ampere-hour. If this energy is represented (top of figure 3) it is possible to see how the battery SOC increases during the charging period till 100% of charge. On the other hand, the SOC of the cell decreases till its minimum value of 0% during the discharging process.

The measurement of temperatures are done with two sensors located at different places of the battery. These parameters vary cyclically depending on the state of the battery (charge, discharge, rest after charge and rest after discharge) and on its voltage. At the bottom of figure 3, it is possible to see the temperature behavior for each operating region.

The dataset has been obtained by carrying out the mentioned test over the power cell. The current and the voltage were registered to study the state of the battery. The parameter SOC was calculated with the current and the time for each test. Also two different temperatures were measured to detect malfunction on the device, if the temperature is far from the predicted one. The data were labeled during the test to know the corresponding state.

3 Model Approach

The scheme of the model approach is shown in figure 4. Taking into account the power cell performance and the test made, it is possible to divide the dataset in four operation ranges. Consequently, four clusters are created and, three regression models (one per output) are implemented for each one. As shown on the figure 4, the global model has two inputs (current and voltage) and three outputs

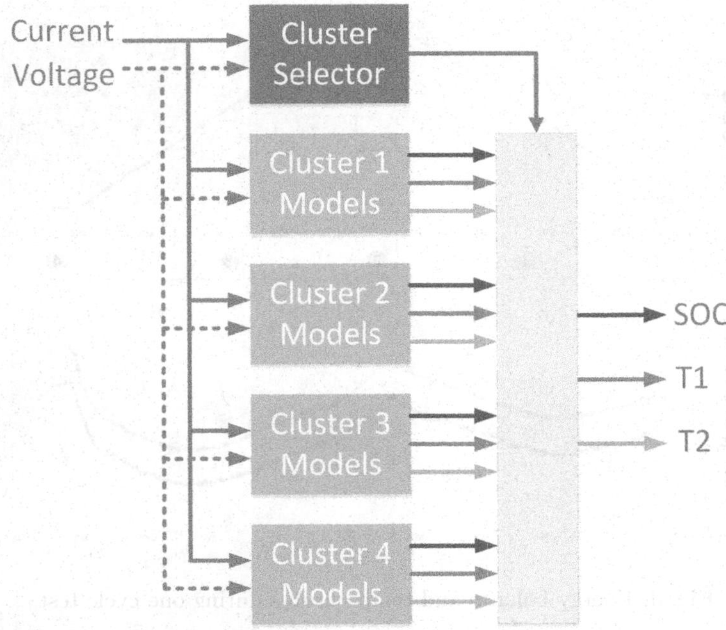

Fig. 4. Model approach

(SOC, T1 and T2). The cluster selector block connects the chosen models with the output.

3.1 Techniques Used

The techniques tested in the study to achieve the best model are described below.

Data Clustering. The K-means Algorithm. Clustering is an unsupervised technique of data grouping where similarity is measured [22,23]. Clustering algorithms try to organize unlabeled feature vectors into clusters or groups, in such a way that samples within a cluster are similar to each other [24]. K-means algorithm is a commonly used partitional clustering algorithm with square-error criterion, which minimizes error function shows in equation 1.

$$e = \sum_{k=1}^{C} \sum_{x \epsilon Q_k} \|x - c_k\|^2 \tag{1}$$

The final clustering will depend on the initial cluster centroids and on the value of K (number of clusters). Choosing K value is the most critical election because it requires certain prior knowledge of the number of clusters present in the data, which is highly doubtful. The K-means partitional clustering algorithm is computationally effective and works well if the data are close to its cluster, and the cluster is hyperspherical in shape and well-separated in the hyperspace.

Polynomial Regression. Generally, a polynomial regression model [25] may also be defined as a linear summation of basis functions. The number of basis functions depends on the number of the model inputs, and the degree of the polynomial used.

With a degree 1, the linear summation could be defined as the one shown in equation 2. The model becomes more complex as the degree increases, equation 3 shows a second polynomial degree for the model.

$$F(x) = a_0 + a_1 x_1 + a_2 x_2 \tag{2}$$

$$F(x) = a_0 + a_1 x_1 + a_2 x_2 + a_3 x_1 x_2 + a_4 x_1^2 + a_5 x_2^2 \tag{3}$$

Artificial Neural Networks (ANN): MultiLayer Perceptron (MLP). A multilayer perceptron is a feedforward artificial neural network [25]. It is one of the most typical ANNs due to its robustness and relatively simple structure. However, the ANN architecture must be well selected to obtain good results.

The MLP is composed by one input layer, one or more hidden layers and one output layer, all of them made of neurons and with pondered connections between the neurons of each layer.

Ensemble Regression. The ensembles are a learning method usually employed for classification tasks [26]. Furthermore, this technique can be used for regression purposes with very satisfactory results when the dataset is large [27]. Regularization is a process for choosing fewer weak learners for an ensemble with the aim to increase predictive performance. Then it is possible to regularize regression ensembles. The method tries to find a set of weights α_t that minimize the expresion 4.

$$\sum_{n=1}^{N} w_n g\left(\left(\sum_{t=1}^{T} \alpha_t h_t(x_n)\right), y_n\right) + \lambda \sum_{t=1}^{T} |\alpha_t| \tag{4}$$

where,

- $\lambda \geq 0$ is the regularization parameter.
- h_t is a weak learner in the ensemble trained on N observations with predictors x_n, responses y_n, and weights w_n.
- $g(f, y) = (f - y)^2$ is the square error.

3.2 Preprocessing the Dataset

The SOC of the battery should be from 0% to 100% and from 100% to 0%. In order to achieve this fact, some incomplete cycles were discarded. Taken this

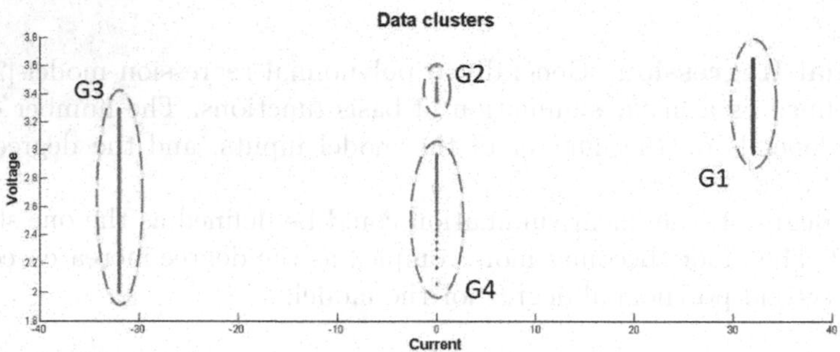

Fig. 5. Dataset clusters

Table 1. Samples assigned to train and test the models

Cluster	Training	Testing	Total
(1) - Charge	4376	2243	6619
(2) - Rest	727	362	1089
(3) - Discharge	4975	2476	7451
(4) - Rest	835	375	1210
Total	10913	5456	16369

fact into account, given that the whole data acquisition has twelve cycles, only nine cycles were included to calculate the model. The data were recorded with a sample time of one second, and with the explained discard, the dataset was reduced from 18130 to 16369 samples.

The first technique applied to the dataset was clustering. To do that, K-means algorithm was applied and four clusters were created. These groups represent the different states of the cell test. In figure 5, it is possible to distinguish these four clusters: blue data correspond to state (1), magenta to state (2), red to (3) and green to (4).

All the dataset was divided in two parts to train and test the models. After this separation, each data was clustered. Table 1 shows the different number of samples for each cluster.

The three mentioned regression techniques were trained for the four clusters, one by each output of the model. As an example, the figure 6 shows the temperature in sensor 2. The four colors indicate the different clusters, as it was mentioned above.

4 Results

The results of the clustering algorithm was compared with the real state asigned during the test. Due to the fact that the dataset has the correct properties to

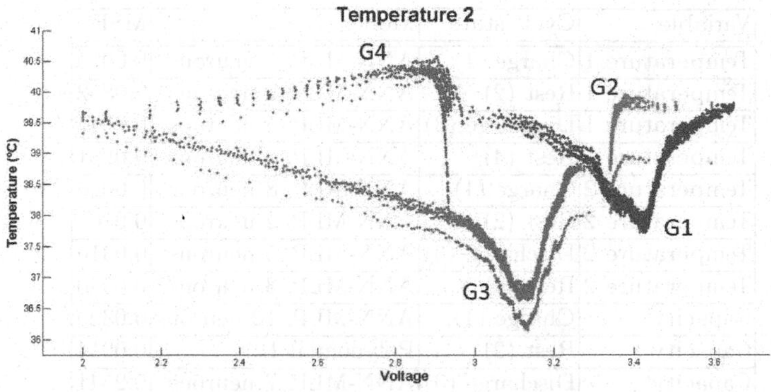

Fig. 6. Temperature 2 vs. Battery voltage

Table 2. Best MSE for each regression algorithm

Variable	Cycle state	ANN-MLP MSE	Polynomial MSE	Ensemble MSE
Temperature 1	Charge (1)	0.0025	0.0413	0.0028
Temperature 1	Rest (2)	0.0862	0.0884	0.1023
Temperature 1	Discharge (3)	0.0344	0.0642	0.0361
Temperature 1	Rest (4)	0.0881	0.1270	0.1024
Temperature 2	Charge (1)	0.0056	0.0413	0.0059
Temperature 2	Rest (2)	0.0761	0.0782	0.0895
Temperature 2	Discharge (3)	0.0316	0.0577	0.0335
Temperature 2	Rest (4)	0.0940	0.1324	0.1098
Capacity	Charge (1)	0.0329	13.7110	0.0516
Capacity	Rest (2)	0.0016	0.0014	0.0016
Capacity	Discharge (3)	0.2541	2.7005	0.2933
Capacity	Rest (4)	0.0021	0.0019	0.0023

use K-Means, the clustering achieved was 100% of correct assignation. This fact allows the model approach not to need to know the cycle state for the data.

14 different ANN-MLP were tested for each cluster, with a number of neurons in the hidden layer from 2 to 15. In all cases, these neurons have a Tan-sigmoidal transfer function, and the output layer neuron has a linear transfer function.

10 different polynomial regressions were tested for each cluster. For this technique, the degrees of the polynomial used were from degree 1 to degree 10.

The ensemble learning method used was 'LSBoost', it was 5000 trained cycles and a regression tree algorithm; one ensemble was training for each cluster.

All the models were compared by using the Mean Square Error (MSE) as the efficiency measurement. The testing data are only used to calculate the MSE, not for training any model.

In table 2 the lowest MSE achieved appears for each algorithm. Table 3 shows the best regression technique and its configuration for each cluster. Even so, the

Table 3. MSE for the best methods

Variable	Cycle state	Model	MSE
Temperature 1	Charge (1)	ANN-MLP, 5 neurons	0.0025
Temperature 1	Rest (2)	ANN-MLP, 2 neurons	0.0862
Temperature 1	Discharge (3)	ANN-MLP, 5 neurons	0.0344
Temperature 1	Rest (4)	ANN-MLP, 3 neurons	0.0881
Temperature 2	Charge (1)	ANN-MLP, 8 neurons	0.0056
Temperature 2	Rest (2)	ANN-MLP, 2 neurons	0.0761
Temperature 2	Discharge (3)	ANN-MLP, 5 neurons	0.0316
Temperature 2	Rest (4)	ANN-MLP, 3 neurons	0.0940
Capacity	Charge (1)	ANN-MLP, 12 neurons	0.0329
Capacity	Rest (2)	Polynomial 1	0.0014
Capacity	Discharge (3)	ANN-MLP, 7 neurons	0.2541
Capacity	Rest (4)	Polynomial 1	0.0019

selection takes the computational cost into account when the MSE for different techniques are close.

It is remarkable that the best MSE achieved without clustering the dataset was, at least, twice worse than the worst result reached with the proposal. In the capacity model, the average MSE with clustering is 0.0726, and without it is over than 236.

5 Conclusions

Very good results have been obtained in general terms with the novel approach proposed in this research. The average of the MSE is 0.0590 varying form 0.0014 and 0.2541 for the different variables depending of the cycle state. It is possible to predict the value of the SOC in real time for the capacity confirmation of the battery test. This model could be used to ensure a good power cell test, for example, by detecting when a test provides wrong results.

The results achieved with the hybrid model increase the whole efficiency of the approach because each model was trained only for a group of the dataset. For the regression, the best approximation has been obtained with MLP in all cases, with the exception of SOC prediction for Rest 2 and 4. For this two cases, the best MSE is reached with Polynomial Regression.

In other terms, the cell temperature is a critical parameter that is so significant of the device health. The temperatures in the battery were included into the model to predict a deviation from the normal settings in the test. Thus, it is possible to detect deviations in this sense, too.

References

1. Chukwuka, C., Folly, K.: Batteries and super-capacitors. In: 2012 IEEE Power Engineering Society Conference and Exposition in Africa (PowerAfrica), pp. 1–6 (July 2012)

2. Qian, H., Zhang, J., Lai, J.S.: A grid-tie battery energy storage system. In: 2010 IEEE 12th Workshop on Control and Modeling for Power Electronics (COMPEL), pp. 1–5 (June 2010)
3. Chaturvedi, N.A., Klein, R., Christensen, J., Ahmed, J., Kojic, A.: Modeling, estimation, and control challenges for lithium-ion batteries. In: American Control Conference (ACC), pp. 1997–2002 (June 2010)
4. Vukosavic, S.: Electrical Machines. Power Electronics and Power Systems. Springer (2012)
5. Konig, O., Jakubek, S., Prochart, G.: Battery impedance emulation for hybrid and electric powertrain testing. In: 2012 IEEE Vehicle Power and Propulsion Conference (VPPC), pp. 627–632 (October 2012)
6. Mark, J., Goldberg, M.A.: Multiple regression analysis and mass assessment: A review of the issues. Appraisal Journal 56(1), 89 (1988)
7. Jin, R., Cho, K., Hyun, C., Son, M.: Mra-based revised CBR model for cost prediction in the early stage of construction projects. Expert Systems with Applications 39(5), 5214–5222 (2012)
8. Ho, L.H., Feng, S.Y., Lee, Y.C., Yen, T.M.: Using modified IPA to evaluate supplier's performance: Multiple regression analysis and DEMATEL approach. Expert Systems with Applications 39(8), 7102–7109 (2012)
9. Cho, Y., Awbi, H.B.: A study of the effect of heat source location in a ventilated room using multiple regression analysis. Building and Environment 42(5), 2072–2082 (2007)
10. Nieves-Acedo, J., Santos-Grueiro, I., Garcia-Bringas, P.: Enhancing the prediction stage of a model predictive control systems through meta-classifiers. Dyna 88(3), 290–298 (2013)
11. Jang, H., Topal, E.: Optimizing overbreak prediction based on geological parameters comparing multiple regression analysis and artificial neural network. Tunnelling and Underground Space Technology 38, 161–169 (2013)
12. Alvarez-Huerta, A., Gonzalez-Miguelez, R., Garcia-Metola, D., Noriega-Gonzalez, A.: Failure detection and prediction in wind turbines by using scada data. Dyna 86(4), 467–473 (2011)
13. Martínez-Rego, D., Fontenla-Romero, O., Alonso-Betanzos, A.: Efficiency of local models ensembles for time series prediction. Expert Syst. Appl. 38(6), 6884–6894 (2011)
14. Cherif, A., Cardot, H., Boné, R.: SOM time series clustering and prediction with recurrent neural networks. Neurocomput. 74(11), 1936–1944 (2011)
15. Ghaseminezhad, M.H., Karami, A.: A novel self-organizing map (SOM) neural network for discrete groups of data clustering. Appl. Soft Comput. 11(4), 3771–3778 (2011)
16. Crespo-Ramos, M.J., Machón-González, I., López-García, H., Calvo-Rolle, J.L.: Detection of locally relevant variables using SOM-NG algorithm. Engineering Applications of Artificial Intelligence 26(8), 1992–2000 (2013)
17. Calvo-Rolle, J.L., Casteleiro-Roca, J.L., Quintián, H., Meizoso-Lopez, M.C.: A hybrid intelligent system for PID controller using in a steel rolling process. Expert Systems with Applications 40(13), 5188–5196 (2013)
18. Wikipedia: Lithium-ion battery - wikipedia, the free encyclopedia (2014) (online; accessed January 30, 2014)
19. Sparacino, A., Reed, G., Kerestes, R., Grainger, B., Smith, Z.: Survey of battery energy storage systems and modeling techniques. In: 2012 IEEE Power and Energy Society General Meeting, pp. 1–8 (July 2012)

20. PNGV Battery Test Manual (February 2001)
21. LiFeBATT X-1P 8Ah 38123 Cell (March 2011)
22. Qin, A., Suganthan, P.: Enhanced neural gas network for prototype-based clustering. Pattern Recogn. 38(8), 1275–1288 (2005)
23. Ye, J., Xiong, T.: SVM versus least squares SVM. Journal of Machine Learning Research - Proceedings Track 2, 644–651 (2007)
24. Kaski, S., Sinkkonen, J., Klami, A.: Discriminative clustering. Neurocomputing 69(1-3), 18–41 (2005)
25. Bishop, C.M.: Pattern Recognition and Machine Learning (Information Science and Statistics). Springer-Verlag New York, Inc., Secaucus (2006)
26. Uysal, I., Gövenir, H.A.: An overview of regression techniques for knowledge discovery. The Knowledge Engineering Review 14, 319–340 (1999)
27. Mozaffari, A., Azad, N.L.: Optimally pruned extreme learning machine with ensemble of regularization techniques and negative correlation penalty applied to automotive engine coldstart hydrocarbon emission identification. Neurocomputing (2013)

Hierarchical Combining of Classifiers in Privacy Preserving Data Mining

Piotr Andruszkiewicz

Institute of Computer Science, Warsaw University of Technology, Poland
P.Andruszkiewicz@ii.pw.edu.pl

Abstract. In privacy preserving classification there are several different types of classifiers with different parameters. We cannot point out the best type of classifiers and its default parameters. We propose the new solution in privacy preserving classification, namely a framework for combinig classifiers trained over data with preserved privacy - the hierarchical combining of classifiers. This solution enables a miner to obtain better results than those achieved with single classifiers.

1 Introduction

Randomisation-based techniques[1] give worse results than solutions without privacy. Furthermore, we cannot choose the best combination of reconstruction algorithms[2] for classification.

Due to many available combinations of reconstruction algorithms we used meta-learning for classification in privacy preserving data mining [3]. The next step in combining results of different classifiers is to create hierarchical classifiers that combine information from different types of classifiers.

Hence, we proposed the new framework for hierarchical combining of classifiers in privacy preserving classification for centralised data distorted with randomisation-based technique in this paper.

The remainder of this paper is organized as follows: Section 3 reviews the randomisation-based methods used in privacy preserving data mining over centralised data. In Section 4, we describe the elements of the privacy preserving classification algorithms which are important in the context of hierarchical combinig of classifiers. Then, in Section 5, we propose how to hierarchically combine privacy preserving classifiers. The experimental results are highlighted in Section 6. Finally, in Section 7, we summarise the conclusions of our study and outline future avenues to explore.

---

[1] For details about randomisation-based technique for continuous and nominal attributes see Section 3, [1], and [2].

[2] Combination of reconstruction algorithms in this paper means always a pair of algorithms for reconstruction of probability distribution, one for continuous attributes and second for nominal attributes.

M. Polycarpou et al. (Eds.): HAIS 2014, LNAI 8480, pp. 573–584, 2014.
© Springer International Publishing Switzerland 2014

2 Related Work

Privacy preserving classification covers various different approaches. As we consider privacy incorporated by randomisation-based techniques for centralised data, we mention only papers that are relevant to this scenario.

The first work that introduced privacy preserving classification task for (centralised) distorted data with privacy incorporated by means of the randomisation-based technique was [1]. It proposed how to build a decision tree over continuous data that was distorted by adding a noise (drawn from a given distribution). The next proposal of the reconstruction algorithm, which was the extension of the aforementioned one, was EM-based reconstruction algorithm. However, this algorithm does not take into account nominal attributes either.

The algorithms for continuous and nominal attributes modified using randomisation-based techniques was proposed in [2] and [4].

The eager approach to privacy preserving classification based on CAEP schema has been presented in [5]. It discovers emerging patterns by finding frequent sets, estimating their supports and selecting emerging patterns. To check the minimal support condition the procedure of estimating an n-itemset support described in [6] and the optimisation presented in [7] to reduce time complexity were used.

The lazy approach to privacy preserving classification has been proposed in [8]. The solution is based on DeEPs algorithm and applies probabilistic intersection of distorted values in order to create binary data.

In [3], meta-learning for decision tree classfiers has been presented. The description of ensembles classifiers and other hybrid methods can be found in [9] [10]. In this paper, we propose the solution for hierarchical combining of classifiers.

3 Randomisation-Based Methods Review

In this section we present the randomisation-based methods (perturbation), which are used to distort original values at random to incorporate a desired level of privacy. In the scheme that we consider, only distorted values are stored in a centralised database.

For nominal attributes we defined **P** matrix of retaining/changing values of an attribute [2] to cover the most general case.

Definition 1. ***P*** *is a matrix of retaining/changing values of a nominal attribute of order k x k:*

$$\mathbf{P} = \begin{pmatrix} a_{1,1} & a_{1,2} & a_{1,3} & \cdots & a_{1,k} \\ a_{2,1} & a_{2,2} & a_{2,3} & \cdots & a_{2,k} \\ \vdots & \vdots & \vdots & \ddots & \vdots \\ a_{k,1} & a_{k,2} & a_{k,3} & \cdots & a_{k,k} \end{pmatrix},$$

where $a_{r,p} = Pr(v_p \to v_r)$ is a probability that a value v_p will be changed to a value v_r and the sum of all elements in each column is equal to 1.

Values of a nominal attribute are distorted according to the probabilities from **P** matrix.

There are three main methods of distorting continuous attributes which do not assume any knowledge about values of attributes of other objects: the additive perturbation method [1], the multiplicative perturbation [11], and the retention replacement perturbation [12].

The *additive perturbation method* is also called *value distortion method* [1]. In this method a random value drawn from a given distribution, e.g., a uniform or normal distribution, is added to an original value of an attribute. Only a modified value is stored.

In the *multiplicative perturbation* an original value of an attribute is multiplied by a random value drawn from a given distribution [11]. In order to distort values of an object, the *rotation perturbation* [13], where the vector of values of attributes for a given object is multiplied by a rotation matrix, can also be used.

In the *retention replacement perturbation* [12], an original value of an attribute is kept with a probability p and with a probability $1 - p$ an original value is replaced with an element selected from a replacing probability distribution function (pdf) $g()$ on a domain of the attribute. The retention replacement perturbation where the replacing pdf is a uniform pdf is called a uniform perturbation.

For all presented randomisation-based methods, the only information a miner gets is a distorted database and parameters of the distorting method, e.g., for the retention replacement the parameters are: p and $g()$.

4 Sample Classifiers in Privacy Preserving Data Mining

We review the classifiers used in privacy preserving data mining that we use in hierarchical combining of classfiers.

4.1 Decision Tree

In the process of building a decision tree in privacy preserving data mining, the most important task, as in building a decision tree without preserving privacy, is to find the best test for a given node of a tree. However, having chosen the best test, we need to split training instances for a given node according to this test. In privacy preserving classification this task is not trivial because training instances are distorted. For more detail about building a decision tree over distorted data please refer to [2].

4.2 Eager Privacy Preserving Classifier with Emerging Patterns, ePPCwEP

In the eager learner schema in the ePPCwEP algorithm that we proposed in [5], EPs are mined once from a training data set and then are used to calculate a category for each test sample. The process of training the eager classifier based on EPs consists of two steps:

Algorithm 1. ePPCwEP, the eager Privacy Preserving Classifier with Emerging Patterns

```
input: 𝒟   // distorted training set (can contain binary, nominal and continuous
           // attributes)
input: 𝒮   // undistorted test set
input: minimumSupport
input: ρ   // threshold for growth rate
  // Training phase
  // 1. Discovering EPs
  transform all continuous and nominal attributes to binary attributes
  partition 𝒟 into 𝒟_i, i = 1, ..., k subsets according to the class labels C_i
  𝒟'_i is the opponent subset to 𝒟_i, 𝒟'_i = 𝒟 \ 𝒟_i, i = 1, ..., k
  for (i = 1; i < k; i++) do begin
    mine frequent sets with the estimated support greater than or equal to
      minimumSupport using MMASK [7] from 𝒟_i and 𝒟'_i
    store supports of frequent sets
    find EPs from 𝒟'_i to 𝒟_i with growth rate greater than or equal to the ρ threshold
       based on frequent sets
    // 2. Calculating statistics
    calculate the aggregate scores [5] for all training instances for class C_i
    calculate the base score baseScore(C_i) [5] for class C_i
  end
  // Testing phase
  for each test instance S ∈ 𝒮 do begin
    calculate aggregate and normalised score of S for each class C_i
    assign to S the class C_j for which S has the largest normalised score
  end
```

1. Discovering EPs.
2. Calculating statistics used for classification of test samples.

Having learned a classifier, a category for test samples is determined based on the statistics calculated during the training phase.

The entire process of building the eager classifier with emerging patterns and classifying a test set is shown in Algorithm 1. For more detail about the two steps of the training phase and the testing process please refer to [5]. Due to limited space, we discuss in this section only the most important to this paper elements of the algorithm.

In order to use nominal attributes in the presented algorithm, these attributes should be transformed into binary attributes and randomisation probabilities for transformed attributes should be also calculated.

We transform a nominal attribute A with k possible values to k binary attributes, A_1 to A_k, in the following way: an attribute A_i has the value of 1 when the attribute A is equal to the i-th value, otherwise the attribute A_i has the value of 0. After the transformation, the probabilities of retaining the original values of attributes need to be calculated. Two approaches to the distortion and probability calculation for nominal attributes are described in [5].

4.3 Lazy Privacy Preserving Classifier with Emerging Patterns, lPPCwEP

The lPPCwEP algorithm that we proposed in [8] utilises the lazy approach to classification and contains of three steps, which are repeated for each test sample:

1. Preparation of binary training data,
2. Discovery of emerging patterns,
3. Calculation of statistics and choice of a final category.

The entire process of classification of a test sample S is shown in Algorithm 2. For more detal please refer to [8]. Due to limited space, we present only the most important for this paper parts of the algorithm.

In order to create binary training data, we need to calculate P_{match} probability for each test sample and each attribute for each training sample.

Definition 2. *P_{match} probability for a test sample S and an attribute X for a training sample L is a probability that an original value of an attribute X for the training sample L matches a value of an attribute X in the test sample S given a value of a modified attribute Z for the training sample L, where the attribute Z is obtained by distorting values of the original attribute X.*

For those attributes and training samples with P_{match} probability greater then a given threshold p_{thr}[3], we assume 1 in the corresponding binary training data. Otherwise, we assign 0.

For a continuous attribute, we define P_{match} probability in the following way: let X be an original attribute and Z is a modified attribute. Let us assume that the attribute Z is equal to the distorted value z for a given training sample L and the value of the attribute X for a test sample S is equal to t.

To estimate P_{match} probability, a neighbourhood-based match with α parameter is used. P_{match} is the probability that an original value of the attribute X for the training sample L belongs to the α-neighbourhood $N(t, \alpha)$ of t given that the value of the distorted attribute Z is equal to z for the training sample L:

$$P_{match}(X \in N(t, \alpha)|Z = z) = P(X \geq t - \alpha \wedge X \leq t + \alpha|Z = z). \quad (1)$$

For more detail about calculation of P_{match} probabilities for continuous attributes distorted with the additive perturbation and nominal attributes please refer to [8].

4.4 Meta-learning in Privacy Preserving Classification

Meta-learning in privacy preserving classification builds several classifiers (in [3], decision tree classifiers were used) and calculates a final category by voiting. For more detail, please refer to [3].

[3] Details about the method of choosing a threshold probability p_{thr} can be found in Section 6.

Algorithm 2. lPPCwEP, the lazy Privacy Preserving Classifier with Emerging Patterns

```
input: D    // distorted training set (can contain binary, nominal and continuous
            // attributes)
input: S    // undistorted test sample
input: minimumSupport
input: ρ    // threshold for growth rate
input: p_thr   // threshold for P_match probability
  for (i = 1; i < k; i++) do begin     // k is the number of classes
    // Prepare binary training data
    D_i = {t ∈ D | t has the class label C_i}
    D'_i = D \ D_i     // D'_i is the opponent subset to D_i
    // transform the set D_i into the binary set B_i and D'_i into the binary set B'_i
    for each set D_i and D'_i do begin
      for each attribute and training sample do begin
       calculate P_match probability
       assign 1 to a binary attribute in either B_i or B'_i if P_match probability is greater
         than p_thr
       assign 0 otherwise
      end
    end
    // Discover emerging patterns
    mine frequent sets with the supports greater than or equal to minimumSupport
      from B_i and B'_i, separately
    store supports of frequent sets
    find EPs from B'_i to B_i with the growth rate greater than or equal to the ρ
       threshold based on frequent sets
    calculate the value of compact summation, that is, the number of samples
      which support at least one EP for a given class C_i
  end
  assign to the test sample S the class C_j for which S has the largest value of
    compact summation
```

5 Hierarchical Combining of Classifiers

In privacy preserving classification there are many available classifiers. Combining results of different classifiers can improve the classification quality. Moreover, there are groups of classfiers that are build on the similar basis. Thus, we want to combine results from different groups and then apply other classifier to make a decision based on results coming from different groups of classifiers. In order to apply, for example the aforementioned scenario, we propose the general framework of hierarchical combining classifiers in privacy preserving classification.

5.1 The Hierarchy

As in the end, we need a simple answer for a given sample, that is a category that a given sample belongs to, thus we assume that classifiers are organised in

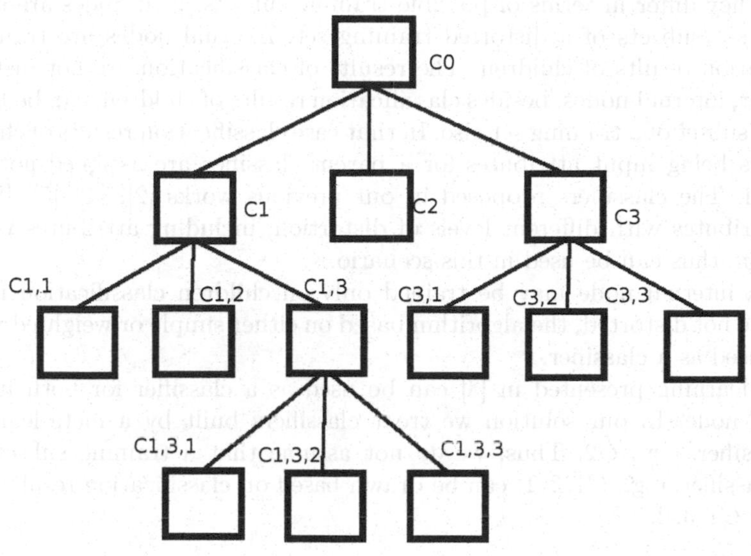

Fig. 1. The example hierarchy of classifiers

a tree. In the root of a tree, there is the last classifier that gives the final answer based on answers from lower level classifiers.

The sample hierarchy of classifiers is presented in Figure 1. A classifier is denoted as a rectangle. We define a classifier as an instance of a given type of classification algorithm, e.g., an instance of a decision tree classifier with given parameters, that is a given algorithm for nominal and continuous attributes distribution reconstruction[4]. The classifier $C0$ is a root classifier, which gives a final answer.

In Figure 1, on the third level we have 3 classifiers, $C1,3,1; C1,3,2; C1,3,3$. These classifiers pass their results to a classifier $C1,3$, which gives the result of classification based on its children results. For instance, classifiers $C1,3,1$; $C1,3,2$; $C1,3,3$ give the following results Y, Y, N (we assume binary classification with Y and N classes). Based on that answers, the classifier $C1,3$ gives the answer Y. $C1,3$ classifier could be a decision tree, Naïve Bayes or even the algorighm based on simple voiting. Classifiers $C1,1; C1,2; C1,3$ constitute the next subtree of classifiers that pass their results to a classifier $C1$. Another subtree consists of $C3,1$; $C3,2$; $C3,3$ classifiers. A classifier $C3$ gives answers based on these classifiers' results. The classifiers from the first level, namely $C1$; $C2$; $C3$ pass their results to the root classifier that gives the final answer.

[4] For more details on algorithms for nominal and continuous attributes distribution reconstruction please refer to [2] and [4].

In the hierarchy, we distinguish two type of nodes: internal nodes and leaf nodes. They differ in terms of possible training subsets. Leaf nodes are trained only on set/subsets of a distorted training set. Internal nodes are trained on classification results of children. The results of classification are not distorted. Moreover, internal nodes, besides classification results of children, can be trained on a set/subset of a training set also. In that case classification results of chilldren classifiers being input attributes for a parent classifier are assigned not to be distorted. The classifiers proposed in our previous works [2], [4], [5], [8] deal with attributes with different levels of distortion, including attributes without distortion, thus can be used in this scenario.

As an internal node may be trained only on children classification results, which are not distorted, the algorithm based on either simple or weighted voiting can be used as a classifier.

Meta-learning presented in [3] can be used as a classifier for both internal and leaf node. In our solution we treat classifiers built by a meta-learner as one classifier, e.g., $C2$. Thus, we do not assume that a training subset for a given classifier, e.g., $C1,3,1$, can be drawn based on classification results of the classifier $C1,3,2$.

6 Experimental Evaluation

This section presents the results of the experiments conducted according to the proposed framework for hierarchical combination of classifiers.

All sets used in our tests can be downloaded from UCI Machine Learning Repository [14]. We used the following sets: *Australian*, *Breast*, *Diabetes*, *Wine*, chosen under the following conditions: at least one set should contain only continuous attributes (e.g., *Diabetes*), at least one set should contain both continuous and nominal attributes (e.g., *Australian*), and at least one of the sets should have a class attribute with multiple values (*Wine*).

In all experiments, we distorted all attributes for a training data set except for a class/target attribute. In order to count supports of itemsets in the eager approach based on EPs, the modified estimation with *reductionTreshold* equal to 3 (empirically chosen) was applied (for details about the estimation procedure please refer to [7]). In order to determine base scores, 75% threshold was set for the eager classifier based on EPs.

In the lazy classifier based on EPs, the reconstruction and calculation of the probability P_{match} for nominal and continuous attributes were performed using only samples with the same class as a training sample, because the empirical results confirmed this was the better approach. Also based on empirical results, we assumed α to be 0 in the interval-based neighbourhood (it means that only an interval within which a value of a given attribute for a test sample lies is treated as a neighbourhood). For nominal attributes, the probability threshold p_{thr} was set as equal to the probability that an original value would be retained. For continuous attributes the probability threshold p_{thr} was chosen arbitrarily.

As a decision tree, we used SPRINT [15] modified to incorporate privacy according to [1,2].

Table 1. The results of classification with the hierarchical combination of classifiers (denoted as h10b), the lazy JEP classifier with the minimal support equal to 0.05, and the decision tree (DT)

Set	Alg.	Priv. [%]	Accuracy	Sensitivity	Specificity	Precision	F	Time [s]
Australian	h10b	100	0.8503	0.8388	0.8598	0.8328	0.8321	23.324
		150	0.8417	0.8350	0.8465	0.8182	0.8227	31.489
		200	0.7552	0.6758	0.8176	0.7574	0.7019	41.223
Australian	lPPCwEP	100	0.7972	0.8235	0.7758	0.7542	0.7807	7.094
		150	0.7797	0.8838	0.6962	0.7086	0.7810	6.401
		200	0.6925	0.8021	0.6036	0.6279	0.6947	4.060
Australian	DT	100	0.8160	0.7866	0.8397	0.8017	0.7902	0.088
		150	0.7702	0.7258	0.8050	0.7537	0.7340	0.100
		200	0.6147	0.4678	0.7328	0.5940	0.5117	0.141
Breast	h10b	100	0.9369	0.8779	0.9708	0.9548	0.9122	12.731
		150	0.9444	0.9103	0.9624	0.9397	0.9223	13.719
		200	0.9390	0.8779	0.9735	0.9603	0.9144	14.292
Breast	lPPCwEP	100	0.9385	0.8879	0.9647	0.9396	0.9109	0.610
		150	0.8918	0.7422	0.9691	0.9442	0.8261	0.691
		200	0.9389	0.9056	0.9512	0.9191	0.9094	0.690
Breast	DT	100	0.9262	0.8552	0.9656	0.9416	0.8925	0.019
		150	0.9258	0.8711	0.9545	0.9191	0.8891	0.015
		200	0.9259	0.8550	0.9647	0.9405	0.8908	0.017
Diabetes	h10b	100	0.7333	0.8594	0.4954	0.7581	0.8038	17.307
		150	0.7201	0.8463	0.4832	0.7512	0.7935	19.280
		200	0.7086	0.8525	0.4377	0.7367	0.7880	20.251
Diabetes	lPPCwEP	100	0.6836	0.7152	0.6182	0.7819	0.7394	0.594
		150	0.6121	0.5391	0.7459	0.8102	0.6285	0.613
		200	0.6506	0.6998	0.5608	0.7574	0.7084	0.711
Diabetes	DT	100	0.6951	0.8212	0.4591	0.7375	0.7742	0.048
		150	0.6762	0.7783	0.4882	0.7382	0.7532	0.048
		200	0.6787	0.8045	0.4477	0.7286	0.7606	0.046
Wine	h10b	100	0.8196	0.9245	0.9314	0.6601	0.6190	6.626
		150	0.8220	0.9254	0.9339	0.6329	0.5880	7.253
		200	0.8307	0.9293	0.9354	0.6524	0.6146	7.940
Wine	lPPCwEP	100	0.6598	0.8601	0.8716	0.5330	0.4593	0.120
		150	0.5798	0.8251	0.8380	0.5903	0.4826	0.126
		200	0.6152	0.8366	0.8523	0.5971	0.5029	0.138
Wine	DT	100	0.7751	0.9080	0.9149	0.6323	0.5818	0.068
		150	0.5396	0.8164	0.8365	0.6496	0.4823	0.042
		200	0.5494	0.8196	0.8346	0.6586	0.5074	0.046

In the experiments, accuracy, sensitivity, specificity, precision and F-measure were calculated (for definitions please refer to [16]). To achieve more reliable results, we applied 10-fold *cross-validation* [5] and calculated the average of 50 multiple runs.

Table 1 shows the accuracy, sensitivity, specificity, precision, and F-measure (F) for the hierarchical combination of classifiers (denoted as h10b), the lazy JEP classifier with the minimal support equal to 0.05[5], and the decision tree for different privacy levels (Priv. [%]).

In order to define *Range Privacy* [3] we used in the experiments, we introduce *differential entropy* [17].

Definition 3. Differential entropy of a random variable A *is:*
$h(A) = - \int_{\Omega_A} f_A(a) \log_2 f_A(a) da$,
where Ω_A *is a domain of a variable* A *and* f_A *is a density function of a variable* A.

Definition 4. Privacy (level) inherent in a random variable A *is:*
$\Pi(A) = 2^{h(A)}$,
where $h(A)$ *is the* differential entropy *of variable* A.

A random variable A distributed uniformly between 0 and a has privacy (level) equal to a. For general random variable C, $\Pi(C)$ denotes the length of the interval over which a uniformly distributed random variable has the same privacy as C.

n% Range Privacy for a random variable A means that we use a distorting random variable Y with privacy measured according to the definition based on differential entropy equal to $n\%$ of the domain range of values of the random variable A, for instance, to achieve 100% level of privacy for a random variable A with the range of its values equal to 10, a distorting random variable Y should have privacy measure equal to 10 (e.g., for the uniform distribution, a random variable distributed between -5 and 5 can be used).

The hierarchical combination of classifiers (denoted as h10b) consists of:

1. lPPCwEP classifier
2. 8 decision trees combined by a simple voter classifier: 4 (combinations of nominal and continuous attributes distribution reconstruction algorithms[6]) * 2 (types of reconstruction - Local, ByClass[7])
3. set of classifiers built according to meta-learning approach with the following number of classifiers: 5 * 2 (bagging, boosting [3]) * 2 (types of reconstruction - Local, ByClass) * 4 (combinations of nominal and continuous attributes distribution reconstruction algorithms)
4. ePPCwEP classifier

[5] We have not presented the results of ePPCwEP algorithm as they were worse than the results of lPPCwEP algorithm.

[6] For more information on nominal and continuous attributes distribution reconstruction algorithms please refer to [2] and [4].

[7] For details about reconstruction types please refer to [1].

The above classifiers were combined by the simple voter.

We empirically have chosen the following parameters to obtain the best accuracy of classification. Thus, for the lazy approach, the JEP classifier with the minimal support equal to 0.05 was used and for the eager EP classifier the following parameters were applied: the minimal support threshold equal to 0.2 and the minimal growth rate equal to 2. For the eager approach to classification, continuous attributes were discretised after distortion into 5 bins with equal number of samples.

Comparing the results of the hierarchical combination of classifiers with lPPCwEP and decision tree classifiers (Table 1) we can notice that the hierarchical combination achieved better results for F-measure for all cases. For accuracy, the hierarchical combination performed better but one case, *Breast* for privacy level equal to 100%. However, the difference is less than 0.5%. Considering precision and specificity for the cases where the hierarchical combination performed worse than the remaining classifier(s), the significant differences are for *Diabetes*. Nevertheless, sensitivity (also called recall) is so high that F-measure is the highest for the hierarchical combination. For sensitivity, the hierarchical combination performed worse 4 times, twice for *Australian* and twice for *Breast*. Though, precision for these cases is so high that F-measure is the highest for the hierarchical combination.

The time of training and testing for the hierarchical combination is the highest because we train more classifiers. Although, the time is higher, the significant overhead is in the training phase. The process of classification takes also longer, nonetheless it is significantly smaller then time of training and does not have such the influence in real applications.

7 Conclusions and Future Work

In this paper, we proposed the new framework for hierarchical combining of classifiers in privacy preserving classification. The proposed hierarchical combination of classifiers framework for privacy preserving classification enabled a miner to combine information from different classifiers and achieve better results than simple classifiers. We experimentally tested the proposed framework and showed that the hierarchical combination of classifiers can perform better than separate classifiers.

In future works, we plan to use also distorted training subset for internal classifiers and check different than voters ans decision tree classifiers for internal nodes. Moreover, we plan to parallelise the process of training and classifying in order to reduce time complexity of the presented solution.

References

1. Agrawal, R., Srikant, R.: Privacy-preserving data mining. In: Chen, W., Naughton, J.F., Bernstein, P.A. (eds.) ACM SIGMOD Conference, pp. 439–450 (2000)
2. Andruszkiewicz, P.: Privacy preserving classification for continuous and nominal attributes. In: Proceedings of the 16th International Conference on Intelligent Information Systems (2008)

3. Andruszkiewicz, P.: Classification with meta-learning in privacy preserving data mining. In: Chen, L., Liu, C., Liu, Q., Deng, K. (eds.) DASFAA 2009. LNCS, vol. 5667, pp. 261–275. Springer, Heidelberg (2009)
4. Andruszkiewicz, P.: Probability distribution reconstruction for nominal attributes in privacy preserving classification. In: ICHIT 2008: Proceedings of the 2008 International Conference on Convergence and Hybrid Information Technology, pp. 494–500. IEEE Computer Society, Washington, DC (2008)
5. Andruszkiewicz, P.: Privacy preserving classification with emerging patterns. In: Saygin, Y., Yu, J.X., Kargupta, H., Wang, W., Ranka, S., Yu, P.S., Wu, X. (eds.) ICDM Workshops, pp. 100–105. IEEE Computer Society (2009)
6. Rizvi, S.J., Haritsa, J.R.: Maintaining data privacy in association rule mining. In: VLDB 2002: Proceedings of the 28th International Conference on Very Large Data Bases, pp. 682–693. VLDB Endowment (2002)
7. Andruszkiewicz, P.: Optimization for MASK scheme in privacy preserving data mining for association rules. In: Kryszkiewicz, M., Peters, J.F., Rybiński, H., Skowron, A. (eds.) RSEISP 2007. LNCS (LNAI), vol. 4585, pp. 465–474. Springer, Heidelberg (2007)
8. Andruszkiewicz, P.: Lazy approach to privacy preserving classification with emerging patterns. In: Ryżko, D., Rybiński, H., Gawrysiak, P., Kryszkiewicz, M. (eds.) Emerging Intelligent Technologies in Industry. SCI, vol. 369, pp. 253–268. Springer, Heidelberg (2011)
9. Abraham, A.: Special issue: Hybrid approaches for approximate reasoning. Journal of Intelligent and Fuzzy Systems 23(2-3), 41–42 (2012)
10. Corchado, E., Wozniak, M., Abraham, A., de Carvalho, A.C.P.L.F., Snásel, V.: Recent trends in intelligent data analysis. Neurocomputing 126, 1–2 (2014)
11. Kim, J.J., Winkler, W.E.: Multiplicative noise for masking continuous data. Technical report, Statistical Research Division, US Bureau of the Census, Washington D.C. (2003)
12. Agrawal, R., Srikant, R., Thomas, D.: Privacy preserving olap. In: SIGMOD 2005: Proceedings of the 2005 ACM SIGMOD International Conference on Management of Data, pp. 251–262. ACM, New York (2005)
13. Chen, K., Liu, L.: Privacy preserving data classification with rotation perturbation. In: ICDM, pp. 589–592. IEEE Computer Society (2005)
14. Asuncion, A., Newman, D.J.: UCI machine learning repository (2007)
15. Shafer, J.C., Agrawal, R., Mehta, M.: Sprint: A scalable parallel classifier for data mining. In: Vijayaraman, T.M., Buchmann, A.P., Mohan, C., Sarda, N.L. (eds.) Proceedings of 22th International Conference on Very Large Data Bases, VLDB 1996, Mumbai (Bombay), India, September 3-6, pp. 544–555. Morgan Kaufmann (1996)
16. van Rijsbergen, C.J.: Information Retrieval. Butterworth-Heinemann, Newton (1979)
17. Agrawal, D., Aggarwal, C.C.: On the design and quantification of privacy preserving data mining algorithms. In: PODS 2001: Proceedings of the Twentieth ACM SIGMOD-SIGACT-SIGART Symposium on Principles of Database Systems, pp. 247–255. ACM, New York (2001)

Classification Rule Mining with Iterated Greedy

Juan A. Pedraza[1], Carlos García-Martínez[2],
Alberto Cano[2], and Sebastián Ventura[2]

[1] I+D Dpt., Yerbabuena Software,
Málaga 29590, España
jantpedraza@gmail.com
[2] Dpt. of Computing and Numerical Analysis, University of Córdoba,
Córdoba 14071, España
{cgarcia,acano,sventura}@uco.es

Abstract. In the context of data mining, *classification rule discovering* is the task of designing accurate rule based systems that model the useful knowledge that differentiate some data classes from others, and is present in large data sets.

Iterated greedy search is a powerful metaheuristic, successfully applied to different optimisation problems, which to our knowledge, has not previously been used for classification rule mining.

In this work, we analyse the convenience of using iterated greedy algorithms for the design of rule classification systems. We present and study different alternatives and compare the results with state-of-the-art methodologies from the literature. The results show that iterated greedy search may generate accurate rule classification systems with acceptable interpretability levels.

Keywords: Classification rule mining, iterated greedy, interpretability.

1 Introduction

Data mining [1] involves the use of data analysis tools to discover useful knowledge from large data sets. Classification is a form of data analysis that extracts models describing important data classes by means of their properties. Classification has been successfully applied to several fields such as medical diagnosis or credit risk evaluation, among others, by means of several approaches of very different nature, for instance, artificial neural networks, support vector machines, or instance-based techniques [2].

Rule-based systems [3] are a representation paradigm that models the knowledge of a specific area of interest by means of sets of rules with an antecedent and one consequent. When applied to classification problems, the antecedents of the rules define some property relations, which are oftenly present in particular sets of patterns, and the consequents emit predictions of the class they belong. Comprehensibility is one of the benefits that rule-based systems possess and have lately attracted the attention of the research community [4,5,6,7].

M. Polycarpou et al. (Eds.): HAIS 2014, LNAI 8480, pp. 585–596, 2014.
© Springer International Publishing Switzerland 2014

Iterated greedy search (IG) is a simple yet effective metaheuristic that has been successfully applied to different combinatorial problems [8,9,10,11,12]. IG explores the solution search space by iterating over a greedy process applied to a single solution and composed by two main phases: *destruction* and *construction.* During the destruction phase, some solutions components are removed, producing a partial solution. Afterwards, the construction phase applies a greedy heuristic to complete this partial solution.

To our knowledge, IG has not previously been applied to the design of rule-based classification systems. In this work, we are interested in analysing the possibility and benefits of generating rule classification systems according to the iterative IG framework. Consequently, we address it as a combinatorial problem where a solution represents a rule based system and undergoes through an iterative process of destruction and construction.

The rest of this work is structured as follows. In Section 2, we address the adaptation of the IG metaheuristic to the problem of generating good rule classification systems. In Section 3, we present several empirical studies aimed at: 1) analysing the influence of the parameters and settings associated with the method that provide accurate rule classification systems, and 2) comparing the resulting IG algorithm for classification rule mining (IG-RMiner) with other prominent approaches from the literature in terms of accuracy and interpretability. Finally, in Section 4, we discuss conclusions and future work.

2 An IG Model for Rule Mining

In this section, we describe our adaptation of the IG model for rule mining. The main framework is presented in Section 2.1, and the alternatives for the construction phase, in Section 2.2.

2.1 General Scheme of the IG for Rule Mining

Figure 1 depicts the outline of our IG metaheuristic for classification rule mining (IG-RMiner). It starts from a single initial solution, a rule-based classification system, generated from scratch by an heuristic construction procedure (steps 1-3; Section 2.2). Afterwards, it iterates through a main loop in which first, a partial solution S_d is obtained at the destruction phase (step 5), and second, a complete candidate solution S_c is reconstructed by applying the same construction procedure to S_d (step 6). A pruning phase is added to improve the constructed solution, if possible (step 7). Before continuing with the next iteration, an acceptance criterion decides whether the solution returned by the pruning phase, S_p, becomes the new current solution (step 11). The process iterates until some termination conditions have been met (e.g. maximum number of iterations, or maximum computation time allotted). The best solution, S_b, generated during the iterative process is kept as the overall result.

The specific features of the IG-RMiner are:

```
Input:
 Greedy-construction(·): Greedy construction procedure
 Acceptance-criterion(·,·): Acceptance criterion
 Stop-condition: Stop condition
 pd: Probability for removing conditions
Output:   Sb: Best solution generated
Sd ← ∅;
S ← Greedy-construction(Sd);
Sb ← S;
while Stop-condition is not reached do
   Sd ←destruction(S, pd);
   Sc ← Greedy-construction(Sd);
   Sp ← pruning(Sc);
   if Sp is better than Sb then
      Sb ← Sp;
   end
   S ← Acceptance-criterion(S, Sp);
end
return Sb;
```

Fig. 1. Pseudocode of the IG-RMiner model

- The method starts with an empty solution with one rule per class and no conditions in their antecedents. When classifying a new pattern, conflicts are resolved according to the rule with higher accuracy.
- The heuristic construction procedure intents to improve the quality of the rules by appending new conditions, one by one, to their antecedents. Section 2.2 specifies the analysed alternatives for selecting the rule to be improved, the condition to be added, and the quality measure to be considered. This phase iterates until there is not any other condition able to improve the quality measure.
- The standard destruction mechanism of IG removes a percentage of random components of the current solution. In our case, the destruction removes a percentage of conditions from some rules, at random.
- The pruning phase revises the conditions in the antecedents of the rules checking whether their individual extraction might improve the global accuracy of the system. If this is the case, the revised condition is removed. This situation may occur, for instance, when the construction phase has included several conditions in the rules step by step, but the last included ones interfere with some others previously inserted.
- Two acceptance criteria, commonly applied in standard IGs, have been studied in this work: replace if and only if the new solution is better than the current one (RB - replace if better) [13], and replace always (RA) [9,14,15].

This latter produces higher diversification in the search process carried out by the algorithm.
- The rule based system that is returned at the end is the one with the highest percentage of correctly classified patterns.

2.2 Construction Phase

Given a partial solution, i.e., a rule system, with some conditions in the antecedents of its rules, this phase intends to improve the quality of the system and/or its rules by iteratively appending new conditions, until no condition producing an improvement is found. To carry out this goal, we have identified three task to be addressed, and analysed different strategies for each one:

Selection of the rule to be improved: We have studied the performance gained when the algorithm tries to optimise either the rule with the lowest accuracy (LAR - lowest accuracy rule) or a randomly selected one (RR - random rule).

Selection of the condition to be inserted: Once the rule has been selected, the set of compatible conditions (those that do not contradict the current antecedent of the rule) is examined. The grammar in Figure 2 specifies the possible conditions to be generated. Then, two strategies are analysed:

- *Best improvement* (BI): This strategy appends the condition that yields the best improvement in the rule, if this condition exists.
- *First improvement* (FI): This strategy scans through the compatible conditions, in a random order, and chooses the first one that improves the quality of the rule, if this condition exists.

Evaluation of the quality improvement: We have studied three quality criteria to evaluate whether the insertion of one condition in the antecedent of the selected rule is or is not favourable (only one at a time):

$$\begin{aligned}
&\langle S\rangle \rightarrow \langle \mathit{condition}\rangle \\
&\langle \mathit{condition}\rangle \rightarrow \langle \mathit{op_num}\rangle\langle \mathit{var_num}\rangle\langle \mathit{value}\rangle \\
&\langle \mathit{condition}\rangle \rightarrow \langle \mathit{op_nom}\rangle\langle \mathit{var_cat}\rangle\langle \mathit{value}\rangle \\
&\langle \mathit{op_num}\rangle \rightarrow \leq \mid \geq \\
&\langle \mathit{op_cat}\rangle \rightarrow = \mid \neq \\
&\langle \mathit{var_num}\rangle \rightarrow \text{Any valid numerical attribute in data set} \\
&\langle \mathit{var_cat}\rangle \rightarrow \text{Any valid categorical attribute in data set} \\
&\langle \mathit{value}\rangle \rightarrow \text{Any valid corresponding value}
\end{aligned}$$

Fig. 2. Grammar used to create single attribute-value conditions

- *Global accuracy Improvement with penalisation for errors* (GI): This measure is defined as the percentage of correctly classified patterns minus the percentage of incorrectly classified ones. Initial experiments reported poor results if only the percentage of correctly classified patterns was evaluated, so this correction was analysed in the study. According to this criterion, new accepted conditions necessarily result in an accuracy improvement of the rule classification system, and no condition that reduced the global accuracy, with regard to the current state, would be inserted.
- *Rule accuracy Improvement* (RI): Rule accuracy is defined as the percentage of patterns correctly classified by the rule, i.e., those covered by its antecedent that belong to the predicted class (true positives - TP) and those not covered that belong to a different class (true negatives - TN) (Equation 1; NP is the number of patterns). This metric is the common accuracy measure for binary classification [16,17]. According to this, new conditions result in an accuracy improvement of the rule, but not necessarily of the global system. Even though, the iterative alternation between construction and destruction phases of IG, with the intention of getting accurate rules, might produce more accurate systems. That is the reason why this criterion is studied.
- *Sensitivity-Specificity Multiplication* (SS): Given a binary classifier (for instance, one rule of our system), its sensitivity is defined as the percentage of correctly classified positive patterns (Equation 2); and its specificity is the percentage of correctly classified negative patterns (Equation 3). Both measures should be maximised. Then, the quality of the condition to be inserted is evaluated as the improvement on the multiplication of both metrics, as it is done in other works [4,18].

$$\text{Rule accuracy} = \frac{TP + TN}{NP} \tag{1}$$

$$\text{Sensitivity} = \frac{TP}{TP + FN} \tag{2}$$

$$\text{Specifity} = \frac{TN}{TN + FP} \tag{3}$$

Therefore, up to 12 combinations of decision strategies for the construction phase, shown in Table 1, are analysed in this work. For instance, the combination referred to by RR-FI-RI accepts the first condition that appended to a randomly chosen rule, improves the accuracy of that rule.

3 Experiments

We have implemented the different IG-RMiner versions in Weka [19] and performed experiments on an Intel Core i7-930 quad-core 2.80GHz computer with 12GB RAM (only one thread per run). Table 2 shows the characteristics of the used 22 datasets from the UCI [20].

Table 1. Construction strategies combinations

			Quality evaluation		
			GI	RI	SS
Rule / Condition	LAR	BI	1. LAR-BI-GI	2. LAR-BI-RI	3. LAR-BI-SS
		FI	4. LAR-FI-GI	5. LAR-FI-RI	6. LAR-FI-SS
	RR	BI	7. RR-BI-GI	8. RR-BI-RI	9. RR-BI-SS
		FI	10. RR-FI-GI	11. RR-FI-RI	12. RR-FI-SS

Table 2. Used datasets

Name	# Patterns	# Attributes	#Classes
1.Australian	690	14	2
2.Balance-scale	625	4	3
3.Breast-cancer	286	9	2
4.Bupa	345	6	2
5.Car	1728	6	4
6.Chess	3196	36	2
7.Contraceptive	1473	9	3
8.Dermatology	366	34	6
9.Flare 2	1066	11	6
10.German	1000	20	2
11.Haberman	306	3	2
12.Ionosphere	351	33	2
13.Iris	150	4	3
14.Lymph	148	18	4
15.Page-blocks	5472	10	5
16.Segment-challenge	2310	19	7
17.Sonar	208	60	2
18.Tae	151	5	3
19.Thyroid	7200	21	3
20.Tic-tac-toe	958	9	2
21.Vehicle	846	18	4
22.Zoo	101	16	7

Non-parametric tests have been used to compare the results of different algorithms or instances [21]. Specifically, we have considered two alternative methods to analyse the experimental results:

- *Iman and Davenport's test* [22] and *Holm's method* [23] as a post hoc procedure. The first test is used to see whether there are significant statistical differences among the results of a certain group of classifiers. If differences are detected, then, Holm's test is employed to compare the best classifier (control classifier) with the remaining ones.
- *Wilcoxon matched-pairs signed-ranks test* [24], which compares the results of two algorithms directly.

In Section 3.1, we address the setting and election of the parameters and decision strategies of IG-RMiner that result in better classifiers. In Section 3.2, we compare the characteristics of the best IG-RMiner instance with regards to state-of-the-art classification techniques.

3.1 Parameter Tuning

Here, we intend to find the combinations, under a full factory design, of acceptance criteria ({RB,RA}), construction components combination (Table 1), and percentage of destructed conditions ($p_d \in \{10\%, 25\%, 50\%\}$) of IG-RMiner, that capacitate it to generate classifiers with high accuracy. The algorithm instances are tested using 5-fold cross-validation on the data sets aforementioned with 5, 50 and 120 seconds as stop conditions for data sets with less than 10, 30, or more attributes, respectively (which are values comparable to those of some algorithms in the following section).

Table 3 shows the mean accuracy levels reached by the best ten IG-RMiner instances (out of 72) on 5 independent runs and all the data sets, together with their mean ranking values. Though Holm's procedure did not find significant differences between the best ranked variant and many others, we observe some commonalities among the best instances:

Table 3. Avg. accuracy, mean ranking and Holm's test on the IG-RMiner variants

IG-RMiner instance	Accuracy	Ranking
IG-RMiner(50%,RR-BI-SS,RA)	**78.2309**	**11.2500**
IG-RMiner(50%,RR-FI-RI,RA)	77.6537	12.1818
IG-RMiner(50%,RR-FI-SS,RA)	77.7715	12.7500
IG-RMiner(50%,RR-BI-RI,RA)	76.9077	15.5455
IG-RMiner(25%,RR-BI-SS,RA)	76.1675	16.8864
IG-RMiner(25%,RR-FI-SS,RA)	76.2823	17.5455
IG-RMiner(25%,RR-FI-RI,RA)	75.9686	18.1136
IG-RMiner(50%,LAR-FI-SS,RA)	72.4367	19.1591
IG-RMiner(50%,LAR-FI-RI,RA)	71.4831	20.4773
IG-RMiner(25%,LAR-FI-SS,RA)	73.0086	20.5000
...	...	...

- All the best variants iterate always from the most recent solution, replacing always the current solution (RA), instead of from the best one.
- Seven variants, the best ranked ones, select a random rule to be improved at the construction phase (RR), not the one with lowest accuracy. On the contrary, there does not seem to exist a clear preference for the condition to be inserted (BI or FI), nor the quality criterion to be evaluated. Regarding this latter, no algorithm between these ten variants considers the global accuracy improvement (GI).
- Most the variants, and the ones in better positions, destroy 50% of the conditions of the rule system per iteration.

Having noticed that the best ranked algorithm, IG-RMiner(50%,RR-BI-SS, RA), satisfies all of previous conclusions, we will compare it with other significant classification techniques in terms of accuracy, interpretability and learning time. From now on, this instance will be referred to by just IG-RMiner.

3.2 Comparison with Salient Classification Techniques

In this Section, we compare IG-RMiner with 10 other significant classification techniques, covering among others, evolutionary based techniques, ant colony optimization, fuzzy rule systems, and classic decision tree generators: ICRM [4], MPLCS [25], ILGA [26], CORE [27], SLAVE [28], GFS-GP [29], DTGA [30], AntMiner+ [31], RIPPER [32], C45R [33]. In particular, ICRM recently proved to be able to generate sufficiently accurate and easily interpretable rule classification systems. In this study, we will analyse the reached accuracy levels of the algorithms, the consumed computation time, and several measures that assess how interpretable the generated systems are, namely, the number of rules, number of conditions (global and mean per rule), and complexity metric [34]. This latter computes the ratio between the number of classes covered and conditions of the rule system (Equation 4):

$$\text{complexity} = \frac{m}{\sum_{i=1}^{r} n_i} \tag{4}$$

where m is the number of classes, r is the number of rules, and n_i is the number of conditions used in the ith rule. This measure returns the value 1 when

Table 4. Algorithms' ranking values per performance measure

Accuracy		Time		#Rules	
MPLCS	3.08	**IG-RMiner**	**3.04**	**IG-RMiner**	**2.48**
DTGA	4.42	C45R	3.29	ICRM	2.56
IG-RMiner	**4.46**	RIPPER	3.56	**CORE*	*3.79*
C45R	4.88	DTGA	4.29	**SLAVE*	*4.63*
ICRM	5.08	**ICRM*	*4.5*	**AntMin+*	*4.65*
RIPPER	5.46	**AntMin+*	*7.1*	**MPLCS*	*5.06*
AntMin+	6.96	**SLAVE*	*7.46*	**C45R*	*7.04*
ILGA	7.67	**MPLCS*	*7.75*	**RIPPER*	*8.13*
SLAVE	7.73	**GFS-GP*	*7.96*	**ILGA*	*8.5*
GFS-GP	7.9	**CORE*	*8.33*	**DTGA*	*8.71*
**CORE*	*8.38*	**ILGA*	*8.71*	**GFS-GP*	*10.46*

#Conds		#Conds/#Rules		Complexity	
**ICRM*	*1.79*	**ICRM*	*1.9*	**ICRM*	*1.43*
IG-RMiner	**3.92**	SLAVE	5.17	**IG-RMiner**	**3.32**
CORE	4.38	CORE	5.29	**CORE*	*4.26*
SLAVE	4.52	AntMin+	5.33	AntMin+	4.56
AntMin+	4.56	C45R	5.58	**MPLCS*	*5.02*
**MPLCS*	*5.25*	MPLCS	6,08	SLAVE	6.06
**C45R*	*6.29*	**IG-RMiner**	**6.19**	**C45R*	*6.23*
**RIPPER*	*7.33*	RIPPER	6.29	**RIPPER*	*7.43*
**DTGA*	*8.75*	GFS-GP	7.31	**DTGA*	*8.58*
**ILGA*	*9.04*	**DTGA*	*7.81*	**ILGA*	*8.97*
**GFS-GP*	*10.17*	**ILGA*	*9.04*	**GFS-GP*	*10.08*

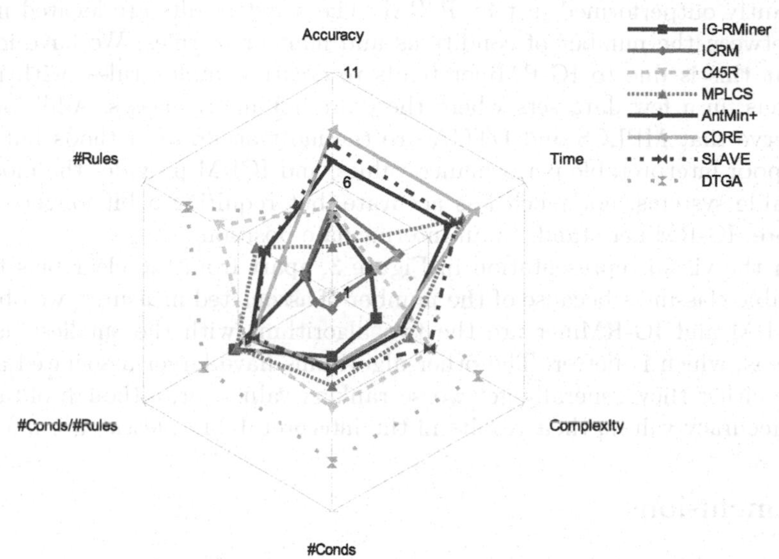

Fig. 3. Algorithms' rankings per performance measure. RIPPER, ILGA, GFS-GP are not represented to make the graph clearer, because they did not get better ranking values than IG-RMiner in neither accuracy nor any interpretability metric

the classifier contains one rule per class using only one condition each and it approaches 0 if there are more rules and conditions. If there are less rules than classes or there exists a default rule without conditions, this measure can be higher. In any case, we have limited the result to 2 times the number of classes.

For these experiments, IG-RMiner was tested using 10-fold cross-validation, the time limits showed in [4] for ICRM, and 5 independent runs. This setting is in accordance with the experimentation in [4], from where the results of previous algorithms were obtained.

Table 4 and Figure 3 summarise the results. The former shows the algorithms and their mean ranking values ordered, over all the datasets and runs, per performance measure. Statistical performance differences between IG-RMiner and the corresponding algorithm according to the Wilcoxon's test and 5% as significance factor are presented in italics with the character '*' at the beginning. IG-RMiner is highlighted in boldface for reference purposes. When IG-RMiner appears higher in the table, that means that IG-RMiner is statistically better than the corresponding algorithm, and vice versa. More detailed results can be consulted at http://www.uco.es/grupos/kdis/kdiswiki/index.php/IG-RMiner.

From the results in Table 4, we can see that IG-RMiner is able to generate accurate rule classification systems very fast, because it is among the best algorithms with regards to accuracy and time and the Wilcoxon's test does not find significant differences with regards to the best one. Additionally, IG-RMiner obtains competitive results in the interpretability performance measures, being significantly outperformed just by ICRM. The worst results are located in the ratio between the number of conditions and number of rules. We have identified that this is due to IG-RMiner tends to create complex rules, with many conditions, in a few data sets where there are not many classes. Additionally, we observe that MPLCS and DTGA are the most accurate methods but they obtain poor interpretable performance values, and ICRM provides the most interpretable systems, not much less accurate, but requiring a bit longer times. Therefore, IG-RMiner stands in an intermediate position.

From the visual representation in Figure 3, apart from the clear bias to interpretable classifiers because of the number of associated measures, we observe that ICRM and IG-RMiner are the two algorithms with the smallest associated areas, which is better. The other algorithms have larger associated areas, because either they generally get worse ranking values, or, although obtaining better accuracy values, their results in the interpretability metrics are inferior.

4 Conclusions

We have studied the application of the IG metaheuristic to the problem of designing rule classification systems. Different alternatives have been tested for the construction phase and acceptation criterion of the IG. The result is a technique that constructs accurate rule classification systems with acceptable interpretability levels, with regards to 10 other methodologies from the literature on 22 data sets from the UCI. In particular, the obtained IG-RMiner algorithm iterates through a process in which conditions are randomly destroyed and inserted into the antecedents of random rules to enhance their sensitivity and specificity values.

In our opinion, this line of research is worthy of further studies. We intend to explore the following avenues of research: 1) to include some interpretability criteria in the search process of IG-RMiner in order to obtain even simpler rule classification systems without a drastic undesirable effect on their accuracy levels; and 2) to analyse the application of IG adaptations to other data mining problems, such as rule association mining [35].

Acknowledgments. This work was supported by the research projects TIN2011-22408 and TIN2012-37930-C02-01.

References

1. Witten, I.H., Frank, E.: Data Mining: Practical Machine Learning Tools and Techniques. Morgan Kaufmann Publishers, San Francisco (2005)
2. Liao, S.-H., Chu, P.-H., Hisao, P.-Y.: Data mining techniques and applications - A decade review from 2000 to 2011. Expert Syst. Appl. 39(12), 11303–113011 (2012)
3. Richards, D.: Two decades of ripple down rules research. Knowl. Eng. Rev. 24, 159–184 (2009)

4. Cano, A., Zafra, A., Ventura, S.: An interpretable classification rule mining algorithm. Inform. Sciences 240, 1–20 (2013)
5. Cano, J., Herrera, F., Lozano, M.: Evolutionary stratified training set selection for extracting classification rules with trade off precision-interpretability. Data Knowl. Eng. 60, 90–108 (2007)
6. García, S., Fernández, A., Luengo, J., Herrera, F.: A study of statistical techniques and performance measures for genetics-based machine learning: accuracy and interpretability. Soft Comput 13, 959–977 (2009)
7. Huysmans, J., Dejaeger, K., Mues, C., Vanthienen, J., Baesens, B.: An empiricial evaluation of the comprehensibility of decision table, tree and rule based predictive models. Decis. Support Syst. 51, 141–154 (2011)
8. Culberson, J., Luo, F.: Exploring the k-colorable landscape with iterated greedy. In: Cliques, Coloring, and Satisfiability: Second DIMACS Implementation Challenge, vol. 26, pp. 245–284 (1996)
9. Ruiz, R., Stützle, T.: A simple and effective iterated greedy algorithm for the permutation flowshop scheduling problem. Eur. J. Oper. Res. 177, 2033–2049 (2007)
10. Lozano, M., Molina, D., García-Martínez, C.: Iterated greedy for the maximum diversity problem. Eur. J. Oper. Res. 214, 31–38 (2010)
11. Rodriguez, F., Lozano, M., Blum, C., García-Martínez, C.: An Iterated greedy algorithm for the large-scale unrelated parallel machines scheduling problem. Comput. Oper. Res. 40(7), 1829–1841 (2013)
12. García-Martínez, C., Rodriguez, F.J., Lozano, M.: Tabu-enhanced iterated greedy algorithm: A case study in the quadratic multiple knapsack problem. Eur. J. Oper. Res. 232, 454–463 (2014)
13. Ying, K.-C., Cheng, H.-M.: Dynamic parallel machine scheduling with sequence-dependent setup times using an iterated greedy heuristic. Expert Syst. Appl. 37(4), 2848–2852 (2010)
14. Lozano, M., Molina, D., García-Martínez, C.: Iterated greedy for the maximum diversity problem. Eur. J. Oper. Res. 214, 31–38 (2011)
15. García-Martínez, C., Rodriguez, F.J., Lozano, M.: Tabu-enhanced iterated greedy algorithm: A case study in the quadratic multiple knapsack problem. Eur. J. Oper. Res. 232, 454–463 (2014)
16. Sokolova, M., Lapalme, G.: A systematic analysis of performance measures for classification tasks. Inform. Process. Manag. 45(4), 427–437 (2009)
17. Ferri, C., Hernández-Orallo, J., Modroiu, R.: An experimental comparison of performance measures for classification. Pattern Recogn. Lett. 30(1), 27–38 (2009)
18. Zafra, A., Ventura, S.: Multi-instance genetic programming for predicting student performance in web based educational environments. Appl. Soft. Comput. 12(8), 2693–2706 (2012)
19. Hall, M., Frank, E., Holmes, G., Pfahringer, B., Reutemannr, P., Witten, I.H.: The WEKA Data Mining Software: An Update. SIGKDD Explorations 11, 10–18 (2009)
20. Bache, K., Lichman, M.: UCI Machine Learning Repository, University of California, Irvine, School of Information and Computer Sciences (2013), `http://archive.ics.uci.edu/ml`
21. Garcia, S., Molina, D., Lozano, M., Herrera, F.: A study on the use of non-parametric tests for analyzing the evolutionary algorithms' behaviour: A case study on the CEC'2005 special session on real parameter optimization. J. Heuristics 15(6), 617–644 (2009)
22. Iman, R., Davenport, J.: Approximation of the critical region of the Friedman statistic. Communications in Statistics, 571–595 (1980)

23. Holm, S.: A simple sequentially rejective multiple test procedure. Scand. J. Stat. 6, 65–70 (1979)
24. Wilcoxon, F.: Individual comparisons by ranking methods. Biometrics 1, 80–83 (1945)
25. Bacardit, J., Krasnogor, N.: Performance and efficiency of memetic Pittsburgh learning classifier systems. Evol. Comput. 17, 307–342 (2009)
26. Guan, S., Zhu, F.: An incremental approach to genetic-algorithms-based classification. IEEE T. Syst. Man. Cy. B 35, 227–239 (2005)
27. Tan, K., Yu, Q., Ang, J.: A coevolutionary algorithm for rules discovery in data mining. Int. J. Syst. Sci. 37, 835–864 (2006)
28. González, A., Perez, R.: Selection of relevant features in a fuzzy genetic learning algorithm. IEEE T. Syst. Man. Cy. B 31, 417–425 (2001)
29. Sánchez, L., Couse, I., Corrales, J.: Combining GP operators with SA search to evolve fuzzy rule based classifiers. Inform. Sciences 136, 175–192 (2001)
30. Carvalho, D., Freitas, A.: A hybrid decision tree/genetic algorithm method for data mining. Inform. Sciences 163, 13–35 (2004)
31. Parpinelli, R., Lopes, H., Freitas, A.: Data mining with an ant colony optimization algorithm. IEEE T. Evolut. Comput. 6, 321–332 (2002)
32. Cohen, W.: Fast effective rule induction. In: Proc. of the 12th International Conference on Machine Learning, pp. 1–10 (1995)
33. Quinlan, J.: C4.5: Programs for Machine Learning (1993)
34. Nauc, D.D.: Measuring interpretability in rule-based classification systems. In: Proc. of the IEEE International Conference on Fuzzy Systems, pp. 196–201 (2002)
35. Luna, J.M., Romero, J.R., Ventura, S.: Design and behavior study of a grammar-guided genetic programming algorithm for mining association rules. Knowl. Inf. Syst. 32(1), 53–76 (2012)

Improving the Behavior of the Nearest Neighbor Classifier against Noisy Data with Feature Weighting Schemes

José A. Sáez[1], Joaquín Derrac[2], Julián Luengo[3], and Francisco Herrera[1]

[1] Department of Computer Science and Artificial Intelligence, University of Granada, CITIC-UGR, Granada, Spain, 18071
{smja,herrera}@decsai.ugr.es

[2] School of Computer Science & Informatics, Cardiff University, Cardiff CF24 3AA, United Kingdom
jderrac@decsai.ugr.es

[3] Department of Civil Engineering, LSI, University of Burgos, Burgos, Spain, 09006
jluengo@ubu.es

Abstract. The Nearest Neighbor rule is one of the most successful classifiers in machine learning but it is very sensitive to noisy data, which may cause its performance to deteriorate. This contribution proposes a new feature weighting classifier that tries to reduce the influence of noisy features. The computation of the weights is based on combining imputation methods and non-parametrical statistical tests. The results obtained show that our proposal can improve the performance of the Nearest Neighbor classifier dealing with different types of noisy data.

Keywords: noisy data, feature weighting, classification.

1 Introduction

The Nearest Neighbor (NN) classifier [4] uses the full training dataset to establish a classification rule, based on the most similar or nearest training instance to the query example. The most frequently used similarity function for the NN classifier is Euclidean distance [1] (see Equation 1, where X and Y are two instances and M is the number of features that describes them).

$$d(X,Y) = \sqrt{\sum_{i=0}^{M} (x_i - y_i)^2} \qquad (1)$$

However, features containing enough noise may lead to erroneous similarities between the examples obtained and, therefore, to a deterioration in the performance of NN, which is known to be very sensitive to noisy data [10]. One way of overcoming this problem lies in modifying the similarity function, that is, the way in which the distances are computed. With this objective, Feature

M. Polycarpou et al. (Eds.): HAIS 2014, LNAI 8480, pp. 597–606, 2014.
© Springer International Publishing Switzerland 2014

Weighting methods [12], [9] try to improve the similarity function, by introducing a weight for each of the features (W_i, usually $W_i \in [0, 1]$). These methods, which are mostly based in the Euclidean distance, modify the way in which the distance measure is computed (Equation 2), increasing the relevance of those features with greater weights associated with them (near to 1.0).

$$d_w(X,Y) = \sqrt{\sum_{i=0}^{M} W_i \cdot (x_i - y_i)^2} \quad (2)$$

These weights W_i can be regarded as a measure of how useful a feature is with respect to the final classification task. The higher a weight is, the more influence the associated feature will have in the decision rule used to compute the classification of a given example. Therefore, an adequate scheme of weights could be used to diminish the worst features of the domain of the problem, which could be those containing the more harmful amount of noise to the classification task. Thus, the accuracy of the classifier could be greatly improved if a proper selection of weights is made.

This contribution proposes a novel approach for weighting features, based on the usage of imputation methods [3], [6], [5]. These are commonly employed to estimate those feature values in a dataset that are unknown, formally known as missing values (MV), using the rest of the data available. Therefore, imputation methods enable us to estimate a new distribution of the original dataset, in which the distribution of each feature is conditioned to the rest of the features or all the data. These conditioned distributions of each feature can be compared with the original ones in order to detect the relevance of each feature, depending on the accuracy of the estimation for that feature performed by the imputation method.

The Kolmogorov-Smirnov statistic [11] may then be used to evaluate the differences between the original distribution of the features and that of the imputed ones. It is thus possible to measure how well the values of each feature can be predicted using the rest of the data. This enables us to give less importance to those features with high changes between their original and estimated value distributions - these features that contain too much noise or the more harmful noise and therefore are not easily predictable using the rest of the data, which increases the effect of those features that are easily predictable, and which have therefore likely a less amount of noise.

The study is completed with an experimentation in which our proposal is compared with the NN classifier, considering 25 supervised classification problems taken from the Keel-Dataset repository [2], into which we will introduce different types and levels of noise.

The rest of this contribution is organized as follows. In Section 2 we describe our proposal. In Section 3 we present the experimental framework, and in Section 4 we analyze the results obtained. Finally, in Section 5 we enumerate some concluding remarks.

2 A Weighting Scheme to Reduce the Effect of Noisy Data

This section describes the weighting method proposed, which is based on three main steps, described in the following subsections. Section 2.1 is devoted to the first step (called *the imputation phase*), whereas Section 2.2 describes the second step (*the computation of the weights*). Finally, Section 2.3 characterizes the third step (*the classification model*).

2.1 Imputation of the Dataset

The first step consists of creating a whole new estimated dataset DS' from the original one DS. In order to do this, an imputation method is used. In this contribution we will consider the following imputation methods (although other imputation methods may be chosen):

1. **KNNI** [3]. Based on the k-NN algorithm, every time an MV is found in a current example, KNNI computes the k ($k = 10$ in our experimentation) nearest neighbors and their average value is imputed. KNNI also uses the Euclidean distance as a similarity function.
2. **CMC** [6]. This method replaces the MVs by the average of all the values of the corresponding feature considering only the examples with the same class as the example to be imputed.
3. **SVMI** [5]. This is an SVM regression-based algorithm developed to fill in MVs. It works by firstly selecting the examples in which there are no missing feature values. In the next step, the method sets one of the input features, some of the values of which are missing, as the decision feature, and the decision feature as the input feature. Finally, an SVM for regression is used to predict the new decision feature.

If the original dataset DS is composed of the features $f_1, f_2, \ldots, f_M$, the imputed dataset DS' will be formed by the features $f'_1, f'_2, \ldots, f'_M$ whose values are obtained by the imputation method.

The procedure to obtain DS' from DS is based on assuming iteratively that each feature value of each example of the dataset DS, that is, $e(f_i)$, is missing. Then, the imputation method IM is used to predict a new value for that feature value. The new dataset DS' is obtained by repeating this process for each feature value, until the whole dataset has been processed. Carrying out this process, it is possible to estimate a distribution of values for each feature, which is conditioned to the rest of the features or the totality of the data. The new dataset DS' will contain these conditioned distributions for each feature.

2.2 Computation of Weights Using the Kolmogorov-Smirnov Test

The next step consists of measuring which features are most changed after the application of the imputation method. Given the nature of the imputation techniques, some features are expected to remain unchanged (or to present only small changes in their values' distribution) whereas other features may present a higher level of disruption when their imputed values are compared with the original ones. Thus, those features that are more difficult to predict with the rest of the features/data will contain the more harmful noise and therefore we will try to make them less important to the classification task. The Kolmogorov-Smirnov test [11] provides a way of measuring these changes. This test works by computing a statistic D_n, which can be regarded as a measure of how different two samples are.

The test is a nonparametric procedure for testing the equality of two continuous, one-dimensional probability distributions. It quantifies a distance between the empirical distribution functions of two samples. The null distribution of its statistic, D_n, is computed under the null hypothesis that the samples are drawn from the same distribution.

Given two samples, X and Y, and their empirical distribution functions F_X and F_Y

$$F_X(x) = \frac{1}{n}\sum_{i=1}^{n} I_{X_i \leq x}, \qquad F_Y(x) = \frac{1}{n}\sum_{i=1}^{n} I_{Y_i \leq x} \tag{3}$$

(where $I_{X_i \leq x}$ is the indicator function, equal to 1 if $X_i \leq x$ and equal to 0 otherwise) the Kolmogorov-Smirnov statistic is

$$D_n = \sup_x |F_X - F_Y| \tag{4}$$

In the approach of this contribution, the D_n statistic provides a valuable way of estimating the degree of change undergone by a feature through the imputation process. By computing the D_n statistic associated with the differences between both samples of the feature (original and imputed), it is possible to measure the greater degree of difference between the expected distribution of both samples. Hence, the greater D_n value obtained, the more different the imputed version of the feature distribution will be (when compared with the original one).

The D_n statistic can be easily transformed into a weight. Since $D_n \in [0, 1]$, features with a lower value of D_n (near to 0.0) it will have little influence on the computation of the similarity function of the NN rule, whereas features with a higher value of D_n (near to 1.0) will be the most influential when computing the distance between two examples. Defining the statistical D_n^i for the feature i as

$$D_n^i = \text{Kolmogorov-Smirnov}(e_{f_i}, e_{f_i'}) \tag{5}$$

(where e_{f_i} and $e_{f_i'}$ are the empirical distributions of the features $f_i \in \mathcal{A}$ and $f_i' \in \mathcal{A}'$ respectively, and $\mathcal{A}$ denotes the set of features of the original dataset DS and $\mathcal{A}'$ denotes the set of features imputed in DS'), then the weights $W_i \in [0, 1]$ computed for a feature $f_i \in \mathcal{A}$ are

$$W_i = (1 - D_n^i)/(\sum_{j=1}^{M} 1 - D_n^j) \tag{6}$$

Therefore, the Kolmogorov-Smirnov test is applied to measure the degree of difference between each attribute f_i and its estimated version f_i'; then, this difference is used to build the weight for the attribute f_i (see Equation 6).

2.3 Final Classification Model

The final classifier considers NN with the weighted Euclidean distance (Equation 2) and the weights computed throughout the Kolmogorov-Smirnov statistic (Equation 6). Since we will consider three different imputation methods (KNNI, CMC and SVMI), three different feature weighting classifiers will be created. Throughout the study, we will denote them as FW-KNNI, FW-CMC and FW-SVMI according to the imputation method used.

Considering weights computed from the D_n statistic, we aim to reduce the effect that changing features have on the computation of the distance. These features, with a larger associated D_n value, will be those easily estimated by the imputation method (whose sample distribution differs poorly if the original and imputed versions are compared). They are preferred since they will contain a less harmful noise, and are the key features describing the dataset.

By contrast, features with a small D_n value will be those whose sample distribution has been greatly changed after the application of the imputation method. Since these features are not easily estimated when the rest of the data is available (the imputation method cannot recover their values properly), they are not preferred in the final computation of the distance, and thus a lower weight is assigned to them.

3 Experimental Framework

Section 3.1 describes the base datasets employed and Section 3.2 shows the noise introduction processes. Finally, Section 3.3 describes the methodology followed to analyze the results.

3.1 Base Datasets

The experimentation considers 25 real-world datasets from the KEEL-Dataset repository [2]. They are described in Table 3, where #EXA refers to the number of examples, #FEA to the number of numeric features and #CLA to the number of classes. For datasets containing missing values (such as *bands* or *dermatology*), the examples with missing values were removed from the datasets before their usage and thus all the attribute values of the datasets considered are known. In this way, the percentage of missing values of each dataset does not influence the results or conclusions obtained. Therefore, the only missing values considered in this contribution are those assumed during the execution of our proposal.

Table 1. Datasets employed in the experimentation

dataset	#EXA	#FEA	#CLA	dataset	#EXA	#FEA	#CLA
banana	5300	2	2	pima	768	8	2
bands	365	19	2	satimage	6435	36	7
bupa	345	6	2	sonar	208	60	2
dermatology	358	34	6	tae	151	5	3
ecoli	336	7	8	texture	5500	40	11
heart	270	13	2	vowel	990	13	11
hepatitis	80	19	2	wdbc	569	30	2
ionosphere	351	33	2	wine	178	13	3
iris	150	4	3	wq-red	1599	11	11
led7digit	500	7	10	wq-white	4898	11	11
mov-libras	360	90	15	wisconsin	683	9	2
newthyroid	215	5	3	yeast	1484	8	10
phoneme	5404	5	2				

3.2 Introducing Noise into Datasets

In order to control the amount of noise in each dataset and to check how it affects the classifiers, noise is introduced into each dataset in a supervised manner. Two different noise schemes, which are proposed in the specialized literature [14], are used in order to introduce a noise level of $x\%$ into each dataset.

- **Random Class Noise.** It supposes that exactly $x\%$ of the examples are corrupted. The class labels of these examples are randomly changed by other one out of the M classes.
- **Random Attribute Noise.** $x\%$ of the values of each attribute in the dataset are corrupted. To corrupt an attribute A_i, approximately $x\%$ of the examples in the dataset are chosen, and their A_i value is assigned a random value from $\mathbb{D}_i$. A uniform distribution is used either for numerical or nominal attributes.

A collection of new noisy datasets are created from the aforementioned 25 base real-world datasets. Both types of noise are independently considered: class and attribute noise. For each type of noise, the noise levels $x = 10\%$ and $x = 30\%$ are studied. Thus, the results of our proposal will be compared with those of NN considering three different scenarios: with the 25 unaltered real-world datasets, with the 25 datasets with a 10% of noise level and with the 25 datasets with a 30% of noise level.

3.3 Methodology of Analysis

The performance estimation of each classifier on each dataset is obtained by means of 3 runs of a 10-fold *distribution optimally balanced stratified cross-validation* (DOB-SCV) [7], averaging its test accuracy results. The usage of this partitioning reduces the negative effects of both prior probability and covariate shifts [8] when classifier performance is estimated with cross-validation schemes.

For the sake of brevity, only the averaged performance results are shown for each classification algorithms at each type and level of induced noise, but it must be taken into account that our conclusions are based on the proper statistical analysis, which considers all the results (not averaged). Thus, in order to properly analyze the results obtained, Wilcoxons signed rank statistical test [13] is used, as suggested in the literature. This is a non-parametric pairwise test that aims to detect significant differences between two sample means; that is, between the behavior of the two algorithms involved in each comparison (which is usually viewed as the the averaged test performance results for each dataset). For each type and noise level, our proposal and NN using the Euclidean distance will be compared using Wilcoxons test and the p-values associated with these comparisons will be obtained. The p-value represents the lowest level of significance of a hypothesis that results in a rejection and it allows one to know whether two algorithms are significantly different and the degree of this difference.

4 Analysis of Results

This section presents the analysis of the results obtained. Each table of results is divided into two different parts. On the left hand of the table the average accuracy results are found, whereas on the right hand of the table the associated Wilconson's test p-values resulting of the comparison of each one of our proposals with the NN method are shown.

Table 2 shows the test accuracy obtained by each classifier on base and class noise datasets.

Table 2. Results on base and class noise datasets and associated p-values

	Accuracy			p-values		
Method	Base	$x = 10\%$	$x = 30\%$	Base	$x = 10\%$	$x = 30\%$
NN	79.37	74.96	65.46	-	-	-
FW-CMC	81.98	77.38	67.46	0.1107	0.1107	0.0787
FW-KNNI	81.97	77.36	67.41	0.1447	0.0827	0.2699
FW-SVMI	81.94	77.30	67.19	0.0626	0.0647	0.4352

From this table, several remarks can be made:

- The performance results of each one of our proposals is better than those of the NN method with the base datasets and also with the class noise datasets (approximately, higher than a 2% in all the cases).

- As the table shows, every proposal obtains low p-values when they are compared with NN: with the base datasets and both levels of class noise in the case of FW-CMC and with the base datasets and the noise level $x = 10\%$ in the case of the methods FW-KNNI and FW-SVMI. Some of these comparisons are also significant at a level of significance 0.1. This shows that the application of our approach to feature weighting improves the performance of the NN classifier with datasets suffering from class noise (sometimes significantly), regardless of the specific imputation method chosen.

On the other hand, Table 3 shows the test accuracy obtained by each classifier on base and attribute noise datasets. The following points are observed from this table:

- Our methods also outperforms the performance of NN with the datasets with different levels of attribute noise (generally they are a 2% better with the base datasets, a 1% better with the noise level $x = 10\%$ and a 0.5% with the noise level $x = 30\%$).
- The Wilcoxon's test p-values are also low, showing and advantage of our three proposals, even though in the case of FW-SVMI against NN with the noise level of $x = 30\%$ the p-value obtained is slightly higher. However, very low p-values are obtained with the two noise levels for the methods FW-CMC and FW-KNNI; they are indeed significant considering a significance level of 0.1.

Table 3. Results on base and attribute noise datasets and associated p-values

	Accuracy			p-values		
Method	Base	$x = 10\%$	$x = 30\%$	Base	$x = 10\%$	$x = 30\%$
NN	79.37	71.69	58.40	-	-	-
FW-CMC	81.98	72.62	59.17	0.1107	0.0067	0.0002
FW-KNNI	81.97	72.58	58.87	0.1447	0.0483	0.0246
FW-SVMI	81.94	72.44	58.61	0.0626	0.1318	0.2414

From the results of Tables 2-3, it is possible to conclude that the proposals presented in this contribution are able to improve the performance of the NN classifier dealing with noisy data, and in some cases, in a significant way.

5 Conclusions

In this contribution we have proposed a new scheme for feature weighting developed to improve the performance of the NN classifier in presence of noisy data, in which the weights are computed by combining imputation methods and the

Kolmogorov-Smirnov statistic. We have assigned a lower weight to that features that were more affected by the presence of noise (those features whose original and imputed distribution of values were more different). In this way, we have reduced the importance of these features that contain the more harmful noise and therefore are not easily predictable using the rest of the data and increased the importance of of those features that are easily predictable, and which have therefore likely a less amount of noise.

The results obtained show that all our approaches enhance the performance of NN in the presence of noise. The statistical analysis performed confirms our conclusions, even though in some cases the differences found are not statistically significant.

Acknowledgment. Supported by the Projects TIN2011-28488, P10-TIC-06858 and P11-TIC-9704. J. A. Sáez holds an FPU grant from the Spanish Ministry of Education and Science.

References

1. Aha, D.W., Kibler, D., Albert, M.K.: Instance-based learning algorithms. Machine Learning 6, 37–66 (1991)
2. Alcalá-Fdez, J., Fernández, A., Luengo, J., Derrac, J., García, S., Sánchez, L., Herrera, F.: Keel data-mining software tool: Data set repository, integration of algorithms and experimental analysis framework. Journal of Multiple-Valued Logic and Soft Computing 17(2-3) (2011)
3. Batista, G.E.A.P.A., Monard, M.C.: An analysis of four missing data treatment methods for supervised learning. Applied Artificial Intelligence 17(5-6), 519–533 (2003)
4. Cover, T., Hart, P.: Nearest neighbor pattern classification. IEEE Transactions on Information Theory 13, 21–27 (1967)
5. Khosla, R., Howlett, R.J., Jain, L.C. (eds.): KES 2005. LNCS (LNAI), vol. 3683. Springer, Heidelberg (2005)
6. Ślęzak, D., Yao, J., Peters, J.F., Ziarko, W.P., Hu, X. (eds.): RSFDGrC 2005. LNCS (LNAI), vol. 3642. Springer, Heidelberg (2005)
7. Moreno-Torres, J.G., Sáez, J.A., Herrera, F.: Study on the Impact of Partition-Induced Dataset Shift on k-fold Cross-Validation. IEEE Transactions on Neural Networks and Learning Systems 23(8), 1304–1312 (2012)
8. Moreno-Torres, J.G., Raeder, T., Alaiz-Rodríguez, R., Chawla, N.V., Herrera, F.: A unifying view on dataset shift in classification. Pattern Recognition 45(1), 521–530 (2012)
9. Paredes, R., Vidal, E.: Learning weighted metrics to minimize nearest-neighbor classification error. IEEE Transactions on Pattern Analysis and Machine Intelligence 28(7), 1100–1110 (2006)
10. Sáez, J., Luengo, J., Herrera, F.: Predicting noise filtering efficacy with data complexity measures for nearest neighbor classification. Pattern Recognition 46(1), 355–364 (2013)

11. Smirnov, N.V.: Estimate of deviation between empirical distribution functions in two independent samples. Bulletin of Moscow University 2, 3–16 (1939) (in Russian)
12. Wettschereck, D., Aha, D.W., Mohri, T.: A review and empirical evaluation of feature weighting methods for a class of lazy learning algorithms. Artificial Intelligence Review 11, 273–314 (1997)
13. Wilcoxon, F.: Individual comparisons by ranking methods. Biometrics Bulletin 1(6), 80–83 (1945)
14. Zhu, X., Wu, X.: Class Noise vs. Attribute Noise: A Quantitative Study. Artificial Intelligence Review 22, 177–210 (2004)

Soft Clustering Based on Hybrid Bayesian Networks in Socioecological Cartography

R.F. Ropero[1], P.A. Aguilera[1], and R. Rumí[2]

[1] Dpt. Biology and Geology, University of Almería, Spain
[2] Dpt. of Mathematics, University of Almería, Spain
{rosa.ropero,aguilera,rrumi}@ual.es

Abstract. The interactions between nature and society need new tools capable of dealing with the inherent complexity and heterogeneity of the territory. Traditional clustering methodologies have been applied to solve this problem. Although these return adequate results, *soft* clustering based on hybrid Bayesian networks, returns more detailed results. Moreover their probabilistic nature delivers additional advantages. The main contribution of this paper, is to apply this tool to obtain the socioecological cartography of a Mediterranean watershed. The results are compared to a traditional agglomerative clustering.

1 Introduction

The aim of socioecological cartography is to identify, characterize and represent in a map different territorial units or sectors in a map, which give information about the relationships between nature and society [1,2]. This information plays an important role as a decision support system in environmental management [3]. The process of obtaining a map involves: i) collecting the socioeconomic and environmental information, ii) its statistical analysis, and iii) incorporating the statistical information in a geographic information system. Different methodologies have been developed to deal with this issue [4,5,6].

Traditional clustering methods are commonly used both in environmental modeling [7] and ecological cartography [6]. Although they provide appropriate results, they can be considered as *hard* clustering approaches, in the sense that clusters are exclusive, *i.e.* each observation is included in a single cluster. In contrast, *soft* clustering yields each observation to belong to one or more clusters, which provides further advantages in natural resource management [8].

One way of dealing with soft clustering is by means of Bayesian networks (BNs)[9], which are a powerful tool for representing complex systems and modeling relationships amongst the variables by means of probability distributions [10].

In the last decades, BNs have been theoretically developed and applied to real problems in fields such as engineering or medicine, but hardly ever in environmental science [11]. Their graphical representation, and the ability to incorporate expert knowledge, make BNs an appropriate tool to deal with the most common

M. Polycarpou et al. (Eds.): HAIS 2014, LNAI 8480, pp. 607–617, 2014.
© Springer International Publishing Switzerland 2014

problems in environmental modeling [12]. However, available environmental data are often continuous or hybrid and, even though they can be managed by BNs, there are some restrictive limitations. For that reason, a widely-used solution is to discretize the variables, but this involves a loss of information [12]. Alternative solutions have been proposed to solve these constraints such as the *Conditional Gaussian* (CG) model [13], the *Mixture of Truncated Exponentials* model (MTE) [14], the *Mixtures of Polynomials* model (MoP) [15] or the *Mixtures of Truncated Basis Functions* (MoTBFs) model [16].

The aim of this paper is to present an application of a probabilistic clustering model based on hybrid BNs in the development of a socioecological cartography in a Mediterranean watershed. Furthermore, this methodology is compared with a hierarchical clustering. The probability distributions of the BNs are modeled using MTEs, allowing to deal this way with discrete and continuous data simultaneously.

2 Hybrid Bayesian Networks Based on the MTE Model

A BN [10] is a statistical multivariate model defined for a set of random variables **X** which is defined in terms of two components:

- A qualitative component defined by a directed acyclic graph (DAG) where each vertex represents one of the variables in the model, and so that the presence of an arc linking two variables indicates the existence of statistical dependence between them.
- A quantitative component specified by a conditional distribution $p(x_i \mid pa(x_i))$ for each variable X_i, $i = 1, \ldots, n$ given its parents in the graph, denoted as $pa(X_i)$.

BNs were originally proposed for handling discrete variables and so a consolidated theory can be found in the literature [10]. Nevertheless, real data, specially environmental data, usually include continuous and discrete variables simultaneously in the so-called *hybrid* Bayesian networks. In such domains, the most common solution in environmental modeling is to discretize the continuous data and treat them as if they were discrete, which allows the existing methodology to be applied [11,17]. However, loss in precision due to discretization explains why other approaches have received much attention over the last few years.

The CG model was the first solution devised for this problem, and it has been widely applied. However, it imposes some restrictions on the network (*e.g.* the joint distribution of the continuous variables has to follow a multivariate Gaussian, and discrete variables cannot have continuous parents).

Another solution is to use the MTE model. This does not impose any restrictions and it is able to deal with any distribution function, because of its high fitting power. For these reasons, the MTE model is used to represent the distributions of the probabilistic clustering in this paper. For more details about learning and inference tasks in MTE models, see [18,19,20].

The last two approaches dealing with hybrid BNs are: MOP model, and a generalization of the MTE and MOP models, the MoTBF model; which have shown recently as a good alternative to MTEs for some problems. However, the probabilistic clustering algorithm using BNs is computationally intensive, so the parameter learning approach for the MTEs, based on a least squares formula known before hand, is more appropriate for this problem than the MoTBF model, in which the parameters are estimated by solving an optimization problem. The inclusion of these models in the algorithms would lead to an exponential increase in computational demands.

3 Probabilistic Clustering Based on Hybrid Bayesian Networks

In this section the probabilistic clustering based on hybrid BNs methodology is presented according to [9], which details the specifics steps and algorithms, implemented in Elvira software [21].

Clustering [22], or unsupervised classification, is understood as a partition of a data set into groups in such a way that the individuals in one group are similar to each other but as different as possible from the individuals in other groups.

BNs can be used to solve both supervised and unsupervised classification tasks if they contain a set of feature variables $X_1, \ldots, X_n$, and a class variable C (in the case of supervised classification), where an individual with observed features $x_1, \ldots, x_n$ will be classified as belonging to a class c^*. The optimal solution is to build a network with no restrictions on the structure, but this is not often feasible due to limited data available. Therefore, fixed and simpler network structures are used such as naïve Bayes or TAN structures [23]. Figure 1 shows a probabilistic clustering based on the hybrid naïve Bayes structure. Note that both continuous and discrete feature variables are allowed.

Unsupervised classification is performed taking into account that no information about class variable C is given. Therefore, a hidden variable H whose values are initially missing is included in the dataset to represent the membership of each case to the different clusters. In the first step, an initial model is learned with 2 clusters (two states for variable H) and the *a priori* probability distribution for H is defined as uniform. Using the *data augmentation* method [24] the initial model is refined to return the 2-clusters model with higher likelihood. This algorithm is an iterative procedure, similar to the Expectation Maximization algorithm [25], in which i) the values for the H variable are simulated for each case in the data set according to the probability distribution for H; ii) the parameters of the probability distribution of the variables in the model are re-estimated according to the new-simulated data. This process is repeated until no improvement in likelihood is achieved.

The following step is to add a new cluster, by dividing in two, one of the existing ones (increasing the number of states of variable H), and to perform again the *data augmentation* method to optimize the parameters. If this new model improves the previous one in terms of likelihood it is accepted, and the process is repeated until the likelihood value of the model with n clusters does not improve with respect to the previous one. In that case, $n-1$ is the optimal number of clusters. Finally, the model is reported and used to perform the data clustering where each observation of the dataset may belong to more than one cluster c^* depending on the probability distribution of H.

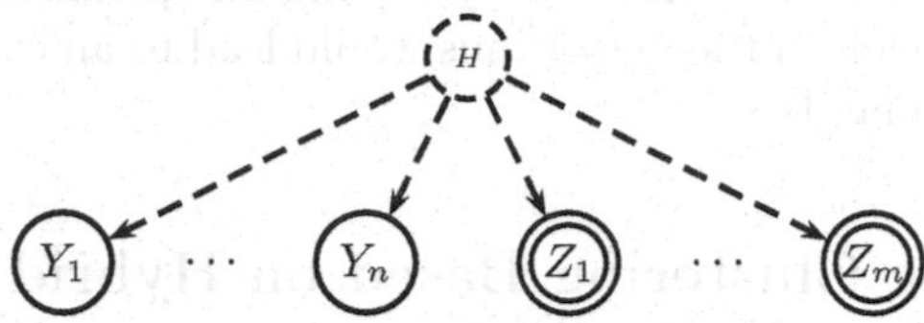

Fig. 1. Probabilistic clustering based on the hybrid naïve Bayes structure. Note that both discrete (**Y**) and continuous (**Z**) variables are allowed. H is the hidden variable which represents the clusters. Adapted from [9].

In this paper, the model is used to assigning the observations of the dataset to the different clusters in the following way: for each case a probability propagation in the model is carried out selecting as evidence all the feature variables of the observation, to compute the updated probability distribution for H. For this new distribution we select the cluster with maximum probability.

4 Traditional Clustering Techniques

We compare the above procedure to a clustering method valid for a dataset of mixed-type variables. From the very few available techniques, an hierarchical agglomerative method using the Gower's distance [26] is selected, from the *cluster* package in the R software [27]. In order to make a fair comparison, we compare the BN-based clustering with its optimal number of clusters to the hierarchical clustering with the same number of clusters; and the hierarchical clustering with its optimal number of clusters to the BN-based clustering with the same number of clusters. To estimate the optimal number of clusters for the hierarchical model, we compute the average silhouette width for the models with 4, 5, 6 and 7 clusters, and select the number of clusters that maximizes it [28].

In this paper we have restricted the possible number of clusters to between 4 and 7. Too few clusters fail to represent the heterogeneity of the territory, whilst more than 7 are excessive, due to the characteristics of the study area (see Sect. 5).

5 Application in Socioecological Cartography

Hierarchical and probabilistic clustering are applied in order to obtain the socioecological cartography of the Andarax watershed, in Almería province, in the

South East of Spain. This area has heterogeneous socioeconomic and environmental features, ranging from highly-populated coastal areas to the top of some mountains peaks 2.000 m after sea level. This tool provides decision makers with information about the delimitation between different socioecological sectors in the territory, and so helps in the design of future management scenarios.

5.1 Data Collection and Pre-processing

Table 1 shows the social, economic and environmental variables available for this problem. Social and economic data were obtained for each municipality for the period 2001 and 2011 from the Andalusian Statistical Institute (Andalusian Regional Government). Environmental variables were collected from the Andalusian Environmental Information Network using ArcGis v.9.3.1 [29] using a 1x1km grid. Environmental variables which occupy less than 1% of the total study area surface were eliminated. The matrix has 44 variables and 2309 observations.

Table 1. Social, economic and environmental variables. Equal frequency method was used to discretize variables where more than 60% of their instances were equal to zero, into 3 intervals (No value, low and high value). The classification into several groups below is designed merely to give a better understanding of the nature of each variable and has no impact on the model.

Group of variables	Variables
Land Use (Discrete)	Forest land, Homogeneous cropland, Heterogeneous cropland, Scrubland, Human infrastructure, Greenhouse
Pedology (Discrete)	Cambisols, Fluvisols, Lithosols, Luvisols, Regosols, Xerosols
Geomorphology (Discrete)	Anthropic, Denudational, Structural, Fluvial, Glacial, Karst
Lithology (Discrete)	Metamorphic, Sedimentary, Plutonic
Climate (Continuous)	Coldest month average temperature, Annual average temperature, Spring average rainfall, Summer average rainfall, Annual average rainfall, Annual number of rainfall days, Spring number of rainfall days, Summer number of rainfall days, Evapotranspiration rate
Social (Continuous)	Population growth, Aging, Primary studies, Secondary studies, Tertiary studies, Emigration, Immigration
Economic (Continuous)	Income per capita, Unemployment, Primary sector employment, Secondary sector employment, Tertiary sector employment
Total	**44**

5.2 Results

Figure 2 shows the results of the average silhouette width for the hierarchical clustering where the optimal number of clusters is equal to four. Figure 3 shows maps from both the hierarchical (Fig. 3a) and probabilistic clustering based on hybrid BN (Fig. 3b) with 4 clusters, which is the optimal number using the hierarchical method. In contrast, Fig. 4, shows the results with 5 clusters, the optimal number using the BNs approach.

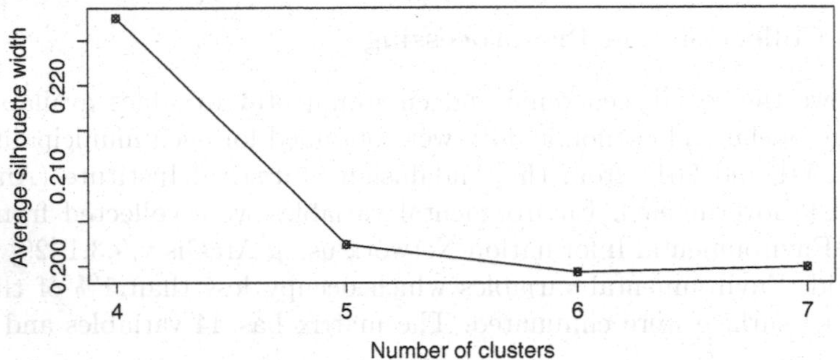

Fig. 2. Average silhouette width results for the different number of clusters

As expected, hierarchical clustering has similar results for 4 and 5 clusters (Fig. 3a) and 4a)). A visual comparison between hierarchical and BN approaches shows that for he south part of the watershed, both methods classify the area in a similar way . However, for the northern part of the watershed, traditional clustering outputs one large sector occupying 61% of the territory. This includes areas of the territory that have very different socioeconomic and environmental characteristics. By contrast, the BN approach separates this unique sector into different ones. Although traditional clustering provides appropriate results, it is not able to deal with the high heterogeneity of this territory. In this case, therefore, th BN approach seems to give more detailed and more easily interpretable results.

The descriptions below relate to the results of the probabilistic clustering with five clusters (Fig. 4ab)).

1. Economical growth sector (First cluster). Densely populated and dedicated to primary and secondary economic sectors, with low unemployment rate and the highest per capita income. Located in the lower river watershed close to the coast. The sedimentary deposits, low relief and warm and dry climate conditions have encourage development of intensive agriculture and a significant population settlement.
2. Mountain foothills sector (Second cluster). This cluster includes two different areas, the foothills of the *Sierra Nevada* and *Sierra Filabres.* They feature extensive agriculture and a high employment rate in the primary sector. Tertiary sector employment is also high due to tourism. However, the unemployment and migration rates are highest in the study area.

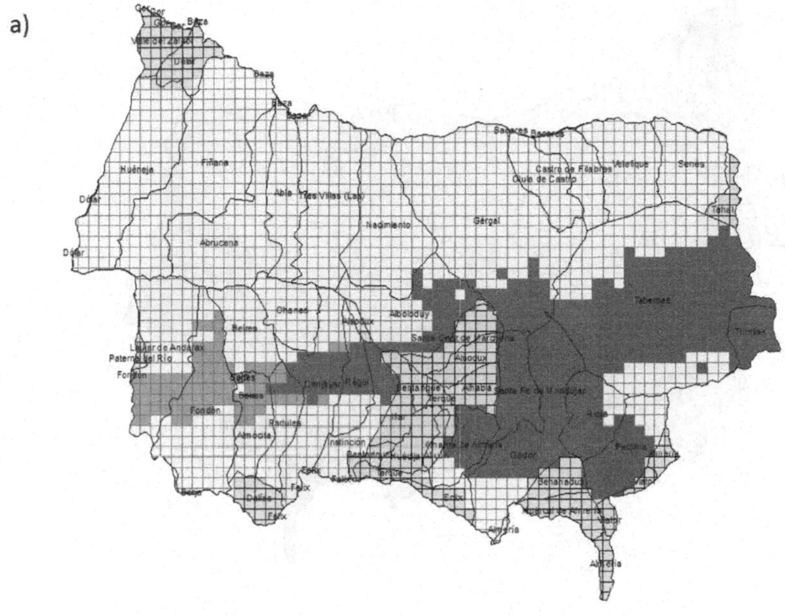

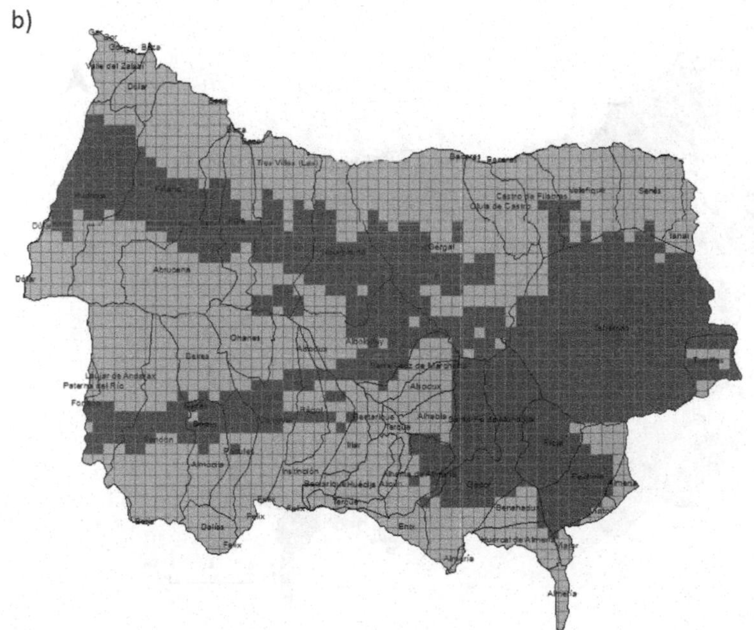

Fig. 3. Hierarchical (a) and probabilistic clustering based on hybrid BNs (b) with 4 clusters, the optimal number of clusters in the hierarchical approach

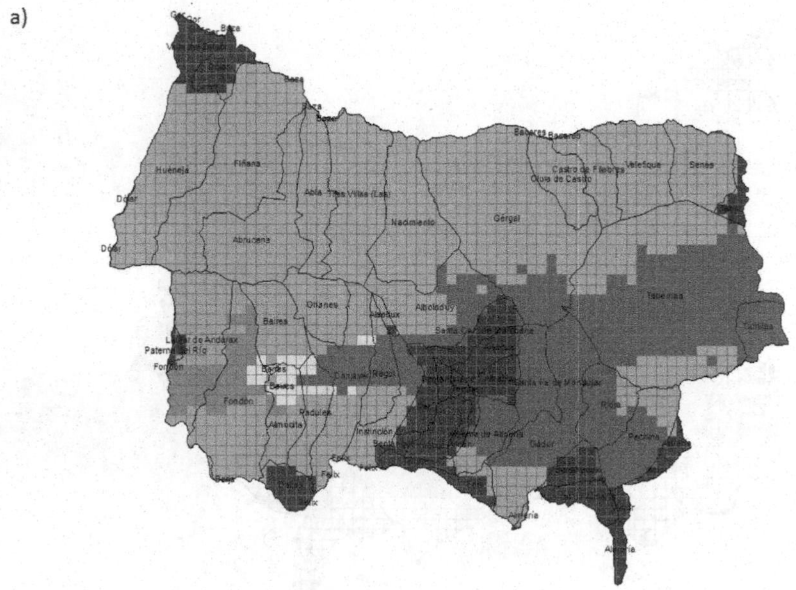

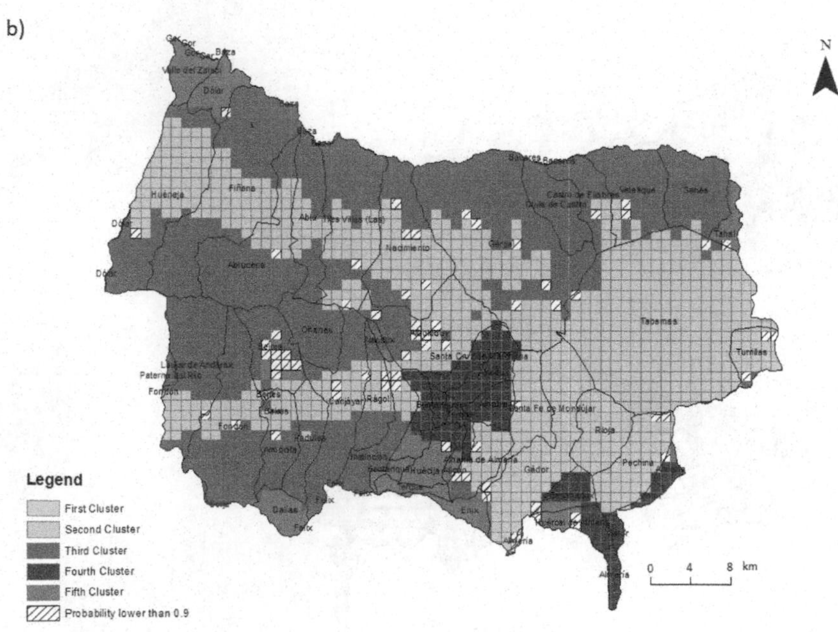

Fig. 4. Hierarchical (a) and probabilistic clustering based on hybrid BNs (b) with 5 clusters, the optimal number of clusters in the probabilistic approach

3. High mountain sector (Third cluster). This cluster features the coldest and rainiest locations on the mountain peaks. Its steep relief is covered by extensive woodland and heterogeneous croplands, and it is peopled by a sparse and ageing population who are dedicated to forestry, agricultural and secondary economic activities. Tourism is important, with the highest value of tertiary sector employment in the study area. Despite this, this landscape is economically depressed, as evidenced by high unemployment, an ageing population and low population growth.
4. Intensive agriculture and populated sector (Fourth cluster). This cluster includes two areas in the south of the study area. The first comprises municipalities close to the provincial capital, Almería, and the second by municipalities in the *Sierra de Gádor* mountains. In both cases, human infrastructure and intensive agriculture occupy the majority of the surface area. In general, the relief is low and the climate is the warm and dry. It is a socioeconomic growth area, with low unemployment and low per capita income, though the population is growing. In spite of the young population, education is mainly to secondary level and employment is mainly dedicated to the primary economic sector.
5. Unpopulated forest sector (Fifth cluster). This cluster includes several patches of territory on the mountain peaks. These are characterized by cold and rainy forest and scrubland landscapes, a sparse ageing population. Cropland is scarce and there is no intensive agriculture. From an economic point of view, employment rate and per capita income are the lowest of the study area.

BNs have some additional advantages compared to traditional clustering methods. In general, in traditional clustering methods it is difficult to find an appropriate distance capable of splitting the data into different clusters when they were collected from several sources with different range and characteristics. In contrast, this data heterogeneity can be easily included in the BN models, specially using MTEs, allowing the main socioecological sectors of the territory to be identified. Moreover, since the variables are defined in terms of probability (including the class variable), an specific threshold can be decided by experts to classify the data into the clusters. In this way, Figure 4b) shows several observations with a probability of less than 0.9 of belonging to any cluster. This gives experts and managers very useful information about those areas which may be considered as problematic, or with have a particular behavior in environmental management. From this perspective, the identification of such areas is really important in order to study in more detail the borders between the different socioecological sectors.

6 Conclusions and Future Work

A soft clustering method based on hybrid BNs was applied in the development of socioecological cartography of a Mediterraneam watershed and compared with an agglomerative method. The BN approach is more efficient at managing the complexity and heterogeneity of the territory, so providing decision makers with more detailed information. Moreover, the probabilistic nature of the class variable makes it possible for experts to establish an specific threshold values that can identify hard-to-classify areas.

Some additional issues could be considered for future work, such as inclusion of the hierarchical order of ecological factors in the BNs approach. This consideration fits perfectly with the BN framework.

References

1. Domon, G., Gariepy, M., Bouchard, A.: Ecological cartography and land-use planning: Trends and perspectives. Geoforum 20, 69–82 (1989)
2. Anderies, J., Janssen, M., Ostom, E.: A framework to analyze the robustness of socio-ecological systems from an institutional perspective. Ecology & Society 9(1), 1–18 (2004)
3. Folke, C.: Resilience: The emergence of a perspective for social-ecological systems analyses. Global Environmental Change 16, 253–267 (2006)
4. Pasqualini, V., Pergent-Martini, C., Clabaut, P., Pergent, G.: Mapping of posidonia oceanica using aerial photographs and side scan sonar: Application of the island of corsica (france). Estuarine, Coastal and Shelf Science 47, 359–367 (1998)
5. Schmitz, M., Pineda, F., Castro, H., Aranzabal, I.D., Aguilera, P.: Cultural landscape and socioeconomic structure. Environmental value and demand for tourism in a Mediterranean territory. Consejería de Medio Ambiente. Junta de Andalucía, Sevilla (2005)
6. Ruiz-Labourdette, D., Martínez, F., Martín-López, B., Montes, C., Pineda, F.D.: Equilibrium of vegetation and climate at the european rear edge. a reference for climate change planning in mountainous mediterranean regions. Int. J. Biometeorol 55, 285–301 (2011)
7. Hawkins, C.V.: Landscape conservation trough residential subdivision bylaws: Explanations for local adoption. Landscape and Urban Planning 12, 141–148 (2014)
8. Jain, A.K., Murty, M.M., Flynn, P.J.: Data clustering: a review. ACM Computing Surveys 31(3), 264–323 (1999)
9. Aguilera, P.A., Fernández, A., Ropero, R.F., Molina, L.: Groundwater quality assessment using data clustering based on hybrid Bayesian networks. Stochastic Environmental Research & Risk Assessment 27(2), 435–447 (2013)
10. Jensen, F.V., Nielsen, T.D.: Bayesian Networks and Decision Graphs. Springer (2007)
11. Aguilera, P.A., Fernández, A., Fernández, R., Rumí, R., Salmerón, A.: Bayesian networks in environmental modelling. Environmental Modelling & Software 26, 1376–1388 (2011)
12. Uusitalo, L.: Advantages and challenges of Bayesian networks in environmental modelling. Ecological Modelling 203, 312–318 (2007)
13. Lauritzen, S.L.: Propagation of probabilities, means and variances in mixed graphical association models. Journal of the American Statistical Association 87, 1098–1108 (1992)
14. Moral, S., Rumí, R., Salmerón, A.: Mixtures of Truncated Exponentials in Hybrid Bayesian Networks. In: Benferhat, S., Besnard, P. (eds.) ECSQARU 2001. LNCS (LNAI), vol. 2143, pp. 156–167. Springer, Heidelberg (2001)

15. Shenoy, P.P., West, J.C.: Inference in hybrid Bayesian networks using mixtures of polynomials. International Journal of Approximate Reasoning 52(5), 641–657 (2011)
16. Langseth, H., Nielsen, T.D., Rumí, R., Salmerón, A.: Mixtures of Truncated Basis Functions. International Journal of Approximate Reasoning 53(2), 212–227 (2012)
17. Dan, L., Yang, H., Liang, X.: Prediction analysis of a wastewater treatment system using a bayesian network. Environmental Modelling & Software 40, 140–150 (2013)
18. Rumí, R., Salmerón, A., Moral, S.: Estimating mixtures of truncated exponentials in hybrid Bayesian networks. Test 15, 397–421 (2006)
19. Rumí, R., Salmerón, A.: Approximate probability propagation with mixtures of truncated exponentials. International Journal of Approximate Reasoning 45, 191–210 (2007)
20. Cobb, B.R., Rumí, R., Salmerón, A.: Bayesian networks models with discrete and continuous variables. In: Lucas, P., Gámez, J.A., Salmerón, A. (eds.) Advances in Probabilistic Graphical Models. STUDFUZZ, vol. 214, pp. 81–102. Springer, Heidelberg (2007)
21. Elvira-Consortium: Elvira: An Environment for Creating and Using Probabilistic Graphical Models. In: Proceedings of the First European Workshop on Probabilistic Graphical Models, pp. 222–230 (2002)
22. Anderberg, M.R.: Cluster Analysis for Applications. Academic Press (1973)
23. Duda, R.O., Hart, P.E., Stork, D.G.: Pattern classification. Wiley Interscience (2001)
24. Tanner, M.A., Wong, W.H.: The calculation of posterior distributions by data augmentation (with discussion). Journal of the American Statistical Association 82, 528–550 (1987)
25. Lauritzen, S.L.: The EM algorithm for graphical association models with missing data. Computational Statistics and Data Analysis 19, 191–201 (1995)
26. Gower, J.: A general coefficient of similarity and some of its properties. Biometrics 27, 857–874 (1971)
27. R Development Core Team: R: A Language and Environment for Statistical Computing. R Foundation for Statistical Computing, Vienna, Austria (2012) ISBN 3-900051-07-0
28. Rousseeuw, P.: Silhouettes: A graphical aid to the interpretation and validation of cluster analysis. J. Comput. Appl. Math. 20, 53–65 (1987)
29. ESRI: ArcMap Version 9.3. Environmental Systems Research Institute (ESRI), Redlands, CA (2006)

Comparison of Active Learning Strategies and Proposal of a Multiclass Hypothesis Space Search

Davi P. dos Santos and André C.P.L.F. de Carvalho

Computer Science Department
Institute of Mathematics and Computer Sciences, University of São Paulo
São Carlos - SP, Brazil
{davips,andre}@icmc.usp.br

Abstract. Induction of predictive models is one of the most frequent data mining tasks. However, for several domains, the available data is unlabeled and the generation of a class label for each instance may have a high cost. An alternative to reduce this cost is the use of active learning, which selects instances according to a criterion of relevance. Diverse sampling strategies for active learning, following different paradigms, can be found in the literature. However, there is no detailed comparison between these strategies and they are usually evaluated for only one classification technique. In this paper, strategies from different paradigms are experimentally compared using different learning algorithms and datasets. Additionally, a multiclass hypothesis space search called SG-multi is proposed and empirically shown to be feasible. Experimental results show the effectiveness of active learning and which classification techniques are more suitable to which sampling strategies.

Keywords: machine learning, classification, active learning.

1 Introduction

Classification techniques are used in a large number of real problems, like face recognition, news filtering, spam detection and others. However, it is common to find applications which require handling of a huge amount of data. These data are frequently unlabeled and the assignment of a class to each instance may have a high cost. A promising way to selectively use this massive unlabeled data for the induction of classification models is by employing active learning, area dedicated to machines that evolve *by asking questions* [31]. One of the core questions is about the class/label of an instance.

It is precisely the means by which this question can be asked the subject of investigation in this document. The idea of selecting the best instances among others is not new, it has appeared in the literature under different perspectives, e.g *Design of the Experiment* [27]. In the context of classification, it dates back to at least the 1970's [26].

When labeled instances are needed to induce a classifier, it is reasonable to acquire labels for only the most important of them, since each label acquisition

M. Polycarpou et al. (Eds.): HAIS 2014, LNAI 8480, pp. 618–629, 2014.
© Springer International Publishing Switzerland 2014

has a cost. Depending on the application domain, this label acquisition process can be categorized in three major settings: *membership query synthesis*, which allows the learner to synthesize the most informative instance to ask for a label [2]; *stream-based query*, which requires immediate learner's decision about querying or discarding each instance that arrive from a stream; and *pool-based query*, formerly known as *selective sampling*, when the learner is given the freedom to choose the most informative instance among several others in a pool, which is the most common scenario and the focus of this work [18].

There are several successful strategies for the pool-based setting [21]. However, this variety poses the problem of choosing the most appropriate to a given task. The main contribution of this work is to empirically demonstrate the effectiveness of active learning and to confront strategies from different paradigms under the same experimental apparatus. The comparison includes an adaptation of one of the strategies to support multiclass problems.

The remainder of this paper is organized as follows. In Section 2, the most common niches of the pool-based query setting are reviewed; in Section 3 we present the experiments performed in this study and discuss about the results obtained; finally, the main conclusions and future directions are presented in Section 4.

2 Related Work

There are not many comprehensive comparative studies in the active learning literature. Those found are specific to strategies for a particular classification algorithm [29], intended for specific tasks [32] or focused on a single niche of strategies [16].

In the following sections, the most common active learning strategies under the pool-based setting are reviewed and experimentally compared: uncertainty sampling, hypothesis space search, expected error reduction, density-weighted sampling and cluster-based sampling. Additionally, *Expected Model Change* is presented, but not included in the experiments due to its incompatibility with the selected techniques. Similarly, *Query by Committee* is also presented, but excluded from the experiments to avoid unfair comparison of accuracies.

All paradigms will be presented along with their characteristic order of complexity referring to the number of (re)trainings needed to perform each query. In the following sections, the number of classes and the initial number of instances in the pool will be denoted by $|Y|$ and $|\mathcal{U}|$, respectively.

2.1 Uncertainty Sampling

Probably, the simplest informativity measure to decide when to select an instance (or a group of instances, in the original proposal) is the maximum posterior probability given by a probabilistic model [18]:

$$P_{max}(\boldsymbol{x}) = \arg\max_{y} P(y|\boldsymbol{x})$$

where $\boldsymbol{x}$ refers to an instance vector sampled from the pool, and $P(y|\boldsymbol{x})$ is the posterior conditional probability of $\boldsymbol{x}$ being of the class y. $P(y|\boldsymbol{x})$ is roughly equivalent, e.g. to the output of a probability-based model. The uncertainty sampling strategy consists of querying the most informative instance, i.e. the instance with the lowest $P_{max}(\boldsymbol{x})$, to explore the decision boundary in the attribute (or parameter) space. The maximum posterior can be substituted by others measures. A similar measure is the *margin* $M(\boldsymbol{x})$ between the two highest posterior probabilities. Given the second most probable class probability P_{2ndmax}, the margin $M(\boldsymbol{x})$ is defined as:

$$M(\boldsymbol{x}) = P_{max}(\boldsymbol{x}) - P_{2ndmax}(\boldsymbol{x})$$

Another measure, which is inversely related to the previous measures is the *Shanon entropy* [34], defined as:

$$E(\boldsymbol{x}) = -\sum_{y} P(y|\boldsymbol{x}) \log P(y|\boldsymbol{x})$$

These three measures depend on a probabilistic model. However, it is possible to roughly approximate such informativity measures or even probability distributions for other families of learning algorithms.

This strategy **requires only a single training** on the labeled instances for all candidates, having $\mathcal{O}(1)$ complexity (a single training per query).

2.2 Hypothesis Space Search

It is possible to perform active learning directly from the hypothesis space perspective. The rationale is to query the most controversial instances when different valid hypotheses are compared with each other, i.e. to query instances that would reduce the *version space* [23] after its inclusion in the training set. One way to search through the hypothesis space is to track the sets S and G of specific and general hypotheses during learning and consider only the most specific $h_S \in S$ and the most general $h_G \in G$ hypotheses.

One important feature of this family of strategies is its **binary decision model**: all instances for which the hypotheses disagree can be queried at once or in any arbitrary order, i.e. there is no precedence among them.

One of the first active learning algorithms is a *query by disagreement*, called *SG-network* [6]. It approximately induces specific/general models θ_S and θ_G by means of generating or sampling random "background" instances and labeling them artificially according to the desired training goal: specificity or generality. Instances are sampled from the region of disagreement between θ_S and θ_G.

The comparison performed in this work is delimited by the pool-based setting, independent on the learning algorithm and the number of classes. Therefore, to fit *SG-network* into the experimental requirements, two sensible adaptations were adopted, *SG-multi* and *SG-multiJS*. The order of complexity of the original work (only binary problems) and the following adaptations is $\mathcal{O}(|Y|)$.

SG-multi. For each class $c \in Y$, there is a pair model/training set $\langle \theta_c, \mathcal{L}_c \rangle$ properly designed to represent the most general hypothesis h_G^c w.r.t. the class c. Initially, all instances $\langle \boldsymbol{x}, y, w \rangle \in \mathcal{L}_c$ are the same instances present in the pool, except for two differences: they are labeled as "positive" to the corresponding class ($y = c$) and weighted to have only a small fraction of the importance of the real labeled instances ($w << 1$), as suggested in the literature [31]. The weight value adopted in this work is $w = \frac{1}{|Y||\mathcal{U}|}$, since it ensures that the summed influence of all background instances is no larger than a single real instance. This measure avoids misleadings due to the scarce initial real training instances.

The prediction function $f(\theta_c, \boldsymbol{x})$ returns the most probable class to a given instance $\boldsymbol{x}$ according to the provided model θ_c. It is possible to determine an instance under disagreement $\boldsymbol{x}^*$ by comparing the outcomes from all different prediction functions. Each prediction function represents the most general concept of each class:

$$\forall a, b \in Y, a \neq b, \exists \boldsymbol{x}^* \mid f(\theta_a, \boldsymbol{x}^*) \neq f(\theta_b, \boldsymbol{x}^*)$$

As soon as the instances from the region of disagreement $\boldsymbol{x}^*$, i.e. those with no consensus, are sampled and queried, they replace their counterparts in all training sets with the real labels and integral weights:

$$\mathcal{L}_c \leftarrow (\mathcal{L}_c - \{\langle \boldsymbol{x}^*, c, w \rangle\}) \cup \{\langle \boldsymbol{x}^*, c, 1 \rangle\} \forall c \in Y$$

In this adapted strategy (*SG-multi*), the decisions based on disagreement were kept binary, i.e. there is no ordering in the sequence of queries, except the precedence of the group of controversial instances over the rest.

SG-multiJS. A real-valued measure of disagreement can be adopted to soften the binary querying criterion of *SG-multi*. It assumes that the probability distributions $P(\theta_c, \boldsymbol{x})$ can be estimated from the models $\theta_c \forall c \in Y$. Besides the constraint on the classification algorithm being able to output probabilities, *SG-multiJS* differs from *SG-multi* in the querying criterion: the Jensen-Shannon divergence [20]. It is an information theoretic measure that compares probability distributions, commonly used in ensembles to assess the degree of agreement between their members. The non-weighted Jensen-Shannon divergence is defined by the entropy of the distributions:

$$JS(\{\theta_c \forall c \in Y\}) = E(\sum_{c \in Y} P(\theta_c, \boldsymbol{x})) - \sum_{c} E(P(\theta_c, \boldsymbol{x}))$$

The higher the JS, the further the members are from a consensus. Therefore, the instance with the highest value should be queried first. This criterion disrupts with the binary decision model underlying its theoretical background inspiration and may be more adequate to select instances from the disagreement area.

2.3 Query by Committee

Committees, also called ensemble-based classifiers, are combinations of models whose united predictions are meant to achieve better accuracy than a single model. Query by Bagging and Query by Boosting are two examples of active learning committees [1]. Depending on the member models output, several measures of disagreement are possible.

In this paper, since the base learning algorithms of all strategies are not ensembles, a comparison that includes *Query by Committee* is deferred to future work. Moreover, a fair comparison between strategies requires the same base learner, otherwise accuracies of classifiers trained on the actively sampled instances could not be compared.

The complexity of Query by Committee is considered here as $\mathcal{O}(1)$, if the ensemble is seen as a single base learner or $\mathcal{O}(M)$, if the number of members M is considered.

2.4 Expected Error Reduction

Probably, the *entropy reduction example* [28] is the first proposal of an *expected error reduction* strategy: the instance that achieves the greatest reduction in the total predicted label entropy is select as the best query.

An important feature of the expected error reduction family of strategies is the possibility to adopt any objective function, like *g-means* or *f-measure* [17] - g-means, e.g. can be employed in the presence of class imbalance, a frequent issue in multi-class problems.

A more recent work [11] presents a method that considers implicitly information about the underlying clustering partitions, instead of relying only on the scarce labeled data. It is the natural choice for the present comparison given its reported superior performance. For each candidate instance $x \in \mathcal{U}$ from the pool, its most probable label y' is calculated optimistically:

$$y' = \arg\min_{y} \sum_{u} H(\boldsymbol{x}_u, \theta_{\mathcal{L} \cup \{\langle \boldsymbol{x}, y \rangle\}})$$

where $H(x, \theta)$ is the objective function. Additionally to the accuracy, and in line with the original work, the entropy on the unlabeled data is also adopted as objective function in this work (amounting two variations of the same strategy: accuracy and entropy).

The high complexity order of the algorithm ($\mathcal{O}(|\mathcal{U}|^2)$) degrades linearly with increases in $|Y|$, which is a major concern in problems with a big number of classes. To alleviate the computational cost, a hundred instances were randomly sampled from $\mathcal{U}$ in each iteration in the experiments of this article.

2.5 Expected Model Change

One can relief the sampling process from the computational complexity of analyzing the expected impact over the pool. This is possible by observing only the expected impact on the model. One such strategy is the Expected Gradient Length [33]. Since the true label is not known in advance, the expected model change is calculated over all possible labels. The differences between two trainings (the previous and the candidate to be the next training) $\Delta C(\boldsymbol{x}, y, \mathcal{L})$ is weighted by the model's posterior probability estimates $P(\boldsymbol{x})$:

$$EMC(\boldsymbol{x}) = \sum_{c \in Y} P(c|\boldsymbol{x}) \Delta C(\boldsymbol{x}, y, \mathcal{L})$$

$$\Delta C(\boldsymbol{x}, c, \mathcal{L}) = |C(\mathcal{L} \cup \{\langle \boldsymbol{x}, c \rangle\}) - C(\mathcal{L})|$$

Expected Model Change is similar to *uncertainty sampling* because it is based on a localized criterion: it is focused on the relation between the current model and the candidate query instead of the rest of the instances.

The complexity of each query is $\mathcal{O}(|Y|.|\mathcal{U}|)$. Like *Expected Error Reduction*, training time can be reduced when the learning algorithm is incremental. Since none of the learning algorithms adopted in this work have an analogous to the gradient length, *Expected Model Change* was not included in the experiments.

2.6 Density-Weighted Sampling

The general contract of the *Density-weighted* strategies is the *information density* measure [30]:

$$ID(\boldsymbol{x}) = H(\boldsymbol{x}) \frac{1}{|\mathcal{U}|} \sum_{\boldsymbol{u} \in \mathcal{U}} sim(\boldsymbol{x}, \boldsymbol{u})$$

or the *training utility* [10], measure adopted by its improved version and used in this work:

$$TU(\boldsymbol{x}) = ID(\boldsymbol{x}) (\sum_{\boldsymbol{l} \in \mathcal{L}} sim(\boldsymbol{x}, \boldsymbol{l}))^{-1}$$

Any similarity $sim(\boldsymbol{x}, \boldsymbol{u})$ and informativity measures $H(\boldsymbol{x})$ can be adopted. In this work, five distances $d(\boldsymbol{x}, \boldsymbol{u})$ were compared (Euclidian, Minkowsky, Manhattan, Chebyshev and Mahalanobis) and transformed into a similarity measure by the formula:

$$sim(\boldsymbol{x}, \boldsymbol{u}) = \frac{1}{1 + d(\boldsymbol{x}, \boldsymbol{u})}$$

Due to publication restrictions concerning space, only the two best distances were kept in the results (Euclidian and Manhattan). The margin $M(\boldsymbol{x})$ was adopted as the informativity measure.

The complexity order is $\mathcal{O}(1)$, but $|\mathcal{U}|^2$ distance calculations are needed for each query. For this reason, their values should be cached in fast access memory to reduce computational costs by taking advantage of the fact that the pool remains the same along the whole process. The main feature of *density-weighted* methods is their sensitivity to the spatial distribution of the data.

2.7 Cluster-Based Sampling

The learning process can exploit natural clusters in the (unlabeled) pool, instead of performing queries that focus the decision boundaries/version space division. One such approach is the hierarchical sampling [7]. Instances are queried with higher probability from the most impure and representative clusters. The original implementation was adopted in the comparison of this work, with the same clustering algorithm: the Ward's average linkage method[1].

Cluster-based strategies are independent from the classification algorithms. Their hierarchical version is statistically sound, since it draws instances at random from each cluster within estimates for the error induced by each pruning. Therefore, it is guaranteed to not perform worse than random sampling. Because of the independence regarding classification algorithms, they are called *agnostic*. Another example of agnostic strategy is Random Sampling.

3 Experiments

In the evaluation of the active learning strategies, it is important to compare different classification algorithms, because non-agnostic strategies depend heavily on the base learner. Therefore, all the evaluated strategies were assessed using four algorithms commonly used in classification problems: C4.5, Naive Bayes (NB) , Very Fast Decision Trees (VFDT) and 5-NN [24,19,9,15]. Specifically, NB, VFDT and 5-NN are well suited for interactive active learning because they accept incremental training. Redundant results, like the similar performance of entropy $E(\boldsymbol{x})$ and uncertainty $P_{max}(\boldsymbol{x})$ were omitted due to space restrictions.

The active learning process is divided in two phases: sampling and training. For each new query, a new model is built/updated and tested against unknown instances previously set apart. Ten runs of 10-fold cross-validation were used for each dataset [5]. Duplicate instances were removed. Each fold was used as the pool of unlabeled instances - as adopted by [22].

In real applications, at least at the first steps, it is expected from the supervisor to perform some kind of *guided active learning* [3] to reduce the risk of incurring into useless labeling. Therefore, in the experiments, it was assumed that one instance from each class had its label revealed before each active learning strategy took place[2]. One or more than one instance per class have been used in literature [12].

3.1 Stopping Criterion

Learning stops after Q queries. Q is dataset-dependent and defined as follows. In the literature, arbitrary values (50, 100, 200, $|\mathcal{U}|$ etc.) have been used [25,12]. However, arbitrary values do not take into account dataset's peculiarities. In this

[1] Clusterer and classifiers implementation, including their default parameters, are from Weka library [14].

[2] Except for the Cluster-based strategy.

work, Q is the average number of queries the best strategy needed to achieve the average *passive accuracy*. The *passive accuracy* was calculated after training the classifier with all available instances in the pool and testing it in the test folds.

To assess the quality of the learned model, its accuracy was averaged along all possible budgets until Q, resulting in the *Area under the Learning Curve* [13].

3.2 Datasets

Twenty-eight labeled data sets from the UCI repository [4] were used in the experiments. They are detailed in Table 1. Datasets with imbalance level larger or equal any of the average passive accuracies were discarded.

Table 1. Dataset details. Last column indicates the proportion of examples from the majoritary class.

Dataset	#Instances	#Numeric	#Nominal	#Classes	%Majoritary class
colon32	62	32	0	2	0.65
bodies	62	3721	0	2	0.55
subject	63	229	0	2	0.56
hayes-roth	84	4	0	3	0.37
accute-i	99	1	6	2	0.56
leukemia-h	100	50	0	2	0.51
breast-t	105	9	0	6	0.21
tae	106	3	2	3	0.36
molecular-p	106	0	57	2	0.50
iris	147	4	0	3	0.34
wine	178	13	0	3	0.40
connection	208	60	0	2	0.53
newthyroid	215	5	0	3	0.70
statlog-h	270	13	0	2	0.56
flare	287	0	11	6	0.30
ionosphere	350	34	0	2	0.64
monk1	432	0	6	2	0.50
breast-c	569	30	0	2	0.63
balance	625	4	0	3	0.46
australian	690	8	6	2	0.56
pima	768	8	0	2	0.65
vehicle	846	18	0	4	0.26
tic-tac-toe	958	0	9	2	0.65
vowel	990	10	0	11	0.09
yeast	1269	8	0	4	0.35
cmc	1358	2	7	3	0.44
wineq-r	1359	11	0	6	0.42
car	1728	0	6	4	0.70

3.3 Experimental Results

In Table 2, all pairs of strategies are compared by the rankings shown in Table 3. Each symbol $s_{r,c}$ in a cell at row r and column c indicates that the strategy r is better than strategy c within the confidence interval 0.05 according to the Friedman test with the Nemenyi post-hoc test [8].

Table 2. Each placed symbol indicates when the strategy at the row is better than the strategy at the column: C4.5 (○), NB (□), 5-NN (△) and VFDT (·)

Active Learning strategy	1	2	3	4	5	6	7	8	9	10
1 - Random Sampling	-									
2 - Uncertainty	△	-					△			
3 - Cluster-based			-							
4 - Margin	△			-			△			
5 - SGmulti	□·	□·	□	□·	-	○	□·	□·		
6 - SGmultiJS	□	□·	□			-	□·	·		
7 - Exp. Error Reduction (entropy)						○	-			
8 - Exp. Error Reduction (accuracy)							△	-		
9 - Density Weighted Training Utility (euclidian)	○□△	○□	○△	○	△	○△	□△·	○△·	-	
10 - Density Weighted Training Utility (manhattan)	○□△	○□·	○△	○·	△	○△	□△·	○△·		-

Table 2 shows that the performances of the strategies are strongly related to the classification algorithm used. The proposed SG-network adaptations were better than almost all other strategies when NB (□) was used. VFDT (·) also presented a positive response under these strategies. The density-weighted strategies achieved similar performance with C4.5 (○) and 5-NN (△); again VFDT was partially well suited, but mostly for the Manhattan variation of the density-based approaches. Uncertainty and Margin sampling using 5-NN were better than random sampling, the baseline of most studies. They were also better than expected error reduction (entropy) when using 5-NN. The worst strategies were based on expected error reduction and random sampling because of the significant losses. Cluster-based was outperformed only by SGmulti and density-based variations, but did not outperformed any strategy with statistical significance.

The expected error reduction strategy was not impacted by the 100-instance subsampling. This is evidenced by noting that its performance was not better even in datasets with less than 100 instances in the pool. The first nine rows of tables 1 and 3 represent the small datasets, which required no subsampling.

Table 3. ALC ranking for the first Q queries (Section 3.1). Lower is better. Strategy numbers are the same given in the Table 2. The last row is the median for all datasets.

	C4.5										VFDT										5-NN										NB									
Strat.	**1**	**2**	**3**	**4**	**5**	**6**	**7**	**8**	**9**	**10**	**1**	**2**	**3**	**4**	**5**	**6**	**7**	**8**	**9**	**10**	**1**	**2**	**3**	**4**	**5**	**6**	**7**	**8**	**9**	**10**	**1**	**2**	**3**	**4**	**5**	**6**	**7**	**8**	**9**	**10**
col.	6	8	5	7	2	0	3	9	1	4	8	5	7	3	2	4	6	9	1	0	9	4	2	3	6	7	8	5	1	0	8	3	9	2	6	4	5	7	1	0
bod.	3	6	9	5	2	4	7	8	1	0	8	7	0	6	4	3	5	9	1	2	8	6	3	5	9	2	7	4	1	0	8	6	9	5	2	0	1	7	4	3
sub.	5	8	3	7	6	9	0	4	2	1	8	7	1	6	5	4	0	9	2	3	9	3	7	4	5	8	6	2	0	1	9	6	7	4	5	0	1	8	2	3
hay.	6	3	8	5	7	9	0	4	1	2	0	8	2	9	1	3	6	4	7	5	4	5	7	6	0	3	9	8	1	2	2	8	3	7	1	0	9	4	6	5
acc.	7	4	5	3	6	9	2	8	0	1	5	7	3	6	1	0	9	8	2	4	8	3	5	2	6	4	9	7	1	0	8	5	6	4	1	2	9	7	3	0
leu.	3	6	9	5	1	8	4	7	2	0	3	7	1	8	0	2	4	9	5	6	8	4	2	3	7	6	9	5	0	1	8	5	1	4	0	2	7	9	3	6
bre.	6	7	5	8	4	2	3	9	0	1	5	7	4	6	1	0	8	9	3	2	8	7	3	5	4	2	9	6	1	0	2	9	3	8	1	0	4	5	7	6
tae	4	0	6	3	1	5	7	9	2	8	5	2	9	7	8	0	4	3	6	1	4	1	8	2	6	7	9	3	0	5	3	9	4	8	2	1	6	0	5	7
mol.	8	3	7	2	5	4	6	9	0	1	3	8	2	9	5	1	6	0	7	4	6	2	1	3	5	8	9	7	4	0	7	9	1	6	4	0	8	5	3	2
iris	8	5	7	4	2	6	3	9	1	0	4	6	3	7	1	0	9	8	5	2	8	2	6	5	4	3	9	7	1	0	6	7	5	8	1	0	9	4	3	2
wine	8	5	3	4	2	7	6	9	1	0	7	5	4	6	2	0	9	8	3	1	8	2	7	3	5	6	9	4	1	0	9	5	8	4	1	0	6	7	3	2
con.	3	9	2	8	6	4	5	7	1	0	5	8	1	7	3	2	6	9	4	0	8	2	5	1	6	7	9	4	3	0	6	9	1	8	0	4	3	2	7	5
new.	5	8	9	7	2	6	4	3	1	0	8	2	4	5	1	0	9	7	6	3	9	2	6	3	7	8	5	4	0	1	9	6	7	5	1	0	8	4	3	2
stat.	5	8	2	7	3	4	6	9	1	0	0	9	1	8	4	3	7	2	5	6	8	3	5	2	6	7	9	4	0	1	5	9	6	7	0	1	8	2	4	3
flare	7	5	2	6	9	8	4	3	0	1	8	5	9	6	1	2	7	4	3	0	8	2	7	3	6	4	9	5	0	1	8	1	9	3	6	0	7	5	2	4
ion.	7	4	6	3	2	9	5	8	1	0	5	7	8	6	0	1	9	4	3	2	7	1	8	0	6	9	3	2	4	5	5	7	4	8	0	1	3	2	9	6
mon.	8	3	6	2	7	9	1	5	0	4	6	4	8	1	3	5	9	7	2	0	6	2	7	3	5	9	8	4	1	0	7	2	8	0	3	5	9	6	4	1
br.c	3	7	4	6	2	8	5	9	1	0	7	6	4	5	1	0	8	9	3	2	7	3	5	2	8	6	9	4	1	0	8	4	6	5	1	0	7	9	3	2
bal.	5	8	6	9	3	7	1	4	0	2	2	9	4	6	0	7	8	5	3	1	6	7	8	4	5	2	9	3	0	1	4	7	6	3	1	8	9	5	2	0
aus.	8	4	1	3	5	9	6	7	2	0	1	9	4	8	0	2	5	3	6	7	6	3	4	2	8	5	9	7	1	0	5	9	3	8	2	0	7	1	6	4
pim.	8	3	9	2	4	7	6	5	1	0	2	8	4	9	0	1	7	3	5	6	7	0	5	2	9	4	8	6	3	1	3	8	4	9	2	1	7	0	6	5
veh.	6	7	8	9	4	3	2	5	1	0	6	5	3	7	2	1	8	9	4	0	8	2	6	3	9	4	5	7	1	0	4	7	1	6	0	3	8	9	2	5
tic.	4	7	2	6	3	9	1	0	8	5	5	4	9	3	0	7	6	8	2	1	8	3	7	2	4	6	9	5	0	1	8	4	9	2	3	5	6	7	1	0
vow.	8	4	7	3	6	9	2	5	1	0	8	7	9	3	2	6	4	5	1	0	8	4	6	2	9	5	7	3	0	1	8	9	7	3	2	6	4	5	1	0
yea.	9	3	4	6	1	2	7	5	8	0	2	8	1	5	0	7	6	9	4	3	9	2	3	4	5	8	7	6	1	0	6	9	3	4	2	8	7	5	0	1
cmc	0	8	2	5	3	6	4	1	9	7	8	6	4	1	3	9	5	7	0	2	1	9	5	6	0	4	3	2	7	8	6	9	5	3	2	4	7	8	1	0
win.r	8	1	9	0	2	6	4	3	5	7	5	4	6	2	1	9	7	8	0	3	2	9	7	3	0	1	4	5	8	6	7	1	8	0	4	9	6	5	2	3
car	8	2	6	3	7	9	4	5	1	0	8	0	7	1	3	9	6	2	4	5	8	5	7	0	4	9	6	3	1	2	8	5	7	4	0	9	6	2	3	1
Med.	6	5	6	5	3	7	4	6	1	0	5	7	4	6	1	2	6	7	3	2	8	3	6	3	6	6	9	4	1	1	7	7	6	4	1	1	7	5	3	2

4 Conclusions

Despite its statistical soundness, sophisticated methods, like the cluster-based, did not perform better than ad hoc approaches, like SGmulti and density-based training utility. Therefore, possibly the *sampling bias* plays an important role in active learning, analogous to the *learning bias* (representation/search bias) of a classifier (learning algorithm): whilst generalization of learning is only possible with a bias, a good choice of queries for a given pair dataset/classifier implies the adoption of a strategy with the correct types of exploration and exploitation, and also the adequate balance between both.

The results obtained in this study suggests that active learning can be effective, but dependent on the classification algorithm. It is worth to mention the good overall results for the first proposed multiclass adaptation of SG-network (SGmulti) and density-based training utility. An investigation of the relationship between dataset features and strategy performance, and the use of other classifiers, with different learning biases, are intended as future works.

Acknowledgments. The authors would like to thank CAPES, CNPq and FAPESP for the financial support.

References

1. Abe, N., Mamitsuka, H.: Query learning strategies using boosting and bagging. In: Shavlik, J.W. (ed.) ICML, pp. 1–9. Morgan Kaufmann (1998)
2. Angluin, D.: Queries and concept learning. Machine Learning 2(4), 319–342 (1987)
3. Attenberg, J., Provost, F.J.: Why label when you can search?: alternatives to active learning for applying human resources to build classification models under extreme class imbalance. In: KDD, pp. 423–432. ACM (2010)
4. Bache, K., Lichman, M.: UCI repository of machine learning databases. Machine-readable data repository, University of California, Department of Information and Computer Science, Irvine, CA (2013)
5. Bouckaert, R.R., Frank, E.: Evaluating the replicability of significance tests for comparing learning algorithms. In: Dai, H., Srikant, R., Zhang, C. (eds.) PAKDD 2004. LNCS (LNAI), vol. 3056, pp. 3–12. Springer, Heidelberg (2004)
6. Cohn, D.A., Atlas, L.E., Ladner, R.E.: Improving generalization with active learning. Machine Learning 15(2), 201–221 (1994)
7. Dasgupta, S.: Two faces of active learning. Theoretical Computer Science 412(19), 1767–1781 (2011)
8. Demsar, J.: Statistical comparisons of classifiers over multiple data sets. Journal of Machine Learning Research 7, 1–30 (2006)
9. Domingos, P., Hulten, G.: Mining high-speed data streams. In: Ramakrishnan, R., Stolfo, S.J., Bayardo, R.J., Parsa, I. (eds.) KDD, pp. 71–80. ACM (2000)
10. Fujii, A., Inui, K., Tokunaga, T., Tanaka, H.: Selective sampling for example-based word sense disambiguation. Computational Linguistics 24(4), 573–597 (1998)
11. Guo, Y., Greiner, R.: Optimistic active-learning using mutual information. In: Veloso, M.M. (ed.) IJCAI, pp. 823–829 (2007)
12. Guo, Y., Schuurmans, D.: Discriminative batch mode active learning. In: Platt, J.C., Koller, D., Singer, Y., Roweis, S.T. (eds.) NIPS. Curran Associates, Inc. (2007)
13. Guyon, I., Cawley, G.C., Dror, G., Lemaire, V.: Results of the active learning challenge. In: Active Learning and Experimental Design @ AISTATS, vol. 16, pp. 19–45. JMLR.org (2011)
14. Hall, M., Frank, E., Holmes, G., Pfahringer, B., Reutemann, P., Witten, I.H.: The WEKA data mining software: an update. SIGKDD Explorations 11(1), 10–18 (2009)
15. Hart, P.E.: The condensed nearest neighbor rule (corresp.). IEEE Transactions on Information Theory 14(3), 515–516 (1968)
16. Körner, C., Wrobel, S.: Multi-class ensemble-based active learning. In: Fürnkranz, J., Scheffer, T., Spiliopoulou, M. (eds.) ECML 2006. LNCS (LNAI), vol. 4212, pp. 687–694. Springer, Heidelberg (2006)

17. Kubat, M., Holte, R.C., Matwin, S.: Learning when negative examples abound. In: van Someren, M., Widmer, G. (eds.) ECML 1997. LNCS, vol. 1224, pp. 146–153. Springer, Heidelberg (1997)
18. Lewis, D.D.: A sequential algorithm for training text classifiers: Corrigendum and additional data. SIGIR Forum 29(2), 13–19 (1995)
19. Lewis, D.D.: Naive (bayes) at forty: The independence assumption in information retrieval. In: Nédellec, C., Rouveirol, C. (eds.) ECML 1998. LNCS, vol. 1398, pp. 4–15. Springer, Heidelberg (1998)
20. Lin, J.: Divergence measures based on the shannon entropy. IEEE Transactions on Information Theory 37(1), 145–151 (1991)
21. McCallum, A., Nigam, K.: Employing EM and pool-based active learning for text classification. In: Shavlik, J.W. (ed.) ICML, pp. 350–358. Morgan Kaufmann (1998)
22. Melville, P., Mooney, R.J.: Diverse ensembles for active learning. In: Proceedings of the Twenty-First International Conference on Machine Learning, p. 74. ACM, New York (2004)
23. Mitchell, T.M.: Machine learning. McGraw Hill Series in Computer Science. McGraw-Hill (1997)
24. Quinlan, J.R.: C4.5: Programs for Machine Learning. Morgan Kaufmann (1993)
25. Raghavan, H., Madani, O., Jones, R.: Active learning with feedback on features and instances. Journal of Machine Learning Research 7, 1655–1686 (2006)
26. Ritter, G.L., Woodruff, H.B., Lowry, S.R., Isenhour, T.L.: An algorithm for a selective nearest neighbor decision rule (corresp.). IEEE Transactions on Information Theory 21(6), 665–669 (1975)
27. Robertson, A.: The sampling variance of the genetic correlation coefficient. Biometrics 15(3), 469–485 (1959)
28. Roy, N., McCallum, A.: Toward optimal active learning through sampling estimation of error reduction. In: Brodley, C.E., Danyluk, A.P. (eds.) ICML, pp. 441–448. Morgan Kaufmann (2001)
29. Schein, A.I., Ungar, L.H.: Active learning for logistic regression: an evaluation. Machine Learning 68(3), 235–265 (2007)
30. Settles, B.: Curious machines: active learning with structured instances. Ph.D. thesis, University of Madison Wisconsin (2008)
31. Settles, B.: Active Learning. Synthesis Lectures on Artificial Intelligence and Machine Learning. Morgan & Claypool (2012)
32. Settles, B., Craven, M.: An analysis of active learning strategies for sequence labeling tasks. In: EMNLP, pp. 1070–1079. ACL (2008)
33. Settles, B., Craven, M., Ray, S.: Multiple-instance active learning. In: Platt, J.C., Koller, D., Singer, Y., Roweis, S.T. (eds.) NIPS. Curran Associates, Inc. (2007)
34. Shannon, C.E.: Communication theory of secrecy systems. Bell System Technical Journal 28(4), 656–715 (1949)

CCE: An Approach to Improve the Accuracy in Ensembles by Using Diverse Base Learners

M. Paz Sesmero, Juan M. Alonso-Weber, German Gutierrez, and Araceli Sanchis

Computer Science Department
Universidad Carlos III de Madrid
Avenida de la Universidad 30, Leganés 28911, Madrid, Spain
{msesmero,ggutierr,masm}@inf.uc3m.es, jmaw@ia.uc3m.es

Abstract. Building ensembles with good performance depends highly on the precision and on the diversity of the base learners that compose them. However, achieving base learners that are both precise and diverse is a complex issue. In this paper we explore the idea of resolving multiclass classification problems using base learners composed of coupled classifiers that are trained with disjoint datasets. The goal is to achieve an accurate ensemble by using base learners that are relatively accurate but highly diverse. The system resulting from this proposal has been validated on the MNIST dataset, which is a good example for multiclass problem.

Keywords: Ensemble of classifiers, Multi-class Classification, Artificial Neural Networks, Feature Selection, Diversity, MNIST.

1 Introduction

An ensemble of classifiers is composed by a group of classifiers that combine their predictions to obtain a system that hopefully is more accurate than every one of its members [1]. To achieve this goal, the members of the ensemble, known as base learners, must be both accurate and diverse. A classifier is accurate if the rate of correctly labelled examples is better than random guessing. Two classifiers are diverse when their errors are not coincident [2]. These two objectives are somewhat conflicting [3] because increasing the accuracy of the classifiers usually is coupled with a higher coincidence in their predictions.

In this paper, we present a preliminary proposal of the Complementary-Complementary Ensemble (CCE), a homogeneous ensemble of classifiers that is designed to resolve multi-class problems. Given that there is a trade-off between accuracy and diversity, in this first approximation, the primary objective is to attain highly diverse base learners, leaving the accuracy as a secondary goal.

The feasibility of the proposed ensemble has been empirically tested on the popular MNIST Database [4]. This research makes a comprehensive analysis of the performance of the proposed ensemble, and the results are compared with other well-known classification methods.

M. Polycarpou et al. (Eds.): HAIS 2014, LNAI 8480, pp. 630–641, 2014.
© Springer International Publishing Switzerland 2014

This paper is organized as follows: Section 2 presents the architecture of CCE. Section 3 describes the MNIST data set, the method and the measures used to evaluate CCE. Section 4 shows the experimental evaluation. Last, Section 5 presents some conclusions that have been derived from this work.

2 Complementary-Complementary Ensemble Architecture

CCE is a classifier ensemble that has been conceived with the objective of attaining an accurate system by using highly diverse base learners. To achieve this aim, we propose building each base learner by using a different training set and a different class codification. So, if the application domain has instances belonging to *k* classes, each base learner is composed by two complementary multiclass classifiers: One of them is trained with the instances that belong to *j* classes ($1<j<k-1$); the other one is trained with the instances that belong to the (k-j) remaining classes. Considering a four class problem ($k=4$; $j=2$) in which the classes are represented by $\{c_1, c_2, c_3, c_4\}$, the possible base learners that can be built are shown in Table 1[1]:

Table 1. Class distribution scheme of CCE for a four-class problem

Base Learner	Classifier #1	Classifier #2
L$_1$	$\{c_1, c_2\}$	$\{c_3, c_4\}$
L$_2$	$\{c_1, c_3\}$	$\{c_2, c_4\}$
L$_3$	$\{c_1, c_4\}$	$\{c_2, c_3\}$

Considering the possible values of *j* and excluding the equivalent combinations, the potential number of different base learners, $L^{(1)}$, is fixed by Eq. (1):

$$L^{(1)} = 2^{k-1} - (k+1) \tag{1}$$

To achieve a higher degree of diversity among the base learners, to balance the time that is required to train each classifier and to reduce the number of ensemble members, the value of *j* is set to *k*/2, if *k* is an even number or to *k*/2+*1* if *k* is an odd number. Consequently, the number of possible base learners that can be built is reduced from $L^{(1)}$ to $L^{(2)}$, with $L^{(2)}$ defined in Eq. (2):

$$L^{(2)} = \begin{cases} \frac{1}{2}\,\frac{k!}{\left(\frac{k}{2}\right)!\left(\frac{k}{2}\right)!}, & \text{if } k \text{ is an even number} \\ \frac{1}{2}\,\frac{(k+1)!}{\left(\frac{k+1}{2}\right)!\left(\frac{k+1}{2}\right)!} & \text{if } k \text{ is an odd number} \end{cases} \tag{2}$$

For example, when the number of classes is 6, the number of base learners is reduced from 25 to 10. Table 2 (left side) shows the class distribution used in the construction of these ten base learners.

---

1 Note that the combination $[\{c_1, c_2\}\in L_1; \{c_3, c_4\}\in L_2]$ is equivalent to $[\{c_3, c_4\}\in L_1; \{c_1, c_2\}\in L_2]$. Therefore, only one of them is considered.

By analogy with the representation scheme proposed by [5], this class distribution will be represented as a $kxL^{(2)}$ matrix (right side of Table 2), where the x_{ij} component indicates if examples belonging to class i are used to train the first ($x_{ij}=0$) or the second ($x_{ij}=1$) classifier of the jth base learner. So, the first row indicates that the classes $\{c_1, c_2, c_3\}$ (labelled with 0) are used to build one of the classifiers that compose the first base learner, and the classes $\{c_4, c_5, c_6\}$ (labelled with 1) to build the second classifier.

Table 2. CCE: class distribution scheme (left) and decomposition matrix (right) for a six-class problem

Base Learner	Classifier #1	Classifier #2	c_1	c_2	c_3	c_4	c_5	c_6
L_1	$\{c_1, c_2, c_3\}$	$\{c_4, c_5, c_6\}$	0	0	0	1	1	1
L_2	$\{c_1, c_2, c_4\}$	$\{c_3, c_5, c_6\}$	0	0	1	0	1	1
L_3	$\{c_1, c_2, c_5\}$	$\{c_3, c_4, c_6\}$	0	0	1	1	0	1
L_4	$\{c_1, c_2, c_6\}$	$\{c_3, c_4, c_5\}$	0	0	1	1	1	0
L_5	$\{c_1, c_3, c_4\}$	$\{c_2, c_5, c_6\}$	0	1	0	0	1	1
L_6	$\{c_1, c_3, c_5\}$	$\{c_2, c_4, c_6\}$	0	1	0	1	0	1
L_7	$\{c_1, c_3, c_6\}$	$\{c_2, c_4, c_5\}$	0	1	0	1	1	0
L_8	$\{c_1, c_4, c_5\}$	$\{c_2, c_3, c_6\}$	0	1	1	0	0	1
L_9	$\{c_1, c_4, c_6\}$	$\{c_2, c_3, c_5\}$	0	1	1	0	1	0
L_{10}	$\{c_1, c_5, c_6\}$	$\{c_2, c_3, c_4\}$	0	1	1	1	0	0

The imposed design constraint reduces the number of possible base learners and, therefore, implies a reduction in the computational cost of the model. Nevertheless, when $k>6$ the number of learners that can be built is still very high (*126* when the number of classes is *10*; *92378* when the number of classes is *20*, and so on). To reduce this quantity, a second design constraint is imposed: The number of base learners, $L^{(3)}$, must be a value between k and $2k$, that is, $L^{(3)} \in [k, 2k]$.

This new restriction on the number of ensemble members implies selecting from the pool of candidates, a specific subset of base learners that makes up the ensemble. A possibility is to use an *over-produce and choose* [6] methodology. That is, to build all the *candidates* for base learners and then to search the subgroup that offers a higher degree of diversity or accuracy. Depending on the value of $L^{(2)}$ –candidates– and $L^{(3)}$ –prefixed ensemble size– either an exhaustive search, or another selection algorithm can be applied [7]. A second possibility is to use an *ad hoc* technique that first heuristically picks the number and the structure (class distribution) of the base learners, and then builds the classifiers. Since using an *over-produce and choose* strategy implies a high computational cost, CCE follows the second approach. In the next epigraph we show how to choose the structure of the base learners to achieve a classification performance as good as possible.

2.1 Base Learner Optimization

One of the main problems of the proposed class decomposition scheme is that most classifiers are forced to classify examples that do not belong to any of the learnt classes. In other words, given an instance that belongs to class c_i, those classifiers that have not been trained using instances belonging to this class give a decision that is always erroneous. In the decomposition matrix shown in Table 2, we can observe that this unfavourable scenario appears in one of the two classifiers that composes each base learner. For example, no pattern belonging to c_2 is correctly classified by *Classifier #2* of $\{L_1, L_2, L_3, L_4\}$ or by *Classifier #1* of $\{L_5, L_6, L_7, L_8, L_9, L_{10}\}$ because no pattern belonging to c_2 is used during the training phase of these classifiers.

Ideally, it is expected that in the combination of a pair of classifiers, the output of the classifier that was trained with examples belonging to class c_i prevails over the fictitious output of the other classifier. As an example, let us consider the MNIST database and a base learner composed by $Cl_{\#1}$ and $Cl_{\#2}$ whose class distribution is given by expression (3):

$$Cl_{\#1} \supset \{c_0, c_5, c_7, c_8, c_9\};\ Cl_{\#2} \supset \{c_1, c_2, c_3, c_4, c_6\} \tag{3}$$

The accuracy of $Cl_{\#1}$ and $Cl_{\#2}$ on the test set is 49.36% and 53.92% respectively, but when both classifiers are combined to form a base learner (see subsection 2.2), the resultant accuracy rate increases to 88.57%. These results demonstrate that, in a great number of cases, the output of the classifier trained with examples belonging to class c_i is the prevailing one. Nonetheless, in a deeper study, we have observed that more of the 90% of the errors made by this base learner are due to the fact that this assumption is not satisfied. After defining the *meta-classes* $C^1=\{c_0, c_5, c_7, c_8, c_9\}$ and $C^2=\{c_1, c_2, c_3, c_4, c_6\}$ and exclusively examining the misclassified instances by our base learner[2], the resulting confusion matrix is shown in Table 3:

Table 3. Confusion matrix for meta-classes C^1 and C^2 on the MNIST test set

	Predicted class	
True Class	C^1	C^2
C^1	33	512
C^2	576	22

The combination of several base learners to make up an ensemble should reduce this mislabeling. Nevertheless, we have realized that an effective way of drastically minimising this type of error is to guarantee that given any two classes there is, at least, a classifier that has been trained using samples from both classes.

In conclusion, CCE is a modular architecture in which:

1. The number of base learners, $L^{(3)}$, is limited to a value between k and $2k$.
2. Each base learner is composed by two complementary multiclass classifiers. Each one of these classifiers is trained with instances that belong to $k/2$ classes.
3. Given any two classes, there is, at least, a classifier that has been trained using examples that belong to both classes.

---

2 On the MNIST database, an accuracy rate of 88.57% is equivalent to 1143 mistakes.

For satisfying the previous requirements and defining the CCE decomposition matrix, a simple *trial and error* algorithm is employed:

1. Build, in a random way, $L^{(3)}$ binary codes ($k<L^{(3)}<2k$) of length k, where the number of *ones* is equal to the number of *zeroes*.
2. Verify that there are neither equal codes nor complementary codes.
3. Check that given any two classes, there is, at least, a classifier that has been trained using examples of both classes.
4. Repeat the process until requirements 2 and 3 are satisfied.

2.2 Design and Integration of the Base Learners

Artificial Neural Networks are one of the most widely used paradigms for solving multiclass classification problems, including the MNIST domain proposed in this paper [8]. For this purpose, different classifiers are designed, based on the combination of multiple elementary ANN, conforming more complex systems [9–11]. Previous work related with this domain (handwritten digit recognition) was also performed using different ANN combinations in order to improve the recognition rates [9, 12].

Once the classifiers that make up a base learner have been built, the next step is to determine the strategy employed for obtaining the output of the base learners and the final decision of the ensemble.

To obtain the output given by a base learner, a parallel combination scheme is applied. The output given by the ith base learner is a vector of k components ($Y_i(x)=[y_1, y_2, ..., y_k]$) in which the y_j component is generated by the first classifier if the x_{ij} element of the decomposition matrix is 0, or by the second classifier if $x_{ij}=1$.

Because the base modules that integrate CCE provide a complete solution to the classification problem, the ensemble decision should be taken in a cooperative way. For both, its simplicity and its effectiveness in large and complex data sets [13] the CCE output is calculated by averaging the outputs that are associated with each class and choosing the class that attains the maximum value. Mathematically, the process is described through Eq. (4):

$$C(\bar{x}) = \arg\max_{j=1;j=k} \left(\frac{\sum_{i=1}^{L} y_{ij}}{L} \right) \tag{4}$$

where: y_{ij} is the jth output of the ith base module, k is the number of categories, and L is the number of base modules.

3 Experimental Setup

This section describes the data set (Sec. 3.1), the method and the measures (Sec. 3.2) used to evaluate CCE.

3.1 MNIST

To evaluate the performance of CCE when solving a problem in which the number of training examples is large and higher than the number of testing examples we have selected the MNIST data collection [4]. This dataset (Figure 1) contains 60000 training examples and 10000 testing examples. Each sample is a handwritten digit, which is represented as a greyscale 28x28 pixel image. Therefore each instance is described by 784 features and belongs to one of ten different classes (digits from 0 to 9).

Fig. 1. Examples from the MNIST database

3.2 Performance Evaluation

To test how well CCE works on solving classification tasks, its performance is compared to that obtained by other well-known classification systems.

The CCE System

Because the number of classes in MNIST is 10, the number of base learners of CCE must be restricted to the [10, 20] interval. To keep the processing time as low as possible, the number of base learners has been reduced to a minimum.

Following the definition made in section 2, the CCE decomposition matrix used in this research for the MNIST problem is shown in Table 4.

Table 1. CCE decomposition matrix for the MNIST problem

Base Learner	C_0	C_1	C_2	C_3	C_4	C_5	C_6	C_7	C_8	C_9
L_1	0	1	1	1	1	0	1	0	0	0
L_2	0	1	1	1	0	1	1	0	0	0
L_3	1	0	1	0	1	1	1	0	0	0
L_4	1	0	1	0	0	0	1	1	0	1
L_5	0	0	0	1	0	1	0	1	1	1
L_6	1	1	0	1	1	0	0	0	1	0
L_7	1	1	1	1	0	0	0	0	0	1
L_8	1	1	0	0	1	1	0	0	0	1
L_9	1	0	1	0	0	0	1	0	1	1
L_{10}	0	0	1	0	0	1	0	1	1	1

Designing the Comparison

To test how well CCE works, its performance is compared to that obtained by the following classification systems:

1. A single one-layer MLP with *10* output units, trained with the *Back Propagation* algorithm. After analyzing the accuracy for several ANN architectures and reaching a compromise between the processing time and the error rate [14], the

number of hidden units has been fixed at 100 and the number of training cycles at 500. The weight initialization is restricted to the [-1, 1] interval, the *learning rate* is set to 0.025 and the activation function for both the hidden and output layer is the *sigmoid* function.
The same configuration and parameters are used for training the MLP's that compose the ensembles in the following sections.

2. An OAA architecture [15] modelled with MLP's. The OAA (*One Against All*) architecture is an ensemble of classifiers based on transforming a multiclass problem into several binary subproblems each of which separates one class from the (*k - 1*) remaining classes. For the MNIST problem, this scheme is composed by 10 ANNs with one output unit. The predicted class corresponds to the unit that attains the highest output value as given in Eq. (5):

$$c(\bar{x}) = F(\bar{x}, y_1, y_2, \dots\dots, y_k) = \arg\max_{i=1,\dots,k}(y_i) \tag{5}$$

where y_i is the output value of the *i-th* neural network.

3. *Bagging* [16] with 20 MLP as base learners. *Bagging* (***B**ootstrapping and **agg**regating*) is a classifier ensemble in which the diversity is achieved using different training data sets to build the individual classifiers. Specifically each base learner is built using a particular data set with the same cardinality as the original training set, but where some instances are repeated while others are omitted.
To avoid errors in the class assignation that are attributable to the integration method [17], the output of *Bagging* is obtained as in CCE, that is using Eq. (4).

4. ECOC [18] with MLP as base classifiers. As well as the OAA architecture, ECOC *-Error Correcting Output Codes-* is a classifier ensemble that was specifically designed to solve multiclass classification problems transforming them into several binary problems. In ECOC, each ensemble member is trained using a different class encoding and the output is computed following Eq (6):

$$C(\bar{x}) = \min_j \sum_{i=1}^{L} \left| f_i(\bar{x}) - w_{ij} \right| \tag{6}$$

where $f_i(x)$ is the output value of the *i-th* binary classifier and w_{ij} = 1/0 if class c_i belongs to one of the categories that the *i-th* classifier considers as positive/negative during the learning phase.
To solve MNIST, ECOC has been constructed using the *15 bit error-correcting output code* for a ten-class problem proposed in [11].

Due to the large amount of attributes that describe the examples, it is probable that a large number of features are either irrelevant or redundant with respect to the class concept. So, all the classification models have been build and tested using: i) The full feature space and ii) The feature subset obtained by applying CFS [19] to all the training subsets.

Ensemble Performance Evaluation

To evaluate the performance of the implemented models and determine if the differences among them are statistically significant, we have used the *McNemar Test*

[20]. This test is regarded as the best alternative whenever the computational cost of the experiment does not allow a cross-validation process [21].

According to the *McNemar Test*, two classifiers, f_i and f_j, are statistically equivalent at a level of significance α when the value given by Eq (7) is less than or equal to the tabulated critical value for the *Chi-square distribution* with one degree of freedom. At a level of significance of *0.05*, this value is equal to *3.841*.

$$\chi^2 = \frac{(|n_{01}-n_{10}|-1)^2}{n_{01}+n_{10}} \tag{7}$$

where n_{ab} is the number of instances classified correctly (*a=1*) or incorrectly (*a=0*) by the classifier *i*, and correctly (*b=1*) or incorrectly (*b=0*) by the classifier *j*.

Finally, to analyse the relationship between the diversity of the base learners and the ensemble accuracy we measure the independence of two base learners, L_i and L_j, using the Yule's *Q* statistic [22, 23]. This value is computed following Eq. (8):

$$Q_{i,j} = \frac{n_{11}n_{00}-n_{01}n_{10}}{n_{11}n_{00}+n_{01}n_{10}} \tag{8}$$

where n_{ab} have the same meaning as in (7). Note that classifiers that tend to recognize the same objects correctly will have high values of *Q*. Classifiers whose errors are not coincident have low values of *Q*.

For an ensemble of *L* base learners, the *Q* statistic is equal to the averaged value over all pairs of classifiers as given in Eq. (9):

$$Q_{av} = \frac{2}{L(L-1)} \sum_{i=1}^{L-1} \sum_{j=i+1}^{L} Q_{i,j} \tag{9}$$

4 Experimental Results

Once the experimental methodology and the implemented classification models have been described, this section shows the obtained experimental results.

As mentioned in section 3.1, *McNemar Test* is used for assessing the statistical significance of the observed differences between each pair of classifiers. To facilitate the comprehension of the analysis, the study is divided into two parts. At first, the results of CCE are compared against the other models when all the features of the input space are used for training. In a second phase, the results are shown for classifiers built with samples on which a feature selection has been performed.

Table 5 shows the Test Errors for the evaluated models (main diagonal). Also shown are the number of shared errors for each pair of classifiers, n_{00} (values above the diagonal) and the values for the *McNemar Test* (values under the diagonal).

The analysis of the errors committed by each model shows that the most accurate model is CCE, followed by those models that decompose the multiclass problem into several binary subproblems, i.e., ECOC and the OAA architecture. Accounting how many times a system is statistically better (win), equivalent (tie) or worse (loss) than another, the best systems are CCE and ECOC (win and tie on two occasions each), being the simple MLP the worst (loss on four occasions).

Table 5. Errors and values for the *McNemar Test.* The values of the diagonal correspond to the errors committed by each model. Values above the diagonal show the shared errors for two classifiers (n_{00}). Values under the diagonal represent the values obtained with eq. (7). A (+) symbol indicates that model M_1 (horizontally) significantly outperforms model M_2 (vertically). A (–) symbol indicates the contrary. A (.) symbol indicates statistically equivalent models.

	ANN	OAA	*Bagging*	ECOC	CCE
ANN	353	148	195	167	152
OAA	36.27 (+)	247	175	153	155
Bagging	28.03 (+)	3.15 (.)	271	194	185
ECOC	45.34 (+)	0.05 (.)	5.78 (+)	243	161
CCE	58.87 (+)	2.72 (.)	16.07 (+)	1.97 (.)	**225**

To estimate the quality of CCE, to check whether it outperforms every one of its members and to verify that the base learners are highly diverse, Figure 2 shows i) the accuracy of the ensemble, ii) the interval defined by the accuracy of all of the base learners, and iii) the ensemble diversity measured using the *Q statistic* –diversity between base learners (Eq. 8) and its averaged value (Eq. 9)–. Additionally, the equivalent values for *Bagging* are shown[3].

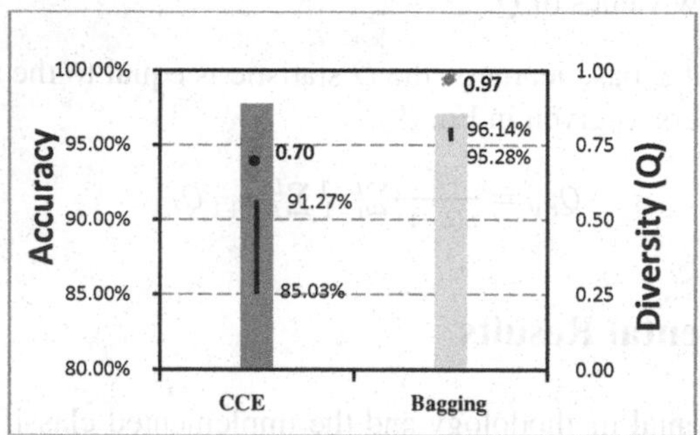

Fig. 2. Ensemble Accuracy (bar), interval defined by the accuracy of the base learners (line) and ensemble diversity (points). Note that low values of Q indicate a high degree of diversity.

The values plotted in Figure 2 show that the base learners of CCE are less accurate than the base learners of *Bagging* but they are considerably more diverse. Given that CCE is more accurate than *Bagging*, it can be deduced that the quality of CCE depends more on the diversity of its base learners than on their accuracy.

Once CCE has been tested on the MNIST dataset and the results have been compared to the other ensemble methods, next we show the results obtained when the base learners of these ensembles are trained with data that are represented by different feature subsets. This strategy is focused on increasing the diversity of the base learners by varying the feature subset used to generate each ensemble member. For this task we have chosen the CFS algorithm [19], which rewards the features with

3 For OAA and ECOC the answer to the classification problem is not complete. Therefore the computation of the diversity values is not possible.

higher correlation with the class labels. Therefore, different combinations of instances and/or classes necessarily give different feature subsets.

Table 6 shows the results obtained when the base learners are trained using a reduced input space.

Table 6. Errors, number of shared errors for each pair of classifiers, and values for the *McNemar Test* when the ensembles are trained with feature selection

	ANN	OAA	Bagging	ECOC	CCE
ANN	377	218	217	196	178
OAA	51.23 (-)	534	192	249	163
Bagging	33.52 (+)	137.03 (+)	288	187	177
ECOC	12.22 (-)	13.81 (+)	71.90 (-)	451	155
CCE	94.30 (+)	221.01 (+)	25.12 (+)	139.93 (+)	224

The values shown in Table 6 indicate that, on the MNIST and with a reduced input space, CCE offers the lowest error rate. What is more, CCE significantly outperforms any of the other implemented models.

On the other hand, comparing the results obtained for each classification system with and without feature selection leads to the conclusion that CCE is the only system without any accuracy loss.

Finally, the values shown in Table 7 prove that, with a reduced input space, the CCE members are more diverse but less accurate than the *Bagging* members. In addition, comparing the values for CCE shown in Figure 2 and in Table 7, it can be observed that the base learners that are trained varying the input space are more diverse than those trained using the full feature space. This result suggests that although the error rate does not differ, combining CCE and CFS improves the ensemble performance in terms of the computational complexity (number of units and weights) and the processing time.

Table 7. Ensemble accuracy and maximum and minimum accuracy of the base learners for CCE and *Bagging* when the ensembles are combined with a feature selection process

	Max Accuracy	Min Accuracy	Ensemble Accuracy	*Q*
CCE	89.69%	86.00%	97.76%	0.639
Bagging	96.26%	95.51%	97.12%	0.969

5 Conclusions

This work shows that the pairwise combination of classifiers that are trained with disjoint subsets is a good approach to achieve diverse base learners. A limitation of this schema is that one of these two classifiers is forced to give a fictitious decision that is always erroneous. Although the combination of these classifiers to make up a base learner corrects a great number of these errors, the accuracy usually remains low.

An effective way of reducing this mislabeling is inducing a high degree of diversity. Therefore, we have defined certain heuristic rules from which derives the CCE architecture.

The experimental analysis that has been performed on the MNIST dataset shows that the base learners of CCE are relatively accurate but highly diverse. This increase in the diversity entails a better performance of CCE versus *Bagging*, ECOC, the OAA architecture and the simple ANN.

On the other hand, when CCE members are trained using data that are represented by different feature subsets, the error rate does not differ from that obtained using the full feature space, but certain characteristics as the computational complexity or the processing time are improved. The good results obtained when CCE is combined with CFS suggest a future in-depth study of the advantages of incorporating this selection process into the CCE design.

Acknowledgments. This research was supported by the Spanish MICINN under projects TRA2010-20225-C03-01, TRA 2011-29454-C03-02, and TRA 2011-29454-C03-03.

References

1. Dietterich, T.G.: Ensemble Methods in Machine Learning. In: Kittler, J., Roli, F. (eds.) MCS 2000. LNCS, vol. 1857, pp. 1–15. Springer, Heidelberg (2000)
2. Kuncheva, L.I.: Combining Pattern Classifiers: Methods and Algorithms. Wiley-Interscience (2005)
3. Chandra, A., Chen, H., Yao, X.: Trade-Off Between Diversity and Accuracy in Ensemble Generation. Multi-objective Mach. Learn. Stud. Comput. Intell. 16, 429–464 (2006)
4. LeCun, Y.: THE MNIST DATABASE of handwritten digits, `http://yann.lecun.com/exdb/mnist`
5. Masulli, F., Valentini, G.: Comparing Decomposition Methods for Classification. In: Fourth International Conference on Knowledge-Based Intelligent Engineering. Systems and Allied Technologies, pp. 188–791 (2000)
6. Roli, F., Giacinto, G., Vernazza, G.: Methods for Designing Multiple Classifier Systems. In: Kittler, J., Roli, F. (eds.) MCS 2001. LNCS, vol. 2096, pp. 78–87. Springer, Heidelberg (2001)
7. Sharkey, A.J.C., Sharkey, N.E., Gerecke, U., Chandroth, G.O.: The "Test and Select" Approach to Ensemble Combination. In: Kittler, J., Roli, F. (eds.) MCS 2000. LNCS, vol. 1857, pp. 30–44. Springer, Heidelberg (2000)
8. Alonso-Weber, J.M., Sanchis, A.: A Skeletonizing Reconfigurable Self-Organizing Model: Validation Through Text Recognition. Neural Process. Lett. 34, 39–58 (2011)
9. Sesmero, M.P., Alonso-Weber, J.M., Gutiérrez, G., Ledezma, A., Sanchis, A.: A New Artificial Neural Network Ensemble based on Feature Selection and Class Recoding. Neural Comput. Appl. 21, 771–783 (2012)
10. Sesmero, M.P., Alonso-Weber, J.M., Gutiérrez, G., Ledezma, A., Sanchis, A.: Specialized Ensemble of Classifiers for Traffic Sign Recognition. In: Sandoval, F., Prieto, A.G., Cabestany, J., Graña, M. (eds.) IWANN 2007. LNCS, vol. 4507, pp. 733–740. Springer, Heidelberg (2007)

11. Sesmero, M.P., Alonso-Weber, J.M., Gutiérrez, G., Ledezma, A., Sanchis, A.: Ensemble of ANN for Traffic Sign Recognition. In: Rabuñal, Dorado, Pazos (eds.) Encyclopedia of Artificial Intelligence, pp. 554–560. IGI Global (2009)
12. Alonso-Weber, J.M., Sesmero, M.P., Gutierrez, G., Ledezma, A., Sanchis, A.: Handwritten Digit Recognition with Pattern Transformations and Neural Network Averaging. In: Mladenov, V., Koprinkova-Hristova, P., Palm, G., Villa, A.E.P., Appollini, B., Kasabov, N. (eds.) ICANN 2013. LNCS, vol. 8131, pp. 335–342. Springer, Heidelberg (2013)
13. Oza, N.C., Tumer, K.: Classifier Ensembles: Select Real-World Applications. Inf. Fusion 9, 4–20 (2008)
14. Sesmero, M.P.: Diseño. Análisis y Evaluación de Conjuntos de Clasificadores basados en Redes de Neuronas (2012), `http://e-archivo.uc3m.es:8080/handle/10016/16177`
15. Allwein, E.L., Schapire, R.E., Singer, Y.: Reducing Multiclass to Binary: A Unifying Approach for Margin Classifiers. J. Mach. Learn. Res. 1, 113–141 (2000)
16. Breiman, L.: Bagging Predictors. Mach. Learn. 24, 123–140 (1996)
17. Duin, R.P.W., Tax, D.M.J.: Experiments with Classifier Combining Rules. In: Kittler, J., Roli, F. (eds.) MCS 2000. LNCS, vol. 1857, pp. 16–29. Springer, Heidelberg (2000)
18. Dietterich, T.G., Bakiri, G.: Solving Multiclass Learning Problems via Error-Correcting Output Codes. J. Artif. Intell. Res. 2, 263–286 (1995)
19. Hall, M.A.: Correlation-based Feature Selection for Machine Learning (1999), `http://www.cs.waikato.ac.nz/~mhall/thesis.pdf`
20. Everitt, B.S.: The Analysis of Contingency Tables. Chapman and Hall, London (1977)
21. Dietterich, T.G.: Machine-Learning Research: Four Current Directions. AI Mag. 18, 97–137 (1997)
22. Kuncheva, L.I., Whitaker, C.J.: Ten Measures of Diversity in Classifier Ensem-bles: Limits for Two Classifiers. In: Proceedings of IEEE Workshop on Intelligent Sensor, pp. 10/1–10/6 (2001)
23. Tsymbal, A., Pechenizkiy, M., Cunningham, P.: Diversity in Search Strategies for Ensemble Feature Selection. Inf. Fusion 6, 83–98 (2005)

A Novel Hybrid Clustering Approach for Unsupervised Grouping of Similar Objects

Kaya Kuru

Gülhane Military Medical Academy, Turkey
kkuru@gata.edu.tr

Abstract. A novel hybrid clustering methodology named CDFISM (Clustering Distinct Features in Similarity Matrix) for grouping of similar objects is implemented in this study to address the unsatisfactory clustering results of current methods. Well-known PCA and a distance measuring method along with a new established algorithm (CISM) are employed to establish CDFISM methodology. CISM embodies both Rk-means method and an agglomerative/contractive/expansive (ACE) method. The CDFISM methodology has been tested on sample face images in three face databases to ensure the viability of the methodology. A high rate of accuracy has been achieved with the methodology, namely 97.5%, 98.75% and 80% respectively regarding the three image databases used in the study, averaging 92%. The hybrid methodology runs effectively for revealing interrelated pattern of similarities among objects.

1 Introduction

Clustering is a classic method that performs grouping of a set of objects in a multidimensional space into classes, such that similar objects are accommodated in same groups nearby. Hierarchical (i.e. SLINK [1], CLINK [2]), centroid-based (i.e. k-means), distribution-based (i.e. EM-clustering [3]) and density-based (i.e. DBSCAN [4], OPTICS [5]) are the main widely used clustering methodologies. One of the drawbacks of current clustering algorithms is that a number of clusters (i.e. k = n [6], n singleton clusters [7]) has to be dictated beforehand and the algorithms execute the calculations to discern groups based on this specified number while centroids of clusters change. The main clustering methods mentioned above may not yield satisfactory results in terms of the distribution of data set to be clustered. Hence, several new approaches specific to the characteristics and the distribution of data have been put into practice to better cluster objects into groups. In this respect, there are many studies specific to image analysis in terms of clustering images as well. Most of these studies have been employed on image segmentation by which several regions in images are discriminated whereas a limited number of them have been established to group face images [8,7,6,9,10,11] with a success rate of about 70%. Interested reader may look at the study of Wolf [9] to refer to some other studies to find out several methods performed for clustering face images.

M. Polycarpou et al. (Eds.): HAIS 2014, LNAI 8480, pp. 642–653, 2014.
© Springer International Publishing Switzerland 2014

In this study, the subject of unsupervised clustering of a data set into groups of similar objects is examined using a hybrid methodology where particularly the expected number of classifiers is not known and dictated beforehand, especially for big databases.

2 Methodology

Conceptual understanding of a novel hybrid methodology named as CDFISM using well-known PCA and k-means methods together with a new algorithm for unsupervised grouping of objects is presented in this section. The methodology is based on the idea that incorporating a new method into several well-known methods with a new hybrid approach may help cluster objects, particularly image objects, better than the current off-the-shelf methods as emphasized by some studies [12,13]. The implementation of the methodology is separated into two interfaces. One interface is developed to both prepare data for further analysis and acquire features and distances between objects, and the other interface is developed to cluster objects using similarities acquired from the first interface. The aim for separating the implementation into two interfaces is to help the users to cluster their objects whose features and distances are acquired using different methods rather than PCA and Euclidean; moreover, by this way, different datasets rather than image datasets can be clustered by employing CISM (clustering in similarity matrix) interface standalone. Thus, CISM interface can be performed for clustering any data set different from image data set. Implementation of PCA eigenface for feature extraction and calculation of distances among objects in data set are carried out by the first interface as mentioned in technical report [14] in more detail. Briefly, first, data set is prepared automatically for further analysis in the first interface: images are converted into grayscale, the method of histogram equalization is applied on these images to acquire better features and these images are cropped to include just faces; the cropping stage is followed by normalizing face images using well known interpolation and extrapolation methods to map face images into same size for comparison. Secondly, PCA eigenface is performed to extract the essential features in face images. Lastly, Euclidean distance is employed to acquire the similarities or distances among the images by considering their eigenface features. The similarity values of each face image to the other images in the data set are calculated and a similarity matrix (SM) that comprises all the pairwise similarity values among the objects in the data set is formed. In the second interface, the clustering is managed by employing a new algorithm named CISM by which most resembling images are brought together while dissimilar images in probable clusters are removed and each image is assigned to a specific nearest group. In CISM, first, k-means, where $k = 4$, is run on SM and the least resembling images are removed from the columns of SM. K-means clustering algorithm is particularly carried out to help reveal the interrelated pattern among objects to some extent as well as to alleviate the cost for further calculations. The notation used throughout the manuscript for performing k-means clustering for removing least resembling objects from the

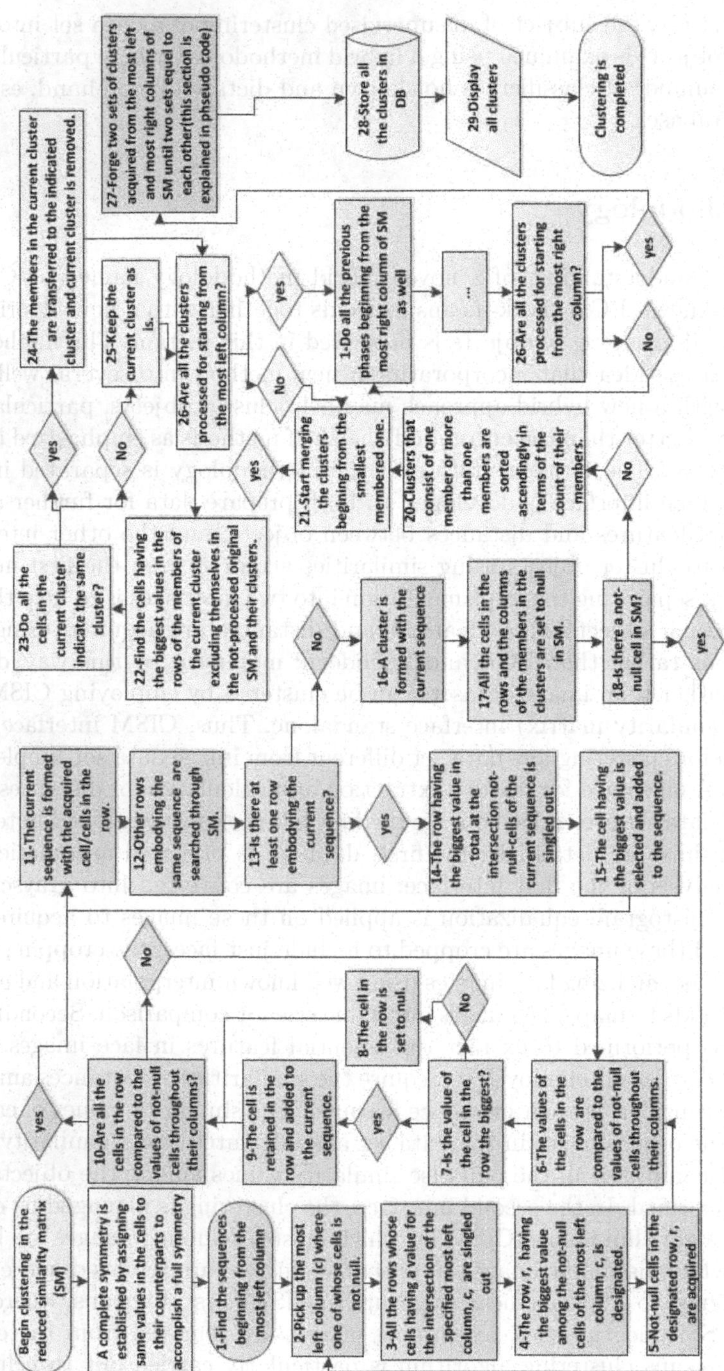

Fig. 1. A part of conceptual framework of CISM Algorithm: clustering begins from the most left of SM

cells of SM is Rk-means. Secondly, a new algorithm (ACE) is embedded in CISM method which carries out the final clustering of objects.

2.1 CISM (Clustering in Similarity Matrix)

CISM embodies Rk-means method and an agglomerative/contractive/expansive (ACE) algorithm. The pseudo code of the CISM algorithm is presented in Algorithm 1. Rk-means algorithm is executed from the command line as >>

```
Data: Similarity matrix acquired following PCA Eigenface and Euclidean distance algorithms are employed.
      Similarity matrix in csv format; number of rows (rows) and columns (cols)
Result: Similarity matrix (SM), S_ij, is reduced after Rk-means method is run; many cells, about 80%, are
      set to null
>> Rk-means.exe -df Similarity_Matrix.csv -k 4 -r 40 -c 40
- >where -df is the similarity matrix in csv format, -k is the desired number of clusters, -r is the number of
rows in SM and -c is the number of columns in SM;
Data: Reduces similarity matrix acquired following Rk-means algorithm. SM processed by Rk_means in csv
      format (main_matrix), number of rows (rows) and columns (cols)
Result: A agglomerative/contractive/expansive (ACE) algorithm. Clusters are constructed while similarity
      matrix (SM), S_ij, is being emptied
- >Variables;
int *embodyingRows= new int[rows]; int * r_one =new int[rows]; int *emptyRow=new int[rows]; int *
r_two =new int[rows]; double val=0; int sR=0; int sC=0;double biggestVal=0;int colNumber=0; int
totalCount=0; double *cmax=new double[cols];int *sequence=new int[cols]; flag
isThereEmbodying=false; int *numberofclusters=new int[rows];int *cindex=new int[cols];int
reference_row=0; int** cluster_matrix = new int*[rows];
- >Create an empty matrix as big as SM to sign clusters;
foreach I_j do
|   cluster_matrix[I_j] = new int[cols];
end
- >initialize cluster_matrix;
foreach I_i do
|   foreach I_j do
|   |   cluster_matrix[I_i][I_j]=0;
|   end
end
- >Establish a full symmetric SM in terms of the diagonal position;
foreach I_i do
|   foreach I_j do
|   |   if main_matrix[I_i][I_j]is null then
|   |   |   main_matrix[I_i][I_j] = main_matrix[I_j][I_i];
|   |   end
|   |   if main_matrix[I_j][I_i] is null then
|   |   |   main_matrix[I_j][I_i] = main_matrix[I_i][I_j];
|   |   end
|   end
end
- >Set diagonal entries to 1, S_(ij) = 1, where i = j which means distances between two identical objects is
0;
foreach I_i do
|   j=i; main_matrix[I_i][I_j] =1;
end
- >Run the procedures;
- >Clusters are created starting from the most left column of SM;
call proce_establish_clusters_in_matrix(ascending);
- >Clusters are created starting from the most right column of SM;
call proce_establish_clusters_in_matrix(descending);
- >Left clusters are established;
call proce_merge_clusters (cluster_matrix_left);
- >Right clusters are established;
call proce_merge_clusters (cluster_matrix_right);
- >Final clusters are established;
call proce_forge_two_sets_clusters_into_one_set (merged_cluster_matrix_left, merged_cluster_matrix_right);
```

Algorithm 1. Pseudo-code of the CISM (Clustering in similarity matrix) algorithm for ultimate clustering of images (Rk-means and ACE): i represent the columns of the similarity matrix whereas j represents the rows.

Rk-means.exe -df Similarity_Matrix.csv -k 4 -r 40 -c 40 where -df is SM in csv format, -k is the desired number of clusters, -r is the number of rows and -c is the number of columns in SM. Output file is Rk_Means.csv whose examples can be

```
PROCEDURE proce_establish_clusters_in_matrix(start_position):
while not similarity matrix, S(ij), empty do
    - >Find the sequences beginning from the most left/right column. Pick up the most left/right column
    where one of whose cells is not null. (In) in S(ij);
    foreach Ii start_position do
        foreach Ij do
            if main_matrix[Ii][Ij]is null then
                - >Clustering begins from the most left of SM; sC: the object from which first and
                following clusters start;
                sC = Ii; break;
            end
        end
    end
    - >Find the object that has the biggest value in OsC column to find the row to go next step;
    foreach Ij do
        if main_matrix[sC][Ii] not null and main_matrix[sC][Ii] >val then
            sR = Ii; val = main_matrix[sC][Ii];
        end
    end
    - >We find the maximum values for each column for further processes;
    foreach Ii do
        cmax[Ii]=-500; /*starting the values with a possible smallest value when compared to the values
        in the cells of SM */;
        foreach Ij do
            if main_matrix[Ii][Ij] not null and cmax[Ii]jmain_matrix[Ii][Ij] then
                cmax[Ii]= main_matrix[Ii][Ij];
            end
        end
    end
    - >Compare the not-null values in the cells of the row in their columns to find whether they are the
    biggest; sign the cell as a member of the current cluster, otherwise set the cell to null value;
    foreach Ii do
        if main_matrix[Ii][sR] not null and main_matrix[Ii][sR] < cmax[Ii] then
            main_matrix[Ii][sR]=null; sequence[Ii]= 0;
        end
        else
            sequence[Ii]= 1; /* The members of the sequence(candidate cluster) are signed with a value
            of 1 in terms of columns*/;
        end
    end
    if func_rows_embodying_sequence is true then
        call proce_find_biggest_in_total_in_embodying_rows; double biggestVal = -500; /* definition to
        find the biggest value in chosen row,bR, different from the cells in current sequence,
        sequence[Ii]*/;
        foreach Ii do
            if sequence[Ii]<>1and biggestVal<main_matrix[Ii][bR] then
                biggestVal= main_matrix[Ii][bR]; bC = Ii; /*column number to be added to the
                current sequence*/;
            end
        end
        foreach Ii and Ii= bC do
            sequence[Ii]= 1; /*new expanding sequence */;
        end
        foreach Ij do
            embodyingRows[Ij]=0; /* reset the array of embodying rows for further sequence*/;
        end
        isThereEmbodying = false; /* reset the control parameter for further analysis*/;
    end
    else
        call proce_clear_cluster_members_in_sm;
        call proce_establish_cluster(start_position);
    end
end
END
```

Algorithm 2. Pseudo-code of the procedure in CISM algorithm for constructing initial clusters.

reached from our technical report [14]. Finally ACE algorithm (second part of Algorithm 1) is performed on the remaining cells in SM to achieve the ultimate clustering using the interrelated similarity pattern among objects.

With ACE algorithm, clusters are singled out one by one beginning from the most left and then from the most right consecutively, and cells in SM are removed from SM as these cells are grouped in clusters; subsequent clusters are searched through the cells of SM until all cells are set to null value. You can download CISM pseudo codes along with its executable files from our technical report [14] and you can test it standalone for your data set; a user manual can be reached from the web page as well. The conceptual framework of the algorithm is depicted in Figure 1. Firstly, ACE algorithm establishes a full symmetry in SM in which Rk-means is previously run by placing the values in cells whose counterparts have values in terms of the symmetry regarding the diagonal position (see the second part of Algorithm 1); the symmetric SM is exerted and in general, objects are assigned to the clusters where their similarity values are biggest based on the pattern they have rather than changing centroids as performed by several well-known methods. The values as well as the position of cells in terms of their interdependency in SM represent a kind of selection criteria desirable for clustering. Secondly, it constructs two sets of clusters independently, one of which is acquired by detecting the pattern beginning from the most left column and the other is acquired by detecting the pattern beginning from the most right column throughout SM based on the position of cells and the values that they accommodate as shown in Algorithm 2. In the algorithm, the distances from one object to the others play a major role for assembling objects in groups for two sets of clusters. In this step, candidate clusters as many as possible are constructed as an agglomerative characteristic of ACE algorithm. The algorithm, regarding the contractive characteristic, proceeds inversely such that members in acquired clusters are evaluated and some of these clusters are merged starting from one-membered clusters depending on the similarity they all have in common in a cluster to ensure the coherency of members in candidate clusters as shown in Algorithm 3. In the first place, members in one-membered clusters are assigned to the nearest cluster from the point of the conceptual understanding of clustering that an object should be grouped by at least another object. The nearest cluster for an object in a single-membered cluster is determined using the cell that has the biggest value in the same row/column where this object is positioned. Thus, these objects in one-membered clusters are assigned to the clusters where their members have the biggest value in the same rows/columns of these objects. In the second place, for the clusters that have more than one member, the distances of elements in one cluster to the distances of the elements in other clusters play a major role to merge some of these clusters. Each member of any two-membered or more-membered cluster is assigned to some other target cluster if and only if each and every member of this cluster indicates the target cluster all together as it is defined for one-membered clusters; otherwise, it is accepted as a cluster in its current state. The execution of the implementation for constructing two sets of clusters, one from the most left and the other from the most right column in SM is >> *smLeftRight.exe -df Rk_means.csv -r 40 -c 40* where -df is the file on which smLeftRight is executed, -r is the number of rows and -c is the number of columns in SM. Output files are full_matrix.csv, cluster_left.csv and cluster_right.csv.

In the last phase of the algorithm having an expansive characteristics to finalize the number of clusters and the elements in them, clusters in two sets get paired up with one from the first set and another from the second set, and the members of these two cluster sets are forged together to yield one set of clusters in terms of the similar clusters in two sets and the degree of coherency

```
PROCEDURE proce_merge_clusters(cluster_matrix):
- >Firstly, members in one_membered clusters are carried to the nearest clusters;
foreach I_j do
|  numberofclusters[I_j]=0; /*assign 0 value to the number of members in clusters*/;
end
foreach I_j do
    foreach I_i do
        if cluster_matrix[I_i][ I_j]=1 then
        |  numberofclusters[I_j]++; /*count the members in clusters*/;
        end
    end
end
foreach I_j do
|  cmax[I_i]=-500;/*starting the values with a possible smallest value when compared to the values in
|  the cells of SM */;
end
foreach I_j do
    if numberofclusters[I_j]=1 then
        biggestVal = -500; colNumber=0; foreach I_i do
            if main_matrix[I_i][I_j]> biggestVal then
                - >Choose the biggest value out of one-membered clusters
                if cluster_matrix[I_i][I_j]<>1 then
                |  biggestVal= main_matrix[I_i][I_j]; colNumber=I_i;
                end
            end
        end
    end
    cmax[I_j]= biggestVal; cindex[I_i]= colNumber;
end
foreach I_j do
    rowNumber = 0; if numberofclusters[I_j]=1 then
        foreach I_j do
            if cluster_matrix[I_j][cindex[I_j]]=1 then
            |  rowNumber = I_j;
            end
        end
        foreach I_i do
            if cluster_matrix[I_i][ I_j]=1 then
                cluster_matrix[I_i][rowNumber]= cluster_matrix[I_i][ I_j]; cluster_matrix[I_i][ I_j]=0;
            end
        end
    end
end
- >Secondly, members in two_membered/more-membered clusters are carried to the nearest clusters if and
only if each member indicates the same cluster just like members in one-membered clusters carried out
previously
END
```

Algorithm 3. Pseudo-code of the procedure in procedures both for main CISM algorithm and for proce_forge_two_sets_clusters_into_one_set (merged_cluster_matrix_left,merged_cluster_matrix_right) for merging similar initial established clusters.

of the elements in these clusters as shown in Algorithm 4. That is to say, an object is accommodated in a cluster where one of its members is more close to it if this object appears in a cluster in the first set different from its counterpart cluster in the second set; thus; members in clusters get thrived regarding grouping the correct objects nearby. The patterns are compared to each other in two sets of clusters to reveal the differences; the objects out of patterns are assigned to the nearest clusters in these two sets of clusters and some new clusters are created to equalize the number of clusters in two sets regarding the expansive feature of ACE; a cluster in one set is divided into two clusters if two clusters in other set indicate this cluster at the same time as a counterpart cluster regarding the most similar cluster embodying the most similar objects. These processes last until two sets equal to each other. Forging two sets of clusters into one is performed with an executable file as >> *smFinalResult.exe -df Rk_means.csv -r 40 -c 40* where -df is the file on which smFinalResult is

```
PROCE proce_forge_two_sets_clusters_into_one_set(merged_cluster_matrix_left,merged_cluster_matrix_right):
- >Forge two sets till they equal to each other. First left matrix will be executed using right matrix;
while merged_cluster_matrix_left = merged_cluster_matrix_right do
    foreach Ix do
        /*numbers of embodying rows are specified; for each row where x = j*/;
        foreach Ij do
            foreach Ii do
                if merged_cluster_matrix_right [Ij][Ix]=1 then
                    if merged_cluster_matrix_right[Ij][ Ix]= merged_cluster_matrix_right [Ij][Ij] then
                        embodyingRows[Ij]=++; /*The cells matching in the rows are counted*/;
                    end
                end
            end
        end
        foreach Ij do
            /*The biggest value of matching, embodyingRows[Ij], throughout the rows are specified;
            if embodyingRows[Ij] > reference_row then
                reference_row = Ij;
            end
        end
        - >The cells matched and singled out with a value of 20 along with not matching cells with a
        value of 1 are counted;
        foreach Ij do
            r_one[Ij] = 0; r_two[Ij] = 0; /*First, previous counted values are set 0 */;
        end
        foreach Ij do
            foreach Ii do
                if merged_cluster_matrix_left [Ii][Ij]=1 then
                    if merged_cluster_matrix_right [Ii][Ix]=1 then
                        r_one[Ii]=++;
                    end
                end
                if merged_cluster_matrix_left [Ii][Ij]=20 then
                    r_two[Ii]=++;
                end
            end
        end
        - >The values specified previously as 20 are changed into 30 if a reference row has been selected
        more than once for not losing the previous calculations (a row in cluster matrix left might
        embrace the biggest value of matching, embodyingRows[Ij] ;
        if r_two [reference_row] > 0 then
            if r_one [reference_row]>= r_two [reference_row] then
                foreach Ii do
                    if merged_cluster_matrix_left [Ii][ reference_row] =20] then
                        merged_cluster_matrix_left [Ii][ reference_row] =30;
                    end
                end
            end
        end
        - >The matching cells in the reference row are singled out by changing the value to another
        value such as 20 different from the value 1;
        foreach Ii do
            if merged_cluster_matrix_right [Ii][ Ix] =1 then
                if merged_cluster_matrix_left [Ii][ reference_row] =1 then
                    merged_cluster_matrix_left [Ii][ reference_row] =20;
                end
            end
        end
        - >Not embodying cells (remaining cells having the value of 1) are carried out to a new row as a
        cluster if their number is greater or equal to the number of embodying cells (cells having the
        value of 20);
        if r_two [reference_row] >0 then
            if r_one [reference_row]>= r_two [reference_row] then
                foreach Ij do
                    totalCount = 0 /*Find first row to carry out them */;
                    foreach Ii do
                        if merged_cluster_matrix_left [Ii][Ij]! =0 then
                            totalCount ++;
                        end
                    end
                    if totalCount>0 then
                        emptyRow = Ij;
                    end
                end
            end
        end
        - >Carry out the cells having the value of 1 in the specified reference row;
        foreach Ij do
            if merged_cluster_matrix_left [Ii][reference_row] =1 then
                merged_cluster_matrix_left [Ii][emptyRow] =1; merged_cluster_matrix_left
                [Ii][reference_row] =0;
            end
            if merged_cluster_matrix_left [Ii][reference_row] =30 then
                merged_cluster_matrix_left [Ii][emptyRow] =30; merged_cluster_matrix_left
                [Ii][reference_row] =0;
            end
        end
        - >One-membered clusters are merged to the nearest clusters if it occurs after the processes;
        call proce_merge_clusters (cluster_matrix);
        - >All the values different from 0 are changed to one to process the left matrix;
        foreach Ij do
            foreach Ii do
                if merged_cluster_matrix_left [Ii][Ij]! =0 then
                    merged_cluster_matrix_left [Ii][Ij]=1;
                end
            end
        end
        - >All the processes above are performed for the merged_cluster_matrix_right using the modified
        merged_cluster_matrix_left and these processes are carried out till left and right matrices equal
    end
end
END
```

Algorithm 4. Pseudo-code of the procedure in CISM algorithm for forging two sets of clusters into one.

executed, -r is the number of rows and -c is the number of columns in SM. Input files are Rk_means.csv, cluster_left.csv, cluster_right.csv (cluster_left.csv and cluster_right.csv files are taken as arg files automatically instead of sending them from command line). Output files are fullsimetrik_matrix.csv, cluster_left_result.csv and cluster_right_result.csv. Clusters presented in these two left and right files are same, but, in different rows since the method runs until two sets are equal. The objects previously accomodated in wrong candidate clusters are placed into the right clusters by forging these two sets into one set. The final number of clusters is specified in terms of the agglomerative/contractive/expansive characteristics of ACE algorithm mentioned above. Readers can reach the sub-procedures/functions (*func_rows_embodying_sequence, proce_find_biggest_in_total_in_embodying_rows, proce_clear_cluster_members_in_sm* and *proce_establish_cluster(start_position)*) from our technical report [14].

3 Data Set and Experimentation

We have tested our approach on sample face images in three face databases, each of which differentiates from the others by various distinctive characteristics to both ensure the viability of the methodology and quantify the results. These are Tarrlab, FEI and Caltech databases. Images in Tarrlab database have no *background noise*. The images in FEI database were captured under *different light variation*. Lastly, images in Caltech face database have different *lighting/expressions/backgrounds*. We incorporated 80 images representing 20 individuals, 4 for each individual, into our study from each of these databases, totally 240 images. The data that we wish to cluster consists of two sets of face images from each of these databases: a set of female and a set of male face images, all of which can be reached from our technical report [14].

User-friendly interfaces have been implemented in C++ programming language to carry out the algorithms mentioned in the previous section. A screenshot of the first interface for acquiring SM is depicted in Fig. 2. With this implementation, a large data set can be trained in several minutes and SM can be acquired by both applying the data set on trained data set and detecting similarities among objects in terms of PC comparison in several minutes. In the first place by employing application, the sample images are cropped using a rectangle as displayed in Fig. 2 as well as delineated in our technical report [14], converted into grayscale and normalization is performed following histogram

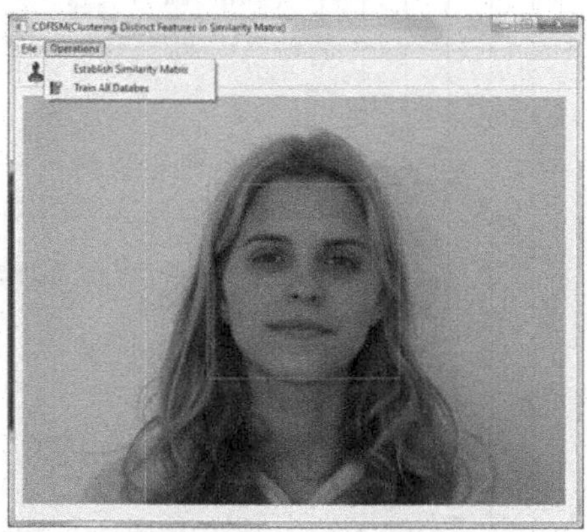

Fig. 2. Interface of the methodology: *Train All Databases* is performed to train the dataset. SM is generated by employing *Establish Similarity Matrix*.

equalization. Then, PCA eigenface method is performed to extract the essential features in face images and Euclidean distance is employed to acquire the similarities or distances among the images by comparing their eigenface features. During this step, one-leave-out cross-validation is carried out. In *leave one out cross validation* we hold one image out as a test image and train the system on all the remaining images. All similarity matrices acquired for the data sets used in the manuscript can be reached from our technical report [14]. The query points of each face image to the other images in the data sets can be seen in SMs. In CISM algorithm regarding the second interface, Rk-means, where k = 4, is employed in the columns of SMs to remove the least resembling images. However, uncertainty in cluster assignment for most of the images is evident; practically, a query point may belong to different clusters with different membership values ranging from 0 to 1. The remaining cells in SM after Rk-means is run is about 20%. Hence, the cost of the calculations is alleviated and finally, the remaining SMs are ready to be analyzed by the algorithm, ACE, as explained in Section 2.1. In-depth analysis through the simplified matrices is carried out and the exact clustering is made employing the ACE algorithm by which most resembling images are brought together and each image is assigned to a specific group. Eventually, clusters are established using the pattern in SM in terms of the positions of not-null cells and the values in these cells without dictating a fixed number beforehand for forming clusters as mentioned in Section 2.1. All the output files of the implementation regarding the three databases can be reached from our technical report [14].

4 Results and Conclusion

The outcomes of ultimate clusters that CISM results in for Tarrlab, FEI and Caltech face images are displayed in Table 1 respectively. A high rate of accuracy has been achieved with the methodology in clustering of objects, namely 97.5%, 98.75% and 80% respectively regarding the three image databases, averaging 92%. Our experimental results show that our model can produce a high rate of accuracy for unsupervised clustering of objects. The methodology runs effectively to reveal interrelated pattern of similarities among objects. Two tailed paired-samples t-test analysis has been performed to evaluate the significance of our results using statistical and computational software tool named SPSS. The findings of the study with the size of our dataset strongly suggest that the outcomes of the study are not coincidental and statistically significant($p < 0.01$). From these results, it has become clear that the proposed hybrid methodology in this study is head and shoulders above the rest. However, there is a large variation in background noise for Caltech database which causes the success rate to reduce significantly, namely from $\approx 98\%$ to $\approx 80\%$ whereas the success rate is not reduced for FEI database in which a large variation of lighting has been applied. We should note that the secrecy of big success rate for FEI database despite huge illumination variations is the result of the histogram equalization method performed on cropped face images to enhance illumination variations

Table 1. Final clustering of images acquired using CDFISM methodology regarding the three databases(objects represented by bold letters are not clustered correctly)

# of clusters	Tarrlab females	Tarrlab males	FEI females	FEI males	Caltech females	Caltech males
1	a1,a2,a3,a4	a1,a2,a3,a4	a1,a2,a3,a4	a1,a2,a3,a4	a1,a2,a3,a4,f1,f2,f3,f4	a1,a2,a3,a4,j1,j2,j3,j4,**h3**,**i2**,**c4**
2	b1,b2,b3,b3	b1,b2,b3,b4,i1,i2,i3,i4	b1,b2,b3,b3	b1,b2,b3,b3	b1,b4	b1,b2,b3,b4
3	c1,c2,c3,c4	c1,c2,c3,c4	c1,c2,c3,c4	c1,c2,c3,c4		c1,c2,c3
4	d1,d2,d3,d4	d1,d2,d3,d4	d1,d2,d3,d4	d1,d2,d3,d4	d1,d2,d3	d2,d3,d4,**h1**
5	e2,e3,e4	e1,e2,e3,e4	e1,e2,e3,e4,**f1**	e1,e2,e3,e4	e1,e3	e1,e2,e3,e4
6	f1,f2,f3,f4	f1,f2,f3,f4	f2,f3,f4	f1,f2,f3,f4		f1,f2,f3,f4
7	g1,g2,g3,g4	g1,g2,g3,g4	g1,g2,g3,g4	g1,g2,g3,g4	g1,g2, g4,**c1**,**e2**, **e4**	g1,g2,g3,g4
8	h1,h2,h3,h4	h1,h2,h3,h4,j1,j2,j3,j4	h1,h2,h3,h4	h1,h2,h3,h4	h2,h3,h4,**b3**,**c2**,**d4**	h2,h4,**d1**
9	i2,i3,i4		i1,i2,i3,i4	i1,i2,i3,i4	i1,i2,i3,i4,**c3**,**c4**,**g3**,**h1**	i1,i3,i4
10	j1,j2,j3,j4,**e1**,**i1**		j1,j2,j3,j4	j1,j2,j3,j4	j1,j2,j3,j4,**b2**	

during data preparation phase; thus, better features are acquired. A background noise reduction method should be employed before training the dataset that has an intensive background noise as in Caltech database. These results are closer to human perception of visual face data discrimination and better than human perception on the basis of clustering a huge amount of data set in archives.

We perform a variety of experiments showing that our hybrid model has been proved to result in clustering objects effectively and efficiently. CDFISM methodology yields a very satisfactory rate of accuracy for clustering of objects by discerning them into correct groups along with achieving a correct number of clusters, 10 in our experiments. To conclude, the proposed methodology in this study leads to improvements in the specific field of clustering different datasets.

Acknowledgement. I would like to thank Prof. Mahesan Niranjan from Southampton University who motivated me to establish the methodology mentioned in the manuscript by discussions during a previous study.

References

1. Sibson, R.: Slink: An optimally efficient algorithm for the single-link cluster method. The Computer Journal 16(1), 30–34 (1973)
2. Defays, D.: Radiology reporting. The Computer Journal 20(4), 364–366 (1977)
3. Bishop, C.M.: Pattern Recognition and Machine Learning. Springer, New York (2006)
4. Ester, M., Kriegel, H.P., Sander, J., Xu, X.: A density-based algorithm for discovering clusters in large spatial databases with noise. In: Simoudis, E., Han, J., Fayyad, U.M. (eds.) Proceedings of the Second International Conference on Knowledge Discovery and Data Mining, pp. 226–231. AAAI Press (1996)
5. Ankerst, M., Breunig, M.M., Kriegel, H.P., Sander, J.: Optics: Ordering points to identify the clustering structure. SIGMOD Rec. 28(2), 49–60 (1999)
6. Kim, T.K., Cipolla, R.: Mcboost: Multiple classifier boosting for perceptual co-clustering of images and visual features. In: Koller, D., Schuurmans, D., Bengio, Y., Bottou, L. (eds.) NIPS, pp. 841–856. Curran Associates, Inc. (2008)
7. Antonopoulos, P., Nikolaidis, N., Pitas, I.: Hierarchical face clustering using sift image features. In: JGuan, L., Hirota, K. (eds.) Computational Intelligence in Image and Signal Processing. IEEE, Honolulu (2007)

8. Perronnin, F., Dugelay, J.L.: Clustering face images with application to image retrieval in large databases (2005)
9. Wolf, L., Hassner, T., Taigman, Y.: Descriptor based methods in the wild. In: Real-Life Images workshop at the ECCV (October 2008)
10. Guillaumin, M., Verbeek, J.J., Schmid, C.: Is that you? metric learning approaches for face identification. In: ICCV, pp. 498–505. IEEE (2009)
11. Mitra, S., Parua, S., Das, A., Mazumdar, D.: A novel data mining approach for performance improvement of EBGM based face recognition engine to handle large database. In: Meghanathan, N., Kaushik, B.K., Nagamalai, D. (eds.) CCSIT 2011, Part I. CCIS, vol. 131, pp. 532–541. Springer, Heidelberg (2011), `http://dx.doi.org/10.1007/978-3-642-17857-3_52`
12. Wozniak, M., Graña, M., Corchado, E.: A survey of multiple classifier systems as hybrid systems. Information Fusion 16, 3–17 (2014)
13. Corchado, E., Wozniak, M., Abraham, A., de Carvalho, A.C.P.L.F., Snásel, V.: Recent trends in intelligent data analysis. Neurocomputing 126, 1–2 (2014)
14. Kuru, K., Niranjan, M.: CDFISM Methodology. Technical report, GATA, Department of IT (December 2013), `http://www.gata.edu.tr/CDFISM`

Fusion of Kohonen Maps Ranked by Cluster Validity Indexes

Leandro Antonio Pasa[1,2],
José Alfredo F. Costa[2], and Marcial Guerra de Medeiros[2]

[1] Federal Technological University of Paraná, UTFPR, Medianeira, Brazil
pasa@utfpr.edu.br
[2] Federal University of Rio Grande do Norte, UFRN, Natal, Brazil
{jafcosta,marcial.guerra}@gmail.com

Abstract. In this study, a new approach to Kohonen Self-Organizing Maps fusion is presented: the use of modified cluster validity indexes as a criterion for merging Kohonen Maps. Computational simulations were performed with traditional dataset from the UCI Machine Learning Repository, with variations in map size, number of subsets to be merged and the percentage of dataset bagging. The fusion results were compared with a regular single Kohonen Map. In some selected parameters, the proposed method achieves a better accuracy measure.

Keywords: Fusion, Self Organizing Maps, Validity Index.

1 Introduction

On several knowledge areas, the amount of information collected and stored increases every day. Due to the volume and dimensionality, these data end up without a proper analysis and interpretation. Ensemble methods may be a useful tool for analysing large amounts of data as well as distributed data.

An ensemble consists of an individual classifiers collection which have differences between each other and lead to a higher generalization than when working separately, a decrease in variance model and higher noise tolerance when compared to a single component [1]. Each classifier operates independently of the others and generates a solution that is combined by the ensemble, producing a single output. The study of ensembles started with Hansen and Salamon's researches [2], combining artificial neural networks, with separate training, resulting in a better system generalization capability.

One of the basic requirements for a successful outcome of the ensemble is that components generalize differently, there is no point combining models that adopt the same procedures and assumptions to solve a problem, it is essential that the errors introduced by each component are uncorrelated [3].

For Kohonen Self-Organizing Maps, this task is relatively simple because different networks can be trained from the same set of feature vectors - varying some training parameters - or different training sets, for example. The main

M. Polycarpou et al. (Eds.): HAIS 2014, LNAI 8480, pp. 654–665, 2014.
© Springer International Publishing Switzerland 2014

difficulty is related to the combination of these maps to generate a single output. The ensemble of Kohonen Maps can be obtained by merging the neurons of the maps to be fused. These neurons must represent the same region of the data input space, in other words, the weight vectors to be fused should be quite similar.

In this study, a new approach to Kohonen Self-Organizing Maps fusion is presented: the use of modified cluster validity indexes as a criterion for merging Kohonen Maps. Also considering the hits in each prototype not the simple mean between weight vectors. The aim of this study was to verify the influence of map size, amount of candidate components and bagging percentage, on the fusion accuracy value.

The remainder of the paper is organized as follows: section 2 presents important concepts about this subject. In Section 3, it is defined all parameters used in this computational simulation. Section 4 shows and discuss the results. Finally, Section 5 presents the conclusions and recommendations for future works.

2 Background

In this section some essentials concepts are presented, such as Kohonen Self-Organizing Maps, Kohonen Maps fusion and a modified version of validity index for use with SOM.

2.1 Self-Organizing Maps

Proposed by Kohonen [4], the Self-Organizing Maps (SOM) consists of an artificial neural network with competitive and unsupervised learning, which performs a non-linear projection of the input space $\Re^p$, with $p \gg 2$, in a grid of neurons arranged in an usually two-dimensional array.

The SOM is organized into an input layer and an output layer. The network inputs x, correspond to the p-dimensional vector space. Each neuron i of the output layer is connected to all the inputs of the network, being represented by a vector of synaptic weights, also in p-dimensional space, $w_i = [wi_1, wi_2, ..., wi_p]^T$. These neurons are connected to adjacent neurons by a neighbourhood relation that describes the topological structure of the map.

In training phase, every time an input pattern x is presented and compared to the neurons of the output layer in a random sequence. A winning neuron, called BMU (Best Match Unit), is chosen through the Euclidean distance criterion and will represent the weight vector with the smallest distance to the input pattern. In other words: the BMU has a great similarity with the input vector.

Assigning the winner neuron index by c, the BMU can be formally defined as the neuron according to the Equation 1.

$$\|x - w_c\| = argmin_i \|x - w_i\| \tag{1}$$

The weights of the BMU and the neighboring neurons, are adjusted according to the Equation 2.

$$w_i(t+1) = w_i(t) + h_{ci}(t)[x(t) - w_i(t)] \tag{2}$$

where t indicates the iteration of the training process, $x(t)$ is the input pattern and $h_{ci}(t)$ is the nucleus of neighbourhood around the winner neuron c.

2.2 Kohonen Maps Fusion

Initially the components candidates to join the ensemble are generated. After this, the components candidates, who will contribute to the better ensemble performance, are selected. Finally, the outputs of each selected component are combined into a output. Special attention should be given to the generation components. If we combine too similar components, there will be no gain to the ensemble. So there must be diversity among them. Some strategies can be adopted to ensure a diversity between de candidates, such as a random initialization of weights for each component, a change in the architecture of single neural network, variation on the training algorithm or a data re-sampling.

In the case of re-sampled data, one of the widely used techniques is bagging [5]. It is a technique to generate different training sets from a single set through re-sampling with replacement. There is the possibility that the components do not generalize satisfactorily, but the ensemble of these components can result in better generalization than the one that would be achieved by the individual component.

It may be that not all components will contribute to the overall ensemble performance. Thus, it is necessary to identify and discard these components, since the inclusion of all candidates in the ensemble may degrade its performance [6].

In this work, the ranking-based selection was used for selecting ensemble components and can be described as: M candidates to compose the ensemble are ordered based on some criteria, such as error, which will measure the individual performance of each component. The candidate who has a better individual performance is the first ensemble component. The next candidate (the second best individual performance) is added to the ensemble. If the performance of the ensemble improves, the committee shall have two components. Otherwise, the newly inserted element is removed. This process is then repeated for all other remaining candidates in the ranked list generated initially.

The combination of the results obtained by each of the components depends on the choice of a consensus function. This function that indicates when the combination may occur directly influences the ensemble performance. In this work, the chosen criterion will be the improvement of the cluster validity index (Generalized Dunn, Davies-Bouldin, CDbw, PBM and Calinski and Harabasz), which will be shown in the next section.

2.3 Validity Indexes

The validity indexes are used to evaluate and validate the results of clustering algorithms, assisting in decision making about the definition of the correct number of clusters formed from a set of data. The literature presents a very wide variety of them, each one suitable for application in datasets with particular characteristics. Some indexes can be applied to datasets that present good separation between clusters, others are designed to high-dimensional data and there also are the ones with no good response in noise presence.

Considering that the majority of cluster validation indices have high computational complexity, which can be a complicating factor in applications involving large volumes of data, Gonçalves [7] has proposed a modification in the validity indexes calculations using a vector quantization produced by Kohonen Map. His research presents the equations for the modified validity indexes used in this work. The synaptic weight vectors (prototypes) are used instead of the original data. Thus, it causes the decrease of the amount of data and therefore the computational complexity for calculating the validity index decreases too. Also to avoid possible differences between the values calculated with all data and only the prototypes, the author proposed that hits should be used in conjunction with the prototypes.

The cluster validity indexes use some calculation related to distance. The modification proposed changes the way these processes are performed. The following example illustrates the proposed change in the calculation of the distance between two clusters, C_i and C_j:

$$\delta_{i,j} = \frac{1}{|C_i|\,|C_j|} \sum_{x \in C_i, y \in C_j} d\,(x, y) \tag{3}$$

In Equation 3, $d\,(x, y)$ is a distance measure, and $|C_i|\,e\,|C_j|$ refers to the clusters' amount of points C_i and C_j, respectively. When the amount of those points is high, the computational complexity is also high. Equation 4 shows the proposed modification:

$$\delta_{i,j}^{SOM} = \frac{1}{|C_i|\,|C_j|} \sum_{w_i \in W_i, w_j \in W_j} h\,(w_i) \cdot h\,(w_j) \cdot d\,(w_i, w_j) \tag{4}$$

Where W_i and W_j are the SOM prototype sets that represent the clusters C_i e C_j, respectively; $d\,(x, y)$ is the same distance measure type (Euclidian, for exemple) of Equation 3, $h\,(w_i)$ is the prototype's hits w_i belonging to W_i and $h\,(w_j)$ is the prototype's hits w_j belonging to W_j.

The Equation 4 presents a lower computational cost, since the quantities involved, w_i and w_j are lower than C_i and C_j. The inclusion of the prototypes' hits $h\,(.)$ leads to error minimization caused by the vector quantization that Kohonen Map produces, since it introduces in the calculation the approach for the points density in the input space, here represented by prototypes.

2.4 Related Works

The interest in ensemble methods applications have grown rapidly. It is possible to find variations in implementations and their applications in diverse knowledge areas.

In the approach of Georgakis *et al.* [8], they compared merged maps with the traditional SOM for document organization and retrieval. As a criterion for combining maps, the Euclidean distance between neurons was used in order to select the neurons were aligned (allowing the merger), working with two maps each time, until all maps are fused into one. The ensemble of SOM obtained a better result than the traditional application.

In work presented in [9], the fusion of neurons was named *Fusion*-SOM and it is based on Voronoi polygons - regions of the input space to which the neurons of the Kohonen map can be associated. The proposed method outperforms the performance of the SOM in MSQE and topology preservation, by effectively locating the prototypes and relating the neighbour nodes.

Corchado [10] used a weighted voting process, called WeVoS-ViSOM, wich pourpose was the preservation of the map topology, in order to obtain the most truthful visualization of datasets. This algorithm was used in a hybrid system to predict business failure [11] This methodology does not outperform single models classification accuracy or quantization error, but it succeeds in reducing the distortion error of single models.

It is possible to find variations in implementations of SOM ensemble methods and their applications in several areas of knowledge as image segmentation [12] robotic [13], identification and characterization of computer attacks [14], unsupervised analysis of outliers on astronomical data [15] and financial distress model [16], among others.

In order to reduce the computational cost of the cluster analysis, the study presented in [7] proposes the simplification of cluster validity indexes using the statistical properties of the SOM, using only the weight vectors and the SOM neurons hits frequency to represent the clusters of the original data set. The proposed methodology was applied in the cluster analysis of remotely sensed images and the experiments indicated that this approach is computationally effective. These modified cluster validity indexes will be utilized in this work as a criterion for maps fusion, as will be shown in the next Section.

3 Experiment Setup

In this approach, the bagging method will be used for generating subsets from the training set, with uniform probability and replacement.

The SOM is applied to each subset produced by bagging. The maps generated are candidates for the ensemble. Since not all the components should be used, because it can affect the final ensemble performance, the way to select these candidates will be through cluster validity index, modified for use with SOM, proposed by Gonçalves [7].

The components will be selected by the construction method, ordering the candidates from their individual performance in relation to the measure of modified validity index. In this paper the validity indexes CDbw [17], Calinski-Harabasz [18], generalized Dunn [19], PBM [20] and Davies-Bouldin [21] were used as parameters in fusion decision process (consensus function).

The fusion process used in this work is based on the work of Georgakis *et al.* [8]. The neurons fusion is obtained by calculating the centroid of the weight vector of the neurons to be merged, as shown in Equation 5

$$w_c = \frac{1}{|W_k|} \sum_{w_i \in W_k} w_i \tag{5}$$

where W_k represents the weight vectors of the neurons to be merged and w_c is the result of the fusion of neurons (centroid).

3.1 Maps Fusion

In this approach, the maps to be merged have the same size, or the same number of neurons. After having generated the maps, the Euclidean distance is calculated between all neurons of the maps to be fused. The fusion occurs between two neurons that have the minimum Euclidean distance between them, indicating that they represent the same region of the input space.

In this study, in order to avoid the influence of dead neurons (neurons without hits) and as the maps are merged in pairs, the Equation 5 is modified to Equation 6.

$$w_c = \frac{w_i \cdot h_i + w_j \cdot h_j}{h_i + h_j} \tag{6}$$

where w_c is the fusion result of neurons w_i and w_j, considering h_i and h_j, the prototype's hits.

3.2 Datasets

The experiments were performed on three datasets from the UCI Repository [22]. They are Iris dataset with 150 instances, 4 attributes and 3 classes, Wine dataset with 178 instances, 13 attributes and 3 classes and Breast Cancer Wisconsin (Original) dataset with 699 instances, 10 attributes and 2 classes.

3.3 Experiments Parameters

In this work, three map sizes were studied: 10x10, 15x15 and 20x20. Through the bagging were generate 10, 50, 100 and 200 subsets. These subsets were created with different data rates: 50%, 70% and 90% of the training set, i.e., for each map size, it has four different numbers of subsets and three different values of percentage of bagging. The datasets were separated in training and test data, in a proportion of 80% and 20% respectively.

For example, for maps size 10x10, the fusion process was tested with 10 subsets with percentage of 50%, 70% and 90% of training set. After this, they were tested with 50 subsets with these same percentages. Following the test for 100 subsets and ending with 200 subsets. This sequence was repeated for map sizes of 15x15 and 20x20. Thus it is possible to evaluate the influences of the number of subsets, the percentage and the map size on the final result.

3.4 Fusion Method

The method consists in the fusion of Kohonen maps formed from fractions of database created by bagging algorithm. The test used to decide whether or not there will be a merger between two subsets is the improved cluster validity index obtained with the result of this merger. The sequence is described below:

1. Generate, through the bagging, subsets from the training set;
2. Apply the SOM to the subsets generated, resulting in N_i $(i = 1, 2, 3, ...)$ maps with the same dimension;
3. Segment the maps, with k-means clustering;
4. Calculate the cluster validity index for each of the N maps and sort them according to this value, from the best index to the worst.
5. The map with the best cluster validity index value is named base map.
6. The base map is fused with the next best map (according to the sorted cluster validity index), according to the Equation 6.
7. Calculate the cluster validity index value of fused map;
8. If there is an improvement in the cluster validity index value, the map resulting from the fusion becomes the base map, then return to step 6 until all maps are fused in this way. If there is no improvement in cluster validity index, the fusion is discarded, then return to step 6 until all maps are fused in this way.

4 Results

The aim of the simulation was to verify in what map size, number of subsets and percentage of bagging configuration, the best value of accuracy could be obtained. Each experiment was run 5 times and was obtained mean values for a 95% confidential interval.

The computational simulations generated 15 tables with the fusion results for each dataset (Iris, Wine and Wisconsin Breast Cancer) ranked by each validity index (Generalized Dunn, Davies-Bouldin, CDbw, PBM and Calinski and Harabasz). It is obvious that not in all situations the model accuracy is greater than that observed in a single SOM. This study has precisely this purpose: to evaluate under what conditions this fusion method gets better results than a unique SOM map.

A table for each dataset (Table 1, 2 and 3) will be presented to give an idea of how the computational simulations were performed. The Tables 4, 5 and 6, summarize, in terms of cluster validity index, the fusion results.

Table 1, shows the accuracy results for Wine dataset, ranked by CDbw Index. The last column shows the regular SOM mean accuracy for each map size. The columns named L and U refers, respectively to lower and upper values for a 95% confidential interval and M column shows the accuracy mean value, for each combination setup.

For exemple, for 10x10 map size, the average value of accuracy for a regular single SOM was 93.71%. After the fusion process, the highest value obtained was 96.18%, considering a bagging with 90% from the training set and 200 subsets components candidates.

Concerning 15x15 map size, the best value of accuracy obtained was 93,93%, considering a bagging with 70% from training set and 10 subsets components candidates. The regular SOM achieved 94,94%. The same result was observed for the 20x20 map size.

Tables 2 and 3, show the results for Breast Cancer Wisconsin and Iris datasets, respectively. The best accuracy values obtained for each map size, compared to single SOM, are highlighted in the tables.

Table 1. Accuracy results for Wine Dataset weighted by CDbw Index

Subsets			10			50			100			200		SOM
Size	(%)	M	L	U	M	L	U	M	L	U	M	L	U	Mean
10x10	50	93.60	91.90	95.29	92.13	89.93	94.34	93.26	88.65	97.87	93.82	90.55	97.09	93.71
	70	93.82	91.83	95.81	95.28	93.66	96.90	95.06	92.93	97.18	96.07	94.64	97.50	93.71
	90	94.72	93.22	96.22	95.84	94.68	97.00	95.62	94.52	96.71	**96.18**	94.92	97.44	93.71
15x15	50	90.70	89.33	92.24	91.69	89.03	94.34	92.47	91.16	93.79	89.78	86.11	93.44	94.94
	70	**93.93**	92.03	95.84	93.48	92.57	94.40	92.58	90.13	95.04	92.36	91.00	93.72	94.94
	90	93.37	91.40	95.34	93.37	91.47	95.27	92.58	91.68	93.49	93.15	91.24	95.05	94.94
20x20	50	91.01	89.06	92.97	91.35	88.12	94.57	93.03	90.87	95.19	90.67	89.83	91.52	94.94
	70	**93.93**	92.84	95.03	93.15	92.05	94.24	92.58	91.49	93.68	91.69	89.39	93.98	94.94
	90	93.15	91.35	94.95	93.60	91.90	95.29	92.36	90.74	93.98	91.57	89.86	93.29	94.94

Table 2. Accuracy results for Breast Cancer Wisconsin Dataset weighted by Calinski and Harabasz Index

Subsets			10			50			100			200		SOM
Map Size	(%)	M	L	U	M	L	U	M	L	U	M	L	U	Mean
10x10	50	96,08	95,30	96,86	**96,57**	96,03	97,12	96,19	95,87	96,52	95,81	95,36	96,26	95,75
	70	95,99	95,79	96,19	96,05	95,63	96,46	96,25	95,98	96,53	96,22	95,99	96,46	95,75
	90	95,84	95,34	96,34	96,25	95,85	96,65	95,93	95,31	96,55	96,14	95,77	96,50	95,75
15x15	50	95,67	95,24	96,09	96,22	95,87	96,58	96,57	96,23	96,92	96,60	96,46	96,75	96,19
	70	95,78	95,35	96,21	95,99	95,15	96,83	96,02	95,50	96,54	96,31	95,80	96,82	96,19
	90	95,87	95,13	96,61	96,22	95,79	96,65	**96,98**	96,75	97,22	96,43	96,16	96,70	96,19
20x20	50	96,02	95,36	96,67	95,81	95,24	96,39	96,14	95,38	96,89	96,22	95,78	96,66	96,34
	70	**96,49**	96,18	96,80	96,28	95,80	96,76	96,19	95,87	96,52	96,14	95,47	96,80	96,34
	90	96,46	95,95	96,96	96,08	95,75	96,40	95,93	95,17	96,69	96,19	95,81	96,58	96,34

Due to the large amount of data generated by the results and to provide a better visualization, the results were summarized in simplified tables - Tables 4, 5 and 6. In these tables it is possible to compare the performance of each cluster validity index used as fusion weighting for each map size, subsets number

Table 3. Accuracy results for Iris Dataset weighted by PBM Index

Subsets		10			50			100			200			SOM
Map Size	(%)	M	L	U	M	L	U	M	L	U	M	L	U	Mean
10x10	50	89,33	86,94	91,73	**93,47**	91,55	95,38	87,07	85,05	89,08	88,00	85,35	90,65	91,47
	70	90,13	86,22	94,05	90,27	88,44	92,09	88,93	85,98	91,89	88,40	85,67	91,13	91,47
	90	89,47	86,58	92,35	90,00	88,53	91,47	88,13	84,90	91,37	88,93	86,67	91,20	91,47
15x15	50	90,27	88,65	91,89	89,47	87,06	91,88	90,67	88,23	93,10	88,93	87,85	90,02	90,00
	70	**91,47**	90,04	92,90	88,53	86,87	90,20	87,60	86,60	88,60	89,73	86,78	92,69	90,00
	90	88,93	86,92	90,95	89,73	88,06	91,41	89,60	88,92	90,28	88,67	86,51	90,83	90,00
20x20	50	89,07	87,45	90,69	90,67	88,16	93,17	89,33	87,30	91,37	89,73	86,33	93,14	90,67
	70	89,33	86,83	91,84	88,53	86,48	90,58	89,60	87,59	91,61	88,27	86,76	89,77	90,67
	90	90,40	87,33	93,47	88,53	87,04	90,03	**91,20**	89,77	92,63	89,33	88,21	90,45	90,67

and bagging percentage. In these tables CH stands for Calinski and Harabasz validity index, DB stands for Davies-Bouldin validity index and Dunn means the Generalized Dunn validity index.

Analysing the first row of the Table 4, for Iris dataset, using the Dunn index as criterion for the maps merging, the 10x10 map size, the best accuracy value was obtained for 50 subsets and bagging of 70% from the training set. With these parameters, the accuracy value (92, 13%) was higher than the accuracy for a single SOM map (91, 47%). The best parameter for Iris dataset (93, 47%) was for PBM index, with 10x10 map size, 50 subsets to be merged bagging of 50% from the training set. This mean that with bagging of 50% of training set, the fusion classification accuracy overcome the accuracy from a single SOM map.

Table 4. Best accuracy for Iris Dataset

				Accuracy	
Index	Map Size	%	Subsets	Single SOM	SOM Fusion
DUNN	10x10	70	50	91,47	92,13
DUNN	15x15	50	200	90,00	92,00
DUNN	20x20	90	100	90,67	90,53
CDBW	10x10	90	200	91,47	91,07
CDBW	15x15	70	10	90,00	91,33
CDBW	20x20	70	100	90,67	91,07
CH	10x10	50	50	91,47	90,67
CH	15x15	70	10	90,00	91,33
CH	20x20	90	100	90,67	91,07
DB	10x10	90	200	91,47	91,07
DB	15x15	50	100	90,00	90,93
DB	20x20	90	10	90,67	90,93
PBM	10x10	50	50	91,47	**93,47**
PBM	15x15	70	10	90,00	91,47
PBM	20x20	90	100	90,67	91,20

In Breast Cancer Wisconsin dataset, Table 5, the best accuracy (96,98%) occurred for Calinski and Harabasz index, with 15x15 map size, 100 subsets to be merged bagging of 90% from the training set.

Table 5. Best accuracy for Breast Cancer Wisconsin Dataset

				Accuracy	
Index	Map Size	%	Subsets	Single SOM	SOM Fusion
DUNN	10x10	50	10	95,75	95,58
DUNN	15x15	90	10	96,19	95,46
DUNN	20x20	90	10	96,34	95,43
CDBW	10x10	50	100	95,75	96,19
CDBW	15x15	90	10	96,19	96,28
CDBW	20x20	90	50	96,34	96,34
CH	10x10	50	50	95,75	96,57
CH	15x15	90	100	96,19	**96,98**
CH	20x20	70	10	96,34	96,49
DB	10x10	50	100	95,75	96,19
DB	15x15	50	10	96,19	96,25
DB	20x20	70	10	96,34	96,52
PBM	10x10	90	100	95,75	96,75
PBM	15x15	90	100	96,19	96,34
PBM	20x20	70	10	96,34	96,57

While in Wine dataset, Table 6, the best accuracy (96, 52%) occurred for PBM index, with 10x10 map size, 50 subsets to be merged bagging of 90% from the training set.

Table 6. Best accuracy for Wine Dataset

				Accuracy	
Index	Map Size	%	Subsets	Single SOM	SOM Fusion
DUNN	10x10	70	100	93,71	95,96
DUNN	15x15	90	200	94,94	96,07
DUNN	20x20	90	50	94,94	95,96
CDBW	10x10	90	200	93,71	96,18
CDBW	15x15	70	10	94,94	93,93
CDBW	20x20	70	10	94,94	93,93
CH	10x10	90	100	93,71	95,51
CH	15x15	70	10	94,94	94,61
CH	20x20	90	200	94,94	94,83
DB	10x10	90	100	93,71	95,73
DB	15x15	90	100	94,94	94,94
DB	20x20	70	50	94,94	94,49
PBM	10x10	90	50	93,71	**96,52**
PBM	15x15	70	100	94,94	95,06
PBM	20x20	70	100	94,94	94,83

5 Conclusion

This work investigated the possibility of merging Kohonen maps ranked by five cluster validity indexes (Generalized Dunn, Davies-Bouldin, CDbw, PBM and Calinski and Harabasz).

In the computer simulations were evaluated different setting for map size, subsets number and different amounts (percentage) of the training set. The results showed that in some situations, merging maps overcame the value of a single SOM network, which works with all data.

The Kohonen Map fusion method achieves values similar or superior to that observed in regular SOM. That is, using a percentage of the training data (not all data), the proposed model achieved satisfactory results compared to SOM, which used all the training set.

Future works involve testing datasets with different characteristics from the ones used in this study. It is also a goal evaluate strategies to enhance visualization of the fused maps, since the fusion Euclidean distance based causes distortion on the map.

References

1. Dietterich, T.G.: Ensemble methods in machine learning. In: Kittler, J., Roli, F. (eds.) MCS 2000. LNCS, vol. 1857, pp. 1–15. Springer, Heidelberg (2000)
2. Hansen, L.K., Salamon, P.: Neural network ensembles. IEEE Transactions on Pattern Analysis and Machine Intelligence 12, 10 (1990)
3. Perrone, M.P., Cooper, L.N.: When networks disagree: ensemble methods for hybrid neural networks. In: Neural Networks for Speech and Image Processing, pp. 126–142. Chapman and Hall (1993)
4. Kohonen, T.: Self-organized maps, 2nd edn. Springer, Berlin (1997)
5. Breiman, L.: Bagging predictors. Machine Learning 24, 123–140 (1996)
6. Zhou, Z.-H., Wu, J., Tang, W.: Ensembling neural networks: many could be better than all. Artificial Intelligence 137(1-2), 239–263 (2002)
7. Gonçalves, M.L., De Andrade Netto, M.L., Costa, J.A.F., Zullo, J.: Data clustering using self-organizing maps segmented by mathematic morphology and simplified cluster validity indexes: an application in remotely sensed images. In: International Joint Conference on Neural Networks, IJCNN 2006, pp. 4421–4428 (2006)
8. Georgakis, A., Li, H., Gordan, M.: An ensemble of SOM networks for document organization and retrieval. In: International Conference on Adaptive Knowledge Representation and Reasoning (2005)
9. Saavedra, C., Salas, R., Moreno, S., Allende, H.: Fusion of self organizing maps. In: Sandoval, F., Prieto, A.G., Cabestany, J., Graña, M. (eds.) IWANN 2007. LNCS, vol. 4507, pp. 227–234. Springer, Heidelberg (2007)
10. Corchado, E., Baruque, B.: WeVoS-ViSOM: an ensemble summarization algorithm for enhanced data visualization. Neurocomputing 75, 171–184 (2012)
11. Borrajo, M.L., Baruque, B., Corchado, E., Bajo, J., Corchado, J.M.: Hybrid neural intelligent system to predict business failure in small-to-medium-size enterprises. International Journal of Neural Systems 21(04), 277–296 (2011)
12. Jiang, Y., Zhi-Hua, Z.: SOM ensemble-based image segmentation. Neural Processing Letters 20(3), 171–178 (2004)

13. Low, K.H., Wee, K.L., Marcelo, H.A.: An ensemble of cooperative extended Kohonen maps for complex robot motion tasks. Neural Computation 17, 1411–1445 (2005)
14. DeLooze, L.L.: Attack characterization and intrusion detection using an ensemble of self-organizing maps. In: 2006 IEEE Information Assurance Workshop, pp. 108–115 (2006)
15. Fustes, D., Dafonte, C., Arcay, B., Manteiga, M., Smith, K., Vallenari, A., Luri, X.: SOM ensemble for unsupervised outlier analysis. Application to outlier identification in the Gaia astronomical survey. Expert Systems with Applications 40(5), 1530–1541 (2013)
16. Tsai, C.-F.: Combining cluster analysis with classifier ensembles to predict financial distress. Information Fusion 16, 46–58 (2014)
17. Halkidi, M., Vazirgiannis, M.: A density-based cluster validity approach using multi-representatives. Pattern Recognition Letters 29, 773–786 (2008)
18. Milligan, G.W., Cooper, M.C.: An examination of procedures for determining the number of clusters in a data set. Psychometrika 50, 159–179 (1985)
19. Bezdek, J.C., Pal, N.R.: Some new indexes of cluster validity. IEEE Transactions on Systems, Man and Cybernetic. B 28, 301–315 (1998)
20. Pakhira, M.K., Bandopadhyay, S., Maulik, U.: Validity index for crisp and fuzzy clusters. Pattern Recognition 37(3), 487–501 (2004)
21. Davies, D.L., Bouldin, D.W.: A cluster separation measure. IEEE Transactions on Pattern Analysis and Machine Intelligence PAMI-1(2), 224–227 (1979)
22. Bache, K., Lichman, M.: Machine Learning Repository. University of California, Irvine, School of Information and Computer Sciences (2013), `http://archive.ics.uci.edu/ml`

Maintaining Case Based Reasoning Systems Based on Soft Competence Model

Abir Smiti and Zied Elouedi

LARODEC, University of Tunis,
Institut Supérieur de Gestion de Tunis,
41 Street of liberty, Bouchoucha, 2000 Le Bardo, Tunisia
smiti.abir@gmail.com,
zied.elouedi@gmx.fr

Abstract. Case-based Reasoning (CBR) is a well known computer reasoning technique. Its deficiency depends on the mass of the case data and the rapidity of the retrieval process that can be wasteful in time. This is due to the number of cases that gets large and the store of cases besieges with ineffective cases, as the noises. This may badly affect the performance of the system in terms of its efficiency, competence and solution quality. Resultantly, maintaining CBR system becomes mandatory.

In this paper, we offer a novel case base maintenance (CBM) policy based on well-organized machine learning techniques, using a soft competence model, in the process of improving the competence of our reduced case base. The intention of our CBM strategy is to shrink the volume of a case base while preserving as much as possible the performance and the competence of the CBR system.

We support our approach with empirical evaluation using different benchmark data sets to show the effectiveness of our method in terms of shrinking the size of the case base and the research time, getting satisfying classification accuracy and improving the competence of the system.

Keywords: Case based reasoning, Case base maintenance, Clustering soft competence model.

1 Introduction

One of the huge ambitions of Hybrid Intelligent Systems is to produce smart methods and systems able to recognize and imitate human way of thinking. Case Based Reasoning (CBR) [1–4] is a well established study scope in Artificial Intelligence that deals with experience-based problem solving. It is a range of reasoning by correspondence. More specifically, CBR uses a database of problems to solve new problems. The database, called the Case Base (CB), is organized from previous cases. The case structure is presented in form of problem description and its solution. In fact, the CBR solves new problems by the four REs CBR cycle [1, 5] (*REtrieve, REuse, REvise, REtain*): The new problem is matched against cases in the case base and one or more related cases are retrieved.

M. Polycarpou et al. (Eds.): HAIS 2014, LNAI 8480, pp. 666–677, 2014.
© Springer International Publishing Switzerland 2014

A solution supported by the matching cases is then reused and checked for success. Except the retrieved case is a close match, the solution will have to be revised generating a new case that can be maintained.

In fact, CBR system can be modernized to keep in mind any novel information exposed in the processing of the new solution. Nevertheless, this would downgrade system performance if the amount of cases has grown exponentially. Consequently, removing superfluous or less useful cases to reach an acceptable error level is one of the most key tasks in maintaining CBR systems.

A range of CBM policies chiefly reflect on two gauges: the size and the accuracy of the Case Base (CB) which touch the performance of the CBR. Or, the quality of CB is not only dedicated to the performance of the system but also to the study of the case base competence which is measured by the range of problems that can be satisfactorily solved. How to make an equilibrium between the performance and competence grow to be a core concern in our study. Hence, we propose a novel case base maintenance policy named Soft Case Base Maintenance (SCBM), which is a multi-objective problem, it can shrink the size of the case base and the retrieval time, improve the accuracy and the competence of the final case base. The rest of the paper is organized as follows: In Section 2, some of strategies for maintenance of the case base will be approached. Section 3 presents our soft competence model. Section 4 describes in detail our new approach for maintaining case base. Section 5 details and analyzes experimental results carried out on data sets from the U.C.I. repository [6]. Finally, Section 6 ends this work and presents future works.

2 Case Base Maintenance Policies: Related Work

An assortment of case base maintenance policies have been proposed to maintain the Case Base (CB), in the literature. Freshly, the case base maintenance topic has drawn more and more consideration to two main measures that deliver to the evaluation of a case base. The first one is the CB's performance [7] which is the answer time that is needed to compute a solution for case targets. This measure can be usually judged by the size of the case base and the accuracy which is the percentage of the problems that can be successfully solved. The second one is the CB's competence [8, 9] which is the range of target problems that can be successfully solved.This last criterion is hard to be measured, so, we need a theoretical model that allows the competence of a case-base to be evaluated and predicted. That's way we create a competence (coverage) model which is able to find some approximations to this set. One branch of CBM research has centered on the partitioning of case base which erects a detailed CB structure and maintains it constantly [10, 11]. We may quote, also, the methods proposed in [5, 12, 13]. They decompose the large case base into small groups of closely related cases using clustering technique and for each small group; they eliminate cases judged to be futile for the CB.

Another branch of research has spotlighted on CBM optimization which exploits an algorithm to erase or revise the entire CB [9]. Besides, we can refer to competence preserving deletion [14]. These methods categorized the cases according to their competence. In the same branch, we can cite selection based data reduction methods that start with an empty set, select a subset of instances from the original set and add it into the new one as Condensed Nearest Neighbor Rule (CNN) [15], Reduced Nearest Neighbor Rule (RNN) [16], Edited Nearest Neighbor Rules (ENN) [17] and the series of Instance Base Learning algorithms (IBL) [18]. These policies aim at reducing a case base by selecting representatives from the training case base.

Nonetheless, there are some troubles when using these CBM methods. In fact, many of them suffer from the diminish of competence especially when it exists some noisy cases, since the system's competence depends on the type of the cases stored. Furthermore, we have also to declare, that the trend in this area of research is to deal with fuzziness of the case base where one case can belong to more than one competence group which can be non-uniform. These last points have been neglected by many CBM strategies.

3 SCM: Soft Competence Model for Case Based Reasoning

To amend these troubles quoted above, we need an efficient model for computing case base competence. This coverage model will help us to build a strong soft case base maintenance strategy. As a result, we portray, in this Section, our model for computing case base coverage, named SCM- Soft Coverage model based on fuzzy Mahalanobis Distance and soft Clustering. The innovation of this work consists of proposing efficient techniques of machine learning to distinguish the important cases, which invoke the quality of the system, whether noisy cases or isolated cases or similar cases, in imprecise context [19].

Hence, we have delineated three central types of cases which should be regarded as the key to achieve a good estimate of coverage computing:

- CN_i: Noisy cases are unpleasant cases. They can decline the performance of the case base because they shrink the classification accuracy. In addition, they give the wrong impression about the estimation of the CBs coverage. Therefore, the CBR's quality can negatively diminish. In analytical tasks, CN_i are cases that do not belong to any set of similar cases. The best option in this circumstance is to identify cases expected to be noisy and give them an empty set as a coverage value
- CS_i: Every case from a group of similar cases presents analogous coverage values, for the reason that they belong to the same competence set, they cover the same group of cases. Consequently, the coverage value of each case equals to the number of cases in this group (n).
- CI_i: There are some cases that are much distant to the other members in one competence group. We can regard them as isolated cases. In analytical tasks, CI_i belongs to a set of similar cases not like those of type CN_i but it is farther than the CS cases. It covers only itself. Accordingly, the coverage of each case of this type equals to one.

Based on these explanations, we obtain a new coverage model named SCM-Soft Competence model for Case based reasoning. Our new plan pinpoints these three sorts of cases and affects the suitable coverage value to each type. To apply this idea, we necessitate first a clustering procedure because it guarantees that each group is small and surrounded similar cases, so it is effortless to spot the different types of cases. After that, for each small cluster: the cases, which are near to the cluster's center and close to each other, are considered as cases of the type of CS_i. The cases, which are considered as cases of the type CI_i. Finally, the cases, which are outside the clusters and have not affected to a determined cluster, are considered as cases of the type CN_i.

3.1 First Step: Clustering

Among the proposed clustering approaches, we should, ideally, use a method that while clustering and creating groups of similar cases, can smooth the discover of the different types of cases in such data sets. So, we prefer to use the fuzzy clustering method named "soft DBSCAN" proposed in [20]. We can resume the basic steps of this clustering technique as follows:

Algorithm 1. Basic Soft DBSCAN Algorithm

1. Begin
2. m: weighting exponent ($m > 2$)
3. ξ: tolerance level
4. Run DBSCAN and find:
   x = number of noises
   k = number of clusters
5. $c \leftarrow x + k$
6. Create the initial fuzzy partition:
   if $x_i \in c_j$ then $u_{ij} \leftarrow 1$
   Else $u_{ij} \leftarrow 0$
7. $t \leftarrow 0$
8. Repeat
   Update U_t as following: $\text{cr}\mu_{ik} = [\sum_{j=1}^{c}(\frac{MD_{ik}}{MD_{jk}})^{\frac{2}{m-1}}]^{-1}$
   Where MD_{ik} is the Mahalanobis distance between x_k and v_k
   Calculate v_t as following
   $v_i = \frac{1}{\sum_{k=1}^{n}\mu_{ik}^{m}}\sum_{k=1}^{n}\mu_{ik}^{m}x_{ik}$ i= 1, 2,...,c
9. Until $\|U_t - U_{t-1}\| \leq \xi$
10. $(U, v) \leftarrow (U_t, v_t)$
11. noisy points = $\{x_{ij}|cj = x_{ij}\}$
12. End

This technique is an appropriate clustering method for our SCM coverage technique because it has a number of good aspects: it can create regions which may have an arbitrary shape and the points inside a region may be arbitrarily distributed, it can detect points expected to be noises and it is able to assign one data point into more than one cluster by affecting to each observation a "degree of membership" to each of the classes in a way that is consistent with the distribution of the data.

3.2 Second Step: Distinguishing the Different Types of Cases

Once we have partitioned the original case memory by soft DBSCAN, we select cases which our clustering technique mentions them as noises. The Soft DBSCAN selects these cases as noises because they have membership degrees values bigger than to belong to other clusters. For these cases (CN_i), we accord them an empty set as coverage value. For each cluster determined by the first step, each case gives weighted value of the cluster, and the weight is given by the membership degree of the fuzzy membership function. Heretofore, the cases which are distant from the core of the cluster are judged as cases of type "Isolated cases" CI. The paramount practice to spot them is the Mahalanobis distance with weighted mean and covariance of the cluster.

$$MD_{x_i,V_i} = ((x_i - V_i)^T F_i^{-1}(x_i - V_i))^{1/2} \tag{1}$$

Where V_i gives weighted mean of the cluster, and the weight is given by the membership degree of the fuzzy membership function and F_n is the fuzzy covariance matrix of the i-th cluster, is defined by:

$$F_i = \frac{\sum_{k=1}^{n}(\mu_{ik})(x_{ik} - V_i)(x_{ik} - V_i)^T}{\sum_{k=1}^{n}(\mu_{ik})} \tag{2}$$

Where μ_{ik} is the membership degree defined in the first step by the soft DBSCAN clustering technique.

Based on our hypotheses, the cases with a large Mahalanobis distance in a cluster are selected as CI type. The brink of bulky distance depends on when the similarity between cases and the center starts raising. For that, we need to compare the MD of each case by the standard deviation of this cluster, in order to measure how closely the cases cluster around the mean and how are spread out in a distribution of the cluster. This last is a good measure of the categorization of CI and CS cases, such the case whose MD is superior to the standard deviation of the cluster, will be consider as CI case, else it will be CS type.

$$Cov(x_i) = \begin{cases} 1 \text{ if } MD(x_i, V_i) > \sigma \\ |CS| \text{ otherwise} \end{cases}$$

As a result, we have affected for each case the appropriate coverage value depending on its type.

4 SCBM: Soft Case Base Maintenance Method Based on Soft Coverage Model

Our endeavor is to pick few cases from a large set of candidates that will correctly classify a given set. In that way, we shrink the size and safeguard maximum the competence of the system. We present a novel approach of case base maintenance based on the machine learning techniques, called SCBM (*S*oft *CBM*aintenance method) to reduce the size of a case base while preserving as much as possible the performance and the competence of the CBR system. The intend of our SCBM is to eradicate cases which have no upshot on competence from CB. SCBM will erect an abridged case base CB' by selecting cases from CB and achieving a good generalization accuracy and CB' coverage.

Our new SCBM strategy is based on the SCM described in the previous section. It responds to this question: which cases can we delete without reducing the quality of the system? From our SCM model, we can discern which case has no aftermath to the competence and the performance of the CBR in order to eliminate it. This type of case has either a poor coverage value, or it exists another case similar to it, that can replace it. Hence, its deletion cannot reduce the quality of our CBR system. Based on this notice, we can delete first the cases which have zero as coverage values, that means the noisy cases (CN). This is totally legitimate, since these cases have no fruitful role in our case base, they just mislead the computation of the CBs coverage and they can drop the competence of the system and also the reduce of the CB accuracy, i.e. the performance of the CBR. So, as a first step of our SCBM method, we have to run our SCM model and delete all cases which have a zero as coverage value (delete cases designed as CN type).

In the second step, we can get rid of cases whose coverage values equal to the number of cases in one competence group. Here, we talk about the cases of type CS mentioned by our SCM model. Since these cases are similar, they play the same role, they share the same coverage set of cases. Hence, deleting any member of this group has no effect on competence since the remaining cases offer the same coverage. Hereafter, for each competence group generated by our SCM model, we can remove these cases and keep only one of them which can replace all this set. This is obvious, by reason of the competence of our CB can not change.

The third step focuses on the type of CI selected by our SCM model, that means the cases which have 1 as coverage value. For this type, we keep these cases because they are reachable by no other case but themselves, their deletion directly reduces the competence of system because there is no other case that can cover them or replace them in the coverage computing.

So, based on these deductions, we can generate a small case base (CB') without reducing the competence of our CB.

5 Experimental Analysis

In this Section, we try to show the effectiveness of our SCBM maintenance approach.

In order to evaluate the performance rate of our SCBM, we test on ten diverse data sets with different sizes. In this paper, we use public datasets obtained from the U.C.I. repository of Machine Learning databases [6]. Details of these databases are presented in Table 1. Different results carried out from these simulations will be presented and analyzed.

Table 1. Description of databases

Dataset	Ref.	#instances	#attributes
IRIS	IR-150	150	4
Ionosphere	IO-351	351	34
Breast-W	BW-698	698	9
Blood-T	BT-748	748	5
Indian	IN-768	768	9
Vehicle	V-846	846	18
Mammographic	MM-961	961	6
Cloud	C-1023	1023	10
Yeast	Y-1483	1483	8
Abalone	AB-4176	4176	8

As we have indicated, the aim of our approach is to diminish the case base while preserving as much as possible the competence and the performance of the system. For that, we use the following criteria:

"**Size (S %)**" the average storage percentage which presents the rate of the reduction of size. It computes how much our SCBM policy can reduce the original Case Base. For that, we adopt this canon:

$$S = \frac{number\ of\ final\ cases}{size\ of\ training\ casebase} \times 100 \tag{3}$$

"**PCC (PCC%)**" the mean percentage of correct classification over stratified ten fold cross validation runs in front of 1-Nearest-Neighbor. We apply the 1-NN algorithm to the same datasets and the same ten-fold cross-validation task to obtain the average accuracy rate.

"**Time**" the retrieval time in seconds exerted in 1-Nearest Neighbor algorithm. The purpose of this criterion is to show the performance of our method in the reducing of the retrieval time.

"**Competence (Comp%)**" is the ratio of the cardinal of the covering set and cardinal of the reachability set. It refers to the range of target problems that a system can successfully solve.

Like that we evaluate our work in multifarious sides namely competence and performance of the CB.

The SCBM technique has been described, which, we claim, benefits from improved efficiency, competence, and quality characteristics. From Table 2, we

Table 2. Comparing our new SCBM to the initial CB for the system CBR

Datasets	CBR				SCBM			
	Performance			*Competence*	*Performance*			*Competence*
	S (%)	*PCC (%)*	*Time (s)*	*Comp (%)*	*S (%)*	*PCC (%)*	*Time (s)*	*Comp (%)*
IR-150	100.00	97.33	0.0163	92.16	53.33	99.97	0.0087	95.6
IO-351	100.00	93.16	0.0724	87.36	48.43	98.82	0.0264	98.29
BW-698	100.00	97.99	0.1043	89.04	14.3	98.8	0.0016	88.84
BT-748	100.00	78.81	0.0902	92.91	13.37	94	0.007	96.79
IN-768	100.00	83.92	0.1581	92.60	18.82	97.72	0.113	82.96
V-846	100.00	82.03	0.2521	94.17	8.27	98.286	0.0079	99.53
MM-961	100.00	84.92	0.3157	89.96	27.47	96.59	0.0223	83.14
C-1023	100.00	61.24	0.5324	92.69	8.5	98.036	0.0069	98.72
Y-1483	100.00	86.16	0.3682	90.36	50.02	97.42	0.2235	75.18
AB-4176	100.00	97.93	0.4023	89.06	33.6	97.809	0.0158	96.293

validate these claims with a comprehensive experimental study, where we compare the rate of performance and competence of the various datasets generated by our SCBM with the ones provided by the original case bases.

Several observations can be made from the results in this table. As we expect, our method defeats the original data editing methods on average. The most obvious result is that "Mammographic" gives good results compared with the original case base, where its size is reduced by 27.47 %, its accuracy shows improvement by more than 96.59 % and for the retrieval time has been reduced 14 times, with keeping approximately the same competence rate, opposed to the initial size of the case base which contains all instances, and the initial accuracy (84.92 %) with original retrieval time (0.3157 seconds).

These high-quality results attest that our SCBM deletion method able to shrink the mass of the CB while safeguarding and even improving the competence of the system. We allege this achievement to the benefit of our SCM model which distinguishes the type of each case, chiefly the cases with higher coverage values and also the assistance of our Soft DBSCAN that improves the accuracy values.

In the ultimate part of our testing, we balance our SCBM with other well known reduction techniques: we run CMCD [5], COID [12], CNN [15], RNN [16], ENN [17] and Instance Based learning IBL schemes [18] on the previous data sets.

It comes as no surprise, that our experimental results in Tables 3, 4, 5, 6 show that IB2, IB3, CNN, ENN and RNN delete many cases, but at a severe cost in accuracy and competence. This is not the case, for our strategy SCBM where it strikes a balance between accuracy and competence, and deletion.

From table 3, our SCBM achieves a great data reduction by more than half for the most datasets, which is inferior to the other policies. For instance, SCBM retains over 50% of the data instances of "Yeast' case base, whereas 70% for IB2, IB3 and ENN, 62 % for CNN. Note that SCBM and CMCD give the best reduction rate for the almost datasets, we can elucidate this truth that the clustering techniques used in these two CBM strategies are proficient in term of giving for each type of case its appropriate value, especially the noisy cases.

Table 3. Comparing storage size (%) of SCBM to well known reduction schemes

Datasets	SCBM	CMCD	WCOID	COID	CNN	RNN	ENN	IB2	IB3
IR-150	53.33	52	57.33	47.3	27.63	93.33	95.33	24	24
IO-351	48.43	29.34	13.39	13.96	15.3	83.91	86.89	25.07	25
BW-698	14.3	25.5	29.46	26.59	26.3	26.87	81.69	35.48	30.46
BT-748	13.37	12.03	20.45	19	37.3	38.72	32.10	26.09	26.00
IN-768	18.828	13.12	15.34	16.00	43.66	42.08	24.39	22.12	21.00
V-846	8.27	17.77	20.80	51.89	43.62	43.63	76.48	46.57	50.73
MM-961	27.47	17.48	51.00	53.18	64.21	54.26	82.52	53.48	53.93
C-1023	8.5	11.57	32.45	39.29	62.3	72.89	58.46	84.85	87.85
Y-1483	50.02	51.3	68.07	68.22	62.34	64.02	69.59	69.79	69.98
AB-4176	33.6	25.86	30.67	35.58	38.5	58.55	87.5	51.92	51.92

From the experimental results in Table 4, we obtain the similar observations as before. This experiment further validates the superiority of our method since it works well for different size of datasets. The accuracies provided by SCBM show better values. For example, the dataset "Cloud", the PCC provided by SCBM (98,03%) is more efficient compared to the one given by the other policies: 97.13 % for CMCD, 96.22% for WCOID, 96.54% for COID, 82.92% for CNN, 89.43% for RNN, 70.4% for ENN, 59% for IB2 and IB3.

Table 4. Comparing classification accuracy (PCC %) of SCBM to well known reduction schemes

Datasets	SCBM	CMCD	WCOID	COID	CNN	RNN	ENN	IB2	IB3
IR-150	99.97	98.98	96.56	96.94	73	94.23	91.6	91.67	91.67
IO-351	98.82	98.572	97.77	98.9	70.83	70.83	98.36	95.45	94.89
BW-698	98.8	98.157	95.45	98.01	68.18	67.05	94.66	69.69	70.56
BT-748	94	93.978	79.56	79.12	67.94	66.65	71.63	74.69	74.21
IN-768	97.72	95.977	94.71	92.06	67.4	69.19	99.14	87.39	88.26
V-846	98.28	95.996	95.45	87.24	57.58	57.45	82.45	74.44	73.73
MM-961	96.59	89.988	89.12	89.31	70.82	78.6	77.04	66.28	66.42
C-1023	98.03	97.132	96.22	96.54	82.92	89.43	70.4	59.16	59.5
Y-1483	97.42	97.566	88.1	86.78	83.56	83.92	88.08	73.82	73.38
AB-4176	97.80	97.618	96.44	96.19	68.75	62.5	96.7	91.2	91.67

For the retrieval time, as shown in table 5, our SCBM outperforms the other policies. Actually, SCBM recorded higher classification accuracies and lower storage requirements than did the other techniques, it is logical to generate the shortest time of research phase. For instance, for Abalone case base, our policy offers less than 0.0158 seconds as retrieval time, whereas more than 0.07 for the other techniques.

Table 5. Comparing retrieval time in seconds of SCBM to well known reduction schemes

Datasets	SCBM	CMCD	WCOID	COID	CNN	RNN	ENN	IB2	IB3
IR-150	0.0087	0.014	0.0244	0.0252	0.0111	0.0101	0.0137	0.0024	0.0026
IO-351	0.0264	0.0352	0.55	0.58	0.0069	0.81	0.616	0.0122	0.102
BW-698	0.0016	0.0341	0.116	0.134	0.43	0.35	0.734	0.244	0.227
BT-748	0.007	0.0078	0.0212	0.076	0.098	0.183	0.1941	0.2035	0.197
IN-768	0.113	0.0044	0.0102	0.0263	0.05	0.067	0.0266	0.0102	0.0092
V-846	0.0079	0.0044	0.0755	0.0771	0.064	0.0604	0.1349	0.0595	0.0581
MM-961	0.0223	0.0607	0.0664	0.0532	0.208	0.199	0.815	0.339	0.0327
C-1023	0.0069	0.0051	0.0671	0.0536	1.802	1.842	0.931	0.2079	0.1746
Y-1483	0.2235	0.3449	0.544	0.771	0.64	0.604	0.1349	0.595	0.581
AB-4176	0.0158	0.0706	0.189	0.157	0.111	0.101	0.137	0.24	0.26

Table 6. Comparing competence rate (comp %) of SCBM to well known reduction schemes

Datasets	SCBM	CMCD	WCOID	COID	CNN	RNN	ENN	IB2	IB3
IR-150	95.6	92.75	89.71	89.71	86.94	87.44	86.26	88.93	88.95
IO-351	98.29	90.47	86.98	86.92	84.41	84.87	83.27	83.54	84.44
BW-698	88.84	98	85.59	85.38	84.75	84.75	88.73	87.33	87.39
BT-748	96.79	88.66	91.00	89.25	91.90	92.46	89.72	92.37	92.60
IN-768	82.96	80	82.50	80.92	83.78	84.41	84.38	78.52	78.52
V-846	99.53	97.33	90.43	92.19	52.67	55.22	84.62	76.34	74.25
MM-961	83.14	89.56	83.70	85.88	79.97	70.11	70.32	89.36	89.57
C-1023	98.72	98.33	85.92	85.87	83.02	83.85	89.74	81.66	80.74
Y-1483	75.18	93.33	89.51	89.03	56.27	57.90	88.45	90.07	89.92
AB-4176	96.29	89.04	88.65	87.09	81.33	81.61	74.18	73.29	81.19

Analogous examinations are achieved comparing to other CBM policies, in which our SCBM has the most excellent competence rates, as shown in Table 6. For instance, the coverage rate for "Blood-T" is 96.79%, which symbolizes a vast difference judged against the one given by CMCD (88.66%), WCOID (91%), COID (89.25%), CNN (91.90%), RNN (92.46%), ENN (89.72%), IB2 (92.37%) and IB3 (92.60%). This is due to our soft competence model and its effectiveness, in terms of affecting the accurate value for each case. Like that, we can eradicate cases with pitiable coverage and produce a new subset of cases with lofty competence rate.

In summary, these results show that SCBM displays superior learning performance on all training sets both in terms of storage requirements and in its ability to filter unskilled cases. Since, our Soft Competence Model successfully detected and eliminated noisy instances from the concept description, due to the efficient of our Soft DBSCAN clustering technique. SCBM recorded higher classification accuracies and lower storage requirements than did the other CBM techniques, when the training instances were corrupted with noise. Besides, due to the performance of our SCM model, our SCBM method benefits from superior efficiency, competence and quality characteristic.

6 Conclusion and Futures Works

In this paper, we have proposed a maintaining case base approach named SCBM - Soft Case Base Maintenance- which is able to maintain the case bases by improving the performance and the competence of the CBR system. It is based on our soft case base competence model which uses Mahalanobis distance and the clustering technique Soft DBSCAN.

This policy is characterized by its performances at solving several purposes once at a time: it can shrink the size of the case base and the retrieval time, improve the accuracy and the competence of the final case-base.

Our deletion policy can be improved in future works by introducing the effects of incremental data on the CBM work. Besides, in order to show the performance of this method, we plan to apply it in the medical domain through the diagnosis which is performed to solve new problems by remembering solutions to problems that are similar to the current problem.

References

1. Aamodt, A., Plaza, E.: Case-based reasoning: Foundational issues, methodological variations, and system approaches. Artificial Intelligence Communications 7(1), 39–52 (1994)
2. Kolodner, J.: An introduction to case-based reasoning. Artificial Intelligence Review 6(1), 3–34 (1992)
3. Baruque, B., Borrajo, M., Corchado, E., Bajo, J., Corchado, J.M.: Hybrid neural intelligent system to predict business failure in small-to-medium-size enterprises. International Journal of Neural Systems 21(4), 277–296 (2011)
4. Abraham, A.: Hybrid approaches for approximate reasoning. Journal of Intelligent and Fuzzy Systems 23(2-3), 41–42 (2012)
5. Smiti, A., Elouedi, Z.: WCOID: Maintaining case-based reasoning systems using Weighting, Clustering, Outliers and Internal cases Detection. In: Proceedings of the eleventh International on Intelligent Systems Design and Applications, ISDA 2011, pp. 37–42 (2011)
6. Asuncion, A., Newman, D.J.: UCI machine learning repository (2007), `http://www.ics.uci.edu/mlearn`
7. Leake, D.B., Wilson, D.C.: Remembering Why to Remember: Performance-Guided Case-Base Maintenance. In: Blanzieri, E., Portinale, L. (eds.) EWCBR 2000. LNCS (LNAI), vol. 1898, pp. 161–172. Springer, Heidelberg (2000)
8. Smyth, B., McKenna, E.: Competence guided incremental footprint-based retrieval. Journal of Knowledge-Based Systems 14, 155–161 (2002)
9. Haouchine, M.K., Chebel-Morello, B., Zerhouni, N.: Competence-preserving case-deletion strategy for case-base maintenance. In: Similarity and Knowledge Discovery in Case-Based Reasoning Workshop, 9th European Conference on Case-Based Reasoning, ECCBR 2008, pp. 171–184 (2008)

10. Yang, Q., Wu, J.: Keep it simple: A case-base maintenance policy based on clustering and information theory. In: Hamilton, H.J. (ed.) Canadian AI 2000. LNCS (LNAI), vol. 1822, p. 102. Springer, Heidelberg (2000)
11. Cao, G., Shiu, S.C.K., Wang, X.: A fuzzy-rough approach for case base maintenance. In: International Conference on Case Based Reasoning, pp. 118–130 (2001)
12. Smiti, A., Elouedi, Z.: COID: Maintaining Case Method Based on Clustering, Outliers and Internal Detection. In: Lee, R., Ma, J., Bacon, L., Du, W., Petridis, M. (eds.) SNPD 2010. SCI, vol. 295, pp. 39–52. Springer, Heidelberg (2010)
13. Smiti, A., Elouedi, Z.: Competence and performance-improving approach for maintaining case-based reasoning systems. In: The International Conference on Computational Intelligence and Information Technology – CIIT, Chennai, India, pp. 37–42 (2012)
14. McKenna, E., Smyth, B.: A competence model for case-based reasoning. In: 9th Irish Conference on Artificial Intelligence and Cognitive Science, pp. 208–220 (1998)
15. Chou, C.H., Kuo, B.H., Chang, F.: The generalized condensed nearest neighbor rule as a data reduction method. In: International Conference on Pattern Recognition, vol. 2, pp. 556–559 (2006)
16. Manry, J., Yu, T., Wilson, D.R.: Prototype classifier design with pruning. International Journal on Artificial Intelligence Tools, 261–280 (2005)
17. Wilson, D.L.: Asymptotic properties of nearest neighbor rules using edited data. IEEE Transactions on Systems, Man and Cybernetics 2(3), 408–421 (1972)
18. Aha, D.W., Kibler, D., Albert, M.K.: Instance-based learning algorithms. Machine Learning, 37–66 (1991)
19. Smiti, A., Elouedi, Z.: Modeling competence for case based reasoning systems using clustering. In: The 26th International FLAIRS Conference, The Florida Artificial Intelligence Research Society, Florida, USA, pp. 399–404 (2013)
20. Smiti, A., Elouedi, Z.: Soft DBSCAN: Improving DBSCAN Clustering method using fuzzy set theory. In: The 6th International Conference on Human System Interaction, HSI 2013, Spot, Poland, pp. 380–385 (2013)

Clustering-Based Ensemble of One-Class Classifiers for Hyperspectral Image Segmentation

Bartosz Krawczyk[1], Michał Woźniak[1], and Bogusław Cyganek[2]

[1] Department of Systems and Computer Networks, Wrocław University of Technology, Wrocław, Poland
{bartosz.krawczyk,michal.wozniak}@pwr.wroc.pl
[2] AGH University of Science and Technology
Al. Mickiewicza 30, 30-059 Krakow, Poland
cyganek@agh.edu.pl

Abstract. In this paper, we propose a new ensemble for an effective segmentation of hyperspectral images. It uses one-class classifiers as base learners. We prove, that despite the multi-class nature of hyperspectral images using one-class approach can be beneficial. One need simply to decompose a multi-class set into a number of simpler one-class tasks. One-class classifiers can handle difficulties embedded in the nature of the hyperspectral data, such as a large number of classes, class imbalance and noisy pixels. For this task, we utilise our novel ensemble, based on soft clustering of the object space. On the basis of each cluster, a weighted one-class classifier is constructed. We show a fast method for calculating weights assigned to each object, and for an automatic calculation of preferred number of clusters. We propose to build such ensemble for each of the classes and then to reconstruct the original multi-class hyperspectral image using Error-Correcting Output Codes. Experimental analysis, carried on a set of benchmark data and backed-up with an extensive statistical analysis, proves that our one-class ensemble is an efficient tool for handling hyperspectral images and outperforms several state-of-the-art binary and multi-class classifiers.

Keywords: machine learning, one-class classification, classifier ensemble, clustering, hyperspectral image, image segmentation.

1 Introduction

Hyperspectral sensors contain hundreds of spectral channel, each one covering a small portion of electromagnetic spectrum. This spectral high-resolution is expected to allow making detailed thematic maps of remote sensing data by means of spectral classification of different materials expected in the sensed scene. However, the classification of hyperspectral data is a challenging task due to the high dimension of the data, the imbalance of the class distributions, and the variety of noise sources that introduce a high variability of spectra within each class.

M. Polycarpou et al. (Eds.): HAIS 2014, LNAI 8480, pp. 678–688, 2014.
© Springer International Publishing Switzerland 2014

So far, significant attention has been paid to the use of machine learning techniques for analysing hyperspectral data [18]. Some works tend to use pixel-based representation, while other search for a more sophisticated approaches, that combinine both spatial and spectral processing, i.e. applying morphological area filtering to the first principal component of the spectral data [7], performing feature extraction from 3-D Gabor wavelet transformation [19], proposing extensions of SVM [15] with spatial terms, following Bayesian approaches [16], and, finally, regularizing pixel spectral classification by a watershed segmentation [20].

To formalize the hyperspectral classification problem, let $S \equiv \{1, ..., n\}$ denote a set of integers indexing the n pixels of a hyperspectral image. Let $\omega \equiv \{\omega_1, ..., \omega_K\}$ be a set of K class labels, and let $x \equiv \{x_1, ..., x_n\} \in \mathbb{R}^{d \times n}$ denote an image in which the pixels are d-dimensional spectral vectors. Let $y \equiv \{y_1, ..., y_n\} \in \omega^n$ denote an image of class labels. The goal of hyperspectral image classification is to infer the class labels $y_i \in \omega$ from the feature vectors $x_i \in \mathbb{R}^d$, for each image pixel $i \in \mathbb{S}$.

As mentioned, hyperspectral segmentation and classification is a non-trivial task, due to the difficulties embedded in the nature of the data. Our previous works with difficult datasets [11] directed our attention towards the one-class classification (OCC) domain [10].

OCC is based on the principle, that during the training stage only objects coming from a single class are available. Such distribution is called the target concept or target class, and is denoted by ω_T. OCC aims at establishing a decision boundary that encloses all relevant target class examples, thus describing the given concept [22]. During the exploitation step, new objects that were unknown during the training, may appear. These may originate from one or more distributions and represent data that do not belong to the target concept. Such objects, denoted by ω_O, are called outliers. OCC is useful in many real-life applications, where positive examples are abundant, but due to the cost, time or legal constraints it is impossible to obtain counterexamples.

Hyperspectral images are multi-class datasets, therefore representatives of all of the classes are present in the training set. Therefore, one may wonder why to use a OCC approach, when all types of examples can be presented to the trained classifier. OCC discards all of the counterexamples and concentrates only on the target class. By this, it has a limited knowledge about other classes and does not take a full advantage of the information being available. Yet recent reports show, that using OCC for multi-class data can be beneficial [12]. One-class classifiers detect unique features of the target class. They are insensitive to imbalanced distribution, robust to class noise and can handle irregular or chunked object distributions. Additionally, they decompose a complex multi-class problem into a set of simpler one-class tasks.

In this paper, we use our novel approach for forming one-class classifier committees, based on data clustering in the object space [13]. OCC models are built based on each of the clusters. This can be seen as an extension of the popular family of ensembles derived from the idea of *clustering and selection* proposed by Kuncheva [14]. In our approach we further extend this concept by utilizing weighted one-class classifiers and proposing a new scheme for calculating their weights. We show, that decomposition of multi-class hyperspectral images with our one-class ensemble leads to an excellent segmentation accuracy.

2 One-Class Clustering Ensemble

In this work, we propose to use a novel scheme for creating ensembles of one-class classifiers - a committee named one-class clustering-based ensemble (OCClustE) [13]. It is based on the clustering of a object space into smaller partitions. OCLustE has proven itself as an efficient algorithm for handling one-class problems and as a useful tool for decomposing multi-class datasets. In this paper, we aim at investigating its usefulness in the task of hyperspectral image segmentation. Let us present shortly the basic concepts behind the OCClustE framework.

This ensemble classifier uses a clustering algorithm to partition the object space into atomic subsets. In the next step each of these clusters is used to train a one-class classifier. This leads to the formation of a pool of K classifiers assigned to the target class, as follows:

$$\Pi = \{\Psi^{(1)}, \Psi^{(2)}, ..., \Psi^{(K)}\}. \quad (1)$$

Such a process of forming a pool of base classifiers assures the initial diversity among learners (as a result of using different inputs in their training) and their complementarity (as classifiers together cover all the decision space), which leads to better performance of the ensemble.

OCClustE uses kernel fuzzy c-means, which is a modification of the fuzzy c-means algorithm that operates in an artificial feature space created by a kernel function [24].

To further improve the performance of OCClustE, aweighted one-class support vector machine (WOCSVM) is used as the base learner [3]. It has been shown, that weighted one-class classifiers can outperform the canonical ones that assume the uniform importance level of all objects in the training set. This is due to controlling the degree of influence that each object has on the shape of the decision boundary. What is worth mentioning, weighted methods are insensitive to internal outliers, that may be present in the target class (as it may contain irrelevant, noisy objects). By assigning them a low weight, they have minimal impact on the process of shaping the decision boundary.

The quality of WOCSVM relies strongly on the proper establishment of weights, which is heuristic and time-consuming process [3]. In OCClustE, we implemented a novel approach for establishing the degree of importance of objects, based on the output of clustering algorithm. A fuzzy clustering algorithm is used, that returns the membership functions for each object in the given cluster. These membership values are then used directly as weights for WOCSVM. With this new weights correspond to the degree of importance of a given object in a cluster and are pre-calculated. This significantly reduce the computational time needed for training each WOCSVM.

Number of clusters on the target class is equal the number of classifiers in the ensemble (as on each cluster we train an individual WOCSVM). This has a strong impact on the performance of the OCClustE. To alleviate this problem, we propose a procedure for an automatic assessment of the number of clusters. The entropy of the membership values is used, which depends on the data and the number of clusters C. Low entropy is a good indicator of the quality of clustering [2]. This is computed as:

$$E(C) = -\sum_{c=1}^{C}\sum_{i=1}^{N} w_{ci}\log w_{ci}, \tag{2}$$

where N denotes the number of data points and w_{ci} is the weight assigned to a given cluster. If the number of clusters C is not known in advance, clustering can be performed for a varying numbers of clusters, and the number with minimal entropy can be chosen to build the ensemble [5]. Although this is not always an optimal solution, it allows to select the number of classifier automatically, without the time-consuming tuning phase.

As hyperspectral data is multi-class, one cannot use one-class classifiers directly. However, one may use them as a decomposition tool. In this case, each of the classes is considered separately. So a M-class task can be decomposed into M one-class problems. In our previous works [12], we have shown that one-class decomposition has some attractive features and can outperform binary decomposition. Additionally, we have shown that OCClustE can easily handle multi-class datasets, with performance similar or better than binary models [13].

In the considered problem, a single OCClustE ensemble is trained separately for each class, and then the outputs of ensembles are fused together with the use of Error-Correcting Output Codes (ECOC) [23] to rebuild the original multi-class problem.

In summary, the approach proposed in this paper leads to several improvements compared with the standard OCC models:

- Boundary-based approaches (such as WOCSVM) were shown to display better generalization abilities than clustering-based (reconstruction) OCC [21], but are highly prone to atypical and complex data distributions. Therefore, a hybrid method utilizing both approaches combines the advantages of each while reducing their drawbacks.
- As each classifier is trained only on a reduced chunk of the data, its computational complexity is reduced in comparison to a single model approach. This reduces the probability of overtraining the one-class learner. Additionally, a number of individual classifiers can easily be applied in a distributed environment, leading to a significant decrease in execution time.
- Using chunks of data as the classifier input reduces the influence of negative effect, known as the empty sphere; that is, the area covered by the boundary in which no objects from the training set are located [9].
- A boundary classifier trained on a more compact data partition usually has a lower number of support vectors.

– By combining the fuzzy clustering with weighting scheme, we are able to obtain good estimation of weights assigned to training objects in a reduced time.
– OCClustE can be easily used for an effective one-class decomposition of multi-class data, when ECOC fuser is applied to combine the one-class outputs into a multi-class final decision.

3 Experimental Evaluation

The aims of the experiments were to establish the quality of the proposed OCClustE method in the task of hyperspectral image segmentation, and to compare it with several state-of-the-art classifiers, dedicated for handling big data with a large number of classes.

3.1 Used Hyperspectral Images

– **Salinas C (Image 1)**
Salinas C dataset was collected over the Valley of Salinas, Southern California, in 1998. It contains 217 x 512 pixels and 224 spectral bands from 0.4 to 2.5 m, with nominal spectral resolution of 10 nm. It was taken at low altitude with a pixel size of 3.7 m. The data include vegetables, bare soils, and vineyard fields. Image is depicted in Figure 1.

Fig. 1. Salinas C: *(left)* source image, *(right)* pixel labels

– **Indian Pines**
This scene was gathered by AVIRIS over the Indian Pines test site in Northwestern Indiana and consists of 145x145 pixels and 224 spectral reflectance bands in the wavelength range 0.4 to 2.5 nm. It, contains two-thirds agriculture, and one-third forest or other natural perennial vegetation. There are two major dual lane highways, a rail line, as well as some low density housing, other built structures, and smaller roads. Since the scene is taken in June some of the crops present, corn, soybeans, are in early stages of growth with less than 5% coverage. Image is depicted in Figure 2.

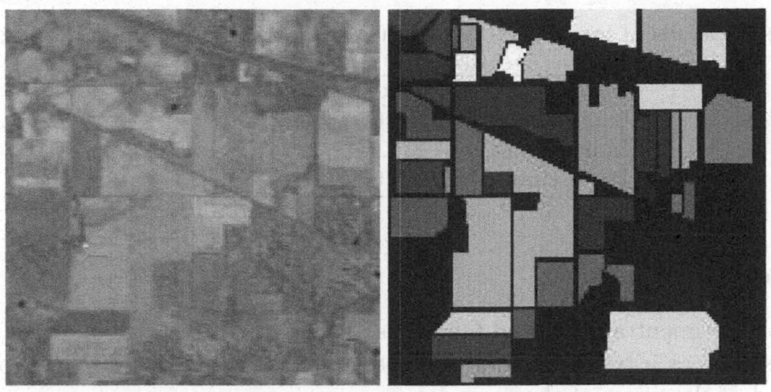

Fig. 2. Indian Pines: *(left)* source image, *(right)* pixel labels

- **Pavia University**
  This is a scene acquired by the ROSIS sensor during a flight campaign over Pavia, Northern Italy. The number of spectral bands is 103 for Pavia University. Pavia University is 610 x 610 pixels image. The geometric resolution is 1.3 meters. Image is depicted in Figure 3.

Fig. 3. Pavia University: *(left)* source image, *(right)* pixel labels

The details of the used datasets, with the respect to the number of pixels (objects), spectral bands (features) and classes, are given in Table 1. As one may see, we deal with datasets with large number of objects and described by a significant number of classes.

Table 1. Details of hyperspectral datasets used in the experimental investigation

Dataset	#Pixels	#Bands	#Classes
Salinas C	111104	224	16
Indian Pines	21025	224	16
Pavia University	372100	103	9

3.2 Set-up

For the experiment a Weighted One-Class Support Vector Machine with a RBF kernel is used as a base classifier. The pool of classifiers were homogeneous, i.e. consisted of classifiers of the same type.

In contemporary machine learning, one cannot say that a given algorithm is superior over another one, without the use of statistical tests. Experimental results must be accompanied by a thorough statistical analysis, to prove that the reported differences between analysed models are significant [6]. To get a full statistical information about the performance of our method, we use three different types of statistical tests:

- For a pairwise comparison, we use a 5x2 combined CV F-test [1]. It repeats five-time two fold cross-validation so that in each of the folds the size of the training and testing sets is equal. This test is conducted by comparison of all versus all.
- For assessing the ranks of classifiers over all examined benchmarks, we use a Friedman ranking test [6]. It checks, if the assigned ranks are significantly different from assigning to each classifier an average rank.
- We use the Shaffer post-hoc test to find out which of the tested methods are distinctive among an n x n comparison. The post-hoc procedure is based on a specific value of the significance level α. Additionally, the obtained p-values should be examined in order to check how different given two algorithms are.

We fix the significance level $\alpha = 0.05$ for all comparisons.

To put the obtained results into a context, we need to compare our method with the state-of-the-art classifiers, dedicated for handling complex and multi-class data. Details about the used reference algorithms are given in Table 2.

Table 2. Details of the reference classifiers used in the experiments

Classifier	Parameters
Random Forest [4]	120 decision trees in the ensemble
Support Vector Machine [17]	RBF kernel, SMO procedure, DDAG for multi-class data
OVO Decomposition [8]	C4.5 as base classifier, pairwise coupling for fusion
OVA Decomposition [8]	C4.5 as base classifier, max confidence strategy for fusion
OCC Decomposition [12]	single WOCSVM delegated to each class

3.3 Results

The results are presented in Table 3. *RF* stands for Random Forest, *SVM* for Support Vector Machine, *OVO* for one-versus-one C4.5 decomposition with pairwise coupling fusion, *OVA* for one-versus-all C4.5 decomposition with max confidence strategy fusion, *OCC* for standard one-class decomposition and *OCCLUSTE* for the proposed method. Small numbers under each method stands for the indexes of models from which the considered one is statistically better. The last row presents ranks according to the Friedman test.

Table 3. Results of the experimental results with the respect to the accuracy [%] and statistical significance

Dataset	RF[1]	SVM[2]	OVO[3]	OVA[4]	OCC[5]	OCClustE[6]
Salinas C	88.56	91.34	92.46	90.78	93.24	95.32
	–	1	1,2,4	1	1,2,3,4	*ALL*
Indian Pines	73.25	80.36	91.05	85.62	91.73	93.65
	–	1	1,2,4	1,2	1,2,4	*ALL*
Pavia	81.23	87.48	92.58	89.74	90.85	92.22
	–	1	1,2,4,5	1,2	1,2,4	1,2,4,5
Rank	6.00	4.67	2.33	4.33	2.34	1.34

Results of the Shaffer post-hoc test between the OCClustE and reference methods are depicted in Table 4

Table 4. Shaffer test for comparison between the OCClustE and reference methods. Symbol '=' stands for classifiers without significant differences, '+' for situation in which the method on the left is superior and '-' vice versa

hypothesis	*p*-value
OCClustE vs RF	+ (0.0041)
OCClustE vs SVM	+ (0.0084)
OCClustE vs OVO	+ (0.0393)
OCClustE vs OVA	+ (0.0127)
OCClustE vs OCC	+ (0.0156)

3.4 Discussion

The experimental results, presented in Table 3 prove the quality of our proposed approach for tackling hyperspectral images. Let us take a detailed look on the performance of the tested methods.

Random Forest, a popular state-of-the-art ensemble for multi-class classification, delivered the worst performance from all of the tested methods. This can be explained by the nature of hyperspectral data - they are characterised by a significant number of classes (from 9 to 16 in our cases). Random Forest could not cope with such high number of unique labels and produced a too complex decision boundary, which in turn lead to a deterioration of the classification accuracy.

Support Vector Machine returned a significantly better performance than Random Forest. This is due to the fact that SVM *de facto* implements a decomposition strategy. As SVM is a binary classifier, it needs to decompose the original multi-class dataset into a set of two-class sub-problems. It has been proven, that for many cases (especially for problems with a large number of classes) binarization can improve the classification accuracy, as it simplifies the original problem.

As SVM is a popular classifier for analysing hyperspectral images, we decided to go further in this direction and check the performance of three other decomposition strategies: OVA, OVO and OCC.

In case of OVA and OVO, we used C4.5 decision trees, as they display beneficial properties when used for the decomposition [8]. Our findings confirmed the reports found in contemporary literature - OVO outperforms OVA despite a larger number of base classifiers [8]. OVA introduces a imbalance in classification (objects from a single class against all of the remaining classes), which in case of hyperspectral data with a large number of classes leads to a drop of accuracy. Additionally, OVO with decision trees was significantly better than decomposition with SVM.

Decomposition with one-class classifiers has been recently introduced as an alternative for handling multi-class data. One-class classifiers adapt to the properties of the target class, as they do not use examples from other classes in the training process. In this standard scenario, a single one-class classifier is delegated to each of the classes in the problem. This means, that for a M-class problem, we will have M individual one-class classifiers. On one hand this leaves them in disadvantage to binary classifiers (as they discard some portion of the information about the considered problem), on the other hand they can deal with difficulties embedded in the data. In the considered case, the OCC decomposition achieves similar performance to the binary OVO.

The proposed method, OCClustE, outperformed all of the reference methods, which is additionally proven by the results of the Shaffer post-hoc test (see Table 4 for details). It follows the decomposition track, thus preserving the beneficial features of simplifying the classification problem. Additionally, it further decomposes each class to atomic sub-groups, being able to capture the complex distribution and reduce the potential overfitting that can appear when using single one-class classifiers for classes with a large inner-spread. The efficient mechanism for establishing weights for each of the base WOCSVM's allows to filter difficult cases and eliminate the non-representative samples present in the training set. This is very important in case of hyperspectral data, where single noisy pixels may disrupt an entire region of objects. By utilising one-class classifiers, we are able to cope with imbalanced distribution of objects in classes and efficiently tackle large number of classes (binary OVO decomposition tends to drops its performance when dealing with a significant number of classes). The proposed ensemble proves, that one-class classifiers can be efficiently used for segmentation and classification of multi-class hyperspectral data.

4 Conclusions

In this paper, we have presented an application of a novel OCClustE classifier in the task of hyperspectral image segmentation. OCClustE is a one-class ensemble classifier, that uses a clustering algorithm for detecting atomic sub-groups in the target class, and trains base classifiers on these clusters. It combines a fuzzy kernel clustering with weighted one-class classifiers. Classifiers use the membership values from the clustering to initialise weights assigned to their objects, which significantly speeds-up the training phase and establishes a link between the clustering and classification steps. We showed how to use OCClustE for handling multi-class datasets. The dataset is decomposed into one-class problems, and for each class a separate OCClustE is being trained. Then with the use of ECOC fuser, we rebuild the original multi-class task.

OCClustE has delivered satisfactory results in the field of hyperspectral image segmentation, significantly outperforming several state-of-the-art binary and multi-class classifiers. This is due to the fact, that OCClustE can cope with difficulties embedded in the nature of hyperspectral data. It works well with datasets with a large number of classes, while using relatively small number of base classifiers. It is insensitive to class imbalance, which is a common problem in hyperspectral data. By using a object-related weight, it is possible to discard noisy and irrelevant pixels. Experimental results prove that one-class decomposition, despite discarding information about other classes during the training phase, is a useful and promising tool for tackling hyperspectral images.

In our future works, we plan to modify OCClustE to deal with semi-supervised hyperspectral data.

Acknowledgment. The work was supported by The Polish National Science Centre under the grant agreement no. DEC-2013/09/B/ST6/02264

References

1. Alpaydin, E.: Combined 5 x 2 cv f test for comparing supervised classification learning algorithms. Neural Computation 11(8), 1885–1892 (1999)
2. Bezdek, J.: Pattern Recognition With Fuzzy Objective Function Algorithms. Plenum Press, New York (1981)
3. Bicego, M., Figueiredo, M.A.T.: Soft clustering using weighted one-class support vector machines. Pattern Recognition 42(1), 27–32 (2009)
4. Breiman, L.: Random forests. Machine Learning 45(1), 5–32 (2001)
5. Cyganek, B.: One-class support vector ensembles for image segmentation and classification. Journal of Mathematical Imaging and Vision 42(2-3), 103–117 (2012)
6. Demsar, J.: Statistical comparisons of classifiers over multiple data sets. Journal of Machine Learning Research 7, 1–30 (2006)

7. Fauvel, M., Chanussot, J., Benediktsson, J.A.: A spatial-spectral kernel-based approach for the classification of remote-sensing images. Pattern Recognition 45(1), 381–392 (2012)
8. Galar, M., Fernandez, A., Barrenechea, E., Bustince, H., Herrera, F.: An overview of ensemble methods for binary classifiers in multi-class problems: Experimental study on one-vs-one and one-vs-all schemes. Pattern Recognition 44(8), 1761–1776 (2011)
9. Juszczak, P.: Learning to recognise. A study on one-class classification and active learning. PhD thesis, Delft University of Technology (2006)
10. Koch, M.W., Moya, M.M., Hostetler, L.D., Fogler, R.J.: Cueing, feature discovery, and one-class learning for synthetic aperture radar automatic target recognition. Neural Networks 8(7-8), 1081–1102 (1995)
11. Krawczyk, B., Woźniak, M.: Combining diverse one-class classifiers. In: Corchado, E., Snášel, V., Abraham, A., Woźniak, M., Graña, M., Cho, S.-B. (eds.) HAIS 2012, Part II. LNCS, vol. 7209, pp. 590–601. Springer, Heidelberg (2012)
12. Krawczyk, B., Woźniak, M.: Diversity measures for one-class classifier ensembles. Neurocomputing 126, 36–44 (2014)
13. Krawczyk, B., Woźniak, M., Cyganek, B.: Clustering-based ensembles for one-class classification. Information Sciences 264, 182–195 (2014)
14. Kuncheva, L.I.: Clustering-and-selection model for classifier combination. In: KES, pp. 185–188 (2000)
15. Li, C.-H., Kuo, B.-C., Lin, C.-T., Huang, C.-S.: A spatial-contextual support vector machine for remotely sensed image classification. IEEE Transactions on Geoscience and Remote Sensing 50(3), 784–799 (2012)
16. Li, J., Bioucas-Dias, J.M., Plaza, A.: Spectral-spatial hyperspectral image segmentation using subspace multinomial logistic regression and markov random fields. IEEE Transactions on Geoscience and Remote Sensing 50(3), 809–823 (2012)
17. Li, K., Huang, H., Tian, S.: A novel multi-class svm classifier based on ddag. In: Proceedings of 2002 International Conference on Machine Learning and Cybernetics, vol. 3, pp. 1203–1207 (2002)
18. Richards, J.A., Jia, X.: Remote Sensing Digital Image Analysis. An Introduction. Springer, Heidelberg (1999)
19. Shen, L., Jia, S.: Three-dimensional gabor wavelets for pixel-based hyperspectral imagery classification. IEEE Transactions on Geoscience and Remote Sensing 49(12), 5039–5046 (2011)
20. Tarabalka, Y., Chanussot, J., Benediktsson, J.A.: Segmentation and classification of hyperspectral images using watershed transformation. Pattern Recognition 43(7), 2367–2379 (2010)
21. Tax, D.M.J., Duin, R.P.W.: Support vector data description. Machine Learning 54(1), 45–66 (2004)
22. Tax, D.M.J.: Robert P. W. Duin. Characterizing one-class datasets. In: Proceedings of the Sixteenth Annual Symposium of the Pattern Recognition Association of South Africa, pp. 21–26 (2005)
23. Wilk, T., Woźniak, M.: Soft computing methods applied to combination of one-class classifiers. Neurocomput. 75, 185–193 (2012)
24. Zhang, L., Zhou, W., Jiao, L.: Kernel clustering algorithm. Jisuanji Xuebao/Chinese Journal of Computers 25(6), 587–590 (2002)

Credal Decision Trees to Classify Noisy Data Sets

Carlos J. Mantas and Joaquín Abellán

Department of Computer Science and
Artificial Intelligence
University of Granada, Granada, Spain
{cmantas,jabellan}@decsai.ugr.es

Abstract. Credal Decision Trees (CDTs) are algorithms to design classifiers based on imprecise probabilities and uncertainty measures. C4.5 and CDT procedures are combined in this paper. The new algorithm builds trees for solving classification problems assuming that the training set is not fully reliable. This algorithm is especially suitable to classify noisy data sets. This is shown in the experiments.

1 Introduction

By using the theory of imprecise probabilities presented in Walley [9], known as the Imprecise Dirichlet Model (IDM), Abellán and Moral [1] have developed an algorithm for designing decision trees, called *credal decision trees* (CDTs). The variable selection process for this algorithm is based on imprecise probabilities and uncertainty measures on credal sets, i.e. closed and convex sets of probability distributions. In this manner, this algorithm considers that the training set is not reliable when the variable selection process is carried out. This method obtains good experimental results, especially when noisy data are classified [3,6].

The theory of credal decision trees and the C4.5 [7] are connected in this paper. So, Credal-C4.5 is presented. We have compared Credal-C4.5 and classic C4.5 when they classify data sets with or without noise and the results are analyzed in this work.

2 Credal Decision Trees

The split criterion employed to build Credal Decision Trees (CDTs) (Abellán and Moral [1]) is based on imprecise probabilities and the application of uncertainty measures on credal sets. The mathematical basis of this procedure can described as follows: Let Z be a variable with values in $\{z_1, \ldots, z_k\}$. Let us suppose a probability distribution $p(z_j), j = 1, .., k$ defined for each value z_j from a data set.

Walley's Imprecise Dirichlet Model (IDM) [9] is used to estimate probability intervals from the data set for each value of the variable Z, in the following way

$$p(z_j) \in \left[\frac{n_{z_j}}{N+s}, \frac{n_{z_j}+s}{N+s} \right], \quad j = 1, .., k;$$

M. Polycarpou et al. (Eds.): HAIS 2014, LNAI 8480, pp. 689–696, 2014.
© Springer International Publishing Switzerland 2014

with n_{z_j} as the frequency of the set of values $(Z = z_j)$ in the data set, N the sample size and s a given hyperparameter.

This representation gives rise to a specific kind of credal set on the variable Z, $K(Z)$ (see Abellán [2]), defined as

$$K(Z) = \left\{ p \,|\, p(z_j) \in \left[\frac{n_{z_j}}{N+s}, \frac{n_{z_j}+s}{N+s} \right], \quad j = 1,..,k \right\}. \tag{1}$$

On this type of sets (credal sets), uncertainty measures can be applied. The procedure to build CDTs uses the maximum of entropy function on the above defined credal set (see Klir [5]). This function, denoted as H^*, is defined as $H^*(K(Z)) = max\{H(p) \,|\, p \in K(Z)\}$, where the function H is the Shannon's entropy function [8]. H^* is a total uncertainty measure which is well known for this type of set [5]. The procedure for H^* in the IDM reaches its lowest cost with $s = 1$ and it is simple (see [2]). For this reason, we will use the value $s = 1$ in the experimentation section.

3 Credal-C4.5

The method for building Credal-C4.5 trees is similar to the Quinlan's C4.5 algorithm [7]. The main difference is that Credal-C4.5 estimates the values of the features and class variable by using imprecise probabilities and uncertainty measures on credal sets. Credal-C4.5 considers that the training set is not very reliable because it can be affected by class or attribute noise. So, Credal-C4.5 can be considered as a proper method for noisy domains.

Credal-C4.5 is created by replacing the *Info-Gain Ratio* split criterion from C4.5 with the *Imprecise Info-Gain Ratio* (IIGR) split criterion. This criterion can be defined as follows: in a classification problem, let C be the class variable, $\{X_1, \ldots, X_m\}$ the set of features, and X a feature; then $IIGR^{\mathcal{D}}(C, X) = \frac{IIG^{\mathcal{D}}(C,X)}{H(X)}$, where *Imprecise Info-Gain* (IIG) is equal to:

$$IIG^{\mathcal{D}}(C, X) = H^*(K^{\mathcal{D}}(C)) - \sum_i P^{\mathcal{D}}(X = x_i) H^*(K^{\mathcal{D}}(C|X = x_i)),$$

with $K^{\mathcal{D}}(C)$ and $K^{\mathcal{D}}(C|X = x_i)$ are the credal sets obtained via the IDM for the C and $(C|X = x_i)$ variables respectively, for a partition $\mathcal{D}$ of the data set (see Abellán and Moral [1]); $P^{\mathcal{D}}(X = x_i)$ $(i = 1, ..., n)$ is a probability distribution that belongs to the credal set $K^{\mathcal{D}}(X)$.

We choose the probability distribution $P^{\mathcal{D}}$ from $K^{\mathcal{D}}(X)$ that maximizes the following expression: $\sum_i P(X = x_i) H(C|X = x_i))$.

It is simple to calculate this probability distribution. Let x_{j_0} be a value for X such that $H(C|X = x_i)$ is the maximum. Then the probability distribution $P^{\mathcal{D}}$ will be

$$P^{\mathcal{D}}(x_i) = \begin{cases} \frac{n_{x_i}}{N+s} & \text{if } i \neq j_0 \\ \frac{n_{x_i}+s}{N+s} & \text{if } i = j_0 \end{cases}.$$

Each node No in a decision tree causes a partition of the data set (for the root node, $\mathcal{D}$ is considered to be the entire data set). Furthermore, each No node has an associated list $\mathcal{L}$ of feature labels (that are not in the path from the root node to No). The procedure for building Credal-C4.5 trees is explained in the algorithm in Figure 1 and its characteristics below.

```
Procedure BuildCredalC4.5Tree(No, L)

1. If L = ∅, then Exit.
2. Let D be the partition associated with node No
3. If |D| < minimum number of instances, then Exit.
4. Calculate P^D(X = x_i) (i = 1, ..., n) on the convex set K^D(X)
5. Compute the value
      α = max_{X_j ∈ M} { IIGR^D(C, X_j) }
   with M = { X_j ∈ L / IIG^D(C, X_j) > avg_{X_j ∈ L} { IIG^D(C, X_j) } }
6. If α ≤ 0 then Exit
7. Else
   8. Let X_l be the variable for which the maximum α is attained
9. Remove X_l from L
10. Assign X_l to node No
11. For each possible value x_l of X_l
   12. Add a node No_l
   13. Make No_l a child of No
   14. Call BuilCredalC4.5Tree(No_l, L)
```

Fig. 1. Procedure to build a Credal-C4.5 decision tree

Split Criteria: *Imprecise Info-Gain Ratio* is employed for branching. As in the C4.5 algorithm, it is selected the attribute with the highest Imprecise Info-Gain Ratio score and whose Imprecise Info-Gain score is higher than the average Imprecise Info-Gain scores of the split attributes.

Labeling leaf node: The most probable value of the class variable in the partition associated with a leaf node is inserted as label.

Stopping Criteria: The branching is stopped when the uncertainty measure is not reduced ($\alpha \leq 0$, step 6) or when there are no more features to insert in a node ($\mathcal{L} = \emptyset$, step 1) or when there are not a minimum number of instances per leaf (step 3).

Handling Numeric Attributes and Missing Values: Both are handled in the same way that classic C4.5 algorithm (using here the IIG criterion).

Post-Pruning Process: Like C4.5, *Pessimistic Error Pruning* is employed in order to prune a Credal-C4.5.

4 Credal-C4.5 versus Classic C4.5

Next, it is commented the situations where Credal-C4.5 and classic C4.5 are different.

a) **Small data sets**. According eq. (1), when imprecise probabilities are used to estimate values of a variable, the size of the obtained credal set is proportional to the parameter s. If $s = 0$ IIGR measure is equal to IGR. If $s > 0$ the size of the credal set is inversely proportional to the data set size N. If N is very high then the effect of the parameter s can be ignored and the measures IIGR and IGR can be considered equivalent. If N is small then the parameter s produces high credal sets and the measures IIGR and IGR can be different. That is, Credal-C4.5 and C4.5 have a different behavior in the nodes with small data set, usually in the lower levels of the tree.

b) **Split criterion can be negative**. It is important to note that for a feature X and a partition $\mathcal{D}$, $IIGR^{\mathcal{D}}(C, X)$ can be negative. This situation does not appear with classical split criteria, such as the IGR criterion used in C4.5. This characteristic enables the IIGR criterion to reveal features that worsen the information on the class variable. Hence, a new stopping criterion is defined for Credal-C4.5 (Step 6 in Figure 1) that is not available for classic C4.5. So, Credal-C4.5 procedure produces smaller trees than classic C4.5.

5 Experimental Analysis

Our aim is to study the performance of Credal-C4.5 as opposed to classic C4.5. An algorithm that is equal to C4.5 by replacing IGR measure by IG is also implemented in order to carry out a more complete comparison. This is called MID3. We used a broad and diverse set of 25 known data sets, obtained from the *UCI repository of machine learning data sets* which can be directly downloaded from http://archive.ics.uci.edu/ml. A brief description of these can be found in Table 1.

We used *Weka* software [10] on Java 1.5 for our experimentation. We use C4.5 algorithm provided by *Weka* software, called *J48* and added the necessary methods to build Credal-C4.5 trees with the same experimental conditions. The parameter of the IDM for the Credal-C4.5 algorithm was set to $s = 1.0$. Using *Weka's* filters, we added the following percentages of random noise to the class variable: $0\%, 10\%$ and 30%, only in the training data set. Finally, We repeated 10 times a 10-fold cross validation procedure for each data set.

Following the recommendation of Demsar [4], we used a series of tests to compare the methods. We used, for a level of significance of $\alpha = 0.1$: a **Friedman test** to check if all the procedures are equivalents and a pos-hoc **Nemenyi test** to compare all the algorithms to each other (see [4] for more references about the tests).

5.1 Results

Tables 2, 3 and 4 present the accuracy results for each method and each level of noise. Tables 5 and 6 present the average result of accuracy and tree size (number of nodes) for each method on each level of noise.

Table 7 shows Friedman's ranks obtained from accuracy results. We remark that the null hypothesis is rejected in all the cases. Table 8 shows the p-values of the Nemenyi test obtained from accuracy results for the methods C4.5, Credal-C4.5 and MID3 in the experimentation. In all the cases, Nemenyi procedure rejects the hypotheses that have a p-value≤ 0.033333.

Table 1. Data set description. "N" is the number of instances, "Feat" is the number of features, "Num" is the number of numerical variables, "Nom" is the number of nominal variables, "k" is the number of states of the class variable and "Range" is the range of states of the nominal variables of each data set.

Data set	N	Feat	Num	Nom	k	Range
arrhythmia	452	279	206	73	16	2
audiology	226	69	0	69	24	2-6
breast-cancer	286	9	0	9	2	2-13
wisconsin-breast-cancer	699	9	9	0	2	-
cmc	1473	9	2	7	3	2-4
horse-colic	368	22	7	15	2	2-6
credit-rating	690	15	6	9	2	2-14
german-credit	1000	20	7	13	2	2-11
dermatology	366	34	1	33	6	2-4
pima-diabetes	768	8	8	0	2	-
hungarian-14-heart-disease	294	13	6	7	5	2-14
heart-statlog	270	13	13	0	2	-
hepatitis	155	19	4	15	2	2
iris	150	4	4	0	3	-
kr-vs-kp	3196	36	0	36	2	2-3
lymphography	146	18	3	15	4	2-8
mfeat-pixel	2000	240	0	240	10	4-6
optdigits	5620	64	64	0	10	-
sick	3772	29	7	22	2	2
soybean	683	35	0	35	19	2-7
Sponge	76	44	0	44	3	2-9
vehicle	946	18	18	0	4	-
vote	435	16	0	16	2	2
waveform	5000	40	40	0	3	-
zoo	101	16	1	16	7	2

Table 2. Accuracy results of C4.5, Credal-C4.5 and MID3 on data sets with level of noise 0%

Dataset	C4.5	Credal-C4.5	MID3
arrhythmia	65.65	67.68	65.15
audiology	77.26	78.94	76.91
breast-cancer	74.28	74.84	71.75
wisconsin-breast-cancer	95.01	95.12	95.35
cmc	51.44	52.80	52.06
horse-colic	85.16	85.18	84.34
credit-rating	85.57	85.43	84.03
german-credit	71.25	71.34	71.98
dermatology	94.10	94.26	93.49
pima-diabetes	74.49	74.15	74.39
hungarian-14-heart-disease	80.22	82.33	76.77
heart-statlog	78.15	80.33	78.81
hepatitis	79.22	79.79	80.33
iris	94.73	94.73	94.73
kr-vs-kp	99.44	99.45	99.42
lymphography	75.84	78.31	75.01
mfeat-pixel	78.66	79.76	77.12
optdigits	90.52	90.83	91.10
sick	98.72	98.79	98.85
soybean	91.78	92.40	89.94
sponge	92.50	92.50	92.50
vehicle	72.28	72.78	72.71
vote	96.57	96.59	96.11
waveform	75.25	76.07	75.83
zoo	92.61	92.42	92.01
Average	82.83	83.47	82.43

Table 3. Accuracy results of C4.5, Credal-C4.5 and MID3 on data sets with level of noise 10%

Dataset	C4.5	Credal-C4.5	MID3
arrhythmia	62.54	65.76	58.44
audiology	77.53	77.39	72.70
breast-cancer	71.13	72.07	70.75
wisconsin-breast-cancer	93.72	94.28	94.06
cmc	49.95	51.36	50.36
horse-colic	84.61	85.10	84.50
credit-rating	84.78	85.23	84.22
german-credit	71.18	71.38	71.72
dermatology	93.31	93.12	91.06
pima-diabetes	72.37	73.83	72.56
hungarian-14-heart-disease	79.78	80.94	77.03
heart-statlog	75.63	78.41	76.04
hepatitis	77.88	80.19	78.62
iris	92.73	93.53	92.47
kr-vs-kp	98.97	98.95	98.80
lymphography	75.11	74.78	76.53
mfeat-pixel	76.77	77.97	74.36
optdigits	88.47	88.94	88.86
sick	98.22	98.24	98.22
soybean	90.54	91.74	85.85
sponge	91.80	91.66	92.50
vehicle	68.51	69.99	68.26
vote	95.74	95.45	95.28
waveform	69.51	75.13	69.50
zoo	92.39	92.10	92.19
Average	81.33	82.30	80.60

Table 4. Accuracy results of C4.5, Credal-C4.5 and MID3 on data sets with level of noise 30%

Dataset	C4.5	Credal-C4.5	MID3
arrhythmia	49.15	62.06	45.09
audiology	70.88	70.68	60.25
breast-cancer	68.65	67.61	67.49
wisconsin-breast-cancer	89.24	92.27	89.43
cmc	46.39	47.70	45.59
horse-colic	79.63	80.48	75.00
credit-rating	74.58	81.41	71.77
german-credit	63.09	63.70	66.05
dermatology	87.64	88.95	86.56
pima-diabetes	69.39	69.67	68.93
hungarian-14-heart-disease	78.16	80.81	74.68
heart-statlog	65.52	72.33	64.70
hepatitis	68.15	73.36	68.63
iris	84.00	89.00	84.07
kr-vs-kp	91.13	90.97	90.53
lymphography	66.33	68.11	68.59
mfeat-pixel	71.98	73.19	68.43
optdigits	76.91	80.77	70.24
sick	95.20	97.14	95.29
soybean	88.45	89.34	72.78
sponge	88.84	86.71	92.50
vehicle	56.06	63.50	55.56
vote	90.99	91.55	91.38
waveform	57.32	70.08	56.59
zoo	87.65	87.74	89.05
Average	74.61	77.56	72.77

Table 5. Average result of accuracy for C4.5, Credal-C4.5 and MID3 on each level of noise

Tree	noise 0%	noise 10%	noise 30%
C4.5	82.83	81.33	74.61
Credal-C4.5	83.47	82.30	77.56
MID3	82.43	80.60	72.77

Table 6. Average result about tree size for C4.5, Credal-C4.5 and MID3 on each level of noise

Tree	noise 0%	noise 10%	noise 30%
C4.5	114.99	132.85	201.66
Credal-C4.5	88.66	94.70	127.91
MID3	105.11	124.12	211.81

Table 7. Friedman's ranks for $\alpha = 0.1$ obtained from accuracy results of C4.5, Credal-C4.5 and MID3 on each level of noise

Tree	noise 0%	noise 10%	noise 30%
C4.5	2.24	2.10	2.20
Credal-C4.5	1.44	1.44	1.32
MID3	2.32	2.46	2.48

Table 8. p-values of the Nemenyi test with $\alpha = 0.1$ obtained from accuracy results for the methods C4.5, Credal-C4.5 and MID3 on each level of noise

i	algorithms	noise 0%	noise 10%	noise 30%
3	Credal-C4.5 vs. MID3	0.001863	0.000311	0.000041
2	C4.5 vs. Credal-C4.5	0.004678	0.019624	0.001863
1	C4.5 vs. MID3	0.777297	0.203092	0.322199

The results shown are analyzed as follows:

- **Average accuracy**: According to this factor, Credal-C4.5 obtains the best result in all the cases. If the level of noise is increased, this difference is higher. This result is reasonable because Credal-C4.5 uses imprecision to estimate the probability values of each variable.
- **Tree size**: Credal-C4.5 obtains the smallest average tree size in all the cases (with and without noise). The reason of this result is the new stopping criterion provided by Credal-C4.5. This criterion is activated when the IIGR measure is negative.
- **Friedman's ranking**: According this ranking, Credal-C4.5 also obtains the best results in all the cases. MID3 is the worst model.
- **Nemenyi test**: According to this test, the differences between Credal-C4.5 and the classic methods (C4.5 and MID3) are statistically significant for data with or without noise. From this result, we think that the use of Credal C4.5 is more recommendable than classic methods, especially when data sets with noise are classified.

6 Conclusion

We have presented a new model with the combination of C4.5 and CDTs. The obtained algorithm uses imprecision in the estimation of the probabilities and has the advantages of C4.5. In an experimental study, we have shown that this new algorithm is especially indicated to classify noisy data sets and obtains the smallest trees.

Acknowledgments. This work has been supported by the Spanish "Consejería de Economía, Innovación y Ciencia de la Junta de Andalucía" under Project TIC-6016, TIC-04813 and Spanish MEC project TIN2012-38969.

References

1. Abellán, J., Moral, S.: Building classification trees using the total uncertainty criterion. International Journal of Intelligent Systems 18(12), 1215–1225 (2003)
2. Abellán, J.: Uncertainty measures on probability intervals from Imprecise Dirichlet model. International Journal of General Systems 35(5), 509–528 (2006)
3. Abellán, J., Masegosa, A.: Bagging schemes on the presence of noise in classification. Expert Systems with Applications 39(8), 6827–6837 (2012)
4. Demsar, J.: Statistical Comparison of Classifiers over Multiple Data Sets. Journal of Machine Learning Research 7, 1–30 (2006)
5. Klir, G.J.: Uncertainty and Information, Foundations of Generalized Information Theory. John Wiley, Hoboken (2006)
6. Mantas, C.J., Abellán, J.: Analysis and extension of decision trees based on imprecise probabilities: application on noisy data. Expert Systems with Applications 41, 2514–2525 (2014)
7. Quinlan, J.R.: Programs for Machine Learning. Morgan Kaufmann series in Machine Learning (1993)
8. Shannon, C.E.: A mathematical theory of communication. The Bell System Technical Journal 423, 379–423, 623–656 (1948)
9. Walley, P.: Inferences from multinomial data, learning about a bag of marbles. Journal of the Royal Statistical Society, Series B 58, 3–57 (1996)
10. Witten, I.H., Frank, E.: Data Mining, Practical machine learning tools and techniques, 2nd edn. Morgan Kaufmann, San Francisco (2005)

YASA: Yet Another Time Series Segmentation Algorithm for Anomaly Detection in Big Data Problems

Luis Martí[1], Nayat Sanchez-Pi[2], José Manuel Molina[3], and Ana Cristina Bicharra Garcia[4]

[1] Dept. of Electrical Engineering, Pontifícia Universidade Católica do Rio de Janeiro, Rio de Janeiro (RJ) Brazil
lmarti@ele.puc-rio.br

[2] Instituto de Lógica, Filosofia e Teoria da Ciéncia (ILTC), Niterói (RJ) Brazil
nayat@iltc.br

[3] Dept. of Informatics, Universidad Carlos III de Madrid, Colmenarejo, Madrid, Spain
molina@ia.uc3m.es

[4] ADDLabs, Fluminense Federal University, Niterói (RJ) Brazil
cristina@addlabs.uff.br

Abstract. Time series patterns analysis had recently attracted the attention of the research community for real-world applications. Petroleum industry is one of the application contexts where these problems are present, for instance for anomaly detection. Offshore petroleum platforms rely on heavy turbomachines for its extraction, pumping and generation operations. Frequently, these machines are intensively monitored by hundreds of sensors each, which send measurements with a high frequency to a concentration hub. Handling these data calls for a holistic approach, as sensor data is frequently noisy, unreliable, inconsistent with *a priori* problem axioms, and of a massive amount. For the anomalies detection problems in turbomachinery, it is essential to segment the dataset available in order to automatically discover the operational regime of the machine in the recent past. In this paper we propose a novel time series segmentation algorithm adaptable to big data problems and that is capable of handling the high volume of data involved in problem contexts. As part of the paper we describe our proposal, analyzing its computational complexity. We also perform empirical studies comparing our algorithm with similar approaches when applied to benchmark problems and a real-life application related to oil platform turbomachinery anomaly detection.

Keywords: Time series segmentation, anomaly detection, big data, oil industry application.

M. Polycarpou et al. (Eds.): HAIS 2014, LNAI 8480, pp. 697–708, 2014.
© Springer International Publishing Switzerland 2014

1 Introduction

The problem of finding patterns in data that do not conform to an expected behavior, is known as the anomaly detection problem[1]. Hence, unexpected patterns or instances are often referred as anomalies [2], outliers [3], faults [4] —just to mention a few— depending on the application domain.

The importance of anomaly detection is a consequence of the fact that anomalies in data translate to significant actionable information in a wide variety of application domains. The correct detection of such types of unusual information empowers the decision maker with the capacity to act on the system in order to correctly avoid, correct, or react to the situations associated with them.

One of such cases is the detection of anomalies in turbomachinery installed in off-shore petroleum extraction platforms from a centralized company control hub. Recent history shows us how important a correct handling of these equipment is as failures in this industry has a dramatic economical, social and environmental impact.

Dealing with this problem calls for a comprehensive approach, as sensor data is frequently noisy, unreliable, inconsistent with a priori problem axioms. Furthermore, the amount of data to process is frequently vast upon as one platform has several turbomachines, that, on average, are monitored by more than 250 sensors, which are sampled at a relatively high-frequency.

Therefore, in this case, we are also facing a big data problem as the idea is to run a detection analysis over these data in an online fashion. In terms of social goods, big data uses concepts from non-linear system identification to reveal interesting patterns about anomaly events, energy usage and mechanical performance which can potentially help performing predictions of outcomes and behaviors to reduce fuel costs, maintenance costs, and improve safety.

One additional characteristic of this problem is these machines have different operational profiles. For example, they are used at different intensities or throttle depending on the platform exploitation profile. Therefore, in order to correctly detect future anomalies it is essential to segment the dataset available in order to automatically discover the operational regime of the machine in the recent past.

In order to deal with such amount of noisy data, time series segmentation has been identified as a necessary technique to be used in a preprocessing step for time series analysis. Segmentation would be responsible for detecting the most recent block of valid data to be used as reference by the anomaly detection algorithm henceforth.

Time series segmentation [5] methods can be classified as explicit, implicit, or hybrid. Implicit methods produce high quality segmentation, but are slow. This type of segmentation method is one in which the application phase calculates the error of a given segmentation. The error is passed back to the segmentation phase and is then used to improve the segmentation. On the other hand, the explicit methods are fast but they produce lower quality segmentation results. The need of a fast and quality method for real-time applications became the motivation of this work.

In this work, we propose a fast and high quality segmentation algorithm to improve results in the anomaly detection problem that is currently used in the oil extraction platform supervision problem described above. The remainder of this paper is organized as following. In the next section, we discuss some related work. Subsequently, we describe our segmentation algorithm proposal in detail. After that, we present a case study for offshore oil platform turbomachinery sensor data segmentation. This case study is used to empirically compare our approach with current state-of-the-art alternatives in terms of segmentation accuracy and computational cost. Finally, on Section 5, some conclusive remarks and directions for future work are presented.

2 Foundations

In the problem of finding frequent patterns, the recent trend is to formulate adaptive nature inspired computational models combining different knowledge representation schemes, decision making models and learning strategies to solve a computational task [6]. In modern data processing, one of the corner stone problems is an effective fault prediction technique. Fault prediction [4] consists on diagnosing faults and predicting failure based on recent data history of machine behavior, that means relying on recent system data, determine if it is probable that the system will fail or malfunction in the near future. In a business application we can find [7] that implements an intelligent system to predict business failure in small-to-medium-size enterprises. In the case of anomalies detection problems in turbomachineries, it is essential to segment the dataset available in order to automatically discover the operational regime of the machine in the recent past. There is a vast work done in time series segmentation. But before start citing them, we state a segmentation definition and describe the available segmentation method classification.

In general terms, a time series can be expressed as a set of time-ordered possibly infinite measurements [8], $\mathcal{S}$, such that,

$$\mathcal{S} = \{\langle s_0, t_0\rangle, \langle s_1, t_1\rangle, \ldots \langle s_i, t_i\rangle, \ldots\}, i \in \mathbb{N}^+; \forall t_i, t_j : t_i < t_j \text{ if } i < j \,. \quad (1)$$

In practice, time series frequently have a simpler definition as measurements are usually obtained at equal time intervals between them. This type of time series is known as regular time series. In this case, the explicit reference to time can be dropped and exchanged a order reference index, leading to a simpler expression

$$\mathcal{S} = \{s_0, s_1, \ldots s_i, \ldots\}, i \in \mathbb{N}^+ \,. \quad (2)$$

The use of regular time series is so pervasive that the remainder of this paper will deal only with them. Henceforth, we the term time series will be used to refer to a regular time series.

Depending on the application, the goal of the segmentation is used to locate stable periods of time, to identify change points, or to simply compress the original time series into a more compact representation. Although in many real-life applications a lot of variables must be simultaneously tracked and monitored, most of the segmentation algorithms are used for the analysis of only one time-variant variable.

There is a vast literature about segmentation methods for different applications. Basically, there are mainly three categories of time series segmentation algorithms using dynamic programming. Firstly, sliding windows [9] top-down [10], and bottom-up [11] strategies. The sliding windows method is a purely implicit segmentation technique. It consists of a segment is grown until it exceeds some error bound. This process is repeated with the next data point not included in the newly approximated segment.

However, like all implicit methods, it is extremely slow and not useful for real-time applications, its complexity is $O(Ln)$. Top-down methods are those where the time series is recursively partitioned until some stopping criteria is met. This method is faster than the sliding window method above, but it is still slow, the complexity is $O(n^2K)$. And the bottom-up starts from the finest possible approximation and segments are merged until some stopping criteria is met. It produces similar results to top-down algorithms but are faster, $O(Ln)$.

There also, more novel methods for instance those using clustering for segmentation. The clustered segmentation problem is clearly related with the time series clustering problem [12] and there are also several definitions for time series [13]. One natural view of segmentation is the attempt to determine which components of a data set naturally "belong together".

There exist two classes of algorithms for solving the clustered segmentation problem: distance-based clustering of segmentations that measure distance between sequence segmentations and we employ a standard clustering algorithm (e.g., k-means) on the pair-wise distance matrix. The second class consists of two randomized algorithms that cluster sequences using segmentations as "centroids". In particular, we use the notion of a distance between a segmentation and a sequence, which is the error induced to the sequence when the segmentation is applied to it. The algorithms of the second class treat the clustered-segmentation problem as a model selection problem and they try to find the best model that describes the data.

There also methods considering multiple regression models.In [14] it is considered a segmented regression model with one independent variable under the continuity constraints and studied the asymptotic distributions of the estimated regression coefficients and change-points. In [15] is considered some special cases of the model studied cited before, and provided more details on distributional properties of the estimators.

Bai [16] considered a multiple regression model with structural changes, the model without the continuity constraints at the change-points, and studied the asymptotic properties of the estimators.

3 YASA: Yet Another Segmentation Algorithm

In this section we introduce a novel and fast algorithm for time series segmentation. Besides the obvious purposed of obtaining a segmentation method that produces low approximation errors another set of guidelines were observed while devising it. They can be summarized as:

- *Low computational cost*: The application context calls for algorithms capable of handling large amounts of data and that scale properly as the those amounts are increased. Most current segmentation algorithms have such a computational complexity that impairs them to correctly tackle the problems of interest.
- *Easy parameterization*: one important drawback of current approaches is that their parameters may be hard so set by end users. In our case we have as main parameter the significance test threshold, which is a very good understood and easy to grasp feature.

The YASA algorithm is presented in Figure 1 in schematic form. It is best understood when presented in recursive form, as it goes by computing a linear regression with the time series passed as parameter. A call to the segmentation procedure first checks if the current level of recursion is acceptable. After that it goes by fitting a linear regression to the time series data. If the regression passes the linearity statistical hypothesis test then the current time series is returned as a unique segment.

If the regression does not model correctly the data it means that it is necessary to partition the time series in at least two parts that should be further segmented. The last part of YASA is dedicated to this task. It locates the time instant where the regression had the larger error residuals. It also warranties that time instant does not creates a too-short time series chunk. Once an adequate time instant is located and used as split point to carry out the segmentation the parts of the time series located at both sides of it.

4 Case Study in Offshore Oil Process Plant

Equipment control automation that includes sensors for monitoring equipment behavior and remote controlled valves to act upon undesired events is nowadays a common scenario in the modern offshore oil platforms. Oil plant automation physically protects plant integrity. However, it acts reacting to anomalous conditions. Extracting information from the raw data generated by the sensors, is not a simple task when turbomachinery is involved.

Turbomachinery, in mechanical engineering, describes machines that transfer energy between a rotor and a fluid, including both turbines and compressors [17]. While a turbine transfers energy from a fluid to a rotor, a compressor transfers energy from a rotor to a fluid. The two types of machines are governed by the same basic relationships including Newton's second Law of Motion and Euler's energy equation for compressible fluids. Centrifugal pumps are also turbomachines that transfer energy from a rotor to a fluid, usually a liquid, while turbines and compressors usually work with a gas.

Any devices that extracts energy from or imparts energy to a continuously moving stream of fluid (liquid or gas) can be called a Turbomachine. Elaborating, a turbomachine is a power or head generating machine which employs the

function SEGMENTDATA($\mathcal{S}^{(j)}_{t_{\max},t_0}$, $\rho_{\min}$, $l_{\max}$, $s_{\min}$, l)
Parameters:
▷ $\mathcal{S}^{(j)}_{t_{\max},t_0}$, time series data of sensor j corresponding to time interval $[t_0, t_{\max}]$.
▷ $\rho_{\min} \in [0, 1]$, minimum significance for statistical hypothesis test of linearity.
▷ $l_{\max} > 0$, maximum levels of recursive calls.
▷ $s_{\min} > 0$, minimum segment length.
Returns:
▷ $\Phi := \{\phi_1, \ldots, \phi_m\}$, data segments.
  if $l = l_{\max}$ **then**
    return $\Phi = \left\{\mathcal{S}^{(j)}_{t_{\max},t_0}\right\}$
  end if
  Perform linear regression,

$$\{m, b\} \leftarrow \text{LINEARREGRESSION}(\mathcal{S}^{(j)}_{t_{\max},t_0}).$$

  if LINEARITYTEST($\mathcal{S}^{(j)}_{t_{\max},t_0}, m, b$) $> \rho_{\min}$ **then**
    return $\Phi = \left\{\mathcal{S}^{(j)}_{t_{\max},t_0}\right\}$.
  end if
  Calculate residual errors,

$$\{e_0, \ldots, e_{\max}\} = \text{RESIDUALS}(\mathcal{S}^{(j)}_{t_{\max},t_0}, m, b)$$

  $t_s \leftarrow t_0$.
  while $\max(\{e_0, \ldots, e_{\max}\}) > 0$ **and** $t_s \notin (t_0 + s_{\min}, t_{\max} - s_{\min})$ **do**
    Determine split point, $t_s = \arg\max_t \{e_t\}$.
  end while
  if $t_s \in (t_0 + s_{\min}, t_{\max} - s_{\min})$ **then**
    Φ_{left} = SEGMENTDATA($\mathcal{S}^{(j)}_{t_s,t_0}$, $\rho_{\min}$, $l_{\max}$, $s_{\min}$, $l+1$).
    Φ_{right} = SEGMENTDATA($\mathcal{S}^{(j)}_{t_{\max},t_s}$, $\rho_{\min}$, $l_{\max}$, $s_{\min}$, $l+1$).
    return $\Phi = \Phi_{\text{left}} \cup \Phi_{\text{right}}$.
  end if
  return $\Phi = \left\{\mathcal{S}^{(j)}_{t_{\max},t_0}\right\}$.
end function

Fig. 1. Pseudocode of the proposed algorithm

dynamic action of a rotating element, the rotor; the action of the rotor changes the energy level of the continuously flowing fluid through the machine. Turbines, compressors and fans are all members of this family of machines.

In contrast to Positive displacement machines especially of the reciprocating type which are low speed machines based on the mechanical and volumetric efficiency considerations, majority of turbomachines run at comparatively higher speeds without any mechanical problems and volumetric efficiency close to hundred per cent.

Turbomachines can be categorized on the basis of the direction of energy conversion:

- Absorb power to increase the fluid pressure or head (ducted Fans, compressors and pumps).
- Produce power by expanding fluid to a lower pressure or head (hydraulic, steam and gas turbines).

4.1 Problem Formalization

Assuming independence between turbomachines we can deal with each one separately. Although, in practice, different machines do affect each other, as they are interconnected, for the sake of simplicity we will be dealing with one at a time.

Using that scheme we can construct an abstract model of the problem. A given turbomachine, $\mathcal{M}$, is monitored by a set of m sensors $s^{(j)} \in \mathcal{M}$, with $j = 1, \ldots, m$. Each of these sensors are sampled at regular time intervals in order to produce the time series

$$\mathcal{S}^{(j)}_{t_{\max},t_0} := \left\{ s^{(j)}_t \right\}, t_0 \leq t \leq t_{\max} \,. \tag{3}$$

Using this representation and assuming that sensors are independent, the problem of interest can be expressed as a two-part problem: (i) predict a future anomaly in a sensor, and; (ii) decision making from anomaly predictions. This can be expressed more formally as:

Definition 1 (Sensor Anomaly Prediction). *Find a set of* anomaly prediction functions, $A^{(j)}(\cdot)$, *such that*

$$A^{(j)} \left(\mathcal{S}^{(j)}_{t,t-\Delta t} \middle| \widehat{\mathcal{S}}^{(j)}_{t_{\max},t_0} \right) = \begin{cases} 1 \textit{ predicted anomaly} \\ 0 \textit{ in other case} \end{cases}, \tag{4}$$

that is constructed using a given reference (training) set of sensor data, $\widehat{\mathcal{S}}^{(j)}_{t_{\max},t_0}$, and determines if there will be a failure in the near future by processing a sample of current sensor data $\mathcal{S}^{(j)}_{t,t-\Delta t}$, with $t_{\max} < t - \Delta t < t$ and, generally, $\Delta t \ll t_{\max} - t_0$.

Using those functions the second problem can be stated as:

Definition 2 (Machine Anomaly Alarm). *For each turbomachine $\mathcal{M}$, obtain a* machine alarm function

$$F_{\mathcal{M}} \left(a^{(1)}_t, \ldots, a^{(m)}_t \middle| \boldsymbol{w}_{\mathcal{M}} \right) = \begin{cases} 1 \textit{ alarm signal} \\ 0 \textit{ in other case} \end{cases}, \tag{5}$$

where $a_t^{(j)} = A^{(j)}\left(\mathcal{S}_{t,t-\Delta t}^{(j)}\right)$ *and the weights vector,* $\boldsymbol{w}_{\mathcal{M}} = \left\{w^{(1)},\ldots,w^{(m)}\right\}$ *represents the contribution —or relevance— of each sensor to an alarm firing decision.*

It must be noted that, although we have expressed these problems in a crisp (Boolean) form they can be expressed in a continuous [0, 1] form suitable for application of fuzzy logic or other forms of uncertainty reasoning methods.

In order to synthesize adequate $A^{(j)}$ and $F_{\mathcal{M}}$ it is necessary to identify the different operational modes of the the machine. Knowing the operational modes of the machine enables the creation of $A^{(j)}$ and $F_{\mathcal{M}}$ functions —either explicitly or by means of a modeling or machine learning method— that correctly responds to each of modes.

4.2 Comparative Experiments

YASA is been currently applied with success to the problem of segmenting turbomachine sensor data of a major petroleum extraction and processing conglomerate of Brazil. In this section we present an part of the experimental comparison involving some of the current state-of-the-art methods and our proposal that was carried out in order to validate the suitability of our approach. Readers must be warned that the results presented here had to be transformed in order to preserve the sensitive details of the data.

In this case in particular we deal with a dataset of measurements taken with a five minute frequency obtained during the first half of 2012 from more than 250 sensors connected to an operational turbomachine. An initial analysis of the data yields that there are different profiles or patterns that are shared by different sensors. This is somewhat expected as sensors with similar purposes or supervising similar physical properties should have similar readings characteristics.

Figure 2 displays the four shared time series profiles found in the dataset. On hand, we have smooth homogeneous time series that are generally associated with slow-changing physical properties. Secondly, we found fast changing/unstable sensor readings that could be a result of sensor noise or unstable physical quantity. There is a third class of time series which exhibit a clear change in operating profile attributable to different usage regimes of the machine or the overall extraction/processing process.

Using this dataset we carried out an study comparing four of the main segmentation algorithms and our proposal. In particular we compare the Bottom-Up [11], Top-Down [18], adaptive Top-Down [10] and Sliding Window and Bottom-up algorithms [5].

The need for comparing the performance of the algorithms when confronted with the different sensor data prompts the use of statistical tools in order to reach a valid judgement regarding the quality of the solutions, how different algorithms compare with each other and their computational resource requirements. Box plots [19] are one of such representations and have been repeatedly applied in our context. Although box plots allows a visual comparison of the results and, in principle, some conclusions could be deduced out of them.

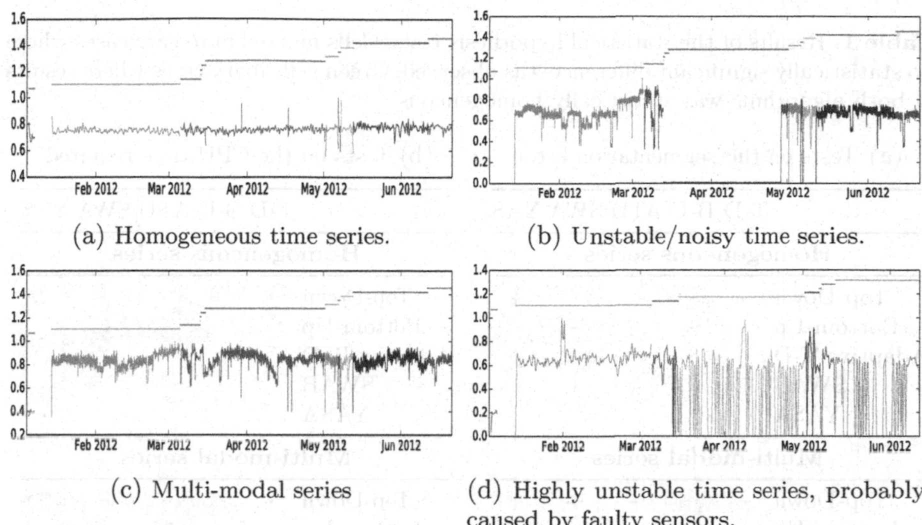

(a) Homogeneous time series. (b) Unstable/noisy time series.

(c) Multi-modal series (d) Highly unstable time series, probably caused by faulty sensors.

Fig. 2. A sample of the four main types of time series contained in the dataset. We have marked with color changes the moments in which the machine was switched on/off. Data has been anonymized and transformed for confidentiality reasons.

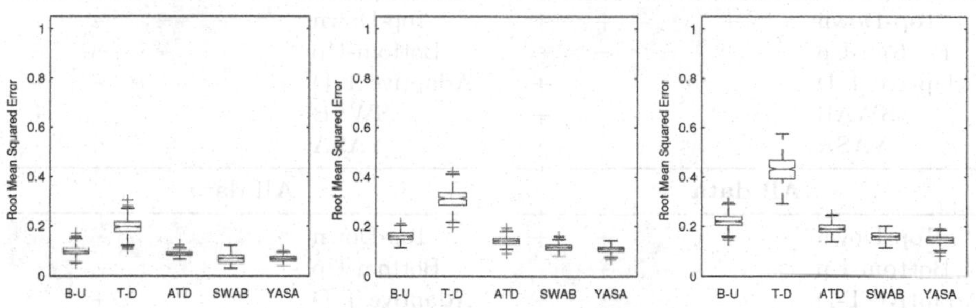

(a) Errors for homogeneous series. (b) Errors for multi-modal series. (c) Errors for noisy series.

Fig. 3. Box plots of the root mean squared errors yielded by the Bottom-Up (B-U), Top-Down (T-D), adaptive Top-Down (ATD), Sliding Window and Bottom-up (SWAB) and our proposal (YASA). Data has been anonymized and transformed for confidentiality reasons.

Figure 3 shows the quality of the results in terms of the mean squared error obtained from the segmentation produced by each algorithm in the form of box plots. We have grouped the results according to the class of sensor data for the sake of a more valuable presentation of results. The main conclusion to be extracted from this initial set of results is that our proposal was able to achieve a similar performance —and in some cases a better performance— when compared with the other methods.

Table 1. Results of the statistical hypothesis tests. Cells marked in red are cases where no statistically significant difference was observed. Green cells mark cases where results of both algorithms was statistically homogeneous.

(a) Tests on the segmentation errors.

	T-D	B-U	ATD	SWA	YAS
Homogeneous series					
Top-Down	·	−	+	+	+
Bottom-Up		·	−	−	−
Adaptive T-D			·	−	+
SWAB				·	+
YASA					·
Multi-modal series					
Top-Down	·	−	+	+	+
Bottom-Up		·	−	−	−
Adaptive T-D			·	−	+
SWAB				·	+
YASA					·
Noisy series					
Top-Down	·	+	−	+	+
Bottom-Up		·	−	−	−
Adaptive T-D			·	−	+
SWAB				·	+
YASA					·
All data					
Top-Down	·	+	−	+	+
Bottom-Up		·	−	−	−
Adaptive T-D			·	−	+
SWAB				·	+
YASA					·

(b) Tests on the CPU time required.

	T-D	B-U	ATD	SWA	YAS
Homogeneous series					
Top-Down	·	−	−	−	−
Bottom-Up		·	−	−	−
Adaptive T-D			·	+	−
SWAB				·	−
YASA					·
Multi-modal series					
Top-Down	·	−	−	−	−
Bottom-Up		·	−	−	−
Adaptive T-D			·	+	−
SWAB				·	−
YASA					·
Noisy series					
Top-Down	·	−	−	−	−
Bottom-Up		·	−	−	−
Adaptive T-D			·	+	−
SWAB				·	+
YASA					·
All data					
Top-Down	·	−	−	−	−
Bottom-Up		·	−	−	−
Adaptive T-D			·	+	−
SWAB				·	−
YASA					·

The statistical validity of the judgment of the results calls for the application of statistical hypothesis tests. It has been previously remarked by different authors that the Mann–Whitney–Wilcoxon U test [20] is particularly suited for experiments of this class. This test is commonly used as a non-parametric method for testing equality of population medians. In our case we performed pair-wise tests on the significance of the difference of the indicator values yielded by the executions of the algorithms. A significance level, α, of 0.05 was used for all tests.

Table 1a contains the results of the statistical analysis which confirm the judgements put forward before.

Comparing performance is clearly not enough as one of the leit motifs of this work is to provide a good and fast segmentation algorithm. That is why we

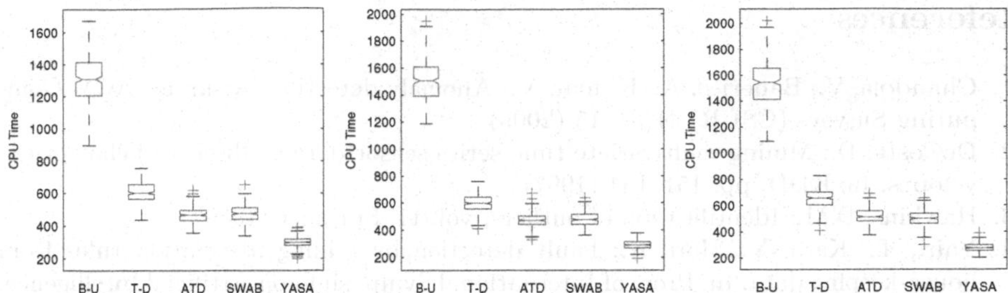

(a) RMS errors for homogeneous series. (b) RMS errors for multimodal series. (c) RMS errors for noisy series.

Fig. 4. Box plots of the CPU time needed by the Bottom-Up (B-U), Top-Down (T-D), adaptive Top-Down (ATD), Sliding Window and Bottom-up (SWAB) and our proposal (YASA). Data has been anonymized and transformed for confidentiality reasons.

carry out a similar study to the previous one, this time focusing on the amount of CPU time required by each algorithm. Figure 4 summarizes this analysis. It is visible how our approach required less computation to carry out the task. Table 1b allows to assert this analysis with the help of statistical hypothesis tests, as explained in the previous analysis.

5 Final Remarks

In this work we introduced a novel segmentation online segmentation method specially devised to deal with massive or big data problems. We have applied this algorithm to the segmentation sensor measurements of turbomachines used as part of offshore oil extraction and processing plants. In the problem under study, our approach was able to yield adequate results at a lower computational cost.

Although we have introduced and presented the YASA algorithm focusing of the segmentation problem itself, it must be pointed out that the algorithm is currently deployed as part of a larger system that rely of the segmentation to train a set of one-class support vector machine classifiers [21]. In this case, YASA is used to detect blocks of homogeneous data segments. If the last of those segments meets some required constraint (length, trend, etc.) it is used as training set of the one-class SVMs.

Currently, these YASA and one-class SVM classifier combination is being applied to detect anomalies in turbomachinery platform operation. The global system is currently in use by a major petroleum industry conglomerate of Brazil and is to be presented as a whole in a forthcoming paper.

Further work in this direction is called for and is currently being actively carried out. An important direction is the formal understanding of the computational complexity of the proposal. We also intend to extend the context of application to other big data application contexts.

References

1. Chandola, V., Banerjee, A., Kumar, V.: Anomaly detection: A survey. ACM Computing Surveys (CSUR) 41(3), 15 (2009)
2. DeCoste, D.: Mining multivariate time-series sensor data to discover behavior envelopes. In: KDD, pp. 151–154 (1997)
3. Hawkins, D.M.: Identification of outliers, vol. 11. Springer (1980)
4. Yairi, T., Kato, Y., Hori, K.: Fault detection by mining association rules from house-keeping data. In: Proc. of International Symposium on Artificial Intelligence, Robotics and Automation in Space, vol. 3. Citeseer (2001)
5. Keogh, E., Chu, S., Hart, D., Pazzani, M.: Segmenting time series: A survey and novel approach. Data Mining in Time Series Databases 57, 1–22 (2004)
6. Abraham, A.: Special issue: Hybrid approaches for approximate reasoning. Journal of Intelligent and Fuzzy Systems 23(2-3), 41–42 (2012)
7. Borrajo, M.L., Baruque, B., Corchado, E., Bajo, J., Corchado, J.M.: Hybrid neural intelligent system to predict business failure in small-to-medium-size enterprises. International Journal of Neural Systems 21(04), 277–296 (2011)
8. Bouchard, D.: Automated time series segmentation for human motion analysis. Center for Human Modeling and Simulation, University of Pennsylvania (2006)
9. Bingham, E., Gionis, A., Haiminen, N., Hiisilä, H., Mannila, H., Terzi, E.: Segmentation and dimensionality reduction. In: SDM. SIAM (2006)
10. Lemire, D.: A better alternative to piecewise linear time series segmentation. In: SDM. SIAM (2007)
11. Hunter, J., McIntosh, N.: Knowledge-based event detection in complex time series data. In: Horn, W., Shahar, Y., Lindberg, G., Andreassen, S., Wyatt, J.C. (eds.) AIMDM 1999. LNCS (LNAI), vol. 1620, pp. 271–280. Springer, Heidelberg (1999)
12. Vlachos, M., Lin, J., Keogh, E., Gunopulos, D.: A wavelet-based anytime algorithm for k-means clustering of time series. In: Proc. Workshop on Clustering High Dimensionality Data and Its Applications. Citeseer (2003)
13. Bollobás, B., Das, G., Gunopulos, D., Mannila, H.: Time-series similarity problems and well-separated geometric sets. In: Proceedings of the Thirteenth Annual Symposium on Computational Geometry, pp. 454–456. ACM (1997)
14. Feder, P.I.: On asymptotic distribution theory in segmented regression problems–identified case. The Annals of Statistics, 49–83 (1975)
15. Hinkley, D.V.: Inference in two-phase regression. Journal of the American Statistical Association 66(336), 736–743 (1971)
16. Bai, J.: Estimation of a change point in multiple regression models. Review of Economics and Statistics 79(4), 551–563 (1997)
17. Logan Jr., E.: Handbook of Turbomachinery, 2nd edn. CRC Press (2003)
18. Duda, R.O., Hart, P.E., et al.: Pattern classification and scene analysis, vol. 3. Wiley, New York (1973)
19. Chambers, J., Cleveland, W., Kleiner, B., Tukey, P.: Graphical Methods for Data Analysis. Wadsworth, Belmont (1983)
20. Mann, H.B., Whitney, D.R.: On a test of whether one of two random variables is stochastically larger than the other. Annals of Mathematical Statistics 18, 50–60 (1947)
21. Ratsch, G., Mika, S., Scholkopf, B., Muller, K.: Constructing boosting algorithms from svms: an application to one-class classification. IEEE Transactions on Pattern Analysis and Machine Intelligence 24(9), 1184–1199 (2002)

Author Index